W9-DFN-760

Introduction to

3 Edition

ABNORMAL CHILD and ADOLESCENT PSYCHOLOGY

Introduction to

ABNORMAL CHILD
and ADOLESCENT
PSYCHOLOGY

3 Edition

ROBERT WEIS
DENISON UNIVERSITY

Los Angeles | London | New Delhi
Singapore | Washington DC | Melbourne

FOR INFORMATION:

SAGE Publications, Inc.
2455 Teller Road
Thousand Oaks, California 91320
E-mail: order@sagepub.com

SAGE Publications Ltd.
1 Oliver's Yard
55 City Road
London EC1Y 1SP
United Kingdom

SAGE Publications India Pvt. Ltd.
B 1/I 1 Mohan Cooperative Industrial Area
Mathura Road, New Delhi 110 044
India

SAGE Publications Asia-Pacific Pte. Ltd.
3 Church Street
#10-04 Samsung Hub
Singapore 049483

Acquisitions Editor: Abbie Rickard
eLearning Editor: Morgan Shannon
Editorial Assistant: Alexander Louis Helmintoller
Production Editor: Libby Larson
Copy Editor: Megan Markanich
Typesetter: C&M Digitals (P) Ltd.
Proofreader: Dennis Webb
Indexer: Will Ragsdale
Cover Designer: Candice Harman
Marketing Manager: Katherine Hepburn

Printed in the United States of America

Library of Congress Cataloging-in-Publication Data

Names: Weis, Robert, 1973- author.

Title: Introduction to abnormal child and adolescent psychology / Robert Weis, Denison University.

Description: Third edition. | Los Angeles : SAGE, [2018] | Includes bibliographical references and index.

Identifiers: LCCN 2016044641 | ISBN 9781506339764 (hardcover : alk. paper)

Subjects: LCSH: Child psychopathology. | Adolescent psychopathology.

Classification: LCC RJ499 .W3925 2018 | DDC 618.92/89—dc23
LC record available at https://lccn.loc.gov/2016044641

This book is printed on acid-free paper.

17 18 19 20 21 10 9 8 7 6 5 4 3 2 1

Brief Contents

Detailed Case Studies

Additional case studies and discussion questions are available to instructors.
Visit abnormalchildpsychology.org.

Detailed Contents

Preface

Now is an exciting time to learn about abnormal child psychology. The field of child psychopathology is rapidly changing. The study and practice of abnormal child psychology began when Lightner Witmer established the first psychological clinic for children in 1896. However, some of the most exciting developments in the field have emerged in the past two decades. For example, the theoretical perspective of developmental psychopathology has shaped the way professionals view children's development (and maldevelopment) across time and from multiple perspectives. Technical advances in clinical neuroscience and neuroimaging have allowed us to better appreciate the genetic and biological underpinnings of childhood disorders. There is also greater importance on evidence-based treatments and the dramatically increased use of psychotropic medications for children with behavioral and social–emotional problems. Changes in the demographic and socioeconomic makeup of the United States also prompt us to view children's development within broader social and cultural contexts.

Most recently, the past 4 years have seen the publication of the new *Diagnostic and Statistical Manual of Mental Disorders, Fifth Edition (DSM-5*; American Psychiatric Association, 2013), Dante Cicchetti's edited volumes of *Developmental Psychopathology,* and advances in the National Institute of Mental Health (NIMH) Research Domain Criteria (RDoC) initiative for the classification and conceptualization of mental disorders. Even the Society of Clinical Child and Adolescent Psychology's creation of the website www.effectivechildtherapy.org is a sign that our field is rapidly changing.

Now is a particularly exciting time for students. There is so much for them to explore! Students can ask relevant, novel questions almost immediately. Important questions such as the following require answers: Why is autism spectrum disorder (ASD) more commonly diagnosed today compared to only 10 years ago? Why are adolescent girls more likely than boys to become depressed? What's the best way to help physically abused children? The field needs curious, motivated students with a solid understanding of psychological science and research methods to ask, and begin to answer, these questions and many more.

There is also much work to be done applying psychological science and evidence-based treatments to help children and families in need. Students often find themselves on the front lines of treatment. Some students work in residential treatment facilities with disruptive adolescents. Others serve as behavior therapists for children with developmental disabilities. Still other students volunteer with at-risk youths; they may tutor children with learning disabilities, serve as Big Brothers or Big Sisters to disadvantaged children in their communities, or facilitate after-school groups for children in high-risk neighborhoods. There is no shortage of people who want to help children in need; the difficulty is finding individuals who are willing to use scientific principles and evidence-based practices to help them. The field desperately needs bright, empathic students who are willing to devote their professional lives to help children, using the principles of psychological science.

GOALS OF THIS BOOK

This book provides an introduction to students interested in abnormal child and adolescent psychology, child psychopathology, children with special needs, or otherwise exceptional children. It adopts a developmental psychopathology approach to understanding youths with behavioral, cognitive, and social–emotional problems. The developmental psychopathology perspective examines the emergence of child and adolescent disorders over time, pays special attention to risk and protective factors that influence developmental processes and trajectories, and examines child psychopathology in the context of typical child development.

This book has four overarching goals: (1) to introduce students to the principles of developmental psychopathology; (2) to help students appreciate the importance of integrating psychological science with real-world clinical practice; (3) to emphasize the need for evidence-based interventions for children and families; and (4) to be relevant to students' lives.

Goal 1: Introduce the Principles of Developmental Psychopathology

The first goal of this book is to introduce students to the principles of developmental psychopathology and to show how this perspective can aid our understanding of childhood disorders. Children's problems are multiply determined and constantly changing. The best understanding of these problems requires us to integrate research from many disciplines and to apply this information to children and families in specific developmental and sociocultural contexts. Beginning students can find this task overwhelming. However, the developmental psychopathology perspective allows us to appreciate the complexity of children's development over time and across contexts, without oversimplifying the research literature or making the field too daunting for students.

In the book, I wanted to go beyond merely describing each disorder. I also wanted to introduce students to the multitude of factors that cause children's problems. Potential etiologies are numerous and complex. To help students organize the research literature, I present each disorder across five broad levels of analysis:

- Genetics and epigenetics (e.g., behavioral and molecular genetics research)
- Biology (e.g., brain structure and functioning, hormones, neuroimaging studies)
- Psychological processes (e.g., the interplay between children's thoughts, feelings, and actions)
- Interpersonal relations (e.g., parent–child attachment, family functioning, peer relationships)
- Social–cultural context (e.g., children's ethnicity, socioeconomic status [SES], and neighborhood)

The causes of childhood disorders can be analyzed at each of these levels. However, the most complete accounts of child psychopathology usually involve interactions across multiple levels of analysis and across time. In reading this book, I hope students will see that the field of abnormal child psychology is interdisciplinary and complex.

Goal 2: Appreciate the Importance of Integrating Science and Practice

I also wanted to convey the value and interdependence of psychological research and human service. Psychological research and clinical practice are not separate professional endeavors. On the contrary, effective clinical work draws upon existing psychological research, while the most meaningful psychological research is often inspired by clinical practice.

Two features of this text will help students apply psychological science to children and families in need. First, the book includes detailed case studies for each major disorder. These case studies are based on real clients (with names and other identifying information altered) to show the complex nature of children's problems. Students are encouraged to use information in the text to develop hypotheses regarding the causes of each child's disorder and to develop possible plans for treatment. Second, sections titled Research to Practice provide transcripts of therapy sessions that illustrate how evidence-based treatments might be implemented with real children and families.

I hope that these case studies and transcripts bring to life my descriptions of the various disorders, their causes, and treatments. I also hope these case studies allow students to focus their attention on children and families, rather than on disorders.

Goal 3: Focus on Evidence-Based Treatments

My third goal was to provide students with an understanding of evidence-based treatments. These treatments include psychosocial and pharmacological interventions as well as primary (universal) and secondary (indicated) prevention techniques. To the extent possible, I try to provide a detailed description of each form of therapy so that students can appreciate both the theory behind the intervention and how the treatment plays out in clinics, hospitals, and schools. Then, I briefly review the efficacy and effectiveness of each form of treatment and limitations in the research literature.

My goal is not to teach students how to conduct therapy. Instead, I hope these vivid descriptions of treatment will help students draw connections between the causes of each disorder and the methods used to treat them. Such connections will help students integrate material within chapters and across disorders. I also hope that my emphasis on evidence-based treatments will help students become better consumers of psychological services. Unfortunately, there are too many interventions available to children and families that lack empirical support and too few evidence-based treatments accessible to families most in need. Perhaps this book will help students discriminate between therapies grounded in science versus well-intentioned treatments that lack empirical support.

Goal 4: Find the Relevance to Students' Lives

Finally, I wanted to show students *why* an understanding of child psychopathology and its treatment might be important to them. Most students will not become psychologists or counselors. However, all students have multiple opportunities to influence the lives and developmental outcomes of children and adolescents. Some students will become physicians, nurses, teachers, librarians, day care providers, occupational or recreational therapists, or other professionals who have immediate, frequent contact with children. Other students will volunteer as coaches, tutors, or mentors in schools or the community. Most students will become parents and have the primary responsibility of raising the next generation of youths. Although few students will become mental health professionals, all can rely on psychological science and critical thinking to make informed decisions about the welfare of our families, schools, neighborhoods, and society.

KEY FEATURES

The third edition of this book offers all of the features instructors and students expected from the second edition, including the following:

- A focus on the principles of developmental psychopathology and the understanding of childhood disorders across multiple levels of analysis
- Comprehensive coverage of all *DSM-5* childhood disorders, their causes, and evidence-based treatments
- Complete *DSM-5* diagnostic criteria for each disorder
- Detailed case studies and therapy transcripts that help students apply empirical evidence and theories to children and families in specific contexts
- Extensive discussion of the ways age, gender, and ethnicity can affect the diagnosis, etiology, and treatment of childhood disorders
- Critical-thinking exercises that encourage students to analyze, apply, and synthesize information from the text
- Ancillary materials for students (e.g., flash cards, practice quizzes) and instructors (e.g., PowerPoint presentations, test banks, videos) to support learning and teaching

CHANGES TO THE THIRD EDITION
A Developmental Structure

The text is organized developmentally in which disorders that typically emerge in infancy and early childhood are presented first, followed by disorders most commonly seen in later childhood, adolescence, and emerging adulthood. Specifically, it includes five parts:

Part I: Evidence-Based Research and Practice

This section introduces students to developmental psychopathology (Chapter 1), reviews major theories of child development and maldevelopment across multiple levels of analysis (Chapter 2), and provides an overview of psychological assessment (Chapter 3) and treatment (Chapter 4).

Part II: Developmental Disorders and Disabilities

This section presents neurodevelopmental disorders that typically emerge in early childhood and reflect underlying cognitive problems: intellectual disability (ID) and developmental disorders (Chapter 5), autism spectrum disorder (ASD; Chapter 6), and communication and learning disorders (Chapter 7).

Part III: Disruptive Disorders and Substance Use Problems

This section includes the externalizing disorders attention-deficit/hyperactivity disorder (ADHD; Chapter 8), oppositional defiant disorder (ODD), and conduct disorder (CD; Chapter 9). It also includes a chapter on child and adolescent substance use and substance use disorders (Chapter 10), which often emerge in children with behavior problems.

Part IV: Emotion and Thought Disorders

Most of this section concerns the internalizing disorders: anxiety, obsessive–compulsive disorder (OCD), and related problems (Chapter 11); trauma-related disorders and child maltreatment (Chapter 12); depressive disorders and suicide (Chapter 13); and bipolar disorders (Chapter 14). The final chapter in this section also covers pediatric schizophrenia.

Part V: Health-Related Disorders

The last section includes feeding and eating disorders (Chapter 15) and elimination disorders, sleep disorders, and pediatric health problems (Chapter 16). These disorders reflect an array of health-related problems that illustrate the connection between physical and mental well-being.

Readers of the previous edition will notice four important changes to this structure. First, there is expanded coverage of psychological assessment (Chapter 3) and evidence-based treatment (Chapter 4). There are also new case studies that illustrate the process of assessment and therapy, respectively.

Second, the section on research methods was removed from the chapter on the causes of childhood disorders (Chapter 2) and placed in an appendix. Most students are already familiar with basic research designs and methods; however, students who need a quick refresher can consult this appendix.

Third, the chapters on communication and learning disorders were shortened and combined into a single chapter (Chapter 7). This organization reflects the close relationship between children's communication and learning problems.

Fourth, each chapter is organized thematically into subsections (e.g., 1.1. The Prevalance of Childhood Disorders; 1.2. What Is a "Mental Disorder"?; 1.3. An Introduction to Developmental Psychopathology). Each subsection serves as a module that can be assigned and presented independently. Therefore, instructors can assign specific subsections on specific days or assign only those subjections they find most important to their class.

Greater Emphasis on Pedagogy

This edition has new features that will help students learn and apply information and skills presented in the text. Extensive case studies presented in the text are designed to help students organize information about specific disorders by providing them with examples of children with each condition. Instructors also have access to a separate collection of case studies online that they can use to guide lectures or stimulate classroom discussion. Each case study is followed by questions that correspond to material presented in the text. For example, questions typically ask students to assign a DSM-5 diagnosis for the child, provide a rationale for the diagnosis, identify one or more possible causes for the child's disorder, or describe an evidence-based treatment for the child or family. These case studies, which I wrote specifically for this text, can be used either for class sessions, homework assignments, or exams.

Perhaps the most salient change to this edition is that the text is organized by questions rather than by subheadings. These questions serve three purposes:

1. *They focus students' reading.* The questions are essentially learning objectives that are placed immediately before their relevant portion of the text rather than at the beginning of each chapter. Consequently, they help student focus on salient topics regarding the definition, epidemiology, etiology, and treatment of each disorder.

2. *They motivate students to read.* Interesting, relevant questions prompt students to read the text and find answers. How common are mental disorders? How does a child's gender affect her likelihood of being diagnosed? Do most children with disorders receive treatment? Questions like these spark interest and motivate students to read on.

3. *They facilitate learning.* Cognitive psychologists have long recognized that taking practice tests and elaborating on one's reading are two of the most effective strategies to promote learning and increase exam performance. On the other hand, the strategies most often used by students (e.g., highlighting, rereading) are least effective (Dunlosky, Rawson, Marsh, Nathan, & Willingham, 2013). The questions allow students to prepare for exams as they read and test their learning by comparing their answers with the section summaries. Students can also use these summaries to quickly review main points prior to class.

Updated and Expanded Research

The third edition also includes expanded coverage on several topics:

- Updated epidemiological information based on new population-wide surveys such as the most recent data from the Autism and Developmental Disabilities Monitoring (ADDM) Network, National Comorbidity Replication Survey and Monitoring the Future (MTF)
- A new section on epigenetics and epigenetic research applied to specific childhood disorders
- Complete coverage of the *DSM-5* conditions and new developments in the National Institute of Mental Health (NIMH) Research Domain Criteria (RDoC) for childhood disorders
- Expanded coverage of psychological assessment and systems of psychotherapy
- Coverage of timely topics such as the effects of lead ingestion or Zika virus exposure on children's cognition or the use of technology to improve the communication skills of children with developmental disabilities
- Expanded coverage of selective mutism in young children
- A new section on the identification, prevention, and treatment of suicide in children and adolescents

This edition also includes new and exciting developments in the research literature. For example, the text includes recent information about disorders that were added to *DSM-5* or experienced major revisions, such as autism spectrum disorder (ASD), disinhibited social engagement disorder (DSED), disruptive mood dysregulation disorder (DMDD), and binge eating disorder (BED). Not only does the text describe research for all of the new *DSM-5* disorders but it also offers hundreds of new references, published in the past 3 years, on already existing conditions. The third edition is not merely an "updated" version of the previous edition; it expands upon its predecessors by discussing emerging topics and research findings.

A FINAL WORD TO INSTRUCTORS

To accompany this text, I have created ancillary material for instructors. This material is designed to facilitate lectures, class discussion, and the creation of exams. I hope that this material will allow instructors greater time and flexibility to engage students in the classroom rather than manage the "nuts and bolts" of their courses. The ancillary instructor material includes the following:

A sample syllabus

PowerPoint slides for each chapter, including tables and figures from the text

Online videos to supplement lectures

A separate set of case studies and discussion questions to prompt class activities and critical thinking

A test bank that includes multiple-choice, short-answer, and essay questions

Students also have access to online materials including flash cards, videos, and web resources. You can access these resources at www.abnormalchildpsychology.org.

ACKNOWLEDGMENTS

I am grateful to many people for their support and encouragement. First, I am thankful for the professional training and mentorship of Dr. Chris Lovejoy and the faculty at Northern Illinois University, who embody the spirit of the scientist–practitioner tradition. Second, I want to acknowledge three clinician–scholars who have greatly influenced my view of developmental psychopathology and the delivery of psychological services to children, adolescents, and families: Dr. Thomas Linscheid and Dr. Joseph Hatcher of Nationwide Children's Hospital in Columbus, Ohio, and Dr. Terry Kaddatz of St. Michael Hospital in Stevens Point, Wisconsin. Third, I would like to thank my colleagues at Denison University for their collegiality and support for this project. I am especially grateful to my former student, Celeste Erickson, who helped edit this new edition.

I also thank the reviewers of this manuscript, who offered many helpful suggestions in its preparation. They are David L. Carlston, Midwestern State University; Christie Karpiak, University of Scranton; Richard Milich, University of Kentucky; Martin Murphy, University of Akron; Wendy J. Nilsen, University of Rochester; Jill Norvilitis, SUNY College at Buffalo; Elizabeth Soliday, Washington State University, Vancouver; Ric Steele, University of Kansas; and Margaret Wright, Miami University of Ohio.

Finally, I am most indebted to my wife, Jennifer, and three wonderful children, Thomas, Marie, and Anne Catherine. My children were infants and toddlers when the first edition of this book was published, and they are now reaching adolescence. It has been a pleasure helping them along their developmental paths, wherever these paths might eventually lead.

Robert Weis
Denison University
Granville, Ohio

About the Author

Robert Weis is a licensed clinical psychologist and associate professor of psychology at Denison University, a liberal arts college near Columbus, Ohio. He earned an AB in psychology from the University of Chicago and a PhD in clinical child psychology from Northern Illinois University. He completed his predoctoral and postdoctoral work in clinical child and pediatric psychology at Nationwide Children's Hospital (Ohio) and Portage County Mental Health Center (Wisconsin). At Denison, he teaches courses in introductory psychology, research methods and statistics, abnormal psychology, children with special needs, and assessment and psychotherapy. He also supervises an undergraduate internship in applied psychology. He is the 2016 recipient of the Charles A. Brickman Teaching Excellence Award at Denison. His research interests are in children's mental health program evaluation and learning disabilities. His work has been published in *Psychological Science*, the *Journal of Personality and Social Psychology*, the *Journal of Abnormal Child and Adolescent Psychology*, *Psychological Assessment*, and *Psychology in the Schools*. When not working, Robert enjoys spending time with his wife, three children, and little dog.

PART I

Evidence-Based Research and Practice

iStockphoto.com/Liderina

CHAPTER 1

The Science and Practice of Abnormal Child Psychology

There once was an old man who lived near the ocean. One morning, the man went for a walk on the beach and found the shore littered with starfish, stretching in both directions. A storm had passed the night before, stranding the starfish upon the sand.

In the distance, the man noticed a young boy walking along the shoreline. As the boy approached, he paused every so often, bent down to pick up an object, and threw it into the sea. When the boy came close enough, the man shouted, "Good morning! May I ask what you are doing?"

The young boy stopped, looked up, and replied, "I'm throwing the starfish into the ocean. The storm has washed them onto the beach, and they can't return to the sea by themselves. They need me to help them."

The old man replied, "But there must be thousands of starfish on this beach. I'm afraid you really won't be able to make much of a difference."

The boy bent down, picked up another starfish, and threw it into the water as far as he could. Then, he turned to the man, smiled, and said, "It made a difference to that one!"

When first learning about psychological disorders in children, it is easy to be pessimistic, like the old man in the story. Approximately 20% of all children and adolescents experience at least one mental health problem prior to adulthood. This percentage means that nearly 15,000,000 youths in the United States alone will encounter problems with their behavioral, cognitive, or social–emotional functioning. These problems include developmental disabilities like Down syndrome or autism spectrum disorder (ASD), externalizing disorders like attention-deficit/hyperactivity disorder (ADHD), internalizing disorders like anxiety and depression, and health-related problems like eating disorders and insomnia. Problems like these are serious; they can affect important aspects of children's development and long-term outcomes, their ability to learn and perform well in school, their relationships with family and friends, and their overall happiness and well-being (Office of Juvenile Justice and Delinquency Prevention, 2016; Perou et al., 2016).

Image 1.1   The little boy and the starfish.

Equally worrisome is the fact that most children and adolescents who require treatment for these disorders receive substandard care or no care whatsoever. Barriers to effective treatment include poor recognition of children's psychological problems; limited access to high-quality, mental health services, especially among children from socioeconomically disadvantaged families; and an overall shortage of mental health professionals who are trained in evidence-based interventions (Garland et al., 2013; Olfson, Druss, & Marcus, 2015).

On the other hand, there is good reason to be optimistic, like the young boy who rescued the starfish. There are many new opportunities for students who are interested in helping children and families in need. The past 20 years have witnessed a remarkable increase in the scientific study of child psychopathology. New theories and empirical studies have advanced the field, enabling researchers to more fully understand the causes of these conditions. Research depends on teams of professionals, working together, to piece together the causes of these disorders across multiple levels of analysis: genetic, biological, psychological, familial, and social–cultural (Cicchetti, 2016a, 2016b). No matter what your interest, there is work that needs to be done!

Similarly, we have made great strides developing evidence-based treatments for children with these disorders (Hamilton, Daleiden, & Youngstrom, 2015). These treatments include new medications, psychotherapies, and prevention strategies that can be delivered in a wide range of contexts: clinics, hospitals, schools, and the community. Furthermore, there is increased effort to tailor these interventions to meet the needs of children and families from diverse cultural, ethnic, linguistic, and socioeconomic backgrounds (Christophersen & Vanscoyoc, 2013; Nathan & Gorman, 2015).

There is, perhaps, no more exciting time to be studying abnormal child psychology than now. Even if you do not intend on becoming a mental health professional, it is likely that you will play a significant role in the life of a child or adolescent (if you haven't already). Not all of us are called to be researchers or therapists, but nearly everyone has the opportunity to promote the welfare of children in some capacity: as a caregiver, parent, teacher, coach, or mentor. This book is intended to introduce you to this intellectually exciting and personally rewarding discipline. Welcome!

1.1 THE PREVALENCE OF CHILDHOOD DISORDERS

How Common Are Mental Disorders in Children?

Overall Prevalence

Epidemiologists are scientists who study the prevalence of medical and psychological disorders in the general population (Maughan & Rutter, 2010). Prevalence refers to the percentage of individuals in a given population who have a medical or psychological condition. To estimate prevalence, epidemiologists collect data from thousands of individuals in the population, recording their current physical or psychological health. To estimate the prevalence of psychological disorders among children and adolescents, epidemiologists usually rely on information gathered from parents, other caregivers, or professionals, such as psychologists, physicians, or teachers. Sometimes, epidemiologists also collect data from children and adolescents themselves, especially when questions deal with feelings (e.g., depression) or behaviors that might be hidden from parents (e.g., alcohol and other drug use). Epidemiologists can use this information to determine *point prevalence*, the percentage of youths with a disorder at a given point in time, and *lifetime prevalence*, the percentage of youths with a disorder at any point in their lifetime.

Sometimes, epidemiologists want to determine the likelihood that someone will develop a disorder in a given period of time. Incidence refers to the percentage of new cases of a disorder in a discrete period of time—usually 1 year. Because incidence only refers to new cases of a disorder, it is typically a much smaller number than prevalence. For example, the lifetime prevalence of ASD is approximately 1.8%; that is, roughly 1.8% of youths in the United States have been diagnosed with autism. However, the incidence of autism is approximately 0.3%; that is, in any given year, approximately 0.3% of children will be diagnosed with autism for the first time (Centers for Disease Control and Prevention, 2016c).

Determining the prevalence of children's mental health problems is challenging for several reasons (Costello & Angold, 2016). First, there is no single agency that tracks the prevalence of mental disorders in children and adolescents. Instead, prevalence must be estimated using data from dozens of individual studies, conducted by different research teams.

Second, epidemiological studies use different methods to collect data, yielding slightly different results. For example, the National Health Interview Survey (NHIS) estimates the prevalence of childhood disorders by interviewing 12,000 parents in their homes each year. In contrast, the National Youth Risk Behavior Survey estimates behavior and substance use problems in adolescents by administering questionnaires to 16,000 high school students annually. These different research methods (e.g., interviewing parents vs. administering questionnaires to teens) can yield different findings. For example, parents are generally better able to comment on children's disruptive behavior but are less accurate in estimating children's difficulties with depression or use of alcohol. In contrast, adolescents may be more accurate reporters of their own mood and substance use, but may underestimate behavior problems (Kamphaus, Reynolds, & Dever, 2014; Stiffler & Dever, 2015).

Third, there are practical problems with epidemiological research. Many people do not want to participate in lengthy surveys, others do not understand questions asked of them, and still others provide inaccurate information. Conducting large-scale interviews or surveys is also costly and time consuming.

Despite these methodological obstacles, researchers have conducted several large epidemiological studies designed to estimate the prevalence of childhood disorders. Collectively, these studies include data from tens of thousands of children and their caregivers, using a variety of research strategies. Altogether, these data suggest that 13% to 15% of youths experience a psychological disorder in any given year. Slightly more than 20% of youths experience a disorder at some point before adulthood (Perou et al., 2016).

Recent data indicate that the overall prevalence of children's mental health problems is on the rise. For example, in the past decade, there has been a 24% increase in the number of children receiving mental health or substance abuse treatment in the United States (Health Care Cost Institute, 2012). The number of youths prescribed medication to treat psychological disorders, such as ADHD, has also increased approximately 28% during that same time (Visser, Danielson, & Bitsko, 2014). Finally, the rate of hospital admissions for children with psychological disorders, such as depression, has increased 80% in the past 20 years (Pfuntner, Wier, & Stocks, 2013).

Table 1.1 shows the prevalence of specific mental disorders among children and adolescents in the United States. As you might suspect, ADHD is the most common condition; approximately 8.9% of youths will be diagnosed with this disorder at some point before adulthood. Anxiety disorders, such as separation anxiety or social phobia, are also relatively common. Certain conditions, such as autism, are more common than previously thought; as many as 1 in 68 children will develop this serious condition (Autism and Developmental Disabilities Monitoring [ADDM] Network, 2016). Other problems, such as eating

Table 1.1   Prevalence of Mental Disorders in Children (Ages 3–15)

Diagnosis	Past 12 Months	Lifetime
Children (3–15 years)		
Any Disorder	**13.1%**	**20.1%**
ADHD	8.1%	8.9%
Anxiety Disorders	4.0%	4.7%
Depression	3.0%	3.9%
Conduct Problems	2.1%	3.9%
Autism Spectrum Disorder	1.1%	1.8%
Eating Disorders	0.2%	0.7%
Bipolar Disorders	0.2%	0.3%
Tics/Tourette Disorder	0.2%	0.3%
Schizophrenia	<0.1%	0.1%

This table shows the median percentage of youths with each disorder from the following US data sets: ADDM Network, National Comorbidity Survey Replication–Adolescent Supplement, NHIS, National Health and Nutrition Examination Survey, National Survey of Children's Health, National Survey on Drug Use and Health, National Youth Risk Behavior Survey (2013–2016).

disorders and tics (i.e., repeated, involuntary vocalizations or movements), are relatively rare in children.

Children's disorders tend to occur together. Comorbidity refers to the presentation of two or more disorders in the same person at the same time. On average, approximately 40% of children and adolescents with one mental disorder have at least one other psychiatric condition (Merikangas & He, 2014). Certain disorders show high comorbidity in children and adolescents. For example, as many as 75% of youths with depression also experience an anxiety disorder that interferes with their daily functioning (Cummings, Caporino, & Kendall, 2014). Similarly, approximately 50% of young children with ADHD also exhibit conduct problems, such as oppositional defiant behavior toward parents or other adults (Pliszka, 2015). For disorders like depression and ADHD, comorbidity is the rule rather than the exception in children.

Psychological disorders have direct, deleterious consequences on the lives of children and their families. The total cost of child and adolescent mental health care in the United States is approximately $247 billion annually (Centers for Disease Control and Prevention, 2016b). Children with mental health problems need evidence-based interventions, such as counseling and/or medication, to help them manage their symptoms and improve their functioning. Children's mental health problems can also compromise their caregivers' well-being, leading to reduced productivity at work and increased tension at home. The cost to communities is also enormous. Societal costs include incarceration and rehabilitation for youths with conduct problems, drug and alcohol counseling for youths with substance abuse and dependence, and family supervision and reunification services for youths who experience maltreatment. School districts must pay for special education services for children with cognitive, learning, and behavior problems that interfere with their ability to benefit from traditional public education. Preventing childhood disorders would spare families suffering and save communities money. Unfortunately, prevention remains an underutilized approach to dealing with child and adolescent psychopathology in the United States (Ghaemi, Khakshour, Abasi, & Hajikhani Golchin, 2015).

Use of Medication

One of the greatest changes in the field of abnormal child psychology in the past two decades has been the increased use of medication to treat childhood disorders. Psychotropic medications are prescription drugs used to treat psychological problems. Today, approximately 7.5% of all school-age children and adolescents are taking at least one psychotropic medication (Howie, Pastor, & Lukacs, 2014; Jonas, Gu, & Albertorio-Diaz, 2013).

The use of psychotropic medication varies as a function of children's age (Figure 1.1). Medication is more frequently prescribed to adolescents than to prepubescent children. The greater use of psychotropic medication among adolescents likely reflects the greater overall prevalence of mental health problems in adolescents compared to younger children. Furthermore, adolescents'

mental health problems tend to be more severe and, consequently, may be more likely to require medication. Although young children are less likely to be prescribed medication, recent research indicates that 1% to 2% of preschoolers are currently taking at least one psychotropic drug (Chirdkiatgumchai et al., 2013; Fontanella, Hiance, Phillips, Bridge, & Campo, 2014).

Medication use also varies by gender. Regardless of age, boys are more likely to receive medication for psychological problems than girls. This gender difference in medication use reflects the fact that boys are approximately 3 times more likely than girls to be diagnosed with ADHD and receive medication for that condition.

The percentage of youths receiving medication to treat psychological problems has more than doubled from 1995 to today. Interestingly, the percentage of children participating in psychotherapy, a nonmedicinal treatment, has remained relatively stable during this same time period (Olfson, Blanco, Wang, Laje, & Correll, 2014; Olfson, He, & Merikangas, 2013).

Two factors seem to be driving this overall rise in the use of psychotropic medication for children. First, clinicians are getting better at recognizing mental disorders in youths. Second, physicians have more medication options for children now than two decades ago (Olfson et al., 2014).

Interestingly, not all types of psychotropic medications have showed the same increase in popularity. Medications used to treat ADHD, such as Ritalin and Adderall, showed a dramatic increase in the past two decades. In contrast, medications used to treat anxiety disorders (i.e., anxiolytics) and

Figure 1.1 Medication use by children and adolescents. Approximately 7.5% of youths use psychotropic medication. Boys are more likely to use medication than girls, and adolescents are more likely to use medication than prepubescent children (Howie et al., 2014).

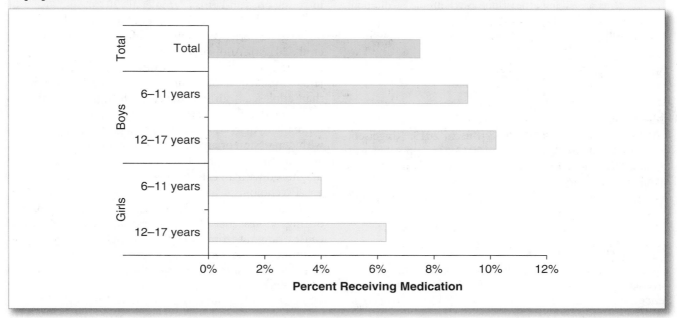

thought disorders like schizophrenia (i.e., antipsychotics) have increased at a slower pace. Only one class of medication for children and adolescents has declined in popularity: antidepressants. In the 1990s, physicians began prescribing antidepressant medications, like Prozac, to youths with depressive symptoms. In 2004, however, the US Food and Drug Administration (FDA) issued a warning to physicians that youths prescribed antidepressants were significantly more likely to experience suicidal thoughts or engage in suicidal behaviors (4%) than youths with depression who took placebo (2%). Because of this warning, antidepressant prescriptions declined. Today, antidepressants are usually reserved for youths who show more serious depressive symptoms and who are not responsive to psychotherapy (Friedman, 2014).

Is medication overprescribed? To answer this question, researchers examined psychological problems and medication use in a large, nationally representative sample of adolescents (Merikangas & He, 2014). In the previous year, approximately 40% of adolescents experienced a mental health problem. However, only 14.2% of adolescents with mental health problems were prescribed medication by their physician. These findings challenge the widespread belief that psychotropic medication is overprescribed to youths. On the contrary, many children and adolescents who might benefit from medication never receive it.

Review:

- Approximately 13% to 15% of youths experience a psychological disorder in any given year; 20% of youths experience a disorder prior to reaching adulthood. The most common disorders among children are ADHD and anxiety disorders.
- Approximately 40% of youths with one disorder have another (comorbid) disorder.
- Approximately 7.5% of school-age children and adolescents are taking at least one psychotropic medication. Although medication can be overprescribed, most youths with psychological disorders do not receive medication.

What Factors Influence the Prevalence of Childhood Disorders?

Mental health problems are not equally distributed across the population (Cook, Barry, & Busch, 2013; Ringeisen, Casanueva, Urato, & Stambaugh, 2015). The prevalence of mental disorders varies across sociodemographic groups. Four sociodemographic factors are especially important: (1) age, (2) gender, (3) socioeconomic status (SES), and (4) ethnicity.

Age

The prevalence of mental disorders varies with age. On average, adolescents are more likely than children to experience mental health problems (Merikangas & He, 2014). The best data that we have regarding the prevalence of mental health problems in adolescents comes from the results of the National Comorbidity Survey Replication–Adolescent Supplement (Kessler et al., 2012a). The researchers who conducted this study interviewed a nationally representative sample of more than 10,000 adolescents ages 13 to 17. They also administered rating scales to parents to gather additional data on adolescents' functioning. Results showed that 23.4% of adolescents reported a mental disorder in the past month and 40.3% reported a mental disorder in the previous year. Although most of the disorders experienced by adolescents were mild to moderate in severity, the overall prevalence of disorders was much higher than in previous studies involving children (Kessler et al., 2012b).

The study also allows us to compare the prevalence of specific disorders across childhood and adolescence (see Figure 1.2). Certain disorders are more common among younger children: autism, separation anxiety, and ADHD. However, the prevalence of most disorders increases with age. For example, adolescents are much more likely to experience problems with social phobia, depression, bipolar disorders, and eating disorders than prepubescent children. Problems with alcohol and other drug use also typically emerge in adolescence and are relatively rare among prepubescent children.

Gender

The prevalence of psychological disorders also varies across gender. In early childhood, many disorders are more typically seen in boys. For example, boys are 4 times more likely than girls to be diagnosed with ASD and 3 times more likely than girls to be diagnosed with ADHD. Boys are also more likely than girls to show disruptive behavior problems, such as oppositional defiant disorder (ODD). The prevalence of other disorders is approximately equal in young boys and girls (Perou et al., 2016).

By adolescence, however, girls are more likely than boys to experience mental health problems (Kessler et al., 2012a). Adolescent boys continue to be at greater risk than adolescent girls for developing behavior problems. Similarly, adolescent boys are slightly more likely than adolescent girls to develop problems with alcohol and other drugs. However, adolescent girls are 2 to 3 times more likely than adolescent boys to experience problems with depression or anxiety. Furthermore, adolescent girls are 5 to 10 times more likely than adolescent boys to be diagnosed with an eating disorder.

Psychologists have struggled to explain why girls show a dramatic increase in mental health problems during adolescence. Researchers have suggested many causes ranging from biological changes during puberty to unreasonable social–cultural expectations placed on girls. Recently, however, researchers have identified two particularly important factors: stressful life events and the way girls think about those events.

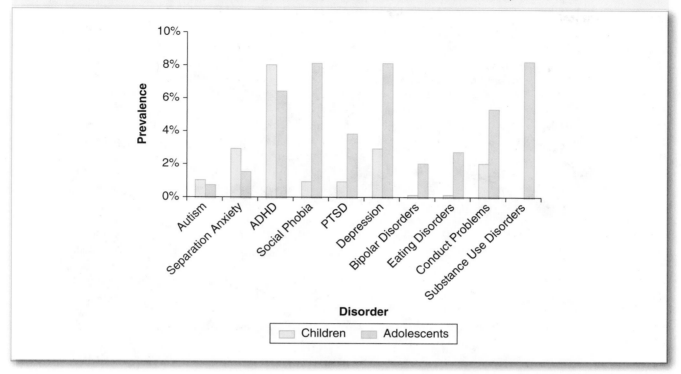

Figure 1.2 Children's mental disorders vary by age. On average, adolescents are more likely to experience disorders than children. However, certain disorders, like autism spectrum disorder and separation anxiety disorder, are more common among younger children than adolescents (Kessler et al., 2012a; Perou et al., 2015).

In one study, researchers followed a large sample of adolescents from late childhood through middle adolescence (Hamilton, Stange, Abramson, & Alloy, 2015). Most adolescents reported increased stress during this time period; however, girls were particularly sensitive to "interpersonally dependent stressors"—that is, stressful events that involved important people or relationships in their lives. For example, girls were especially likely to report difficulties with parents, peers, or romantic partners. Perhaps more importantly, the way girls thought about these interpersonally dependent stressors affected their mood. For example, adolescents who believed they were responsible for these interpersonal problems (e.g., "It's my fault my mom is angry with me") were more likely to experience depression than adolescents who did not blame themselves (e.g., "My mom is just grouchy after working all day"). Similarly, adolescents who tended to ruminate, or dwell upon and overthink these events (e.g., "I wonder why my friends are mad at me? Was it something I said?"), were also more likely to experience problems with depression. These findings suggest that girls' thoughts about interpersonal events can greatly determine their well-being. In fact, cognitive therapists help adolescents change their ways of thinking to alleviate these negative moods (Image 1.2).

Socioeconomic Status

Socioeconomic status (SES) is one of the best predictors of children's mental health. SES is a composite variable that reflects three aspects of a child's environment: (1) parents' levels of education, (2) parents' employment, and (3) family income. As you might expect, these three variables are correlated; parents with more education tend to work more complex, higher-paying jobs. Overall, children from lower-SES families are at greater risk for developing mental disorders than children from middle- or high-SES families (Kessler et al., 2012a).

There are at least two explanations for the association between SES and risk for psychological disorders. First, higher-SES parents may be less likely to experience psychological problems themselves. They pass on genes conducive to better mental health to their children. Second, higher-SES parents may be better able to provide environments for their children that protect them from psychological problems. For example, parents with higher incomes may be better able to afford higher-quality health care, nutrition, or schooling for their children. These early experiences, in turn, can protect their children from the emergence of mental health problems.

A related predictor of children's mental health is family composition. Recent research indicates that youths living with only one biological parent are twice as likely to develop an anxiety or mood disorder as youths living with both biological parents. Furthermore, adolescents living in single-parent homes may be 6 times more likely to develop

Image 1.2   Slumber Party Nightmare. Imagine that you go to a slumber party and the other girls ignore you. Is it your fault? Will it happen again in the future? Will it affect other parts of your life? Researchers found that the way girls think about events like these predicted their likelihood of depression (Hamilton, Stange, Abramson, & Alloy, 2015).

Source: monkeybusinessimages

a behavior or substance use disorder as youths living in a two-parent household (Kessler et al., 2012a). The association between single-parent families and increased mental health problems is partially explained by SES; single parents often earn lower family incomes than two-parent families. However, single parents also report greater stress and may have more difficulty monitoring their children's behavior than two-parent families. These factors, in turn, can contribute to their children's behavior problems (Frick, 2013).

Ethnicity

The relationship between ethnicity and childhood disorders is complex. Certain disorders are more commonly diagnosed in non-Latino, White families. For example, the prevalence of ASD is approximately twice as high among non-Latino, White children (1.1%) compared to Latino (0.5%) or African American (0.4%) youths. Similarly, ADHD is more frequently diagnosed in non-Latino, White youths (9.1%) than in African American (8.0%) or Latino (4.1%) children. Anxiety disorders are also slightly more common among White youths compared to their non-White classmates (Perou et al., 2016).

On the other hand, African American youths are more likely to develop conduct problems than White youths. Specifically, approximately 8.1% of African American youths will develop oppositional defiant behavior or conduct problems at some point in childhood, compared to 4.2% of White and 3.9% of Latino youths (Perou et al., 2016).

What explains these differences? One possibility is that differences in SES partially explain these differences in mental disorders across ethnicities. Sadly, members of many minority groups disproportionately come from lower-SES families (Taylor & Wang, 2013). Consequently, minority families often face many of the same risks confronted by low-SES families: reduced access to high-quality health care and nutrition, less optimal child care, impoverished educational experiences, and higher family stress. Immigrant families also face special risks, such as stress associated with language differences and acculturation (Coll & Magnuson, 2014). These risk factors might explain the higher prevalence of conduct problems among African American youths. Indeed, when researchers control for SES, there are often few differences in the percentage of children diagnosed with mental disorders across ethnic groups (Hayden & Mash, 2014).

Another possibility is that children's racial or ethnic background might partially determine the likelihood that their disorders are identified and treated. For example, African American and Latino children tend to be diagnosed with ASD much later than non-Latino, White children (Ratto, Reznick, & Turner-Brown, 2015). Research indicates that minority parents are often less able to recognize the early signs of autism; consequently, their children's disorder may remain unrecognized (Magaña, Lopez, Aguinaga, & Morton, 2013). Similarly, recent research has found that many Latino parents regard the hyperactive–impulsive symptoms of ADHD to be developmentally normative. Consequently, they may be less likely to view their children's symptoms as problematic and less likely seek treatment (Gerdes, Lawton, Haack, & Hurtado, 2014).

A third possibility is that these differences reflect divergent parenting practices and cultural values across racial and ethnic groups. For example, African American adolescents are much less likely to develop alcohol and other drug use problems that non-Latino, White adolescents (Kessler et al., 2012a). Some experts have argued that African American culture, which tends to discourage heavy alcohol use, protects many of these youths from substance use disorders (Zapolski, Pedersen, McCarthy, & Smith, 2014). Furthermore, the more African American adolescents endorsed these cultural beliefs, the more likely they were to avoid substance use problems (Stock et al., 2013).

Review:

- Adolescents are more likely than children to experience psychological disorders.
- Boys are more likely to be diagnosed with psychological disorders in early childhood, especially ASD and ADHD. Girls are more likely to be diagnosed in adolescence, especially anxiety and depression.
- Children from low-SES families are at greater risk for psychological disorders than children from higher-SES families.
- The prevalence of certain disorders, such as ADHD and ASD, is higher among non-Latino, White children than children of other ethnicities. The prevalence of other disorders, especially disruptive disorders, is higher among certain minority youths.

Do Most Youths With Mental Disorders Receive Treatment?

Access to Treatment

Although 20% of children and adolescents will develop a mental disorder at some point prior to adulthood, only about one-half of these youths receive treatment. The most recent, epidemiological studies indicate that approximately 51% of children and 45% of adolescents with mental disorders receive any form of treatment (Centers for Disease Control and Prevention, 2016b; Costello, He, Sampson, Kessler, & Merikangas, 2014). The likelihood that a youth will receive treatment depends on his or her disorder. For example, youths with ADHD are most likely to receive treatment, usually in the form of stimulant medication (e.g., Adderall, Ritalin). In contrast, youths with anxiety disorders are least likely to receive medication or therapy.

Children and adolescents with mental health problems are most likely to receive treatment at school (24%),

a specialized mental health clinic (23%), or a medical facility (10%). Some children receive services through other social service agencies (8%), clinics that offer complementary or alternative medicine (5%), or the juvenile justice system (5%). As we might expect, youths with ADHD and learning disabilities are most likely to receive treatment at school, whereas youths with certain high-risk conditions such as eating disorders and substance use problems are more likely to visit specialized mental health facilities. Children and adolescents with anxiety and mood disorders are most likely to be treated by their pediatricians.

Not all children have equal access to high-quality mental health care. Parents of higher SES are most likely to obtain specialty mental health care for their children. In contrast, youths from lower-SES backgrounds disproportionately receive treatment through public schools, human-service agencies, and the juvenile justice system. Furthermore, African American youths are less likely than non-Latino, White youths to receive treatment (Costello et al., 2014).

Altogether, these data indicate that only 50% of youths with mental health problems receive the treatment they need. Furthermore, when children are able to access treatment, it is often not delivered by mental health specialists. Instead, many youths receive care from paraprofessionals such as school personnel, juvenile justice officers, nurses, and pediatricians. We desperately need students to devote their careers to providing specialized mental health services to children and adolescents, either by delivering evidence-based treatment themselves, or by removing sociocultural barriers to families' access to high-quality treatment.

Barriers to Treatment

Researchers and policy experts have identified several barriers to families' access to high-quality mental health interventions (Garland et al., 2013; Santiago, Kaltman, & Miranda, 2013). First, financial hardship often interferes with children's access to comprehensive treatment. In the United States, mental health treatment and medical treatment do not receive equal coverage from insurance companies, despite evidence that mental health problems cost families and society considerable financial expense. Families may find themselves unable to pay for high-quality treatment. Families who lack adequate insurance face the additional challenge of obtaining treatment from a public social service system that is often overburdened and underfunded.

Second, even if families can pay for high-quality mental health services, they may be unable to find these services. As we will see, evidence-based high-quality mental health treatments are not available in most communities. For example, Multisystemic Therapy (MST) is an evidence-based treatment for older adolescents with serious conduct problems. Many well-designed studies have shown MST to reduce adolescents' disruptive behavior problems, improve their social and academic functioning, reduce their likelihood of arrest and incarceration, and save money (Dopp, Borduin, Wagner, & Sawyer, 2014; van der Stouwe, Asscher, Stams, Deković, & van der Laan, 2014). However, few clinicians are trained in providing MST, and MST is available in only a small number of communities. Consequently, many clinicians rely on other, less well-supported interventions.

Third, there are simply not enough experts in child and adolescent mental health to satisfy the need for services. Our current mental health system is able to address the needs of only about 10% of all youths with psychological problems. Furthermore, only 63% of counties in the United States have a mental health clinic that provides treatment for children and adolescents (Cummings, Wen, & Druss, 2013). Youths who receive treatment are typically those who show the most serious distress or impairment. Youths with less severe problems, such as moderate depression, mild learning disabilities, or unhealthy eating habits, often remain unrecognized and untreated until their condition worsens. Inadequate mental health services are especially pronounced in disadvantaged communities.

Finally, stigma can interfere with children's access to mental health treatment (O'Driscoll, Heary, Hennessy, & McKeague, 2012). Stigma refers to negative beliefs about individuals with mental disorders that can lead to fear, avoidance, and discrimination by others or shame and low self-worth in oneself (Corrigan, Bink, Schmidt, Jones, & Rüsch, 2016). Many caregivers are reluctant to refer their children for therapy because of the negative connotations associated with diagnosis and treatment. In fact, roughly 25% of all pediatrician visits involve behavioral or emotional problems that could be better addressed by mental health professionals (Horwitz et al., 2002). Parents often seek help from pediatricians and family physicians to avoid the stigma of mental health treatment. Stigma associated with the diagnosis and treatment of childhood disorders causes many at-risk youths to receive less-than-optimal care (Bowers, Manion, Papadopoulos, & Gauvreau, 2013).

Review:

- Only about one-half of children with psychological problems receive treatment. Non-Latino, White children and youths from higher-SES families are most likely to receive care.
- Barriers to treatment include (a) financial problems, (b) a lack of evidence-based treatment in the community, (c) an absence of well-trained clinicians, and (d) stigma.

1.2 WHAT IS A MENTAL DISORDER?

How Do We Identify "Abnormal" Behavior in Children?

There is no consensus on how to define abnormal behavior in children and adolescents, and no agreement on how best to differentiate abnormality from normal functioning. However, mental health practitioners and researchers have proposed several criteria to identify children with behavioral and social–emotional problems (Cicchetti, 2016a; Dulcan, 2015; Hayden & Mash, 2014).

One approach to defining abnormality is based on *statistical deviancy*. Using this approach, abnormal behaviors are defined by their relative infrequency in the general population. For example, transient thoughts about death are fairly common among adolescents. However, recurrent thoughts about killing oneself are statistically infrequent and could indicate a mood disturbance, such as depression. Advocates of the statistical infrequency approach might administer a rating scale to clients and identify youths who show symptoms well beyond the range of normality, compared to other children and adolescents of the same age and gender (Achenbach, 2015).

The chief limitation of the statistical deviancy approach to defining abnormality is that not all infrequent behaviors are indicative of mental disorders. Imagine a child who is tearful, prefers to stay in her room, does not want to play with friends, and is having problems completing schoolwork. From the statistical deviancy perspective, we might diagnose this girl with depression because she shows mood problems that are rare among children her age. However, if we learn that her grandfather died a few days before her assessment, we would likely interpret her behavior as a normal grief reaction, not as an indicator of major depressive disorder (MDD). Although statistical infrequency may be an important component of a definition of abnormality, it is insufficient. Statistical deviancy does not take into account the context of children's behavior.

Another approach to defining abnormality is based on disability or degree of *impairment*. From this perspective, abnormal behavior is defined by thoughts, feelings, or actions that interfere with a person's social, academic, or occupational functioning. For example, an adolescent who feels sad because she broke up with her boyfriend would not be diagnosed with depression, as long as she is able to maintain relationships with friends, get along with parents, and perform adequately in school. However, her behavior might be considered abnormal if her functioning deteriorates in any of these areas.

Defining abnormality by level of impairment has a serious drawback: Many people with mental disorders do not show overt impairment in functioning. For example, 15-year-old Dorothy Dutiel shot and killed herself and a classmate at her high school in Glendale, Arizona. Dorothy obtained a gun from another classmate who did not know that she was depressed and intended a murder–suicide. After the incident, first responders found a handwritten note in Dorothy's pocket that read, "I would like to clarify that (the student) and his family are in no way affiliated with my actions. (The student) was under the absolute impression I needed the gun for self-defense.

I lied to receive this gun." Dorothy's classmate was unaware that she was depressed. Not all mental health problems are accompanied by overt impairment.

Yet another definition of abnormality incorporates a person's degree of *psychological distress*. People can show psychological distress through depressed mood, irritability, anxiety, worry, panic, confusion, frustration, anger, or any other feeling of dysphoria. Psychological distress is one of the central features of most anxiety and mood disorders.

One limitation of defining abnormality in terms of psychological distress is that distress is often subjective. Some signs of distress can be observed by others, such as sweaty palms and flushed face. However, distress is usually assessed by asking clients to report their feelings. Subjective assessment of distress in children is especially problematic. Many young children are not aware of their mood states. For example, some youths express anxiety or depression in terms of physical complaints, like headaches or stomachaches, instead of experiencing negative emotions. Other children have trouble differentiating their feelings. For example, young children often confuse negative emotions, such as "fear" and "anger." Finally, children's ratings of distress often cannot be compared against an objective criterion. For example, a child who reports feeling "bad" might be experiencing more distress than another child who reports feeling "terrible."

A second limitation to defining abnormality based on distress is that many youths with serious behavior problems do not experience negative emotions. For example, adolescents with conduct problems often show no signs of anxiety or depression. They may only express remorse when they are caught and punished. Similarly, younger children with oppositional and defiant behavior toward adults rarely express psychological distress. Instead, their disruptive behavior causes distress to their parents and teachers (see Image 1.3).

Abnormal behavior might also be defined by actions that violate society's standards or rules. Put another way, abnormality may be defined in terms of *cultural deviancy*. For example, conduct disorder (CD) is characterized by a persistent pattern of behavior that violates the rights of others or the rules of society. Adolescents with CD often have histories of disruptive behavior problems that clearly go against cultural norms and mores: shoplifting, robbery, violence toward others, and truancy.

The chief limitation of defining abnormal behavior exclusively by the degree to which it violates social norms is that these norms can vary considerably from culture to culture. For example, in Western societies, parents often require young children to sleep in their own beds, usually in separate rooms. Children who refuse to sleep in their own beds may be classified as having a sleep disorder. However, in many non-Western societies, requiring young children to sleep alone is considered cruel and detrimental to their social and emotional development.

Image 1.3 Psychological disorders are often defined by psychological distress. Often, however, children with mental health problems cause distress to others rather than experience it themselves.

Source: bowdenimages

Some experts define abnormality in terms of *behavioral rigidity*. From this perspective, abnormal behavior is characterized by the repeated and inflexible display of certain actions, thoughts, or emotions in response to psychosocial stressors. Consider a child who shows fear at the prospect of separating from his mother. Under some circumstances, clinginess to parents is adaptive, for example, when the child is in an unfamiliar and potentially dangerous setting, such as a crowded airport. Under other circumstances, however, separation anxiety is clearly maladaptive, such as when a child is unwilling to leave his parents to attend school. Whereas mental health is characterized by flexibility and adaptation to changing circumstances, abnormality may be characterized by the persistent use of the same behavior in all situations, regardless of the context (Millon, 2014).

A final way to differentiate abnormality from normality is based on the notion of harmful dysfunction. According to Jerome Wakefield (1992), a disorder exists when two criteria are met. First, the person must show a *dysfunction*—that is, a failure in some internal mechanism to work in the correct manner. Second, the dysfunction *must cause harm,* or it must limit or threaten the person in some way.

The harmful dysfunction criteria can be applied to the field of medicine. For example, heart disease is a disorder because (1) it involves an abnormality in the functioning of the pulmonary system and (2) this underlying dysfunction can cause disability or death. Similarly, the harmful dysfunction criteria can be used to identify mental health problems. For example, depression is a mental disorder because (1) it involves an abnormality in the functioning of people's capacity for emotion regulation and (2) this underlying dysfunction causes great distress and impairment.

When applying the harmful dysfunction criteria to the field of abnormal child psychology, we must remember to consider the child's behavior in the context of her development and social–cultural surroundings (Wakefield, 1997). Many behaviors that are objectively dysfunctional may be appropriate or adaptive given the context. For example, Sarah is a girl who lives with her parents on a military base in California. Upon hearing that her mother will soon be deployed to a combat area, Sarah becomes excessively clingy with both parents, has problems eating and sleeping, and refuses to go to school. She may meet diagnostic criteria for an anxiety disorder because of her problematic behavior and degree of impairment. However, her anxiety might be justified given her social context—that is, the imminent deployment of her mother. Behavior can only be understood in the context of a person's life and social context.

Review:

- Abnormal behavior can be defined in terms of (1) statistical infrequency, (2) associated impairment, (3) associated distress, (4) cultural deviancy, and (5) behavioral rigidity. Each characteristic, however, has limitations.
- Andrew Wakefield proposed that abnormal behavior is characterized by an underlying medical or psychological dysfunction that causes the person harm and/or limits the person's functioning in some way.

How Does *DSM-5* Define a Mental Disorder?

In the United States, most mental health practitioners and researchers use the *Diagnostic and Statistical Manual of Mental Disorders, Fifth Edition (DSM-5;* American Psychiatric Association, 2013) to diagnose mental disorders. *DSM-5* is published by the American Psychiatric Association and reflects a medical approach to identifying mental health problems in children and adults.

The *DSM-5* definition of a mental disorder not only reflects Wakefield's notion of harmful dysfunction but also emphasizes the role of impairment and psychological distress in differentiating normal versus abnormal behavior:

> A mental disorder is a syndrome characterized by clinically significant disturbance in an individual's cognition, emotion regulation, or behavior that reflects a dysfunction in the psychological, biological, or developmental processes underlying mental functioning. Mental disorders are usually associated with significant distress or disability in social, occupational, or other important activities. An expectable or culturally approved response to a common stressor or loss, such as the death of a loved one, is not a mental disorder. Socially deviant behavior (e.g., political, religious, sexual) and conflicts that are primarily between the individual and society are not mental disorders unless the deviance or conflict results from a dysfunction in the individual, as described above. (American Psychiatric Association, 2013, p. 20)

DSM-5 adopts a *medical approach* to mental disorders in which psychological problems have underlying causes that reside within the individual (Stein, Phillips, et al., 2010). For example, if someone is diagnosed with a medical illness, such as smallpox, we assume that this illness is caused by a virus that has infected the person's body. Similarly, practitioners who adopt the medical model for mental disorders assume that if a child exhibits behavioral or social–emotional problems, those problems are caused by some underlying dysfunction within the child.

There are two limitations with the *DSM-5* medical conceptualization of mental disorders, especially when applied to children. First, some childhood disorders are relational in nature and are best understood in an interpersonal context (Heyman et al., 2009). For example, young children with ODD argue with their parents, refuse to comply with parental requests, and throw tantrums when they do not get their way. Interestingly, their defiant behavior is often directed at some adults (e.g., parents) but not others (e.g., teachers). Therefore, the disorder seems to be dependent on the relationship between people and does not merely reside within the child. Relationships may be especially important to mental disorders in children and adolescents, who are highly dependent on other people for their well-being.

A second limitation of the medical approach to mental disorders is that we often do not know the underlying cause for children's psychological problems. When smallpox was first described by physicians in the 15th century, it was assigned a diagnostic label based on its symptoms: small blisters (i.e., "pox") on the skin. We now know that smallpox is caused by a virus, not the blisters themselves. Today, however, we are only beginning to understand the underlying causes of mental disorders. When we say that a child has ADHD, we are describing his symptoms, not their underlying cause. In fact, ADHD probably has multiple underlying causes that have yet to be fully identified (Pliszka, 2016). Therefore, we must avoid attributing a child's symptoms to his diagnostic label since these labels describe symptoms, not causes. Instead, we must look at the scientific research literature to determine the underlying causes of childhood disorders. For example, we should not say, "My son has problems with attention because of his ADHD" because ADHD is defined by problems with attention. Instead, we might say, "My son has problems with inattention because of underactivity of his prefrontal cortex," which more accurately reflects the cause of his behavior problems, rather than merely describes his symptoms.

The *DSM-5* definition also claims that all mental disorders have an underlying dysfunction that is typically biological in nature. Indeed, some disorders are associated with specific biological causes. For example, many adolescents who develop schizophrenia experience progressive deterioration of the frontal lobes of their brain shortly before their first symptoms (Giedd et al., 2015). However, requiring an underlying biological cause for childhood disorders is problematic in at least three ways.

1. First, researchers have not yet identified specific biological causes for most childhood disorders (Frances, 2009). For example, autism is a highly heritable condition that leads to serious impairment in social communication and behavior. However, researchers have been unable to identify which genes cause this disorder.

2. Second, when specific abnormalities have been identified in research studies, not all children with the disorder show these abnormalities. For example, some children with autism show reduced synaptic density and abnormalities in their limbic system; however, these differences in brain structure cannot be used to identify children with the disorder. The brains of most children with autism are not different than the brains of typically developing peers.

3. Third, even when children show specific biological abnormalities, we usually cannot conclude that these abnormalities cause the disorder. For example, some children with autism show underactivity in a brain region responsible for processing human faces. However, we do not know if underactivity in this brain region causes autism or whether their autistic symptoms lead to deterioration in this brain region. Alternatively, a third variable, such as exposure to environmental toxins during pregnancy, may cause abnormalities in both brain and behavior (see Figure 1.3).

It is worth noting that *DSM-5* describes people with mental disorders as "usually" experiencing significant distress *or* disability (i.e., impairment)—they may not always show both characteristics. As we have seen, some seriously depressed adolescents experience tremendous emotional pain, but they do not show marked impairment in their social or academic functioning. Other youths who show serious conduct problems have been arrested and have dropped out of school, but they report no problems with anxiety, depression, or low self-esteem.

Figure 1.3 Correlation does not imply causality.

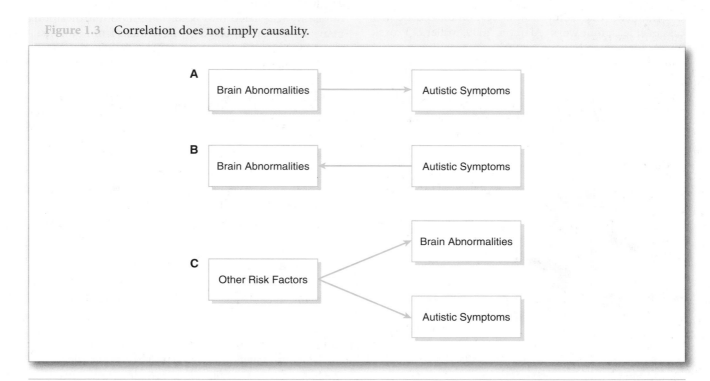

Source: Based on Baron-Cohen (2005) and Lawrence, Lott, and Haier (2005).

Note: Although there is a correlation between brain structure and autistic symptoms, we do not know if (a) brain abnormalities cause autistic behaviors, (b) autistic behaviors lead to abnormal brain development, or (c) other risk factors, like exposure to toxins, cause both brain abnormalities and autism.

Although most youths with mental health problems experience distress *and* impairment, both features are usually not required for a *DSM-5* diagnosis.

Review:

- The *DSM-5* definition of *mental disorder* reflects Wakefield's notion of a "harmful dysfunction." According to *DSM-5*, a disorder reflects a biological, developmental, or psychological dysfunction that causes distress or disability in the individual.
- *DSM-5* adopts a medical approach to disorders. Limitations of this approach include (1) we cannot always identify the underlying cause of children's disorders, and (2) many childhood disorders are best understood in an interpersonal context rather than within an individual.

How Does Culture Affect the Identification of Childhood Disorders?

According to *DSM-5*, clinicians must carefully differentiate symptoms of a mental disorder from behaviors and psychological states that are sanctioned in a given culture. Differentiating abnormal symptoms from culturally sanctioned behavior is especially challenging when clinicians are asked to assess youths from other cultural backgrounds. Consider the case of Julia (below).

Ethnicity and culture can affect the diagnostic process in at least four ways (Alarcon, 2009; Miller & Prosek, 2013). First, members of minority groups living in the United States often have different cultural values that affect

their views of children, beliefs about child-rearing, and behaviors they consider problematic. For example, non-Latino, White parents often place great value on fostering children's social–emotional development and encouraging child autonomy. These parents often provide warm and responsive behavior during parent–child interactions. In contrast, many African American parents place relatively greater value on children's compliance; consequently, they may adopt less permissive and more authoritarian socialization tactics. Clinicians need to be aware of cultural differences in socialization goals and parents' ideas about appropriate and inappropriate child behavior.

Second, recent immigrants living in the United States often encounter psychosocial stressors associated with acculturation. Acculturation stressors can include assimilation into the mainstream culture, separation from extended family and friends, language differences, limited educational and employment opportunities, and prejudice. Some immigrants do not share the same legal status as members of the dominant culture. For these reasons, the sheer number of psychosocial stressors encountered by these families is greater than those encountered by families who are members of the dominant culture.

Third, language and cultural differences can cause problems in the assessment and diagnosis of minority youths. The assessment and diagnostic process was designed predominantly for English-speaking individuals living in the United States and other Western societies. The words that describe some psychological symptoms are not easily translated into other languages. Furthermore, many symptoms reported by individuals from other cultures do not readily map onto *DSM-5* diagnostic criteria. Psychological tests are almost always developed with

CASE STUDY

CULTURAL CONTEXT

Culture Matters

Source: ©iStockphoto.com/FangXiaNuo

Julia was a 16-year-old Asian American girl who was referred to our clinic by her oncologist after she was diagnosed with a rare form of cancer. Julia refused to participate in radiation therapy or take medications for her illness. Her physician suspected that Julia was paranoid because she attempted to attack him when he tried to examine her in his office.

With the help of a translator, Julia's therapist learned that Julia was a second-generation Hmong immigrant from Southeast Asia who lived with her parents and extended family. Julia and her family had limited contact with individuals outside the Hmong community and refused to participate in Western medicine. Instead, Julia and her parents practiced traditional Eastern folk medicine.

Because Julia's therapist doubted that folk medicine alone would help her cancer, she suggested that Julia's community shaman talk with her physician to identify which aspects of medical treatment might be acceptable to Julia and her family. Over time, Julia was able to successfully participate in Western medical treatment by having the shaman attend all of the radiation therapy sessions, bless the medications prescribed by the oncologist, and perform other remedies important to Julia and her family.

English-speaking children and adolescents in mind. For example, children raised in Columbus, Ohio, will likely find the following question on an intelligence test fairly easy: "Who was Christopher Columbus?" However, immigrant children who recently moved to the city might find the question extremely challenging. Psychologists must be aware of differences in language and cultural knowledge when interpreting test results.

Fourth, ethnic minorities are often underrepresented in mental health research. Over the past two decades, researchers have made considerable gains in understanding the causes and treatment for a wide range of child and adolescent disorders. However, researchers know relatively little about how differences in children's ethnicity and cultural backgrounds might place them at greater risk for certain disorders or affect treatment. Furthermore, researchers have only recently begun to create treatment programs designed specifically for minority youths. For example, narrative therapies have been developed to help Spanish-speaking children and adolescents overcome mood and anxiety problems, using culturally relevant storytelling (Costantino, Malgady, & Cardalda, 2005). Youths listen to, write, and sometimes enact stories in which the main characters model adaptive responses to stressful life experiences in a manner that is consistent with social–cultural attitudes and values. Clearly, more research needs to be done to investigate the interplay between psychopathology and culture.

Review:

- Children's ethnicity can affect their likelihood of being identified with a disorder in at least four ways: (1) the cultural values of the child's family may be different from those of the clinician; (2) immigrant families may experience increased stress due to acculturation; (3) language differences can cause communication problems between the clinician and the family; and (4) minority children are often underrepresented in mental heath research.

1.3 AN INTRODUCTION TO DEVELOPMENTAL PSYCHOPATHOLOGY

What Is Developmental Psychopathology?

Development Over Time

Developmental psychopathology is a broad approach to studying adaptive and maladaptive development across the life span. Developmental psychopathologists believe that development is shaped by the complex interaction of biological, psychological, and social–cultural factors over time. An adequate understanding of development depends on the appreciation of each of these domains,

how they interact, and how they affect the person from infancy through adulthood (Achenbach, 2015; Rutter & Sroufe, 2000).

Developmental psychopathologists study human development across several levels of analysis. These levels include the person's (1) genetics, (2) brain structure and functioning, (3) psychological development (i.e., actions, thoughts, and emotions), (4) family interactions and peer relationships, and (5) the broader social–cultural context in which the person lives. Each of these levels can be used to describe and explain the emergence of children's disorders. More importantly, however, factors on each of these levels interact with each other, over time, to shape children's developmental outcomes (Cicchetti, 2016a, 2016b). Developmental psychopathologists call this process of unfolding probabilistic epigenesis.

To understand epigenesis, consider Nina, a child with Down syndrome (see Figure 1.4). As you probably know, this genetic disorder places Nina at increased risk for low cognitive functioning. Nina's disorder was caused by a genetic mutation on chromosome 21, probably acquired through an abnormality in her mother's egg cell (Level 1: genetics). This genetic mutation caused Nina's brain and central nervous system to develop in an abnormal fashion. Specifically, she showed abnormalities in her hippocampus, a brain region important for memory and learning (Level 2: biology). These abnormalities, in turn, shaped her psychological functioning during early childhood. Nina's parents reported delays in her motor development (e.g., sitting up, walking), use of language, and acquisition of daily living skills (e.g., toilet training, dressing). In school, she showed problems learning to read, write, and count (Level 3: psychology). These psychological characteristics affected the type of care she received from parents and teachers. Nina's mother was understandably very protective, and her teachers often offered Nina extra attention in school. Nina's cognitive functioning also affected her relationships with peers. Nina preferred to play with younger children rather than her classmates (Level 4: parents and peers). By the time Nina reached junior high school, she was well behind her peers academically. However, Nina was able to spend half the school day in a regular sixth-grade classroom, assisted by an aide. She spent the remainder of the day in a special education class. These extra services offered by her school district enabled Nina to begin a part-time job during high school (Level 5: social–cultural factors).

Nina's story illustrates the unfolding of development over time. Each level of development affects the one beyond it. Epigenesis is also a bidirectional process. Genetic and biological factors certainly affect psychological and social functioning; however, psychological and social factors can also determine the effects of genes and biology on development. Many experts use the term *transactional* to refer to the way factors across levels affect each other over time (Kerig, 2016; Sameroff, 2000).

Figure 1.4 Probabilistic epigenesis refers to the unfolding of children's development. Outcomes are "probabilistic," not predetermined. The long-term outcome of a child with Down syndrome will depend greatly on the severity of his cognitive impairment, his parents' involvement, and the quality of his education and life experiences.

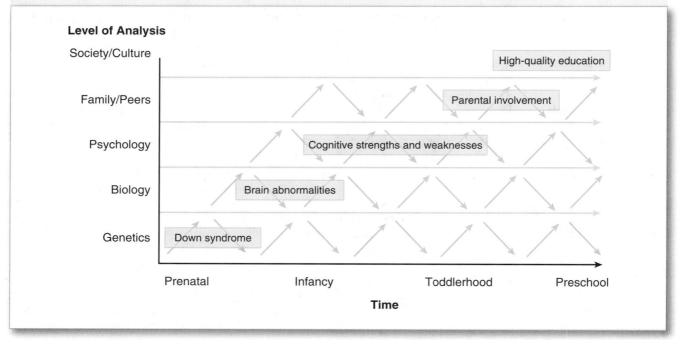

To understand the transactional nature of development, consider Anthony, another child with Down syndrome. Anthony's mother, Anita, was heartbroken when her obstetrician told her that Anthony had Down syndrome (see Image 1.4). Rather than despair, Anita decided that she was going to maximize her son's cognitive, social, and behavioral potential by giving him the most enriching early environment that she could provide. Anita spent countless hours talking to Anthony, reading books, listening to music, playing games, and going on outings. Anita also learned to capitalize on Anthony's strengths. For example, she noted that Anthony acquired skills best through hands-on learning rather than verbal instruction. Although Anthony acquired language and daily living skills slowly, Anita had high expectations for him. She remained patient and tried to provide structure and help so that Anthony might learn these skills independently. Anita enrolled Anthony in a special needs preschool and was heavily involved throughout his education. Anthony developed fairly good language and daily living skills and was able to graduate with his high school class. Today, Anthony is employed full-time in the mailroom of a large company, lives independently, and has several friends and hobbies.

Understanding and predicting child development is extremely difficult for two reasons. First, development is influenced by many factors across multiple levels: genes, biology, psychology, family, and society. Second, these factors are constantly changing over time, each interacting with the others. Consequently, the unfolding of development is

not predetermined by one's genes, biology, or any other factor. Instead, the unfolding of development is probabilistic; a person's developmental outcome can vary depending on the interplay of many biological and environmental factors. Developmental psychopathologists use the term *probabilistic epigenesis* to refer to the complex transaction of biogenetic, psychological, familial, and social–cultural factors that shape development over time (Gottlieb & Willoughby, 2006; Rutter & Sroufe, 2000).

Adaptive vs. Maladaptive Development

From the perspective of developmental psychopathology, normal and abnormal behavior is determined by the degree to which it promotes children's competence. Behaviors that allow children to develop social, emotional, and behavioral competence over time and meet the changing demands of the environment are regarded as adaptive. Examples of adaptive behavior include toddlers learning to understand other people's emotional states, school-age children learning to think before acting, and adolescents using moral reasoning to solve interpersonal problems. These behaviors are adaptive because they allow children to understand and interact with their environment in effective and flexible ways (Sroufe, 1997).

Behaviors that interfere with children's social, emotional, and behavioral competence or do not meet the changing demands of the environment are regarded as maladaptive behaviors. Examples of maladaptive behaviors

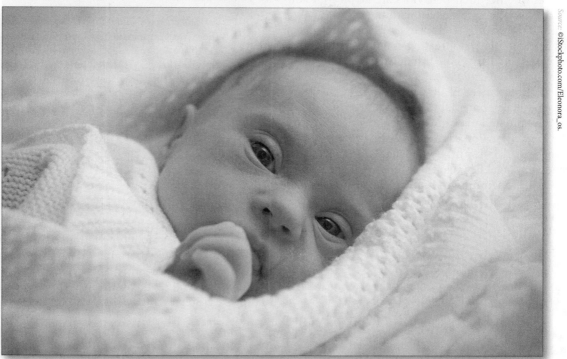

Image 1.4 The development of this infant with Down syndrome will depend on the interaction of biological, psychological, and social-cultural factors over time. Developmental psychopathologists use the term epigenesis to refer to this process.

Source: ©iStockphoto.com/Eleonora_os.

include toddlers who do not understand others' emotional expressions and withdraw from social interactions, school-age children who impulsively hit others when they are angry, and adolescents who fail to show respect to peers. These behaviors are considered maladaptive because they indicate a failure to develop social competencies and they interfere with children's social–emotional well-being (Sroufe, 1997).

Normal behavior is determined by the degree to which children's actions are adaptive, given their age and level of development. Consequently, normality and abnormality are dependent on children's *developmental context*. Consider a 2-year-old child who stubbornly refuses to dress in the morning and tantrums when told that he cannot have cookies for breakfast. Although these oppositional behaviors cause parents grief, they are usually not considered abnormal in 2-year-olds. In fact, defiance and stubbornness can reflect toddlers' developmentally appropriate bids for autonomy. However, the same behaviors shown by a 6-year-old child would likely be considered maladaptive and abnormal. In the context of his age and level of development, these behaviors likely reflect problems balancing needs for autonomy with respect for parental authority (Burt, Coatsworth, & Masten, 2016).

Normal and abnormal behaviors are also determined by the degree to which they are adaptive given the child's surroundings. Consequently, normality and abnormality

are dependent on children's *environmental context*. Consider Xavier, a 13-year-old boy who has a history of running away from home, staying out all night, skipping school, and earning low grades. Clearly, Xavier's behavior is problematic. However, if we discover that Xavier is also experiencing physical abuse at home, we might see how his problematic behavior reflects an attempt to cope with this psychosocial stressor. Specifically, Xavier stays out at night and runs away from home to escape physical maltreatment. Furthermore, he likely has difficulty completing assignments and attending school because of his stressful home environment. Although Xavier's behavior deserves the attention of caring professionals, his actions are best understood in terms of his environmental context.

Developmental psychopathologists view abnormal development as a deviation from normality. Our ability to recognize, understand, and treat childhood disorders depends on our knowledge of normal child development. Consider George, a 14-year-old boy who begins drinking with friends at parties. Approximately once every month for the past 6 months, George has drunk at least five or more alcoholic beverages while partying with friends. He drinks in order to "have fun" and has never gotten into trouble or put himself in dangerous situations while intoxicated. Consider also a 14-year-old girl, Maria, who is dieting to lose weight. Although Maria's weight is average for a girl her age and height, she is very dissatisfied with her body and feels like she needs to lose at least 15 lbs. Whether we regard George and Maria's actions as abnormal depends partially on whether their behaviors are atypical of adolescents their age or inconsistent with the environmental demands they face. Knowledge of normal development can assist us in identifying and treating children's problems.

Developmental psychopathologists also believe that abnormal behavior can shed light on normal child and adolescent development. Youths who clearly show delays in mastering developmental tasks or failures in meeting environmental demands can teach us how development typically proceeds. For example, children with autism show unusual deficits in perceiving and interpreting other people's social behavior. By studying these deficits, researchers are beginning to understand how the ability to process social information develops in typically developing infants and children (Burt et al., 2016; Masten & Cicchetti, 2016).

Review:

- Developmental psychopathologists believe that development is shaped by multiple factors (e.g., biological,

psychological, social), it is probabilistic rather than predetermined, and it is transactional (i.e., the result of factors influencing each other over time).
- Developmental psychopathologists view behavior as either adaptive or maladaptive. Thoughts, feelings, and actions that promote children's competence, and help them meet important developmental tasks, are adaptive.
- Adaptive and maladaptive behaviors can be understood only in the child's developmental and environmental context. A behavior that was adaptive in one situation, or in the past, may be maladaptive in another situation or at another time.

Are Childhood Disorders Stable Over Time?

Developmental Pathways

Developmental psychopathologists liken child development to a journey along a path. Indeed, they often refer to children as following certain developmental pathways, or trajectories, toward either healthy or unhealthy outcomes (Pickles & Hill, 2006). Consider Carter, a boy heading down a problematic developmental pathway (see below).

CASE STUDY

DEVELOPMENTAL PATHWAYS

A Pathway to Trouble

Source: ©iStockphoto.com/luammonino

Carter was a 13-year-old boy who was referred to the psychologist at his school because of fighting. Although Carter's most immediate problem was getting into fights with other boys at lunch and after school, the psychologist knew that Carter's problems began much earlier. As a preschooler, Carter was physically abused by his mother's live-in boyfriend. Like many children who experience maltreatment, Carter developed problems trusting adults—especially men. He was reluctant to develop close emotional ties with others or to rely on others when he was sad, scared, or in need of comfort and reassurance. Instead, Carter became mistrustful of others and often expected others to be angry or hurtful toward him. These early experiences placed him on a developmental path strewn with many obstacles toward a healthy view of himself and others.

Carter's early experience of maltreatment also taught him that physical aggression can be an effective, short-term strategy for expressing anger and solving interpersonal problems. Instead of learning to avoid arguments or to regulate his emotions, Carter tended to solve disputes by yelling, pushing, or punching. These aggressive actions interfered with his ability to develop more adaptive, prosocial problem-solving strategies and led him further along a path to long-term problems.

Now in middle school, Carter has few friends and is actively disliked by most of his peers. Because of his social rejection, Carter spends time with other peer-rejected youths who introduce him to more serious, disruptive behavior: truancy, vandalism, and alcohol use. Carter is following a path blazed by many youths who show conduct problems and antisocial behavior in adolescence.

Luckily, it is not too late for Carter. His school psychologist might help him find ways to reconnect with prosocial peers. Maybe Carter can join a sports team or after-school club? The psychologist might also be able to teach Carter new strategies to regulate his emotions and solve social problems so that he does not have to rely on fighting. Most importantly, perhaps the psychologist's actions and empathy can convince Carter to trust other adults. Interventions like these can help Carter find a new path to adulthood that is characterized by behavioral, social, and emotional competence.

As children grow, they face certain developmental tasks or challenges along their paths (see Table 1.2). These tasks depend largely on the age and developmental level of the child. Erik Erikson (1963) outlined some of the most important social and emotional tasks facing individuals as they progress from infancy through old age. For example, the primary developmental task facing infants is to establish a sense of trust in a loving and responsive caregiver. Infants must expect their caregivers to be sensitive and responsive to their physical, social, and emotional needs and to see themselves as worthy of receiving this care and attention from others. A primary developmental task of adolescence is to establish a sense of identity. Adolescents must develop a coherent sense of self that links childhood experiences with goals for adulthood. Adolescents usually accomplish this task by trying out different social roles during the teenage years.

Developmental tasks present forks in life's path. The child can either successfully master the developmental task or have problems with its successful resolution. Mastery of developmental tasks leads to social, emotional, and behavioral competence, placing children on course for optimal development. For example, infants who establish a sense of basic trust in caregivers may have greater ability to make and keep friends in later childhood (Image 1.5). Unsuccessful resolution of developmental tasks, however, can lead to problems in later development. For example, failure to establish a sense of trust in caregivers during infancy

Table 1.2 Developmental Tasks in Childhood and Adolescence
Infants, Toddlers, and Preschool-Aged Children
• Attachment (basic trust) to one or more specific caregivers
• Learning to sit, stand, walk, and jump
• Acquiring functional language
• Obedience to simple commands and instructions of adults
• Toilet training
• Appropriate play with toys and other people
• Achieving a sense of autonomy from parents
School-Aged Children
• Learning reading, writing, mathematics
• Attending and behaving appropriately at school
• Following rules for behavior at home, at school, and in public places
• Getting along with peers at school
• Making friends with peers
Younger Adolescents
• Attending and behaving appropriately at school
• Learning to solve advanced problems with numbers, algebra
• Learning required language, history, and other subjects
• Completing secondary schooling
• Getting along with peers in school
• Making and maintaining close friendships
• Obeying the laws of society
Older Adolescents
• Working or preparing for future higher education
• If working, behaving appropriately in the workplace
• If in school, meeting academic standards for courses or degrees
• Forming and maintaining romantic relationships
• Obeying the laws of society
• Transitioning from parents, living independently

Source: Based on Masten, Burt, & Coatsworth (2006).

Image 1.5   At each stage of life, children are confronted with developmental tasks that they must master. This infant must develop a sense of trust in her primary caregivers. Mastery of early tasks can set the stage for competence later in development.

Source: ©iStockphoto.com/AngiePhotos

may interfere with children's abilities to develop close peer relationships later in childhood (Masten & Cicchetti, 2016).

Progress along developmental pathways, therefore, builds upon itself over time. Early developmental experiences set the groundwork for later experiences. If children show early social, emotional, and behavioral competence, they can use these early skills to master later developmental tasks. However, failure to master early developmental tasks can interfere with the development of later skills and abilities. For example, a preschool child who learns to control his behavior and emotions during play will likely have an easier time making friends when he enters first grade. However, a preschooler who continues to tantrum or act aggressively when he does not get his way may be ostracized by peers in the first-grade classroom.

To understand the hierarchical nature of development, consider another analogy: Development is like a building. Our genetic endowment might form the foundation of the building, providing us with our physical attributes, raw neurobiological potentials, and behavioral predispositions. The ground floor might consist of early environmental experiences, such as our prenatal surroundings or the conditions of our gestation and delivery. Subsequent floors might consist of postnatal experiences, such as our nutrition and health care, the relationships we develop with our parents, the quality of our education, and the friends we make in school. The integrity of the upper levels of our "building" is partially determined by the strength of the lower levels. For example, problems with the foundation will place additional challenges on the formation of higher levels. However, especially well-developed higher levels can partially compensate for difficulties in the foundation.

The building does not exist in a vacuum, however. The context in which the structure is created is also important.

Just as temperature, wind, and rain can affect the construction of a building, so, too, can the child's social–cultural climate affect his development. Certain social and cultural conditions can promote the child's psychological integrity: high-quality schools, safe neighborhoods, and communities that protect and value children and families. Other social and cultural factors, such as exposure to poverty and crime, can compromise child development.

Continuity vs. Change

When children are first diagnosed with a mental disorder, parents often want to know this: How long will it last? Some disorders tend to be developmentally transient; they rarely persist into adolescence or adulthood. For example, most children with elimination disorders (e.g., bed-wetting and soiling), experience problems only during their school-age years. In contrast, other disorders show homotypic continuity—that is, they persist into adolescence or adulthood relatively unchanged. For example, young children with intellectual disability or autism will likely continue to show these disorders as adults (Maughan & Rutter, 2010).

Most childhood disorders, however, show heterotypic continuity—that is, children's symptoms change over time, but their underlying pattern of behavior remains the same. To understand heterotypic continuity, consider Ben, a 6-year-old boy recently diagnosed with ADHD. Like most young boys with ADHD, Ben's most salient problem is hyperactivity; he frequently leaves his seat during class, talks with his neighbors, and fidgets with his clothes and belongings. By middle school, however, Ben shows more problems with inattention than hyperactivity. He has difficulty staying focused during class, remembering to complete homework assignments, and ignoring distractions during exams. Finally, as a young adult, Ben continues to experience underlying symptoms of ADHD, but he is most bothered by problems with organization, planning, and prioritizing activities at home and at work. Although Ben's most salient symptoms have changed, his underlying problems with attention and inhibition have persisted over time (Barkley, 2016).

Another example of heterotypic continuity can be seen in Emma, an extremely shy preschooler. Approximately 15% of infants inherit a temperament that predisposes them to become shy and inhibited when placed in unfamiliar situations (Fox, Snidman, Haas, Degnan, & Kagan, 2015). Emma, who inherited this tendency, developed extreme anxiety when separated from her mother. She would cry, tantrum, and become physically ill when her mother would leave her at preschool. Although Emma's separation anxiety gradually declined, she began experiencing problems with chronic worrying in middle school. Now, as a young adult, Emma continues to experience problems with both anxiety and depression. Although Emma's symptoms have changed over time, her pattern of underlying distress has persisted into adulthood.

Of course, not all childhood disorders persist into adulthood. Why do some youths show continuity whereas others do not? Developmental psychopathologists are very interested in individual differences in child and adolescent development—that is, they want to discover what causes children's divergent developmental outcomes. Predicting individual differences in development is extremely difficult because, as we have seen, many factors interact over time to affect children's outcomes. The interactions between factors, over time, produce two phenomena: equifinality and multifinality (Hinshaw & Beauchaine, 2015).

Equifinality occurs when children with different developmental histories show similar developmental outcomes. For example, imagine that you are a psychologist who conducts evaluations for a juvenile court. As part of your duties, you assess adolescent boys who have been arrested and convicted of illegal activities, such as theft, assault, and drug use, in order to make recommendations to the court regarding probation and treatment. All of the boys that you assess have similar developmental outcomes—that is, they all show conduct problems. However, after interviewing many of the boys, you discover that their developmental histories are quite different. Some boys have long histories of antisocial behavior, beginning in early childhood. Other boys have no histories of conduct problems until their recent arrest. Still other boys' conduct problems are limited to times when they were using drugs and alcohol. Your discovery illustrates the principle of equifinality in child development: There are many different paths to the same developmental outcome (see Figure 1.5).

The principle of multifinality refers to the tendency of children with similar early experiences to show different social, emotional, and behavioral outcomes. For example, imagine that you are a clinical social worker who evaluates children who have been physically abused. During the course of your career, you have assessed a number of children who have been abused by their caregivers. You notice, however, that some of these children show long-term emotional and behavioral problems while others seem to show few adverse effects. Your observation reflects the principle of multifinality: Children with similar early experiences show different outcomes.

The principle of equifinality makes definitive statements about the *causes* of psychopathology extremely difficult. Because of equifinality, we usually cannot infer the causes of children's problems based on their current symptoms. For example, many people incorrectly believe that all adolescents who sexually abuse younger children were, themselves, sexually abused in the past. In actuality, adolescents engage in sexual abuse for many reasons, not only because they were victimized themselves.

The principle of multifinality limits the statements we can make about children's *prognoses*. For example, many people erroneously believe that if a child has been sexually abused, she is likely to exhibit a host of emotional

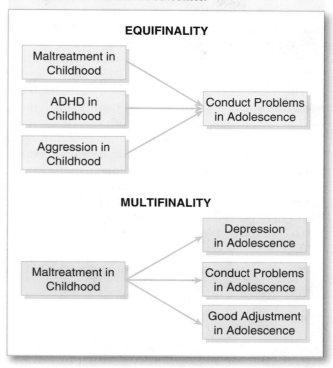

Figure 1.5   Equifinality occurs when children with different histories show the same outcomes; multifinality occurs when children with the same histories show different outcomes.

and behavioral problems later in life, ranging from sexual deviancy and aggression to depression and anxiety. In fact, the developmental outcomes of boys and girls who have been sexually abused vary considerably. Some children show significant maladjustment while others show few long-term effects. Their diversity of outcomes illustrates the difficulty in making predictions regarding development (Hinshaw & Beauchaine, 2015).

Summary:

- Developmental pathways reflect the manner by which children face important developmental tasks over time. Common developmental tasks include establishing a sense of trust (in infancy), developing basic academic competence (in elementary school), and forming close friendships (in adolescence).
- Mastery of early developmental tasks (e.g., trust in infancy) can promote mastery in later developmental tasks (e.g., friendships in adolescence).
- Some disorders, such as autism, show homotypic continuity; they remain relatively stable over time. Most disorders, such as anxiety and mood disorders, show heterotypic continuity; the overt signs and symptoms of the disorder change over time, but the underlying problem remains relatively constant.
- Equifinality occurs when children with different histories show the same outcomes; multifinality occurs when children with the same histories show different outcomes.

What Determines the Course of Children's Development?

What explains equifinality and multifinality? Why is there such great variability in children's developmental pathways? The answer is that child development is multiply determined by the complex interplay of genetic, biological, psychological, familial, and social–cultural factors. Some of these factors promote healthy, adaptive development, whereas other factors increase the likelihood that children will follow less-than-optimal, more maladaptive, developmental trajectories.

Developmental psychopathologists use the term *risk factors* to describe influences on development that interfere with the acquisition of children's competencies or compromise children's ability to adapt to their environments. Risk factors occur across levels of functioning: They can be genetic, biological, psychological, familial, or social–cultural (Cicchetti, 2016a; Luthar, 2006).

In general, the more risk factors experienced by children, the greater their likelihood of developing a mental disorder. In one study, researchers counted the number of environmental risks experienced by a large sample of adolescents (McLaughlin et al., 2012). Approximately 58% of adolescents experienced at least one risk factor such as parental divorce (28%), parental mental illness (16%), or economic hardship (16%). Regardless of race, ethnicity, or gender, the more risks experienced, the greater the likelihood of a mental disorder. Certain risk factors were especially predictive of mental health problems, such as parental criminal involvement, parental mental health problems, family violence, and child maltreatment.

It is noteworthy, however, that not all youths who experience these risk factors develop mental disorders. Psychologists use the term *protective factors* to refer to influences on development that buffer the negative effects of risks on children's development and promote adaptive functioning (see Table 1.3).

Table 1.3 Some Risk and Protective Factors in Childhood and Adolescence

Level	Possible Risk Factors	Possible Protective Factors
Genetic	• Genetic disorders • Genetic predisposition toward behavioral, cognitive, emotional, or social problems	• Genetic screening to identify potential problems • Genetic predisposition toward behavioral, cognitive, emotional, or social competence
Biological	• Inadequate prenatal health care • Complications during pregnancy or delivery • Inadequate postnatal health care, immunizations • Malnutrition • Exposure to environmental toxins, teratogens • Childhood illness or injury • Abnormalities in brain development • Speech, language, vision, hearing problems	• Good access to prenatal and postnatal care • High-quality nutrition • Early recognition of medical and developmental delays or deficits • Early intensive treatment for medical problems and developmental delays
Psychological	• Cognitive delays or deficits • Hyperactivity, inattention, learning problems • Problems regulating emotions • Problems in social interactions	• Enriched learning, environmental experiences • High-quality special educational services • Help from therapist, school counselor, parents to remedy problems in emotional control or social functioning
Familial	• Parental death, separation, or abandonment • Parental divorce, marital conflict • Cold, distant, intrusive, or harsh parenting • Child abuse or neglect • Placement into foster care, group home • Parental substance abuse or mental illness • Parental antisocial behaviors	• Close relationship with at least one caregiver • Sensitive, responsive parenting behavior • Consistent use of parental discipline • Adequate parental monitoring • Good relationships with peers, extended kin • Adoption by loving parents
Social–Cultural	• Low socioeconomic status (SES) • Dangerous, high-crime neighborhood • Inadequate educational opportunities • Rejected by peers or association with deviant peers • Discrimination	• Peer acceptance, close friends • Involvement in prosocial activities (e.g., sports, clubs) • Relationships with adult mentors (e.g., coaches) • Adequate educational opportunities

Source: Adapted from Hayden and Mash (2013).

Diverging Developmental Paths

Source: ©iStockphoto.com/Feverpitched

Ramon and Rafael are brothers growing up in the same low-income, high-crime neighborhood. Ramon, the older brother, begins showing disruptive behavior at a young age. He is disrespectful to his mother, defiant toward his teachers, and disinterested in school. By late elementary school, he has been suspended a number of times for fighting and being truant. In junior high school, Ramon associates with peers who introduce him to other antisocial behaviors, such as shoplifting and breaking into cars. By adolescence, Ramon rarely attends school and earns money selling drugs. At 15, Ramon is removed from his mother's custody because of his antisocial behavior and truancy.

Rafael, the younger brother, also shows early problems with defiance and aggression. However, these problems do not persist beyond the early elementary school years. Although Rafael does not enjoy school, he befriends an art teacher who recognizes his talent for drawing. The teacher offers to tutor him in art and help him show his work. Rafael also takes art classes at a local community center to learn new mediums. Through these classes, he meets other adolescents interested in drawing and painting. Rafael's grades in high school are generally low; however, he excels in art, music, and draftsmanship. He graduates with his class and studies interior design at community college.

Like risk factors, protective factors can occur across the genetic, biological, psychological, familial, or social–cultural levels. For example, parental divorce is a risk factor for the development of behavioral and emotional disorders in young children, especially in families experiencing chronic stress and economic adversity (Hetherington, 2014). However, certain factors protect children of divorcing parents from developing problems. These protective factors include the child's temperament or innate emotional disposition (a biological factor), the quality of the parent–child relationship (a familial factor), and the degree to which parents can rely on others for social and tangible support (a social–cultural factor).

The salience of a risk factor depends on the child's age, gender, level of development, and environmental context. For example, child sexual abuse is a risk factor for later psychosocial problems. However, the effects of sexual abuse depend on the gender of the child and the age at which the abuse occurs. Boys often show the greatest adverse effects of sexual victimization when they are abused in early childhood, whereas girls often show the poorest developmental outcomes when abuse occurs during early adolescence.

Similarly, the ability of protective factors to buffer children from the harmful effects of risk depends on context. For example, many children who experience sexual abuse report considerable psychological distress and show marked behavioral impairment. However, children who are able to rely on a caring, nonoffending parent are often able to cope with this stressor more effectively

than youths without the presence of a supportive parent (Heflin & Deblinger, 2003).

Protective factors are believed to promote resilience in youths at risk for maladaptive development. Resilience refers to the tendency of some children to develop social, emotional, and behavioral competence despite the presence of multiple risk factors (Hayden & Mash, 2014). Consider the case of Ramon and Rafael (above), two brothers growing up in the same impoverished, high-crime neighborhood but experiencing different outcomes.

What accounts for Ramon's struggles and Rafael's resilience? Although there is no easy answer, a partial explanation might be the presence of protective factors at just the right time in Rafael's development. Ramon's path to antisocial behavior was probably facilitated by peers who introduced him to criminal activities. In contrast, Rafael's peer group encouraged prosocial activities and the development of artistic competence. If Rafael's teacher did not encourage the development of his art talents until later in Rafael's development, perhaps after he developed friendships with deviant peers, would he have followed the same developmental pathway as Ramon? Although we do not know for sure, we can speculate that these protective factors played an important role in his ability to achieve despite multiple risks (Masten & Cicchetti, 2016).

Most protective factors occur spontaneously: A teacher nurtures a special talent in an at-risk youth, a coach encourages a boy with depression to join a team, or a girl who has been abused is adopted by loving parents. Sometimes, however, protective factors are planned to

A PORTRAIT OF RESILIENCE

Malala Yousafzai

Source: Photo courtesy of Wikimedia Commons: UK Department for International Development.

Malala was a Sunni Muslim girl living in the Swat Valley of Pakistan. As a child, Malala's region was invaded by the Taliban, a religious extremist group. The Taliban killed more than 2,000 people in her region and initiated a war with the Pakistani army that brought chaos to the area. The Taliban also prohibited television, music, and the education of girls and women.

With the help of her parents, Malala became a human rights advocate, speaking out against the Taliban. In her first speech, 11-year-old Malala questioned, "How dare the Taliban take away my basic right to education?" Several months later, she began writing a blog that described her experiences living under Taliban oppression:

I had a terrible dream yesterday with military helicopters and the Taliban. I have had such dreams since the launch of the military operation in Swat. My mother made me breakfast and I went off to school. I was afraid of going to school because the Taliban had issued an edict banning all girls from attending schools. Only 11 students attended the class out of 27. The number decreased because of Taliban's edict.

Malala's activism angered the Taliban. In 2012, a Taliban gunman shot her three times as she traveled to school. After her recovery, Malala continued to advocate for female education and human rights. She received the Nobel Peace Prize in 2014, at the age of 17, making her the youngest recipient of that award.

---

prevent the emergence of disorders. For example, communities may offer free infant and toddler screenings to identify children with developmental disabilities at an early age. Identification of developmental delays in infancy or toddlerhood can lead to early intensive intervention and better prognosis. Similarly, schools may offer prevention programs for girls who might develop eating disorders. Volunteers might teach girls about healthy eating, risks of dieting, and stress management. Even psychotherapy can be seen as a protective factor. Therapy helps children and adolescents alter developmental trajectories away from maladaption and toward adaptation (Masten & Cicchetti, 2016). Consider Malala Yousafzai, a girl who demonstrated remarkable resilience in the face of incredible risks (see above).

As we have seen, developmental psychopathology is an emerging approach to understanding abnormal child behavior in the context of normal child development, in relation to the environment, and across time. Developmental psychopathology offers a rich and multifaceted perspective on abnormal child psychology across a number of different levels: genetic, biological, psychological, familial, and social–cultural. Throughout this book, we will use the principles of developmental psychopathology to explore the causes and treatment of child and adolescent disorders across these levels and within various developmental contexts.

Review:

- Risk factors are influences that interfere with the acquisition of children's competencies or children's ability to adapt to their surroundings. Protective factors are influences that buffer children from these risks.
- Resilience occurs when children develop behavioral, emotional, and social competencies despite the presence of multiple risk factors.

1.4 INTEGRATING SCIENCE AND PRACTICE

What Is Evidence-Based Practice?

Definition

Imagine that you experience unusual pain in your stomach that does not go away with the help of over-the-counter medication. You make an appointment with your physician in the hope that she might be able to identify the cause of your ailment and prescribe an effective treatment. You would hope that your physician's assessment, diagnostic, and treatment strategies are evidence-based—that is, that they reflect the scientific research and best available practice (Rousseau & Gunia, 2016).

Psychologists and other mental health professionals who work with children and families also strive for evidence-based practice. According to the American Psychological Association (APA; Brown et al., 2008), evidence-based practice is "the integration of the best available research with clinical expertise in the context of patient characteristics, culture, and preferences." The purpose of evidence-based practice is to deliver the highest-quality mental health services to children, adolescents, and families and to promote mental health in the community (Hamilton, Daleiden, et al., 2015).

Clinicians who adopt an evidence-based approach to their practice consider the following three factors:

1. Scientific research: According to the research literature, what methods of assessment and forms of treatment work best for a child with this disorder?

2. Clinical expertise: According to my own professional experience and judgment, what is the best way for me to assess and treat this child?

3. Patient characteristics: How might the child's age, gender, and sociocultural background, or the family's expectations and preferences for therapy, affect the way I help them?

Evidence-based practice, therefore, begins with consideration of the scientific research literature. If parents request treatment for their son with ADHD, which form of treatment is most likely to be helpful? Fortunately, professional organizations have identified various evidence-based treatments that have been shown in research studies to reduce children's symptoms and improve their functioning. For example, the Society of Clinical Child and Adolescent Psychology (2016) maintains an excellent website, effectivechildtherapy.org, that describes the most efficacious psychosocial treatments for childhood disorders. Similarly, the American Academy of Child and Adolescent Psychiatry (2016) issues guidelines to help physicians identify medications and psychosocial treatments that are effective for childhood disorders.

Evidence-based treatments are typically categorized into one of five levels, depending on how well they are supported by research (Southam-Gerow & Prinstein, 2014). Figure 1.6 shows each level and its degree of research support. For example, behavior parent training is a "well-established" treatment for children with ADHD; it has been shown to reduce symptoms in several randomized controlled studies. Behavior parent training, in which parents learn to monitor their children's behavior and reinforce appropriate actions, is considered a first-line psychosocial treatment. Neurofeedback training, on the other hand, is considered "possibly efficacious" because it has less empirical support. Although one large and well-designed study suggests that this treatment can help children regulate brain activity and behavior, the study needs to be replicated before it can be considered a first-line treatment. Finally, the research literature suggests that social skills training is not effective in reducing children's

ADHD symptoms. Most children with ADHD already know how to behave in social situations; their main problem is inhibiting their behavior long enough to implement this knowledge (Evans, Owens, & Bunford, 2014).

Evidence-based practice does not simply mean using evidence-based treatments. Clinicians must also use their expertise and experience to tailor interventions to meet the social–emotional needs of children and families. For example, imagine that a mother brings her son with ADHD to their first therapy session. The therapist might initially decide to use behavior parent training. However, the therapist soon senses that the mother needs time in the initial session to describe her own frustration with her son's behavior and her ex-husband's lack of interest in sharing caregiving responsibilities. The skillful therapist knows that evidence-based treatments must be modified to meet the immediate needs of families. Consequently, the therapist might see her initial goal as providing empathy and building an alliance with a mother who feels powerless or isolated as a caregiver (Rajwan, Chacko, Wymbs, & Wymbs, 2014).

Finally, evidence-based practice requires clinicians to consider the characteristics and sociodemographic backgrounds of the children and families they serve (Gonzales, Lau, Murray, Pina, & Barrera, 2016). For example, therapists sometimes have difficulty engaging fathers in parent training. Consequently, researchers have modified traditional parent training to better address the interests of fathers. A treatment called COACHES (Coaching Our Acting-Out Children: Heightening Essential Skills) allows fathers to practice parent management techniques as they play soccer with their children (see Image 1.6). Several studies show that the COACHES program not only engages fathers who might otherwise avoid therapy but also improves children's behavior on the playing field and at home (Isaacs, Webb, Jerome, & Fabiano, 2015).

Importance

Evidence-based practice is important to provide effective, ethical care to children and families (Society of Clinical Child and Adolescent Psychology, 2016). Ethics refers to the principles and standards of a profession that (1) ensure high-quality care and (2) protect the rights and dignity of others (Hill, 2014). Two important ethical principles in psychology are *beneficence* and *nonmaleficence*. Beneficence is the ethical principle that guides psychologists to help and promote the welfare of others. Nonmaleficence is the related principle that instructs psychologists to "do no harm" (APA, 2010). Evidence-based practice is important because it increases the likelihood that psychologists' interventions will be helpful and decreases the likelihood that their actions will be harmful (Hamilton, Daleiden, et al., 2015).

Evidence-based practice is also important to the scientific practice of psychology. Psychology is a science that

1. Well-Established Treatment

At least two, large randomized controlled studies, conducted by independent researchers, showing treatment is better than placebo or an existing treatment

2. Probably Efficacious Treatment

At least two, large randomized controlled studies showing treatment is better than placebo or an existing treatment

3. Possibly Efficacious (Promising) Treatment

At least one, well-designed study showing treatment is better than no treatment; or, several studies with methodological limitations

4. Experimental Treatment

At least one study showing treatment is helpful, but with methodological limitations

5. Ineffective Treatment

Treatment does not work better than no treatment or is harmful

has its roots in empirical evidence and objective evaluation (McFall, 1991). Indeed, the distinction between psychological science and clinical practice is artificial. The only way clinicians can help their clients in a competent and ethical manner is to base their interventions on the research literature and on empirical investigation. Before practicing any form of assessment or treatment, clinicians must ask, "What is the empirical evidence supporting my practice?" Whenever possible, clinicians must rely on assessment strategies and therapy techniques that have scientific support.

Unfortunately, some clinicians do not ground their interventions in the research literature or empirical data (Garb & Boyle, 2004). Instead, they may base their clinical practice on other factors, including theory, clinical experience, and anecdotal information provided by others. Although theories, experience, and anecdotes can

be useful when combined with empirical evidence, they are insufficient guides for clinical practice by themselves. Psychological scientists believe that empirical data provide the best evidence either for or against specific clinical interventions.

Without empirical data, clinicians might intervene in ways that are not effective. Ineffective interventions can harm clients and their families in at least three ways. First, ineffective interventions can *cost significant time and money*—resources that might be better spent participating in treatment with more empirical support. For example, available treatments for childhood disorders include listening to certain types of music, wearing special glasses, taking large doses of vitamins, avoiding certain textured foods, riding on horseback, swimming with dolphins, reenacting the birth experience, and doing a host of other therapies with little systematic support. Although most of

Image 1.6 COACHES is an evidence-based treatment designed specifically for fathers of young children. The best evidence-based treatments are tailored to meet the needs of children and families.

Source: ©monkeybusinessimages

these interventions do not cause physical or psychological harm to clients, they can cost significant time, energy, and money. Furthermore, when insurance companies compensate individuals for participating in these therapies, resources available for more evidence-based interventions are diminished.

Second, families who participate in ineffective treatment can *lose hope* in the therapeutic process and in psychological treatment more generally. For example, many parents of oppositional and defiant children seek help to manage their children's behavior. Although a number of well-supported interventions exist to treat children's disruptive behavior, many families are given therapy that lacks empirical support. Consequently, families meet with limited success. As a result, many parents come to believe that psychological interventions will not help their children. Some parents simply give up on treatment.

Third, interventions that lack empirical support *can be harmful* to clients, families, and society. The history of psychology is marked by examples of clinicians harming individuals and society by practicing without empirical basis. Perhaps nowhere is this more obvious than in the treatment of autism. In the 1960s, Bruno Bettelheim suggested that autism was caused by parents who were cold and rejecting toward their children. Bettelheim's erroneous theory placed unnecessary blame on parents and resulted in a host of interventions that were completely ineffective at alleviating autistic symptoms.

Later, sociologist Douglas Biklen (1993) recommended that individuals with autism and severe intellectual disability might be able to communicate with others if facilitated by a trained therapist. The subsequent practice of "facilitated communication" involved the therapist guiding the client's hand as the client supposedly typed messages on a keyboard. In one case, a client participating in facilitated communication supposedly reported that he had been abused by his family. As a result, the client was removed from his family's custody, despite no corroborating evidence of maltreatment. Later, the technique of facilitated communication was discredited by showing that the messages typed by clients actually reflected knowledge and information provided by therapists, not by the individuals with developmental disabilities themselves.

Even more recently, physician Andrew Wakefield and colleagues (1998) suggested that the measles, mumps, and rubella (MMR) vaccine caused autism in some children susceptible to the disorder. Although his assertion was unfounded, it caused a dramatic reduction in the percentage of vaccinated children in the United States and a dangerous increase in these childhood illnesses (Taylor, Swerdfeger, & Eslick, 2014). Even today, 57% of parents have concerns that vaccinations cause autism and 2% to 3% of parents refuse to vaccinate their children because of these concerns (Miller, 2015; Smith et al., 2011; see Image 1.7).

Psychologists and other mental health professionals who are engaged in evidence-based practice approach their professional activities using the principles of psychological science. From this perspective, clinical work is analogous to a research study in which the practitioner's sample size consists of one individual (i.e., the client). The clinician generates hypotheses about the source of the client's problem and the best form of treatment, based on data gathered from the client and information presented in the research literature. Then, the clinician administers treatment and evaluates the client's outcomes using objective criteria. Finally, the clinician modifies her intervention based on information from the client and his family, in order to improve effectiveness.

Psychological science informs clinical practice by helping psychologists use the most accurate assessment techniques and effective therapeutic methods possible. At the same time, the practice of assessment and therapy guides research by helping scientists focus their efforts on discovering principles and practices that have real-world applications (Drabick & Goldfried, 2000).

Review:

- Evidence-based practice refers to the integration of high-quality research and clinical expertise to promote the welfare of children and families, in the context of their characteristics, culture, and preferences for treatment.
- Evidence-based treatments have been shown in high-quality research studies to be efficacious in reducing children's problems and improving their functioning.
- Evidence-based practice is important because it increases the likelihood that clinicians will be helpful to their clients while avoiding harm. Evidence-based practice is also essential to the scientific practice of psychology, a discipline based on empirical evidence and objective evaluation.

Image 1.7   The claim that the MMR vaccine causes autism has been discredited. Nevertheless, approximately 2% to 3% of parents refuse to vaccinate their infants.

Source: ©bowdenimages

How Can Students Help Children in an Evidence-Based Manner?

Psychology students often find themselves providing services to children and adolescents in distress. Students sometimes act as aides for individuals with developmental disabilities; behavior therapists for youths with autism; tutors for children with learning disabilities; or psychological technicians in residential treatment facilities, juvenile detention centers, and hospitals. Students can also provide paraprofessional services through volunteer experiences. For example, many students mentor at-risk youths, provide in-services to grade school and high school students, monitor telephone crisis hotlines, and help local community mental health centers.

Because students often provide frontline services, they have enormous potential for improving the functioning of children, adolescents, and families. However, students can also contribute to the propagation of inaccurate information and the dissemination of ineffective and unsupported treatments. Although psychology students are not in a position to direct interventions, they can approach treatment from the perspective of psychological science. Specifically, students can ask the following questions:

1.   What is the evidence for the intervention or service that I am providing? Is there a theoretical and empirical basis for my work? Are there alternative services that might provide greater benefits to the people I serve?

2.   Am I effective? Am I monitoring the effectiveness of the services I provide to determine whether I am helping my clients? Is there any possibility that I might be harming them?

3.   Am I providing ethical, time-effective, and cost-effective services? During my work, do I respect the rights and dignity of others, conduct myself in a responsible and professional manner, and represent the field of psychology with integrity? Are my activities being supervised by someone who practices in an ethical and scientifically mindful manner?

As you read this book, consider how you might use the empirical literature to inform your own understanding of child and adolescent disorders. A scientific approach to child psychopathology is not reserved for licensed psychologists or university professors. Instead, all students, parents, teachers, and individuals who work with youths are called upon to use empirical data to help improve the functioning of others.

Review:

- Students often find themselves providing services to children in need. They can rely on evidence-based practice to guide their work in a scientific and ethical fashion.

Adaptive behavior: Thoughts, feelings, and actions that allow children to develop social, emotional, and behavioral competence over time and meet the changing demands of the environment

Comorbidity: The presentation of two or more disorders in the same person at the same time

Developmental pathways: Possible courses or trajectories of children's behavioral, cognitive, or social–emotional development over time, ranging from adaptation to maladaptation

Developmental psychopathology: A multidisciplinary approach to studying adaptive and maladaptive development across the life span. According to this perspective, development is shaped by the complex interaction of biological, psychological, and social–cultural factors over time

Diagnostic and Statistical Manual of Mental Disorders, Fifth Edition (DSM-5): A compendium of mental disorders and diagnostic criteria adopted by the American Psychiatric Association and used by most professionals in the United States

Epidemiologists: Scientists who study the prevalence of medical and psychological disorders in the general population

Equifinality: Describes the phenomenon in which children with different developmental histories show similar developmental outcomes

Ethics: Principles and standards of a profession that ensure high-quality care and protect the rights and dignity of others

Evidence-based practice: The integration of empirical research with clinical expertise to help children and families in the context of their characteristics, culture, and preferences

Evidence-based treatments: Psychotherapies and medications that have been shown in well-designed research studies to reduce children's symptoms and improve their functioning

Harmful dysfunction: A definition of abnormal behavior characterized by (1) a failure in some internal mechanism to perform a function for which it was naturally selected and (2) the failure causes harm

Heterotypic continuity: The phenomenon in which symptoms change over time, but their underlying pattern remains the same (e.g., a boy's ADHD symptoms change from childhood to adulthood, but he still has underlying problems with inhibition)

Homotypic continuity: The phenomenon in which disorders persist over time relatively unchanged (e.g., a boy with intellectual disability continues to have this disorder as an adult)

Incidence: The percentage of new cases of a disorder in a discrete period of time, usually 1 year

Individual differences: Deviations among children on some psychological attribute, behavior, or disorder

Maladaptive behaviors: Thoughts, feelings, and actions that interfere with children's social, emotional, and behavioral competence or do not meet the changing demands of the environment

Mental disorder: "A syndrome characterized by clinically significant disturbance in an individual's cognition, emotion regulation, or behavior that reflects a dysfunction in the psychological, biological, or developmental processes underlying mental functioning" (DSM-5)

Multifinality: Describes the phenomenon in which children with similar early experiences show different social, emotional, and behavioral outcomes

Prevalence: The percentage of individuals in a given population who have a medical or psychological condition

Probabilistic epigenesis: A principle of developmental psychopathology; refers to the manner in which genetic, biological, and social–cultural factors interact over time to influence (but not absolutely determine) development

Protective factors: Influences on development that buffer the negative effects of risks on children's development and promote adaptive functioning

Psychotropic medications: Prescription drugs used to treat psychological disorders, such as anxiety, depression, and schizophrenia

Resilience: The tendency of some children to develop social, emotional, and behavioral competence despite the presence of multiple risk factors

Risk factors: Influences on development that interfere with the acquisition of competencies or compromise children's ability to adapt to their environments

Socioeconomic status (SES): A composite variable that reflects three aspects of a child's environment: (a) parents' levels of education, (b) parents' employment, and (c) family income

Stigma: Negative beliefs that can lead to fear, avoidance, and discrimination by others or shame and low self-worth in oneself

CRITICAL THINKING EXERCISES

1. According to *DSM-5*, a mental disorder is a pattern of behavior characterized by distress or disability (impairment) that resides within the individual. What might be some limitations to this definition of "mental disorder"—especially when it is applied to children and adolescents?

2. Approximately 50% of youths in the general population who have a mental disorder have at least one other comorbid condition. However, the prevalence of comorbidity among children referred to mental health clinics is much higher—between 70% and 80%. What might explain this difference?

3. Mrs. Johnson referred her 5-year-old son, Billy, to a psychologist because Billy showed problems with oppositional and defiant behavior (e.g., crying, throwing tantrums, sassing back). The psychologist observed Mrs. Johnson and Billy during a 20-minute play session in the clinic. During the session, Mrs. Johnson repeatedly yelled at Billy, threatened to spank him, and lost her temper. How might Billy's behavior problems be explained by the *transaction* between Billy and his mother?

4. Vincente is a 14-year-old boy who was sent to the emergency department (ED) of a children's hospital following a suicide attempt. Vincente, a recent immigrant, does not speak English. After Vincente was medically stable, the psychologist at the hospital interviewed him through a translator, in order to determine whether he met diagnostic criteria for depression or another mental disorder. If you were the psychologist, what considerations might you keep in mind while interviewing Vincente?

5. Why do developmental psychopathologists describe children's behavior as "adaptive" or "maladaptive" rather than as "good" or "bad?"

TEST YOURSELF AND EXTEND YOUR LEARNING

Videos, flash cards, and links to online resources for this chapter are available to students online. Teachers also have access to PowerPoint slides to guide lectures, case studies to prompt classroom discussions, and exam questions. Visit www.abnormalchildpsychology.org.

iStockphoto.com/Liderina

CHAPTER 2

The Causes of Childhood Disorders

A Levels of Analysis Approach

LEARNING OBJECTIVES

After reading this chapter, you should be able to do the following:

2.1. Explain how genetic and epigenetic factors can contribute to the emergence of childhood disorders.

2.2. Describe the structure and function of major brain regions and their relationship to childhood disorders.

2.3. Use learning theory to explain how certain childhood disorders develop and are maintained over time.

2.4 Explain the importance of social cognition and emotion regulation in children's development.

2.5. Understand the way parents, families, and friends can contribute to childhood problems or protect youths from developing disorders.

2.6. Analyze the way social and cultural factors can influence child development proximally and distally.

There is an old story about six blind men who came upon an elephant. Each man touched a different part of the beast in order to determine what it was. The man who felt a leg said the elephant is like a pillar; the one who felt the tail said the elephant is like a rope; the man who felt the ear said the elephant is like a fan, and so on (see).

The men quarrelled with each other over the identity of the elephant until the king, who was not blind, approached and said, "All of you are right, but only partially. The reason for your disagreement is that each of you is touching a different part of the animal. You must work together to get the complete picture."

Like the men in the story, psychologists can try to understand childhood disorders using a range of approaches. Some psychologists study the biological underpinnings of behavior; others focus on children's thoughts or emotions; and still others investigate the impact of family, friends, or society on development. Although each approach is helpful, it yields only part of the picture. For example, a psychologist who tries to understand autism spectrum disorder (ASD) in terms of genetics or brain abnormalities alone, ignores the role conscientious parents and high-quality schools can play in the developmental outcomes of children with that condition. Conversely, a psychologist who looks for the causes of eating disorders in the way the media portray women, may overlook the way operant conditioning can be used to explain dangerous behaviors like bingeing and purging. Children's disorders are complex and multiply determined; they can be most fully understood using multiple perspectives.

Developmental psychopathologists study the potential causes of childhood disorders from multiple levels of analysis. These levels include children's (1) genes; (2) brain structure and functioning; (3) psychological processes—that is, their thoughts, feelings, and actions; (4) family environment; and (5) broader social–cultural experiences. Researchers must integrate data from multiple levels to understand children's disorders and find the best way to treat them (Hinshaw & Beauchaine, 2015). Because the research methods and theories differ at each level, it can be difficult for professionals who study abnormal behavior at different levels to communicate with one another. It can be even more challenging

for students, who are new to the field of abnormal child psychology, to understand these diverse approaches.

This chapter is designed to help you understand the causes of children's disorders, by briefly reviewing some of the principles and theories used by researchers who study disorders at each of these levels of analysis. Some concepts, such as classical and operant conditioning, will likely be familiar to you. This chapter will begin to show you how these ideas can be applied to abnormal child psychology. Other concepts, like epigenetics, may be unfamiliar. This chapter will introduce you to these concepts and demonstrate their usefulness in explaining childhood disorders. Altogether, this chapter will lay the groundwork for later sections of this book when we explore the causes of specific disorders.

The theories described in this chapter are supported by decades of empirical research. It is likely that you are already familiar with the basic research designs in psychology, such as experiments and correlational studies. If you'd like a review, you can find a primer on research in abnormal child psychology in the appendix of this book.

2.1 GENETIC AND EPIGENETIC INFLUENCES ON DEVELOPMENT

How Do Genes Affect Development?

Genes, Chromosomes, and Alleles

Our body contains approximately 50 trillion cells; each cell contains our complete genetic code. The code is written using deoxyribonucleic acid (DNA). DNA is shaped like a twisted ladder, or double helix. The "ropes" of the ladder are made

up of sugars (deoxyribose) and phosphates. The "rungs" of the ladder consist of pairs of purine and pyrimidine bases held together by hydrogen bonds. Their structures allow them to combine only in certain ways, forming our unique code (Frommlet, Bogdan, & Ramsey, 2016).

A nucleotide consists of one base pair "rung," a deoxyribose "rope," and a phosphate "rope." Three nucleotides arranged together in the ladder form a trinucleotide, sometimes called a codon. Each trinucleotide instructs the cell to build a specific amino acid. These amino acids are used to build proteins, which form the structure and characteristics of the person. Thousands of trinucleotides form a gene. A single human cell contains approximately 20,000 genes. If the genes in each cell were connected together, end-to-end, they would be approximately two meters long. To save space in the cell, genes wrap around proteins called histones. Histones are important because they can turn genes "on" and "off" by binding to them in certain ways (Rutter & Thapar, 2015).

As you might recall from high school biology class, our genes are organized into strands called chromosomes (see Image 2.2). In typically developing humans, each cell contains 23 pairs of chromosomes, for a total of 46. Twenty-two of these pairs, called autosomes, look the same in both males and females. The 23rd pair, the sex chromosomes, differs in males and females. Females have two X chromosomes, whereas males have one X and one Y chromosome.

Most cells form in a process called *mitosis*. In this process, chromosome pairs split in two and duplicate themselves. Then, the cell divides, forming two cells with 23 pairs of chromosomes each. The resulting (daughter) cells are identical to the original (parent) cell. Each cell contains the entire genetic code, but certain segments of the code are switched on or off, telling the cell its function: to serve as lung tissue, heart tissue, or other parts of the body.

Sex cells (i.e., sperm and ova) form differently, in a process called *meiosis*. Just as in mitosis, chromosome pairs split and duplicate themselves. Unlike in mitosis, however, chromosome pairs line up and exchange genetic material with each other, a process called recombination. Finally, the recombined chromosomes split into two daughter cells that are genetically different from the parent cell and divide again into sex cells. The result is that the sex cells have slightly different genetic information than the parent cells and only one-half the number of chromosomes. When sex cells combine during fertilization, each parent contributes one set of chromosomes and his or her genetic diversity to the offspring (Frommlet et al., 2016).

As we will see in Chapter 4, many genetic disorders arise when problems occur during meiosis. For example, children may inherit too many or two few chromosomes from each parent. Down syndrome typically occurs when children inherit an extra 21st chromosome during fertilization. In other instances, however, parts of chromosomes are lost or rearranged inappropriately during meiosis. For example, a rare disorder known as Williams syndrome

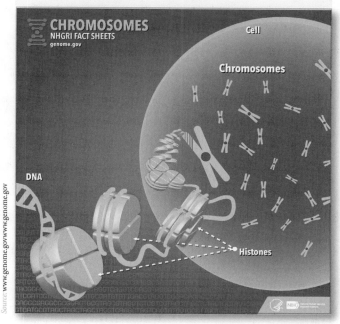

Image 2.2 Each cell contains 23 pairs of chromosomes. Each chromosome contains genes, which consist of DNA and proteins called histones, around which the DNA is wrapped.

(WS) usually occurs when genetic material on the 7th chromosome is accidentally deleted. Children with this condition tend to be extremely friendly and endearing, have trouble with abstract and spatial reasoning, and may experience heart problems (Magee, 2016).

All typically developing people have the same genes; the differences in people's appearance come from slight variations in these genes, called alleles. For example, all people have genes that determine their hair color. Different alleles influence whether someone will be a blonde, redhead, or brunette. These alleles are usually inherited from parents or develop spontaneously as a genetic mutation (Nussbaum, 2016).

Many people erroneously believe that genes determine behavior. For example, newscasters may incorrectly report that researchers have discovered a gene responsible for sexual orientation or a gene that makes people behave aggressively. Nothing could be further from the truth. Genes merely form a blueprint for the body's creation of proteins. Some of these proteins partially determine our hair color, eye color, or skin pigmentation. Others influence our height, body shape, and (sadly) our cholesterol. No gene directs behavior. However, genes can lead to certain structural and functional changes in our bodies that predispose us to behave in certain ways (Jaffee, 2016).

Behavioral Genetics

Behavioral genetics is an area of research that examines the relationship between genes and behavior. Behavioral geneticists use three approaches to identifying the relative contributions of genetic and environmental influences on child development. The first, and simplest, approach is by conducting a *family study*. In a family study, researchers determine whether a certain behavior or mental disorder is shared by members of the same family. If the disorder is partially determined by genetics, biologically related individuals will be affected more frequently than unrelated individuals.

For example, researchers have examined the heritability of children's intelligence using family studies. If we look at the light gray bars on Figure 2.1, we see that the correlation of children's IQ scores is higher among biological relatives than among nonbiological relatives. Behavioral concordance is expressed as the correlation between individuals, ranging from 1.0 (i.e., perfect similarity) to 0 (i.e., no similarity). The mean correlation between two biological siblings' IQ scores is approximately .45, whereas the mean correlation between two unrelated children's IQ scores is only about .27. These findings suggest that genetic factors play a role in children's intelligence.

The primary limitation of family studies is that they do not adequately control for environmental effects. Although it is true that biological relatives share similar genes, they also usually live in similar environments. Most family members share the same house, live in the same neighborhood, enjoy similar pastimes, and come from similar socioeconomic and cultural backgrounds. Therefore, when family studies indicate that closely related relatives are more likely to have a disorder than more distant relatives, we cannot determine whether this similarity is due to common genes or similar environments.

To tease apart the relative effects of genes and environment on behavior, behavioral geneticists conduct *adoption studies*. In an adoption study, researchers examine children who were separated from their biological families shortly after birth. If a behavioral attribute is influenced by genetics, we would expect children to show greater similarity to their biological relatives than to their adoptive relatives.

For example, the mean correlation between parents and their biological children's IQ scores is approximately .40. In contrast, the mean correlation between parents and their adoptive children's IQ scores is only .25. Because children show greater similarity to their biological parents than their adoptive parents, we can conclude that genetic factors play unique roles in the development of children's intelligence.

The primary weakness of adoption studies is that parents who adopt children are often not typical of parents in the general population. Adoption agencies carefully screen prospective adoptive parents before placing a child in their custody. Consequently, adoptive parents are less likely to have mental health problems and are more likely to have higher income and educational backgrounds than other parents. Furthermore, parents who offer their children for adoption often have higher rates of mental illness and come from more disadvantaged backgrounds than parents

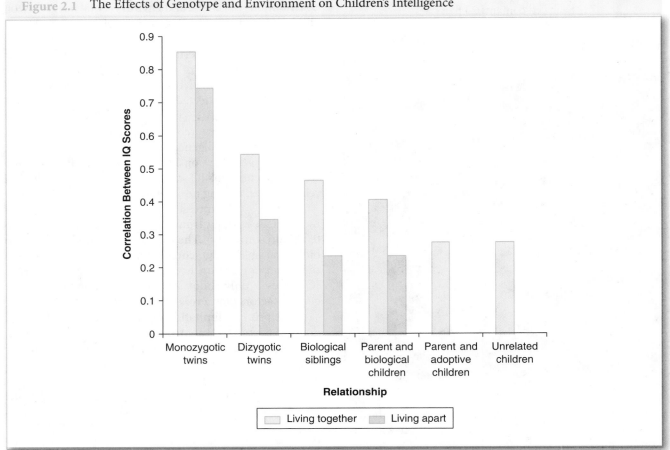

Figure 2.1 The Effects of Genotype and Environment on Children's Intelligence

Correlation Between IQ Scores (y-axis, 0 to 0.9)

Relationship (x-axis): Monozygotic twins, Dizygotic twins, Biological siblings, Parent and biological children, Parent and adoptive children, Unrelated children

Legend: Living together, Living apart

Source: Based on Sattler (2001).

in the general population. These differences between biological and adoptive families may partially account for the greater similarity between children and their biological parents compared to their adoptive parents.

A third way that behavioral geneticists identify the relative contributions of genes and environment on behavior is by conducting a *twin study*. In a twin study, researchers compare the concordance between monozygotic (MZ; identical) and dizygotic (DZ; fraternal) twins. MZ twins are the products of the same egg and sperm cell; consequently, they have 100% genetic similarity. DZ twins are the products of different egg and sperm cells; consequently, they share only 50% of their genes, like other biologically related siblings. The correlation between IQ scores for MZ twins is .85, whereas the correlation for DZ twins is only .55. The higher concordance for MZ twins than DZ twins indicates that intelligence is at least partially genetically determined.

In some cases, twin and adoption studies are combined by examining twins who both live with their biological parents (e.g., the light bars in Figure 2.1) and twins separated at birth (e.g., the dark bars in Figure 2.1). For example, the mean correlation in IQ for MZ twins reared together is .85, whereas the mean correlation for MZ twins reared apart is .75. The high correlations for twins reared together or apart indicate that genetic factors play important roles in the development of intelligence. Even twins separated shortly after birth have remarkably similar IQs.

Behavioral geneticists often divide environmental influences on behavior into two types: shared environmental factors and nonshared environmental factors. Shared environmental factors are experiences common to siblings. For example, siblings usually are reared by the same parents, grow up in the same house, attend the same schools, and belong to the same church. Shared environmental experiences make siblings more alike. In contrast, nonshared environmental factors are experiences that differ among siblings. For example, siblings may have different friends, play different sports, or enjoy different subjects in school. Siblings may also have different types of relationships with their parents. For example, a girl and boy might have different relationships with their father. These nonshared environmental factors often account for more of the variance in children's behavior than do shared experiences. Nonshared environmental factors help to explain why siblings can be so different even though they grow up in the same home (Caspi & Shiner, 2010).

Another way to study the effects of genes on behavior is to examine children's genes at the molecular (rather than the behavioral) level. Recent advances in our knowledge of the human genome and in gene research technology have allowed scientists to search for specific genes that might be partially responsible for certain disorders (Kornilov & Grigorenko, 2016).

Recall that in typically developing individuals, genes show natural variation, called alleles. Molecular geneticists can attempt to link the presence of specific alleles with certain attributes, behaviors, or disorders.

One way to identify which alleles might be responsible for specific disorders is to conduct a *linkage study*. In a linkage study, researchers search the entire genetic structure of individuals (i.e., perform a "genome scan"), looking for the presence of certain alleles and the existence of a specific disorder. If researchers find certain alleles in individuals with the disorder and do not find these alleles in people without the disorder, they hypothesize that the allele is partially responsible for the disorder (Dick & Todd, 2006).

Researchers tend to use linkage studies when they do not know exactly where to look for genes responsible for the disorder. Given the magnitude of the human genome, it is extremely difficult to identify links between certain alleles and specific disorders. However, researchers have successfully used linkage studies to identify alleles responsible for disorders caused by single genes, such as Huntington's disease. Linkage studies have been less successful in identifying the causes of disorders that depend on the presence or absence of multiple genes.

An alternative technique is to conduct an *association study*. In an association study, researchers select a specific gene that they believe might play a role in the emergence of a disorder. Then, they examine whether there is an association between a particular allele of this "candidate" gene and the disorder (Jaffee, 2016).

For example, researchers hypothesized that a specific gene, which affects the neurotransmitter dopamine, might play a role in the development of attention-deficit/hyperactivity disorder (ADHD). They suspected this particular gene because abnormalities in dopamine have been identified as a specific cause for ADHD. Furthermore, medications that affect dopamine in the brain can reduce ADHD symptoms. The researchers identified a group of children with and without ADHD. Then, they examined whether the two groups of children had different alleles for the candidate gene. The researchers found that a certain allele for this gene was much more common among youths with ADHD compared to youths without the disorder. Consequently, they concluded that the gene may be partially responsible for ADHD (Rende & Waldman, 2006).

Of course, molecular genetics research is much more complicated than has been described here. Nearly all mental disorders are influenced by multiple genes; there is almost never a one-to-one relationship between the presence of a specific allele and the emergence of a given disorder. Furthermore, genes never affect behavior directly; their influence on behavior is always influenced by environmental experience (Kornilov & Grigorenko, 2016).

Review:

- Each cell in our body contains 20,000 genes. Genes direct the creation of proteins, which affect the structure and functioning of each person. Genes are organized into 23 pairs of chromosomes.
- Most cells reproduce in a process called mitosis, resulting in identical daughter cells. Sex cells reproduce in a process called meiosis, resulting in daughter cells that are not genetically identical to their parent cell.
- Genes come in different versions, called alleles. The alleles we inherit from our parents can influence our physical attributes (e.g., eye and hair color) as well as our risk for developing certain disorders.
- Behavioral geneticists conduct family, adoption, and twin studies to determine the heritability of intelligence, personality, and disorders.
- Molecular geneticists conduct linkage and association studies to identify specific genes that may underlie certain disorders.

How Do Genes Interact With the Environment to Shape Development?

The Diathesis–Stress Model

Genes guide our maturation, but they do not determine our development. Our genotype refers to the genetic code that we inherit from our parents. In contrast, our phenotype is the observable expression of our genetic endowment. Our phenotype is determined by the complex interaction between our genes and our environment (Caspi & Shiner, 2010).

We should not think of genes and environment as independently influencing children's development. Rather, children's genotype and the quality of their environmental experiences interact over time to shape development (Grigorenko et al., 2016).

The diathesis–stress model can be used to explain the way genes and environments affect development. According to this model, a child exhibits a disorder when an underlying genetic risk for the disorder is triggered by a stressful environmental experience or life event. Both genetic risk and an environmental stressor are necessary for the disorder to emerge; the genetic risk or environmental experience alone is insufficient (Goforth, Pham, & Carlson, 2011).

We can see the usefulness of the diathesis–stress model in a famous study conducted by Avshalom Caspi and colleagues (2003). The researchers followed a large group of children from early childhood through early adulthood in order to examine the relationship between child maltreatment and depression later in life. As we might expect, children exposed to maltreatment were at risk for depression in adulthood. However, whether a maltreated child developed depression depended on his or her genotype.

The results of the study are shown in Figure 2.2. Children who did not experience maltreatment were at low risk for depression later in life, regardless of their genotype. However, children exposed to severe maltreatment displayed different outcomes, depending on their genotypes. Specifically, children who inherited one or two short alleles of the serotonin transporter gene were likely to develop depression in adulthood. Interestingly, this gene regulates the neurotransmitter serotonin, a chemical that plays an important role in mood regulation. The short version of this gene seems to place children at risk for depression if they also experience maltreatment. In contrast, children who inherited two long alleles of the serotonin transporter gene were not more likely to develop depression in adulthood, even if they were exposed to maltreatment. The long version of this gene seems to protect children from the effects of stressful life events.

The diathesis–stress model is especially helpful in explaining multifinality, the tendency of children exposed to the same

environmental stressor to show different developmental outcomes. In Caspi and colleagues' (2003) study, abused and neglected children showed divergent outcomes depending on whether they were at genetic risk for depression.

Gene–Environment Correlation

The diathesis–stress model shows that both genes and environment influence development. A second influential model, developed by Sandra Scarr and Kathleen McCartney (1983), shows genes and environments are not independent. According to the gene–environment correlation model, we sometimes select environments that complement our genotypes. Specifically, there are three types of gene–environment correlations: passive, evocative, and active.

Passive Gene–Environment Correlation

Although our biological parents determine our genotype, they also determine the quality of our early environmental experiences. Our genes and early experiences are related. For example, parents with high intelligence may pass on this genetic predisposition to their children. At the same time, because of their high intelligence and (perhaps) income, these parents have access to higher quality medical care, more nutritious meals, excellent child care, and better schools. Intelligent parents speak and read to their children frequently, provide stimulating educational toys, and take their children on outings to museums and zoos. In this

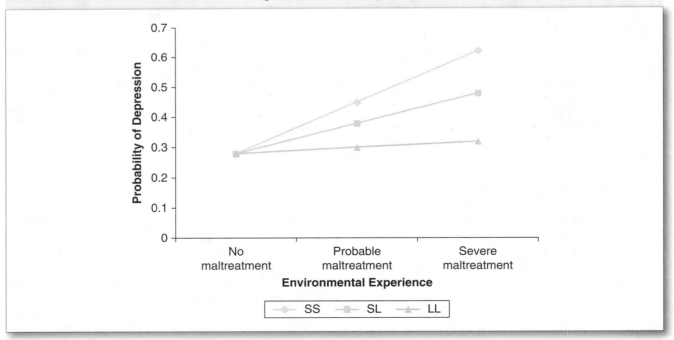

Figure 2.2   Example of the diathesis-stress model. Whether a child developed depression depends on genetic risk (i.e., one or two short alleles of the serotonin transporter gene) and an environmental stressor (i.e., maltreatment). SS = two short alleles, SL = one short, one long allele, LL = two long alleles. Based on Caspi et al. (2003).

manner, their children *passively* receive genotypes and early environmental experiences conducive to high intelligence.

Evocative Gene–Environment Correlation

As children develop, their phenotype gradually emerges from the interaction between their genotype and early environment. Like their parents, they may begin to show signs of above-average intelligence. They show well-developed verbal skills, learn more quickly than their peers, perform more tasks independently, and are curious about a wide range of topics. These behaviors *evoke* certain responses in others. School personnel may identify these children as "gifted" and provide them with more enriched educational experiences. They may be admitted into accelerated classes in high school and gain academic scholarships to highly selective colleges.

Active Gene–Environment Correlation

As children continue to develop, they *actively select* environmental experiences conducive to their genotype. For example, they might develop friendships with other bright children with similar interests and hobbies; seek out extracurricular activities that satisfy their curiosity in science, music, or art; and select challenging but rewarding majors in college. Children's tendency to select environmental experiences conducive to their genotypes is sometimes called niche-picking. As children gain more autonomy, niche-picking plays an increasingly important role in shaping their development. In a sense, youths select their own environments based on the cumulative influence of their genes and early environmental experiences.

Now that you know the basics of gene–environment correlation, consider Kirby (below). Kirby's problems include poor academic skills, disruptive behavior at school, and rejection by peers.

Kirby's problems can be explained using the three types of gene–environment correlation. First, Kirby's parents pass their genes on to him—genes that may have placed him at risk for low academic achievement. Furthermore, his parents also provide him with an early environment that is not conducive to good grades. They may not be able to afford high-quality schools and do not seem involved in his education. Consequently, Kirby struggles with reading and acts out in class.

Second, Kirby's poor academic skills and appearance evoke negative reactions in others. His teacher is frustrated with his antics, and his classmates dislike him.

Finally, Kirby is beginning to actively select surroundings that are conducive to his genes and emerging disruptive behaviors. Rejected by children his age, Kirby associates with older boys who introduce him to smoking cigarettes and drinking alcohol.

If you were Kirby's therapist, how might you use the concept of gene–environment correlation to intervene and help Kirby establish a new developmental trajectory?

CASE STUDY

GENE–ENVIRONMENT CORRELATION

Kirby

Source: ©iStockphoto.com/bodnarchuk

Kirby is a 10-year-old boy who attends the third grade at a local public school. Kirby failed first grade and will likely fail again this year. Kirby's reading is well below average, and he makes frequent mistakes in math. His writing skills are also poor. The school psychologist did not find evidence of a learning disability; however, psychological testing revealed below-average intelligence.

Kirby is frequently disruptive and inattentive during class. His teacher stated that Kirby's parents "just don't care." She has tried to contact his mother by telephone, but she usually does not return her calls and rarely follows through with her suggestions for home tutoring. Kirby will likely be sent to a remedial "special ed" class next year if improvements are not made.

Socially, Kirby is awkward. He is larger and taller than his classmates. He is teased because of his size, his poor grades, and the frequent reprimands he receives from teachers. Classmates also make fun of Kirby because of his name, his old "Wal-Mart clothes," his poorly cut hair, and the fact that he always "smells like hot dogs"—due to his family's wood burning stove.

Kirby has few friends in his class. After school, he often hangs around with older kids at the junior high school. Kirby has been caught smoking on a few occasions and teachers also suspect some alcohol use. He is also beginning to pick on younger children after school.

- The diathesis–stress model posits that both (1) a genetic risk and (2) an environmental stressor are necessary for a disorder to arise. The model is helpful in explaining multifinality—that is, why children with similar genes or experiences have different outcomes.
- The gene–environment correlation model assumes that people's genotypes and their environments are not independent. Sometimes, people actively select environments that are conducive to their genes.
- There are three types of gene–environment correlations: passive, evocative, and active. Their relative importance changes with development.

How Can Epigenetics Help Explain Children's Development?

The diathesis–stress model posits that genes predispose children to certain disorders given the presence of an environmental stressor. Similarly, gene–environment correlations show that our genotypes and our surroundings are not independent; we sometimes select environments that are conducive to our genes. An emerging field called epigenetics shows that environmental factors can also directly affect our genotype, contributing to long-term risk of psychopathology that may be passed on from one generation to the next (Hill & Toth, 2016).

Recall that DNA sequences wrap around histones and other chemical structures in each cell. These histones and chemical structures are not part of the person's genetic code; consequently, scientists call them epigenetic (i.e., above the genome). Epigenetic structures can turn genes "on" or "off" by directing the production of their proteins (see Image 2.3).

Behavioral epigenetics is an emerging field that seeks to understand the relationships between epigenetic structures, the expression of genes, and behavior. Recently, geneticists made two striking discoveries. First, epigenetic structures can change based on experience. Certain environmental factors, such as diet, smoking, and exposure to disease, have been shown to alter structures, leading to different expressions of the genetic code. Second, epigenetic structures are heritable. Although much of the epigenome is reset when parents pass their genes to their children, some structures persist and affect the child's phenotype (Hill & Toth, 2016).

Researchers at McGill University first demonstrated the effects of epigenetics on behavior in rats (Weaver et al., 2004). Rat pups have a certain gene that regulates their stress response. This gene is wrapped tightly around a histone that prevents it from becoming active. The researchers found that nurturing behaviors of the mother toward the pups shortly after birth (e.g., licking, grooming) caused this portion of the gene to unwind from the histone, allowing it to be expressed. When these pups reached adulthood, they

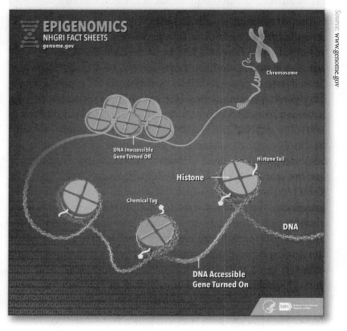

Image 2.3　Behavioral epigenetics helps to explain how histones and other chemical structures, which are not part of the genome itself, affect the expression of individual genes and, ultimately, children's behavior.

Source: www.genome.gov

were better able to cope with stress than rats whose mothers were less nurturing. Subsequent research showed that these epigenetic changes affected the care these rats gave their own offspring, thus passing on this stress response to the next generation of pups (Masterpasqua, 2009).

Researchers are only beginning to understand how epigenetics might help explain the development of disorders in children. In one recent study, researchers examined the caregiving behaviors of three groups of mothers: depressed mothers taking antidepressant medication, depressed mothers not prescribed medication, and non–depressed mothers. As we might expect, depressed mothers (with and without medication) showed more anxious behavior toward their infants than non–depressed mothers. Surprisingly, however, the infants of depressed mothers showed different epigenetic structures than the infants of non–depressed mothers, suggesting that these early caregiving experiences might affect epigenetic activity. Longitudinal research is needed to determine whether these epigenetic changes, brought on by early experience, might affect children's subsequent behavior (Moore, 2015).

Other research has begun to examine the epigenetic structure of children with existing behavior problems. In one of the largest studies so far, researchers examined children and adolescents referred to mental health clinics because of disruptive behavior problems. The researchers found that children's stress hormones and their severity of behavior problems were associated with changes in their epigenetic structure, specifically, structures associated with the expression of the cortisol receptor gene. This finding is interesting because cortisol is the body's main stress hormone; furthermore, the cortisol receptor gene plays a role in regulating the body's stress response. Epigenetic changes to the expression of this gene might underlie some of the problems shown by these youths (Dadds et al., 2016).

Clearly, we are only beginning to appreciate how behavioral epigenetics can help us understand the emergence of childhood disorders. Perhaps equally as important, epigenetic research might someday be helpful in developing medications that can affect epigenetic structures, genetic expression, and behavior (Nigg, 2016b).

Review:

- Epigenetic structures include histones and other chemicals that can turn genes "on" or "off." These structures, which are not part of the child's genotype, can be changed by environmental factors and passed down from one generation to the next.
- Behavioral epigenetics is an emerging field of research that seeks to understand relationships between epigenetic structures and psychological traits or disorders.

2.2 THE BRAIN AND NEUROTRANSMITTERS

How Is Neuroimaging Used to Study Childhood Disorders?

We have witnessed considerable advances in our understanding of brain development in the past 30 years. Beginning in the 1970s, clinicians and researchers used *computed tomography (CT)* to obtain more detailed images of the brain. In CT scanning, multiple images are taken using a movable X-ray device. A computer integrates these images to provide a clearer picture of the brain. Unfortunately, CT scanning, like older X-ray imaging, exposed individuals to radiation. Consequently, it was used sparingly with children.

In the 1980s, a new tool was developed: *magnetic resonance imaging (MRI)*. MRI technology is based on the fact that when body tissues are placed in a strong magnetic field and exposed to a brief pulse of radiofrequency energy, cells from the tissue give off a brief signal, called a magnetic resonance. Different types of tissue give off slightly different signals. In the brain, neurons (i.e., gray matter), myelin (i.e., white matter), and cerebral spinal fluid give different signals. A computer can use these different signals to generate a digital image of the brain. MRI machines generate two-dimensional images of brain tissue that can be integrated by the computer (i.e., "stacked" on top of one another) to create a

three-dimensional picture (Picon, Volpe, Sterzer, & Heinz, 2016).

MRI has a number of advantages over CT and most other imaging techniques. First, MRI does not subject individuals to radiation; it is believed to be safe and has even been used to obtain images of the brains of developing fetuses. Second, because it is safe, MRI can be used with healthy children and administered repeatedly over time. Consequently, MRI technology allows us to study the same children's brains across development. Third, MRI yields clearer and more precise pictures of the brain than older neuroimaging methods (Giedd & Denker, 2015).

MRI can allow us to detect structural abnormalities in the brains of youths with mental disorders. In a typical MRI study, researchers scan the brains of youths with and without a specific disorder. For example, Castellanos and colleagues (2002) scanned the brains of children with and without ADHD. The researchers compared the volumes of the frontal cortex of children in the two groups. They found that children with ADHD showed an average 4% reduction in volume of the frontal cortex compared to children without ADHD. These results are important because underactivity in portions of the frontal cortex is believed to account for some ADHD symptoms.

Functional magnetic resonance imaging (fMRI) is a relatively new technique used to measure brain activity (Pine, 2006). The techniques used in fMRI greatly resemble MRI. However, the fMRI device measures changes in oxygenated hemoglobin concentrations in the brain. When the individual engages in mental activity, oxygenated hemoglobin concentrations increase in brain regions that become active. Consequently, fMRI yields a picture of the individual's brain showing regions most active during certain mental activities (Sadock & Sadock, 2015).

To perform fMRI, researchers typically obtain an image of the individual's brain, using traditional MRI. Then, researchers ask the individual to perform a series of mental activities while they collect fMRI data. For example, researchers might ask adolescents with autism to describe the emotional expression on pictures of people's faces or ask children with learning disabilities to read or solve math problems. These fMRI images are then superimposed over the traditional MRI to show brain regions that are most active during the mental tasks (see Image 2.4).

Tamm, Menon, and Reiss (2006) used fMRI to determine which brain regions might be responsible for the deficits in attention shown by youths with ADHD. They asked 14 adolescents with ADHD and 12 adolescents without ADHD to perform a test of attention while they collected fMRI data. In this task, youths were presented with a series of either circles or triangles. They were asked to press one button when they saw a circle and a different button when they saw a triangle. As expected, youths with ADHD made significantly more errors than youths without ADHD. Furthermore, youths with ADHD showed significantly less activity in certain brain areas

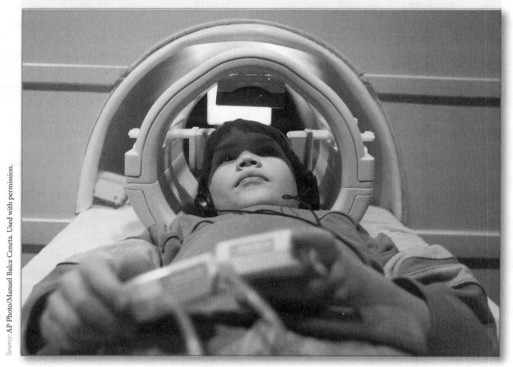

Image 2.4   Nine-year-old Patrick is shown participating in an fMRI study of children with ADHD.

(i.e., their parietal lobes) compared to their healthy peers. The researchers concluded that these brain regions may play a role in people's ability to direct and regulate attention.

Neuroimaging studies involving children and adolescents often yield inconsistent results. The primary reason for the inconsistent results of many neuroimaging studies is that children show enormous variability in their brain volumes and rates of brain development. For example, total brain volumes can differ by as much as 20% based on factors such as children's age, gender, and environment. Researchers wishing to identify structural abnormalities in the brains of children with specific disorders need to carefully control for these factors. A second reason for inconsistent findings is that many studies have been unable to detect structural abnormalities in children because of low-image resolution. Even today, with better technology, many children find it uncomfortable to remain in MRI devices for long enough periods of time to obtain the clearest images possible (Sadock & Sadock, 2015).

Perhaps the most important reason for the inconsistent findings is that disorders in children and adolescents rarely have single causes that can be traced to specific brain regions. For example, ADHD appears to be caused by a complex relationship between biological, psychological, and environmental factors. It would be a mistake to think that a specific brain abnormality would account for all (or even most) cases of ADHD or any other disorder. Instead,

it is likely that early differences in brain structure interact with environmental experiences to produce symptoms (Johnson & de Haan, 2006).

Review:

- MRIs provide information about brain structure, whereas fMRIs provide information about brain functioning while performing specific tasks.
- Neuroimaging studies often yield inconsistent findings because children show great variability in brain structure and functioning.

How Does the Brain Change Across Childhood and Adolescence?

Advances in neuroimaging have given us increasingly more detailed pictures of the brain in infancy, childhood, and adolescence. Most recently, scientists have conducted prospective, longitudinal studies, examining children's brains over time, to chart maturation across development. These studies have yielded at least five principles of brain development.

1.   The brain consists of 100 billion neurons.

A **neuron** is a nerve cell that is typically very narrow and very long. Most neurons are small; you could place

50 neurons side by side within the period that ends this sentence. Neurons vary in length from one millimeter to more than one meter. Neurons are also very numerous; if you counted each neuron in your brain, one neuron per second, it would take you more than 3,000 years to finish.

The structure of a neuron can tell us something about its function (see Image 2.5). The center of most neurons contains the cell body; its main purpose is to carry on basic metabolic functions for the cell—to keep the cell alive. The neuron also has dendrites, fingerlike appendages that receive information from either outside stimuli (e.g., light, pressure) or other neurons. Finally, the neuron has a longer axon, which relays information from the dendrites and cell body to the terminal ending of the neuron. Neurons relay information electrically, by controlling the positively and negatively charged particles that are allowed to enter the cell. Information is conducted down the axon in a manner analogous to electricity flowing down a wire. Mammalian axons are wrapped in a fatty substance called myelin, which increases conduction and speeds the electrical impulse.

2. *Neurons communicate with each other using chemical messengers.*

Each neuron typically forms many connections with other neurons, forming a complex neurological network.

Although information travels within neurons electrically, it travels between neurons chemically. When an impulse reaches the axon terminal, it triggers the release of a chemical messenger called a neurotransmitter. The neurotransmitter is released into the synapse, a small cleft between neurons. In the synapse, neurotransmitters can be detected by other neurons, causing them to change their electrical charge. Sufficient stimulation by neurotransmitters can cause other nerve cells to become active, thus propagating the impulse to the next neuron.

Neurotransmitters have different functions. Some are excitatory—that is, they increase the positive charge of neurons making them more likely to become active. For example, dopamine is a major excitatory neurotransmitter that is important to attention and concentration. Insufficient dopamine in certain brain regions is associated with ADHD. Other neurotransmitters are inhibitory—that is, they increase the negative charge of neurons making them less likely to become active. For example, GABA is a major inhibitory neurotransmitter. Alcohol causes an increase in GABA, thus slowing reaction time and impairing judgment and decision-making. Most psychotropic medications (and drugs) affect behavior by enhancing or attenuating the effects of neurotransmitters.

3. *Brain development consists of periods of growth and periods of pruning.*

Image 2.5   The neuron consists of three main parts: the dendrites, the cell body, and the axon. Neurons communicate within themselves electrically and between each other chemically using neurotransmitters.

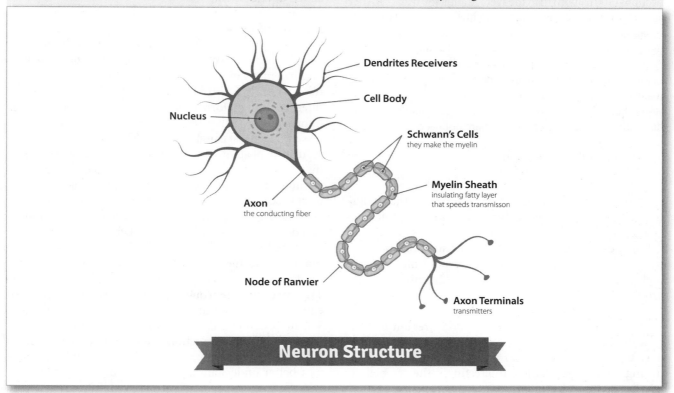

The development of the central nervous system begins shortly after conception and continues well into adulthood. During the first month after conception, the *neural tube* is formed. This tissue will later become the basis for the brain and spinal cord. During the second and third months of gestation, the brain gradually begins to take shape at the top of the neural tube, with the foremost part of the brain becoming prominent. Shortly after the first trimester, there is a rapid proliferation of neurons and an increase in neural density. From Month 3 to Month 5 of gestation, these neurons gradually make their way from the center of the brain to the outmost areas, a process called migration. These neurons, which migrate to the outermost shell of the brain, will later form the cortex. At the beginning of the second trimester, the brain experiences a period of rapid cell death. Approximately 50% of neurons will die during this process, presumably to make way for more important neural connections and increased brain organization (Sadock & Sadock, 2015).

During the remainder of gestation, there is a dramatic increase in myelin. Increased myelination is believed to speed up neural activity and make brain processes occur more quickly and efficiently. This increase in myelination continues at a rapid rate until age 2 years. Myelination then slows, but continues through adolescence.

Also during the third trimester of gestation, there is a dramatic increase in the number of neurons and connections between neurons. This rapid increase in synaptic connections continues until approximately age 2. Indeed, the average 2-year-old child has approximately 50% more synaptic connections (100 trillion) than the average adult (50 trillion). After age 2, however, there is a gradual reduction in the number of synaptic connections. Many of the connections that are not needed simply die off, in a process called synaptic pruning. Although pruning might seem like a waste of neural connections, it is actually a normal and healthy process. Pruning makes the brain process information more efficiently, by strengthening neural connections that are frequently used and discarding neural connections that are not necessary.

4.   *The brain is built and organized from the bottom up, with lower-order regions developing first.*

Longitudinal neuroimaging studies show that evolutionarily older areas of the brain develop first, followed by more complex, higher-order brain regions (see Figure 2.3). For example, the brain stem consists of the medulla, pons, and midbrain and is largely responsible for basic metabolic functions such as heart rate, respiration, and arousal. It is developed at birth and is necessary for life (Ganzel & Morris, 2016).

Similarly, the cerebellum is a brain region located near the back of the brain; it is chiefly responsible for balance and coordinated motor activity. It develops rapidly during the first year of life. Interestingly, the cerebellum

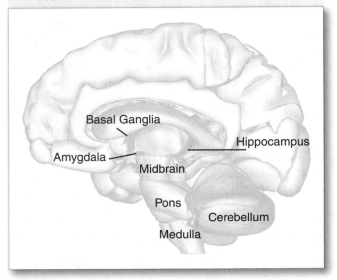

Figure 2.3   Cross-section of the brain showing the brain stem (medulla, pons, midbrain), cerebellum, basal ganglia, and portions of the limbic system (amygdala, hippocampus)

undergoes a second round of synaptic pruning during early adolescence. Researchers now believe the cerebellum plays a role in mental gracefulness and efficiency in addition to adroitness in physical movement. Maturation of the cerebellum during adolescence might explain the increased physical gracefulness exhibited by older adolescents as well as a general increase in mental efficiency across development.

Just above the brain stem, in the center of the brain, are two important regions that also mature relatively early. The basal ganglia are located between the brain stem and the higher-level cortical regions. The basal ganglia perform many important functions. One of their primary roles is to help control movement. Another function is to filter incoming information from the senses and relay this information to other brain regions where it can be processed. The basal ganglia have also been implicated in the regulation of attention and emotions. Researchers believe that structural changes in the basal ganglia, especially the pruning that occurs during childhood and adolescence, might account for children's increased motor functioning, attention, and emotional processing across development (Giedd, Shaw, Wallace, Gogtay, & Lenroot, 2006).

Finally, the limbic system is located deep inside the brain, behind the cortex. Two important components of the limbic system are the amygdala and hippocampus. The amygdala aids in our understanding and expression of emotions, especially negative feelings, such as fear and rage. The hippocampus also plays a role in emotional processing, especially the formation of emotion-laden memories. Although neuroimaging studies are just beginning to give us a better understanding of these elusive brain regions, most data indicate dramatic growth and pruning of neurons in the limbic system between 8 months and 2 years of age (Giedd et al., 2006).

5. *Higher-order brain regions take longer to develop; they are sometimes not mature until adulthood.*

The cortex is the outermost shell of the brain. It is divided into four lobes (see Figure 2.4). The occipital lobe, located near the back of the brain, is primarily responsible for visual processing. This brain region appears to undergo the most change from birth through age 2. In contrast, the volume of the parietal lobe (located on the sides and top of the brain) peaks around age 6 and then gradually decreases in size. The parietal lobe is primarily responsible for integrating visual, auditory, and tactile information. Pruning in this region may account for improved sensory and motor functioning that occurs during childhood. The temporal lobe (located on the sides and bottom of the brain) shows peak growth during the first six years of life, with gradual pruning into adolescence. The temporal lobe has multiple functions, including hearing, language, and the expression and regulation of emotions. Pruning of the temporal lobe may underlie adolescents' abilities to understand and regulate their feelings.

The volume of the frontal lobe peaks in late childhood, at approximately age 11 or 12. The frontal cortex plays an important role in language production, problem-solving, and memory—skills that develop rapidly during the childhood years. A particular region of the frontal lobe, the prefrontal cortex, shows peak growth in late childhood with gradual pruning and reorganization into early adulthood. This brain region is responsible for executive functioning: planning, organizing, and prioritizing activity to meet long-term goals. Just as an executive of a company makes decisions and allocates resources to achieve the company's long-term objectives, the executive areas of the brain direct our attention and activities to achieve long-term goals. Development of the prefrontal cortex is believed to underlie young adults' increased capacity for attention, inhibition, and overall behavioral regulation (de Haan & Johnson, 2016).

Review:

- The brain consists of 100 billion neurons that form trillions of synaptic connections with each other. Neurons relay information within themselves electrically; however, they communicate between one another using chemical messengers called neurotransmitters.
- Brain development is characterized by periods of rapid neural growth followed by periods of neural pruning. Development begins in evolutionarily "older" brain regions (e.g., brain stem, limbic system, basal ganglia) and ends in regions responsible for higher-order functions (e.g., the cortex).

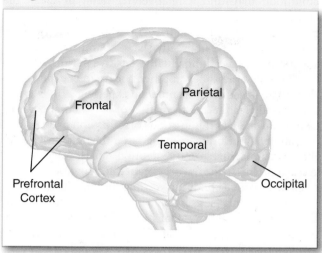

Figure 2.4   Lobes of the Brain

Frontal

Parietal

Temporal

Prefrontal Cortex

Occipital

How Can Experience Affect Brain Development?

Although it may seem that brain maturation determines development, the relationship between maturation and behavior is bidirectional. Some of the most exciting research in the past 20 years has shown that the brain can change in response to experience. Biological maturation and environmental experiences can interact in three ways to shape the developing brain (Fox, Levitt, & Nelson, 2010; Greenough & Black, 2013).

First, certain aspects of brain development are *gene-driven*. These aspects are largely impervious to the effects of experience and almost entirely determined by the person's genetic code. For example, the development of the neural tube and migration of neurons from the center of the brain to the cortex is believed to be genetically preprogrammed and largely insensitive to experience. Developmental psychologists sometimes refer to this importance of genes over experience in embryonic development as canalization (Blair, Raver, & Finegood, 2016).

Second, some aspects of brain development are *experience-expectant*—that is, the formation of the brain region is partially dependent on information received from the environment. Infants have an overabundance of neural connections, many of which they do not need. Connections that are used are maintained and strengthened while connections that are not used atrophy and die. Whether a connection is maintained or pruned depends on experience. For example, an infant exposed to the Japanese language during the first few years of life may strengthen neural connections responsible for processing the sounds used in Japanese. However, infants not exposed to Japanese during this early period of development may lose neural connections that play a role in processing the Japanese language. Consequently, children who are not exposed to Japanese in infancy and early childhood may find it relatively difficult to speak the language without an accent later in life. Developmental psychologists often refer to periods of development in which experience can greatly shape neural structure and functioning as developmentally sensitive periods.

Third, brain development can be *experience-dependent*—that is, environmental experiences in later life can actually lead to the formation of new neural connections or to changes in the brain's organization or structure. The ability of the brain to change after the first few years of life was unimaginable one generation ago. However, recent research points to the ways the brain can change in response to environmental conditions throughout the life span.

Neuroscientists use the term plasticity to refer to the brain's malleability—that is, its capacity to change its structure and/or functioning in response to environmental experiences. These environmental experiences can be either internal or external. Internal experiences alter the immediate environment of the brain and nervous system. For example, exposure to too much testosterone or stress hormone can lead to structural changes in various brain regions. In contrast, external experiences come from outside the organism. For example, an infant exposed to environmental toxins can experience brain damage (Cicchetti, 2015).

Neuroscientists have discovered that the brain is remarkably adaptive to environmental stressors, especially when these stressors occur early in life. Perhaps the most striking example of brain plasticity is seen following a surgical procedure called a functional hemispherectomy. Functional hemispherectomy is performed on some children who have medically intractable epilepsy that arises in one hemisphere of the brain. These seizures cause severe impairment, occur very frequently, and are not responsive to medication. To perform a functional hemispherectomy, the surgeon removes the entire parietal lobe of the non-functional hemisphere (which is often the origin of the seizures) and severs the corpus callosum (which allows the seizure to travel from one hemisphere to the other; van Schooneveld, Braun, van Rijen, van Nieuwenhuizen, & Jennekens-Schinkel, 2016).

Despite removal or disconnection of several brain regions, children usually show remarkable recovery from the procedure. Children often experience motor deficits on the side of the body opposite the hemisphere that was removed. Furthermore, if the left hemisphere is removed, most children experience temporary disturbance in language. However, children usually recover much of this lost functioning within 6 to 12 months after surgery, as the remaining hemisphere gradually assumes many of these lost functions. In fact, most children who undergo this surgery are able to return to school 6 to 8 weeks later (Jonas et al., 2004; van Empelen, Jennekens-Schinkel, Buskens, Helders, & van Nieuwenhuizen, 2004).

Environmental experiences need not be as dramatic as a hemispherectomy to produce changes in the organization of the brain. Rats reared in isolation show dramatic increases in stress hormone. These chronic elevations in stress hormone seem to alter the rats' stress response. As a result, isolated rats often show long-term propensities toward aggression as adults. Similarly, some children who are repeatedly exposed to physical or sexual abuse show dysregulation of certain brain regions responsible for the body's stress response. This dysregulation, in turn, can cause problems with anxiety and mood later in life.

Positive environmental experiences can also lead to the formation of new neural connections. Long ago, the neuropsychologist D. O. Hebb (1949) proposed that the simultaneous activation of neurons can cause the neurons to form new synaptic connections. Hebb suggested that neurons that "fire together, wire together." Recently, neuroscientists have been able to show synaptogenesis—that is, the formation of new neural connections due to experience. For example, rats reared in enriched living environments (e.g., given extra space and access to toys and mazes) show differences in brain structure and functioning compared to rats reared in typical cages. Humans who receive extensive training in Braille show growth in brain regions responsible for processing the sense of touch. Even skilled musicians show a reorganization of brain regions responsible for controlling the finger positions of their instruments (Cicchetti & Curtis, 2006)!

Review:

- Some aspects of development are gene-driven; they are largely directed by biological factors (e.g., the physical maturation of the brain). Other aspects are experience-expectant; they require stimuli from the environment to emerge properly (e.g., the acquisition of language). Experience-expectant processes emerge during sensitive periods in development.
- Still other aspects of development are experience-dependent; environmental experiences can lead to synaptogenesis, the formation of new neural connections. Brain plasticity refers to the ability of the nervous system to reorganize based on experience.

2.3 LEARNING THEORY

How Is Classical Conditioning Important to Understanding Childhood Disorders?

Researchers who study the psychological causes of child psychopathology are interested in explaining maladaptation at the behavioral level. The term *behavior* encompasses three important facets of children's functioning: their thoughts, feelings, and actions. Psychologists recognize that thoughts, feelings, and actions are closely connected; each partially influences, and is influenced by, the others.

Psychologists often use learning theory to explain and predict children's overt actions. From the perspective of learning theory, children's actions are chiefly determined by environmental contingencies. Learning occurs in three principal ways: (1) through classical conditioning, (2) through operant conditioning, and (3) through social imitation or modeling.

In classical conditioning, learning occurs when the child associates two stimuli paired together in time. One stimulus is initially called the neutral stimulus (NS) because it does not elicit a response. The other stimulus is initially called an unconditioned stimulus (UCS) because it naturally elicits an unconditioned response (UCR). The child may come to associate the NS with the UCS if the two stimuli are presented together.

Pavlov demonstrated that dogs would associate the sound of a metronome (NS) with the presentation of meat powder (UCS) if the two stimuli were presented contiguously. After repeated presentations, the metronome alone elicited salivation. After conditioning, the previously neutral stimulus (e.g., metronome) is referred to as the conditioned stimulus (CS), whereas the resulting response (e.g., salivation) is referred to as the conditioned response (CR).

Classical conditioning can be used to explain the emergence of certain childhood disorders. For example, a boy who is bitten by a dog might associate the sight of a dog (NS) with the experience of being bitten (UCS). The dog bite, in turn, naturally causes a fear response (UCR). Later, the presence of any dog (CS) may elicit a similar fear response (CR). The boy might develop a phobia for dogs.

Consider another example. A girl is taking notes in her high school math class when she suddenly experiences a panic attack (i.e., an intense episode of fear, racing heartbeat, and rapid breathing). The attack is so severe that she immediately leaves class and runs to the bathroom for privacy and safety. The girl associates her math classroom (NS) with the panic attack (UCS), which naturally causes intense negative emotions (UCR). Later, any thought of reentering her math classroom (CS) might elicit feelings of apprehension or anxiety (CR). She might develop agoraphobia or a fear of going to school.

One way of decreasing behaviors acquired through classical conditioning is to use extinction. Extinction involves repeatedly presenting the CS until it no longer elicits the CR. Extinction is usually accomplished gradually, in a process called *graded exposure*. For example, a therapist might recommend that a girl with a fear of dogs gradually expose herself to dogs, in order to extinguish this fear. Initially, the girl might simply look at pictures of dogs, then remain in a room with a dog on a leash, and finally pet a dog. After the girl is repeatedly exposed to the dog, the dog's presence no longer elicits an intense fear response.

Extinction can also occur rapidly, through a procedure called *flooding*. For example, the girl with agoraphobia might enter her math classroom with her therapist. Initially, she might experience intense anxiety. Over time, however, her anxiety will gradually decrease. Usually,

Image 2.6   Graded exposure is like dipping your toe into cold water until you get used to its temperature. Flooding is like jumping in!

flooding is a more rapid treatment than graded exposure; however, flooding is less frequently used with children because it typically elicits greater distress (see Image 2.6).

Review:

- Learning theory posits that behaviors are acquired through classical conditioning, operant conditioning, or modeling.
- Classical conditioning occurs when children associate two stimuli together in time. Behaviors acquired through classical conditioning can be extinguished using graded exposure or flooding.

How Is Operant Conditioning Important to Understanding Childhood Disorders?

Whereas classical conditioning occurs when children associate two stimuli together in time, operant conditioning occurs when children associate a behavior with a consequence in the environment. Operant conditioning is based on the notion that the consequences of our actions determine the likelihood that the actions will be repeated. If the consequences of our actions increase the likelihood that we will repeat the behavior in the future, these consequences have *reinforced* our behavior. If the consequences of our actions decrease the likelihood that we will repeat our behavior in the future, these consequences have *punished* our behavior. Reinforcement increases the likelihood of future behavior, whereas punishment decreases the likelihood of future behavior (see Figure 2.5).

Reinforcement can be positive or negative. Positive reinforcement occurs when an individual is presented with a stimulus that increases the likelihood of behavior. For example, a father might give his daughter ice cream after she eats her vegetables at dinner. If the presentation of ice cream following the meal increases the likelihood that the girl eats her vegetables in the future, we say that the ice cream positively reinforced the child's eating.

Many people mistakenly believe that the adjective "positive" in the term *positive reinforcement* refers to the pleasantness of the reinforcer. In fact, the term *positive* simply refers to the fact that the stimulus is *presented* to the individual. Some presumably pleasant stimuli are not positively reinforcing to all children. For example, providing a 2-year-old with one piece of candy for using the toilet may increase the likelihood that he will use the toilet in the future. However, providing one piece of candy to a 14-year-old for completing his math homework will likely not increase the likelihood that he will complete his math homework.

Additionally, some presumably unpleasant stimuli can be positively reinforcing. For example, a teacher may reprimand her student for disrupting class. If the teacher's reprimand results in an increase in the student's disruptive behavior, the teacher's behavior is positively reinforcing, no matter how aversive it appears.

Negative reinforcement occurs when the withdrawal or avoidance of a stimulus increases the likelihood of behavior. For example, a father might allow his daughter to leave the dinner table only after she finishes her vegetables. If escaping the dinner table by eating vegetables increases the likelihood that the girl eats her vegetables in the future, we say that the father's action negatively reinforced the child's eating.

Negative reinforcement often underlies childhood behavior problems. For example, a mother might ask her son to turn off the television and clean his room. The son might ignore his mother because he prefers to watch his favorite TV program. The mother might withdraw her request and clean her son's room herself. If the mother's behavior (i.e., withdrawal of her request) increases the likelihood that her son will ignore her requests in the future, we say that her actions are negatively reinforcing his disobedience. She is teaching him to disobey.

In contrast to reinforcement, punishment always *decreases* the probability of future behavior. There are two types of punishment: positive and negative. Positive punishment involves a stimulus *presentation* that decreases the likelihood of behavior. For example, a mother might spank her son for his disobedience. If spanking results in a decrease in her child's defiance, then the mother's action was a form of positive punishment. Negative punishment

Figure 2.5   Operant Conditioning

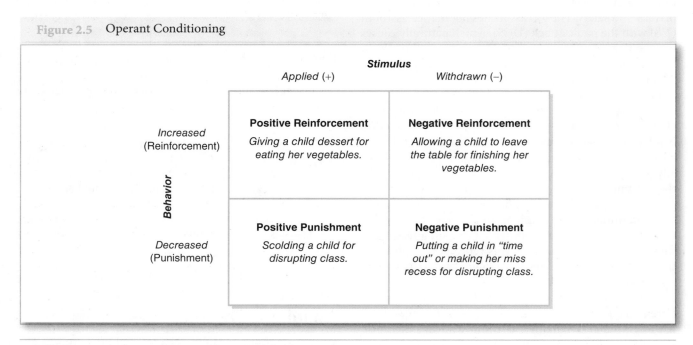

Note: Reinforcement leads to an increase in behavior; punishment leads to a decrease in behavior.

involves *avoidance or removal* or a stimulus that decreases the likelihood of behavior. For example, a teacher might remove a child from a desirable classroom activity following his disruptive behavior in class. If the teacher's action results in a decrease in the student's disruptive behavior, then the teacher's behavior was a form of negative punishment.

Clinicians prefer to use reinforcement, instead of punishment, to correct behavior problems. In some cases, however, punishment can be used therapeutically. For example, a therapist might teach a parent to use positive punishment to correct her son's bed-wetting. Specifically, every time the boy wets the bed, the parent might require the boy to perform a series of actions designed to correct the problem behavior. These actions might include stripping the bed, taking the bedding to the washing machine, helping to start the wash, putting on new sheets, and sitting on the toilet. Similarly, a therapist might teach a parent to use time-out as a form of negative punishment for her disruptive preschooler. Time-out involves removing the child from all potentially reinforcing stimuli for a period of time, in an attempt to decrease the child's defiance. The child might be required to sit in a special chair for 3 minutes with no access to toys, television, or other stimuli.

Review:

- Operant conditioning occurs when children associate a behavior with a consequence in the environment.
- Reinforcement always increases the likelihood of future behavior, whereas punishment always decreases the likelihood of future behavior. Reinforcement and punishment can be positive (i.e., involve the presentation of a stimulus) or negative (i.e., involve the avoidance or removal of a stimulus).

How Is Social Learning Important to Understanding Childhood Disorders?

Behaviors can also be acquired through the observation of others. Albert Bandura and colleagues (Bandura, Ross, & Ross, 1961) demonstrated that children who watched adults behaving aggressively toward an inflatable doll often imitated the adults' aggressive actions. Bandura believed that learning through imitation, or modeling, was a primary mechanism of behavioral acquisition. Social learning was especially likely when models were similar to children in age and gender and when models were reinforced for their actions.

Modeling is also used to explain and to treat other child behavior problems. For example, parents who model anxiety to their children can increase their children's likelihood of developing an anxiety disorder. A mother who is afraid of social situations might model fear to her daughter. Specifically, she might avoid attending social gatherings and express her worry about appearing foolish in public. She might also convey to her daughter that other people are often critical and judgmental, thereby increasing her daughter's fears of social situations. As a result, her daughter might develop anxiety in social situations and a tendency toward social withdrawal.

A therapist might also use modeling as a means to reduce the daughter's social phobia. Specifically, the therapist might ask the child's teacher to pair the girl with a "classroom buddy"—a female classmate who shows well-developed social skills and is willing to model appropriate social behavior. By watching her "buddy," the girl might discover that social situations are often pleasant and are rarely catastrophic. Consequently, her social anxiety may decrease.

Review:

- Social learning occurs when children acquire behaviors through imitation or modeling.
- Modeling can be used to explain the acquisition of problematic behaviors, or it can be used in treatment.

2.4 COGNITION AND EMOTION REGULATION

How Does Cognition Change Across Development?

Cognitive development refers to the emergence of more complex perception, thought, language, and problem-solving over time. Jean Piaget's stage theory provides a framework for thinking about cognitive development in children and adolescents. According to this theory, development progresses through series of four broad stages in an invariant sequence. Each stage is characterized by greater sophistication in children's cognition (Barrouillet, 2015; Carey, Zaitchik, & Bascandziev, 2015).

Infants in the *sensorimotor stage* (0–2 years) develop an understanding of themselves and their surroundings largely through happenstance and trial and error. This stage is marked by the emergence of object permanence, the notion that objects exist even when the child cannot see them; pretend play, acting "as if" one object (e.g., a doll) is another (e.g., a real baby); and increased use of language. Problems with pretend play and language characterize many communication disorders that can emerge in this stage.

Preschoolers in the *preoperational stage* (2–6 years) engage in increasingly more sophisticated use of language and representational thought. They form more complex understanding of their world and can begin to plan their actions before engaging in them. Gradually, two phenomena emerge. First, children develop theory of mind—that is, the notion that other people have experiences, thoughts, and feelings (i.e., "minds") that can be different from their own. Second, children develop greater capacity for empathy, or the ability to experience others' feelings. Certain disorders, such as ASD and social communication disorder, are characterized by delays in theory of mind and empathic understanding.

School-age children (6–12 years) fall in the stage of *concrete operations*. Throughout elementary school, these children develop greater capacity for conservation—that is, understanding that objects may change in appearance, but their amount or quantity remains constant. Conservation is tied to the physical world rather than to abstractions or ideas. Consequently, children in this stage can learn about subjects connected to the physical world (e.g., arithmetic, reading) but are typically not ready for more abstract subjects (e.g., algebra, literary analysis).

Finally, most adolescents (≥12 years) achieve the stage of *formal operations*, characterized by logical-deductive reasoning. At this stage, adolescents can begin to use general principles to determine specific truths enabling them to engage in more abstract thought. For example, an adolescent can reason the following:

You must be 21 to legally drink alcohol.

Monica is 21.

Therefore, Monica can legally drink alcohol.

Formal operational thought allows adolescents and young adults to comprehend algebra and geometry, psychology and sociology, or philosophy and political science, subjects that children typically have trouble understanding.

Social cognition is an important aspect of cognitive development that concerns our capacity to think about social situations. Social cognition is based on social information processing theory, a general model for how humans perceive, judge, store, and retrieve social information. Central to the notion of social cognition is the idea that we form schemas, or mental models, about ourselves and others in social relationships. These schemas are based on prior interpersonal experiences, and they guide and direct future social behaviors. For example, a child with well-developed social skills and many friends might expect a new classmate to be friendly. He might approach the new classmate and ask him to play during recess. In contrast, a child who is socially awkward and rejected by her peers might anticipate that a new classmate would also reject her. Consequently, she might avoid the new classmate (Bargh, 2013; Fiske & Taylor, 2013).

Problems with social information processing underlie many childhood disorders. For example, children who engage in aggressive behavior toward peers typically have negative schemas regarding themselves and others. Furthermore, when confronted with social problems, they tend to perceive others' actions as hostile or rejecting and have difficulty generating peaceful problem-solving strategies (Dodge, Godwin, & Conduct Problems Prevention Research Group, 2013). Similarly, children with depression often view themselves as ineffective in social situations. When confronted with social problems, they tend to shy away from others, often leading others to reject them, confirming their low self-worth. Fortunately, therapies have been developed to improve children's social information-processing skills and alleviate children's behavioral and emotional problems (Michl, McLaughlin, Shepherd, & Nolen-Hoeksema, 2013).

Review:

- Piaget described four stages of cognitive development. These stages help us understand the emergence of childhood disorders involving thinking, problem-solving, or language.
- Social cognition refers to a child's ability to think about social situations and solve interpersonal problems. Some childhood disorders are associated with social problem-solving biases or deficits.

How Do Children's Emotion-Regulation Skills Change Across Development?

Emotional development is the emergence and refinement of a child's experience, expression, understanding, and regulation of emotions (Odle, 2016). The process of emotional development reflects the child's physical maturation, increasing cognitive sophistication, and experiences with others (Cole, 2016).

Emotional expression begins in infancy. Crying is a powerful means of communication for newborns. Distress, pleasure, anger, fear, and interest are among the earliest emotions that infants display. Young infants occasionally laugh and smile, although smiling deliberately at other people typically does not emerge until age 4 to 6 months. Emotions such as sadness and fear are typically seen in the second half of the first year of life.

Toddlerhood is characterized by rapid development of the brain's limbic system and frontal lobe and increased independence from parents. Consequently, toddlers begin to show more complex feelings such as pride (in asserting autonomy) and shame (in taking risks and failing). Between the ages of 3 and 5, children develop greater capacity for empathy. Empathy is dependent on their ability to attend to other's emotional expressions, label them correctly, and take their perspective. Children eventually diagnosed with ASD typically show delays in their emotional expression and understanding of others' emotional experiences.

Advances in cognition, especially language, allow preschoolers and young school-age children to label and differentiate their own emotions. For example, kindergarteners can begin to distinguish feeling "mad" from feeling "sad." Young children also become better able to share their feelings verbally, rather than expressing them through aggression, crying, or throwing tantrums. Young children also learn how to alter their emotional expressions in different contexts. For example, the emotions a child can express at home might be different than the emotions he might show in the classroom or playground.

A major developmental task during childhood and adolescence is the development of emotion regulation. Emotion regulation refers to children's capacity to recognize, label, and control the expression of their emotions in ways that are consistent with cultural expectations (Odle, 2016). Emotion regulation is critical for children to achieve long-term goals. For example, children must be able to control their anger if they want to make and keep friends or avoid problems at school.

Several child and adolescent disorders reflect problems with emotion regulation. For example, disruptive mood dysregulation disorder (DMDD) is seen in young children who exhibit chronic irritability and severe temper outbursts. A critical component of treatment for this disorder is to teach children to avoid situations that might trigger inappropriate emotional displays and find new ways to cope with negative emotions. Eating disorders also sometimes reflect underlying problems with emotion regulation. Some adolescents engage in bingeing or purging as a maladaptive means to reduce anxiety. Finally, self-injurious behaviors (SIBs; e.g., burning, cutting) can also be seen as a problematic attempt to regulate emotions. The treatment of these latter disorders typically involves replacing these maladaptive emotion-regulation strategies with healthier, more effective methods.

Review:

- Early emotional development is chiefly concerned with emotional expression and accurately understanding the emotions of others. Children with ASD often show problems in developing these skills.
- Later emotional development is characterized by greater capacity for emotion regulation—that is, the ability to recognize, label, and control emotional expression. Children with disruptive behavior and mood disorders often show difficulty with emotion regulation.

2.5 PARENTS, FAMILIES, AND FRIENDS

Children's emotional development is heavily influenced by their interpersonal relationships. Parents, families, and peers can help children achieve developmental tasks or hinder the development of cognitive, emotional, and social competence. In this section, we will examine four important influences on social development: temperament, attachment, parenting behavior, and peers.

What Is Temperament?

Temperament refers to the way infants and young children organize their behavior in response to environmental stimuli (Kagan, 2014). Temperament is relatively stable over time and across situations. Temperament reflects one aspect of personality that is believed to be largely innate—that is, independent of experience. Children enter the world with a particular temperament that helps them make sense of their experiences. These experiences, in turn, interact with their temperament and shape their personalities (Stifter & Dollar, 2016).

Parents of two or more children can appreciate differences in temperament. One child may be relatively quiet, easy to calm when upset, yet timid in new situations. His sibling, however, may cry at the slightest provocation, be a poor sleeper and picky eater, and act like a daredevil on the playground. Temperament helps to explain why biological siblings, who share 50% of their genes in common and are raised by the same parents, can think, feel, and act so differently.

The New York Longitudinal Study provides us with the best data regarding temperament in infancy and personality later in life. In this study, Stella Chess, Alexander Thomas, and Herbert Birch (1965) identified nine dimensions of temperament that could be reliably observed during parent–child interactions. These dimensions included (1) the infant's degree of motor activity; (2) the regularity of their eating, sleeping, and daily schedules; (3) their response to new people and situations; (4) their ability to adapt to changes in their environment; (5) their emotional reactivity, or sensitivity to stimuli; (6) their intensity of responses to stimuli; (7) their general mood or disposition, such as acting happy or irritable; (8) their tendency to become distracted during activities; and (9) their attention span. Infants tended to show stability in these dimensions of temperament as early as 2 to 3 months of age.

The researchers were able to categorize most children into one of three temperament clusters based on their relative strengths and weaknesses on these dimensions:

1. *Easy children* tended to show a high degree of positive affect during parent–child interactions, engaged in regular daily routines, and were at ease with new people and situations. Furthermore, they could be soothed easily when upset. These children were classified as "easy" because they presented fewer problems to their caregivers.

2. *Difficult children* tended to display more negative affect and irritability during parent–child interactions; showed more intense emotional reactions to environmental stimuli; and experienced problems establishing regular eating, sleeping, and toileting schedules. Furthermore, they were more easily upset by changes to their routines or surroundings. These children were labeled "difficult" because their behavior presented challenges to their caregivers.

3. *Slow-to-warm-up children* tended to show low levels of activity and emotion during parent–child interactions and appeared apprehensive when confronted with new people or situations. These children were considered "slow-to-warm-up" because they were slower to adapt to changes in their surroundings.

The researchers discovered that the same dimensions of temperament could be observed in children of all ethnicities and socioeconomic groups. Furthermore, by studying children from infancy through adulthood, the researchers determined that temperament was relatively stable over time and influenced the development of personality. Perhaps most important, however, was the *goodness-of-fit* between the infant's temperament and the demands and expectations of his or her environment. For example, a "difficult" baby raised by a single parent who is experiencing a high degree of stress herself might show more problems than a "difficult" baby raised by a single parent who has a safe home, a flexible job, and the support of family and friends (see Figure 2.6).

Developmental psychopathologists explore the degree to which temperament might place children at risk for disorders later in life. For example, Jerome Kagan studied one dimension of temperament, emotional reactivity, which can be observed in 4-month-old infants. When presented with a novel stimulus, such as dangling mobile, emotionally reactive infants engage in a high degree of movement and appear distressed. In contrast, infants with low reactivity remained calm when presented with the same stimulus. When tested again at 14 and 21 months, highly reactive infants often displayed inhibition and fear in novel situations (e.g., when a clown entered the room), whereas infants low in reactivity tended to be more outgoing and engaging. Furthermore, children who were reactive in infancy and fearful as toddlers were at increased risk for developing anxiety disorders in later childhood (Fox, Snidman, Haas, Degnan, & Kagan, 2015).

It is important to remember that temperament does not determine personality or a child's risk for psychopathology. However, temperament can affect children's personality and subsequent interactions with others. For example, Nathan Fox conducted an impressive longitudinal study investigating the relationship between difficult temperament in infancy and the emergence of psychological disorders in adolescence and early adulthood. The study, which took more than 15 years to conduct, showed that infants and young children with inhibited temperament were at increased risk for anxiety problems as young adults. However, children's peer networks during adolescence largely explained the relationship between early temperament and later anxiety. Inhibited children who avoided social contact and developed smaller peer networks tended to develop anxiety disorders; in contrast, inhibited children who were able to establish supportive peer networks did not show increased anxiety. These findings suggest that temperament can place children on certain developmental trajectories, but temperament does not determine children's outcomes (Frenkel et al., 2015).

Review:

- Temperament refers to the way infants and young children organize their behavior in response to

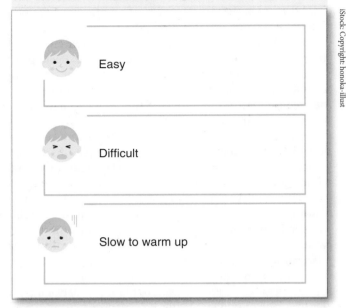

Figure 2.6 Chess, Thomas, and Birch (1965) identified three temperaments. The goodness-of-fit between the infant's temperament and her caregiver influenced the infant's developmental outcomes.

environmental stimuli. It is largely innate and influences personality development.

- Chess et al. (1965) identified three district temperament clusters in infants across ethnic and socioeconomic groups: easy, difficult, and slow-to-warm-up.
- The goodness-of-fit between the child's temperament and his or her caregiver is important to the child's social–emotional development.

How Can Parents and Families Influence Children's Development?

Parent–Child Attachment

Attachment refers to the affective bond between caregiver and child that serves to protect and reassure the child in times of danger or uncertainty (Grossman, Bretherton, Waters, & Grossman, 2016). According to John Bowlby (1969, 1973, 1980), the parent–child attachment relationship has three basic functions. Most important, the attachment relationship serves to protect the child from danger. Infants and young children are biologically predisposed to seek contact and proximity to their parents when scared, upset, or unsure of their surroundings. At the same time, parents are predisposed to respond to their infant's bids for attention and care (Pasco Fearon, Groh, Bakermans-Kranenburg, van IJzendoorn, & Roisman, 2016).

Second, the attachment relationship is designed to provide dyads with an avenue for sharing positive emotional experiences. Through interactions with parents, infants learn about the natural reciprocity of social interactions and the give-and-take of interpersonal relationships.

Third, the attachment relationship helps the infant learn to regulate negative emotions and behaviors. Initially, the infant controls anxiety and distress by directly relying on comfort from his parent. Over time, the child develops an internal working model, or mental representation of his parent, that helps him cope with psychosocial stress. The infant learns to use this mental representation of his parent as a "secure base" from which to explore his surroundings and control his emotions and actions.

The quality of parent–child interactions over the first few years of life influences the initial quality of the attachment relationship. Parents who provide sensitive and responsive care to their children, by meeting their children's needs in a consistent and developmentally appropriate fashion, usually develop *secure attachment relationships* with their children. Their children, in turn, come to expect sensitive and responsive care from their parents. At the same time, these children come to view themselves as worthy of receiving sensitive and responsive care from others.

In contrast, parents who do not provide sensitive and responsive care in a consistent fashion are likely to foster *insecure attachment relationships* with their children. When scared or upset, these children do not expect their parents to effectively meet their needs and help them regulate their emotions. They adopt internal working models of their parents as unavailable or inconsistent. At the same time, they may view themselves as unworthy of receiving attention and care from others.

Ainsworth, Blehar, Waters, and Wall (1978) identified three patterns of attachment that develop over the first few months of life. These patterns can be observed in the behavior of 12-month-old infants using the strange situation,

a laboratory-based test of infant–mother attachment. The strange situation occurs in a laboratory playroom and involves separating infants from their parents for short periods of time (see Table 2.1). Most infants experience distress when separated. However, researchers are primarily interested in how infants respond to their parents when they are reunited. Specifically, researchers observe whether infants are able to use their parents as a means to reduce distress and return to play.

Most children who participate in the strange situation show secure attachment relationships with their parents. These children use their parents as a secure base from which to regulate their emotions, control their behavior, and return to play. Although they usually show considerable distress during separation, they seek comfort and physical contact with their parents when they are reunited. After a little while, reassurance from caregivers soothes these infants, and they can return to play and exploration.

In contrast, some infants develop *insecure–avoidant attachment* relationships with their parents. When reunited with their mothers, these infants show passivity and disinterest. In fact, many of these infants actively avoid their parents' bids for attention by turning away or ignoring them. Although these infants might be upset by separation, they appear uninterested or resentful of their parents when they return. Instead of using their parents as a secure base from which to regulate their emotions and return to play, these infants attempt to rely on themselves to cope with the stress of separation. Attachment theorists reason that parents who consistently dismiss their children's bids for attention foster insecure–avoidant attachment relationships with their infants.

Other infants develop *insecure–ambivalent attachment* relationships with their parents. When separated, these infants usually show considerable distress. However,

Table 2.1	The Strange Situation		
Episode	Persons Present	Duration	Description of Events
1	Mother, infant	30 secs	Parent and infant are introduced to the experimental room.
2	Mother, infant	3 min	Parent and infant are alone. Parent does not participate while infant explores.
3	Mother, infant stranger	3 min	Stranger enters, converses with parent, then approaches infant. Parent leaves.
4	Stranger, infant	3 min	First separation episode. Stranger tries to play with infant.
5	Mother, infant	3 min	First reunion episode. Parent greets and comforts infant then leaves again.
6	Infant alone	3 min	Second separation episode.
7	Stranger, infant	3 min	Stranger enters, tries to play with infant.
8	Mother, infant	3 min	Second reunion episode. Parent enters, greets infant, and picks up infant; stranger leaves inconspicuously.

Source: Based on Ainsworth et al. (1978).

when reunited with their parents, these infants alternate between seeking and resisting their caregivers' support. For example, an infant might initially motion to be picked up by her mother and then immediately push away. The behavior of these infants conveys the notion that they desperately want comfort from their parents but that they do not expect their parents to adequately provide for their needs. Attachment theorists reason that parents who alternate between providing care and ignoring their children foster this insecure–ambivalent pattern of attachment.

Ainsworth and her students noticed that some infants could not be classified into any of the three original attachment patterns. In the strange situation, these infants tended to show repetitive, stereotyped behaviors when separated from their caregivers, such a jerky movements of their arms, neck, or back. Moreover, when reunited with their caregivers, these infants tended to freeze, stare off into space, or act fearfully. Mary Main, a student of Ainsworth, classified these children as *insecure–disorganized/disoriented* because their attachment did not seem organized like those of other infants (Main & Solomon, 1986). Subsequent research showed that insecure–disorganized/disoriented attachment is associated with histories of neglect. Furthermore, many caregivers who developed insecure–disorganized/disoriented attachment relationships with their infants experienced a major loss or trauma shortly before or after their child's birth.

A landmark project called the Minnesota Longitudinal Study of Parents and Children examined relationships between mother–child attachment in infancy and children's developmental outcomes. Beginning in 1974, this study (and others like it) provided some of the best data regarding the role attachment plays in later social-emotional development. Overall, results showed that the development of secure attachment relationships in infancy and early childhood is associated with later social-emotional competence. For example, infants who formed secure attachment relationships tended to be popular with peers, resilient, resourceful, and cooperative in preschool. By age 6, they were more compliant, responsive, self-reliant, and empathic than children with insecure attachment histories.

In contrast, infants who developed insecure–avoidant attachment relationships were more likely to display behavior problems such as stealing, lying, or cheating. Others were at risk for mood problems, such as irritability, anger, depression. They were likely to provoke adults and peers into rejecting them than those who were in secure relationships during infancy.

Infants who developed insecure–ambivalent attachments tended to show excessive dependency on caregivers and teachers in preschool. During the school-age years, they often acted frustrated, passive, or helpless. They often required reassurance, at the expense of taking risks and engaging in other activities.

Finally, infants who showed insecure–disorganized/disoriented attachment were at greatest risk for behavior problems in childhood. Specifically, many of these children showed oppositional, defiant, or spiteful behaviors toward their caregivers. In childhood, these children were most likely to develop aggressive behavior and conduct problems. In adolescence, these children were also at risk for dissociative symptoms, such as unexpected lapses in awareness or memory.

Although early parent–child attachment seems to place children on developmental trajectories toward either competence or adversity, it does not determine children's destiny. Many children change their patterns of attachment from infancy to adolescence because of experiences with other attachment figures. Supportive relatives, teachers, coaches, and friends can provide corrective emotional experiences to children who were initially insecure, causing them to modify their working models for relationships. Indeed, researchers have identified a subset of infants who changed their attachment patterns from insecure (in infancy) to secure (in childhood) largely because of sensitive and responsive care from adults in their lives. These children tend to show better peer relationships and family functioning in adolescence (van IJzendoorn & Bakermans-Kranenburg, 2014). Indeed, psychotherapy can be seen as a way to alter individual's schemas for relationships from ones based on rejection or inconsistency to ones based on sensitivity and trust.

Parenting Behavior

Although parenting practices differ considerably across families and cultures, psychologists have identified at least two dimensions of parenting that are important to most children's cognitive and social–emotional development (Kerig, 2016). The first dimension, *parental responsiveness*, refers to the degree to which parents display warmth and acceptance toward their children, orient their behavior to meet their children's needs in a sensitive and responsive fashion, and engage their children through shared activities and positive emotions. The second dimension, *parental demandingness*, refers to the degree to which parents have age-appropriate expectations for their children's behavior, clearly establish and consistently enforce rules governing their behavior, and supervise their children (Bornstein, 2016).

Diana Baumrind (1991) has classified caregivers into four parenting types, based on the degree to which they endorse responsiveness and demandingness in their usual interactions with their children (see Figure 2.7).

1. **Authoritative** parents are both responsive and demanding toward their children. These parents set high, but age-appropriate, expectations for their children's behavior and help their children meet these expectations by providing them with nurturance and support. They are assertive in their interactions with their children but not intrusive. They use discipline to support their children and to teach them how to control their own behavior; they do not use discipline punitively. They value responsibility but also recognize children's needs for sensitive and responsive care.

Figure 2.7   Baumrind's Parenting Typology

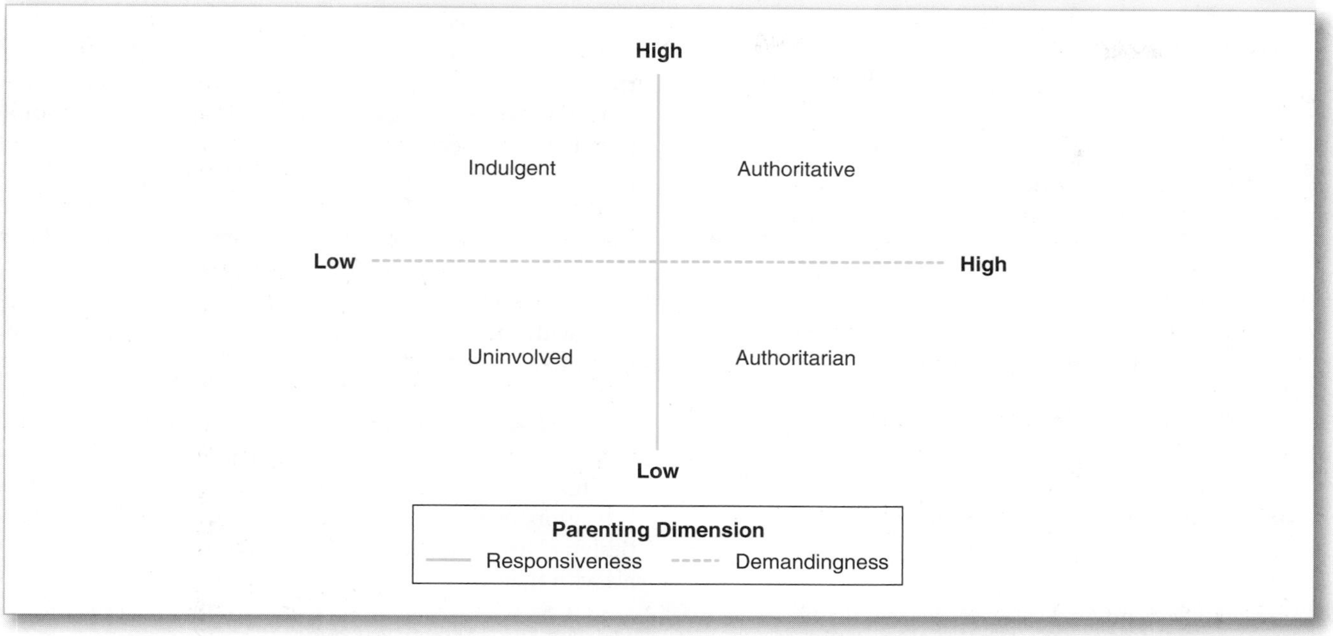

2.   Authoritarian parents show high levels of demandingness but low levels of responsiveness. These parents value obedience and achievement in their children. They set high standards for their children and firm limits on their children's behaviors. They establish clear rules and expect them to be obeyed without question. These parents are highly involved in their children's lives, providing them with organized, structured, and supervised educational, extracurricular, and social experiences. They strive to teach self-reliance and responsibility to their children, but they may give their children little support and encouragement to live up to these responsibilities.

3.   Indulgent parents show high levels of responsiveness but low levels of demandingness. These parents are described as lenient, nondirective, and permissive. They value autonomy and exploration in their children. They place few limits on their children's behaviors and are reticent to discipline.

4.   Uninvolved parents show low levels of both responsiveness and demandingness. These parents display infrequent or inconsistent interactions toward their children, often because they are distracted by other psychosocial stressors (e.g., working multiple jobs, caring for an elderly relative).

Prospective longitudinal research has shown that children's social–emotional outcomes are related to parenting style (Baumrind, 1991; Weiss & Schwarz, 1996). Overall, children of authoritative parents display the best developmental outcomes. On average, these children show well-developed social skills,

emotional competence, and capacity for self-regulation and self-direction. Children of authoritarian parents tend to perform well academically but are at risk for low self-esteem and peer problems, especially in late childhood and early adolescence. Children of indulgent parents often display high levels of self-esteem and well-developed social skills, but they are susceptible to behavior problems during childhood and substance use problems during adolescence. Children of uninvolved parents display the poorest outcomes. These children are at particular risk for low academic achievement, behavior problems, and emotional difficulties across development.

Psychologists have also identified a third dimension of parenting, *hostility or coercion*, which is especially relevant to the development of children's behavior problems. Hostile/coercive parenting reflects tactics that express negative affect or indifference toward children or involve the use of threat, harsh physical punishment, or psychological manipulation (Lovejoy, Weis, O'Hare, & Rubin, 1999). Examples of hostile or coercive parenting behavior include threatening to hurt or abandon a child, slapping or handling a child roughly, and using guilt or ridicule to control a child's behavior. Prospective longitudinal research indicates that hostile or coercive parenting behavior may contribute to the development of disruptive behavior problems in childhood and adolescence, especially problems with defiance and aggression (Dishion & Patterson, 2016).

Review:

●   Attachment refers to the emotional bond between caregiver and child that serves to promote safety and security. The development of attachment is innate; however, the quality of attachment can be secure or insecure depending on the sensitivity and responsiveness of the caregiver.

- Children form internal working models, or social–emotional schemas, based on their interactions with caregivers over the first few years of life. These models guide (and are influenced by) future interpersonal relationships.
- Four patterns of attachment have been identified using the strange situation: secure, insecure–avoidant, insecure–ambivalent, and insecure–disorganized/disoriented. Whereas secure attachment promotes social–emotional competence later in development, insecure attachment can contribute to problems in some children.
- Baumrind identified four parenting types each associated with different developmental outcomes in children: authoritative, authoritarian, indulgent, and uninvolved.

How Do Peers Influence Children's Development?

Interpersonal Theory

Harry Stack Sullivan (1953) was an influential psychiatrist who developed one of the first comprehensive theories regarding the importance of friendships to our social–emotional development. He believed that close, trusting friendships were vital to people's sense of self and their overall well-being. In contrast, Sullivan believed that loneliness is the most painful human experience possible.

Sullivan thought that intimacy is the hallmark of satisfying interpersonal relationships. According to Sullivan, intimate relationships are characterized by closeness and vulnerability between two people who value each other and regard each other as equals in the relationship. Intimate relationships foster love and ward off feelings of anxiety, isolation, and loneliness. Sullivan identified several stages of interpersonal development, from infancy through adulthood, characterized by a greater capacity for intimacy in interpersonal relationships.

Young children's relationships (2–6 years) tend to be low in intimacy. Relationships are either between two people of unequal standing (e.g., parent and child) or two equals who do not have emotional closeness (e.g., two preschoolers playing with the same toys). Children's main task is to learn to delay gratification (e.g., taking turns, sharing toys) in order to maintain relationships over time. Some children will develop imaginary friends with whom they will "practice" these skills.

Slightly older children (6–9 years) begin to establish intimate relationships in their selection of peer groups. Sullivan saw these friendships (or "chumships") as critical for all later relationships. In the classroom and on the playground, school-age children decide which peers they like and dislike. By accepting another child into one's play group, the child is saying, "I like and value you." Acceptance establishes a sense of self-worth in children.

Sullivan described preadolescence (9–12 years) as a "quiet miracle" in which children begin to develop intimate friendships with one or more "best" friends. These friends act as a source of security and support in times of trouble. Sullivan believed these relationships can begin to foster love, a feeling that occurs when another person's happiness and security becomes as important as the happiness and security of oneself. Sullivan believed that loving relationships allowed preadolescents to share their feelings without fear of rejection or humiliation and to take risks in exploring their identities and values.

Adolescence begins with puberty (12–14 years) and ends with the establishment of a loving relationship with one other person (14+ years). Sullivan saw early adolescence as a time of insecurity and self-doubt that can be managed through the emotional support of peers. In time, however, adolescents use their increased capacity for intimacy to initiate romantic relationships. Part of this transition involves viewing romantic partners not as objects designed to gratify their needs but as autonomous individuals with their own identities, values, and intrinsic worth.

Peer Acceptance and Psychopathology

The formation of interpersonal relationships depends on cognitive, emotional, behavioral, and social factors (Hay, 2016; Prinstein & Giletta, 2016).

First, the ability to form friendships depends on children's cognitive development. Young children must be able to attend to the activities of others, imitate others' actions, understand cause-and-effect relationships, and have basic competence with language. Children with autism, communication disorders, learning disorders, and developmental disabilities may have trouble gaining acceptance from peers because of deficits in these areas.

Second, interpersonal relationships depend on the ability to accurately interpret others' emotions, the capacity to regulate one's own emotional expression, and the ability to empathize with others. As we have seen, youths with autism have difficulty understanding emotions and showing empathy. Children and adolescents with mood disorders also typically have problems with emotion regulation. Irritability, sadness, or social withdrawal can compromise their relationships with family and friends.

Third, children must be able to regulate their own behavior to make and keep friends. Children with ADHD and other disruptive behavior disorders are often rejected by peers because of their aversive, high-rate, or aggressive actions.

Finally, children need adequate social skills to form intimate relationships with others (McGinnis, 2011a, 2011b). These skills include basic modes of social communication (e.g., how to introduce yourself to a stranger), strategies for solving social problems (e.g., how to avoid a fight with a friend), and more advanced coping skills (e.g., how to deal with group pressure). Inadequate social skills can lead to peer rejection. Some peer-rejected youths develop depression and other mood problems, whereas other rejected youths associate with deviant peers who introduce them to antisocial behavior.

Review:

- Sullivan believed that intimate friendships are critical to feelings of security and social–emotional competence. Friendships in childhood form the basis for future adult relationships based on mutuality, closeness, and love.
- Peer acceptance depends on cognitive, emotional, behavioral, and social competence. Problems in any area can contribute to peer rejection and psychological problems.

2.6 CULTURE AND SOCIETY

How Can Culture and Society Shape Children's Development?

Until now, we have focused chiefly on the immediate causes of child psychopathology. These causes include the child's genotype, biological structure and functioning, learning experiences, and interpersonal relationships. These immediate determinants of children's functioning are often referred to as proximal risk factors because they can directly affect children's well-being. For example, a genetic disorder can lead to low intellectual functioning whereas exposure to hostile or coercive parenting can contribute to oppositional and defiant behavior. The overwhelming majority of research addressing the causes of child psychopathology focuses on proximal risk factors because they are typically the easiest to study (Wade & Cairney, 2006).

Researchers have increasingly turned their attention to other, distal risk factors for child behavior problems. Distal risk factors are social, cultural, and broader environmental influences on child development that do not directly affect children's functioning but can affect their social, emotional, and behavioral competence (Toolan, 2016).

One important distal risk factor is socioeconomic status (SES), a construct that reflects parents' educational attainment, income, employment status, and living conditions. Children from low-SES families are at increased risk for developing behavioral and emotional disorders compared to youths from middle- and high-SES backgrounds. Another frequently studied distal risk factor is ethnicity. For example, some ethnic minority youths show greater likelihood of developing a mental or behavioral disorder than their White counterparts. Other distal risk factors include family structure (e.g., single-parent families), neighborhood quality (e.g., population density, crime), and broader social norms and mores (Wadsworth, Evans, Grant, Carter, & Duffy, 2016).

How do distal factors contribute to child psychopathology? According to Wade and Cairney (2006), risk factors like poverty and neighborhood disadvantage can affect child development in at least three ways. First, distal risk factors can *directly influence* child development. For example, infants and toddlers who ingest lead are at risk for developing behavioral and learning problems in early childhood. Typically, youths are exposed to lead from lead-based paint that flakes off the walls of older homes. Children from low-SES families are disproportionately exposed to lead-based paint because they often live in older, more dilapidated homes. Consequently, rates of lead poisoning, and subsequent neurological impairment, are much greater among low-SES youths than among middle-class children (Jennings & Fox, 2015).

Second, proximal factors can *mediate* the effects of distal risks on child development. In this case, distal risk factors undermine parents' abilities to provide optimal care for their children. This less-than-optimal care, in turn, can lead to children's behavioral or emotional problems. For example, Conger, Ge, Elder, Lorenz, and Simons (1994) discovered that the degree to which parents argued over financial concerns predicted the extent to which they showed hostile and coercive behaviors toward their children. Their hostile and coercive parenting behaviors, in turn, predicted the development of their children's behavior problems.

Third, distal risk factors can *moderate* the effects of proximal factors on children's outcomes. For example, the effects of parenting behavior (e.g., a proximal factor) on children's development might differ depending on whether the child is from a low- or high-SES background (e.g., a distal factor). Lundahl, Risser, and Lovejoy (2006) found that psychotherapy that involves teaching parents to reduce hostile or coercive behavior toward their children is often associated with a reduction of children's behavior problems. However, the effects of psychotherapy on children's behavior depend on parents' SES. Psychotherapy is more effective among middle-class parents than low-SES parents. Social and economic disadvantage might interfere with parents' abilities to participate in treatment and, consequently, reduce its benefits.

Review:

- Risk factors can be proximal or distal. Proximal risk factors directly affect children's development.
- Distal risk factors include the broader social and cultural influences that usually affect children indirectly, though parents, other family members, schools, and peers.

What Is Bronfenbrenner's Bioecological Systems Theory?

Perhaps the most influential and comprehensive account for the way social and contextual factors affect child development has been offered by the developmental psychologist Urie Bronfenbrenner (see Figure 2.8). According to Bronfenbrenner's (1979, 2000) bioecological systems theory, children's environment can be viewed as a hierarchy of four nested social systems, each encompassing the others like Russian dolls.

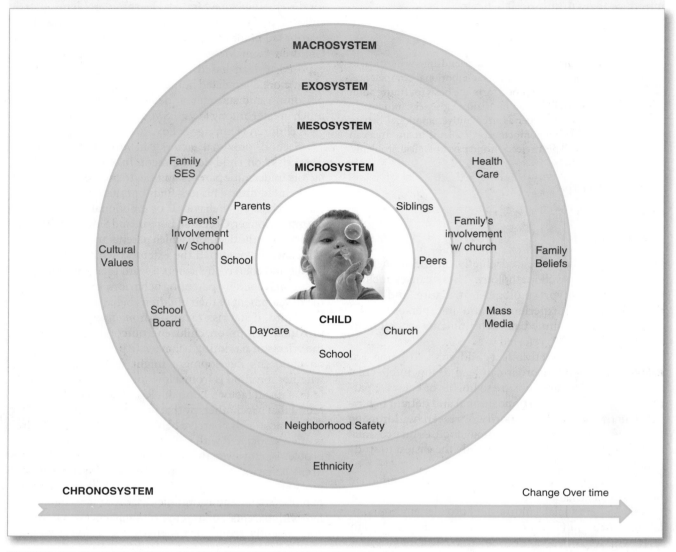

MACROSYSTEM

EXOSYSTEM

MESOSYSTEM

MICROSYSTEM

Family SES

Health Care

Parents

Siblings

Parents' Involvement w/ School

Family's involvement w/ church

Cultural Values

School

Peers

Family Beliefs

School Board

Mass Media

Daycare

Church

CHILD

School

Neighborhood Safety

Ethnicity

CHRONOSYSTEM

Change Over time

Source: Adapted from Bronfenbrenner (1979, 2000)

The microsystem reflects children's immediate surroundings and proximal influences on their development. Factors within the microsystem include children's genetic inheritance, biological functioning, psychological processes, and interactions with parents and family. The microsystem also includes children's other significant relationships (e.g., with teachers, coaches, peers) and the various social roles they adopt (e.g., student, athlete, friend). The microsystem is the "primary engine of development," and children's interactions with caregivers and friends are typically the most important proximal determinants of development (Bronfenbrenner & Morris, 1998).

The mesosystem refers to the connections between microsystems. For example, children's relationships at home and school are important determinants of their overall functioning. However, the quality of interactions *between* home and school also influences children's

well-being. Children whose parents take an active role in their educational and extracurricular activities will likely show different outcomes than children whose parents show less interest in their activities.

The exosystem reflects contextual influences that affect microsystems but do not affect children directly. For example, a father might be required to change work schedules or to work longer hours to keep his job. These work-related changes might influence the amount of time he is able to spend with his child. Similarly, the school board might decide to reduce funding for certain extracurricular activities, causing a child to give up a favorite sport or club. The parent's change in work schedule and the school board's change in funding can alter children's daily experiences and, consequently, their development.

The macrosystem refers to broad social, economic, and cultural influences on children's development. Chief among these factors are socioeconomic disadvantage, neighborhood quality, and media exposure. Other broad influences can include the family's religious beliefs, cultural values, and mores (Toolan, 2016).

Bronfenbrenner recognized that the effects of all four systems on development change over time. In fact, he considered time to be a fifth system in his model—the "chronosystem." Time shaped development in two ways. First, the importance of various systems depends on children's age and developmental level. For example, the relative importance of peers to child development increases across childhood and early adolescence. Second, the nature of proximal and distal risk factors changes across generations. For example, the degree to which children are exposed to violent crime and other social–cultural risk factors has increased dramatically in recent decades (Bronfenbrenner, McClelland, Wethington, Moen, & Ceci, 1996). A full understanding of child development, therefore, depends on an appreciation for children's interactions with these environmental systems and how these interactions vary across time.

Summary:

- Bronfenbrenner's bioecological systems theory views child development as occurring within a series of nested social systems ranging from the microsystem (e.g., immediate influences) to the macrosystem (e.g., distal, indirect influences).
- Development also occurs in the context of time (i.e., the chronosystem).

KEY TERMS

Alleles: Alternate forms of a gene that are inherited or arise because of a mutation

Attachment: The affective bond between caregiver and child that serves to protect and reassure the child in times of danger or uncertainty

Authoritarian [parenting]: A parenting type characterized by low responsiveness and high demandingness; sometimes associated with high achievement but mood problems

Authoritative [parenting]: A parenting type characterized by high responsiveness and demandingness; often associated with good developmental outcomes

Behavioral concordance: The probability that a pair of individuals (e.g., identical twins) will have the same trait given that one of them has that trait; can range from 0 to 1.0

Behavioral epigenetics: A scientific field of study that seeks to understand the relationships between epigenetic structures, the expression of genes, and behavior

Basal ganglia: Brain regions located under the cortex; they help to regulate movement, filter incoming information, relay information to other regions, and regulate attention and emotions

Behavioral genetics: An area of scientific study that examines the relationship between genes and behavior; chiefly interested in determining the heritability of traits or disorders

Bioecological systems theory: A theory of child development that consists of concentric nested systems, each progressively more distal from the child: microsystem, mesosystem, exosystem, macrosystem, chronosystem

Brain stem: An evolutionarily old region of the brain responsible for many basic life-sustaining functions; consists of the medulla, pons, and midbrain

Cerebellum: A brain region located posteriorly (back) chiefly responsible for balance and coordination

Chromosomes: Threadlike strands of genes organized in 23 pairs in typically developing humans

Chronosystem: In bioecological systems theory, the effects of time on children's development

Conservation: The understanding that objects may change in appearance, but their amount or quantity remains constant; develops between ages 6 and 12

Diathesis–stress model: A broad theory that posits that a child will exhibit a disorder when she has both (1) an underlying genetic risk for the disorder and (2) an environmental experience or life event that triggers its onset

Distal risk factors: Risks to child development that are removed from the child's direct experience (e.g., family SES, high-crime neighborhoods, problems with acculturation)

DNA (deoxyribonucleic acid): The hereditary material in humans; found in each cell and codes for creation of proteins that make up our physical structure

Emotion regulation: The capacity to recognize, label, and control the expression of feelings in ways that are consistent with cultural expectations

Epigenetics: A scientific field of study that examines the ways environmental experiences can affect genetic expression and be passed from one generation to the next

Exosystem: In bioecological systems theory, contextual influences that indirectly affect children's development (e.g., parent's work-related stress)

Extinction: A term used in learning theory; involves the repeated presentation of a CS until it no longer elicits a CR

Frontal lobe: A region located in the anterior (front) portion of the brain primarily responsible for language production, problem-solving, memory, and executive functioning (e.g., planning, prioritizing, organizing)

Gene–environment correlation: A model that refers to the idea that our environments are partially influenced by our genotypes; there are three types of correlations: (1) passive, (2) evocative, and (3) active

Gene: Thousands of nucleotides that form part of a chromosome; they are transferred from parent to offspring and influence the characteristics of those offspring

Genotype: The genetic code that we inherit from our parents

Histones: Proteins found in cells; they act as spools around which DNA winds; they regulate the expression of portions of genes, turning genes "on" or "off"

Indulgent [parenting]: A parenting type characterized by high responsiveness and low demandingness; sometimes associated with high self-esteem but behavior problems

Internal working model: In attachment theory, a mental representation (i.e., schema) of a caregiver that helps an individual cope with psychosocial stress

Learning theory: A broad explanation for the causes of behavior that relies on classical conditioning, operant conditioning, and modeling

Limbic system: Located deep within the brain, responsible for emotional processing and memory; consists of the amygdala, hippocampus, and several other structures

Macrosystem: In bioecological systems theory, broad social, economic, and cultural influences on children's development (e.g., an economic downturn affecting overall SES)

Mesosystem: In bioecological systems theory, the connections between microsystems (e.g., parents involvement with the child's extracurricular activities or school)

Microsystem: In bioecological systems theory, proximal influences on children's development (e.g., parents, teachers)

Modeling: In learning theory, refers to behaviors that are acquired by observing others

Myelination: The process that occurs during development in which axons become coating with a white, fatty substance that increases their conductivity

Negative punishment: In operant conditioning; refers to the avoidance or withdrawal of a stimulus that decreases the likelihood of future behavior

Negative reinforcement: In operant conditioning; refers to the avoidance or withdrawal of a stimulus that increases the likelihood of future behavior

Neuron: Nerve cell; consist of dendrites, a cell body (soma), an axon, and terminal endings; relay information within themselves using electrical signals

Neurotransmitters: Chemical messengers that allow neurons to communicate with each other; examples are dopamine, norepinephrine, and serotonin

Niche-picking: The tendency to select environmental experiences conducive to one's genotype

Nonshared environmental factors: Experiences that differ between siblings (e.g., different age, gender, friends, sports, or hobbies)

Nucleotide: Smallest portion of DNA; three of them (i.e., a trinucleotide) code for the production of an amino acid, the building block for proteins

Occipital lobe: A region located in the posterior (back) of the brain that is primarily responsible for visual processing

Parietal lobe: A region located on superior (top) portions of the brain that is primarily responsible for integrating visual, auditory, and tactile information

Phenotype: The observable expression of our genetic endowment

Plasticity: A term used to describe the brain's capacity to change its structure or functioning in response to environmental experience

Positive punishment: In operant conditioning; refers to the presentation of a stimulus that decreases the likelihood of future behavior

Positive reinforcement: In operant conditioning, refers to the presentation of a stimulus that increases the likelihood of future behavior

Proximal risk factors: Immediate risks to children's development (e.g., genetic disorder, teratogen exposure, child maltreatment)

Schemas: Mental models or cognitive "blueprints" about ourselves, others, and the world; acquired and revised through experience

Shared environmental factors: Environmental experiences common to siblings (e.g., same parents, house, school)

Social cognition: Refers to a person's capacity to think about social situations (e.g., how to perceive, interpret, and solve interpersonal problems)

Strange situation: A laboratory-based test of infant–caregiver attachment; can be used to determine attachment security

Synapse: The small cleft between neurons; neurotransmitters transverse the cleft and relay chemical signals to other neurons

Synaptic pruning: The natural atrophy and death of neural connections across development, especially connections not regularly used

Synaptogenesis: An increase in the number of neurons and connections between neurons; arises partially from maturation and partially from experience

Temperament: An inborn tendency to organize behavior in response to environmental stimuli

Temporal lobe: A region located on the lateral (side) and inferior (bottom) of the brain, primarily responsible for hearing, language, and the expression and regulation of emotions

Theory of mind: The notion that other people have experiences, thoughts, and feelings that can be different from one's own; develops around age 3 or 4

Uninvolved [parenting]: A parenting type characterized by low responsiveness and demandingness; often associated with poor developmental outcomes

CRITICAL THINKING EXERCISES

1. Are you and your biological siblings alike? Although you and your brother or sister might have been raised by the same parents and grew up in the same home, you might have different personalities, interests, and goals for the future. Use the concept of shared and nonshared environmental factors to explain why two biologically related siblings, who grow up in the same household, can be so different.

2. The American Academy of Pediatrics has urged parents to monitor young children's access to television and to limit infants' exposure to electronic media altogether. Their recommendation is based on the understanding that the infant and toddler brain is developing rapidly. What is the evidence that brain development extends *beyond* early childhood? Should parents also monitor and limit their adolescents' media consumption?

3. Savannah is a 12-year-old girl who is extremely shy in social situations. She loves computer programming and graphic design and wants to take a class this summer to develop her skills. However, she is afraid to go. How might you use graded exposure or flooding to help Savannah overcome her anxiety about attending the class?

4. Bruno is a 14-month-old infant who participates in the strange situation. When left alone, Bruno becomes greatly upset and cries considerably. However, when his mother returns to the room, he runs to her, motions to be picked up, and sinks into her arms. An observer comments, "Bruno doesn't seem to be securely attached. He's so easily upset when his mother leaves!" Is this statement accurate?

5. Diana Baumrind discovered that children from authoritative families often show the best developmental outcomes. However, most research supporting this conclusion has been conducted with middle-class, predominantly White families. How might ethnicity affect the relationship between parenting behavior and children's outcomes?

TEST YOURSELF AND EXTEND YOUR LEARNING

Videos, flash cards, and links to online resources for this chapter are available to students online. Teachers also have access to PowerPoint slides to guide lectures, case studies to prompt classroom discussions, and exam questions. Visit www.abnormalchildpsychology.org.

iStockphoto.com/Liderina

CHAPTER 3

Assessment and Diagnosis

LEARNING OBJECTIVES

After reading this chapter, you should be able to do the following:

3.1. Describe the purpose of psychological assessment and the importance of including information from multiple informants and multiple methods.

Understand the basic techniques used to assess children and families, such as diagnostic interviewing, behavioral assessment, intellectual assessment, and personality assessment.

Explain the importance of standardization, reliability, and validity in psychological testing.

3.2. Describe the *DSM-5* approach to diagnosing mental disorders.

Evaluate the benefits and limitations of diagnosing children and adolescents.

3.1 PSYCHOLOGICAL ASSESSMENT

Mental health practitioners spend most of their time engaged in three types of professional activities: *assessment, diagnosis*, and *treatment* (Trierweiler & Stricker, 2013). Assessment refers to the process of gathering information about children and families in order to gain an accurate understanding of their psychosocial functioning. Diagnosis refers to the task of describing the client's functioning, usually by matching the client's behavior to descriptions of psychiatric conditions recognized by other practitioners. Treatment involves the use of psychosocial and/or medicinal therapies to alleviate distress or impairment and promote children's well-being. In this chapter, we will examine the first two activities: assessment and diagnosis.

What Is Psychological Assessment?

Purpose

Psychological assessment refers to the process of gathering data about children and families in order to reach valid conclusions about their current functioning and future well-being. The assessment of children and adolescents can have several purposes (Sattler, 2014). First, assessment can be conducted *to screen* children for possible behavior problems or developmental delays. For example, a pediatrician might ask a psychologist to screen a toddler who is showing delays in language acquisition and social skills despite normal sensory and motor functioning. The psychologist might conduct a brief evaluation to determine whether the child has a significant delay that needs attention. Early screening can prevent more severe problems later in development (Briggs-Gowan, Godoy, Heberle, & Carter, 2016).

Second, assessment can be used *to reach a diagnosis.* For example, parents might refer their child to a psychologist because the child is showing a wide range of emotional and disruptive behavior problems. The psychologist would likely conduct a detailed evaluation of the child's strengths and weaknesses in order to identify the nature of the child's problems. The clinician would likely assign one or more diagnostic labels to describe the child's main problem areas. Diagnosis might help parents understand their child's functioning, allow the clinician to estimate the child's prognosis, and help the clinician identify treatment options (Achenbach & Rescorla, 2016).

Third, some assessments are conducted *to plan treatment.* For example, a third-grade teacher might ask a school psychologist to assess a student who repeatedly bullies younger children during recess. In this case, the purpose of the assessment is not to assign a diagnosis. Instead, the purpose of assessment is to identify potential causes of the bullying and to plan an intervention. After careful observation of the bully's behavior, the school psychologist might notice that the boy initiates fights only with certain peers. She might recommend that the bully be separated from these peers during recess in order to avoid the problem in the future.

A fourth purpose of assessment is *to monitor progress in treatment.* For example, a pediatrician might prescribe methylphenidate (Ritalin) to a boy with attention-deficit/hyperactivity disorder (ADHD). She might ask the child's teachers to rate the boy's ADHD symptoms for 3 weeks. During the first week, the boy might not take any medication. During the

second week, the boy might take a low dose of the medication. During the third week, the boy might take a slightly higher dose. The pediatrician might use teachers' ratings over the 3 weeks to determine whether the medication reduced the boy's symptoms and which dose was more effective.

Psychological assessment involves much more than administering a test or assigning a diagnosis. Instead, assessment involves appreciating children's strengths and weaknesses within the context of their surroundings and drawing valid conclusions regarding how to help them improve their lives and the well-being of their families.

Psychological assessment is a *process.* From a scientific perspective, each assessment is analogous to a research study with a sample size of one. The clinician listens to the family's presenting problem and begins to formulate hypotheses about the child's functioning. For example, if a mother reports that her child is earning low grades at school, possible hypotheses might be (a) the child has ADHD or a learning disorder that interferes with his academic performance; (b) the child has an emotional problem, such as depression, that distracts him from his work; or (c) the child has high intelligence and is bored with traditional classroom instruction.

The clinician systematically tests each of these hypotheses by gathering data from parents, teachers, and the child. Hypotheses that are supported by data are retained; hypotheses not supported by data are revised or discarded. For example, after careful testing, the clinician might find little evidence of ADHD, a learning problem, or

CASE STUDY

PSYCHOLOGICAL ASSESSMENT

Stubborn Sara

Source: ©iStockphoto.com/Peopleimages

Fourteen-year-old Sara was referred to our clinic by her pediatrician because of chronic problems with her physical health. Since the beginning of the academic year, Sara has complained of recurrent headaches, stomachaches, and nausea that have interfered with her ability to attend school. Sara experiences symptoms when she wakes in the morning, she begs her mother to allow her to stay home, and then she appears better by midday. After a thorough evaluation, her pediatrician determined that there was nothing physically wrong with Sara and suggested that she be evaluated by a psychologist to determine the source of her complaints.

"Last week was the breaking point," exclaimed her mother. "My husband needed to attend an appointment, and I was already late for work when Sara again reported being sick. She begged to stay home and when I refused, because I had no one to watch her, she had a tantrum like a 2-year-old."

Sara's absences have begun to interfere with her academic performance. "She's missed a lot of work and is falling behind her classmates in math," reported her teacher. "She's such a sweet, caring girl. I really hope that we can find out how to help her."

above-average intelligence. However, while interviewing the child, the clinician might find evidence of mood problems, perhaps associated with difficulty making friends in school. The clinician might revise her hypothesis, asserting that the child's academic problems are due to symptoms of depression caused by a lack of peer acceptance.

The process of psychological assessment, therefore, involves generating and systematically evaluating clinical hypotheses using empirical data. To illustrate this process, consider the case of Sara (see previous page). What initial hypotheses can you generate to explain Sara's problems? How might you test these hypotheses using empirical data?

Principles

Jerome Sattler (2014) has identified four components of psychological assessment that are optimal for obtaining an accurate understanding of children and families. These four "pillars" of psychological assessment are (1) diagnostic interviews, (2) behavioral observations, (3) norm-referenced tests, and (4) informal data gathering.

From Sattler's perspective, the process of psychological assessment is analogous to the process of erecting a building. The conclusions and treatment recommendations that clinicians make regarding child and family functioning are supported by the four assessment methods. Removal of any of these pillars can compromise the integrity of clinician's inferences, just as removal of one of the support beams of a building can adversely affect its stability.

The most accurate understanding of children's functioning is based on multimethod assessment. Multimethod assessment involves gathering data in a number of different ways to obtain a more complete picture of children and families. Under ideal conditions, multimethod assessment involves all four assessment pillars: (1) interviews, (2) observations, (3) norm-referenced testing, and (4) informal data gathering.

Multimethod assessment would be extremely helpful in identifying the cause of Sara's physical complaints and school refusal. First, we would probably want to interview Sara and her mother to learn more about her family, school, and developmental history. Is Sara reluctant to attend school because she is bullied by classmates? Second, we might want to observe Sara's school refusal firsthand. Perhaps we could find a way to intervene and make mornings go more smoothly for her family. Third, we might want to administer some norm-referenced tests to evaluate Sara's functioning. It is possible that Sara has a learning disability that is causing academic problems. Perhaps she refuses to attend school because she is embarrassed by her delays in math. Multi-informant assessment is equally necessary to provide a complete picture of a child's functioning. Data should be gathered from many different people, especially parents, teachers, other caregivers, and the child herself. Previous research has shown low correlations between parents, teachers, and children's ratings of child behavior.

Correlations between informants tend to range from .30 to .40. In general, parents and teachers tend to report more disruptive behavior problems than do children, whereas children tend to report more anxiety and mood problems than do parents and teachers. Consequently, a clinician who relies only on information provided by one informant will likely obtain an inaccurate picture of a child's functioning (Achenbach, McConaughy, & Howell, 1987; Kamphaus & Frick, 2002).

Why do informants disagree so much in their reports? The answer is twofold. First, informants are privy to different types of information about children's functioning. For example, parents have access to information about children's overt behavior at home, whereas teachers are usually better able to comment on children's academic and behavioral functioning at school. Children themselves are often more accurate than parents and teachers in reporting emotional problems, like anxiety and depression. Second, children's behavior can vary dramatically across settings. For example, children may appear anxious at school but appear relaxed at home. Similarly, children may be defiant and disrespectful toward parents but be courteous and compliant toward teachers. Disagreement between informants, therefore, often reflects differences in informants' knowledge of the child and variability in the child's behavior across settings.

Multi-informant assessment would be useful to test our initial hypotheses regarding the source of Sara's problems. For example, we might decide to administer questionnaires to Sara's parents and teacher to evaluate her behavior at home and school, respectively. Her parents might report significant problems with physical complaints, sleep, and anxiety, whereas her teacher might report no such problems at school. In fact, her teacher might report that Sara has well-developed social skills and several friends at school. Such data might suggest that bullying is not the cause of Sara's school refusal. We need to revise our hypotheses and look elsewhere.

Review:

- Psychological assessment is a process that has several purposes: (a) to screen for problems, (b) to reach a diagnosis, (c) to plan treatment, and (d) to monitor progress in treatment.
- Sattler (2014) identifies four pillars of child assessment: (1) diagnostic interviewing, (2) behavioral assessment, (3) norm-referenced testing, and (4) informal data-gathering.
- Ideally, assessment should involve multiple methods (e.g., self-reports, observations, testing) and multiple informants (e.g., children, parents, teachers).

What Is a Diagnostic Interview and Mental Status Exam?

Perhaps the most important component of psychological assessment is the diagnostic interview. The interview usually occurs during the first session, and it can sometimes extend across multiple sessions. The interview usually involves the child and his or her parents, and it can sometimes include extended family members, teachers, and other people knowledgeable about the child's functioning. Some clinicians prefer to interview children and parents together, whereas other clinicians separate adults and children (Saywitz & Camparo, 2014).

One purpose of the interview is to identify the family's presenting problem and to begin to establish rapport. The *presenting problem* is the primary reason(s) the family is seeking treatment. Sara's presenting problem is recurrent physical complaints that lead to school refusal. The clinician pays special attention to the degree to which all family members, especially the child, want to participate in treatment. The clinician begins to establish rapport with the child and parents by empathically listening to their concerns, accurately reflecting their thoughts and feelings, and offering an initial plan to address their problems.

Another purpose of the interview is to obtain information about the child's psychosocial history and current functioning. Typically, clinicians interview the child, parents, and teachers to gain information about the history and current status of the presenting problem; the developmental history of the child; relationships between the child, family, and school; and the child's strengths and weaknesses (see Table 3.1). Many clinicians will also ask families to bring in the child's school and medical records to help them fill in details regarding the child's history.

During the course of the interview, some clinicians also conduct a mental status examination of the child

Table 3.1   Assessing Psychosocial History and Current Functioning

Domain	Sample Questions
Presenting Problem	
Description	*What brings you in today?*
Onset	*When did this problem begin?*
Course	*Has it changed, become better, or become worse?*
Duration	*How long has it lasted?*
Antecedents	*Were there any stressors before the problem began?*
Consequences	*Are there any factors that might maintain the problem over time?*
Attempts to Solve	*Have you found anything that helps alleviate the problem?*
Family	
Structure	*How many people are in your family?*
Parents	*What are your occupations? Educational backgrounds?*
Siblings	*What is the child's relationship to his/her siblings?*
SES	*How is the family's financial security? Housing situation?*
Culture	*What language do you speak at home?*
Psychiatric History	*Has anyone in your family had a problem similar to your child's problem?*
Developmental History	
Gestation/Delivery	*Were there any medical problems during pregnancy?*
Early development	*Did your child walk/talk on time?*
Medical history	*Has your child had any serious injuries or illnesses?*
Physical health	*Does your child take any medications?*
Academic History	
Achievement	*How is your child doing academically?*
Problems	*Has your child's teacher ever reported academic problems?*
Involvement	*Are you satisfied with your child's teachers?*
Goals	*Will your child graduate from high school/attend college?*
Social History	
Parents	*How is your relationship with your child?*
Peers	*Does your child have friends at school/in the neighborhood?*
Social Skills	*How good is your child at listening/taking turns/sharing?*
Behavioral History	
Interests	*Is your child involved in afterschool activities?*
Substance Use	*Does your child use cigarettes, alcohol, or other drugs?*
Sexual Behavior	*Is your child sexually active?*
Psychiatric History	
Previous Problems	*Has your child ever been diagnosed in the past?*
Psychotherapy	*Has your child ever received counseling/been hospitalized?*
Medications	*Was your child ever prescribed medication?*

Source: Adapted from Garcia-Barrera and Moore (2013).

(Sadock & Sadock, 2015). The mental status examination is a brief assessment of the child's current functioning in three broad areas: (1) appearance and actions, (2) emotion, and (3) cognition. (see Table 3.2)

With respect to *appearance and actions,* the clinician examines the child's overt behavior during the session. She is especially interested in the child's general appearance, posture, degree of eye contact, quality of interactions with parents, and attitude toward the therapist.

With respect to *emotion,* the clinician assesses the child's mood and affect. Mood refers to the child's long-term emotional disposition. Mood is usually assessed by asking the child and his parents about the child's overall emotional functioning. Moods can range from shy and inhibited, to touchy and argumentative, to sanguine and carefree. Affect refers to the child's short-term emotional expression. Affect is usually inferred by watching the child's facial expressions, posture, and body movements during the session. Affect can include tearfulness, anger, and withdrawal. Some children show a range of affective displays, whereas others show very little emotional expression. The clinician is especially interested in whether the child's affect is appropriate to the given situation. For example, a child who laughs while talking about a parent's death displays inappropriate affect.

The clinician assesses the child's *cognition* in several ways. One aspect of cognition is thought content—that is, the subject matter of the child's cognition. For example, some children are preoccupied with certain topics or hobbies, whereas other children's thoughts are plagued by persistent worries or fears. In severe instances, children have delusions or bizarre thoughts that do not correspond to reality. Another aspect of cognition is thought process—that is, the way in which the child forms associations and solves problems. Thought process is usually inferred from the child's speech. For example, the clinician observes whether the child's speech is coherent, whether it is rapid and difficult to follow, or whether the child abruptly stops speaking in mid-conversation.

Other aspects of cognition include the child's overall intelligence, attention and memory, and orientation. Orientation refers to the child's awareness of himself, his surroundings, and current events. For example, a child involved in a car accident might become disoriented; lack of orientation to person, place, and time can indicate serious impairment.

Finally, clinicians assess the child's insight and judgment. Insight refers to the degree to which the child recognizes that he might have a social, emotional, or behavioral problem. Youths with eating disorders and conduct problems often show poor insight; they often deny having any problems whatsoever. Judgment refers to the child's understanding of the seriousness of his behavior problem and its impact on himself and others. Judgment also refers to the child's ability to consider the consequences of his behavior before acting. Disorders such as ADHD are usually characterized by poor judgment.

Table 3.2 Assessing a Child's Mental Status

1. Appearance and Actions
   - General appearance
   - Posture, eye contact, body movements, activity level
   - Behavior toward clinician and caregivers
2. Emotion
   - Mood
   - Affect
   - Appropriateness of Emotions
3. Cognition
   - Thought content
   - Thought process
   - Intelligence
   - Attention
   - Memory
   - Orientation to person, place, and time
   - Insight
   - Judgment

Source: Based on Garcia-Barrera and Moore (2013).

Very often, a final purpose of the interview is to arrive at an initial diagnosis for the child. Most clinicians review diagnostic criteria informally during the course of the interview. Other clinicians conduct more structured diagnostic interviews to review criteria with children and parents. In a structured diagnostic interview, the clinician systematically reviews all of the major psychiatric diagnoses with children and parents to determine whether the child meets criteria for any diagnosis (Angold et al., 2012). For example, the Diagnostic Interview Schedule for Children (DISC; Shaffer, Fisher, Lucas, Dulcan, & Schwab-Stone, 2000) contains approximately 3,000 questions that can be administered to children and parents to review the diagnostic criteria for anxiety, mood, behavior, substance use, and thought disorders. The interview takes about 1.5 to 2 hours to complete, but it provides a comprehensive assessment of the child's functioning.

Let's imagine that we interview Sara and her mother during her first session. Sara presents as an attractive although somewhat emotionally withdrawn girl who participated in the session only with reassurance from her mother. She lives with her mother, a dental hygienist, and her father, a former professional chef who has been unable to work because of a stroke several months ago. Sara's developmental history was unremarkable, although her mother described her as a "shy" and "needy" child who has always been reluctant to try new things. Sara's physical health had been excellent until the beginning of this school year, when she began to experience physical symptoms.

Academically, Sara has always lagged behind her classmates. She received special reading instruction in the first grade because of moderate delays in reading acquisition. However, she has never been tested for a learning disability. Sara admitted that she feels "uncomfortable" going to school but would not elaborate. However, she was able to identify several friends at school and described her teacher as "okay." Sara was a member of her school's soccer team but has been ineligible to play because of her absences. She has never been referred for therapy or prescribed psychotropic medication.

Review:

- In a diagnostic interview, the clinician collects data regarding the child and family's presenting problem, history, and current functioning.
- Some clinicians assess children's mental status, which reflects three broad aspects of their current psychological functioning: (1) appearance and actions, (2) emotions, and (3) cognitions.

How Do Psychologists Assess Children's Behavior?

Observation Methods

Behavioral observations are essential to child assessment. Although parental reports of child behavior are important, there is no substitute for the rich amount of information that can be gathered from watching children. Clinicians observe children in three ways (Groth-Marnat, 2003). First, most clinicians observe children *as they participate in the diagnostic interview*. Clinicians might note children's activity level, speech and language, emotional expressions, quality of interactions with parents, and other overt actions. The shortcoming of informal observation is that children's behavior in the clinic may not be representative of children's behavior at home and school.

Second, many clinicians observe children performing *analog tasks* in the clinic. Analog tasks are designed to mimic activities or situations in which children engage in daily life. For example, a clinician might want to observe the interactions between a mother and her preschool-age child. The clinician might ask the dyad to play in the clinic playroom for 20 minutes. At the end of the play session, the clinician might ask the mother to tell the child to stop playing and to clean up the room. This analog task allows the clinician to observe firsthand how the mother issues commands to her child, how the child responds to her commands, and how the mother disciplines her child. Information gathered from analog observation can help the clinician understand how the pattern of interactions between parent and child might contribute to the child's behavior problems. Observational data might also be used to plan treatment.

A third approach involves *naturalistic observation*. Naturalistic observations are most frequently used by mental health professionals who work in schools. During math class, a school psychologist might monitor the activity level of a child suspected of having ADHD. The frequency of ADHD symptoms shown by the target child might be compared to the frequency of ADHD symptoms shown by other children in the class. The primary strength of naturalistic observation is that it permits clinicians to examine children's behavior in natural settings. The chief weakness of naturalistic observation is that it is time consuming. A second shortcoming of naturalistic observation is reactivity—that is, children might react to the fact that they are being observed and act in *un*natural ways.

Functional Analysis

Some clinicians perform a functional analysis of children's behavior. Functional analysis of behavior involves the identification of the antecedents and consequences of a child's behavior based on either direct observation or detailed reports from parents or teachers. Functional analysis is based on the notion that children's behavior is purposeful—that is, their behavior serves a function (Sattler, 2014). In most cases, behavior serves to maximize rewards and to minimize punishment. By carefully observing events that occur immediately before and immediately after a behavior, clinicians can determine the behavior's purpose. Then, the clinician can use information about the behavior's purpose to plan treatment (Beavers, Iwata, & Lerman, 2013; Kratochwill, 2014).

To perform a functional analysis of behavior, the clinician operationally defines the child's behavior problem in clear, observable terms. For example, a mother might complain that her preschool-age child is "defiant." However, terms like "defiant" are vague and not easily observed. Consequently, the clinician might operationally define the term "defiant" as the child's failure to comply with his mother's commands within 10 seconds. By defining the child's behavior in clear, observable terms, the clinician can more easily observe the child's problem behavior and identify its purpose (O'Brien, Haynes, & Kaholokula, 2015).

Next, the clinician gathers data regarding the antecedents and consequences of the target behavior. *Antecedents* refer to environmental conditions that immediately precede the target behavior, whereas *consequences* refer to conditions that immediately follow the behavior. Clinicians conceptualize the situation in the following terms: A (antecedent), → B (behavior), → and C (consequence). For example, the clinician might observe the parent–child dyad during an analog play session. She might notice that the child refuses to obey his mother's commands when her commands are vague. Specifically, the child obeys his mother when she tells him to perform a single, clear action (e.g., "Pick up *that* toy"), but he often fails to comply when his mother issues a vague or complex command (e.g., "Clean up"). The clinician discovers that vague or complex commands often precede the child's noncompliance. Furthermore, the clinician might notice that the mother often backs down from her commands when her child ignores her or when he refuses to obey. Therefore, the consequence of the child's noncompliance is that the mother stops issuing her request and allows the child to continue playing.

The clinician can use information about the antecedents and consequences of the child's behavior to plan treatment. Because vague and complex commands often precede the child's noncompliance, the clinician might help the mother issue clearer, more concrete commands to her child—commands that the child is more likely to obey. Similarly, because the child's noncompliance is often reinforced by the mother's backing down from her commands, the clinician might teach the mother to be more consistent and insist that her child obey her commands (see Figure 3.1).

Let's perform a functional analysis of Sara's school refusal based on detailed reports from her mother. We can operationally define "school refusal" as Sara's requests to avoid school because of at least one physical complaint (e.g., headache, nausea). Then, we will ask her mother to report the antecedents of her refusal. As we might imagine, Sara experiences physical problems only on school days (never on weekends) and only in the morning (never during school in the middle of the day). Finally, we will try to identify the consequences of her refusal. How do her parents respond to her begging and tantrums? Her mother reports that she usually gives in to Sara's requests and allows her to stay home. Her acquiescence quiets Sara, who tends to feel "better" by midday. These findings suggest that her parents' decision to allow Sara to stay home negatively reinforces her behavior by allowing her to avoid an unpleasant stimulus (i.e., going to school). Consequently, Sara is more likely to refuse school in the future.

Review:

- Clinicians can observe children during the diagnostic interview, while performing analog tasks (e.g., in a clinic playroom), or in naturalistic settings (e.g., home, school).

- Functional analysis of behavior adopts the following model: (A) antecedents → (B) behavior → (C) consequence.
- Functional analysis seeks to identify the antecedents that prompt a specific behavior or the consequences that maintain the behavior over time. Clinicians can either alter the antecedents or consequences to change problematic behaviors.

How Do Psychologists Assess Children's Cognitive Functioning?

Intelligence

Children are often referred for testing because of questions regarding their cognitive functioning. For example, a parent might ask a psychologist to assess the intellectual functioning of a child with a developmental disability to determine the child's cognitive strengths and weaknesses. A teacher might refer her struggling student to determine if he has a learning disability. A physician might request testing for her patient who was involved in a bicycle accident and now experiences problems with short-term memory. In these cases, assessment will likely involve an intelligence test (Wadsworth, Evans, Grant, Carter, & Duffy, 2016).

Over the past century, considerable effort has gone into defining intelligence and developing tests to measure it. Nearly all theorists recognize that intelligence reflects some aspects of the person's mental functioning that has its origins in genetics and biology but is shaped by experience and education. Albert Binet and Theodore Simon (1916), the developers of the first intelligence test, defined *intelligence* as the ability "to judge well, to comprehend well, and to reason well" (pp. 42–43). Years later, another important figure in the history of intelligence testing, David Wechsler (1958), described intelligence as "the capacity of the individual to act purposefully, to think rationally, and to deal effectively with his environment" (p. 7). Even more recently, John Carroll (1997) claimed that intelligence is "the degree to which, and the rate at which, people are able to learn and retain in long-term

Figure 3.1 Functional analysis of behavior involves identifying the antecedents that prompt behavior problems and the consequences that maintain them over time.

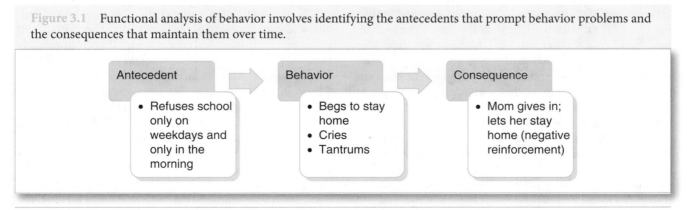

Source: Based on Beavers and colleagues (2013).

memory the knowledge and skills that can be learned from the environment, that is, what is taught in the home and in school, as well as things learned from everyday experience" (p. 44).

Intelligence, therefore, is a broad construct that is related to people's abilities to adapt to their environments, to solve problems, and to learn and use information accurately and efficiently. According to a survey of experts, the most important components of intelligence include the capacity for reasoning and abstract thinking, problem-solving, knowledge acquisition, memory, adaptation to one's surroundings, speed of processing information, adroitness with language and mathematics, general knowledge, and creativity (Snyderman & Rothman, 1987).

The Wechsler Intelligence Scale for Children–Fifth Edition (WISC–V; Wechsler, Raiford, & Holdnack, 2014) is the most frequently used intelligence test for children and adolescents. Wechsler began developing tests in the 1930s in an attempt to measure facets of adults' intelligence and problem-solving abilities. His first intelligence test, the Wechsler-Bellevue Intelligence Scale, was designed for adults. Later, he created a simplified version of his adult scale to measure children's intellectual functioning. The first version of the WISC was created in 1949; subsequent revisions were published in 1974, 1991, 2003, and 2014. The test is appropriate for children 6 and 16 years of age. The WISC–V consists of a series of short subtests that are individually administered to children, either in paper format or digitally. It takes approximately one hour to administer the test (Wadsworth et al., 2016).

The WISC–V yields a full scale IQ (FSIQ) score, an estimate of the child's overall intelligence (Kaufman & Raiford, 2016). FSIQ reflects the child's performance on all domains of the test; therefore, it gives an overall picture of the child's cognitive abilities. Very often, children show areas of strength and weakness that can be missed if we look only at their FSIQ. Consequently, most psychologists examine performance on the five WISC–V indices to obtain a more detailed picture of the child's functioning (see Figure 3.2).

- Verbal comprehension reflects the child's word knowledge and her ability to use verbal information to express herself and to solve word or story problems. Everyday tasks that require verbal comprehension include sharing facts and information, knowing the meaning of words and phrases, and understanding verbal analogies.
- Fluid reasoning reflects the child's ability to solve novel, largely nonverbal problems; to detect underlying patterns or relationships among objects; and to engage in abstract thinking. Everyday tasks that require fluid reasoning include the ability to detect patterns in numbers or objects and to use abstract thought to solve new problems.
- Visual-spatial reasoning reflects the child's ability to attend, organize, and interpret visually presented material and to use visual information to solve immediate problems. Everyday tasks that involve visual-spatial reasoning include the ability to solve puzzles and mazes.

- Working memory reflects the ability to attend to information, retain and manipulate visual or auditory information in memory, and apply information when necessary. Everyday tasks that require working memory include remembering someone's telephone number and solving arithmetic problems in one's head.
- Processing speed reflects the capacity to visually scan visual information, to make quick and accurate decisions, and to rapidly implement one's decisions. Tasks that require processing speed include scanning a supermarket aisle for a specific product or activities that require matching and sorting.

Psychologists examine the child's score on each composite and note areas of relative strength and weakness. For example, a child might show an FSIQ within the average range, but his verbal comprehension score might be much lower than his perceptual reasoning and visual–spatial reasoning scores. The psychologist might predict that the child will have difficulty with traditional verbal instruction in school. He might recommend that teachers use visual demonstrations and hands-on practice to help this child learn.

Intelligence test scores are normally distributed, with a mean of 100 and a standard deviation of 15. The distribution of test scores in the general population is bell shaped, with most people earning scores relatively close to 100 and fewer people earning scores at the extremes (see Figure 3.3). Approximately 95% of people earn IQ scores within two standard deviations about the mean (e.g., IQ = 70–130). The remaining 5% earn IQ scores at the extremes. Approximately 2.2% have IQ scores less than 70, and they may qualify for the diagnosis of intellectual disability. Approximately 2.2% earn IQ scores greater than 130, indicative of extremely high intellectual functioning, which some school districts consider "gifted" (Cohen, Swerdlik, & Sturman, 2013).

Academic Achievement

Academic achievement refers to the knowledge and academic skills that children learn through formal and informal educational experiences. Some clinicians distinguish between tests of intelligence, which measure a person's intellectual ability or capacity to learn, and tests of achievement, which measure information that the person has already learned and retained (Flanagan, Ortiz, & Alfonso, 2013).

Tests of academic achievement generally measure three broad skills: (1) reading, (2) mathematics, and (3) written expression. These three areas reflect the main types of learning disabilities recognized by public schools. They are also the three dimensions included in the *Diagnostic and Statistical Manual of Mental Disorders* (*DSM-5*; American Psychiatric Association, 2013) definition of a learning disorder. Some tests assess a fourth dimension of academic functioning, oral language, which

Figure 3.2 Items similar to those on the WISC-V.

Verbal Comprehension:	
Reflects the development of verbal reasoning based on word knowledge	
Similarities	In what way are a dog and a cat alike?
	In what way are orange juice and water alike?
Vocabulary	What is a *camera*?
	What does the word *walking* mean?

Visual-Spatial:	
Reflects spatial reasoning ability and analysis of visual details	
Block Design	Use colored blocks such as the ones on the left to create designs such as the one on the right. 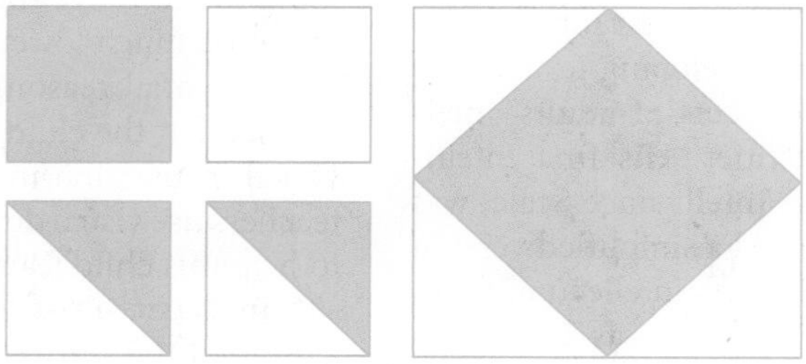

Fluid Reasoning:	
Reflects the ability to apply visual details to abstract reasoning and knowledge	
Matrix Reasoning	Select one of the choices below to complete the matrix pattern. 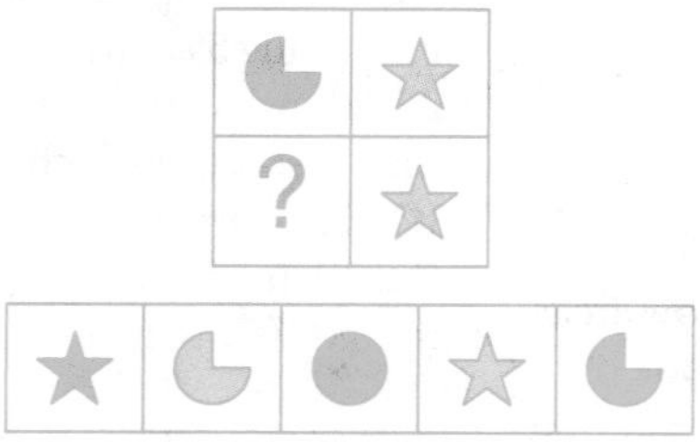
Figure Weights	Select the response that keeps the second scale balanced. 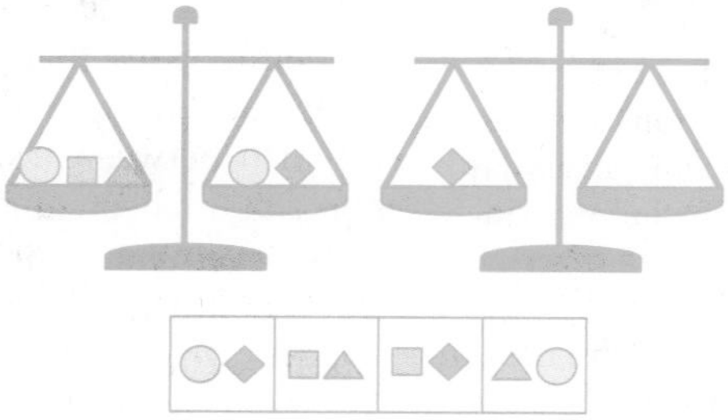

Working Memory:	
Reflects the ability to perceive visual and auditory information and temporarily store it for use in problem-solving	
Digit-Span	Repeat a string of 8 numbers from memory.
	Repeat the numbers 1 through 10 backwards.

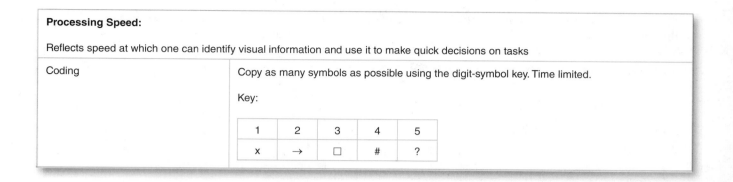

Processing Speed:					
Reflects speed at which one can identify visual information and use it to make quick decisions on tasks					
Coding	Copy as many symbols as possible using the digit-symbol key. Time limited. Key:				

1	2	3	4	5
x	→	□	#	?

Figure 3.3 The standard normal distribution or "bell curve." Most children earn IQ scores near the mean with fewer children earning scores at the extremes.

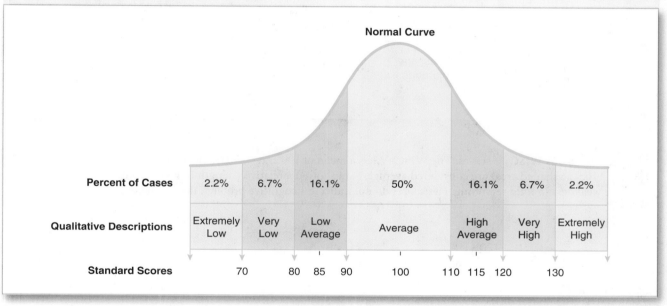

Normal Curve

Percent of Cases	2.2%	6.7%	16.1%	50%	16.1%	6.7%	2.2%
Qualitative Descriptions	Extremely Low	Very Low	Low Average	Average	High Average	Very High	Extremely High
Standard Scores	70	80 85	90	100	110 115 120		130

reflects the child's listening and speaking skills. Problems with oral language are usually diagnosed as communication disorders in *DSM-5*.

The Woodcock-Johnson IV Tests of Achievement (WJ-IV; Schrank et al., 2014) are the most widely used, comprehensive tests of academic achievement. The WJ-IV assesses academic achievement in reading, math, and written language. Within each domain, psychologists can assess children's basic skills, fluency (i.e., speed and accuracy), and advanced applications (see).

For example, children's math skills can be assessed by asking them to calculate math problems (i.e., basic skills), to solve as many simple math problems as possible in a short period of time (i.e., math fluency), or to correctly answer increasingly more difficult math story problems (i.e., applied problem-solving). Similarly, children's written language can be assessed by asking them to spell certain words (i.e., basic skills), to write as many simple sentences

as possible in a brief time period (i.e., writing fluency), or to write more complex sentences according to specific prompts (i.e., applied writing).

The WJ-IV yields standardized scores on each of the three achievement domains with a mean of 100 and standard deviation of 15. Scores more than one standard deviation below the mean (i.e., < 85) can indicate delays in a particular area of achievement, and scores more than 1.5 standard deviations below the mean (i.e., < 78) might indicate a specific learning disability. Usually, clinicians examine children's IQ and achievement test scores together in order to obtain a more complete picture of children's cognitive strengths and weaknesses.

On the WISC–V, Sara earned an FSIQ of 98, which is squarely in the average range (see Figure 3.5). She showed a relative strength in verbal comprehension and a relative weakness in fluid reasoning; however, all of her scores fell within normal limits for a child her age. On

Figure 3.4   The Woodcock-Johnson IV Tests of Achievement (WJ-IV) assess reading, math, and writing skills in three ways: (1) basic skills, (2) fluency (speed and accuracy), and (3) applications.

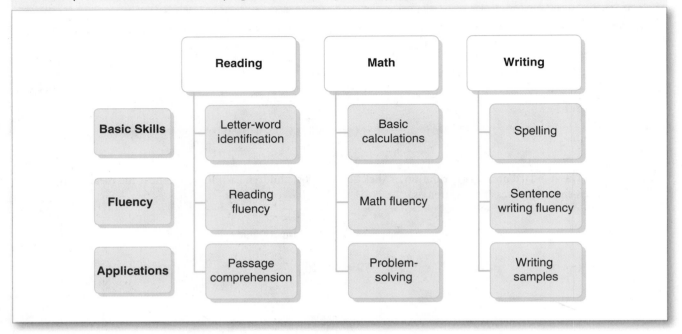

Figure 3.5   Sara's WISC–V scores. The WISC–V has a mean of 100 and standard deviation of 15. Scores between 90 and 110 (the shaded area) are considered average. Sara showed a relative strength in verbal comprehension but a relative weakness in fluid reasoning. Her scores do not indicate a cognitive problem that would explain her school refusal.

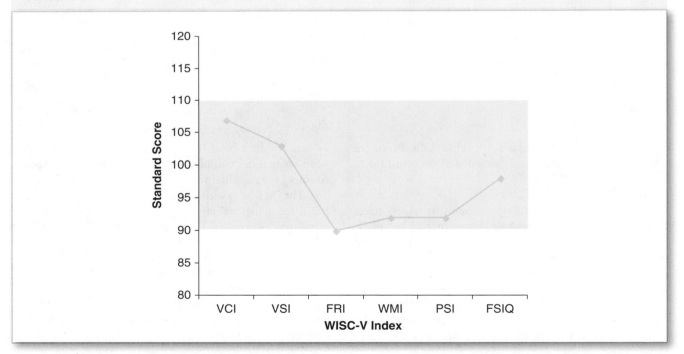

the WJ-IV, Sara's reading and math scores were 93, in the lower end of the average range. Her scores placed her at the 32nd percentile compared to other children her age. Altogether, her scores were average and suggested that her school refusal is not due to a cognitive problem or learning disability.

Review:

- Intelligence is a broad construct that reflects children's ability to adapt to their environments, to solve problems, and to learn and use information accurately and efficiently.
- The WISC–V yields an FSIQ score and measures of (a) verbal comprehension, (b) fluid reasoning, (c) visual–spatial reasoning, (d) working memory, and (e) processing speed.
- Academic achievement refers to knowledge and academic skills that children learn through formal and informal educational experiences. The WJ-IV yields achievement scores on three broad dimensions: (1) reading, (2) math, and (3) written language.
- Scores on most IQ and achievement tests are normally distributed with a mean of 100 and standard deviation of 15.

How Do Psychologists Assess Children's Personality and Social–Emotional Functioning?

Personality Testing

Personality refers to an individual's relatively stable pattern of thoughts, feelings, and overt actions. Because children are in a stage of life characterized by development in all three domains, psychologists are often reluctant to make definitive statements regarding their personality functioning. Instead, clinicians often seek to understand children's functioning in terms of thoughts, feelings, and actions in the context of their maturation and changing environment (Sattler, 2014).

The most frequently used self-report measure of personality in older adolescents and adults is the Minnesota Multiphasic Personality Inventory (MMPI). Despite its name, the MMPI is better viewed as a test of psychopathology and social–emotional functioning than personality per se. The original MMPI consists of true/false items that assess several domains of functioning. The most recent version of the MMPI, developed specifically for adolescents, is the MMPI-Adolescent-Restructured Form (MMPI-A-RF; Archer, 2016). This self-report test assesses three higher-order domains of adolescents' functioning: (1) emotional/internalizing dysfunction, (2) behavioral/externalizing dysfunction, and (3) thought dysfunction. Furthermore, it generates a personality profile based on adolescents' self-reports on nine restructured clinical (RC) scales:

- Demoralization: dissatisfaction, hopelessness, self-doubt (RCd)
- Somatic Complaints: physical complaints such as headaches and stomachaches (RC1)
- Low Positive Emotions: depression, lack of pleasure in life (RC2)

- Cynicism: beliefs in the general badness or selfishness of others (RC3)
- Antisocial Behavior: conduct and substance use problems (RC4)
- Ideas of Persecution: Suspiciousness or mistrust of others (RC6)
- Dysfunctional Negative Emotions: Anxiety, irritability, feelings of vulnerability (RC7)
- Aberrant Experiences: Unusual perceptions or thoughts (RC8)
- Hypomanic Activation: Impulsiveness, grandiosity, and high energy (RC9)

The MMPI-A-RF yields scores (called T scores) with a mean of 50 and standard deviation of 10. Scores >65 can indicate clinically significant problems in social-emotional functioning. Clinicians usually plot the adolescent's T scores on a profile to graphically represent the most salient aspects of the adolescent's functioning.

Sara's MMPI-A-RF profile showed elevations on the emotional/internalizing dysfunction domain (see Figure 3.5). Her scores were particularly high on scales assessing somatic complaints (RC1) and dysfunctional negative emotions like anxiety and worry (RC7).

The Behavior Assessment System for Children, Third Edition (BASC-3; Reynolds & Kampaus, 2014) Self-Report of Personality is a commonly used instrument that can assess personality in children. The BASC-3 can assess personality in two ways: (1) as a semistructured interview or (2) as a self-report questionnaire. The BASC-3 assesses several dimensions of children's personality functioning. These dimensions include areas of potential problems (e.g., anxiety, depression) and areas of strength and adaptation (e.g., self-esteem, self-reliance). The BASC-3 also yields T scores with a mean of 50 and standard deviation of 10. Problem scores >60 or adaptive scores <40 can indicate maladaptive functioning.

Table 3.3 shows Sara's results on the BASC-3. Compared to other girls her age, Sara reported significant somatic complaints, high levels of anxiety, and a tendency to perceive the world as a dangerous place in which she has little control. Sara also reported low self-reliance indicating a general lack of confidence in her ability to cope with stressors in her life. Interestingly, Sara did not report a negative attitude toward teachers, her school, or her classmates. These data indicate that anxiety or worry might underlie Sara's physical complaints and school refusal.

Parent and Teacher Rating Scales

Many clinicians ask parents and teachers to rate children's functioning using behavioral checklists or rating scales. Perhaps the most frequently administered behavior rating scale is the Achenbach System for Empirically Based Assessment (ASEBA; Achenbach, 2009). The ASEBA includes child behavior checklists that can be completed by parents and teachers for children 6 to 18 years of age. There is also a separate version of the test for preschoolers.

Table 3.3 Sara's scores on the BASC-3 Self-Report of Personality

Dimension	T Score	Interpretation
CLINICAL SCALES		
Attitude to School	55	Feels satisfied with school and schoolwork
Attitude to Teachers	45	Views teachers as warm and supportive
Atypicality	41	No unusual thoughts or actions
Locus of Control	**70***	Feelings that situations are often out of one's control
Social Stress	53	Feels reasonably comfortable in social situations
Anxiety	**71***	Excessive anxiety, worries, or fear
Depression	61	Feeling sad, dejected, or misunderstood by others
Inadequacy	61	Moderate feeling of being a failure
Somatization	**73***	Excessive health complaints
Attention Problems	57	No problems with inattention, forgetfulness
Hyperactivity	51	No problems with inhibiting behavior
Sensation Seeking	44	No excessive risk-taking or aggression
ADAPTIVE SCALES		
Relations w/ Parents	60	Views parents as close and supportive
Interpersonal Relations	61	Feels likes and respected by classmates
Self-Esteem	50	Average self-respect and self-acceptance
Self-Reliance	**37***	Problems with confidence and decision-making

Compared to other girls her age, Sara reported significant health problems, anxiety, and lack of control in her life. She also reported significantly low self-reliance and confidence in her ability to cope with stressors.

* Problem scores >60 and adaptive scores <40 suggest significant problem areas.

Figure 3.6 Sara's Minnesota Multiphasic Personality Inventory-Adolescent-Restructured Format (MMPI-A-RF) profile. She shows significant problems on the emotional/internalizing dysfunction scale. Her problems are somatic complaints (RC1) and dysfunctional negative emotions (RC7).

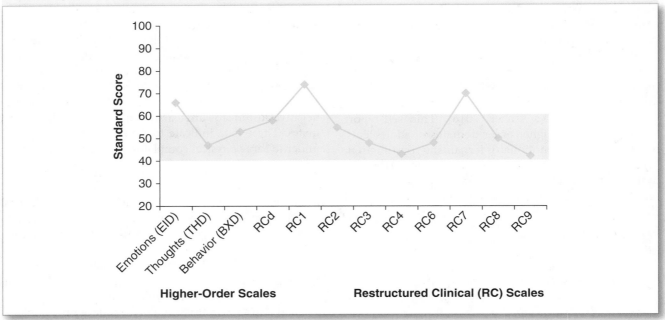

The ASEBA assesses eight types of behaviors across settings: (1) anxiety, (2) depression, (3) somatic complaints, (4) social problems, (5) thought problems, (6) attention problems, (7) rule-breaking behavior, and (8) aggression. The test is norm-referenced, yielding T scores that compare the child's behavior with other children of the same age and gender. Recent revisions to the ASEBA also allow clinicians to compare their clients to children of various cultural backgrounds and to examine the degree to which parent and teacher ratings suggest specific *DSM-5* diagnoses (Achenbach, 2016).

Results of the ASEBA child behavior checklist confirm that Sara is experiencing significant problems with anxiety and somatic complaints at home but few problems at school (see Figure 3.7). Whereas her mother reported significant problems, her teacher largely denied these concerns. These data indicate that Sara might manifest anxiety in terms of physical problems, like headaches and stomachaches, and that she might be worried about her family.

Specific Symptom Inventories

Clinicians can also administer other tests to assess specific disorders. For example, the Autism Spectrum Rating Scales (ASRS; Goldstein & Naglieri, 2015) are widely used to screen children suspected of autism spectrum disorder

(ASD). Clinicians administer the scales to parents and teachers who rate *DSM-5* symptoms of the disorder. The ASRS also assesse the child's communication and socialization skills; tendency to engage in rigid, repetitive, or unusual behaviors; sensitivity to sensory stimuli (e.g., certain tastes or noises); and capacity for self-regulation. The ASRS are norm-referenced; scores allow clinicians to compare the child to other youths of approximately the same age as well as children previously diagnosed with autism.

The *Conners 3* (Conners, 2015) is a behavior rating scale used to screen children for ADHD and disruptive behavior disorders. The test assesses *DSM-5* symptoms of ADHD and can be administered to parents, teachers, and older children to provide multi-informant data regarding the child's functioning at home and school. The test also assesses other potential problems such as oppositional behavior toward adults, learning difficulties, and peer rejection. The test is norm-referenced; it yields T scores that allow clinicians to compare children to youths of the same age and gender.

The *Revised Children's Anxiety and Depression Scale* (Weiss & Chorpita, 2011) might be administered to girls like Sara who show internalizing problems. This self-report questionnaire assesses five *DSM-5* anxiety disorders commonly seen in children and adolescents as well as children's symptoms of depression. The scale

Figure 3.7 Sara's parent and teacher ratings on the ASEBA Child Behavior Checklist. Although her mother reported significant problems with anxiety and somatic complaints at home, her teacher denied these problems at school.

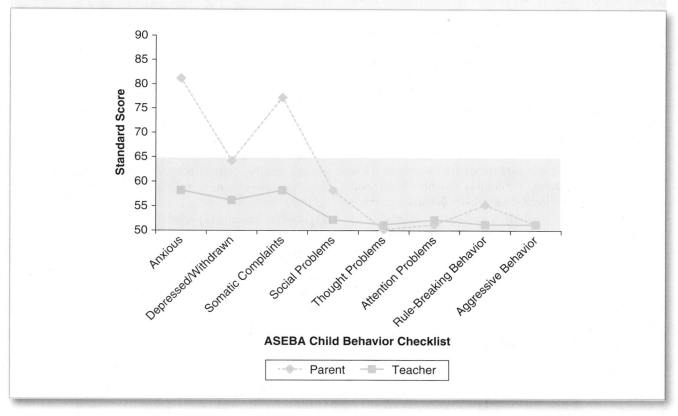

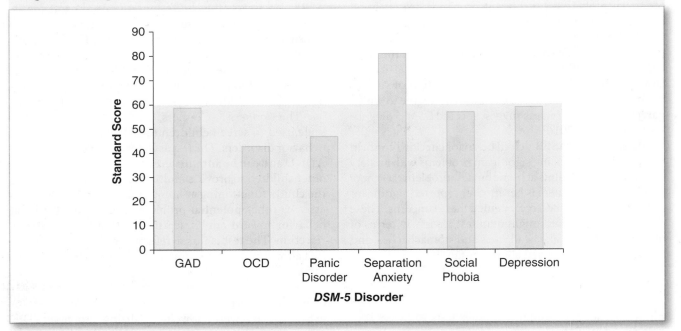

yields T scores, which allow clinicians to compare a child's score with other children of the same age and gender. Sara reported significant problems with separation anxiety compared to other girls her age (see Figure 3.8). Specifically, she reported marked fears about leaving her parents and persistent worries about her parents when separated from them for an extended period of time.

Altogether, data from the diagnostic interview, observations, and norm-referenced tests indicate that Sara's somatic symptoms and school refusal are caused by underlying anxiety about separating from her parents. During the first few sessions, her therapist learned that Sara's symptoms developed shortly after her father's stroke. Because of her mother's busy work schedule, she cared for her father as he recovered over the summer. However, as the academic year approached, Sara became preoccupied by thoughts that he might experience another stroke if she left him to attend school. Her anxiety about her father and fears of separation increased until she began to develop physical symptoms: headaches, stomachaches, and nausea. By allowing her to stay home from school, her mother inadvertently reinforced these symptoms and helped to maintain Sara's school refusal over time.

Review:

- The MMPI-A-RF is a broad, self-report measure of adolescents' social–emotional functioning. It assesses (a) emotional/internalizing dysfunction; (b) behavioral/externalizing dysfunction; and (c) thought, as well as nine clinical scales.

- The BASC-3 Self-Report of Personality assesses problems and areas of strength and adaptation in older children and adolescents.
- The ASEBA can be completed by parents, teachers, or older youths to assess a wide range of externalizing and internalizing symptoms.
- Most tests of personality and social–emotional functioning yield T scores with a mean of 50 and standard deviation of 10.

What Makes a Good Psychological Test?

Although there are many kinds of psychological tests, not all tests are created equal. The accuracy of clinician's diagnoses and decisions regarding treatment depend greatly on the quality of the tests they select than the manner in which they use them. In this section, we will discuss three of the most important features of evidence-based testing: (1) standardization, (2) reliability, and (3) validity.

Standardization

Most tests used in clinical settings follow some sort of standardization—that is, they are administered, scored, and interpreted in the same way to all examinees. For example, all 7-year-old children who take the WISC–V are administered the same test items. Items are presented in the same way to all children according to specific rules described in the test manual. These rules include where participants must sit, how instructions must be presented, how much time is allowed, and what sort of help (if any) examiners can provide. Children's answers are scored in the same way, using specific guidelines presented in the manual (Wechsler et al., 2014).

Standardized test administration and scoring allow clinicians to compare one child's test scores with the performance of his or her peers. Two children who obtain the same number of correct test items on an intelligence test are believed to have comparable levels of overall intellectual functioning *only* if they were administered the test in a standardized fashion. If one child was given extra time, additional help, or greater encouragement by the examiner, comparisons would be inappropriate.

Most standardized tests used in clinical settings, like the WISC–V, are norm-referenced. Norm-referenced tests allow clinicians to quantify the degree to which a specific child is similar to other youths of the same age, grade, and/or gender. These tests are called norm-referenced because the child is compared to a normative sample of children, a large group of youths whose demographics reflect a larger population of interest (e.g., all children in the United States; all children with ADHD). Examples of norm-referenced tests include intelligence tests, personality tests, and behavior rating scales (Achenbach, 2015).

Children's scores on norm-referenced tests are compared to the performance of other children, in order to make these scores more meaningful. Imagine that a 9-year-old girl correctly answers 45 questions on the WISC–V. A clinician would record her "raw score" as 45. However, a raw score of 45 does not allow the clinician to determine whether the girl is intellectually gifted, average, or cognitively delayed. To interpret her raw score, the clinician needs to compare her score to children in the normative sample, that is, other children who have already completed the WISC–V. If the mean raw score for 9-year-olds in the norm group was 45 and the girl's raw score was 45, the clinician might conclude that the girl's intellectual functioning is within the average range. However, if the mean raw score for 9-year-old children was 30 and the girl's raw score was 45, the clinician might conclude that the girl has above-average intellectual functioning.

The results of norm-referenced testing, therefore, depend greatly on the comparison of the individual child with the norm group. At a minimum, comparisons are made based on children's age. For example, on measures of intelligence, 9-year-old children must be compared to other 9-year-old children, not to 6-year-old children or 12-year-old children. On other psychological tests, especially tests of behavior and personality, comparisons are made based on age and gender. For example, boys tend to show more symptoms of hyperactivity than do girls. Consequently, when a clinician obtains parents' ratings of hyperactivity for a 9-year-old boy, he compares these ratings to the ratings for other 9-year-old boys in the norm group (Achenbach, 2015).

Usually, clinicians want to quantify the degree to which children score above or below the mean for the normative sample. To quantify children's deviation from the mean, clinicians transform the child's raw test score to a standard score. A standard score is simply a raw score that has been changed to a different scale with a designated mean and standard deviation. For example, most intelligence tests have a mean of 100 and a standard deviation of 15. A child with an IQ of 100 would fall squarely within the average range compared to other children his age, whereas a child with an IQ of 115 would be considered above average.

Reliability

Reliability refers to the consistency of a psychological test (Anastasi & Urbina, 1997). Reliable tests yield consistent scores over time and across administrations. Although there are many types of reliability, the three most common are test–retest reliability, inter-rater reliability, and internal consistency.

Test–retest reliability refers to the consistency of test scores over time. Imagine that you purchase a Fitbit to help you get into shape. You wear the Fitbit each morning while walking to your first class. If the number of steps estimated by the Fitbit is approximately the same each day, we would say that the Fitbit shows high test–retest reliability. The device yields consistent scores across repeated administrations. Psychological tests should also have high test–retest reliability. For example, a child who earns an FSIQ of 110 should earn a similar FSIQ score several months later.

Inter-rater reliability refers to the consistency of test scores across two or more raters or observers. Imagine that you are affluent enough to own a Fitbit *and* Garmin to measure your daily activity, one on each wrist. If the number of steps were similar for each device, we would say that the devices showed excellent inter-rater reliability; they agree with each other. Similarly, psychological tests should show high inter-rater reliability. For example, on portions of the WISC–V, psychologists assign points based on the thoroughness of children's answers. If a child defines an elephant as an animal, she might earn 1 point, whereas if she defines it as an animal with four legs, a trunk, and large ears, she might earn 2 points. Different psychologists should assign the same point points for the same response, showing high inter-rater reliability.

Internal consistency refers to the degree to which test items yield consistent scores. Imagine that you want to obtain an estimate of your physical activity using your Fitbit. You decide to measure activity in three ways: (1) using an activity tracker, (2) using GPS data, and (3) by manually recording your activity. If you exercise a lot that day, all three scores should be high, because they all measure the same construct (i.e., activity). On the other hand, if you are sedentary that day, all three scores should be low. Such data would indicate good internal consistency;

items measuring the same construct should yield consistent results.

Psychological tests should also high good internal consistency. For example, the WISC–V verbal comprehension tests show very high internal consistency. Children with excellent verbal skills tend to answer most test items correctly whereas children who show verbal comprehension deficits tend to struggle on most test times. High internal consistency suggests that this index measures the same construct (e.g., verbal comprehension) and not other constructs such as the child's reading ability or memory.

Reliability can be quantified using a coefficient ranging from 0 to 1.0. A reliability coefficient of 1.0 indicates perfect consistency. What constitutes "acceptable" reliability varies depending on the type of reliability and the construct the test is measuring. For example, tests that assess constructs that are believed to be stable over time, such as IQ, should have high test–retest reliability. In contrast, tests that measure constructs that are likely to change over time, such as depressive symptoms, will likely have lower test–retest reliability.

Validity

Validity refers to the degree to which a test measures the construct it is designed to measure. Tests of intelligence should measure intelligence, tests of depression should measure depression, and so forth.

Whereas reliability reflects consistency, validity refers to accuracy. Imagine a poor archer whose arrows are scattered across a target in a random pattern (see Figure 3.9). The poor archer shows low reliability (as evidenced by his scattered arrows) and low validity (because he missed the bull's-eye). Now imagine a better archer whose five arrows are clustered together but distant from the bull's-eye. The better archer displays high reliability (as evidenced by

his consistent pattern) but low validity (because he also missed the bull's-eye). Finally, imagine Katniss Everdeen, whose arrows are clustered together within the bull's-eye. Katniss shows high reliability and validity, like the ideal psychological test.

Technically speaking, validity is not a property of tests themselves but, rather, validity is a property of using a test for a specific purpose. Imagine that you record your daily physical activity with your Fitbit for one month. Your daily activity level is very high (10,000 steps) and relatively consistent (i.e., reliable) each day. Consequently, you might conclude that you are in excellent health. However, when you visit your doctor, she tells you that you have high blood pressure and cholesterol. The Fitbit may be a reliable measure of activity, but in your case, it is not a valid measure of your overall health. Similarly, a child's WISC–V fluid reasoning score may provide an accurate estimate of her nonverbal reasoning, but it is probably not a valid indicator of her reading or writing skills.

The validity of psychological tests can be examined in at least three ways. First, psychologists examine the content validity of the test. Specifically, the content of test items should be relevant to the test's purpose. For example, the Children's Depression Inventory, Second Edition (CDI-2; Kovacs, 2011) is the most widely used instrument to assess depression in children. The test includes items that reflect many of the diagnostic criteria for depression including, "I am sad all the time," "I am cranky all the time," and "I have trouble sleeping every night." The CDI-2 has excellent content validity because these items are consistent with the *DSM-5* symptoms of major depressive disorder (MDD) and expert opinion.

Psychologists also examine the construct validity of the test (Cronbach & Meehl, 1955). Construct validity refers to the degree to which test scores reflect hypothesized behavioral attributes, or constructs. Most psychological variables are constructs: intelligence, depression,

Figure 3.9 Reliability refers to consistency; validity refers to accuracy. The best psychological tests yield consistent scores that accurately measure the construct they are designed to measure.

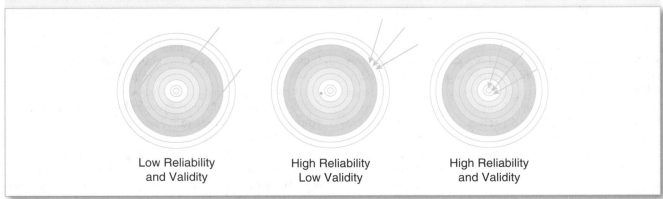

Low Reliability
and Validity

High Reliability
Low Validity

High Reliability
and Validity

Source: Based on Cohen and colleagues (2013).

anxiety, aggression. Constructs cannot be measured directly; instead, they must be inferred from overt actions or people's self-reports. For example, intelligence might be inferred from excellent grades in school, depression might be inferred from frequent crying, and aggression might be inferred from a history of physical fighting.

To investigate the construct validity of a test, psychologists examine the relationship of test scores to other measures of similar and dissimilar constructs. Evidence of *convergent validity* comes from significant relationships between test scores and theoretically similar constructs. In contrast, evidence of *discriminant validity* comes from nonsignificant relationships between test scores and theoretically dissimilar constructs. For example, the convergent validity of the CDI-2 is supported by high correlations with other measures of childhood depression and relatively low correlations with measures of other childhood problems such as anxiety and aggression.

Finally, psychologists examine the test's criterion-related validity. Criterion-related validity refers to the degree to which test scores can be used to infer a probable standing on some external benchmark or criterion (Anastasi & Urbina, 1997). One measure of criterion-related validity is called *concurrent validity*, the degree to which test scores are related to some criterion at the same point in time. For example, children with depression should score significantly higher on the CDI-2 than children without depression. Another aspect of criterion-related validity is called *predictive validity*. Predictive validity refers to the ability of test scores to predict theoretically expected outcomes. For example, children who earn high CDI-2 scores may be at risk for suicidal thoughts and actions in the future.

One aspect of criterion-related validity that is especially important in clinical psychology is a test's predictive power (see Table 3.4). Predictive power refers to the ability of test results to predict the actual presence or absence of a disorder. For example, if a child shows high scores on the CDI-2, what is the likelihood that he has depression? Positive predictive power (PPP) refers to the likelihood that an elevated score accurately indicates that the person has the disorder. The PPP of the CDI-2 is 77%, indicating that 77% of children who score highly on the test really have depression. In contrast, negative predictive power (NPP) indicates the likelihood that a low score accurately indicates that the person does not have the disorder. The NPP of the CDI-2 is 83%, indicating that 83% of children who earn low scores on the test do not have depression. Ideally, diagnostic tests have high PPP and NPP. Sometimes, however, test scores yield false positives (a high score in someone without the disorder) or false negatives (a low score in someone with the disorder).

Review:

- Standardized tests are administered, scored, and interpreted in the same way to all children. Consequently,

Table 3.4 Positive predictive power (PPP) is the probability that a positive test result accurately indicates a disorder. Negative predictive power (NPP) is the probability that a negative test result accurately indicates no disorder.

	Actual Disorder	
	Present	Absent
Test Result: Positive (High)	**True Positive**	False Positive
Test Result: Negative (Low)	False Negative	**True Negative**

they allow clinicians to compare a child to youths of the same age, grade, and/or gender.
- Most standardized tests are norm-referenced. They yield standard scores that quantify the degree to which a child's performance on the test is similar to that of her peers.
- Reliability refers to a test's consistency. Types of reliability include (a) test–retest, (b) inter-rater, and (c) internal consistency reliability.
- Validity refers to a test's ability to accurately reflect a desired construct. Types of validity include (a) content, (b) construct, and (c) criterion-related validity.

3.2 *DSM-5* DIAGNOSIS

What Is the *DSM-5* Approach to Diagnosis?

DSM-5 is a compendium of mental disorders published by the American Psychiatric Association (2013). It is organized into 20 broad categories based on each disorder's presentation. Each disorder is defined using specific signs and symptoms. A sign is an overt feature of a disorder whereas a symptom is a subjective experience associated with a disorder. For example, a sign of depression is weight loss or psychomotor retardation (i.e., sluggish behavior). In contrast, a symptom of depression is a subjective lack of appetite or energy. To be diagnosed with a given disorder, the individual must show the diagnostic features described in the manual.

To illustrate the diagnostic approach used in *DSM-5*, consider the diagnostic criteria for Sara's condition, separation anxiety disorder (SAD; see Figure 3.10). This disorder is characterized by developmentally inappropriate and excessive fear about separating from a loved one, such as a parent. Children with this disorder, like Sara, are preoccupied with fear that something bad will happen to themselves, or their loved one, if they are separated. Consequently, they avoid periods of prolonged separation, or endure them with great distress, and experience impairment in their academic or social functioning (American Psychiatric Association, 2013).

Figure 3.10 The *DSM-5* Diagnostic Approach

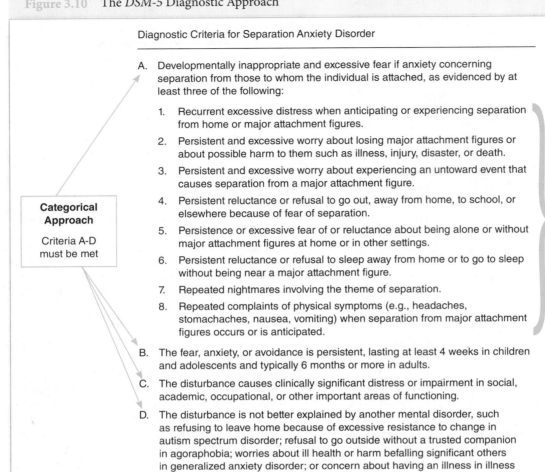

Diagnostic Criteria for Separation Anxiety Disorder

Categorical Approach

Criteria A-D must be met

A. Developmentally inappropriate and excessive fear if anxiety concerning separation from those to whom the individual is attached, as evidenced by at least three of the following:

1. Recurrent excessive distress when anticipating or experiencing separation from home or major attachment figures.

2. Persistent and excessive worry about losing major attachment figures or about possible harm to them such as illness, injury, disaster, or death.

3. Persistent and excessive worry about experiencing an untoward event that causes separation from a major attachment figure.

4. Persistent reluctance or refusal to go out, away from home, to school, or elsewhere because of fear of separation.

5. Persistence or excessive fear of or reluctance about being alone or without major attachment figures at home or in other settings.

6. Persistent reluctance or refusal to sleep away from home or to go to sleep without being near a major attachment figure.

7. Repeated nightmares involving the theme of separation.

8. Repeated complaints of physical symptoms (e.g., headaches, stomachaches, nausea, vomiting) when separation from major attachment figures occurs or is anticipated.

B. The fear, anxiety, or avoidance is persistent, lasting at least 4 weeks in children and adolescents and typically 6 months or more in adults.

C. The disturbance causes clinically significant distress or impairment in social, academic, occupational, or other important areas of functioning.

D. The disturbance is not better explained by another mental disorder, such as refusing to leave home because of excessive resistance to change in autism spectrum disorder; refusal to go outside without a trusted companion in agoraphobia; worries about ill health or harm befalling significant others in generalized anxiety disorder; or concern about having an illness in illness anxiety disorder.

Prototypical Approach

≥ 3 signs or symptoms must be present

Categorical Classification

DSM-5 uses a hybrid of three different approaches to classification: (1) categorical, (2) prototypical, and (3) dimensional. Categorical classification involves dividing mental disorders into mutually exclusive groups, or categories, based on sets of essential criteria. The categorical approach is the oldest approach to diagnosing mental disorders, and is also used predominantly in biology and medicine. For example, in the field of biology, an animal is classified as a mammal if it (a) has vertebrae, (b) has hair, and (c) feeds its young with mother's milk. An animal that does not possess these essential features is not a mammal. In the field of medicine, a person is diagnosed with diabetes mellitus if she has significant problems regulating her blood glucose. A person without significant dysregulation of blood sugar is not diagnosed with diabetes. Similarly, each mental disorder is defined by the presence of essential diagnostic criteria listed in the *DSM-5*. A person without those criteria would not be diagnosed with a given disorder.

You can see the categorical approach to classification in the diagnostic criteria for SAD. The disorder has four essential features (labeled A, B, C, and D); all four are required for the diagnosis. A child would not be diagnosed with SAD if she does not meet all criteria.

Prototypical Classification

Prototypical classification is based on the degree to which the individual's signs and symptoms map onto the ideal, or prototypical, picture of the disorder (Westen, 2012). This approach assumes that individuals with a given disorder may show some variability; not all people with the disorder will manifest it in exactly the same way. For example, if you were asked to generate a mental picture of a bird, you would likely conjure an image of a small, flying animal with a beak that looks like a sparrow or robin. It is much less likely that your initial image of a bird would be something like a penguin or ostrich. A sparrow or robin is closer to the prototype of bird than a penguin or ostrich, although the latter two animals are certainly birds. Similarly, *DSM-5* recognizes that most people with a specific disorder show signs and symptoms similar to the prototype for that disorder; however, *DSM-5* also allows for some variability in the way people can manifest these diagnostic features.

You can also see elements of the prototypical approach to classification in the *DSM-5* criteria for SAD. Although there are four essential features of the disorder, children can manifest the signs and symptoms of the disorder in eight different ways. Only three of these signs or symptoms are required for the diagnosis. For example, some children with the disorder, like Sara, worry about harm befalling a loved one, whereas other children fear harm befalling themselves. The prototypical approach allows flexibility in the way children experience each disorder.

Dimensional Classification

Dimensional classification assumes that disorders fall along a continuum of severity ranging from slight to severe. It involves describing the severity of the individual's distress and/or impairment on this continuum. One advantage of dimensional classification is that it conveys more information than simple categorical or prototypical classification. For example, rather than merely diagnosing a child with ASD, a clinician can describe the child as having mild impairment in social communication (e.g., problems with the normal give-and-take of conversations) but severe impairment associated with his behavior (e.g., repetitive actions and difficulty adjusting to changes in routine). A second advantage of the dimensional approach to classification is that it allows clinicians to monitor changes in children's functioning across time. For example, a child may continue to meet diagnostic criteria for ASD after several years of behavior therapy; however, his repetitive behavior might improve from "severe" to "mild."

Previous versions of the *DSM* were criticized for their exclusive reliance on the categorical and prototypical approaches to classification. Consequently, the developers of *DSM-5* attempted to incorporate aspects of dimensional classification into the newest edition of the manual. Dimensional classification is most easily seen in the *DSM-5* Cross-Cutting Symptom Measure (American Psychiatric Association, 2013), a rating scale that can be used to evaluate the severity of children's signs and symptoms. The rating scale allows dimensional classification on ten broad domains including somatic symptoms and sleep problems, anxiety and depression, anger and irritability, and mania and psychotic symptoms. Children's severity on each domain can be described on a 5-point continuum ranging from "none/not at all" to "severe/nearly every day."

Table 3.5 shows Sara's ratings on two relevant dimensions: somatic complaints and anxiety. The ratings provide additional data, above and beyond her SAD diagnosis. Specifically, they show that Sara is experiencing severe problems with somatic complaints and moderate symptoms with anxiety. These ratings can be used as a baseline from which to assess Sara's progress in treatment.

Some *DSM-5* disorders also allow clinicians to provide additional information about their clients using diagnostic specifiers. A specifier is a label that describes a relatively homogenous subgroup of individuals with a given disorder. Usually, specifiers are created based on the person's symptom presentation. For example, because of the *DSM-5* prototypical approach to classification, children with ADHD can show considerable heterogeneity of symptoms. Some children are primarily hyperactive and impulsive but listen to their parents and teachers, others daydream in class but remain quiet and still, and others show a combination of hyperactive–impulsive and inattentive symptoms. Although all of these children are diagnosed with ADHD, clinicians might assign the specifier "predominantly hyperactive-impulsive presentation," "predominantly inattentive presentation," or "combined presentation" to children in the first, second, or third groups, respectively.

Table 3.5   *DSM-5* Cross-Cutting Symptom Measure (Child Ages 6–17)

During the past **TWO (2) WEEKS**, how much (or how often) has the child….	**None** Not at all	**Slight** Rare, less than a day or two	**Mild** Several days	**Moderate** More than half the days	**Severe** Nearly every day
Somatic Complaints					
Complained of stomachaches, headaches, or other aches and pains?	0	1	2	3	(4)
Said he/she was worried about his/her health or about getting sick?	0	1	2	3	(4)
Anxiety					
Said he/she felt nervous, anxious, or scared?	0	1	2	(3)	4
Has not been able to stop worrying?	0	1	2	(3)	4
Said he/she couldn't do things he/she wanted to do because they made him/her feel nervous?	0	1	2	(3)	4

Specifiers can also be used to indicate symptom onset. For example, children with conduct disorder (CD) show a persistent pattern of behavior that violates the rules of society (e.g., truancy, vandalism) and disregards the rights of others (e.g., fighting, theft). Prospective longitudinal studies show that children who develop this pattern of behavior in childhood tend to have worse prognoses than youths who first show these behaviors in adolescence (Poulton, Moffitt, & Silva, 2015). Consequently, *DSM-5* allows clinicians to specify whether youths have the "childhood-onset" or "adolescent-onset" type of this disorder.

Review:

- *DSM-5* uses a categorical approach to classification because it requires children to meet specific criteria to be diagnosed with a disorder. Youths who do not meet all criteria are not diagnosed with the disorder.
- *DSM-5* also uses a prototypical approach to classification for many disorders, allowing children to show a subset of possible signs and symptoms of a disorder that reflect the ideal (i.e., prototypical) case of the disorder.
- *DSM-5* uses a dimensional approach to classification for several disorders. Clinicians are allowed to indicate the severity of children's distress or impairment on a continuum ranging from mild to severe.

How Is *DSM-5* Different Than Its Predecessors?

DSM-IV (the edition before *DSM-5*) was published in 1994 with minor revisions in 2000. Since that time, our understanding of the causes, correlates, and treatment of mental disorders changed because of advances in the research literature. The primary impetus for *DSM-5* was to update the manual to reflect the current research base and the way knowledge is applied in clinical practice.

Psychiatrists, psychologists, and other mental health professionals were invited to serve on work groups to propose changes for *DSM-5*. Each work group focused on a specific class of disorders (e.g., neurodevelopmental disorders, mood disorders). Each group used the scientific literature to determine which disorders were most closely associated with one another and how each disorder differed from the others. To accomplish this task, they gathered information in four ways. First, they conducted extensive literature reviews to gain the most up-to-date understanding of each disorder. Second, they reanalyzed data to determine the effect altering diagnostic criteria might have on the prevalence of each disorder. Third, they asked clinicians to conduct field trials—that is, to use the proposed diagnostic criteria in their practice and report on their reliability, validity, and usefulness in clinical settings. Fourth, they asked for feedback from mental health professionals and members of the public.

Based on this information, the *DSM-5* developers organized disorders using three broad criteria (Robins & Guze, 1970):

1. Do disorders show similar *antecedents*? For example, disorders caused by similar genetic, sociodemographic, or environmental risks should be grouped together.

2. Do disorders show similar *concurrent variables*? Disorders that tend to co-occur with each other or are associated with the same underlying biological abnormalities should be grouped together.

3. Do disorders show similar *outcomes*? Disorders that predict the same outcomes later in life or respond to the same treatments should be grouped together.

The result of their work was a new organization, or "metastructure," for *DSM-5*. Although the number of diagnoses did not change markedly from *DSM-IV* to *DSM-5*, disorders were grouped into broad areas based largely on similar biological and psychological risks, correlates, and outcomes. Certain disorders were grouped together into a single diagnostic category because there was little evidence for their differentiation. For example, autistic disorder and Asperger's disorder were combined into a single diagnostic category, ASD, because of limited evidence that the two disorders differed from each other in terms of causes, correlates, or outcomes. Other disorders that were formerly lumped together into a single diagnostic group were separated because they showed different causes, correlates, or outcomes. For example, *DSM-5* includes two slightly different diagnoses for posttraumatic stress disorder (PTSD) to reflect that preschoolers manifest the disorder differently than older children or adults. Finally, *DSM-5* includes several new disorders, to reflect recent advances in the research literature. For example, binge eating disorder (BED) was added to *DSM-5* after several studies showed it to be a relatively prevalent and serious eating disorder affecting children and adults.

DSM-5 also attempted to correct some of the limitations of its predecessors (Maser et al., 2009). These problems included the following:

- *A high frequency of co-occurring disorders:* Many people met diagnostic criteria for multiple disorders at the same time (Krueger & Bezdjian, 2009). Often, the co-occurrence of disorders reflected actual comorbidity—that is, the presence of two distinct disorders in the same person. For example, approximately 30% to 40% of youths with ASD also have intellectual disability, a condition characterized by low intellectual functioning and deficits in daily living skills. In some cases, however, this co-occurrence was artificial; it occurred when same signs or symptoms act as criteria for different disorders. For example, "irritable mood" was a symptom of more than eight disorders in *DSM-IV*; it was not specific to a particular disorder. A person with irritability, therefore, might qualify for several disorders simply because of the way *DSM-IV* was written (Hyman, 2011). To remedy this problem, the developers of *DSM-5* revised the diagnostic criteria to make them more specific and thereby reduce artificial comorbidity (Helzer, 2011).

- *Little developmental focus:* DSM-IV included a category of disorders titled Disorders Usually First Diagnosed in Infancy, Childhood, or Adolescence. These disorders included many conditions often first experienced early in life, such as autism and ADHD. However, it excluded many disorders frequently shown by children and adolescents such as anxiety and depression. By creating a separate childhood category, *DSM-IV* implied that disorders outside this category were reserved for adults. It also implied that disorders such as ADHD were rare in adulthood (Rutter, 2011).

The developers of *DSM-5* attempted to remedy this problem in three ways (Pine et al., 2011). First, they changed the order of the manual to emphasize the development of psychopathology over the life span. They dropped the childhood disorders category and, instead, present disorders in the order in which they typically emerge. For example, disorders such as intellectual disability, ASD, and learning disorder are presented in the first section of the manual, whereas personality disorders and neurocognitive disorders (e.g., Alzheimer's disease) occur near the end. Second, the diagnostic criteria vary depending on whether they are applied to children or adults. For example, the symptoms of PTSD are different for preschool-age children than for older children and adults, because preschoolers often have difficulty describing their thoughts and feelings. Third, *DSM-5* describes how children might manifest disorders differently than adults. For example, young children with SAD might have a tantrum to avoid separation from parents whereas older children and adolescents might become "clingy" or avoid peer interactions to avoid separation.

- *Frequent use of the "NOS" category:* In *DSM-IV*, clinicians were allowed to use the term *not otherwise specified (NOS)* to diagnose people who showed features of a particular disorder but did not meet all of the diagnostic criteria. For example, many children who showed persistent problems with irritable and angry moods were incorrectly diagnosed with bipolar disorder, NOS because some of their mood problems resembled bipolar disorder. The overuse of the NOS category caused confusion because, for some disorders, more children were diagnosed with NOS than the actual disorder itself. To remedy this problem, the developers of *DSM-5* discouraged the use of NOS as a generic, "catch-all" diagnostic category.

- *International agreement:* A final limitation of *DSM-IV* was that it did not align with the International Classification of Diseases (ICD), the manual used internationally to classify individuals with medical and psychiatric disorders. Many disorders appearing in the *ICD-10* did not appear in *DSM-IV* and vice versa. Furthermore, disorders with the same title often had different criteria in *DSM-IV* and *ICD-10*. Consequently, the manuals diagnose individuals consistently for some disorders, like depression (87% agreement) but not for others like PTSD

(35%) or substance use problems (33%; Andrews, Slade, & Peters, 2009). These differences caused problems when researchers wanted to compare the results of studies conducted in different countries.

To remedy this problem, the developers of *DSM-5* attempted to align diagnostic criteria with the creation of *ICD-11*. Although there are still points of divergence, the names and criteria for the diagnoses show greater concordance.

Review:

- *DSM-5* reflects recent advances in the research literature.
- The disorders in *DSM-5* are organized into a new "meta-structure" based on similar (a) antecedent risks, (b) co-occurring variables, and (c) outcomes or treatments (Robins & Guze, 1970).
- *DSM-5* also corrected several limitations of previous versions by reducing artificial comorbidity and the use of the generic "NOS" diagnosis, providing greater focus on the development of disorders over time, and making *DSM-5* consistent with *ICD-11*.

What Are the Advantages and Disadvantages of Diagnosing Children?

Possible Benefits

Diagnosis has a number of benefits. Perhaps the most obvious benefit to diagnostic classification is *parsimony*. Imagine that you are a psychologist who has just assessed a 3-year-old child with suspected developmental delays. You discover that the child shows severe and pervasive problems with social communication and repetitive behavior. Instead of describing each of these symptoms, you can simply use the appropriate diagnostic label: ASD. Diagnostic classification is used for the sake of parsimony in medicine, too. Physicians do not describe children as having mild fever, upset stomach, sweaty palms, flushed face, gastrointestinal upset, vomiting, diarrhea, dizziness, and fatigue; instead, they simply say the child has influenza.

A second advantage to diagnosis is that it can aid in professional *communication*. Another mental health professional who sees your diagnosis knows that your client exhibits signs and symptoms described in *DSM-5*. The second professional does not need to conduct her own assessment of the child to arrive at an independent diagnosis to know something about the child's functioning.

A third advantage of diagnostic classification is that it can aid in *prediction*. If you know that your client has ASD, you can use the existing research literature to determine prognosis. For example, most children with autism show chronic impairment in social and communicative functioning; however, prognosis is best among children with higher intelligence and more developed language skills before age 5. The research literature also indicates that children who participate in treatment before age 4 often have the best developmental outcomes. You might use this information to provide parents with realistic expectations regarding their child's future so that they can make more informed decisions regarding treatment.

A fourth and closely related benefit of diagnostic classification is that it can help plan *treatment*. If you know that your client has ASD, you can also use the existing research literature to plan an intervention. For example, a number of studies have indicated that early, intensive behavioral interventions can be effective in improving the social and communication skills of young children with autism. Other forms of treatment, such as art and music therapy, have far less empirical support. Consequently, you can use knowledge gained from research studies involving other children with autism to help your client.

Fifth, diagnostic classification can help individuals *obtain social or educational services*. For example, the Individuals With Disabilities Education Improvement Act (IDEIA; 2004) is a federal law that entitles children with ASD to special education because of their developmental disability. Special education might involve enrollment in a special needs preschool, early intensive behavioral training paid by the school district, provision of a classroom aide or tutor, academic accommodations, life skills training, and other services. Children may be entitled to receive these services only if they are diagnosed with autism or another developmental disorder. Consequently, diagnostic classification is sometimes a means to obtaining educational or social benefits.

Sixth, diagnostic classification can be *helpful to caregivers*. Although no parent is happy when his or her child is diagnosed, many parents feel relieved when their child's disorder is finally identified. After hearing that her 3-year-old child had autism, one parent said, "Well, I finally know what's wrong. I always suspected it and now I know. I suppose we can finally move forward." Diagnostic labels can also facilitate communication between caregivers of children with similar disorders in order to share information and gain social support.

Finally, diagnostic classification can *facilitate scientific discovery*. Researchers who conduct studies on the causes and treatment of ASD can compare the results of their investigations with the findings of others. Indeed, many studies are conducted by teams of researchers across multiple locations. As long as researchers use the same diagnostic criteria and procedures to classify children, results can be combined to generate a more thorough understanding of the disorder.

Potential Limitations

The *DSM-5* classification system also has some inherent disadvantages and risks (Hyman, 2011; Rutter, 2011).

The first main drawback of the *DSM-5* classification system is that it often *gains parsimony at the expense of detailed information*. Although a diagnostic label can convey considerable information to others, it cannot possibly convey the same amount of information as a thorough description of the individual. As we have seen, children assigned the same diagnosis can display different patterns of behavior. We must not overlook the ways each child manifests the disorder in order to plan effective treatment.

A second criticism of the *DSM-5* diagnostic system is that it *does not adequately reflect the individual's environmental context*. Recall that developmental psychopathologists seek to understand children's mental health problems in the context of their developmental level and surroundings. Many maladaptive behaviors exhibited by children and adolescents can be seen as attempts to adapt to stressful environments at specific points in time. For example, some physically abused children attempt to cope with their maltreatment by developing internal working models based on mistrust and defensiveness. Although these models may help to psychologically protect them when they are experiencing the abuse, they may interfere with the development of interpersonal relationships later in life.

A third drawback of the *DSM-5* lies in its *focus on individuals*. *DSM-5* conceptualizes psychopathology as something that exists within the person. However, childhood disorders are often relational in nature. For example, children with SAD, like Sara, experience fear or worry associated with separating from a caregiver. Similarly, youths with oppositional defiant disorder (ODD) show patterns of noncompliant and defiant behavior toward others, especially adults in positions of authority. Considerable research indicates that the quality of parent–child interactions plays an important role in the development of both disorders. Furthermore, treatment for both disorders relies heavily on parental involvement. However, in the *DSM-5* system, both SAD and ODD are diagnosed in the child. The *DSM-5* approach to diagnosis can overlook the role caregivers, other family members, and peers play in the development and maintenance of children's problems.

A fourth limitation of the *DSM-5* system is that *distinctions between normality and abnormality are sometimes arbitrary*. In the categorical approach used by *DSM-5,* individuals either have a disorder or they do not. For example, to be diagnosed with ADHD, a child needs to show at least six symptoms of inattention or hyperactivity–impulsivity. If the child displays only five of the required six symptoms, he would not qualify for the ADHD diagnosis. Although his lack of diagnosis might seem like a good thing, it could mean that he does not receive the treatment or support services that he needs. However, as we will see, many youths with subthreshold symptoms experience significant distress and impairment and often do not differ appreciably from children who fully meet diagnostic criteria.

A fifth criticism of the *DSM-5* classification system is that sometimes *boundaries between diagnostic categories are still unclear*. Categorical classification systems, like *DSM-5,* work best when all members of a diagnostic group are homogeneous, when there are clear boundaries between two different diagnoses, and when diagnostic categories are mutually exclusive. Unfortunately, these conditions are not always met. When two disorders include the same signs or symptoms, children can be diagnosed with both disorders, causing artificial comorbidity. For example, bipolar disorder is a serious mood disorder seen in approximately 1% to 2% of youth. Some studies indicate that 80% to 90% of youths with bipolar disorder also meet diagnostic criteria for ADHD. In most cases, children with bipolar disorder clearly show symptoms of ADHD, even when they are not having mood problems. In some instances, however, the high co-occurrence of bipolar disorder and ADHD is caused by the same signs and symptoms included in the diagnostic criteria for both disorders: an increase in activity, short attention span, distractibility, talkativeness, and impulsive behavior. Some children with bipolar disorder may be incorrectly diagnosed with ADHD because of this overlap in signs and symptoms.

Finally, diagnostic classification can lead to *stigma*. Recall that stigma occurs when people view individuals (or themselves) in a negative light because of a diagnostic label (Corrigan, Bink, Schmidt, Jones, & Rüsch, 2016). Stigmatization of mental illness comes in many forms. During casual conversation, people use terms like *crazy*, *wacked*, *nuts*, and *psycho* without giving much thought to the implications these words have for people with mental illness. Children may use the derogatory term *retard* to describe peers who behave foolishly. Parents of children with psychological and behavioral disorders often report discrimination from school and medical personnel because of their child's illness. Some insurance companies discriminate against individuals with mental disorders by not providing equal coverage for mental and physical illnesses. Movies and television shows unfairly depict people with mental illness as violent, unpredictable, deranged, or devious. Even children with mental illness are portrayed in a negative light (Martinez & Hinshaw, 2016).

Stigma can negatively affect youths and their families in several ways. First, it can cause a sense of shame or degradation that decreases self-esteem and lowers self-worth. The negative self-image generated by the social judgments of others, in turn, can exacerbate symptoms or hinder progress in therapy. Second, stigmatization can lead to self-fulfilling prophecies. Youths may believe that they are deviant, "damaged," or "deranged" because of their diagnostic label. In some cases, children may alter their behavior to fit the diagnostic label or use the diagnosis to excuse their behavior problems. Third, stigmatization can decrease the likelihood that families will seek psychological services because they want to avoid the shame of a diagnostic label. Indeed, many youths who show significant behavioral, emotional, and learning problems do not receive treatment because parents do not want them to receive a diagnosis (Martinez & Hinshaw, 2016).

Research Domain Criteria

The National Institute of Mental Health (NIMH) is attempting to move beyond the current *DSM-5* system of classifying mental disorders based on descriptions of signs and symptoms (Insel & Lieberman, 2013). Specifically, NIMH has launched the Research Domain Criteria (RDoC) initiative to identify the genetic and biological causes of each disorder. The RDoC are based on the assumption that mental disorders are "biological disorders involving brain circuits that implicate specific domains of cognition, emotion, or behavior." The goal of this initiative is to use genetic and biomedical research to identify the underlying causes of these disorders in order to provide more effective treatments. Specifically, research targets several levels of analysis: genes, molecules, cells, neural circuits, physiology, and behavior.

Critics of *DSM-5* argue that instead of being a "bible" of mental disorders, it functions more like a dictionary—providing mere definitions in terms of observable actions and self-reported symptoms. Instead, advocates of the RDoC argue that a new system is needed that addresses the underlying genetic and neurological causes for each disorder.

The *DSM-5* and RDoC reflect different approaches to conceptualizing mental disorders (Lilienfeld & Treadway, 2016). Time will tell if classification based on underlying genetic risk and neural circuitry increases diagnostic validity and leads to more effective treatment than one based on description. In the meantime, psychologists should not forget the rich information that is gained from approaching childhood disorders from multiple levels of analysis in the context of youths' development and surroundings. Recent advances in mental health research indicate that psychological, familial, and sociocultural influences are at least as important in explaining the cause and maintenance of childhood disorders as the genetic and biological factors emphasized by these other diagnostic systems (Cicchetti, 2016a, 2016b). Furthermore, most evidence-based treatments for these disorders operate that these "higher" levels, by improving the psychological, familial, and sociocultural functioning of children and families (Christophersen & Vanscoyoc, 2013). We must not neglect these psychosocial interventions for helping at-risk youths while simultaneously looking to the future.

Review:

- *DSM-5* diagnosis is parsimonious; it facilitates professional communication and permits prediction and treatment planning. Diagnosis can also help children gain access to educational or professional services, be helpful to caregivers, and facilitate research.
- *DSM-5* diagnosis may gain parsimony at the expense of detailed information, may not adequately reflect children's environmental context, and may focus too much on individual children rather than on dyads or families. Diagnosis can also lead to stigma.
- Whereas *DSM-5* diagnosis is based largely on descriptions of children's signs and symptoms, the proposed RDoC seek to classify children based on underlying causes.

KEY TERMS

Academic achievement: Knowledge and skills that children learn through formal and information educational experiences; typically reflects reading, math, and written language

Achenbach System for Empirically Based Assessment (ASEBA): Behavior checklists that can be completed by parents, teachers, and children to assess children's externalizing symptoms, internalizing symptoms, and social–emotional functioning

Affect: A child's short-term emotional expression; usually assessed by observation

Behavior Assessment System for Children, Third Edition (BASC-3) Self-Report of Personality: A broad, self-report measure of problems and areas of strength and adaptation for older children and adolescents

Categorical classification: Diagnostic approach in which disorders are divided into mutually exclusive groups based on sets of essential criteria

Content validity: The degree to which test items (i.e., questions) are relevant to the construct of interest; usually supported by asking experts to rate the quality of each item

Construct validity: The degree to which test scores assess the construct of interest; usually supported by strong correlations with similar constructs (convergent validity) and weak/absent correlations with dissimilar constructs (discriminant validity)

Criterion-related validity: The degree to which test scores can be used to infer a probable standing on some external variable of interest; usually supported when test scores are associated with outcomes at the same point in time (concurrent validity) or in the future (predictive validity)

Diagnostic interview: The most common assessment technique in which the clinician collects data regarding the child and family's presenting problem, history, and current functioning

Dimensional classification: Diagnostic approach in which the severity of the individual's distress and/or impairment is described on a continuum

Fluid reasoning: A component of intelligence; the child's ability to solve novel, largely nonverbal problems; to detect underlying patterns or relationships among objects; and to engage in abstract thinking

Functional analysis of behavior: An assessment technique in which the clinician attempts to identify the antecedent events that elicit a behavior and the environmental consequences that maintain it over time

Insight: During a mental status exam, the degree to which the child recognizes that he might have a psychological problem

Intelligence: A broad construct related to people's abilities to adapt to their environments, to solve problems, and to learn and use information accurately and efficiently

Inter-rater reliability: The consistency of test scores across two or more raters or observers

Internal consistency: The degree to which items on the same test are consistent with each other

Judgment: During a mental status exam, the child's ability to consider the consequences of behavior before acting

Mental status examination: A brief assessment of the child's current functioning in three broad areas: (1) appearance and actions, (2) emotion, and (3) cognition

MMPI-Adolescent-Restructured Form (MMPI-A-RF): A broad self-report measure of adolescents' social–emotional functioning; assesses emotional/internalizing dysfunction; behavioral/externalizing dysfunction; and thought, as well as nine clinical scales

Mood: A child's long-term emotional disposition; usually assessed by self-report

Multi-informant assessment: The process of gathering data from several different people (e.g., parents, teachers, child) to obtain an estimate of children's functioning across settings

Multimethod assessment: The process of gathering data in a number of different ways (e.g., self-report, observation, testing) to obtain a more complete picture of children's functioning

Negative predictive power (NPP): The likelihood that a low score on a test accurately indicates that the person does not have a disorder

Norm-referenced tests: Tests that yield scores that quantify the degree to which a child's performance on the test is similar to that of her peers

Normally distributed: A bell-shaped distribution of scores in which most children earn scores near the mean and fewer earn scores at the extremes

Orientation: During a mental status exam, the child's awareness of person, place, and time

Personality: A broad construct that refers to a person's relatively stable pattern of thoughts, feelings, and overt actions

Positive predictive power (PPP): The likelihood that an elevated score on a test accurately indicates that the person has a disorder

Predictive power: The ability of test results to predict the presence or absence of a disorder

Processing speed: A component of intelligence; the child's capacity to visually scan visual information, to make quick and accurate decisions, and to rapidly implement your decisions

Prototypical classification: Diagnostic approach that is based on the degree to which the individual's signs and symptoms map onto the ideal picture of the disorder

Psychological assessment: The process of gathering data about children and families in order to reach valid conclusions about their current functioning and future well-being

Psychosocial history: A portion of the diagnostic interview in which the clinician gathers information about the child's developmental, educational, medical, and psychological past

Reliability: The consistency of scores generated by a psychological test

Sign: An observable feature of a disorder (e.g., hyperactivity, sluggishness)

Specifier: A label that describes a relatively homogenous subgroup of individuals with a given disorder

Standard score: A child's raw score on a test that has been changed to a different scale with a designated mean and standard deviation (e.g., IQ tests have a mean of 100 and standard deviation of 15)

Standardization: A property of evidence-based tests; indicates that tests are administered, scored, and interpreted in the same way to all examinees

Structured diagnostic interview: An assessment process in which the clinician systematically reviews all of the major psychiatric diagnoses with children and/or parents to determine whether the child meets criteria for any diagnosis

Symptom: A subjective experience associated with a disorder (e.g., anxiety, depressed mood)

Test–retest reliability: The consistency of test scores over time; temporal stability

Thought content: During a mental status exam, the subject matter of the child's cognitions

Thought process: During a mental status exam, the manner in which the child forms associations and solves problems

Validity: A test's ability to accurately reflect a desired construct

Verbal comprehension: A component of intelligence; the child's word knowledge and her ability to use verbal information to express herself and solve word or story problems

Visual–spatial reasoning: A component of intelligence; the child's ability to attend, organize, and interpret visually presented material and to use visual information to solve immediate problems

Wechsler Intelligence Scale for Children–Fifth Edition (WISC–V): The most frequently used intelligence test for children; yields a full scale IQ (FSIQ) score and scores on five broad composites

Woodcock-Johnson IV Tests of Achievement (WJ-IV): The most frequently used achievement test for children; yields scores for reading, math, and written language

Working memory: A component of intelligence; the child's ability to attend to information, retain and manipulate visual or auditory information in memory, and apply information when necessary

CRITICAL THINKING EXERCISES

1. Imagine that you are a psychologist who wants to assess an 8-year-old boy for ADHD. From whom might you gather information about the boy's behavior?

2. How might a psychologist use naturalistic observation to assess an 8-year-old boy suspected of ADHD?

3. Can a psychological test be reliable but not valid? Can a test be valid but not reliable?

4. Terry is a 9-year-old boy diagnosed with a learning disability. His guidance counselor explained to his teacher, "Terry has trouble with reading because he has a learning disability." Is the guidance counselor correct? Does Terry's diagnosis actually *explain* his learning problems? What might be the benefit of this diagnostic label?

5. The proposed RDoC emphasize the genetic, neurological, and biobehavioral causes of mental disorders. What might be one limitation of classifying childhood disorders based chiefly on these underlying causes?

TEST YOURSELF AND EXTEND YOUR LEARNING

Videos, flash cards, and links to online resources for this chapter are available to students online. Teachers also have access to PowerPoint slides to guide lectures, case studies to prompt classroom discussions, and exam questions. Visit www.abnormalchildpsychology.org.

Treating Children, Adolescents, and Families

LEARNING OBJECTIVES

After reading this chapter, you should be able to do the following:

4.1. Identify some common medications used to treat childhood disorders and the neurotransmitters they affect.

4.2. Differentiate the major systems of psychotherapy used to treat children, adolescents, and families.

4.3. Be familiar with the research literature on the efficacy and effectiveness of psychotherapy for children.

4.4. Apply the APA Ethical Principles to clinical situations involving children and families.

Mental health professionals hold positions of authority and trust. Clients usually come to therapists when they are experiencing emotional distress and marked problems with daily life. Clients are often vulnerable, and they seek care that is sensitive and responsive to their needs. The provision of evidence-based and ethically mindful treatment is especially important when clients are juveniles. Parents and other caregivers place their most valuable assets—their children—in the care of therapists, with the expectation that clinicians will help their children overcome problems and achieve the highest levels of behavioral, cognitive, and social–emotional functioning possible.

In this chapter, we will examine the use of medication and psychotherapy to treat youths with mental disorders. We will also learn why ethics is important in the helping professions and explore some special ethical considerations when clinicians work with children and families. To illustrate these aspects of treatment, consider the case of Anna.

CASE STUDY

SYSTEMS OF PSYCHOTHERAPY

Anna's Secret

Sixteen-year-old Anna first disclosed her habit of bingeing and purging in the most unlikely of places: the dentist's office. During a routine cleaning, the hygienist noticed a marked deterioration of her dental enamel and an overall yellowish-gray hue of her teeth. These signs, combined with slight inflammation of her salivary glands, suggested repeated vomiting.

"When the hygienist asked if I made myself vomit on purpose, I felt really strange: a mix of terror and relief," Anna later explained to her therapist. "I was so embarrassed, but it also made me feel a little better that I could now talk about it."

With the help of the hygienist, Anna agreed to tell her mother about her pattern of bingeing and purging. Her behavior began 18 months ago and had waxed and waned depending on Anna's stress level. She was most likely to binge when upset about her family, friends, or school and when she was feeling lonely or left out. She tended to binge on snack foods, especially chips, cereal, and ramen noodles. On average, Anna would binge 4 to 5 times per week.

"I wasn't really surprised when Anna told me," her mom added. "She's tried to hide it from us by running the water in the bathroom sink, taking a lot of showers, and using air fresheners and mints. It was like the elephant in the living room that we all saw but no one talked about."

"Well, it's out in the open now," Anna's therapist replied. "Let's see if we can find a way to make things better."

4.1. MEDICATION
How Is Medication Used to Treat Children and Adolescents?

Psychotropic medications are usually prescribed to children by physicians: pediatricians, family practitioners, or child psychiatrists. In most jurisdictions, psychologists (who are not physicians) cannot prescribe medication.

The medications used to treat childhood disorders are the same as those prescribed to adults. Children are not merely "little adults," however; they process medication differently. For example, children are less efficient than adults at absorbing medications into their digestive systems. They also metabolize and excrete medications more rapidly than do adults. Consequently, children often require higher and more frequent doses (relative to their height and weight) than adults. Some medications that are effective for adults are ineffective for children (Lee & Findling, 2015).

Most research supporting the safety and efficacy of psychotropic medications has involved adults; relatively few medications have been approved by the US Food and Drug Administration (FDA) for use with children. Two federal laws, the Best Pharmaceuticals for Children Act and the Pediatric Research Equity Act, provide incentives to pharmaceutical companies to test these medications with youths. Consequently, there has been an increase in the number of studies investigating the safety and efficacy of medication for children and adolescents. Nevertheless, many medications are prescribed to children "off label"— that is, without formal FDA approval (US Food and Drug Administration, 2012).

Pharmacological treatment involves three phases: (1) initiation, (2) maintenance, and (3) discontinuation. First, the physician selects a low starting dose to determine if the child can tolerate it. The physician gradually titrates (i.e., increases) the dosage until it yields beneficial results. If the child fails to respond to the medication or if the medication causes excessive side effects, the physician may try a different medication. Even medications in the same class have slightly different chemical structures, resulting in different effects on children's behavior. Consequently, a child who does not respond positively to the first medication may benefit from a different one (Lee & Findling, 2015).

After an effective medication and dosage has been identified, the physician monitors the child's response during the maintenance phase of treatment. Many physicians will ask other adults, who are blind to the child's medication status, to complete rating scales regarding the child's functioning. For example, a teacher might be asked to complete a short attention-deficit/hyperactivity disorder (ADHD) symptom checklist before and after a child is prescribed stimulant medication to see if the medication affects his behavior at school. In some cases, physicians must periodically monitor children's blood and cardiovascular health to make sure that the medication does not cause rare, but dangerous side effects. Physicians also work with caregivers to make sure that there is an adherence to treatment by children. For example, some children refuse to take medication because they have difficulty swallowing pills, dislike the medication's side effects, or are oppositional toward adults more generally. Some adolescents abuse psychotropic medications or distribute their medication to peers, a practice known as diversion. For example, some stimulant medications used to treat ADHD can be abused to produce a euphoric effect or sold to classmates to help them study.

Finally, the physician must supervise the discontinuation of medication. Rapid discontinuation can produce rebound effects, which are typically a rapid increase in symptoms the medication was meant to reduce. In rare cases, unsupervised discontinuation can also lead to more serious health problems (Dulcan & Ballard, 2015).

Review:

- In most cases, medication is prescribed by physicians.
- Relatively few psychotropic medications are FDA approved for children or adolescents; nevertheless, nonapproved medications are frequently prescribed off label to youths.
- Pharmacotherapy involves three stages: (1) initiation, (2) maintenance, and (3) discontinuation.

What Medications Are Most Frequently Prescribed to Children?

Table 4.1 summarizes the most commonly prescribed psychotropic medications for childhood disorders. They are organized into five classes: (1) stimulants and non-stimulants for ADHD, (2) anxiolytics, (3) antidepressants, (4) mood stabilizers and anticonvulsants, and (5) antipsychotics.

Stimulants and Nonstimulants for Attention-Deficit/Hyperactivity Disorder

The most frequently prescribed medications for children are the psychostimulants. These medications are used to treat ADHD by increasing activity of dopamine (and to a lesser extent, norepinephrine) in brain areas responsible for attention, concentration, and behavioral inhibition. The two broad types of stimulants, the amphetamines and methylphenidates, have different chemical structures and augment dopaminergic activity in slightly different ways. These medications take immediate effect; children usually experience increased attention and decreased hyperactivity approximately twenty to thirty minutes after ingestion. Effects last approximately four hours for the short-acting version of these medications (e.g., Adderall, Ritalin). However, extended release versions of these medications have been developed that last 8 to 12 hours (e.g., Concerta, Vyvanse). Stimulant granules can also be sprinkled onto food (e.g., Metadate CD) or administered using a transdermal patch (e.g., Daytrana) for children who cannot swallow pills. The most common side effects are appetite suppression and insomnia, which can usually be corrected by adjusting the time the medication is administered (Spencer, Biederman, & Wilens, 2015).

The nonstimulant medication for ADHD, atomoxetine (Strattera), was developed as an alternative form of treatment. Atomoxetine is a specific norepinephrine reuptake inhibitor that can regulate attention and behavioral inhibition in the 30% of children with ADHD who do not respond to stimulants. The medication takes 1 to 4 weeks to produce maximum benefits. Because it is not a stimulant, and because it does not produce immediate effects, it is less likely to be abused or distributed to others. It also has fewer side effects (Spencer et al., 2015).

Anxiolytics

Anxiolytics are medications that are used to reduce anxiety, panic, or worry. Behavioral and cognitive therapy is typically recommended as a first-line treatment for children with anxiety. However, medication can be used if children's symptoms interfere with their ability to participate in therapy or if therapy is not effective by itself. *Selective serotonin reuptake inhibitors (SSRIs)* are typically the first medication used to treat anxiety disorders and obsessive–compulsive disorder (OCD). These medications regulate the reuptake of serotonin in the synaptic cleft, thus alleviating negative affect. They take approximately two to four weeks to achieve maximum benefits. Common side effects include nausea, diarrhea, headaches, dizziness, and changes in appetite or weight.

Serotonin norepinephrine reuptake inhibitors (SNRIs) have also been shown to reduce anxiety in older children and adolescents. As their name implies, these medications affect both serotonin and norepinephrine reuptake. They appear to be especially useful in decreasing chronic worry, a key symptom of generalized anxiety disorder (GAD; Connolly, Suarez, Victor, Zagoloff, & Bernstein, 2015).

Other medications used to treat anxiety in adults do not have sufficient evidence demonstrating their efficacy and safety in children. For example, benzodiazepines reduce anxiety in adults by enhancing the inhibitory neurotransmitter gamma-aminobutyric acid (GABA). Few studies indicate that benzodiazepines are effective to treat childhood anxiety. Furthermore, these medications can lead to sedation, cognitive impairment, and (with prolonged use) dependence. Most physicians only prescribe these medications to children to help them cope with a short-term stressor or traumatic event (Connolly et al., 2015).

Antidepressants

Some SSRIs are effective in reducing depression in children and adolescents. Antidepressants fluoxetine (Prozac) and sertraline (Zoloft) have repeatedly been shown to reduce depressive symptoms in children and adolescents, and both are FDA approved for children with certain anxiety or mood problems. Side effects include nausea, diarrhea, headaches, dizziness, and appetite disturbance. SSRIs are also associated with increased suicidal ideation (but not suicide attempts) in some children. The FDA found that approximately 4% of children taking SSRIs reported increased suicidal thoughts compared to 2% of children taking placebo. Therefore, SSRIs must be used judiciously, and children taking these medications should be monitored by their physicians and caregivers (Emslie, Croarkin, Chapman, & Mayes, 2015).

Older, *tricyclic antidepressants* are generally not regarded as first-line medications for child or adolescent depression. These medications regulate the reuptake of either serotonin and norepinephrine (e.g., amitriptyline; Elavil) or norepinephrine alone (e.g., nortriptyline; Pamelor). Randomized controlled studies have not shown these medications to be effective in reducing depression among youths. Furthermore, they are associated with cardiovascular problems in children and adolescents

Table 4.1   Common Psychotropic Medications for Children and Adolescents

Medication (Examples)	Effects	Side Effects
ADHD Medications		

Short-Acting Stimulants
    Amphetamine (Adderall, Dexedrine)
    Methylphenidate (Ritalin, Focalin)
Long-Acting Stimulants
    Amphetamine (Vyvanse)
    Methylphenidate (Concerta)
Nonstimulants
    Atomoxetine (Strattera)
	Enhances dopamine and norepinephrine;
	
	Reduces ADHD symptoms; improves social and academic problems caused by ADHD
		Reduced appetite, sleep problems, headaches, abdominal problems, abuse & diversion (for stimulants)

Anti-Anxiety Medications		

SSRIs
    Fluoxetine (Prozac)
    Sertraline (Zoloft)
SNRIs
    Duloxetine (Cymbalta)
    Venlafaxine (Effexor)
	Regulates the reuptake of serotonin and norepinephrine; SSRIs are first-line medication for anxiety & OCD; SNRIs are effective in reducing generalized anxiety (worry)	Nausea, diarrhea, headaches, dizziness, sleepiness

Antidepressants		

SSRIs
    Fluoxetine (Prozac)
    Sertraline (Zoloft)
	Regulates the reuptake of serotonin; Some SSRIs are effective in decreasing depression in youths	Nausea, diarrhea, headaches, dizziness, sleepiness; increase in suicidal thoughts in some youths

Mood Stabilizers & Anticonvulsants		

Mood Stabilizers
    Lithium (Eskalith)
Anticonvulsants
    Valproate (Depakote)
    Carbamazepine (Tegretol)
    Oxcarbazepine (Trileptal)
	Decreases duration and severity of mania, prevents future manic or depressive episodes	Nausea, diarrhea, sedation, tremor, weight gain, acne; can cause toxicity, heart, and liver problems if not monitored

Antipsychotics		

First generation
    Haloperidol (Haldol)
    Molindone (Moban)
Second generation
    Olanzapine (Zyprexa)
    Risperidone (Risperdal)
Third generation
    Aripiprazole (Abilify)
	Blocks dopamine receptors; Decreases delusions and hallucinations of schizophrenia; can reduce aggressive behavior in children with developmental disorders and autism, often used to decrease mania in children with bipolar disorder	Sedation, cognitive problems, weight gain, agitation/restlessness, metabolic problems, prolactin (hormone) abnormalities; in rare cases neuroleptic malignant syndrome

Source: From Correll (2015); Dulcan & Ballard (2015); Emslie, Croarkin, Chapman, & Mayes (2015); Gracious, Danielyan, & Kowatch (2015); Lee & Findling (2015); and Spencer, Biederman, & Wilens (2015).

that can cause sudden death. In contrast, the newer *atypical (i.e., non-SSRI) antidepressants* like bupropion (Wellbutrin) and mirtazapine (Remeron) are effective in reducing depression in adults, but there have not been sufficient studies demonstrating their efficacy and safety with youths (Emslie et al., 2015).

Mood Stabilizers and Anticonvulsants

The mood stabilizer *lithium* (Eskalith) has considerable evidence supporting its efficacy in treating bipolar disorders in adults. Over the past 20 years, randomized controlled studies have shown that lithium is moderately effective in reducing the duration and severity of manic symptoms in children and adolescents. It may also be effective in preventing future manic or depressive episodes in youths with bipolar disorder. Lithium is a naturally occurring salt that affects various receptors in the central nervous system. It is FDA approved for use in adolescents with bipolar disorder although recent randomized controlled studies indicate it is probably also effective for children with the disorder (Findling et al., 2013). Side effects include nausea, diarrhea, sedation, tremor, weight gain, and acne. Some patients can develop more severe reactions including toxicity, heart problems, or liver failure. Consequently, physicians must monitor patients carefully (Gracious et al., 2015).

Physicians have also discovered that anticonvulsants, medications used to treat seizures, are helpful in decreasing mania in adults. These medications include older anticonvulsants such as valproate (Depakote) and the newer anticonvulsants carbamazepine (Tegretol) and oxcarbazepine (Trileptal). Emerging evidence suggests that these medications are also effective in reducing mania in children and adolescents and in decreasing aggressive episodes in children. Side effects are similar to those associated lithium. In rare instances, youths can experience inflammation of the pancreas or liver failure; careful monitoring is warranted (Gracious et al., 2015).

Antipsychotics

All antipsychotics block the activity of dopamine in the central nervous system. Consequently, they have an overall inhibitory effect on patients, decreasing behavior and cognition. They have long been recognized to be effective in reducing delusions and hallucinations (i.e., psychotic symptoms) in adults with schizophrenia and mania. Consequently, in recent years they have been increasingly prescribed to children and adolescents with early onset schizophrenia and bipolar disorders (Correll, 2015).

There are different "generations" of antipsychotic medications that allow us to loosely group them based on their chemical structure and effects on patients. The older, first-generation medications bind strongly to dopamine receptors in the brain. They are particularly useful in treating schizophrenia but tend to produce more severe side effects such as sluggishness, erratic movements, or feelings of agitation or restlessness. The newer antipsychotics are more frequently prescribed to children and adolescents. Risperidone (Risperdal) and aripiprazole (Abilify) are surpassing lithium as first-line medications for youths with bipolar disorders. Risperidone (Risperdal) has also been shown to reduce aggressive outbursts in children with developmental disorders and autism spectrum disorder (ASD). The main drawback to these medications is their tendency to produce sedation and weight gain in children. In rare instances, they can also produce metabolic problems, blood problems, and neuroleptic malignant syndrome (NMS) that can cause fever, racing heart, and motor rigidity. These side effects can usually be controlled by reducing the dosage of the medication (Elbe, McGlanaghy, & Oberlander, 2016).

Anna would most likely be diagnosed with bulimia nervosa (BN), an eating disorder characterized by a recurrent pattern of binge eating followed by inappropriate behaviors (like purging) to avoid gaining weight. Older adolescents and adults with BN often report significant symptoms of anxiety and depression. Anna said that negative moods tend to prompt binges, which make her feel better in the short-term but lead to long-term psychological and health-related problems. Antianxiety or antidepressant medication is sometimes an effective component of treatment because it can reduce these negative mood states (von Ranson & Wallace, 2014). Fluoxetine (Prozac) is the only FDA-approved medication for treating BN, although most of the research demonstrating its effectiveness has involved adults. Adolescents prescribed this medication seem to experience benefits for 4 to 6 months; consequently, it should probably not be the only form of therapy that Anna receives (Levine, Piran, & Jasper, 2015). If Anna is willing, and with the consent of her parents, her physician might suggest a trial of fluoxetine and refer her to a psychotherapist who might teach her more adaptive ways to cope with stress in her life.

Review:

- Psychostimulants, used to treat ADHD, are the most frequently prescribed class of medication for children and adolescents. Some nonstimulant medications are also efficacious in treating ADHD.
- Anxiolytics and antidepressants regulate negative emotions by affecting serotonin and (often) norepinephrine.
- Mood stabilizers and anticonvulsants are used to reduce mania and aggressive behaviors in some youths.
- Antipsychotic medications reduce symptoms of mania and schizophrenia by regulating dopamine.

4.2 SYSTEMS OF PSYCHOTHERAPY
What Is Psychotherapy?

Description

Most mental health professionals spend the majority of their time practicing psychotherapy. However, no one has provided a definition of psychotherapy that satisfies all practitioners. One influential definition of psychotherapy has been offered by Raymond Corsini (2005), an expert in clinical interventions:

> Psychotherapy is a formal process of interaction between two parties . . . for the purpose of amelioration of distress in one of the two parties relative to any or all of the following areas of disability or malfunction: cognitive functions (disorders of thinking), affective functions (suffering or emotional discomforts), or behavioral functions (inadequacy of behavior). . . . The therapist [has] some theory of personality's origins, development, maintenance and change along with some method of treatment logically related to that theory and professional and legal approval to act as a therapist. (p. 1)

According to this definition, psychotherapy is an interpersonal process. Therapy must involve interactions between at least two individuals: a therapist and a client. The therapist can be any professional who has specialized training in the delivery of mental health services. Therapists can include psychologists, psychiatrists, counselors, and social workers; however, therapists can also include teachers and other paraprofessionals who have received training and supervision in the use of psychosocial interventions. The therapist uses a theory about the causes of psychopathology to develop a means of alleviating the client's psychological distress. The client is an individual experiencing some degree of distress or impairment who agrees to participate in the therapeutic interaction to bring about change (Hill, 2014).

Common Factors

The purpose of psychotherapy is to alter the thoughts, feelings, or overt actions of the client. Change occurs primarily through interactions with the therapist. Specifically, the therapist provides certain conditions, consistent with his or her theory of psychopathology, to improve the functioning of the client. Jerome Frank (1973) has suggested that certain factors are common to all forms of psychotherapy. These factors include the presence of a trusting relationship between the client and therapist, a specific setting in which change is supposed to take place, a theory or explanation for the client's suffering, and a therapeutic ritual in which the client and therapist engage to alleviate the client's suffering. Frank argues that these "common factors" of psychotherapy have been primary components of psychological and spiritual healing since ancient times (Frank & Frank, 2004).

The famous psychologist Carl Rogers (1957) argued that there are three necessary and sufficient conditions for therapeutic change. Rogers developed person-centered psychotherapy as an approach to treatment that focused chiefly on these three factors. First, the therapist must provide the client with *unconditional positive regard*—that is, the therapist must be supportive and nonjudgmental of the client's behavior and characteristics in order to establish a relationship built on trust and acceptance. Second, the therapist must respond to the client with *congruence*—that is, the therapist must show his or her genuine feelings toward the client and avoid remaining emotionally detached, distant, or disengaged. Rogers described the ideal therapeutic relationship as "transparent"—that is, the client should easily witness the clinician's genuine feelings during the therapy session. The therapist does not try to hide her feelings or put on airs. Third, the therapist must show *empathy* toward the client. Specifically, the therapist must strive to understand the world from the client's perspective and take a profound interest in the client's thoughts, feelings, and actions. Rogers believed that clients whose therapists provided them with these three conditions would experience the greatest benefits from treatment.

Few practitioners dispute the importance of the psychotherapeutic factors identified by Frank (1973) and Rogers (1957). However, most clinicians regard these common factors as necessary but *not* sufficient to bring about change. Most therapists supplement these common factors with specific strategies and techniques consistent with their theories of the origins of psychopathology. The specific therapeutic methods they use depend on the system of psychotherapy they practice and the presenting problem of the client (Frank & Frank, 2004).

Review:

- Psychotherapy is a professional relationship between at least two people with the goal of alleviating distress or impairment, and promoting growth and adaptation, in one person (the client). This goal is usually achieved by altering the client's thoughts, feelings, or actions.
- Jerome Frank believed that certain factors were common to all psychotherapies, such as a the presence of a trusting relationship, a theory that explains the client's presenting problems, and plausible techniques to improve functioning.
- Carl Rogers posited three necessary and sufficient conditions for therapeutic change: (1) unconditional positive regard, (2) congruence, and (3) empathy. Most therapists view these conditions as the starting point for all therapies.

What Are the Major Systems of Psychotherapy?

There are hundreds of systems or "schools" of psychotherapy. They can be loosely categorized in terms of the level at which they approach clients' presenting problems. These levels include (a) the client's overt behaviors and symptoms, (b) the client's patterns of thinking, (c) the client's family relationships, (d) the client's other interpersonal relationships, and (e) the client's knowledge of himself and his intrapersonal functioning (Prochaska & Norcross, 2009).

Behavior Therapy

Behavior therapy focuses primarily on the client's overt actions and maladaptive patterns of behavior. Behavior therapy has its origins in the work of Joseph Wolpe (1958), Hans Eysenck (1959), and B. F. Skinner (1974). Behavior therapists address clients' problems at the symptom level. Behavior therapists do not assume that underlying personality traits or intrapsychic conflicts influence behavior. Instead, behavior is determined by environmental contingencies—that is, conditions in the person's surroundings that reinforce or punish certain actions. The goal of behavior therapy is usually to alter these environmental contingencies to increase the likelihood that clients will engage in more adaptive patterns of action.

Behavior therapists typically perform a functional analysis of their client's problematic behavior in order to determine situations that elicit the behavior (antecedents) or conditions that reinforce it over time (consequences). Then, behavior therapists work with clients to find ways to avoid these environmental triggers or alter their schedule of reinforcement (Miltenberger, Miller, & Zerger, 2015).

Recall that Anna's most problematic behavior is her tendency to binge and purge. A behavior therapist would carefully note the frequency of Anna's bingeing. Then, the therapist would try to identify situations that often precede a binge. For example, Anna might report that she tends to binge after school, when she is feeling lonely, and when she is hungry. The therapist would also try to determine how Anna's bingeing is maintained over time. Anna might report feeling less lonely and hungry immediately after bingeing; thus, bingeing is negatively reinforced by the withdrawal of these unpleasant feelings.

Over the course of treatment, a behavior therapist might teach Anna to monitor her binge eating, its antecedents, and its consequences. Then, the therapist might help Anna avoid antecedents that trigger binges. For example, the therapist might help Anna eat more regular, balanced meals to avoid feelings of intense hunger. Similarly, the therapist might help Anna identify ways to avoid the loneliness and boredom that often trigger her binges. The therapist might encourage Anna to become more involved in after-school activities or teach her to develop more satisfying peer relationships. By altering environmental factors that elicit or reinforce her binges, Anna should be able to decrease their frequency.

Cognitive Therapy

Cognitive therapy focuses primarily on the client's patterns of thinking about herself, others, and the future. One cognitive therapist, Aaron Beck (1976), argued that people experience psychological distress and impairment when they engage in systematic errors in thinking called cognitive biases and cognitive distortions. A **cognitive bias** occurs when someone selectively attends to negative aspects of her environment rather than looking at situations in a more balanced, realistic way. For example, a girl with social anxiety might focus exclusively on her classmate's laughs or snickers while giving a speech rather than her teacher's nods of approval. Similarly, a boy with depression might attend to the fact that only one classmate sits with him during lunch instead of feeling supported by his friend who chose to spend lunchtime with him.

A **cognitive distortion** occurs when someone twists reality to fit her negative worldview. For example, the girl with social anxiety might misperceive her classmate's giggles during her speech as a sign of criticism. She might think, "They're laughing at me. They think I'm stupid." These distorted thoughts, in turn, might interfere with her ability to give a good speech and lead to actual criticism from others, thus confirming her expectations. Similarly, the boy with depression might misperceive the fact that few friends sat with him during lunch as a sign that he is worthless. He might think, "No one likes me. I'm such a loser." His distorted thoughts, in turn, might cause him to act mopey or avoid others, thus leading his classmates to reject him and confirming his negative view of himself.

An initial goal of cognitive therapy is to help clients recognize the close connection between our thoughts, feelings, and actions (Beidel & Reinecke, 2015). Often, we have little direct control over our feelings. In contrast, however, we can control what we think or do. If we change the way we think or act, we can often improve the way we feel (see the following Research to Practice section).

Later, cognitive therapists help clients identify and challenge cognitive biases and distortions and adopt more accurate ways of thinking. A primary technique in cognitive therapy involves asking clients for evidence to support their maladaptive beliefs. For example, a therapist might ask the girl with anxiety, "How do you know that your classmates thought you were stupid? What evidence do you have to support your belief? Is there any evidence to the contrary, that maybe they actually liked your speech?" Similarly, a therapist might ask the boy with depression, "What's the evidence that no one wanted to sit with you during lunch? I thought you said one boy did sit with you? If you saw a kid sitting alone during lunch, would you think he was worthless or a loser?" The goal of therapy is not to teach clients to think positively, but rather, to help them see themselves, others, and the world more realistically rather than in a biased or distorted fashion.

Another cognitive therapist, Albert Ellis, claimed that **irrational beliefs** contribute to psychological distress and maladaptive ways of acting (Ellis, 2005; Ellis & Harper, 1961). When people engage in absolute, black-or-white thinking, they often place considerable pressure on themselves leading to depression, anxiety, or anger. For example, people who make dogmatic demands on themselves (e.g., "I *must* get into graduate school") often set themselves up for failure and increase their likelihood of low self-worth. Similarly, people who place rigid demands on others (e.g., "My teacher *should* have given me a higher grade on the exam") can experience anger and frustration. According to Ellis, cognitive therapists challenge clients'

CONNECTING THOUGHTS AND FEELINGS

Cognitive therapists teach children that the way we think affects how we feel. The picture of the elephant and the mouse can be helpful when working with anxious children.

Source: Istockphoto: 8613053

Therapist:	How is the elephant feeling?
Child:	He's scared.
Therapist:	Why?
Child:	He thinks the mouse will hurt him.
Therapist:	Will the mouse really hurt him?
Child:	No. The mouse is so little.
Therapist:	If the elephant had a different thought like, "Look at that cute little mouse" would he feel differently?
Child:	Yes. Maybe he'd be happy and want to play with the mouse.
Therapist:	So the way we think about situations affects our feelings.

absolute, dogmatic, and rigid beliefs and teach clients to think more flexibly and logically (Ellis, 2011).

A cognitive therapist would focus her attention on the thoughts associated with Anna's bingeing and purging. A therapist adopting Beck's (1976) approach to cognitive therapy might help Anna identify cognitive distortions that occur before she vomits. Specifically, Anna might think, "I'm afraid of becoming fat. If I become fat, then no one will love me." The therapist might help Anna challenge this belief to determine whether it is true or whether it is a distortion of reality. For example, the therapist might ask Anna, "If you become fat, what's the likelihood that *no one* will love you?" Then the therapist might help Anna think more realistically about her eating behavior. For example, the therapist might encourage Anna to adopt a different thought, like, "I know I feel terrible right now, but if I don't throw up I'll feel OK in a little while."

A therapist adopting Ellis's (2005) perspective of cognitive therapy might help Anna identify irrational beliefs that contribute to her purging. For example, Anna might hold the irrational belief, "I need to be thin and beautiful so that people will love me." The therapist would likely challenge this belief, arguing that Anna does not necessarily *need* to be thin or beautiful in order to be loved. Furthermore, the therapist would help Anna identify more logical ways of thinking. For example, the therapist might encourage Anna to think, "I'd *like* to be thin and beautiful, but it wouldn't be terrible if I gained some weight."

Both Beck's (1976) and Ellis's (2005) approaches to cognitive therapy emphasize the connection between thoughts, feelings, and actions. As clients learn to think in more realistic, flexible ways, they may experience fewer negative emotions and behave in a more adaptive manner. Usually, cognitive therapists incorporate elements of behavior therapy into their treatments. Cognitive–behavioral therapy (CBT) refers to the integrated use of cognitive and behavioral approaches to treatment (Beidel & Reinecke, 2015).

Interpersonal Therapy

Interpersonal therapy (IPT) focuses primarily on the quality of clients' relationships with others and their ability to cope with changes in those relationships over time. IPT is based on the theoretical writings of the attachment theorist John Bowlby and the psychiatrist Harry Stack Sullivan, whose ideas are presented in Chapter 2. Recall that Bowlby (1969, 1973) believed that people form internal working models of interpersonal relationships through their interaction with caregivers and other significant individuals in their lives. Internal working models built on trust and expectations for care promote later social–emotional adjustment. However, models based on mistrust and inconsistent care can interfere with the development of social–emotional competence. Sullivan (1953) believed that interpersonal relationships are essential for mental health. Friendships in childhood help youngsters develop a sense of identity and self-worth and form the basis for more intimate relationships in adulthood. Problems in interpersonal relationships can interfere with social–emotional functioning and self-concept.

Interpersonal therapists conceptualize psychopathology as arising from disruptions or problems in interpersonal relationships (Klerman & Weissman, 1993). First, interpersonal relationships can be disrupted due to *death* or extended separation. Second, relationship problems can arise when a person experiences an *interpersonal transition* or change in social roles (e.g., problems adjusting from middle school to high school). Third, problems can occur when a person experiences an *interpersonal conflict*—that is, when her social role conflicts with the expectations of others (e.g., parents and adolescents disagree about dating or the importance of attending college). Finally, problems can occur when an individual has *interpersonal deficits* that interfere with his ability to make and keep friends (e.g., excessive shyness or lack of social skills).

An interpersonal therapist attempts to identify and correct relationship problems that might contribute to the client's primary diagnosis. The strategies that the therapist selects depend on the nature of the client's interpersonal problems. For example, a therapist might help an adolescent cope with the death of her parent by giving her time to mourn during the therapy session. Then, the therapist might help the client find ways to cope with her parent's death and develop a plan for adjusting to life without the parent. Alternatively, a therapist might help an excessively shy, lonely adolescent develop social skills so that he can expand his peer network and social support system.

An interpersonal therapist might notice that Anna's eating problems occurred shortly after her father changed jobs and the family moved to a new neighborhood and school district. The therapist might interpret Anna's eating disorder as a maladaptive attempt to lose weight, appear attractive to others, and gain acceptance by peers at her new school. Through a combination of support and suggestions, the therapist would help Anna grieve the loss of her old neighborhood and friends, cope with her move to a new school, and find more effective ways to make new friends (Rudolph, Lansford, & Rodkin, 2016).

Family Systems Therapy

Family systems therapy seeks to improve patterns of communication and interaction among family members (Bitter, 2013). Although there are many types of family therapies, all family therapists view the family as a *system*—that is, a network of connected individuals who influence and partially direct each other's behavior. Viewing the family as a system has several important implications for therapy. First, no member of the family can be understood in isolation. A family member's behavior is best understood in the context of all other members of the family. Second, family therapists see the entire family as their "client," not just the person who is identified

by certain family members as "the one with the problem." Finally, a systems approach to treatment assumes that change in one member of the family will necessarily affect all members of the family. Consequently, family therapists believe that helping one or two family members improve their functioning can lead to symptom reduction in the family member with the identified problem (Kerig, 2016).

The famous family therapist Salvador Minuchin (1974) developed *structural family therapy*. Structural family therapists are chiefly concerned with the structure of the relationships between family members and between the family and the outside world. In healthy families, parents form strong social–emotional bonds, or alliances, with each other that are based on mutual respect and open lines of communication. Furthermore, in healthy families, parents form boundaries between themselves and their children. Specifically, parents respect children's developing autonomy and provide for their social–emotional needs, but they also remain figures of authority.

In unhealthy families, alliances are formed between one parent and the children, leaving the other parent disconnected or estranged from the rest of the family. For example, a mother might encourage her daughter to form an alliance against her father because of the father's excessive alcohol use. The alliance between the mother and daughter might leave the father feeling alienated from his family while the mother and daughter might grow to resent the father. This phenomenon is sometimes called *triangulation*, because an alliance is formed between two family members, leaving a third member feeling isolated or rejected.

Furthermore, in unhealthy families, boundaries between parents and children are often overly rigid or excessively diffuse. For example, *disengaged families* are characterized by overly rigid boundaries, in which open communication between family members is stifled, and members feel disconnected from one another. In contrast, *enmeshed families* are characterized by diffuse boundaries where family members lack autonomy and constantly intrude into one another's lives (Wendel & Gouze, 2015).

Adlerian family therapy is an alternative, contemporary approach to family systems therapy that helps parents manage their children's behavior problems (Sherman & Dinkmeyer, 2014). An Adlerian family therapist believes that all family members, including children, seek lives based on meaning, effectiveness, and purpose. They view children's disruptive behavior as a maladaptive attempt to achieve meaning or purpose in the family. Specifically, disruptive behavior can occur for four reasons: (1) to gain attention, (2) to assert autonomy from the parent, (3) to extract revenge or "to get even," or (4) to avoid others and be left alone. The therapist's task is to identify the purpose of the child's misbehavior and help parents find more adaptive ways for children to derive meaning in the family.

Most family therapists would insist on seeing Anna and her parents together, for at least part of treatment. The therapist would likely pay attention to alliances and boundaries in Anna's family and the way Anna's eating disorder might help to maintain the family system in a maladaptive way. For example, the therapist might discover that Anna's parents frequently argue with one another and are considering a divorce. The therapist might notice that the onset of Anna's symptoms coincided with her parents' marital problems. The therapist might hypothesize that Anna's eating symptoms serve to maintain the family system by distracting her parents from their marital disputes (Wendel & Gouze, 2015).

A family therapist might also notice that Anna's parents are overprotective and excessively demanding. The therapist might interpret Anna's desire to lose weight as a maladaptive attempt to gain the approval of her parents. The therapist might refer Anna's parents to a marriage counselor to help them improve the quality of their relationship. At the same time, the therapist might work with Anna and her parents to help improve communication at home. One goal of therapy might be to help Anna's parents give her more autonomy over her day-to-day behavior.

Psychodynamic Therapy

Psychodynamic therapy focuses chiefly on intrapsychic conflict—that is, conflict within the self. Psychodynamic therapy is based on the theoretical and clinical work of Sigmund Freud (1923/1961), Anna Freud (1936), and a host of neo-Freudian theorists. Although there are a vast number of psychodynamic approaches to therapy, almost all believe that unconscious thoughts, feelings, dreams, images, or wishes influence our behavior.

According to Freud's *topographic theory*, the mind can be divided into two levels: (1) conscious and (2) unconscious. Unconscious mental activity cannot be directly accessed. However, unconscious mental processes influence and direct our day-to-day actions. Freud believed that behavior is not random; actions are influenced by both conscious will and unconscious processes. From the psychodynamic perspective, psychological symptoms often reflect these unconscious mental processes (Terr, 2015).

The primary goal of psychodynamic therapy is to provide *insight*—that is, to make the person aware of unconscious mental conflict that contributes to his psychological symptoms. Insight is believed to result in symptom alleviation and more adaptive behavior.

One way therapists help clients gain insight is by paying attention to the client's transference, the attitude and patterns of interaction that the client develops toward the therapist. Transference is believed to reflect the client's history of interpersonal relationships and unconscious fantasies projected onto the therapist. For example, an adolescent who has been physically abused or neglected by her parents might express mistrust and hostility toward the therapist in the therapeutic relationship. The client might unconsciously expect the therapist to abandon, reject, or mistreat her in a way similar to her abusive parents. The therapist can use transference to help the client gain awareness of these unconscious thoughts and feelings. For example, the therapist might interpret the client's

transference by suggesting, "I notice that whenever we talk about ending treatment, you get very angry and resentful toward me. I wonder if you're afraid that I'm going to abandon you?" Over the course of therapy, as clients gain greater insight into the causes of their distress, they may experience symptom reduction, develop more effective means of coping with anxiety, and achieve more satisfying relationships with others (Terr, 2015).

A psychodynamic therapist might focus on Anna's transference. Over the course of multiple sessions, the therapist might notice that Anna often acts helpless and childlike during therapy sessions, as if she wants the therapist to tell her what to do. Furthermore, Anna might become frustrated and angry toward the therapist when the therapist remains nondirective and insists that Anna solve problems for herself. The therapist might interpret Anna's transference as an unconscious desire to remain in a childlike state. The therapist might suggest that as long as Anna remains helpless and childlike, she does not have to assume adult responsibilities that cause her considerable distress: getting a part-time job, going to college, or leaving home. The therapist might suggest that Anna's eating disorder ensures that her parents will coddle her and provide her with attention and sympathy, rather than insist that she develop more autonomous, age-appropriate behavior.

Review:

- Behavior therapists focus on children's overt actions. They usually try to change behavior by altering environmental contingences that either elicit the behavior or maintain it over time.
- Cognitive therapists focus on children's thoughts about self, others, and the future. They may identify and challenge cognitive biases, distortions, or irrational beliefs that contribute to maladaptive actions or emotions.
- Interpersonal therapists focus on the quality of children's relationships with others and help them cope with changes to these relationships over time.
- Family systems therapists view the entire family as their "client." They believe that improvement in one member's behavior will necessarily change all members of the family.
- Psychodynamic therapists focus largely on unconscious thoughts and feelings that affect children's functioning. Therapists often attend to transference—that is, the client's attitude and patterns of responding to the therapist.

4.3 PSYCHOTHERAPY EFFICACY AND EFFECTIVENESS
How Does Child Psychotherapy Differ From Adult Psychotherapy?

Child psychotherapy and adult psychotherapy differ in several ways. First, there are often *motivational differences* between child and adolescent clients and their adult counterparts. Most adults refer themselves to therapy; by the time they make the initial appointment, they are at least partially motivated to change their behavior. Indeed, some evidence suggests that the very act of seeking treatment and making an initial appointment is itself therapeutic (Howard, Kopta, Krause, & Orlinsky, 1986; Kopta, 2003). In contrast, children and adolescents are almost always referred by others (e.g., parents, teachers). Youths seldom recognize their behavioral, emotional, and social problems and typically show low motivation to change. Indeed, many youths with psychiatric disorders show very little psychological distress; instead, distress is usually experienced by parents, teachers, and other people in their lives. Most therapists initially try to increase children's willingness to trust the therapist and participate in treatment.

Second, *cognitive and social–emotional differences* between children, adolescents, and adults can influence the therapeutic process. Most forms of child and adolescent therapy are downward extensions of adult therapeutic techniques. However, by virtue of their youth, children and adolescents often lack many of the cognitive, social, and emotional skills necessary to fully benefit from these techniques. For example, cognitive therapy depends greatly on clients' ability to engage in metacognition, that is, to think about their own thinking. However, metacognitive skills develop across childhood and adolescence; some youths may find cognitive therapy too abstract and difficult. Similarly, cognitive and insight-oriented therapies often rely heavily on verbal exchanges between client and therapist. Young children, with immature verbal abilities, may not benefit from these types of "talk" therapy.

Third, the *goals of therapy* often differ for children compared to adults. In adult psychotherapy, the primary objective of treatment is usually symptom reduction. Most therapists and clients consider treatment to be successful when clients return to a previous state of functioning. In therapy with children and adolescents, return to previous functioning is often inadequate. Instead, the goal of child and adolescent therapy is to alleviate symptoms while simultaneously promoting children's development. For example, a child with ADHD might participate in behavior therapy and take medication to alleviate his hyperactivity and inattention. However, these behavior problems have likely alienated him from classmates. Consequently, the therapist might have an additional goal of helping the child gain acceptance in the classroom and overcome a history of peer rejection.

Fourth, children and adolescents often have less *control over their ability to change* than do adults. Adults usually have greater autonomy over their behavior and environmental circumstances than do children. For example, a woman who is depressed might decide to exercise more, join a social support group, practice meditation, change jobs, or leave her boyfriend. However, a child who is depressed because of his parents' martial conflict is less able to alter his environment. Although he might decide to exercise or participate

in extracurricular activities, he is unable to leave home or get new parents. Instead, the boy's social–emotional functioning is closely connected to the behavior of his parents. Consequently, the boy's capacity to change is directly associated with his parents' involvement in therapy.

Finally, children and adolescents are more likely to have *multiple psychiatric conditions* compared to adults. In fact, comorbidity is the rule rather than the exception among children and adolescents with mental health problems. Among youths in the community, approximately 50% who have one disorder also have a second disorder. Among youths referred to clinics, rates of comorbidity range from 50% to 90%, depending on the age of the child and the specific problem. Clinicians who treat children and adolescents must address multiple disorders simultaneously, often without the zealous participation of their young clients (Weisz, 2014).

Review:

- Children are often less motivated than adults to participate in therapy and can lack the cognitive, emotional, or social skills necessary to participate in treatment.
- The goals of therapy for children include not only symptom reduction but also the promotion of children's development.
- Children are more likely than adults to experience comorbid problems and may be less able to alter their life circumstances to improve their functioning.

Does Child Psychotherapy Work?

One way to examine the efficacy of child psychotherapy is to use meta-analysis. In a meta-analysis, researchers combine the results of several empirical studies. To perform a meta-analysis, researchers locate all of the research examining the efficacy of child and adolescent psychotherapy. Each study typically compares at least one group of children who received treatment with another group of children who served as controls. Then, for each study, researchers calculate a number that indicates the difference between the two groups' scores on some measure of functioning after treatment. Many researchers use the following formula:

$$ES = (M_{\text{treatment group}} - M_{\text{control group}})/SD_{\text{control group}}$$

In this formula, we subtract the mean score for the control group from the mean score for the treatment group to tell us the difference between groups after treatment. Positive scores indicate that the treatment group fared better than the control group after treatment—that is, the therapy worked. Negative scores indicate that the control group fared better than the treatment group—that is, the therapy was harmful. Next, we take this difference between groups and divide it by the standard deviation of the control group. This tells us how many standard deviations apart the two groups are after treatment. We call this value the effect size (ES), it tells us the overall effect of treatment.

Since the ES is in standard units, we can combine the ES of many studies, even if they used different measures to evaluate therapy outcomes. Specifically, we might calculate the average ES across all studies that have investigated the efficacy of some form of psychotherapy. Most researchers consider the ES of 0.20 to be small, 0.50 to be medium, and 0.80 to be large (Cohen, 1988).

Four large meta-analyses have investigated the efficacy of child and adolescent psychotherapy (Casey & Berman, 1985; Kazdin, Bass, Ayers, & Rodgers, 1990; Weisz, Weiss, Alicke, & Klotz, 1987; Weisz, Weiss, Han, Granger, & Morton, 1995). Results of these four meta-analyses are quite consistent. Average ESs ranged between 0.71 and 0.88 and are considered moderate to large. These average ESs are similar to the average ESs obtained from studies involving psychotherapy for adults (Shapiro & Shapiro, 1982; Smith & Glass, 1977). These findings suggest that psychotherapy for children and adolescents

works, that youngsters who participate in therapy often fare much better than youngsters in control groups, and that the efficacy of child and adolescent therapy is comparable to the efficacy of therapy for adults (see Figure 4.1).

Review:

- Meta-analysis allows researchers to combine the results of multiple quantitative studies to reach overall conclusions regarding the efficacy of psychotherapy.
- Overall, the ES for therapy with children and adolescents is moderate to large. Youths who participate in therapy tend to have better outcomes than youths who do not receive treatment.

What Therapies Work Best?

Efficacy

Although it is encouraging to know that therapy works, we probably want to know *which* system of therapy works best.

Figure 4.1 Does psychotherapy work?

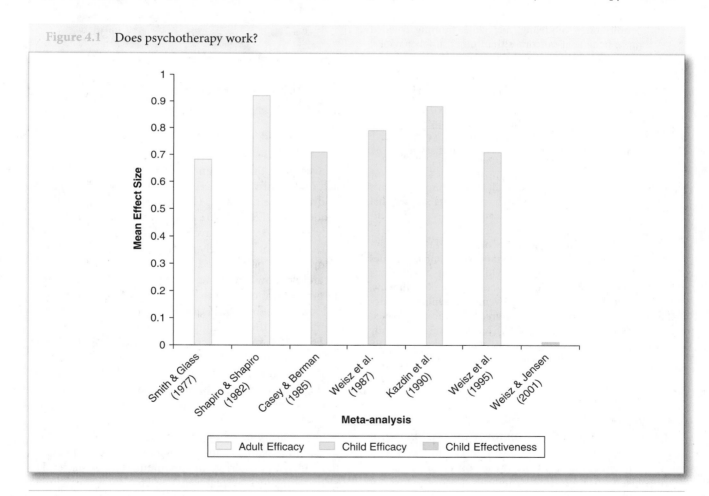

Source: Based on Weisz, Jensen, & McLeod (2005).

Note: Large meta-analyses indicate that adults (light gray) and youths (medium gray) who receive psychotherapy show greater improvement than controls who do not receive therapy. These findings indicate that both adult and child therapy is efficacious. Studies investigating the effectiveness of child therapy (dark gray; final bar only) have yielded more disappointing results in real-life situations.

Researchers who examine the efficacy of adult psychotherapy have generally concluded that all forms of therapy are equally effective. No single system of psychotherapy works best under all circumstances (Lambert, 2013; Lambert & Ogles, 2004). Some researchers have referred to this phenomenon as the dodo verdict (Parloff, 1984; Rosenzweig, 1936). In *Alice in Wonderland,* Alice watches a race in which each contestant starts in a different position, each races in a different direction, and all contestants win. One of the characters in the book, the dodo bird, concludes, "Everybody has won, and all must have prizes." So, too, in adult psychotherapy, there is little evidence that any form of therapy is superior to any other form of therapy, overall (see Image 4.1).

Weisz and colleagues (1995) performed a meta-analysis to investigate whether the dodo verdict applies to child and adolescent therapy. Their meta-analysis yielded three important results:

1. Behavioral therapies tended to yield greater ESs (ES = 0.76) than nonbehavioral therapies (ES = 0.35). Behavioral techniques, such as classical and operant conditioning, modeling, and skills training, yielded more beneficial outcomes than other, nonbehavioral techniques (e.g., psychodynamic treatments).

2. Children's age and gender predicted their response to therapy. Treatment tended to work better for adolescents than for children and was more efficacious for girls than boys. On the other hand, therapy was equally efficacious for both externalizing (e.g., disruptive behavior problems) and internalizing disorders (e.g., depression, anxiety).

3. Children showed global and specific improvements in therapy. Previous research with adults showed that therapy often has global effects on clients. Adult clients often experience improvement in a wide range of thoughts, feelings, and behaviors, even if these behaviors were not the focus of therapy. Weisz and colleagues (1995) found that children, like adults, experience some global benefits from participating in therapy. However, the greatest improvement in children's functioning occurs in problem areas specifically targeted for treatment. The average ES for problems specifically addressed in therapy was 0.60, whereas the average ES for problems not a focus of treatment was 0.30.

Effectiveness

We might conclude from the results of the meta-analyses that psychotherapy usually improves the well-being of children and adolescents who are referred to treatment. However, we must keep in mind the source of the information used in these meta-analyses (Weisz, Doss, & Hawley, 2005). First, the researchers who conducted these meta-analyses tended to calculate the average ES across all studies. If the ESs were 0.50, 0.70, and 0.90 in three studies, respectively, their average ES would be 0.70. Calculating

Image 4.1 *In Alice in Wonderland,* the dodo bird holds a race in which "everybody has won, and all must have prizes." In adult psychotherapy, the dodo verdict refers to the finding that all therapies work equally well, on average. However, the dodo verdict may not be true for child and adolescent therapies.

Source: Image courtesy Project Gutenberg.

the average in this way ignores the number of children in each of the three studies. For example, if there were 100 children in the first study (ES = 0.50), 20 children in the second study (ES = 0.70), and only 10 children in the last study (ES = 0.90), the average ES for the three studies, 0.70, would not accurately reflect the overall outcome for children who participated in the studies. Consequently, researchers now tend to weight the ESs of studies, assigning greater importance to studies with larger samples. If we look at the overall ES of child and adolescent psychotherapy using the weighting method, we see that the average ES is 0.54, much lower than 0.70 (Weisz et al., 1995). We can conclude that the effects of therapy on children and adolescents are probably "moderate" rather than "large."

Perhaps more importantly, the meta-analyses reported previously examined only psychotherapy efficacy studies. Efficacy studies examine the effects of therapy under optimal conditions. They are usually conducted by university-based research teams with well-trained, supervised clinicians administering the treatments. Clinicians tend to use only one form of treatment, which is carefully planned and followed, using a therapy manual. Participants in efficacy studies are voluntary; they agree to participate in the research project. Participants are also carefully selected. They are screened to make sure they have the disorder or problem that the researcher is interested in studying, and they typically do not have comorbid disorders.

In contrast, most child and adolescent psychotherapy is not administered under ideal conditions. Typically, therapy is conducted in clinics, hospitals, and schools. Clinicians are usually not trained in any one specific form of therapy; rather, they rely on an array of therapy techniques (Weisz, Jensen, & McLeod, 2005). Their approaches tend to be based on the clinician's experience as a therapist. Clinicians tend to have large caseloads with little time for careful review and preparation. They may also be limited by insurance companies in the number and kinds of therapies they provide. In most clinical settings, clients are not hand selected; clinicians treat almost anyone who seeks help. Furthermore, children and adolescents are often unwilling to participate in treatment; they are brought to therapy by their parents. Finally, clients tend to have multiple, often poorly defined problems that sometimes do not fit neatly into *DSM-5* diagnostic categories.

What is the effectiveness of child psychotherapy; does it work under real-world conditions? Surprisingly little research has been directed to answer this question. Lee, Horvath, and Hunsley (2013) found only 20 studies examining the effectiveness of psychotherapy for children and adolescents under real-world conditions. With respect to internalizing disorders, 80% of youths participating in behavioral, cognitive, or IPT for anxiety or depression completed treatment. Furthermore, 65% of youths responded to treatment; after completion, their functioning was similar to youths without internalizing problems. With respect to externalizing disorders, 81% of families who participated in behavior therapy completed treatment. On average, 69% of youths who received therapy had better outcomes than youths who did not receive treatment. Outcomes varied considerably, however, with some studies showing large improvements in behavior and other showing no symptom reduction.

Altogether, these findings suggest that child psychotherapy is effective under real-world conditions. It is noteworthy, however, that all of the studies showing the effectiveness of therapy examined treatments that had previously been shown to be efficacious under optimal conditions. As long as clinicians rely on evidence-based treatments in their practice, they have reasonable expectations that their therapies will help their clients. However, therapies that have not been shown to be efficacious under ideal conditions will probably also not be effective under real-world conditions. Indeed, a previous meta-analysis examining the effectiveness of unsupported therapies in the community (i.e., usual clinical care) yielded an overall ES of −.001 (Weisz & Jensen, 2001). Now, more than ever, it is important for clinicians to rely on evidence-based interventions to help children and families in need.

Review:

- Efficacy refers to the effects of treatment under optimal, research-based conditions; effectiveness refers to the effects of treatment in real-world circumstances where it is typically delivered (e.g., clinics, hospitals, schools).
- Although the dodo verdict suggests that all therapies are equally efficacious for adults, most data suggest that behavior therapy is most efficacious for children. Therapy is also most efficacious for older children/adolescents and girls.
- Evidence-based therapies developed in research settings can be effectively used in the community. On average, approximately 80% of families complete treatment, and most youths show significant improvement.

4.4 PROFESSIONAL PRACTICE AND ETHICS
Who Treats Children and Families?

Because childhood disorders are multiply determined, their treatment often requires coordinated care from professionals with different educational backgrounds and training (see Image 4.2; Landrum & Davis, 2014; Metz, 2016; Norcross & Sayette, 2016).

Psychologists assess, diagnose, and treat individuals with mental disorders. They hold doctoral degrees (PhD or PsyD) in clinical or counseling psychology. Psychologists are not physicians; consequently, most do not prescribe medication but instead rely on psychotherapy and other nonmedicinal interventions. Child psychologists complete a 4- or 5-year graduate program and a 1-year internship accredited by the American Psychological Association (APA). Some also receive postdoctoral specialization in assessment, therapy, or neuropsychology. They work in hospitals, clinics, residential treatment facilities, private practice, and colleges/universities.

School psychologists assess, diagnose, and treat children with behavioral, cognitive, and social–emotional problems that interfere with their functioning at school. Most specialize in the identification and treatment of developmental and learning disabilities, deliver school-based mental health services, and act as liaisons between children's families and the school. Most have specialist degrees in education (EdS) or doctoral degrees in education or psychology (EdD or PhD) and are accredited by the National Association of School Psychologists or the APA.

Psychiatrists are physicians (MD or DO) who specialize in the assessment, diagnosis, and treatment of mental disorders. They complete medical school, a four-year residency in psychiatry, and are certified by the American Board of Psychiatry and Neurology. Child psychiatrists specialize in mental disorders in children and adolescents. Most of their work involves prescribing psychotropic medications and monitoring children's response to treatment.

Pediatricians are physicians (MD or DO) who treat children and adolescents with medical illnesses. They may also prescribe psychotropic medications to children with disorders such as ADHD, anxiety, and depression.

Because childhood disorders are multiply determined, treatment often requires coordinated care from professions with different educational backgrounds.

Source: Stock photo ID:82691459

They complete medical school, a three-year pediatric residency, and are certified by the American Board of Pediatrics. Developmental–behavioral pediatricians have specialization in evaluating and treating children with developmental disorders and behavior problems. They work in hospitals and clinics.

Psychiatric–mental health nurses are nurses who specialize in the treatment of individuals with mental disorders. Psychiatric–mental health nurse practitioners earn either a master's or doctoral degree and, in many states, can practice independently of a physician. They tend to work in hospitals, clinics, and residential treatment facilities.

Marriage and family therapists are mental health professionals trained in psychotherapy and family systems. They are licensed to diagnose and treat mental and emotional disorders within the context of a couple or family. Most have master's degrees and work in clinics and private practice.

Social workers are professionals who provide counseling and support to individuals and families experiencing psychosocial stress. Most licensed social workers (LSWs) have bachelor or master's degrees and provide case management services to children and families. Licensed clinical social workers (LCSWs) typically have master's degrees and can also provide therapy. They work in hospitals, clinics, residential treatment facilities, social service agencies, and schools.

Speech–language pathologists assess, diagnose, and treat communication disorders in children, such as language delays, articulation problems, and stuttering. They may help children who have language problems because of injury, a developmental disability, or autism. Most have master's degrees and work in schools, clinics, and hospitals.

Occupational therapists treat sick, injured, or disabled children through the therapeutic use of everyday activities and exercises. They help children develop, recover, and improve the skills needed for play, education, and daily living. They typically have a master's degree and work in schools, clinics, and hospitals.

Special education teachers help students with cognitive, emotional, and physical disabilities. They adapt lessons to meet the needs of these students. Some also teach basic communication and daily living skills to students with severe disabilities. They typically have bachelor's degrees in education with a teaching license and work in schools.

School counselors help students develop academic and social skills to succeed in school. Career counselors also assist youths with the process of making career decisions by helping them develop skills or choose a career or educational program. Most have master's degrees in school counseling and work in schools.

Child life experts are professionals who help children and families cope with psychosocial stressors through activities and play. They may help children separated from their families because of trauma or children hospitalized because of illness or injury. Most have a bachelor's degree with a background in child development and family systems. They work in clinics, residential treatment facilities, and hospitals.

Creative arts therapists are professionals who use the arts to improve children's communication skills, recognition and expression of emotions, and overall social–emotional functioning. Typically, they earn master's degrees in art therapy, music therapy, or dance therapy. Each profession has its own accreditation process, usually involving supervised training.

Review:

- The treatment of children and adolescents often involves coordinated services from psychologists, physicians, teachers, and other professionals.

What Is the APA Ethics Code?

Ethics refers to the standard of behavior that is determined to be acceptable for a given profession. Ethics should not be confused with a person's morality—that is, his personal beliefs in the rightness or wrongness of a given behavior. Ethical behavior is determined by group consensus; morality is determined by one's personal convictions (Knapp, Gottlieb, & Handelsman, 2015). All mental health professionals adhere to a code of ethics that guides their professional practice. Different professional organizations have different ethics codes. These codes include the APA (2010) *Ethical Principles of Psychologists and Code of Conduct*, the National Association of School Psychologists (2010) *Principles for Professional Ethics,* the American Counseling Association (2014) *Code of Ethics,* and the American School Counselor Association (2010) *Ethical Standards for School Counselors.* Because the APA Ethics Code is the most frequently used system, we will examine it in greater detail.

The APA Ethics Code provides a common set of principles and standards upon which psychologists build their professional and scientific work (APA, 2010). The primary purpose of the APA Ethics Code is to protect the welfare of individuals with whom psychologists work (e.g., clients, research participants, students). The secondary purpose of the Ethics Code is to educate psychologists, students, and the general public about the ethical practice of psychology. Because the Ethics Code is endorsed by the APA, all APA members and student affiliates are required to be familiar with the code and adhere to its rules. Failure to adhere to the Ethics Code can result in sanctions from the APA, psychology licensing boards, and other professional organizations.

The APA Ethics Code consists of four parts: (1) an introduction, (2) a preamble, (3) five general principles, and (4) specific ethical standards. The introduction and preamble describe the purpose, organization, and scope of the Ethics Code. The five general ethical principles are broad ideals for the professional behavior of psychologists. The general principles are aspirational in nature; they are not enforceable rules. Instead, the general principles

describe the highest ideals of psychological practice toward which all psychologists should strive (APA, 2010):

- *Beneficence and nonmaleficence:* Psychologists strive to benefit those with whom they work, and they take care to do no harm.
- *Fidelity and responsibility:* Psychologists establish relationships of trust, . . . are aware of their professional and scientific responsibilities, . . . uphold professional standards of conduct, clarify their professional roles and obligations, [and] accept appropriate responsibility for their behavior.
- *Integrity:* Psychologists seek to promote accuracy, honesty, and truthfulness in science, teaching, and the practice of psychology.
- *Justice:* Psychologists recognize that fairness and justice entitle all persons to access to and benefit from the contributions of psychology.
- *Respect for people's rights and dignity:* Psychologists respect the dignity and worth of all people and the rights of individuals to privacy, confidentiality, and self-determination.

Review:

- Ethics refers to the standards of behavior that is acceptable for a given profession. The primary purpose of ethical rules is to protect the welfare of others.
- The APA Ethics Code consists of five general ethical principles toward which all psychologists should aspire, and many ethical standards (rules) that determine appropriate professional behavior.

What Are the Four Cs of Child/Family Ethics?

The bulk of the Ethics Code consists of the ethical standards: specific rules that guide professional practice. The ethical standards govern all major professional activities including assessment, therapy, research, and teaching. Although there are too many ethical standards to describe here, we will examine some of the rules that are most relevant to the treatment of children and adolescents. These rules fall into four categories (Koocher, 2008), sometimes called the Four Cs of ethics when working with children and families: (1) competence, (2) consent, (3) confidentiality, and (4) conflicts of interest.

Competence

According to the APA Ethics Code (2010), "psychologists provide services, teach, and conduct research with populations and in areas only within their boundaries of competence" (Standard 2.01). Competence refers to the use of education, training, and professional experience to deliver evidence-based services to individuals and the community. In general, psychologists achieve and maintain competence in three ways. First, psychologists have the educational background necessary to assess, diagnose, and treat the individuals, families, and groups with whom they work. Second, psychologists seek additional training and supervised experiences to maintain their awareness of evidence-based practice and, perhaps, expand their clinical work to new populations. Third, psychologists monitor their own mental and physical health and sociocultural awareness to make sure that these factors do not limit their ability to deliver effective care (Nagy, 2011).

Practicing within the boundaries of competence is important because it protects the welfare of clients. Psychologists who practice outside their areas of training will likely be less effective than therapists who are more knowledgeable and skillful. Therapists who practice outside the boundaries of their competence also risk harming their clients.

Competence is especially relevant to the assessment and treatment of children and adolescents. There is a shortage of clinicians who have received formal education and training in diagnosing and treating childhood disorders. Many clinicians, whose educational and clinical experiences largely focused on adults, may be tempted to provide care outside their boundaries of competence. Consider the case of Dr. Williams:

CASE STUDY

PROFESSIONAL ETHICS: COMPETENCE

Well-Intentioned Dr. Williams

Source: ©iStockphoto.com/m-imagephotography

Dr. Williams is a clinical psychologist who has 15 years of experience treating adults and couples with psychological problems, especially alcohol abuse. In fact, Dr. Williams has gained recognition in her community for her expertise in helping adults with chronic alcohol use problems. One day, she receives a telephone call from a mother who requested an appointment for her 15-year-old son. The son was recently suspended for bringing alcohol to a school athletic event and has been arrested for underage alcohol possession. Should Dr. Williams accept this client?

Dr. Williams is an expert in treating substance use disorders in adults. However, she lacks specialized training and supervision in the treatment of adolescent substance use disorders. It would likely be unethical for her to offer services to adolescents without first receiving additional training. Ideally, Dr. Williams would participate in some additional coursework on adolescent substance use disorders and receive supervision from a colleague who has expertise in this area.

Competence is also relevant to psychology students. Students often serve on the front lines of mental health treatment for children. For example, some students deliver behavioral interventions to children with autism, others help administer summer treatment programs for youths with ADHD, and still others work in group homes or residential treatment facilities. Because of their status as students, they must receive supervision from psychologists or other licensed mental health professionals who accept responsibility for their work. Students should always feel comfortable with their level of supervision and never feel pressured to accept more responsibility than they have received training to provide. Equally as important, students should never feel embarrassed to ask for help from their supervisor.

Consent

Perhaps the best way to avoid ethical problems is to make sure that children and families know what they are agreeing to before they decide to participate in therapy. The Ethics Code requires psychologists to obtain consent from individuals before assessment, treatment, or research (Standard 3.10). The person must have the ability to understand the facts and consequences of participating in treatment. The person also must voluntarily agree to participate. Consent protects people's right to self-determination (Nagy, 2011).

Informed consent to therapy includes a number of components. First, individuals are entitled to a description of treatment, its anticipated risks and benefits, and an estimate of its duration and cost. Second, the psychologist must discuss alternative treatments that might be available and review the strengths and weaknesses of the recommended treatment approach. Third, psychologists must remind clients that participation is voluntary and that they are free to refuse treatment or withdraw from therapy at any time. Finally, psychologists should review the limits of confidentiality with their clients (APA, 2010).

Informed consent is especially important when treating children and adolescents. Children, unlike adults,

Resentful Rachel

Source: ©iStockphoto.com/pabham

Rachel was a 11-year-old girl referred to our clinic by her guidance counselor for disruptive behavior at school. Rachel had been increasingly moody and recently initiated two loud arguments with teachers. Her parents admitted that Rachel showed similar outbursts at home and has alienated herself from many of her former friends at school and in the neighborhood.

During the first session, Rachel's mother reported, "Rachel has been really touchy. She flies off the handle so easily, snaps at us, and then hides in her room for the rest of the evening." Her father added, "We're hoping you might be able to talk with her and identify the problem." At that point, Rachel uncrossed her arms, stood up, pointed at her parents, and yelled, "I'll tell you what the problem is! Him and her!" She exited the room, slamming the door behind her.

---

rarely refer themselves to therapy. Instead, children and adolescents are usually referred to therapy by parents, teachers, other school personnel, pediatricians, or (sometimes) the juvenile court. Although these adults may want the child to participate in treatment, the child's motivation might be low. Consider the case of Rachel.

Children and adolescents, by virtue of their age and legal status as minors, are usually not capable of providing consent. Consent implies that individuals both understand and freely agree to participate. Young children may not fully appreciate the risks and benefits of participation in treatment. Older children and adolescents, like Rachel, may not freely agree to participate because they may feel pressured by others. Instead, proxy consent is obtained from parents or legal guardians. Then, psychologists obtain the assent of children and adolescents before providing services. To obtain assent, psychologists typically describe treatment using language that youths can understand, discuss goals for therapy that might be acceptable to the child or adolescent, and ask the youth for tentative permission to initiate treatment (Shumaker & Medoff, 2013). Although Rachel's parents provide consent for therapy, a skillful therapist knows that obtaining Rachel's assent is essential. Assent gives Rachel a voice in the initial stages of therapy and allows her to set goals (and parameters) for therapy that are important to her, not only to her parents and teachers (Knapp et al., 2015).

In rare cases, children can receive treatment without parental consent (Hecker & Sori, 2010). For example, clinicians can provide therapy to children who are in a state of crisis (e.g., thinking about killing themselves). Similarly, clinicians can delay obtaining parental consent if youths seek treatment because of suspected abuse, neglect, or endangerment. Psychologists who work in clinics and schools may also provide short-term mental health services to youths who are pregnant or experience sexual health concerns (Jacob &

Kleinheksel, 2012). Parental consent is delayed in these special cases to provide immediate care to children in need or to allow youths to access services they might avoid if parental consent was required (Gustafson & McNamara, 2010).

Confidentiality

Confidentiality refers to the expectation that information that clients provide during the course of treatment will not be disclosed to others. The expectation of confidentiality serves at least two purposes. First, it increases the likelihood that people in need of mental health services will seek treatment. Second, it allows clients to disclose information more freely and facilitates the therapeutic process (Smith-Bell & Winslade, 2008).

In most cases, confidentiality is an ethical and legal right of clients. Therapists who violate a client's right to confidentiality may be sanctioned by professional organizations and held legally liable. Most psychologists consider protecting clients' confidentiality one of the most important ethical standards (Sikorski & Kuo, 2015).

Although clients have the right to expect confidentiality when discussing information with their therapists, clients should be aware that the information they disclose is not entirely private. There are certain limits of confidentiality that therapists must make known to clients, preferably during the first therapy session. First, if the client is an *imminent danger to self or others*, the therapist is required to break confidentiality to protect the welfare of the client or someone he or she threatens. For example, if an adolescent tells his therapist that he plans on killing himself after he leaves the therapy session, the therapist has a duty to warn the adolescent's parents or guardians to protect the adolescent from self-harm. The psychologist's duty to protect the health of the adolescent supersedes the adolescent's right to confidentiality.

Second, if the therapist *suspects child abuse or neglect,* the therapist is required to break confidentiality to protect the child. For example, if during the course of therapy a 12-year-old girl admits to being maltreated by her step-father, the psychologist would have a duty to inform the girl's mother and the authorities to protect the child from further victimization.

Third, in exceptional circumstances, a judge can issue a *court order* requiring the therapist to disclose information provided in therapy. For example, a judge might order a psychologist to provide information about an adolescent client who has been arrested for serious criminal activity.

Fourth, therapists can disclose limited information about clients in order *to obtain payment* for services. For example, therapists often need to provide information about clients to insurance companies. This information typically includes the client's name, demographic information, diagnosis, and a plan for treatment. Usually, insurance companies are the only parties who have access to this information.

Fifth, therapists can disclose limited information about clients to colleagues *to obtain consultation* or supervision. It is usually acceptable for psychologists to describe clients' problems in general terms in order to gain advice or recommendations from other professionals. However, therapists only provide information to colleagues that is absolutely necessary for them to receive help, and they avoid using names and other identifying information.

Therapists also have a duty to protect children and adolescents from harm when they know youths are engaging in potentially dangerous behaviors. Frequently, ethical dilemmas arise when the therapist's duty to protect children comes into conflict with the therapist's responsibility to protect confidentiality. Consider the case of Renae.

CASE STUDY

PROFESSIONAL ETHICS: CONFIDENTIALITY

Risky Renae

Source: ©iStockphoto.com/101dalmatians

Renae was a 16-year-old high school sophomore who was participating in therapy for long-standing problems with depression. During one session, Renae tells her therapist that her parents are leaving for an overnight trip that weekend and she intends on having sex with her boyfriend while they are gone. She explains that this decision is "huge" because she has never had sex with anyone before.

Renae's therapist asks questions about Renae's sexual health and access to birth control. She also wants to know if Renae is experiencing any pressure to initiate a sexual relationship. Should Renae's decision to have sex remain confidential, between she and her therapist, or do her parents have a right to know her plans?

When therapists face decisions about confidentiality, they must weigh two factors: (1) the frequency, intensity, and duration of the potentially harmful or maladaptive behavior and (2) the importance of maintaining the therapeutic process (Sullivan, Ramirez, Rae, Razo, & George, 2010). In general, therapists are more likely to break confidentiality as the risk of harm increases. For example, if Renae's decision to have sex was made freely, and if she was at low risk for pregnancy or illness, most therapists would respect her confidentiality. However, if we learned that Renae's "boyfriend" was a 25-year-old man that she met online, we would have greater reason to take steps to protect her from harm. In any case, therapists place considerable importance on maintaining the therapeutic relationship. Would Renae ever trust her therapist (or any other therapist) if the therapist disclosed this information to Renae's parents? What might the implications of disclosure be on Renae's long-term mental health?

According to the Health Insurance Portability and Accountability Act (HIPAA), the right to confidentiality is held by children's parents, not by children themselves. From a legal standpoint, parents have the right to the information their children disclose in therapy. In most cases, parents recognize the importance of respecting the confidentiality of their children and do not solicit information from therapists. However, parents (and therapists) have the duty to protect children from harm. Therefore, therapists will often talk with parents and children together, to discuss what information will be shared (see the following Research to Practice section). Initiating conversations about confidentially can prevent future problems (Sikorski & Kuo, 2015).

Conflicts of Interest

Usually, when parents seek treatment for their children, they have their children's best interests at heart.

PROFESSIONAL ETHICS: CONFLICTS OF INTEREST

Margaret's Mournful Mother

Source: ©iStockphoto.com/Wavebreakmedia

Margaret was a 12-year-old girl who was referred to our clinic for oppositional and defiant behavior. Although Margaret was largely compliant at school, she would frequently disrespect her mother and throw tantrums to avoid responsibilities at home.

The therapist met with Margaret's mother to gain additional information. During the course of the conversation, it became clear that Margaret's mother was very depressed and was experiencing considerable marital problems with Margaret's father. She said she was having a hard time caring for Margaret and performing her other responsibilities at home and work. She also admitted to thoughts of suicide.

The therapist believed that Margaret's disruptive behavior was connected to her mother's depressed mood. She offered to counsel Margaret's mother individually, in addition to providing therapy for Margaret's disruptive behavior. Was this a good decision?

Occasionally, however, ethical issues arise when it is unclear whether psychologists are providing services to children or to their parents. The Ethics Code indicates that psychologists must avoid such conflicts of interest—that is, instances in which the psychologist engages in relationships that impair her objectivity, competence, or effectiveness with her client (Standard 3.06).

Conflicts of interest can arise in child and adolescent therapy in several ways. One conflict occurs when a therapist is in a professional role with the child and then (inadvertently) enters into another role with the child's parent. Consider the case of Margaret (above).

Although well-intentioned, the therapist entered into a multiple relationship with Margaret and her mother. A multiple relationship occurs when a psychologist, who is in a professional role with a client, enters into another relationship with the same individual or a person closely associated with that individual. Multiple relationships are problematic when they impair the services that psychologists provide (Campbell, Vasquez, Behnke, & Kinscherff, 2010). Would the therapist be able to effectively treat Margaret while also simultaneously providing services to her mother? Might it be better for the therapist to refer Margaret's mother to another provider?

Conflicts of interest can also occur in situations of separation and divorce (Shumaker & Medoff, 2013). Imagine that Margaret's family situation goes from bad to worse:

Margaret's father decides to divorce Margaret's mother and seek custody of Margaret. Her father requests Margaret's psychological records, which include information about her mother's depressed mood and difficulty caring for Margaret. He intends on using this information to gain custody of his daughter.

The therapist now finds herself serving as a therapist for Margaret, a therapist for her mother, and a potential witness for her father. Clearly, the therapist's objectivity is threatened! At this point, the therapist must make this conflict known to both adults and explain the importance of limiting access to Margaret's records.

Therapists can avoid conflicts of interests by asking this question: Who is my client? In most instances, therapists identify the child or the entire family as their client. In these instances, the therapist does not provide services to other members of the family independently. If parents present goals in therapy that are separate from those of their child or family, the therapist will acknowledge those goals but refer the parent to another provider to avoid a multiple relationship (Koocher & Daniel, 2012).

Review:

- Psychologists must practice within the boundaries of competence.
- Custodial parents consent to therapy for their children. Children cannot legally provide consent because of their minor status; instead, they give assent.
- In most jurisdictions, parents have a legal right to access their child's medical and psychological records. Other limits to confidentiality include a danger to self or others and suspected child maltreatment.
- Psychologists avoid multiple relationships—that is, they do not knowingly enter into a relationship with someone closely associated with their client.

PROTECTING ADOLESCENTS' CONFIDENTIALITY

Source: Stock photo ID:46005644

Psychologists who work with adolescents must balance parents' rights with adolescents' expectations for confidentiality in therapy. On one hand, parents have the right to the medical and psychological records of their children; on the other hand, adolescents are unlikely to fully participate in therapy if they feel their thoughts and feelings will be shared with others without their permission. Most psychologists try to prevent future problems by raising the issue of confidentiality with parents and teens early in treatment. Here is one strategy:

Psychotherapy works best when adolescents have confidence in the privacy of their conversations. At the same time, parents want to feel confident about their adolescent's well-being and safety. Since you (parents) were once teenagers, you certainly know that an adolescent may want to use therapy to talk about sex, alcohol, or other activities. Let's discuss about how we can assure your child's confidentiality so she can talk openly about what's on her mind, and at the same time assure you (parents) about your adolescent's safety.

Based on Koocher and Daniel (2012)

Adherence: The degree to which a client or patient follows treatment recommendations prescribed by his or her clinician

Anticonvulsants: Medications used to treat seizures, mania, and (sometimes) aggression; valproate (Depakote) and carbamazepine (Tegretol) are examples

Antidepressants: Medications used to treat depressed mood and negative affect; often regulate serotonin and norepinephrine; fluoxetine (Prozac) and sertraline (Zoloft) are examples

Antipsychotics: Medications that block the activity of dopamine in the brain; useful for reducing mania and schizophrenia; risperidone (Risperdal) and aripiprazole (Abilify) are examples

Anxiolytics: Medications that are used to reduce anxiety, panic, or worry

APA Ethics Code: Consists of five general ethical principles toward which all psychologists should aspire and many ethical standards (rules) that determine appropriate professional behavior

Assent: Agreement to participate in therapy given by legal minors

Behavior therapy: A system of psychotherapy that focuses on children's overt actions; tries to change behavior by altering environmental contingences that either elicit the behavior or maintain it over time

Cognitive bias: In cognitive therapy, it occurs when someone selectively attends to negative aspects of the environment rather than looking at situations in a more balanced, realistic way

Cognitive distortion: In cognitive therapy, it occurs when someone misperceives or twists reality to fit a negative worldview

Cognitive therapy: A system of psychotherapy that focuses on children's thoughts; identifies and challenges cognitive bias, distortions, or irrational beliefs that contribute to maladaptive actions or emotions

Competence: The use of education, training, and professional experience to deliver evidence-based services to individuals and the community

Confidentiality: The expectation that information that clients provide during the course of treatment will not be disclosed to others without their permission

Conflicts of interest: Situations in which the psychologist engages in relationships that impairs her professional objectivity, competence, or effectiveness with her client

Consent: A person's ability to understand the facts and consequences of participating in treatment and his or her voluntary decision to do so; protects people's right to self-determination

Diversion: The practice of distributing prescription medications to peers

Dodo verdict: A term used to describe the fining that all no single system of psychotherapy works best under all circumstances for adults

Effect size (ES): A statistic used in many meta-analyses that tells the number of standard deviations apart that the means of the treatment and control groups are; larger ESs indicate greater effects for therapy

Efficacy studies: Research studies that examine the effects of therapy under optimal conditions (e.g., well-trained therapists with carefully selected clients)

Ethics: The standards of behavior that are acceptable for a given profession

Family systems therapy: A system of psychotherapy that views the entire family as the "client"; improvement in one member's behavior will necessarily change all members of the family

Interpersonal therapy (IPT): A system of psychotherapy that focuses on the quality of children's relationships with others and helps them cope with changes to these relationships over time

Irrational beliefs: In rational emotive behavior therapy, absolute and rigid demands on self, others, or the world that lead to negative emotions; usually begin with *should, must,* or *ought*

Limits of confidentiality: Situations in which a psychologist is ethically and/or legally required to break confidentiality; examples include cases of possible suicide, homicide, or child maltreatment

Meta-analysis: A statistical technique in which researchers combine the results of several studies into a single analysis; can be used to determine psychotherapy efficacy

Mood stabilizer: Medication to reduce mania and regulate emotional fluctuations in people with bipolar disorders; lithium (Eskalith) is one example

Multiple relationship: Occurs when a psychologist, who is in a professional role with a client, enters into another relationship with the same individual or a person closely associated with that individual

Nonstimulant medication for ADHD: Medications used to treat ADHD that are not stimulants; atomoxetine (Strattera) is one example

Necessary and sufficient conditions: According to Carl Rogers, three conditions that lead to improvement in therapy are (1) unconditional positive regard, (2) congruence, and (3) empathy

Psychodynamic therapy: A system of psychotherapy that focuses on unconscious thoughts and feelings that affect children's functioning; often attends to transference—that is, the client's attitude and pattern of responding to the therapist

Psychostimulants: A class of mediations often used to treat ADHD; stimulate portions of the frontal lobe and striatum responsible for attention and inhibition

Psychotherapy: A professional relationship between at least two people with the goal of alleviating distress or impairment, and promoting growth and adaptation, in one person (the client). This goal is usually achieved by altering the client's thoughts, feelings, or actions

Transference: In psychodynamic therapy, the attitude and patterns of interaction that the client develops toward the therapist; reflects the client's history of interpersonal relationships and unconscious thoughts/feelings

CRITICAL THINKING EXERCISES

1. A boy in Mrs. Lewandowski's fifth-grade class frequently bullies other children during recess. Mrs. Lewandowski observes the boy, Rufus, initiating fights with younger children. How might Mrs. Lewandowski perform a functional analysis of Rufus' behavior to identify the antecedents and consequences of his bullying?

2. Allison is a psychology major interested in a career involving counseling for children and adolescents. However, Allison does not want to earn a doctoral or medical degree. Identify some of her career options. How might she find more information about these careers?

3. Maddy is a 14-year-old girl who is experiencing depression following the death of her father. How might her counselor use (a) behavior therapy, (b) cognitive therapy, and (c) interpersonal therapy to help Maddy?

4. Mr. Fox's teenage daughter has depression. Her pediatrician recommended that she see a therapist. Mr. Fox was disappointed, saying, "I don't believe in therapy. Depression is caused by neurochemistry—no amount of talk therapy will help." Evaluate Mr. Fox's claim. What is the evidence that psychotherapy for adolescents is efficacious? Effective?

5. Taylor is an undergraduate who is interning at a community mental health center. During her internship, she suspects that one of her clients, a 9-year-old boy, may be physically abused by his parents. His parents engage in "rough discipline" such as hard spanking. The boy has never complained, and there has never been any marks left on his body. What should Taylor do?

TEST YOURSELF AND EXTEND YOUR LEARNING

Videos, flash cards, and links to online resources for this chapter are available to students online. Teachers also have access to PowerPoint slides to guide lectures, case studies to prompt classroom discussions, and exam questions. Visit www.abnormalchildpsychology.org.

PART II

Developmental Disorders and Disabilities

CHAPTER 5

Intellectual Disability and Developmental Disorders

Once there was a craftsman who used all his skill and effort to create a wonderful new pot. The pot was made of clay, crafted by his weathered hands, and baked into a beautiful form. The man glazed and decorated the pot, using colors and designs that were as unique as they were beautiful. When it was finished, the man carried the pot to a nearby well to fetch some water for his home. To his surprise, he discovered the pot had developed a small crack from the kiln, which caused water to leak from the bottom. At first, the crack was small, but over time it became larger and more noticeable.

One day, the man's friend said, "That pot has a crack. By the time you get home, you've lost half of your water. Why don't you throw it away and get a new one?" The man paused, turned to his friend, and replied, "You don't understand. Yes, it's true that this pot leaks more and more every day. But every day it also waters more and more flowers on the path from the well to my home." Sure enough, along the path had sprung countless wildflowers of all varieties, while in other areas, the land was barren. His friend simply nodded in approval (see Image 5.1).[1]

The story of the broken pot illustrates the dignity and value of every person. Each person has unique gifts and talents, although sometimes they are hard to recognize. When studying children with developmental disabilities, it's easy to focus on limitations and lose sight of the children themselves. Many of these youths face significant challenges performing everyday activities like bathing and dressing. Others have difficulty with communication and language. Still others struggle in school or exhibit challenging behaviors in social settings. Too often, these problems overshadow their abilities.

Regardless of his or her disability, disorder, or diagnosis, each of these children has intrinsic worth. A challenge facing parents, teachers, and all people who interact with these youths is to not lose sight of the child when we focus on

---

[1]Adapted from a story by Kevin Kling.

Image 5.1 Sure enough, along the path had sprung countless wildflowers of all varieties, while in other areas, the land was barren.

his or her problem. One of my clients, Will, was born with Down syndrome. Although he struggled with reading and math, he taught his classmates to be patient, to act with empathy, and to respect others who are different. Another client, Camden, a boy with intellectual disability (ID) and attention-deficit/hyperactivity disorder (ADHD), could not stay focused in class; however, he had an excellent sense of humor and loved to play soccer. Still another client, Chloe, had Williams syndrome (WS). Although she had serious cognitive deficits and health problems, she was also one of sweetest girls I have ever met. Consider Rosa, a girl with Down syndrome, whose family changed the way we think about ID today.

5.1 DESCRIPTION AND EPIDEMIOLOGY

What Is Intellectual Disability?

Intellectual disability (ID) is a term that describes the behavior of an extremely diverse group of people. They range from children with severe developmental disabilities who need constant care to youths with only mild delays

---

CASE STUDY

INTELLECTUAL DISABILITY (DOWN SYNDROME)

The Family Who Got Rid of the "R-Word"

We all know the old saying: Sticks and stones may break my bones, but words will never hurt me. Nina Marcellino begged to differ. "It's not true that words won't hurt you. You can't call someone something terrible and treat them in a different way."

Nina's family is largely responsible for changing the way we describe people with intellectual disability (ID). Her story began when she met with school officials to discuss the educational plan for Rosa, her 9-year-old daughter with Down syndrome. School officials had changed Rosa's special education status from *other health impaired* to *mentally retarded*. "It was bad," Nina remembered. "They called the meeting to change her code, and I was blindsided." Rosa's 14-year-old brother added, "We're not allowed to use the words (mentally retarded) at my house. It would be like saying a curse word. We are not allowed to use words that are hurtful."

The Marcellino family spent the next 2 years urging lawmakers to remove the term *mentally retarded* from all federal laws, enactments, and regulations because of its negative connotation. Rosa's parents met with politicians, her two sisters organized a petition, and Nick spoke before the Maryland General Assembly.

Rosa's Law (Public Law No. 111-256) was enacted on October 5, 2010, replacing *mental retardation* with the term *intellectual disability* in all federal documents. Rosa described the ceremony: "We went to the White House together. And he is president, and he is handsome to me. And so we went to his house to [see] my law be signed. And I got a big hug."

During the ceremony, President Obama quoted Nick: "What you call people is how you treat them. If we change the words, maybe it will be the start of a new attitude toward people with disabilities" (Cyphers, 2015).

who are usually indistinguishable from their peers. These children also have diverse outcomes. Most are integrated into general education classrooms, many participate in educational and recreational events in their communities, and some raise families of their own. In this chapter, we will explore this heterogeneous group of individuals, explore the causes of their disabilities, and learn evidence-based strategies to help them achieve their highest potentials (Witwer, Lawton, & Aman, 2014).

All individuals with ID have significantly low intellectual functioning (see Table 5.1). They experience problems perceiving and processing new information, learning quickly and efficiently, applying knowledge and skills to solve novel problems, thinking creatively and flexibly, and responding rapidly and accurately. In children approximately 5 years of age and older, intellectual functioning is measured using a standardized, individually administered intelligence test. Recall that IQ scores are normally distributed with a mean of 100 and a standard deviation of 15. IQ scores approximately two standard deviations below the mean (i.e., IQ < 70) can indicate significant deficits in intellectual functioning. The measurement error of most IQ tests is approximately 5 points; consequently, IQ scores between 65 and 75 are recommended as cutoffs in determining intellectual deficits (American Psychiatric Association, 2013). IQ scores below this cutoff are seen in approximately 2% to 3% of the population.

Individuals with ID also show significant deficits in adaptive functioning. Adaptive functioning refers to how effectively individuals cope with common life demands and how well they meet the standards of personal independence expected of someone in their particular age group, social–cultural background, and community setting (American Psychiatric Association, 2013). Whereas intellectual functioning refers to people's ability to learn information and solve problems, adaptive functioning refers to their typical level of success in meeting the day-to-day demands of society in an age-appropriate manner (Sturmey, 2014b).

The *Diagnostic and Statistical Manual of Mental Disorders* (*DSM*-5; American Psychiatric Association, 2013) identifies three domains of adaptive functioning: conceptual, social, and practical. To be diagnosed with ID, individuals must show impairment in at least one domain. Usually, children with ID experience problems in multiple areas:

Conceptual skills: understanding language, speaking, reading, writing, counting, telling time, solving math problems, having the ability to learn and remember information and skills

Social skills: having interpersonal skills (e.g., making eye contact when addressing others), following rules (e.g., turn-taking during games), engaging in social problem-solving (e.g., avoiding arguments), understanding others (e.g., empathy), making and keeping friends

Practical skills: activities of daily living including taking personal care (e.g., getting dressed, grooming), practicing safety (e.g., looking both ways before crossing street), doing home activities (e.g., using the telephone), having school/work skills (e.g., showing up on time), participating in recreational activities (e.g., clubs, hobbies), and using money (e.g., paying for items at a store)

Table 5.1   Diagnostic Criteria for Intellectual Disability (Intellectual Developmental Disorder)

Intellectual disability (intellectual developmental disorder) is a disorder with onset during the developmental period that includes both intellectual and adaptive functioning deficits in conceptual, social, and practical domains. The following three criteria must be met:

A. Deficits in intellectual functions, such as reasoning, problem solving, planning, abstract thinking, judgment, academic learning, and learning from experience, confirmed by both clinical assessment and individualized, standardized intelligence testing.

B. Deficits in adaptive functioning that result in failure to meet developmental and socio-cultural standards for personal independence and social responsibility. Without ongoing support, the adaptive deficits limit functioning in one or more activities of daily life, such as communication, social participation, and independent living, across multiple environments, such as home, work, and community.

C. Onset of intellectual and adaptive deficits during the developmental period.

Specify current severity: Mild, Moderate, Severe, Profound*

Source: Reprinted with permission from the *Diagnostic and Statistical Manual of Mental Disorders, Fifth Edition,* (Copyright 2013). American Psychiatric Association.

*Table 5.2 provides a description of each type of severity.

Adaptive functioning can be assessed by interviewing caregivers about children's behavior and comparing their reports to the behavior of typically developing children of the same age and cultural group (Tassé et al., 2012).

Often, psychologists administer a norm-referenced interview or rating scale to caregivers to collect information about children's adaptive functioning. For example, the Diagnostic Adaptive Behavior Scale (DABS) is a semistructured interview that is administered to caregivers of children with developmental disabilities (see the following Research to Practice section). Based on caregivers' reports, the interviewer rates children's adaptive behavior across the conceptual, social, and practical domains. The DABS provides standard scores, much like IQ scores, which indicate children's adaptive functioning relative to their peers. Scores more than two standard deviations below the mean (i.e., < 70) on at least one domain could indicate significant impairment in adaptive functioning (Balboni et al., 2014; Schalock, Tassé, & Balboni, 2015).

Note that ID is characterized by low intellectual functioning *and* problems in adaptive behavior. Many people incorrectly believe that ID is determined solely by IQ; however, deficits in adaptive functioning are equally necessary for the diagnosis. A child with an IQ of 65 but with no problems in adaptive functioning would not be diagnosed with ID (Sturmey, 2014a).

Finally, all individuals with ID show limitations in intellectual and adaptive functioning early in life. Although some people are not identified as having ID until they are adults, they must have histories of intellectual and daily living problems beginning in childhood. This age-of-onset requirement differentiates ID from other disorders characterized by problems with intellectual and adaptive functioning.

Review:

- ID is characterized by significant deficits in intellectual and adaptive functioning that emerge early in life. Both intellectual and adaptive functioning deficits are necessary for the diagnosis.
- Adaptive functioning refers to a person's ability to cope with day-to-day tasks. *DSM-5* identifies three dimensions of adaptive functioning: (1) conceptual, (2) social, and (3) practical.

How Does Intellectual Disability Differ Based on Severity?

Clinicians specify the severity of ID based on the person's level of adaptive functioning. Children with mild deficits in adaptive functioning (i.e., standard scores 55–70) in only

RESEARCH TO PRACTICE

HOW DO CLINICIANS ASSESS ADAPTIVE FUNCTIONING?

Clinicians assess adaptive functioning by administering semistructured interviews to caregivers of children suspected of intellectual disability (ID). Adaptive functioning scales allow clinicians to assess children's conceptual, social, and practical skills. Caregivers' reports are converted to standard scores, which can be used to determine if children have deficits compared to typically developing children.

Here are some areas of adaptive functioning that might be assessed in younger children, older children, and adolescents.

	Younger Children	*Older Children*	*Adolescents*
Conceptual	Can count 10 objects, one by one; Knows day, month, year of birth	States value of penny, nickel, dime; Uses mathematical operations	Sets a watch or clock to correct time; Can complete a job application
Social	Says "hi" and "bye" when coming and going; Asks for help when needed	Reads and obeys common signs (e.g., stop, do not enter); Knows topic of group conversations	Has satisfying friendships; Keeps personal information private
Practical	Uses the restroom; Drinks from a cup without spilling	Answers the telephone; Can safely cross busy streets	Travels to school or work by themselves; Washes clothes, dishes

Based on the DABS (Schalock et al., 2015).

one domain would presumably need less support from caregivers than children with profound deficits in adaptive functioning (i.e., standard scores <25) across multiple domains. Furthermore, by specifying the domains most in need of support, clinicians can begin to plan interventions to improve children's adaptive functioning or compensate for deficits that might be less responsive to treatment. Table 5.2 provides an overview of children's adaptive functioning at each level of severity

Mild Intellectual Disability (Adaptive Functioning Scores 55–70)

As infants and toddlers, children with mild ID usually appear no different than other children (Jacobson & Mulick, 1996). They achieve most developmental milestones at expected ages, learn basic language, and interact with family members and peers. Their intellectual deficits are usually first identified when they begin school. Teachers may notice that they require more time and practice to master academic skills, such as letter and number recognition, reading, and math. As they progress in school and their schoolwork becomes more challenging, these children fall further behind and may repeat a grade. Some children grow frustrated with traditional education and display behavior problems in class. By middle school, these children master basic reading and math but seldom make further academic progress. After school, they typically blend back into society, perform semiskilled jobs, and live independently in the community. They usually require only occasional support from others to overcome their intellectual deficits. For example, they may need help

Table 5.2   Describing the Severity of Intellectual Disability

Severity	Conceptual Domain	Social Domain	Practical Domain
Mild	Preschoolers may show no obvious conceptual differences. School-aged children show difficulties in acquiring academic skills (e.g., reading, writing, arithmetic, telling time, using money). Abstract thinking and planning may be impaired; thinking tends to be concrete.	Communication, conversation, and language are more concrete or immature than the skills of peers. The child may have difficulty accurately understanding the social cues of others. There may be difficulties regulating emotion and behavior compared to peers.	The child may function in an age-expected manner with regard to personal care. In adolescence, assistance may be needed to perform more complex daily living tasks like shopping, cooking, and managing money.
Moderate	Preschoolers' language and pre-academic skills develop slowly. School-age children show slow progress in academic skills. Academic skill development is usually at the elementary school level.	The child shows marked differences in social and communicative skills compared to peers. Spoken language is simplistic and concrete. Social judgment and decision making are limited. Friendships with peers are often affected by social or communicative deficits.	The child needs more time and practice learning self-care skills, such as eating, dressing, toileting, and hygiene, than peers. Household skills can be acquired by adolescent with ample practice.
Severe	The child generally has little understanding of written language or numbers. Caretakers must provide extensive support for problem solving throughout life.	There are limited spoken language skills with simplistic vocabulary and grammar. Speech may be single words/phrases. The child understands simple speech and gestures. Relationships are with family members and other familiar people.	The child needs ongoing support for all activities of daily living: eating, dressing, bathing, elimination. Caregivers must supervise at all times. Some youths show challenging behaviors, such as self-injury.
Profound	Conceptual skills generally involve the physical world rather than symbols (e.g., letters, numbers). Some visual-spatial skills, such as matching and sorting, may be acquired with practice. Co-occurring physical problems may greatly limit functioning.	The child has limited understanding of symbolic communication. The child may understand some simple instructions and gestures. Communication is usually through nonverbal, non-symbolic means. Relationships are usually with family members and other familiar people. Co-occurring physical problems may greatly limit functioning.	The child is dependent on others for all aspects of physical care, health, and safety, although he or she may participate in some aspects of self-care. Some youths show challenging behaviors, such as self-injury. Co-occurring physical problems may greatly limit functioning.

Source: Based on *DSM-5*, 2013.

completing a job application, filing a tax return, or managing their finances.

Moderate Intellectual Disability (Adaptive Functioning Scores 40–55)

Children with moderate ID often show signs of their intellectual and adaptive impairments as infants or toddlers (Jacobson & Mulick, 1996). Their motor skills usually develop in a typical fashion, but parents often notice delays in learning to speak and interacting with others. These children often seem less interested in their surroundings compared to their age mates. They are often first identified as having ID as toddlers or preschoolers, when they show little or no language development. Instead, they rely mostly on gestures and single word utterances. By the time they begin school, these children usually speak in short, simple phrases and show self-care skills similar to typically developing toddlers. However, they display problems mastering basic reading, writing, and mathematics. By adolescence, these children are able to communicate effectively with others, have basic self-care skills, and have simple reading and writing abilities. They may continue to have trouble with reading a newspaper, performing arithmetic, or handling money. As adults, some may perform unskilled jobs if they are given training and supervision. They usually live with family members or in residential care facilities.

Severe Intellectual Disability (Adaptive Functioning Scores 35–40)

Children with severe ID are usually first identified in infancy (Jacobson & Mulick, 1996). They almost always show early delays reaching early developmental milestones, such as sitting up and walking. They also usually show one or more biological anomalies that are indicative of a genetic or medical disorder. They require ample supervision from parents and caregivers. By the time they begin school, they may be able to move on their own and perform some basic self-care skills, such as feeding, dressing, and using the toilet. They may communicate using single words and gestures. As adults, their speech continues to be limited and difficult to understand, although their ability to understand others is often better developed. They are usually unable to read or write, but they may be able to perform simple daily living tasks under close supervision. They typically live with family or in residential care.

Profound Intellectual Disability (Adaptive Functioning Scores <25)

Children with profound ID are first identified in infancy (Jacobson & Mulick, 1996). They almost always show multiple biological anomalies and health problems indicative of neurological damage. By the time they reach school age, their skills are similar to those of typically developing 1-year-olds. They may be able to sit up, imitate sounds, understand simple commands, and recognize familiar people. About half of the children with profound ID will continue to require help from others throughout their lives. The other half will show slow development of adaptive skills. They may learn to walk, develop some communication skills, and be able to perform some self-care activities. As adults, they usually continue to require constant support and supervision from family and caregivers. They may also show chronic medical problems and sensory impairments.

Remember that the diagnosis of ID is determined by the child's intelligence and adaptive functioning. Two people can show ID but look and act very differently. For example, one person might be a child with Down syndrome. Another child with the same IQ might have no identifiable cause of their impairments. The label "ID" tells us only about a person's general intellectual and adaptive functioning; the diagnosis says nothing about causes, course, or outcomes (Witwer et al., 2014).

Needed Supports

The American Association on Intellectual and Developmental Disabilities (AAIDD) is the oldest professional organization devoted to the study and assistance of individuals with impairments in intellectual and adaptive functioning. The AAIDD consists of professionals and laypersons who research, help, and advocate on behalf of people with IDs. Since 1910, they have offered guidelines for the identification of ID and the best methods to help children and adults with this condition. In years past, the *DSM* and AAIDD definitions of ID had differed considerably. Currently, however, the *DSM-5* and AAIDD definitions overlap to a great degree, which will likely improve communication between members of these two professional organizations (Harris & Greenspan, 2016).

One remaining difference in the AAIDD conceptualization of ID is its emphasis on needed supports (Schalock & Luckasson, 2015). Needed supports refer to a broad array of assistance that helps the individual function effectively in society (see Image 5.2). Supports can be formal assistance provided by health care providers, mental health professionals, teachers, educational specialists, professional caregivers, or human service agencies. Supports can also refer to informal help from parents, friends, or members of the community. The AAIDD designates four possible levels of supports, based on how much and how long assistance is needed: intermittent (i.e., occasional, in time of crisis), limited (i.e., short-term), extensive (i.e., long-term), and pervasive (i.e., constant).

Rather than categorize clients into mild, moderate, severe, and profound impairment, the AAIDD recommends that professionals describe individuals' need for supports across various areas of functioning. For example, a child with ID might be described as needing "extensive"

Image 5.2   The AAIDD conceptualization of Intellectual Disability emphasizes needed supports — assistance from others that helps the person with a disability function effectively in society.

Source: ©iStockphoto.com/izusek.

educational support, such as a full-time classroom aide for all academic activities, but only "intermittent" support in areas of social functioning, such as one-time training to help him learn to make friends.

The AAIDD has published a semistructured interview to help clinicians identify the type and intensity of supports needed for adolescents and adults with ID (Buntinx, 2016). The Supports Intensity Scale measures support needs in the areas of home living, community living, lifelong learning, employment, health and safety, social activities, and protection and advocacy. It ranks each activity according to *frequency* (e.g., none, at least once a month), *amount* (e.g., none, less than 30 minutes), and *type* (e.g., monitoring, verbal gesturing) of support needed.

The AAIDD approach to classifying individuals with ID in terms of needed supports has two main advantages (Schalock & Luckasson, 2015). First, this approach conveys more information about clients than simply classifying them with ID alone. Second, it focuses on clients' abilities rather than on their impairments. The main drawback to the AAIDD approach is that it is complex. Describing clients on so many dimensions of functioning is cumbersome and can hinder communication among professionals. The AAIDD approach can also make research difficult; with so many combinations of needed supports and areas of functioning, it is difficult to identify homogenous groups of individuals for study.

Review:

- *DSM-5* allows clinicians to classify individuals with ID based on their adaptive functioning: mild, moderate, severe, or profound.

- In contrast, the AAIDD classifies individuals with ID based on their needed supports—that is, assistance that helps these individuals function in society.
- Levels of needed supports include intermittent, limited, extensive, or pervasive.

What Is Global Developmental Delay?

Description

The diagnosis of ID requires significant deficits in intellectual and adaptive functioning. Typically, intellectual functioning is assessed using norm-referenced IQ tests. Although assessing IQ is relatively straightforward among school-age children, it can be tricky in toddlers and preschoolers—especially those children suspected of developmental delays.

Clinicians who want to measure the intellectual ability of very young children have several options (Witwer et al., 2014). The Bayley Scales of Infant and Toddler Development, Third Edition (BSID-III) are appropriate for children aged 1 to 42 months. However, the BSID-III is usually considered a measure of children's cognitive, motor, and social development rather than intelligence per se. The Stanford-Binet Intelligence Scales, Fifth Edition is a true IQ test that can be administered to children as young as two-years old. Similarly, the Wechsler Preschool and Primary Scale of Intelligence, Fourth Edition (WPPSI-IV) can be given to children as young as 2.5 years. However, IQ scores assessed prior to age 4 or 5 are often not good predictors of intelligence in later childhood or adolescence (Tirosch & Jaffe, 2011). How, then, should infants and toddlers with delays be classified?

Global developmental delay (GDD) is a neurodevelopmental disability that is only diagnosed in children less than 5 years of age. GDD is diagnosed when the infant or child fails to meet developmental milestones in several areas. The infant or child's physician or psychologist suspects ID; however, because the child is so young, an individually administered IQ test cannot be administered. Consequently, GDD is assigned as a temporary diagnosis to indicate developmental delays until the child is old enough to participate in IQ testing (American Psychiatric Association, 2013).

GDD is usually diagnosed in infants and toddlers who show significant delays in two or more of the following developmental domains: (1) fine/gross motor skills, (2) speech/language, (3) social/personal skills, and (4) daily living. *Significant delays* are defined by scores two or more standard deviations below the mean (see Table 5.3). Typically, children with GDD show delays across most or all domains of functioning (Shevell, 2010).

Children with GDD are usually identified in the first year of life. Some children show physical abnormalities at birth indicative of a developmental disorder. Other children's delays become apparent only when caregivers notice that their children are not developing in the same way as their peers. For example, a parent might wonder, "Why is my son not sitting up by himself at 9 months or walking at 15 months? Why hasn't my daughter learned to say 'mama' and ask for her cup by 18 months?" (Shevell et al., 2003). Consider the case of Sam, a preschooler with GDD (see next page).

The word *delay* in the name GDD implies that children will eventually catch up to their typically developing peers. Unfortunately, longitudinal studies of children with GDD indicate that is not always the case (Shevell, 2008). Many infants and toddlers initially diagnosed with GDD eventually meet criteria for ID by the time they begin preschool. Furthermore, retrospective studies indicate that most older children with ID showed delays in early development that would have merited the diagnosis of GDD. Consequently, some researchers consider GDD to be a "placeholder" diagnosis for children too young to be diagnosed with ID (Shevell, 2010).

Not all children with GDD have concurrent deficits in intellectual functioning, however. In one recent study, researchers examined the WPPSI scores of preschoolers

Table 5.3 Developmental Milestones Shown by Infants and Toddlers

Age	Motor	Language	Social	Daily Living
2 mo.	Raises head up in prone position	Differentiated cries	Smiles, follows caregiver w/ eyes	—
3 mo.	Raises head and chest; grasps object	Coos	Laughs	—
4 mo.	Rolls, stretches	—	Social smile in response to others	—
6 mo.	Sits up with support	Babbles, turn to sounds	—	Mouths objects
8 mo.	Sits up without support	Turn to the sound of own name	Stranger anxiety	—
10 mo.	Pincer grasp, crawls	Waves "bye-bye"	Peek-a-boo	Holds bottle with both hands
12 mo.	Walks but falls easily	First words	Separation anxiety	Drinks from a cup
15 mo.	Walks steadily, scribbles	Points to objects, uses single words	—	Uses spoon, helps to dress self
18 mo.	Walks up/down stairs with help; throws ball	Points to body parts when asked, two-word phrases	Plays with others	Builds small tower with blocks
24 mo.	Walks up/down stairs, kicks ball	Uses pronouns, three-word phrases	Says "no" frequently	Tries to feed self without help

Source: Based on Centers for Disease Control (2012).

Note: A pediatrician may consult a table of developmental milestones to determine if an infant is delayed in motor, language, social, or daily living skills. If she suspects delays in a particular domain, she might administer a norm-referenced test to determine the severity of the delay.

Silent Sam

Source: ©iStockphoto.com/AkilinaWinner

Sammy was a 34-month-old boy who was referred to our clinic by his pediatrician because of significant language delays. "I'm mostly concerned about his speech," his mother said. "Sammy has never been much of a talker. He only says a handful of words. Most of the kids his age in the neighborhood speak in complete sentences and he doesn't."

Dr. Baer learned that Sammy was born approximately six weeks' premature and continues to be small for his age. His motor skills tended to lag behind his peers throughout his life. When other children were learning to walk, Sammy was just beginning to crawl; when his peers began using a spoon and fork during meals, Sammy used his fingers.

Dr. Baer administered the Bayley Scales of Infant and Toddler Development (BSID) to Sammy. She observed Sammy complete a series of tasks to assess his functioning and asked questions of Sammy's mother about his development and behavior at home.

Sammy's performance on the BSID showed delays in language, motor, and social–emotional skills. Overall, Sammy's functioning was more than two standard deviations lower than other children his age. Sammy's most prominent delays were in language. He showed problems with receptive vocabulary; for example, he could not correctly point to the parts of his body that Dr. Baer named or demonstrate how to use a cup, shoe, or scissors when asked. Sammy also showed delays in expressive language; he usually spoke in two-word sentences, had difficulty naming pictures of common objects (e.g., apple, bed, car), and did not use pronouns when speaking. Testing also showed similar delays in fine motor skills (e.g., putting coins in a slot), gross motor skills (e.g., climbing stairs, kicking a ball) and social–emotional functioning (e.g., pretend play, interest in peers).

"I'm really glad that you brought Sammy to see me," Dr. Baer said to Sammy's mother. "His language and motor skills are lower than what we'd expect from a boy his age. Let's work together to find some ways we can help him develop these skills."

with GDD. Children's scores ranged widely, and nearly 20% of children earned scores within the average range (Riou, Ghosh, Francoeur, & Shevell, 2009).

Furthermore, some young children with GDD do not develop ID later in life. For example, cerebral palsy is a life-long, developmental disorder that causes marked delays in fine motor skills, gross motor skills, and (sometimes) eating, speech, and cognition (Hanna et al., 2009). Children with cerebral palsy usually show abnormal muscle tone (e.g., slouching), muscle spasms (e.g., rapid tightening of muscles that control the limbs), involuntary movements (e.g., jerks of the head, facial expressions), unsteady gait, poor balance, and noticeable joint or bone deformities. The disorder ranges in severity from mild clumsiness to a lack of coordinated motor activity. Although many children with cerebral palsy also show intellectual deficits, approximately one-third of children show normal intelligence (Shevell et al., 2003).

Similarly, children exposed to social deprivation or severe economic hardship can show early delays in motor, language, and cognitive development. For example, some infants adopted from developing countries have been raised in orphanages or "baby centers" with very high caregiver-to-child ratios (van IJzendoorn et al., 2011). Many of these children were provided with inadequate nutrition, cognitive stimulation (e.g., access to books, toys), and interactions with others. Their opportunities to develop motor skills through play and exploration may also be limited. Many of these infants and toddlers show marked delays in development across multiple domains. However, sensitive and responsible care, especially if provided before age 9 months, can remedy these deficits.

Identification

Between 1% and 3% of infants and toddlers have GDD (Srour & Shevell, 2014). In some cases, the cause of GDD can be determined based on physical examination. For example, children with Down syndrome can be identified by certain physical attributes, such as enlarged and rounded face and wide nasal bridge. In most cases, however, pediatricians must order blood tests to screen for genetic disorders. The American Academy of Pediatrics recommends chromosomal microarray (CMA) as a standard test for infants with GDD (Moeschler et al., 2014). This test identifies copy number variants (i.e., unusual

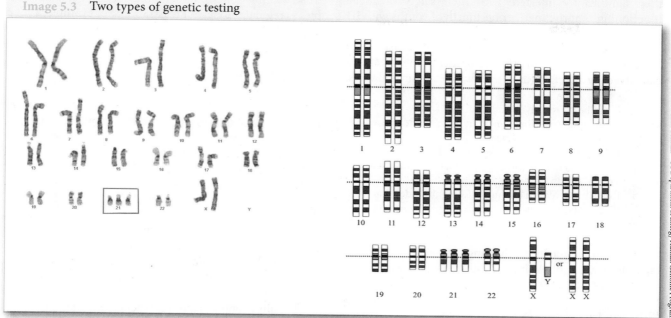

Source: Public Domain - from National Institutes of Health, Courtesy of the National Human Genome Research Institute Public domain - US Department of Energy Human Genome Program

Note: Genetic testing is used to determine the cause of GDD. G-banded karyotyping (*left*) produces a stained image of the child's chromosomes; it is useful for detecting gross genetic abnormalities. In contrast, chromosomal microarray (CMA; *right*) screens the child's genome and generates a high-resolution "virtual karyotype" that can detect small repetitions or deletions of genetic material. The tests above show a child with three (rather than two) 21st chromosomes, a feature of Down syndrome.

duplications or deletions) in major regions of the genome. CMA can be used to create a "virtual karyotype" of the child's chromosome structure to identify abnormalities (Flore & Milunsky, 2012). CMA has replaced older forms of genetic testing, such as G-banded karyotyping, which has poorer resolution and may be unable to detect more subtle chromosomal abnormalities (see Image 5.3). The most common genetic disorders that cause GDD are Down syndrome, Fragile X syndrome, Rett syndrome (another X-linked disorder), and subtle translocations or deletions of portions of the genome. Approximately 4% of children with GDD have an identifiable genetic disorder that explains their delays (Stevenson, Schwartz, & Rogers, 2012).

Physicians may also order blood or urine tests to screen for metabolic disorders that can cause developmental delays. Some metabolic disorders are phenylketonuria (PKU; described later), hypothyroidism, and lead poisoning. These disorders are relatively rare; only about 1% of youths with GDD have identifiable metabolic problems (Gilissen et al., 2014).

If the results of genetic and metabolic testing are negative, physicians may try to determine the source of children's delays using neuroimaging. Magnetic resonance imaging (MRI) is usually able to locate structural abnormalities in 30% to 40% of children with GDD. These abnormalities include central nervous system malformation, cerebral atrophy, problems with myelination, or cellular damage and lesions.

Of course, physicians must also rule out the possibility that sensory deficits underlie children's developmental delays. Approximately 13% to 25% of children with GDD also show vision problems, whereas 18% of children with GDD display significant hearing problems (Shevell et al., 2003). Untreated visual and auditory deficits can greatly interfere with the acquisition of children's speech, language, and social skills (Shevell, 2008).

Review:

- GDD is characterized by significant delays in several developmental domains (e.g., motor, language, social, or daily living skills) prior to age 5 years. It is a temporary diagnosis used when clinicians suspect ID but the child it too young to administer an intelligence test.
- Between 1% to 3% of infants and toddlers meet criteria for GDD.
- The American Academic of Pediatrics recommends CMA as a first-line test to identify genetic abnormalities in children with GDD.

What Challenging Behaviors Are Associated With Intellectual Disability?

Experts in the field of developmental disabilities use the term *challenging behavior* to describe children's actions, which are of such intensity, frequency, or duration that they significantly interfere with their safety or social functioning. Approximately one-fourth of youths with ID engage in challenging behavior (Didden et al., 2012).

Challenging behavior is problematic because it can affect children's health and development. Specifically, it can adversely affect children and families in several ways:

- It can be physically harmful.
- It can strain relationships with parents and cause children to be rejected by peers.
- It can limit children's access to developmentally appropriate social experiences, such as birthday parties, sleepovers, and sports.
- It can interfere with learning and cognitive development.
- It can place a financial burden on families and the public.

Given its seriousness, challenging behavior is a main target for treatment. Although children with ID can show many types of challenging behavior, we will focus on the most common: stereotypies, self-injurious behaviors (SIBs), and aggression (Sturmey, 2014b).

Stereotypies

Some children with ID show stereotypies, behaviors that are performed in a consistent, rigid, and repetitive manner and that have no immediate, practical significance (Vollmer, Bosch, Ringdahl, & Rapp, 2014). Stereotypies often involve repeated movements of the hands, arms, or upper body. For example, some children flap their hands, repeatedly move their fingers, twirl, fidget with objects, or rock back and forth. Other common stereotypes are facial grimacing, face and head tapping, self-biting, and licking.

Typically developing infants and toddlers sometimes show stereotyped behaviors, such as arm waving, kicking, or swaying. Some healthy older children and adolescents continue to engage in repetitive behaviors, such as hair twirling, body rocking, and repetitive object manipulation (e.g., twirling a pencil). These behaviors are not problematic unless they come to dominate the youths' behavior, persist over time, and interfere with functioning. *DSM-5* permits clinicians to diagnose children with stereotyped movement disorder when stereotypies become sufficiently impairing (Machalicek et al., 2016).

Stereotypies are fairly common among children with ID. In one large study, 18% of higher-functioning and 31% of lower-functioning children with developmental disabilities also displayed stereotypies. Moreover, 71% of youths with both ID and autism spectrum disorder (ASD) showed stereotyped behaviors.

Children engage in stereotypies for many reasons (Didden et al., 2012). Certain genetic disorders are characterized by stereotyped movements. More commonly, children engage in stereotypies because these behaviors are self-reinforcing. For example, spinning in place or rocking back and forth can be pleasurable, especially in situations that might otherwise be boring (e.g., sitting at a

desk, waiting in line). Other children engage in stereotypies to regulate anxiety or frustration. For example, a child might suck his fingers or flap his arms to soothe himself or express agitation or excitement.

Self-Injurious Behaviors

Self-injurious behaviors (SIBs) involve repetitive movements of the hands, limbs, or head in a manner that can, or do, cause physical harm or damage to the person. SIBs can be classified in three ways. First, they can be described in terms of their *severity*, from mild (e.g., head rubbing, finger picking, thigh slapping) to severe (e.g., eye gouging, self-scratching, head banging). Second, SIBs can be described in terms of their *frequency*, from low-occurrence acts with high potential for harm (e.g., head banging once per day) to high-occurrence acts that may cause harm over time (e.g., hand rubbing). Third, SIBs can be classified in terms of their *purpose*. Some actions seem reinforced by the responses they elicit from others. For example, a child might gain attention from his teacher by picking his skin. Other actions appear to be reinforcing by themselves. For example, a child might insert objects into his mouth or ears because they produce pleasant sensations (Sigafoos, O'Reilly, Lancioni, Lang, & Didden, 2014).

Approximately 10% to 12% of children with ID engage in SIBs (Didden et al., 2012). The prevalence of SIBs, like stereotypies, is directly related to the severity of children's intellectual and adaptive impairments. SIBs are most commonly seen in children with severe and profound impairments, children in institutional settings, and children with autism (Thompson & Caruso, 2002). Indeed, children with ID and autism may be 5 times more likely than children with ID alone to show SIBs. Head banging and self-biting/scratching are the two most common SIBs (Kahng, Iwata, & Lewin, 2002).

SIBs usually occur in episodes or "bouts" several times each day. Children with SIBs usually show the same behaviors in each episode (Kahng et al., 2002). In some children, episodes last only for a few seconds. These episodes are usually triggered by the environment, such as when a child with ID is reprimanded by a caregiver. In other children, episodes last for minutes or hours, more or less continuously. During these episodes, the child may not eat or sleep. Although these episodes may be triggered by environmental events, they are usually maintained over time by biological factors (Machalicek et al., 2016).

There are at least three possible explanations for SIBs in children with ID (Thompson & Caruso, 2002). One explanation is that children show SIBs because these behaviors serve a certain purpose or function. For example, some youths with ID engage in SIBs because they lack communication skills (Sigafoos et al., 2014). Head banging may be a way of communicating "I don't like this!" or "I'm bored!" To test this hypothesis, Hanley, Iwata, and McCord (2003) reviewed 536 cases of SIB or problematic behavior among people with ID. In 95.9% of cases, the SIBs

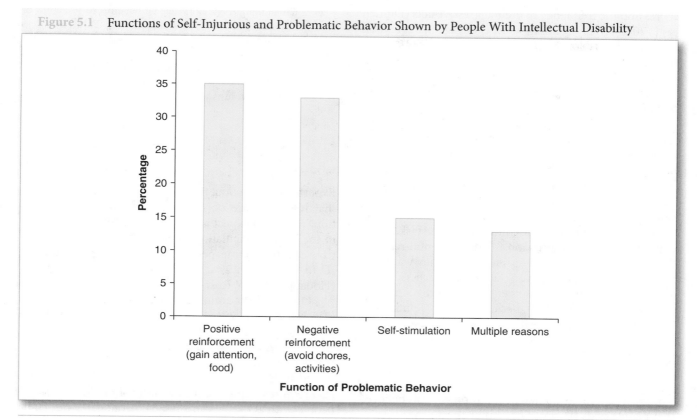

Function of Problematic Behavior

Source: Based on Hanley et al. (2003).

Note: More than 95% of cases of problematic behavior have some identifiable function.

served some identifiable purpose. These purposes included (a) gaining attention, food, or specific items; (b) escaping a chore, activity, or social interaction that they disliked; (c) providing stimulation or enjoyment; or (d) some combination of these three functions (see Figure 5.1).

A second explanation is that SIBs are caused by a hypersensitivity to the neurotransmitter dopamine. Three lines of evidence support this hypothesis. First, destroying dopamine receptors in the brains of neonatal rats causes them to develop a hypersensitivity to dopamine. If these rats are then injected with drugs that activate dopamine in the brain, they display severe self-injury. Second, healthy rats given high dosages of dopamine also show self-injury. Third, some antipsychotic drugs, which bind to dopamine receptors, decrease SIBs in humans.

A final possibility is that SIBs are maintained by high levels of endogenous opioids or endorphins (Schroeder et al., 2001). These naturally occurring chemicals bind to certain receptors in the brain and produce analgesia and feelings of pleasure. Children and adults who show SIBs may be better able to tolerate the pain because of these analgesic properties. Some individuals who show SIBs may actually derive pleasure from self-injury.

Evidence for the endorphin hypothesis comes from three sources. First, people with ID who show SIBs display a dramatic increase in endorphins immediately after engaging in self-harm; this increase is much faster than in individuals who do not show SIBs. Second, many people with ID and SIBs have abnormalities in the functioning of endorphin receptors and levels in their brains. Third, some studies indicate that SIBs can be reduced by administering drugs that block endorphin receptors (Thompson & Caruso, 2002).

Physical Aggression

Youths with ID, like their typically developing peers, sometimes engage in aggression (Farmer & Aman, 2011). Physical aggression refers to behavior that causes (or can cause) property destruction or harm to another person. Aggressive acts include throwing objects, breaking toys, ruining furniture, hitting, kicking, and biting others. By definition, aggressive acts are done deliberately, not by accident. However, it is sometimes difficult to determine the intentions of children with severe or profound ID (Didden et al., 2012).

Approximately 20% to 25% of youths with ID show chronic problems with aggression. Aggressive acts are most common among boys, children with comorbid autism, and youths with poor communication skills (Healy, Lydon, & Murray, 2014). Furthermore, there is often an inverse relationship between children's IQ scores and the frequency of their aggressive acts (Didden et al., 2012). Many children with ID engage in aggression because they lack communication skills to share their thoughts and feelings in more prosocial ways (Kanne & Mazurek, 2011). Indeed, interventions that help children improve their communication skills are frequently effective in reducing aggression (Sturmey, 2014a).

Matson and colleagues (2011) reviewed the published literature on the causes of aggression in individuals with ID. Most individuals showed aggression in order to avoid or escape a task, assignment, or chore. For example, a child might push, throw an object, or yell at his teacher because she asked him to put on his coat. Often, the child's aggression is negatively reinforced by the teacher withdrawing her request and allowing the child to avoid the task. Other children engage in aggression for instrumental reasons, that is, to obtain an item or privilege that they want. For example, a child might shove a classmate to access a toy. To a lesser degree, children might engage in aggression, especially property destruction, because it is self-reinforcing. Some youths find it pleasurable to destroy objects, toys, and furniture (Machalicek et al., 2016).

Comorbid Disorders

Until recently, many mental health professionals believed that people with ID could not suffer from other psychiatric disorders. Some experts believed that low intellectual functioning somehow immunized these individuals against depression, anxiety, and psychological distress. Other professionals simply did not differentiate ID from mental illnesses. Gradually, clinicians became aware that people with ID could suffer from the full range of psychiatric disorders (Pandolfi & Magyar, 2016).

Experts use the term *dual diagnosis* to refer to the presence of mental disorders among individuals with ID. Emerging evidence suggests that approximately 40% of children and adolescents with ID have a dual diagnosis. The most common co-occurring disorders are disruptive behavior disorders (25%), ADHD (9%), and anxiety (9%; Witwer et al., 2014).

Unfortunately, clinicians frequently overlook the presence of mental disorders in youths with ID, a phenomenon called diagnostic overshadowing. Why might clinicians miss anxiety, depression, and even psychotic symptoms in people with ID? Some mental health professionals simply do not have much experience in assessing and treating people with ID. Others erroneously attribute psychiatric problems to the person's low intelligence or problems in adaptive functioning (Einfeld et al., 2006; Koskentausta, Iivanainen, & Almqvist, 2007).

Review:

- Approximately 25% of youths with ID exhibit challenging behaviors such as stereotypies, SIBs, or physical aggression.

- Challenging behaviors can be harmful to the child or others, strain social relationships, limit children's access to educational or social opportunities, and place a financial burden on families.
- Approximately 40% of youths with ID have a comorbid mental disorder. Comorbid conditions are easily overlooked in youths with ID.

How Common Is Intellectual Disability?

Experts disagree about the prevalence of ID. If we assume that IQ scores are normally distributed in the population, we would expect approximately 2.2% of individuals in the general population to earn IQ scores less than 70. Consequently, some people estimate the prevalence of ID to be between 2% and 3% of the general population (Hodapp, Zakemi, Rosner, & Dykens, 2006).

Other experts argue that the prevalence of ID is lower (Tirosch & Jaffe, 2011). A meta-analysis suggested that approximately 1.83% of individuals have ID (Yeargin-Allsop, Boyle, & van Naarden, 2008). There are several reasons for this lower estimate. First, ID is not determined by the individual's IQ score alone; the diagnosis also requires impairment in adaptive functioning. Many people with IQ scores in the 55–70 range do not show significant deficits in adaptive functioning. Consequently, they are not diagnosed with ID.

Second, a person's IQ can fluctuate over time. Although IQ scores are quite stable for people with severe and profound impairments, IQs are less stable for individuals scoring on the higher end of the ID continuum (i.e., IQ 55–70). Someone might earn an IQ score below 70 when assessed as a child but earn a score above 75 in adolescence. Consequently, he or she would no longer qualify for the diagnosis.

Third, the life expectancy of individuals with severe and profound impairment is less than the life expectancy of typically developing individuals. Because of this reduced longevity, the number of people with ID is likely lower than expected based on the normal curve.

The prevalence of ID varies by age. ID is more frequently diagnosed among school-age children and adolescents than among adults (Hodapp & Dykens, 2006). If all adults in a town are screened for ID, the prevalence is approximately 1.25% (McLaren & Bryson, 1987); if only school-age children are assessed, the prevalence increases to 2.5% (National Center for Educational Statistics, 2015). Why are more school-age children classified as having ID than people in the general population? The answer seems to be that the cognitive impairments associated with ID are more noticeable when people are in school. After a person leaves school, these impairments are less noticeable, and people with them are less likely to be identified.

ID is slightly more common in males than in females. The gender ratio is approximately 1.3:1. Experts disagree on why males are more likely to show ID than females. Some people believe the male central nervous system is more susceptible to damage. Others believe that males are more likely to show ID than females because some forms of ID are caused by abnormalities on the X chromosome. Because boys have only one X chromosome, they may be more susceptible to disabilities caused by damage to this chromosome (Hodapp et al., 2006; Stromme & Hagberg, 2000).

Review:

- Meta-analyses indicate that approximately 1.8% of the population has ID.
- ID is more commonly diagnosed in school-age children (compared to adults) and boys (compared to girls).

5.2 CAUSES

What Is the Difference Between Organic and Cultural–Familial Intellectual Disability?

Zigler's Classification

Edward Zigler (1969) proposed one of the first methods to classify children with ID based on the cause of their impairments. Zigler divided children with ID into two groups (see Table 5.4). The first group consisted of children with identifiable causes. He classified these children with organic ID

because most of the known causes of ID at that time involved genetic disorders or biological abnormalities, such as Down syndrome. As a group, children with organic ID had IQ scores less than 50, physical features indicating neurological problems, and medical complications. Children with organic ID usually had parents and siblings with normal intellectual functioning and came from families of all socioeconomic backgrounds (Iarocci & Petrill, 2012).

Children in the second group showed no clear cause for their cognitive and adaptive impairments. They tended to earn IQ scores in the 50 to 70 range, had normal physical appearance, and showed no other health or medical problems. They were more likely to have parents, siblings, and other biological relatives with low intellectual functioning. Furthermore, they often came from low-income families. Zigler referred to individuals in this second group as experiencing "familial" ID because relatives often had low levels of intellectual and adaptive functioning. Today, many experts refer to people in this category as experiencing cultural–familial ID because children in this group are believed to experience ID due to a combination of environmental deprivation (e.g., low levels of cognitive stimulation, poor schools) and genetic diathesis toward low intelligence (Iarocci & Petrill, 2012).

The terms *organic* and *cultural–familial* can be misleading. A child with organic ID does not necessarily have a genetic cause for his impairments. Similarly, the deficits shown by a child with familial ID are not necessarily caused by environmental factors. The organic/familial

Table 5.4   Intellectual Disability Classified Into Organic Versus Cultural-Familial Types

	Organic	*Cultural-Familial*
Definition	• Child shows a clear genetic or biological cause for his/her Intellectual Disability	• Child shows no obvious cause for his/her Intellectual Disability • Biological relatives may have low IQ
Diagnosis	• Usually diagnosed at birth or infancy • Frequent comorbid disorders	• Usually diagnosed after beginning school • Few comorbid disorders
Intelligence and Adaptive Functioning	• IQ usually ≤ 50 • Siblings with normal IQ • Greater impairment in adaptive functioning • Often dependent on others	• IQ usually > 50 • Siblings with low IQ • Lesser impairment in adaptive functioning • Can live independently with support
Associated Characteristics	• Similar across ethnicities and SES groups • Associated with health problems and physical disabilities • Higher mortality rate • Unlikely to mate, often infertile • Often have facial abnormalities	• More prevalent in ethnic minorities and low-SES groups • Usually few health problems and no physical disabilities • Normal mortality rate • Likely to marry and have children with low IQ • Normal appearance

Source: Based on Iarocci and Petrill (2012).

Note: Although these names are somewhat misleading, they are useful for broadly differentiating people with intellectual disabilities.

distinction is based solely on whether we can identify the cause of the child's ID. For example, some cases of organic ID are caused by environmental factors, such as mothers' alcohol use during pregnancy. Similarly, some types of familial ID may be due to genetic anomalies that we have not yet identified. For example, the cause of Fragile X syndrome, the second-most common genetic cause of ID, was not identified until 1991. Even today, as many as 80% of people with Fragile X do not know they have the disorder. As genetic and medical research advances, it is likely that more causes of ID will be uncovered (Karmiloff-Smith, Doherty, Cornish, & Scerif, 2016).

Similar Sequence and Similar Structure Hypotheses

Typically developing children progress through a series of cognitive stages in a reliable order (Carey, Zaitchik, & Bascandziev, 2015). Infants learn to represent people in their minds and engage in pretend play, preschoolers show mastery of language, school-age children develop knowledge of conservation and concrete problem-solving, and adolescents show higher level abstract thinking. Zigler (1969) suggested that the sequence of cognitive development among children with ID is similar to the sequence of cognitive development seen in typically developing children. His similar sequence hypothesis posits that children with ID progress through the same cognitive stages as typically developing children, albeit at a slower pace.

Zigler (1969) also suggested that the cognitive structures of children with ID are similar to the cognitive structures of typically developing children of the same mental age. His similar structure hypothesis indicates that two children of the same mental age (one with ID and the other without ID) will show similar abilities. According to the similar structure hypothesis, a 16-year-old with ID whose intellectual functioning resembles that of a 5-year-old child should show the same pattern of cognitive abilities as a typically developing 5-year-old child.

Subsequent research on children with cultural–familial ID has generally supported the similar sequence and similar structure hypotheses. Children with cultural–familial ID show the expected sequence of cognitive development, although they reach stages at a slower rate than typically developing children (Zigler, Balla, & Hodapp, 1986). Furthermore, children with cultural–familial ID generally show similar cognitive abilities as children without ID of the same developmental age (Weisz, 1990).

Subsequent research involving children with organic ID has yielded mixed results. The cognitive development of children with organic ID does follow an expected sequence, similar to the development of typically developing children. However, children with organic ID often show different cognitive abilities than typically developing children of the same mental age. Specifically, children with organic ID often show characteristic strengths and weaknesses in their cognitive abilities; their cognitive abilities are not uniformly low. Furthermore, these cognitive strengths and weaknesses depend on the cause of the child's ID. For example, children with Down syndrome often show one pattern of cognitive abilities, whereas children with Fragile X syndrome show different cognitive profiles.

Behavioral Phenotypes

The finding that children with different types of organic ID show characteristic patterns of cognitive abilities is important. If scientists could identify the cognitive and behavioral characteristics associated with each known cause for ID, this information could be used to plan children's education and improve their adaptive functioning (Carlier & Roubertoux, 2015).

Consequently, researchers have moved away from lumping all children with known causes of ID into one large "organic" category. Instead, researchers study children with ID in separate groups in order to better understand the strengths and weaknesses associated with each disorder. For example, some researchers study the abilities of children with Down syndrome while others focus on the strengths and weaknesses of children with Fragile X syndrome (Hodapp et al., 2006).

Stated another way, researchers are interested in determining a behavioral phenotype for children with each known cause of ID. According to Dykens (1995), a behavioral phenotype involves "the heightened probability or likelihood that people with a given syndrome will exhibit certain behavioral or developmental sequelae relative to those without the syndrome" (p. 523). Behavioral phenotypes include the appearance, overall intellectual and adaptive functioning, cognitive strengths and weaknesses, co-occurring psychiatric disorders, medical complications, and developmental outcomes of children with specific causes for their ID. Behavioral phenotypes are probabilistic. Although not every child will show all of the features associated with the disorder, a general description might help organize and guide research and assist practitioners in developing evidence-based interventions (Carlier & Roubertoux, 2015).

Review:

- The term *organic ID* was used to describe children who had identifiable causes for their intellectual and adaptive disabilities. Usually, they had genetic disorders, earned very low IQ and adaptive functioning scores, experienced medical complications, and had no family history of ID.
- The term *cultural–familial ID* was used to describe children with no identifiable cause for their intellectual and adaptive disabilities. Usually, they earned IQ and adaptive scores in the 50–70 range, were physically healthy, and had family members with ID.
- Most research supports the similar sequence hypothesis—that is, youths with ID progress through the same stages of cognitive development as typically developing peers, albeit at a slower pace.

- In contrast, there is limited support for the similar structures hypothesis. Some causes of ID are associated with behavioral phenotypes—that is, specific patterns of behavior and cognitive strengths and weaknesses.

How Can Chromosomal Abnormalities Cause Intellectual Disability?

Researchers have identified more than 800 unique causes of ID. They can be loosely organized into five categories: (1) chromosomal abnormalities, (2) X-linked disorders, (3) metabolic disorders, (4) embryonic teratogen exposure or illness, and (5) complications during or after delivery. Altogether, these conditions explain approximately 70% of cases of ID (see Figure 5.2).

Down Syndrome

Down syndrome is a genetic disorder characterized by moderate to severe ID, problems with language and academic functioning, and characteristic physical features. The disorder was first described by John Langdon Down in 1866. It occurs in approximately 1 per 1,000 live births. The likelihood of having a child with Down syndrome depends on maternal age (see Figure 5.3).

Approximately 95% of cases of Down syndrome are caused by an extra 21st chromosome. This form of the disorder is sometimes called trisomy 21 because the child shows three chromosome 21s rather than the usual two. Trisomy 21 is not inherited. Instead, it is due to a *nondisjunction*—that is, a failure of the chromosome to separate during meiosis. In most cases, the mother contributes two chromosomes instead of one, but cases of paternal nondisjunction have also been reported.

Down syndrome can also occur when the child inherits one chromosome 21 from each parent and an abnormally fused chromosome (usually consisting of chromosomes 21 and 15) from one of the parents. This abnormality, called a *translocation*, results in additional genetic material passed on to the child. It occurs in approximately 3% of youths with Down syndrome. Down syndrome caused by translocation is inherited. Usually, the parents are unaffected carriers of abnormally fused chromosomes, and they unknowingly pass them on to their children.

Finally, Down syndrome can occur when some cells fail to separate during mitosis. This causes the child to have some normal cells and some cells with an abnormal amount of genetic information. The mix of normal and abnormal genetic information is called *chromosomal mosaicism*. Just as a mosaic is made up of different colored tiles, people with chromosomal mosaicism have cells of different genetic makeups. Chromosomal mosaicism accounts for approximately 2% of cases of Down syndrome.

Children with Down syndrome have characteristic facial features including flattened face, slanting eyes, wide nasal bridge, and low-set ears (see Image 5.4). Other physical features include short stature and poor muscle tone. Children with Down syndrome show small overall brain size and fewer folds and convolutions than in the brains of typically developing children. Fewer folds suggest reduced surface area of the cortex and may be partially responsible for low intelligence (Key & Thornton-Wells, 2012).

Children with Down syndrome are almost always diagnosed with ID; few of these children earn IQ scores greater than 60. Cognitive development progresses in a typical fashion for the first few months of life. After the child's first birthday, however, intellectual development slows and falls further behind typically developing peers.

Figure 5.2   The Causes of Intellectual Disability. Genetic and metabolic disorders explain 50% of cases.

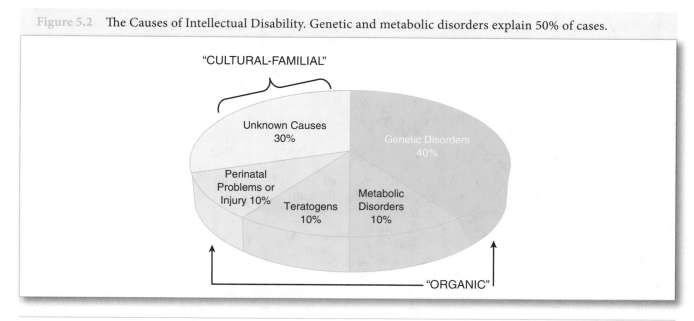

Source: Based on Toth, deLacy, and King (2015).

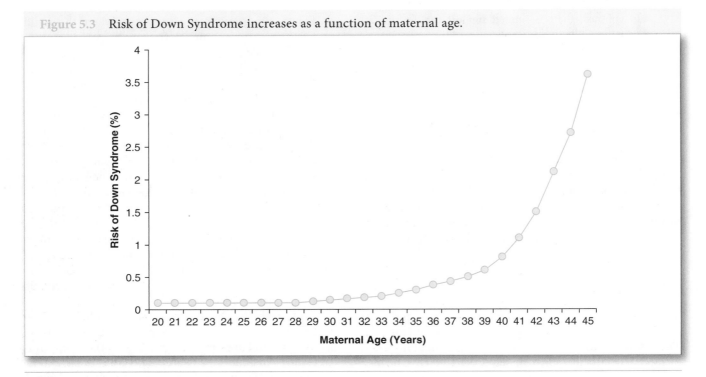

Figure 5.3   Risk of Down Syndrome increases as a function of maternal age.

Source: Based on Cuckle, Wald, and Thompson (1987).

Note: After a woman reaches age 35, most physicians recommend prenatal screening due to increased risk.

As a result, the delays of children with Down syndrome become more pronounced with age.

Children with Down syndrome show significant deficits in language (Dykens & Hodapp, 2001). They often have simplistic grammar, limited vocabulary, impoverished sentence structure, and impaired articulation. In fact, 95% of parents report difficulties understanding the speech of their children with Down syndrome (Kumin, 1994). These children also show problems with auditory learning and short-term memory. Consequently, they often struggle in traditional educational settings where teachers present most lessons verbally (Chapman & Bird, 2012).

In contrast, children with Down syndrome show relative strengths in visual–spatial reasoning (Dykens & Hodapp, 2001). For example, these children can repeat a series of hand movements presented visually more easily than they can repeat a series of numbers presented verbally (Dykens, Hodapp, & Evans, 2006). Some experts have suggested that teachers should capitalize on these children's visual–spatial abilities in the classroom. For example, Buckley (1999) taught children with Down syndrome how to read by having children visually match printed words with pictures, play word-matching games with flash cards, and manipulate flash cards with words printed on them into sentences. These techniques, which relied heavily on their propensity toward visual learning, led to increased reading skills. Furthermore, their advances in reading extend into other areas, such as speech and language.

Young children with Down syndrome are usually described as happy, social, and friendly. It is extremely rewarding to volunteer as a tutor for a child with Down syndrome because these children are often socially outgoing and affectionate. Children with Down syndrome are less likely to develop psychiatric disorders than other children with ID (Dykens et al., 2006). However, in adolescence they may experience emotional and behavioral problems due to social isolation or increased recognition of their impairments (Reiss, 1990).

Medical complications associated with Down syndrome include congenital heart disease, thyroid abnormalities, respiratory problems, and leukemia (Chase, Osinowo, & Pary, 2002). After age 40, many adults with Down syndrome show early symptoms of Alzheimer's disease (Coppus et al., 2006). Postmortem studies of their brains have shown a high incidence of neurofibrillary tangles and plaques, similar to those shown by older adults with Alzheimer's disease. The life expectancy for individuals with Down syndrome is approximately 65 years.

Prader-Willi Syndrome

Prader-Willi syndrome (PWS) is a noninherited genetic disorder characterized by mild ID, overeating and obesity, oppositional behavior toward adults, and obsessive–compulsive behavior (see Image 5.5). PWS occurs in 1 per 20,000 live births (Dykens & Shah, 2003).

Image 5.4   Michelle is a 7-year-old girl with Down syndrome, preparing for her first communion. She attended religious education classes with other children her age and received communion with her classmates.

Image 5.5   This boy has Prader-Willi syndrome (PWS), a genetic disorder than can cause intellectual disability, behavior problems, and unique facial characteristics like a prominent nose, absent philtrum, and thin upper lip.

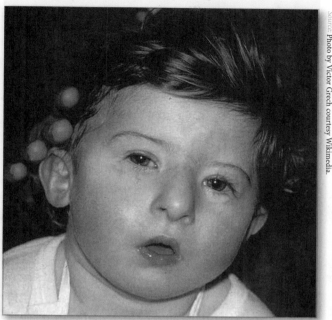

PWS is usually caused by the deletion of genetic information on portions of chromosome 15. In 70% of cases, the father's information is deleted, so the child inherits only one set of genetic information, from the mother. In most of the remaining cases, the mother contributes both pairs of chromosome 15. In both instances, the father does not contribute the significant portion of chromosome 15, resulting in missing paternal genetic information.

Individuals with PWS show either mild ID or borderline intellectual functioning. Average IQs range from 65 to 70 (Dykens & Shah, 2003). Children with PWS show relatively strong visual–spatial skills. Indeed, some children with PWS may be able to solve jigsaw puzzles faster than the psychologists who test them (Dykens & Cassidy, 1999). On the other hand, these children show weaknesses in short-term memory. Furthermore, their adaptive behavior is usually much lower than their IQ.

The most striking feature of many children with PWS is their intense interest in food (Dykens, 2003; Dykens & Cassidy, 1999). Infants with the disorder show problems with sucking, feeding, and gaining weight. However, between 2 and 6 years of age, children with PWS eat enormous amounts of food (i.e., hyperphagia). Some evidence suggests that these children have abnormal neural functioning in the paraventricular nucleus of the hypothalamus, the area of the brain that controls hunger and satiety. Since these children never feel full, they eat to excess and are often preoccupied by food. Some children steal food, hoard food, or obtain food from the garbage in an attempt to satisfy themselves. If their diet is not monitored, they will become obese. Medical complications associated with obesity are a leading cause of death among adults with PWS (Dykens & Shah, 2003). Consider the case of Dontrell, a boy with ID caused by PWS (see next page).

The onset of hyperphagia is also associated with changes in behavior. Many (70%–95%) children with PWS become argumentative, defiant, and throw temper tantrums (Dykens & Kasari, 1997). Approximately 42% of children with PWS destroy property during their disruptive outbursts, and 34% physically attack others (Dykens, Cassidy, & King, 1999).

Most (71%–98%) children with PWS show obsessive thoughts or ritualistic, compulsive behaviors (Dykens & Cassidy, 1999). The most common obsessions concern food (Dykens & Cassidy, 1999). They may eat foods in

INTELLECTUAL DISABILITY (PRADER-WILLI SYNDROME)

Obsessed With Food

Source: ©iStockphoto.com/tuanmonino

Dontrell was a 6-year-old boy referred to our clinic by his pediatrician because of significant delays in language and self-care skills. Dontrell recently entered the public school system after his maternal grandmother assumed caregiving responsibilities for him. His mother, a migrant worker, returned to Mexico but wanted Dontrell to remain in the United States and attend school.

Dontrell was slow to reach many developmental milestones. Whereas most children learn to sit up by age 6 months and walk by their first birthday, Dontrell showed delays mastering each of these developmental tasks. Most striking were Dontrell's marked delays in language. He had limited vocabulary in English and Spanish, struggled to recite the alphabet or recognize letters, and had difficulty counting. He also had problems performing self-care tasks typical of children his age, such as dressing, bathing, and grooming. School officials attributed these developmental delays to a history of poor medical care and nutrition and impoverished learning experiences as a toddler and preschooler.

Dontrell also showed significant problems with his behavior. First, he was hyperactive and inattentive. Second, Dontrell showed serious problems with defiance and aggression. When he did not get his way, he would throw a tantrum. Third, Dontrell's grandmother said that he had "an obsession for food." Dontrell apparently had an insatiable appetite and was even caught hoarding food under his bed and stealing food from relatives. Indeed, Dontrell weighed nearly 85 lbs!

Dr. Valencia, the psychologist who performed the evaluation, recognized that many of Dontrell's behaviors were consistent with a genetic disorder called Prader-Willi syndrome (PWS). Although most children with this disorder are recognized in infancy or toddlerhood, Dontrell was likely overlooked because he did not receive regular medical care. She suggested genetic testing to confirm her diagnosis.

a certain order or according to color, texture, type, or caloric content (Dykens, 2003). Children with PWS often show compulsive behaviors, too. They may hoard paper and pens; order and arrange toys and household objects by color, size, or shape; repeat information or questions; or be overly concerned with symmetry (Dimitropoulos, Feurer, Butler, & Thompson, 2001).

In early adulthood, some individuals with PWS show psychotic symptoms, including distorted thinking and hallucinations. In one study, 12.1% of parents of children with PWS reported auditory or visual hallucinations in their children (Stein, Keating, Zar, & Hollander, 1994). Life expectancy among adults with PWS is usually reduced because of obesity.

Angelman Syndrome

Angelman syndrome is a genetically based developmental disorder characterized by ID, speech impairment, happy demeanor, and unusual motor behavior. The disorder was identified by the physician Harry Angelman when three children (later diagnosed with the syndrome) were admitted to his hospital at the same time. All three children showed severe ID, an inability to speak, and problems with gait and balance. Their movements were sporadic, jerky, and irregular. They tended to walk with arms uplifted, sometimes on their toes, lurching forward with abrupt starts and stops. Most strikingly, all three children frequently smiled and laughed (see Image 5.6). Later, while visiting the Castelvecchio Museum in Verona, Angelman saw a painting titled *Boy With a Puppet* that reminded him of the happy disposition of his three young patients. Angelman subsequently wrote a scientific paper describing his three "Puppet Children," which slowly attracted the attention of clinicians throughout the world (Angelman, 1965). Today, professionals refer to the disorder as Angelman syndrome. Approximately 1 per 15,0000 to 20,000 children have the disorder.

Both PWS and Angelman syndrome are caused by abnormalities on portions of chromosome 15. Healthy children inherit two chromosome 15s, one from each parent. PWS occurs when children inherit genetic information on chromosome 15 only from the mother. In contrast, Angelman syndrome occurs when children inherit genetic information on chromosome 15 only from the father. In 70% of cases of Angelman syndrome, genetic information from the mother is deleted. In another 3% to 5% of cases, the father contributes two chromosome 15s and the mother contributes none. In the remaining cases of Angelman syndrome, the child shows other genetic mutations in chromosome 15 or the cause is unknown.

Image 5.6   This little girl has Angelman syndrome, a genetic disorder characterized by intellectual disability, speech problems, and hypo-pigmentation.

Image 5.7   Mary is a preschool-age girl with Williams syndrome. She shows strong verbal skills, characteristic of children with the disorder.

The most striking feature of Angelman syndrome is the persistent social smile and happy demeanor shown by children with the disorder. Many infants with Angelman syndrome begin this persistent smiling between 1 and 3 months of age. Later in development, it is accompanied by laughing, giggling, and happy grimacing. Facial features of children with Angelman syndrome often include a wide smiling mouth, thin upper lip, and pointed chin (Williams, 2005).

Despite children's social smiling, Angelman syndrome is usually not recognized until toddlerhood. Parents and physicians often suspect the disorder when children continue to show cognitive impairment, lack of spoken language, and movement problems. By childhood, intellectual functioning is generally in the range of severe or profound ID. Youths with the disorder show levels of functioning similar to a 2.5- to 3-year-old child. Most children with Angelman syndrome are unable to speak, although some can use a few words meaningfully. They usually can understand other people and are able to obey simple commands.

Nearly all children with Angelman syndrome show hyperactivity and inattention. Parents usually describe them as "on the go." Children may flap their arms, fiddle with their hands, and become easily excited. Hyperactivity often interferes with their ability to sleep. Children with Angelman syndrome often have difficulty sustaining their attention on one person or task for long periods of time. Problems with hyperactivity and inattention continue throughout childhood but decrease somewhat with age.

Some children with Angelman syndrome have hypopigmentation—that is, they may appear pale and have light-colored eyes. Hypopigmentation occurs when the gene that codes for skin coloring is deleted along with other information on chromosome 15.

More than 90% of children with Angelman syndrome have seizures. Sometimes, seizures are difficult to notice because of these children's sporadic movements. In most cases, physicians prescribe anticonvulsant medications to reduce the number and severity of seizures. Adults with Angelman syndrome have life expectancies approximately ten to fifteen years shorter than typically developing individuals. Life expectancy is dependent on the severity of comorbid medical problems, especially seizures.

Williams Syndrome

Williams syndrome (WS) is a genetic disorder characterized by low overall intellectual functioning, hyperactivity, impulsivity, inattention, and unusual strengths in spoken language and sociability (Elsabbagh & Karmiloff-Smith, 2012). Children with WS can be identified by their facial features. They often have broad foreheads; full lips; widely spaced teeth; star-shaped patterns in their irises; and elfin-like noses, eyes, and ears (see Image 5.7). Their facial features suggest a mixture of joy and mischievousness. WS is caused by a small deletion in a portion of chromosome 7. The disorder occurs in approximately 1 per 20,000 live births.

Despite their low IQ scores, children with WS show curious strengths in certain areas of language (Mervis, 2012). They have unusually well-developed lexicons (Hodapp & Dykens, 2006). They can tell relatively complex stories with advanced vocabulary and sophisticated grammar. They may even use sound effects when telling stories to add emphasis. Some children with WS show relative strengths in auditory memory and music (Hodapp & DesJardin, 2002). Teachers sometimes alter their instructional methods to play to the strengths of children with WS. For example, children with WS might respond best to verbal instruction rather than to reading and may prefer to work with partners or in groups, rather than independently (Hodapp & DesJardin, 2002).

Children with WS do poorly on visual–spatial tasks. They have great difficulty copying pictures or figures. This relative deficit in visual–spatial abilities is likely due to the genetic deletion that causes WS. Specifically, the portion of chromosome 7 that is deleted contains a gene that codes for an enzyme called LIM kinase. This enzyme is necessary for brain development and functioning, especially in brain regions responsible for visual–spatial processing. Deficits in this enzyme likely underlie the visual–spatial problems shown by children with the disorder (Elsabbagh & Karmiloff-Smith, 2012).

Children with WS are described as friendly and sociable. They are especially good at remembering faces and inferring a person's mental state and emotions based on his or her affect. Sometimes, they are overly trusting of strangers, placing them at risk for exploitation by others.

Children with WS often show problems with high-rate behavior and are easily excitable. They display inattention, hyperactivity, and impulsivity; many are diagnosed with ADHD (Einfeld, 2005). Furthermore, children with WS show hyperacusis—that is, an unusual sensitivity to loud noises. Truck engines, fire alarms, and school bells can cause them considerable distress.

Most children with WS show problems with anxiety. Like typically developing children, young children with WS fear ghosts, storms, and vaccinations. However, unlike typically developing children, older children with WS continue to fear these stimuli and show a marked increase in generalized anxiety with age. In particular, older children with WS often worry that something bad is about to happen. Many are extremely sensitive to failure and criticism by others (Dykens, 2003). In a sample of 51 individuals with WS, 35% showed phobias for objects or social situations while 84% showed subthreshold problems with anxiety. In contrast, the prevalence of phobias among children with other types of ID is only about 1% (Landau, 2012).

Dykens and Hodapp (2001) have suggested that the characteristic features of WS may place them at increased risk for developing anxiety problems. For example, their hyperacusis may place them at risk for developing fear of loud noises. Early problems with balance and gait might contribute to fears of falling from high places. Their social sensitivity may place them at increased risk for social anxiety. Consequently, the fears of children with WS may stem from the interaction of genotype, early experiences, and the behavioral characteristics of the disorder.

Children with WS are at risk for cardiovascular problems. The portion of chromosome 7 that is deleted in WS also contains a gene that codes for elastin. Elastin is used by the cardiovascular system to give connective tissue its elastic, flexible properties. Insufficient elastin can cause hypertension and other heart problems.

22q11.2 Deletion Syndrome

Children with 22q11.2 DS are at risk for developing ID because of missing genetic material on a portion of one pair of the 22nd chromosome. In approximately 10% of cases, the child inherits an abnormal chromosome from a parent. In most instances, however, genetic information is lost during fertilization. Approximately 1 in 2,000–4,000 children have this condition (Toth, deLacy, & King, 2015).

Children with 22q11.2 DS can show a wide range of physical and behavioral features (see Image 5.8). Physical characteristic usually include cleft lip and/or palate, small ears, and small mouth and chin. These youths often experience health problems including congenital heart problems, middle ear infections or hearing loss, immune problems, and seizures. The cleft lip and/or palate and hearing loss often cause these children to experience language delays and learning problems. Their average IQ is approximately 70 with significantly higher verbal skills than nonverbal skills (Butcher et al., 2012).

Children with 22q11.2 DS are at risk for psychiatric disorders. Young children with this condition often experience problems understanding social situations and show impaired social problem-solving. Some develop autistic-like symptoms. Older children with 22q11.2 DS often display problems with attention and may be diagnosed with ADHD. Approximately one-half of these youths

Image 5.8   Children with 22q11.2 DS often have cleft palate and small ears. Their average IQ is 70 with higher verbal than nonverbal skills. They are at risk for ADHD in childhood and schizophrenia in adulthood.

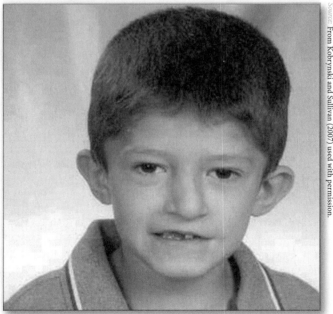

develop schizophrenia or psychotic symptoms, making 22q11.2 DS one of the few known causes for schizophrenia (Vorstman et al., 2015).

Review:

- Down syndrome (trisomy 21) is associated with moderate ID, characteristic appearance, weakness in verbal skills and language, strength in visual–spatial reasoning, and sociability.
- PWS is caused by missing paternal genetic material on chromosome 15. It is associated with mild ID, weakness in short-term memory, strength in visual–spatial reasoning, hyperphagia, and obsessive–compulsive behavior.
- Angelman syndrome is caused by missing maternal genetic material on chromosome 15. It is associated with moderate to severe ID, sporadic/jerky movements, lack of spoken language, hyperactivity, and persistent social smile.
- WS is caused by deletions on chromosome 7. It is associated with mild ID, well-developed spoken language, strengths in auditory memory, weakness in visual–spatial reasoning, hyperactivity, anxiety, and friendly demeanor.
- 22q11.2 DS is caused by deletions on chromosome 22. It is associated with mild to moderate ID, cleft lip/palate, ADHD, and risk for schizophrenia later in life.

How Can X-Linked Disorders Cause Intellectual Disability?

X-linked disorders are a specific class of genetic abnormalities that occur on the X-chromosome. Because girls have two X chromosomes and boys have only one, these disorders typically manifest differently across gender.

Fragile X Syndrome (FMR-1 Disorder)

Fragile X syndrome is an inherited genetic disorder that is associated with physical anomalies, moderate to severe intellectual impairment, and social/behavioral problems. It occurs in 1 per 4,000 boys and 1 per 8,000 girls (Toth et al., 2015).

Fragile X syndrome is caused by a mutation in a gene on the X chromosome, called the Fragile X mental retardation 1 (FMR1) gene (Cornish, Cole, Longhi, Karmiloff-Smith, & Scerif, 2013). In healthy individuals, this gene contains a three-nucleotide sequence of cytosine-guanine-guanine (CGG) that repeats a small number of times. It produces Fragile X mental retardation protein (FMRP), which assists in normal brain maturation and cognitive development. Children with Fragile X syndrome show an unusually high number of CGG repeats. Children who inherit 50 to 200 repeated sequences usually show no symptoms. They are typically unaware that they carry the genetic mutation, but they may pass this mutation on to their offspring. Children who inherit more than 200 repeated sequences usually show symptoms. The repeated sequences interfere with the functioning of the FMR1 gene and, consequently, decrease the amount of FMRP produced. In general, the less FMRP produced, the more severe children's cognitive impairments. Brain scans of children with Fragile X show abnormalities of the prefrontal cortex, caudate nucleus, and cerebellum, presumably from less FMRP production. The disorder is called Fragile X because the X chromosome appears broken (Stevenson et al., 2012).

Boys and girls differ in their presentation of Fragile X syndrome, with boys showing greater intellectual impairment, more severe behavior problems, and more physical anomalies. Boys show relatively greater impairment because their only X chromosome is affected. Girls, on the other hand, inherit one affected X chromosome and a second X chromosome, which is typically unaffected. The additional unaffected X chromosome produces normal amounts of FMRP and contributes to higher cognitive functioning (Cornish et al., 2013).

Boys with Fragile X tend to have elongated heads, large ears, hyperflexible joints, and large testicles after puberty (Sadock & Sadock, 2015). They also tend to be shorter than other boys. Medical problems sometimes associated with Fragile X include heart murmur and crossed eyes (see Image 5.9).

Boys with Fragile X syndrome tend to show moderate to severe ID (Abbeduto, McDuffie, Brady, & Kover, 2012). Additionally, they show a curious pattern of strengths and weaknesses in the way they process information and solve problems. They perform relatively well on tasks that require *simultaneous processing*—that is, perceiving, organizing, and interpreting information all at once. Solving puzzles or completing mazes demands simultaneous

Image 5.9   Blake is a preschool-age boy with Fragile X syndrome. His parents describe him as "a sweet and spunky little guy."

processing. Alternatively, boys with Fragile X syndrome show relative deficits in *sequential processing*, or the capacity to arrange and process information in a certain order. Reading a sentence or following instructions on how to assemble a toy requires sequential processing. These boys also show weakness in planning and organizing activities in an efficient manner (Karmiloff-Smith et al., 2016).

Boys with Fragile X also tend to show characteristic patterns of behavior. Most notably, many show autistic-like behavior, such as a reluctance to make eye contact or be touched by others. However, only about 25% of boys with Fragile X meet diagnostic criteria for autism. The rest appear extremely shy in social situations. Many boys with Fragile X also display hyperactivity and inattention. As many as 90% have ADHD (Dykens & Hodapp, 2001; Sullivan, Hooper, & Hatton, 2007).

Girls with Fragile X tend to have higher IQs, less noticeable physical anomalies, and less severe behavior problems than do boys with the disorder. Like boys, girls may have problems with attention. They may also show excessive shyness, gaze aversion, and social anxiety (Hodapp & Dykens, 2006).

Rett Syndrome (MECP-2 Disorder)

Rett syndrome is the most common cause of severe ID in girls. It is almost always caused by a genetic mutation in the MECP-2 gene of the X chromosome; it is rarely inherited. The disorder is almost always seen in girls; boys with the condition often die during or shortly after fertilization. The disorder affects 1 in 8,500 to 10,000 children (Toth et al., 2015).

Infants with Rett syndrome display normal development for the first 6 to 18 months of life. Then, they usually show a rapid deterioration in their language, motor, and social skills. Most will display social withdrawal and develop stereotypic hand-wringing movements (see Image 5.10). Many will also show health problems such as growth failure, breathing problems, loss of movement, and scoliosis (i.e., curvature of the spine). As toddlers, many develop emotion-regulation problems such as episodes of crying and screaming. Approximately 90% have seizures. Youths with Rett syndrome can live into adulthood with support from caregivers (Lyst & Bird, 2015).

Review:

- Fragile X syndrome is an inherited, X-linked disorder that adversely affects boys more than girls. It is characterized by mild to moderate ID, characteristic appearance, strengths in simultaneous processing, weakness in sequential processing, and social deficits.
- Rett syndrome is usually caused by a genetic mutation in a portion of the X chromosome. It almost always affects girls. It is characterized by typical development in early infancy followed by rapid deterioration in social functioning and language, severe ID, hand-wringing stereotypies, and seizures.

Image 5.10   Individuals with Rett syndrome often show severe intellectual disability, stereotyped hand movements, and health problems. This image shows the same person with Rett syndrome at age 9 and 24.

How Can Metabolic Disorders Cause Intellectual Disability?

Phenylketonuria (PKU) is the most well-known metabolic disorder that can lead to ID if untreated. In most cases, PKU is characterized by the body's inability to convert phenylalanine, an essential amino acid found in certain foods, to paratyrosine. In PKU, the enzyme that breaks down phenylalanine (phenylalanine hydroxylase) is not produced by the liver. As the child eats foods rich in phenylalanine, such as dairy, meats, cheeses, and certain breads, the substance builds up and becomes toxic. Phenylalanine toxicity eventually causes brain damage and ID.

PKU is caused by a recessive gene (see Figure 5.4). In order for a child to show PKU, he must inherit the gene from both mother and father. Children who inherit the gene from only one parent are carriers of the disorder but do not display symptoms. If a carrier mates with another carrier, each offspring has a 25% chance of showing PKU. The disorder occurs in approximately 1 per 11,500 children.

Newborns are routinely screened for PKU through a blood test conducted shortly after birth. If the disorder is detected, the child is placed on a diet consisting of foods that are low in phenylalanine. The diet decreases the chances of toxicity; consequently, adherence to the diet results in normal intellectual development. Most physicians suggest the diet should be continued indefinitely. Since phenylalanine is an essential amino acid, children on the diet must be monitored by their pediatricians. They are at risk for low red blood cell count (anemia) and low blood glucose levels (hypoglycemia).

Youths with PKU who do not diet show symptoms several months after birth. By childhood, they often develop severe ID and they lack spoken language. Children with untreated PKU are also hyperactive, show erratic movements, and throw tantrums. Additionally, they may experience gastrointestinal problems and have seizures. These impairments are irreversible, even if a phenyl-free diet is initiated later in childhood.

Review:

- PKU is an inherited disorder characterized by an inability to break down phenylalanine, an amino acid in many foods (e.g., dairy, meats).
- Restricting phenylalanine can prevent severe ID, seizures, and other medical problems.

Figure 5.4 PKU Is an Autorecessive Metabolic Disorder

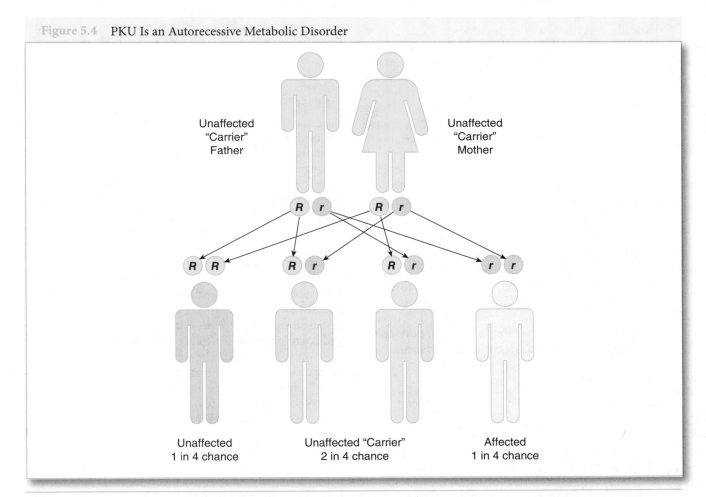

Note: Children must inherit the recessive gene from both parents to develop the disorder. If children inherit only one recessive gene, they will carry the disorder but not show symptoms.

How Can Maternal Illness or Environmental Toxins Cause Intellectual Disability?

Maternal Illness

Infections acquired by mothers during pregnancy can result in preterm birth; low birth weight; and, in some instances, ID (Silasi et al., 2015). The five main classes of maternal illnesses that can contribute to cognitive problems in children are represented by the acronym TORCH.

T: *Toxoplasma* infection is caused by a parasite that exists in warm-blooded animals throughout the world. In developed countries, pregnant women are most likely to acquire this parasite by consuming undercooked meat or handling animal droppings. Consequently, pregnant women should avoid cleaning cat boxes. Toxoplasmosis affects the development of the central nervous system. Symptoms may not appear until late infancy or toddlerhood in some children.

O: *Other infections* that can cause ID include the varicella zoster virus (which causes chicken pox), syphilis, hepatitis B, and HIV/AIDS. Mothers can avoid varicella infection with the chicken pox vaccine or by limiting contact with affected individuals. The other conditions can often be avoided by altering sexual behavior. If a mother becomes infected, syphilis can be treated with penicillin. Although there is no cure for hepatitis B or HIV/AIDS, several strategies can reduce the likelihood that the virus will be transmitted to the fetus: the use of antiviral medications during gestation, delivery by Caesarian section, and bottle-feeding rather than breastfeeding. For example, the likelihood of mother-to-infant transmission of HIV is 25% and <1% with and without these prevention strategies, respectively.

R: *Rubella* is a virus that causes German measles. Although maternal symptoms are relatively minor (i.e., a rash), infants infected with rubella typically show moderate to severe cognitive impairment. Infection is most serious during the first trimester of gestation. With the widespread use of the rubella vaccine, fetal infection is relatively rare in developed countries. However, women who refuse vaccination or who live in countries where vaccination is not practiced continue to be at risk.

C: *Cytomegalovirus (CMV)* is an extremely common virus that most people acquire during adolescence or early adulthood. It causes mononucleosis, an illness characterized by a high fever, chills, sore throat, and fatigue. CMV can be transmitted to a fetus if the mother acquires the illness for the first time during gestation. The illness can cause significant damage to the fetal nervous system, hearing loss, ID, and death.

Consequently, pregnant women should avoid individuals who experience symptoms of mononucleosis.

H: *Herpes simplex virus type 2 (HSV-2)* is an infection that is typically acquired through sexual contact. Approximately 20% of women aged 14 to 49 have the illness. Fetuses typically acquire the virus in two ways: (1) if a mother first acquires the infection during the final trimester of pregnancy or (2) if a mother has an active herpes lesion that comes into contact with the infant during delivery. Infants who acquire the virus can experience severe damage to their central nervous system, blindness, seizures, and ID. Although there is no cure for HSV-2, mothers can prevent fetal transmission by using antiviral medication and delivering by Caesarian section.

One final illness deserves special mention: *Zika virus disease* (Rasmussen, Jamieson, Honein, & Petersen, 2016). The disease is caused by the Zika virus and is usually acquired through infected mosquitoes or sexual contact. The disease causes fever, rash, joint pain, and conjunctivitis in adults. Symptoms are usually minor. Unfortunately, fetuses can acquire the virus during gestation. Zika can cause severe damage to the developing central nervous system, microcephaly (i.e., small head circumference), cognitive impairment, and death (see Image 5.11; Brasil et al., 2016; Centers for Disease Control and Prevention, 2016f).

Lead Exposure

Lead is a neurotoxin that can cause developmental disabilities in children. Fetuses are at risk for lead toxicity if their mothers are exposed to lead during gestation. For example, pregnant women may inadvertently ingest lead through contaminated drinking water or by working in industrial facilities. In high amounts, ingested lead can pass through the placenta and affect fetal development. A mother's history of lead exposure can also place her fetus at risk. For example, a mother exposed to lead during her childhood and adolescence may store it in her bones. If she does not consume sufficient calcium during pregnancy, her body may substitute this stored lead for the calcium her baby needs. In either case, newborns exposed to lead during gestation are at risk for premature birth, low birth weight, and cognitive problems (Shah-Kulkarni et al., 2016),

Young children can be exposed to lead in three ways. First, children can drink contaminated tap water that contains high lead levels (see Figure 5.5). Second, children can be exposed to lead from playing near industrial sites that use lead in manufacturing. Third, and most commonly, children can ingest lead-based paint. Although lead-based paint was banned in the United States in 1978, approximately 24 million older homes and apartments still contain lead-based paint. Eventually, this paint can chip or flake. Infants may eat paint chips on the floor and children may inadvertently inhale paint dust containing lead (Eid & Zawia, 2016).

Image 5.11   This mother had the Zika virus while pregnant. Her 2.5-month-old son has microcephaly, a birth defect characterized by a small head and severe intellectual disability.

Source: Courtesy NPR.

Figure 5.5   Lead exposure places children at risk for developmental problems. African American children, youths living in poverty, and children living in older homes are most often exposed.

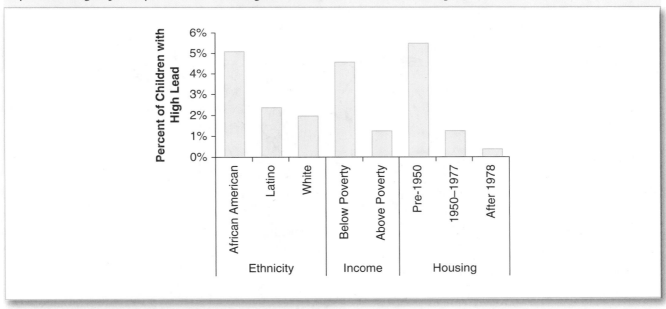

Source: Centers for Disease Control and Prevention, 2016d.

Lead exposure is typically measured with a blood test. Levels greater than 5 micrograms per deciliter (>5µg/dL) are considered "elevated" (Centers for Disease Control and Prevention, 2016a). However, no level of lead exposure is considered safe. Even lower lead levels are associated with neurodevelopmental problems in some children.

The effects of lead on development vary as a function of the child's age and the amount and duration of exposure. In general, lead is most dangerous to youths 0 to 5 years, because of the rapid development of the nervous system that occurs during this developmental period. Lead is strongly associated with cognitive problems, especially lower intelligence and increased risk for learning disabilities. Recent longitudinal studies indicate that every 1μg/dL increase in lead is associated with a 1- to 2-point IQ reduction. These cognitive deficits typically persist into adulthood (Mazumdar et al., 2011).

Infants and toddlers exposed to lead are also at risk for behavior problems. Most commonly, children experience problems with attention and concentration, hyperactivity, and disruptive behavior including aggression. Early lead exposure is also associated with increased risk for conduct problems in adolescence.

Unfortunately, most children do not show clear signs of lead toxicity until their lead levels approach 40 to 50μg/dL. Symptoms of lead toxicity in young children include cognitive delays and learning problems, irritability, sluggishness, loss of appetite, and gastrointestinal problems. Children with very high levels can receive chelation therapy. Chelation is injected into the child's bloodstream, where it binds to lead and helps remove it from the body. Chelation therapy is used only in extreme instances of lead toxicity because it can cause kidney damage, heart problems, and other metabolic difficulties.

How can families prevent lead exposure? First, families who live in older homes can inspect walls, windows, and porches for chipping or flaking paint. Deteriorating surfaces can be professionally treated and repainted to protect children (see Image 5.12). Second, parents should regularly clean floors and other surfaces of their home as well as their children's hands and toys. Parents should limit their children's exposure to toys that might contain lead-based paint. Third, families should remove their shoes before entering the house to prevent them from bringing in lead-contaminated soil. Children should also avoid playing outside while barefoot. Finally, families whose tap water comes from a public water system can check with their water supplier for information about lead levels. Water suppliers are required to provide customers with a consumer confidence report that describes water quality each year. Families with a private water supply (e.g., a well) can check lead levels using a kit (Centers for Disease Control and Prevention, 2016d).

Alcohol and Other Drugs

Many drugs, if ingested by pregnant women, are associated with low birth weight, reduced head circumference, and increased risk for behavioral and learning problems in childhood. Interestingly, "hard" drugs, such as heroin and

Image 5.12   The Centers for Disease Control and Prevention (2012) publishes a coloring book to teach children about the risks of lead exposure.

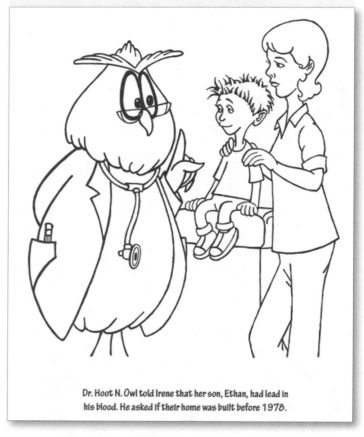

Dr. Hoot N. Owl told Irene that her son, Ethan, had lead in his blood. He asked if their home was built before 1978.

cocaine, are not as consistently associated with ID as are more socially accepted drugs like alcohol.

Fetal alcohol spectrum disorder (FASD) is caused by maternal alcohol consumption during pregnancy. FASD is characterized by lower intellectual functioning, learning disabilities, hyperactivity, and slow physical growth as well as characteristic craniofacial anomalies. Some children with FASD have cardiac problems. FASD is called a spectrum disorder because the severity of symptoms range from mild to severe, depending on the mother's use of alcohol during gestation (Popova et al., 2016).

The prevalence of FASD is approximately 1 to 3 per 1,000 live births. However, among children of women who have alcohol use disorder, the prevalence is approximately 1 in 3. Experts disagree on how much alcohol must be consumed to produce FASD. Some data indicate that FASD can occur from only 2 to 3 oz. of alcohol per day during gestation. Furthermore, binge drinking during pregnancy greatly increases the chance of FASD. Although occasional consumption of alcohol during pregnancy may not produce severe symptoms, it may lead to subtle cognitive, behavioral, and physical abnormalities, such as mild learning problems, reduced attention span, or short stature. Consequently, the American Academy of Pediatrics states that no amount of alcohol during pregnancy is safe and that women should abstain from alcohol during gestation (Williams, Smith, & Committee on Substance Abuse, 2015).

The intellectual functioning of children with FASD varies considerably. Most children with FASD show mild to moderate ID, although some earn IQ scores within the borderline to low-average range. These children usually have academic problems and may drop out of school. Many have learning disabilities. The most common behavioral problems associated with FASD are hyperactivity, impulsivity, and inattention. Young children with FASD are often diagnosed with ADHD. Older children and adolescents with FASD report feelings of restlessness and difficulty sustaining attention on reading and homework.

Children with FASD are at risk for conduct and mood problems as they enter late childhood and adolescence. They may experience peer problems and teasing because of their cognitive impairment. Furthermore, they may become depressed because of their academic deficits, behavior problems, or stigmatization associated with the disorder (Popova et al., 2016). Consider the case of Andrew, a boy with moderate FASD.

Review:

- The acronym TORCH reflects the five most common maternal illnesses that can cause ID.
- Lead exposure during gestation or early childhood is associated with behavior and learning problems. In high elevations, lead toxicity can cause ID.
- FASD is associated with lower intellectual functioning, learning disabilities, hyperactivity–impulsivity, inattention, and characteristic facial appearance. High exposure to alcohol during gestation can cause mild ID.

CASE STUDY

FETAL ALCOHOL SPECTRUM DISORDER

Tough Love

Andrew was a 14-year-old boy referred to our clinic because of a marked increase in disruptive behavior at school. Andrew was a large boy, approximately 5 feet 10 inches and more than 160 lbs. He displayed many of the physical features of youths with FASD including wide-spaced eyes, upturned nose, low-set ears, and broad face. Andrew's mother had an extensive history of alcohol and other drug use. She drank throughout her pregnancy and was intoxicated at the time of his delivery.

Andrew had long-standing academic problems. His IQ was 67. His reading and mathematics scores were comparable to those of a second- or third-grade child. Andrew received special education services, including remedial tutoring; however, he felt humiliated about receiving these special services.

Since beginning junior high school the previous year, Andrew's behavior became increasingly disruptive. He would often "clown around" in class, play pranks on teachers and other classmates, and get into fights on the playground. Andrew admitted to being teased by classmates because of his appearance, his academic problems, and his family history. "I know I'm slow," he said. "I don't need the other kids to tell me."

Andrew met with a psychologist at our clinic for weekly therapy sessions. Andrew was initially silly and disruptive during the sessions, but he gradually came to trust his therapist and share his feelings.

During one session, Andrew commented, "You know, if it wasn't for my mom, I wouldn't have all of the problems that I'm having right now." His therapist replied, "I guess you're right. Your mom makes you pretty upset when you visit her. That causes you to get into trouble." Andrew replied, hesitantly, "No. That's not what I mean. I mean, if it wasn't for my mom's drinking—when I was inside her—I wouldn't be so dumb. If only she could have loved me more than drinking."

How Can Perinatal or Postnatal Problems Cause Intellectual Disability?

Complications With Pregnancy and Delivery

Complications that occur during gestation or delivery can contribute to ID. Maternal hypertension or uncontrolled diabetes during pregnancy is sometimes associated with ID in children. Delivery complications that interfere with the fetus's ability to obtain oxygen for extended periods of time (anoxia) can also lead to central nervous system damage and ID. Anoxia can occur when the umbilical cord wraps around the fetus's throat, interfering with oxygen intake.

One of the greatest predictors of cognitive problems in children is premature birth and/or low birth weight. Children born before 36 weeks' gestation are at risk for deficits in intellectual and adaptive functioning in infancy and early childhood. Two meta-analyses have shown an inverse relationship between premature birth and children's subsequent IQ (see Figure 5.6). Furthermore, a very large, community-based study found that the risk of developmental delays increased exponentially with decreasing gestational age. Approximately 4.2% of full-term infants showed motor, language, social, or daily living delays compared to 37.5% of infants born at 24 to 25 weeks' gestation. Controlling for other biological and social factors, such as mother's age and education, did not affect this relationship between prematurity and developmental risk (Kerstjensk, DeWinter, Bocca-Tjeertes, Bos, & Reijnveld, 2013).

Preterm birth is a risk factor because of the rapid growth of the central nervous system during the third trimester. Between 24 and 40 weeks' gestation, the fetus's cortical volume increases fourfold. There is a dramatic increase in the number of neurons, axons, and synapses; increased myelination; and more complex brain activity. Although maturation can (and does) continue after delivery, optimal development occurs in utero (Volpe, 2008).

Childhood Illness or Injury

The two childhood illnesses most associated with the development of ID are *encephalitis* and *meningitis*. Encephalitis refers to the swelling of brain tissue, whereas meningitis refers to an inflammation of the meninges, the membrane that surrounds the brain and spinal cord. Both illnesses can be caused by bacteria or viral infections, although viral infections are more serious because they are resistant to treatment.

All serious head injuries have the potential to cause ID. An obvious source of injuries is car accidents; however, most childhood head injuries occur around the home. Falls from tables, open windows, and stairs account for many injury-related cognitive impairments. Similarly, children who almost drown in swimming pools or bathtubs can experience brain damage and corresponding cognitive problems (Appleton & Baldwin, 2006).

Children exposed to certain types of physical maltreatment are also at risk for ID and other cognitive problems (Shaahinfar, Whitelaw, & Mansour, 2015). Abusive head trauma (more commonly called shaken baby syndrome)

Figure 5.6   Preterm Birth Places Infants at Greater Risk for Delays

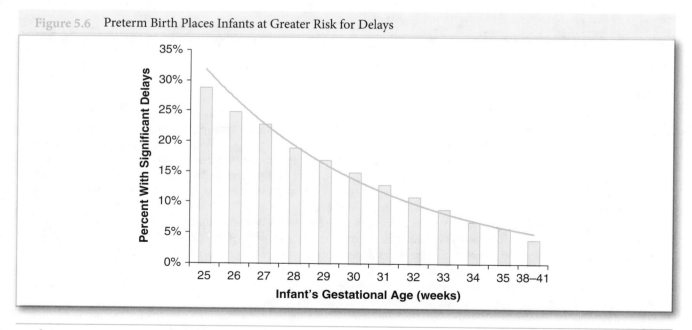

Source: From Kerstjenks and colleagues (2013).

Note: Preterm infants are at much greater risk for delays in motor, language, social, and daily living skills than full-term infants. Risk increases exponentially with decreased gestational age.

occurs when caregivers induce brain injury by forcefully shaking an infant or toddler. Very young children have weak neck muscles; therefore, any amount of back-and-forth shaking can cause trauma to the brain. Usually, caregivers engage in this behavior when frustrated by their baby's crying. Children's symptoms range from irritability, lethargy, and poor appetite to vomiting, tremors, and death. Infants who survive such shaking frequently experience cognitive deficits such as ID, learning disabilities, and attention and memory problems.

Review:

- Anoxia during gestation or delivery and preterm birth are risk factors for ID and learning problems in childhood.
- Encephalitis, meningitis, and high fever in childhood can also contribute to ID.
- Head injuries during infancy and childhood, especially abusive head trauma (i.e., shaken baby syndrome) are risk factors for ID.

What Causes Cultural–Familial Intellectual Disability?

Cultural–familial ID results from the interaction of the child's genes and environmental experiences over time. Some children inherit a genetic propensity toward low intelligence. When these children also experience environmental deprivation that interferes with their ability to reach their cognitive potentials, they are at risk for below-average intelligence and adaptive functioning. Environmental deprivation might include poor access to health care, inadequate nutrition, lack of cognitive stimulation during early childhood (e.g., parents talking, playing, and reading with children), low-quality early education, and a general lack of cultural experiences during early childhood (e.g., listening to music, trips outside the home). Over time, the interaction between genes and environment can contribute to ID.

Cultural–familial ID is more prevalent among children from low-income families than middle-class families. The correlation between socioeconomic status (SES) and children's intelligence is approximately .33. Furthermore, the relationship between SES and children's IQ increases when children experience extreme poverty or socioeconomic disadvantage (Turkheimer & Horn, 2015).

Both genetic and environmental factors explain this association between SES and children's intelligence. With respect to genetics, low-income parents tend to have lower IQ scores than middle-class parents. Individuals with higher IQs complete more years of schooling and assume more challenging and higher paying jobs. The children of high-income parents inherit their parents' genotypes that predispose them to a higher range of intellectual and adaptive functioning (Stromme & Magnus, 2000).

Furthermore, children from low-income families are exposed to environments that may restrict their intellectual potential. For example, low-income children are more likely to experience gestational and birth complications, have limited access to high-quality health care and nutrition, have greater exposure to environmental toxins such as cigarette smoke or lead, receive less cognitive stimulation from their home environments, and attend less optimal schools. These environmental deficits or risk factors can limit their cognitive and adaptive skills (von Stumm & Plomin, 2015).

Brain imaging studies confirm the risk of poverty on children's cognitive development (Luby, 2015). In one of the largest studies conducted to date, researchers used MRI to measure brain size in a large group of school-age children. Children living in poverty showed an 8% to 10% reduction in brain volume compared to youths not living in poverty. Reductions were greatest in areas responsible for problem-solving and memory, especially the frontal lobe and hippocampus. Furthermore, these reductions were associated with a 6-point decrease in IQ and a 4- to 7-point decrease in academic achievement (Hair, Hanson, Wolfe, & Pollak, 2015; von Stumm & Plomin, 2015).

Many studies suggest a relationship between the quality of the home environment and children's intellectual development. After reviewing the data, Sattler (2014) identified two broad ways parents can enrich their children's home environment and help them achieve their intellectual potentials. First, families who provide their children with ample verbal stimulation, model and provide feedback regarding language, and give many opportunities for verbal learning foster greater intellectual development in their children. Parents should take every opportunity to interact with their children through talking, playing, and reading. Second, encouraging academic achievement, curiosity, and independence in children is associated with increased intellectual functioning. Parents should encourage creative play, arts and crafts, and homemade games and activities, especially with young children, in order to help them develop novel and flexible problem-solving skills.

Review:

- Cultural–familial ID is associated with a genetic predisposition toward lower intellectual functioning and environmental experiences that restrict the development of intelligence and adaptive functioning (e.g., low-quality nutrition, health care, schooling).
- Caregivers can promote their children's intellectual functioning by providing verbal stimulation and encouraging academic achievement, curiosity, and independence at home.

5.3 PREVENTION AND TREATMENT

How Do Professionals Screen for Developmental Disabilities?

Shortly after birth, newborns are routinely administered a series of blood tests to detect genetic and metabolic disorders that cause ID. For example, all infants are screened for PKU. If PKU is found, a genetic counselor and nutritionist will meet with parents to discuss feeding options for the child.

If parents are at risk for having children with ID or other developmental delays, a physician may recommend genetic screening during gestation. Parents who may be carriers of specific genetic disorders, parents who have other children with developmental delays, or mothers older than age 35 often participate in screening.

At 15 to 18 weeks' gestation, mothers can undergo serum screening (Cuckle, Pergament, & Benn, 2015). This procedure is usually called the triple test or triple screen because it involves testing mother's blood for three serum markers: alpha-fetoprotein, unconjugated estriol, and human chorionic gonadotropin. These serums are produced by the fetus's liver and the placenta. If the child has Down syndrome, alpha-fetoprotein and unconjugated estriol may be unusually low, while human chorionic gonadotropin levels may be unusually high. Significant elevations can be a sign of a genetic disorder, but this test has a high rate of false positives. Consequently, if results are positive, the physician will usually recommend that the mother participate in additional testing.

Amniocentesis is a more invasive screening technique that is usually conducted during weeks 15 to 20 of gestation. The procedure involves removing a small amount of amniotic fluid with a needle inserted into the abdomen of the mother. The amniotic fluid contains fetal cells, which can be cultured and examined for genetic abnormalities. Amniocentesis is invasive; it carries a 0.5% risk of fetal death. Amniocentesis can also be conducted before 15 weeks' gestation, at the beginning of the second trimester, but the risk of fetal death increases to 1% to 2%.

Chorionic villus sampling (CVS) is another genetic screening technique that can be done earlier, usually between 8 and 12 weeks' gestation. In CVS, the physician takes a small amount of chorionic villi, the wisplike tissue that connects the placenta to the wall of the uterus. This tissue usually has the same genetic and biochemical makeup as the developing fetus. The tissue can be analyzed to detect genetic or biological anomalies. CVS is usually performed only when there is greatly increased risk of the fetus having a developmental disorder. The risk of miscarriage associated with CVS is 0.5% to 1.5%.

Finally, physicians can use ultrasound to detect structural abnormalities in the fetus that might indicate the presence of a developmental disorder (Rissanen, Niemimaa, Suonpää, Ryynänen, & Heinonen, 2007). Ultrasound is believed to be a relatively safe procedure for both mother and fetus. Between 11 and 14 weeks' gestation, embryos with Down syndrome often show flatter facial profile and shorter (or absent) nasal bones than typically developing fetuses. The presence of these physical abnormalities, revealed by ultrasound, could indicate the presence of a genetic disorder (see Image 5.13).

Review:

- Serum screening is a maternal blood test that can be conducted 15 to 18 weeks' gestation to detect the presence of some developmental disorders.

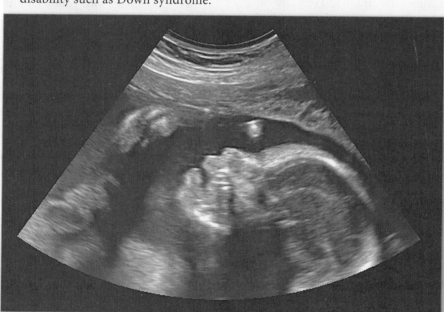

Image 5.13 Ultrasound can be used between 11 and 14 weeks' gestation to detect physical abnormalities that might indicate a developmental disability such as Down syndrome.

Source: iStock 69235923

- Amniocentesis and CVS are more invasive procedures that may be used when there is an elevated possibility of a developmental disability.
- Physicians can use ultrasound to detect structural abnormalities in the fetus that might indicate Down syndrome.

Can Early Education Programs Prevent Intellectual Disability?

Infants and Toddlers

A number of state- and locally administered programs have been developed to prevent the emergence of ID in infants at risk for below-average intelligence. The Infant Health and Development Program (IHDP) is one of the largest. Participants in the IHDP were 985 premature, low birth weight infants. Previous research indicated that these children were at increased risk for developmental delays, including ID (Baumeister & Bacharach, 1996). Infants were randomly assigned to either an early intervention group or a control group. The parents of children in the intervention group received regular home visits from program staff. During these visits, staff taught parents games and activities that they could play with their infants to promote cognitive, linguistic, and social development. Staff also helped parents address problems associated with caring for a preterm, low birth weight infant. When infants turned 1, parents were invited to enroll them in a high-quality preschool program. The program was free and transportation to and from the preschool was provided. The preschool ran year round, 5 days per week, until children were 3 years old. Families assigned to the control group were not given home visits or offered the preschool program.

To evaluate the success of the intervention, children's cognitive development was assessed at the end of the preschool program (age 3), at age 5, and at age 8. Children who participated in the program earned slightly higher IQs than children in the control group at age 3. However, by age 5, these differences in IQ disappeared.

The results of the IHDP indicate that early intervention programs can boost IQ scores in at-risk children, but increases in IQ are not maintained over time. Experts have disagreed on how to interpret the findings. Critics of the IHDP argue that early intervention programs do not prevent ID and they should be discontinued (Baumeister & Bacharach, 2000). Instead, the money and time used for early intervention programs could be spent on primary prevention, such as providing at-risk families with better access to health care and nutrition.

Advocates of the program believe the data speak to the importance of continuing educational enrichment for high-risk children beyond the preschool years. If the program had been extended through elementary school, children in the intervention group might have continued to show higher IQ scores than controls. Furthermore, simply offering intervention services to high-risk families does not mean that they will take advantage of these services. In fact, 20% of children in the intervention group attended the preschool program less than 10 days in 2 years, and 55 children never attended at all (Hill et al., 2003). Since gains in IQ are directly related to participation in treatment, motivating families to participate in treatment seems to be a critical goal of any effective prevention program.

Head Start and Preschool Prevention

Other studies have investigated whether providing early intensive preschool education might improve children's cognitive outcomes (Yoshikawa et al., 2013). Early studies focused largely on young children at risk for lower intelligence and academic problems because of socioeconomic disadvantage. For example, the Perry Preschool Project was administered to low-income children. Most children participated in a high-quality, daily preschool program for 2 years taught by well-trained teachers. Teachers also visited families in their homes to encourage parents to take a greater role in their children's preschool education. Similarly, the Abecedarian Project delivered high-quality, year-round child care and preschool to disadvantaged children. The intervention emphasized language development, literacy, and problem-solving.

Perhaps the best-known prevention program is Head Start, an intervention that provides comprehensive early childhood education, health, nutrition, and parent-involvement services to lower-income preschoolers and their families. Head Start was originally designed as a summer program for at-risk preschoolers to give them a "head start" before beginning kindergarten. Today, Head Start provides preschool services to 1,000,000 children in the United States including preschoolers in Native American communities, the children of migrant workers, and homeless youths.

Most recently, communities have begun to offer universal early childhood education programs—that is, preschool programs designed for all children regardless of socioeconomic risk. For example, the Tulsa (Oklahoma) and Boston Pre-K Programs offered free, voluntary preschool education for one or two years. On average, these programs deliver intensive, high-quality educational programs to approximately 75% of youths in their communities.

Do preschool prevention programs boost children's IQ? Overall, results have been mixed (Yoshikawa et al., 2013). The available data from many different evaluations suggest the following:

1. Early childhood interventions can significantly increase children's cognitive skills. Recent meta-analyses indicate that children who participate in these preschool programs earn IQ scores 4 to 5 points higher than controls. Furthermore, youths (especially girls) who participate in these programs earn higher reading and math achievement scores than controls. On average,

youths who participate in preschool programs are approximately one-third of an academic year ahead of their kindergarten classmates who did not attend these programs. The benefits of preschool are greatest for minority children, youths from low-SES backgrounds, and youths at risk for developmental disability (Magnuson et al., 2016).

2. The highest-quality preschool programs were associated with the greatest increase in children's cognitive skills. For example, children who participated in the high-quality Tulsa and Boston Pre-K programs earned reading scores approximately one academic year ahead of other children who did not participate in these programs (see Figure 5.7). The highest-quality programs were characterized by stimulating interactions between teachers and children; a curriculum that focused on language, literacy, and math; and an emotionally supportive learning environment. Furthermore, teachers received ongoing training and supervision (Phillips & Meloy, 2016).

3. The effects of preschool programs on other aspects of children's functioning were mixed. Overall, these programs were not associated with large improvements in children's behavior. However, programs that targeted specific aspects of children's social–emotional functioning were associated with modest improvement

in behavioral inhibition and attention. Furthermore, Head Start, which specifically targets children's health outcomes, is associated with increases in child immunizations. Immunizations, in turn, can prevent serious childhood illnesses that hinder cognitive development or cause youths to miss school.

4. The benefits of preschool programs fade over time. Although children who participate in preschool programs show early gains, most of these gains are lost in elementary school. Although experts do not agree what causes this loss, many believe it is due to low-quality primary education, especially in disadvantaged school districts (Hill, Gormley, & Adelstein, 2015; Yoshikawa et al., 2013).

5. Some children show long-term benefits from preschool prevention programs, however. Recent, longitudinal studies indicate that at-risk boys who participate in preschool programs are less likely to repeat a grade in school, less likely to be referred for special education, and more likely to graduate than boys who do not participate in preschool programs (Magnuson et al., 2016).

Altogether, these data indicate that preschool programs can give young children a head start for kindergarten. However, their effects are typically modest, may disappear over time, and depend on sufficient resources to deliver high-quality services (Jenkins, Farkas, Duncan, Burchinal, & Vandell, 2016).

Review:

- The IHDP showed that early childhood prevention programs can boost IQ among high-risk youths, but most gains are not maintained over time.
- Preschool prevention programs (e.g., Tulsa and Boston Pre-K, Head Start) show boosts of 4 to 5 IQ points compared to controls. Prevention programs are most effective for girls, ethnic minority children, youths from low-SES backgrounds, and children at risk for developmental disabilities.
- Most studies indicate that the IQ benefits of preschool programs fade over time. However, youth who participate in these programs may be less likely to repeat a grade, be referred to special education, or drop out of school than controls.

What Services Are Available to School-Age Children?

Mainstreaming and Academic Inclusion

In 1975, Congress passed the Education of All Handicapped Children Act (Public Law 94–142). This act mandated a "free and appropriate public education" for all children with disabilities aged 3 to 18. From its implementation in 1977 through the mid-1980s, the practice of mainstreaming became more common in public school systems across the United States. Mainstreaming involved placing children with ID in classrooms alongside typically developing peers,

Figure 5.7 Can preschool boost children's academic skills? The Tulsa Pre-K program improved the reading scores for typically developing children and youths with special needs. On average, children in the program were 8 to 9 months ahead of their peers who did not participate in the program. The effects on math skills were more modest (Phillips & Meloy, 2016).

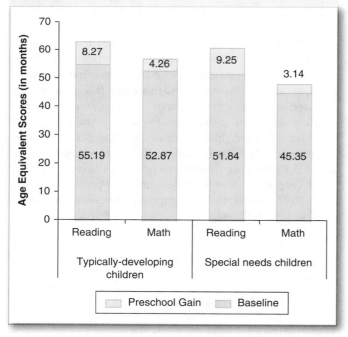

to the maximum extent possible. At first, mainstreamed children with ID were allowed to participate in physical education, art, and music with typically developing children. For other subjects, they attended self-contained special education classes for children with developmental delays (Verhoeven & Vermeer, 2006).

Unfortunately, subsequent research showed that children with ID who were assigned to special education classes actually earned lower academic achievement scores and had poorer adaptive functioning than children with ID who spent most of the school day with typically developing peers (Sturmey, 2014a). Consequently, many parents argued that children with ID and other disabilities had the right to attend all regular education classes. This movement, called the regular education initiative, gradually led to the practice of inclusion. Inclusion involves the education of children with ID alongside typically developing peers for all subjects, usually with the support of a classroom aide.

In 1997, Congress passed the Individuals With Disabilities Education Act (IDEA; PL 105–17). IDEA codified the practice of inclusion by demanding that children with disabilities be educated in the least restrictive environment possible:

> To the maximum extent appropriate, children with disabilities . . . are educated with children who are not disabled, and special classes, separate schooling, or other removal of children with disabilities from the regular educational environment occurs only when the nature or severity of the disability of a child is such that education in regular classes with the use of supplementary aids and services cannot be achieved satisfactorily. (p. 61)

In addition to providing services for children with disabilities, IDEA also required local educational systems to identify all infants, toddlers, and children with disabilities living in the community, whether or not they attended school. Once children are identified, a team of educational professionals (e.g., regular education teachers, special education teachers, school psychologists) conducts a comprehensive evaluation of the child's strengths and limitations and designs a written plan for the child's education. Infants and toddlers, 0 to 3 years, are provided with an *Individualized Family Services Plan (IFSP)*. In contrast, preschoolers and school-aged children receive an *Individualized Education Program (IEP)* in consultation with parents. Typically, IEPs provide extra support to children while at school; children may be given special education services or a classroom aide. IEPs can also grant accommodations to children with disabilities that help them achieve their cognitive, social, emotional, or behavioral potentials. IDEA was revised in 2004 as the Individuals With Disabilities Education Improvement Act (IDEIA; PL 108–446).

Empirical studies show that inclusion improves the functioning of children with developmental disabilities, especially children with mild or moderate impairments.

Inclusion seems to work best when (a) students with ID can become active in the learning process and (b) these children frequently interact and cooperate with typically developing classmates. Inclusion may also have benefits for typically developing peers. Specifically, inclusion may teach typically developing children greater tolerance and understanding of individuals with developmental delays and increase students' willingness to welcome children with delays into their peer groups.

Universal Design in the Classroom

In recent years, universal design has been a primary method of including children with intellectual and physical disabilities. Universal design is an educational practice that involves creating instructional materials and activities that allow learning goals to be achievable by all children—with and without disabilities (Schalock et al., 2010).

The clearest example of universal design can be seen in accommodations for people with physical disabilities. Many sidewalks now have "curb cuts" or sidewalk ramps that allow people who use wheelchairs to more easily cross the street. Similarly, buses are often built with low floors, rather than steep steps, to allow people with orthopedic problems easier access. These specially designed sidewalks and buses are used by all people; even people without physical disabilities often find them easier to use (Goldsmith, 2012).

Similarly, teachers can design assignments and activities that are universally accessible. These assignments and activities offer alternatives to traditional lecturing, reading, and writing. Universally designed materials can affect (a) the way teachers introduce content to students, (b) the format of instructional material, and (c) the way students demonstrate their learning (Coyne, Pisha, Dalton, Zeph, & Smith, 2012).

First, a teacher might use a wide variety of instructional strategies to match the diversity of students' skills and abilities. For example, a fourth-grade science teacher might find that all children (with and without disabilities) can learn about human anatomy by tracing their bodies on large sheets of paper and then drawing and labeling major organs. Similarly, a fourth-grade English teacher might demonstrate the steps involved in writing a book report using pictures, symbols, and arrows (i.e., graphic organizers) to help all students understand the temporal relationship of elements in a story.

Second, a teacher might modify the instructional technology she uses to present material. *Instructional technology* refers to the educational materials instructors use to teach ideas and concepts. For example, the science teacher might supplement her lessons with a child-friendly website about human anatomy. The website might allow children to enlarge the size of text, to read text aloud, and to access diagrams, pictures, and videos. Similarly, the English teacher might use digital media that allow children to simultaneously listen to and read books online.

Third, teachers can measure students' learning in ways that do not penalize them for their disability. One way to accomplish this task is to rely on assistive technology when assessing student learning. *Assistive technology* refers to educational tools students use to compensate for their disabilities. For example, students with mild deficits in writing might be allowed to use text-to-speech software. Children with more profound problems with writing might use software that allows them to use symbols and pictures to create sentences. Children with impairments in cognitive processing or fluency might be given extra time to complete tests. Indeed, if speed is not an important skill for a given learning domain (e.g., history), all children might be given extra time.

Overall, instructional strategies that adopt principles of universal design are effective. Students with mild to moderate impairments in intellectual and adaptive functioning seem to benefit the most from modifications to instructional methods and materials (Coyne et al., 2012).

Review:

- Academic inclusion is the practice of educating children with ID and other disabilities alongside typically developing classmates for all subjects possible, usually with the support of a classroom aide.
- IDEIA requires school systems to identify infants and children with disabilities and prepare an IFSP (for infants/toddlers) or IEP (for school-age children) to promote their development.
- Universal design is an educational practice that involves creating instructional materials and activities that allow learning goals to be achieved by children, regardless of their abilities and skills.

How Can Clinicians Reduce Challenging Behaviors in Children With Intellectual Disabilities?

Approximately 25% of children with ID show challenging behavior, such as stereotypies, SIBs, or aggression. These behaviors are the primary reason children with ID are referred for treatment (Matson et al., 2011).

Applied Behavior Analysis

Applied behavior analysis (ABA) is a scientific approach to identifying a child's problematic behavior, determining its cause, and changing it (Feeley & Jones, 2006). The principles of ABA are based largely on the work of B. F. Skinner (1974), who believed that the study of behavior should be based on observable, quantifiable data. Skinner asserted that psychologists do not need to rely on latent (unobservable) constructs to explain and predict behavior. Instead, behavior can be understood in terms of overt actions and environmental contingencies. Rather than viewing behavior as originating from within the person, applied behavior analysts understand behavior primarily as a function of environmental antecedents and consequences (Vollmer et al., 2014).

A behavior analysts' first job is to operationally define the child's problem behavior—that is, to describe the behavior in a way that it can be observed and measured. For example, if a child repeatedly behaves "aggressively" in the classroom, the behavior analyst might operationally define the child's behavior in terms of one or two discrete actions, such as "throws objects" or "pushes classmates." Whereas *aggression* is a vague term that cannot be easily observed or measured, *throwing* and *pushing* are easily observed and measured.

Next, the behavior analyst will carefully observe and record the child's challenging behavior. Several methods of behavioral observation are available (Hurwitz & Minshawi, 2012). One technique is to use *event recording*: The clinician observes the child and records the number of times the problem behavior occurs in an allotted period of time (e.g., 15 minutes). Event recording is suitable for behaviors that occur frequently and have a clear beginning and ending. For example, a school psychologist might record the number of times a child blurts out answers during class. Another technique is *interval recording*. In interval recording, the clinician divides the observation period into brief time segments (i.e., intervals) usually less than 30 seconds in length. Then, the clinician observes the child and notes whether the problem behavior occurred during each interval. Interval recording is useful for frequently occurring behaviors without clear beginnings or endings. For example, a psychologist might use interval recording to determine the percentage of class time a child engages in stereotyped rocking or swaying. A third technique, *duration recording*, is most appropriate for behaviors that take a long time to resolve. A clinician using this technique would record the duration of a continuously occurring behavior, such as the length of a temper tantrum or the time a child spent out of seat during class.

Observations of children's behavior can help identify the environmental conditions that elicit it or the consequences that maintain it (Lancioni, Singh, O'Reilly, Sigafoos, & Didden, 2012). Is the child's challenging behavior prompted only by certain people or situations? Is it followed by consequences that might be positively or negatively reinforcing? Does the behavior tend to occur at certain times during the day?

Finally, the behavior analyst conducts a functional analysis of the child's behavior in order to identify and alter its causes (Matson et al., 2011). Functional analysis of behavior involves carefully specifying the child's challenging behavior, identifying the environmental contingencies that immediately precede the behavior (i.e., the antecedents), and identifying the environmental events that occur immediately after the behavior (i.e., the consequences) that likely maintain it. To change the child's behavior, the therapist can either alter the antecedents that prompt the undesirable behavior or change the consequences of the behavior so that it is no longer reinforced.

Brian Iwata and colleagues (1994) have developed a method of functional analysis to determine the causes of children's challenging behavior. This method involves observing the child in four conditions and noting the effect of each condition on the child's behavior:

Attention condition: Whenever the child engages in challenging behavior in this condition, the therapist provides attention by reprimanding him or showing concern. For example, if the child throws an object, the therapist might respond, "Don't do that."

Demand condition: In this condition, the therapist asks the child to engage in a moderately difficult task (e.g., sorting objects, cleaning a room).

Alone condition: The child waits in a room with no people or toys present.

Play condition: The therapist and the child play together.

The frequency and intensity of children's challenging behavior across the four sessions can indicate the behavior's purpose (see Figure 5.8). Relatively high levels of challenging behavior in the attention condition, compared to the other conditions, might suggest that the behavior is maintained by *positive social reinforcement*—that is, to get attention from others.

Relatively high levels of challenging behavior in the demand condition, compared to the other conditions, suggests that the behavior is maintained through *negative reinforcement*—that is, it allows the child to avoid or escape undesired tasks. It is likely that caregivers negatively reinforce the challenging behavior by backing down from requests.

Relatively high rates of challenging behavior in the alone condition compared to the other conditions indicate that the behavior may be *automatically reinforced*.

Children may engage in challenging behavior while alone because the behaviors themselves are reinforcing.

Once the purpose of the child's challenging behavior has been identified, the therapist can either alter the antecedents that elicit the behavior or the consequences that follow the behavior. Typically, therapists rely on reinforcement to accomplish the second objective (O'Brien, Haynes, & Kaholokula, 2015).

Positive Reinforcement

Whenever possible, therapists use positive reinforcement to strengthen desirable behavior at the same time they reduce undesirable behavior. In a technique called differential reinforcement, therapists provide positive reinforcement only for behaviors that are desirable, while they ignore unwanted actions.

The two most common forms of differential reinforcement are (1) differential reinforcement of incompatible behavior (DRI) and (2) differential reinforcement of zero behavior (DRO). In differential reinforcement of incompatible behavior (DRI), the therapist provides positive reinforcement when the child engages in a behavior that is incompatible with the problematic behavior. For example, if a child engages in hand flapping or skin picking, the therapist might reinforce him for keeping his hands in his pockets or holding onto a special toy or blanket. Since the child cannot flap his hands and keep them in his pockets at the same time, the hand flapping should decrease. In differential reinforcement of zero behavior (DRO), the therapist reinforces the child for not engaging in the problematic behavior for a certain period of time. For example, a therapist might give a child a small piece of candy every 30 seconds he does not engage in hand flapping or skin picking.

Figure 5.8   Clinicians can use functional analysis to identify the cause of a child's challenging behavior. In this case, 6-year-old Jeoffrey engaged in rocking only when alone. This indicates that his behavior is automatically reinforced. Attention, differential reinforcement, and exercise might be helpful to reduce this behavior. Adapted from Vollmer and colleagues (2014).

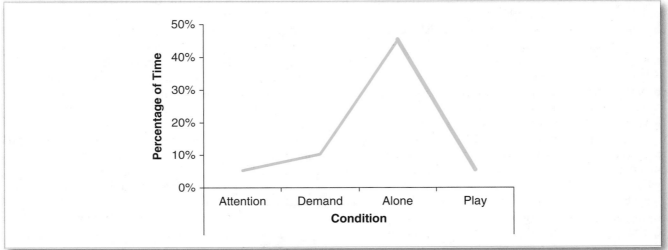

Positive Punishment

Reinforcement increases behavioral frequency; punishment decreases it. Positive punishment involves the presentation of a stimulus that decreases the frequency of a behavior. Since positive punishment techniques are aversive, they are only used under certain conditions such as when children's behaviors are dangerous or life threatening and other methods of treatment have been ineffective at reducing the problematic behavior. Punishment is only used in combination with positive reinforcement, and its use is carefully reviewed and monitored by independent experts. Parents must consent to the use of punishment before it is used to correct their children's behavior problem.

Salvy and colleagues (2004) describe the use of *punishment by contingent stimulation* to reduce SIB in a toddler with ID. The girl, Johanna, would bang her head against her crib and other hard surfaces approximately 100 times each day. She had bruises on her forehead because of her behavior. Nonaversive interventions were not effective in reducing Johanna's head banging. The therapists and Johanna's mother decided to use punishment to reduce SIBs. The punisher was a brief electric shock that was administered by a device attached to Johanna's leg. The therapists could administer the shock remotely using a handheld activator. The shock was unpleasant (like being snapped by a rubber band), but it did not cause injury.

Treatment involved two phases. In the first phase (hospital implementation), Johanna and her mother played in an observation room in the hospital. Observers counted the frequency of her head banging during the first 10 minutes. This provided a baseline of Johanna's behavior to evaluate the effectiveness of the punishment. Then, the shock device was attached to Johanna's leg but shocks were not administered. Observations continued for another 10 minutes to see whether Johanna's behavior would change merely because she wore the device. Next, therapists began administering a brief electrical shock contingent on Johanna's head banging. As before, observations were conducted for an additional 10 minutes. Finally, the shock device was removed, and Johanna's behavior was observed for another 10 minutes. Results showed that the frequency of Johanna's head banging decreased from 30 times during baseline observation to 4 times after punishment.

During the second phase of treatment (home implementation), Johanna's mother was taught to punish Johanna's behavior at home. Therapists observed Johanna's behavior in the home for 2 days to obtain baseline data. On the third day, the shock device was attached to Johanna's leg. When Johanna began banging her head, her mother said, "No hit, Johanna"; retrieved the activator from her purse; and immediately issued a brief shock. The frequency of Johanna's behavior was recorded over the next month, at which time the shock device was removed from the home. Results showed that the frequency of Johanna's head banging at home decreased from 117 times per day at baseline to zero times per day after the contingent administration

of shocks. Johanna's mother discovered that the verbal prompt "No hit, Johanna" combined with the action of walking toward her purse was sufficient to stop Johanna's head banging. At one-year follow-up, her mother reported no SIBs and no need to use the shock device.

Another form of positive punishment is called overcorrection. In overcorrection, the therapist requires the child to correct his problematic behavior by restoring his surroundings to the same (or better) condition than that which existed prior to his disruptive act. Overcorrection is often used when children show chronic problems using the toilet, wetting the bed, or destroying property. In the case of bed-wetting, the therapist might require the child to strip his bedding, take his bedding and wet clothes to the laundry, help wash the clothes, and assist in making the new bed. For most children, this procedure is aversive because it is tedious and takes time away from sleep or enjoyable activities.

Overcorrection is often combined with a technique called positive practice. In positive practice, the therapist makes the child repeatedly practice an acceptable behavior immediately following his unacceptable act. In the case of bed-wetting, the child might be required to sit on the toilet five times to practice appropriate urination. Positive practice can be aversive to children, but it also teaches children alternative, appropriate behavior.

Negative Punishment

Negative punishment occurs when the therapist withdraws a stimulus from the child, which decreases the recurrence of the child's behavior. Usually, the stimulus that is withdrawn is pleasant to the child. Consequently, the child experiences distress over its removal. Negative punishment is usually less aversive than positive punishment, so it is more often used to reduce problematic behavior.

The most benign form of negative punishment is extinction. In extinction, the therapist withdraws reinforcement from the child immediately following an unwanted behavior. Hanley and colleagues (2003) found that some children with developmental delays tantrum in order to obtain attention from caregivers. Caregivers would unknowingly reinforce their children's tantrums by looking at, talking to, and holding them. To extinguish these tantrums, caregivers can withdraw this reinforcement—that is, they can simply ignore their children's bids for attention. This strategy is sometimes called planned ignoring.

When caregivers begin to extinguish behavior, the rate of children's behavior may temporarily increase. This phenomenon is called an extinction burst. Children will usually escalate their problematic behavior in an attempt to gain the reinforcement that was previously provided. Over time, the behavior's frequency and intensity will decrease, as long as reinforcement is withheld. Extinction is a slow, but effective, means of reducing behavior problems.

A second form of negative punishment is time-out. In time-out, the therapist limits the child's access to reinforcement for a certain period of time. Time-out can take a number of forms, but it must involve the complete absence of reinforcement. Children should not be allowed to play, avoid tasks, or gain attention from others while in time-out. Time-out is usually accomplished by physically removing the child from the reinforcing situation for several minutes.

A final form of negative punishment is response cost. In response cost, the therapist withdraws reinforcers from the child immediately following a problematic act. Each problematic behavior "costs" the child a number of tangible reinforcers, such as candy, points, tokens, or other desired objects or privileges. Response cost is similar to time-out. In time-out, reinforcement is withdrawn *for a specific amount of time*. In response cost, reinforcement is withdrawn *in a specific quantity*. Response cost is often used in combination with token economies. Children may be reinforced with tokens or points for each desirable behavior and give up a certain number of tokens or points for each problematic behavior.

Behavioral treatment for people with ID has considerable empirical support. Kahng and colleagues (2002) reviewed 35 years of published research on the effectiveness of behavior therapy to treat SIBs. Data from 706 individuals showed an overall reduction in SIBs of 83.7%. The most effective treatments tended to involve punishment (e.g., overcorrection, time-out) with 83.2% effectiveness, followed by extinction (e.g., planned ignoring) with 82.6% effectiveness, and positive reinforcement with 73.2% effectiveness. Combining behavioral interventions usually resulted in slightly higher effectiveness than the use of any single intervention alone.

Medication

Two medications are frequently prescribed to reduce challenging behavior shown by youths with ID: aripiprazole (Abilify) and risperidone (Risperdal). These medications are atypical antipsychotics that were originally intended to treat disorders like schizophrenia and bipolar disorder. However, several double-blind, placebo-controlled studies showed that these medications are also effective in reducing aggression and irritability among youths with low intellectual functioning. In one of the first studies, the Risperidone Disruptive Behavior Study Group (Aman et al., 2002) examined 118 children ages 5 to 12 who showed both low intellectual functioning and significant behavior problems. Children were randomly assigned to either an experimental group whose members received a low dose of risperidone or to a control group whose members received placebo. Six weeks later, 77% of the children in the experimental group showed significant improvement in their behavior, compared to only 33% of children in the control group. Other studies have yielded similar results (Roth & Worthington, 2015).

Atypical antipsychotics may also be effective in reducing SIBs among youths with ID. Previous studies showed that some youths who displayed SIBs also had hypersensitivity to dopamine. When they engaged in SIBs, they may experience a certain degree of pleasure or reinforcement. Atypical antipsychotics, which block dopamine receptors, likely reduce the reinforcing properties of SIBs, making children less likely to engage in them (Szymanski & Kaplan, 2006).

Antidepressants are often used to treat anxiety and mood disorders in adolescents with ID. Unfortunately, most of the research supporting the efficacy of antidepressants on these disorders was conducted on typically developing youths. Because behavioral interventions are effective in reducing both anxiety and depressive symptoms in older children and adolescents with ID, these behavioral treatments should be used first (Sturmey & Didden, 2014; Sturmey, Lindsay, Vause, & Neil, 2014).

Review:

- Clinicians can use functional analysis to identify and alter the antecedents or consequences of challenging behavior. Most challenging behavior is maintained by positive social reinforcement, negative reinforcement, or automatic reinforcement.
- Differential (positive) reinforcement is usually the first-line behavioral treatment to reduce challenging behavior in youths with ID. Negative punishment strategies include extinction, time-out, and response cost. Positive punishment is used only when other interventions are unsuccessful, when the behavior is very problematic, and when parents consent to treatment.
- Atypical antipsychotics like aripiprazole (Abilify) and risperidone (Risperdal) are effective in reducing aggression in some youths with ID.

How Can Clinicians Help the Caregivers of Children With Intellectual Disability?

Clinicians should also help support the caregivers of children with ID. After children are initially diagnosed with GDD or ID, parents are at increased risk for mood problems. They often report a sense of loss or disappointment associated with their child's diagnosis and apprehension about their child's future or their ability to raise a child with special needs. Over time, however, parents' dysphoria usually decreases (Glidden, 2012). Nevertheless, challenges associated with caring for a child with a developmental disability remain. In one large study of parents of children with GDD, nearly 42% reported a significant elevation in parenting stress (Tervo, 2012).

Parenting stress can take its toll on the family system (Al-Yagon & Margalit, 2012). Parents of children with developmental disabilities often experience disruptions in the quality of their marriage and family life. However, the effect of having a child with a disability on marital and life satisfaction is complex. Parents who report socio-economic stress, a high degree of work and interpersonal hassles, and low support from their spouse often report a marked deterioration in marital and family life after the birth of a child with special needs. In contrast, parents who feel supported by their spouse and who use active, problem-focused coping techniques to deal with family-related stress often report no change in marital satisfaction or quality of life. Indeed, some families report greater cohesion and satisfaction after the birth of a child with a developmental disability (Glidden, 2012).

Some developmental disorders are not strongly associated with increased parental stress. For example, the parents of children with Down syndrome often report only moderate levels of stress, perhaps because children with this condition typically show mild cognitive impairment and are usually described by others as affectionate and social. There may be less stigma associated with caring for a child with Down syndrome; most people can easily recognize a child with this condition and generally have some understanding of the disorder. Support groups for families are also available in many communities (Witwer et al., 2014).

Other developmental disorders are associated with higher levels of parenting stress. Parents can experience considerable stress when the cause of their child's developmental delay cannot be identified. Parents might blame themselves for their child's limitations or feel uncertain about their child's prognosis. When the cause of children's delays is unknown, or when the disorder is uncommon, parents may also feel misunderstood or alienated. Regardless of etiology, certain child behaviors seem to increase parenting stress: poor behavioral control, social deficits, and aggression (Tervo, 2012).

Therapists can help children with developmental disabilities by supporting parents in times of difficulty and uncertainty. Besides providing informational support about their children's development and suggestions for symptom management, therapists can offer emotional support through their willingness to listen to and empathize with parents' concerns. Therapists can also encourage the use of active, problem-focused strategies to deal with parenting stress (Al-Yagon & Margalit, 2012). Parents who are able to cope with their own stress may be better able to care for their children and implement many of the interventions that will promote their children's intellectual and adaptive functioning.

Review:

- Caring for a child with a developmental disability can be stressful. Parents report greater stress when children with ID show challenging behaviors or comorbid disorders.
- Clinicians can support parents by providing evidence-based treatment to their children and encourage problem-focused coping strategies to deal with stress.

KEY TERMS

Abusive head trauma: A form of maltreatment in which a caregiver induces brain injury by forcefully shaking an infant or toddler; can cause learning disabilities, memory problems, ID, irritability, lethargy, vomiting, tremors, and death (sometimes called shaken baby syndrome)

Adaptive functioning: A term used to refer to a person's ability to cope with common life demands and meet the standards of independence expected of someone in their particular age group and social–cultural background

American Association on Intellectual and Developmental Disabilities (AAIDD): The oldest professional organization devoted to the study and assistance of individuals with ID

Amniocentesis: A moderately invasive procedure to screen for developmental disabilities 15 to 20 weeks' gestation; involves collecting amniotic fluid from the mother

Angelman syndrome: A genetic disorder caused by missing maternal genetic material on chromosome 15; associated with moderate to severe ID, sporadic/jerky motor movements, lack of spoken language, hyperactivity, and persistent social smile

Anoxia: The absence of oxygen; a potential cause of ID

Applied behavior analysis (ABA): A scientific approach to identifying a child's problematic behavior, determining its causes, and altering environmental contingencies to change it

Behavioral phenotype: Characteristic features (e.g., appearance, cognitive strengths/weaknesses, comorbid disorders) associated with specific causes for ID

Challenging behavior: Actions shown by some youths with ID that are physically hazardous or that limit their access to educational or social opportunities

Chorionic villus sampling (CVS): A moderately invasive technique to screen for developmental disabilities 8 to 12 weeks' gestation; involves collecting tissue that connects the placenta to the wall of the uterus

Chromosomal microarray (CMA): A genetic test that identifies copy number variants (i.e., unusual duplications or deletions) in major regions of the genome; used to identify causes of GDD

Cultural–familial ID: A term used by Zigler to describe children with no identifiable cause for their intellectual and adaptive disabilities; associated with IQ and adaptive functioning scores in the 50–70 range, no health problems, and a family history of ID or low intellectual functioning

Diagnostic overshadowing: A term used to describe the tendency of some clinicians to overlook the presence of mental disorders in people with ID

Differential reinforcement: A form of positive reinforcement in which therapists reinforce only behaviors that are desired, while they ignore unwanted actions

Differential reinforcement of incompatible behaviors (DRI): The therapist provides positive reinforcement when the child engages in a behavior that is incompatible with the problematic behavior

Differential reinforcement of zero behavior (DRO): The therapist reinforces the child for not engaging in the problematic behavior for a certain period of time

Down syndrome: Trisomy 21; associated with moderate ID, characteristic appearance, weakness in verbal skills and language, strength in visual–spatial reasoning, and sociability

Dual diagnosis: A term used to refer to the presence of mental disorders among individuals with ID

Education of All Handicapped Children Act: Federal law that mandated "free and appropriate public education" for all children with disabilities aged 3 to 18

Extinction: A form of negative reinforcement; the therapist withdraws reinforcement from the child immediately following an unwanted behavior; sometimes called planned ignoring

Extinction burst: A term used to describe a temporary increase in the rate or intensity of children's behavior immediate after therapists use extinction or "planned ignoring"

Fetal alcohol spectrum disorder (FASD): A disorder caused by maternal alcohol consumption during gestation; characterized by lower intellectual functioning or mild ID, learning disabilities, hyperactivity, and characteristic craniofacial anomalies

Fragile X syndrome: An inherited, X-linked disorder that adversely affects boys more than girls; characterized by mild to moderate ID, characteristic appearance, strengths in simultaneous processing, weakness in sequential processing, and social communication deficits

Global developmental delay (GDD): A *DSM-5* disorder, diagnosed in children < 5 years, and characterized by significant delays in several developmental domains (e.g., motor language, social, or daily living skills); a temporary diagnosis used when clinicians suspect ID but the child is too young to determine IQ

Inclusion: A term used to describe the education of children with ID alongside typically developing peers for all subjects, usually with the support of a classroom aide

Individuals With Disabilities Education Act (IDEA): Federal legislation that extended disability rights to infants and toddlers, mandated IFSP for young children and IEPs for school-age children with disabilities

Intellectual disability (ID): A *DSM-5* disorder characterized by deficits in intellectual and adaptive functioning deficits in conceptual, social, and practical domains that emerge during infancy or childhood

Mainstreaming: Involved placing children with ID in classrooms with typically developing peers, to the maximum extent possible

Needed supports: Assistance that helps an individual with ID function effectively in society; an important component of the AAIDD definition of ID

Organic ID: A term used by Zigler to describe children who had identifiable causes for their intellectual and adaptive disabilities; associated with genetic disorders, very low IQ and adaptive functioning, medical complications, and no family history of ID

Overcorrection: A form of positive punishment in which the therapist requires the child to correct his problematic behavior by restoring his surroundings to the same (or better) condition than that which existed prior to his disruptive act

Phenylketonuria (PKU): A recessive disorder characterized by an inability to break down phenylalanine, an amino acid; dieting can prevent severe ID, seizures, and other medical problems

Physical aggression: Actions that cause, or can cause, property destruction or injury/harm to another person

Positive practice: Usually a form of positive punishment; the therapist makes the child repeatedly practice an acceptable behavior immediately following an unacceptable act; usually paired with overcorrection

Prader-Willi syndrome (PWS): A genetic disorder caused by missing paternal genetic material on chromosome 15; associated with mild ID, weakness in short-term memory, strength in visual–spatial reasoning, hyperphagia, and obsessive–compulsive behavior

Response cost: A form of negative reinforcement; the therapist withdraws reinforcers from the child immediately following a problematic act

Rett syndrome: A genetic disorder usually caused by a mutation on a portion of the X chromosome; almost always affects girls; characterized by typical development in early infancy followed by rapid deterioration in social functioning and language, severe ID, and stereotypies

Self-injurious behaviors (SIBs): Repetitive movements of the hands, limbs, or head in a manner that can, or do, cause physical harm or damage to the person

Serum screening: A blood test conducted between 15 and 18 weeks' gestation to screen for possible developmental disorders in the fetus

Similar sequence hypothesis: Posits that children with ID progress through the same cognitive stages as typically developing children, albeit at a slower pace; generally supported by research

Similar structure hypothesis: Posits that two children of the same mental age (one with ID and the other without ID) will show similar abilities; has mixed support

Stereotypies: Actions performed in a consistent, rigid, and repetitive manner and that have no immediate, practical significance

Time-out (from positive reinforcement): A form of negative reinforcement; the therapist limits the child's access to positive reinforcers (e.g., attention, toys) for a certain period of time, usually by placing the child in a specific setting

TORCH: An acronym that represents the main maternal illnesses that can cause ID in offspring

Universal design: An educational practice that involves creating instructional materials and activities that allow learning goals to be achievable by children with different abilities and skills

Williams syndrome (WS): A genetic disorder caused by deletions on chromosome 7; associated with mild ID, well-developed spoken language, strengths in auditory memory, weakness in visual–spatial reasoning, hyperactivity, anxiety, and friendly/social demeanor

22q11.2 DS: A genetic disorder caused by deletions on chromosome 22; associated with mild to moderate ID, cleft lip/palate, social communication deficits, and risk for schizophrenia later in life

CRITICAL THINKING EXERCISES

1. When many people think of ID, they think about a child with Down syndrome. To what extent do children with Down syndrome reflect all children with IDs?

2. How does the treatment for PKU illustrate the interaction of genes and environment in child development?

3. Why are children of lower-SES backgrounds at greater risk for certain types of ID? Why might low-SES children with IDs have poorer prognoses than middle-class children with IDs?

4. Why would clinicians probably not use extinction (i.e., planned ignoring) to reduce SIBs in a young child with a developmental disorder?

5. What might be the benefits and drawbacks of academic inclusion on a typically developing child?

TEST YOURSELF AND EXTEND YOUR LEARNING

Videos, flash cards, and links to online resources for this chapter are available to students online. Teachers also have access to PowerPoint slides to guide lectures, case studies to prompt classroom discussions, and exam questions. Visit www.abnormalchildpsychology.org.

iStockphoto.com/Liderina

CHAPTER 6

Autism Spectrum Disorder

LEARNING OBJECTIVES

After reading this chapter, you should be able to do the following:

6.1. Describe the key features of autism spectrum disorder (ASD) and explain how the disorder exists along a "spectrum."

Show how the prevalence of ASD varies as a function of children's gender, socioeconomic status (SES), and ethnicity.

6.2. Identify the genetic, epigenetic, and brain abnormalities associated with ASD in young children.

List and describe early deficits in social cognition typically shown by infants and toddlers who are later diagnosed with ASD.

6.3. Describe several evidenced-based treatments for ASD and differentiate these treatments from interventions that lack empirical support.

Provide examples of evidence-based techniques to improve the communication skills of children with ASD.

6.1 DESCRIPTION AND EPIDEMIOLOGY

Aristotle called humans "social animals." He recognized the importance of social interactions and interpersonal relationships in the quality of our lives. Autism spectrum disorder (ASD) is one of the most serious, and interesting, childhood disorders because it affects this important dimension of our humanity: our ability to effectively interact with others.

Autism spectrum disorder (ASD) is characterized by (a) marked impairments in social communication and (b) the presence of restricted, repetitive patterns of behavior, interests, or activities. Most children with ASD begin showing signs and symptoms of the disorder in infancy or toddlerhood, although some are not diagnosed until they begin school. Their problems—interacting with others, communicating their thoughts and feelings, and developing relationships—greatly impair their social functioning. Furthermore, their tendency to engage in repetitive behaviors, their adherence to routines, their preoccupation with idiosyncratic topics, or their unusual reactivity to sensory stimulation (e.g., sights, sounds, smells) can appear strange or off-putting to others (Realmuto, 2015).

As its name implies, ASD reflects a "spectrum" of signs and symptoms, ranging in severity. Some children show complete disinterest in interactions with others; have few verbal or nonverbal communication skills; and persistently engage in stereotyped, rigid behaviors or rituals. Their intellectual functioning may be low or they may have comorbid intellectual disability (ID). Children at the opposite end of the ASD spectrum are extremely awkward or rigid in their interactions with others, engage in rituals or repetitive behaviors that cause them to be rejected by peers, and need support from others to function in social situations. Their IQ scores may fall within normal limits and they may even have special talents, skills, or abilities. To say that someone has ASD merely implies that he has marked problems in social communication and behavior. The ASD label does not tell us much about the child's unique strengths and challenges. As we discuss children and adolescents with ASD in this chapter, we need to be mindful of their heterogeneity. There is no such thing as a "typical" child with ASD. Consider the case of Kylie and Thomas.

What is Autism Spectrum Disorder?

ASD was described in the research literature by Leo Kanner (1943) more than 70 years ago. Kanner used the term *early infantile autism* to describe 11 children who showed difficulty relating to other people and adjusting to new situations. Kanner identified two features that he believed were especially salient in these children. First, the children showed "autistic aloneness" or a tendency toward extreme self-isolation and an apparent lack of interest in social interaction. Second, they displayed an "obsessive

CASE STUDY

AUTISM SPECTRUM DISORDER

Kylie and Thomas

When I found out I was pregnant, Matt and I were over the moon. Then I had a scan which confirmed that we were having twins. At 37 weeks, I gave birth by C-section to Kylie, who weighed 5 lbs 9 oz, and then Thomas, who was 6 lbs 3 oz. It was hard at first, but then we learned to cope . . . with the lack of sleep at least! By 14 months, Kylie was walking and talking. However, Thomas was a lot slower. Our doctor said he was just the slower twin and not to worry. At 18 months, Thomas finally began to walk, but he never played with his twin sister and wasn't talking. I asked the nurse, who was also beginning to be concerned about him. She got in contact with a local child development center and a lady came to see us.

Thomas

Source: Used with permission of his mother.

Kylie

Source: Used with permission of her mother.

Penny came to our house to watch Thomas. I remember he sat on the floor lining his bricks in a row and making unusual sounds. He was disinterested in the rest of us. Penny sat writing in her book. Then she looked at us and said, "I think Thomas may have autism." I actually had an idea that she might say that. I had looked on the Internet and came across a Web site which explained to me what the symptoms were. To be honest, the shock wasn't so bad when we were told. After his assessment, Thomas was diagnosed with severe autism.

The twins are now eight. Thomas is still nonverbal and still in diapers. Kylie is his big sister and always will be. She sits with him and tries so hard to teach him words. I used to be really upset at the stares that Thomas would get from others. But now I just take no notice. I hate the word "normal." Thomas is normal to us.

Source: Reproduced with permission of Kylie and Thomas's mother.

insistence on sameness" or a strong desire to avoid changes to their daily routine (Volkmar & Pelphrey, 2015).

Kanner also noticed that his patients showed marked delays or deficits in language. All were slow in learning to speak, and most showed unusual characteristics in their language use. For example, many of these children repeated words or phrases. Others reversed or misused pronouns. Still others spoke in an awkward, rigid manner (Witwer & Lecavalier, 2008).

Several years before Kanner's publication, the Viennese physician Hans Asperger described children with behavioral characteristics that resembled Kanner's patients. Asperger used the term *autistic psychopathy* to describe their symptoms. Like Kanner's patients, Asperger's patients showed difficulty interacting with others. Asperger noticed that they had considerable problems approaching others and engaging them in conversation, looking others in the eye while speaking, and displaying emotions. The children also tended to be preoccupied with singular topics about which they knew a great deal of information (Feinstein, 2010).

Unlike the children described by Kanner, however, Asperger's patients showed good vocabularies and basic language skills. Indeed, many of these children were very talkative and would carry on lengthy discourses on their favorite subjects.

The deficits observed by both Kanner and Asperger remain the essential features of ASD today (see Table 6.1). Specifically, ASD is defined by (a) persistent deficits in reciprocal social communication and social interaction and (b) restricted, repetitive patterns of behavior, interests, or activities. These symptoms are present in early childhood and impair everyday functioning (American Psychiatric Association, 2013). Although some children with ASD show dramatic deficits in verbal communication, like Kanner's patients, other children with ASD show only mild problems with expressive and receptive language, like Asperger's patients. Children's language skills, therefore, need not be impaired for the child to be diagnosed with ASD, although most children with the disorder show marked problems with verbal communication (Volkmar & Pelphrey, 2015).

Deficits in Social Communication

Perhaps the most salient feature of ASD is the child's persistent deficits in social communication and social interaction. Specifically, children with ASD display deficits in three areas:

1. *Social–emotional reciprocity*: the normal back-and-forth of conversation and social interactions through the sharing of interests, affect, or emotions

---

Table 6.1   Diagnostic Criteria for Autism Spectrum Disorder

A. Persistent deficits in social communication and social interaction across multiple contexts, as manifested by the following:

1. Deficits in social–emotional reciprocity ranging from abnormal social approach and failure of normal back-and-forth conversation; to reduced sharing of interests, emotions, or affect; to failure to initiate or respond to social interactions.

2. Deficits in nonverbal communicative behaviors used for social interaction ranging from poorly integrated verbal and nonverbal communication; to abnormalities in eye contact and body language or deficits in understanding and use of gestures; to a total lack of facial expressions and nonverbal communication.

3. Deficits in developing, maintaining, and understanding relationships ranging from difficulties adjusting behavior to suit various social contexts; to difficulties in sharing imaginative play or in making friends; to absence of interest in peers.

Specify current severity: Level 1, Level 2, Level 3*

B. Restrictive, repetitive patterns of behavior, interests, or activities as manifested by at least two of the following:

1. Stereotyped or repetitive motor movements, use of objects, or speech (e.g., simple motor stereotypies, lining up toys, echolalia, idiosyncratic phrases).

2. Insistence on sameness, inflexible adherence to routines, or ritualized patterns of verbal or nonverbal behavior (e.g., extreme distress at small changes, difficulties with transitions, rigid thinking patterns, greeting rituals, need to take same route or eat same food every day).

3. Highly restricted, fixated interests that are abnormal in intensity or focus (e.g., strong attachment to or preoccupation with unusual objects, excessively circumscribed or perseverative interests).

(Continued)

Table 6.1   (Continued)

4. Hyper- or hyporeactivity to sensory input or unusual interest in sensory aspects of the environment (e.g., apparent indifference to pain/temperature, adverse response to specific sounds or textures, excessive smelling or touching of objects, visual fascination with lights or movement).

   Specify current severity: Level 1, Level 2, Level 3*

C. Symptoms must be present in the early developmental period (but may not become fully manifest until social demands exceed limited capacities, or may be masked by learned strategies in later life).

D. Symptoms cause clinically significant impairment in social, occupational, or other important areas of current functioning.

E. These disturbances are not better explained by Intellectual Disability or Global Developmental Delay. Intellectual Disability and Autism Spectrum Disorder frequently co-occur; to make comorbid diagnoses of Intellectual Disability and Autism Spectrum Disorder, social communication should be below that expected for general developmental level.

Specify: With or without accompanying intellectual impairment

   With or without accompanying language impairment

   Associated with a known medical or genetic condition or environmental factor

   Associated with another neurodevelopmental, mental, or behavioral disorder

Source: Reprinted with permission from the *Diagnostic and Statistical Manual of Mental Disorders, Fifth Edition* (Copyright 2013). American Psychiatric Association.

*Severity levels are described in Table 6.2.

2. *Nonverbal communication*: the effective use of eye contact, gestures, and facial expressions

3. *Interpersonal relationships*: showing an interest in others and the capacity to make and keep friends.

Each of these deficits can range from moderate to severe, depending on the amount of support children require during social interactions (Bernier & Dawson, 2016).

Many toddlers and young children with ASD are often described as being "in their own world" and largely uninterested in social interactions. They may avoid eye contact with others and seem uninterested in others' activities or reactions to their behavior. They may not respond to the sound of their name, hand clapping and waving, or other bids for their attention. Young children with ASD may not assume an anticipatory posture before being picked up. Indeed, they are often reluctant to let others touch them. They may not respond to hugs and other signs of affection from others, and they may show little emotion. They seldom, if ever, initiate social interactions and usually do not participate in imitative games like "peekaboo" or "the itsy-bitsy spider" (Joseph, Soorya, & Thurm, 2015).

As children with ASD develop, they often begin to show greater tolerance for social interactions with family members. For example, they may allow parents to place them on their laps or let caregivers touch and cuddle with them. Some seem to enjoy being tickled or held in affectionate ways. Nevertheless, children with ASD rarely initiate social interactions or engage in novel activities.

They appear relatively uninterested in playing with other children and have great difficulty forming friendships. They may interact with others, but their communication and social relationships seem artificial and one-sided (Klinger, Dawson, Barnes, & Crisler, 2014).

Older children and adolescents with ASD usually continue to show marked impairments in social functioning. They tend to have few friends and social interests, and they may be ostracized by peers. Some older children with ASD are able to engage in rigid, scripted play in which they direct activities. For example, high-functioning youths with ASD might enjoy playing the role of "banker" in Monopoly. These youths generally avoid unscripted activities, such as "hanging out" with friends. Some of these children and adolescents develop narrow interests or become obsessed with specific hobbies, such as collecting trading cards or certain types of rocks. However, they infrequently join clubs or play spontaneously with peers (Volkmar, Reichow, Westphal, & Mandell, 2015).

Some older, high-functioning children with ASD like to spend time with family and desire to be accepted by peers. Unfortunately, their social deficits interfere with their abilities to interact with others and make friends. These high-functioning youths with ASD usually appear awkward or insensitive to others during social interactions. For example, they might want to join their classmates in a game of soccer during recess but do not know how. Instead of making an appropriate bid to join (e.g., "Hey, can I be on someone's team?"), they might intrude on the activity or insist on directing play around their own interests. Over time, the awkward and inappropriate social behavior displayed by these children can cause peer rejection. Sometimes, these youths develop anxiety and depression because they want friends, but they are ostracized by peers (Bellini, Gardner, & Markoff, 2015).

Restricted, Repetitive Behaviors, Interests, or Activities

Children with ASD also show restricted, repetitive patterns of behavior, interests, or activities that interfere with their ability to interact with others (Powers et al., 2015). Specifically, they show at least two of the following:

1. Stereotyped or repetitive behaviors including speech (e.g., repeating words or phrases), movements (e.g., hand gestures), or use of objects (e.g., lining up toys)
2. Excessive adherence to routines or resistance to change (e.g., need to dress, eat, or bathe at a certain time or in a certain manner)
3. Restricted, fixated interests that are abnormal in intensity or focus (e.g., constantly talking about idiosyncratic hobbies)
4. Hyper- or hyporeactivity to sensory input (e.g., indifference to pain, unusual sensitivity to certain tastes, textures, or sounds).

Each of these problems can be moderate to severe, depending on the amount of support children require to overcome them (Bernier & Dawson, 2016).

The most common stereotyped behaviors among lower-functioning children with ASD include rocking, hand flapping, whirling, and making unusual repetitive mannerisms with hands and fingers (Volkmar et al., 2015). Roughly one half of younger children with ASD show at least one of these repetitive behaviors. Stereotypies are most common among younger children with ASD and among individuals with lower intellectual functioning.

Approximately 85% of children with ASD and ID show echolalia—that is, they repeat words that they hear others speak or overhear on television and radio. Oftentimes, these words are taken out of context or repeated at inappropriate times, so they seem nonsensical to others.

Complex ritualistic behaviors are more common among older children with ASD and among individuals with higher intellectual functioning. Some children spend hours each day sorting and arranging toys, clothes, or collectables. Other children have food rituals. For example, one child with ASD insisted on eating his foods in a certain order, according to color and texture. Still other children with ASD show compulsive behaviors, such as ritualistic patterns of walking around the room or turning light switches on and off.

A common feature of many children with ASD is their strong desire for daily routines. Many of these children insist on the same day-to-day schedules and become extremely distressed when daily routines are altered or broken. For example, one boy with ASD became argumentative because he was unable to watch his favorite television program during a power outage (Strang, 2016).

Many higher functioning children with ASD develop a fascination with idiosyncratic topics. Some children show intense preoccupation with the batting averages of baseball players, the birth and death dates of US presidents, or the history of certain weather patterns. These highly specialized interests are often appropriate in *content*, but they are always unusual in their *intensity* (Klinger et al., 2014). For example, it is not uncommon to see a 5-year-old fascinated by trains or a 10-year-old interested in baseball statistics. These idiosyncratic interests become problematic when they preoccupy the child's time to the extent they interfere with other activities or social relationships. For example, the 5-year-old might spend hours each day playing with and talking about trains, exhausting his parents' patience. He might tantrum if denied access to trains. Similarly, the 10-year-old may be ostracized by classmates and reprimanded by teachers because of his obsessive interest in earned run averages.

Longitudinal studies indicate that restricted, repetitive behaviors or interests usually emerge *after* deficits in social communication (Klinger et al., 2014). Some experts have suggested that children develop these repetitive behaviors in response to their impairment in social functioning. For example, children with ASD and severe ID might use stereotyped rocking or hand flapping to escape boredom or alleviate anxiety. Higher-functioning youths with ASD might insist on daily rituals in order to gain a sense of control over their otherwise stressful daily lives. Other youths might develop circumscribed interests in response to peer rejection (Strang, 2016).

Many children with ASD show unusual sensitivity to sensory stimulation (Grapel, Cicchetti, & Volkmar, 2015). Some children display hyposensitivity to light, sound, temperature, or pain. For example, there are anecdotal reports of children with ASD not hearing a fire alarm or not experiencing pain from falling off a chair or bicycle. Other children show oversensitivity to stimuli. For example, some youths with ASD tantrum when made to wear certain clothing because they cannot tolerate its texture. Still other children with ASD become fixated on certain stimuli, such as flashing lights or running water (see Image 6.1).

Specifying Symptoms

The *Diagnostic and Statistical Manual of Mental Disorders* (*DSM*-5; American Psychiatric Association, 2013) allows clinicians to describe the functioning of children with ASD using various specifiers. Given the heterogeneity of youths with ASD, these specifiers provide other professionals a better picture of the child's strengths, challenges, and needs for support (American Psychiatric Association, 2013).

First, the clinician indicates whether the child's symptoms of ASD are associated with a known medical

Image 6.1   Shaun is a boy with ASD. He is fascinated with the sound of water hitting the pavement outside his house.

condition or genetic disorder. For example, Rett syndrome can cause ASD, severe ID, and serious impairment in motor control. Using the *DSM-5* system, a child might be diagnosed with "Autism spectrum disorder associated with Rett syndrome."

Second, the clinician describes the severity of the child's symptoms for each of the two broad domains of ASD: (1) social communication and (2) restricted, repetitive behavior or interests. *DSM-5* provides a rating scale to describe severity based on the level of support the child needs in each domain (see Table 6.2). The clinician describes each domain separately.

Third, the clinician specifies whether or not the child has language impairment and describes the nature of the impairment. Finally, the clinician specifies any co-occurring neurodevelopmental, mental, or behavioral disorders. For example, some older children with ASD develop problems with depression; they may want friends, but their social communication deficits interfere with the ability to develop peer relationships. By specifying coexisting depression, the clinician can communicate to other professionals this important dimension of the child's social–emotional functioning that might otherwise be overlooked (Pandolfi & Maygar, 2016).

Review:

- ASD is a disorder that emerges in early childhood and is characterized by deficits in social communication and the presence of restricted or repetitive behaviors, interests, or activities.
- Deficits in social communication include (a) a lack of reciprocity in social interactions, (b) problems with nonverbal communication such as poor eye contact, and (c) a lack of interest in interpersonal relationships or problems making and keeping friends.
- Restricted or repetitive behaviors include (a) stereotyped speech or movement, (b) resistance to change, (c) fixated interests, and (d) unusually high or low sensitivity to sensory stimulation.
- When diagnosing ASD, clinicians can specify the severity of social communication deficits and restricted or repetitive behaviors, the presence of language impairment, or coexisting medical or mental disorders.

Table 6.2   Severity Levels for Autism Spectrum Disorder

Severity Level	Social Communication	Restricted, Repetitive Behavior
Level 3 *Requiring very substantial support*	Severe deficits in verbal and nonverbal social communication skills cause severe impairments in functioning, very limited initiation of social interactions, and minimal response to social overtures from others.	Inflexibility of behavior, extreme difficulty coping with change, or other restricted/repetitive behaviors markedly interfere with functioning in all spheres. Great distress/difficulty changing focus or attention.
Level 2 *Requiring substantial support*	Marked deficits in verbal and nonverbal social communication skills; social impairments apparent even with supports in place; limited initiation of social interactions; and reduced or abnormal responses to social overtures from others.	Inflexibility of behavior, difficulty coping with change, or other restricted/repetitive behaviors appear frequently enough to be obvious to the casual observer and interfere with functioning in a variety of contexts. Distress and/or difficulty changing focus or attention.
Level 1 *Requiring support*	Deficits in social communication cause noticeable impairments without supports in place. Difficulty initiating social interactions, and clear examples of atypical or unsuccessful responses to social overtures of others. May appear to have decreased interest in social interactions.	Inflexibility of behavior causes significant interference with functioning in one or more contexts. Difficulty switching between activities. Problems of organization and planning hamper independence.

What Disorders Frequently Occur With Autism Spectrum Disorder?

Although not part of the diagnostic criteria for ASD, many youths with this disorder also experience low intellectual functioning or language problems. As we will see, some youths with ASD have severe cognitive disabilities and are mute. In contrast, other children with ASD have average or above-average intelligence and show adequate language skills. Just as children's ASD symptoms exist along a spectrum, their intellectual and linguistic functioning also falls on a continuum ranging from severely limited and requiring extensive support to above average or gifted! Consider Alex and Benji, two boys with ASD who have different cognitive and linguistic abilities.

Intellectual Disability

ID is not part of the diagnostic criteria for ASD. However, a sizable minority of youths with ASD also have low intelligence. One decade ago, as many as 70% of youths with ASD earned IQ scores consistent with the diagnosis of ID (Fombonne, 2005). Today, however, large population-based studies indicate that most youths with ASD earn below-average, but not deficient, IQ scores (Peters-Scheffer, Didden, & Lang, 2016).

For example, researchers examined the IQ scores of 8-year-old children with ASD from several research centers across the United States (Christensen et al., 2016). Overall, 44% of children with ASD earned IQ scores <70. Approximately 24% of children earned intelligence scores in the borderline range (i.e., IQ 71–85) and 32% earned scores in the average or above average range (i.e., IQ >85). Girls with ASD (46%) were more likely than boys with ASD (37%) to have scores consistent with an ID (see Figure 6.1).

Experts are not sure why a smaller percentage of children with ASD meet criteria for ID today than in the past. It is possible that as the definition of ASD has been expanded to include high-functioning children, a smaller percentage of children with ASD have ID (Levy et al., 2010).

Communication Disorders

Communication disorders are the most common comorbid condition shown by children with ASD. In one large population-based study, approximately two-thirds of children with ASD also showed deficits in speech or language (Levy et al., 2010). The severity of these communication problems ranges considerably. Approximately 25% of children with ASD are mute—that is, they have no functional

---

CASE STUDY

AUTISM SPECTRUM DISORDER WITH INTELLECTUAL DISABILITY

Alex

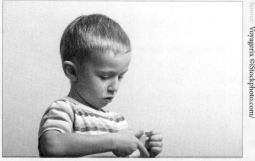

Source: Voyagerix @iStockphoto.com/

Alex was born 4 weeks premature and experienced significant complications with delivery. Labor continued for most of the day and forceps were required. Alex was born listless, with low blood oxygen levels, and was hospitalized for several days.

As an infant, Alex lagged behind his age-mates in terms of sitting up and walking. His mother became especially concerned when he did not show any signs of talking by 24 months and seemed more interested in objects than in people. Alex was a reluctant eater and poor sleeper. His pediatrician attributed his delays to complications at birth.

Near his second birthday, Alex began showing great interest in certain objects and activities. He had a box of toy farm animals; however, he never played with them in an imaginary way (e.g., "mooing" and "oinking"). Instead, he would drop each one on the floor, watching them fall and listening to the sounds they made. Alex would also spend hours lining them up or spinning them. During his play, he frequently rocked back and forth.

At age 3, Alex was largely unable to communicate verbally. He spent most of his time engaged in solitary activities or with his parents. He showed little interest in playing with his brother and actively disliked playdates with peers. Alex would not feed himself, get dressed, or perform other self-care skills. When forced to perform these activities, he would tantrum loudly. He was eventually diagnosed with ASD and intellectual disability (ID) at age 3.5 and referred to a special needs preschool, which helped to improve his communication and self-care skills.

AUTISM SPECTRUM DISORDER WITHOUT INTELLECTUAL DISABILITY

Benji

Source: ©iStockphoto.com/MilicaStankovic

Benji was a full-term baby who experienced no complications during gestation or delivery. He showed slight delays in learning to sit up and walk but nothing that caused his parents concern. His eating and sleeping were typical for an infant his age.

Benji's parents suspected problems when he did not show much progress acquiring language between 12 and 24 months of age. At his 3-year birthday, Benji was largely mute. He communicated with cries, grunts, and gestures and only when he wanted something from his parents.

About this same time, his parents noticed Benji's odd social behavior. Whereas most preschoolers where affectionate toward their parents, Benji never liked to cuddle. He seemed content playing by himself for hours each day, usually with blocks or toy cars, or drawing in a notebook. He also developed picky eating habits; during one summer, he seemed to live on a diet of fish-shaped crackers and chicken nuggets. Other peculiarities were his intense fear of the vacuum clearer, a tendency to walk on his toes, and irritability when forced to wear "scratchy" clothes—all of which caused tantrums.

Benji showed a dramatic increase in language skills shortly before preschool. Although he spoke in simple sentences, he would rarely initiate conversations with others. Instead, he used language instrumentally, to obtain what he wanted or to avoid activities he disliked. He also tended to repeat words and phrases the he heard others say or from TV and movies.

In preschool, he showed problems developing age-appropriate social skills like making eye contact, waiting his turn, and sharing with others. He was formally diagnosed with ASD shortly after his fifth birthday. Intelligence testing showed IQ in the average range. Although Benji's parents were initially disheartened by his diagnosis, they admit that in retrospect "it helps explain so many things."

Figure 6.1 Intellectual functioning of children with ASD. Approximately 44% of school-age children with ASD have intellectual disability. However, one-third of youths with ASD have average or above-average intelligence.

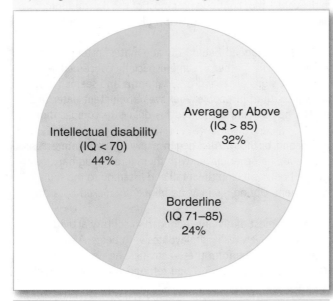

Source: Adapted from Christiansen and colleagues (2016).

verbal language. On the other hand, another 25% of children with ASD are able to carry on lengthy conversations using sophisticated vocabularies. The severity of these language problems is usually associated with children's verbal intelligence; children with higher verbal IQs tend to show superior language skills, although they almost always display some deficits in the use of language during social interactions (Kim, Paul, Tager-Flusberg, & Lord, 2015)

Although most children with ASD develop language, their use of language is often odd, rigid, or peculiar. First, many children with ASD show *pronoun reversal*. For example, a child with ASD might state, "You are hungry" when he wants to say, "I am hungry." Other children with ASD refer to themselves in the third person, saying, "He wants some water" when they mean to say, "I want some water."

Second, many children with ASD show abnormal *prosody*—that is, their tone or manner of speech is atypical or awkward. For example, some children with ASD speak mechanically. Other children speak with an unusual rhythm or intonation, using a singsong voice. Still others talk loudly or stress the wrong syllables when speaking.

Third, almost all children with ASD who are able to speak show *problems with pragmatic language*. *Pragmatics* refers to the use of language in specific social contexts, especially the natural give-and-take that occurs during conversation and the ability to tell coherent stories with appropriate background information. Although youths with ASD may speak in grammatically correct sentences, their sentences do not fit the social situation. For example, many children with ASD do not provide appropriate context for their statements. A boy with ASD might begin a conversation saying, "*We* enjoyed *that* yesterday" without explaining to his friend that he is referring to a movie that he saw with his family earlier in the week. Another example of poor pragmatics is tangential conversation. For example, a schoolmate might ask a girl with ASD, "How are you today?" The girl might respond in an off-topic, tangential manner, saying, "I ate a hot dog for lunch." Still, other children with ASD inappropriately switch topics in the middle of conversations, often confusing and frustrating listeners.

Fourth, the verbal communication of many children with ASD is often *one-sided*. These children communicate primarily to express their needs or to gain information. They seldom talk to others to share their thoughts, experiences, or feelings. In general, children with ASD do not show the natural reciprocity that characterizes most dialogue. They seem to be talking *to* others rather than talking *with* others. Some high-functioning children with ASD talk constantly. Their discussions are usually described as pedantic ramblings that exhaust their listeners. Often, these children do not seem to care whether anyone is listening to them at all.

Some children show problems using language in social situations, but they do not engage in restricted, repetitive behaviors. Consequently, they cannot be diagnosed with ASD. Instead, these youths are diagnosed with social (pragmatic) communication disorder, a disorder characterized by persistent problems with verbal and nonverbal communication in everyday situations. We will learn more about social (pragmatic) communication disorder in the next chapter.

Behavioral and Emotional Disorders

Children with ASD are more likely than their typically developing peers to experience other mental health problems (Strang, 2016). Approximately 70% of youths with ASD in the community have at least one behavioral or emotional disorder and almost 50% have two or more comorbid conditions. The most common co-occurring disorders are ADHD (40% to 50%), an anxiety disorders (30% to 40%), and obsessive–compulsive disorder (OCD; 15% to 20%).

It can be difficult to tease apart the symptoms of ASD and the symptoms of these other disorders. For example, children with ASD or social anxiety disorder tend to experience distress when placed in social situations. However, children with ASD usually do not show anticipatory anxiety about social situations, as do youths with social anxiety disorder. Similarly, both ASD and OCD are characterized by repetitive thoughts and actions. However, the thoughts and actions exhibited by children with ASD tend to involve touching, moving,

or ordering whereas the repetitive behaviors of children with OCD tend to involve cleaning, checking, or counting. The cognitive and language impairments shown by many children with ASD can also limit their ability to describe their symptoms accurately to clinicians. Many professionals rely on the Schedule for the Assessment of Psychiatric Problems Associated with Autism (SAPPA) to help differentiate ASD from other disorders. Nevertheless, it takes considerable knowledge and skill to differentiate ASD from these other conditions (Ameis & Szatmari, 2016).

Medical Problems

Youths with ASD are also more likely than typically developing youths to experience medical problems (Walton & Coury, 2016). Approximately 70% of children with ASD experience gastrointestinal problems (e.g., acid reflux, constipation, nausea/vomiting) compared to 42% of children with other developmental disabilities and 28% of typically developing children. Sleep difficulties are also more likely among youths with ASD (44% to 86%) than youths without ASD (20% to 30%).

Perhaps the most serious medical problem associated with ASD is epilepsy. Seizures are much more likely among children with ASD and ID (21.5%) than among children with ASD alone (8%). Most of the evidence indicates that underlying malformation of the brain is responsible for children's intellectual impairments, ASD symptoms, and seizures. However, in some cases, it is possible that seizures in the developing brain contribute to the development of ASD (Bernard & Benke, 2015).

Review:

- Approximately 44% of school-age children with ASD may meet criteria for ID.
- Approximately 25% of children with ASD are mute and approximately 50% more youths with ASD show problems with speech or language.
- Children who show deficits in social communication but do not display restricted or repetitive interests or behaviors would be diagnosed with social (pragmatic) communication disorder rather than ASD.
- Approximately 70% of youths with ASD have a comorbid mental disorder (e.g., ADHD, anxiety) and 70% have an associated medical problem (e.g., GI problems, seizures).

How Common Is Autism Spectrum Disorder?

Overall Prevalence

The Centers for Disease Control and Prevention established the Autism and Developmental Disabilities Monitoring (ADDM) Network to collect data regarding the prevalence of ASD at various locations in the United States. The network reviews records in pediatric health clinics and hospitals, specialized programs for children with developmental disabilities (e.g., early intervention preschools), and special education programs in public schools. Although the ADDM Network cannot identify all youths with ASDs, the data it gathers provide one of the best estimates of the disorder's prevalence. The ADDM Network's most recent data indicate that 14.6 per 1,000 children (approximately 1 in 68) have ASD (ADDM Network, 2016).

Although the ADDM Network gathers the most thorough data regarding the prevalence of ASD, it gathers data from only 11 geographic locations. These data may not be representative of youths across the entire country, and some children with ASD might be missed by the researchers.

The National Health Interview Survey (NHIS) assesses ASD by randomly sampling 12,000 parents from across the United States, asking them if their child was ever diagnosed with ASD or another developmental disability. Results showed that 20.8 per 1,000 children (approximately 1 in 48) have been diagnosed with ASD (Zablotsky, Black, Maenner, Schieve, & Blumberg, 2015). This prevalence is somewhat higher than the estimate obtained by the ADDM Network. On the other hand, the NHIS data are based exclusively on parental reports rather than official medical or educational records. It is possible that some parents inaccurately report ASD in their children.

Epidemiological data from other countries also show a high prevalence of ASD, ranging from approximately 1% to 2% of children in the general population. Prevalence estimates from Southeast Asia, Australia, Western Europe, and the Middle East are similar to those obtained in the United States (Centers for Disease Control and Prevention, 2016e).

Regardless of the survey methods, all data indicate that the prevalence of ASD is increasing. The first epidemiological data, collected in 1978, suggested that ASD was a rare disorder, occurring in approximately 4 per 10,000 children (Rutter, 1978). By 1997, the first year of the NHIS, prevalence had increased to 2 per 1,000 youths. In 2000, the first year of the ADDM Network, prevalence was estimated at 1 in 150 children. By 2008, the prevalence had jumped to 1 in 88. Today, their estimated prevalence is approximately 1 in 68. If this trend continues in a similar manner (which is unlikely), approximately 10% of children will be diagnosed with ASD within the next 45 years (Dowrick, 2015).

Several explanations have been offered to explain the increased prevalence of ASD. Some experts have posited that the United States is experiencing an ASD "epidemic." It is possible that there is a real increase in the disorder. Some researchers attribute the recent increase in ASD, food allergies, metabolic disorders, and subtle neurological problems to unidentified environmental factors (e.g., foods additives, environmental toxins, or other teratogens) or changes in lifestyle (e.g. delaying pregnancy until later in life).

Alternatively, the increased prevalence of ASD may be explained by a greater number of children being diagnosed with the disorder, rather than an actual increase in the disorder itself (McPartland, Reichow, & Volkmar, 2012). First, parents, teachers, and pediatricians have become more aware of the signs and symptoms of ASD over the past 10 years, making them more likely to refer youths to mental health practitioners for diagnosis and treatment. Second, mental health professionals may be more willing to assign the ASD diagnosis now, than in the past, to help families gain access to behavior therapy, special education, or vocational services. Third, in the past decade, there has been a broadening of the conceptualization of ASD to include youths who do not meet full *DSM* criteria for the disorder but who do show abnormalities in social communication or stereotyped behaviors. Indeed, in one large epidemiological study, the greatest increase in ASD diagnoses was seen among youths with subthreshold symptoms (Rosenberg, Daniels, Law, Law, & Kaufmann, 2009).

Gender, Socioeconomic Status, and Ethnicity

Nearly every large, epidemiological study indicates that ASD is much more common in boys than in girls. For example, the ADDM Network demonstrated that ASD is 4.5 times more prevalent in boys (1 in 42) than in girls (1 in 189). The NHIS data revealed a similar gender ratio of 4:1 favoring boys (Christensen et al., 2016).

Overall, boys and girls with ASD show only minor differences in their cognition and behavior (Hartley & Sikora, 2009). Studies involving older children with ASD indicate that girls earn lower average IQ scores than boys and are more likely to have severe or profound deficits in intellectual functioning. Studies involving younger children with ASD have found that girls show greater problems with social communication than boys, whereas boys display greater severity of restricted, repetitive, and stereotyped behavior than girls. Young girls with ASD are also more likely than boys to experience sleep and mood problems, although the magnitude of this difference is small. In general, boys and girls with ASD show more similarities than differences.

Experts are not sure why boys are more likely than girls to have ASD. One explanation is that girls, in general, have an advantage in social and linguistic functioning compared to boys. Therefore, girls with ASD would need to show greater levels of impairment before they would be diagnosed. Evidence for this explanation comes from studies showing that girls, on average, display superior social and communicative functioning at various times in development. For example, across the life span, girls are better than boys at interpreting other people's facial expressions, emotions, and nonverbal behavior. Similarly, girls show greater tendency to use language to convey emotions and share feelings than do boys. It is possible that these strengths in social communication make ASD less noticeable in girls (Kirby, 2015).

An alternative explanation is that male hormones lead to the development of ASD disproportionately in boys. Considerable evidence suggests that high levels of male hormones during gestation can affect the developing brain. In particular, prenatal hormones have been shown to affect the limbic system and frontal cortex. This is important because the limbic system and frontal cortex are involved in perceiving, processing, and responding to social information. Furthermore, these brain regions may be underactive in youths with ASD. It is possible that excessive exposure to male sex hormones in utero affects brain development, which, in turn, increases the likelihood of autistic behaviors (Koenig & Tsatsanis, 2005).

The prevalence of ASD also varies as a function of socioeconomic status (SES). In general, mothers who complete college or who live in households with higher incomes are 1.4 to 2 times more likely to have a child diagnosed with ASD than mothers who do not complete high school or who live in poverty (Boyle et al., 2011). These findings are somewhat counterintuitive, given that lower parental educational attainment and lower family income is typically associated with increased likelihood of childhood disorders.

The increased prevalence of ASD among higher-SES families may be partially attributable to higher-SES families' ability to obtain medical, educational, and behavioral services for their children (Durkin et al., 2010). In one epidemiological study, researchers found a higher prevalence of ASD among families earning >$90,000 (17.2 per 1,000) compared to families earning <$30,000 (7.1 per 1,000) annually (Thomas et al., 2012). The researchers also discovered that high-income families participated in a greater number of diagnostic evaluations (e.g., pediatric visits, psychological assessments, school-based evaluations) than lower-income families. The children from higher-income families were also diagnosed with ASD at an earlier age than the children from lower-income families. These data suggest that in higher-SES areas, the signs and symptoms of ASD may come to the attention of parents, pediatricians, and mental health professionals sooner than in lower-SES areas. Furthermore, high-SES families may be more likely to advocate for the needs of their children than lower-SES families, obtaining the ASD diagnosis and access to treatment. Interestingly, studies conducted in Europe typically show no association between ASD and family income or maternal education, presumably because access to health care and education is less dependent on SES (Kirby, 2015).

In the United States, the prevalence of ASD varies across ethnicities. Most data show the highest prevalence among non-Latino, White children. For example, the most recent ADDM Network data indicate that non-Latino, White children are 1.2 times more likely to be diagnosed with ASD than African American children and 1.5 times more likely to be diagnosed than Latino children. It is likely that the increased likelihood of ASD classification among non-Latino, White children is partially attributable to SES. In some studies, when SES is taken into account, there is no difference in prevalence across White, African American, and Latino families (Christensen et al., 2016).

Review:

- The ADDM Network, which reviews medical and school records, estimates the prevalence of ASD as 1 in 68 youths. Data from the NHIS, which is based on parent reports alone, estimates prevalence at 1 in 48 youths. These data suggest that ASD occurs in 1.5% to 2.1% of children.
- Boys are 4.0 to 4.5 times more likely than girls to be diagnosed with ASD. Girls with ASD tend to show greater impairment than boys.
- ASD is disproportionately diagnosed in non-Latino, White youths and children from higher-SES families. Recognition of ASD and access to high-quality educational and medical services may partially explain these demographic differences in prevalence.

What Is the Course and Prognosis for Children With Autism Spectrum Disorder?

Parents of children with ASD often report that their children's symptoms began during the first two years of life. Many parents remember feeling that something was "different" or unusual about their infant's social behavior. Some parents describe their infants as aloof, distant, or avoidant (Chawarska, Macari, Volkmar, Kim, & Shic, 2015).

Prospective studies of infants later diagnosed with ASD largely confirm parents' reports. Early signs of ASD are sometimes present by age 18 months. For example, 18-month-olds later diagnosed with ASD spend less time looking at others' faces and initiating social interactions with caregivers. They often do not respond when others call their names and do not share interesting toys with caregivers. Young children later diagnosed with ASD seldom direct their attention when other people point to objects or events, and they show delays in make-believe social play (Davis & Carter, 2015).

Most parents first seek professional advice shortly after their children's second birthday (Klinger et al., 2014). They usually consult a pediatrician or psychologist because their child shows significant delays in language. Whereas typically developing children are able to speak in simple two-word phrases by their second birthday (e.g., "Give drink" or "Me cookie"), most children later diagnosed with ASD speak few, if any, words by age 2.

On the other hand, one-third of children with ASD do not show early signs of the disorder. Instead, this sizable minority of children seems to show relatively normal social and linguistic development up to age 2. After age 2, however, these children display a lack of social initiative and interpersonal skills, a loss of language, and an increase in stereotyped behaviors.

Experts used to believe that the prognosis of ASD was extremely poor. Recent research, however, indicates that prognosis depends on three factors (Howlin, 2015):

1. Children's *intellectual ability* predicts their long-term outcomes. Infants and toddlers who show interest in a wide range of play materials, who engage others in play, and who begin showing the ability for symbolic play tend to fare well. In contrast, infants and toddlers with restricted interests or repetitive, stereotyped behaviors tend to have worse prognoses.

2. Children's *language ability* predicts their social outcomes and later capacity for independent living. Children with ASD who have functional language skills by age 5 tend to have much better outcomes than their counterparts who lack functional language by the time they begin school.

3. Children's *social engagement* in early childhood predicts their long-term social and emotional outcomes. Young children with ASD who show some capacity for shared attention, imitation, and social engagement tend to have better outcomes than children with ASD who show low motivation for social engagement.

Evidence-based treatments for ASD, therefore, tend to target one or more of these three areas: intellectual ability, language, and/or social engagement (Odom, Boyd, Hall, & Hume, 2015; Rogers & Vismara, 2015).

Review:

- Approximately two-thirds of children eventually diagnosed with ASD display signs of the disorder by age 18 months. Early indicators include a lack of eye contact, failure to initiate social interactions, and problems with joint attention.
- Approximately one-third of children eventually diagnosed with ASD do not show signs of the disorder until after age 2, when social communication deficits and restrictive, repetitive behaviors or interests emerge.
- Prognosis for youths with ASD is variable. The best outcomes are seen in children with (a) higher intellectual ability, (b) better language skills, and (c) greater social engagement.

6.2 CAUSES

The earliest explanations for ASD placed considerable blame on families. Kanner (1943) believed that the parents of his patients were emotionally distant. He described these parents as showing little interest in their children's behavior, as socially aloof, and as overly intellectual. Extending these observations, the philosopher and writer Bruno Bettelheim (1967) suggested that cold and rejecting parents *caused* their children to develop autism. In his book, *The Empty Fortress,* Bettelheim blamed cold, emotionally distant "refrigerator mothers" who caused their children to retreat into themselves in response to their dismissive

parenting practices. Bettelheim and others suggested that ASD could be treated by helping parents become warmer toward their children (Feinstein, 2010).

In the 1960s and 1970s, researchers began challenging the theories of Bettelheim and others regarding the etiology of ASD. Bernard Rimland (1964) first suggested that ASD might have a neurological cause. Empirical data also showed that ASD was not caused by cold or rejecting parents. In fact, parents of children with ASD were extremely involved in their children's development and care. Unfortunately, many parents assumed that they were somehow responsible for having a child with ASD. New theories, which implicated genetics and neurodevelopment, slowly alleviated some of this guilt.

Today, we still do not know exactly what causes ASD. However, most of the evidence points to a combination of genetic, neurobiological, and early environmental factors.

Is Autism Spectrum Disorder Heritable?

Genetics

ASD has a strong genetic component (Rutter & Thapar, 2015). There is clear evidence that ASD runs in families. For example, if parents have one child with ASD, their risk of having a second child with the disorder is approximately 20% (compared to 1% to 2% in the general population). If parents have two children with ASD, their risk of having a third child with the condition increases to 1 in 3 (Huguet, Benabou, & Bourgeron, 2016).

Twin studies confirm the heritability of ASD. On average, concordance for monozygotic (MZ) twins ranges from 60% to 90%; in contrast, concordance for dizygotic (DZ) twins falls between 5% to 20%. The drop in concordance between MZ and DZ twins suggests that genes play an important role in ASD (Klinger et al., 2014).

On the other hand, recent research indicates that environmental factors are at least as important in the development of ASD as genetics. For example, a large twin study showed that roughly 55% of the variance in children's ASD symptoms could be attributed to environmental factors, such as health, diet, and the early home environment. In contrast, in this study, genes explained only 40% of the variance in children's ASD symptoms (Chaste & Devlin, 2016).

Today, researchers believe that no single gene causes ASD. Instead, multiple genes predispose individuals to a wide range of autism spectrum behaviors. Geneticists have attempted to determine which genes might play a role in ASD (see Figure 6.2). In the largest study so far, the Autism Genome Project, researchers in 19 countries studied approximately 1,200 families in which two or more members had ASD. By looking at family members' DNA, researchers have been able to identify underlying genetic abnormalities associated with ASD. On average, 15% of children with ASD have small deletions or duplications of genetic material

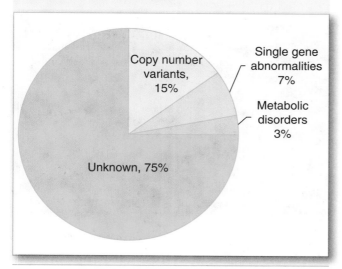

Figure 6.2 Genetic causes of ASD. In approximately 75% of cases, a genetic or metabolic cause cannot be identified.

Copy number variants, 15%

Single gene abnormalities 7%

Metabolic disorders 3%

Unknown, 75%

Source: Based on Wang and colleagues (2015).

on specific chromosomes (i.e., copy number variants). An additional 7% of cases are caused by a genetic abnormality or mutation on a single portion of one gene. Usually, this portion of the genetic code is responsible for early brain maturation. For example, some people with ASD showed an absence of a particular gene called neurexin 1, located on chromosome 2, a gene that produces proteins important to early brain maturation and neural connections. Finally, approximately 2% to 3% of cases are attributable to metabolic disorders, such as untreated phenylketonuria (PKU). This leaves roughly 75% of cases of ASD unexplained. Clearly, there is much work to do (Wang et al., 2015)!

Geneticists are continuing this work with MSSNG, a project to scan the genomes of 10,000 individuals with ASD. MSSNG is unique for two reasons. First, the study involves the largest number of participants with ASD to have their DNA mapped. Second, the data will be shared by researchers worldwide so that scientists can work together to find the genetic underpinnings of the disorder (MSSNG, 2016).

Epigenetics

Researchers have known for some time that advanced maternal age was associated with ASD. Recently, however, studies have confirmed that older fathers are more likely to have children with ASD than their younger counterparts. Men 50 years of age and older are more than twice as likely to have a child with ASD than men younger than 30. What is perhaps more surprising is that grandpaternal age (on both sides of the family) also increases children's risk for ASD. For example, if your father or your partner's father was older when you were born, your offspring may be at elevated risk for ASD (Milekic et al., 2015).

Two factors likely explain the association between paternal age and ASD. First, older men are more likely to experience genetic mutations to the DNA in their sperm cells than younger men. These mutations may be spontaneous or the result of accumulated exposure to environmental toxins over their life span. Researchers believe these mutations could contribute to ASD in their offspring. Second, environmental stressors over the man's life span could lead to epigenetic changes that are passed down from one generation to the next. For example, chronic stress, illness, or traumatic experiences might cause changes to the way in which genes are expressed. These epigenetic changes are inherited by both the man's son and grandson, who might be at increased risk for ASD (Peter, Reichenberg, & Akbarian, 2015).

Review:

- ASD is heritable; approximately 40% of the variance in children's ASD symptoms is attributable to genetic causes.
- The Autism Genome Project has identified several causes for ASD: deletions or duplications of genetic material (15%), specific genetic mutations (7%), and metabolic disorders (2% to 3%). Unfortunately, the causes of 75% of cases of ASD cannot be determined at this time.
- Older men are at greater risk for offspring with ASD than younger men. Explanations for their increased risk include genetic mutations in sex cells, exposure to environmental toxins over the man's life span, and epigenetic effects.

What Brain Abnormalities Are Associated With Autism Spectrum Disorder?

Youths with ASD often have abnormalities in the structure and functioning of certain brain regions. First, many show a pattern of rapid brain growth and synaptic density in infancy and early childhood, followed by a period of deterioration and a loss of neural connectivity in later childhood and adolescence. Furthermore, three brain regions are specifically implicated in ASD: the amygdala, the fusiform gyrus, and portions of the prefrontal cortex. These three areas play important roles in the perception of, processing of, and responses to social information. There is also a neural pathway connecting these brain regions. Collectively, this pathway is called the *social brain* because it is critical to our functioning in social situations (Elsabbagh & Johnson, 2016).

Synaptic Density and Neural Connections

Longitudinal studies indicate that infants later diagnosed with ASD show an unusual pattern of head growth. At birth, their head circumference is similar to typically developing neonates. However, beginning at age 4 months, children later diagnosed with ASD tend to show a rapid increase in head circumference. By age 12 months, the average head circumference of these children is typically one standard deviation larger than their healthy peers. Then, head growth tends to decelerate, such that the circumferences of children with and without ASD are again similar by late childhood (McKeague et al., 2015).

This unusual pattern of head growth corresponds to abnormalities in brain density and volume. Several studies have documented increased brain density beginning in early childhood. For example, in one study, researchers scanned the brains of children with ASD between 6 and 15 years of age (Mak-Fan, Taylor, Roberts, & Lerch, 2012). Compared to youths without ASD, children with ASD showed increased brain volume, surface area, and cortical thickness in early childhood but normal structure in later childhood and early adolescence.

Together, these findings support the growth dysregulation hypothesis of ASD. According to this hypothesis, infants and young children later diagnosed with ASD show unusual maturation of the cortex, characterized by large head circumference, brain volume, and synaptic density. Whereas typically developing infants experience a period of dramatic brain growth followed by synaptic pruning, infants later diagnosed with ASD show only rapid growth. Their brains may form too many neural connections, thus, reducing the efficiency of brain activity. By late adolescence or early adulthood, however, many of these individuals show an abnormal decline and possible deterioration in neural connections (Sacco, Stefano, & Persico, 2015).

Recent neuroimaging studies have found that many of the abnormalities shown by children with ASD are in the neural connections *between* brain regions in addition to abnormalities within brain regions. Scientists study connections between brain regions using a technique called diffusion tensor imaging (DTI). DTI is similar to functional magnetic resonance imaging (fMRI), but it measures the diffusion of water molecules in brain tissue (Emsell, Van Hecke, & Tournier, 2016). DTI provides a high-resolution image of the strength or integrity of brain tissue. DTI is especially good at generating images of the brain's white matter—that is, the myelinated axons that form the connections between neurons. By measuring the structural integrity of white matter, scientists can estimate the strength of connections between brain regions (Baribeau & Anagnostou, 2015).

DTI has revealed two important findings (Solso et al., 2016). First, children with ASD often show weakened connections between brain regions responsible for social communication, language, and movement. Second, researchers used DTI to study the brains of the younger siblings of children with ASD. They found that these siblings often showed abnormalities in brain connectivity six months before they began developing ASD symptoms themselves (Koyama et al., 2016). Longitudinal data, like these, suggest that abnormal brain connectivity in infancy might be an important predictor for ASD during the toddler and preschool years (see Image 6.2).

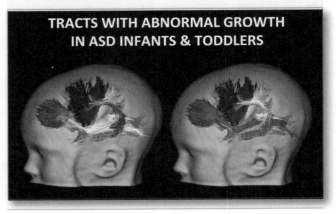

Image 6.2 Diffusion tensor imaging (DTI) shows abnormalities in brain connectivity (white matter) in infants and toddlers who are later diagnosed with ASD.

TRACTS WITH ABNORMAL GROWTH IN ASD INFANTS & TODDLERS

Source: Used with permission from Solso and colleagues (2016).

Abnormalities of the Limbic System

A second brain area that sometimes differs in individuals with and without ASD is the amygdala (Baron-Cohen, 2005; Lawrence, Lott, & Haier, 2005). The amygdala is located deep in the brain in a region known as the limbic system, an area important to our social and emotional functioning. It becomes highly active when we watch other people's social behaviors and attempt to understand the motives for their actions or emotional displays. Abnormalities in the structure or functioning of the amygdala might underlie some of the deficits shown by youths with ASD. For example, Baron-Cohen, Lombardo, Tager-Flusberg, and Cohen (2013) compared the brain activity of individuals with and without ASD as they attempted to infer the mental states of others. Compared to typically developing individuals, people with ASD showed significant reductions in amygdala activity.

A second line of evidence comes from structural studies of the brains of individuals with ASD. Individuals with ASD often show reduced amygdala volume or neural density relative to healthy controls (Schumann & Amaral, 2006).

A third line of evidence suggesting the amygdala plays a role in the etiology of ASD comes from studies of animals and humans with damage to this brain region. Humans with damage to the amygdala often show deficits in social understanding that resemble those deficits displayed by high-functioning individuals with ASD. For example, they have problems recognizing and responding to others' facial expressions, detecting social faux pas, and understanding other people's intentions based on their overt behavior. Furthermore, intentional damage to the amygdala in monkeys causes autistic-like behaviors, such as social isolation, lack of eye contact, and stereotypies (Schultz & Robins, 2005).

Another brain region that may be important to the development of ASD is the right fusiform gyrus. This brain region is located on the underside of the temporal lobe, near the occipital lobe. For a long time, this brain area was believed to play a specific role in processing human faces. When healthy adults are asked to view images of human faces, especially faces displaying emotions, they show strong activation of their right fusiform gyrus. In contrast, children and adolescents with ASD who are asked to process facial expressions do not show increased activation in this brain region (see Image 6.3). Instead, people with ASD use a different brain area, the inferior temporal gyri, to process facial information. Interestingly, the inferior temporal gyri are usually used to process information about objects, not people. These findings indicate that people with ASD process facial information using parts of their brains that most people use to process information about objects. This abnormality in information processing may help explain the difficulty that people with ASD have understanding other people's emotions and social behavior (Critchley et al., 2000; Schultz et al., 2003).

The fusiform gyrus does much more than process human faces. It is also important in understanding human social behavior. In a clever experiment, Castelli, Happe, Frith, and Frith (2000) showed healthy individuals simple cartoons of geometric shapes engaging in humanlike social behavior. For example, one cartoon showed a circle entering a schematic of a house and playing hide-and-seek with a triangle. Another cartoon showed two shapes "fighting" or "chasing" each other. People without ASD almost always described these shapes as having human intentions that motivated their behavior. For example, they reported that the shapes were "playing," "chasing," or "fighting." In contrast, people with ASD usually did not view the shapes as behaving in a social manner. Instead, they reported that the shapes were simply "bumping into" each other (Klin, 2000).

More important, people with and without ASD showed different levels of activity in their fusiform gyri when watching the shapes. As you might expect, people without ASD showed greater activity of the right fusiform gyrus compared to people with ASD. These findings indicate that the right fusiform gyrus is important to understanding social interactions in general, not just faces. Hypoactivation of this brain region in people with ASD might impair their understanding of social situations and contribute to their social deficits (Schultz et al., 2003).

Why do children with ASD frequently show hypoactivation of the right fusiform gyrus? Emerging data indicate that underactivity is partially due to a lack of attention, motivation, or interest in faces and social interactions (Pierce & Redcay, 2009). For example, when children with ASD are shown faces of familiar people, like their mothers, their activity level in this brain region becomes close to normal. Furthermore, if researchers increase children's attention by placing a dot on the face they are asked to process, activation of the right fusiform gyrus significantly increases. These data suggest that the right fusiform gyrus can function in children with ASD,

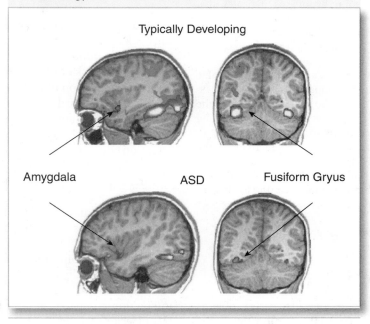

Image 6.3 When processing faces, children with ASD show less activation in brain areas responsible for social and emotional functioning, like the amygdala and fusiform gyrus.

Source: Used with permission from Pierce and Redcay (2009).

but its performance depends on other factors like the child's motivation to engage in social stimuli.

Prefrontal Cortex

A final brain area that may play a role in ASD is the prefrontal cortex (Klinger et al., 2014). Considerable evidence suggests that this brain region is responsible for higher order cognitive activities, such as regulating attention, extracting information from the environment, organizing information, and using information to solve problems. The prefrontal cortex acts like the chief executive officer of the brain: directing, organizing, and planning mental activity and behavior. For this reason, psychologists say that the prefrontal cortex is responsible for executive functioning.

Children with ASD often show deficits in executive functioning. Although their short-term, rote memory is intact (and sometimes exceptional), children with ASD often have difficulty paying attention to important aspects of their environment. For example, when watching a television program, they may pay greater attention to objects in the background than to the activities of the main characters. Their lack of attention to salient social information could interfere with their ability to correctly perceive and respond to social situations (Klin, 2000; Klin, Jones, Schultz, & Volkmar, 2003). Even high-functioning children with ASD show deficits in organization and planning. Specifically, they tend to have difficulty processing information in flexible ways and solving problems on the spot. Ozonoff and colleagues (2004) have suggested that their rigid cognitive style might explain their strong desire for sameness and repetitive, stereotyped behaviors. Indeed, some people with damage to their prefrontal cortex show a desire for sameness and a propensity for stereotyped behaviors like individuals with ASD (Klinger et al., 2014).

Review:

- The growth dysregulation hypothesis indicates that youths with ASD show abnormal maturation of the cortex and poor neural connectivity, especially in brain regions responsible for social communication and language.
- Some youths with ASD show smaller and less active functioning of the amygdala, a portion of the limbic system responsible for emotional processing.
- Children with ASD often show underactivity of the right fusiform gyrus, a region responsible for processing human faces and interpreting social behavior.
- Many youths with ASD display underactivity of the prefrontal cortex, a region responsible for executive functioning. These youths have difficulty attending to important social information and adapting to changes in their environment.

What Deficits in Social Cognition Are Associated With Autism Spectrum Disorder?

Abnormalities in the social brain can lead to early problems in the development of children's social cognition, that is, the way children think about social interactions (Baron-Cohen et al., 2013). Specifically, children with ASD perceive, interpret, and respond to social information in a manner differently than their typically developing peers. Problems with social cognition emerge in infancy and may lead to the development of serious deficits in social functioning.

Lack of Joint Attention

One of the chief ways infants learn about other people and the world around them is through joint attention (Mundy, 2016). Joint attention refers to the infant's ability to share attention with his caregiver on a single object or event. In typically developing infants, joint attention gradually emerges between 6 and 18 months of age.

To understand joint attention, imagine that an 8-month-old child is sitting in her high chair. Her mother points to a bowl on the table and says, "Do you want some cereal?" The girl follows her mother's pointing finger, gazes in the direction of the cereal, and squeals. The infant shows *responding joint attention*; she is able to follow the gaze or gesture of her mother. Imagine, also, a 10-month-old girl sitting on the floor inspecting some toys. By chance, the girl swipes at a toy frog and it "ribbits." The girl is surprised by the noise and momentarily shifts her gaze from the toy to her mother. The mother looks at the girl, smiles, and says reassuringly, "That's a frog!" The child smiles at her mother and turns her attention back to the toy. In this case, the child shows a more complex skill, *initiating joint attention*. Specifically, the infant initiates a social interaction with her mother through their shared attention on the frog.

Through joint attention, infants learn about the world around them. At the very least, the 8- and 10-month-old girls learn about "cereal" and "frogs," respectively. Although this seems trivial, without joint attention, the child would miss out on countless learning opportunities. As her parent tried to teach her about cereal, frogs, and other objects in her environment, she would not be focusing her attention on the same objects or events. As a result, the flow of information to the child would be greatly reduced. The lack of joint attention might cause problems with the acquisition of language, general knowledge, and intelligence (Pickard & Ingersoll, 2015).

Children diagnosed with ASD often show marked problems with joint attention (especially initiating joint attention) during the first two years of life. Psychologists have documented these early deficits in three ways. First, researchers have asked parents of children with ASD to recall their children's social functioning when they were infants. Most parents remembered that their children had marked problems with shared attention and eye contact between 12 and 18 months of age. Second, psychologists have reviewed home movies of infants later diagnosed with ASD. Even during their first birthday parties, these children showed deficits in joint attention and social interaction compared to their typically developing peers (Van Hecke, Oswald, & Mundy, 2016).

Finally, several recent studies have shown that deficits in joint attention during infancy are associated with problems with language acquisition and social functioning. For example, researchers tested the joint attention skills of preschoolers with and without ASD (Falck-Yttr, Fernell, Hedvall, von Vofsten, & Gillberg, 2012). Specifically, they showed preschoolers silent movies of three toys positioned on the left-hand, center, or right-hand portion of a table. Next, a woman in the movie (a) looked, (b) gestured, or (c) looked and gestured to one of the toys (see Image 6.4). The researchers tracked the preschoolers' eye movements to determine if they were able to look at the same toy as the woman in the film. As we might expect, preschoolers with ASD were much less likely than healthy preschoolers to follow the woman's gaze or gesture and look at the correct toy. More importantly, however, the number of errors they made was negatively correlated with their social communication skills and verbal intelligence. The more errors they showed, the lower their skills. These findings support the idea that joint attention is an important component of children's social functioning (van Hecke et al., 2016).

Problems With Social Orientation

Social development also depends on young children's capacity for social orientation—that is, their ability to attend to, and interact with, important aspects of their social environment. Typically developing infants show well-developed capacities for social orientation. For example, if we gave a 12-month-old child a new toy car, he might smile, play with the car briefly, and show the car to his mother. Although the child lacks language, he communicates his enjoyment to his mother by showing her the car and smiling. His mother might acknowledge her son's enjoyment by meeting his gaze, smiling, and enthusiastically saying, "What a great car!"

Early parent–child exchanges teach children about social interactions. Even at 12 months, the infant is learning that social communication occurs between people, that people take turns signaling and responding to one another, that the social exchange is usually centered on

a common theme, and that effective communication involves eye contact and emotional expression (Nele, Ellen, Petra, & Herbert, 2015).

Unfortunately, young children who are eventually diagnosed with ASD show problems with social orientation. Although they might be extremely pleased with a new toy car, they are less likely to share this pleasure with another person. Similarly, these children often do not respond when family members call their names, clap their hands, or otherwise try to attract their attention. Instead, these children may appear distant or aloof (Klinger et al., 2014).

A lack of responsiveness causes these children to miss out on important social information, especially information from people's faces. Researchers asked 2-year-olds with ASD to watch videos of a caregiver and measured the percentage of time the children gazed at the caregiver's eyes, mouth, body, or surrounding objects (Jones, Carr, & Klin, 2008). Toddlers with ASD spent the greatest amount of time looking at the caregiver's mouth. In contrast, typically developing toddlers, and toddlers with developmental disorders but not ASD, spent the greatest amount of time looking at the caregiver's eyes (see Figure 6.3). Whereas the eyes provide a rich source of information regarding the emotional quality and intent of others, the mouth conveys less important information about social interactions. By attending to others' mouths, rather than eyes, children with ASD may miss facial cues important to understanding social situations. Indeed, less time spent gazing at the caregiver's eyes was associated with the degree of social impairment shown by the 2-year-olds with ASD.

Delays in Symbolic Play

Between 18 and 24 months of age, children develop the capacity for symbolic play. Symbolic play refers to the child's ability to allow one object to represent (i.e., symbolize) another object. Children show symbolic play in two ways. First, they can pretend that one object (e.g., a rectangular block) represents another object (e.g., a phone). Thus, a 2-year-old can pretend to talk to her father on the telephone while holding the block up to her ear. Second, children can

Image 6.4   Preschoolers with ASD have problems with joint attention. They make more errors following the woman's gaze (*left*), gesture (*right*), or gaze and gesture (*center*). The number of errors they make is associated with deficits in social communication and verbal intelligence.

Source: From Falck-Yttr et al. (2012). Used with permission.

Figure 6.3   Toddlers With ASD Show Deficits in Social Orientation.

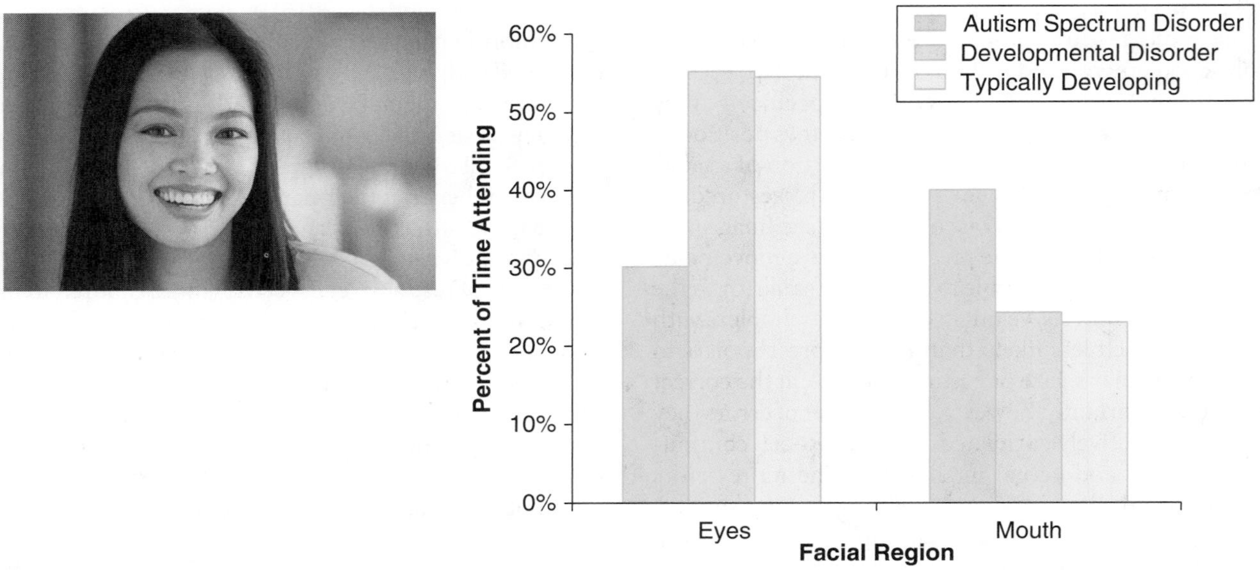

Source: Based on Jones et al. (2008).

Note: When asked to watch a video of a caregiver (left), 2-year-olds with ASD spent less time looking at the caregiver's eyes and more time looking at her mouth than did typically developing toddlers or toddlers with developmental disorders. Furthermore, less time spent gazing at the caregiver's eyes was associated with greater social impairment.

pretend that an inanimate object represents a living thing. For example, the child might decide to give his teddy bear a drink of water and lay him down for a nap. Symbolic play is often called pretend play because children are able to pretend that one object represents another object.

Children who are eventually diagnosed with ASD show delays in symbolic play. When children with ASD begin to show symbolic play, it is usually simplistic and mechanical. For example, typically developing children often show elaborate pretend play involving creative and flexible scripts. My son routinely hosted dinner parties for his toy dinosaurs, complete with appetizers, a main course, and dessert. In contrast, the pretend play of children with ASD tends to be more repetitive and without flexible, elaborative themes (Chaudry & Dissanayake, 2015).

Why is it important that children with ASD show deficits in pretend play? First, a lack of pretend play by 24 months of age can be an early sign of ASD. Although parents and physicians often overlook other signs, such as delays in joint attention or social orientation, the absence of pretend play can be a useful indicator that there might be a problem in the child's development. Since the treatment for ASD is most effective when it is initiated early, recognition and treatment of the disorder during the toddler years can lead to better prognosis.

Second, pretend play is a precursor to language acquisition. Jean Piaget believed that children begin to show pretend play when they develop the capacity for complex mental representations. In the case of pretend play, an object (e.g., a block) is allowed to mentally represent another object (e.g., a phone). A similar process occurs in verbal language. The child learns that a certain utterance (e.g., the sound "cup") represents a particular object (e.g., a cup). Words are, after all, symbols that represent objects and events. Delays in the development of symbolic play, therefore, may be associated with the delays in language shown by many people with ASD (Lam, 2015).

Deficits in Theory of Mind and Empathy

Imagine that you are standing in the hallway of a building on campus and you notice another student suddenly leave a nearby classroom. She quickly exits the classroom, shuts the door behind her, leans her head against the wall, and begins to cry. What just happened? Based on your observations, you might infer that the student received a low grade on an important exam or that her professor chastised her in front of the class. In either case, you would likely feel sorry for her and maybe try to comfort her.

Empathy is the ability to take the perspective of another person in order to understand her thoughts, intentions, and feelings. As the scenario illustrates, our ability to react in an empathic manner depends on two social skills. First, we need to understand that the person's mental state (e.g., cognitions, emotions) motivated her behavior. By understanding her mental state, we can infer that she either received a low grade on the exam or was humiliated in front of the class. Second, we need to have an appropriate emotional reaction to her crying. We would probably feel troubled by the incident and want to help her in some way. Our ability to empathize allows us to interpret social situations accurately and respond to people in sensitive and appropriate ways (Koehne, Hatri, Cacioppo, & Dziobek, 2016).

During the preschool years, most children develop theory of mind, the notion that other people have mental states (e.g., thoughts, beliefs, intentions, and desires) that motivate their behavior. Moreover, the mental states of others can be different than our own. Theory of mind allows children to interpret social situations accurately and act with empathy.

Psychologists measure theory of mind using a false belief task (see Figure 6.4). In one study, the psychologist introduced preschool-age children to a puppet named Sally who hid a toy in a basket and then left the room. While Sally was away, another puppet moved the toy to a different location (a box). The children were asked where Sally would look for her toy when she returned. Young children, without theory of mind, responded that Sally would search for the toy in the box because that is where the toy was moved. These children did not appreciate that Sally's behavior would be motivated by beliefs that differed from their own. Older children, with theory of mind, answered correctly: They responded that Sally would search for the toy in the basket because Sally believed the

Figure 6.4 Children with ASD have deficits in theory of mind. Youths with ASD often fail the false belief task whereas typically developing children, and youths with Down syndrome usually pass.

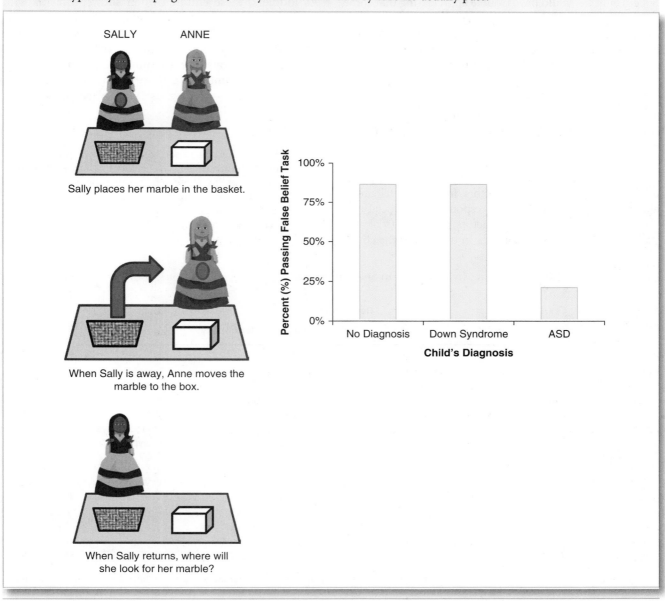

Source: Based on Baron-Cohen and colleagues (1985).

toy was still in its original location (Baron-Cohen, Leslie, & Frith, 1985).

In typically developing children, theory of mind emerges between 3 and 5 years of age. However, children with ASD show marked deficits in theory of mind. In one study, 85% of typically developing preschoolers successfully passed a false belief task compared to only 20% of preschoolers with ASD.

Why is this deficit in theory of mind important to understanding ASD? The answer is that a well-developed theory of mind is necessary for most complex social interactions. Children with ASD display "mind-blindness"— that is, they are often unable to appreciate that other people have mental states that motivate and direct their actions (Baron-Cohen et al., 1985). If a child with ASD witnessed a student abruptly leaving a classroom and crying, he would likely have difficulty understanding the student's behavior. Specifically, he would have trouble appreciating that some antecedent event and mental state (e.g., failing a test, feeling embarrassed) motivated the student's actions. Because he is unable to infer the student's mental state, he may not respond to the situation in an appropriate way.

The Emergence of Autism Spectrum Disorder Over Time

Taken together, the available evidence indicates that ASD is a neurodevelopmental disorder that emerges well before most children receive the ASD diagnosis. Its primary causes are genetic, although in approximately 75% of cases, diagnosticians cannot find a clear genetic cause of the disorder. Genetic and early environmental risk factors, in turn, contribute to abnormalities in brain regions responsible for social and emotional development. Risk factors may lead to abnormalities in the social brain, which, in turn, affect the child's ability to perceive, process, interpret, and respond to social situations. Genetic and early environmental risk factors can also interfere with the connections between brain areas that affect social cognition, language, and overt behavior.

Many experts believe that these neurological abnormalities prompt a cascade of social and emotional deficits that build upon one another and contribute to the signs and symptoms of ASD in early childhood (Joseph et al., 2015; see Figure 6.5). Indeed, the abnormal cortical growth seen in many toddlers eventually diagnosed with ASD often precedes or coincides with the emergence of early social cognitive deficits. The early deficits include a lack of interest in others' faces, deficits in joint attention, and delays in social orientation. Instead of interacting with others, these young children miss out on a great deal of social and linguistic information that, in turn, can contribute to deficits in higher order social cognitive skills. As toddlers, these children often show problems with symbolic play, theory of mind, and language.

During the preschool years, deficits in social orientation and language often prompt parents to seek help for their children. Consequently, most children are not diagnosed with ASD until age 3. However, the cascade of events that contributed to this diagnosis likely began much earlier.

Review:

- Infants later diagnosed with ASD often show delays in joint attention and social orientation during the first 24 months of life. These deficits cause them to miss out on social and linguistic information.
- Toddlers diagnosed with ASD often show delays in symbolic (pretend) play. Symbolic play is a precursor to later language development.

Figure 6.5   A Developmental Model of Autism Spectrum Disorder

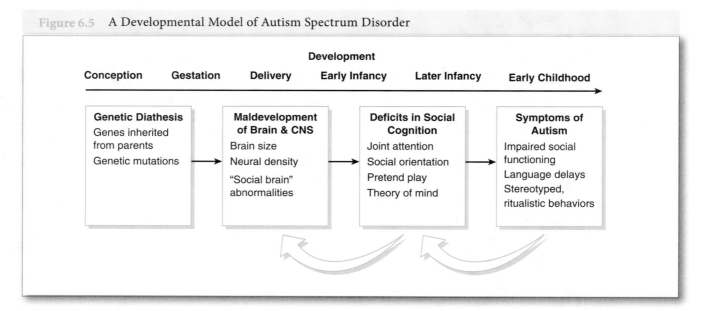

Note: In this general model, individuals show genetic risk for the disorder, which can lead to structural and/or functional differences in the developing brain. Brain abnormalities, in turn, can lead to problems in the development of social cognition during infancy. Social cognitive abnormalities also affect developing brain structure. By early childhood, deficits can be severe enough to merit the diagnosis of autism.

- Many 3- and 4-year-olds later diagnosed with ASD show deficits in theory of mind—that is, the ability to appreciate the mental states of others. These deficits likely contribute to problems interpreting others' social behaviors and problems with empathy.

6.3 IDENTIFICATION, PREVENTION, AND TREATMENT

How Is Autism Spectrum Disorder Identified and Diagnosed?

Early intervention is critical for children with ASD (Ibanez, Stone, & Coorod, 2015). Children who begin behavior therapy between 18 and 36 months of life have better long-term outcomes than youths who start receiving treatment as preschoolers. In practice, however, identifying the early signs of ASD is challenging. Infants can show great variability in their social communication and behavioral development. Furthermore, the earliest signs of ASD can be subtle and easily overlooked (Tanguay & Lohr, 2015).

Most children with ASD do not show significant signs of the disorder prior to 6 months of age (Ozonoff et al., 2014). Between 6 and 12 months, however, children who are eventually diagnosed with ASD tend to show delays in social skills, communication, and behavior (see Figure 6.6). For example, 9-month-old babies later diagnosed with ASD are much less likely to follow another's gaze, show interest in social games (e.g., peekaboo), and point to interesting objects than their typically developing peers. Many parents first become concerned when their children show delays in language acquisition between 12 and 18 months and an absence of creative, pretend play. During this same time period, children who are later diagnosed with ASD may begin to show repetitive behaviors and a general preference for objects over interactions with people. Clinicians can use these signs as "red flags" that might indicate the need for more thorough assessment (Klinger et al. 2014).

Figure 6.6   Early Signs of Autism Spectrum Disorder

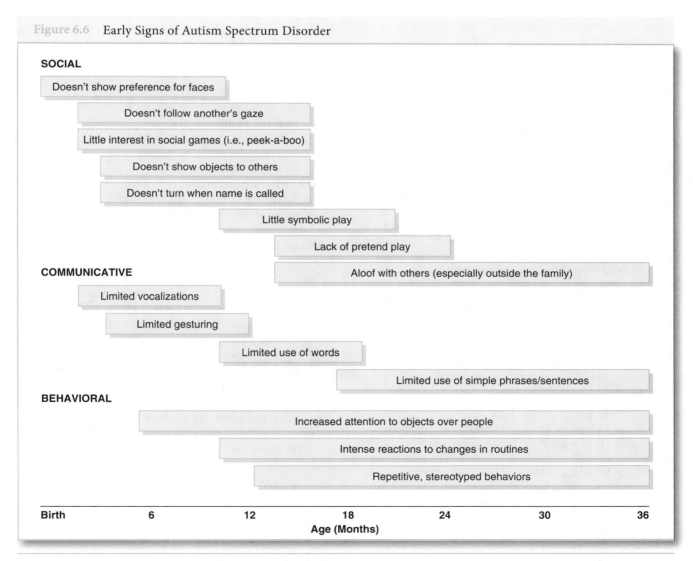

Source: Based on Klinger and colleagues (2014), Penner and colleagues (2015), and Tanguay and Lohr (2015). Age ranges are approximate.

The American Academy of Pediatrics recommends that physicians routinely screen all infants for ASD at 18 months (Myers, Mackintosh, & Goin-Kochel, 2009). Most physicians administer the Modified Checklist for Autism in Toddlers, Revised with Follow-up (M-CHAT-R/F; Robins et al., 2014), a 20-item questionnaire that screens for early signs of the disorder. The questionnaire is norm-referenced so that the physician can compare parents' responses to those of the parents of toddlers in the general population. Toddlers who earn high scores on the questionnaire can be referred to mental health professionals for more thorough assessment.

Formal ASD assessment requires collaboration by families, psychologists, physicians, and teachers or day care providers (Penner , Zwaigenbaum, & Roberts, 2015). Frequently, speech–language pathologists or occupational therapists may be consulted when children show language or movement delays. Data from multiple informants will be collected using interviews, observations, and questionnaires. For example, the Autism Diagnostic Interview, Revised (ADI-R; Rutter, Lecouteur, & Lord, 2015) is a structured interview that assesses children's reciprocal social interactions, language/communication, and restricted or repetitive behaviors and interests. It can be supplemented with the Autism Diagnostic Observation Schedule, Second Edition (ADOS-2; Lord, Rutter, et al., 2015), a procedure in which the clinician delivers age-appropriate social cues to the child and notes how he responds. For example, the clinician may greet the child and observe eye contact or present the child with play materials and look for symbolic play. The ADOS-2 assesses several domains of ASD including social interaction, communication, play, and stereotyped/restricted behaviors (Lord, Corsello, & Grzadzinski, 2015).

The chief limitation of the ADI-R and ADOS-2 is that they take considerable time and experience to administer. Consequently, many clinicians will administer questionnaires to parents, caregivers, and teachers. Some of the most frequently used rating scales are the Social Responsiveness Scale, Second Edition (SRS-2), the Childhood Autism Rating Scale, Second Edition (CARS-2), and the Autism Spectrum Rating Scales (ASRS). Assessment of ASD will also include testing the child's intelligence, language, and adaptive skills to determine if he also has ID (Weeks, 2016).

Review:

- Although deficits in social communication usually emerge between 6 and 12 months, most parents become concerned when their children show delays in language and symbolic play between 12 and 18 months of age.
- The American Academy of Pediatrics recommends universal screening for ASD at 18 months. The M-CHAT-R/F is a frequently used screening instrument.
- Formal ASD diagnosis is made by an interdisciplinary team of professionals. Clinicians tend to rely on interviews, such as the ADI-R, and observations, such as the ADOS-2.

What Treatments Are Effective for Preschoolers and School-Age Children?

Early Intensive Behavioral Intervention

Many experts regard early intensive behavioral intervention (EIBI) as the gold standard in the treatment of young children with ASD (Maglione, Gans, Das, Timbie, & Kasari, 2012). EIBI is a behavioral treatment in which children are taught skills on a one-on-one basis, using principles of operant conditioning and observational learning. Although there are a number of different EIBI programs, they have several features in common (Smith & Bryson, 2015).

First, the focus of EIBI is on children's *overt behavior*. Behavior therapists view ASD as consisting of a pattern of behavioral deficits and excesses. Deficits include problems in communication and social interaction. Excesses include stereotypies and tantrums. Treatment is designed to improve areas of deficit and reduce areas of excess. Behavior therapists do not focus primarily on constructs that are not readily observable, such as the parent–child attachment relationship or the way the child integrates or processes information. Instead, they focus on children's overt actions (Miltenberger, Miller, & Zerger, 2015).

Second, behavior therapists rely on *learning theory* to guide their interventions. They use modeling, prompting, and positive reinforcement to teach children new skills and to shape appropriate behavior.

Third, behavior therapists *structure the child's environment* to maximize learning. Typically developing children are constantly learning from their surroundings through their observation and imitation of others, dialogue, and exploratory play. However, children with ASD show deficits in all three areas, making it difficult for them to learn like other children. Put another way, there is a mismatch between the abilities of the child with ASD and his environment. To compensate for this mismatch, learning experiences are structured so that there is a high probability that children will succeed at learning, rather than fail.

Therapists use discrete trial training to simplify the learning experience and increase the probability of skill acquisition. Skills are taught systematically. Behaviors are selected by the therapist and are designed to build upon one another to gradually improve the child's functioning. One of the first behaviors a child may learn is to sit when prompted by the therapist. Another behavior frequently taught in initial training sessions is to maintain eye contact with the therapist. These behaviors are essential for the acquisition of more complex behaviors.

Discrete trial training typically occurs in a distraction-free setting. First, the therapist gets the child's attention, usually with a verbal prompt (e.g., calling the child's name) or physical prompt (e.g., gently positioning the child's head). Then, the therapist issues a clear and succinct verbal command, such as "Sit down." The therapist structures the environment so that it is relatively easy for the child to comply: A chair might be located immediately behind the child. Additionally, the therapist might physically prompt (e.g., nudge) the child backward so that she sits. Immediately after the child complies, she is positively reinforced. The choice of reinforcer depends on the child. Frequently used reinforcers include touching/hugging, verbal praise/smiling, or food/drink. The entire procedure is repeated multiple times, and prompting is gradually faded. The learning trial ends when the child successfully displays the behavior 85% to 90% of the time. Parents are then asked to practice the behavior at home (Wilczynski, McIntosh, Tullis, Cullen, & Querim, 2016).

The most well-known EIBI program is the UCLA Young Autism Project, developed by O. Ivar Lovaas. The program accepts children under 4 years of age who have ASD but no other major medical problems. The children participate in intensive behavioral training, approximately 40 hours per week, for about three years. Each child is trained individually; four or five therapists are assigned to each child. Training is typically conducted in the child's home (see Image 6.5).

Lovaas's EIBI program consists of six stages. As children progress through the stages, they acquire greater capacity for social interaction, language, and behavioral regulation. The first goal of training (Stage 1) is to establish a teaching relationship between the therapist and child. Discrete trial training is used almost exclusively to teach children basic skills necessary for later learning, such as how to sit down and maintain eye contact. Once children are able to attend to the therapist, training focuses on increasing the child's receptive vocabulary and imitation skills (Stage 2). The child is taught how to obey simple commands (e.g., "Pick up the cup") and discriminate between two commands (e.g., "Pick up the cup" when presented with a cup and a crayon). The child is also taught to imitate the therapist's actions, such as waving or clapping. Imitation is one of the easiest ways for children to acquire new skills or combine behaviors in novel ways. In Stage 3, the therapist increases the child's expressive vocabulary. Initially, the child is reinforced for imitating speech sounds (e.g., "aaahhh"), then words, then phrases, and finally simple sentences. The child is also reinforced for correctly labeling objects. Only about half of the children in the program are able to adequately imitate speech (Lovaas & Smith, 2003; Smith, Groen, & Wynn, 2000).

For those who show signs of emerging language, training focuses on expanding communication skills and using language during social interactions (Stage 4). At this stage, the child may begin preschool for typically developing children. The therapist focuses on improving the child's social skills. In Stage 5, the focus of training is on peer interactions. The therapist typically works with the child at home and at school, teaching skills such as initiating play with peers, asking for help in the classroom, and taking turns. Finally (Stage 6), children may be ready to enter a regular kindergarten classroom, and their training is discontinued. These children tend to have the best developmental outcomes. Other children will

Image 6.5   Three-year-old Joey has Autism Spectrum Disorder. He is participating in an early intensive behavior treatment program to help him improve his social communication skills. His therapist provides clear prompts; when he responds correctly, he is reinforced with praise and his favorite snack.

repeat preschool in order to acquire needed linguistic or social skills. Children who repeat preschool and continue to show marked delays usually need ongoing support services throughout their development (Lovaas, 1987; Lovaas & Smith, 2003).

A number of studies have examined the effectiveness of EIBI (Odom et al., 2015). Lovaas (1987) evaluated 59 children with ASD who were referred to the UCLA Young Autism Project. Children were assigned to three treatment groups, depending on the availability of therapists: (1) an experimental group that received 40 hours per week of training, (2) a control group that received less than 10 hours per week of training, and (3) a second control group that was referred to other professionals in the community for treatment. Most children referred to professionals in the community participated in special education. Results showed that children in the experimental group earned higher IQ scores than children in the control groups at age 7 years. Furthermore, 47% of children in the experimental group were identified as "best outcome" because they showed IQ scores above 85 and were placed in classrooms with typically developing peers. In contrast, only 3% of children in the control groups were described as "best outcome." Follow-up testing showed that the gains children displayed during preschool were maintained at age 12 (Lovaas, 1987; McEachin, Smith, & Lovaas, 1993; see Table 6.3).

These findings suggest that EIBI can be efficacious in improving the intellectual functioning of children with ASD. However, parents should not routinely expect the remarkable changes in IQ initially reported by Lovaas (1987). Programs that provide fewer hours of training per week are associated with more modest gains in IQ and perhaps no apparent gains in adaptive functioning (Smith et al., 2000).

Pivotal Response Training

Although discrete trial training can be effective, it has some limitations. One limitation is that discrete trial training may not increase children's spontaneous social or linguistic behavior. For example, a child with ASD might be taught to say, "Hello. How are you?" when introduced to a stranger, but she may not spontaneously ask questions or engage others unless prompted by caregivers. Many children with ASD often appear to have a low motivation to engage in spontaneous social or linguistic interactions, even after they have participated in extensive discrete trial training (Bottema-Beutel, Yoder, Woynaroski, & Sandbank, 2015).

A second limitation of discrete trial training is that the skills that children acquire via this method do not automatically generalize to new situations or people. For example, a child with ASD may be able to draw or color when prompted and monitored by her therapist, but she may have difficulty initiating and sustaining the behavior alone. Many children who learn behaviors through discrete trial training may become overly dependent on others to guide and regulate their activities; they often have problems with self-direction.

Pivotal response training is designed to increase the motivation and self-regulation skills of children with ASD (Bradshaw, Steiner, Gengoux, & Koegel, 2015). In pivotal response training, *parents* are taught behavioral techniques to improve children's motivation and self-regulation. Then, parents use these techniques in the home and community. Ideally, parent-guided treatment leads to improvement in children's functioning and the generalization of skills outside the therapy setting.

Pivotal response training differs from discrete trial training in several ways (Mohammadzaheri, Koegel, Rezaei, & Bakhshi, 2015). First, pivotal response training is conducted in naturalistic settings, like the home and community. The diversity of settings fosters generalization of skills. Second, the child, not the therapist, selects the focus of the social interaction. For example, if a child is playing with a certain toy, the therapist takes the child's lead and begins an interaction addressing aspects of the toy. This technique maximizes the child's interest in learning. Third, the therapist uses reinforcers that are naturally tied to the learning experience or the child's behavior. For example, giving the child access to a toy car is a natural reinforcer for saying the word *car*. In contrast, giving the child food or drink for saying the word *car* is not directly related to the child's behavior. The use of natural reinforcers strengthens

Table 6.3   The Efficacy of Early Intensive Behavioral Intervention

Group	Mean IQ Score			Best Outcome (%)	
	Pretreatment	Age 7	Age 12	Age 7	Age 12
EIBI (40 hrs/wk)	63	83	85	47	42
Minimal treatment (< 10 hrs/wk)	57	52	55	0	0
Special education	60	59	–	5	–

Source: Based on Lovaas and Smith (2003); Lovaas (1987); and McEachin et al. (1993).

Note: EIBI = Early intensive behavioral intervention. Best Outcome = IQ score > 85 and unassisted placement in regular education classroom.

the child's understanding of the behavior-consequence relationship and more closely resembles events in the real world. Finally, the therapist reinforces children for their *attempts* at social or linguistic interaction, rather than for successfully engaging in the behavior. If the therapist reinforces attempts, the child is more likely to initiate novel behaviors in the future.

Pivotal response training can also be used to increase children's *motivation* to verbally engage others (Koegel, Koegel, & Brookman, 2005). For example, parents teach children simple questions, such as "What is that?" "Where is it?" and "Whose is it?" Then, parents model, prompt, and reinforce children's use of the questions in naturalistic settings. As children gradually master the use of these questions, prompts can be faded. Reinforcement comes from the child's interactions with the environment, not from the parents. Indeed, simple questions and verbal statements can replace functionally equivalent disruptive behaviors. For example, a child with ASD might tantrum during a meal because his parents do not give him much attention. To correct these tantrums, the child might be taught to use functionally equivalent questions (e.g., "Am I being good?") or statements (e.g., "Talk to me") that attract the parents' attention in more appropriate ways.

Parents use a similar procedure to increase children's self-direction. First, they select a target behavior. For example, parents may want their children to be able to play independently for 30 minutes so that they can perform

household chores. Second, parents identify a natural reinforcer for the target behavior. If the child enjoys playing with toy cars, access to the cars can be contingent on independent play. Third, parents demonstrate appropriate and inappropriate independent play to the child. For example, appropriate play might be sitting in the living room, playing with cars on the floor. Inappropriate play might be leaving the room, playing with the cars on the piano, or engaging in stereotypies or disruptive behavior. Fourth, parents teach the child to self-monitor the target behavior. Initially, parents can prompt children every few minutes by asking, "Are you playing quietly?" Appropriate play could be reinforced with access to an additional toy car. Eventually, the prompts are given less often, the schedule of reinforcement is decreased, and children are able to monitor and reinforce their own behavior.

Data supporting the use of pivotal response training comes from both randomized controlled trials and single-subject studies. Overall, approximately 80% of studies show large improvements in children's social communication, play, and language skills (Bozkus-Genc & Yucesoy-Ozkan, 2016). Furthermore, these benefits persist after treatment (Gengoux et al., 2015). Other studies have shown that pivotal response training can be effectively applied in community settings (Smith, Flanagan, Garon, & Bryson, 2015) and, when administered correctly, can be as effective as traditional EIBI (Mohammadzaheri et al., 2015; see the following Research to Practice section).

TEACCH

The Treatment and Education of Autistic and Related Communication-Handicapped Children (TEACCH) approach was developed by Eric Schopler, a student of Bettelheim. Schopler disagreed with Bettelheim's assertion that cold and rejecting mothers caused autism. Schopler and colleagues developed a comprehensive program for youths with ASD that stressed understanding and compassion for these children and their families (Mesibov, Howley, & Naftel, 2015).

TEACCH relies heavily on principles of operant conditioning and observational learning. It is administered in a specialized classroom environment. The focus of treatment is to help children with ASD fit comfortably and effectively in the classroom. This is accomplished in two ways. First, therapists try to expand children's behavioral repertoire by teaching them new social, communicative, and daily living skills. Second, therapists attempt to structure the child's environment to increase the likelihood that the child can complete activities successfully and independently (Mesibov, Shea, & Schopler, 2005; Siegel & Ficcaglia, 2006).

TEACCH practitioners used a method of instruction called structured teaching. As its name implies, structured teaching involves a variety of structures and supports to help children understand and master the classroom environment. The technique capitalizes on the developmental principle of scaffolding. Just as a physical

scaffold supports a building as it is being constructed, a behavioral scaffold guides and supports the developing child as he learns new skills through interactions with his environment (Vygotsky, 1978).

Scaffolding can be seen in the classroom setting. The classroom itself is highly organized and predictable. Activity stations are clearly partitioned, color-coded, and labeled so that children can understand what behavior is to be performed in each location. Stations are also structured to minimize distractions. Within each station, therapists use colors, pictures, shapes, and other prompts so that children can complete activities successfully. For example, in the bathroom area, the soap, water faucet, and towel might be assigned the same color to remind children to use all three objects when washing. In the closet, silhouettes of children's coats might be painted on the wall under pegs, to prompt children to hang up their coats when entering the classroom. Children's desks or work stations might be labeled with their pictures or names (Mesibov et al., 2005).

Scaffolding of daily activities can also be seen in the use of visual schedules. Since many young children with ASD have limited language, therapists rely heavily on pictures and symbols to organize and direct children's behavior. A visual schedule might consist of a list of pictures outlining the child's activities for the day. Children can refer to visual schedules throughout the day to help them transition from one activity to the next with minimal help. Children can also monitor their progress in daily activities by checking off tasks as they complete them.

Scaffolding is also used to help children perform individual activities. Imagine that the therapist wants to teach the child to brush his teeth. The therapist avoids using verbal instruction. Instead, the therapist teaches the skill by first breaking the activity into small, easy steps and labeling these steps using a visual prompt. The steps required to brush teeth might be presented in picture form on a card placed near the sink. Then, the therapist clearly and slowly demonstrates each step. Next, the therapist helps the child perform each step using hand-over-hand assistance (i.e., the therapist guides the child's hands with her own). The therapist gradually replaces her physical prompts with gestures (e.g., pointing to the water faucet) or simple verbal prompts (e.g., "turn off"). The activity is periodically repeated until the child can perform it independently.

Scaffolding is also used to improve communication. First, the therapist teaches the child to associate single objects with specific activities. For example, a spoon might represent "eating lunch," a roll of toilet paper "using the bathroom," and a small plastic shovel "going outside for recess." Children learn to use these physical objects to communicate a desire to engage in their corresponding activities. A child who wants to use the bathroom might bring the roll of toilet paper to the teacher. Later, physical objects are gradually replaced by more abstract representations for these activities. For example, the child might communicate a desire to use the toilet by presenting the teacher with a photograph or drawing of the toilet.

Techniques used by therapists in the classroom are also taught to parents, so that skills can generalize to the home. Each family is assigned two therapists; one works primarily with the child while the other serves chiefly as a "parent consultant." The consultant helps parents learn about ASD and the basic principles of learning and scaffolding. The therapist then teaches parents the techniques used in the classroom. In most cases, the therapist watches parents use these same techniques with their own children and coaches parents to help them use the techniques most effectively. Consultants may also conduct home visits to help parents structure the home in an organized, predictable way (Mesibov et al., 2015).

Several randomized controlled trials and quasi-experimental studies support the efficacy of TEACCH. On average, children who participate in TEACCH show large improvements in social communication and reductions in problem behavior. The effects of TEACCH on children's cognitive skills, spoken language, and motor functioning, although significant, are more modest (Virues-Ortega, Julio, & Pastor-Barriuso, 2013).

Review:

- EIBI relies on discrete trial training to improve the social communication and language skills of young children with ASD. EIBI is associated with increases in IQ and social functioning when administered by well-trained therapists on a frequent basis.

- Pivotal response training is a behavioral intervention in which parents use natural reinforcers to increase children's motivation to engage in social interactions. A secondary goal of the program is to improve children's ability to direct their own behavior.
- TEACCH is a classroom-based intervention that relies on a highly structured environment and scaffolding to improve social communication and reduce challenging behaviors in children with ASD.

What Treatments Are Effective for At-Risk Infants and Toddlers?

Social communication prevention and treatment programs typically target older infants and toddlers who begin to show signs of ASD (Rogers & Vismara, 2015). These interventions systematically teach early social communication skills that are often delayed in children with the disorder. Skills include children's capacity for joint attention, social imitation, and pretend play. Nonverbal social communication skills are taught in naturalistic settings by clinicians or parents and tailored to the developmental needs of the child. The hope is that improvements in these early social communication skills will lead to corresponding improvements in later social functioning (Berger & Ingersoll, 2015).

For example, Ingersoll (2010b) has developed reciprocal imitation training (RIT), a naturalistic intervention designed to improve imitation skills in toddlers and preschoolers with ASD. RIT is administered by a therapist in a

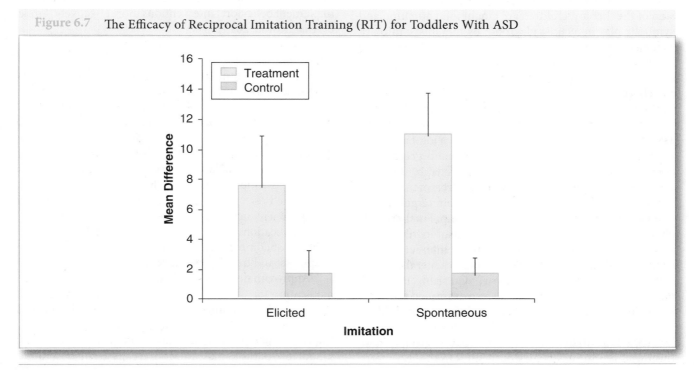

Figure 6.7   The Efficacy of Reciprocal Imitation Training (RIT) for Toddlers With ASD

Source: From Ingersoll (2010a). Used with permission.

Note: RIT increases elicited and spontaneous imitations in toddlers and preschoolers with ASD. Children learn to imitate play with objects and imitate the therapist's gestures.

clinic playroom. As children play, the therapist imitates the child's action with a duplicate toy. For example, if the child plays with a toy dog, the therapist might imitate the child's action by "walking" another toy dog across the table. As children play, the therapist teaches them to imitate gestures by modeling actions associated with their play activities. For example, if the child plays with a baby doll, the therapist might put her hands to her lips and gesture "shh" as if the baby is sleeping. Therapists also prompt children to imitate therapists' own actions and gestures and praise children for using imitation during therapy sessions.

Ingersoll (2010a) randomly assigned young children with ASD to receive either 30 sessions of RIT or to participate in treatment as usual in the community. After 10 weeks of treatment, children who received RIT showed a greater increase in elicited and spontaneous imitation of objects and gestures than children in the control group (see Figure 6.7). A second randomized controlled trial (Ingersoll, 2012) also showed that children who received RIT showed better social–emotional functioning after treatment than controls. However, increased imitation did not seem to explain the corresponding increase in social–emotional functioning. Nevertheless, these findings provide initial evidence for the usefulness of RIT in improving early social communication skills.

A second naturalistic intervention for young children is joint attention symbolic play engagement and regulation (JASPER). As its name implies, JASPER was designed to improve the joint attention and symbolic play abilities of 3- and 4-year-olds with ASD (Kasari, Gulsrud, Paparella, Hellemann, & Berry, 2015). In the original version of the therapy, children are taught joint attention and symbolic play in a clinic playroom by therapists. Initially, therapists use principles of applied behavior analysis to prompt, model, and reinforce a desired behavior. Later, however, therapists follow the child's play activities, imitate the child's actions, and look for opportunities to model, prompt, and reinforce joint attention and symbolic play.

In one evaluation study, researchers randomly assigned preschoolers with ASD to either a joint attention treatment group, a symbolic play treatment group, or a control group (Kasari, Freeman, & Paparella, 2006). After 6 weeks of treatment, children in the treatment groups showed significant improvement in their targeted skill compared to children in the control group. Furthermore, children in the treatment groups also exhibited an increase in their targeted behavior while interacting with parents, indicating that they were able to generalize these behaviors to new people. Kasari, Gulsrud, Freeman, Paparella, and Hellemann (2012) also examined the long-term outcomes of these children. Five years later, children who participated in the treatment groups showed better language skills than children in the control group. These findings support the efficacy of JASPER in the short term (i.e., improving social communication skills) and long term (i.e., improving language).

Since the initial validation study, JASPER has been developed so that it can be administered by parents (Kasari, Gulsrud, Wong, Kwon, & Locke, 2010) and teachers (Lawton & Kasari, 2012) with minimal training. It has also demonstrated efficacy in improving social communication skills in nonverbal preschoolers with ASD (Goods, Ishijima, Chang, & Kasari, 2013).

Review:

- Prevention programs seek to improve the early social communication skills of children at-risk for ASD.
- RIT teaches imitation skills. Therapists imitate children's play and reinforce children for imitating gestures and other actions.
- JASPER relies on discrete trial training to improve joint attention and symbolic play in young children with ASD. Treatment can be delivered by therapists, parents, or teachers.

Is Medication Effective for Youths With Autism Spectrum Disorder?

Only behavioral interventions, like EIBI and pivotal response training, are effective at reducing the core symptoms of ASD. However, physicians frequently prescribe medications to reduce other behavior problems that might interfere with treatment. Overall, 64% of children with ASD have been prescribed at least one psychotropic medication, 35% use two medications, and 15% use three or more (Spencer et al., 2014). The goal of pharmacotherapy is to remove barriers to treatment so that parents, teachers, and therapists can implement behavioral interventions more effectively (Smile & Anagnostou, 2015).

Children with ASD and ID frequently display challenging behaviors, such as irritability, self-injury, and/or aggression (Machalicek et al., 2016). Ideally, challenging behaviors can be identified using functional analysis and reduced using operant conditioning (see Chapter 5). In some cases, medications can be used to supplement behavior therapy. The FDA has approved two medications, aripiprazole (Abilify) and risperidone (Risperdal), for children with ASD who exhibit challenging behaviors. These medications are atypical antipsychotics, which block dopamine receptors in the brain. On average, 50% to 70% of youths with ASD show a reduction in challenging behavior while taking these medications, compared to 12% to 35% taking placebo. Their most common side effects are weight gain, daytime sleepiness, and tremors (Smile & Anagnostou, 2015).

Approximately 16% of youths with ASD receive medication for ADHD (Dalsgaard, Nielsen, & Simonsen, 2013). Several randomized controlled studies indicate that the stimulant medication methylphenidate (Concerta, Ritalin) reduces hyperactivity and inattention at home and school for youths with ASD. More recent studies also show the nonstimulant medication atomoxetine (Strattera) to be effective. Side effects include insomnia and appetite suppression (especially for stimulants) and gastrointestinal problems (Smile & Anagnostou, 2015).

As many as 80% of youths with ASD experience sleep problems. Sleep problems may be caused by children's heightened sensitivity to stimuli, comorbid behavior problems (e.g., ADHD), or the effects of medication (e.g., stimulants). Because no medications are approved for treating sleep problems in children with ASD, behavioral interventions are the first-line treatment (see Chapter 16). However, some physicians prescribe melatonin to alleviate insomnia. Melatonin is a naturally occurring hormone that regulates the body's sleep–wake cycle. A synthetic version can be taken as a dietary supplement. Melatonin has been shown to help children with ASD fall asleep faster and stay asleep longer (Greydanus, Kaplan, & Patel, 2015).

Review:

- Medication is typically used to reduce challenging behaviors and comorbid mental disorders experienced by youths with ASD.
- The atypical antipsychotic medications aripiprazole (Abilify) and risperidone (Risperdal) are useful in reducing irritability, self-injury, and physical aggression in children with ASD.
- Medications are also sometimes prescribed to children with ASD for comorbid ADHD or sleep problems.

How Can Clinicians Improve Communication in Youths With Autism Spectrum Disorder?

Augmentative and Alternative Communication

Approximately 25% of children with ASD have considerable difficulty speaking to others; many of these children are functionally mute. To help these youths communicate, professionals have developed augmentative and alternative communication (AAC) systems (Sturmey, 2014a).

Augmentative and alternative communication (AAC) systems compensate for the language deficits shown by some children with ASD and facilitate their communication skills. AAC systems can be used to temporarily augment children's communication as they acquire greater language skills, or they may be used as a permanent means to compensate for language deficits. In either case, AAC systems are meant to complement, not replace, children's verbal language (Lynch, 2016).

There are four components of all AAC systems: (1) *symbols*, (2) *aids*, (3) *strategies*, and (4) *techniques* (American Speech-Language-Hearing Association, 2016).

1. Symbols are the representations of objects or actions that the child uses to communicate. For example, a symbol of someone waving might be used to communicate "hello." Symbols can be rudimentary (e.g., a stick figure) or complex (e.g., a photograph).

2. Aids are the devices that children use to send or receive messages. Some aids use little technology, such as cards containing single drawings, which are used to communicate important objects and actions. Other aids are highly sophisticated, such as tablet devices that contain pictures that, when pressed, indicate the desired object or action.

3. Strategies refer to the way in which symbols and aids are organized. For example, some AAC systems rely on a color-coding strategy, in which symbols that represent similar objects or actions are grouped together using the same color (e.g., line drawings that represent "hungry," "thirsty," and "bathroom" are colored similarly). Other, high-tech AAC systems use prediction strategies to speed communication. For example, electronic devices may try to predict the children's desired word or phrase based on the first few letters he types, much like a search engine.

4. Techniques refers to the methods that the child uses to communicate. Techniques include pointing at a symbol, pressing a button, or scanning through symbols and verbally indicating a choice.

Therapists and families choose from the wide range of the available symbols, aids, strategies, and techniques to build an AAC system for their child. Selection depends mostly on the needs of the child and preferences of the family. Because there are so many options, we will focus on two of the most popular systems (Lofland, 2016).

Picture Exchange Communication System

Frost and Bondy (2002) developed the Picture Exchange Communication System (PECS) as a means to improve the communicative functioning of children with language deficits. PECS is a low-tech AAC system that consists of a series of line drawings or simple pictures printed on cards (see Figure 6.8). These symbols represent common objects or actions that children can present to caregivers to communicate their needs. For example, a line drawing of a toilet might be used to communicate "bathroom." Later, children learn to combine cards to ask questions and convey more complex ideas.

Practitioners of PECS use positive reinforcement to associate picture symbols with objects or activities in the environment. To accomplish this task, therapists teach children to exchange a picture–symbol of an object or activity for a desired item or action (Lynch, 2016).

Training consists of six phases that can occur over several days to several weeks. In the first phase, the child learns to exchange pictures of commonly used objects in his environment for primary reinforcers, like a favorite food or drink. The child is seated at a table in front of a 2 in. x 2 in. laminated drawing. The drawing represents a common object in the child's environment such as a cup. Two therapists provide the training. One therapist serves as the child's communicative partner. She tells the child to give her "cup." The second therapist sits behind the child and physically guides the child to pick up the card and hand it to the first therapist. The first therapist immediately

Figure 6.8   Using PECS to Help Children Communicate

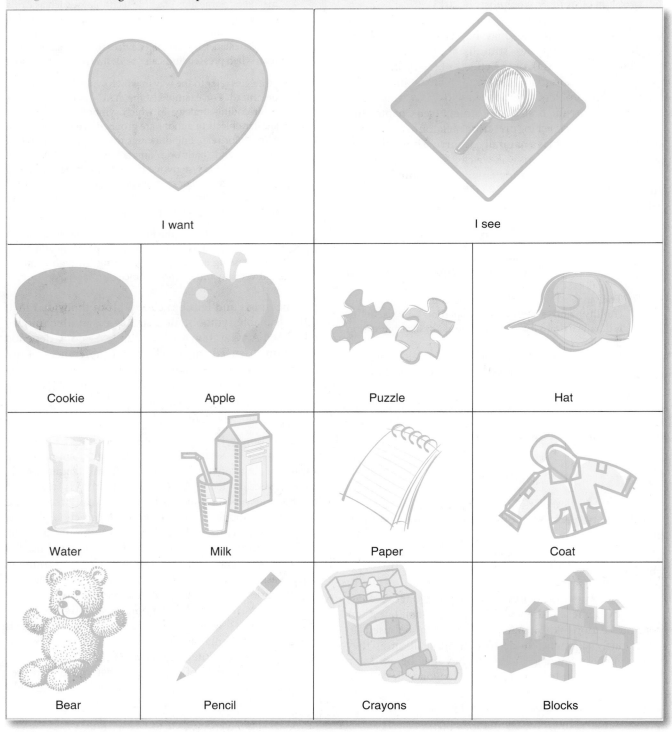

| I want | I see |

Cookie	Apple	Puzzle	Hat
Water	Milk	Paper	Coat
Bear	Pencil	Crayons	Blocks

Note: Children can use the Picture Exchange Communication System (PECS) to communicate. They might point to "I want" and "water" to request a drink.

reinforces the child. The procedure is repeated several times, with the second therapist gradually fading the amount of help she provides. The training session continues until the child is able to independently exchange the picture for the reinforcer 80% of the time.

After the child learns basic exchanges, he develops more complex, expressive language skills. In Phase 2, the child is taught to initiate social interactions by getting the attention of adults and handing them a picture card. In Phase 3, the child learns to discriminate among many pictures in an array. For example, if the child is presented with pictures of a tree, a car, and a house, the child learns to successfully give the picture of the house when asked. In Phases 4 and 5, children learn to form sentences and answer questions using the pictures. In the final phase, children expand on previously mastered skills to express more complex needs and desires using the picture–symbols (Nelson, 2016).

Many studies have investigated the effectiveness of PECS and other low-tech AACs for children with limited verbal language. Overall, these systems yield large effects on children' functional communication skills. Furthermore, they may also be helpful in reducing challenging behavior by allowing youths to convey their

thoughts and feelings rather than act out (Heath, Ganz, Parker, Burke, & Ninci, 2015).

Speech-Generating Devices

Tablets, smartphones, and other mobile touchscreen devices have given youths with ASD and their families new options for communication (Durand, 2015). Many youths with limited verbal skills rely on applications that allow them to press icons on their device to convey their needs or share their feelings. Once pressed, the device emits speech that is easily understood by others. Frequently used speech-generating apps include Pic a Word, PixTalk, and Proloquo2Go (see Image 6.6). Users can customize the app to include frequently used objects and places (e.g., pencil,

Image 6.6   Proloquo2Go is an app that allows children with ASD and language impairment to communicate by pressing icons. In this case, a child can use an iPhone or tablet to order lunch.

Source: From Sennott and Bowker (2009). Used with permission.

bathroom), favorite foods, and customized pictures of family members and friends. Children can also learn to combine icons to convey more complex thoughts. For example, a child who wants to play with his brother, Joseph, and his toy trains can select icons for "I want," "Joseph," and "trains."

Other youths augment their communication using visual scene displays (VSDs). Whereas most systems organize symbols semantically (e.g., by word meaning), VSDs organize them schematically in the context of a picture. For example, a girl's tablet device might include a schematic of her classroom. She might press various "hot spots" on the schematic to communicate. Pressing the image of the teacher might communicate "I need help" whereas pressing the image of "pencil" on the desk in the picture might indicate "I want my pencil." Different visual scenes can be used in different contexts (e.g., school, mealtime, bedroom). VSDs are especially useful with toddlers who have trouble using more complex pictures or symbols. Indeed, VSDs have been effectively used with children as young as 2 years of age (Lofland, 2016).

Researchers are just beginning to systematically investigate the effectiveness of touch screen communication systems for youths with ASD. The available research, involving mostly single-subject studies, indicate that most youths with ASD can learn to use these systems, even children with comorbid ID. Furthermore, they can be as effective as low-tech systems such as PECS (Boesch, Wendt, Subramanian, & Hsu, 2015; Stephenson & Limbrick, 2015).

Review:

- AAC systems can be used to supplement the communication skills of children with ASD.
- PECS is a low-tech AAC system in which children communicate by pointing to or exchanging cards with symbols or pictures that represent actions, feelings, ideas, or objects.
- Many youths with ASD and language deficits rely on speech-generating devices or VSDs to communicate with others.

What Interventions Have Limited Empirical Support?

Table 6.4 provides a partial list of popular treatments for ASD that have limited empirical support. These treatments include interventions designed to increase children's social skills (e.g., "holding therapy" and "pet therapy"), communication skills (e.g., "facilitated communication"), emotional and behavioral functioning (e.g., "art/music therapy"), and sensorimotor functioning (e.g., "sensory integration training"). Other treatments include the use of mental telepathy, the consumption of fish oil and thyme, and the injection of stem cells (Dowrick, 2015)!

There are at least three reasons parents might select treatments with limited empirical support. First, many parents are not aware of the scientific data regarding treatments

Table 6.4   Treatments for Autism With Limited Empirical Support

Therapy	Description
Holding therapy	Based on the incorrect notion that children with autism have disturbed attachment to their mothers and that autistic behaviors are the child's way of withdrawing from the mother's rejection; therapist encourages "mother-child holding" to repair the broken attachment bond
Pet therapy	Contact with animals such as cats, dogs, horses, and dolphins is believed to reduce children's anxiety, improve social and communicative skills, and teach decision making and responsibility; some advocates believe dolphins' use of sonar and echolocation causes physiological changes in children's bodies, leading to improvement in functioning
Facilitated communication	Based on the incorrect notion that individuals with autism who are unable to communicate verbally can communicate when assisted by trained professionals; professionals facilitate communication by guiding the patient's hand as he points to symbols/pictures or types messages; evaluations of facilitated communication indicate that "messages" from individuals with autism are likely sent by the professionals who assist them, not by the patients themselves
Auditory integration training	Based on the idea that children with autism have extremely sensitive hearing and that autistic signs are caused by auditory discomfort; children receive auditory training by listening to specialized recordings of music on headphones
Art/music therapy	Art therapy is believed to allow nonverbal expression through drawing, painting, and sculpting; music therapy involves listening to specific musical pieces or playing instruments to reduce anxiety, reinforce positive behavior, and permit self-expression
Megavitamin/diet therapies	Based on the notion that nutritional deficiencies underlie autism; some advocates recommend supplements of B6 and magnesium, other dietary supplements, or avoidance of certain foods
Irlen lenses	Based on the belief that autism is caused by a perceptual disturbance related to difficulties processing light, called scotopic sensitivity; children wear tinted glasses

Source: Based on Simpson et al. (2005).

for ASD. Most parents do not have access to reputable journals and professional newsletters. Even if they did, published empirical studies are often difficult to read and evaluate. Consequently, most parents might rely on advice from doctors, paraprofessionals, or well-meaning friends—advice that might not be based in scientific research.

Second, most parents have turned to therapists in their communities for help but did not see improvements in their children. Unfortunately, many practitioners do not rely on evidence-based treatments for ASD, such as EIBI or pivotal response training. Those that do may not be able to deliver the intensive, highly structured services that yield the best outcomes for children. Parents who try these less-than-optimal interventions and who meet with limited success may turn to other, less-supported therapies in the hope that these treatments might help their children.

Finally, these pseudo-scientific "treatments" have seductive appeal (Miller, Schreck, Mulick, & Butter, 2012). For example, an increasingly popular intervention is "equine assisted therapy," in which youths with ASD and other disabilities interact with horses. Some practitioners claim their therapy can cure anything from sensory deficits and physical health problems to ASD and posttraumatic stress disorder (PTSD; see Image 6.7). Websites also make broad, unsupported claims like, "Equine-assisted work often helps clients change and grow more effectively and quickly than traditional clinical and psycho-educational approaches" (EAGALA, 2016).

To help parents and practitioners identify evidence-based interventions for ASD, the Society of Clinical Child and Adolescent Psychology maintains a website (effectivechildtherapy.org) that describes treatment options with the greatest empirical support. Furthermore, the National Professional Development Center on Autism Spectrum Disorders (2016) has identified six components of evidence-based treatment for ASD that are most likely to yield benefits to children and families:

1. Effective treatment involves *early identification and intervention*. The best outcomes occur when treatment begins before age 3. Infants, toddlers, and preschool-age children in the community should be periodically screened for ASD to identify the disorder and intervene early.

2. Second, treatment must be *intensive*. Children with the best outcomes participate in full-time educational treatment all year long. Some research suggests a dose-response effect for treatment—that is, children who received full-time treatment (i.e., 40 hours per week) showed significantly greater improvement than children who received less intensive treatment (e.g., 20 hours per week). The committee recommended a minimum of 25 hours of instruction per week, extended across the entire calendar year.

3. Treatment must involve *repeated, planned, and structured learning opportunities*. Examples of learning opportunities include discrete trial training, pivotal response training, or structured teaching. Regardless

Image 6.7 Equine Therapy

Note: Equine therapy is sometimes recommended for children with ASD and other psychiatric conditions. Proponents argue that children's functioning improves as they interact with horses. No randomized controlled studies support this claim.

of the approach, training should be geared toward the needs of the child.

4. Treatment programs should have *low student-to-teacher ratios*. Ideally, instruction occurs on a 1:1 basis. However, treatment programs for very young children should not have more than two children for each therapist. Ideally, each child should have only a limited number of therapists, to maintain consistency in treatment.

5. *Parents must be active* in their children's treatment. Parents' participation in treatment is strongly associated with their children's outcomes. Parental participation in the program increases generalization of children's skills from school to home and provides children with more opportunities to practice skills across contexts.

6. Programs must *monitor children's progress* in treatment and alter intervention strategies to meet children's needs and developing skills. No two children with ASD are alike. Consequently, not all children with ASD will respond to any single intervention. Intervention strategies need to be tailored to individual children and modified during the course of treatment in order to produce the greatest benefits.

Review:

- Many popular interventions for ASD, such as special diets, sensory integration training, and equine assisted therapy have limited empirical support.
- Parents may select therapies with limited support because they are not familiar with the research literature, because their child did not improve in traditional therapy, or because evidence-based treatments are not available in their communities.
- Best practices include early identification and treatment, intensive and structured learning opportunities, low student-to-teacher ratios, and high parental involvement.

Amygdala: A brain region located in the limbic system; important to emotional processing

Augmentative and alternative communication (AAC) systems: Techniques used to supplement the communication skills of children with ASD as they acquire spoken language or compensate for spoken language in children who are mute

Autism and Developmental Disabilities Monitoring (ADDM) Network: A group of programs funded by the Centers for Disease Control and Prevention to estimate the number of children with ASD in the United States, using medical and educational records

Autism Genome Project: The largest private/public partnership studies, involving researchers from 19 countries, investigating the genetic causes of ASD

Autism spectrum disorder (ASD): A *DSM-5* disorder characterized by persistent deficits in social communication and the presence of restricted, repetitive patterns of behavior, interests, or activities that begin in early life and cause significant impairment in social functioning

Diffusion tensor imaging (DTI): A neuroimaging technique that provides a high-resolution image of white matter; allows researchers to determine the strength of neural connections

Discrete trial training: A behavioral technique to teach skills to children; each skill is broken into component parts; each part is systematically introduced, modeled, practiced, and reinforced; parts are combined to produce more complex behaviors

Early intensive behavioral intervention (EIBI): A behavioral treatment for ASD that relies on intensive use of direct instruction to teach and reinforce social communication and language skills

Echolalia: The repetition of words uttered by others

Empathy: The ability to take the perspective of another person in order to understand her thoughts, intentions, and feelings

Executive functioning: Activities such as planning, prioritizing, and delaying gratification to meet long-term goals; believed to be regulated by the prefrontal cortex

False belief task: A laboratory-based test of theory of mind using dolls

Growth dysregulation hypothesis: Posits that youths with ASD show abnormal maturation of the cortex, large head circumference, and high synaptic density in early childhood but poor neural connectivity, especially in brain regions responsible for social communication and language

Hand-over-hand assistance: A scaffolding technique to help children acquire new skills; the therapist guides the child's hands with her own

Joint attention symbolic play engagement and regulation (JASPER): An intervention for young children at-risk for ASD; relies on discrete trial training to improve joint attention and symbolic play in young children

Joint attention: An infant's ability to share attention with a caregiver on a single object or event in the outside world; often delayed in children with ASD

MSSNG: A project involving the genetic mapping of 10,000 individuals with ASD with the goal of determining the genetic risk factors for the disorder; data are shared with scientists using a public platform

National Health Interview Survey (NHIS): Annual survey that provides nationally representative estimates on a wide range of disorders in the United States; child prevalence estimates are based on caregivers' reports

Picture Exchange Communication System (PECS): A low-tech AAC in which children communicate by pointing to or exchanging cards with symbols or pictures that represent actions, feelings, ideas, or objects

Pivotal response training: A behavioral intervention usually administered by parents in naturalistic settings; designed to increase the motivation and self-regulation skills of children with ASD

Pragmatics: The use of language in specific social contexts, especially the natural give-and-take that occurs during conversation and the ability to tell coherent stories with appropriate background information; often impaired in youths with ASD

Prosody: The pattern of stress or intonation in a person's speech; sometimes atypical in children with ASD

Reciprocal imitation training (RIT): An intervention for young children at risk for ASD; teaches imitation skills through modeling and natural reinforcers

Restricted, repetitive patterns of behavior, interests, or activities: A problem shown by all youths with ASD; characterized by (a) stereotyped or repetitive behaviors, (b) excessive adherence to routines or resistance to change, (c) restricted, fixated interests, or (d) hyper- or hyporeactivity to sensory input

Right fusiform gyrus: A brain region responsible for processing human faces and interpreting social behavior; often underactive in youths with ASD

Scaffolding: A term used by Vygotsky to describe guidance and support provided to help children learn new skills as they interact with the environment

Social communication: A deficit shown by all youths with ASD; reflects problems with (a) social–emotional reciprocity, (b) nonverbal communication, or (c) interpersonal relationships

Social orientation: A child's ability to attend to, and interact with, important aspects of interpersonal interactions (e.g., eyes, faces, emotional expressions, interactions between people); often delays in children with ASD

Structured teaching: A component on TEACCH; the use of structures and supports to help children understand and master the classroom environment

Symbolic play: The child's ability to allow one object to represent another object; important for language acquisition; often delayed in children with ASD

Theory of mind: The understanding that people have mental states (e.g., thoughts, beliefs, intentions) that motivate their behavior; often deficient in children with ASD

Treatment and Education of Autistic and Related Communication-Handicapped Children (TEACCH): A classroom-based intervention that relies on a highly structured and scaffolding to improve the social communication and reduce challenging behaviors in children with ASD

UCLA Young Autism Project: An EIBI study conducted by Lovaas and colleagues that relied on discrete trial training for young children with ASD who were largely nonverbal; demonstrated gains in IQ and language

Visual schedules: A chart containing pictures and symbols to organize and direct children's daily behavior at home or school

CRITICAL THINKING EXERCISES

1. What does it mean when professionals refer to autism as existing on a "spectrum"?

2. In retrospect, many parents recall that their children with ASD exhibited problems with social communication and behavior in infancy and toddlerhood. However, in most cases, ASD is not diagnosed until the preschool years. Why?

3. Explain the concept of discrete trial training. How might a therapist use discrete trial training to teach a child with ASD and ID to identify a penny, a nickel, and a dime?

4. Imagine that you are a third-grade teacher. You have learned that a transfer student, a boy with ASD and ID, will be beginning your class in 2 weeks. What might you do with the other students in your class to prepare them for their interactions with this newcomer?

5. Your neighbor has a son with ASD. She is considering flying herself and her son to another state to participate in a 1-week sensory integration therapy program that promises to improve his social functioning. What might you say to your neighbor regarding her plan?

TEST YOURSELF AND EXTEND YOUR LEARNING

Videos, flash cards, and links to online resources for this chapter are available to students online. Teachers also have access to PowerPoint slides to guide lectures, case studies to prompt classroom discussions, and exam questions. Visit www.abnormalchildpsychology.org.

CHAPTER 7

Communication and Learning Disorders

7.1 COMMUNICATION DISORDERS

Communication and learning disorders are among the most common, and most overlooked, neurodevelopmental disorders experienced by children (Bishop & Rutter, 2010). Whereas most people are familiar with Down syndrome and autism spectrum disorder (ASD), relatively few people have heard of language disorder or know much about the causes of learning disabilities. Despite their "Cinderella status" among early childhood disorders, approximately 15% of youths have one or more of these conditions. Furthermore, longitudinal studies indicate that these disorders can lead to short- and long-term problems with children's academic attainment, behavior, and social functioning (Cortiella & Horowitz, 2014).

What Is Language Disorder?

Description

Language refers to communication in which beliefs, knowledge, and skills are experienced, expressed, and shared. It involves the complex manipulation and organization of auditory or visual symbols according to a system of rules that is determined by one's culture. Language can be spoken, signed, or written. Between 6 and 8 million people in the United States have some form of language impairment that interferes with their ability to communicate with others (Angell, 2009).

Language disorder is diagnosed when children show marked problems in the acquisition and use of language due to deficits in comprehension or production. Children with language disorder have trouble with grammar or sentence structure or have more general problems sharing their thoughts and feelings. By definition, language disorder is not explained by intellectual disability (ID) or a physical disability, such as hearing loss (see Table 7.1; American Psychiatric Association, 2013).

Table 7.1 Diagnostic Criteria for Language Disorder

A. Persistent difficulties in the acquisition and use of language across modalities (i.e., spoken, written, sign language) due to deficits in comprehension or production that include the following:

1. Reduced vocabulary (word knowledge and use).

2. Limited sentence structure (ability to put words and word endings together to form sentences based on the rules of grammar and morphology).

3. Impairments in discourse (ability to use vocabulary and connect sentences to explain or describe a topic or series of events or have a conversation).

B. Language abilities are substantially and quantifiably below those expected for age, resulting in functional limitations in effective communication, social participation, academic achievement, or occupational performance, individually or in combination.

C. Onset of symptoms is in the early developmental period.

D. The difficulties are not attributable to hearing or other sensory impairment, motor dysfunction, or another medical or neurological condition and are not better explained by Intellectual Disability or Global Developmental Delay.

Source: Reprinted with permission from the *Diagnostic and Statistical Manual of Mental Disorders, Fifth Edition* (Copyright 2013). American Psychiatric Association.

The *Diagnostic and Statistical Manual of Mental Disorders (DSM-5;* American Psychiatric Association, 2013) does not specify how language disorder should be assessed and identified. In practice, however, language disorder is typically diagnosed in toddlers and preschool-age children who earn language scores more than 1.25 standard deviations below the mean on standardized language tests (e.g., <80), have nonverbal IQ scores within with the average range (e.g., >85), and otherwise appear healthy. Children with language disorder, therefore, show impairment that is specific to their language skills rather than general intellectual impairments or global developmental delay (GDD).

Children with language disorder can show problems with receptive language, expressive language, or both aspects of communication. Receptive language is the ability to listen to and understand communication. One test of receptive language is the Peabody Picture Vocabulary Test, Fourth Edition. On this test, the psychologist presents four pictures to the child and asks her to point to the picture that shows a specific word or idea. The test assesses receptive vocabulary because the child indicates her understanding by pointing, not by speaking or writing. In contrast, expressive language refers to the ability to share beliefs, knowledge, and skills with others. One test of expressive language is the Expressive One-Word Picture Vocabulary Test, Fourth Edition. On this test, the psychologist presents a picture to the child and asks her to name it. This test assesses expressive vocabulary because the child must recognize the picture and state its name (Shipley & McAfee, 2015).

Language disorder is characterized by overall delays in language acquisition or skills. The diagnosis serves as a "red flag," which warns professionals to monitor the child's language development and, if necessary, to intervene early to prevent more serious language deficits. Typically, professionals specify the type of language problem the child displays: (a) late language emergence or (b) specific language impairment (SLI).

Late Language Emergence

Late language emergence is a type of language disorder characterized by significant delays in receptive or expressive language. It is typically diagnosed when children are between 18 and 36 months of age yet show marked delays in understanding language or speaking (see Figure 7.1). For example, a 24-month-old who cannot follow simple directions (e.g., "Pick it up") or a 36-month-old who cannot combine words to form simple sentences (e.g., "Give me the doll") might show late language emergence.

Late language emergence is important because it can be an indicator of later, more serious language problems (e.g., SLI) or an early sign of ASD. Therefore, children diagnosed with late language emergence need to be monitored and, if appropriate, provided with early intervention to improve their language skills (MacWhinney & William, 2015). Consider the case of Cody, a boy with language disorder characterized by late language emergence.

Prolonged delays in language acquisition can be an indicator of more pervasive neurodevelopmental problems. Buschmann, Jooss, and Rupp (2008) assessed a large sample of 24-month-old children with late language emergence. Approximately 22% showed at least one other developmental delay. For example, 12% showed borderline significant deficits in nonverbal cognitive functioning, like

Figure 7.1   Expressive Vocabulary Increases Dramatically in Typically Developing Children

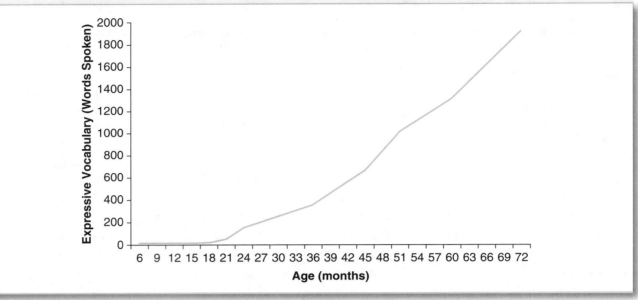

Source: Based on National Institute on Child Health and Human Development (NICHD, 2010), data.

Note: Most children show a marked increase in words between 18 and 36 months of age. Children with Late Language Emergence do not.

CASE STUDY

LANGUAGE DISORDER (LATE LANGUAGE EMERGENCE)

Cody's Problems With Language Acquisition

Cody was a physically healthy 26-month-old boy referred to our clinic by his pediatrician because of language delays. Cody's mother reported that he was only able to speak a few words clearly, such as *mama, dada,* and *cup.* He usually communicated by gesturing and crying. A physical exam indicated that Cody was healthy; his head circumference and weight were within normal limits. He showed no problems with vision or hearing. His motor and social skills were also appropriate for a child his age.

A psychologist at our clinic tested Cody's cognitive functioning and language skills. Although his fluid IQ fell within the average range (101), his verbal IQ score indicated marked delays (75). Cody's receptive language skills were approximately one standard deviation below his peers. For example, he was able to follow simple one-word commands, but he had difficulty pointing to pictures of common objects when instructed to do so. Cody's expressive language skills were also delayed. His vocabulary consisted of only about 20 to 25 words, most of which served a function (e.g., up, more, mama). He did not combine words to form simple, two-word sentences.

"I'm not sure if Cody really has a language problem or if he's just a late bloomer," said his mother. "I thought I'd just give him a few more months to catch up to the other kids, but his doctor suggested I have him tested right away."

Cody, 6% showed significant deficits in nonverbal intelligence, and 4% met diagnostic criteria for ASD. Although most children with late language emergence eventually develop language skills similar to their peers, a sizable minority of these children have potentially serious developmental delays that require treatment (Pierce, 2015).

Specific Language Impairment

Although most youths with late language emergence catch up to their peers, 25% to 40% develop more serious problems with language (Kaderavek, 2014). Specific language impairment (SLI) is characterized by marked deficits in language that are not better explained by ID or another medical or psychiatric condition (MacWhinney & William, 2015).

Children with SLI are usually diagnosed in preschool or kindergarten, when their language skills continue to lag behind those of their peers. Overall, their language is short, simplistic, and filled with errors characteristic of much younger children. Older children with SLI make the same linguistic errors, in roughly the same sequence, as much younger children without language problems. For example, a 7- or 8-year-old child with SLI speaks like a typically developing 3- or 4-year-old preschooler (Cupples, 2011). Consider the case of Bernadette, a girl with language disorder characterized by SLI.

Children with SLI typically show problems in four domains of language: (1) phonology, (2) morphology, (3) grammar, and (4) semantics (Brookshire & McNeil, 2014). Phonology refers to the sounds of a language and the rules for combining these sounds. English has 42 basic sounds, or phonemes. As children acquire language, they typically make certain errors in phonological processing and articulation. For example, it is common for 3-year-old children to say "ephant" for *elephant* or "sghetti" for *spaghetti*. However, children with SLI often continue to make these characteristic phonological errors into their early school years.

Children with SLI often show a lack of phonemic awareness—that is, the ability to hear, identify, and manipulate these sounds. For example, separating the spoken word "cat" into three distinct phonemes, /k/, /a/, and /t/, requires phonemic awareness. Children with SLI show problems with phonemic awareness in their language when they transpose, substitute, or mispronounce word sounds. For example, they may say "ting" instead of *thing*, "tu" instead of *zoo*, and "dob" instead of *job*. As we will see, a lack of phonemic awareness underlies both communication and learning disorders.

Morphology refers to the study of word structures—quite literally, how words are built from phonemes (Pindzola, Plexico, & Haynes, 2015). A morpheme is the smallest unit of language that has meaning. Some morphemes

CASE STUDY

LANGUAGE DISORDER (SPECIFIC LANGUAGE IMPAIRMENT)

Bernadette's Problems With Expression

Bernadette was a 5-year-old girl referred to our clinic by her parents because of deficits in expressive language. She had a history of late language emergence. She did not begin talking until 24 months of age and only began speaking in short two- or three-word sentences the previous year. Her pediatrician initially suspected that Bernadette had ID; however, her nonverbal intelligence and adaptive functioning were within the average range for a girl her age. Indeed, Bernadette was a friendly, outgoing girl whose main limitation was her difficulty expressing herself.

The speech–language pathologist at our clinic showed Bernadette a series of pictures and asked her to tell a story with them. The exchange went as follows:

Therapist:	Here's the first picture. Tell me what's going on.
Bernadette:	(Pointing to the girl in the picture.) Who her?
Therapist:	Her name is Sally.
Bernadette:	Sally. Her going shopping. Sally hold . . . (long pause) bag and . . . (pause)—
Therapist:	What is she holding?
Bernadette:	I don't know.
Therapist:	OK. Let's try the next picture. What's going on here?
Bernadette:	Her goed into house. Sally. Her eat with mom.
Therapist:	What did they eat?
Bernadette:	Her eated apple. Her eated . . . (pause) . . . I don't know.
Therapist:	It looks like they ate an apple and some grapes.
Bernadette:	(Smiles.) Yeah.

"She often can't remember the names of objects," Bernadette's mother reported. "There might be a problem with her memory." The therapist replied, "That is possible. I'll need to assess her more thoroughly to be sure. But I think her main difficulty is expressive language. Luckily, there are some things you and I can do to help Bernadette express herself better."

are "free"—that is, they carry meaning on their own as whole words (e.g., tie, walk, dog). Other morphemes are "bound"—that is, they carry meaning only when combined with other morphemes, as in the case of prefixes or suffixes (un– as in "untie"), endings (–ed as in "walked"), or plurals (–s as in "dogs").

Typically developing children follow a relatively consistent pattern in their mastery of morphemes. For example, the use of the –ing ending (e.g., swimming) and certain prepositions (e.g., in the box) usually develop first. Later, children begin to master the plural –s ending (e.g., hats), the possessive –s ending (e.g., Mommy's hat), and the uncontractible copula "be" (e.g., She is my mom. I am her son.) Some of the last morphemes that children master include the past tense –ed ending (e.g., walked), the first-person singular –s ending (e.g., The bird chirps), and the uncontractible auxiliary "be" followed by a verb (e.g., She is playing. I was running).

Children with SLI show marked deficits in their mastery of morphemes, especially the morphemes that are typically learned later in development (see Table 7.2). For example, many youths with SLI omit past-tense endings; they may say, "I walk to school" instead of "I walked to school." Another common error is to omit the third person singular –s ending: "My friend walk with me" instead of "My friend walks with me." A third common error is difficulty with conjugations involving be, such as "Mommy bes nice" instead of "Mommy is nice." Although these errors are developmentally normative in 2- and 3-year-old children, children with SLI continue to make these errors in preschool and kindergarten (Pindzola et al., 2015).

Grammar describes the rules that govern the use of morphemes and the order of words (syntax) in a sentence. Children with SLI often make serious grammatical errors. For example, they might say "Me go there" instead of "I went there" or "Why he like me?" instead of "Why does he like me?" They may also not appreciate differences in word order. For example, they may have difficulty using puppets to act out the sentence "The dog is chased by the boy" because they are not sure who is chasing whom (Kaderavek, 2014).

Semantics refers to the meaning of language. Semantics can refer to the meaning of individual words (lexical semantics) or sentences (sentential semantics). Word meaning is important because it allows children to verbally represent their world, understand others, and convey their thoughts with precision. Children with SLI often show delays in word acquisition and word knowledge. Whereas most 2-year-old children have vocabularies of approximately 200 words, 2-year-olds later diagnosed with SLI typically know only 20 (Owens, 2013).

Children with SLI typically have semantic skills similar to those of much younger children. For example, preschoolers with SLI often show errors of overextension and

Table 7.2 Morphological and Grammatical Errors Often Shown by Children With Specific Language Impairment

Error	Example
Regular past tense (–ed)	He push him. (He pushed him.)
Present possessive verb –ing	Cat eat him food. (The cat is eating his food.)
Plural /s/	Me got two toy. (I have two toys.)
Possessive 's	That mommy hat. (That is Mommy's hat.)
Simple pronoun errors	He running. (She is running.)
Pronoun case markings	Her do it. (She can do it.)
Omitted copula be verb	The bear big. (The bear is big.)
Errors in copula be verb	Me happy today. (I am happy today.)
Omitted articles (e.g., a, the)	Give me drink. (Give me a drink.)
Omitted prepositions in and on	Daddy, put table my paper. (Daddy, put my paper on the table.)
Omitted auxiliary verbs (e.g., is, do, can)	Janie do it. (Janie can do it.)
Overuse of vague demonstratives (e.g., this, that, these, those)	This mine! (This toy is mine.)
Third person singular verbs	Mommy teach me. (Mommy teaches me.)
wh questions	What we can make? (What can we make?)
Embedded clauses with wh questions	What do you think what Janie broke? (What do you think that she broke?)

Source: Based on Kaderavek (2011).

underextension similar to 2- and 3-year-olds. *Overextension* is inappropriately generalizing a word (e.g., calling all adult men "daddy") whereas *underextension* is failing to generalize a word (e.g., using the word "cat" to refer only to the family's pet and not to other cats). Children with SLI may also have difficulty with pronouns (e.g., mixing up he/she or him/her). They almost always have underdeveloped vocabularies and experience trouble expressing themselves with precision. Like Bernadette, they may appear to have word retrieval problems, use words incorrectly, invent novel words that have no meaning (e.g., neologisms), or rely on vague, simplistic words (e.g., *thing, this, stuff;* Cupples, 2011).

Causes

Genes and Brain Structure

Language impairments are greatly influenced by genetics. Heritability estimates for language disorder range between .50 and .75. Whereas the prevalence of language disorder is approximately 7% in the general population, the prevalence increases to 40% for children with at least one family member with the disorder. Furthermore, when the siblings of children with language disorder do not meet criteria for the disorder, they often show subtle difficulties with phonemic awareness and grammar. Altogether, these data suggest a common set of genes that predispose youth toward language problems. The greater the genetic similarity, the greater the risk for language impairment (Kornilov et al., 2016).

Some studies have found brain abnormalities in children with language disorder (Hedge & Maul, 2006). These studies have focused on the region surrounding the lateral sulcus. The lateral sulcus, also known as the sylvian fissure, is a large gyrus (groove) in the left hemisphere of the brain (see Image 7.1). In this area are several brain regions responsible for language including Broca's area, Wernicke's area, and the primary auditory cortex. Most right-handed children show a normal enlargement of this area—that is, this area of the left hemisphere, which is specialized for language, is larger than the corresponding area in the right hemisphere. However, many children with language disorder do not show this typical asymmetry. Instead, both hemispheres may be of equal size, suggesting a lack of linguistic specialization.

Unfortunately, there is not a direct relationship between abnormality of the lateral sulcus and language disorder. Many children with language disorder do not show this lack of asymmetry, and many children with no language impairments show this abnormality. Therefore, this structural difference cannot explain all cases of language disorder.

Auditory Perception Problems

Auditory perception is the ability to identify and differentiate sounds. It can be measured by asking children to detect differences between two tones with different pitch or two

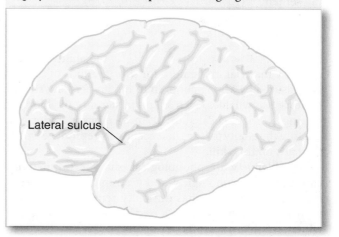

Image 7.1   The lateral sulcus, or sylvian fissure, is a large gyrus (groove) in the left hemisphere of the brain. Abnormalities near this brain region likely play a role in the development of language disorder.

Lateral sulcus

phonemes with slightly different sounds (e.g., the /th/ and /d/ sounds). Auditory perception is important because children must detect subtle differences between phonemes in order to develop phonemic awareness. Typically developing children gradually acquire the ability to differentiate subtle differences in auditory information over the first years of life. However, children with language disorder do not. Delays in auditory perception may lead to problems in both speech and language. For example, a child who does not differentiate the /l/ and /r/ sounds may have difficulty accurately producing these sounds (e.g., the word *ring* sounds like "ling."). Furthermore, a child who does not differentiate the word *sing* from the word *sings* may not produce the plural /-s/ ending when speaking (Weismer, 2008).

Deficits in Rapid Temporal Processing

Rapid temporal processing is the ability to quickly and accurately process sensory information. Rapid temporal processing is assessed by asking children to discriminate between stimuli presented quickly. For example, children might be asked to discriminate between two computer-generated sounds (e.g., /ba/ and /pa/) or two multisyllabic words that are presented in rapid succession. When stimuli are presented slowly, all children perform well. However, when stimuli are presented rapidly, children with language disorder perform much worse than their peers without language impairments.

Rapid temporal processing is important when auditory information is presented briefly or in rapid succession, such as when a parent speaks quickly to a child. In order for a child to develop phonemic awareness, to learn the names of objects and to understand sentences, she must be able to encode this auditory information quickly. However, children who have deficits in rapid temporal processing take in and process less fine-grained auditory information. They simply miss out on linguistic input. Problems with rapid temporal processing, therefore, can contribute to delays in children's awareness of phonemes, underdeveloped vocabularies, and difficulty understanding sentences (Richards & Goswami, 2015).

Delays in Short-Term Memory

Phonological short-term memory is the ability to hold auditory material in memory for short periods of time. It is measured by asking children to remember long strings of nonsense syllables, such as "perplisteronk" or "blonter-staping." Phonological short-term memory is important, because the ability to learn and accurately reproduce words depends on this skill.

Problems with phonological short-term memory can lead to morphological and grammatical errors. For example, a child who has difficulty remembering auditory information may omit a past-tense or plural ending when completing a sentence (e.g., Yesterday, I walk[ed] to school; Today, John ride[s] his bike.) Similarly, children with phonological short-term memory deficits may have underdeveloped vocabularies or show problems understanding sentences. For example, they may have trouble determining whether "The boy chased the dog" and "The dog was chased by the boy" have the same meaning (Gathercole & Baddeley, 2014).

Impoverished Parent–Child Communication

A great deal of research has focused on the verbal interactions between children with language disorder and their parents. Overall, studies have shown that the quality of these interactions is impoverished, compared to the verbal exchanges between parents and typically developing children (Hedge & Maul, 2006). On average, the parents of children with language disorder do the following:

- Interact with their children less often
- Ask their children fewer questions
- Use shorter and less complex sentences
- Show less variation in their language toward their children
- Respond less often to their children's utterances

It is unknown whether these parenting behaviors are a cause or consequence of language disorder. It is possible that impoverished parent–child communication contributes to children's language delays. Alternatively, recent data suggest that the parents of children with language disorder may use less complex language in response to their children's communication problems (Blackwell, Harding, Babayiğit, & Roulstone. 2015).

Evidence-Based Treatments

The treatment of language disorder is tailored to the needs of the child. Some children, such as those with late language emergence, need help expanding their expressive vocabularies and combining words to form sentences. Other children, such as those with SLI, need to correct morphological and grammatical errors in their language, such as problems using the past tense or the omission of articles and prepositions. Treatment, therefore, capitalizes on children's linguistic strengths to overcome or compensate their weaknesses (Roth & Worthington, 2015).

Discrete Trial Training to Increase Language Production

Individual Words. The expressive vocabularies of many young children with language disorder lag far behind their typically developing peers. A primary goal of therapy is to increase these children's expressive vocabularies, capacity for multiword utterances, and overall language production.

For children with limited expressive language, discrete trial training may be used. As we have seen, discrete trial training is an individually administered instructional approach used to teach specific behaviors in a planned, controlled, and systematic manner. Skills are taught, one at a time, using a series of repeated trials. Each trial has three parts: (1) the presentation of the stimulus, (2) the child's action, and (3) reinforcement for engaging in the desired action.

First, the therapist presents the target word. For example, the therapist might want to teach a child to say "cookie." The therapist might present a cookie to the child and ask, "What is this?" If the child does not respond to the therapist's question, the therapist will prompt the child by saying, "This is a cookie. Say 'cookie.'" The goal is for the child to produce the desired verbal response so that the therapist can reinforce it.

Second, the therapist watches for the child to respond correctly. In this case, the child replies "cookie" with or without the therapist's prompt. If the child answers incorrectly, the therapist corrects the child, saying, "No, this is a cookie. Say 'cookie.'" Then, the therapist waits for the correct response.

Third, the therapist provides positive reinforcement, contingent on the child's production of the correct utterance. For example, the therapist might reinforce the child's reply of "cookie" by smiling, saying "Good. This is a cookie," and giving the child a bite.

Each trial is repeated multiple times until the child correctly produces the desired behavior with minimal prompting. Then, a new behavior is introduced which usually builds upon previously acquired skills.

Requests and Comments. Discrete trial training can also be used to help children combine words into phrases and simple sentences. One important type of phrase that children learn to use is mands, or requests. Mands are important because they allow children to obtain objects, information, or privileges. Mands are also fairly easy to teach because they specify their own reinforcers. For example, a 2-year-old who says "Give drink" can be given a sip of his favorite juice to reinforce his request.

Initially, therapists use discrete trial training to teach simple mands. For example, the therapist might produce a cup of juice and prompt the child's request by saying "You want a drink. Say, 'Give me a drink.'" The therapist would continue to prompt the child until the child produces the request. Then, the therapist would reinforce the mand. Trials would be repeated until the child makes the request with little prompting. Eventually, all prompting would be decreased (or faded) until the child requests on his own.

Children can also be taught to use tacts—that is, comments and descriptions. Tacts allow children to combine nouns and verbs to describe their experiences and surroundings. Examples of tacts include the following:

- Descriptions of objects (e.g., The dog is black and white)
- Descriptions of parts of objects (e.g., The dog has two ears and a nose)
- Descriptions of the function of objects (e.g., His nose is for smelling)
- Descriptions of actions (e.g., The dog runs fast)
- Action sequences (e.g., He runs outside. Then, he gets his ball)
- Expression of feelings (e.g., He likes to play).

To teach a child to use tacts, a therapist might show her client a picture of a dog and say, "Here is a picture of my dog. I want you to tell me about him. You may tell me what he looks like, about the parts of his body, or anything else. For example, say, 'He is black and white.'" The therapist would then praise the child's response and continue with a second trial, saying, "Very good. The dog is black and white. Tell me more about how he looks. Say, "He has big ears.'" Over the course of several sessions, the therapist would gradually fade her prompts so the child can describe objects on his own.

Questions. Therapists also teach children with limited expressive vocabularies to ask questions. Questions are important because they allow children to gather information about their surroundings and expand their semantic knowledge. The therapist structures a situation that encourages the child to ask a question. Then, the therapist models the question and reinforces the child's attempts to ask the question.

For example, the therapist might present a magnifying glass to the child, saying, "Look what I have. You don't know what this is. Ask me, 'What is it?'" When the child responds correctly, the therapist reinforces his question, saying, "Great! You asked a good question. It is a magnifying glass. You see with it. Let's try it."

The therapist might introduce other objects, gradually fading her verbal prompt until the child can ask questions independently. The therapist might use other approaches to teach *who, when, where,* and *why* questions (see Table 7.3). In each case, the therapist initially relies heavily on verbal prompts. Later, the therapist fades the prompts as the child begins to produce questions independently.

Complex Sentences. Older children with language disorder usually have difficulty forming complex sentences. For example, they often have trouble generating compound sentences (e.g., "Orville climbed aboard the airplane *and* Wilbur started the engine"), dependent clauses (e.g., "*After the engine had started,* Wilbur gave his brother the signal to start"), and embedded clauses (e.g., "The airplane, *which was made of wood and fabric,* went into the air").

Table 7.3 Discrete Trial Training to Teach Children to Ask Questions

Question	Example
Who	If you don't know someone, you ask a question that starts with *who*. [Holds up a picture of a boy.] Look at this picture. You don't know this boy. Ask me, "Who is that boy?"
What	If you want to know something, you ask a question that starts with *what*. [Shows a picture of two children playing chess.] Look at this picture. You don't know what the children are doing. Ask me, "What are they doing?"
When	When you want to know when something will happen, you ask a question that starts with the word *when*. Let's pretend that your mother tells you that your grandma is going to visit. You don't know when. Ask, "When is grandma going to visit?"
Where	When you can't find someone or something, you ask a question that starts with *where*. Let's pretend that you want to put on your shoes to go outside, but you can't find them. Ask, "Where are my shoes?"
Why	When you don't understand something, you ask a question that starts with *why*. Let's pretend that your mother gives you a toy car for your birthday, but the car doesn't work. Ask, "Why doesn't the car work?"
How	If you don't know the way to do something, you ask a question that starts with *how*. Here is a new game that you've never played before. Ask, "How do we play the game?"

Source: Based on Hegde and Maul (2006).

Therapists can encourage children to use longer and more elaborate sentences using discrete trial training. Specifically, therapists systematically model, prompt, and reinforce complex sentence structures.

- Here is a picture of two men. We can tell about these men in one big sentence. Say, "One man is tall *and the other is short*."
- Here is a picture of a happy girl. She just won a race. Let's make one sentence telling why the girl is happy. Say, "The girl is happy *because* she won a race."
- Here is a picture of two dogs. The dog with the red collar is dirty. Let's make one sentence telling which dog is dirty. Say, "The dog, *with the red collar*, is dirty."

The therapist gradually fades these prompts until the child can produce complex sentences independently.

Conversational Recast Training to Correct Language Errors

Children with language disorder often show specific deficits in morphology and grammar. For example, children may have difficulty using the *to be* form, omit the plural /s/, or leave off the –ed ending of the past tense. Therapists need to target these deficits by modeling, reinforcing, and practicing appropriate language skills. A commonly used technique to achieve these goals is conversational recast training (Cleave, Becker, Curran, Van Horne, & Fey, 2015).

In conversational recast training, the therapist structures the child's environment in ways that are likely to elicit the desired verbal behavior. Then, the therapist prompts the child to practice the desired language skill, each time correcting mistakes and reinforcing appropriate language use with eye contact, smiles, attention, and verbal praise. The following Research to Practice section provides one example of this intervention.

Ample practice is critical to the success of conversational recast training. Mistakes must be corrected immediately and proper use of the desired language skills must be reinforced to maintain its use over time.

Milieu Training to Generalize Skills

Although discrete trial training is very effective at introducing and reinforcing language skills, therapists must

RESEARCH TO PRACTICE

RECAST TRAINING: PRACTICING SPECIFIC LANGUAGE SKILLS

A therapist wants the child to practice the /s/ ending of the third person singular. The therapist might invite the child to play "zoo" with toy animals (Kaderavek, 2011):

Therapist: The animals are hungry and tired. Let's help the zookeeper feed them and put them to bed. Here is the zookeeper. [Moves human toy figure to giraffe.] He feeds the giraffe every day. What does he do?

Child: He feed giraffe.

Therapist: He feeds the giraffe doesn't he? Let's ask the giraffe what he eats. What do you want to eat, giraffe? You ask the giraffe what he wants to eat?

Child: What you eat?

Therapist: What do you eat, giraffe? Oh, he says he eats hay. He eats hay. Does he eat bananas? No, he eats hay. The monkey eats bananas, doesn't he? Who do you think eats and eats the banana?

Child: Monkey eats bananas.

Therapist: Great! The monkey eats and eats the yellow bananas. What does the giraffe eat?

Child: Giraffe eats hay.

Therapist: Very good. The monkey eats bananas and the giraffe eats hay. Now let's put the giraffe to bed. Where does the giraffe sleep? Does the giraffe sleep in the pond?

Child: No, the giraffe sleep under the tree.

Therapist: Oh, I see. The giraffe sleeps under the tree. He sleeps and sleeps all night. Here is the zookeeper asking the giraffe, "where do you sleep?" Where does the giraffe sleep?

Child: He sleeps under the tree.

Therapist: Exactly! He sleeps under the tree.

rely on other strategies to help generalize these skills to children's homes and schools. Milieu training is a treatment approach that uses behavioral principles in contexts that approximate children's real-life environments and experiences. *Milieu* simply means the physical setting in which events typically occur. A young child's milieu might include her home, preschool, day care, and family outings (e.g., shopping, going to the playground). In milieu training, children practice language skills in natural contexts (Wright & Kaiser, 2016).

Milieu training relies chiefly on contingency management. The therapist observes the child engage in everyday tasks, such as coloring, eating, and playing with toys, and looks for situations in which the child might be able to practice language skills. When such situations arise, the therapist prompts the child to practice the language skill, models the skill (if necessary), and reinforces the child's attempts to use the skill.

The *mand-model technique* is commonly used in milieu training. The therapist observes the child approach a desired object, such as a toy car, and immediately prompts (mands) the child to ask for the object (e.g., "Tell me what you want."). If necessary, the therapist models the correct statement (e.g., "Say, 'I want the car.'"), and reinforces the child's request (e.g., "Good. I'm glad you told me what you wanted. Here, take it.").

Another strategy is to use the *delay technique*. This technique is similar to the mand-model approach, but the therapist waits, with an expectant facial expression, for the child to ask for the desired object. The goal of the delay technique is for the child to request the object without the therapist asking "What do you want?" or providing a similar verbal prompt. The delay strategy is designed to increase independent verbal output.

A third strategy is *incidental teaching*. In this technique, the therapist simply waits for the child to initiate a topic and then prompts the child to elaborate on that topic. After elaboration, the therapist reinforces the child's verbal output. For example, the child might ask, "Where daddy?" The therapist would capitalize on the child's question and respond, "You want to know where daddy is. Say, 'Where *is* daddy?'" When the child asks correctly, the therapist provides reinforcement, saying, "Very good! You asked a good question. Let's find him" (Kaderavek, 2014).

Review:

- Language disorder is characterized by persistent difficulties with the acquisition or use of language that include (a) reduced vocabulary, (b) limited sentence structure, or (c) impairments in discourse. Two broad types are late language emergence and SLI.
- Language disorder is heritable and associated with deficits in auditory processing, rapid temporal processing, and short-term memory. It is unclear if impoverished parent–child communication is a cause or consequence of children's language problems.
- Evidence-based treatments include discrete trial training to increase vocabulary, conversational recast training to correct language errors, and milieu training to generalize skills to home and school.

What Is Speech Sound Disorder?

Description

Speech is produced when young children learn to modulate their voice to produce specific, discernible sounds that have meaning in a particular language. Speech is complex; it depends on the maturation of the central nervous system; cognitive development; and coordination of head, neck, mouth, chest, and diaphragm muscles. Over the first five years of life, most children transition from unintelligible voice sounds, to idiosyncratic utterances that only their parents understand, to clear and fluid word production. However, 3% to 5% of first-grade students show speech problems that interfere with their ability to communicate (Stemple & Fry, 2010).

Speech sound disorder (SSD) is diagnosed when children are unable to produce the expected speech sounds appropriate for their age (see Table 7.4). Children with

---

Table 7.4   Diagnostic Criteria for Speech Sound Disorder (SSD)

A. Persistent difficulty with speech sound production that interferes with speech intelligibility or prevents verbal communication of messages.

B. The disturbance causes limitations in effective communication that interfere with social participation, academic achievement, or occupational performance, individually or in any combination.

C. Onset of symptoms is in the early developmental period.

D. The difficulties are not attributable to congenital or acquired conditions, such as cerebral palsy, cleft palate, deafness or hearing loss, traumatic brain injury, or other medical or neurological conditions.

Source: Reprinted with permission from the *Diagnostic and Statistical Manual of Mental Disorders, Fifth Edition* (Copyright 2013). American Psychiatric Association.

SSD omit, substitute, distort, add, or otherwise incorrectly produce sounds in such a manner that others have difficulty understanding their speech (American Psychiatric Association, 2013).

Five sound production problems are common among children with SSD.

- Omission errors occur when children leave off phonemes, usually at the beginning or end of words. For example, children may say "at" for "cat" or "ba" for "ball."
- Substitution errors occur when children replace one phoneme with another. For example, they may say "wed" instead of "red" or "thoup" instead of "soup."
- Sound distortions occur when a phoneme is not produced correctly, usually resulting in a "slushy" sound. Children with SSD most frequently distort the /r/, /l/, /z/, /sh/, and /ch/ sounds. Sylvester the Cat displays distortions when he says "thuffering thuccotash."

- Addition errors occur when children include an extra phoneme, usually the short /u/ sound, into words. For example, children may say "farog" instead of "frog" or "salow" instead of "slow."
- A lisp is a specific and relatively common speech error that usually results in indistinct /s/, /sh/, and /ch/ sounds. Central lisps occur when the tongue is allowed to protrude beyond the front teeth (e.g., "thun" instead of "sun"). Lateral lisps occur when air is allowed to pass between the tongue and the molars, resulting in a slushy /s/ sound.

Some children show more pervasive problems with speech sound production, beyond simple articulation. Furthermore, their speech errors follow a pattern that reflects underlying problems with phonology. For example, these children may consistently add phonemes to words (e.g., "eggi" for "egg"), reverse sounds (e.g., "peek" for

"keep"), replace one sound for another (e.g., "hoop" for "soup"), blend or glide sounds (e.g., "yewo" for "yellow"), or delete sounds (e.g., "pu" for "pool"). Unlike most children with SSD, their deficits are caused by phonological processing problems rather than difficulties with articulation. Needless to say, these phonological processing problems make them very difficult to understand. Consider the case of Amie and Paul, two children with SSD but different problems with speech production (see previous page).

Typically developing children often show speech production errors when they are young. For example, many toddlers say *wabbit* for *rabbit*, *dis* for *this*, *pasgehti* for *spaghetti*. SSD is only diagnosed when children's errors are developmentally unexpected—that is, when children make significantly more errors (or more severe errors) than might be expected for their age.

Clinicians must be attentive to children's ethnicity and cultural background when diagnosing SSD. SSD is not diagnosed in children who adopt regional dialects. For example, some African American children use phonemes differently than European American children (e.g., lessening of /l/ phoneme, such as "too" for "tool"; reversals, such as "aks" for "ask"). Similarly, SSD is not diagnosed in bilingual children whose speech sound production reflects their first language. For example, Spanish-speaking children may substitute Spanish language phonemes for English phonemes (e.g., "Yulie" for "Julie") or insert sounds following the rules of Spanish phonology (e.g., "eskate" for "skate"). These cultural differences reflect linguistic variations and not disorders (Hedge, 2008).

SSD is the most common reason young children are referred to speech-language pathologists. Approximately 10% of preschoolers have a communication disorder; as many as 80% of these children have SSD. By first grade, approximately 3.8% of all children meet diagnostic criteria for SSD. Most of these children show articulation problems only; some also show underlying difficulties with phonological processing (Eadie et al., 2015).

Causes

Phoneme acquisition follows an ordered sequence from infancy through age 7.5 years. However, typically developing children show a great deal of variability in their speech sound production. Children in the same preschool class may vary in their phonemic production by as much as 3 years. Usually, vowel sounds are mastered by age 3, simple consonants sounds (/p/, /m/, /n/, /k/) by age 5, and consonant clusters and blends by age 7.5. Because of the wide variability among children, SSD is usually not diagnosed until children's speech skills fall more than one standard deviation behind their classmates (Pena-Brooks & Hedge, 2007).

Most explanations for SSD are based on the notion that children's articulation problems reflect a failure to transition from immature speech to more mature speech production. These theories assume that speech is a complex task that takes children several years to master. Very young children imitate speech sounds generated by parents. These children may initially imitate speech sounds using simplistic, yet incorrect, phonemes. For example, a child who initially learns to produce the /s/ sound by thrusting her tongue beyond her front teeth may find this an effective form of communication. Her parents and other family members may understand her and reinforce this habit. This immature speech usually fades as children gain greater cognitive and motor control over their speech production. However, in some cases, simplified or immature phoneme production persists beyond an age at which it is developmentally expected. Although a lisp may be acceptable at age 3, it becomes problematic at age 7 when most peers speak clearly (Waring & Knight, 2013).

More pervasive cases of SSD often reflect underlying phonological processing problems. Some experts believe these children have difficulty perceiving and differentiating phonemes, rather than merely articulating them. The phonological theory of SSD asserts that children develop underlying mental representations for phonemes as they become exposed to language over their first few years. Children who produce speech sounds normally have formed accurate mental representations of these sounds. However, subtle neurological impairments may interfere with the ability of some children to accurately perceive, differentiate, and mentally represent phonemes, thus leading to impairments in speech production (Dodd, 2013).

SSD is heritable. Approximately 35% to 40% of children with SSD have a family member with a history of the disorder. It is likely that this familial association is caused by shared genes. However, because parents and other family members usually model speech production to children, this association may also be partially explained by shared environmental experiences. Indeed, parents with poor articulation often have children with similar articulation deficits. SSD is also highly comorbid with language disorder. As many as 40% to 80% of children with SSD may also have language disorder. It is possible that early deficits in phonological processing underlie children's speech and language problems (Dodd, 2014).

Evidence-Based Treatments

The treatment of SSD involves teaching children how to correctly generate speech sounds. The goals of therapy depend on the specific deficits evidenced by the child. For example, one child might need to improve her articulation of the /r/ sound at the beginning of words, another might need to focus on the /s/ sound at the end of words, and a third might need to correct a lateral lisp. In any case, the therapist uses a combination of modeling and reinforcement to teach children how to produce phonemes in a developmentally appropriate manner. Because children with SSD have never acquired the capacity to produce these word sounds correctly, and may habitually use less complex (and incorrect) sounds, therapy takes considerable effort on the part of therapist and child.

Speech therapy often relies on direct instruction. Therapists break down correct speech into component parts. Then, they model each part and allow the child to practice its correct use. Over time, basic skills build upon each other until the child is able to correctly produce speech sounds in more complex, flexible ways (Dwight, 2006). The following Research to Practice section describes the use of direct instruction to help Angie, a girl with SSD.

Subsequent sessions focus on producing *syllables* that either begin (i.e., la, le, li, lo, lu) or end (i.e., al, el, il, ol, ul) with the /l/ phoneme. Then, the therapist and child practice naming *objects* that either begin (e.g., lion), end (e.g., apple), or contain (e.g., balloon) the /l/ phoneme. Still later, sessions focus on blends containing the target phoneme (e.g., clown). Then, words are combined to form phrases, sentences, and stories that the therapist models and the child repeats (see Image 7.2). Finally, the child and therapist practice correct phoneme production during semistructured play. The therapist looks for opportunities to model and reinforce correct sound production and immediately corrects the child's mistakes (Raz, 1995).

Considerable evidence supports the effectiveness of speech therapy in helping young children overcome SSD. Most children show an 80% reduction in speech–sound errors in 20 sessions, especially if skills are practiced at home by parents. Children who show underlying phonological processing problems or language impairments tend to show gains in therapy more slowly, however (Brumbaugh & Smit, 2013).

Review:

- SSD is characterized by persistent difficulty with clear and articulate speech production that limits children's communication. Examples include sound omissions, substitutions, distortions, and lisps.
- Most children with SSD continue to use immature speech production into middle childhood. Some children with the disorder have underlying phonological problems that cause them to mentally represent and process speech sounds incorrectly.
- Direct instruction can be used to systematically introduce, model, and reinforce correct speech production. Most youths show an 80% reduction in errors.

What Is Childhood-Onset Fluency Disorder?

Description

Speech fluency refers to the ease and automaticity of speech. It has several components, including *rate* (the speed at which people speak), *duration* (the length of time of individual speech sounds), *rhythm* (the flow and fluidity of sounds), and *sequence* (the order of sounds). Fluency is important to speech because it increases the likelihood that listeners will understand speakers' utterances and respond appropriately (Ratner & Tetnowski, 2014).

Childhood-onset fluency disorder reflects a marked impairment in speech fluency (see Table 7.5). It is commonly called stuttering. Stuttering reflects an underlying problem with speech production rather than a language

---

SPEECH THERAPY FOR SPEECH SOUND DISORDER

Six-year-old Angie incorrectly produced the /l/ sound. First, her therapist must model and reinforce the correct tongue position to produce the /l/ phoneme:

Therapist: (Sitting next to child, facing a mirror.) Look at my tongue. Watch me lift my tongue and put it right behind my front teeth like this. (Demonstrates.) Now you try it. Let's practice lifting our tongues in front of the mirror five times. Each time we do it correctly, we'll color in a happy face circle.

The therapist helps the child attain the correct tongue position and praises correct positioning. In another session, the therapist teaches the child to make the /l/ sound with the tongue in the correct position:

Therapist: Today, I'm going to open my mouth and raise my tongue just behind my front teeth like before. But this time, I'm going to make the /l/ sound. Listen: /l/. (Repeats). Now you try it after me.

Child: wwwlah.

Therapist: That's not exactly it. See how I smile when I make the /l/ sound with my tongue. Raise your tongue just behind your front teeth like me, smile, and make the /l/ sound like this (smiles): /l/.

Child: /l/.

Therapist: Very good /l/ sound. Let's practice it again. Each time we do it right, we'll color a little piece of this picture.

Lucy is a black lab.	She is not too little or too large.
Lucy likes to play with her ball.	Lucy plays ball with her pal Lena.
The ball fell into a yellow pail.	The pals laugh and laugh.

problem. Children who stutter know what they want to say but they have problems saying it. As a result, their speech is disfluent and difficult to comprehend.

Common disfluencies include sound repetitions (e.g., *l-l-l-l . . . listen to me*), broken words (e.g., com—puter), and silent blocking (e.g., problems with word production producing large pauses in speech). Other common problems are sound extensions ("mmmmmy dog") and visible tension while speaking. Consider Davis, a child who stutters (see next page).

Many typically developing children, especially preschoolers, exhibit problems with speech fluency. However, children who stutter exhibit fluency problems more frequently than their typically developing peers. Childhood-onset fluency disorder is diagnosed only when it is developmentally inappropriate—that is, when the number of disfluencies exceeds the number expected based on the child's age and gender (Yairy & Seery, 2016).

Approximately 5% of youths have problems with stuttering at some point during childhood. Boys are more likely to stutter than girls. Furthermore, the gender ratio for stuttering increases with age. For example, in preschool, boys outnumber girls approximately 2:1. However, by adolescence, the gender ratio increases to 5:1. This gender disparity is probably due to the fact that girls are more likely to naturally recover from stuttering than boys (Yairy & Seery, 2016).

Stuttering typically emerges between 24 and 48 months of age and rarely emerges after age 6 years. It usually has an abrupt onset in young children. In one large study, 40% of children who stuttered had their symptoms emerge in less than 2 or 3 days. An additional 33% of children showed intermediate speed of onset, with symptoms emerging over the course of 1 or 2 weeks. Only 28% of children showed gradual symptom onset (Yairi & Seery, 2016).

Table 7.5   Diagnostic Criteria for Childhood-Onset Fluency Disorder (Stuttering)

A. Disturbances in the normal fluency and time patterning of speech that are inappropriate for the individual's age and language skills, persist over time, and are characterized by frequent and marked occurrences of one (or more) of the following:

   1. Sound and syllable repetitions

   2. Sound prolongations of consonants as well as vowels

   3. Broken words (e.g., pauses within a word)

   4. Audible or silent blocking (filled or unfilled pauses in speech)

   5. Circumlocutions (word substitutions to avoid problematic words)

   6. Words pronounced with an excess of physical tension

   7. Monosyllabic whole-word repetitions (e.g., "I-I-I-I see him")

B. The disturbance causes anxiety about speaking or limitations in effective communication, social participation, or academic or occupational performance, individually or in any combination.

C. The onset of symptoms is in the early developmental period.

D. The disturbance is not attributable to a speech-motor or sensory deficit, dysfluency associated with neurological insult (e.g., stroke, tumor) or another medical condition and is not better explained by another mental disorder.

Source: Reprinted with permission from the *Diagnostic and Statistical Manual of Mental Disorders, Fifth Edition* (Copyright 2013). American Psychiatric Association.

CASE STUDY

CHILDHOOD-ONSET FLUENCY DISORDER

Davis's Stuttering

Four-year-old Davis was referred to our clinic by his pediatrician because of problems with stuttering. His father explained, "It started about two months ago. He's always been a good talker. He began saying words at 10 months and could speak in sentences by his second birthday. Recently, however, I noticed he's having more trouble getting the words out."

His mother added, "At first, Davis just repeated the first syllable of certain words. Then, it occurred more often. Recently, he's been having trouble beginning his sentences." The therapist turned to Davis:

Therapist:	Davis, do you like the toys I have in my office?
Davis:	(Puts down action figure.) Y-y-y-y-es. (Pauses as if he wants to speak.) B-b-b-b-ut I l-l-l-ike Thomas the Tank Engine b-b-b-etter.
Therapist:	What's your favorite Thomas train?
Davis:	(Pause.) I l-l-l-l-ike . . .
Father:	(Interrupts). Davis. Try starting again, this time clearly.
Davis:	(Frustrated.) I l-l-l-ike . . .
Mother:	Percy's your favorite, isn't he?
Davis:	Y-y-y-es.

His father explained. "That's pretty typical. He just can't get the words out. We make him start over to practice speaking correctly. We don't want him to practice stuttering." The therapist replied, "If you like, I can show you some other strategies that might work better."

Most young children who stutter eventually recover. In several longitudinal studies, 65% to 80% of preschool and young school-age children who stuttered showed either complete or significant symptom reduction within 4 or 5 years. Recovery is most common among girls, younger children, and youths with a family member who recovered from stuttering as a child. Unfortunately, approximately 20% of children who stutter experience long-term fluency problems that persist into adolescence or adulthood.

Often, older children and adolescents who stutter can engage in certain behaviors that reduce the severity of their symptoms. For example, nearly all children report a dramatic reduction in stuttering when they sing, speak to a pet, talk to themselves, read aloud when no one is else is present, speak in time to the rhythmic swaying of their arm, or read in unison with a large group of students. Other techniques that decrease stuttering for some children include speaking in a singsong manner, speaking in monotone, whispering, acting a part in a play, repeating sentences after someone else, or simply speaking more slowly. It is unclear why these strategies are helpful in reducing stuttering and why some strategies work for some children but not others (Yairi & Seery, 2016).

Causes

We do not yet have a comprehensive explanation for the causes of stuttering. Models based on neurobiology, learning theory, emotional processing, and cognition likely explain some, but not all, instances of stuttering in children. As is the case with most disorders, stuttering is multidetermined.

Genetics and Neurobiology

Stuttering is heritable. On average, 28% of children who stutter have a parent who stuttered as a child, 43% have at least one immediate family member with a history of stuttering, and 71% have at least one extended family member with a history of the disorder. Twin studies support the notion that genes can contribute to stuttering in some children. On average, if one identical twin stutters, the likelihood that the other twin will also stutter is approximately 67% (Yairi & Seery, 2016).

Several studies have indicated possible functional differences in the brains of people who do and do not stutter. When speaking, most people show greater activation of left-hemisphere brain regions responsible for language, especially Broca's and Wernicke's areas. However, individuals who stutter often show excessive activity of the right (not left) hemisphere. It is possible that this abnormality in brain functioning explains some instances of stuttering (see Image 7.3). Indeed, at least one study has demonstrated changes in brain activity following therapy for stuttering (De Nil, Kroll, Lafaille, & Houle, 2003).

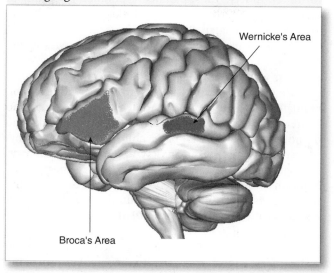

Image 7.3   Regions of the Brain Responsible for Language

Wernicke's Area

Broca's Area

Unfortunately, there are several limitations to the neurobiological data regarding the causes of stuttering. First, most studies show only small differences in brain structure and functioning between individuals who do and do not stutter, and many studies show no differences whatsoever. Second, the results of studies have been inconsistent; findings often lack replication. Third, very few neuroimaging studies have involved children who stutter, and almost no studies have involved preschoolers—the age group most likely to exhibit the disorder. Because nearly all imaging studies have involved adults, it is unclear whether brain abnormalities are a cause or consequence of stuttering (Yairi & Seery, 2016).

Learning and Emotion

The two-factor theory of stuttering posits that both classical and operant conditioning play roles in the onset and maintenance of stuttering (Brutten & Shoemaker, 1967). Specifically, children begin stuttering when normal speech disfluencies are paired with parental disapproval (e.g., classical conditioning). Children may associate these negative parenting behaviors with disfluent speech and, consequently, develop tension and apprehension when speaking. Later, children's stuttering is reinforced by the reactions of others (e.g., operant conditioning). For example, parents may give children attention (positive reinforcement) and teachers may excuse children from assignments (negative reinforcement) because of stuttering.

Support for the two-factor theory of stuttering comes from children's self-reports. Older children and adolescents who stutter report tension and apprehension in speaking situations. Furthermore, parents, teachers, and peers can exacerbate children's apprehension by interrupting them, scolding them, ridiculing them, or punishing them when they exhibit disfluencies. On the other hand, there is little evidence that parents cause their children to stutter. Indeed, most parents respond empathically to their children's speech problems (Jackson, Yaruss, Quesal, Terranova, & Whalen, 2015).

Anxiety can also play a role in stuttering (Messenger, Packman, Onslow, Menzies, & O'Brian, 2015). Young children who stutter may have temperaments that predispose them to anxiety, such as problems with emotion regulation and self-soothing. Adolescents and adults who stutter report higher anxiety levels than individuals who do not stutter. Nearly all older children and adolescents report intense feelings of anxiety, apprehension, and psychological tension associated with speaking. The negative emotions most commonly reported are fear, dread, feeling trapped, embarrassment, shame, humiliation, resentment, and frustration (Yairi & Seery, 2016).

The anticipatory-struggle theory of stuttering suggests that older children and adolescents with speech disfluencies expect speaking to be anxiety-provoking and difficult (Garcia-Barrera & Davidow, 2015). Certain situations tend to elicit the most anxiety: public speaking, answering the telephone, and saying one's own name. Children who stutter experience very low self-efficacy in these situations; they may doubt their ability to speak without mistakes, hesitations, or repetitions. Furthermore, they often report negative thoughts associated with these situations, such as "I won't be able to speak clearly," "I'll make a fool of myself," or "Other people will think I'm stupid." These negative automatic thoughts, and the anxiety they elicit, may increase the severity of the individual's stuttering.

It is unlikely, however, that anxiety is sufficient to explain all (or even most) instances of stuttering. Recall that stuttering typically emerges between 24 and 48 months of age. Young children who stutter are largely unaware of their symptoms. Most children who stutter do not report anxiety about public speaking until age 4 or 5 years.

Psycholinguistics

A final explanation for the causes of stuttering comes from the field of psycholinguistics, the study of the psychological and neurocognitive underpinnings of language. Although there are many psycholinguistic theories of stuttering, they are all based on the premise that fluency depends on three processes: (1) conceptualization, (2) formulation, and (3) articulation. First, children must think about what they want to communicate. Next, they must formulate the appropriate mental representations for their message. Formulation involves encoding the appropriate sounds (phonological representations) and word order (grammatical representations) for the message. Finally, they must articulate these representations through manipulation of the mouth, lips, tongue, and vocal cords. Usually, these three processes occur rapidly and outside children's awareness. Most children perform these steps automatically while speaking.

Stuttering occurs when there is a breakdown in one or more of these basic psycholinguistic processes. Most often, breakdowns occur during formulation. Although children who stutter know what they want to say, they may have difficulty planning out the sound sequence needed to say it (i.e., phonological encoding). Consequently, they may be able to utter only the first phoneme or single-syllable word. Alternatively, children may know what they want to say, but be unable to find the correct word or phrase to communicate their message (i.e., grammatical encoding). Consequently, they may show unusual pauses and repetitions as they struggle to generate the proper mental representations for these words.

According to the covert-repair hypothesis, children who stutter show more frequent disruptions in phonological and grammatical formulation than their non-stuttering peers (Buhr, Jones, Conture, & Kelly, 2015). They are also highly sensitive to these disruptions and closely monitor their own speech. When they encounter a problem, they attempt to correct it midspeech. Unfortunately, their covert attempts to repair breakdowns in phonological and grammatical encoding lead to speech disfluencies: They show sound and word repetitions, unusual pauses, and other retrieval problems. Just as traffic stops and starts during road repairs, so, too, does speech stop and start as children attempt to repair disruptions in speech formulation (Yairi & Seery, 2016).

Evidence-Based Treatments

Treatment for Younger Children

Most preschoolers who stutter do not require treatment. As many as 75% of these youths will naturally recover from their disfluencies. Clinicians often recommend waiting several months after the onset of stuttering to see if the problem will spontaneously resolve itself. Although some parents are concerned about delaying treatment, longitudinal data indicate that a brief delay does not affect the severity of the disorder or the efficacy of treatment once it is initiated (Jones, Onslow, Harrison, & Packman, 2000; Kingston, Huber, Onslow, Jones, & Packman, 2003). Treatment is usually warranted if stuttering persists for more than 6 to 12 months, if the child shows other speech or language problems, if the child has a family member who stutters, or if the child's stuttering causes distress or embarrassment (Ratner & Tetnowski, 2014).

Most treatments involve at least one of the following three components: (1) modifying children's speech motor patterns, (2) increasing fluency and decreasing stuttering through operant conditioning, and (3) supporting parents (Ratner & Guitar, 2006).

First, therapists must modify children's speech motor behaviors—behaviors that increase the likelihood that children will pause, repeat, or otherwise linguistically stumble when producing speech sounds. Children are systematically trained to (a) use a soft or "easy" voice when speaking, (b) speak at a slower rate, and (c) relax muscles of their mouth and throat and control their breathing.

Initially, children might be taught to whisper when speaking. Then, children are asked to utter one-syllable words and to elongate (i.e., draw out) the vowel sounds of these words to increase the likelihood that they will utter them without pauses or repetitions. Later, children might be asked to practice two-syllable compound words (e.g., school bus, hot dog) at a very slow rate of speech (60 words/min), elongating vowel sounds and speaking in a soft voice. Still later, children increase the length of utterances (i.e., phrases and sentences) and gradually increase their volume and rate of speech. All the while, therapists model slow speech, controlled breathing, and soft voice.

Most therapists also rely heavily on operant conditioning to improve children's speech motor behaviors. In an early experiment, Martin, Kuhl, and Haroldson (1972) asked young children who stuttered to talk with a puppet. The puppet interacted with the children as long as they spoke fluently. However, when the children stuttered, the puppet stopped interacting with the children for 10 seconds. At the end of the study, the children showed significant decreases in stuttering, both in the laboratory and at home.

Parental involvement in treatment is important. Parents often have many questions about the causes of stuttering and the prognosis for their children. Therapists can answer parents' questions and provide support and reassurance. Therapists can teach parents how to model soft, slow speech at home and reinforce their children's fluency (Yairi & Seery, 2016).

Treatment for Older Children

Therapy for older children and adolescents involves three components: (1) identification, (2) modification, and (3) generalization. Identification involves helping children recognize instances of stuttering when they occur. Although older children are aware that they stutter, they may not be aware of the frequency of their stuttering, physical behaviors associated with their stuttering (e.g., facial tension, blinking), and speaking situations that are most likely to elicit stuttering. Initially, therapists might use mirrors or video recordings to help children identify instances of stuttering. Later, therapists and children work to identify situations that elicit stuttering, such as answering the telephone or being called upon in class (Ratner & Tetnowski, 2014).

Next, children begin modifying their speech. The goal of this phase of treatment is similar to the treatment of preschool-age children; children must learn to switch from "hard speech" to relaxed, slow, "easy speech." Typically, speech modification is taught during the course of conversations between the child and therapist, using a technique called in-block modification. When the child or therapist notices a disfluency (i.e., a "block"), he or she points it out, and the child must correct it.

The third component of treatment is generalization. Children practice their language skills at home and at school. Initially, home and school settings that elicit stuttering might be role-played during sessions. Later, parents and teachers prompt children to use "easy speech" at home and school and reinforce them for their attempts. Children can also develop communication strategies with their teachers to reduce stuttering in the classroom; for example, if the child raises his hand with an open palm, he signals "I know the answer and want to be called." In contrast, a raised hand with a closed palm might signal, "I know the answer but please don't call on me right now."

Therapists will also address the social and emotional consequences of stuttering on older children and adolescents. Two consequences are particularly salient: teasing from peers and anxiety in speaking situations. With respect to teasing, therapists might work with teachers to identify and rectify situations in which the child is most often teased. Because school personnel cannot monitor all situations, therapists often teach children coping strategies to deal with teasing. For example, some children use humor: "I guess you noticed that I stutter . . . " or "Don't get too close, or you might catch it too." Other children need to learn problem-solving skills, such as how to deal with embarrassment or avoid fights with peers.

Although stuttering is more difficult to treat in older children and adolescents than in preschoolers, therapy can be effective. Overall, interventions that involve the identification, modification, and generalization of children's speech are associated with 85% to 90% reductions in stuttering. These data provide hope to older youths and their families with this problem (Yairi & Seery, 2016).

Review:

- Childhood-onset fluency disorder (stuttering) is a persistent problem with the normal rate, efficiency, and timing pattern of children's speech, often characterized by sound or syllable repetitions, broken or blocked words, or tension while speaking. Problems with speech fluency cause anxiety about speaking or interfere with children's communication.
- Stuttering is heritable and is sometimes acquired through classical conditioning, as children associate speaking with anxiety. Psycholinguistic theories suggest that stuttering is also caused by covert attempts to fix language problems.
- Speech therapies to reduce stuttering emphasize (a) adopting a soft or "easy" voice when speaking, (b) speaking at a slower rate, and (c) relaxing the throat and controlling breathing. Older children can learn mechanisms to cope with anxiety in speaking situations.

What Is Social (Pragmatic) Communication Disorder?

Description and Causes

Some children show no obvious problems with language or speech. Their fluency, phonological processing, morphology, grammar, and semantics are all well developed.

However, they still show marked impairments in their ability to communicate with others. Social (pragmatic) communication disorder is characterized by deficits in pragmatics—that is, the use of language in specific social contexts (see Table 7.6). Children with social communication disorder have an appreciation for the sounds and structure of language, they speak in complete sentences, and their vocabulary may be well developed. However, they lack the ability to communicate with others effectively in social settings (Norbury, 2014).

Children with social communication disorder show deficits in four broad areas of social communication. First, they display deficits in using communication for social purposes. For example, they may have problems greeting others, joining a conversation that is in progress, or sharing information. Second, they have problems switching their communication style to meet the demands of the situation. For example, they may speak the same way with their classmates on the playground as they do with their teacher in the classroom. Third, these youths have marked problems carrying on conversations. They may have problems taking turns, identifying when their conversational partner does not understand them, and rephrasing their statements when they are not understood. Fourth, older children and adolescents often have great difficulty understanding information that is not explicitly stated but is instead communicated based on context. Puns, jokes, idioms, and double meanings often go over their heads (American Psychiatric Association, 2013).

Youths with social communication disorder often experience problems in their peer relationships. For example, these children may not know how to begin a conversation with a peer or follow the subtle rules of taking turns during a conversation. They may also have difficulty maintaining the flow of a conversation without speaking off topic. These children may not pick up on nonverbal cues from others during conversations—cues that might indicate that others don't want to talk about a certain topic or that a particular topic carries a great deal of interest or importance. Consequently, children with social communication disorder may not draw correct inferences from their social interactions or may behave in socially inappropriate ways (Swineford, Thurm, Baird, Wetherby, & Swedo, 2015). Consider Willem, a boy with social communication disorder (see next page).

Children with social communication disorder often show deficits in two areas that are especially noteworthy: (1) narration and (2) conversational repair. Narrative skills are used to relate personal experiences. Children might rely on narrative skills to describe their favorite movie or their week at summer camp. Narratives are stories; they have a beginning, a middle, and an end. Narratives also include effective vocabulary to convey ideas and events, and they relate events in logical order. Unfortunately, children with social communication disorder have problems with narratives.

Table 7.6 Diagnostic Criteria for Social (Pragmatic) Communication Disorder

A. Persistent difficulties in the social use of verbal and nonverbal communication as manifested by all of the following:

1. Deficits in using communication for social purposes, such as greeting and sharing information, in a manner that is appropriate for the social context.

2. Impairment of the ability to change communication to match context or the needs of the listener, such as speaking differently in the classroom than on the playground, talking differently to a child than to an adult, and avoiding use of overly formal language.

3. Difficulties following rules for conversation and storytelling, such as taking turns in conversation, rephrasing when misunderstood, and knowing how to use verbal and nonverbal signals to regulate interaction.

4. Difficulties understanding what is not explicitly stated (e.g., making inferences) and nonliteral or ambiguous meanings of language (e.g., idioms, humor, metaphors, multiple meanings that depend on the context for interpretation).

B. The deficits result in functional limitations in effective communication, social participation, social relationships, academic achievement, or occupational performance, individually or in combination.

C. The onset of symptoms is in the early developmental period (but deficits may not become fully manifest until social communication demands exceed limited capacities).

D. The symptoms are not attributable to another medical or neurological condition or to low abilities in the domains of word structure and grammar, and are not better explained by Intellectual Disability, Global Developmental Delay, Autism Spectrum Disorder, or another mental disorder.

Source: Reprinted with permission from the *Diagnostic and Statistical Manual of Mental Disorders, Fifth Edition* (Copyright 2013). American Psychiatric Association.

SOCIAL (PRAGMATIC) COMMUNICATION DISORDER

Willem's One-Sided Conversation

The following is a transcript between Willem, a boy with social communication disorder, and his classmate, Mike:

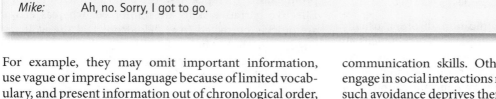

Willem: Hey, Mike, what did you get on the last test?

Mike: I didn't do too well. I studied really hard, but only got a C–.

Willem: Oh. Well, I got an A. I thought it was pretty easy.

Mike: Ah, yeah, good for you. I think my mom and dad are going to be disappointed with me.

Willem: I didn't even study that hard for it.

Mike: Yeah, I'm glad you did well. I'm mostly worried that they may not let me go to the basketball game on Tuesday because they'll want me to study.

Willem: Yeah. I love basketball. Did you see the game yesterday on TV?

Mike: Ah, no. Sorry, I got to go.

For example, they may omit important information, use vague or imprecise language because of limited vocabulary, and present information out of chronological order, thus, making their stories difficult to follow.

Children with social communication disorder are also frequently deficient in conversational repair skills. These children fail to recognize and take action when others do not follow their conversations. Conversational repair skills might include repeating or rephrasing information, providing additional information or examples, or giving background information or context. Children with social communication disorder often have difficulty implementing these skills or are altogether unaware that their communication is not understood by others.

Children with social communication disorder, like children with higher-functioning ASD, show problems with social reciprocity and understanding social interactions. They seem to talk *at* others rather than talk *with* others and show a lack of awareness for others' feelings. However, children with social communication disorder do not show repetitive behaviors and restricted interests like people with ASD. If a child meets diagnostic criteria for ASD, he would not be diagnosed with social communication disorder as well.

Evidence-Based Treatments

Initiating and Maintaining Conversations

Many children with social communication disorder avoid conversations because they lack confidence in their communication skills. Other children are reluctant to engage in social interactions more generally. Unfortunately, such avoidance deprives them of opportunities to practice their social skills and improve their use of language in social situations. Over time, the communication skills of these children decline (Ingersoll & Dvortcsak, 2010).

The therapist's first job is to teach children to initiate conversations. A critical component of beginning a conversation is to maintain eye contact with the conversational partner. The therapist might give instructions on the importance of eye contact, model appropriate eye contact, prompt its use, and reinforce the child's attempts to achieve and maintain it.

Second, the therapist must encourage the child to initiate a conversation. To accomplish this goal, the therapist might tempt the child to begin speaking by strategically placing pictures and objects in her office that require the child to ask questions (e.g., What is this toy? How does it work? Will you play it with me?). Alternatively, the therapist might prompt the child to begin a conversation or tell a story by asking him to complete a sentence stem (e.g., Yesterday, I _____. One of my favorite things is _____.) The therapist reinforces all initiations with eye contact and praise, "Oh, I am so happy you told me that. Thanks for sharing it."

Third, the therapist encourages children to maintain conversations. Some children provide only brief responses to questions whereas others prematurely end conversations. The therapist teaches children to maintain the conversation with prompts, such as "Tell me more?" "What happened next?" and "What did you like best about it?"

Other children include off-topic information or switch topics abruptly. To encourage children to stay on topic, the therapist might gently interrupt and redirect the child, by saying, "Stop! I liked how we were talking about your trip to the circus. Tell me more about that trip."

A final component of pragmatics is turn taking. Children must learn the natural reciprocity of language in which both members of the conversational pair exchange verbal information. Children must attend to their conversational partners, avoid interruptions, and respond to social cues to talk. The therapist can teach turn-taking skills through verbal, symbolic, and physical prompts. Verbal prompts might be specifically telling children when to listen and when to speak (e.g., "It's your turn now"). Symbolic prompts might include gestures (e.g., pointing, motioning) to indicate who is speaking and who is listening. The therapist might even pass a physical prompt, like a microphone, between herself and the child to indicate whose turn it is to speak. The therapist reinforces appropriate turn taking and gradually fades prompts (Ingersoll & Dvortcsak, 2010).

Conversational Repair and Narratives

Children with social communication disorder usually have poor conversational repair skills. Their deficits in conversational repair are understandable for at least three reasons. First, most people, even people without social communication disorder, are very reluctant to interrupt speakers, and ask for more information when they do not understand something. Often, people simply continue the conversation in an attempt to avoid offense or embarrassment. Second, children with social communication disorder often do not understand slang and nonliteral phrases (i.e., figures of speech). Third, children with social communication disorder often have more global deficits in social functioning, making higher-order social communication skills (such as conversational repair) challenging.

One aspect of teaching conversational repair skills is to systematically instruct children how to ask for clarification from speakers. The therapist can teach clarification by deliberately giving ambiguous commands to the child. For example, the therapist might strategically place three toy cars on a table and say, "Please give me the car." When the child gives the "wrong" car to the therapist, she might respond, "You don't know which one I want. Ask, 'Which car do you want?'" Later, the therapist will teach appropriate ways to interrupt the speaker, such as by saying "Excuse me . . ." and "I'm sorry, but . . ."

Another aspect of conversational repair skill training is to help children recognize when listeners do not understand them and to take appropriate action. For example, the therapist might show pictures of people who look confused so that children can more easily detect this emotion in others. Then, the therapist might model appropriate ways to ask for more information from speakers. For example, she might pretend not to understand the child

and model appropriate responses: "I don't understand," "Can you say it differently?" "I don't know what (X word) means." Finally, the therapist reinforces conversational repair skills by saying, "Oh, now I get it. Thanks!"

Narrative skills are among the most important, and challenging, aspects of social communication. Narratives are children's capacity to tell a story that involves a beginning, middle, and end. Stories can be autobiographical (e.g., what I did after school yesterday) or about others (e.g., the plot of the book I finished reading). Good narratives provide descriptive information, avoid extraneous details, convey a main point, and present elements of the story in an organized fashion. Children with social communication disorder have difficulty with narratives. Their stories often leave out important information, present distracting or irrelevant details, lack a "main point," or present details out of chronological order.

Initially, narrative skills can be introduced, modeled, prompted, and reinforced by using the tell–retell procedure. Specifically, the therapist might tell a familiar story, such as *The Three Little Pigs*, using the aid of picture prompts. Then, with the help of the pictures and verbal prompts, the therapist asks the child to retell the story. Effective narrative skills are reinforced, whereas errors are quickly corrected (e.g., "Hold on! Did the wolf say anything to the pig before he blew down the house?").

Later, the therapist encourages the child to practice narrative skills using autobiographical information. For example, the therapist might first model a simple autobiographical narrative: "Each night, before I go to sleep, I get ready for bed. First, I put on my pajamas . . . " Then, she might encourage the child to recount his own bedtime routine, prompting him if necessary, correcting errors, and reinforcing appropriate narrative skills.

A final technique to teach narrative skills is to use scripts. Scripts are descriptions of social interactions in which people routinely engage. Ordering food at a restaurant, shopping at a grocery store, or visiting the doctor for a checkup are examples of scripts. Scripts can either be written down verbatim, represented using pictures, or improvised. In individual therapy, the therapist and child take turns acting out the parts of the main characters in a script (e.g., the child plays the role of waiter and the therapist plays the role of customer). The therapist asks the child to generate the script by explaining the next sequence of events that should occur (e.g., we sit, then we read the menu, and then we order). Then, therapist and child role-play the events and practice other pragmatic language skills (e.g., eye contact, turn taking, conversational repair). Finally, therapist and child switch roles to reinforce the interactive nature of social communication.

Social Skills Training and Videotaped Modeling

Children with social communication disorder also benefit from social skills training, a behavioral intervention in which frequently used social skills are systematically introduced, modeled, practiced, and reinforced (Wilczynski, McIntosh, Tullis, Cullen, & Querim, 2016). Skillstreaming (McGinnis, 2011a, 2011b) is a popular curriculum in which clinicians can teach skills such as how to begin a conversation, how to ask a question, and how to join a group activity. Each skill is broken down into steps that are modeled and practiced in small groups.

Alternatively, the Program for the Education and Enrichment of Relational Skills (PEERS), is a 16-week group intervention for middle and high school students with social communication deficits. Youths learn skills such as how to find common interests by sharing information with others, how to appropriately use humor, how to make phone calls to friends, and how to be a good host at get-togethers (Laugeson, Gantman, Kapp, Orenski, & Ellingsen, 2015; Laugeson & Park, 2014).

Recent data indicate that social skills training programs are effective in improving children's social communication skills (Durand, 2015; Smith & Bryson, 2015). For example, Thomeer and colleagues (2012) randomly assigned children to either a social skills training summer camp or to a control condition. After 5 weeks of training, children who attended the camp showed improvements in communication, social interactions, and understanding nonliteral language (i.e., idioms) compared to controls (see Figure 7.2).

An especially effective way to demonstrate social skills is through videotaped modeling (Cardon, 2016). Social skills are clearly modeled by therapists, family members, or other children and recorded. Children with social communication deficits can then review these skills outside of therapy using a tablet device or smartphone.

Emerging data indicate that videotaped modeling helps generalize children's social skills to home and school settings (Acar, Tekin-Iftar, & Yikmis, 2016; O'Handley, Radley, & Whipple, 2015; Vandermeer, Beamish, Milford, & Lang, 2016).

Review:

- Social communication disorder is characterized by persistent difficulties in the use of verbal and nonverbal communication in social contexts (i.e., pragmatics). Features include problems (a) greeting others and sharing information; (b) changing communication style to meet the needs of listeners in different contexts; (c) maintaining conversations or telling stories; or (d) understanding inferences, idioms, metaphors, or humor.
- Youths with social communication disorder show deficits in social communication but they do not display the restrictive, repetitive patterns of behavior seen in children with ASD.
- Treatment involves helping youths initiate and maintain eye contact and conversations, develop conversational repair skills, and improve storytelling abilities. Social skills training, either in group therapy or while watching videotaped models, is also effective in improving pragmatic communication skills.

7.2 LEARNING DISABILITIES AND SPECIFIC LEARNING DISORDER

Learning disabilities are serious conditions that can adversely affect children's academic functioning, career

Figure 7.2   In social skills training, children learn and practice the steps for effective social interaction. In one study, children randomly assigned to a Skillstreaming summer camp showed improvements in social communication and nonliteral language skills compared to controls.

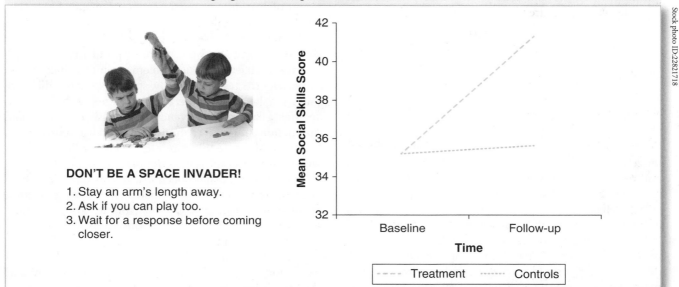

DON'T BE A SPACE INVADER!
1. Stay an arm's length away.
2. Ask if you can play too.
3. Wait for a response before coming closer.

Stock photo ID:22821718

Source: Based on Smith and Bryson (2015).

attainment, and self-concept (Pierce, 2015). Although there is disagreement as to the exact definition of learning disabilities, most experts agree children with learning disabilities have the following characteristics:

- Children with learning disabilities have marked deficits in basic academic skills: reading, math, and/or written expression. These academic problems are due to dysfunction in underlying psychological processes.
- Learning disabilities are heritable. Genes are believed to cause subtle abnormalities in brain structure, functioning, perception, memory, and information processing, which, in turn, interfere with learning.
- If untreated, learning disabilities persist over time. Children with learning disabilities are not simply "slow learners" or "late bloomers."
- Although children's intelligence and academic achievement are correlated, learning disabilities are not caused by low intelligence or ID.
- Learning disabilities are also not caused by emotional problems (e.g., test anxiety, depression), socioeconomic deprivation (e.g., malnutrition, poverty), or impoverished educational experiences (e.g., low-quality schools). Although these factors can exacerbate children's learning problems, they do not cause learning disabilities.

There is currently no consensus regarding the best way to identify children with serious learning problems. Indeed, the definition of learning disabilities varies across disciplines. Professionals who work in clinics, hospitals, and other health care facilities (e.g., clinical psychologists, physicians) tend to adopt the medical definition of learning disabilities outlined in *DSM-5*. These professionals diagnose children with specific learning disorder. In contrast, professionals who work in educational settings (e.g., school psychologists, special education teachers) tend to rely on the legal definition of learning disabilities outlined in federal and state laws. These professionals typically classify children with "specific learning disabilities" (Lewandowski & Lovett, 2014).

What Is Specific Learning Disorder?

Learning Disorder

Specific learning disorder is a *DSM-5* condition characterized by a current, normative deficit in reading, writing, and/or mathematics (see Table 7.7). Children with specific learning disorder earn reading, writing, and/or math scores well below their peers on standardized measures of academic achievement. "Well below" is usually considered at least 1.5 standard deviations below the mean. Because most achievement tests have a mean of 100 and a standard deviation of 15, a score < 78 might indicate low achievement. These academic skill deficits must be normative, that is, they must be low compared to other children in the general population. Relative deficits in academic skills, such as a lower score in math compared to reading, do not indicate a specific learning disorder (American Psychiatric Association, 2013).

Children with specific learning disorder must meet three other criteria. First, they must have a history of academic problems. In most instances, children's academic problems emerge during the early elementary or middle school years and significantly affect school performance. In some cases, however, problems begin in early childhood, but youths are able to compensate for these problems in some way. For example, a child with reading problems who has excellent short-term memory might compensate for these problems by memorizing frequently occurring words. His problems may not manifest themselves until later childhood or adolescence, when academic demands (e.g., more complex reading vocabulary) exceed his compensatory strategy.

Second, the deficits shown by people with specific learning disorder must interfere with their academic achievement, work functioning, or everyday life activities. It is not sufficient for children to score low on an achievement test; their academic deficits must also affect their functioning in the real world. For example, children with specific learning disorder might have difficulty meeting educational benchmarks for their grade, adolescents might have trouble maintaining their eligibility to play sports, or young adults may experience problems reading instruction manuals, balancing checkbooks, or writing resumes (Weis, Speridakos, & Ludwig, 2014).

Third, academic deficits shown by children with learning disorder must be "specific" to one or more academic domains—they must not reflect overall low cognitive ability. Children's overall intellectual functioning should be within normal limits with specific deficits in reading, writing, and/or math. Furthermore, specific learning disorder must not be due to other mental or neurological disorders or sensory impairments, such as vision or hearing problems. Professionals must rule out these other potential causes for low academic achievement, such as anxiety at school, medical problems that might interfere with learning, or problems seeing the blackboard or hearing the teacher. Finally, specific learning disorder must not be attributable to sociodemographic factors, such as a lack of proficiency in English or inadequate instruction in school (American Psychiatric Association, 2013). To illustrate this condition, consider Daniel, a boy with a specific learning disorder in the domain of reading.

When diagnosing specific learning disorder, clinicians specify the area of impairment: reading, written expression, or mathematics. Then, for each area identified, clinicians indicate the nature of the child's weakness. For example, Daniel might be diagnosed with specific learning disorder with impairment in reading. He seems to have moderate problems reading words accurately and fluently. Some clinicians use the term *dyslexia* to describe these deficits. In contrast, another child might be able to read words accurately and quickly but he might show

Table 7.7 Diagnostic Criteria for Specific Learning Disorder

A. Difficulties learning and using academic skills, as indicated by the presence of at least one of the following symptoms that have persisted for at least 6 months, despite the provision of interventions that target those difficulties:

1. Inaccurate or slow and effortful word reading (e.g., reads single words aloud incorrectly or slowly and hesitantly, frequently guesses words, has difficulty sounding out words).

2. Difficulty understanding the meaning of what is read (e.g., may read text accurately but not understand the sequence, relationships, inferences, or deeper meanings of what is read).

3. Difficulties with spelling (e.g., may add, omit, or substitute vowels or consonants).

4. Difficulties with written expression (e.g., makes multiple grammatical or punctuation errors within sentences; employs poor paragraph organization; written expression of ideas lack clarity).

5. Difficulties mastering number sense, number facts, or calculation (e.g., has poor understanding of numbers, their magnitude, and relationships; counts on fingers to add single-digit numbers instead of recalling the math fact as peers do; gets lost in the midst of arithmetic computation and may switch procedures).

6. Difficulties with mathematical reasoning (e.g., has severe difficulty applying mathematical concepts, facts, or procedures to solve quantitative problems).

B. The affected academic skills are substantially and quantifiably below those expected for the individual's chronological age, and cause significant interference with academic or occupational performance, or with activities of daily living, as confirmed by individually administered standardized achievement measures and comprehensive clinical assessment.

C. The learning difficulties begin during school-age years but may not become fully manifest until the demands for those affected skills exceed the individual's limited capacities (e.g., as in timed tests, reading or writing complex reports for a tight deadline, excessively heavy academic loads).

D. The learning difficulties are not better accounted for by Intellectual Disability, uncorrected visual or auditory acuity, other mental or neurological disorders, psychosocial adversity, lack or proficiency in the language of academic instruction, or inadequate educational instruction.

Note: The four diagnostic criteria are to be met based on a clinical synthesis of the individual's history (developmental, medical, family, educational), school reports, and psycho-educational assessment.

Specify all academic domains and subskills that are impaired. When more than one domain is impaired, each one should be coded individually according to the following specifiers:

Specific Learning Disorder with Impairment in Reading:

Word reading accuracy

Reading rate of fluency

Reading comprehension

Specific Learning Disorder with Impairment in Written Expression:

Spelling accuracy

Grammar and punctuation accuracy

Clarity or organization of written expression

Specific Learning Disorder with Impairment in Mathematics:

Number sense

Memorization of arithmetic facts

Accurate fluency calculation

Accurate math reasoning

Source: Reprinted with permission from the *Diagnostic and Statistical Manual of Mental Disorders, Fifth Edition* (Copyright 2013). American Psychiatric Association.

SPECIFIC LEARNING DISORDER

Waiting to Fail

Source: ©iStockphoto.com/qhoto

Daniel was a 9-year-old boy referred to our clinic because of low academic achievement. He began struggling in kindergarten. He had trouble recognizing and writing letters and numbers, answering questions about stories, and following instructions. A medical examination showed that he was healthy. Daniel repeated kindergarten the following year, but his academic problems continued.

In the first grade, Daniel was tested to determine if he had a learning disability. Daniel's IQ score was 103, indicating average intellectual functioning. His standardized scores on tests of reading (80) and writing (81) were significantly below most of his peers. However, Daniel's reading, writing, and math test scores were not low enough for him to receive special education services.

At the time of the evaluation, Daniel was attending a regular third-grade classroom. He showed significant trouble in reading. He often confused letters with similar appearances and had trouble differentiating similar-looking words, such as *that, this, those,* and *these*. Daniel could not sound out unknown words; instead, he usually guessed at their pronunciation. Daniel also read very slowly.

Daniel hated school. He was especially embarrassed to read out loud in front of the class. He resented the teacher for correcting him when he misread a word. Daniel would often try to avoid schoolwork by averting his eyes in class, volunteering to do chores in the classroom, or charming the teacher. At home, Daniel would whine when his mother asked him to complete his homework.

Daniel explained, "I'm not dumb or lazy. I just have a hard time with reading." The psychologist at the clinic suggested that Daniel be assessed for a possible learning disability. His mother responded, "Okay. But didn't they already test him when he was in the first grade and find out that he wasn't dyslexic? Besides, can't Ritalin work for these sorts of problems?"

poor comprehension. Finally, clinicians rate the severity of children's academic problems. Severity ranges from "mild" (i.e., difficulties that can be compensated by academic accommodations and support services) to "severe" (i.e., difficulties in multiple academic domains that greatly interfere with skill acquisition).

Learning Disabilities

Professionals working in schools tend to use the term *specific learning disability*, rather than specific learning disorder, to describe children with serious deficits in academic skills (Peacock & Ervin, 2012). The term *learning disability* was coined by Samuel Kirk (1962) to describe children who showed significant delays in the development of reading, writing, math, or oral language. Kirk suggested that these delays interfered with children's ability to learn and were likely caused by structural abnormalities of the brain. Kirk differentiated learning disabilities from other psychological conditions that often interfere with learning, such as low intelligence and sensory impairment (Courtad & Bakken, 2011).

Today, the legal definition of a learning disability is provided by the Individuals With Disabilities Education Improvement Act (IDEIA, Public Law 5-17). This definition borrows heavily from Kirk's original conceptualization:

The term "specific learning disability" refers to a disorder in one or more of the basic psychological processes involved in understanding or in using language, spoken or written, which may manifest itself in the imperfect ability to listen, think, speak, read, write, spell, or do mathematical calculations. The term includes such conditions as perceptual disabilities, brain injury, minimal brain dysfunction, dyslexia, and developmental aphasia. It does not include a learning problem that is primarily the result of visual, hearing, or motor disabilities, of intellectual disability, of emotional disturbance, or of environmental, cultural, or economic disadvantage.

IDEIA is noteworthy in several ways. First, it applies to all children with disabilities. Although the majority of school-age children receiving special education have specific learning disabilities, IDEIA also applies to children with ID, ASD, and physical/sensory impairments (see Table 7.8). Second, IDEIA entitles all children with disabilities to a "free appropriate public education (FAPE)." Youths with disabilities have a right to receive an education that allows them to learn and achieve their academic potentials. Third, children with disabilities must be taught in the "least restrictive environment"—that is, they should be educated alongside students without disabilities in regular education classrooms whenever possible. Fourth, children with disabilities are entitled to Individualized

Table 7.8	Percent of Children With Disabilities in U.S. Schools
Disability	Percentage of All Children
Any Disability	**13.1**
Learning disability	4.9
Speech/language impairment	2.9
Other health impairments	1.4
Intellectual disability	0.9
Emotional disturbance	0.8
Autism	0.8
Developmental delay	0.7
Multiple disabilities	0.3
Hearing impairments	0.2
Visual impairments	0.1
Orthopedic impairments	0.1
Traumatic brain injury	0.1

Source: Based on U.S. Department of Education, National Center for Education Statistics (2012).

Note: Learning disabilities and speech/language impairments (i.e., communication disorders in *DSM-5*) are the most common types of disabling conditions. Other health impairments include chronic or acute health problems, such as a heart condition, asthma, sickle cell anemia, hemophilia, epilepsy, or leukemia.

Education Programs (IEPs) that specify what services will be provided to them to help them achieve. Finally, IDEIA entitles parents to take an active role in planning and implementing their children's education (Walter, 2015).

Review:

- Specific learning disorder is a *DSM-5* diagnosis characterized by difficulties learning or using reading, math, or writing skills. These academic skill deficits are significantly low, compared to other people of the same age, and cause impairment in school or other activities.
- *Specific learning disability* is a legal term that reflects problems in the basic psychological processes involved in using spoken or written language. These processing problems cause impairment in reading, math, spelling, writing, or oral language.
- The academic problems shown by children with learning disorders or disabilities are not due to sensory impairments, impoverished educational experiences, socioeconomic disadvantage, or children's cultural or linguistic background.

How Are Learning Disabilities Identified in Children?

Response to Intervention

Most school personnel identify learning disabilities using response to intervention (RTI). RTI gets its name because children are identified with learning disabilities when they fail to respond to scientific, research-based educational interventions. Children who are provided with high-quality, evidence-based reading, math, and writing instruction, but who fail to show academic progress, may be classified with learning disabilities using the RTI approach (Reschly & Coolong-Chaffin, 2016).

School systems that use RTI usually rely on a three-tier system to identify children with learning disabilities (Jimerson, Burns, & VanDerHeyden, 2016; see Figure 7.3). Tier I is characterized by universal or "primary preventative" screening; all children in a class are evaluated to assess their acquisition of basic academic skills. Typically, screenings are brief and administered periodically over the course of the academic year. Furthermore, screening often relies on curriculum-based assessment. Curriculum-based assessment involves measuring children's progress toward academic benchmarks established by the teacher or school district. Rather than comparing children's scores to a norm group (like standardized achievement testing), children are evaluated based on whether they are meeting these learning goals.

For example, many school districts use the Dynamic Indicators of Basic Early Literacy Skills (DIBELS) to identify children with delays in word reading (Smolkowski & Cummings, 2016). The DIBELS consists of a series of very brief tests that require students in early elementary school to read words or short passages. Testing takes only a few minutes and is repeated across the school year to monitor students' reading acquisition. Children's performance on the DIBELS is compared to other students in their class and evaluated based on the school district's learning objectives.

Approximately 85% of all children show adequate progress in reading, writing, and math. However, the remaining 15% who lag behind their peers or fall short of the district's standards are considered "nonresponsive" to treatment and progress to Tier II. This tier is called secondary prevention because interventions in this tier are administered to children who show academic delays but have not yet been identified with learning disabilities. Children in Tier II typically receive supplemental, small-group instruction in the academic domain in which they show delays. For example, children struggling with reading might receive regular reading instruction in the classroom and additional, small-group instruction several times per week. Reschly and Bergstrom (2009) recommend that Tier II interventions last 10 to 20 weeks. In practice, the frequency and duration of group interventions range considerably, from weekly sessions lasting a few months to daily sessions lasting most of the academic year (McKenzie, 2009). After

Figure 7.3   Response to Intervention (RTI)

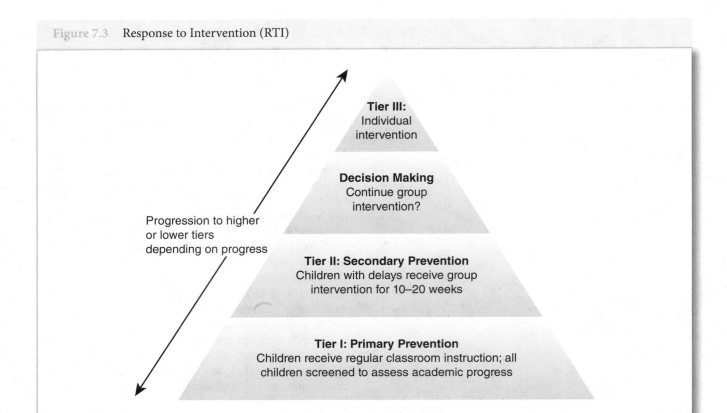

Tier III:
Individual
intervention

Decision Making
Continue group
intervention?

Tier II: Secondary Prevention
Children with delays receive group
intervention for 10–20 weeks

Tier I: Primary Prevention
Children receive regular classroom instruction; all
children screened to assess academic progress

Progression to higher
or lower tiers
depending on progress

Source: Based on Reschly and Bergstrom (2009).

Note: RTI usually consists of three tiers of increasingly more individualized and intensive instruction. Children who fail to respond progress up the tiers and may eventually receive special education services and be classified with a learning disability.

small-group instruction, schools reevaluate children's need for continued services in Tier II. Children who meet learning benchmarks may return to Tier I, students who show some improvement may remain in Tier II, and children who do not respond to group intervention may progress to Tier III (Reschly & Bergstrom, 2009).

Between 5% and 10% of school-age children continue to show academic deficits even when provided with supplemental group instruction. These youths may progress to Tier III of RTI (Jimerson et al., 2016). The services delivered to children in Tier III vary from school to school. In most instances, Tier III involves individualized instruction or one-on-one tutoring, targeting children's academic deficit. Some experts regard Tier III as "special education" whereas others believe that children should only be placed in special education if they fail to show progress in Tier III (Clemens, Keller-Margulis, Scholten, & Yoon, 2016). To see the three-tier system at work, consider the case of Rafe and Ricky.

The chief benefit of RTI is that it allows school personnel to identify and help children with learning disabilities at an earlier age (Yssledyke, Burns, Scholin, & Parker, 2010). Children with potential learning problems can be identified based on classroom

observations, and primary and secondary prevention strategies can be implemented immediately. Early identification and remediation might also decrease the number of children referred to special education. Because RTI uses a tiered approach to identification and treatment, only children who fail to respond to lower level interventions are referred for more intensive (and costly) special education services (Walter, 2015).

Comprehensive Assessment

Comprehensive assessment is an alternative approach to learning disability identification (Flanagan, Fiorello, & Ortiz, 2010; Flanagan, Ortiz, & Alfonso, 2013). It involves integrating classroom observations of academic performance with norm-referenced testing that includes measures of academic achievement, intellectual ability, and cognitive processing. Advocates of comprehensive assessment point out that children can fail to respond to evidence-based academic instruction for many reasons— only one of which is a learning disability (Hale et al., 2010). Alternative reasons might include low intellectual functioning, attention problems, anxiety or mood disorders, low motivation, poor parental involvement or support,

Rafe, Ricky, and Rti

Rafe and Ricky are 7-year-old boys in the same first-grade class. Both boys had problems with letter recognition and basic word reading in kindergarten and have continued to lag behind their peers this year as well. Periodic screenings conducted by their teacher indicated that they could read only about 8 to 10 words/minute, compared with their classmates who read 20 to 25 words/minute on average. Because the boys were not making adequate progress with regular classroom instruction, they progressed to Tier II of their school's RTI program. Tier II consisted of regular reading class and supplemental small-group instruction, designed to improve the boys' ability to sound out words. Their group met approximately 20 minutes each day for 20 weeks.

Figure (a) shows Rafe's progress. The dark line shows the school's benchmark criterion for first graders; that is, it shows how many words a first-grade child should be able to read at each point in the school year. Rafe's reading specialist set the goal (light line) that he should be able to read three more words/minute each week over the course of the intervention. As the dotted line shows, Rafe was able to meet his goals and catch up to his peers. Because he responded to Tier II intervention, it was discontinued, and he continued to receive only regular reading instruction with his class.

Figure (b) shows Ricky's progress. Although Ricky and Rafe had the same goals, Ricky did not respond to the group-based intervention (dotted line). Ricky's parents, teacher, and reading specialist decided that Ricky should receive Tier III services, which consisted of individual reading instruction for the remainder of the academic year. Their goal is to help Ricky catch up to his classmates before transitioning to the second grade.

Figures (a) and (b) Rafe (a) Responded to Group-Based Reading Intervention in Tier II of RTI but Ricky (b) Did Not

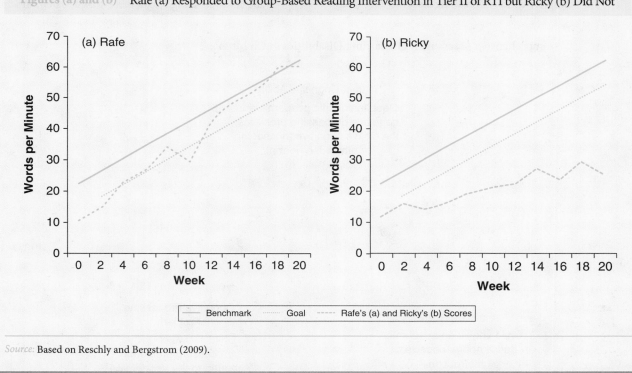

Source: Based on Reschly and Bergstrom (2009).

linguistic or cultural differences, health or nutritional problems, or other difficulties stemming from social–cultural disadvantage (Tannock, 2013). Although all children with learning disabilities have academic delays, all children with academic delays do not necessarily have learning disabilities. Comprehensive assessment permits clinicians to differentiate learning disabilities caused by underlying cognitive processing problems from low achievement caused by these other factors (Mascolo, Alfonso, & Flanagan, 2014).

The first part of the comprehensive model capitalizes on the strengths of RTI. Children who show delays in academic skills compared to their peers (Tier I) are provided with additional group-based instruction (Tier II). If children continue to lag behind their classmates, they may receive individualized instruction and practice (Tier III). If children continue to show deficits despite individual instruction, they might have a learning disability. Determination is based on the following four criteria (see Figure 7.4):

1. The child shows a *normative deficit in academic skills*. According to *DSM-5*, the child's reading, math, or writing achievement score is <85 (lowest 16th percentile).

2. The child shows a *cognitive processing problem* that is related to his or her academic skill deficit. For example, cognitive testing might show that a child with poor reading fluency displays underlying problems with processing speed. Alternatively, a child with poor math calculation skills might have underlying deficits in working memory.

3. The child *does not have generally low intelligence*. Although the child shows specific cognitive processing problems, his or her intellectual functioning is intact. For example, a child with reading disability might have

underlying problems with processing speed. However, his verbal IQ should be within normal limits and most of his other cognitive processing scores should fall into the average range. An otherwise normal cognitive profile allows the clinician to differentiate children with learning disabilities from children who experience learning problems because of low intelligence.

4. *Alternative explanations for the child's academic deficit are ruled out*. For example, the clinician must determine that the child's achievement deficit is not due to language differences or problems with acculturation, socioeconomic disadvantage, test anxiety, or sensory deficits.

Children who meet criteria for learning disabilities according to the comprehensive model may be referred for high-intensity, individualized instruction to help them overcome their academic deficits. More importantly, the results of comprehensive assessment provide information to school personnel that might help them tailor interventions to suit children's cognitive strengths and weaknesses (Flanagan & Harrison, 2012).

Review:

• Learning disabilities are usually identified in school-age children using RTI, a three-tiered system in which

Figure 7.4 Comprehensive Assessment of Learning Disabilities in Children

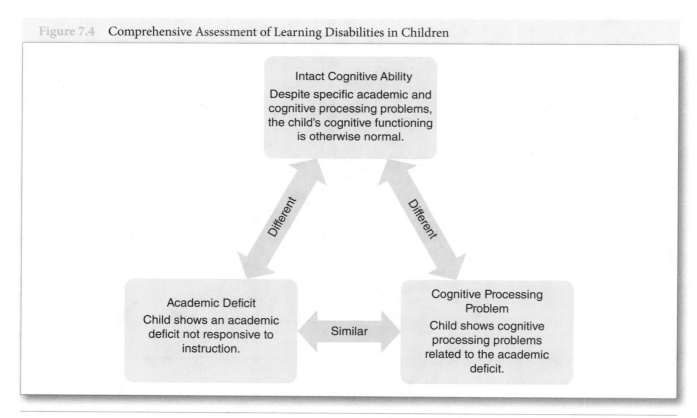

Source: Based on Flanagan and colleagues (2010).

Note: Children with learning disabilities show (a) an academic skill deficit, (b) underlying cognitive processing problems associated with that academic deficit, and (c) otherwise normal cognitive functioning (IQ). Furthermore, alternative explanations for the child's academic problem (e.g., cultural or economic disadvantage) must be ruled out.

children receive progressively more intense, individual services to help them acquire academic skills. Failure to respond to these interventions may indicate a disability.

- RTI relies on curriculum-based assessment, the measurement of children's academic progress toward standards or benchmarks.
- In comprehensive assessment, children are diagnosed with a learning disability when they show (a) normative deficits in academic skills, (b) underlying cognitive processing problems that might explain these deficits, and (c) otherwise average intelligence. Furthermore, alternative causes for their achievement problems must be ruled out.

How Common Are Learning Disabilities?

Prevalence

Approximately 5% of children have been classified with learning disabilities and are receiving special education services in US schools (Cortiella & Horowitz, 2014). This percentage has remained relatively stable for the past decade. This percentage likely underestimates the actual number of children with learning disabilities because not all youths receive a formal disability classification and receive services. An alternative way to estimate prevalence is to ask parents if their child has even been diagnosed with a learning disability, either by school officials or by private practitioners. Results of the National Health Interview Survey (NHIS), a very large epidemiological study, revealed that 7.5% of parents report that their child has a learning disability (Centers for Disease Control and Prevention, 2016b).

Reading disability is the most common learning disability; as many as 80% of children with diagnosed learning disabilities have reading problems. The prevalence of writing disabilities (8%–15%) and math disabilities (5%–8%) is much lower. Many children with learning disabilities experience problems in two or more academic domains. For example, roughly half of all youths with math-related problems also show difficulty reading. Furthermore, children with both math and reading problems show greater impairment in each of these areas than do children with math or reading problems alone (Cortiella & Horowitz, 2014).

Gender, Ethnicity, and Culture

Studies examining gender differences in the prevalence of learning disabilities have yielded mixed results. Most data indicate that boys are more likely than girls to be classified with a learning disability and receive special education services. For example, data from the NHIS (Centers for Disease Control and Prevention, 2016b) indicated that approximately 9% of boys and 5.9% of girls have been identified with a learning disability. Boys may be more likely to receive learning disability classification

because they also tend to show more disruptive behavior than girls. Their disruptive behavior may increase the likelihood that they will be referred for testing and, consequently, receive special education.

Ethnically diverse children in the United States are more likely to be classified with learning disabilities than non-Latino, White children. For example, Shifrer, Muller, and Callahan (2011) found that African American, Latino, and American Indian children were approximately 1.5 times more likely than non-Latino, White children to be diagnosed with learning disabilities. According to the researchers, these differences are largely attributable to socioeconomic status (SES). Low family income consistently predicted a child's likelihood of disability classification; furthermore, when the researchers controlled for SES, differences in the prevalence of learning disabilities across ethnicities disappeared. The researchers hypothesized that low family income, low parental education, and barriers to high-quality schools, nutrition, and health care place children at risk for learning disabilities (see Figure 7.5).

Children whose primary language is not English are *not* more likely than native English speakers to be diagnosed with learning disabilities (Shifrer et al., 2011). However, children who do not gain proficiency in English by the time they begin school or children who are placed in an English as a second language class in school are at increased likelihood of learning disability classification. This increased risk is not explained by ethnicity or SES. The researchers suggest that school personnel may misinterpret these children's difficulty with English as evidence of a learning disability. These findings speak to the importance of being sensitive to children's native language and cultural background when assessing their academic skills (Lewandowski & Lovett, 2014).

Review:

- Between 5% and 7.5% of school-age children have been identified as having a learning disability. Reading disabilities account for approximately 80% of youths with these conditions.
- Boys are more likely than girls to be identified with a learning disability.
- Children from minority backgrounds are more likely to be identified with a learning disability than non-Latino, White youths. These differences in identification are partially attributable to SES.

What Causes Reading Disabilities?

Basic Reading Problems

Reading is a complex task that children do not acquire naturally. As children learn to read, they progress along a continuum of reading skills. First, children learn to recognize individual letters by their names and sounds. For example, preschool-age children learn to recognize the letter *s* from a list of printed letters, to name the letter *s*, and to tell a parent that the *s* makes the /s/ sound. Letter

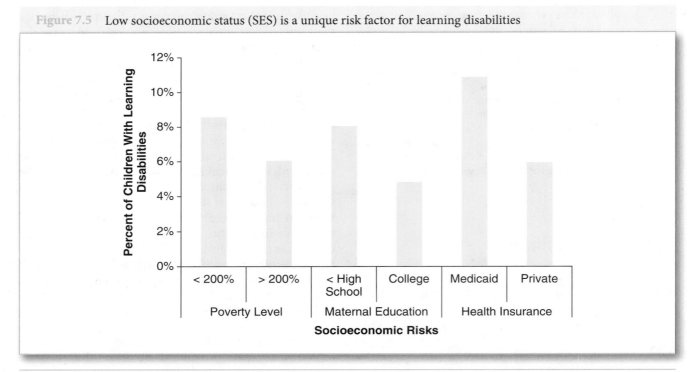

Source: Based on Boyle and colleagues (2011).

Note: Children who live in poverty, whose mothers did not complete high school, or who receive Medicaid are at increased risk for developing learning disabilities.

recognition is essential to the development of all other reading skills.

After letter recognition, children must develop phoneme awareness. First, children must learn to isolate phonemes (i.e., the first sound in "car" is /c/), segment phonemes (e.g., there are three sounds in "shop": /sh/ /o/ /p/), blend phonemes (e.g., the sounds /s/ /t/ /r/ /ee/ /t/ make "street"), and manipulate phonemes (e.g., "car" with a /f/ instead of a /c/ is "far"). Later, they are able to use these phonemic skills to phonetically sound out new words (e.g., the letters C-A-T spell /c/ /a/ /t/ or "cat"). Most children need systematic instruction to develop phoneme awareness. Indeed, a considerable percentage of time in preschool and kindergarten is devoted to learning phoneme awareness and developing phonics skills (Samms-Vaughn, 2006).

Children with adequate phoneme awareness are able to engage in phonemic mediation—that is, the ability to sound out novel words. Consider the following sentence: *Cat has a snack* (see Image 7.4). A beginning reader might know the first three words in the sentence but be unfamiliar with the word *snack*. He might use phonics skills to sound out the word by translating each letter into its corresponding phoneme: /s/ - /n/ - /a/ - /k/. Then, he examines whether the resulting combination of phonemes corresponds to his existing spoken vocabulary. For example, he might think to himself, "The word sounds like

snack. I know what a *snack* is. The word *snack* makes sense in the sentence, so the word must be *snack*."

Most children with reading disabilities have marked deficits in phoneme awareness (Johnson, Humphrey, Mellard, Woods, & Swanson, 2010). Consequently, they have difficulty sounding out novel words. Instead, they may try to infer words based on their appearance, other words in the sentence, or contextual cues (e.g., pictures). In the sentence, *Cat has a snack*, a young child with a reading disability might guess at the meaning of the word *snack* based on its length or beginning letter. Then, he might use pictures to test whether his inference is correct. In some cases, these strategies lead to reading errors. For example, a child might incorrectly read the sentence as *Cat has a sack* because he sees a picture of the cat holding a bag of candy.

Brain abnormalities may underlie children's problems with basic reading. Three areas of the brain are important to reading (see Image 7.5). The first area is the left occipitotemporal cortex, located near the back of the brain near our visual processing area. Functional MRI (fMRI) studies indicate that this region helps us recognize familiar printed words (i.e., common "sight" words). It is likely that this brain region is especially involved in our ability to read rapidly and accurately. Damage to this region renders people unable to recognize familiar words. Instead, people with damage to this brain region must sound out

Image 7.4   Children with adequate phonics skills can sound out the word "snack" to read the sentence. Children with reading disabilities who lack phonics skills may guess the word based on its appearance.

Cat has a snack.

Image 7.5   Abnormalities in brain areas associated with processing of words underlie many children's problems with basic reading.

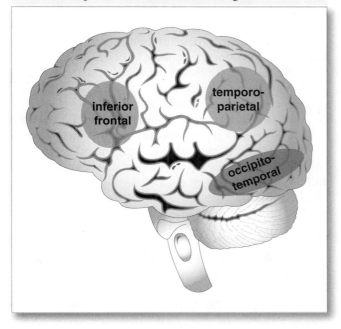

even simple, frequently occurring words. Their reading is slow and laborious (Kovelman et al., 2012).

The second brain region is a portion of the left temporoparietal cortex known as Wernicke's area. This brain region is responsible for sounding out words. Individuals with damage to this brain region can read common words quickly and automatically, but struggle with unfamiliar words.

The final brain region is a portion of the left inferior frontal lobe known as Broca's area. This region helps us understand a word's meaning and its association with other words in the sentence. Individuals with damage to this brain area are often able to read common words and sound out novel words, but have poor reading comprehension.

Children with reading problems often show abnormal functioning of the left inferior frontal and left temporoparietal cortices (i.e., Broca's and Wernicke's areas). Instead of relying on these regions in the left hemisphere, children with reading disabilities often use portions of their right hemispheres—regions responsible for processing visual information. Interestingly, older children with reading disabilities show greater reliance on right hemisphere brain regions than younger children with the disorder. These findings indicate that older children with reading disabilities may learn to compensate for their poor phonics skills by memorizing words based on their appearance or relying on contextual cues. Although these strategies can be effective for early readers, they are inadequate to read complex material and to read with high comprehension (Kovelman et al., 2012).

Surprisingly, children with reading disabilities who receive instruction in phonics show a significant increase in activity in the left frontal and temporoparietal areas. In several studies, 2 to 8 months of phonics instruction caused significant increases in left hemisphere activity. After instruction, the brain activity and reading skills of children with reading disabilities were similar to those of typically developing readers. Phonics instruction may normalize brain activity among children with reading disabilities, helping these children process words like their classmates (Aylward, Bender, Graves, & Roberts, 2003; Shaywitz et al., 2004).

Reading Fluency and Comprehension Problems

Reading fluency refers to the ability to read rapidly, accurately, and with proper expression. Fluent readers recognize words quickly, attend to important words in sentences more than unimportant words, and emphasize critical words so that sentences make sense.

Children become fluent readers through extensive practice. Initially, children must sound out almost all words in order to gain familiarity with the irregularities of the English language. Over time, children begin to recognize frequently occurring words on sight. Consequently, their speed and accuracy increases. As children accumulate reading experience, they encounter more novel words, which gradually become familiar "sight" words. Practice allows children to make reading automatic—that is, practice lets children "turn low-frequency words into high-frequency words" (Rayner, Foorman, Perfetti, Pesetsky, & Seidenberg, 2001, p. 40).

Reading comprehension refers to children's ability to read text for meaning, to remember information from the text, and to use information to solve problems or to share with others. Reading comprehension is an active process in which children construct meaning from what they read. Reading comprehension, therefore, depends on the interaction between the reader and the text. The reader's understanding of the text will depend on her basic reading skills, reading fluency, and prior knowledge.

Children with reading fluency and comprehension problems often have histories of poor phoneme awareness. Many of these children never developed the basic reading skills necessary to sound out novel words. Consequently, their exposure to novel words and practice with reading is limited. Problems reading novel words often lead to an overall reduction in the rate of reading (i.e., fluency) and accuracy with which children can answer questions about the passages they read (i.e., comprehension).

Reading fluency and comprehension problems are also associated with specific cognitive processing deficits (Johnson et al., 2010). Processing speed refers to a child's cognitive efficiency—that is, her ability to quickly and accurately perform relatively simple tasks without expending a high degree of effort. Children with above-average processing speed can perform simple cognitive tasks automatically and, therefore, can devote cognitive resources to high-level thinking and reasoning. Because these children can read quickly and accurately, they can spend more energy thinking about the meaning of the text. Children with below-average processing speed find cognitive tasks slow and effortful; consequently, they have fewer resources available for higher order mental activity. Often, these children read slowly and spend a great deal of energy sounding out words; as a result, they have less energy to spend on comprehension.

Working memory is the ability to simultaneously hold and manipulate multiple pieces of information in short-term memory to solve problems. Verbal working memory is a specific kind of working memory for verbal information (e.g., words, sentences). Children with above-average verbal working memory can keep verbal information in short-term memory long enough so that it can be used to solve immediate problems. When reading, these children can keep details about the early part of a sentence or paragraph in mind while simultaneously reading the later part of a sentence. Their verbal working memory permits greater reading comprehension. Children with below average verbal working memories have difficulty maintaining and manipulating information in short-term memory. When reading, these children may forget important information presented earlier in the text and, consequently, show poor comprehension (Swanson & Stomel, 2012).

Finally, rapid automatized naming (RAN) refers to the ability to recall the names of a series of familiar items as quickly as possible (Denckla & Rudel, 1976). In everyday life, RAN might be measured by counting the number of songs on your smartphone that you can name in one minute. In clinical settings, RAN is measured by counting the number of items in a certain category that children can name while working against a time limit (e.g., "Name as many foods as possible in one minute"). It can also be assessed by presenting an array of pictures, colors, letters, or numbers in random order and asking children to name each stimulus in the array while working against a time limit.

Experts are not certain why RAN is important to reading. It is possible that RAN depends on both verbal working memory (e.g., the recall of words) and processing speed (e.g., the automaticity of processing), which are, themselves, important to language. Whatever the reason, considerable research has shown that children's capacity for RAN predicts their reading achievement. Furthermore, deficits in RAN are associated with reading disabilities (Norton & Wolf, 2012).

Children with reading disability can be differentiated into three groups based on the nature of their reading problems and underlying cognitive processing deficits (O'Brien, Wolf, & Lovett, 2012). Wolf and Bowers (1999) developed the double-deficit model to explain these differences. Some children show problems with word reading. These children often have deficits in phonological processing. In early elementary school, they may rely on sight words and context cues to read. However, by middle school, these children experience problems with word reading and reading comprehension because of the greater frequency of novel words (e.g., *chlorophyll, diffusion, photosynthesis*). Their deficits in phonemic mediation catch up to them.

A second group of children shows few problems with word reading or phonemic awareness but does display poor reading fluency. These children often have underlying deficits in processing speed, verbal working memory, and/or RAN. They can read words accurately, but their reading is slow and laborious. These children may also have poor reading comprehension skills because of their slow reading speed and working memory deficits. They often have difficulty remembering information from the beginning of the passage by the time they reach the end of the passage.

A third, small group of children shows impairments in both basic reading skills and reading fluency. These children with double-deficits show the greatest level of reading problems overall (Frijters et al., 2011).

Review:

- Children with basic reading problems often display poor phonemic awareness, which interferes with their ability to decode unfamiliar words. Underactivity of the left hemisphere language areas of the brain are associated with these deficits.
- Youths with reading fluency and comprehension problems often have underlying deficits in processing speed, working memory, or RAN.
- The double-deficit model indicates that children can have problems with (a) basic word reading, (b) reading fluency and comprehension, or (c) both. Youths with double deficits are most resistant to treatment.

What Treatments Are Effective for Children With Reading Disabilities?

Basic Reading

Empirical studies confirm the importance of systematic instruction in phoneme awareness and phonics to treat problems with word reading (see Table 7.9). Explicitly teaching children to recognize and manipulate phonemes has a large and direct effect on their phoneme awareness skills. Explicit training in phoneme awareness is also associated with significant gains in reading and spelling. Similarly, children who receive systematic instruction in phonics show significantly greater gains in reading than children who do not receive phonics instruction. Phonics programs that encourage children to convert letters (graphemes) into sounds (phonemes) and combine or blend sounds into recognizable words are associated with the greatest improvement in reading. Systematic phonics instruction is most effective when it is administered individually or in small groups and when it is initiated before second grade. Phonics-based reading instruction is also associated with gains in children's reading comprehension (Adams & Carnine, 2003; Carlson & Francis, 2002; National Reading Panel, 2000).

Reading Fluency

Reading fluency depends on practice; therefore, interventions designed to increase reading fluency provide children with ample exposure to text and frequent feedback regarding accuracy. One evidence-based approach is guided oral reading. In guided oral reading, the child reads and rereads a text aloud until she becomes proficient. Teachers or peers listen to the child, provide assistance sounding out words, and correct reading errors. Sometimes, children read along with audiotapes, videos, or computer programs.

A variant of guided oral reading is digitally assisted reading, in which children read text on a tablet or computer as a voice models proper pronunciation, speed, and inflection. For example, Literacy by Design offers "echo reading" in which children can read a story while a digital narrator demonstrates proper reading accuracy, speed, and inflection (see Image 7.6; Coyne, Pisha, Dalton, Zeph, & Smith, 2012).

Children who participate in these interventions show increased reading accuracy, speed, and comprehension compared to children who do not receive treatment. Furthermore, these interventions are effective for typically developing readers and children with reading disabilities (National Reading Panel, 2000).

What about children who struggle with reading fluency despite ample practice? Interventions for these children target underlying deficits in cognitive processing such as working memory and RAN. Wolf, Miller,

Table 7.9   Using Direct Instruction to Teach Reading
Step 1: The teacher explicitly states the goals for the lesson.
Today, we are going to learn how to read words that contain the letters "st" and make the sound /st/. By the end of the lesson, you will be able to read words that have /st/ in them.
Step 2: The teacher breaks down material into small steps, giving students the chance to practice each step.
Here are the letters "st." What are the letters? (Child answers "st.")
They make the /st/ sound. What sound do they make? (Child answers /st/.)
Step 3: Teacher provides clear and detailed instructions.
Let's practice some words that start with /st/. All of these words begin with the /st/ sound. Ready? (Teacher gives examples.)
Step 4: Teacher provides guidance during initial practice.
Start with this word. (Teacher points to each part of the word as child reads it.)
Step 5: Teacher provides systematic feedback and corrects child's mistakes immediately.
Now read this word. (Child correctly reads the word "stop.")
Good. Now this one. (Child incorrectly reads the word "stem.")
No. The word is "stem." Read it again with me.
Step 6: Teacher gives additional practice, either during seatwork, homework, or during the next lesson.
During the last lesson, we learned about words that begin with /st/. Today, we're going to review and practice more /st/ words.

and Donnelly (2000) have developed a program to improve the reading fluency of children with these deficits. Their intervention is called retrieval, automaticity, vocabulary, elaboration, and orthography (RAVE-O), an intensive program designed to improve children's ability to automatically decode, identify, and understand words (Wolf, Gottwald, & Orkin, 2009).

To help children read words more quickly, and with less effort, teachers emphasize certain "core words" that form the basis of their reading vocabulary (Wolf, Barzillai, et al., 2009). These words are organized in groups based on similar rhymes. For example, "hat," "mat," and "cat" share the /at/ rhyme. Children learn to recognize related core words each week as well as common rhyme patterns. They also begin to recognize words quickly based on their beginnings and endings (e.g., –at).

Teachers try to improve children's word recognition by improving their reading vocabularies. One method to increase children's semantic knowledge is to use image cards to help children learn and recall frequently encountered words quickly and easily. Image cards contain pictorial representations of common words designed to help children with memory deficits recall them. Multiple meanings for each word might be displayed on the card, to help children

Image 7.6 Literacy by Design

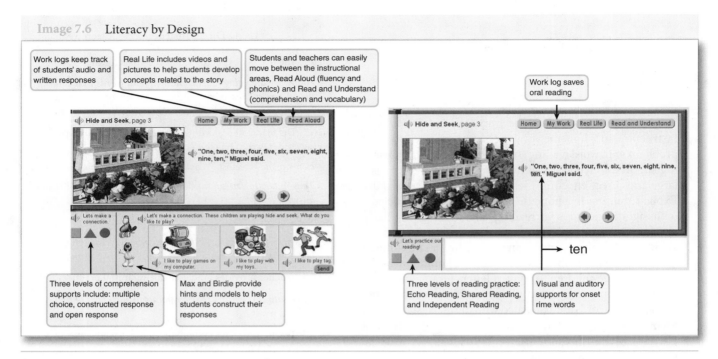

Source: From Coyne and colleagues (2012). Used with permission.

Note: Literacy by Design is a universal design approach to teaching reading comprehension. Children can read along with the narrator (i.e., echo reading), read with a partner, or read to themselves. Children can click on text to hear words or access pictures and videos. Children can demonstrate their comprehension by taking a multiple-choice test, typing their answers, or speaking their answers aloud.

appreciate the flexibility of language. For example, the word *jam* might be shown as "a topping for toast" and as "a child in trouble."

A final component of treatment involves improving children's word recall strategies. Recall that children with RAN deficits have difficulty retrieving words. One technique to improve word recall is the detective game. Children are taught to be "word detectives" who retrieve words that might be "on the tip of their tongues."

The efficacy of RAVE-O was investigated in a randomized controlled study of 279 children with reading disabilities (Morris et al., 2012). Youths were randomly assigned to one of four conditions: (1) traditional phonemic awareness and word identification skills training, (2) RAVE-O, (3) phonemic awareness training plus study skills training, or (4) controls. All interventions were conducted 5 days per week for 70 sessions. At the end of treatment, children in the three active treatment groups showed significantly more improvement in word reading than children in the control group. More importantly, children who participated in RAVE-O showed the greatest improvement in reading fluency and comprehension.

Reading Comprehension

Children with reading disability will not develop adequate reading comprehension on their own. Reading comprehension skills must be systematically introduced and modeled in the classroom. Children who are provided with systematic training in reading comprehension show significant improvements compared to youths who do not receive explicit instruction. Systematic instruction is associated with increases in children's memory for information, speed of reading, understanding, and ability to apply information to answer questions or solve problems (National Reading Panel, 2000; Therrien, Wickstrom, & Jones, 2006).

Many children with reading disabilities have deficits in story grammar (Mason & Hagaman, 2012). Story grammar refers to knowledge of the components and structure of stories, such as their characters, setting, conclusion or resolution, and tone or emotion. Children with reading disability are often unaware of many of these aspects of story grammar and recall fewer of them than typically developing children. Furthermore, they exhibit deficits in story grammar regardless of whether they are listening to or reading stories.

Interventions teach children to recognize and retain information about story grammar (Mason & Hagaman, 2012). For example, *story mapping* is a technique suitable for younger readers. As children read stories aloud, the teacher emphasizes aspects of story grammar when they occur. Then, she represents each aspect with a picture to aid children's recall (e.g., straw, sticks, and bricks to represent events in *The Three Little Pigs*). With practice, children learn to recognize aspects of story grammar independently and complete their own story maps. Another technique, appropriate for older children, is *self-questioning*. Although skillful readers naturally ask questions about story grammar while reading a narrative, poor readers need to be taught this skill. In self-questioning, children are initially prompted by teachers to ask questions about purpose, characters, plot, and resolution while they are reading. With practice, children begin to ask (and answer) these questions independently.

Children with reading disabilities also struggle with nonfiction. Text that conveys facts and information tends to use relatively unfamiliar structure (e.g., lists, compare-and-contrasts), adopts complex vocabulary, and assumes prior knowledge, which children might lack (Mason & Hagaman, 2012). To understand nonfiction writing, children need to be taught to break down and reorganize the text, using text enhancements. Text enhancements are visual aids or routines that assist students in identifying, organizing, understanding, and recalling important information (see Image 7.7). Some of the most effective text enhancements are graphic organizers (i.e., diagrams, figures, or timelines to make abstract ideas concrete), cognitive maps (i.e., arrows, flowcharts, or lines that show relationships between ideas), mnemonics (i.e., memory aids like HOMES to help you recall the Great Lakes), and computer-assisted instruction (i.e., embedded digital media such as hyperlinks or videos). Youths with learning disabilities who use text enhancements show moderate improvements in reading comprehension (Berkeley, Scruggs, & Mastropieri, 2010; Kellems et al., 2016).

Review:

- Children with reading fluency or comprehension problems caused by poor word reading skills may benefit from phonics-based instruction.

- Guided oral reading, digitally assisted reading, and the RAVE-O program are effective at increasing the rate and accuracy of children's reading.
- Interventions to improve reading comprehension for fiction often focus on teaching story grammar—that is, the components and structure of stories. Interventions for nonfiction often involve text enhancements, such as diagrams, flowcharts, or mnemonics.

What Causes Disabilities in Written Expression?

Like reading, writing is a complex task that takes years to master. For most children, the writing process involves three steps: planning, translating, and reviewing (Hayes & Flower, 1980). *Planning* involves determining the purpose of the writing, generating a main topic and supporting ideas, and organizing these ideas so that they make sense. *Translating* involves converting ideas into text. It depends on children's phoneme awareness, their knowledge of vocabulary and spelling, and the mechanics of writing (e.g., how they hold a pencil, typing skills). *Reviewing* involves rereading their stories, identifying mistakes, and making changes.

Children with writing disabilities spend less time on all three tasks than their typically developing classmates. First, children with writing disabilities spend little time planning and organizing. Consequently, their writing becomes a stream of consciousness in which ideas are disjointed and arguments are difficult to follow. Second, children with writing disabilities make frequent spelling errors and have poor handwriting. Although these problems may seem minor, they hinder the writing process. Third, children with writing disabilities seldom review their work. When they do edit, their changes tend to be superficial (e.g., correcting a spelling or punctuation

Image 7.7   A timeline is one example of a text enhancement that can help children with reading comprehension. This fifth-grader's timeline shows events leading up to the American Revolution.

error) rather than focus on the coherence and quality of the composition.

Children with and without writing disability differ greatly in the quality of their writing. Specifically, they differ in six areas (Graham, Harris, & Chambers, 2016; MacArthur, 2016; MacArthur, Philippakos, & Graham, 2016)

- *Productivity.* Children with writing disability simply write fewer words than their typically developing classmates. On average, their compositions are one-third shorter than those of children with average writing skills. Their lack of productivity is seen in both narrative and expository writing.
- *Lexical diversity.* Lexical diversity is typically assessed by counting the number of different root words in a composition. Children with writing disability write fewer words and use language that is less varied and more redundant.
- *Grammar.* Grammatical errors are the most noticeable and common problem shown by children with writing disability. They often omit essential parts of a sentence, have difficulty with subject–verb agreement, or mistakenly use pronouns and contractions (e.g., *their* vs. *they're*).
- *Sentence complexity.* Children with writing disability use less descriptive sentences than their peers. Sentence complexity is typically assessed by determining the average length of main clauses and dependent clauses in the child's writing. Consider the following lines of text:
   I followed the rabbit all day until it ran into its hole.
   I followed the rabbit all day. It ran into its hole.
   Although both lines have the same meaning, the first is more complex.
- *Spelling accuracy.* Children with writing disability often make spelling errors. Children with underlying phonological processing problems and reading disability often make dysphonetic spelling errors—that is, there is little relationship between the sound of their words and the way they spell them. For example, a young child with adequate phonemic processing might spell "telephone" as "telafone." However, a child without adequate phonemic processing might spell the word *talnofe*, which does not correspond to the sound of the word. Dysphonetic spelling errors make children's compositions extremely difficult to read.
- *Story content.* Children with writing disability also receive lower ratings for overall story content than do their typically developing classmates. Specifically, they have difficulty (a) relating experiences or presenting information in a clear and focused manner, (b) structuring their writing in such a way that their main idea is clear and supported, (c) using an appropriate tone of voice and degree of formality for the purpose of the writing and the audience, and (d) adopting writing conventions such as punctuation and capitalization.

Review:

- Youths with disabilities in written expression spend less time than their typically developing peers planning, translating, and reviewing their writing.
- Youths with writing disabilities also produce less text, use simpler and less diverse words and sentences, and make frequent mistakes in grammar or sentence structure.

What Treatments Are Effective for Children With Disabilities in Written Expression?

Children with writing disability need systematic instruction, ample practice, and frequent feedback (MacArthur, Philippakos, Graham, & Harris, 2012; Mather & Wendling, 2011). One of the most effective methods of teaching writing skills is Self-regulated strategy development (SRSD). SRSD is based on the notion that poor writers lack effective strategies for planning, implementing, and evaluating their work. Teachers introduce, model, and reinforce writing strategies, give specific feedback regarding the quality of children's writing, and offer ample opportunities to practice and improve their writing over time (Harris & Graham, 2016).

The SRSD model consists of a series of stages that children learn to implement, practice, and evaluate (Harris et al., 2012; Reid, Harris, Graham, & Rock, 2012):

1. *Develop and activate background knowledge*: The teacher explains or models any skills or information needed to complete the writing assignment. For example, if the assignment involves autobiographical writing, the teacher might explain the term *autobiography* and provide a short example of an autobiographical narrative.

2. *Discuss the strategy*: The teacher suggests a specific strategy for completing the writing task.

3. *Model the strategy*: The teacher presents each step in the strategy, emphasizing why it is important. The teacher "thinks aloud," explaining her thought process behind each step. Modeling is extremely important because it makes normally covert processes overt and accessible to students.

4. *Memorize the strategy*: Students memorize each step in the strategy through repetition and variation. The more practice they receive, the easier they will recall the strategy when necessary.

5. *Support the strategy*: Teachers use scaffolding to make sure students are successful implementing the strategy. Initially, teachers offer a great deal of assistance. As students become more familiar with the strategy, teachers reduce their level of support until students can implement it independently.

6. *Independent performance*: The teacher continues to monitor students' use of the strategy and help them modify it, when necessary, to suit different writing assignments.

The specific strategies used in the SRSD model vary depending on the writing task (Common Core State Standards, 2016). For example, when teaching narrative writing (i.e., storytelling), teachers might introduce the POWER strategy: planning, organizing, writing, editing, revising. First, the student *plans* her story. What is the purpose of the story? What background information or knowledge do I need to write it? Second, the student *organizes* her thoughts before writing. She completes a worksheet that prompts her to identify the main characters, the setting, the problem, and the resolution. Third, the teacher models the *writing* process using the think-aloud technique. The teacher shows how he uses the students' ideas to create sentences and why the order of events is important to a story's coherence. Fourth, the student *edits* her own writing. She reads her story, stars portions that she likes, and marks sections that need improvement. She also receives feedback from classmates. Fifth, the teacher models ways to *revise* the story to make it better. The student ultimately decides which changes she will make based on feedback from the teacher and peers (Harris, Graham, & Adkins, 2015).

Another strategy, DEFENDS (i.e., decide, examine, form, expose, note, drive, search) is useful in expository writing, when children must defend a thesis statement. Using the SRSD approach, the teacher introduces, models, and supports each step in the strategy. First, the child *decides* on an exact position (e.g., *Geckos make the best pets for fourth-grade boys.*) Second, he examines possible reasons for his position, perhaps by generating them on his own or consulting other people or books (e.g., *They are interesting to feed*). Third, the student *forms* a list of points that explains each reason (e.g., *They eat live crickets and mealworms. They shake their tails before attacking their prey. Their food crunches in their mouths*). Fourth, the child is ready to begin writing. He *exposes* his position in the first sentence of the essay. Fifth, he *notes* each reason for his position and supporting points. Sixth, the student *drives* home his main idea in the final sentence. Finally, he *searches* for mistakes and makes necessary corrections.

Overall, children with and without disabilities who use SRSD show improvement in grammar, length, and quality of their writing (see Figure 7.6). Furthermore, the benefits of SRSD are maintained over time and generalize to other writing assignments. For example, children who are initially taught to write essays also improve in writing book reports and short stories. The benefits of SRSD are attributed to the fact that teachers systematically introduce and model planning and reviewing strategies and encourage students to actively participate in the writing process (Graham, McKeown, Kiuhara, & Harris, 2012).

Review:

- SRSD involves introducing, modeling, and reinforcing strategies for improving written expression.

- Children are explicitly taught steps to plan, implement, and evaluate the quality of their written expression, and they are given frequent feedback as they practice their writing skills.

What Causes Math Disabilities?

Delays in Number Sense

Some experts have argued that children are biologically predisposed to understand and process mathematics information. Infants may have inherent number sense—that is, they may be aware that a group of stimuli can be understood in terms of their quantity (Geary, 2010). For example, Karen Wynn (1992) demonstrated that 5-month-old infants could differentiate between a correct numerical expression (1 + 1 = 2) and an incorrect expression (1 + 1 = 1). Similarly, Starkey and Cooper (1980) showed that 4- through 7-month-old infants could differentiate groups of dots presented in different numbered clusters. More recent research has shown that young infants can also discriminate between sounds of different numbers (Lipton & Spelke, 2003), and older infants can order sets of items from largest in number to smallest (e.g., A > B > C; Xu & Spelke, 2000). By the time most children begin school, their ability to discriminate small quantities is greatly refined. Six-year-olds can easily tell that a basket containing 25 pieces of candy has more candy than another basket containing only 20 pieces of candy. By late childhood, this capacity for numerosity is similar to that of adults (Geary, 2013).

Number sense permits the development of all other math abilities (Geary, 2010). It allows very young children to subitize—that is, to estimate the number of objects in a small group, rapidly and accurately, without counting them. For example, young children can quickly differentiate between a plate with three cookies and a plate with five cookies. Number sense also allows them to mentally represent quantities. For example, young children learn the correspondence between Arabic numerals and discrete quantities (e.g., 3 = ■ ■ ■). At about the same time, children also begin to mentally represent quantities along a number line. Young children easily understand that numbers are positioned in ordinal fashion—that is, first, second, third, and so on. Over time, children also learn that the intervals between numbers are equal. The capacity to mentally represent quantities permits basic math calculation in early elementary school, like addition and subtraction.

Children with mathematics disabilities tend to show delays in the development of number sense. The Number Sets Test (see Figure 7.7) is a brief test of number sense that consists of a series of numerals (e.g., 1, 3) or groups of objects (e.g., ■, ◆ ◆ ◆) that children must group to

Figure 7.6   Effects of SRSD on Children's Writing

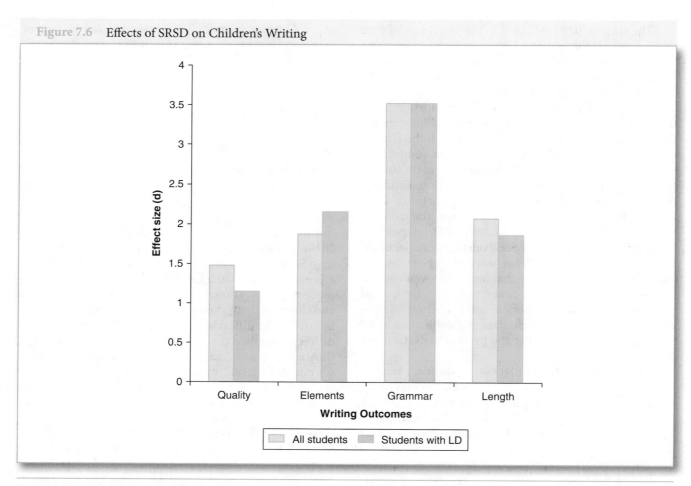

Source: Based on Graham and Harris (2003).

Note: Children who participate in SRSD show improvements in four areas of writing compared to youths who receive traditional writing instruction. SRSD is associated with improvements in both typical readers and children with learning disabilities.

Figure 7.7   The Numbers Sets Test

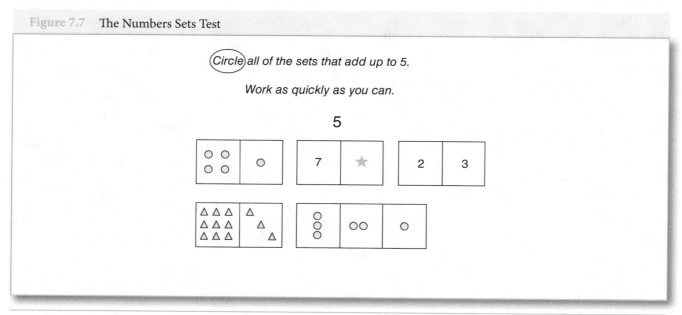

Source: Based on Geary and colleagues (2011).

Note: This test can be used to predict mathematics disorder in young children. Children with mathematics disorder are 3 years behind their typically developing classmates in their capacity for numerosity.

Figure 7.8 Children with math disability lag behind their classmates throughout elementary school.

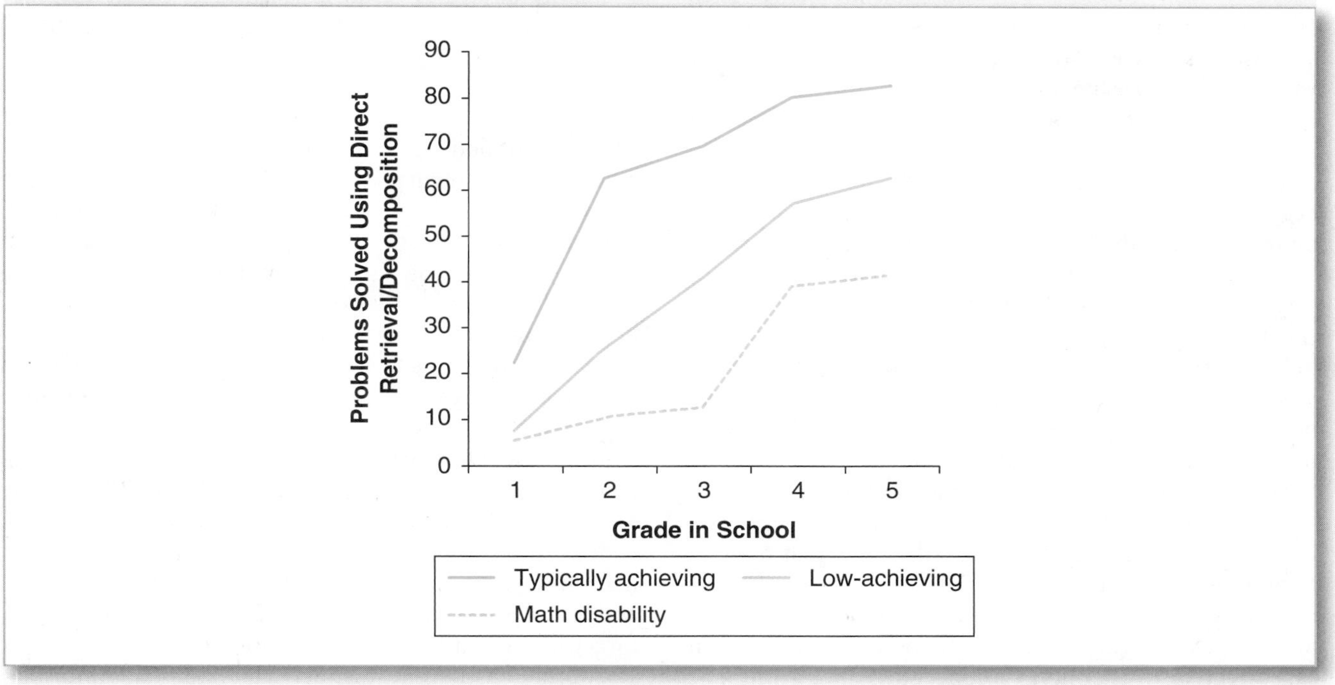

Source: Based on Geary and colleagues (2012).

Note: In this longitudinal study, children with math disabilities used direct retrieval or decomposition less frequently than did typically achieving children and low-achieving children. Instead, youths with math disability relied heavily on immature (i.e., counting) strategies.

match a target number presented at the top of the page. Children can use subitizing, counting, or a combination of both strategies to group the stimuli as fast and as accurately as possible. Typically developing children show improvement on this test from first through fourth grade. However, children with mathematics disabilities perform more slowly and make more errors than their classmates. On average, they lag approximately three years behind their peers (Geary, Bailey, & Hoard, 2009). Furthermore, children's performance on the Number Sets Test at the beginning of first grade (before most children even know how to add and subtract) predicts their likelihood of developing mathematics disability by the time they reach third grade. In fact, first graders' scores on the Number Sets Test predict later math skills better than their intelligence, memory, and baseline knowledge of math!

Counting and Calculation Errors

Children's ability to count develops between the ages of 2 and 5. Young children obey certain principles of counting that follow a fixed sequence (Gelman & Gallistel, 1978).

- *One-to-one correspondence:* One number is assigned to each object.
- *Stable order:* Numbers are counted in a specific order.

- *Cardinality:* The last number stated reflects the quantity of the items counted.
- *Abstraction:* Objects of any kind can be grouped and counted.
- *Order irrelevance:* Objects can be counted in any order.

Preschoolers later diagnosed with math disability make two types of counting errors not often shown by their classmates (Geary, Hoard, & Bailey, 2011; Geary, Hoard, Nugent, & Bailey, 2012). To study these errors, researchers ask children to help a puppet learn to count objects. On some counts, the puppet deliberately makes mistakes. The researchers record whether the child detects the mistake and corrects the puppet. First, children with math disability often become confused when counting occurs from right to left, rather than in the typical left-to-right order. They do not seem to understand the principle of order irrelevance. Second, they often fail to detect errors when the puppet double-counts the first object in the row (e.g., the puppet points to the first object and counts "one, two" and then points to the second object and counts "three"). It seems that these children have difficulty remembering one-to-one correspondence.

Beginning in elementary school, children's math skills become more complex, as children transition from counting to arithmetic. Addition depends greatly on children's counting abilities. For example, young children use fairly immature strategies to add numbers. Initially, they might count on their fingers to solve addition problems. Later, addition is performed verbally or mentally. Young children also use less efficient strategies to add. For example, very young children use the *counting-all strategy*; when asked to add 7 + 4, they first count from 1 to 7 and then count four more numbers until they arrive at the correct answer. In contrast, older children use the *counting-on strategy*; they begin with the larger number (i.e., 7) and then count four more digits until they arrive at the answer. Similar shortcuts are used for subtraction and other mathematical operations (Augustyniak, Murphy, & Phillips, 2006).

With experience, children learn to store math facts in long-term memory. For example, children begin to use direct retrieval to recall that 7 + 6 = 13; they no longer need to count to arrive at the correct answer. Alternatively, they may use a process called decomposition to solve the same problem; they might break up the problem into smaller components that are more easily remembered. For example, children might directly recall that 6 + 6 = 12 and then add one to this partial sum to obtain the correct answer. Direct retrieval and decomposition permit more rapid and automatic math computation. Children can direct their attention to conceptualizing arithmetic problems rather than to counting. Direct retrieval and decomposition also free short-term memory, allowing children to perform more complex calculations in their heads (Geary, 2011).

Children with math disabilities show deficits in math calculation skills. They calculate more slowly and make more errors than their typically developing classmates (see Figure 7.8). Several studies indicate that memory deficits underlie many of their difficulties with math calculations (Geary et al., 2011). Specifically these children have trouble remembering math facts (Geary et al., 2012). Whereas most fourth graders can effortlessly recall 4 + 5 = 9, children with mathematics disability often need to count to recall the correct answer. Consequently, they spend greater cognitive resources performing basic calculations and fewer resources conceptualizing the problem itself (Andersson, 2010).

Youths with mathematics disabilities also have difficulty remembering math procedures. For example, when presented with a problem such as 41 − 29 = ?, children with disabilities may forget how to "borrow" and, consequently, they provide an incorrect answer (Temple & Sherwood, 2002).

Because of their difficulty retrieving math facts and procedures from long-term memory, children with mathematics disabilities often rely on immature strategies to solve math problems. For example, many first graders count on their fingers to solve addition problems. However, children with mathematics disabilities often continue to rely on this immature tactic into the third and fourth grades. Furthermore, when young children with disabilities count, they often count all digits rather than rely on more advanced "add-on" strategy. These immature strategies result in slow, error-prone calculations (Swanson, 2015; Swanson, Lussier, & Orosco, 2015).

Deficits in Math Reasoning

By late childhood, children begin to develop more complex math problem-solving skills. These skills include the ability to solve story problems, to interpret charts and graphs, and to perform mathematical operations with complex sets of numbers (i.e., borrowing, long division, fractions).

Children's ability to solve higher order math problems depends on their capacity for working memory (Toll, van der Ven, Kroesbergen, & van Luit, 2011). Many children with mathematics disabilities have problems with *verbal or phonological* working memory. Some children have reading disabilities that interfere with their ability to comprehend math story problems. Other children have difficulty with auditory working memory, attention, and concentration; they are unable to hold mathematical information in short-term memory long enough to process it and arrive at the correct answer. For example, they may forget important bits of information at the beginning of story problems, become distracted by extraneous information, or transpose digits when converting a story problem to a math calculation (Toll et al., 2011).

Other children with mathematics disorder have problems with *visual–spatial* working memory. Poor visual–spatial working memory can lead to difficulty interpreting charts and graphs. Many complex math calculations, like adding three-digit numbers or performing long division, also depend on visual–spatial skills. Deficits in visual–spatial working memory can cause children to misalign numbers, leading them to use the wrong digits for their calculations (Geary et al., 2015).

Review:

- Deficits in number sense that persist into first grade predict math disabilities.
- Youths later diagnosed with math disabilities often show characteristic mistakes in counting and math calculation skills. They often rely on immature strategies to perform math computations.
- Some youths have deficits in math reasoning because of poor verbal working memory, which causes them to forget important information in story problems. Other children have deficits in visual–spatial working memory, which leads to mistakes interpreting graphs and figures.

What Treatments Are Effective for Children With Math Disabilities?

Clinicians generally rely on one of three methods for math instruction: (1) direct instruction, (2) self-instruction, or (3) mediated/assisted instruction (Steedly, Dragoo, Arafeh,

& Luke, 2008; see Table 7.10). Direct instruction in mathematics, like direct instruction for other skills, involves the systematic presentation of math calculation and problem-solving strategies. The teacher introduces and demonstrates the skill following a carefully designed script. Then, the skill is broken down into specific steps, which children perform. Teachers provide help and feedback regarding children's performance, correcting children's mistakes. Gradually, assistance is faded as children gain mastery of the skill. Children are given repeated opportunities to practice the skill and extend it to new problems. Direct instruction tends to be most effective in improving basic math computation skills in younger children.

Self-instruction is a second method to improve children's math skills. In self-instruction, teachers systematically present a series of verbal prompts that children can use to solve math problems. Teachers model the use of these prompts as they complete problems. Then, children are encouraged to use the prompts when solving their own problems, while the teacher monitors their use. Initially, teachers provide careful assistance to children in using the prompts. Eventually, assistance is faded until children can use the prompts to solve problems on their own. Self-instruction tends to be most effective for higher order math problem-solving.

Teachers who use mediated or assisted instruction begin with the child's understanding of the mathematical problem. Then, they offer assistance and guidance to help the child solve the problem correctly. Mediated or assisted instruction does not involve the use of a

---

Table 7.10   Three Methods for Teaching Mathematics Skills

Problem: Anne had 9 apples. She gave 4 apples to her friend. How many apples does Anne have left?

Direct Instruction[a]

Step A
Read the problem with me. *Teacher reads the problem.*
What kind of problem is it? *Answer: Subtraction*

Step B
Good. It's subtraction. Is the big number given? *Answer: yes*

Step C
Let's read the problem again. *Teacher reads the problem again.*
Is 9 the big number or the small number? *Answer: The big number.*
What kind of number is 4? *Answer: the small number.*

Step D
Good. Now let's take 9 and subtract 4. Watch me. Nine minus four is five.
Now you say "Nine minus four is five." *Child repeats.*
Good. What is the answer? *Answer: Five*

Step E
Good. Now let's read the next problem.

Self-Instruction[b]

Teacher introduces and demonstrates the following steps to solve story problems. Teacher encourages children to use the steps (first aloud, then silently) as she monitors.

What are you asked?	*How many apples does Anne have left?*
What numbers do you have?	*9 and 4*
What number(s) do you need to know?	*How many left?*
What must you do?	*Subtract, 9 − 4*
What is the answer?	*5*
Check your answer.	*4 + 5 = 9, so it checks out!*

Mediated/Assisted Instruction[c]

Teacher provides a structured sequence of hints to help the child complete the problem. Hints become gradually more specific and content-related until the child is able to arrive at the correct answer.

Hint Strategy	Example
Simple negative feedback: Teacher asks child to check answer.	Your answer is not quite right. Try again.
Working memory refresher: Teacher reminds child of important parts of the problem.	Remember, she has 9 and gives away 4.
Numerals as memory aids: Teacher asks child to write down important parts of problem.	Let's write it down in numbers: 9 − 4.
Enumeration: Teacher uses a series of verbal instructions and numbers to guide child.	Nine apples [points to nine] minus four apples [points to four] is what?
Complete demonstration: Teacher completes problems for child, giving rationale.	See. Nine minus four is five.

a. Based on DISTAR Arithmetic (Engelmann & Carnine, 1975).

b. Based on Fleischner and Manheimer (1997).

c. Based on Goldman (1989).

script (as direct instruction) or a series of prompts (as self-instruction). Instead, the teacher offers increasingly detailed hints until the child is able to complete the problem successfully. In this way, children are encouraged to derive their own way of solving problems, rather than rely on a formal set of rules.

Meta-analyses support the use of all three strategies for children with and without math disabilities (Gersten et al., 2009). Children with disabilities who receive direct instruction or self-instruction show large improvements in calculation and reasoning skills compared to controls. Mediated or assisted instruction is associated with moder-ate improvement in math reasoning, especially for older children and adolescents.

Review:

- Three effective treatments for math disabilities are direct instruction, self-instruction, and mediated or assisted instruction. These strategies also improve math skills in youths without disabilities.
- Direct and self-instruction are most effective with younger children whereas mediated or assisted instruction is recommended for older children.

KEY TERMS

Anticipatory-struggle theory of stuttering: A theory used to explain stuttering; suggests that children expect speaking to be anxiety-provoking; these cognitions interfere with speech production

Auditory perception: The ability to accurately identify and differentiate sounds

Childhood-onset fluency disorder: A *DSM-5* disorder characterized by a persistent problem with the normal rate, efficiency, and timing pattern of speech; causes anxiety and/or interferes with communication

Comprehensive assessment: A method of learning disability assessment in which children are classified when they show (a) normative deficits in academic skills, (b) underlying cognitive processing problems that might explain these deficits, and (c) otherwise average intelligence

Conversational recast training: A therapy for SLI, the therapist structures the child's environment to elicit verbal behavior; then, the therapist prompts the child to practice the behavior, correcting mistakes and reinforcing appropriate use

Conversational repair skills: Techniques used to help listeners regain an understanding of information conveyed during discourse; examples include providing additional background information or context

Covert-repair hypothesis: An explanation for stuttering; children who stutter show frequent disruptions in language formulation; their stuttering occurs when they try to correct these formulations while speaking

Curriculum-based assessment: A technique use in schools to measure children's academic progress in terms of their ability to reach academic goals or "benchmarks"

Decomposition: A technique used to solve math calculation problems in which the problem is broken into smaller steps that are more easily recalled and performed. In math calculation, to break up complex problems into smaller components which are more easily remembered or solved

Digitally assisted reading: A technique to improve fluency using technology; children read text on a tablet or computer as a voice models fluent reading

Direct instruction: The systematic introduction, modeling, practice, and reinforcement of appropriate skills

Direct retrieval: In math calculation, the immediate recall of math facts (e.g., 3 x 3 = 9)

Double-deficit model: A model that indicates that children can have problems with (a) basic word reading, (b) reading fluency and comprehension, or (c) both

Dyslexia: A term used by some clinicians to refer to deficits in basic word reading and reading fluency

Expressive language: The ability to share beliefs, knowledge, and skills with others

Guided oral reading: A technique to improve fluency in which children read aloud and teachers provide assistance and feedback regarding mistakes

Grammar: The rules that govern the use of morphemes and the order of words (syntax) in a sentence

Immature speech: Developmentally less sophisticated speech production that might be adaptive at early ages but is considered inarticulate and maladaptive at later ages

Individuals With Disabilities Education Improvement Act (IDEIA): A federal law that entitles children with disabilities to free, appropriate public education

Language: Spoken, signed, or written communication in which beliefs, knowledge, and skills are experienced, expressed, or shared; involves the manipulation and organization of auditory or visual symbols according to a system of rules that is determined by one's culture

Language disorder: A *DSM-5* disorder characterized by persistent difficulties with the acquisition or use of language that include (a) reduced vocabulary, (b) limited sentence structure, or (c) impairments in discourse

Late language emergence: A subtype of language disorder characterized by significant delays in receptive or expressive language; usually identified between 18 and 36 months

Lateral sulcus: Also known as the sylvian fissure, a large gyrus (groove) in the left hemisphere of the brain; near important areas for language

Mands: A term used by speech-language therapists to refer to requests

Mediated or assisted instruction: A technique to improve math reasoning in which teachers help students comprehend math problems and offer assistance as children work through the problems themselves

Milieu training: A treatment for SLI; uses behavioral techniques to encourage children's language use in real-life environments and experiences

Morphology: The structure of words; usually the combination of several phonemes; can be fixed or free

Narrative skills: Communication skills used to tell stories or relate personal experiences; often deficient in youths with social communication disorder

Number sense: An early awareness that a group of stimuli can be understood in terms of their quantity

Number Sets Test: A test of number sense in which children must match numerals or objects with a target number; predicts math disabilities in young children

Phonemic awareness: The ability to hear, identify, and manipulate these phonemes (i.e., the sounds of a language)

Phonemic mediation: The ability to use phonemic awareness and phonics skills to sound out novel words

Phonological short-term memory: The ability to hold auditory material in memory for short periods of time

Phonological theory of SSD: Asserts that children develop SSD when they develop incorrect mental representations for phonemes during the first few years of life

Phonology: The sounds of a language and the rules for combining these sounds

Processing speed: The ability to quickly and accurately perform relatively simple cognitive tasks without expending a high degree of effort

Psycholinguistics: The study of the psychological and neurocognitive underpinnings of language

Rapid automatized naming (RAN): The ability to recall the names of a series of familiar items as quickly as possible

Rapid temporal processing: The ability to quickly and accurately process sensory information

RAVE-O: A program to improve reading fluency; involves instruction in retrieval, automaticity, vocabulary, elaboration, and orthography

Reading comprehension: The ability to read text for meaning, to remember information from the text, and to use information to solve problems or share with others

Reading fluency: The ability to read rapidly, accurately, and with proper expression

Receptive language: The ability to listen to and understand communication

Response to intervention (RTI): A method of learning disability identification in which children are classified when they persistently fail to respond to scientific, research-based educational interventions

Scripts: Detailed descriptions of social interactions in which people routinely engage; can be used to practice social communication skills

Self-instruction (in mathematics): Teachers systematically present a series of verbal steps or "prompts" that children can use to solve math problems by themselves

Self-regulated strategy development (SRSD): A technique to improve written expression; involves introducing, modeling, and reinforcing writing strategies for specific types of assignments

Semantics: The meaning of individual words (lexical) or sentences (sentential) in a sentence

Social (pragmatic) communication disorder: A *DSM-5* disorder characterized by persistent difficulties in the use of verbal and nonverbal communication in social contexts; interferes with communication and/or social functioning

Specific language impairment (SLI): A subtype of language disorder characterized by significant deficits in morphology, syntax, and/or grammar that are not better explained by ID or another medical or mental disorder

Speech: The modulation of one's voice to produce specific, discernible sounds that have meaning in a particular language

Speech fluency: The ease and automaticity of speech; includes rate, duration, rhythm, and sequence

Speech sound disorder (SSD): A *DSM-5* disorder characterized by persistent difficulty with clear and articulate speech production; include sound omissions, substitutions, distortions, and lisps

Skillstreaming: A social skills training program that systematically introduces, models, practices, and reinforces social skills; useful in teaching social communication

Specific learning disability: A legal term usually used in educational settings to describe problems in the basic psychological processes involved in spoken or written language; causes impairment in reading, math, spelling, writing, or oral language

Specific learning disorder: A *DSM-5* disorder characterized by difficulties learning or using reading, math, or writing skills; emerges in childhood or adolescence; skill deficits are significantly low, compared to other people of the same age, and cause impairment in school or daily activities

Story grammar: Knowledge of the components and structure of stories (e.g., characters, setting, plot); often deficient in children with poor reading comprehension

Tacts: A term used by speech-language therapists to refer to a comment or description

Text enhancements: Visual aids or routines that assist students in identifying, organizing, understanding, and recalling important information; important to nonfiction reading comprehension

Two-factor theory of stuttering: Posits that stuttering arises because of classical conditioning and is maintained through operant conditioning

Working memory: The ability to simultaneously hold and manipulate multiple pieces of information in short-term memory to solve problems

CRITICAL THINKING EXERCISES

1. Tom and Kelly are parents of a 2-year-old girl with late language emergence. At 24 months, their daughter is able to say only a handful of words and communicates mostly through gestures. Tom and Kelly are wondering if their daughter will eventually catch up to other children her age or if her language delays are a sign of a more serious problem. How might you respond to their concerns? What other information might you need?

2. Children's language problems are sometimes associated with impoverished parent–child interactions. Why can't we conclude that the quality of parent–child interactions *causes* these language problems?

3. Some adults try to help children who stutter by encouraging them to "relax" during conversations. Why isn't this strategy usually effective? What might be a more effective intervention for older children and adolescents who stutter?

4. Why aren't children who meet diagnostic criteria for ASD also diagnosed with social communication disorder? How might these two disorders be differentiated?

5. Children from low-SES families are at disproportionate risk for being classified with a learning disability. How might school psychologists and other professionals avoid misdiagnosing these children?

TEST YOURSELF AND EXTEND YOUR LEARNING

Videos, flash cards, and links to online resources for this chapter are available to students online. Teachers also have access to PowerPoint slides to guide lectures, case studies to prompt classroom discussions, and exam questions. Visit www.abnormalchildpsychology.org.

PART III

Disruptive Disorders and Substance Use Problems

iStockphoto.com/Liderina

CHAPTER 8

Attention-Deficit/Hyperactivity Disorder

LEARNING OBJECTIVES

After reading this chapter, you should be able to do the following:

8.1. Describe the key features of attention-deficit/hyperactivity disorder (ADHD) and how the signs and symptoms of this disorder vary from early childhood through adulthood.

Identify problems associated with ADHD and how these problems vary as a function of children's age and gender.

8.2. Discuss some of the main causes of ADHD and differentiate among the three neural pathways that underlie the disorder.

Summarize Barkley's neurodevelopmental model for ADHD.

8.3. Evaluate the relative strengths and weaknesses of medication and psychosocial therapy for the treatment of ADHD in children, adolescents, and young adults.

8.1 DESCRIPTION AND EPIDEMIOLOGY

We might think of attention-deficit/hyperactivity disorder (ADHD) as a truly "modern" illness, a by-product of 21st-century life. In the age of smartphones, social media, and multitasking, it is probably no surprise that 8% of children and adolescents have significant problems with hyperactivity, impulsivity, or inattention and approximately 7% of American youths are taking medication to manage these symptoms. We live in a fast-paced world where distractions are everywhere (Pliszka, 2015).

ADHD is not a new disorder, however. Read the poems *Johnny Head-In-Air* and *Fidgety Phillip*, written by a German pediatrician more than 150 years ago (see Figure 8.1). They describe children with significant inattention and hyperactivity–impulsivity, respectively—the two core dimensions of the disorder we now call ADHD.

In the 1800s, problems with attention and impulse control were attributed to poor upbringing. By 1902, however, the British physician George Still provided the first scientific description of 20 children with a deficit in "volitional inhibition." He believed that these problems with inattention and impulse control were caused by subtle brain abnormalities; consequently, the disorder was initially labeled "minimal brain damage" and later "minimal brain dysfunction."

One generation later, and almost by accident, the American psychiatrist Charles Bradley (1937) discovered that stimulant medication could reduce hyperactivity and improve attention in boys with histories of disruptive behavior (Strohl, 2011). He wrote the following:

> The most striking change in behavior occurred in the school activities of many of these patients. There appeared a definite "drive" to accomplish as much as possible. Fifteen of the 30 children responded to (medication) by becoming distinctly subdued in their emotional responses. Clinically in all cases, this was an improvement.

Figure 8.1 Inattention and hyperactivity–impulsivity are not new childhood problems. These pictures and poems are from a 19th century book for children.

Johnny Head-In-Air

As he trudged along to school,

It was always Johnny's rule

To be looking at the sky

And the clouds that floated by;

But what just before him lay,

And the things in his way,

Johnny never thought about;

So that everyone cried out,

"Look at little Johnny there,

Little Johnny Head-In-Air!"

Fidgety Phillip

Let me see if Philip can

Be a little gentleman;

Let me see if he is able

To sit still for once at table.

Phil wriggled, giggled,

And, I declare,

Swung backward and forward

In his chair,

Just like any rocking horse, --

Father now is getting cross!"

Source: From Hoffmann (1845). Images courtesy of Project Gutenberg and Wikipedia commons.

Although Bradley's observations were not noticed by the medical community for several decades, stimulant medication continues to be a first-line treatment for ADHD today.

The disorder now known as ADHD first appeared in *DSM-II* (1968) as "hyperkinetic reaction of childhood." In *DSM-III* (1980), it was renamed *attention-deficit disorder (ADD)* a term still used by some people today. Subsequent research showed that problems with inattention and hyperactivity–impulsivity were *both* important features of the disorder; consequently, the disorder received its current name in a revised version of *DSM-III-R* (1987): attention-deficit/hyperactivity disorder. As we will see, the *Diagnostic and Statistical Manual of Mental Disorders (DSM-5;* American Psychiatric Association, 2013) has continued to refine our conceptualization of ADHD and influence the way mental health professionals think about this condition (Nigg & Barkley, 2014).

What Is Attention-Deficit/Hyperactivity Disorder?

Description

ADHD is a neurodevelopmental disorder characterized by significant symptoms of inattention and/or hyperactivity–impulsivity (American Psychiatric Association, 2013). *DSM-5* lists behavioral symptoms that define problems in each of these domains (see Table 8.1). Children with significant *attention problems* show persistent and developmentally unexpected difficulties with attention to detail, sustaining attention over time, listening to others and following through with assignments, organizing tasks, staying focused, and remembering information and the location of important objects. Children who have significant problems with *hyperactivity* fidget and squirm, have difficulty remaining seated and staying still when expected, show

A. A persistent pattern of inattention and/or hyperactivity-impulsivity that interferes with functioning or development, as characterized by (1) and/or (2):

1. **Inattention:** Six (or more) of the following symptoms have persisted for at least 6 months to a degree that is inconsistent with developmental level and that negatively impacts directly on social and academic/occupational activities[1]:

   a. Often fails to give close attention to details or makes careless mistakes in schoolwork, at work, or during other activities (e.g., overlooks or misses details, work is inaccurate).

   b. Often has difficulty sustaining attention in tasks or play activities (e.g., has difficulty remaining focused during lectures, conversations, or lengthy readings).

   c. Often does not seem to listen when spoken to directly (e.g., mind seems elsewhere, even in the absence of any obvious distraction).

   d. Often does not follow through on instructions and fails to finish schoolwork, chores, or duties in the workplace (e.g., starts tasks but quickly loses focus and is easily sidetracked).

   e. Often has difficulty organizing tasks and activities (e.g., difficulty managing sequential tasks; difficulty keeping materials and belongings in order; messy, disorganized work; has poor time management; fails to meet deadlines).

   f. Often avoids, dislikes, or is reluctant to engage in tasks that require sustained mental effort (e.g., schoolwork or homework; for older adolescents and adults, preparing reports, completing forms, reviewing lengthy papers).

   g. Often loses things necessary for tasks or activities (e.g., school materials, pencils, books, tools, wallets, keys, paperwork, eyeglasses, mobile telephones).

   h. Is easily distracted by extraneous stimuli (for older adolescents and adults, may include unrelated thoughts).

   i. Is often forgetful in daily activities (e.g., doing chores, running errands; for older adolescents and adults, returning calls, paying bills, keeping appointments).

2. **Hyperactivity and impulsivity:** Six (or more) of the following symptoms have persisted for at least 6 months to a degree that is inconsistent with developmental level and that negatively impacts directly on social and academic/occupational activities:[1]

   a. Often fidgets with or taps hands or feet or squirms in seat.

   b. Often leaves seat in situations when remaining seated is expected (e.g., leaves his or her place in the classroom, in the office or other workplace).

   c. Often runs about or climbs in situations where it is inappropriate. (Note: In adolescents or adults, may be limited to feeling restless.)

   d. Often unable to play or engage in leisure activities quietly.

   e. Is often "on the go," acting as if "driven by a motor" (e.g., is unable to be or is uncomfortable being still for extended time, as in restaurants, meetings; may be experienced by others as being restless or difficulty [sic] to keep up with).

   f. Often talks excessively.

   g. Often blurts out an answer before a question has been completed (e.g., completes people's sentences; cannot wait for turn in conversation).

   h. Often has difficulty waiting his or her turn (e.g., while waiting in line).

   i. Often interrupts or intrudes on others (e.g., butts into conversations, games, or activities; may start using other people's things without asking or receiving permission; for adolescents and adults, may intrude into or take over what others are doing).

B. Several inattentive or hyperactive-impulsive symptoms were present prior to age 12 years.

C. Several inattentive or hyperactive-impulsive symptoms are present in two or more settings (e.g., at home, school, or work; with friends or relatives; in other activities).

D. There is clear evidence that the symptoms interfere with, or reduce the quality of, social, academic, or occupational functioning.

E. The symptoms do not occur exclusively during the course of Schizophrenia or another psychotic disorder and are not better explained by another mental disorder.

Specify whether:

Combined presentation: If both Criterion A1 (inattention) and Criterion A2 (hyperactivity-impulsivity) are met for the past 6 months.

Predominantly inattentive presentation: If Criterion A1 (inattention) is met but Criterion A2 (hyperactivity-impulsivity) is not met for the past 6 months.

Predominantly hyperactive/impulsive presentation: If Criterion A2 (hyperactivity-impulsivity) is met but Criterion A1 (inattention) is not met for the past 6 months.

Source: Reprinted with permission from the *Diagnostic and Statistical Manual of Mental Disorders, Fifth Edition* (Copyright 2013). American Psychiatric Association.

[1]The symptoms of inattention and/or hyperactivity-impulsivity are not solely a manifestation of oppositional behavior, defiance, hostility, or failure to understand tasks or instructions. For older adolescents and adults (age 17 and older), at least five symptoms are required.

problems playing quietly, are talkative, and are "on the go." They often exhaust others' patience with their high-rate behavior or annoy others with their restlessness. Children who have significant problems with *impulsivity* act without forethought; they may blurt out answers in class, have trouble waiting their turn in line, and intrude into others' conversations or activities. They often have problems delaying gratification in order to achieve long-term goals. Older children and adolescents may also make decisions or begin tasks without first considering the long-term consequences of their actions (Taylor & Sonuga-Barke, 2010).

Children can be diagnosed with ADHD if they show significant symptoms of inattention *or* hyperactivity–impulsivity. By definition, children must show at least six out of a possible nine symptoms of *either* inattention *or* hyperactivity–impulsivity to be diagnosed with the disorder.

The fact that children can be diagnosed with ADHD if they show either significant hyperactivity–impulsivity or significant inattention means that two children diagnosed with ADHD can have qualitatively different symptoms. A fourth grader with predominantly hyperactive–impulsive symptoms might wander about the classroom, talk excessively with peers, interrupt the teacher, and disrupt learning. In contrast, his classmate with predominantly inattentive symptoms might sit quietly at her desk, look out the classroom window, think about events occurring in the hallway, and daydream. The diagnostic label ADHD reflects a mix of children (Nigg & Barkley, 2014).

After reading the diagnostic criteria for ADHD, you may think, "Maybe I have ADHD?" Don't all students sometimes have difficulty attending to lectures, experience time management problems, forget appointments or assignments, and dislike long and complex tasks? In fact, nearly all of the symptoms of ADHD are also seen in typi-

cally developing individuals from time to time. However, people with ADHD can be differentiated from their peers without ADHD in three ways.

First, people with ADHD show a *persistent pattern* of inattention and/or hyperactivity–impulsivity that lasts for at least 6 months. The signs and symptoms of ADHD are relatively enduring; they are not occasional problems with distractibility or transient feelings of restlessness.

Second, people with ADHD show symptoms *in multiple settings.* Typically, individuals with ADHD have problems with inattention and/or hyperactivity–impulsivity at home, at school, and in other settings (e.g., work, with friends). Symptoms may be less noticeable or impairing during some activities (e.g., playing sports) than others (e.g., attending class), but they are present. By definition, a child cannot be diagnosed with ADHD if he shows symptoms only in one setting.

Third, people with ADHD show inattention and/or hyperactivity–impulsivity that *is inconsistent with their developmental level.* All children show problems with inattention and hyperactivity–impulsivity from time to time. Younger children generally have more frequent problems than older children. To qualify for a diagnosis of ADHD, individuals must show symptoms that greatly exceed the inattention and/or hyperactivity and impulsivity shown by people of the same age.

Psychologists can compare a person suspected of having ADHD with other individuals of the same age by using norm-referenced rating scales. For example, a psychologist might administer an ADHD rating scale, like the Conners 3, to a child's parents and teachers to assess the child's behavior at home and school, respectively. The rating scale would ask informants to evaluate the severity of the child's *DSM-5* ADHD symptoms. If the parents' and teacher's ratings indicate that the child's symptoms exceed

95% or 97% of children his age in the norm group, the child might qualify for a diagnosis of ADHD (Taylor & Sonuga-Barke, 2010).

Children's symptoms must also interfere with their everyday functioning. To be diagnosed with ADHD, children must show clear impairment in academic, social, or occupational activities. For example, inattentive symptoms might interfere with their ability to pay attention in class and do well in school. Alternatively, hyperactive–impulsive symptoms might lead to peer rejection. Adolescents might get into trouble at work because of careless mistakes, rushing through activities, or forgetting important tasks.

Finally, *DSM-5* conceptualizes ADHD as a disorder that emerges in childhood. In order to be diagnosed with ADHD, individuals must have at least some symptoms of inattention *or* hyperactivity–impulsivity before age 12 (American Psychiatric Association, 2013).

DSM-5 instructs clinicians to specify the severity of ADHD symptoms. Individuals with "mild" ADHD have few, if any, symptoms in excess of the required number for the ADHD diagnosis and only minor impairment in social, academic, or occupational functioning. In contrast, people with "severe" ADHD have many more symptoms beyond the number required for the ADHD diagnosis and

marked impairment in functioning. Clinicians can also rate severity as "moderate"—that is, severity between mild and severe (American Psychiatric Association, 2013).

Presentations

When clinicians diagnose ADHD, they specify children's current symptom presentation in one of three ways: (1) predominantly hyperactive–impulsive presentation, (2) combined presentation, or (3) predominantly inattentive presentation (Coghill & Seth, 2011; Tannock, 2013).

Children with ADHD, predominantly hyperactive–impulsive presentation show significant hyperactive and impulsive symptoms but only subthreshold problems with inattention. These children may have problems with attention and concentration, but their inattention is not severe enough to merit a combined specification. These children are usually described as "driven by a motor" or "constantly on the go" (van Ewijk & Oosterlaan, 2015).

Children with predominantly hyperactive–impulsive symptoms tend to be younger children and are disproportionately boys. Their symptoms tend to emerge between 3 and 4 years of age and interfere with their interactions with caregivers, family members, and peers. Most young children

CASE STUDY

ATTENTION-DEFICIT/HYPERACTIVITY DISORDER, COMBINED PRESENTATION

The Energizer Bunny

Source: ©iStockphoto.com/ungaryanu

Corey was an 8-year-old boy who was referred to our clinic by his mother. Corey showed significant problems with hyperactivity and impulsiveness at home. "Most second-grade boys are active, but Corey is always on the go," his mother reported. "Watching him tires me out." According to his mother, Corey had difficulty remaining seated during meals, constantly fidgeted with objects around the house, talked incessantly, and engaged in high-rate behavior. "He's very impulsive," she added. "As soon as I let him out of the car, I know he'll run into the parking lot. He's constantly doing dangerous stunts with his bike. He just doesn't think things through."

Corey also had difficulty sustaining his attention on any activity that required concentration or effort. "He can't focus on his homework for more than a few minutes at a time," his mother said. "I tried to reward him for completing his work, but then he rushes through it sloppily." Corey was also extremely forgetful. He often neglected his chores, forgot to complete school assignments, and lost belongings. His mother said, "This is the third schoolbag he's had this year. He'd forget to put on his underwear if I didn't remind him."

Corey showed similar problems with hyperactivity, impulsivity, and inattention at school. Corey completed assignments quickly, making careless mistakes. His work was often difficult to read. His grades were slightly below average because he often forgot to turn in assignments, lost his work, or rushed through tests without reading directions. "When I remind him to obey the class rules, he's always apologetic," his teacher said. "He wants to be good, but he just can't follow through."

A psychologist in our clinic interviewed Corey in her office. "You have a hard time doing what you're supposed to do at home and in school?" she asked. "Yeah," admitted Corey, "I'm always getting into trouble because I'm so hyper. My mom calls me her 'Energizer Bunny.'"

with predominantly hyperactive–impulsive symptoms will eventually develop attention problems as well. Between the ages of 6 and 12, most of these children will transition form hyperactive–impulsive presentation to combined presentation. Indeed, hyperactive–impulsive presentation is so rare among older children and adolescents, some experts believe it should be viewed as a developmental precursor for combined presentation (Nigg & Barkley, 2014).

Children with ADHD, combined presentation show significant inattentive and significant hyperactive–impulsive symptoms for the past six months. When most people think of ADHD, they probably envision a child with combined presentation. Parents and teachers describe these children as careless, forgetful, sloppy, distractible, rushed, irresponsible, or restless (Barkley, 2013c). Children with combined presentation have underlying problems with behavioral inhibition—that is, the ability to control or regulate immediate impulses to achieve long-term goals. Disinhibition causes them to have difficulty with sustained attention and to show over-activity and impulsiveness at school and home. Most children diagnosed with ADHD in clinics and hospitals display combined symptoms. Consider Corey, a boy with combined presentation.

Children with ADHD, predominantly inattentive presentation show significant problems with inattention but subthreshold symptoms of hyperactivity and impulsivity. These children are typically described as "distractible, forgetful, and disorganized." They may not pay attention to teachers at school or parents at home and may get into trouble because of their distractibility and lack of focus.

Although predominantly inattentive presentation is the second most common presentation in clinical settings, it is the most common presentation in the community. Children with predominantly hyperactive-impulsive symptoms are more likely than children with predominantly inattentive symptoms to be referred for treatment because of their high-rate, overactive behavior. In contrast, children with predominantly inattentive symptoms are often overlooked by parents and teachers, despite their higher frequency in the general population. Consider Brandy, a well-behaved girl with serious inattentive symptoms.

Predominantly inattentive presentation is usually seen in older children and adolescents and is disproportionately diagnosed in girls. Youths diagnosed with ADHD, predominantly inattentive presentation usually do not have a history of significant hyperactive–impulsive symptoms in early childhood. Their inattentive symptoms usually emerge between the ages or 8 and 12 years and are noticed by others when they interfere with daily activities, especially schoolwork.

CASE STUDY

ATTENTION-DEFICIT/HYPERACTIVITY DISORDER, PREDOMINANTLY INATTENTIVE PRESENTATION

Well-Behaved Brandy

Source: ©iStockphoto.com/princigalli

Brandy was a 10-year-old girl with a history of low academic achievement. She was referred to our clinic for psychological testing by her pediatrician, who suggested that she might have a learning disability.

Brandy's academic problems emerged 2 years earlier, when she was in the third grade. She began making careless mistakes on homework and often asked teachers to repeat instructions on assignments. In class, Brandy had difficulty listening and often daydreamed. "Brandy always seems to be off in her own little world," her teacher reported. "She seems more interested in doodling or staring out the window than in listening to me. I called her mother to make sure that Brandy was getting enough sleep, but she assured me that wasn't the problem."

Brandy's mother reported similar trouble with inattention at home: "She never listens to me. It's not that she's being disrespectful; it's just that I have to remind her a thousand times to do something." Brandy's mother also remarked about her daughter's forgetfulness: "She's always asking, 'Where's my shoes, where's my homework?'" Brandy was generally compliant, except during homework time. Her mother explained, "I'll tell her to go upstairs and to do her homework, but when I check on her, she's listening to music or drawing. She says she'll get to work, but she never does."

A psychologist at our clinic administered an IQ and academic achievement test. Brandy's scores indicated average intelligence and academic skills. The psychologist shared his findings with Brandy's mother: "I don't think your daughter has a learning disability. I need a little more information, but I think that she might have ADHD." Her mother replied, "ADHD? That can't be. She's such a quiet, well-behaved girl."

The diagnostic criteria for ADHD were developed for young children. Consequently, many of these criteria seem inapplicable to adolescents and adults. It is hard to envision a college student with ADHD who "blurts out answers" in class, "has difficulty sustaining attention on play activities," or "runs about or climbs" in a lecture hall. For these reasons, *DSM-5* describes several ways that older children, adolescents, and adults might manifest these symptoms. For example, whereas children might display hyperactive–impulsive symptoms by leaving their seat in class or blurting out answers, college students are more likely to experience subjective feelings of restlessness during lectures or have difficulty waiting their turn while in line at the registrar's office. Whereas children might display inattention by not listening to parents or being easily distractible in school, college students might show inattention by daydreaming during lectures, forgetting to keep appointments, or submitting late assignments (Tannock, 2013). Clinicians can also consult tables, like Table 8.2, which show the way inattentive, hyperactive, and impulsive symptoms might manifest themselves across development.

The diagnostic criteria for ADHD are slightly modified for older adolescents and adults. *DSM-5* requires older adolescents and adults ($\geq$17 years of age) to show only five, rather than six, symptoms of either inattention or hyperactivity–impulsivity to be diagnosed with the disorder. The reduced symptom count is allowed because, on average, adults with significant impairments due to ADHD often endorse fewer symptoms than children with the disorder. Indeed, as many as 50% of adults with persistent problems with inattention and hyperactivity–impulsivity fall short of the six-symptom criterion established for

children. Adults who exhibit only five symptoms tend to have equal levels of impairment in tasks requiring attention or behavioral control as adults who meet six or more symptoms (Solanto, Wasserstein, Marks, & Mitchell, 2013).

Review:

- ADHD is a *DSM-5* neurodevelopmental disorder characterized by significant inattention and/or hyperactivity–impulsivity that emerges prior to age 12 years, is present in two or more settings, and interferes with academic or social functioning.
- ADHD can be differentiated from normal functioning because ADHD is persistent over time and has signs and symptoms that are present across multiple settings. In addition, people with ADHD show behavior that is developmentally atypical.
- Individuals can be diagnosed with ADHD, predominantly hyperactive–impulsive presentation, predominantly inattentive presentation, or combined presentation. Presentations differ across age and gender.

What Problems Are Associated With Attention-Deficit/ Hyperactivity Disorder?

Conduct and Substance Use Problems

Comorbid psychiatric disorders are common among children with ADHD. In community-based samples, 44% of children with ADHD have at least one other mental disorder. Among youths referred to mental health clinics, approximately 85% have a comorbid condition (Willcutt et al., 2012).

Table 8.2   The core symptoms of ADHD are the same for children, adolescents, and adults. However, these symptoms manifest themselves differently across development.

	Preschool	School-Age	Adolescence	College
Inattention	Child plays for short periods of time (<3 min)	Activities are brief (<10 min); forgetful, disorganized, easily distracted	Less persistent in tasks than peers (<20-30 min); doesn't focus on details; forgets assignments	Forgets appointments or assignments; doesn't plan ahead for long-term projects
Hyperactivity	Overactive; can't be settled, acts like a "whirlwind"	Restless, excessive movement, leaving seat in school	Fidgets with object; squirms in seat; movement of legs and limbs	Subjective sense of restlessness
Impulsiveness	Doesn't listen to adults' warnings; no sense of danger	Blurts out answers in class; interrupts others; gets into many accidents	Speaks or acts before thinking; doesn't plan ahead; risk taking	Quick and unwise decision-making; impatient; reckless driving

Source: Based on Taylor and Sonuga-Barke (2010).

Conduct Problems

Many youths with ADHD develop significant conduct problems at some point in their lives. Approximately 54% to 67% of children with ADHD show oppositional defiant disorder (ODD), a condition characterized by persistent stubbornness and noncompliance toward adults. Children with ODD refuse to obey, talk back, throw tantrums, and are otherwise spiteful or argumentative toward caregivers.

Approximately 20% to 50% of children and 44% to 50% of adolescents with ADHD show conduct disorder (CD), a behavioral disturbance characterized by a persistent disregard for the rules of society. Youths with CD show a wide range of disruptive and destructive behaviors, including physical fighting, theft, vandalism, and truancy.

Approximately 12% to 21% of adolescents with ADHD will develop antisocial personality disorder (ASPD) in adulthood. ASPD is a serious personality disturbance defined by a persistent disregard for the rights and dignity of others. Adults with ASPD often have histories of aggression and illegal behavior. Overall, the presence of ADHD in childhood increases the likelihood of developing ODD, CD, and/or ASPD tenfold (Nigg & Barkley, 2014).

Longitudinal research indicates that ADHD is causally related to the emergence of these conduct problems. Some experts believe ADHD acts like a "motor" that can drive children toward oppositional, defiant, and aggressive or destructive behavior (Kimonis et al., 2014). Other research suggests that children with ADHD have underlying problems with emotion regulation (e.g., excessive anger and irritability); emotional dysregulation, in turn, contributes to arguments with caregivers and other adults, peer problems, aggression, and antisocial behavior (Barkley, 2010; Biederman et al., 2012).

Although ADHD and conduct problems frequently co-occur, they are considered separate disorders. Indeed, *DSM-5* specifically warns clinicians that ADHD symptoms are not solely a manifestation of oppositional, defiant, or antisocial behaviors (American Psychiatric Association, 2013). Most children with ADHD are hyperactive, impulsive, and/or inattentive but do not talk back to parents, fight with classmates, or skip school. Other children and adolescents show serious patterns of defiant and aggressive behavior toward family and peers but show no problems with hyperactivity or inattention (Nigg & Barkley, 2014).

Substance Use Problems

Children with ADHD are also at increased risk for substance use problems in adolescence and adulthood (Bukstein, 2011). On average, children with ADHD are 6 times more likely than typically developing peers to misuse nicotine, alcohol, or other drugs later in life. Approximately 22% of children with ADHD develop substance use problems during adolescence and as many as 24% show substance use problems as adults. The drug most frequently used by adolescents and young adults with ADHD is nicotine, although the abuse of alcohol, marijuana, prescription pain medications, and inhalants is also common (Charach, Yeung, Climans, & Lillie, 2011; Lee, Humphreys, Flory, Liu, & Glass, 2011).

Why are adolescents with ADHD at increased risk for substance use problems? The answer depends on the type of substance that adolescents use. Most studies indicate that the association between ADHD and alcohol and other drug use problems is mediated by comorbid conduct problems (e.g., ODD, CD). Youths with ADHD are at risk for peer rejection because of their high-rate, aversive behavior. They may associate with other rejected, deviant peers who might introduce them to alcohol and other drugs. Children with ADHD may succumb to pressure from these youths in order to gain acceptance and to avoid further rejection (Bukstein, 2011).

In contrast, ADHD is a specific, unique predictor for smoking. Even after controlling for comorbid conduct problems, adolescents with ADHD are approximately twice as likely to smoke as their typically developing peers. Youths with ADHD begin smoking at an earlier age, have more difficulty quitting the habit, and have higher relapse rates after they quit. In one large, population-based study, there was a linear relationship between the number of ADHD symptoms reported by youths and their risk of smoking: the more symptoms, the greater the risk. Adolescents and young adults with ADHD often report that nicotine improves their concentration and behavioral inhibition. It is likely that many youths use nicotine to regulate their attention and behavior (Bukstein, 2011).

One early study suggested that stimulant medication, the primary treatment for ADHD, might predispose children with the disorder to substance use problems later in life (Lambert & Hartsough, 1998). Longitudinal research conducted since that time has not replicated that finding. In fact, some studies have found that stimulant medication protects children with ADHD from future substance use problems (Molina et al., 2013).

Academic Problems

Children with ADHD often show difficulties across academic domains, with particular problems in reading and math (Langberg, Dvorsky, et al., 2016). A recent review indicated that children with ADHD showed significantly lower academic achievement scores and school performance than their typically developing classmates (Arnold, Hodgkins, Kahle, Madhoo, & Kewley, 2016). Youths with ADHD often require special tutoring (56%), are referred for special education because of a learning disability (45%), repeat a grade (30%), and do not complete high school (10%; Bernard et al., 2012). Children with inattentive presentation are most at risk for these deleterious outcomes. Furthermore, these negative outcomes remain even after taking into account children's intelligence and socioeconomic backgrounds (DuPaul, Gormley, & Laracy, 2013).

Longitudinal data suggest that underlying problems with attention and memory contribute to the academic deficits shown by youths with ADHD (Tamm et al., 2016). Children with ADHD often have cognitive processing problems that interfere with their ability to learn in traditional academic settings. For example, these children may miss information presented by teachers and opportunities to practice newly learned academic skills. Missed learning experiences may contribute to a generally lower fund of information (Buckley et al., 2006). Similarly, children with ADHD often have deficits in working memory that interfere with their ability to perform multistep academic tasks (Renz et al., 2003). They may have problems holding information in working memory long enough to use this information effectively to solve academic problems. They may also show difficulty organizing information and relaying it to others. These deficits interfere with their ability to learn new skills and to perform well on homework and exams.

Problems With Parents and Peers

Parent–Child Interactions

Children with ADHD often have problematic interactions with their parents. One way psychologists study parent–child interactions in young children is to observe dyads playing or performing a structured task (e.g., reading a book, cleaning up after play). During these interactions, children with ADHD are more talkative, negative, and defiant; less compliant and cooperative; and more demanding of their parents' attention and assistance. Their parents, in turn, are more hostile and less sensitive and responsive than are parents of children without ADHD. Researchers believe that these parent–child behaviors are reciprocal: Parents engage in more hostile–intrusive parenting tactics because they are frustrated by their children's high-rate behavior; children engage in more disruptive behavior because of their parents' punitive discipline. Negative parent–child interactions in early childhood, like these, predict the emergence of oppositional behavior and conduct problems through adolescence (Babinski, Waxmonsky, & Pellham, 2014; Webster-Stratton, Reid, & Beauchaine, 2013; Zisser & Eyberg, 2012).

Parents of children with both ADHD and conduct problems are at particular risk for problematic parent–child interactions. These parents report high levels of parenting stress, low confidence in their abilities to control their children's behavior, and less positive interactions with their children and family. Indeed, the parents of children with ADHD and conduct problems are more likely to have high levels of couple or marital conflict, to separate, or to divorce than the caregivers of children with ADHD alone or youths without behavior problems (Nigg & Barkley, 2014).

Interestingly, children's ADHD and conduct problems can prompt some parents to drink. In a series of studies, researchers asked adults to interact with a young boy during three short activities (Kashdan, Adams, Kleiman, Pelham, & Lang, 2013). The first activity consisted of drawing a picture using an Etch A Sketch with the adult and child each controlling one knob on the device. For the second activity, the adult was required to balance a checkbook while the child completed math problems. The final activity was a free play session in which the adult was required to gain the child's assistance in cleaning up. Unknown to the adult participants, the boy in the sessions was actually a confederate who was told to either act in a compliant or hyperactive–defiant manner. After these sessions, adults were asked to complete questionnaires and offered alcoholic beverages. The researchers discovered that a subgroup of parents used alcohol to cope with the child's aversive behavior. These adults tended to experience high levels of trait anxiety and depression and had poor coping strategies to deal with negative affect. These findings suggest that some parents, particularly those with a genetic diathesis toward alcohol abuse, may use alcohol to cope with their children's disruptive behavior.

Peer Rejection and Neglect

It is important for school-age children to be accepted by peers and to develop friendships with children their age (Sullivan, 1953). These peer relationships are believed to contribute to children's self-esteem, to serve as models for adult interpersonal relationships, and to promote the development of children's identity and capacity for intimacy later in life. Indeed, the degree to which we are liked and accepted by peers in early elementary school is one of the best predictors of our social and emotional well-being in adolescence (Rubin & Asendorpf, 2014).

Unfortunately, children with ADHD are frequently disliked by peers. Their hyperactive and impulsive behavior often interferes with their ability to behave appropriately during peer interactions. Children's ADHD symptoms often cause peers to reject them quickly. In one study, unfamiliar children rated children with ADHD as less desirable play partners after only two brief play sessions. In another study, children at a summer camp rejected children with ADHD after only 3 days. Once children are rejected by some of their peers, they often develop negative reputations among the rest of the peer group. As many as 70% of children with ADHD may not have a single friend in school (Mrug et al., 2012).

Hoza and colleagues (2005) used sociometric ratings to determine the peer status of school-age children with and without ADHD. All children in a class were asked to privately identify the children with whom they most and least enjoyed playing. Then, researchers tallied children's nominations to determine the peer status of each child. Children were categorized into one of five groups based on their peer nominations. *Popular* children received the greatest number of positive nominations. *Rejected* children received the greatest number of negative nominations. *Controversial* children received a large number of both positive and negative nominations. *Neglected* children received few nominations altogether. *Average* children received an average number of nominations, both positive and negative.

Hoza and colleagues (2005) discovered that children with the hyperactive–impulsive symptoms of ADHD were not only unpopular but they were also actively rejected by their classmates (see Figure 8.2). Indeed, 52% of children with ADHD were rejected. Although children with ADHD sought friendships, popular children were *most* likely to reject and avoid them. The tendency for children with ADHD to be rejected was not merely due to comorbid problems, such as oppositional or defiant behavior. Children were rejected based on their ADHD symptoms alone. Even children as young as 6 years old were rejected because of their ADHD symptoms.

Subsequent research has shown that peer rejection can also exacerbate children's ADHD symptoms and lead to the development of conduct problems. For example, in one longitudinal study, researchers found that children's hyperactive–impulsive symptoms at age 4 predicted peer rejection by age 6. Peer rejection at age 6, in turn, was associated with an increase in ADHD symptom severity and continued peer rejection 2 years later. Once children develop this pattern of behavior, their developmental pathway is resistant to change (Stenseng, Belsky, Skalicka, & Wichstrøm, 2016).

Children with ADHD, predominantly inattentive presentation are at risk for peer neglect, rather than outright rejection. Because these children frequently are passive and withdrawn in social situations, they may be overlooked by peers as potential playmates or friends (Marshall, Evans, Eiraldi, Becker, & Power, 2014).

Stimulant medication is associated with improvements in the social interactions of children with ADHD. Specifically, medication is useful in decreasing hyperactive, impulsive, and disruptive behaviors that peers find aversive. However, medication does not seem to improve children's social skills or positive interactions with peers. Furthermore, once children gain negative reputations at school or in their neighborhoods, it is often difficult for them to gain acceptance \ (Gardner & Gerdes, 2015).

Sleep Problems

Approximately 50% of children with ADHD experience sleep problems (Owens et al., 2013). Most of these problems are mild in severity or occur only occasionally.

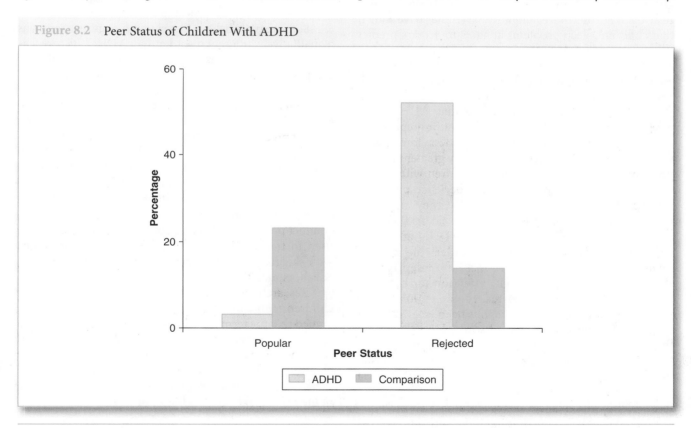

Figure 8.2   Peer Status of Children With ADHD

Source: Based on Hoza et al. (2005).

Note: Compared to healthy children, youths with ADHD are less popular and more frequently rejected by classmates. Peer rejection can lead to association with deviant peers and more severe behavior problems later in childhood.

However, nearly 20% of youths with ADHD experience moderate to severe sleep disorders, compared to only 13% of youths with other psychiatric disorders, and less than 6% of children in the general population.

The sleep problems experienced by children with ADHD fall into three general categories. First, some children experience *dyssomnias*, such as refusing to go to sleep, problems falling asleep, or difficulty waking in the morning. These sleep problems are most frequently seen in youths with ADHD and comorbid conduct problems. Second, some children develop *movement disorders* associated with sleep, such as sleep talking, teeth grinding, and excessive tossing and turning. These involuntary movements are most often seen in youths with ADHD who display significant hyperactive–impulsive symptoms. Third, some youths develop *parasomnias*, such as night wakings, recurrent nightmares, or night terrors. These sleep problems occur about as frequently in youths with ADHD as in youths with other psychiatric disorders and may not be unique to ADHD (Nigg & Barkley, 2014).

Sleep problems may be partially responsible for children's ADHD symptoms. When researchers deliberately restrict children's sleep by 1 or 2 hours per night, problems with attention and hyperactivity–impulsiveness often increase. Increased ADHD symptoms are even observable by teachers who are unaware that children's sleep is restricted. Furthermore, longitudinal studies have shown that children's sleep problems at age 2 to 4 years predict the emergence of ADHD symptoms at age 5. However, children whose early sleep problems subsided show fewer ADHD symptoms in later childhood than children with persistent sleep problems (Gruber et al., 2012).

Alternatively, there is evidence that ADHD may interfere with children's sleep. Several studies report that children with ADHD exhibit more restless, low-quality sleep. Their sleep is also characterized by greater physical movement of the torso and limbs. Children with hyperactive–impulsive symptoms often experience problems settling into bed at night; consequently, they may have delayed sleep onset or refuse to go to bed altogether.

A third possibility is that both ADHD and sleep problems are caused by the same underlying mechanism. Like children with ADHD, children deprived of sleep often exhibit problems with attention and behavior regulation. The prefrontal cortex, a brain region largely responsible for these functions, has been implicated in both ADHD and several sleep disorders. Furthermore, the neurotransmitter dopamine is also implicated in both ADHD and some sleep disorders. Dopaminergic underactivity has been suggested as a cause of ADHD whereas low levels of dopamine have been implicated in problems with arousal and wakefulness.

Taken together, these findings indicate a bidirectional association between sleep and ADHD. It is likely that sleep problems exacerbate ADHD symptoms and these symptoms threaten the quality of children's sleep (Schneider, Lam, & Mahone, 2016).

Sluggish Cognitive Tempo

Most children with ADHD, predominantly inattentive presentation show at least six inattentive symptoms and a moderate (but still subthreshold) number of hyperactive–impulsive symptoms. However, a subset of children with predominantly inattentive presentation show few or no symptoms of hyperactivity–impulsivity (Langberg, Becker, & Dvorsky, 2014). These children are sometimes described as having sluggish cognitive tempo (see Table 8.3). They often daydream, appear drowsy, and act confused. Interpersonally, they are described as lethargic, hypoactive, or passive. In school, they often appear spacey and disoriented, as if their minds were constantly wandering from topic to topic. They may not be aware of events around them and take a long time to respond when called upon by others. These children usually do not get into trouble at school, but they may have problems making friends and getting along with classmates (Becker, Leopold, & Burns, 2016).

Empirical studies have shown a close relationship between children with sluggish cognitive tempo and youths with ADHD, predominantly inattentive presentation. Approximately 60% of children with sluggish cognitive tempo also meet criteria for ADHD. Conversely, nearly 40% of youths with ADHD also show sluggish cognitive tempo (Barkley, 2013b).

Some experts believe that sluggish cognitive tempo is a qualitatively different disorder than ADHD. Its core features—poor concentration and memory, lethargy and general passivity, and impaired academic performance—seem distinct from ADHD, predominantly inattentive presentation (Tamm et al., 2016). Indeed, children with sluggish cognitive tempo often show different cognitive processing problems than other children with ADHD, such as slow processing speed and working memory deficits. Children with sluggish cognitive tempo are also more likely to show problems with internalizing disorders (e.g., anxiety, depression, social withdrawal), whereas other children with ADHD are more likely to develop externalizing disorders (e.g., conduct problems, substance abuse). Finally, medications used to treat ADHD are often less effective for youths with sluggish cognitive tempo (Garner, Mrug, Hodgens, & Patterson, 2012).

Researches even disagree on how best to describe children with these features. Russell Barkley (2016) has argued that the term *concentration deficit disorder* is more appropriate, given the negative connotation of "sluggish cognitive tempo." Researchers are continuing to study children with sluggish cognitive tempo to determine if there is a need for a separate disorder in future versions of the *DSM* (Saxbe & Barkley, 2014).

Review:

- Many children with ADHD develop comorbid conduct problems or substance use problems. ADHD is a specific risk factor for cigarette smoking. Youths with

Table 8.3 Sluggish Cognitive Tempo

Approximately 40% of children with ADHD show sluggish cognitive tempo. Common features include the following:

- Daydreams often
- Has trouble staying awake and alert
- Is mentally foggy and easily confused
- Stares a lot
- Acts spacey/mind is elsewhere
- Is lethargic
- Is underproductive
- Is slow-moving/sluggish
- Doesn't process questions accurately
- Has drowsy/sleepy appearance
- Acts apathetic or withdrawn
- Is lost in thoughts
- Is slow to complete tasks
- Lacks initiative; can't sustain effort

Source: ©iStockphoto.com/monkeybusinessimages

ADHD may use nicotine to regulate their attention and actions.

- Approximately 45% of children and adolescents with ADHD are also diagnosed with a learning disability. Approximately 50% of youths with ADHD have sleep problems and 20% have a sleep–wake disorder.
- Youths with ADHD are at risk for hostile parent–child interactions and peer rejection. Both factors predict the emergence of conduct problems later in childhood or adolescence.
- Sluggish cognitive tempo is characterized by daydreaming, mind-wandering, drowsy appearance, lethargy, social passivity, and concentration problems. It is unclear whether sluggish cognitive tempo is distinct from ADHD, predominantly inattentive presentation.

How Common Is Attention-Deficit/Hyperactivity Disorder?

Prevalence

Researchers can estimate the prevalence of ADHD by reviewing medical records. These data show that ADHD affects approximately 5.29% to 7.1% of children and adolescents and from 3.4% to 5.0% of adults, worldwide. Prevalence appears to be highest in South America and Africa and lowest in the Middle East. Prevalence among children and adolescents in North American and Europe is approximately equal, ranging from 5% to 7% of youths (Centers for Disease Control and Prevention, 2016a).

The prevalence of ADHD in the Unites States is significantly higher based on caregiver reports, however (see Table 8.4). Approximately 11.5% of caregivers report having a child previously diagnosed with ADHD, 9% report having a child with a current ADHD diagnosis, and 6-7% report

having a child currently receiving treatment for ADHD (Centers for Disease Control and Prevention, 2016a).

The prevalence of ADHD in the United States has increased dramatically (Nigg & Barkley, 2014). Approximately 1% of children were diagnosed with ADHD in the late 1980s (Olfson, Gameroff, Marcus, & Jensen, 2003) compared to approximately 7% to 9% today. The largest increase in ADHD has been seen in African American children and youths from lower-socioeconomic status (SES) backgrounds (Akinbami, Liu, Pastor, & Reuben, 2011).

There are at least four explanations for the increase in ADHD. First, the Individuals With Disabilities Education Improvement Act (IDEIA), a federal law that addresses the education of children with disabilities, began recognizing ADHD as a potential disability in 1990. Consequently, many parents sought diagnoses for their children in order to gain educational accommodations and services. Second, the number of school-based health clinics increased during this time period, giving low-income children greater access to mental health services. Third, the 1990s witnessed advances in the assessment of ADHD, leading to better identification of children with the disorder. Fourth, there was a general increase in public awareness of the disorder and, perhaps, a decrease in stigma. Organizations such as Children and Adults With Attention-Deficit/Hyperactivity Disorder (CHADD) and the Attention Deficit Disorder Association (ADDA) advocate for the rights of individuals with ADHD and their families.

Gender

ADHD is more common in boys than in girls. Among clinic-referred children, the gender ratio is approximately 10:1 in favor of boys. In community samples, however, the

Table 8.4   Prevalence of ADHD

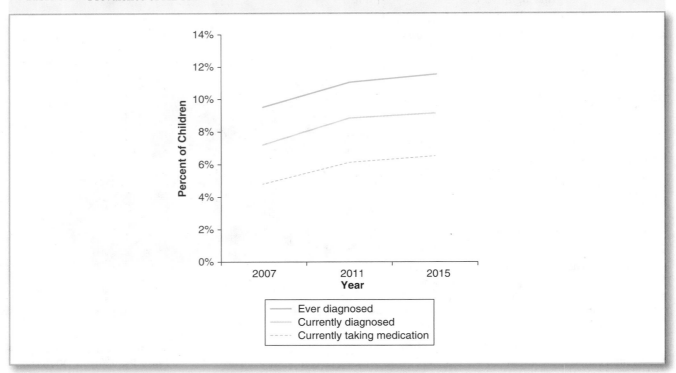

gender ratio favors boys by only 3:1. The large gender ratio among clinic-referred children is partially due to referral bias. Boys with ADHD are more likely than girls to have co-occurring conduct problems; consequently, they are more likely to be referred for treatment. Girls with ADHD, on the other hand, are less likely to show oppositional and defiant symptoms than boys, and are often overlooked by parents, teachers, and other adults (Simon, 2016).

On average, girls with ADHD show fewer hyperactive–impulsive symptoms and more inattentive symptoms than boys. Girls are also more likely than boys to be diagnosed with ADHD at a later age and to be classified with predominantly inattentive presentation (Chacko et al., 2016).

Boys and girls with ADHD show similar impairment in behavior and social functioning. Whereas boys are more likely than girls to develop conduct problems, girls are more likely than boys to experience academic difficulties. These school-related problems are often attributable to underlying problems with executive functioning and working memory that leads to both inattentive symptoms and difficulty with acquiring reading, writing, and math skills (Elkins, Malone, Keyes, Iacono, & McGue, 2011).

Course

Several prospective, longitudinal studies have examined the course of ADHD by following individuals with the disorder from early childhood through early adulthood (see Figure 8.3). These studies indicate that ADHD is a neurodevelopmental disorder that emerges early in life,

can persist into adulthood, and has the potential to affect academic, behavioral, and social–emotional functioning (Nigg & Barkley, 2014).

Hyperactive–impulsive symptoms usually emerge between the ages of 3 and 4 years. Although these symptoms cause caregivers distress, children are usually not referred to pediatricians or mental health care providers until they begin formal schooling. Between the ages of 5 and 8, problems with inattention often increase, leading to a diagnosis of ADHD, combined presentation (Willcutt et al., 2012).

Between the ages of 8 and 12, some children begin to show only predominantly inattentive symptoms. These youths are disproportionately girls and often have no history of hyperactivity–impulsivity in early childhood. Most are brought to the attention of clinicians because of academic problems. These youths are typically diagnosed with predominantly inattentive presentation.

School-age boys and girls with ADHD are at risk for a wide range of academic, behavioral, and social problems. These problems include low academic achievement and behavior problems at school, peer rejection, oppositional behavior toward parents, conduct problems, and substance use in adolescence.

Between 50% and 80% of children with ADHD continue to meet diagnostic criteria though adolescence. Overtly hyperactive symptoms tend to be replaced by subjective feelings of restlessness. Nevertheless, these youths continue to experience marked problems with impulsivity, as evidenced by poor decision-making and planning. For

Figure 8.3   Course of Attention-Deficit/Hyperactivity Disorder.

AGE 3–4 | AGE 5–6 | AGE 7–8 | AGE 9–12 | AGE 13–20 | AGE 21+

Hyperactive-impulsive symptoms emerge | Symptoms become problematic as child begins school | Inattentive symptoms emerge; Combined Presentation often diagnosed | Problems with school, parents, and peers; conduct problems may emerge | At risk for academic problems, substance use problems, and auto accidents | Approximately 2/3 continue to experience inattention and feelings of restlessness

Stock vector ID-491133758

example, rates of accidental injury, speeding tickets, and auto accidents are significantly greater among adolescents with ADHD than their typically developing peers. Adolescents continue to experience attention and concentration problems; indeed, their inattentive symptoms are likely their most salient concern during their high school years.

Although most youths with ADHD do not meet diagnostic criteria in adulthood, the vast majority do experience persistent, subthreshold symptoms. For example, Biederman and colleagues (Biederman, Petty, Clarke, Lomedico, & Faraone, 2010; Biederman, Petty, Evans, Small, & Faraone, 2011) studied a large sample of boys with ADHD from childhood through early adulthood. Although only 35% continued to meet diagnostic criteria in adulthood, 53% showed subthreshold ADHD symptoms, and 80% reported school or work impairment because inattention or impulsivity. Clearly, ADHD is not merely a childhood disorder.

Review:

- Medical records indicate that between 5% and 7% of school-age children have ADHD. However, parental reports indicate that 7% to 9% of youths have ADHD. Prevalence has increased significantly in the past 30 years.
- ADHD is more common in boys than girls. Boys show more severe hyperactive–impulsive symptoms and conduct problems, whereas girls show more severe inattentive symptoms and academic problems.
- Hyperactive–impulsive symptoms tend to emerge during the preschool years, usually followed by inattentive symptoms in elementary school. Most (50% to 80%) children with ADHD continue to meet diagnostic criteria in adolescence.

8.2 CAUSES

Is Attention-Deficit/ Hyperactivity Disorder Heritable?

Behavioral Genetics

ADHD is a neurodevelopmental disorder with a strong genetic basis. Although the exact genes that underlie ADHD have not been identified, genetic factors explain 70% to 90% of the variance in ADHD symptoms among children with the disorder. Concordance between monozygotic (MZ) twins is 50% to 80%, whereas concordance between dizygotic (DZ) twins is only 33%. Concordance is higher for hyperactivity–impulsivity symptoms than for symptoms of inattention (Thapar, Cooper, Eyre, & Langley, 2013).

ADHD also runs in families. Children with ADHD are more likely to have a biological parent with the disorder (18%) than children without ADHD (3%). Adults with ADHD have a 57% chance of having at least one child with the disorder. Furthermore, the siblings of children with ADHD are 3 to 5 times more likely to have the disorder compared to controls. Adoption studies consistently show that children show a much greater similarity in ADHD symptoms with their biological parents than their adoptive parents (Asherson & Gurling, 2011).

Molecular Genetics

Genes associated with the dopamine and serotonin neurotransmitter systems play a primary role in the development of ADHD. Evidence for their involvement comes from four sources. First, dopamine and serotonin receptors are especially prevalent in brain regions responsible for regulating attention and inhibiting behavior, especially the striatum and prefrontal cortex. Second, people with lesions to these areas (and presumably damage to the dopamine and serotonin systems) often show ADHD symptoms. Third, medications used to treat ADHD stimulate the dopamine system and enhance attention. Fourth, mice lacking genes that code for dopamine receptors in the brain show hyperactivity and impulse-control problems (Pliszka, 2015).

Unfortunately, genome-wide scans have been unable to identify specific genes responsible for ADHD. Instead, it seems that ADHD is caused by small deletions or duplications on several chromosomes (i.e., copy number variants). Most of the genes that have been implicated so far regulate dopamine. For example, the dopamine transporter gene (DAT1) located on chromosome 5, codes for proteins that pump dopamine out of the synaptic cleft back into the presynaptic neuron. Some children with ADHD show mutations of this gene, such as an unusual repetition of gene sequences. Mutations like these may cause disruption in the dopamine reuptake process. Medications like Adderall inhibit the reuptake of dopamine, allowing dopamine to remain in the synaptic cleft longer and be detected by the postsynaptic neuron. The result is better synaptic activity and behavioral control (Asherson & Gurling, 2011).

The dopamine D4 and D5 receptor genes are also likely involved in ADHD. These genes code for proteins that act as receptors for dopamine in postsynaptic neurons. Some children with ADHD show mutations in these genes. For example, the "D4 long variant mutation" occurs when portions of the D4 gene incorrectly repeat seven times. Certain stimulant medications, such as Ritalin, bind to D4 receptors in frontal brain regions, stimulating these regions, and producing greater attention and behavioral control (Asherson & Gurling, 2011).

Genes and Early Environment

Although genetics accounts for the lion's share of the variance of ADHD symptoms, environmental factors also play important roles. Nonshared environmental factors—experiences unique to individual children—seem especially important in predicting the development of ADHD. Three risk factors are especially salient. Interestingly, all of these risk factors are associated with restricted oxygen intake at different times in development (Millichap, 2010; Sedky, Bennett, & Carvalho, 2014).

Prenatally, fetuses exposed to cigarette smoke are significantly more likely than nonexposed fetuses to develop ADHD, lower intelligence, and other neuropsychological problems later in life. Cigarette exposure may cause neurological damage by restricting oxygen during gestation. Risk for ADHD remains even after controlling for mothers' age, intelligence, SES, and other drug use.

Perinatal risks include premature birth, low birth weight, and complications with delivery involving hypoxia (i.e., temporary lack of oxygen). Medical conditions that deprive the fetus or neonate of oxygen for extended periods of time present the greatest risk. Areas of the brain responsible for behavioral inhibition and executive functioning (i.e., the frontal–striatal regions) seem to be highly susceptible to damage caused by hypoxia.

Postnatally, children with breathing problems during sleep are at elevated risk for ADHD. Furthermore, there is a moderate relationship between the severity of children's breathing problems during sleep and their ADHD symptoms. Medical correction of these breathing problems is associated with a decrease in ADHD symptoms.

Of course, genetic diathesis and environmental risks interact to produce the signs and symptoms of ADHD. Even MZ twins, who have 100% of their genes in common, show less than 80% concordance in their ADHD symptoms (Nigg, 2016b).

Review:

- ADHD is highly heritable. Concordance for MZ twins approaches .80 whereas concordance for DZ twins is only .33.
- Genes that regulate the neurotransmitter dopamine likely play a role in the development of ADHD.
- Restricted oxygen intake places fetuses, infants, and toddlers at risk for ADHD later in development.

What Brain Abnormalities Are Associated With Attention-Deficit/ Hyperactivity Disorder?

The Mesolimbic Neural Circuit (Heightened Reward Sensitivity)

Years ago, Jeffrey Gray (1982, 1987, 1994) hypothesized the existence of two systems that govern our actions. The first system, the behavioral inhibition system (BIS), is responsible for slowing or stopping behavior in response to punishment or a lack of reinforcement. Imagine a child who engages in high-rate behavior on the playground. At recess, boisterous behavior is appropriate; however, when recess ends, the child must reduce the frequency and intensity of his behavior to meet the expectations of the classroom. The BIS is responsible for inhibiting his behavior and making it conform to environmental expectations.

Children with ADHD show underactivity of the BIS. These children are unable to adjust their behavior to meet the demands of new situations, such as the transition from recess to the classroom. They may show difficulties inhibiting their boisterous play even when classmates no longer reciprocate (i.e., a lack of reinforcement) or the teacher becomes angry (i.e., punishment). Although children with ADHD know how they should behave in class, their underactive BIS interferes with their ability to follow classroom rules (Costa Dias et al., 2013).

Children with ADHD also show problems with the second system, the behavioral activation system (BAS). The BAS is responsible for approaching stimuli and adjusting behavior to achieve reinforcement. Imagine that a boy is playing on his school's basketball team. In order to be successful, the boy must follow the rules of the game, pass the ball to other players, and play good defense. To win the game, the boy must delay immediate gratification in order to work with the team. If the boy is able to engage in these behaviors, he is likely to enjoy playing the game, to be liked by his teammates, and to be praised by his coach.

Youths with ADHD often show overactivity of the BAS (Costa Dias et al., 2015). Their behavior is governed by a strong need for immediate reinforcement. Indeed, some theorists have argued that these children have a greater sensitivity to immediate rewards than other children (Shaw, Stringaris, Nigg, & Leibenluft, 2014). Consequently, a boy with ADHD might behave impulsively on the basketball court in order to achieve immediate gratification, rather than work with his teammates. For example, he might ignore the referee, refuse to share the ball with other players, and avoid parts of the game that are less exciting, like defense.

Structural and functional neuroimaging studies have largely confirmed Gray's theory regarding dysregulation of the BIS and BAS (Nigg, 2016a). Our response to reinforcement and punishment is mediated by a brain pathway called the mesolimbic neural circuit. This pathway consists of three areas (see Figure 8.4):

- the ventral tegmental area (VTA) and nucleus accumbens (located in the middle of the brain)
- the amygdala and hippocampus (located in the limbic system)
- the prefrontal cortex

The mesolimbic pathway is rich in dopamine receptors and involves areas of the brain responsible for learning, memory, and emotion. It has long been considered the brain's "pleasure pathway" and is important to understanding most addictive behaviors.

However, the mesolimbic pathway is also responsible for motivating us to engage in tasks for which we anticipate rewards. Evidence supporting this claim comes from two sources. First, animals with damage to this pathway lack motivation to work for food rewards they previously found reinforcing. Second, adolescents and adults with ADHD often show underactivity of this brain pathway. These individuals respond to immediate reinforcement, but they have problems delaying gratification to attain long-term goals or objectives (Snyder, 2016).

Taken together, these data indicate that individuals with ADHD might not be sensitive to reinforcement in the same way as their typically developing peers (Luman, van Meel, Oosterlaan, & Geurts, 2012). Specifically, they may be highly sensitive to reinforcement that is immediate and pleasurable and relatively insensitive to reinforcement that

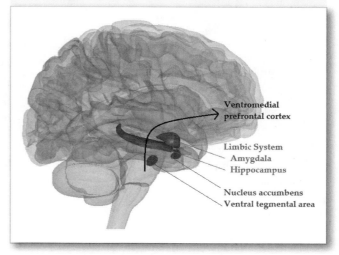

Figure 8.4 The mesolimbic circuit connects reward centers in the middle of the brain with emotion and memory areas of the limbic system. It is associated with reward sensitivity and immediate pleasure-seeking.

is less salient, due to underactivity of the mesolimbic circuit. Dysregulation of the mesolimbic pathway might explain why many children with ADHD can play video games for hours (i.e., a task with immediate, salient reinforcement) but cannot sustain their attention on math homework for more than a few minutes (i.e., a task with delayed, less salient reinforcement). This difference in reinforcement sensitivity has implications for treatment: To influence the behavior of children with ADHD, parents and teachers must reinforce appropriate behavior immediately and frequently.

The Frontal–Striatal Neural Circuit (Impaired Inhibition)

The second pathway implicated in ADHD is the frontal–striatal neural circuit (see). The striatum is part of the basal ganglia, located near the center of the brain. The striatum itself consists of three smaller regions: the caudate, the putamen, and the globus pallidus. Together, these three regions regulate behavior in response to feedback from the environment. They are also rich in dopamine. Dopaminergic activity in the striatum prompts us to seek out pleasure, excitement, novelty, and potential rewards. For example, the striatum is active when we are about to watch an exciting movie, spend time with friends, or indulge in our favorite dessert. Unfortunately, the striatum also becomes active when we are enduring a boring lecture and notice birds outside the classroom window, a conversation in the hallway, or the interesting way light reflects off our cell phone or calculator.

The second part of this pathway, the right prefrontal cortex, is located just behind the forehead. It consists of two subregions important to ADHD: the *orbitofrontal cortex* and the *dorsolateral cortex*. The orbitofrontal cortex is largely responsible for inhibition and impulse control. It

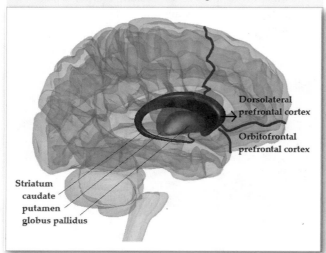

Figure 8.5   The frontal–striatal path connects the striatum with the prefrontal cortex. It regulates attention and executive functioning.

is the brain region that tells us to "stop" and resist the urge to act upon our immediate desires. The dorsolateral cortex is responsible for regulating our attention, organizing our behavior, and planning future actions. It is the brain region that tells us to "stay focused" and engage in activities to meet our long-term goals. The neurotransmitter norepinephrine plays a major role in these areas.

Together, the orbitofrontal and dorsolateral cortices are responsible for executive functioning. Just as an executive of a company plans, prioritizes, organizes, and implements the company's activities, the executive regions of the brain allow us to ignore distractions, focus on the steps needed to achieve long-term goals, and enact these steps in an organized way. These regions tell us to avoid engaging in our immediate impulses—the birds outside, the conversation, the reflections—and attend to what is important: the teacher!

Youths with ADHD show three abnormalities with the frontal–striatal neural circuit that likely contribute to their ADHD symptoms. First, they show a *maturational delay* in the development of regions along this pathway. Researchers discovered this delay by scanning the brains of the same children with and without ADHD for several years, from childhood through adolescence. Typically developing children show a dramatic increase in the size and thickness of the striatum, peaking at about 8 years of age, followed by a normal process of synaptic pruning. Then, typically developing children show growth and pruning of the prefrontal cortex, continuing through early adulthood. In contrast, youths with ADHD lag behind their typically developing peers by approximately 3 years. Even in adolescence, these regions are smaller and thinner. It is likely that delayed brain maturation underlies some of adolescents' problems with impulse control and executive functioning (van Ewijk & Oosterlaan, 2015).

Second, youths with ADHD show *dysregulation of the major neurotransmitters* involved in the frontal-striatal circuit. Compared to typically developing children, youths with ADHD show increased dopaminergic activity in the striatum and decreased norepinephrine and dopaminergic activity in the right prefrontal cortex. Researchers believe these abnormalities partially explain why children with ADHD are unusually sensitive to environmental stimuli and have difficulty ignoring these stimuli and staying on task. Interesting, the medications that affect these neurotransmitters are most effective for ADHD (Simon, 2016).

Third, recent data indicate that youths with ADHD show *reduced neural connectivity* between the striatum and right prefrontal cortex. Specifically, diffusion tensor imaging (DTI) has shown ADHD is associated with reduced integrity of the white matter (myelinated axons) along this pathway. Reduced connectivity is believed to interfere with children's ability to suppress immediate impulses and engage in more adaptive behavior (van Ewijk et al., 2014).

The Default Mode Network (Daydreaming and Mind-Wandering)

A final neural circuit that has gained attention by researchers is the default mode network. The network consists of three major brain regions: the medial prefrontal cortex, the medial parietal cortex, and the medial temporal cortex (see Figure 8.6). The default mode network gets its name because it is a brain pathway that becomes active by "default"—that is, when we are in a relaxed, resting state and not thinking about anything in particular. Although it seems like our brain is inactive when we are at rest, the default mode network is highly active during this time. Most experts believe this network underlies experiences like daydreaming, mind-wandering, and

Figure 8.6   The default mode network connects the medial frontal, temporal, and parietal cortices. It is active during daydreaming and mind-wandering.

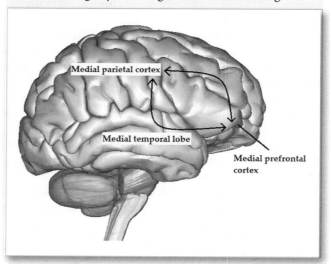

reflecting about activities that occurred earlier in the day or in our autobiographical memories (Weyandt et al., 2013).

The neural connections along the default mode network are strengthened in early childhood. By middle childhood, most youths can effectively inhibit the default mode network when they need to engage in an important task. For example, if a child is daydreaming about last night's soccer game, and her teacher directs her attention to a math lesson, she can effectively switch the default network off and get to work. However, children with ADHD have difficulty suppressing the default mode network. This inability to turn the network "off" may explain their inattention, daydreaming, and distractibility (Querne et al., 2016). Interestingly, medications used to treat ADHD enhance children's ability to inhibit the default mode, allowing them to focus (Liddle et al., 2011).

Review:

- The mesolimbic neural circuit consists of the (a) ventral tegmental area (VTA) and nucleus accumbens, (b) amygdala and hippocampus, and (c) prefrontal cortex. Dysregulation may cause heightened sensitivity to immediate rewards.
- The frontal–striatal neural circuit consists of the (a) striatum and (b) prefrontal cortex. Dysregulation may cause problems with inhibition and executive functioning.
- The default mode network consists of the (a) prefrontal, (b) parietal, and (c) temporal cortices. Dysregulation may cause inattention and daydreaming.

How Do Deficits in Executive Functioning Underlie Attention-Deficit/Hyperactivity Disorder?

Barkley's Neurodevelopmental Model

So far, we have seen that genetic, biological, and early environmental factors are associated with the development of ADHD. Now, we will examine the mechanism by which these risk factors lead to the disorder. One of the most influential explanations for the development of ADHD in children has been offered by Russell Barkley. According to Barkley's neurodevelopmental model (Barkley, 2014; Nigg & Barkley, 2014), problems in neural development, caused primarily by genetic and early biological risks, lead to problems with behavior later in life.

According to Barkley, the chief problem with ADHD is not inattention; instead, the fundamental deficit in ADHD is a lack of behavioral inhibition. Behavioral inhibition refers to the ability to inhibit immediate responses, especially responses that usually provide immediate gratification. Children show behavioral inhibition when they resist the impulse to act, when they stop responding in the middle of an action, or when they ignore a distracting stimulus in order to complete another behavior. Behavioral inhibition allows children time to consider other, more adaptive ways of responding.

For example, children show behavioral inhibition when they resist the urge to blurt out answers in class. Although blurting out answers might provide them with immediate reinforcement (e.g., teacher gives them attention, classmates laugh), it may not be the most beneficial way of responding. By inhibiting this behavior, children can consider alternative ways of responding (e.g., raising their hands) that could be more reinforcing in the long term (e.g., teacher provides praise for correct answer).

According to Barkley, children with ADHD show fundamental deficits in their capacity for behavioral inhibition (see Figure 8.7). These deficits arise from the combination of genetics and early environmental experiences (e.g., prenatal distress, birth complications). In typically developing children, behavioral inhibition gives children time to develop more sophisticated cognitive processes that allow them to regulate behavior and solve complex problems.

The Development of Executive Functions

Barkley asserts that the capacity for behavioral inhibition permits the development of four basic executive functions (Antshel, Hier, & Barkley, 2014). Each of these executive functions begins as an overt, observable behavior. Gradually, each function is internalized into mental representations or thoughts.

The executive functions serve three primary purposes. First, they allow children *to determine their own behavior*, rather than to be controlled by environmental stimuli. For example, the executive functions allow schoolchildren to ignore noises in the hallway and, instead, to focus on their teacher. Second, the executive functions allow children *to be influenced by delayed reinforcers* rather than by immediate gratification. For example, the executive functions allow children to resist the temptation to play video games (i.e., an immediate reinforcer) and, instead, complete their homework to earn a high grade (i.e., a delayed reinforcer). Third, executive functions allow children *to set long-term goals*. For example, executive functions allow children to plan and organize their behaviors (e.g., setting sequential short-term tasks) to accomplish long-term goals (e.g., completing a class presentation).

The first executive function to emerge is working memory. Recall that working memory involves holding information in short-term memory; analyzing this information to detect useful patterns, principles, or rules; and applying this information to solve future problems. Stated another way, working memory allows us to remember past experiences and use these experiences to plan for the future. Children with ADHD often have difficulty with working memory. They are forgetful, do not listen to others or learn from past experiences, and do not consider the consequences of their behaviors before they act. Instead, their behavior is tied largely to the here and now. They are influenced primarily by stimuli in their immediate

Figure 8.7   Barkley's Neurodevelopmental Model for ADHD

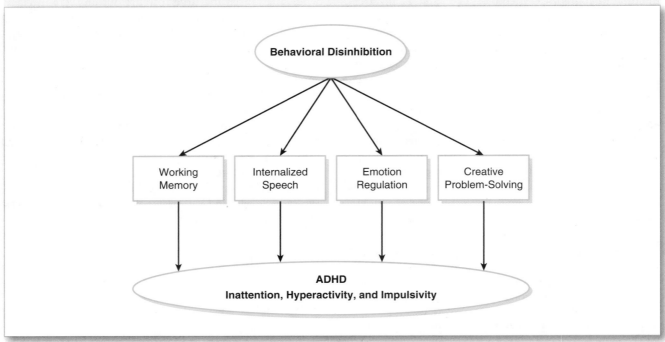

Note: Early problems with behavioral inhibition can adversely affect the development of the four executive functions. Executive functioning deficits underlie symptoms of ADHD.

environments rather than by past events or future consequences (Fried et al., 2016).

The second executive function to emerge is internalized speech. Children's inner speech guides and directs their overt behavior, giving them increased control over their actions (Vygotsky, 1978). As toddlers, children use speech primarily to communicate with others. As preschoolers, children begin to speak to themselves while performing tasks. This "self-directed" speech helps organize their actions and regulate their behavior. By the early school years, self-directed speech becomes even less overt, perhaps noticeable only when the child learns new behaviors or when he is trying to solve particularly difficult problems. By middle childhood, self-directed speech is completely internalized. In essence, self-directed speech becomes thought. Thoughts, or private speech, allow children to guide their behavior in logical and organized ways (Aro, Poikkeus, Laakso, Tolvanen, & Ahonen, 2015).

A lack of behavioral inhibition interferes with the internalization of speech. Children with ADHD have difficulty organizing and directing their behavior, following rules, and obeying others' instructions. Instead of being motivated by internalized speech and thoughts, their surroundings largely dictate their actions.

The third executive function to develop is emotion regulation. As children become better at inhibiting immediate behaviors, they also gain greater capacity to control the emotions that would normally follow those behaviors.

Consequently, they are less influenced by immediate, transitory emotions and more influenced by expectations for long-term rewards. For example, children become better at suffering through the short-term boredom of studying for a test in order to achieve future rewards associated with the studying (e.g., good grades, praise from parents). In short, children's motivation becomes less extrinsic and more intrinsic (Calkins & Perry, 2016).

Children with ADHD, however, continue to show problems with emotion regulation. They have difficulty regulating their moods, show reduced ability to maintain their motivation on tasks that require sustained effort, and appear heavily dependent on immediate reinforcement from the environment to direct their behavior. Consequently, children with ADHD can spend hours engaged in tasks that provide immediate reinforcement, but they quickly lose interest in other activities that depend on intrinsic motivation (e.g., reading, drawing, collecting).

The fourth and most complicated executive function to develop is the capacity for creative problem-solving. Initially, children learn about their surroundings by physically manipulating objects in their environment. During play, children discover the properties of objects by disassembling them, performing simple experiments, and combining objects in new and creative ways (e.g., a child playing with Legos). Later in development, objects can be mentally manipulated, analyzed, and combined in novel ways in order to solve problems. Whereas younger children might build a "fort" in their living room out of pillows and blankets through trial and error, older children can mentally plan the "fort" before beginning actual construction.

By late childhood, children can also combine words, images, information, and ideas in novel ways. This allows them to organize information, plan strategies, and solve increasingly more complex problems before acting. For example, middle school students arranging a Halloween party can plan the guest list, refreshments, entertainment, and each person's responsibilities for the party well in advance. Children with ADHD, however, show difficulty with organization, planning, and problem-solving.

In summary, Barkley's neurodevelopmental model posits that the underlying problem with ADHD is a deficit in behavioral inhibition. Problems with behavioral inhibition are primarily determined by genetics and early environmental risks. Difficulty with behavioral inhibition interferes with the development of the executive functions during infancy and early childhood. Children show impairments in working memory, internalized speech (thinking), emotional regulation, and creative problem-solving. Over time, these impairments in executive functioning can interfere with subsequent brain development and lead to the emergence of ADHD (Barkley, 2014; Nigg & Barkley, 2014).

Review:

- Barkley's neurodevelopmental model suggests that ADHD is caused by underlying deficits in behavioral inhibition, which impair the development of executive functioning.
- The four basic executive functions are (1) working memory, (2) internalized speech, (3) emotion regulation, and (4) creative problem-solving.
- Problems with the development of the executive functions lead to the symptoms of ADHD.

8.3 EVIDENCE-BASED TREATMENT

What Medications Are Effective for Attention-Deficit/ Hyperactivity Disorder?

Psychostimulants

Psychostimulants are the most commonly prescribed medications for ADHD. These medications affect the neurotransmitters dopamine and norepinephrine and cause increased attention and behavioral inhibition (Pliszka, 2015). There are two broad classes of psychostimulants: (1) amphetamines and (2) methylphenidates. The most frequently prescribed amphetamines are Adderall, Dexedrine, and Vyvanse. The most commonly prescribed methylphenidates are Concerta, Daytrana, Focalin, and Ritalin. Approximately 7% of all school-age children and 2% of all preschoolers take one of these medications, totaling more

Figure 8.8 Percentage of children ages 4 to 17 currently taking medication for ADHD. Prevalence ranges from 2% (Nevada) to 10.4% (Louisiana).

≤ 3.0%   3.1%–5.0%   5.1%–7.0%
7.1%–9.0%   ≥ 9.1%

Source: From Centers for Disease Control and Prevention (2016a).

than 3 million children in the United States (see Figure 8.8; Visser, Danielson, & Bitsko, 2014).

Amphetamine and methylphenidate have slightly different chemical structures and mechanisms of action (Heal, Smith, & Findling, 2011). Both medications stimulate the central nervous system by increasing dopamine and norepinephrine levels in the synaptic cleft. Amphetamine works primarily by increasing the release of dopamine from presynaptic storage vesicles, resulting in more dopamine output to the cleft. Methylphenidate slows the dopamine transporter system that removes dopamine from the cleft, thereby allowing dopamine to remain in the cleft for longer periods of time. The overall effect of both of these medications is a net increase in dopamine activity in brain regions that are typically underactive in children and adolescents with ADHD, particularly the frontal–striatal circuit. This increase in dopamine activates the regions that are responsible for executive control, behavioral inhibition, and working memory (Greenhill, 2005). Youths taking these medications experience increased ability to attend, ignore distractions, inhibit behavior, and engage in organization, planning, and problem-solving.

The various medications for ADHD also target different brain regions (Heal et al., 2011; Spencer, Biederman, & Wilens, 2015). For example, Adderall and Ritalin are older stimulants that bind to dopamine receptors in the prefrontal cortex. In contrast, Focalin is a newer stimulant that binds to dopamine receptors in the striatum. Medications also differ in their method of delivery. For example, Adderall begins binding to dopamine receptors soon after ingestion; children usually show peak effects in 30 to 40 minutes, lasting approximately 4 to 5 hours. In contrast, Adderall XR (extended release) consists of a 50:50 ratio of immediate-release and delayed-release capsules, resulting in effects that last 6 to 8 hours. Children who refuse to swallow pills can use a methylphenidate transdermal patch, Daytrana, which is applied to the skin once daily and produces effects that last 6 to 10 hours.

What would happen if youths without ADHD took stimulant medication? Neuroimaging studies suggest that the same brain circuitry is used to regulate attention and achieve behavioral inhibition, regardless of a person's diagnostic status. Specifically, the frontal–striatal neural circuit seems to be largely responsible for attention and inhibition, with other brain regions playing important supportive roles. Stimulant medication seems to activate frontal–striatal brain regions, by increasing dopamine and norepinephrine (see Figure 8.9). Consequently, low doses of stimulant medication reduce impulsivity and increase attention in individuals with and without ADHD (Pliszka, 2015).

Because stimulant medication affects individuals with and without ADHD, it has high potential for misuse. In the United States, psychostimulants are Schedule II drugs that are restricted by the Controlled Substances Act. (Other drugs on this list include cocaine, morphine, and pentobarbital.)

They can be misused in two ways. First, adolescents without ADHD may use these medications as "study enhancers" by orally ingesting other people's medications. These medications improve students' attention and concentration while studying. Approximately 15% of adolescents with ADHD report giving away their medication to friends, 7% admit to selling their medication, and 4% indicate that their medication was stolen in the previous 12 months. Second, immediate-release medications can be crushed and inhaled, producing a short-lasting euphoric effect. Approximately 2.7% of eighth graders and 5% of 12th graders admit to abusing stimulant medication in this manner (Bukstein, 2011).

Nonstimulant Medication

Not all ADHD medications are stimulants. Atomoxetine (Strattera) is a selective norepinephrine reuptake inhibitor (SNRI). Like the stimulants, Strattera seems to affect the norepinephrine system; unlike the stimulants, it appears to have little effect on dopamine activity. Effects tend to occur 2 to 3 weeks after first administration. Several randomized clinical trials have shown Strattera to be superior to placebo and comparable to methylphenidate in reducing ADHD symptoms. For example, Spencer et al. (2002) found that 69% of children responded to atomoxetine, compared to 73% taking methylphenidate and 31%

Figure 8.9   Immediate-release D-amphetamine (Dexedrine) increases dopamine in the striatum.

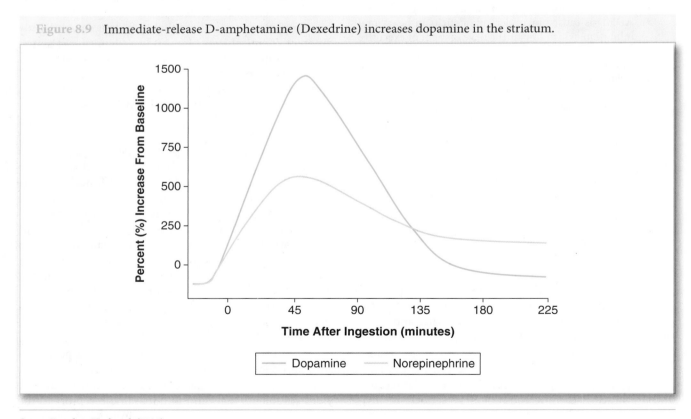

Source: Based on Heal at al. (2011).

Note: Immediate-release D-amphetamine (Dexedrine) increases dopamine in the striatum by 1500% and norepinephrine in the prefrontal cortex by 500% approximately 45 minutes after ingestion.

taking placebo. Because atomoxetine is not a stimulant, it has lower risk of misuse (Spencer et al., 2015).

Atomoxetine is often prescribed to the 20% to 30% of children who do not respond to stimulants. It can also be given to children with other behavioral or medical conditions that might be exacerbated if administered stimulant medication. For example, some children with tics or heart conditions may experience increased symptoms when taking stimulants. Finally, atomoxetine may be appropriate for adolescents with a history of conduct problems or substance abuse who might misuse stimulants if they were prescribed (Millichap, 2010).

A final medication that is used to treat ADHD in children and adolescents is guanfacine (Intuniv). This medication is a α₂ receptor agonist, a class of medication usually used to treat hypertension in adults. We do not know exactly how this medication works to reduce ADHD symptoms; however, it appears to affect brain areas responsible for impulse control and emotion regulation. Randomized controlled studies show that it is effective for children and adolescents, especially youths aged 6 through 12 (Newcorn et al., 2016).

Guanfacine can be administered either as first-line medication for ADHD or (more commonly) used in combination with stimulant medication to help children who do not respond to stimulants alone. Because guanfacine is not a stimulant, it does not have the same risks as stimulant medications. Side effects are generally sedation and daytime sleepiness. Abrupt discontinuation should be avoided because it can cause a potentially dangerous drop in blood pressure (Bernknopf, 2011).

Efficacy and Limitations

More than 250 placebo-controlled studies have demonstrated the effectiveness of medication in reducing ADHD symptoms in school-age children (Pliszka, 2015). One way to examine the efficacy of these medications is through meta-analysis. Recall that meta-analysis allows us to combine the results of many studies to generate an effect size (ES), a measure of how much better participants in the treatment group were than participants in the control group at the end of the study. Faraone (2009) conducted a meta-analysis of randomized controlled studies, examining the relative effects of four classes of ADHD medications to placebo: amphetamines, methylphenidates, atomoxetine, and guanfacine.

Results showed that all medications improved ADHD better than placebo. The largest effects were for the stimulant medications (see Figure 8.10). Across studies, approximately 60% to 70% of children with ADHD respond to medication compared to only 15% to 20% taking placebo. The response rate increases to 85% if children try a second type of stimulant medication if they do not respond to the first type (Pliszka, 2015).

Medication seems to affect ADHD symptoms and reduce other disruptive behavior problems, such as oppositional behavior, defiance, and some conduct problems. Stimulant medication is also associated with improvements in children's academic, cognitive, and social functioning (Spencer et al., 2015). Several studies have demonstrated better academic performance and productivity as well as improvements in working memory and executive functioning. For example, Barnard and

Figure 8.10 Medications for ADHD are significantly better than placebo in randomized controlled studies. On average, amphetamine and methylphenidate yields the largest effects.

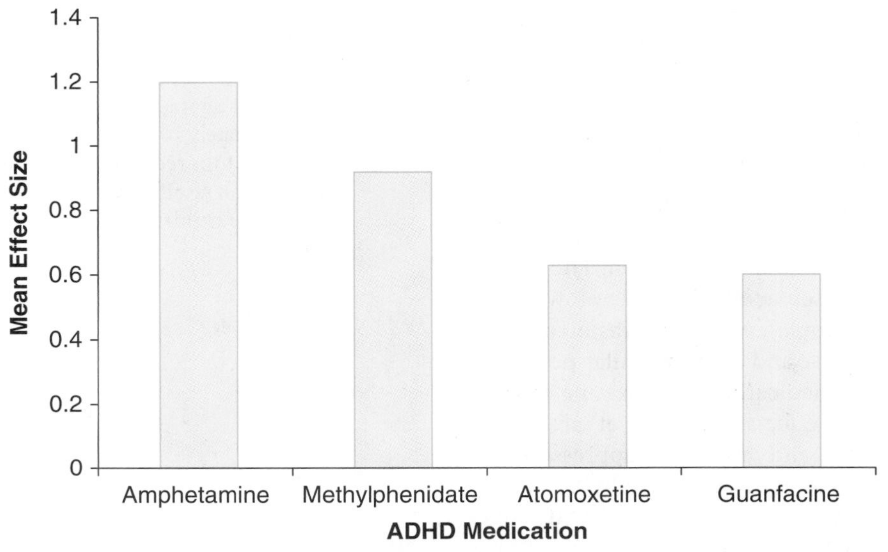

Source: Based on Faraone (2009).

colleagues (Barnard, Stevens, To, Lan, & Mulsow, 2010) examined the effects of stimulants on the academic achievement of 2,844 children with ADHD. Their analyses showed that medication was associated with higher achievement test scores across the duration of the four-year study.

Recent research also indicates that stimulants can be effective for preschoolers (Spencer et al., 2015). In the Preschool ADHD Treatment Study (PATS), 3.5- to 5-year-old children with ADHD were randomly assigned to receive various doses of immediate-release methylphenidate or placebo for 8 weeks. Results showed significant improvement in ADHD for children in the medication conditions, except those taking the lowest dose. In contrast, there was no improvement in children prescribed placebo. Only 21% of preschoolers who took medication achieved complete symptom remission, however. Furthermore, 30% of parents reported that their children experienced significant side effects (e.g., sleep or behavior problems). These findings indicate that medication can be helpful for preschoolers with ADHD.

The most common side effects of stimulants are insomnia, decreased appetite, stomachache, headache, and dizziness. These side effects are usually minor and go away when dosage is reduced. Early research indicated that children who take stimulant medication may experience a slowdown in their physical growth. However, more recent research suggests that children with ADHD who do not take stimulant medication also show slower growth rates, so the exact effects of stimulants on children's growth is still debated.

There had been concern that stimulants might be associated with cardiovascular problems in children. The Canadian Department of Health temporarily prohibited certain extended-release amphetamines for children with ADHD, following anecdotal reports of sudden death, heart attack, and stroke. In the United States, several regulatory agencies recommended black-box warning for stimulants frequently prescribed to children. Indeed, the American Heart Association suggested that children taking stimulants participate in periodic electrocardiograms (ECGs) to monitor their safety. Recently, however, a large epidemiological study indicated that these concerns are unwarranted. Researchers analyzed health records of 1,200,438 children and young adults, including 373,667 individuals prescribed stimulant medication. They found that the risk of a cardiovascular event was very low overall (i.e., 81 people in the sample), and there was no association between stimulant use and cardiovascular problems.

The nonstimulant medication atomoxetine is associated with fewer side effects (Spencer et al., 2015). For example, insomnia and appetite suppression are less common with atomoxetine than methylphenidate. Furthermore, atomoxetine is not associated with appetite suppression and slowed growth. However, because axomoxetine affects norepinephrine, like many antidepressant medications, it carries a black-box warning that indicates that children who take this medication may be at increased risk for suicidal ideation. In one large study, 0.4% of children taking atomoxetine showed increased suicidal ideation compared to 0% of children taking placebo. Although risk of suicidal ideation is low, clinicians and parents must weigh this risk against the potential benefits of atomoxetine when deciding to use this medication.

Medication for ADHD has several limitations. First, not all children respond to medication. Even in carefully controlled research studies, as many as 15% to 30% of children with ADHD do not show improvement. Clearly, medication is not a panacea for ADHD (Chacko et al., 2016).

Second, discontinuation of medication almost always results in the return of ADHD symptoms. Consequently, most physicians view stimulant medication as a long-term treatment for ADHD. Longitudinal studies indicate that stimulant medications remain safe and effective for at least 2 years, but their effects after that duration are largely unknown (Simon, 2016).

Third, stimulant medications should be used cautiously in children with tics or Tourette's syndrome. Overall, there is little evidence that stimulant medications elicit tics. However, very high doses of stimulants may exacerbate tics in certain children who already have them. These children may be prescribed atomoxetine instead of stimulants, which is not associated with motor control problems (Pringsheim & Steeves, 2012).

Finally, many families are reluctant to use medications to manage their children's ADHD symptoms. For these families, psychosocial interventions offer an alternative avenue of treatment.

Review:

- The stimulant medications, amphetamine and methylphenidate, are most effective in reducing ADHD symptoms in children and adolescents. These medications enhance dopamine and (to a lesser extent) norepinephrine leading to improved attention and inhibition.
- Alternative medications for ADHD include atomoxetine (Strattera), an SNRI, and guanfacine (Intuniv) an α_2 receptor agonist.
- Approximately 70% of youths with ADHD show significant symptom reduction with medication. Medication is slightly less effective for preschoolers compared to school-age children and adolescents.

What Psychosocial Treatments Are Effective for Attention-Deficit/Hyperactivity Disorder?

Clinical Behavior Therapy

Clinical behavior therapy is the most frequently used nonpharmacological treatment for ADHD. This treatment is called clinical behavior therapy because clinicians typically administer treatment in clinics and hospitals, rather than in homes or schools. The focus of therapy is on children's overt behavior. Clinical behavior therapy has three main components: (1) parent consultation, (2) school consultation, and (3) a combined home–school reward system (Young & Amarasinghe, 2010).

Parent consultation, sometimes called parent training, involves helping the caregivers of children with ADHD learn more effective ways to manage their children's behavior. Typically, the therapist meets with parents on a weekly basis, over the course of 2 to 3 months. Each week, the therapist introduces a new parenting principle or tactic designed to improve the quality of parents' interactions with their children or help parents manage their children's high-rate behaviors. Early sessions focus on teaching parents how to attend to children's positive behavior and reinforce children for obeying rules. These sessions help parents acknowledge and strengthen desirable aspects of their children's behavior—aspects that are often overshadowed by children's ADHD symptoms (Mendenhall, Arnold, & Fristad, 2015).

Later sessions focus on setting clear expectations for children and administering consistent discipline for children's misbehavior. Clinicians usually teach parents of young children to use time-out to address disruptive behavior problems. Parents of older children may be taught how to use tokens or points to reinforce appropriate behavior and penalize inappropriate actions. The purpose of these sessions is to help parents address their children's misbehavior without yelling, threatening, or resorting to hostile and coercive interactions.

In addition to meeting with parents, clinicians consult with teachers and other school personnel and implement a home–school reward system. Clinicians usually help teachers identify situations when the child is most often off task. Then, clinicians help teachers change the environment to reduce disruptive behavior and encourage on-task activities. Clinicians also encourage teachers to keep a daily report card of children's appropriate behavior at school, which can be monitored and rewarded by parents at home. Finally, clinicians may help teachers develop a classroom-wide token economy or point system to encourage students' attention and compliance. Tokens can be exchanged for privileges enjoyed by all students in the class.

Clinical behavior therapy is effective in improving the functioning of children with ADHD and their families (Lundahl, Risser, & Lovejoy, 2006). A meta-analysis of 68 studies showed that parent training was associated with moderate improvements in children's behavior (ES = .42), parents' behavior (ES = .47), and parents' perceptions of their children (ES = .53). Up to one year after treatment, gains made in therapy remained significant. Children who showed the most severe behavior problems tended to benefit the most from parent training. Parent training was much more effective when it was administered to individual families rather than to groups of parents. However, parent training was least effective for families from disadvantaged backgrounds. It is possible that socioeconomic hardships interfere with parents' abilities to attend therapy

sessions, to learn strategies taught during sessions, and to practice these strategies at home. The researchers suggest that disadvantaged families might benefit from individual parent-training sessions, during which the therapist might tailor interventions to each family's needs.

Clinical behavior therapy for ADHD also has several limitations. First, the efficacy of behavior therapy is strongly related to parents' involvement in the program. For example, in one study of kindergarten children with ADHD, clinical behavior therapy led to improvements in children's behavior at school, but not at home (Barkley et al., 2000). The failure of treatment to improve home behavior was probably due to the fact that most parents did not consistently attend the parent training program. When parents consistently attended training sessions, treatment was associated with improvements across home and school contexts (Anastopoulos, Shelton, & Barkley, 2005).

Second, parent training is typically effective only as long as parents actively implement strategies and tactics learned in therapy. Although most children show symptom reduction immediately after their parents' completion of the training program, the effects of therapy tend to be reduced 6 to 12 months later (Hinshaw, Klein, & Abikoff, 2002).

Third, parent training does not always normalize child behavior. Normalization refers to whether, at the end of treatment, children cannot be distinguished from children without significant behavior problems. Even after behavior therapy, children tend to show symptoms of ADHD and continue to merit the ADHD diagnosis. In fact, only about 25% of children whose parents participate in treatment no longer meet diagnostic criteria for ADHD (Hinshaw et al., 2002).

Fourth, behavior therapy programs are less effective for adolescents than for children (Barkley, 2014). Therapy works best when parents have a high degree of control over their children's environment. However, parents have much less control over adolescents than over school-age children. Consequently, some clinicians supplement traditional parent consultation with parent–adolescent problem-solving and communication training. Specifically, clinicians teach parent-adolescent dyads how to solve problems and handle disputes constructively—rather than by resorting to yelling, sarcasm, criticism, or "shutting down." Unfortunately, supplementing traditional parent training with communication training does not seem to be more effective than traditional parent training alone. Only about 23% of adolescents show reliable improvement in their behavior, and 17% of dyads actually showed a worsening of family disputes, perhaps because they were encouraged to discuss conflicts openly rather than to avoid them.

Summer Treatment Programs

A second form of behavioral treatment for ADHD is direct contingency management. Direct contingency management is used in schools and specialized classroom settings, in which therapists have a great deal of control over children's surroundings. In direct contingency management, therapists alter children's environments to maximize the frequency of desired actions. They rely heavily on systematic rewards and punishments to shape behavior. Usually, environmental contingencies are used to increase attention, reduce disruptive behavior in the classroom, and improve the quality of children's interactions with peers (Fabiano, Schatz, & Pelham, 2014).

One of the best-known examples of a direct contingency management program for children with ADHD is the Summer Treatment Program (STP) developed by William Pelham. The STP provides comprehensive treatment for children with ADHD over the summer months, a time during which most children do not receive school-based treatment for their ADHD symptoms. The STP is an 8-week program for children aged 5 through 15 with ADHD and other disruptive behavior problems (Pelham, Fabiano, Gnagy, Greiner, & Hoza, 2005).

Children are divided into age-matched teams led by staff members, usually college students who are trained as behavior therapists. Teams stay together throughout the summer in order to foster friendships and improve the social functioning of members. Each group spends 3 hours per day in a modified classroom setting, led by special education teachers. Children participate in 1 hour of academic instruction, 1 hour of computer-assisted instruction, and 1 hour of art class. Children spend the rest of the day in recreational group activities that are highly structured, such as soccer, softball, and swimming. These activities are designed to improve children's social and motor skills.

STP differs from traditional summer camps; staff members use direct contingency management to modify children's behavior. The tactics used by staff members resemble the strategies taught to parents during clinical behavior therapy. The low staff-to-child ratio allows staff to closely monitor children's behavior throughout the day and provide immediate reinforcement contingent on children's appropriate actions. The intervention is intensive and comprehensive.

First, staff members issue brief, clear, and specific commands to children. Clear directions reduce the chance that children will not comply with the command because of inattention, ambiguity, or distraction. Second, staff members provide immediate and liberal reinforcement contingent on desirable behavior. Social reinforcers include eye contact and smiles, touch (e.g., a high five), or recognition (e.g., buttons, stickers). Third, staff members use tokens with younger children or a point system with older children to foster desirable behavior. Staff award tokens or points for appropriate behavior in the classroom (e.g., attending to the teacher, working quietly) and during recreation (e.g., listening to coaches, following pool safety rules). Tokens or points can be exchanged for privileges. Response cost is used to reduce inappropriate behavior. Staff members take away tokens or deduct points contingent on unwanted actions (e.g., excessive talking in class, teasing peers on the

soccer field). For more serious rule violations, staff members use time out. For example, children who deliberately hurt others or destroy property are removed from positive reinforcement (e.g., no swim or computer time).

The behavioral interventions used by STP staff are supplemented by social skills training, parent training, and medication assessment and management. First, all children participate in 10 minutes of formal social skills training each day. Staff members initially introduce a social skill (such as raising your hand before speaking in class) by talking about it, demonstrating it, and breaking it down into steps. Then, children are encouraged to practice the skill during role play. Staff members remind children to use the new skill throughout the day and reward them liberally for its use. Second, caregivers participate in weekly group parent training sessions designed to teach them how to use behavioral principles at home. Staff members give parents a daily report card and encourage them to reward their children for appropriate behavior at camp. Finally, children in the STP are assessed to determine the appropriateness of medication to treat their ADHD symptoms. If medication is warranted, the effectiveness of the medication is monitored during camp.

Direct contingency management greatly improves ADHD symptoms and other disruptive behaviors (Fabiano et al., 2014). Chronis and colleagues (2004) performed one of the first controlled studies of the effectiveness of STP for children with ADHD. In their study, children participated in an 8-week STP. All children had ADHD, and 85% also had conduct problems. The researchers used a within-subjects design to evaluate the effectiveness of the STP. For the first five weeks of camp, staff used direct contingency management to modify children's behavior. For 2 days during Week 6, staff refrained from using direct contingency management. For the final 2 weeks of the STP, direct contingency management procedures were reinitiated. Independent observers rated children's behavior during all three phases of the evaluation. Children showed a significant increase in disruptive behavior when treatment was removed compared to when direct contingency management was used (see Figure 8.11).

Subsequent studies indicate that programs using direct contingency management increase attention and appropriate social behavior, reduce disruptive behavior and aggression, and improve children's self-esteem. Parents can be taught to implement the behavior management strategies used in these programs to improve children's behavior at home, especially when completing homework. Parental participation is associated with reduced parent-child conflict and a high degree of satisfaction with treatment (Graziano, Slavec, Hart, Garcia, & Pelham, 2014; Sibley et al., 2013).

Behavioral Classroom Management

Behavioral classroom management is a school-based intervention for children with ADHD. Behavioral

Figure 8.11   Summer Treatment Program for Youths With ADHD

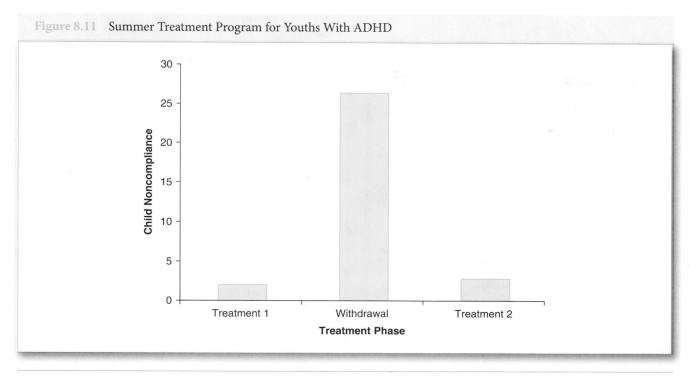

Source: Based on Chronis et al. (2004).

Note: Chronis and colleagues (2004) used direct contingency management during treatment phases 1 and 2, but withdrew contingencies between treatment phases. Children's noncompliance increased during treatment withdrawal, indicating that treatment was effective.

classroom management relies on the same interventions used in clinical behavior therapy and summer treatment. The unique characteristic of behavioral classroom management is that it is administered by teachers and other education specialists in classroom settings. Although programs vary, interventions rely heavily on monitoring appropriate child behavior, administering frequent positive reinforcement contingent on appropriate behavior, structuring the classroom environment to elicit appropriate behavior, and developing a daily report card so that parents can reinforce appropriate behavior at home.

Several randomized controlled studies support the efficacy of behavioral classroom management. On average, 40% to 60% of school-age children with ADHD show significant improvement in ADHD symptoms at school as a result of their participation in this program. With few exceptions, however, these interventions have been studied with school-age children only; much less in known about their efficacy when used with adolescents (Evans, Owens, & Bunford, 2014; Nissley-Tsiopinis, Krehbiel, & Power, 2016).

One noteworthy variation of traditional behavior classroom management is the Challenging Horizons Program (Evans et al., 2016). This program combines school-based behavioral interventions with an afterschool program designed to increase academic engagement and performance. Previous research has shown that older children and adolescents with ADHD tend to have negative attitudes toward school and little engagement in their academic work and extracurricular activities. The Challenging Horizon afterschool groups teach organization and social skills to middle school students with ADHD. Several sessions offer parent training to caregivers and opportunities for consultation with classroom teachers. Evaluation studies indicate that the program yields moderate to large effects compared to children in regular classroom environments (Langberg, Evans, et al., 2016).

A second innovative approach to classroom behavior management is MOSAIC (Making Socially Accepting Inclusive Classrooms), a brief group intervention designed to improve the social functioning of youths with ADHD. Recall that children with ADHD are at-risk for peer rejection because of their high-rate, aversive actions or peer neglect because of their off-task, inattentive behavior. Over time, children with ADHD may develop negative reputations, which place them on developmental pathways toward conduct problems or social isolation and loneliness. MOSAIC seeks to change their paths by (a) improving their behavior toward peers in the classroom and (b) helping their classmates become more accepting and forgiving of their hyperactive–impulsive or inattentive actions (see Figure 8.12). Evaluation studies indicate that MOSAIC is as effective as traditional classroom behavior management in improving children's disruptive behavior at school. Furthermore, youths who participate in MOSAIC are less rejected by their peers and have more reciprocated friendships than youths in traditional programs (Mikami et al., 2013; Mikami, Jia, & Na, 2014).

Figure 8.12 MOSAIC improves the classroom behavior and social functioning of children with ADHD.

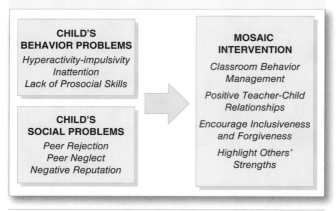

Source: Based on Mikami and Normand (2015).

Potentially Effective Treatments

Special Diets

Many parents believe that certain foods or food additives can exacerbate hyperactivity and impulsivity in children with ADHD. The notion that diet might be related to ADHD began in 1973 when Benjamin Feingold, chief of the Department of Allergy at the Kaiser Permanente Foundation Hospital, suggested that certain foods might increase symptoms. He suggested restricting foods containing salicylic acid, such as apples, berries, green peppers, oranges, and tomatoes, as well as artificial preservatives. He claimed that 60% to 70% of children with ADHD improved on the Kaiser Permanente diet. Similar diets recommend avoiding artificial colors and flavors and restricting foods containing dairy or wheat.

Studies investigating the effects of special diets on ADHD have been plagued by methodological problems. For example, most studies have not recruited participants through random selection. Instead, they have typically relied on parent–volunteers who are willing to carefully monitor and restrict their children's food intake. These volunteers might be different from parents in the general population. Furthermore, children fed special diets in these studies tend to receive more attention than youths in comparison groups, perhaps affecting their outcomes. Finally, many parents report symptom improvement after implementing special diets, but these improvements are typically not observed by clinicians or teachers. It is likely that placebo effects account for some of benefits attributed to these diets (van Ewijk & Oosterlaan, 2015).

Do special diets help children with ADHD? On average, the difference between children with ADHD who adopt special diets versus children in comparison groups is small (ES = .28). However, there appears to be a subset of children with ADHD (approximately 30%) who do show

symptom improvement following dietary changes. Usually, these children have a history of sensitivity to certain foods or additives. Two types of dietary changes are helpful for these children. Some children respond to diets that restrict synthetic food coloring (Heilskov Rytter et al., 2015). Other children seem to benefit from dietary supplementation of omega-3 acids, such as fish (Gillies, Sinn, Lad, Leach, & Ross, 2012; Sonuga-Barke et al., 2013). Overall, these dietary changes are associated with moderate improvements in ADHD symptoms but only for this subset of youths (ES = .54). Dietary changes will likely have little to no effect on most other children (Stevens, Kuczek, Burges, Hurt, & Arnold, 2011).

Sleep and Exercise

Another promising strategy to reduce ADHD symptoms is to make sure children get enough sleep. Recall that children with ADHD often experience sleep disturbance; they may be reluctant to go to bed at night, have difficulty falling or staying asleep, and show more restless sleep than their typically developing classmates (Alfano & Gamble, 2009). Furthermore, most children (with or without ADHD) show an increase in inattentive and hyperactive–impulsive symptoms when deprived of sleep. Consequently, researchers speculated that sleep might be a mechanism by which ADHD symptoms could be alleviated in certain children.

Gruber and colleagues (2012) randomly assigned children to two conditions. Parents in the first condition were asked to put their children to bed 1 hour earlier than usual; parents in the second condition were asked to put their children to bed 1 hour later. On average, children in the sleep enhancement condition gained an extra 27 minutes of sleep per night, whereas children in the sleep restriction condition lost 54 minutes per night. Teachers, who were blind to the children's condition, reported improvements in the behavior of children in the sleep enhancement condition; they noted less daytime sleepiness, better emotional stability, and fewer restless and hyperactive behaviors at school. In contrast, teachers reported increased behavior problems in children whose sleep was restricted. Altogether, these results indicate that sleep enhancement might be a free, no-risk strategy that parents can implement to improve their children's behavior.

A second strategy to improve children's attention is physical exercise. Pontifex and colleagues (Pontifex, Saliba, Raine, Picchietti, & Hillman, 2012) asked children to perform two simple tasks (1) read a book while seated for 20 minutes or (2) run on a treadmill for 20 minutes. All children performed both tasks in counterbalanced order (i.e., some children read first whereas others exercised first). After each task, children completed tests of attention and concentration, reading, and math. Regardless of the order of the tasks, children showed better attention after exercising than after sitting (see Figure 8.13). Furthermore,

Figure 8.13 Children with ADHD showed more brain activity *(lighter gray)* indicative of attention and concentration after 20 minutes of cardiovascular exercise than after 20 minutes of reading. After exercising, children also showed better performance on standardized tests of reading and math. Exercise might be a no-cost, no-risk means of improving attention and academic performance in children with ADHD.

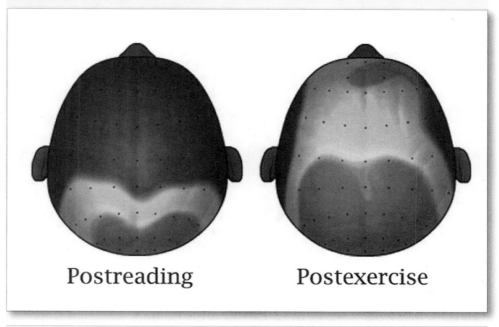

Postreading   Postexercise

Source: Based on Pontifex and colleagues (2012). Used with permission.

children's reading and math scores were significantly higher after exercising than after sitting. Interestingly, electroencephalograms (EEGs), performed during the study, indicated that exercise was associated with greater allocation of resources to areas of the brain responsible for attention and concentration—areas typically underactive in children with ADHD. Exercise might stimulate those brain areas and improve attention and concentration.

Working Memory Training

Recall that working memory refers to the ability to temporarily hold information in short-term memory, manipulate it, and use it to solve problems. Working memory is important to many cognitive tasks including remembering instructions, planning work, and completing assignments. Working memory is one of several executive functions believed to be underdeveloped in children with ADHD (Barkley, 2014). Furthermore, children and adolescents with ADHD often show deficits in working memory compared to typically developing peers. For example, children with ADHD often forget to complete a chore at home because they are distracted by a telephone call, or they forget an important step in a math problem because they were eavesdropping on a conversation between two classmates. Deficits in working memory likely contribute

to children's inattention and academic problems. Indeed, working memory deficits often underlie learning disabilities (Geary, Hoard, Nugent, & Bailey, 2012).

Although stimulant medication can improve the behavior of children with ADHD, its effects on working memory are less robust. Consequently, Beck, Hanson, Puffenberger, Benninger, and Benninger (2010) have developed an intervention program designed to improve the working memory skills of youths with ADHD (see Figure 8.14). The computer-based program is administered at home and is supervised by parents. It consists of 25 sessions, each lasting 30 to 40 minutes, administered over the course of 6 weeks. Each session consists of activities designed to strengthen children's working memory skills. Some activities involve verbal working memory (e.g., remembering names or objects), whereas other activities are designed to strengthen visual–spatial working memory (e.g., remembering patterns, shapes, or puzzles). The computer adjusts the difficulty of items based on children's performance, so they are neither bored nor overwhelmed by the activities.

A randomized controlled study of the working memory intervention yielded promising results. The parents of children who participated in the program reported significant reductions in their children's inattentive symptoms over time. Furthermore, these gains were maintained 4 months later. Teachers reported borderline-significant

Figure 8.14 Working memory training can reduce inattentive symptoms in some children with ADHD.

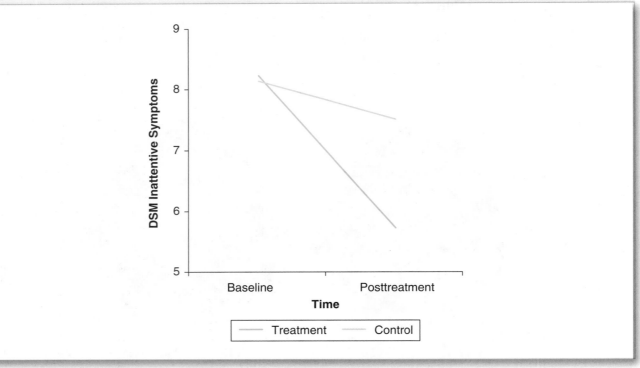

Source: Based on Beck and colleagues (2010).

Note: This brief and easy-to-use program led to a significant reduction in parent-reported symptoms.

improvement in children's inattentive symptoms as well. No such improvement was seen among youths in the comparison group. These findings are noteworthy because this program was relatively brief, easy to administer, and did not involve the use of medication.

Review:

- Clinical behavior therapy relies on parental monitoring and positive reinforcement. Key components are parent consultation, school consultation, and a combined home–school reward system.
- STP is a form of direct contingency management in which children receive positive reinforcement for appropriate behavior in the classroom, during social activities, and while playing sports.
- Clinicians who use behavioral classroom management administer positive reinforcement to foster appropriate behavior at school. It can be combined with peer interventions to improve social functioning.

Which Is More Effective: Medication or Psychosocial Treatment?

Multimodal Treatment

Both stimulant medication and behavior therapy can effectively reduce ADHD symptoms in children. Is one

treatment better than the other? Should we combine treatments to produce the greatest effects?

Fortunately, several studies have compared the efficacy of pharmacological and psychosocial treatments. In one of the first, large-scale studies, researchers randomly assigned 103 children with ADHD to one of three treatment groups. The first group received only methylphenidate. The second group received methylphenidate plus clinical behavior therapy. The third group received methylphenidate plus an attention placebo. The children in this third condition worked on projects with staff members, received help with homework, and participated in nondirective therapy with a counselor about day-to-day problems. Their parents also attended a support group but did not receive parent training. Parents, teachers, psychiatrists, and independent observers rated children's behavior every 6 months for 2 years. The researchers were interested in whether children who received both medication and behavior therapy would fare better than children in the other two groups (Abikoff et al., 2004a, 2004b; Hechtman et al., 2004a, 2004b).

Results yielded three important findings. First, all three groups of children showed improved functioning from the beginning of the study to the time the study ended. For example, children in all three treatment groups showed fewer disruptive behavior problems, improved academic functioning, better social skills, and improved parent–child interactions over the course of treatment. Most of the gains in children's behavior occurred during the first six months of treatment. The second important finding was that all three groups of children showed generally equivalent outcomes at 1- and 2-year follow-up. The third finding was most surprising of all: children who received methylphenidate plus behavior therapy fared no better than children who received methylphenidate alone or methylphenidate plus placebo.

The largest study examining the relative effects of medication and behavior therapy on ADHD was the Multimodal Treatment Study of Children With ADHD (MTA). In this study, researchers randomly assigned 579 children with ADHD to one of four treatment groups:

1. *Medication alone.* Youths in this group received 14 months of medication, usually methylphenidate, which was carefully administered by researchers.

2. *Behavior therapy alone.* Youths in this group participated in 8 months of clinical behavior therapy during part of the academic year and an STP during the summer. These youths did not receive medication.

3. *Combined treatment.* Youths in this group received both medication and behavior therapy, both administered by the researchers.

4. *Community care.* Youths in this group were referred to mental health professionals (e.g., physicians, psychologists) in their communities. They were free to receive any treatment recommended by these professionals, but they did not receive treatment from the researchers. Most (67%) children who received community care were prescribed medication. Youths in this group served as a "treatment as usual" control condition.

Researchers examined children's outcomes after 14 months (MTA Cooperative Group, 1999; Swanson et al., 2001). Results indicated that all four treatments were effective at reducing children's ADHD symptoms. Children who received combined treatment or medication alone showed the best outcomes. In fact, youths who received combined treatment or medication alone were approximately twice as likely to improve than youths who received behavior therapy alone or community care. Finally, the combination of medication and behavior therapy yielded only small benefits above and beyond medication alone (see Figure 8.15).

Taken together, these studies seem to suggest that medication should be the first-line treatment for ADHD in children. After all, medication alone was superior to behavior therapy alone for children's ADHD symptoms. Furthermore, adding behavior therapy to medication leads to a statistically significant, but small, improvement in children's functioning over medication alone (Molina et al., 2009; Murray et al., 2008).

Other research, however, demonstrates the importance of including behavior therapy in treatment protocols for

Figure 8.15 Results of the MTA Study

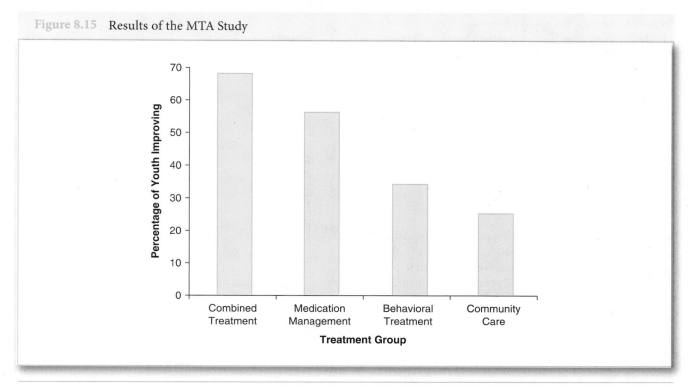

Source: Based on Swanson et al. (2001).

Note: Combining medication with behavior therapy, or using medication alone, is superior to behavior therapy alone to treat ADHD.

ADHD. Recall that in the MTA, researchers compared children's outcomes after 14 months. At posttest, children in the medication groups were still taking medication whereas children in the behavior therapy groups stopped receiving therapy several months earlier. When researchers compared the functioning of children when they were both actively receiving treatment, they found similar improvements in children receiving medication versus behavior therapy. Behavior therapy may work as well as medication as long as both are maintained over time (Pelham et al., 2000).

Fabiano and colleagues (2009) reviewed 175 studies, involving more than 2,000 participants, investigating the usefulness of psychosocial interventions for ADHD. Overall, the effect of these interventions was large. For example, in between-group studies, participants who received psychosocial treatment showed greater symptom reduction than approximately 80% of controls. Similarly, in within-group studies, children who received psychosocial interventions showed an average of 2.64 standard deviations improvement from pretest to posttest.

Furthermore, not all children respond to pharmacological treatments for ADHD. Psychosocial interventions offer an alternative form of treatment to nonresponders. Pelham and colleagues (2016) randomly assigned children with ADHD to two treatment groups: methylphenidate alone or behavior therapy alone. Children who did not respond sufficiently to their initial treatment were provided the other treatment, too. The researchers found that youths who received behavior therapy first and medication second showed better outcomes than youths who received medication first and behavior therapy second. Behavior therapy increased parents' involvement in their children's treatment, thus strengthening the effects of that treatment on children's outcomes.

Finally, survey data indicate that parents strongly prefer behavioral treatments over pharmacological ones for their children. Parents are understandably wary of administering medications to their children, especially those for which we have limited data regarding their long-term impact. Parents also report higher satisfaction with behavior therapy than with medication (Barkley, 2014; Evans et al., 2014).

Best Practices

Several professional organizations, such as the American Academy of Pediatrics and the Society of Clinical Child and Adolescent Psychology, have issued best-practice guidelines for the evidenced-based treatment of ADHD in children, adolescents, and adults (American Academy of Pediatrics Subcommittee on ADHD, 2011; Evans et al., 2014; Nathan & Gorman, 2015). Collectively, these guidelines recommend behaviorally based interventions and medication to treat individuals with this disorder. However, the relative emphasis of behavior therapy versus medication varies as a function of age.

- Preschool-age children should receive behavior therapy as a first-line treatment for ADHD. Preschoolers who do not respond to behavior therapy may be prescribed medication with consent of their caregivers.
- School-age children and adolescents should receive a combination of behavior therapy and medication as a first-line treatment. Behavior therapy can be administered either in a clinic (with parents), school (with teachers), or across settings. Medication should only be used with the consent of caregivers and assent of youths.
- Adults with ADHD should consider medication and (if possible) participate in a behavior therapy program to help them manage symptoms in everyday life. For example, adults may learn strategies to improve executive functioning such as planning and prioritizing work, remembering important tasks, and setting and achieving long-term goals.

Unfortunately, the treatment that most youths receive does not meet these best practices (see Figure 8.16). Researchers from the Centers for Disease Control and Prevention examined the treatments provided to children and adolescents with ADHD and other health-related problems. Only about one-half of preschoolers with ADHD received behavior therapy, even though behavior therapy is regarded as the first-line treatment for preschool-age children. Furthermore, only 35% of

Figure 8.16 Most youths with ADHD receive treatment; however, only about one-third receive the recommended combination of medication and behavior therapy.

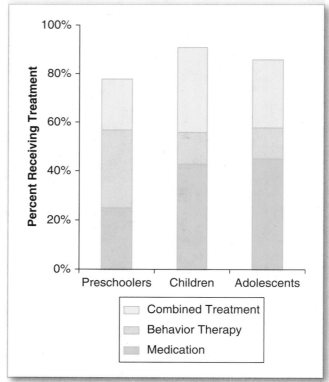

school-age children and 28% of adolescents with ADHD received combined behavioral and pharmaceutical treatment, the recommended practice (Visser, 2016; Visser et al., 2014, 2015).

Data from the MTA also indicate that the community-based treatment that most children receive is less than optimal. Recall that one group of children in the MTA were assigned to community care—the type of care children are likely to receive if their families seek treatment from physicians or mental health practitioners in the community. Although these children showed symptom reduction, their likelihood of improvement was lower than any of the other treatment conditions (Pliszka, 2015).

These data emphasize the need for evidence-based care. Although youths with ADHD desperately need treatment, they deserve high-quality interventions, grounded in science, which maximize their likelihood of improvement.

Review:

- The MTA indicated that combined medication and behavior therapy yielded the greatest benefits to children with ADHD. Medication alone was superior to behavior therapy alone, however.
- Most professionals recommend behavior therapy as a first-line treatment for preschoolers with ADHD and combined behavior therapy and medication for children and adolescents with ADHD.
- Only one-third of youths with ADHD receive the recommended treatment.

KEY TERMS

α₂ receptor agonist: A class of medications sometimes used to treat ADHD in children; originally developed to treat hypertension in adults; guanfacine (Intuniv) is an example

Amphetamines: A class of stimulant medications used to treat ADHD; increases the release of dopamine from presynaptic storage vesicles, resulting in more dopamine output to the synapse; Adderall and Dexedrine are examples

Attention-deficit/hyperactivity disorder (ADHD): A *DSM-5* neurodevelopmental disorder characterized by significant inattention and/or hyperactivity–impulsivity that emerges prior to age 12 years, is present in two or more settings, and interferes with academic or social functioning

ADHD, combined presentation: A presentation of ADHD characterized by significant inattentive and significant hyperactive–impulsive symptoms

ADHD, predominantly hyperactive–impulsive presentation: A presentation of ADHD characterized by significant hyperactive–impulsive symptoms but subthreshold problems with inattention; usually seen in younger children only

ADHD, predominantly inattentive presentation: A presentation of ADHD characterized by significant problems inattentive symptoms but subthreshold problems with hyperactivity–impulsivity

Barkley's neurodevelopmental model: A model for ADHD; suggests that ADHD is caused by underlying deficits in behavioral inhibition which impair the development of executive functioning

Behavioral activation system (BAS): According to Gray, a neuropsychological system is responsible for approaching stimuli and adjusting behavior to achieve reinforcement

Behavioral classroom management: An evidence-based treatment for ADHD in which teachers or educational specialists administer positive reinforcement to foster appropriate behavior at school; can be combined with peer interventions to improve social functioning

Behavioral inhibition: The ability to inhibit immediate responses, especially responses that usually provide immediate gratification

Behavioral inhibition system (BIS): According to Gray, a neuropsychological system is responsible for slowing or stopping behavior in response to punishment or a lack of reinforcement

Challenging Horizons Program: A classroom behavior therapy that combines school-based behavioral treatment with an afterschool program designed to increase the academic engagement of middle school students

Clinical behavior therapy: An evidence-based, behavioral treatment for ADHD in children; relies on monitoring and positive reinforcement for appropriate actions; consists of parent consultation, school consultation, and a combined home–school reward system

Creative problem-solving: The capacity to analyze, manipulate, and combine ideas or objects in a novel way; an executive function important to directing one's own behavior in anticipation of long-term reinforcement

Daily report card: A daily record of children's appropriate behavior at school, which can be monitored and rewarded by parents at home

Default mode network: A neural pathway implicated in ADHD; consists of the medial prefrontal cortex, medial parietal cortex, and medial temporal lobe; active during daydreaming and mind-wandering

Dopamine D4 and D5 receptor genes: Genes that code for proteins that regulate receptor cites for dopamine on postsynaptic membranes; implicated as genes partially responsible for some cases of ADHD

Dopamine transporter gene (DAT1): A gene codes for proteins that regulate the reuptake of dopamine in the brain; implicated as a gene partially responsible for some cases of ADHD

Four basic executive functions: In Barkley's neurodevelopmental model of ADHD: working memory, internalized speech, emotion regulation, and creative problem-solving

Frontal–striatal neural circuit: A brain pathway associated with ADHD; consists of the (a) striatum and (b) right prefrontal cortex

Internalized speech: According to Vygotsky, the development of thought that occurs when children internalize the speech of others as they engage in overt actions; an executive function important to regulating one's own behavior

Mesolimbic neural circuit: A brain pathway associated with ADHD; consists of the (a) VTA and nucleus accumbens, (b) amygdala and hippocampus, and (c) prefrontal cortex

Methylphenidate: A class of stimulant medications used to treat ADHD; slows the dopamine transporter system that removes dopamine from the cleft, allowing dopamine to remain in the cleft longer; Concerta and Ritalin are examples

Multimodal Treatment Study of Children With ADHD (MTA): A large study comparing the effects of medication and behavior therapy for children with ADHD; results suggested the best outcomes of youths who participated in combined treatment

MOSAIC (Making Socially Accepting Inclusive Classrooms): A brief classroom behavior management program designed to improve the social functioning of youths with ADHD

Nonshared environmental factors: Environmental factors experienced by one child but not his or her siblings (e.g., anoxia during gestation or delivery, peer rejection in elementary school)

Normalization: A term used to the functioning of children who receive treatment and whose functioning is similar to that of typically developing children

Parent consultation: Sometimes called parent training, involves helping the caregivers learn more effective ways to manage children's ADHD signs and symptoms

Preschool ADHD Treatment Study (PATS): A randomized controlled study showing that stimulant medication is efficacious in reducing ADHD symptoms in children 3 to 5 years

Psychostimulants: The most commonly prescribed medications for ADHD; affect dopamine and norepinephrine; cause increased attention and behavioral inhibition

Right prefrontal cortex: An anterior brain region responsible for inhibition and impulse control (orbitofrontal region) and attending, organizing, and planning (dorsolateral region)

Selective norepinephrine reuptake inhibitor (SNRI): Nonstimulant medication used to treat ADHD; regulates the reuptake of neurotransmitter and regulates attention, behavior, and mood; atomoxetine (Strattera) is an example

Sluggish cognitive tempo: A term used to describe a pattern of behavior characterized by daydreaming, mind-wandering, drowsy appearance, lethargy, social passivity, concentration problems, and problems with attention; frequently co-occurs with ADHD, predominantly inattentive presentation

Sociometric ratings: A method used to assess peer status among school-age children; youths rate classmates with whom they would most and least like to play

Striatum: Part of the basal ganglia; consists of the caudate, putamen, and globus pallidus; regulates behavior in response to feedback from the environment

Summer Treatment Program (STP): An evidence-based, behavioral treatment for children with ADHD; consists of immediate, positive reinforcement for appropriate behavior in the classroom, during social skills activities, and while playing sports in a summer camp environment

CRITICAL THINKING EXERCISES

1. Nearly all young children show occasional problems with inattention and hyperactivity–impulsivity. How might a psychologist differentiate developmentally expected inattention or hyperactivity–impulsivity from ADHD?

2. Why are children with ADHD at risk for problematic parent–child interactions? Why are children with ADHD at risk for peer rejection? If you were a clinician, how might you prevent these social problems in young children with ADHD?

3. Barkley claims that ADHD is not primarily a disorder of inattention; rather, it is a disorder caused by a lack of behavioral inhibition. How does behavioral inhibition play a critical role in Barkley's model for ADHD?

4. Under what circumstances might a physician decide to prescribe a nonstimulant medication, such as Strattera, to a child or adolescent with ADHD?

5. Philip is an 8-year-old boy who was recently diagnosed with ADHD, combined presentation. His mother is reluctant to use medication to manage his symptoms; instead, she wants Philip to participate in "talk therapy" with a counselor to help him "learn how to behave." What might you say to Philip's mother regarding (a) the merits and limitations of medication for ADHD and (b) the benefits and drawbacks of psychosocial treatments?

TEST YOURSELF AND EXTEND YOUR LEARNING

Videos, flash cards, and links to online resources for this chapter are available to students online. Teachers also have access to PowerPoint slides to guide lectures, case studies to prompt classroom discussions, and exam questions. Visit www.abnormalchildpsychology.org.

CHAPTER 9

Conduct Problems in Children and Adolescents

After reading this chapter, you should be able to do the following:

9.1. Describe the key features of oppositional defiant disorder (ODD) and conduct disorder (CD).

Explain how conduct problems vary as a function of children's age of onset, gender, and capacity for prosocial emotions.

9.2. Discuss some of the main causes of children's conduct problems across genetic, biological, psychological, familial, and social–cultural levels of analysis.

Outline three main developmental pathways to conduct problems in youths.

9.3. Describe evidence-based psychosocial treatments for childhood conduct problems.

9.1 OPPOSITIONAL DEFIANT DISORDER AND CONDUCT DISORDER

If you were asked to generate a mental picture of a child with "conduct problems," what image would come to mind? You might think about the 5-year-old boy you saw at the checkout aisle of the grocery store who was screaming at his mother because she wouldn't buy him a candy bar. You might recall a middle school classmate, who deliberately bullied other kids and picked fights after school. A third image might be of an adolescent gang member who has been arrested twice by the age of 15. These mental images depict the many facets of conduct problems in youths.

The *Diagnostic and Statistical Manual of Mental Disorders, Fifth Edition (DSM-5)* recognizes two categories of conduct problems that typically emerge in childhood or adolescence: oppositional defiant disorder (ODD) and conduct disorder (CD). Both disorders bring children into significant conflict with caregivers and other authority figures, strain relationships with parents and teachers, and can lead to acts that violate the standards of society and the rights and dignity of others (American Psychiatric Association, 2013). Equally important, these disorders can adversely affect children's behavioral and social–emotional development and place them at risk for interpersonal and occupational problems later in life.

Conduct problems are also some of the most common disorders experienced by children and adolescents. In fact, 40% of children referred for mental health treatment by their pediatricians are diagnosed with a conduct problem. This percentage is surpassed only by attention-deficit/hyperactivity disorder (ADHD; Kimonis et al., 2015).

Fortunately, over the past 30 years, researchers have identified several factors that contribute to the development of conduct problems and have found effective ways to treat children with these disorders. One study estimated that preventing a single child from developing long-term conduct problems could result in a savings of more than $3.2 million (Cohen & Piquero, 2009). Understanding conduct problems, their causes, and their evidence-based treatment is important to children, families, and communities alike.

What Are Oppositional Defiant Disorder and Conduct Disorder?

Oppositional Defiant Disorder

Oppositional defiant disorder (ODD) reflects a pattern of noncompliant, defiant, and/or spiteful behavior toward others. The signs and symptoms of the disorder fall into three dimensions: (1) angry or irritable mood, (2) argumentative or defiant behavior, and (3) vindictiveness toward others (see Table 9.1). The disorder causes distress to the child or (more likely) to his parents, caregivers, teachers, or other adults. In most instances, ODD interferes with the child's relationships with others and negatively impacts the quality of his parent–child interactions, education, and social activities (American Psychiatric Association, 2013).

All young children show oppositional or defiant behaviors from time to time. After all, nearly everyone has heard of children entering "the terrible twos" or "the horrible threes." Usually, children show a developmentally normative increase in oppositional and defiant behavior during the toddler and early preschool years. Two-year-olds may insist on selecting their own clothes in the morning, even though they prefer to wear shorts and a T-shirt in the middle of winter. Three-year-olds may tantrum when told to go to bed. Four-year-olds may stubbornly refuse to eat their vegetables and sit at the table for an hour to see whether their parents will acquiesce to their demands to be excused. In one study, 97% of toddlers initially ignored or refused to obey adults' requests to clean up after play (Klimes-Dougan & Kopp, 1999).

How can we distinguish normative child behavior from childhood behavior problems? Although there is no easy answer to this question, *DSM-5* suggests that differentiating normal from abnormal behavior must be determined based on (1) symptom number and frequency and (2) children's overall development context (American Psychiatric Association, 2013). First, children with ODD show *a greater number of problematic behaviors*, and they show these behaviors more frequently than their typically developing peers. Whereas many children occasionally defy their parents' requests or complain when they do not get their way, children with ODD repeatedly tantrum, defy parents, argue with adults, or act in mean and spiteful ways (Bufferd, Dyson, Hernandez, & Wakschlag, 2016).

Indeed, empirical research has consistently shown that children with ODD show more frequent and severe behavior problems than other children their age. For example, Keenan and Wakschlag (2004) compared the frequency of disruptive behaviors of young children referred for psychiatric treatment with the behavior of children in the community (see Figure 9.1). Among clinic-referred children, oppositional behavior was common. Approximately 70% of referred children repeatedly denied an adult's requests or threw tantrums. In contrast, such oppositional behavior was relatively rare among children in the community; only about 4% to 8% showed these disruptive behaviors. Although strong-willed behavior is common among preschoolers, symptoms of ODD are not (Frick & Shirtcliff, 2016).

Second, children with ODD engage in disruptive behaviors that are *developmentally unexpected*. These actions persist beyond an age at which they are developmentally normative. For example, when a 2-year-old tantrums because his father asks him to clean up his toys, we might consider the child's behavior as developmentally normative. However, when a 5- or 6-year-old child

---

Table 9.1 Diagnostic Criteria for Oppositional Defiant Disorder

A. A pattern of angry/irritable mood, argumentative/defiant behavior, or vindictiveness lasting at least 6 months as evidenced by at least four symptoms from any of the following categories, and exhibited during interaction with at least one individual who is not a sibling.

Angry/Irritable Mood

1. Often loses temper.
2. Is often touchy or easily annoyed.
3. Is often angry and resentful.

Argumentative/Defiant Behavior

1. Often argues with authority figures or, for children and adolescents, with adults.
2. Often actively defies or refuses to comply with requests from authority figures or with rules.
3. Often deliberately annoys others.
4. Often blames others for his or her mistakes or misbehavior.

tantrums when asked to put away his toys, we would likely consider the behavior as atypically oppositional (Curtis et al., 2016). Consider Davidson, a boy with ODD.

How do clinicians determine if a child's behavior is uncharacteristic for his or her age? Clinicians typically administer norm-referenced behavior rating scales to children's parents and teachers in order to compare the severity of their conduct problems with other children. Elevated ratings, beyond the 93rd or 95th percentile, would likely indicate significant oppositional or defiant symptoms. Furthermore, *DSM-5* provides guidelines to clinicians to differentiate developmentally expected oppositional and defiant behavior from actions that merit professional attention. Specifically, children under 5 years of age should show symptoms most days for at least 6 months to be diagnosed with ODD. Children 6 years and older may show symptoms less often (i.e., at least once per week) for at least 6 months to be diagnosed with ODD. In all cases, symptoms must cause impairment in children's social or educational functioning (American Psychiatric Association, 2013).

The three dimensions of ODD can be reliably differentiated from each other. The first dimension refers chiefly to problems regulating emotions (i.e., angry or irritable mood), the second dimension principally describes difficulties regulating overt actions (i.e., argumentative and defiant behavior), and the third dimension reflects problems controlling both emotions and overt actions (i.e., vindictiveness). These dimensions are important because they predict different developmental outcomes. For example, the angry–irritable mood dimension predicts later depressive disorders. In contrast, the argumentative–defiant behavior dimension is associated with comorbid ADHD. Finally, the presence of vindictiveness predicts the emergence of CD in adolescence (Burke, 2012; Burke, Hipwell, & Loeber, 2010).

Children can be diagnosed with ODD if they show symptoms in only one setting. For example, some children with ODD are defiant toward parents but appear compliant and respectful toward teachers, coaches, and other adults. In fact, some children with ODD only show symptoms toward one parent but not the other. The fact that children with ODD can show symptoms in certain situations or with specific people suggests that environmental factors greatly influence the development and maintenance of the disorder. ODD differs from ADHD, in which symptoms must be present across multiple settings (Lindheim, Bennett, Hipwell, & Pardini, 2015).

Clinicians classify children's ODD symptoms based on their severity. Mild symptoms occur in only one setting (e.g., at home, at school, or with peers), moderate symptoms occur in two settings, and severe symptoms occur in three or more settings. ODD symptoms are almost always directed at parents (96%) or teachers (85%). Less commonly, they are directed toward peers (67%). Most children with ODD (62%) show symptoms at home, school, and with peers (Youngstrom, van Meter, & Algorta, 2010).

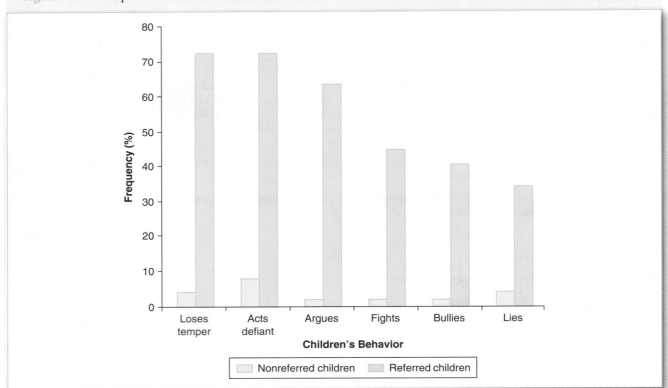

Source: Based on Keenan and Wakschlag (2004).

Note: Most young children in the community do not show serious conduct problems like physical fighting, bullying, and lying.

Conduct Disorder

Conduct disorder (CD) is a serious condition character-ized by a repetitive and persistent pattern of behavior in which the basic rights of others or major age-appropriate societal norms or rules are violated (see Table 9.2).

The symptoms of CD can be grouped into four cat-egories: (1) aggression to people and animals, (2) destruc-tion of property, (3) deceitfulness or theft, and (4) serious violations of rules. Aggression to people and animals involves initiating physical fights, physical cruelty, assault, and robbery. Destruction of property involves intention-ally damaging others' belongings through vandalism, arson, or other reckless acts. Deceitful behaviors include breaking and entering, stealing, or lying to earn a reward or to avoid a responsibility. Other serious rule violations include staying out all night, running away from home, or being truant. Consider Brandyn, a boy with CD.

Notice that the 15 signs and symptoms of CD reflect a range of antisocial behaviors. To be diagnosed with CD, youths must show at least three signs or symptoms in the previous year. Because the criteria reflect such diverse behaviors, two children with CD can show dramatically different behavioral profiles. Consider the following

15-year-old boys, each of whom might be diagnosed with CD:

- Anthony has run away from home, is frequently truant from school, and stays out all night without his parents' permission.
- Brett initiates physical fights with peers, uses a knife to rob others, and forces girls into sexual activity.
- Charles deliberately vandalizes school property, sets fires, and tortures animals.
- Dean breaks into others' homes, shoplifts, and steals credit cards.

Although all of these boys might be diagnosed with CD, each shows a different pattern of symptoms. The diagnostic label CD reflects a large and heterogeneous group of youths.

Review:

- ODD is a *DSM-5* disorder characterized by a pattern of (a) angry or irritable mood, (b) argumentative or defi-ant behavior, and/or (c) vindictiveness toward others.
- Children with ODD differ from typically developing children in two ways: (1) they show a greater number

OPPOSITIONAL DEFIANT DISORDER

Davidson's Escape

"If you don't sit down and behave this minute, your dad will hear about it when we get home!" Upon listening to those words, Dr. Driscoll knew that 7-year-old Davidson and his mother, Mrs. Lepper, had arrived for their 9:30 appointment. Dr. Driscoll invited them into her office and asked how she might help.

"Davidson's a handful, and I don't know what to do. He won't listen to anything I say, and he seems to enjoy giving me grief." As Mrs. Lepper explained Davidson's defiance at home, Davidson interrupted, saying, "Hey, Mom, this is boring, can I have some gum?" Mrs. Lepper replied harshly, "Not now." Dr. Driscoll added, "I have some coloring books on the table. Let's see if we can find one for you."

Davidson remained interested in coloring for only a few minutes; then, he returned to nagging his mother and interrupting her conversation. His mother explained, "It's like this all the time. I can't talk on the telephone without him bothering me. I can't shower in the morning; he'll scream outside the bathroom door or walk in on me if I don't lock it. I can't go shopping with him because he won't stop grabbing things from the shelves or embarrassing me."

By this time, Davidson grew impatient and walked to Dr. Driscoll's office door. After checking to make sure that the adults were watching, Davidson slowly turned the door handle and opened the door slightly. His mother replied, "If you leave this room, you're going to get it when we get home." With an ever-widening smile, Davidson opened the door a bit more and placed one foot in the hallway. His mother stood up and began to count, "1 . . . 2 . . . Davidson." Her son responded by bolting down the hallway, slamming the office door behind him.

Mrs. Lepper leaped toward the door with an angry expression. Dr. Driscoll interjected, "Mrs. Lepper, please have a seat." Exasperated, Mrs. Lepper replied, "I need to get him." Dr. Driscoll said, "Why? This end of the hallway is empty, and he can't enter the rest of the clinic without a key card. He's safe and can't get into any trouble. Davidson decided he doesn't want to color and that's fine. Now he can sit in the hallway for a while." For the first time, a smile flickered across Mrs. Lepper's face.

CONDUCT DISORDER

Making Mom Miserable

Brandyn was a 9-year-old boy who was referred to our clinic by his third-grade teacher because of defiant and aggressive behavior at school. According to his teacher, Mrs. Miller, Brandyn became angry and resentful whenever she placed limits on him. For example, he would tantrum, throw objects, and hit her when she asked him to pick up his belongings. Brandyn also bullied and intimidated other children in the class in order to obtain toys and to get his way. Mrs. Miller explained, "Brandyn seeks out the younger kids and torments them until he gets what he wants. If they stand up to him, he pushes or pinches them. He even choked a classmate because he wouldn't give him a scented pencil that he wanted."

Brandyn engaged in other acts of aggression designed to get attention from others. For example, he cut a girl's ponytail off during class and repeatedly destroyed other students' belongings. On two occasions, he was caught stealing items from lockers and desks. Classmates often avoided playing with Brandyn because of his aggressive acts. Mrs. Miller commented, "I don't know what to do with him. He doesn't seem bothered when we reprimand him and we can't keep him in the time-out chair."

Brandyn's mother reported similar problems with aggression and defiance at home. "He doesn't listen to me at all," she explained. "He seems to enjoy making my life miserable." She addeed, "It's hard enough being a single mother and working a crummy job. Then, I have to come home and deal with him. I love him, but I don't know what to do. It scares me sometimes because I see him heading down the same road as his father. I guess the apple doesn't fall too far from the tree."

Table 9.2   Diagnostic Criteria for Conduct Disorder

A. A repetitive and persistent pattern of behavior in which the basic rights of others or major age-appropriate societal norms or rules are violated, as manifested by the presence of at least three of the following 15 criteria in the past 12 months from any of the categories below, with at least one criterion present in the past 6 months:

Aggression to People and Animals

1. Often bullies, threatens, or intimidates others.

2. Often initiates physical fights.

3. Has used a weapon that can cause serious physical harm to others (e.g., a bat, brick, broken bottle, knife, gun).

4. Has been physically cruel to people.

5. Has been physically cruel to animals.

6. Has stolen while confronting a victim (e.g., mugging, purse snatching, extortion, armed robbery).

7. Has forced someone into sexual activity.

Destruction of Property

1. Has deliberately engaged in firesetting with the intention of causing serious damage.

2. Has deliberately destroyed others' property (other than by firesetting).

Deceitfulness or Theft

1. Has broken into someone else's house, building, or car.

2. Often lies to obtain goods or favors or to avoid obligations (e.g., "cons" others).

3. Has stolen items of nontrivial value without confronting a victim (e.g., shoplifting, but without breaking and entering; forgery).

Serious Violations of Rules

1. Often stays out at night despite parental prohibitions, beginning before age 13 years.

2. Has run away from home overnight at least twice while living in the parental or parental surrogate home, or once without returning for a lengthy period.

3. Is often truant from school, beginning before age 13 years.

B. The disturbance in behavior causes clinically significant impairment in social, academic, or occupational functioning.

C. If the individual is age 18 years or older, criteria are not met for Antisocial Personality Disorder.

Specify whether:

Childhood-onset type: Individuals show at least one symptom characteristic of Conduct Disorder prior to age 10 years.

Adolescent-onset type: Individuals show no symptom characteristic of Conduct Disorder prior to age 10 years.

Unspecified onset: Criteria for a diagnosis of Conduct Disorder are met, but there is not enough available to determine whether the onset of the first symptom was before or after age 10 years.

Specify current severity:

Mild: Few if any conduct problems in excess of those required to make the diagnosis are present, and conduct problems cause relative minor harm to others (e.g., lying, truancy, staying out after dark without permission, other rule breaking).

Moderate: The number of conduct problems and the effect on others are intermediate between those specified in "mild" and those in "severe" (e.g., stealing without confronting a victim, vandalism).

Severe: Many conduct problems in excess of those required to make the diagnosis are present, or conduct problems cause considerable harm to others (e.g., forced sex, physical cruelty, use of a weapon, stealing while confronting a victim, breaking and entering).

Source: Reprinted with permission from the *Diagnostic and Statistical Manual of Mental Disorders, Fifth Edition* (Copyright 2013). American Psychiatric Association.

and severity of behavior problems and (2) their behaviors are developmentally unexpected.

- CD is a *DSM-5* disorder characterized by a repetitive and persistent pattern of behavior in which the basic rights of others or societal norms are violated. Behaviors include (a) aggression, (b) property destruction, (c) deceitfulness or theft, and (d) serious rule violations.

How Do Professionals Identify Subtypes of Conduct Problems?

Because of the diverse symptoms of CD, researchers have been interested in categorizing children and adolescents into groups based on the pattern of symptoms they show. Researchers have attempted to classify youths with CD based on four characteristics:

1. The nature of their conduct problems: covert or overt

2. Their type of aggression: reactive or proactive

3. Their age of symptom onset: childhood or adolescence

4. Their capacity for prosocial emotions.

We will now examine each of these four characteristics.

Overt vs. Covert Problems

The diagnostic criteria for CD can be loosely divided into two broad clusters: (1) overt symptoms and (2) covert symptoms. Overt symptoms of CD refer to observable and confrontational antisocial acts, especially acts of physical aggression. Examples of overt symptoms include physical assault, robbery, and bullying. In contrast, covert symptoms of CD refer to secretive antisocial behaviors that usually do not involve physical aggression. Examples of covert symptoms include breaking into someone's home, burglarizing, lying, skipping school, and running away from home (Hess & Scheithauer, 2015).

Although most youths with CD show both overt and covert symptoms, these two symptom clusters can be differentiated. Some children, especially boys, tend to show mostly overt symptoms of CD, whereas other children, especially girls, are more likely to show covert symptoms (Frick, 2013).

Frick and colleagues (1993) used factor analysis to identify conduct problems that often occurred together. The researchers reviewed data from 60 studies involving more than 24,000 youths. They discovered that children's conduct problems could be grouped into four factors based on two independent dimensions: (1) their degree of overtness versus covertness and (2) their degree of destructiveness versus nondestructiveness (see Figure 9.2). When children's conduct problems were plotted along these two dimensions, four factors emerged:

- *Property violations*. These behaviors are covert and destructive. They generally include the *DSM-5* CD

symptoms labeled destruction of property (e.g., vandalism, firesetting) and deceitfulness or theft (e.g., breaking and entering, shoplifting).

- *Aggression*. These behaviors are overt and destructive. They generally include the *DSM-5* CD symptoms labeled aggression to people and animals (e.g., bullying, being cruel, fighting).

- *Rule violations*. These behaviors are covert and usually nondestructive. They generally include the *DSM-5* CD symptoms labeled serious violations of rules (e.g., running away, being truant) and comorbid substance use problems.

- *Oppositional and defiant behavior*. These behaviors are overt and usually nondestructive. They include most of the *DSM-5* symptoms for ODD.

Altogether, these data indicate that children's conduct problems can be differentiated in reliable and meaningful ways based on their degree of overtness and destructiveness.

Reactive vs. Proactive Aggression

Overt conduct problems can further be divided into two types of aggression: (1) reactive and (2) proactive. Children show reactive aggression when they engage in physical violence or property destruction in response to a threat, a frustrating event, or provocation. For example, a child might shove a classmate because the classmate stole his pencil (Dickson et al., 2015; Frey, Higheagle Strong, & Onyewuenyi, 2016).

Reactive aggression usually occurs because children act impulsively and automatically, without considering alternative, prosocial ways of responding (e.g., asking a teacher for help, finding another pencil). Certain children are at risk for engaging in reactive aggression. First, younger children and youths with ADHD may show reactive aggression, because they have difficulty inhibiting their impulses. Second, youths with emotion-regulation problems, who lack coping skills to reduce feelings of frustration and anger, may rely on reactive aggression. Third, children with deficits in social problem-solving may use reactive aggression to resolve interpersonal dilemmas. Instead of using cognitive strategies to negotiate disputes with peers, these children might yell, kick, or hit other children to solve social problems. Finally, youths with a history of physical abuse and/or bullying may engage in reactive aggression. At one time, aggression may have been adaptive to help them escape maltreatment; however, the aggression becomes problematic when it persists into new contexts and interferes with relationships at home and school (Kimonis et al., 2015).

Children show proactive aggression when they deliberately engage in an aggressive act in order to obtain a desired goal. For example, a child might shove a classmate and steal his pencil because he wants it (Dickson et al., 2015; Frey et al., 2016).

Most experts believe that children learn to use proactive aggression. Learning occurs through modeling and

Figure 9.2 Children's conduct problems can be grouped into four clusters based on their degree of overtness and destructiveness: (1) property violations, (2) aggression, (3) rule violations, and (4) opposition-defiant symptoms.

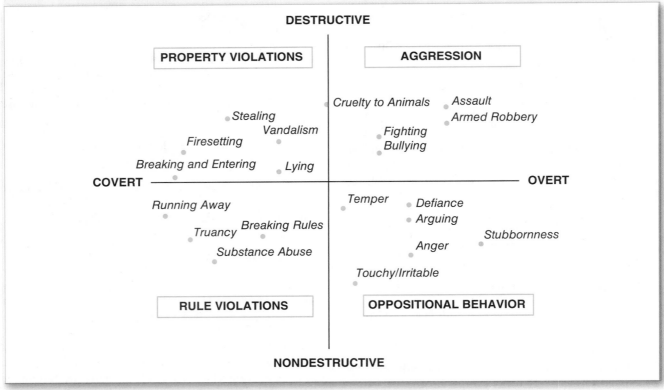

Source: Based on Frick and colleagues (1993) and Frick (2012).

reinforcement. First, parents model proactive aggression when they use hostile behaviors in the home (e.g., spanking, yelling) to force children to comply with their commands. By observing their parents, children learn that proactive aggression is a legitimate and effective way of achieving one's short-term objectives. Second, children's use of proactive aggression is strengthened through positive reinforcement. Children learn that they can acquire objects, money, and social status through fighting or bullying. In fact, children who engage in proactive aggression tend to be unusually sensitive to reinforcement. These children overestimate the rewards that they will receive by engaging in aggressive actions and underestimate the probability of getting punished for their behavior.

Although occasional aggressive outbursts are common during childhood, repeated displays of reactive or proactive aggression are uncommon. Approximately 7% of children show recurrent problems with reactive aggression, 3% show patterns of proactive aggression, and 10% show a mixture of reactive and proactive aggression. As we might expect, youths who frequently engage in both reactive and proactive aggression are at greatest risk for delinquency in adolescence and criminal behavior in adulthood (Kimonis et al., 2015).

Childhood-Onset vs. Adolescent-Onset Problems

A third method of differentiating childhood conduct problems is based on age of onset. When diagnosing CD, *DSM-5* urges clinicians to indicate whether children's symptoms first emerged in childhood (i.e., at least one symptom prior to age 10 years) or adolescence (i.e., no symptoms prior to age 10 years; American Psychiatric Association, 2013).

The differentiation between childhood-onset and adolescent-onset CD is based on a 40-year longitudinal study of 1,000 New Zealand youths called the Dunedin Multidisciplinary Health and Development Study (Moffitt, 2003; Moffitt, Caspi, Rutter, & Silva, 2001; Poulton, Moffitt, & Silva, 2015). The island country of New Zealand was an excellent location for such a prospective, longitudinal study; even after several decades, nearly 96% of the children originally recruited for the study were still living locally and could participate in follow-up testing. Results of the study showed two developmental pathways for conduct problems: (1) the child-onset path and (2) the adolescent-onset path.

Individuals with childhood-onset conduct disorder (CD) first show symptoms in preschool or early elementary school. Some children displayed problems as early as age 4.5 years. These youths showed problems with emotional control in infancy and early childhood, neurological abnormalities and delayed motor development in preschool, lower IQ and reading problems in school, and later neuropsychological deficits—especially in the areas of decision-making, judgment, and memory. More importantly, children with childhood-onset conduct problems showed an increase in aggressive and disruptive behavior throughout childhood and adolescence. As adults, they were at risk for antisocial behaviors, mental health and substance use problems, work and financial difficulties, domestic abuse, and incarceration.

Youths with childhood-onset CD are at particular risk for developing antisocial personality disorder (ASPD) in adulthood (Dishion & Patterson, 2016). ASPD is a serious disorder characterized by a pervasive pattern of disregard for and violation of the rights of others. Adults with ASPD typically show impulsive, irritable, and aggressive behavior; engage in reckless or illegal actions; fail to live up to their responsibilities or social obligations; and feel little remorse for mistreating others (American Psychiatric Association, 2013). Approximately 40% of adolescent boys with CD will develop ASPD by early adulthood. A boy's likelihood of developing ASPD depends on two factors. First, the sheer number of covert (but not overt) symptoms that the boy shows in adolescence predicts his likelihood of showing future antisocial behavior. Deceitfulness, property destruction, and theft are some of the best predictors of the development of ASPD. Second, adolescents with CD who come from low-income families are at particular risk for developing ASPD in adulthood. In one study, adolescents with CD from low socioeconomic backgrounds (65%) were much more likely to develop ASPD than adolescents with CD from families not exposed to socioeconomic disadvantage (20%; Shiner & Tackett, 2014).

In contrast, youths with adolescent-onset conduct disorder (CD) show their first symptoms after puberty. They usually do not show psychosocial risk factors for the disorder (e.g., emotional control problems, neurological deficits). However, they do endorse a strong need for autonomy and resentment of "traditional" values. These youths tend to engage in covert antisocial acts (e.g., stealing, truancy, running away) rather than acts of overt aggression. Their behavior problems tend to persist into middle adolescence and then gradually taper off.

Limited Prosocial Emotions

A final method of differentiating children with conduct problems is based on the presence of callous and unemotional traits (Golmaryami & Frick, 2015). Recent research suggests that there is a subgroup of children with childhood-onset conduct problems who show callousness in interpersonal interactions, characterized by a lack of empathy, absence of guilt, and a generally uncaring attitude toward others. These youths might bully a classmate or steal from a parent with little concern for their feelings. They

might experience regret for getting caught and punished, but not remorse for the misbehavior itself. These youths also show a general lack of emotions in interpersonal interactions or a shallowness and superficiality in their emotional expression. For example, these youths appear emotionally cold and are unlikely to trust or confide in caregivers or peers in ways that make themselves vulnerable (Kahn, Frick, Youngstrom, Findling, & Youngstrom, 2012).

This persistent disregard for the rights of others, combined with the presence of callous and unemotional traits, places children on trajectories toward long-term antisocial behavior and criminal activity (Kimonis et al., 2015). These traits are so predictive of persistent conduct problems that *DSM-5* allows clinicians to specify their presence in children with CD. Because the *DSM-5* developers believed that the label "callous-unemotional" was pejorative and potentially stigmatizing, they substituted the specifier "with limited prosocial emotions." Specifically, youths who have CD with limited prosocial emotions show two more of the following:

- *A lack of remorse or guilt.* When these children and adolescents do something wrong, they do not feel "sorry" for their behavior. They might regret "getting caught," but they do not show remorse for the act itself.
- *Callousness or a lack of empathy.* These children and adolescents are unconcerned about the feelings of others. They experience little discomfort when witnessing others' misfortune.
- *Lack of concern about performance.* These children and adolescents do not care about their performance in school, work, or sports. They are not bothered even when failing a class or being fired from a part-time job.
- *Shallow or deficient affect.* These children and adolescents show only superficial emotions and do not confide in others or express their feelings in emotionally vulnerable ways. They may only express emotions to manipulate or "con" others and frequently show emotions that are incongruent with their actions (e.g., smiling or laughing while hurting others).

Consider Cade, a boy who has childhood-onset CD with limited prosocial emotions.

By definition, the characteristics of limited prosocial emotions must exist for at least 12 months and must be displayed across settings. Consequently, it is necessary for clinicians to gather data from multiple people (e.g., parents, teachers, other adults involved in the child's life) to assess these features. It is especially important for clinicians to supplement youths' self-reports with data from other informants, because children and adolescents with limited prosocial emotions often deny or minimize the number and severity of their problems (Ansel, Barry, Gillen, & Herrington, 2015).

Youths with limited prosocial emotions have many characteristics of adults with psychopathy. Psychopathy is a syndrome characterized by antisocial behavior, impulsivity, shallow affect, narcissism, and disregard for the suffering

CONDUCT DISORDER WITH LIMITED PROSOCIAL EMOTIONS

Callous Cade

Source: ©iStockphoto.com/Photobuff

Cade was a 14-year-old boy who was referred to our clinic by his caseworker from the juvenile court. Cade had a history of disruptive behavior. His mother remembered, "As a toddler, he was a handful. He was always getting into mischief, disobeying me, and throwing tantrums. When he was 5, he cut all of the whiskers off our cat and set our living room rug on fire."

By the time Cade was in second grade, he had been suspended twice for physical aggression. Once, he stuck a nail from the inside of his shoe through the toe and kicked classmates on the playground. On another occasion, he shoved a classmate down the stairs. Cade got in trouble for playing pranks, such as "mooning" other children in gym class, spraying classmates with a bottle of urine, and pulling the fire alarm on several different occasions.

By the time Cade reached the sixth grade, he had few friends his own age. He preferred to spend time with older boys at the nearby junior high school who introduced him to more serious antisocial behaviors. Cade began using alcohol and marijuana and skipping school. He was arrested for the first time in seventh grade for vandalizing school buses, causing several thousand dollars of damage.

At the time of the referral, Cade was attending an eighth-grade classroom for youths with behavior problems. He had gotten into trouble earlier in the year for making sexually suggestive and racially offensive comments to two girls at the school. Most recently, he injured a classmate during a fight with a box cutter. One teacher said, "Cade deliberately tries to provoke others—calling people names, swearing, making offensive remarks. He seems to take delight in hurting others, and he doesn't care about being punished."

The psychologist who interviewed Cade was most concerned about Cade's fascination with fire and explosives. Cade said proudly, "About two years ago, I began building bombs in my house. I use cigarette lighters, aerosols, gasoline, fireworks, batteries, Styrofoam containers . . . whatever I can get my hands on. My friends and me build them and set them off in the field."

Cade's mother commented, "I know Cade has made a lot of trouble, but he's really not a bad kid. I think if his father played a larger role in his life, he'd be okay."

---

of others. Like these children, adults with psychopathy usually show callousness and a lack of emotional vulnerability. However, they can also be superficially charming and manipulative in order to gain others' trust or to obtain favors. These adults are often highly motivated to seek out exciting and pleasurable activities and give little regard for the potentially negative consequences of their actions. Adults with psychopathy often have histories of coerciveness, manipulation, and serious violations of the rights and dignity of others (Cooke, Forth, & Hare, 2012).

Psychopathy is not a *DSM-5* disorder; it is a term used by some clinicians and researchers to describe a subset of adults with serious conduct problems who are at risk for harming others. Psychopathy is similar to ASPD; both conditions are characterized by antisocial behavior, violation of others' rights, impulsive and irresponsible actions, and (often) illegal activity. However, psychopathy differs from ASPD in its interpersonal and emotional characteristics: shallow affect, superficial charm, manipulation, and lack of empathy (Forth, Kosson, & Hare, 2014).

Children and adolescents are usually not classified with psychopathy because of the potentially stigmatizing effects of this label. Furthermore, youths are still developing their capacity for empathy, emotion regulation, and prosocial behavior. Most clinicians avoid the psychopathy label, which implies relatively stable impairment in social–emotion functioning and a disposition toward antisocial actions (Frick, Wall, Barry, & Bodin, 2015).

Children with limited prosocial emotions are at risk for long-term behavior problems beyond what might be expected by CD alone (Frick & Moffitt, 2010). For example, Kahn and colleagues (2012) assessed conduct problems in 1,700 children from the community and mental health clinics. They classified children into three groups: (1) youths with CD and limited prosocial emotions, (2) youths with CD alone, and (3) youths without conduct problems. Results showed that 32% of children in the community and 50% of children from the clinics who met criteria for CD also showed limited prosocial emotions. These youths displayed the highest rates of aggression and cruelty toward people and animals—even higher than youths with CD alone (see Figure 9.3).

A second, large community-based study examined conduct problems in boys across a 2-year timespan

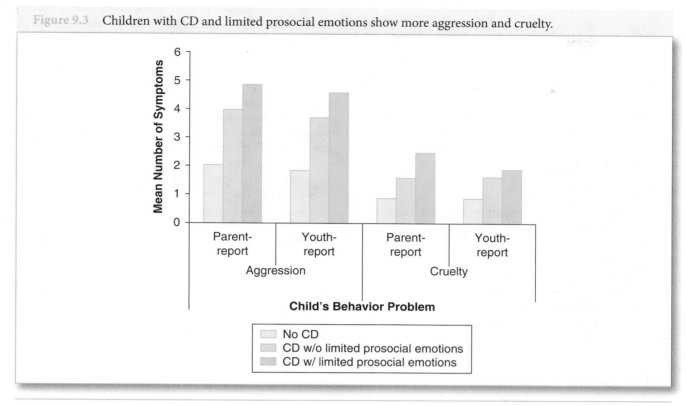

Figure 9.3 Children with CD and limited prosocial emotions show more aggression and cruelty.

Source: Based on Kahn and colleagues (2012).

Note: Children with CD and limited prosocial emotions are more likely to show physical aggression and cruelty toward people and animals than clinic-referred children without CD or clinic-referred children with CD but without limited prosocial emotions. Limited prosocial emotions predict aggression and cruelty as reported by both parents and children themselves.

(Pardini & Fite, 2010). Approximately 5.9% of boys met criteria for CD, almost all of whom showed symptom onset in childhood. Youths with CD and limited prosocial emotions were significantly more likely to engage in serious criminal activity than youths with CD alone. Interestingly, limited prosocial emotions predicted only serious, violent crime rather than less serious activities like shoplifting and truancy.

Perhaps most alarmingly, longitudinal studies indicate that limited prosocial emotions in childhood predict long-term antisocial and criminal behavior. McMahon, Witkeiwitz, and Kotler (2010) followed a large sample of high-risk children from middle school through early adulthood. Youths with limited prosocial emotions in seventh grade showed increased likelihood of engaging in antisocial and criminal behavior in adulthood, even after controlling for other disruptive behavior problems such as ADHD, ODD, and CD.

Finally, studies have shown that a lack of prosocial emotions is associated with poorer response to treatment (Frick & Moffitt, 2010). Although CD is difficult to treat in general, children and adolescents who show both CD and limited prosocial emotions are especially resistant to treatment. Treatment seems to be less effective for two reasons. First, children with limited prosocial emotions

may be less willing to establish a relationship with a therapist based on trust and may be reluctant to disclose thoughts or feelings that make themselves emotionally vulnerable. Second, youths with limited prosocial emotions seem to be less sensitive to punishment than other children; consequently, behavioral interventions may be less effective for them (Hawes, Price, & Dadds, 2014).

Review:

- Children's conduct problems fall into four factors: (1) oppositional and defiant behaviors, (2) aggression, (3) property violations, and (4) rule violations. These factors are identified based on the overtness and destructiveness of the child's actions.
- Aggression can be reactive (in response to threat, frustration, or provocation) or proactive (to achieve some goal).
- The Dunedin study showed two pathways for CD based on the onset of conduct problems. Childhood-onset CD was associated with more severe and lasting problems, and placed youths at risk for ASPD in adulthood.
- Limited prosocial emotions include (a) a lack of remorse or guilt, (b) callousness or lack of empathy, (c) minimal concern about performance, and (d) shallow or deficient affect. These characteristics overlap with the construct of psychopathy in adults.

What Disorders Are Associated With Conduct Problems?

Most youths with conduct problems show other cognitive, behavioral, or emotional disorders. In fact, it is more common to see a child with conduct problems and some other disorder than conduct problems alone (Thomas, 2015).

The Relationship Between Oppositional Defiant Disorder and Conduct Disorder

The relationship between ODD and CD is complex and has been a matter of controversy. Some experts believe that ODD is simply an early manifestation of CD—that is, the two disorders reflect the same underlying problem at different periods of development. Indeed, the previous version of the *DSM* prohibited professionals from diagnosing children with ODD if they also met criteria for CD, because CD was considered the more serious disorder.

Recent research, however, supports the notion that ODD and CD are qualitatively different disorders that often co-occur. First, as we have seen, the symptoms of ODD can be reliability differentiated from the symptoms of CD. Meta-analysis has repeatedly shown that many children who show oppositional and defiant behaviors do not also display aggression, property violations, or serious rule-breaking (Frick, 2012).

Second, children can meet diagnostic criteria for CD without also having significant symptoms of ODD. In the Pittsburgh Youth Study, researchers assessed behavior problems shown by a very large sample of boys from the community. Overall, 13.4% of boys had ODD and 5.9% had CD. However, approximately 31% of boys who met criteria for CD *did not* meet criteria for ODD. This result was surprising to the researchers who considered CD to be a more serious manifestation of ODD (Pardini & Fite, 2010).

Third, ODD predicts different outcomes in children than CD. Whereas CD is often associated with other externalizing behavior problems and substance use, ODD is associated with both externalizing and internalizing symptoms. Even after controlling for coexisting CD, youths with ODD continue to show these problems later in development. For these reasons, *DSM-5* allows children to be diagnosed with both ODD and CD if they meet criteria for each disorder separately (Frick & Nigg, 2012; Kimonis et al., 2015).

Attention-Deficit/Hyperactivity Disorder

Community studies indicate that approximately 41% of youths with conduct problems also have ADHD. On average, ADHD affects 36% of boys and 57% of girls with conduct problems. ADHD is more common among youths with CD (75%) than youths with ODD (27%; Waller, Hyde, Grabell, Alves, & Olson, 2015).

Although there is little disagreement that ADHD and conduct problems co-occur, there is considerable debate regarding the nature of their association. Some experts believe that shared genes explain the association between conduct problems and ADHD. The mechanism by which genes influence behavior is unknown. One possibility is that genes directly predispose children to both ADHD and conduct problems. Another possibility is that genes predispose children to show symptoms of ADHD, which, in turn, evoke hostile behavior by parents, teachers, and peers. These hostile behaviors can lead to the emergence of conduct problems (Cohn & Adesman, 2015; Pliszka, 2015).

An alternative explanation is that the hyperactive–impulsive symptoms of ADHD act as the "motor" that drives youths to engage in aggression and other antisocial acts. Children's high-rate and impulsive behaviors in early childhood elicit negative reactions from caregivers and lead to problems in caregiver–child interactions. These problems, in turn, often contribute to the development of oppositional and defiant behaviors (Lahey, McBurnett, & Loeber, 2000).

A third possibility is that children with ADHD have underlying problems with emotion regulation. Difficulties controlling emotional outbursts contribute to the development of both ODD and CD (Barkley, 2014).

Substance Use Problems

Adolescents with conduct problems are at increased risk for substance use (Elliott, Huizinga, & Menard, 2012). Youths with conduct problems often begin using nicotine, alcohol, and other drugs at earlier ages than children without conduct problems. For example, approximately 42% of youths with conduct problems have tried alcohol and 23% have tried marijuana by their 14th birthday. In contrast, only 27% and 7% of 14-year-olds without conduct problems have tried alcohol and marijuana, respectively.

Conduct problems also place children and adolescents at increased risk for substance use disorders. In one large epidemiological study, researchers examined the emergence of substance use disorders from childhood through adolescence (Yoshimasu et al., 2016). They found that children with ADHD were 3.5 times more likely than children without ADHD to develop substance use problems. However, children with conduct problems (with or without ADHD) were nearly 6 times more likely than youths without conduct problems to develop substance use disorders (see Figure 9.4). Another population-based study showed that ODD or CD completely explained the relationship between childhood ADHD and later substance use disorders. Together, these findings indicate that ODD and CD may be important, unique predictors of adolescent substance use problems.

What causes adolescents with conduct problems to use alcohol and other drugs? First, there seems to be a common set of genes that predispose individuals to both conduct problems and substance use disorders. Studies of twins and adopted children reared apart indicate a significant association between children's genes and the

Figure 9.4 Data from the Rochester Epidemiology Project indicate that children with ODD or CD are almost 6 times more likely than youths without conduct problems to develop substance use disorders.

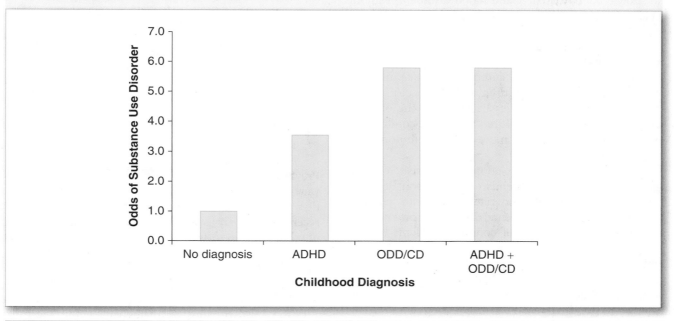

Source: Yoshimasu et al., 2016.

emergence of both conduct and substance use problems. Some researchers have suggested that children inherit a sensitivity to rewards. This sensitivity might predispose them to both conduct problems (e.g., to obtain excitement) and substance use (e.g., to obtain pleasure from the drug).

Second, disruptive children are typically first introduced to alcohol and other drugs by older, deviant peers. Deviant peers provide access to these substances, model their use, and reward adolescents with acceptance into their peer group. Substance use problems, therefore, are typically part of a larger spectrum of CD symptoms fostered by deviant peers (Kimonis et al., 2015; Wilens & Zulauf, 2015).

Academic Problems

Youths with conduct problems usually experience difficulties in school. They are more likely to earn low grades, to repeat a grade, and to be referred for special education than youths without conduct problems. Disruptive youths usually show problems in critical areas of academic achievement, especially reading and math. Approximately 25% of children with conduct problems show academic underachievement—that is, their academic performance is significantly lower than what might be predicted by their intelligence. Academic underachievement is especially likely when children have both ADHD and conduct problems (Frick, 2012).

By middle childhood, children's academic difficulties often lead to negative attitudes toward school and teachers. Youths with conduct problems often devalue education, put less effort and time into their schoolwork, and show reduced confidence in their academic abilities. These negative attitudes can cause them to distance themselves from school, teachers, and prosocial peers.

Schools, too, sometimes play a role in the development of conduct problems. Schools that place little emphasis on academic work, hold low expectations for students' academic achievement and classroom behavior, and provide students with poor learning environments can contribute to children's disruptive behavior. Unfortunately, these characteristics are often seen among schools in impoverished neighborhoods.

Recent prospective, longitudinal studies indicate that early conduct problems and academic difficulties can place children on a negative developmental path. Brennen and colleagues (Brennan, Shaw, Dishion, & Wilson, 2012) examined a large sample of youths from preschool through adolescence. Academic and conduct problems in first grade predicted low achievement, special education placement, referral to mental health services, and dropout throughout children's school years. Longitudinal studies like these suggest that early intervention programs are critical to prevent long-term problems.

Anxiety and Depression

In community-based samples, approximately one-third of youths with conduct problems also have comorbid anxiety or depression. Among clinic-referred youths, the prevalence of anxiety or depression among youths with conduct problems is 75%. Girls are approximately twice as likely as boys to show comorbid anxiety and mood disorders (Kimonis et al., 2015).

Research investigating the anxiety symptoms of children with conduct problems has yielded conflicting results (McMahon & Frick, 2005). Some studies have shown that children with comorbid anxiety disorders are less impaired than children with conduct problems alone, whereas other studies have shown the opposite effect, specifically, that children with both conduct and anxiety problems display more severe symptoms and impairment.

It is likely that the relationship between conduct problems and anxiety depends on the personality characteristics of the child. Moderate levels of anxiety allow children to benefit from parental discipline. Some children may display lower levels of conduct problems because they fear parental disapproval or punishment. For these children, comorbid anxiety problems decrease the severity of their conduct symptoms. However, certain children and adolescents have personality traits that make them slow to respond to punishment. For these children and adolescents, comorbid anxiety might be associated with an increase in conduct problems, especially hostile and aggressive behaviors (Frick & Loney, 2002).

Expert opinion about depression in children with conduct problems has also changed in light of new research. Years ago, experts believed that depression and feelings of low self-worth caused children's conduct problems. Some people believed that depressive symptoms were masked by children's disruptive and aggressive behavior. Subsequent research has not supported this theory of masked depression (Toolan, 1962).

Instead, longitudinal studies indicate that children's conduct problems usually precede, and often cause, their symptoms of depression. Patterson and Capaldi (1991) have offered the dual failure model to explain the association between conduct problems and depression. According to this model, conduct problems cause children to experience failure in two important areas: (1) peer relationships and (2) academics. Peer rejection and academic problems, in turn, can cause depression and feelings of low self-worth. The relationship between conduct problems and depression is especially strong for girls. Disruption of family and peer networks may be particularly stressful for girls, causing depressed mood and increased disruptive behaviors (van Lier et al., 2012).

Review:

- ODD and CD are distinct disorders that frequently co-occur. Most youths with ODD do not develop CD; approximately 31% of youths with CD do not have a history of ODD.
- ADHD places children at risk for ODD and CD. Underlying problems with inhibition or emotion regulation could explain the comorbidity of ADHD and these disorders.
- Youths with conduct problems begin using substances at an earlier age than typically developing youths and are 6 times more likely to develop a substance use disorder.
- As many as 75% of older children and adolescents with conduct problems have anxiety or depression. The dual failure model posits that conduct problems cause academic and peer difficulties that, in turn, contribute to depression.

What Is the Prevalence of Children's Conduct Problems?

Prevalence estimates for childhood conduct problems vary considerably, depending on participants' age, location (e.g., community or clinic), and gender. The most recent meta-analysis indicates that approximately 3.3% of youths aged 6 to 18 meet diagnostic criteria for ODD and 3.2% meet criteria for CD (Canino, Polanczyk, Bauermeister, Rohde, & Frick, 2010).

The prevalence of conduct problems depends on gender. With respect to ODD, prevalence for boys ranges from 1.9% to 13.3%, with most estimates being within the 4% to 6% range. For girls, the prevalence of ODD ranges from 1.1% to 9.4%, with most estimates being approximately 2% to 3%. With respect to CD, prevalence estimates for boys range from 1.7% to 14%, with most estimates being within the 5% to 10% range. For girls, prevalence ranges from approximately 1% to 8%, with most estimates being within the 2% to 4% range. Altogether, these data indicate that conduct problems are approximately 2 to 3 times more likely in boys than girls.

Prevalence also varies as a function of age. In preschoolers, rates of ODD and CD are typically low and rates are similar for boys and girls. Gradually, the prevalence of conduct problems increases. By the middle school years, the gender ratio for conduct problems reaches 3:1 favoring boys. By late adolescence, however, the gap narrows to approximately 2:1 (Kimonis et al., 2015).

Until recently, many experts believed that girls were infrequently diagnosed with CD because they usually showed less aggression than boys. However, subsequent data suggest that girls aggress in different ways than boys—ways that can be easily overlooked. Specifically, girls often use relational aggression—that is, they harm other people's mood, self-concept, or social status by damaging or manipulating interpersonal relationships (Crick & Grotpeter, 1995). Relational aggression can occur in a number of ways. Girls can spread rumors; ostracize another girl from a social network; share another girl's secrets without her consent; steal another girl's online identity; or make fun of another girl's weight, clothes, or general appearance. These tactics can be used either reactively (e.g., because the girl is angry at something another girl did) or proactively (e.g., because the girl wants to gain popularity or social status by harming a peer).

Girls may show relational aggression more than boys for at least three reasons. First, parents socialize girls differently than boys. From an early age, girls are discouraged to show anger through physical aggression. They may learn to use relational aggression to express anger, frustration, and discontent. Whereas physical aggression by girls is usually punished, relational aggression is often overlooked or may even be modeled by parents (Kuppens, Laurent, Heyvaert, & Onghena, 2013).

Second, relational aggression may be more effective than physical aggression at harming other girls. Because girls' moods and identities are so connected with their social relationships, damage to these relationships might be more hurtful than physical assault. In fact, girls view relational aggression as extremely distressing and comparable to physical bullying (Crick, 1995, 1997; Kawabata, Tseng, & Crick, 2014).

Third, girls' relatively more advanced language skills make relational aggression possible. Relational aggression does not typically emerge until late childhood and adolescence, when children's verbal skills are developed enough to engage in these complex, socially aggressive acts. Since young girls' verbal skills are often better developed than those of boys, girls may be able to show relational aggression at younger ages than boys (Murray-Close, Nelson, Ostrov, Casas, & Crick, 2016).

Experts have wondered whether the diagnostic criteria for CD should be modified to take into account the manner in which girls might manifest the disorder. Two proposals have gained recent attention. One option is to decrease the number of symptoms required by girls for the diagnosis. A second option is to broaden the diagnostic criteria to include relational aggression as a sign of CD. Additional research is needed to determine how such modifications might affect this diagnosis (Crapanzano, Frick, & Terranova, 2010; Frick & Nigg, 2012).

Review:

- Approximately 3.3% of youths have ODD and 3.2% have CD.
- On average, conduct problems are appropriately 2 to 3 times more likely in boys compared to girls. The gender gap is greatest during middle childhood.
- Girls are more likely than boys to engage in relational aggression—that is, harming others' mood, self-concept, or social status through rumors, lies, and the manipulation of interpersonal relationships.

9.2 CAUSES

Are Conduct Problems Heritable?

Conduct problems run in families. Youths with ODD or CD often have first-degree relatives with histories of conduct problems or antisocial behavior. However, family studies do not tell us whether the transmission of conduct problems from parent to child is due to shared genes or shared environments.

The results of twin studies have yielded inconsistent findings. Across all studies, genetic factors account for approximately 40% to 50% of the variance in children's conduct problems, broadly defined. If we assume that approximately 50% of the variance in children's conduct problems is attributable to genetics, then the remaining variance must be attributable to environmental causes.

Behavioral geneticists believe that nonshared environmental factors explain most of the remaining variance in children's conduct problems. These factors include the child's gender, his unique temperament and cognitive functioning, his interactions with parents, and his peer group and afterschool activities and interests. As we will see, these nonshared factors play important roles in most models explaining the development of conduct problems in youths. Nonshared factors are especially important when predicting physical aggression (see Figure 9.5; Tackett, Krueger, Iacono, & McGue, 2005).

In contrast, shared environmental experiences typically account for very little of the variance in conduct problems, with estimates ranging from 0% to 37% (Tackett et al., 2005). Although factors like health care, nutrition, and housing are important to determining the emergence of conduct problems, they seem less important than other factors.

The genes that place children at risk for ODD and CD have remained elusive. It is likely that children inherit a genetic risk for developing a difficult temperament, a tendency toward emotion-regulation problems, or a predisposition toward hyperactive–impulse behavior. These attributes, in turn, elevate the child's risk for developing conduct problems later in childhood or adolescence.

It is also likely that the development of conduct problems depends on both genetic risk and an environmental stressor. For example, Caspi and colleagues (2003) examined the gene that coded for the production of monoamine oxidase A (MAOA), an enzyme that regulates dopamine, serotonin, and norepinephrine—neurotransmitters important to behavior and emotion regulation. Boys who had a mutation of the MAOA gene, and consequently produced low levels of the enzyme, were at risk for developing conduct problems, but only if they experienced maltreatment. More than 80% of boys exposed to maltreatment who also had the genetic mutation developed CD (Snyder, 2016; Thomas, 2015).

Review:

- Genes account for 40% to 50% of the variance in children's conduct problems. Nonshared environmental factors account for most of the remaining variance.
- Mutations to the MAOA gene, in combination with environmental stressors such as child maltreatment, place children at increased risk for conduct problems.

Figure 9.5 The Effect of Genetic and Environmental Factors on Children's Conduct Problems

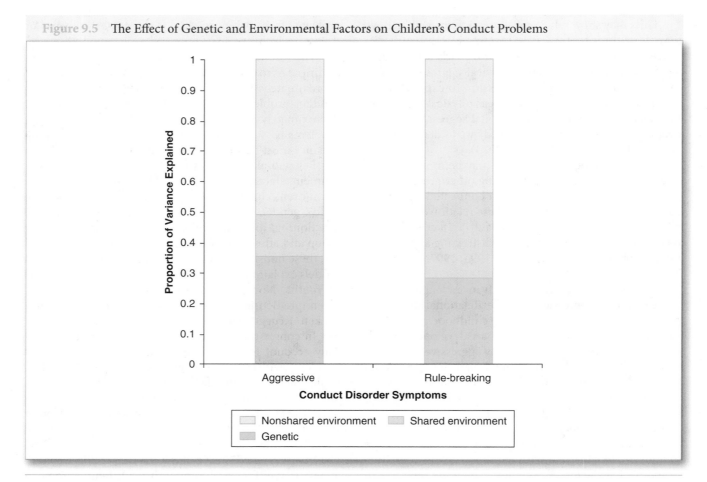

Source: Based on Tackett et al. (2005).

Note: The type of disruptive behavior that children show determines how important genetic and environmental factors are in children's conduct problems. Genetic and nonshared environmental factors account for most of the variance in children's aggressive symptoms. However, nonaggressive conduct symptoms (e.g., stealing, lying, truancy) are explained by genetic, nonshared, *and* shared factors.

How Can Temperament and Early Neurological Development Contribute to Conduct Problems?

Youths with childhood-onset conduct problems often have certain temperamental characteristics that contribute to their disruptive behavior. Recall that temperament refers to children's typical physiological, emotional, and behavioral responses (Nigg, 2006). A child's temperament is chiefly determined by genetic factors; temperament can be observed in infancy. Children with early onset conduct problems often show difficult temperaments in infancy and early childhood. They display either extremely high or extremely low levels of emotional activity, are quick to cry and fuss at novel stimuli, are easily frustrated, and have difficulty adjusting to change (Frick, 2012; Waller et al., 2015).

Recently, researchers have begun examining *how* difficult temperament can contribute to the development of conduct problems. So far, two underlying aspects of

children's neurocognitive functioning have been identified: (1) problems with emotion regulation and (2) overall low emotional arousal.

Emotion-Regulation Problems

Some children with difficult temperament show problems with excessive emotional reactivity. When confronted with an environmental stressor, these children display intense, negative emotional reactions and take an unusually long time to soothe. Keenan and Shaw (2003) believe this tendency is caused by an underlying problem with emotion regulation. These children have difficulty controlling negative emotions and responding to stressors in adaptive, flexible, and age-appropriate ways. When frustrated, these children often react with outbursts, anger, and aggression. Problems with emotion regulation emerge between 6 and 24 months of life and likely contribute to the development of both ADHD and conduct problems in young children (Frick, 2012; Musser, Galloway-Long, Frick, & Nigg, 2013).

Difficulty with emotion regulation can lead to the development of conduct problems in several ways. First, young children's early emotional displays can interfere with the development of more effective emotion-regulation skills. Most infants and toddlers learn to control negative emotions by relying on parents for comfort, support, and reassurance. However, the parents of these at-risk children may have difficulty responding sensitively and appropriately because of their children's outbursts. Consequently, their children may enter their preschool years with diminished capacity for emotional control (Keenan & Shaw, 2003).

Second, emotion-regulation problems can compromise the quality of parent–child interactions during the preschool years. Crying, yelling, and aggression interfere with children's abilities to internalize and follow rules. These emotional displays also lead parents to adopt hostile and angry disciplinary tactics that can model aggression or inadvertently reinforce children's disruptive acts (Kochanska & Kim, 2013; Snyder, 2016).

Third, excessive emotional reactivity can interfere with the development of social problem-solving skills in early childhood. As we will see, children with social problem-solving deficits have difficulty negotiating social disputes in logical and flexible ways. Instead, they rely on impulsive decision-making and aggressive actions to resolve interpersonal dilemmas (Crick & Dodge, 1996; Dodge, Godwin, & Conduct Problems Prevention Research Group, 2013).

Finally, intense displays of negative emotion can lead to peer rejection. Children with emotion-regulation difficulties may associate with other peer-rejected children who introduce them to antisocial behaviors (Chen, Drabick, & Burgers, 2015; Frick & Shirtcliff, 2016).

Low Emotional Arousal

Other children with difficult temperament show low emotional arousal. These youths have a reduction in overall autonomic activity: low resting heart rate, reduced brain activity, low skin conductivity. Because of their low arousal, these children need more intense stimulation to experience the same feelings as typically developing children. Consequently, they tend to engage in high-rate, high-risk activities and may be less responsive to punishment (Kimonis et al., 2015).

Toddlers with low emotional arousal are slow to react to pleasurable stimuli, appear less afraid of frightening or dangerous situations, and do not adjust their behavior when punished. By middle childhood, these youths often show an inability to feel empathy for others' suffering or distress, a lack of remorse for misbehavior, a desire to use others for personal gain, and a lack of response to discipline. Adolescents who show limited prosocial emotions often display a fascination with impulsive, dangerous, or delinquent behaviors (Thomas, 2015).

Early problems with low emotional arousal can contribute to the development of conduct problems in at least three ways. First, children with low emotional arousal do not seem to experience typical patterns of *fear and guilt* when they are reprimanded by parents. This reduced fear and guilt interferes with their ability to internalize parental rules and prohibitions, the development of conscience, and the capacity for advanced moral reasoning. Consequently, these children often show premeditative, aggressive behaviors without regard for the rights of others (Essau, Sasagawa, & Frick, 2006; Frick, 2012).

Second, children with low emotional arousal show an overall reduction in autonomic reactivity that renders them *less sensitive to punishment*. Consequently, they do not correct their misbehavior when disciplined. Indeed, traditional punishments often have little effect on these children, making the process of socialization challenging (Frick, 2012; Gatzke-Kopp, Greenberg, & Bierman, 2015).

Third, children's low autonomic arousal may render them *less able to experience pleasure*, excitement, and exhilaration. Whereas typically developing children and adolescents derive pleasure from moderate levels of stimulation (e.g., playing sports, going to the movies), children with low autonomic activity need to engage in high-rate, novel, and sometimes dangerous activities to obtain the same pleasurable sensations (e.g., reckless skateboarding, driving). Many people describe these youths as "unusually daring," "sensation seeking," or "risk takers" (Essau et al., 2006; Frick, 2012).

Children who show limited prosocial emotions are at increased risk for aggression in late childhood and adolescence. For example, low emotional activity predicts future antisocial behavior, delinquency, and violent criminal offenses. The presence of low emotional reactivity may be a better predictor of future antisocial behavior than the presence of CD alone (Frick, Ray, Thornton, & Kahn, 2014). For example, Frick and colleagues (Frick, Cornell, Barry, Bodin, & Dane, 2003) studied 98 school-age children, separated into four groups based on the presence or absence of conduct problems and low emotional arousal. As we might expect, children with conduct problems at the beginning of the study were more likely than children without conduct problems to show disruptive behaviors 4 years later. However, children who showed limited emotional arousal at the beginning of the study, regardless of whether they also showed conduct problems, displayed the greatest likelihood of aggressive and delinquent behavior at follow-up (see Figure 9.6).

Taken together, research indicates that the presence of difficult temperament in infancy can predispose children toward conduct problems in later childhood and adolescence. Problems with high emotional reactivity or low emotional arousal can independently contribute to later behavior problems. Although difficult temperament is largely determined by genetic factors, the emergence of later conduct problems is caused by a complex interplay of temperamental and environmental risks (Frick et al., 2014).

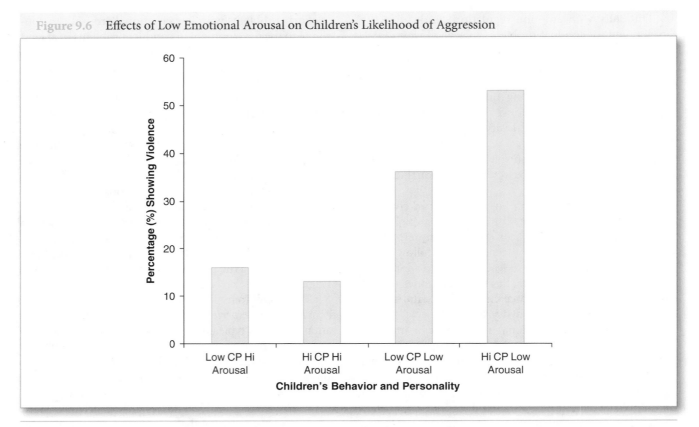

Note: Frick, Cornell, Barry, and colleagues (2003) divided children into four groups based on the presence or absence of conduct problems (CP) and low emotional arousal. Four years later, they assessed children's aggressive behavior. Children with low emotional arousal showed more aggressive behavior, regardless of whether they also had histories of conduct problems.

Review:

- Problems with emotional reactivity in early childhood can interfere with the development of emotion-regulation skills, compromise the quality of parent–child interactions, hinder the development of social problem-solving, or lead to peer rejection.
- Some youths with conduct problems show low emotional arousal. They may be more likely to engage in high-risk, pleasurable activities and have reduced sensitivity to punishment.

How Can Parenting Behavior Contribute to Children's Conduct Problems?

Coercive Parent–Child Interactions

Although genetic and temperamental factors can predispose children to conduct problems, the development of ODD and CD depends greatly on early learning experiences. Chief among these experiences is the quality of parent–child interactions (Snyder & Dishion, 2016).

Hostile–coercive parenting behavior is associated with the development of children's conduct problems. Hostile–coercive parenting behavior includes harsh disciplinary tactics, such as yelling, arguing, spanking, hitting, or criticizing. Hostile parenting can also involve using guilt and shame to correct children's misbehavior or relying on parental power to make children comply with requests or commands. Usually, hostile parenting is administered in an inconsistent fashion. Parents are often unwilling to hit or yell at their children for every misbehavior. Instead, parents tend to rely on hostile practices only when other tactics have proved ineffective or when they have become increasingly frustrated. Consequently, hostile parenting is almost always associated with anger and resentment (Stover et al., 2016; Weis & Toolis, 2010).

Gerald Patterson and colleagues (Patterson, Reid, & Dishion, 1992) have identified a particularly problematic pattern of parent–child interactions known as the coercive family process (see Figure 9.7). The coerceive process describes a pattern of parent–child interactions that predispose children to act in oppositional and defiant ways. The cycle is based on learning theory, especially principles of operant conditioning (Patterson, 2016).

Coercive parent–child interactions often begin when the parent issues a command to the child. For example, a girl might be playing in the living room and her mother might ask her to set the table for dinner. The girl might

Figure 9.7 According to Gerald Patterson, coercive parent–child interactions underlie oppositional and defiant behavior. Parents and children negatively reinforce each other's problematic actions.

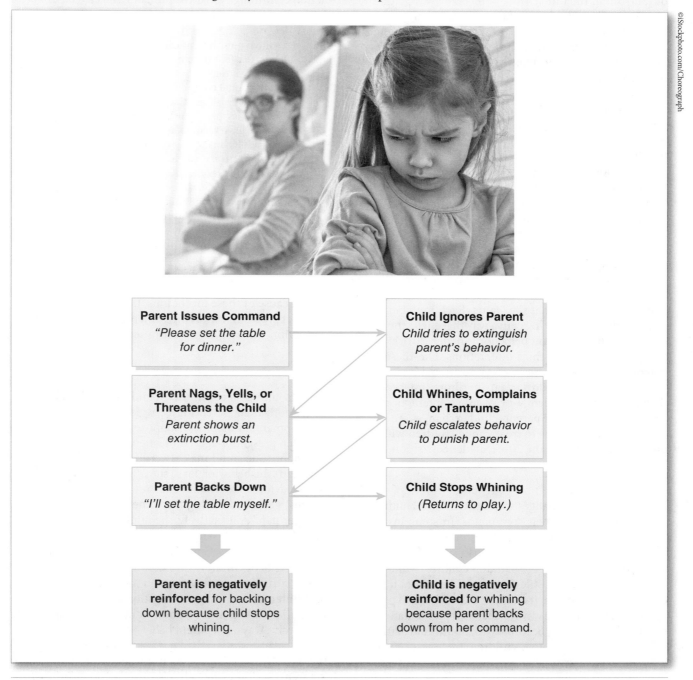

Source: Based on Patterson and colleagues (1992) and Smith and colleagues (2014).

initially ignore her mother's request. In behavioral terms, she is attempting to *extinguish* her mother's behavior by not reinforcing it with compliance.

The mother will probably repeat her request, this time more forcefully. She might nag, yell, or threaten the girl with punishment. In behavioral terms, the mother is showing an *extinction burst*—that is, a marked increase in the frequency or intensity of a behavior that occurs when the behavior is not reinforced. In response to her mother's nagging, the girl might issue a more forceful refusal; she might whine, yell, or throw a tantrum to avoid setting the table.

Eventually, her mother decides that it is too much trouble to argue with her daughter and resolves to set the table herself. She withdraws her request and stops nagging. In behavioral terms, the mother *negatively reinforces* her daughter for whining; she withdraws an aversive stimulus (e.g., nagging) in response to her daughter's whines, making it more likely that her daughter will whine or tantrum in the future.

At the same time, her daughter *negatively reinforces* the mother's acquiescence; the child stops whining or complaining in response to her mother's decision to "give in" and leave her alone. Consequently, her mother will be more likely to give in in the future.

The coercive process can also begin with the child. For example, a girl and her father might be in the checkout aisle of the grocery store when the girl asks her father for some candy. Her father denies her request, saying that the candy will spoil her dinner. The girl may exhibit an extinction burst, in this case, a dramatic increase in whining, crying, or throwing tantrums in response to her father's refusal to purchase the candy. Embarrassed and frustrated, the father might acquiesce and give her daughter the candy. The daughter is positively reinforced for her tantrums; she learns that throwing tantrums allows her to obtain candy. Her father, in turn, is negatively reinforced for giving in to his daughter's tantrums; he learns that he can avoid embarrassment and frustration in a crowded store by giving her what she wants. Each member of the dyad teaches the other to act in a way that elicits the child's oppositional and defiant behavior (Snyder, 2016).

Coercive parent–child interactions, like these, contribute to the development of oppositional and defiant behavior in young children. Furthermore, interventions that reduce the frequency of coercive interactions and promote more positive parent–child exchanges are among the most effective ways to treat young children with conduct problems (Patterson, 2016; Snyder & Dishion, 2016).

Modeling Physical Aggression

In most coercive exchanges, parents reinforce children for ignoring or defying their commands. In some instances, however, parents become angry and insist on compliance. In these cases, parents may engage in hostile behaviors, such as yelling, threatening, or spanking children while angry. Parents may model hostile–aggressive behaviors for their children. They show their children that verbal and physical aggression are effective ways to deal with problematic social situations (Kochanska & Kim, 2013; Smith et al., 2014).

Parents of disruptive children frequently alternate between overly permissive and hostile–coercive parenting behaviors. Typically, parents are lax on discipline, perhaps because they want to avoid stress associated with correcting their children's misbehavior. However, when parents feel frustrated or threatened by children's misbehavior, they may respond in a hostile or aggressive fashion: yelling, threatening, grabbing, or hitting. Parents' reliance on overly permissive and hostile–coercive parenting behaviors is one of the best predictors of conduct problems in young children. Furthermore, harsh discipline is one of the best ways to predict whether a child with ODD will develop CD as an adolescent.

Nevertheless, many parents rely on positive punishment (e.g., yelling, spanking) to stop children's aversive actions. Although positive punishment can be effective in the short term, it has several long-term disadvantages:

- Positive punishment can model hostile and aggressive behaviors to children. Children learn that yelling and spanking are appropriate and effective ways to deal with interpersonal conflict.
- Positive punishment does not teach children new, prosocial behaviors. Punishment teaches children what not to do (e.g., cry, complain) rather than what to do (e.g., obey adults, make appropriate requests).
- To be effective, positive punishment must be used consistently; however, parents usually use it only intermittently (especially when they are angry).
- If punished often, children learn to avoid or escape these punishments through negative reinforcement. For example, they may avoid interacting with parents.
- Positive punishment, when administered when parents are angry or frustrated, can lead to verbal and physical abuse.

Because of these limitations, treatment for children's conduct problems relies chiefly on positive reinforcement, extinction, and negative punishment such as time-out.

Parents' Cognitions and Mental Health

Parents' thoughts about their children's misbehavior can affect both their parenting behavior and their children's developmental outcomes. Suppose that a mother notices that her preschool-age child often tantrums in the late afternoon. She could make two different attributions for her child's misbehavior. First, she might attribute her child's misbehavior to *external* and *unstable* causes, saying, "Oh, she just gets tired during that time of the day. She needs a longer nap." Alternatively, she might attribute the child's tantrum to *internal* and *stable* causes, saying, "Oh, she's such a bad girl. She seems to enjoy making me upset."

Parents of children with conduct problems are more likely to attribute misbehavior to internal and stable factors. Internal and stable attributions increase the likelihood that parents will respond to misbehavior in hostile or coercive ways. If a parent believes that her child misbehaves because she is "a bad girl" or "deliberately naughty," the parent is prone to anger and resentment. However, if a parent attributes her child's misbehavior to transient, situational factors (e.g., fatigue, hunger, boredom), the parent is more likely to respond in a problem-focused, rational way (Colalillo, Williamson, & Johnston, 2014; Webster-Stratton, 2016).

The way parents think about their own parenting skills can also affect their disciplinary tactics. The parents of disruptive children frequently feel powerless over their children, and they often report little confidence in their caregiving abilities. Parents who feel powerless over their children's behavior may give up trying to discipline their children. In one study, the parents of disruptive preschoolers disciplined their children *less* often than the parents of nondisruptive preschoolers, despite the fact that children in the former group showed more behavior problems (Cunningham & Boyle, 2002; Johnston, 2005).

We need to remember that the relationship between parenting behavior and child misbehavior is transactional; parents and children influence each other over time. For example, a child who has difficulty regulating his emotions might engage in more crying, throwing tantrums, and engaging in disruptive behavior than most children his age. His aversive emotional displays might cause his mother to adopt hostile–coercive strategies to manage his behavior. These less-than-optimal parenting strategies might, in turn, contribute to more severe oppositional and defiant behaviors and future conduct problems. In fact, children with difficult temperaments and affect regulation problems seem to elicit hostile–coercive behaviors from their parents. These parenting behaviors, in turn, contribute to the development of conduct problems throughout childhood (Lochman, Boxmeyer, Powell, & Dishion, 2016).

Parental psychopathology is also a strong predictor of children's conduct problems. Maternal depression, paternal antisocial behavior, and parental substance abuse are especially associated with oppositional, defiant, and aggressive behavior in offspring. Furthermore, marital or partner conflict also predicts children's conduct problems.

Caregivers' mental health problems can contribute to children's disruptive behavior by interfering with the quality of parent–child interactions. For example, mothers with depression are often less supportive and more coercive toward their children than mothers without depression; their emotional distress and low energy interferes with the care and discipline they give their children. Similarly, fathers who engage in harsh or inconsistent disciplinary strategies can inadvertently model and reinforce aggression at home. As we will see, many effective treatments for children's conduct problems provide support to parents, to help them overcome emotional difficulties, alleviate parenting stress, and learn more effective ways to manage their children's behavior (McGilloway et al., 2014; Webster-Stratton, 2016).

Low Parental Monitoring

By late childhood and early adolescence, children assume greater autonomy over their behavior. They are given greater freedom to plan their day, and they are able to participate in more activities without parental supervision. However, the increased autonomy that children enjoy also provides them with more opportunities to engage in disruptive and antisocial acts.

Low parental monitoring is strongly associated with the development of conduct problems in late childhood and adolescence (see Figure 9.8). Parental monitoring has three components. First, parents must know children's whereabouts, activities, and peers. Second, parents must set developmentally appropriate limits on children's activities. Third, parents must consistently discipline children when they fail to adhere to rules (Snyder, Reid, & Patterson, 2003). Children whose parents fail to monitor or supervise their activities show increased likelihood of conduct problems; however, children whose parents set firm limits on afterschool activities show decreased rates of delinquency (Kimonis et al., 2015).

Recent research indicates that many adolescent-onset conduct problems are associated with low parental monitoring. Adolescents are able to engage in acts like theft, truancy, and vandalism when parents do not monitor their activities or peer groups. Researchers encourage parents to set clear expectations on their children's behavior, to supervise their children's activities, and to administer consequences for their children's rule violations. Although these are wise suggestions, these tactics are more easily said than done. Adolescents are adroit at keeping parents in the dark about potentially delinquent activities (Frick, 2012; Lopez-Tamayo, LaVome Robinson, Lambert, Jason, & Ialongo, 2016).

Review:

- Coercive family process describes interactions in which parents negatively reinforce children for noncompliance or defiance while children negatively reinforce parents for giving in to their demands or tantrums. It predicts the emergence of conduct problems.
- Parents who rely extensively on positive punishment may model aggression to their children.
- The parents of children with conduct problems often attribute misbehavior to internal and stable causes and see themselves as less able to manage children's behavior.
- Parental monitoring involves the degree to which caregivers are aware of their child's activities, set appropriate limits, and consistently enforce these limits. Low parental monitoring predicts the emergence of conduct problems in older children and adolescents.

How Can Children's Social Information Processing Contribute to Conduct Problems?

Children with conduct problems often show characteristic biases in their social information processing—that is, the way they perceive, interpret, and solve social dilemmas and interpersonal disputes. Crick and Dodge (1994, 1996) developed a social information–processing model to explain how children solve interpersonal dilemmas. According to this model, the way children think and feel about social situations influences their actions (Dodge et al., 2013).

To understand the social information–processing model, imagine that an 11-year-old boy is waiting in line in the school lunchroom. He is suddenly struck from behind and notices milk running down his back. He

Figure 9.8 Low parental monitoring predicts children's conduct problems.

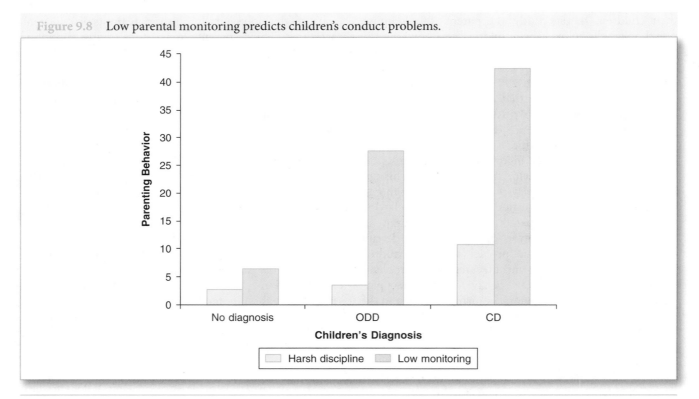

Source: Based on Rowe et al. (2002).

Note: The parents of youths with ODD and CD engage in more harsh discipline and less parental monitoring than do the parents of youths without conduct problems.

further notices that a larger, older boy is standing behind him, looking sheepish, while other children in the lunchroom are beginning to snicker. The younger boy feels embarrassed and confused (see Figure 9.9).

According to the model, the younger boy must perform six problem-solving steps to resolve this social situation. First, he must *encode cues* about the social situation—that is, he must take in information about the situation in order to understand it. Cues can include external information about the situation itself or internal information about the child. For example, the boy might attend to the facial expression of the larger boy behind him, the discomfort of the milk dripping down his back, or his feelings of embarrassment.

In the second step of the model, the boy must *interpret cues* so that they make sense. The boy in the story might infer that his classmate spilled milk down his back on accident and that he wants to apologize. Alternatively, the boy might make a hostile attribution for the older boy's behavior, believing that he deliberately spilled the milk to humiliate him.

Third, the child must *clarify his goals* for the social situation—that is, the child must decide what he wants to accomplish in the situation. One goal might be to avoid further embarrassment and to get cleaned up. An alternative goal might be to take revenge on the older classmate. The goals that he identifies will influence his actions.

In the fourth step, *response access or construction*, the child generates possible plans for action. He can either create a new solution to the problem or draw upon past experiences in similar situations. Ideally, the child generates multiple possible solutions. For example, he might consider walking away from the situation, laughing over his misfortune with the rest of his peers, or punching the older boy in retaliation.

In the fifth step, *response decision*, the boy evaluates his options and selects the best course of action. This step involves weighing the costs and benefits of each potential solution and reaching a decision about how to act. For example, hitting the boy might make him feel better in the short-term but could lead to physical injury or suspension from school.

Finally, the child *enacts the solution* that he believes is the best. Then, the cycle begins anew, as the child begins to process others' reactions to his solution. The way in which other children in the lunchroom respond to his behavior will likely influence his next course of action.

According to Crick and Dodge (1994, 1996), the information-processing steps occur rapidly, usually without children knowing that they are engaging in them. The child's history of social interactions, or "social database," forms the center of the model. Each social interaction contributes new information to the database. Furthermore,

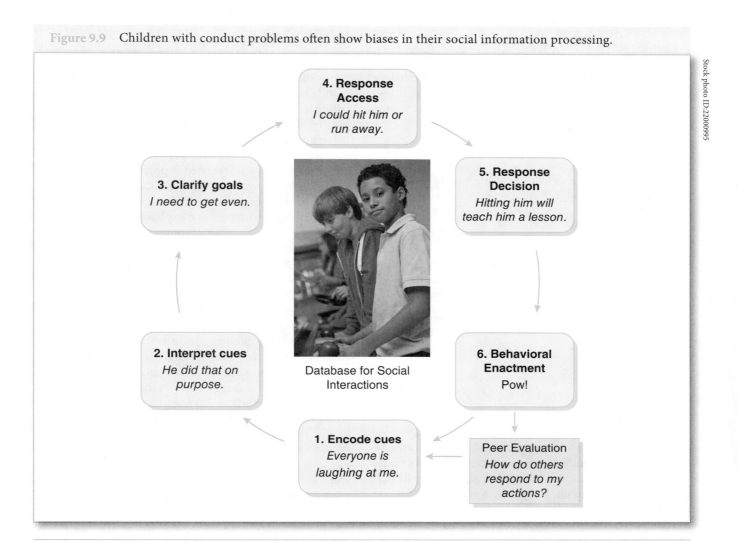

Source: Based on Crick and Dodge (1996) and Dodge and colleagues (2013).

children can draw from experiences in the database to navigate new social problems.

Aggressive children tend to show biases in their social information processing. Furthermore, these biases differ depending on whether children show reactive or proactive aggression.

Children who show *reactive aggression* tend to have problems with the first two steps: (1) encoding and (2) interpreting cues. Specifically, they take in less information about the situation. For example, they might attend to one or two salient features of the situation (e.g., the milk, the other children laughing) and ignore other potentially important cues (e.g., the boy behind saying, "I'm sorry"). These children also have difficulty understanding their own emotional reactions to the situation. For example, they might mistake feelings of embarrassment for feelings of anger. Consequently, children who engage in reactive aggression usually show a hostile attribution bias for others' behavior; they are likely to interpret others' benign

actions as hostile or threatening (Dodge, 2003; Dodge & Pettit, 2003; Dodge et al., 2013).

Children who show *proactive aggression* tend to have difficulty with the next three steps: (3) clarifying goals, (4) response access, and (5) response decision. First, children who engage in proactive aggression tend to select instrumental goals rather than relational goals. Their objective is often to get something that they want rather than to make a friend or to maintain a relationship. Consequently, they often act out of self-interest rather than out of respect for the feelings of others.

Second, when evaluating potential courses of action, children who show proactive aggression emphasize the positive aspects of aggression (e.g., it will allow me to get what I want) and minimize the negative aspects of aggression (e.g., I might get in trouble). Indeed, these children seem to focus excessively on potential rewards (e.g., stealing a candy bar or a car) rather than on possible punishment (e.g., getting grounded or arrested). Consequently, they frequently select solutions that allow them to get what they want with little forethought about the consequences of their actions (Barry et al., 2000; Frick et al., 2003; Dodge et al., 2013).

Although these social information–processing biases are automatic, they are not immutable. As we will see, therapists can help children avoid these biases and reduce the frequency of their aggression.

Review:

- The social information–processing model has six steps: (1) encode cues, (2) interpret cues, (3) clarify goals, (4) response access or construction, (5) response decision, and (6) enactment.
- Youths with reactive aggression tend to adopt hostile attribution biases in this model; they view others' benign actions as hostile or threatening (Steps 1–2).
- Youths with proactive aggression generate fewer prosocial methods for responding, emphasize the potentially positive aspects of aggression, and minimize the potential costs of aggression (Steps 3–5).

How Can Peers and Neighborhoods Contribute to Conduct Problems?

Peer Rejection and Deviancy Training

Across childhood and adolescence, friends gradually assume greater importance to children's self-concepts and emotional well-being. Older children and adolescents develop identities through interactions with their friends; friends influence their thoughts, feelings, and actions. Prosocial peers can protect youths from stressors by providing them with a social support system independent of their families. Deviant peers, however, can contribute to children's behavior problems (Frick, 2012; Simon & Olson, 2014).

Boys who show academic problems and disruptive behavior in school are often rejected by prosocial peers. Children with low academic achievement are seldom selected for group projects and may be teased by classmates. Even in kindergarten, children avoid classmates who are hyperactive or highly disruptive (Lacourse, et al., 2006). Youths who show problems with emotion regulation, anger, or aggression are actively avoided because of their impulsive and aversive displays. Interestingly, children who show angry reactive aggression are more likely to be rejected by peers than children who show proactive aggression. Some bullies are popular (Hess & Scheithauer, 2015).

Socially ostracized boys may seek out other boys who are socially rejected, a tendency known as selective affiliation (Dishion & Snyder, 2016). These deviant peers introduce boys to more serious antisocial behaviors, such as physical aggression, vandalism, truancy, theft, and alcohol use.

Boys learn to engage in antisocial behavior from peers through a process called deviancy training (Snyder, Schrepferman, Bullard, McEachern, & Patterson, 2012).

In deviancy training, peers positively reinforce boys for talking about antisocial activities and ignore prosocial behavior. For example, researchers compared the conversations of disruptive and nondisruptive peer groups. Nondisruptive boys tended to reinforce each other for telling jokes and interesting stories. In contrast, disruptive boys reinforced each other for discussions about antisocial behavior, such as getting into trouble at school, shoplifting, or bullying. Furthermore, disruptive boys rarely engaged in discussions related to prosocial activities, such as movies and sports (Dishion, Kim, & Tein, 2015).

Over time, boys engage in increasingly more severe antisocial behaviors in order to obtain further reinforcement from the deviant peer group. Deviant conversations among peer group members in late childhood predict delinquency, aggression, and substance use problems by early adolescence. Deviant peers, therefore, amplify boys' emerging behavior problems, leading them to engage in more severe and problematic antisocial acts. The process of deviancy training begins early. In fact, deviant discussions with peers predict future behavior in children as young as 6 years old (Snyder et al., 2005; Snyder, 2016).

For girls, the emergence of conduct problems tends to coincide with puberty. Early menarche places girls at risk for later conduct problems (Burt, McGue, DeMarte, Krueger, & Iacono, 2006). Among girls who already show conduct problems before puberty, the stressors of puberty seem to exacerbate disruptive behavior, leading to a general increase in the severity and frequency of problems (see Figure 9.10). However, even girls without prepubertal problems are at risk for conduct problems following early menarche. The physical changes of puberty can attract older boys who introduce early maturing girls to antisocial and sexually precocious behavior.

Neighborhood Risk

Children's neighborhoods may also affect their likelihood of conduct problems (Tolan, 2016). Specifically, youths from disadvantaged, high-crime neighborhoods are more likely to develop ODD and CD than children from middle-class communities (Jocson & McLoyd, 2015; Rudolph, Stuart, Glass, & Merikangas, 2014).

Neighborhoods can influence child development in several ways. First, neighborhoods may lack institutional resources to meet the needs of children in the community. For example, poor neighborhoods often have lower-quality day care and public schools. Children who attend these schools may not receive optimal educational services, especially if they show a developmental or learning disability. As a result, they may experience academic difficulties, devalue learning, and show problematic behavior in and out of school (Ray, Thornton, Frick, Steinberg, & Cauffman, 2016).

Second, neighborhoods may provide inadequate monitoring of children's activities, especially after school. For example, children living in low-income neighborhoods often have limited access to prosocial activities. High-quality

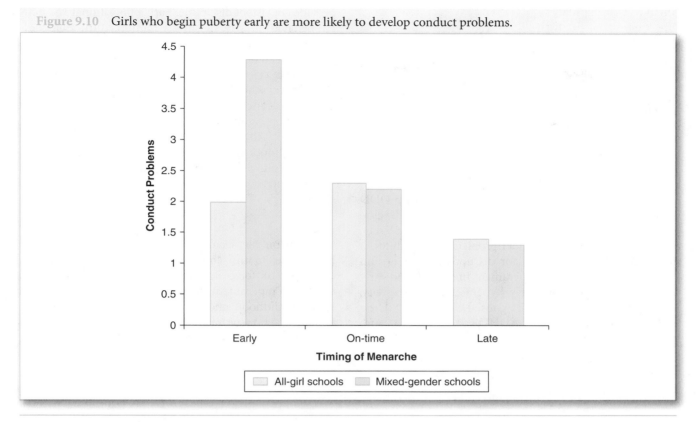

Source: From Caspi, Lynam, Moffitt, and Silva (1993). Used with permission.

Note: Early-maturing girls may associate with older, deviant boys who introduce them to antisocial behaviors. However, early-maturing girls who attend all-girl schools do *not* show increased risk of conduct problems.

recreation centers, afterschool programs, and organized athletics tend to be disproportionately available in middle- and upper-class neighborhoods. In the absence of prosocial programming, youths from disadvantaged neighborhoods may engage in unsupervised, antisocial acts (Chang, Foshee, Reyes, Ennett, & Halpern, 2015).

Third, low-income, high-crime neighborhoods often have weak social control networks; that is, these neighborhoods often lack organizations and community members that encourage prosocial behavior and limit antisocial activity. For example, in middle- and upper-class neighborhoods, children's disruptive behavior is kept in check by police, neighborhood watch groups, and concerned community members. Adolescents who wander the neighborhood at night or vandalize property are quickly brought to the attention of authorities. In contrast, community members living in poorer neighborhoods often tolerate higher levels of antisocial behavior among youths. After all, in high-crime neighborhoods, adolescents wandering the streets at night or engaging in petty acts of vandalism do not merit as much attention as people who engage in other, more serious criminal activities (Chang, Wang, & Tsai, 2016).

Of course, not all children who grow up in disadvantaged neighborhoods develop conduct problems. Certain factors can protect children from environmental risks posed by their surroundings. One protective factor is family cohesion and parental monitoring. Children whose parents set high expectations for their behavior, support their prosocial activities, and monitor their whereabouts are more likely to have positive developmental outcomes, regardless of neighborhood risk (Jennings & Fox, 2015).

A second protective factor is the availability of prosocial afterschool activities. For example, Samek and colleagues (Samek, Elkins, Keyes, Iacono, & McGue, 2015) examined conduct problems in a large sample of youths from early adolescence through early adulthood. Youths who participated in high school sports were less likely to develop conduct problems than nonathletes, regardless of gender.

Review:

- Youths who are rejected by prosocial peers may seek out other rejected, deviant peer groups. These deviant peers may introduce them to antisocial behaviors.
- Deviant peers may reinforce antisocial behavior and ignore prosocial actions, a phenomenon known as deviancy training.
- Neighborhoods place children at risk for conduct problems when they lack institutional resources to promote prosocial development (e.g., clubs, sports), inadequately monitor youths' activities, and have inadequate social control networks (e.g., neighborhood watch, police).

What Are Three Developmental Pathways Toward Conduct Problems?

The sheer number of risk factors makes it difficult to understand the emergence of conduct problems across childhood and adolescence. Fortunately, developmental psychopathologists have identified three main pathways toward conduct problems that can help us organize these risk factors (Frick, 2012; Kimonis, 2015).

Oppositional Defiant Disorder Only Pathway

The first pathway describes children who develop ODD in childhood or early adolescence but do not develop comorbid CD later in development (see Figure 9.11). Like most youths with conduct problems, these children likely inherit a genetic risk for disruptive behavior and often display difficulty temperament in infancy and early childhood. Many show early hyperactivity–impulsivity, and approximately 50% are diagnosed with ADHD. Their difficult temperaments and ADHD symptoms can cause parenting stress and compromise caregivers' abilities to attend to positive aspects of their functioning and

provide consistent discipline. Early oppositional and defiant behavior may be negatively reinforced through coercive parent–child interactions.

Children on this developmental pathway often meet diagnostic criteria for ODD sometime during their elementary school years. ODD symptoms can persist into adolescence; however, youths on this pathway do not develop significant CD symptoms, such as physical aggression. Although ODD symptoms decline during late childhood and adolescence, many of these youths continue to experience behavior and mood problems as young adults.

Childhood-Onset Conduct Disorder Pathway

Children on the second pathway often show the same histories as youths who develop ODD alone. They have a genetic risk for conduct problems, which manifests as difficult temperament, hyperactive–impulsive behaviors in early childhood, and a propensity toward oppositional, defiant, and noncompliant actions toward adults. Between 50% and 75% of these youths will meet diagnostic criteria for ODD.

Figure 9.11 Three pathways to childhood conduct problems.

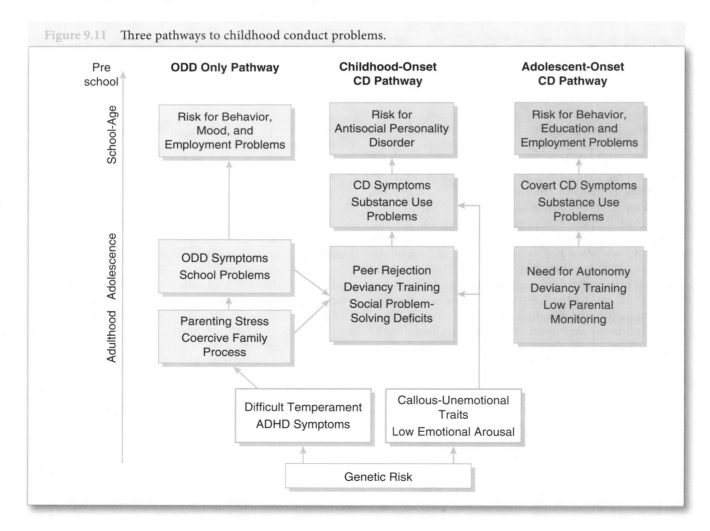

The disruptive behaviors and academic problems shown by these children can lead to peer rejection and affiliation with older, deviant youths. Deviant peers may introduce and reinforce antisocial behaviors of increasing seriousness. Youths on this pathway also frequently show social problem-solving deficits, which contribute to their tendency to use aggression to solve interpersonal disputes. Most of these youths meet diagnostic criteria for CD by late childhood or early adolescence. As many as 60% will also develop substance use problems.

Approximately one-third of youths who develop childhood-onset CD also have limited prosocial emotions. In early childhood, they exhibit low emotional arousal, a disposition that makes them seek our high-risk, pleasurable activities. They also display callous-unemotional traits such as a lack of empathy, guilt, and concern about their academic performance. Consequently, they are slow to respond to typical methods of discipline, such as parental disapproval. This subset of youths with callous-unemotional traits is likely to engage in more overt, aggressive, and destructive behavior (Golmaryami & Frick, 2015).

Childhood-onset CD is a stable condition. Approximately, 90% of children with CD continue to meet diagnostic criteria for the disorder 3 to 4 years later. Their adult outcomes vary, however. Approximately 25% of youths with childhood-onset CD do not experience behavioral or emotional problems in adulthood. However, most youths with this condition continue to engage in antisocial acts as adults. Approximately 40% will meet diagnostic criteria for ASPD. Youths with limited prosocial emotions are at particular risk for showing signs of psychopathy in adulthood (Dishion & Patterson, 2016).

Adolescent-Onset Conduct Disorder Pathway

The final pathway is shown by youths with adolescent-onset CD. By definition, these youths do not show significant conduct problems prior to puberty. Then, they typically engage in property destruction, deceitfulness and theft, and rule violations. These adolescents are typically rebellious, resent limitations imposed upon them by parents and other authority figures, and have a strong need to assert their independence. Their antisocial behavior may reflect maladaptive attempts to assert their autonomy (Dandreaux & Frick, 2009; Frick, 2012). Typically, these adolescents are rejected by prosocial peers and subsequently develop affiliations with deviant peers who introduce them to antisocial acts. These adolescents also frequently have poor parental supervision, which enables them to engage in antisocial actions.

Researchers used to think that conduct problems that emerged in adolescence were simply exaggerations of normal "adolescent rebellion." In fact, researchers used to call this pathway "adolescence-limited CD" because most youths stopped engaging in antisocial actions in early adulthood. Unfortunately, recent research paints a less optimistic picture. Although most individuals with

adolescent-onset CD do not meet criteria for any conduct problem in adulthood, many continue to engage in antisocial behaviors well into their 20s and early 30s. They also frequently experience other difficulties, such as substance use problems, health impairments, and financial hardship. Finally, their opportunities to participate in higher education, job training, and employment are often limited because of their previous antisocial acts. Collectively, these data suggest that adolescent-onset CD places these youths on a developmental trajectory that limits their potentials (Kimonis et al., 2015).

Review:

- The ODD pathway is often characterized by difficult temperament in early childhood, the emergence of hyperactive–impulsive behavior or ADHD, and coercive parent–child interactions. Youths are at risk for behavioral and emotional problems in adolescence.
- The childhood-onset CD pathway is often characterized by ADHD and ODD in childhood, peer rejection, affiliation with deviant peers, and more serious conduct problems in adolescence. Approximately 75% of children on this path continue to show behavior problems as adults; 40% meet criteria for ASPD.
- The adolescent-onset CD pathway is characterized by a strong need for autonomy, the emergence of covert antisocial behavior in early adolescence, and a gradual reduction in behavior problems. Youths on this path often continue to show academic, occupational, and substance use problems in young adulthood, however.

9.3 EVIDENCE-BASED TREATMENT
What Evidence-Based Treatment Is Available for Younger Children?

Parent Management Training

Parent management training (PMT) is the most widely used and best supported treatment for conduct problems in young children. PMT is a behavioral intervention that is based on the notion that children's disruptive behaviors often develop in the context of hostile–coercive parent–child interactions (Patterson, 2016). The clinician assesses the quality of parent–child interactions and notes how parents might inadvertently reinforce or model oppositional, defiant, or aggressive behavior. During the course of therapy, the clinician teaches parents to interact with their children in more adaptive ways and to avoid coercive parent–child exchanges (Pfiffner & Kaiser, 2015). Although there are several effective PMT programs, two with strong empirical support are the Parent Management Training–Oregon Model (PMTO), developed by Gerald Patterson and colleagues, and the Defiant Children program, developed by Russell Barkley (Simon, 2016).

All PMT programs have certain elements in common. In most cases, parents participate in weekly PMT sessions without their children. Parents learn new child management skills each week and practice these skills at home. For example, there are 10 steps in the Defiant Children program (Barkley, 2013a). Each step consists of a principle or skill that parents learn in the session and apply in their home during the course of the week (see Table 9.3). Some parents can complete one step each week, but most parents require multiple weeks to master some steps. The steps can be loosely categorized into four phases of treatment.

In the first phase (Step 1), parents learn about the causes of children's disruptive behavior. Although parents frequently blame themselves for their children's misbehavior, therapists show how children's misbehavior is influenced by parent, child, and environmental factors.

Table 9.3   Parent Management Training

Step	Topic/Description
1	Why do children misbehave?
	The therapist teaches parents the causes of child misbehavior, how these causes interact, and what parents can do to identify these causes in their own families.
2	Pay attention!
	Many parents of disruptive children focus primarily on their children's misbehavior. In this session, the therapist teaches parents to attend to and appreciate their children's appropriate actions.
3	Increasing children's compliance
	After parents learn to attend to their children's appropriate behavior, the therapist teaches them to contingently reinforce their children's appropriate actions, using praise and attention. The therapist especially encourages parents to attend to and reward their children when they are not interrupting or bothering them, such as when they are playing quietly.
4	Using token economies
	Parents are taught how to implement a token economy in the home to increase child compliance with commands, rules, and chores.
5	Using time-out at home
	The therapist teaches parents how to use the token system as a form of punishment using response cost; tokens are withdrawn for inappropriate actions. Parents also learn how to use time-out in the home. Initially, time-out is used for only one or two problem behaviors.
6	Practicing time-out
	Parents gradually expand their use of time-out to other behavior problems. During the session, the therapist and parents address problems using the time-out procedure.
7	Managing children in public places
	Parents are taught how to use modified versions of time-out to discipline children outside the home in stores, restaurants, church. Parents are also taught how to "think ahead" and plan for children's misbehavior in public.
8	Using the daily school behavior report card
	Teachers are asked to complete a daily report card regarding the child's behavior at school. Parents use the home token economy to reinforce appropriate behavior at school, based on teachers' reports on the card.
9	Handling future behavior problems
	The therapist and parents discuss how to deal with future behavior problems and challenging situations. Parents are shown how to use the skills they acquired in the parent training course to address future behavior problems.
10	Booster session and follow-up meetings
	The therapist asks parents to attend a follow-up "booster" session one month after the training ends to check on the family's progress. Parents can use this session to troubleshoot new problems or discuss ways to fade the token system. Follow-up visits may be scheduled every 3 months as needed.

Source: Based on Barkley (1997b).

In phase two (Steps 2–4), parents are taught basic learning principles, with an emphasis on positive reinforcement. Parents who seek treatment for their disruptive children usually attend predominantly to their children's misbehavior. Consequently, therapists teach parents how to attend to and praise appropriate behavior. Initially, parents learn to attend to children's desirable behavior. Then, parents learn to use positive reinforcement to increase the frequency of children's compliance. Parents are taught that in order for reinforcement to be effective, it must be contingent on appropriate behavior—that is, it must occur *immediately* following the appropriate behavior, and it must be *consistently* provided.

Parents are also taught to use Premack's principle, a rule of thumb that can be used to motivate children to engage in appropriate behaviors. It states that a child will be more likely to perform a low base-rate (undesired) activity if she knows that she will be able to partake in a more desirable activity as a consequence. Consequently, parents can use highly desired activities as positive reinforcement for less-desired activities. For example, if a child wants to watch television, her mother might require her to clean her room first. The Premack principle is sometimes called grandma's rule because it seems to be based on old-fashioned common sense; nevertheless, it is sometimes overlooked by caregivers (Russo, 2015; Thomas, 2015).

Later, parents learn to extinguish many of their children's inappropriate behaviors through selective ignoring. That is, parents systematically ignore unwanted behaviors that are aversive but not dangerous (e.g., tantrums, interruptions while parents are on the phone). Finally, parents learn to establish either a token economy (for younger children) or a point system (for older children) in the home. Children earn tokens or points contingent on specific appropriate behaviors, such as compliance with parental requests or homework completion.

In phase three (Steps 5–7), parents learn how to reduce children's disruptive behavior using discipline and environmental structuring. First, parents learn how to use time-out for serious rule violations. Time-out is first practiced at home, with a single behavior problem. Later, time-out is used for other behavior problems at home. Finally, parents extend time-out to public settings (e.g., restaurants, shopping trips). Parents also learn how to avoid behavior problems by structuring the environment to help their children behave. For example, before going grocery shopping, a parent might decide to bring snacks and a few small toys for the child so that she does not fuss or tantrum during the trip.

The fourth phase (Steps 8–10) involves generalizing children's appropriate behavior to the school setting and maintaining behavioral gains in the future. Teachers are asked to complete a daily report card on children's behavior at school. Parents use the report card to monitor children's school behavior and they reward children at home. Later, parents and therapists plan for other potential

behavior problems. Many therapists encourage parents to attend a follow-up session sometime after training has ended, to check in on the family's long-term outcomes.

PMT has received considerable empirical support (Mendenhall, Arnold, & Fristad, 2015). Meta-analyses show large effect sizes (ESs) for children whose families receive PMT compared to controls (ES = .80). Specifically, youths whose parents participate in PMT show more prosocial behavior at home, get into fewer disciplinary problems at school, and are less likely to show serious disruptive behavior problems in the future. After treatment, their functioning is similar to peers without conduct problems. Most longitudinal studies have shown that the effects of treatment last at least 1 to 3 years; however, some studies have shown that treatment gains are maintained 10 to 14 years after the end of treatment (Capaldi & Eddy, 2015; Curtis et al., 2016).

PMT also has some limitations. First, PMT is less effective for parents experiencing high stress. Single parents, low-income parents, parents experiencing marital conflict, and parents who have substance use or mental health problems tend to drop out of PMT or progress slowly. Psychosocial stressors can interfere with parents' abilities to attend sessions, practice skills, and persevere in the face of environmental challenges. Second, PMT has received less empirical support when used with adolescents. Adolescents typically show more severe conduct problems than children, perhaps making them more resistant to treatment. Furthermore, parents tend to have less control over their adolescents' environments and, consequently, have less ability to change environmental contingencies to alter their adolescents' behavior. Third, most clinicians in the community have not received formal training in PMT. Parents who want to participate in PMT may be unable to find a skilled therapist (Capaldi & Eddy, 2015; Pfiffner & Kaiser, 2015).

Parent–Child Interaction Therapy

Parent–child interaction therapy (PCIT) is a variant of PMT designed for families with disruptive preschoolers and young school-age children. As with PMT, the focus of PCIT is on the way parents interact with their children and address child misbehavior. Unlike PMT, parents and children attend therapy sessions together. Clinicians observe parent–child interactions and teach parents techniques for managing their children's behavior during the sessions (Funderberk & Eyberg, 2011; Hembree-Kigin & McNeil, 2013).

PCIT is divided into two phases. In the first phase, *child-directed interaction*, the goal of treatment is to increase parents' sensitivity and responsiveness toward their children and to improve the quality of the parent–child relationship. Children select a play activity and parents follow their lead. One component of this phase of treatment is to help parents develop a set of skills—praising, reflecting, imitating, describing, and enthusiasm—that spell the acronym PRIDE. While playing with their children,

Table 9.4 Parent–Child Interaction Therapy: PRIDE Skills

Skill	Reason	Examples
PRAISE appropriate behavior	Causes your child's good behavior to increase	Parent: Good job putting the toys away!
REFLECT appropriate talk	Shows your child that you are listening	Child: I drew a tree.
IMITATE appropriate play	Lets your child lead; shows your child that you approve of his or her game	Child: I put a nose on the potato head.
DESCRIBE appropriate behavior	Shows your child that you are interested in what he or she does	Parent: You're making a tower with Legos.
ENTHUSIASM Show it!	Lets your child know that you are enjoying the time you are spending together	Parent: You are a REALLY hard worker!

Source: Based on T. Patterson and Kaslow (2002).

parents practice praising, reflecting, imitating, and describing their children's appropriate behavior in an enthusiastic way (see Table 9.4). Furthermore, parents are discouraged from assuming too much control over the play situation, from asking questions or making demands to being critical of their child's behavior. In this way, parents strengthen children's appropriate actions and convey acceptance and warmth (Eyberg, 2006).

In the second phase of PCIT, *parent-directed interaction*, the goal of treatment is to help parents create more realistic expectations for their children's behavior, to reduce hostile and coercive parent–child exchanges, and to promote fair and consistent use of discipline. An important component of this phase of therapy is learning how to give effective commands to children. Commands must be given when children are paying attention. They must be stated clearly and concretely. They must also be followed up immediately by consequences, either praise (for compliance) or discipline (for noncompliance; Eyberg, 2006).

In PCIT, the therapist meets with the parent and child together. The therapist acts as the parent's teacher and coach. The therapist demonstrates all of the skills to the parent in the therapy session. Then, the therapist coaches the parent, during the session, until the parent has performed the skill adequately with her child. The therapist also troubleshoots specific behavior problems as they arise in the session and helps the parent tailor treatment to meet her child's specific needs. In general, PCIT is a hands-on approach to PMT.

PCIT is effective at reducing disruptive behavior in very young children, both at home and in the classroom. Furthermore, PCIT improves the sensitivity and care parents show to their children, decreases parental hostility and criticism toward their children, and reduces parenting stress. Improvements in children's behavior are maintained for at least 1 to 2 years after treatment and possibly up to 6 years after treatment (Curtis et al., 2016; Hembree-Kigin & McNeil, 2013; Simon, 2016).

Unfortunately, relatively few therapists are trained in PCIT. Consequently, PCIT has been adapted so that a greater number of families can access this form of treatment. For example, one version of PCIT allows groups of families to participate together and learn from each other. Another variation is delivered over the Internet, to families who live in communities where PCIT is not available (Niec, Barnett, Prewett, & Shanley, 2016; Simon, 2016).

Videotaped Modeling and the Incredible Years Program

A final variation of traditional PMT is videotaped modeling. Carolyn Webster-Stratton (2016) has developed a comprehensive program for young children with emerging conduct problems that relies on this method. The Incredible Years program consists of separate treatment modules for parents, teachers, and children. The program was designed especially for low-income, high-stress families—families most likely to drop out of traditional PMT.

The *Incredible Years BASIC* parent training program resembles PMTO and the Defiant Children program, with certain modifications made for children aged 2 to 10. The program consists of 14 parent training sessions, each approximately two hours long. Parents learn to attend to children's behavior, to reinforce appropriate actions, and to punish inappropriate actions using noncoercive methods. Parents watch videotaped vignettes of parent–child interactions. These vignettes are designed to illustrate the problematic parent–child interactions that underlie children's conduct problems and to teach alternative, effective parenting strategies. Parents watch the vignettes with other parents and then discuss the child management principles and parenting skills with each other and the therapist. The therapist acts as a collaborator and supporter rather than as a teacher. The therapist encourages parents to decide for themselves how to implement each parenting principle to tailor the program to meet their family's needs.

The *Incredible Years ADVANCE* parent training program is offered to parents as a supplement to the BASIC program. Webster-Stratton realized that parents with high levels of stress and conflict in the home have difficulty implementing the BASIC program and avoiding hostile–coercive exchanges with their children. The ADVANCE program consists of 14 additional sessions that teach parents self-control and anger management strategies, communication skills, interpersonal problem-solving skills, and techniques to strengthen their social support network. These skills are designed to improve parents' mood states, to decrease family tension, and to provide parents with the support they need to effectively implement the BASIC program.

The *Incredible Years Academic Skills Training (SCHOOL)* and *Teacher Training (TEACHER)* programs were developed as adjuncts to BASIC and ADVANCE. These programs were designed to improve children's school functioning. The SCHOOL program consists of four to six sessions attended by groups of parents. It focuses on improving parents' involvement in their children's education, fostering parental collaboration with teachers, and increasing parents' monitoring of children's activities with peers. The TEACHER program is a workshop for teachers. Topics in this program include classroom management strategies, strengthening children's social skills and avoiding peer rejection, improving communication with parents, monitoring children's activities, and reducing physical aggression and bullying.

The Incredible Years child training program was developed for 4- to 8-year-old children with emerging conduct problems. This 22-week program is administered to small groups of children and uses a series of videotaped vignettes, puppets, and role play activities to improve children's behavior at school. The main puppet is Dina Dinosaur; consequently, this program is often called the Classroom Dinosaur Curriculum. The program consists of empathy training, problem-solving skills training (PSST), anger control, friendship skills, and communication skills training. The overall goal is to teach children how to behave in class, how to make and keep friends, and how to play appropriately with peers.

The Incredible Years BASIC program is efficacious in improving parents' attitudes toward child-rearing, their quality of parent–child interactions, and their children's behavior. Parents who participate in the program display fewer hostile–coercive behaviors toward their children, and their children display fewer conduct problems over time. Parents who also participate in the ADVANCE program report more harmonious interactions with their spouses, better communication and problem-solving skills, and greater satisfaction with treatment than do parents who participate only in the BASIC program. These improvements in marital quality, communication, and problem-solving are associated with better parent–child interactions, especially for fathers (Gridley, Hutchings, & Baker-Henningham, 2015; Lees & Fergusson, 2015; Leijten, Raaijmakers, Orobio de Castro, van den Ban, & Matthys, 2015; Simon, 2016; Webster-Stratton, 2016).

The efficacy of the entire program has been evaluated on children with emerging conduct problems and low-income children at risk for developing conduct problems, Overall, children whose families participate in either parent-based, school-based, or child-based interventions show greater improvement in behavior than children whose families do not participate in treatment. Furthermore, children whose families participate in more of the treatment components (e.g., parent, teacher, *and* child training) fare better than families that participate in only one component. Across studies, the BASIC program tends to be most effective. However, the ADVANCE program is especially efficacious for mothers with depression, fathers with histories of substance abuse, and families experiencing psychosocial stress.

Despite the success of the Incredible Years program, approximately one-fourth of parents report significant child behavior problems 3 years after completing treatment (Webster-Stratton, 2016). The best predictors of continued child behavior problems are high marital distress or spousal abuse, single-parent status, maternal depression, low socioeconomic status, high life stress, or a family history of substance abuse. These findings speak to the importance of programs like ADVANCE, which are designed to improve the social–emotional functioning of parents. Improvements in parents' mood and social functioning might help them respond to their children's needs and discipline in a consistent and noncoercive fashion.

Review:

- PMT is a behavioral intervention designed to (1) help parents attend to and reinforce adaptive child behaviors and (2) reduce noncompliant or defiant actions using noncoercive discipline.
- PCIT is a variation of PMT in which parents and young children are coached by therapists as they interact in the clinic. PCIT focuses on PRIDE skills to improve the quality of positive interactions and the use of time-out to reduce defiance.
- The Incredible Years program is a series of modules designed for children with conduct problems, parents, and/or teachers. Participants watch videos that model skills while therapists lead in-session activities and group discussion.

What Evidence-Based Treatment Is Available for Older Children and Adolescents?

Problem-Solving Skills Training

Problem-solving skills training (PSST) is based on the notion that youths with disruptive behavior problems show characteristic biases in the way they perceive, interpret, and respond to interpersonal problems. These social information–processing biases interfere with their ability to respond to dilemmas in prosocial ways and increase the likelihood that they will show hostile and aggressive behaviors (Kazdin, 2010).

Recall that social information processing consists of six steps: (1) encoding cues about the social situation, (2) interpreting these cues, (3) clarifying goals, (4) generating possible plans for action, (5) evaluating, and (6) implementing the best plan to solve the problem. PSST attempts to correct the biased information-processing styles of aggressive children by teaching them how to systematically progress through these social problem-solving steps.

The therapist initially teaches the child a simplified social problem-solving strategy (see Table 9.5). Each step prompts the child to attend to certain aspects of the interpersonal problem and helps the child solve the problem in prosocial ways.

First, the child asks himself, "What am I supposed to do?" This requires the child to identify the problem and determine how he should act in the situation. Second, the child asks, "What are all my possibilities?" This step reminds the child to generate as many courses of action as possible. Third, the child says, "I'd better concentrate and focus in." This step encourages the child to evaluate the possible courses of action. Fourth, the child says, "I need to make a choice." This step requires the child to select the best response. Fifth, the child evaluates his actions and concludes either "I did a good job" or "I made a mistake." The steps slow the problem-solving process and help the child consider more information before acting.

The therapist usually begins each session by describing an interpersonal problem that the child might encounter in everyday life: an argument during recess, a problem on the bus, or a dispute in the hallway at school. The therapist then shows the child how to use the steps to solve the problem. Next, the therapist and child role-play the situation. In the first few sessions, the child says each step aloud as he works through the problem. After the child becomes more familiar with the steps, he can solve the problem silently. Throughout each session, the therapist coaches the child in the use of the steps and provides praise and encouragement. Some therapists also use a token economy during sessions. They reinforce the child's attention and participation in the session and withdraw tokens for inattentive, disruptive, or inappropriate behavior. If possible, parents are taught the problem-solving steps, too, and encouraged to prompt and reward the child for using the steps at home (Kazdin, 2010).

PSST is effective in reducing aggressive and disruptive behavior in school-age children. In several studies, children who participated in PSST showed greater symptom reduction than children who participated in an attention control group. Both inpatient and outpatient children showed improved functioning, relative to controls, and treatment gains were maintained 1 year later. Furthermore, children who participated in both PSST and PMT showed better outcomes than children who received either treatment alone (Kazdin, 2005, 2010; Michelson, Sugai, Wood, & Kazdin, 2013).

Multisystemic Therapy

Multisystemic Therapy (MST) is an intensive form of family- and community-based treatment that is especially effective for adolescents with serious conduct problems. Whereas PMT is frequently used for children and adolescents who show oppositional and defiant behaviors, MST is used most often used with adolescents who show more serious antisocial and violent behavior. In fact, MST has been used successfully with adolescents exhibiting chronic juvenile delinquency, violent crime, substance abuse, psychiatric crisis, and sexual offenses. In short, MST is one of the most successful interventions for adolescents with long-standing and serious behavior problems (Henggeler & Lee, 2003; Henggeler & Schaeffer, 2016).

Table 9.5   Problem-Solving Steps and Self-Statements

Step	Self-Statement	Purpose
1.	What am I supposed to do?	This step requires the child to identify and define the problem.
2.	I have to look at all my possibilities.	This step asks the child to generate alternative solutions to the problem.
3.	I'd better concentrate and focus in.	This step instructs the child to concentrate and evaluate the solutions he has generated.
4.	I need to make a choice.	In this step, the child chooses the best action.
5.	I did a good job. [or] I made a mistake.	In the final step, the child verifies whether the solution was the best among those available, whether the problem-solving process was correctly followed, or whether a less-than-desirable solution was selected.

Source: Based on Kazdin and Weisz (2003).

Note: Problem-solving steps are taught and practiced during role play. The child and therapist alternate turns practicing the steps. The therapist prompts and shapes the child's use of the steps using reinforcement. As the child learns the steps, prompts are gradually faded. The child also progresses from saying the steps aloud (overt), to saying them silently (covert).

Practitioners of MST target three systems essential to the adolescents' welfare: (1) family, (2) school, and (3) peers. In the *family*, therapists might help parents develop more effective skills for interacting with their adolescents. For example, therapists might administer a parent training program, teach parents how to monitor their adolescents' whereabouts after school, or help parents learn to avoid conflict situations with their adolescents. Therapists also try to remove obstacles that interfere with parents' abilities to provide supportive and consistent care. For example, therapists might address parents' marital discord, assist a parent in overcoming alcohol dependence, or increase the social support network of a single parent. Therapists see themselves as resources and allies for parents. Therapists hope that by improving the skills and well-being of parents, these parents will more effectively manage their adolescents' behavior.

A second realm of intervention is the adolescent's *school*. Most MST practitioners seek to increase parental involvement in their adolescents' education. Therapists might serve as liaisons between parents and teachers or help parents advocate for their children's educational needs. Therapists might teach parents to monitor their adolescents' attendance at school and behavior in the classroom. Again, therapists try to remove obstacles to the adolescents' academic achievement. For example, therapists might help to resolve conflicts between parents and teachers or deal with practical problems, like helping parents find time to attend parent–teacher conferences.

A third avenue of intervention involves the adolescent's *peers*. Association with deviant peers is one of the best predictors of adolescent behavior problems. Consequently, therapists attempt to limit adolescents' opportunities for interactions with deviant peers and increase opportunities for interactions with prosocial youths. At the very least, therapists encourage parents and other people involved in the adolescent's life (e.g., family members, teachers, police) to closely monitor his whereabouts, especially after school. At the same time, therapists might help the adolescent develop new peer networks. For example, a therapist might encourage an adolescent to try out for a sports team, join a club at school, or volunteer in the community. The therapist might also help the adolescent improve his social skills, in order to increase the likelihood that he will be accepted by prosocial classmates (Saldana & Henggeler, 2006).

MST is an intense, flexible, and family-focused intervention. Therapists usually work in teams of three to five, and they are available 24 hours a day, 7 days a week. Therapists usually meet with family members in their home or in the community, rather than in an office, in order to increase the family's attendance and involvement. MST usually lasts 3 to 5 months.

There is considerable evidence supporting the efficacy of MST for adolescents with conduct problems (Hart, Nelson, & Finch, 2006; Saldana & Henggeler, 2006). Across a number of randomized controlled trials, adolescents whose families participate in MST are 25% to 70% less likely to be rearrested and 47% to 64% less likely to be removed from their homes than are adolescents of families who do not participate in MST. Treatment appears to improve family functioning and parenting skills, which, in turn, decrease adolescents' association with deviant peers and their disruptive behavior (Henggeler & Schaeffer, 2016).

Researchers have also examined the long-term outcomes of adolescents who participated in MST. In one study, 176 adolescents previously arrested for serious crimes were randomly assigned to receive either MST or traditional supportive therapy (Schaeffer & Borduin, 2005). The adolescents in the study averaged 3.9 arrests for felonies, and 47.8% had at least one arrest for violent crime (e.g., sexual assault, assault and battery with intent to kill). Researchers examined arrest records approximately 13 years after treatment. Results showed that adolescents who participated in MST were less likely than adolescents who participated in supportive therapy to be arrested for a future serious offense (see Figure 9.12). Furthermore, adolescents who participated in MST committed half as many offenses overall as adolescents who participated in supportive therapy. These results suggest that MST is not only effective in reducing adolescent antisocial behavior, but it may also have long-term effects on adolescents' developmental outcomes.

Interestingly, the siblings of adolescent offenders also benefit from the family therapy component of MST. In one study, researchers examined the outcomes of the siblings of young offenders who participated in MST. Approximately 25 years after their parents participated in MST, 43% of siblings had been arrested compared to 72% of the siblings of youths who participated in traditional, supportive therapy. These findings suggest that MST helps the entire family system, not only the adolescent with the identified problem (Wagner, Borduin, Sawyer, & Dopp, 2014).

Unfortunately, MST programs are available to only about 1% of adolescents with serious conduct problems. Most therapists do not have formal training in MST. Hopefully, continued research supporting MST will prompt individuals and agencies to develop programs in their communities (Capaldi & Eddy, 2015; Wu et al., 2016).

Aggression Replacement Training

Aggression Replacement Training (ART) is a multimodal treatment designed for adolescents with histories of disruptive, aggressive, and antisocial behavior (Glick & Gibbs, 2011). ART is founded on the premise that adolescents who engage in antisocial acts lack the behavioral, affective, and cognitive skills that underlie prosocial actions. Instead, these adolescents show delays in social skills, social problem-solving, emotion regulation, and moral reasoning that interfere with their ability to engage in compliant, constructive behaviors. Furthermore, disruptive and aggressive behavior is sometimes modeled and

Figure 9.12   The Efficacy of Multisystemic Therapy (MST)

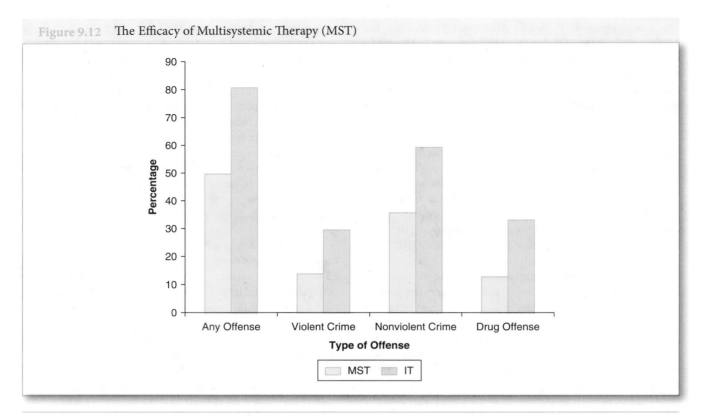

Source: Based on Schaeffer and Borduin (2005).

Note: Researchers compared the behavioral outcomes of adolescents with conduct problems who participated in MST versus interpersonal therapy (IT), a nonbehavioral form of treatment. Adolescents who participated in MST were less likely to show future antisocial behavior.

reinforced by other people in these adolescents' lives, especially family members and peers (Brännström, Kaunitz, Andershed, South, & Smedslund, 2016).

In ART, adolescents engage in structured group activities designed to teach behavioral, emotional, and cognitive skills (Goldstein & Martens, 2000). Specifically, ART consists of three components: (1) Skillstreaming, (2) anger control training, and (3) moral reasoning training.

The goal of *Skillstreaming*, the behavioral component of ART, is to enhance prosocial skills that help adolescents avoid arguments and aggressive displays and promote social competence (McGinnis, 2011a, 2011b). These skills are taught in small groups through a combination of modeling, role play, reinforcement and feedback. Skills fall into six categories: (1) beginning social skills (e.g., listening), (2) advanced social skills (e.g., apologizing), (3) skills related to feelings (e.g., understanding the feelings of others), (4) alternatives to aggression (e.g., keeping out of fights), (5) skills for dealing with stress (e.g., dealing with group pressure), and (6) skills related to planning (e.g., setting a goal).

First, a skill is introduced by the facilitator and defined by the group. Second, the skill is broken down into component parts and each part is modelled by the facilitator. Third, facilitator then prompts each group member to identify how he might utilize the skill in his everyday life. Finally,

volunteers from the group take turns role playing situations in which they might use the skill. Each group member practices the skill and receives feedback from the other group members. The role play and feedback process is repeated until all group members have the opportunity to practice the skill. Then, the facilitator asks each group member to practice the skill outside the group and reflect on the outcome of this practice.

Anger control training comprises the emotion-regulation component of ART (Feindler & Engel, 2011; Novaco, 1975). A primary goal of anger control training is to help adolescents understand the angry behavior cycle—a model for the external triggers and internal cues that prompt adolescents' anger. First, group members identify situations that might trigger anger. Then, the facilitator encourages group members to recognize what physiological markers serve as cues that they are angry. Markers might include sensations (e.g., feeling "hot"), indicators of physiological arousal (e.g., sweatiness, muscle tension) or actions (e.g., yelling). Next, anger-reducing techniques, such as deep breathing, are presented and practiced. Members are also taught to use "reminders"— self-statements designed to decrease arousal, such as "Take it easy, he didn't mean to bump into me on purpose." Group members are also encouraged to identify and use Skillstreaming techniques to solve social problems and avoid angry or aggressive displays. In later sessions, facilitators teach "self-evaluation," in which adolescents review their handling of a conflict, reward themselves for successfully avoiding anger, or find ways to deal with social problems more effectively in the future.

The final element of ART is *moral reasoning training* (Arbuthnot & Gordon, 1986; Gibbs, 2010). Facilitators provide the group with a relatable story in which an adolescent encounters a moral dilemma (e.g., cheating, stealing, fighting). Group members discuss questions posed by facilitators, which highlight cognitive distortions, moral values, and the rights and feelings of others. During the course of discussion, facilitators challenge group members to adopt more mature, less egocentric moral decision-making.

Overall, youths who participate in ART show improvements in their ability to learn and apply social skills compared to comparison youths who do not receive ART. Furthermore, in most studies, youths who receive ART also show increased anger control, improved moral reasoning, and decreased recidivism. Currently, ART is classified as a model program by the United States Office of Juvenile Justice and Delinquency Prevention (Glick & Gibbs, 2011; Weis & Pucke, 2013).

Review:

- PSST is a cognitive intervention in which disruptive youths learn ways to perceive, interpret, and respond to interpersonal problems in more systematic, less biased ways.
- MST is an intensive form of family- and community-based treatment for adolescents with serious conduct problems. It consists of family therapy, academic/school support, and increased parental monitoring.
- ART is a multimodal, cognitive–behavioral treatment designed for adolescents with disruptive, aggressive, and antisocial behavior. It consists of Skillstreaming, anger control training, and moral reasoning training.

KEY TERMS

Adolescent-onset conduct disorder (CD): A developmental pathway in which youths show conduct problems prior to age 10 years; associated with conduct problems during adolescence which decreases in adulthood; associated with long-term behavior and employment problems

Aggression Replacement Training (ART): A multimodal, cognitive-behavioral treatment designed for adolescents with histories of disruptive, aggressive, and antisocial behavior; consists of (1) Skillstreaming, (2) anger control training, and (3) moral reasoning training

Antisocial personality disorder (ASPD): A *DSM-5* personality disorder characterized by a pervasive pattern of disregard for and violation of the rights of others; signs and symptoms include impulsive, irritable, and aggressive behavior; reckless or illegal acts, lack of remorse, and failure to live up to social obligations

Attributions: Reasons that an individual gives for observed causal relationships

Callous and unemotional traits: A term used by some researchers to describe a lack of empathy, absence of guilt, and generally uncaring attitudes toward others; in *DSM-5* largely replaced by the specifier "with limited prosocial emotions"

Childhood-onset conduct disorder (CD): A developmental pathway in which youths first begin showing CD symptoms prior to age 10 years; associated with persistent conduct problems through adolescence and risk of antisocial behavior in adulthood

Coercive family process: A type of parent–child interaction in which parents negative reinforce children for noncompliance or defiance while children negative reinforce parents for giving in to their demands or tantrums; associated with the emergence of conduct problems

Conduct disorder (CD): A *DSM-5* disorder characterized by a repetitive and persistent pattern of behavior in which the basic rights of others or major age-appropriate societal norms or rules are violated; signs and symptoms include (1) aggression, (2) property destruction, (3) deceitfulness or theft, and (4) serious rule violations

Limited prosocial emotions: A specifier used in *DSM-5* to describe youths with CD who also show two of the following: (1) lack of remorse or guilt, (2) callousness or lack of empathy, (3) lack of concern about performance, and (4) shallow or deficient affect

Covert symptoms of CD: Secretive antisocial behaviors that usually do not involve physical aggression; examples include breaking and entering, burglarizing, lying, skipping school, and running away from home

Deviancy training: A tendency for peers to reinforce antisocial behavior and ignore, or not reinforce, prosocial behavior

Dual failure model: Posits that conduct problems cause children to experience failure in two important areas of functioning: peer relationships and academics; failure in these areas contributes to depression

Dunedin Multidisciplinary Health and Development Study: A 40-year prospective, longitudinal study investigating the long-term mental health outcomes of New Zealand youths

Emotional reactivity: Intense, negative emotional reactions followed by problems with self-soothing; associated with reactive aggression

Hostile attribution bias: Biased social information processing shown by some youths with conduct problems characterized by a tendency to interpret others' benign behavior as hostile or threatening

Hostile–coercive parenting behavior: Harsh disciplinary tactics, such as yelling, arguing, spanking, hitting, criticizing or using guilt and shame

Incredible Years program: A series of behavioral modules designed for parents, teachers, and children with conduct problems; relies on instruction by the therapist, in-session activities, and videos modeling desired skills or behaviors

Low emotional arousal: Low autonomic activity in response to environmental stimuli (e.g., low resting heart rate, reduced brain activity, low skin conductivity); associated with a willingness to engage in high-risk, pleasurable activities and reduced sensitivity to punishment

MAOA gene: A gene that codes for an enzyme that regulates dopamine, norepinephrine, and serotonin; mutations are associated with the emergence of conduct problems if triggered by stressor life events

Masked depression: A largely discredited theory that assumed that children's conduct problems were caused by underlying, hidden feelings of depression

Multisystemic Therapy (MST): An intensive form of family- and community-based treatment effective for adolescents with more serious conduct problems; consists of (a) family therapy, (b) academic/school support, and (c) increased parental monitoring to avoid deviant peers

Oppositional defiant disorder (ODD): A *DSM-5* disorder characterized by a pattern of (1) angry of irritable mood, (2) argumentative or defiant behavior, and/or (3) vindictiveness toward others; lasts at least 6 months and causes impairment or distress to self or others

Overt symptoms of CD: Observable and confrontational antisocial acts; examples include physical assault, robbery, bullying

Parent–child interaction therapy (PCIT): A variation of PMT in which parents and children are coached by therapists as they interact; focuses on PRIDE skills to improve the quality of positive interactions

Parent management training (PMT): A behavioral intervention designed to help parents attend to and reinforce adaptive child behaviors and reduce noncompliant or defiant actions using noncoercive discipline; examples include PMTO and Defiant Children

Parental monitoring: The degree to which caregivers (a) are aware of their child's whereabouts, activities, and peers; (b) set appropriate limits on their child's activities; and (c) consistently discipline their children when they violate these limits

Premack's principle: A behavioral heuristic that asserts that a child will be more motivated to perform an undesirable activity if he knows that he will be able to partake in a more desirable activity as a consequence

Proactive aggression Physical violence or property destruction deliberately enacted to obtain a desired goal

Problem-solving skills training (PSST): A cognitive intervention in which disruptive youths learn ways to perceive, interpret, and respond to interpersonal problems in more effective (less biased) ways

Psychopathy: A term used by some mental health professionals to describe a syndrome characterized by antisocial behavior, impulsivity, shallow affect, narcissism, and disregard for the suffering of others; also associated with callousness, a lack of emotional responsiveness, and superficial charm

Reactive aggression: Physical violence or property destruction in response to threat, a frustrating event, or provocation

Relational aggression: A form of aggression, disproportionately shown by girls, in which youths harm others' mood, self-concept, or social status by damaging or manipulating interpersonal relationships

Selective affiliation: A tendency of peer-rejected children to seek out other rejected youths for their peer network

Social information–processing model: A series of six steps that children use to solve social dilemmas or disputes; aggressive youths often show biases or deficiencies in these steps

CRITICAL THINKING EXERCISES

1. Why is CD more commonly diagnosed among adolescent boys than adolescent girls? Are the diagnostic criteria for CD gender biased? Should they be changed?

2. In what way can spanking be a form of positive punishment? Positive reinforcement?

3. David is a 10-year-old boy. During recess, David is hit in the head by a kickball, leaving mud and grass stains on his face and shirt. He notices that the ball was kicked by Goliath, an older and larger boy who was playing kickball with his friends nearby. According to social information–processing theory, what steps will David go through to solve this social problem? If David showed a hostile attributional bias in his problem-solving, how might he interpret and respond to the situation?

4. Imagine that you have received a grant from your city to revitalize and redevelop an impoverished neighborhood. What three changes might you make to decrease the prevalence of conduct problems among youths who live there?

5. Monica participated in 20 sessions of PCIT with her 5-year-old son, Augustine. After treatment, Augustine showed a marked decrease in behavior problems at home but *not* at school. Why?

TEST YOURSELF AND EXTEND YOUR LEARNING

Videos, flash cards, and links to online resources for this chapter are available to students online. Teachers also have access to PowerPoint slides to guide lectures, case studies to prompt classroom discussions, and exam questions. Visit www.abnormalchildpsychology.org.

CHAPTER 10

Substance Use Disorders in Adolescents

10.1 SUBSTANCE USE AND SUBSTANCE USE DISORDERS

Adolescents' involvement with alcohol and other drugs falls on a continuum from complete abstinence to chronic use and dependence. Many teens experiment with cigarettes, alcohol, and (perhaps) marijuana; relatively few develop problematic patterns of use that lead to distress or impairment (Bukstein, 2015).

When they do occur, substance use problems carry immediate and delayed risks to adolescents' health and well-being. In the short-term, problematic use of alcohol and other drugs can lead to motor vehicle accidents, risk-taking, victimization, and unintentional injuries. More prolonged use can contribute to relationship problems with parents and peers; withdrawal from sports, clubs, and other extracurricular activities; and poor school performance. Long-term risks include chronic health problems, educational and employment problems, and anxiety and mood disorders (Heath, Lynskey, & Waldron, 2010).

Adolescence is an important developmental period for the emergence of substance use disorders. Youths who develop moderate to severe substance use disorders by age 18 show higher lifetime consumption of alcohol and other drugs, more risky patterns of substance use, and poor social–emotional and occupational outcomes. In contrast, individuals who avoid substance use problems during adolescence and early adulthood have very low rates of developing such problems later in life (Bukstein, 2015).

In this chapter, we will focus on the *Diagnostic and Statistical Manual of Mental Disorders, Fifth Edition* (DSM-5; American Psychiatric Association, 2013) conceptualization of substance use disorders. We will then focus on two substances often used by adolescents, alcohol and marijuana, and use them as models for understanding the other substance use disorders. We will examine the effects of these substances on adolescents' development and learn about ways to prevent and treat alcohol and cannabis use disorders in adolescents.

What Are Substance Use Disorders?

Overview

People are diagnosed with substance use disorder when they show a problematic pattern of alcohol or other drug use that interferes with their daily functioning or causes significant psychological distress. Each substance is associated with a particular cluster of behavioral, cognitive, and physiological signs and symptoms. People with substance use disorders show these signs and symptoms yet persist in using the substance(s) that causes them (American Psychiatric Association, 2013).

DSM-5 uses the term *substance* to refer to alcohol, drugs, and medications that can be abused. People can develop a substance use disorder for several different classes of substances:

Alcohol is a depressant that enhances gamma-aminobutyric acid (GABA), the brain's primary inhibitory neurotransmitter. Alcohol also blocks glutamate, a major excitatory neurotransmitter. It produces a biphasic effect on the nervous system, resulting in euphoria and sociability in low doses and slurred speech, coordination problems, and cognitive impairment in higher doses.

Cannabis is a naturally occurring drug that contains delta-9-tetrahydrocannabinol (THC). When ingested, it affects a wide range of neurotransmitters and brain areas. Its effects can include euphoria, anxiety reduction, unusual perceptions and thoughts, slowed reaction time, increased appetite, and low motivation for goal-directed activity.

Hallucinogens include substances such as lysergic acid diethylamide (LSD), psilocybin ("mushrooms"), and 3, 4-methylenedioxymethamphetamine (MDMA, "ecstasy"). These medications typically bind to serotonin receptors and stimulate the locus coeruleus, an area of the brain that regulates many other brain regions. These substances typically cause unusual perceptions and thoughts, distortions in sense of time, disorientation, and anxiety reduction. They can also elicit anxiety, depression, paranoia, and impaired judgment and decision-making.

Inhalants include substances, such as gasoline, glue, paint thinners, spray paints, and household cleansers. When ingested, ingredients in these substances produce a wide range of effects on the brain and central nervous system. Effects include euphoria, anxiety reduction, and passivity. However, they can also produce disorientation, slurred speech, slow reaction time, poor judgment, and death.

Opioids include natural opioids (e.g., morphine), semisynthetics (e.g., heroin), and synthetic drugs that act like these substances (e.g., codeine, oxycodone, fentanyl). Synthetic opioids are often prescribed for pain reduction. Besides alleviating pain, they may produce euphoria, reduce anxiety, or cause disorientation. Tolerance can develop quickly. Withdrawal symptoms can be severe and include dysphoria, nausea and vomiting, insomnia, muscle aches, and fever.

Sedatives, hypnotics, and anxiolytics include medications used to treat anxiety and insomnia (e.g., benzodiazepines, barbiturates). They tend to augment GABA, the brain's primary inhibitory neurotransmitter. Their immediate effect is drowsiness and anxiety reduction. Tolerance can develop quickly. Withdrawal symptoms include autonomic hyper-arousal (e.g., sweating, rapid pulse), hand tremor, insomnia, agitation, and anxiety.

Stimulants include medications and drugs that typically enhance dopaminergic activity in the central nervous system. They include medications used to treat ADHD, such as amphetamine and methylphenidate, as well as illegal drugs, such as cocaine. Stimulants have immediate effects on the central nervous system, producing extreme euphoria, energy, and sociability. However, they can also produce anxiety, agitation, and anger; racing heart; shallow breathing; and cognitive problems.

Tobacco contains the chemical nicotine, which has both stimulating and anxiety-reducing effects. Short-term use can result in pleasure, enhanced concentration, reduced tension and anxiety, and decreased restlessness and agitation. Prolonged use is associated with health problems and dependence.

People are diagnosed with a substance use disorder for each drug that causes distress and/or impairment (Chassin, Colder, Hussong, & Sher, 2016). For example, an adolescent who abuses alcohol might be diagnosed with alcohol use disorder whereas another adolescent who abuses marijuana might be diagnosed with cannabis use disorder. Individuals can be diagnosed with multiple substance use disorders. The diagnostic criteria for substance use disorders are the same for alcohol, cannabis, and other substances. Consequently, in this chapter, we will focus on alcohol and marijuana use in adolescents as a model for understanding and treating substance use disorders more generally.

Substance Use Disorders

According to *DSM-5*, a substance use disorder is a maladaptive pattern of substance use leading to clinically significant impairment or distress (see Table 10.1). Individuals with substance use disorders, including children and adolescents, show at least 2 of 11 possible symptoms within a 12-month period. The symptoms can be organized into four clusters: (1) impaired control, (2) social impairment, (3) risky use, and (4) pharmacological criteria (American Psychiatric Association, 2013).

Impaired Control

- *Use in large amounts.* Adolescents might initially try alcohol or marijuana at a party or with friends. Over time, they might use more frequently or consume greater amounts of these substances than originally intended.
- *Problems cutting down.* Adolescents experience problems stopping or reducing their substance use despite a desire to do so. They may find themselves drinking on

Table 10.1   Diagnostic Criteria for Substance Use Disorder

A. A problematic pattern of substance use leading to clinically significant impairment or distress, as manifested by at least two of the following, occurring within a 12-month period:

1. The substance is taken in larger amounts or over a longer period than was intended.

2. There is a persistent desire or unsuccessful efforts to cut down or control substance use.

3. A great deal of time is spent in activities necessary to obtain the substance, use the substance, or recover from its effects.

4. Craving, or a strong desire to use the substance.

5. Recurrent substance use resulting in a failure to fulfill major role obligations at work, school, or home.

6. Continued substance use despite having persistent or recurrent social or interpersonal problems caused by or exacerbated by the effects of the substance.

7. Important social, occupational, or recreational activities are given up or reduced because of substance use.

8. Recurrent substance use in situations in which it is physically hazardous.

9. Substance use is continued despite knowledge of having a persistent or recurrent physical or psychological problem that is likely to have been caused or exacerbated by the substance.

10. Tolerance, as defined by either of the following:

    a. A need for markedly increased amounts of the substance to achieve intoxication or desired effect.

    b. A markedly diminished effect with continued use of the same amount of the substance.

11. Withdrawal, as manifested by either of the following:

    a. The characteristic withdrawal syndrome for the substance.

    b. The substance (or a closely related substance) is taken to relieve or avoid withdrawal symptoms.

Specify if:

In early remission: After full criteria for a substance use disorder were previously met, none of the criteria for a substance use disorder have been met for at least 3 months but for less than 12 months (with the exception that criterion A4 , "craving, or a strong desire to use the substance," may be met).

In sustained remission: After full criteria for a substance use disorder were previously met, none of the criteria for a substance use disorder have been met at any time during a period of 12 months or longer (with the exception that criterion A4 , "craving, or a strong desire to use the substance," may be met).

Specify current severity:

Mild: Presence of 2-3 symptoms.

Moderate: Presence of 4-5 symptoms.

Severe: Presence of 6 or more symptoms.

Source: Reprinted with permission from the *Diagnostic and Statistical Manual of Mental Disorders, Fifth Edition* (Copyright 2013). American Psychiatric Association.

days they did not want to (e.g., before an important test) or be unable to refuse drinks at parties.

- *Time spent obtaining the substance or recovering from its effects.* Adolescents spend a great deal of time acquiring alcohol or recovering from its effects. Time spent in alcohol-related activities begins to interfere with their day-to-day school, peer, and extracurricular activities.

- *Craving.* Adolescents might experience a strong desire or intense urge to drink or use other drugs. Certain people (e.g., friends who drink), places (e.g., a party where alcohol is available), or situations (e.g., a stressful day) can prompt these cravings.

Social Impairment

- *Recurrent failure to fulfill major role obligations.* Adolescents who abuse alcohol or other drugs may miss school or work because of their substance use. They may forget to complete assignments or neglect to study for tests, resulting in low grades. They may be suspended from school for alcohol or other drug use or possession.

- *Continued use despite recurrent interpersonal problems.* Adolescents who abuse alcohol and other drugs may argue with parents about their substance use or problems in school. Adolescents may experience deterioration in their peer relationships. They may physically fight with others while intoxicated.
- *Important activities are given up.* Adolescents might feel as though they have no time for sports, clubs, or hobbies they formerly enjoyed. They may also experience decreased energy or motivation for these activities. They may abandon peers who do not drink or use other drugs.

Risky Use

- *Recurrent use in physically hazardous situations.* Adolescents might drink and drive or repeatedly place themselves in risky social situations while under the influence of alcohol or other drugs.
- *Continued use despite physical or psychological problems.* In some cases, adolescents recognize the negative effects that their drinking and other drug use has on their health, mood, relationships, and academic functioning. Nevertheless, they may continue to drink or use other drugs despite these problems.

Pharmacological Criteria

- *Tolerance.* Tolerance occurs when the person (a) needs more of the substance to achieve intoxication or (b) the same amount of the substance produces diminished effects over repeated use. Adolescents might discover that they need to drink more beer to achieve a "buzz" at parties or smoke more marijuana to experience a reduction in anxiety.
- *Withdrawal.* Withdrawal occurs when the person (a) experiences negative physiological symptoms when they stop or reduce substance use or (b) takes a different substance to avoid these negative symptoms. For example, adolescents who use marijuana for many years may develop withdrawal symptoms if they discontinue use. Symptoms might include increased anxiety, agitation, irritability, and concentration problems.

The pharmacological criteria for substance use disorders can vary considerably, depending on (a) the class of substance and (b) the person using the drug. For example, depressants, like alcohol, often produce withdrawal symptoms of anxiety, agitation, and insomnia. In contrast, stimulants, like methamphetamine, often produce withdrawal symptoms of daytime drowsiness and fatigue. Furthermore, people show great variability in their sensitivity to various classes of substances and their likelihood of developing tolerance and withdrawal symptoms. Some people use for years without developing tolerance whereas others develop tolerance almost immediately (American Psychiatric Association, 2013).

If someone meets diagnostic criteria for a substance use disorder, clinicians specify the severity of the problem. Severity is determined by the number of criteria met: two to three criteria (mild), four to five criteria (moderate), or six or more criteria (severe). Clinicians can also indicate if the person's symptoms are in remission—that is, symptoms used to be present but no longer exist. A person in "early remission" has remained symptom free (except for cravings) for 3 to 11 months. A person in "sustained remission" has remained symptom free (except for cravings) for 12 months or more.

Substance use disorders are diagnosed only when adolescents repeatedly use alcohol and other drugs in a manner that causes significant distress or impairment. Substance use disorders, therefore, can be differentiated from substance use by their (a) recurrence and (b) effects on adolescents' functioning. A single episode of "drinking and driving," although serious, is not sufficient to diagnose an adolescent with alcohol use disorder. The behavior must be *recurrent* and at least one other symptom must be present to merit the diagnosis. Similarly, repeated marijuana use with friends, although concerning, is probably not sufficient to diagnose an adolescent with cannabis use disorder. The behavior must *impair* the adolescent's health or social–emotional functioning to merit a diagnosis (Heath et al., 2010). Consider Erica, a girl with an emerging alcohol use disorder.

Substance-Induced Disorders

Substance use disorders are characterized by the persistent use of alcohol and other drugs despite behavioral, cognitive, and physiological symptoms that cause distress or impairment. By definition, substance use disorders describe symptoms that emerge only after continued substance use.

In contrast, substance-induced disorders describe substance-specific syndromes caused by either the ingestion of alcohol/drugs or their withdrawal. *DSM-5* recognizes three substance-induced disorders: (1) substance intoxication, (2) substance withdrawal, and (3) substance-induced mental disorder.

Intoxication is defined as "a disturbance of perception, wakefulness, attention, thinking, judgment, psychomotor and/or interpersonal behavior" caused by the ingestion of a substance (American Psychiatric Association, 2013, p. 485). Usually, intoxication does not cause distress or impairment, such as when a person experiences a sense of relaxation and gregariousness after a few drinks at a party. However, if intoxication causes distress or impairment, the person can be diagnosed with substance intoxication. The specific symptoms of substance intoxication differ based on the drug. Table 10.2 presents common symptoms of alcohol and cannabis intoxication.

Withdrawal is defined as a "substance-specific problematic behavioral change . . . that is due to the cessation of, or reduction in, heavy and prolonged substance use" (American Psychiatric Association, 2013, p. 486). Withdrawal symptoms

Erica's Emerging Alcohol Problem

Erica is a 16-year-old girl who was referred to our clinic by the juvenile court after she was arrested for driving a car while intoxicated. Two weeks earlier, Erica had attended a party at her friend's house. She consumed approximately six alcoholic beverages and drove home. A police officer noticed Erica driving errati-cally, pulled her over, and determined that her blood alcohol level was .10. Erica was arrested. Her father made her spend the night in jail "to teach her a lesson."

Erica resented having to meet with her substance abuse counselor, Randy. She explained, "I don't know why I'm here. I'm not an addict, I don't use hard drugs, and I didn't do anything that a million other kids my age haven't done." Nevertheless, the judge ordered Erica to participate in a substance abuse eval-uation, 12 sessions of counseling, and community service.

Erica began drinking alcohol, at parties and on weekends with friends, when she was 14 years old. She said that she hated beer but liked sweet drinks. "I drink to relax and have fun with my friends," Erica said. "They call me Captain Cook because that's the kind of champagne I like. Drinking helps me unwind and have a good time." Erica admitted to also using marijuana at parties and other social gatherings but denied using other drugs.

"Has your drinking ever gotten in the way of your daily life?" asked Randy. Erica replied, "Not really, although I have been hungover a few times this year." Randy asked, "What about school?" Erica responded, "I guess my grades are lower now than when I started high school. But I think that's because I hang around with different kids than I used to. I don't think it's the drinking."

"What's your relationship with your mom and dad?" asked Randy. Erica replied, "It's fine. My mom's a doctor and my dad's an investment advisor, so they're pretty busy. As long as I bring home good grades and stay out of trouble, they leave me alone. Now they're on my case because of the arrest."

After the initial session, Erica stated, "I know I have to be here, and I'm really sorry for what I did, but I obviously don't have a drinking problem. Besides, I'm sure you have people worse off than me who really need your help." Randy responded, "Let's schedule an appointment for next week and talk some more."

can include changes in overt actions (e.g., pacing), emotions (e.g., anxiety), cognitions (e.g., unpleasant dreams), and physiological functioning (e.g., rapid heart rate, nausea). By definition, withdrawal symptoms are always problematic, causing distress or impairment in academic, occupational, or social functioning. The specific symptoms of substance withdrawal depend on the drug used.

Finally, a substance-induced mental disorder occurs when someone develops a mental health problem that is caused by the use or withdrawal of a substance. Any of the classes of substances can induce a mental disorder. Two are most common. First, depressants, such as alcohol, sedatives, and hypnotics (e.g., sleep medications), sometimes elicit depressive disorders after prolonged use, and anxiety dis-orders and insomnia upon withdrawal. Second, stimulants, such as amphetamine and cocaine, sometimes elicit psychotic disorders after their use and depressive disorders upon with-drawal. Indeed, certain adolescents are at risk for developing psychotic disorders, such as schizophrenia, after using stimu-lant medication (American Psychiatric Association, 2013).

Review:

- Substance use disorders are characterized by prob-lematic patterns of substance use leading to distress or impairment and characterized by (a) impaired control, (b) social problems, (c) risk-taking, and/or (d) tolerance or withdrawal. In *DSM-5*, individu-als are diagnosed based on the type of substance they use (i.e., alcohol use disorder, cannabis use disorder).
- Two features of substance use disorders are tolerance and withdrawal. Although many adolescents show tolerance for substances like cigarettes, alcohol, and marijuana, withdrawal symptoms are relatively rare in adolescents for these substances.
- Substance-induced disorders are a group of *DSM-5* disorders that describe syndromes caused by either the ingestion or withdrawal of specific substances. They include (1) substance intoxication, (2) sub-stance withdrawal, and (3) substance-induced mental disorders.

Table 10.2   Symptoms of Alcohol and Cannabis Intoxication and Withdrawal

	Alcohol	*Cannabis*
Intoxication	Psychological changes: labile mood, impaired judgment, inappropriate sexual/aggressive behavior	Psychological changes: euphoria, anxiety, sensation of slowed time, impaired coordination, impaired judgment, social withdrawal
	Slurred speech	Conjunctival injection[2]
	Incoordination	Increased appetite
	Unsteady gait	Dry mouth
	Nystagmus[1]	Tachycardia (i.e., increased heart rate)
	Impaired attention/memory	
	Stupor or coma	
Withdrawal	Autonomic hyperactivity	Irritability, anger, or aggression
	Increased hand tremor	Nervousness or anxiety
	Insomnia	Sleep difficulty
	Nausea or vomiting	Decreased appetite or weight loss
	Hallucinations	Restlessness
	Psychomotor agitation	Depressed mood
	Anxiety	Physical symptoms: abdominal pain, shakiness, sweating, fever, headaches
	Generalized tonic-clonic seizures	

Source: American Psychiatric Association (2013).

[1]Involuntary movement of the eyes resulting in jerky or saccadic movements while tracking an object.

[2]Reddening of the eyes due to increased prominence of the conjunctival blood vessels.

How Are Substance Use Disorders Different in Adolescents Than in Adults?

Key Differences

It is noteworthy that the *DSM-5* conceptualization of substance use disorder was developed with adults in mind. Recent research suggests that adolescent substance use and misuse differ in important ways from that of adults. Consequently, some experts have pointed out several limitations of the *DSM-5* criteria when they are applied to children and adolescents (Bukstein, 2015; Weis & Ross, 2015).

One criticism is that the *DSM-5* criteria are *developmentally insensitive*. Two of the most frequently occurring signs of alcohol use problems among adolescents are low grades and truancy. However, neither sign is included in the *DSM-5* diagnostic criteria. Consequently, some researchers have developed more developmentally appropriate criteria for adolescent substance use problems. These criteria include breaking curfew, lying to parents, showing a reduction in grades, and engaging in truancy (Wagner & Austin, 2006; Winters, Martin, & Chung, 2011).

A second concern is the possibility that some criteria are *overidentified in adolescents*, compared to adults.

Two studies (Harford, Grant, Yi, & Chen, 2005; Harford, Yi, Faden, & Chen, 2009) have compared the frequency of *DSM-5* symptoms in adolescents (12–17 years) versus adults (>25 years). Three symptoms were much more likely to be reported by adolescents and their families compared to adults: (1) tolerance, (2) time spent obtaining substances, and (3) substance use in hazardous situations (see Figure 10.1).

In adults, tolerance tends to occur after years of frequent drinking. The amount of alcohol adults need to consume to achieve the same level of intoxication gradually increases. However, because adolescents are typically new to drinking, tolerance may develop more rapidly. For example, a 14-year-old who drinks at a party might become intoxicated after only one or two beers. If his drinking persists for several weeks or months, he might need three or four beers to achieve the same euphoric mood state. "Tolerance" in adolescence, therefore, may be more easily achieved than tolerance in adulthood, leading to over-endorsement of this symptom by youths.

Similarly, adults who spend a great deal of time on substance-related activities tend to have chronic alcohol and other drug problems. For example, an adult who is dependent on prescription pain medication may spend considerable time convincing physicians to prescribe the

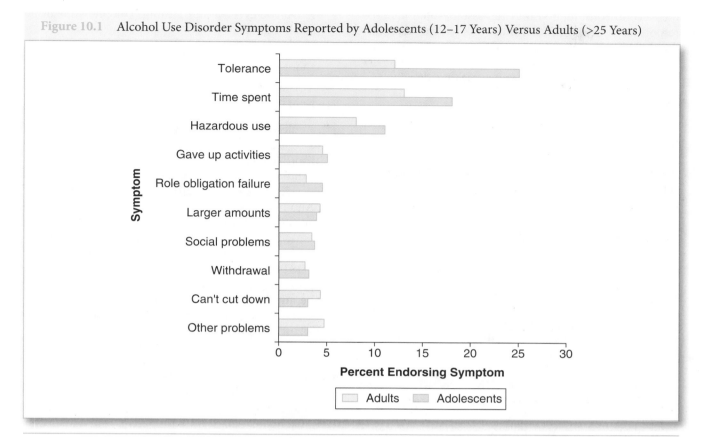

Source: Based on Harford and colleagues (2009).

Note: Adolescents are more likely than adults to report problems with tolerance, time spent acquiring alcohol, and hazardous alcohol use. Consequently, some experts worry that *DSM-5* criteria may overdiagnose adolescents.

medicine to him, steal and sell items to raise money to buy the drug, or purchase the medicine illegally. In contrast, adolescents who endorse this symptom tend to have less severe problems with alcohol and other drugs. Typically, adolescents endorse this criterion because they spend considerable time trying to access alcohol. For example, they may make fake IDs, try to find older friends who will buy alcohol for them, or steal alcohol from parents. These youths are much less likely to have serious substance use problems than adults who endorse this symptom.

Youths are also more likely than adults to report substance use in situations that might be hazardous. It is likely that youths are more likely to use substances in hazardous situations because of their increased probability of engaging in impulsive, high-rate behaviors in general. Youths may be more likely than adults to drive or engage in other high-risk behaviors while intoxicated because of their underdeveloped capacities for considering the long-term consequences of their actions (Leukefeld et al., 2015).

A third criticism of *DSM-5* criteria is that adolescents often show *different patterns of alcohol and other drug use* than adults (Ray & Dhawan, 2011; Wagner & Austin, 2006). For example, adolescent substance use, especially

alcohol use, is more episodic than alcohol use by adults. Most adolescents tend to drink in binges, especially at parties. They usually do not drink every day.

Adolescents also typically use a greater number of substances simultaneously than do adults. It is more common for adolescents to misuse alcohol and marijuana together than to misuse either substance alone. In contrast, most adults who show substance use problems have a single substance of choice.

Adolescents with substance use disorders are also more likely to show comorbid behavior problems than are adults with substance use disorders. Furthermore, adolescents are more likely to show disruptive and antisocial behaviors, whereas adults are more likely to develop mood and anxiety disorders associated with their substance use.

Finally, adolescents are more likely than adults to "outgrow" their substance use problems. Because of the great number of physiological and psychosocial changes that occur during adolescence, many adolescents show a gradual reduction in substance use by the time they reach early adulthood. For example, many older adolescents use alcohol fairly regularly, especially during their late teens and early 20s. However, most young adults dramatically reduce their alcohol consumption after they assume more adultlike responsibilities (e.g., gain full-time employment, have children). Although all serious substance use problems merit treatment regardless of the person's age, adolescents usually show a different course of substance use than do adults.

Assessing Substance Use Disorders in Adolescents

Clinicians often rely on questionnaires or semistructured interviews to assess substance use. One simple screening measure, often used with adults suspected of alcohol use problems, is the CAGE acronym (Ewing, 1984). The acronym CAGE reminds clinicians of the four domains of alcohol use problems:

> C: Have you ever tried to CUT DOWN on your drinking?
>
> A: Have people ANNOYED you by criticizing your drinking?
>
> G: Have you ever felt GUILTY about your drinking?
>
> E: Have you ever felt you needed a drink first thing in the morning (as an EYE-OPENER) to steady your nerves or get rid of a hangover?

Adults who respond affirmatively to two or more CAGE questions should be further assessed for an alcohol use disorder.

Although the CAGE questionnaire is an effective screening measure for substance use problems in adults, it is less applicable for adolescents suspected of substance use problems. Indeed, CAGE does not assess many features of adolescent substance use, such as binge drinking, drinking in hazardous situations (e.g., while driving), or experiencing academic or peer problems because of continued alcohol use (Rumpf, Wohlert, Freyer-Adam, Grothues, & Bischof, 2012). Consequently, clinicians might use a different screening tool to assess adolescent substance use.

One option is the CRAFFT assessment method (Knight, Shrier, Bravender, Farrell, Vander Bilt, & Shaffer, 1999). The CRAFFT questionnaire assesses substance use problems most likely to be exhibited by adolescents and includes questions about alcohol, marijuana, and other drugs.

First, the questionnaire asks if the adolescent has consumed alcohol, smoked marijuana, or other drugs in the past 12 months. Then, the adolescent answers a series of questions reflecting the acronym CRAFFT:

> C: Have you ever ridden in a CAR driven by someone (including yourself) who was "high" or had been using alcohol or drugs?
>
> R: Do you ever use alcohol or drugs to RELAX, feel better about yourself, or fit in?
>
> A: Do you ever use alcohol or drugs while you are ALONE?

> F: Do you ever FORGET things you did while using alcohol or drugs?
>
> F: Do your family or FRIENDS ever tell you that you should cut down on your drinking or drug use?
>
> T: Have you ever gotten into TROUBLE while you were using alcohol or drugs?

Adolescents who answer yes to any of the six CRAFFT items should be more carefully assessed for a substance use disorder. Overall, the CRAFFT has adequate reliability and validity as a brief screening measure for adolescents (Dhalla, Zumbo, & Poole, 2011).

Another questionnaire that is useful in assessing adolescent substance use disorders is the Alcohol, Smoking, and Substance Involvement Screening Test (ASSIST; National Institute on Drug Abuse, 2013). One advantage of ASSIST is that it screens for a wide range of substance use problems. A second strength of ASSIST is that it can be administered to both youths and their parents. Gathering data from both parents and adolescents is important because youths sometimes deny or minimize the frequency and severity of their alcohol and other drug use. Furthermore, parents are sometimes not knowledgeable about the extensiveness of their child's substance use. Indeed, the overall agreement between parent-reported and adolescent-reported alcohol use is approximately 22%. Therefore, data from both parents and adolescents are necessary to obtain the most complete picture of youths' use of substances (Delaney-Black et al., 2010).

The ASSIST asks parents and adolescents to independently report the frequency of adolescents' alcohol and other drug use over the previous 2 weeks (see Table 10.3). Elevated ratings could indicate a substance use disorder (Humeniuk, Henry-Edwards, Ali, Poznyak, & Monteiro, 2010).

Review:

- Adolescents with substance use problems tend to have academic difficulties and engage in truancy. However, these signs are not part of the *DSM-5* criteria for substance use disorder.
- Adolescents are more likely than adults to show tolerance, to spend large amounts of time obtaining substances, and to use substances in hazardous situations.
- Adolescents are more likely than adults to use substances episodically, and to use multiple substances simultaneously.
- The CRAFFT and ASSIST are useful to screen adolescents for substance use problems.

What Disorders Are Associated With Adolescent Substance Use Problems?

Approximately 50% of adolescents in the community with substance use disorders show at least one other mental disorder. Among adolescents referred to treatment, comorbidity ranges from 60% to 90% (Bukstein, 2015).

Table 10.3   Dimensions of the Alcohol, Smoking, and Substance Involvement Screening Test (ASSIST)

During the past 2 weeks, how often did you/your child . . .

    Have an alcoholic beverage?

    Have four or more drinks in a single day?

    Smoke a cigarette or use chewing tobacco?

During the past 2 weeks, how often did you/your child use any of the following medicines without a doctor's prescription or in greater amounts or longer than prescribed?

    Painkillers (like Vicodin)?

    Stimulants (like Ritalin, Adderall)?

    Sedatives or tranquilizers (like sleeping pills)?

During the past 2 weeks, how often did you/your child use any of the following drugs . . .

    Steroids?

    Marijuana?

    Cocaine or crack?

    Club drugs (like ecstasy)?

    Hallucinogens (like LSD)?

    Heroin?

    Inhalants (like glue)?

    Methamphetamine (like speed)?

Source: Based on National Institute on Drug Abuse (2013).

Behavior Problems

ADHD is the most frequently occurring psychiatric condition shown by adolescents with substance use disorders (Dennis et al., 2002, 2004). Approximately 15% to 30% of adolescents with ADHD eventually develop a substance use disorder. Conversely, most (50%–75%) adolescents with substance use disorders have ADHD. Adolescents with ADHD and substance use problems show more severe symptoms of both disorders and greater impairment in overall functioning. Their substance use tends to be longer and more resistant to treatment than that of individuals without ADHD. After treatment for substance use problems, youths with ADHD are more than twice as likely to relapse compared to adolescents without ADHD (Latimer, Ernst, Hennessey, Stinchfield, & Winters, 2004).

At least three hypotheses have been offered to explain the high comorbidity of substance use disorders and ADHD (Wilson & Levin, 2005). First, ADHD and substance use problems can have a common genetic or biological cause. For example, adolescents with both disorders display problems with executive functioning and behavioral inhibition that could stem from their genetic makeup. Second, both ADHD and substance use problems are correlated with other disruptive behavior disorders. For example, children with ADHD show increased likelihood of developing ODD and CD later in their development. ODD and CD, in turn, are associated with adolescent substance use problems. It is possible that ADHD, ODD and CD, and substance use problems are part of a spectrum of externalizing behavior that unfolds across development. Third, symptoms of ADHD could increase the probability of substance use problems. For example, individuals with ADHD often show poor decision-making, social problem-solving, and peer relations. These problems can cause peer rejection, social isolation, and depression. Rejected children with ADHD might use substances to gain acceptance from peers or to cope with feelings of loneliness.

Depression and Anxiety

Approximately 25% to 50% of adolescents with substance use problems are depressed. Longitudinal data indicate that most adolescents do not use alcohol and other drugs primarily to cope with depression. Instead, mood disorders often develop after the onset of adolescents' substance use problems. Comorbid depression and substance use problems can sometimes be explained by shared genetic and psychosocial risk factors, as well (Goodwin, Fergusson, & Horwood, 2004).

Adolescents with substance use problems show greater likelihood of suicidal thoughts, suicide attempts, and suicide completion than their counterparts without substance use disorders (Kaminer & Bukstein, 2005). Mood problems, especially depression, associated with substance use partially account for the relationship between substance use and suicidal ideation. However, at least one study showed that the likelihood of suicide attempts remained elevated even after controlling for co-occurring depression (Wu et al., 2005). It is possible that alcohol and other drugs increase the likelihood of adolescent suicide by producing feelings of dysphoria, by lowering adolescents' inhibitions against self-harm, and by increasing impulsive and risky decision-making.

Approximately 10% to 40% of adolescents with substance use problems have comorbid anxiety (Kaminer & Bukstein, 2005). The relationship between substance use and anxiety is complex. Some anxiety disorders usually precede the development of adolescents' substance use problems. For example, some adolescents use alcohol and other drugs to cope with social anxiety or unwanted memories of trauma. Other anxiety disorders usually develop after the onset of substance use problems. For example, chronic use of alcohol can produce a gradual increase in worry and generalized anxiety.

Psychotic Disorders

Three large community-based studies have demonstrated an association between adolescent marijuana use and psychotic symptoms later in life (Crome & Bloor, 2005). Adolescents who regularly used marijuana were more likely to report psychotic symptoms (e.g., hallucinations, delusions) or develop schizophrenia in late adolescence or early adulthood compared to adolescents who did not use marijuana. The association between marijuana use and psychotic symptoms could not be explained by adolescents' levels of psychological distress. Therefore, it is unlikely that adolescents who eventually showed psychotic symptoms used marijuana to treat early symptoms of psychosis. Instead, the data suggest that repeated marijuana use may increase the likelihood of psychotic symptoms, especially among those adolescents who have a genetic predisposition toward schizophrenia.

Review:

- ADHD is the most frequently occurring comorbid disorder. Between 15% and 30% of youths with ADHD develop substance use problems, whereas 50% to 75% of adolescents with substance use problems have a history of ADHD.
- Between 25% and 50% of youths with substance use problems have depression. Usually, depression arises after the onset of adolescents' substance use problems.
- Marijuana use may elicit psychotic symptoms in some individuals who have a high genetic risk for developing schizophrenia.

How Common Are Substance Use Problems Among Adolescents?
Prevalence of Adolescent Substance Use

The best data regarding adolescent substance use comes from the Monitoring the Future study (MTF; Johnston, O'Malley, Miech, Bachman, & Schulenberg, 2016b; Miech, Johnston, O'Malley, Bachman, & Schulenberg, 2016). In this study, researchers collect data regarding adolescents' attitudes about alcohol and other dugs as well as their overt behavior. In recent years, approximately 50,000 youths in 8th, 10th, and 12th grades have completed anonymous surveys. Their data allow us to determine normative substance use throughout adolescence and see trends in adolescents' substance use over the past 30 years.

Recent data indicate that adolescent alcohol use is common. By their senior year in high school, nearly 75% of adolescents have used alcohol at some point in their lives, approximately 58% have used alcohol in the past year, and almost one-third have used alcohol in the past 30 days. A sizable minority of younger adolescents also report alcohol use. Approximately 35% of students in eighth grade report trying alcohol at some point in their lives, while 10% report alcohol use in the previous month (see).

Marijuana use is also fairly widespread, especially among older adolescents. Approximately one-third of high school seniors have tried marijuana in the past year; almost 21% have used it within the past month. Marijuana use is less common among younger adolescents. The prevalence of cigarette smoking resembles that of marijuana.

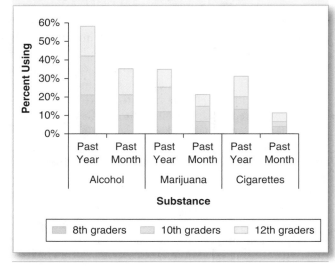

Figure 10.2 Although occasional alcohol consumption is normative for older adolescents, only about one-third of high school seniors have used alcohol in the past month. Similarly, only 20% have used marijuana and 10% have used cigarettes in the past month.

Source: From Miech and colleagues (2016).

Although many adolescents report having tried alcohol and marijuana, most adolescents do not try other illicit drugs. Figure 10.3 shows the percentage of 12th graders who report using other illicit substances in the past year. Notice that the x-axis of this graph extends from 0% to 8%; relatively few high school seniors report using these "harder" drugs.

Interestingly, adolescents are more likely to misuse prescription medication than other illicit drugs. The most frequently misused prescription medications are amphetamines used to treat ADHD (e.g., Adderall, Dexedrine) and prescription pain medications. Adolescents typically obtain these medications from peers or parents, respectively.

In general, adolescent alcohol use has decreased over the past two decades (Johnston, O'Malley, Miech, Bachman, & Schulenberg, 2016a). Among high school seniors, the prevalence of alcohol use in the previous month decreased from 51% in 1995 to 35% today. Similarly, the prevalence of cigarette smoking among high school seniors has decreased dramatically from 33% in 1995 to 11% today.

In contrast, the prevalence of other drug use has remained relatively stable from 23% in 1995 to 24% today. Closer inspection shows a moderate decline in most "hard" drug use, a slight increase in marijuana use in jurisdictions where it has been made legal for adults, and a modest increase in the misuse of prescription medication (Boyd, Veliz, & McCabe, 2015).

Altogether, data from MTF indicate that alcohol use during adolescence is developmentally normative. Furthermore, marijuana use by older adolescents is fairly common, with almost half of 12th-grade students admitting to trying marijuana. Besides alcohol and marijuana, the illicit drugs most frequently used by adolescents appear to be prescription medications. Use of other drugs, such as hallucinogens, cocaine, and heroin, is uncommon. These findings show that adolescent substance use is largely opportunistic. Most adolescents obtain alcohol, marijuana, and prescription drugs from friends, classmates, and family.

Prevalence of Adolescent Substance Use Disorders

What about substance use disorders? Studies assessing prevalence have yielded inconsistent findings. Results vary depending on the sample of adolescents studied, the method of questioning, and the researcher's definition of "problematic" use.

One method of defining substance use problems is to use *DSM* criteria. When researchers use *DSM* criteria, the prevalence of mild substance use disorder among adolescents in the community ranges from 2% to 9%, while the

Figure 10.3 Few high school seniors have used illicit drugs (other than marijuana) in the past year. Amphetamines (e.g., Adderall, Dexedrine) are the most frequently misused prescription medication followed by prescription narcotics (e.g., pain killers).

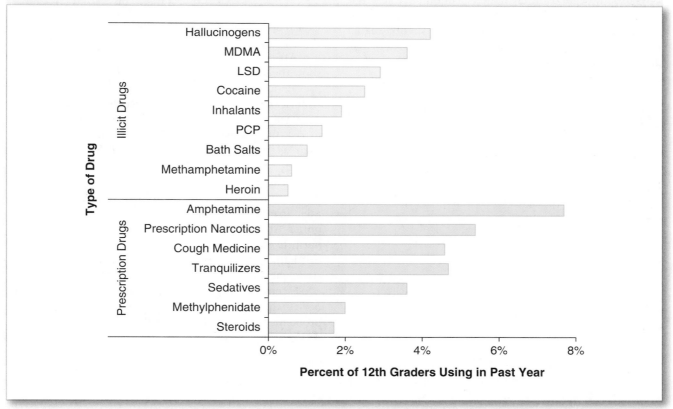

Source: From Johnston and colleagues (2016b).

prevalence of moderate or severe substance use disorder among adolescents in the community ranges from 1% to 5% (Bukstein, 2015; Weis & Ross, 2015).

A second method of identifying substance use problems is to base classification on the frequency of use (see Figure 10.4). For example, many researchers believe that daily use of alcohol or marijuana for 1 month or longer indicates a substance use disorder. Using this criterion, almost 3% of high school seniors have alcohol use problems and 3% to 4% report problems with marijuana or cigarettes, respectively.

We can also define alcohol use problems in terms of binge drinking. Binge drinking is often associated with increased intoxication, risk-taking behavior, and many of the harmful effects of alcohol. Unfortunately, binge drinking is fairly common among adolescents. Approximately 18% of high school seniors admit to binge drinking in the past 2 weeks, while 5% of eighth-grade students admit to bingeing (see Figure 10.4). Interestingly, there is a moderate, inverse relationship between binge drinking and perceived risk associated with bingeing. Adolescents who binge the most are least likely to view their binges as dangerous (Johnston et al., 2016a; Miech et al., 2016).

Gender and Ethnic Differences

Gender

Patterns of substance use differ slightly for boys and girls. Boys usually begin using cigarettes, alcohol, and marijuana at earlier ages than girls. At any age, the percentage of boys who have tried any of these substances is slightly higher than the percentage of girls. Boys are also more likely than girls to binge drink, to engage in dangerous activities as a result of their substance use, and to get into trouble at school because of alcohol or other drugs (Johnston et al., 2016b).

Gender differences in the rates of substance use disorders are less clear. Some research indicates that adolescent boys show greater prevalence of substance use disorders than girls. For example, approximately 23% of adolescent boys report binge drinking compared to only 15% of adolescent girls (Johnston et al., 2016b).

The presentation of substance use problems is different for adolescent boys and girls. Boys with substance use disorders show high rates of impulsivity, aggression, and antisocial behaviors. They are also more likely than girls to experience legal problems associated with their substance use. For boys, substance use disorders usually reflect a more general problem with conduct and antisocial behavior.

Girls with substance use problems often report greater emotional disturbance than boys. These girls often show comorbid problems with depression, anxiety, and physical complaints. Girls with substance use problems are also more likely than boys to have histories of family conflict and sexual abuse (Weis & Ross, 2015).

Ethnicity

Substance use differs by ethnicity. Native American youths show the highest rates of substance use disorders overall, followed by White and Latino adolescents. Native American and non-Latino, White adolescents also begin using alcohol and other drugs at earlier ages and may show greater comorbid mental health problems than most other youths living in the United States (Johnston et al., 2016b; Wu & Blazer, 2015; Wu et al., 2013).

African American and Asian American adolescents show the lowest rates of substance use problems. The low prevalence of substance use problems among African American adolescents is remarkable because African American adolescents are disproportionately exposed to risk factors associated with substance use disorders, such as low socioeconomic status (SES; Gil, Vega, & Turner, 2002). It is possible that certain aspects of African American culture somehow protect these youths from developing substance use problems. For example, involvement in extended family kinships or church activities may buffer African American youths against the potentially harmful effects of socioeconomic hardship.

Latino adolescents usually show prevalence rates somewhere between those of White and African American adolescents (see Figure 10.5). However, Latino adolescents born in the United States show greater rates of substance use problems than Latino adolescents born in other countries. Among foreign-born adolescents, acculturation and ethnic identity seem to influence their likelihood of using alcohol and other drugs.

Course

Adolescents tend to use substances in an orderly, predictable fashion. Among adolescents who use alcohol and

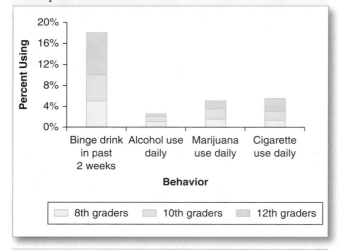

Figure 10.4 Potentially problematic substance use by adolescents. Between 3-5% of high school seniors report daily alcohol, marijuana, or cigarette use. Approximately 18% report binge drinking in the past two weeks.

Source: From Johnston and colleagues (2016b)

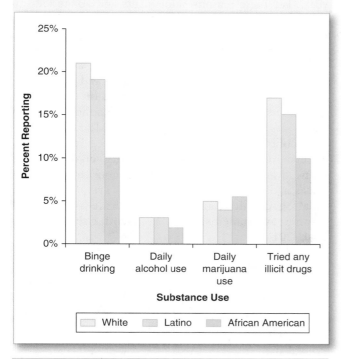

Figure 10.5 Ethnic differences in adolescent substance use. On average, White and Latino adolescents are more likely to engage in problematic alcohol and other drug use than African American adolescents.

Source: From Johnston and colleagues (2016a).

other drugs, a typical pattern of use begins in late childhood with cigarettes. Then, sometime during adolescence, youths may begin to use alcohol and try marijuana. Some individuals subsequently try other illicit drugs, such as stimulants or prescription medications. This progression from "soft" to hard drugs has led some people to suggest that marijuana is a "gateway drug" that introduces youths to other illicit substances (Leukefeld et al., 2015).

Evidence supporting the gateway hypothesis is limited, however. On the one hand, longitudinal data indicate that the vast majority of adolescents who abuse stimulants and prescription medications have also used cigarettes, alcohol, and marijuana. On the other hand, most adolescents who use cigarettes, alcohol, and marijuana *do not* use other illicit substances. We might conclude, therefore, that the abuse of hard drugs is almost always dependent on the use of cigarettes, alcohol, and marijuana; however, use of these softer drugs does not imply an escalation to other illicit substances (Tucker, Ellickson, Orlando, Martino, & Klein, 2005).

Why do most youths stop at alcohol and marijuana while some youths progress to using other illicit substances? Several longitudinal studies have shed some light on this question (Stice, Kirz, & Borbely, 2002; Wagner & Austin, 2006). At least three factors seem to predict escalation in substance use.

First, adolescents with *histories of impulsive and disruptive behavior* are more likely to escalate their use of alcohol and other drugs and develop substance use disorders. Their substance use may be part of a larger problem with disruptive and antisocial activity.

Second, adolescents whose *parents model excessive substance use* in the home are at increased risk of developing substance use problems. Parents who drink or use other drugs to excess may provide adolescents with access to these substances and model their use.

Third, and most important, *friends' use of alcohol and other drugs* strongly predicts the adolescents' likelihood of escalated substance use. Peers introduce adolescents to illicit substances then model and reinforce their use (Kessler, Berglund, Dernier, Jin, & Walters, 2005; O'Brien et al., 2005).

Adolescents who develop substance use disorders are at risk for a host of deleterious outcomes. First, substances carry direct risks to adolescents' health. For example, excessive use of alcohol can cause transient illness; impairment in cognitive functioning; and, in rare cases, coma and death. Substance use can also place adolescents in hazardous situations. For example, adolescents who binge drink may drive while intoxicated, practice risky sexual behavior, or engage in aggressive or antisocial activity. Substance use also carries psychosocial risks. Adolescents with substance use problems show increased conflict and decreased communication with parents, greater likelihood of school-related problems and academic difficulties, and poorer peer relationships. Certainly, problems with family, school, and peers are partly responsible for adolescents' substance use. However, adolescents who use alcohol and other drugs likely exacerbate these social difficulties and compound their substance use problems (Tucker et al., 2005).

Most adolescents who use alcohol and other drugs continue to use these substances after high school. Recent data indicate that substance use typically increases after adolescents leave high school, regardless of whether they drop out of high school, graduate and enter the workforce, or graduate and attend college (White, Labouvie, & Papadaratsakis, 2005). Risk for problematic substance use peaks between the ages of 18 and 22 years. By age 25 years, there is usually a dramatic decline in substance use and misuse, especially among people who attended college. This decrease in substance use with age is probably caused by young adults entering the workforce, assuming more adultlike responsibilities, marrying, and having children (Rohrbach, Sussman, Dent, & Sun, 2005; White et al., 2005).

Most youths who use alcohol and other drugs during adolescence *do not* continue to show substance use problems as adults, especially if the onset of their substance use was in later adolescence. However, some youths, especially those who begin using substances before age 14, show long-term substance use problems. These adolescents are also likely to display lower levels of social competence, decreased employment, and increased likelihood of depression and criminal behavior (Caspi, Harrington, Moffitt, & Milne, 2002).

Review:

- Although occasional alcohol use is normative for older adolescents, only one-third have tried marijuana or smoke cigarettes regularly. Misuse of prescription medications or other illicit substances (e.g., cocaine, heroin) is much less common.
- The prevalence of substance use disorders among adolescents in the general population ranges from 1% to 5%. Approximately 3% to 4% of high school seniors report daily alcohol, marijuana, or cigarette use. Nearly one-fifth of high school seniors report binge drinking in the past 2 weeks.
- Boys are more likely than girls to develop substance use problems. Native American and non-Latino, White adolescents are more likely to develop substance use problems than youths of other ethnicities. On average, African American adolescents show the lowest prevalence of substance use problems.

10.2 CAUSES

What Are the Effects of Alcohol?

Psychological Effects

Alcohol is the drug most widely used by adolescents. Alcohol is often overlooked as a possible drug of abuse because of its widespread availability in the United States. Alcohol is legal in nearly all parts of the country, and it is heavily advertised on television and in magazines. Furthermore, many adolescents and parents regard alcohol consumption as part of adolescent culture. After all, most adolescents drink alcohol at least occasionally at some point during their high school years. For these reasons, adolescents and adults tend to minimize the risks associated with alcohol use (Johnston et al., 2016b).

Alcohol is technically a sedative, a drug that slows nervous system activity. It falls into the same class of drugs as benzodiazepines, barbiturates, and most sleeping pills. The effects of alcohol depend on the amount consumed. Experts usually describe alcohol as having a biphasic effect (see Figure 10.6). Mild to moderate alcohol use produces one set of (largely desirable) effects: increased arousal, sociability, euphoria, and reduced anxiety. Extended alcohol consumption produces a different cluster of (largely aversive) effects: sedation, cognitive and motor impairments, heart and respiratory problems, and other health risks (Schrieks et al., 2014).

Moderate alcohol consumption usually produces pleasurable effects. Consequently, many adolescents will continue to drink in order to maintain or enhance these subjective feelings of well-being. Some people use the term "chasing the high" to describe this attempt to achieve greater euphoria with continued drinking.

Figure 10.6 The biphasic effect of alcohol. Our expectation that "more is better" may not apply to alcohol. At a certain point, people begin to experience diminished returns from continued drinking and more negative effects.

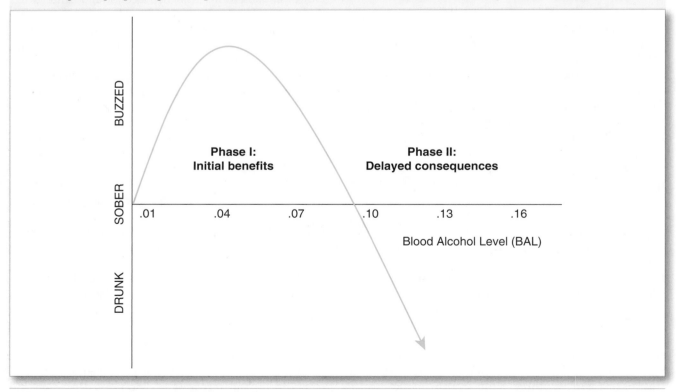

Source: Based on Ray, Bujarski, and Roche (2016).

Unfortunately, at a certain point, individuals reach a state of diminishing returns. Usually continued alcohol consumption produces less-than-desirable effects. Excessive alcohol use can result in binge drinking. Binge drinking can cause fatigue, dizziness, nausea, and blackout. Bingeing may also produce impairment in judgment and problem-solving. Binge drinking is associated with disturbances in balance and coordination, slurred speech, restlessness and irritability, and problems with heart rate and respiration. In rare cases, excessive alcohol consumption can cause coma and death (Madson, Moorer, Zeigler-Hill, Bonnell, & Villarosa, 2013; Marshall, 2014).

Physiological Effects

Alcohol is rapidly absorbed by the gastrointestinal tract and quickly diffuses throughout the bloodstream. It is metabolized primarily by the liver. The exact mechanisms by which alcohol affects mood, cognition, and behavior are unknown. However, alcohol seems to affect the functioning of at least five major neurotransmitters: norepinephrine, glutamate, dopamine, opioids, and GABA (Kosten, George, & Kleber, 2005; Jacobus & Tapert, 2013).

First, low doses of alcohol stimulate the norepinephrine system, causing increased feelings of arousal and excitation. Alcohol seems to target a brain region known as the reticular formation, located in the brain stem. The reticular formation is responsible for alerting us to important information in the environment and initiating attention and arousal. Norepinephrine activity in this brain area is probably responsible for the increase in alertness, sociability, and talkativeness shown by most people after one or two alcoholic beverages.

At the same time, alcohol affects glutamate functioning. Glutamate is a major excitatory neurotransmitter in the central nervous system. Alcohol acts to inhibit the neurotransmission of glutamate, thereby slowing neuronal activity. Specifically, alcohol interferes with certain glutamate receptor sites. Consumption of one or two alcoholic beverages can begin to decrease glutamate activity, producing feelings of relaxation and stress reduction. Reduced glutamate activity might partially explain the negatively reinforcing properties of alcohol; alcohol can alleviate anxiety. Glutamate is also partially responsible for associative learning and memory. Excessive alcohol use, therefore, can lead to memory problems including difficulty forming new memories and periods of memory loss (i.e., blackouts).

Moderate alcohol consumption affects dopamine activity. Researchers have identified a neural pathway that they believe is responsible for the pleasurable effects of most addictive drugs, including alcohol. This "reward pathway" extends from the ventral tegmental area (VTA) of the midbrain to the nucleus accumbens, amygdala, and hippocampus, located in the limbic system (see Image 10.1). This neural pathway responds primarily to dopamine, a neurotransmitter responsible for feelings of pleasure, positive affect (i.e., energy, sociability), and increased

Image 10.1   In the brain, dopamine plays an important role in the experience of pleasure. As part of the reward pathway, dopamine is manufactured in nerve cell bodies located within the ventral tegmental area (VTA) and is released in the nucleus accumbens and the prefrontal cortex.

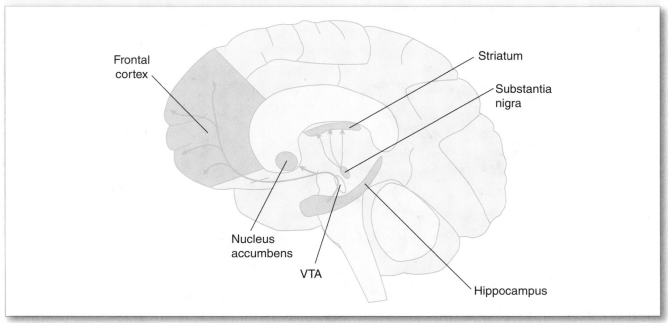

Source: Image courtesy of the National Institutes of Health.

motor activity. Because this dopamine-rich pathway extends from the midbrain (VTA) to the limbic system, it is called the dopaminergic mesolimbic pathway.

How does the dopaminergic mesolimbic pathway operate? Alcohol stimulates dopaminergic neurons in the VTA. The VTA, in turn, increases dopamine levels in a nearby brain area, the nucleus accumbens, producing subjective feelings of euphoria, pleasure, and emotional well-being (see Image 10.2). These pleasant effects constitute the first phase of the "biphasic" response to alcohol, and they are the primary reason most people, especially adolescents, drink. Furthermore, these pleasurable feelings also positively reinforce alcohol use, making the person consume more of the drug. Alcohol also increases neuronal activity in the amygdala and hippocampus, brain areas responsible for processing emotions and forming new memories. The increased activity of these brain regions may account for the highly emotional memories associated with alcohol consumption and the "cravings" for alcohol experienced by chronic drinkers.

Alcohol produces other pleasurable effects through its activity on the body's production of endorphins, natural opioids. Researchers have discovered opioid receptors throughout the brain. These receptors are primarily responsible for subjective feelings of satisfaction and alleviation of pain. Typically, the body makes natural opioids to cope with stressful or painful situations. These opioids are produced by the pituitary gland and released into the bloodstream to circulate throughout the body. Alcohol consumption increases the release of endogenous opioids, producing these pleasurable effects.

Finally, moderate alcohol consumption affects GABA (gamma-aminobutyric acid), a major inhibitory neurotransmitter. Alcohol enhances the effects of GABA, producing a rapid decrease in neuronal activity. This decreased neuronal activity is partially responsible for many of the sedating effects of alcohol: relaxation, cognitive sluggishness, and slowed reaction time.

Most adolescents who use alcohol experience tolerance—that is, they report needing more alcohol to achieve previous levels of euphoria (Chung, Martin, Armstrong, & Labouvie, 2002). Researchers distinguish between two types of tolerance (Meyer & Quenzer, 2005). First, adolescents can experience acute tolerance during a single drinking episode. Specifically, people experience the greatest effects of alcohol after only a few drinks, with diminishing effects after each successive drink. Many adolescents often try to "chase the high" by continuing their alcohol use after reaching this period of diminishing returns. Unfortunately, continued use results in increased sedation rather than increased pleasure.

Second, chronic alcohol use is associated with pharmacodynamic tolerance (Koob & LeMoal, 2006). Over sustained periods of time, the number or sensitivity of the neuroreceptors that respond to alcohol gradually decreases. For example, long-term alcohol use is

Image 10.2   This rat can stimulate his nucleus accumbens by pressing a lever in his cage. The nucleus accumbens is part of the dopamine-rich mesolimbic pathway, the brain's pleasure center. Most addictive drugs stimulate the nucleus accumbens. The rat will press the lever to exhaustion. He will also transverse an electric grid, enduring painful shocks, to access the lever and stimulate his brain.

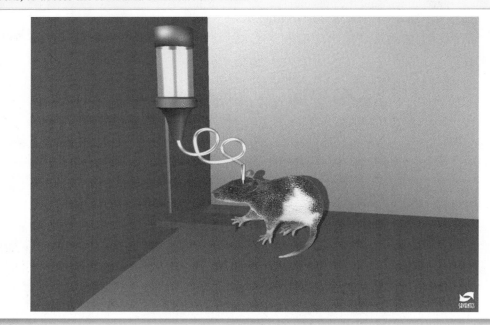

Source: Image courtesy of the National Institute of Mental Health.

associated with decreased sensitivity of GABA and dopamine receptors. Individuals who drink frequently may not exhibit the same sedating effects of alcohol due to this decrease in sensitivity to GABA. Frequent drinkers may also require more alcohol to achieve a state of euphoria due to decreased sensitivity of dopamine receptors. Decreased receptor sensitivity is believed to be a homeostatic mechanism, that is, a way for the body to compensate for the individual's chronic alcohol use.

Because of this decrease in sensitivity, abrupt discontinuation of alcohol can produce withdrawal symptoms in chronic users. Without alcohol, the body's sensitivity to GABA and dopamine is diminished. Consequently, chronic drinkers who stop using alcohol may experience negative effects due to the relative underactivity of these neurotransmitters. Decreased GABA sensitivity can produce feelings of anxiety, excitability, irritability, restlessness, and excessive motor activity. Some adults experience delirium tremens, a cluster of symptoms that include tremors, seizures, confusion, and visual and tactile hallucinations. Decreased dopamine activity can cause low energy, fatigue, and depression.

Review:

- Alcohol has a biphasic effect on most people. Initial consumption produces largely pleasurable effects such as euphoria and anxiety reduction whereas continued consumption largely produces unwanted effects such as sedation.
- Alcohol use is maintained physiologically through activation of the reticular formation (arousal) and the mesolimbic pathway (reward). Norepinephrine and dopamine are the primary neurotransmitters involved in each pathway, respectively.
- Alcohol acts as a GABA agonist, slowing activity of the central nervous system. It causes a reduction in autonomic arousal and sedation with prolonged consumption.

What Are the Effects of Marijuana?

Psychological Effects

Marijuana is a complex substance that contains dozens of compounds known to affect the functioning of the central nervous system. These compounds fall into a certain class called cannabinoids. The most powerful cannabinoid is delta-9-tetrahydrocannabinol (THC; O'Brien et al., 2005).

When someone smokes marijuana, approximately half of the THC enters the lungs and is rapidly absorbed. Within seconds of the first puff, THC enters the brain and affects mood, cognition, and behavior.

Moderate doses of marijuana usually produce mild intoxication. Within seconds of use, people often feel light-headed and dizzy. Some people report tingling sensations in their limbs. After a few minutes, most people experience feelings of euphoria, disinhibition, and increased energy and sociability. Continued use (10–30 minutes) produces reductions in anxiety, a general sense of relaxation, and a state of emotional well-being or contentment. Cognitive and motor processes are usually slowed. For example, marijuana users may show slowed movements, speech, or problem-solving ability. Slowed cognitive and motor responses can interfere with people's abilities to perform complex mental activities (e.g., complete homework) and motor activities (e.g., drive a car). Effects typically last a few hours. Larger doses of marijuana can cause paradoxical effects: increased anxiety and agitation, perceptual distortions or visual hallucinations, and paranoia.

Physiological Effects

THC is detected by cannabinoid receptors located throughout the brain. The largest concentrations of these receptors are in the basal ganglia, cerebellum, hippocampus, and cortex. When THC is detected by these receptors, it causes a reduction in the cell's metabolic activity and the activity of neurotransmitters. The specific effects of THC depend on where it is detected. For example, THC detected by the basal ganglia affects movement and coordination, whereas THC detected by receptors in the cortex affects thinking, judgment, and problem-solving.

THC is known to affect a wide range of neurotransmitters, including norepinephrine, dopamine, glutamate, GABA, and serotonin. The multiple brain areas and neurotransmitters affected by THC likely account for the diverse effects of the substance on people's behavior.

Experts disagree about the long-term physiological risks of repeated marijuana use. People who frequently use marijuana often show impairments in attention, memory, and problem-solving ability relative to individuals who do not use the drug. Some researchers, but not all, have found that these cognitive impairments persist for weeks or months after discontinuing marijuana use. Many chronic users show decreased motivation and goal-directed behavior, a phenomenon called amotivational syndrome. However, experts are unsure whether this lack of motivation is caused by the physiological effects of the drug or by environmental factors associated with drug use (Volkow et al., 2016).

Perhaps the most serious effect of chronic marijuana use is health impairment. Smoking marijuana is associated with the same health risks as smoking cigarettes: respiratory problems, circulatory problems, and cancer. Marijuana can also suppress immune functioning. Finally, the effects of marijuana can impair people's sensory and motor functioning, increasing their likelihood of injury (Volkow, Baler, Compton, & Weiss, 2014).

Most people show acute tolerance to marijuana. During the course of a single marijuana episode, most people need to use more of the drug to achieve the initial state of intoxication. Animal studies demonstrate pharmacodynamic tolerance to marijuana. Long-term use causes reductions in the number and sensitivity of cannabinoid receptors in animals. There is less evidence for pharmacodynamic tolerance in humans; however, many people who frequently use marijuana report needing more of the drug after months or years of use (Karila et al., 2014; Volkow et al., 2016).

Frequent marijuana use can cause dependence. Individuals who are dependent on marijuana report cravings for the drug and show a characteristic pattern of withdrawal symptoms associated with abstinence. Frequent users who are denied the drug can experience sleep and appetite disturbance, anxiety, agitation, restlessness, and irritability. Sometimes, marijuana withdrawal is also associated with physical symptoms, such as sweating, chills, and nausea. Chronic marijuana users show more severe withdrawal symptoms including intense cravings for the drug, depression, anger, bizarre dreams, and headaches. Withdrawal symptoms typically last only a few days (Karila et al., 2014).

Review:

- The effects of marijuana on adolescents include euphoria and disinhibition, anxiety reduction and relaxation, and slowed movement and problem-solving. High doses can produce paradoxical effects (e.g., agitation).
- THC is detected by cannabinoid receptors throughout the brain, especially the basal ganglia, cerebellum, hippocampus, and cortex.
- Chronic use of marijuana can impair adolescents' respiratory health and may lead to amotivational syndrome.

What Developmental Pathways Predict Substance Use Disorders?

The development of substance use disorders is complex. A model that explains the emergence of substance use problems must take into account a wide range of genetic, biological, psychological, and social–cultural factors. One biopsychosocial model has been offered by Kenneth Sher and colleagues to explain the development of alcohol use problems (Chassin, Sher, Hussong, & Curran, 2013; Chassin et al., 2016; Sher, 1991; Sher, Grekin, & Williams, 2005).

Sher's model suggests that alcohol use disorders can emerge along three possible developmental pathways. First, alcohol problems can develop when people inherit a genetic or biological sensitivity to the effects of alcohol and derive a great deal of pleasure from its use (the enhanced reinforcement pathway). Second, alcohol problems can arise when people rely on alcohol to cope with depression or anxiety. In this case, alcohol use is negatively reinforced by the alleviation of psychological distress (the negative affect pathway). Third, alcohol problems can emerge as part of a larger pattern of antisocial behavior (the deviance-prone pathway).

These three pathways to substance use problems are not mutually exclusive; many people abuse alcohol and other drugs for multiple reasons. However, these pathways are useful for organizing our understanding of the etiology of substance use disorders (Chassin et al., 2013).

Enhanced Reinforcement Pathway

Genetic Risk

At the beginning of all three pathways lies a biological diathesis toward developing substance use disorders (see Figure 10.7). Considerable research has shown an association between problematic substance use in parents and the development of substance use disorders in their offspring. Approximately two-thirds of adolescents who show substance use problems have at least one biological parent with a history of substance use disorders. Substance use disorders are especially common among biological fathers (Kendler et al., 2012).

Having a parent with a history of substance use disorders increases one's likelihood of developing a substance use disorder two- to ninefold. Twin and family studies indicate that this association between parent and child substance use is at least partially heritable, with 60% of the variance of alcohol use and 33% of other drug use attributable to genetics. Genetic factors predict the likelihood of using alcohol and other drugs, the age at which people first begin using substances, and the overall probability of a substance use disorder (Chassin et al., 2013).

Molecular geneticists have recently identified one group of genes that likely play a role in the transmission of substance use problems from parents to children: the $GABA_A$ receptor genes. Recall that alcohol, and several other substances, reduce anxiety by enhancing GABA, the body's main inhibitory neurotransmitter. The $GABA_A$ receptor genes code for proteins that regulate the postsynaptic neuron's sensitivity to GABA and, consequently, its response to alcohol (Li et al., 2014).

Positive Expectations and Pleasurable Effects

The enhanced reinforcement pathway assumes that this genetic risk makes offspring unusually sensitive to

Figure 10.7 The Enhanced Reinforcement Pathway Toward Substance Use Problems

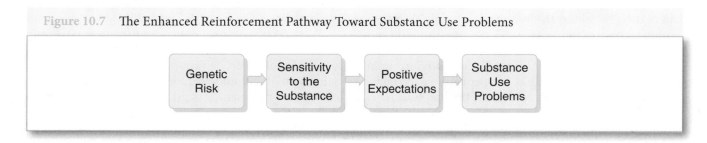

the pharmacological effects of the substance. For example, individuals who have this genetic risk may respond more intensely to the effects of alcohol, may experience more pleasure from drinking, or may have fewer negative side effects from drinking excessively (Finegersh & Homanics, 2014).

At the same time, as adolescents experiment with alcohol and other drugs, they learn about the effects of these substances on their behavioral, social, and emotional functioning. Eventually, they come to expect substances to be beneficial. As use increases, the substances assume reinforcing properties by either bringing about pleasure (i.e., positive reinforcement) or alleviating distress or boredom (i.e., negative reinforcement; Samek, Keyes, Iacono, & McGue, 2013).

A biological sensitivity to the effects of the substance and an expectation that the substance will have positive effects can lead to problematic use. For example, adolescents at risk for substance use disorders often have unusually positive expectations for substance use—that is, they expect substances to produce a great number of benefits with few drawbacks. Indeed, distorted beliefs in the positive effects of alcohol can increase the frequency or amount of drinking. In contrast, adolescents who have negative experiences with alcohol and other drugs or adolescents who are anxious about substance use are less likely to develop substance use problems (Margret & Ries, 2016; Sauer-Zavala, Burris, & Carlson, 2014).

Negative Affect Pathway

The **negative affect pathway** assumes that adolescents can also develop substance use problems in response to stress and negative mood states (see Figure 10.8). Stress can arise from adverse early childhood experiences, such as growing up in an abusive or neglectful home. Stress can also be caused by later environmental factors, such as witnessing marital conflict, experiencing disruptions in family and interpersonal relationships, or encountering school-related difficulties (Bond, Toumbourou, Thomas, Catalano, & Patton, 2005; Libby et al., 2004; Libby, Orton, Stover, & Riggs, 2005). These stressors, in turn, can cause anxiety, depression, and low self-worth. Adolescents who are unable to cope with these negative emotions may use alcohol and other drugs to alleviate psychological distress. Substance use, therefore, is negatively reinforced by the reduction of anxiety or depression. Over time, substance use can increase and lead to substance use disorders.

The negative affect pathway has not enjoyed widespread empirical support as an explanation for substance use problems among adolescents. Most cross-sectional studies show only moderate associations between adolescents' ratings of negative affect and their alcohol use. Furthermore, most longitudinal studies have shown that adolescents' symptoms of anxiety and depression usually *do not* precede the emergence of their substance use problems. Instead, some data indicate the opposite effect: Adolescent substance use often leads to social and academic problems that elicit dysphoria. When mood and anxiety problems predict later substance use, the relationship between mood and substance use is usually weak or attributable to other factors such as disruptive behavior problems (Goodman & Capitman, 2000; Goodwin et al., 2005; Patton et al., 2002; Rao, Daley, & Hammen, 2000).

On the other hand, the negative affect pathway might apply to a subset of adolescents who experienced child maltreatment. Physically abused boys and sexually abused girls show increased likelihood of developing mood problems associated with their victimization. They may rely on alcohol and other drugs to cope with these mood problems (Goldstein, Faulkner, & Wekerle, 2013; Herrenkohl, Hong, Klika, Herrenkohl, & Russo, 2013).

Furthermore, specific mood and anxiety disorders may place children at risk for substance use problems. For example, adolescents who experience extreme anxiety in social situations often use alcohol to cope with anticipatory anxiety. These adolescents might drink *before* going to a party, in order to relax (i.e., "pre-gaming"). Their repeated alcohol use can lead to more lasting problems (Black et al., 2015).

Finally, the negative affect pathway might apply to youths from affluent families. Suburban children living in affluent households may use alcohol and other drugs to cope with stress. Furthermore, affluent adolescent boys use alcohol to gain social standing with peers. Luthar and Latendresse (2005) suggest that affluent adolescents lead overly scheduled lives and experience considerable pressure to excel academically, athletically, and socially. At the same time, their parents are often less involved in their lives because of career and social demands. This combination of high stress and low parental supervision places affluent youths at risk.

Deviance-Prone Pathway

The **deviance-prone pathway** offers a third explanation for the development of adolescent substance use problems.

Figure 10.8   The Negative Affect Pathway Toward Substance Use Problems

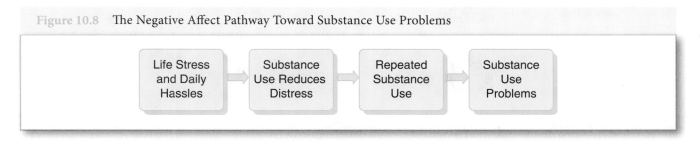

According to this model, problems arise in the context of antisocial behavior (see Figure 10.9).

According to the deviance-prone model, the causes of adolescent substance use are similar to the causes of other disruptive behavior problems. These causes include (a) early problems with neurobehavioral disinhibition, (b) disruptive behavior and academic problems, and (c) peer rejection and affiliation with deviant peers.

Neurobehavioral Disinhibition

Young children who show neurobehavioral disinhibition are at increased risk for developing substance use problems later in life (Zuckerman, 2007). Neurobehavioral disinhibition is characterized by three features: (1) behavioral undercontrol, (2) emotional reactivity, and (3) deficits in executive functioning.

First, children with neurobehavioral undercontrol engage in high-rate, risky, and impulsive actions. These children have a strong need for excitement and are often described as "sensation-seekers" or "daredevils." The tendency toward behavioral undercontrol is likely inherited; twin and family studies show strong heritability for risk-taking and sensation-seeking behavior. Adults with substance use disorders often display behavioral undercontrol, and they may genetically predispose their children to similar behaviors. Indeed, behavioral undercontrol is a strong predictor of later disruptive behavior problems and substance use (Chassin, 2015).

Second, children with neurobehavioral disinhibition display a high degree of emotional reactivity. As young children, they display difficult temperaments. Their caregivers describe them as irritable and fussy. Later in childhood, these children often overreact to stress and display a tendency toward irritability, anger, and aggression.

Third, children with neurobehavioral disinhibition show deficits in executive functioning. Executive functioning allows children to inhibit immediate impulses, plan and prioritize behavior, and achieve long-term goals. Children with deficits in executive functioning display problems with inattention, hyperactivity, and impulsivity.

Disruptive Behavior and Academic Problems

Problems with neurobehavioral disinhibition can adversely affect children's interactions with peers. Peers often find these children's high-rate, disruptive behavior aversive. They may avoid interacting with them in the classroom and during recess. Furthermore, children who display emotional reactivity, especially aggression, are often rejected by peers.

Problems with neurobehavioral disinhibition can also interfere with children's academic performance. Specifically, children who show problems with behavioral undercontrol may have difficulty attending to teachers and adhering to classroom rules. They may also have trouble staying on task and completing exams. Deficits in executive functioning can also interfere with children's abilities to complete assignments in a timely fashion, to plan and organize academic activities, and to finish long-term projects. Children with neurobehavioral disinhibition often have negative views of school, earn low grades, and struggle academically (Chassin et al., 2013; Chassin, 2015).

Peer Rejection and Deviancy Training

Academic problems and peer rejection can cause children to distance themselves from classmates and mainstream peer groups. Instead of associating with prosocial peers, these disruptive children associate with other rejected youths. Typically, rejected peers display similar histories of academic and disruptive behavior problems (Frick, 2012).

Figure 10.9 The Deviance-Prone Pathway Toward Substance Use Problems

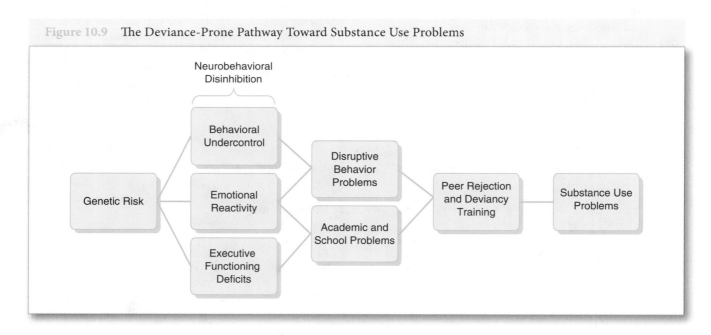

Early substance use often occurs when deviant peers introduce children to alcohol and other drugs. Peers model substance use, encourage experimentation, and reinforce continued use over time. Rejected children might initially engage in substance use to gain acceptance into the deviant peer group. Over time, repeated use can lead to an exacerbation of social and academic problems and the development of substance use disorders (Mrug et al., 2012; van Ryzin, Fosco, & Dishion, 2012).

The relationship between deviant peers and substance use may be different for boys and girls. Some girls associate with deviant peers for the same reasons as boys: They are ostracized by prosocial peers because of their behavioral and academic problems. However, early pubertal maturation also increases the likelihood that girls will associate with deviant peers. Older boys, in particular, may introduce early maturing girls to alcohol and other drugs, encourage antisocial behavior, and pressure them to engage in sexual activity. Despite their appearance, these early maturing girls may lack the maturity to resist social pressures. Indeed, early maturing girls show greater consumption of alcohol and other drugs than typically maturing girls. Furthermore, they are more likely to develop substance use problems than their typically maturing peers (Hedges & Korchmaros, 2016; Hendrick, Cance, & Maslowsky, 2016).

Review:

- According to the enhanced reinforcement pathway, substance use disorders emerge due to (a) genetic risk, (b) unusual sensitivity to the effects of the substance, and (c) positive expectations for substance use.
- The negative affect pathway assumes that substance use is negatively reinforced by the alleviation of psychological distress.
- According to the deviance-prone pathway, substance use disorders emerge due to (a) neurobehavioral undercontrol, (b) disruptive behavior and academic problems, and (c) peer rejection and affiliation with deviant peers.

10.3 EVIDENCE-BASED TREATMENT

Can We Prevent Adolescent Substance Use Disorders?

Primary Prevention: D.A.R.E.

Drug Abuse Resistance Education, or D.A.R.E., is the best-known school-based program designed to prevent substance use problems. D.A.R.E. originated in Los Angeles in 1983. It was originally intended to increase contact between police and school-age children. The program consisted of weekly visits by uniformed police officers to fifth- and sixth-grade classrooms. Officers discussed the dangers of substance use, ways to avoid peer pressure to use alcohol and other drugs, and techniques to promote abstinence. It has since been expanded to elementary and junior high school classrooms across the United States.

Despite its popularity, D.A.R.E. does not appear to be effective in reducing alcohol and other drug use. The first meta-analysis of D.A.R.E., funded by the National Institute of Justice, revealed that children who did and did not participate in D.A.R.E. had equal rates of substance use by early adolescence (Ennett, Tobler, Ringwalt, & Flewelling, 1994). Other randomized controlled studies showed that D.A.R.E. increased children's knowledge of substance use problems but did not reduce children's substance use (Clayton, Cattarello, & Johnstone, 1996; Dukes, Stein, & Ullman, 1997; Rosenbaum, Gordon, & Hanson, 1998).

Although D.A.R.E. is not effective in preventing alcohol use, nearly 80% of public schools in the United States continue to offer the program. Birkeland and colleagues (Birkeland, Murphy-Graham, & Weiss, 2005) interviewed school and community officials who continued to offer D.A.R.E. despite being aware of its shortcomings. School and community leaders gave three reasons for continuing to use D.A.R.E. First, many leaders claimed that they never expected D.A.R.E. to prevent substance use problems in the first place; consequently, they were not surprised when they discovered that the program was ineffective. Second, many supporters acknowledged that D.A.R.E. might not be effective in reducing substance use, but it might be beneficial in other ways. For example, D.A.R.E. might improve relationships between school-age children and the police. Third, some school and community leaders dismissed the research findings altogether. They claimed that, based on personal experience, D.A.R.E. was highly effective at reducing substance use problems in their community.

Secondary Prevention Programs

Secondary prevention programs are designed for youths at risk for developing substance use problems. Most secondary prevention programs are ecologically based prevention—that is, they target at-risk youths in everyday settings, such as schools and neighborhood community centers. Programs are usually designed for middle-school students who are about to transition from childhood to early adolescence. Program developers reason that a successful transition from preadolescence to adolescence can protect youths from developing substance use problems (Leukefeld et al., 2015).

Ecologically based prevention programs target multiple risk factors simultaneously. First, information is provided to *adolescents* about substance use and misuse. Adolescents are also taught techniques to avoid substance use with peers. Second, *parents* are taught about adolescent substance use problems and steps that they can take to decrease the likelihood that their adolescents will use alcohol and other drugs. Many programs emphasize the importance of improving parent-child communication, monitoring children's friends and activities, and setting clear but developmentally appropriate limits on children's behavior. Third, ecologically based programs address the child's *larger social system*: school, peers, and the community. Some programs offer afterschool activities to promote abstinence to entire peer groups. Other programs work with community officials and police to limit adolescents' access to alcohol and other drugs.

Researchers evaluated the effectiveness of 48 secondary prevention programs involving 10,000 adolescents (Sambrano, Springer, Sale, Kasim, & Hermann, 2005). Roughly half of the sample participated in a prevention program, while the remaining adolescents served as controls. Results of the evaluation were disappointing. Overall, adolescents who participated in the prevention programs did not differ in their alcohol and marijuana use compared to controls. However, when researchers looked at the data more carefully, they noticed that the programs that provided high-intensity, comprehensive services reduced substance use more among participants than controls. These findings indicate that all prevention programs are not equal. To be effective, prevention programs must target multiple risk factors in the adolescent's life and teach skills to avoid substances and develop positive relationships with peers.

Review:

- Despite their popularity, older primary prevention programs have shown limited effectiveness in reducing substance use problems.
- Some intensive secondary prevention programs are effective in reducing both substance use and substance use problems. These programs focus on (a) providing education and refusal skills to adolescents, (b) improving parent–child communication and parental monitoring, and (c) improving schools and communities.

Is Medication Effective?

Medication is often used in the treatment of substance use disorders in adults (Bukstein & Deas, 2010). Furthermore, approximately one-half of adolescents who receive treatment for substance use disorders are prescribed at least one medication (Bukstein, 2015). Medication can be used in at least five ways.

First, substitution therapy involves administering a medication that is designed to eliminate cravings for alcohol or other drugs. For example, adolescents and adults who are addicted to opioids, like heroin, might be prescribed methadone, a synthetic opioid that binds to receptors and produces mild analgesia and anxiety reduction. Adults can gradually wean off heroin with methadone as they participate in treatment.

Second, medication can be used during *detoxification* to help patients cope with withdrawal symptoms. For example, adolescents and adults who are addicted to opioids might be prescribed clonidine, a medication that reduces heart rate, blood pressure, and physiological arousal. Clonidine can reduce some of the arousal symptoms associated with opioid withdrawal. Similarly,

adolescents and adults who are addicted to alcohol might be prescribed benzodiazepines, medications that reduce anxiety and agitation. Benzodiazepines are often useful in reducing withdrawal symptoms.

Third, some clinicians use medications that *block the effects* of alcohol and other drugs, reducing their pleasurable consequences. For example, naltrexone is an opioid receptor antagonist, which significantly reduces the euphoric effects of alcohol after it is consumed. Similarly, bupropion is an atypical antidepressant that affects dopamine and norepinephrine and blocks the pleasurable effects of nicotine.

Fourth, some physicians use medication as part of aversion therapy. For example, disulfiram (Antabuse) is a medication that prohibits alcohol from being metabolized. Several minutes after alcohol is consumed, the person experiences accelerated heart rate, shortness of breath, vomiting, nausea, and headache (i.e., symptoms of a hangover). This aversive reaction may help individuals decrease their alcohol consumption.

Fifth, and most commonly, medication is used to treat *comorbid disorders*. Double-blind controlled studies have demonstrated that medication can be useful in alleviating comorbid ADHD, anxiety, and mood disorders in adolescents with comorbid alcohol use disorder. Although these medications can be useful in reducing other conditions, they usually have little effect on alcohol consumption itself (Humphreys, Eng, & Lee, 2013).

It is noteworthy that many psychotropic medications have potential for abuse. For example, some adolescents with ADHD will sell stimulant medication used to treat their disorder, a practice known as "diversion." Alternatively, some psychostimulants can be crushed and ingested to produce euphoria and a rush of energy. Benzodiazepines have high potential for dependence given their antianxiety properties. Consequently, physicians, therapists, and parents must carefully monitor youths with substance use disorders who are prescribed these medications (Cortese et al., 2013).

Review:

- Medication is typically used to treat comorbid behavioral or emotional disorders in adolescents with substance use problems.
- Substitution therapy or aversion therapy can be used to decrease chronic substance use problems. However, these therapies are typically used with adults rather than adolescents.

What Psychosocial Treatments Are Effective for Adolescents?

Psychotherapy is typically regarded as the treatment of choice for adolescents who show substance use problems. Overall, youths with substance use disorders who participate in therapy experience better outcomes than youths who do not participate in therapy. Psychosocial interventions are associated with reductions in substance use and improvements in emotional and social functioning. In some studies, therapy is also associated with gains in academic performance (Stevens & Morral, 2014).

Despite its effectiveness, most youths with substance use disorders never participate in psychotherapy. In one population-based study, 5% of adolescents exhibited a significant alcohol or drug use problem that merited treatment. However, less than 12% of these youths were referred to an inpatient or outpatient treatment program for their substance use problem (Substance Abuse and Mental Health Services Administration, 2007). Clearly, there is much work to be done in the identification and provision of services to youths with alcohol and other drug problems.

Inpatient 12-Step Programs

Some adolescents with serious substance use disorders participate in 28-day inpatient treatment programs. Although inpatient treatment programs vary, most have three goals: (1) to attend to the adolescent's immediate medical needs and to detoxify her body, (2) to help the adolescent recognize the harmful effects of the substance on her health and functioning, and (3) to improve the quality of the adolescent's relationships with others.

To accomplish these goals, nearly all inpatient programs require adolescents to abstain from alcohol and other drug use during treatment. Staff members educate adolescents about the process of substance dependence and the physiological, psychological, and social effects of substance use. Inpatient programs typically provide individual and group therapy to adolescents. Staff members also offer family therapy sessions designed to improve parent-adolescent communication and problem-solving. Before the end of treatment, staff members help the adolescent and family members prepare for a return to school and home.

Most inpatient programs incorporate 12-step philosophies into their treatment package. Some 12-step programs include Alcoholics Anonymous (AA) and Narcotics Anonymous (NA). Proponents of these programs conceptualize alcohol and other drug use as a disease. From this perspective, substance use disorders are medical conditions that develop because of genetics, are maintained because of biology and "brain chemistry," and deleteriously affect the person's social, emotional, and spiritual life. Proponents of 12-step programs argue that individuals must first acknowledge that they have the disease and that they are powerless to overcome its effects (Mendola & Gibson, 2016).

Participants progress through a series of 12 steps designed to help them cope with their substance use and remain abstinent. At some point in their participation, they must recognize their inability to overcome their substance use problem, and they must surrender themselves to a "higher power." Indeed, they are taught to rely on spirituality and support from others to cope with urges to drink or use

other drugs. Participants attend group meetings to gain the support of other people struggling with substance use disorders. Each participant also selects a mentor who provides individual support and advice to help her maintain sobriety.

Twelve-step programs are the most frequently used means of treating substance use disorders in the United States. Typically, 12-step programs are initiated during inpatient treatment. After the individual completes inpatient treatment, he or she is encouraged to continue participating in 12-step programs in the community. Very often, individuals participate in 12-step group meetings while simultaneously meeting with an individual therapist.

Twelve-step programs have demonstrated efficacy among adults with substance use problems. However, less information is available regarding the efficacy of 12-step treatment for adolescents (Kelly et al., 2016). Twelve-step programs that are administered as part of inpatient treatment tend to be highly effective, probably because adolescents are living in controlled environments with limited opportunities for substance use. Some participants are able to maintain treatment gains 6 to 12 months after program completion (Winters et al., 2011). However, adolescents released from these inpatient programs have high rates of relapse. Approximately 60% relapse within 3 months of discharge and as many as 80% relapse within 1 year (Galanter, Kleber, & Brady, 2014; Margret & Ries, 2016).

Cognitive–Behavioral Therapy

Cognitive–behavioral therapy (CBT) for substance use disorders has gained considerable popularity in recent years. Practitioners of CBT view problematic substance use as a learned behavior that is acquired and maintained in four ways (Nathan & Gorman, 2015).

First, people often learn to use alcohol and other drugs through *operant conditioning*. For example, alcohol can be positively reinforcing to the extent that it gives people a subjective sense of satisfaction and well-being or enhances enjoyment during social interactions. Alcohol can also be negatively reinforcing to the extent that it reduces tension or alleviates pain. By definition, the reinforcing properties of alcohol lead to increased use.

Second, through *classical conditioning*, people learn to associate substance use with certain situations or mood states. For example, an adolescent might use marijuana with a certain group of friends. He discovers that smoking with these friends allows him to relax and have a good time. Through classical conditioning, he associates this group of friends with marijuana use. In the future, these friends might serve as a trigger or "stimulus cue" for him to use again.

Third, substance use is often maintained through *social learning*. For example, family members sometimes model substance use. Adolescents might view substance use as an acceptable means to cope with stress or facilitate social interactions. Similarly, peers often model and reinforce drug and alcohol use, communicating that to gain social approval, drug and alcohol use is not only acceptable but also expected.

Fourth, adolescents' *beliefs* mediate the relationship between events that trigger substance use and consumption of alcohol and other drugs (Barlow, 2014; Graham & Reynolds, 2013). Strictly speaking, events do not cause people to use substances; rather, people's interpretations and thoughts about events lead to either substance use or abstinence. Adolescents often hold distorted beliefs about situations that prompt their substance use (see). These distorted beliefs elicit drinking or other drug use.

To understand the way beliefs mediate the relationship between events and behavior, consider the following example. Sam is a shy tenth grader who has been invited to a party. When his friends pick him up to go to the party, they offer him some beer to help him relax. Sam's decision to drink or abstain will depend largely on his thoughts about the situation. Beliefs, such as "Having a couple of drinks will help me relax and get into a good mood," will increase his likelihood of accepting the drink. Alternatively, beliefs, such as "I'll be okay without the drink; Jim isn't having any," may lead him to decline the drink.

The techniques used in CBT target each of the four ways substance use problems develop and are maintained: (1) operant conditioning, (2) classical conditioning, (3) social learning, and (4) ways of thinking. First, the therapist asks the adolescent to monitor her substance use and note environmental factors or mood states that precede substance use. For example, an adolescent might discover that she only drinks when she is nervous before a party. With this information, the therapist and adolescent try to find ways for her to avoid feelings that trigger alcohol use. The adolescent might decide to ask a friend to go to parties with her so that she does not experience as much anticipatory anxiety.

Second, the therapist encourages the adolescent to consider the consequences of her substance use. Specifically, the therapist and adolescent might conduct a cost–benefit analysis of using alcohol or other drugs (see Figure 10.11). For

Figure 10.10   Cognitive Model for Adolescent Alcohol Use

Activating Event
- Going to a party
- Feeling uptight
- Friends offer a drink

Beliefs
- "A drink will help me relax."
- "I'll have more fun with my friends."

Consequence
- Accepting the drink

Note: Cognitions mediate the relationship between events and people's overt behavior. Adolescents who believe that alcohol will facilitate social interactions or help them have more fun are more likely to drink than adolescents who believe that alcohol will not produce pleasurable effects.

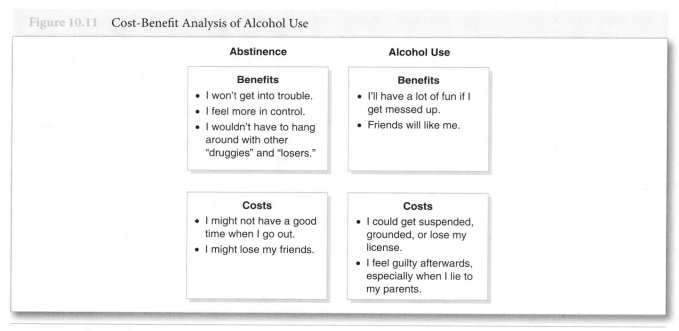

Figure 10.11   Cost-Benefit Analysis of Alcohol Use

Abstinence

Benefits
- I won't get into trouble.
- I feel more in control.
- I wouldn't have to hang around with other "druggies" and "losers."

Costs
- I might not have a good time when I go out.
- I might lose my friends.

Alcohol Use

Benefits
- I'll have a lot of fun if I get messed up.
- Friends will like me.

Costs
- I could get suspended, grounded, or lose my license.
- I feel guilty afterwards, especially when I lie to my parents.

Source: Based on J. S. Beck et al. (2005).

Note: Cognitive-behavioral therapists often ask adolescents to consider the pros and cons of (a) abstinence and (b) continued drinking.

example, the adolescent might list certain benefits of drinking before attending a party: It helps her relax; it allows her to have a good time. However, these benefits might be overshadowed by potential drawbacks: She drinks too much and gets sick; she feels guilty afterward; her parents become angry.

Third, to help adolescents avoid substance use, therapists teach their clients specific skills to reduce the reinforcing effects of alcohol. The skills that they teach depend largely on the adolescents' reasons for using. Adolescents who consume alcohol to reduce anxiety before a party might benefit from relaxation or social skills training. If they felt more relaxed or confident before the party, they might experience less desire to drink. Adolescents who drink in order to gain peer acceptance might be taught alcohol refusal skills. During the session, the therapist and adolescent might generate and practice ways to refuse alcohol when peers offer it.

Fourth, most cognitive–behavioral therapists examine the beliefs that adolescents have about substances and challenge distorted cognitions that lead to problematic use. Many adolescents overestimate the benefits of alcohol and dismiss its potentially harmful effects. An adolescent might reason, "It's fun to get wasted with my friends; we always have a great time." The therapist might encourage the adolescent to look at his alcohol use more objectively, by considering the negative consequences of use.

Similarly, an adolescent might overestimate the frequency with which peers use alcohol and other drugs,

CHALLENGING DISTORTED THOUGHTS ABOUT DRINKING

Therapist:	We've been talking for quite a while, and I've noticed that you put a lot of pressure on yourself to drink when you're hanging out.
Adam:	Well, sort of. It's more like the other guys put a lot of pressure on me. I'm fine when I'm with them most of the time. It just gets a little hard when I go to parties or things like that.
Therapist:	So, when you go to one of these parties, what's it like?
Adam:	Well, I usually see a lot of my friends and the other kids from school. They look like they're drinking and having a good time. It's like they expect me to drink too. And I want to have a good time, too—to have fun. I also don't want to let them down and ruin their fun.
Therapist:	You mean if you don't drink, you might be ruining their good time?
Adam:	Yeah, I guess. I just think that they'd think, "What's the matter with him. Doesn't he want to have fun? Does he think he's better than the rest of us?" It makes me nervous.
Therapist:	And *how do you know* that's what's going through their minds? What's the evidence?
Adam:	I don't know. I can just tell, you know. I get real nervous about the situation, and I can just tell that's what they're thinking.
Therapist:	It sounds to me like you're reasoning with your emotions, not with your head. This can sometimes get us into a lot of trouble and cause us to feel nervous. Let's see if we can look at the situation a little more objectively. Was everyone else at the party drinking?
Adam:	Yeah, most people.
Therapist:	But not everyone?
Adam:	No, there were a few guys who weren't drinking.
Therapist:	Did the other kids make fun of these other guys?
Adam:	No. Everyone was OK with it.
Therapist:	And did you think these kids (who didn't drink) were somehow weird or strange or better than you?
Adam:	No. I guess I didn't think anything of it. Everyone just wanted to have a good time.
Therapist:	So no one at the party was really interested in who drank and who didn't. They were more interested in having fun themselves.
Adam:	Yeah. I guess so, now that I think about it.

claiming, "I drink about as much as everybody else." In response, the therapist might share data regarding typical alcohol use among adolescents of the same age and gender. The following Research to Practice section illustrates the process of challenging cognitive distortions.

Within the past 15 years, a number of randomized controlled studies involving adolescents with substance use problems have shown CBT to be efficacious. Adolescents who participate in CBT show greater reductions in substance use than adolescents who receive individual supportive therapy, group therapy, or information about substance use problems alone (Graham & Reynolds, 2013; Nathan & Gorman, 2015).

Motivational Enhancement Therapy

Another method of treatment is motivational enhancement therapy, sometimes referred to as "motivational interviewing" (Arkowitz, Miller, & Rollnick, 2015). The primary goal of motivational enhancement therapy is to increase the adolescent's desire to reduce his alcohol consumption. Practitioners of motivational enhancement therapy recognize that most adolescents are referred to therapy by parents, teachers, or other adults; rarely do adolescents seek treatment themselves. Consequently, adolescents usually have low motivation to participate in treatment and less motivation to change their drinking habits.

Practitioners of motivational enhancement therapy help adolescents increase their willingness to change (see Figure 10.12). Adolescents progress through a series of steps, or stages of change, as they move from a state of low motivation to change to a state of high readiness to change (Connors, DiClemente, Velasquez, & Donovan, 2012; Prochaska, 2013). The stages are precontemplation (not recognizing that their alcohol use is a problem), contemplation (considering the possibility that their alcohol use is problematic), action (taking initial steps to change, such as scheduling an appointment with a therapist), and maintenance (avoiding relapse).

To increase the adolescent's motivation to change, the therapist uses five principles of motivational interviewing (Miller & Rollnick, 2012; Velasquez, Crouch, Stephens, & DiClemente, 2015). First, she approaches the adolescent in an accepting and nonjudgmental way. The therapist *expresses empathy, warmth, and genuine concern* for the adolescent and avoids signs that she disapproves of the adolescent's alcohol use or disagrees with his attitudes about drinking. She actively listens to the adolescent's point of view in order to understand his perspective. The therapist's initial goal is to accept the adolescent, not to persuade him to adopt others' beliefs about drinking. Second, the therapist *develops discrepancies* between the adolescent's long-term goals and his current alcohol use. For instance, the therapist might surmise that athletic achievement is important to the adolescent.

Figure 10.12   Practitioners of motivational enhancement therapy help adolescents increase their willingness to change.

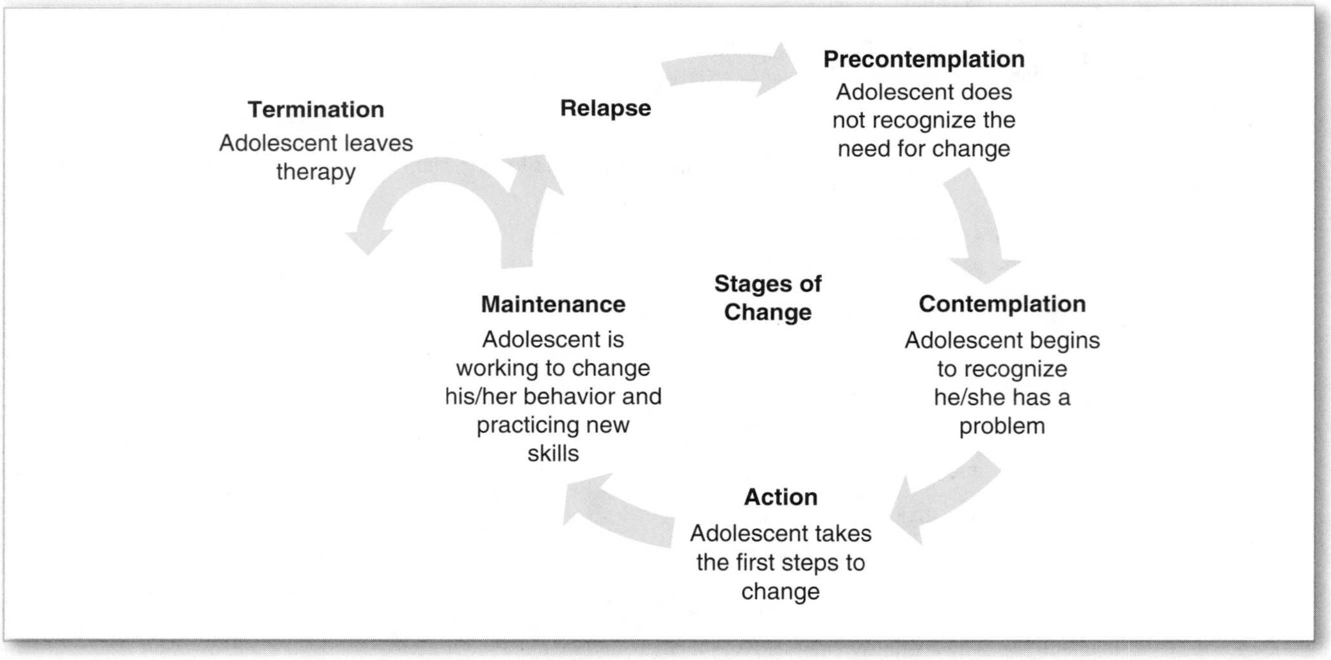

Source: Based on Prochaska, DiClemente, and Norcross (1992).

Note: Adolescents progress through a series of steps, or stages of change, as they move from a state of low motivation to change to a state of high motivation to change.

She might ask him whether drinking, which jeopardizes his eligibility to compete on his high school team, is consistent with his love for sports. Third, the therapist *rolls with resistance and avoids argumentation*. If the adolescent becomes defensive, angry, or avoidant, the therapist assumes it is because she is not adequately understanding and appreciating the adolescent's perspective. Fourth, the therapist *supports any commitment to change*, no matter how small. The therapist sees herself as being "in the adolescent's corner"—that is, supporting and encouraging his decisions regardless of whether they agree with her own. For example, the therapist might support the adolescent's decision to cut back on his drinking, even if this falls short of complete abstinence. Fifth, the therapist promotes the adolescent's *self-efficacy*, by pointing out successful change no matter how small (see Figure 10.13).

Practitioners of motivational enhancement therapy usually do not see abstinence as the primary goal of therapy. Instead, these practitioners often adopt a harm reduction approach to treatment (Boyd, Howard, & Zucker, 2013; Marlatt, Larimer, & Witkiewitz, 2012). According to the harm reduction perspective, the primary goal of therapy is to help adolescents identify and avoid alcohol use that has great potential for harm. For example, a therapist might support the adolescent's decision to drink fewer than four beers at a party, even if this decision might not make the adolescent's parents very happy. Any reduction in alcohol use that decreases risk or harm to the adolescent is viewed as successful. Consider the therapy of Erica, the girl with an emerging alcohol use problem.

Some people question the ethics of using a harm reduction approach with adolescents under 18 years of age (Bukstein, 2015). After all, is it appropriate for therapists to support an adolescent's decision to engage in an illegal behavior?

Although ethical questions like these cannot easily be answered, we should consider three points. First, therapists who adopt a harm reduction perspective must obtain parental consent prior to treatment. Although adolescents have basic rights to autonomy and self-determination, parents have the ultimate responsibility for their children's welfare and development. The therapist cannot ethically proceed with a harm reduction approach to therapy without parental consent. Second, most therapists who adopt a harm reduction perspective would probably argue that abstinence is the *ideal* goal of therapy. To the extent that abstinence has low probability, any reduction in alcohol use can be seen as beneficial. Finally, practitioners need to consider empirical data, in addition to personal beliefs, when they judge the merits of a harm reduction approach to treatment. If harm reduction works and clinicians do not use it, can they defend their practice (Maziak, 2014; McKeganey, 2012)?

Emerging data indicate that motivational enhancement therapy can be effective for high school students at risk for substance use problems. In two studies, adolescents who presented to a hospital emergency department (ED) because of an alcohol-related event were randomly assigned to either one session of motivational enhancement therapy or usual care. At 6-month follow-up, adolescents who participated in motivational enhancement therapy showed

Figure 10.13   Principles of Motivational Interviewing

Develop a discrepancy between goals and current behavior.

Roll with resistance; don't argue.

Express empathy, warmth, and concern through active listening.

Support the client's efforts to change, no matter how small.

Success should be acknowledged to build the client's self-efficacy.

ALCOHOL USE DISORDER

Erica's Treatment

Source: ©iStockphoto.com/spfoto

Erica met diagnostic criteria for alcohol use disorder of mild severity. Erica was at particular risk for more severe and long-standing substance use problems because her friends often encouraged her to drink at parties and her parents did not monitor her behavior.

Her therapist, Randy, continued to meet with Erica for 12 sessions of outpatient treatment. He used the principles of motivational enhancement therapy to help Erica increase her readiness to change her drinking behavior. Both Randy and Erica agreed that it was probably unrealistic for her to avoid drinking at parties altogether. However, Randy helped Erica weigh the benefits of drinking (e.g., having fun) with the potential costs of earning lower grades in school and getting arrested.

Erica completed mandated therapy and community service. Several months after finishing therapy, Erica called Randy to thank him for being her counselor. Apparently, one of Erica's friends was injured in an alcohol-related car accident. "I suppose that could have just as easily been me," said Erica.

lower rates of alcohol-related problems and physical injuries than controls. Furthermore, adolescents with the lowest motivation to change before treatment showed the greatest benefits from their participation in treatment (Monti et al., 1999; Monti, Barnett, O'Leary, & Colby, 2001).

Additional studies examined the efficacy of motivational enhancement among high school students who frequently used alcohol and marijuana (Nagy & Armstrong, 2015). Adolescents received either one session of motivational enhancement therapy or no intervention. Three months later, adolescents who participated in motivational enhancement therapy showed significant reductions in alcohol and marijuana use. Furthermore, reductions were greatest among adolescents who showed the most frequent use before treatment (see Figure 10.14).

Family Therapy

The most extensively studied treatment for adolescent substance use problems is family therapy (Bitter, 2013; Sexton & Lebow, 2015). Practitioners of family therapy view adolescent substance abuse as a family problem. The causes of adolescent substance abuse must be understood in light of the adolescent's family and her surrounding social system. Consequently, family therapists are interested in how the adolescent's relationships with parents, home environment, and school influence her substance use. Since all three ecological factors are interconnected, change in any one factor can affect all of the others. For example, increasing parents' involvement in the adolescent's academic activities could improve the adolescent's commitment and attitude toward school. Helping the

adolescent manage anger could enhance her relationship with parents and decrease her likelihood of seeking support from deviant peers.

Although the tactics used by family therapists vary, they usually share two objectives. One objective is *to help parents manage their adolescent's substance use*. This component of treatment typically involves education about normal and atypical adolescent development, the causes and consequences of adolescent substance abuse, and the role parents play in their adolescent's alcohol and/or other drug use. Therapists usually stress the importance of placing developmentally appropriate limits on adolescents' behavior, disciplining adolescents in a manner that is fair and consistent, and monitoring adolescents' activities.

The second objective of family therapy is *to improve the quality of family functioning*. Typically, therapists meet with adolescents and parents together and observe the quality of family interactions. Most therapists are chiefly interested in patterns of communication among family members. For example, some families avoid direct confrontation with each other and rarely talk about topics that make them angry, worried, or upset. Other families show frequent emotional outbursts and criticism toward each other, behaviors that often leave family members feeling isolated or rejected. Therapists often point out these communication patterns and teach family members to use different, more effective strategies (Hogue & Dauber, 2013; Hogue et al., 2015).

Family therapists are usually interested in the way parents and adolescents solve problems. They want to know how parents balance the adolescent's needs for autonomy with their desire to direct their adolescent's activities. Some

Figure 10.14 Efficacy of Motivational Enhancement Therapy for Adolescents With Alcohol or Marijuana Use Problems

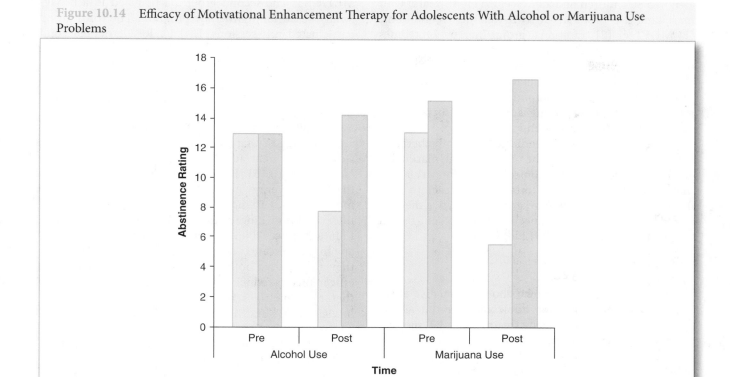

Source: Based on McCambridge and Strang (2004).

Note: Individuals in the treatment group received only one session of motivational enhancement. Three months later, they were less likely to use drugs than adolescents who served as controls.

parents adopt authoritarian practices that deny adolescents appropriate self-determination. Excessive parental control can cause adolescents to defy parental commands and use substances excessively. Other parents are overly permissive. These parents place too few constraints on their adolescents' activities. Permissive parenting increases adolescents' opportunities to associate with deviant peers and engage in substance use (Bitter, 2013; Sexton & Lebow, 2015).

One type of family therapy that has been used for adolescents with substance use problems is multidimensional family therapy (MDFT; Liddle, 2016). MDFT targets four dimensions of family functioning that are relevant to the adolescent's well-being: (1) the adolescent's substance use, (2) the caregiving practices of the adolescent's parents, (3) the quality of the parent–child relationship, and (4) other social factors that can influence the adolescent's substance use, such as his peer relationships or involvement in school.

MDFT involves a series of individual sessions with the adolescent, individual sessions with the parents, and combined family sessions over the course of several months. Individual sessions with the adolescent focus on

increasing the adolescent's social skills and involvement with prosocial peers, helping the adolescent recognize and manage negative emotions, and reducing the adolescent's contact with deviant peer groups.

Individual sessions with parents include teaching parents about the causes of adolescent substance use disorders, outlining ways parenting behaviors can contribute to these disorders, and helping parents monitor adolescent behavior. The therapist also tries to stress the importance of parental involvement in their adolescents' activities.

Family sessions are dedicated primarily to improving communication and problem-solving skills. Near the end of treatment, family sessions are meant to help maintain treatment gains and develop a plan in case of relapse. Throughout the course of treatment, therapists can help families manage specific problems, involving systems outside the family. For example, the therapist might facilitate the adolescent's participation in court-ordered substance counseling or his return to school after suspension.

Family therapy for adolescent substance use problems has been supported by a number of randomized controlled trials. For example, Liddle (2004) randomly assigned 80 children and adolescents (11–15 years) with marijuana use problems to two treatment conditions: (1) MDFT or (2) traditional group therapy. Outcomes were assessed 6 weeks into treatment and at the end of treatment. Results showed that adolescents in both groups displayed reductions in marijuana use. However, MDFT produced more rapid results and was more effective than group therapy in improving adolescents' social, emotional, behavioral, and academic functioning.

Results of other studies indicate that family therapies are efficacious in reducing the use of alcohol, marijuana, and other drugs relative to controls. Furthermore, family therapies have been shown to be more efficacious than individual supportive therapy, group supportive therapy, and education about substance use (Henderson, Dakof, Greenbaum, & Liddle, 2010; Liddle, 2016).

Treatment Comparison

Until recently, little was known about the relative effectiveness of treatments for adolescent substance use problems. The most promising treatments, CBT, motivational enhancement therapy, and family systems therapy, had been studied independently. Then, the Center for Substance Abuse Treatment conducted the first large-scale comparison study to determine which treatment reduced adolescent substance use in the most time- and cost-effective manner (Dennis et al., 2002). This comparison study, the Cannabis Youth Treatment Study, has provided researchers and clinicians with new information about the treatment of adolescent substance use problems.

Dennis and colleagues (2004) conducted two studies administered at four treatment centers across the country. Participants were 600 adolescents with marijuana use problems and their parents. Most adolescents reported daily or weekly marijuana use; almost 20% also reported daily or weekly alcohol use.

In the first study, adolescents were randomly assigned to one of three treatment conditions (Diamond et al., 2002). The first group received five sessions of motivational enhancement therapy and CBT (MET/CBT 5). The second group received 12 sessions of the same treatments (MET/CBT 12). The third group received 12 sessions of motivational enhancement therapy and CBT and an additional 6 sessions of family therapy (MET/CBT 12 + family). The parent–family sessions were designed to improve parents' behavior management skills, improve parent–adolescent communication, and increase parents' involvement in their adolescents' treatment. Researchers assessed adolescent outcomes 12 months after treatment. Results of the first study showed that all three forms of treatment were equally efficacious in reducing adolescent substance use. Five sessions of MET/CBT was the most time- and cost-efficient treatment.

In the second study, adolescents were randomly assigned to one of three treatment conditions (Diamond et al., 2002). The first group received five sessions of MET/CBT. The second group participated in a behaviorally based family therapy program. The third group participated in 15 sessions of MDFT. Results of the second study yielded similar findings. Adolescents in all three treatments showed similar reductions in substance use. In this study, however, five sessions of MET/CBT and the behaviorally based family therapy program were the most time- and cost-effective interventions.

Results of the Cannabis Youth Treatment Study seem to suggest that five sessions of MET/CBT can be sufficient to treat adolescent substance use disorders (see Figure 10.15). However, other research indicates that family therapy may be an important supplement to motivational enhancement and cognitive–behavioral interventions. Liddle and colleagues (Liddle, 2016; Liddle & Rowe, 2006) compared CBT with family therapy for adolescents with alcohol use problems. Overall, they found that both CBT and family therapy were efficacious in reducing substance use; however, family therapy sometimes produced more rapid reductions in alcohol use and more lasting abstinence than CBT. The superiority of family therapy over CBT is attributable to its greater emphasis on decreasing family conflict, improving parent–adolescent communication, and strengthening parenting skills (Hogue, Liddle, Dauber, & Samuolis, 2004). Indeed, most professional organizations recommend including families in the treatment of adolescent substance use disorders, regardless of therapists' usual approach to treatment (Bukstein, 2005; Henderson et al., 2010).

Review:

- Inpatient treatment for substance use disorders typically involves (a) abstinence and detoxification, (b) participation in individual therapy using a 12-step model, and (c) brief individual and family therapy.
- CBT focuses largely on altering environmental factors that elicit or reinforce substance use and changing maladaptive beliefs that contribute to continued use.
- Motivational enhancement therapy seeks to increase an adolescents' willingness to change his or her pattern of substance use. It often adopts a harm reduction approach in which any decrease in use is seen as positive and is reinforced by the clinician.
- MDFT is effective in reducing adolescent substance use problems. It addresses (a) the adolescent's substance use, (b) parenting behavior, (c) the quality of parent–adolescent interactions, and (d) school climate and peer relationships.

What Is Relapse Prevention?

Results of the Cannabis Youth Treatment Study highlighted a glaring problem in the treatment of adolescent substance use disorders: Most adolescents who respond to treatment will eventually relapse. In the cannabis study, 66% to 83% of adolescents who participated in treatment had either not

Figure 10.15   The Cannabis Youth Treatment Study

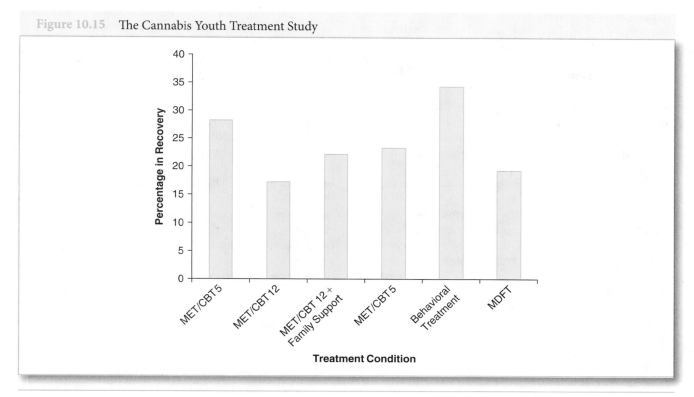

Source: From Dennis et al. (2004). Used with permission.

Note: All groups of adolescents who participated in treatment showed similar rates of recovery. Five sessions of MET/CBT or behavioral treatment were most time- and cost-effective. Notice, however, that only 20% to 30% of youths remained abstinent after treatment. Most relapsed.

responded to therapy or had relapsed within 12 months of completing treatment (Diamond et al., 2002). Across other studies of adolescents with alcohol use problems, approximately 50% of youths relapse within 3 months after treatment, 66% relapse after 6 months, and between 75% to 80% relapse after one year (Wagner & Austin, 2006).

Because relapse is so common, many therapists now decide to openly talk about relapse during treatment. Indeed, Alan Marlatt and colleagues (Hendershot, Witkiewitz, George, & Marlatt, 2011; Witkiewitz & Marlatt, 2011) developed a relapse prevention component to therapy for adults with substance use problems. This approach has subsequently been adapted for use with adolescents (Catalano, Hawkins, Wells, Miller, & Brewer, 2009; Patterson & O'Connell, 2003).

Relapse prevention is most often used with motivational enhancement and CBT. After the adolescent has shown a decrease in substance use, the therapist begins to discuss the possibility of relapse. The therapist might mention that relapse is likely when the adolescent encounters any high-risk situations. High-risk situations usually involve stimulus cues that trigger substance use. Cues might include certain people (e.g., friends who expect the adolescent to drink), situations (e.g., parties or being alone), and negative mood states (e.g., feeling depressed or bored). The strongest stimulus cues seem to be exposure to family members and friends who use substances.

Stimulus cues can trigger relapse even if adolescents have been abstinent for long periods of time. Often, adolescents feel shame and guilt after breaking a period of abstinence, an experience referred to as the abstinence violation effect (Collins & Witkiewitz, 2013). Adolescents may attribute their relapse to internal, stable, and global causes—that is, they blame their relapse on their weak morals, their lack of will power, or their general inability to control their lives. Consequently, many adolescents continue to drink or use other drugs, believing that abstinence is impossible.

Adolescents' thoughts about the relapse greatly affect their ability to maintain sobriety. After having one drink, many adolescents show a number of cognitive distortions that make them more likely to continue their alcohol use. For example, many adolescents engage in catastrophic thinking—that is, they expect the worst possible consequences from "falling off the wagon." They might reason, "Well, now that I've had one drink, everything is ruined. My parents are going to kill me, I'm going to get kicked out of school, and I'm probably not going to graduate." As a result of catastrophic thinking, adolescents conclude, "I guess there's no use; I might as well get drunk."

Therapists who incorporate relapse prevention into their treatment not only help clients develop a plan for responding to a possible relapse but they also teach youths to learn from the relapse experience. First, the therapist encourages the client to identify stimulus cues that might lead to relapse and generate ways to avoid these cues. Second, the therapist and client might create a concrete strategy for dealing with relapse. For example, if the adolescent uses alcohol, she might agree to contact the therapist or a support group member immediately, before she has another drink. The therapist or friend might then encourage her to avoid the situation that triggered the relapse and take steps to maintain sobriety. The therapist might help the client to attribute the relapse to external, transient causes (e.g., a stressful day, pressure from friends) rather than to personal weakness.

Similarly, the therapist might challenge the adolescent's catastrophic thoughts or other cognitive distortions that could increase his likelihood of drinking even more. The Research to Practice section illustrates this process.

As the narrative suggests, the therapist encourages the adolescent to view the lapse as a possible learning experience rather than as a sign of failure. If the adolescent views the lapse as an indicator that she is "back at rock bottom," then she might drink even more heavily. Alternatively, the therapist and client might analyze the antecedents and consequences of the lapse and develop ways to avoid another lapse in the future.

Researchers are only beginning to study factors that affect the likelihood of relapse among high school students. Our current knowledge of relapse among adolescents can be summarized as follows. First, adolescents seem to relapse for different reasons than adults. Adolescents are more likely than adults to relapse because of exposure to substance-using peers, pressure or encouragement from friends, and a desire to enhance mood or enjoy the pleasurable effects of the drug. In contrast, adults often relapse when depressed, anxious, or otherwise distressed (Curry et al., 2012; Ramo, Anderson, Tate, & Brown, 2005). Second, adolescents' self-efficacy regarding their ability to abstain is inversely related to their likelihood of relapse. Adolescents who are confident that they can resist the pleasurable effects of substances and avoid social pressures are more likely to maintain abstinence (Burleson & Kaminer, 2005). Third, adolescents who do not regard their substance use as problematic are far more likely to relapse than adolescents committed to long-term behavior change (Callaghan et al., 2005; Ramo et al., 2005). Since both situational (e.g., peers) and cognitive (e.g., beliefs, readiness to change) factors affect likelihood of relapse, both are targets of relapse prevention.

Review:

- Relapse prevention is a therapeutic strategy wherein the clinician and adolescent anticipate relapse and develop a plan for responding if relapse should occur.
- Relapse prevention is designed to reduce the abstinence violation effect—that is, feelings of guilt, shame, and negative affect following relapse. Instead, adolescents are encouraged to learn from the relapse experience.

RESEARCH TO PRACTICE

LEARNING FROM RELAPSE

Mike:	Before I knew it, I had had five or six beers at the party and I was doing a lot of stupid stuff. At first, I felt really good. But then I just thought, "What a loser." I'd been so good not drinking for those months and now I just threw that all away.
Therapist:	You felt as if all your work had been for nothing?
Mike:	Exactly. Like, no matter what I do, I'm going to end up a drunk like my dad. I figure, what's the use?
Therapist:	It sounds like you're being a little too hard on yourself. Just because you had a few drinks at the party that night, does that really mean you're going to be a drunk? After all, wasn't there a lot of encouragement from friends to drink that night?
Mike:	Well, yeah. I really wanted to have a good time with everybody else.
Therapist:	And you didn't get into any serious trouble like last time [when you drove off the road and hit a tree]?
Mike:	No, I made it home fine.
Therapist:	Then maybe we can look at the situation a little more closely and learn from it. Maybe we can see what triggered your decision to drink and figure out how to avoid these triggers in the future.

12-step programs: A treatment approach that conceptualizes substance use problems as a disease and emphasizes the need for the person to rely on humility and social support to achieve abstinence; involves attending regular meetings with other individuals with substance use problems (e.g., AA or NA) 323

28-day inpatient treatment: An inpatient treatment program for youths with substance use problems usually characterized by (a) abstinence and detoxification, (b) 12-step facilitation, and (c) brief individual and family therapy 323

Abstinence violation effect: Feeling shame and guilt after breaking a period of abstinence; often results in continued substance use to alleviate these negative emotions 331

Acute tolerance: A decrease in a person's response to alcohol after a small quantity of the substance 318

Alcohol, Smoking, and Substance Involvement Screening Test (ASSIST): A measure administered to adolescents and parents to screen for a wide range of substance use problems in adolescents 308

Amotivational syndrome: Decreased motivation and goal-directed behavior associated with chronic marijuana use 317

Aversion therapy: Pharmaceutical treatment for substance use disorders that involves administering a medication that produces a negative effect when the person ingests the illicit substance; usually administered only to adults with chronic substance-use problems 322

Biphasic effect: A description of the effects of alcohol on individuals; mild to moderate alcohol use produces largely desirable effects whereas extended use produces largely adverse effects 314

CAGE acronym: An acronym used to screen for substance use disorders in adults: cut down, annoyed, guilty, eye-opener 308

Cannabinoid receptors: A type of neurotransmitter receptor that regulates appetite, pain sensation, mood, and memory 317

Cannabis Youth Treatment Study: A large, study that examined the relative efficacy of psychosocial treatments for marijuana and alcohol use problems in adolescents 330

Cost–benefit analysis: A technique used by some cognitive behaviorists to increase a client's willingness to change his or her behavior; the client identifies positive and negative aspects of changing versus maintaining current substance use 324

CRAFFT assessment method: A method to screen for substance use disorders in adolescents: car, relax, alone, forget, friends, trouble 308

Delta-9-tetrahydrocannabinol (THC): The most powerful cannabinoid found in marijuana 317

Deviance-prone pathway: A developmental pathway used to explain the emergence of substance use disorders; includes (a) neurobehavioral undercontrol, (b) disruptive behavior and academic problems, and (c) peer rejection and deviant peers who introduce and reinforce substance use 319

Ecologically based prevention: Secondary prevention programs that are administered in settings where children are naturally located such as schools and neighborhood community centers

Endorphins: Naturally occurring chemicals that activate the body's opiate receptors causing an analgesic effect 316

Enhanced reinforcement pathway: A developmental pathway used to explain the emergence of substance use disorders; includes (a) genetic risk, (b) sensitivity to the effects of the substance, and (c) positive expectations for substance use 318

GABA (gamma-aminobutyric acid): A major inhibitory neurotransmitter; regulates arousal or the autonomic nervous system 318

Gateway hypothesis: Posits that adolescents who use marijuana are at increased risk of using other "harder" illicit substances; has received mixed support in the research literature 313

Glutamate: A major excitatory neurotransmitter in the central nervous system; plays a role in arousal, learning, and memory 315

Harm reduction: Asserts that the primary goal of therapy is to help clients identify and avoid substance use that has high potential for harm; the goal is not necessarily abstinence 327

Intoxication: A disturbance of perception, wakefulness, attention, thinking, judgment, psychomotor, and/or interpersonal behavior caused by the ingestion of a substance 304

Mesolimbic pathway: The brain's primary reward neural pathway; extends from the VTA of the midbrain to the nucleus accumbens, amygdala, and hippocampus in the limbic system 312

Monitoring the Future (MTF): An annual study conducted by the University of Michigan Institute for Social Research of approximately 50,000 adolescents in 8th, 10th, and 12th grades; used to estimate substance use, problems, accessibility, and attitudes 310

Motivational enhancement therapy: A brief therapy in which the client uses active listening and supportive questioning to help increase a client's willingness to change his or her substance use 326

Multidimensional family therapy (MDFT): A type of family-based treatment that addresses (1) the adolescent's substance use, (2) parenting behavior, (3) parent–child interactions, and (4) peers/school 329

Negative affect pathway: A developmental pathway used to explain the emergence of substance use disorders; assumes that substance use is negatively reinforced by the alleviation of stress or negative affect 319

Neurobehavioral disinhibition: A composite variable characterized by (a) behavioral undercontrol, (b) emotional reactivity, and (c) deficits in executive functioning; part of the deviance-prone pathway for the emergence of substance use problems 320

Pharmacodynamic tolerance: A decrease in a person's response to alcohol after repeated ingestion over a long period of time; caused by decreased number or sensitivity of the neuroreceptors that respond to alcohol 318

Principles of motivational interviewing: Overarching strategies to increase a client's willingness to reduce his or her substance use: (a) develop discrepancies, (b) roll with resistance, (c) fast empathy, (d) support the client, and (e) success should be acknowledged to build self-efficacy *326*

Reticular formation: Area of the brain stem responsible for alerting the individual to important information in the environment and initiating attention and arousal *315*

Relapse prevention: A component of CBT for substance use problems in which the therapist and client anticipate possible relapse and develop a plan for responding *331*

Remission: A term used to describe substance use symptoms that used to be present but now no longer exist *304*

Stages of change: A trans-theoretical model for a client's readiness to change that applies to most schools of psychotherapy; includes (a) precontemplation, (b) contemplation, (c) action, and (d) maintenance *326*

Stimulus cues: People, situations, or mood states that trigger relapse *331*

Substance-induced disorders: A group of *DSM-5* disorders that describe specific syndromes caused by either the ingestion or withdrawal of specific substances; includes (a) substance intoxication, (b) substance withdrawal, and (c) substance-induced mental disorder *301*

Substance use disorder: A problematic pattern of substance use leading to distress or impairment and characterized by (a) impaired control, (b) social problems, (c) risk-taking, and/or (d) tolerance or withdrawal; in *DSM-5*, individuals are diagnosed based on the type of substance (i.e., alcohol use disorder, cannabis use disorder) *302*

Substitution therapy: Pharmaceutical treatment for substance use problems that involves administering a medication designed to eliminate cravings for alcohol or other drugs *322*

Tolerance: Occurs when a person (1) needs more of a substance to achieve intoxication or (2) the same amount of a substance produces diminished effects over repeated use *304*

Withdrawal: Occurs when a person (a) experiences negative physiological symptoms when they stop or reduce substance use or (b) takes a different substance to avoid these negative symptoms *334*

CRITICAL THINKING EXERCISES

1. What physiological changes explain the biphasic effect of alcohol? How can the biphasic effect lead adolescents to binge drink?

2. Charlie is a 17-year-old high school student. Charlie drinks beer and other alcoholic beverages at parties with friends. He has also used marijuana on several occasions with friends during social gatherings. Charlie's substance use has never led to academic, family, social, or legal problems. To what extent is Charlie's behavior developmentally normative? If you were Charlie's parents, would you be concerned?

3. In the 1980s, First Lady Nancy Reagan initiated an antidrug campaign toward school-age children called Just Say No! The campaign consisted of speeches and rallies, television commercials, and school-based programs. During the 1980s and early 1990s when this campaign was in effect, the use of alcohol and marijuana among older children and adolescents decreased. Why *can't* we conclude that the Just Say No! campaign caused this reduction in substance use?

4. Ringo was suspended from high school for possession of alcohol and marijuana on campus. He was ordered by school administrators to participate in therapy. If you were Ringo's therapist, how might you involve his *family* in treatment?

5. Some clinicians who treat substance use disorders adopt a harm reduction approach with adults. Why might harm reduction be controversial when it is used with adolescents?

TEST YOURSELF AND EXTEND YOUR LEARNING

Videos, flash cards, and links to online resources for this chapter are available to students online. Teachers also have access to PowerPoint slides to guide lectures, case studies to prompt classroom discussions, and exam questions. Visit www.abnormalchildpsychology.org.

PART IV

Emotion and Thought Disorders

CHAPTER 11

Anxiety Disorders and Obsessive–Compulsive Disorder

LEARNING OBJECTIVES

After reading this chapter, you should be able to do the following:

11.1. Describe key features of the *DSM-5* anxiety disorders and explain how children might manifest these disorders differently across childhood and adolescence.

Identify and give examples of some of the major causes of anxiety disorders in youths.

11.2. Describe the key features of obsessive–compulsive disorder (OCD) in children and adolescents, its primary causes, and related conditions.

11.3. Show how behavioral and cognitive interventions are used to treat pediatric anxiety and OCD.

Evaluate the strength and limitations of medication, psychotherapy, and combined treatment for pediatric anxiety disorders and OCD.

11.1 ANXIETY DISORDERS IN CHILDHOOD AND ADOLESCENCE

What Is the Difference Between Normal Anxiety and an Anxiety Disorder?

Adaptive vs. Maladaptive Anxiety

We all know what it is like to be anxious. Think about how you felt before your last important exam or job interview. You probably experienced physiological symptoms like butterflies in your stomach, a rapid heartbeat, or sweaty palms. You might have also shown anxiety through your behavior, by fidgeting with your clothes, pacing about the room, or acting restless and agitated. You probably also had certain thoughts that accompanied your physiological and behavioral symptoms. These thoughts might have included self-statements like, "I really *need* to do well on the test" or "I *have* to get the job" or "*What if* I fail?" Anxiety is a complex state of psychological distress that reflects emotional, behavioral, physiological, and cognitive reactions to threatening stimuli (Barlow, Conklin, & Bentley, 2015).

Psychologists often differentiate between two types of anxiety: (1) fear and (2) worry (Weems, Graham, Scott, Banks, & Russell, 2013). Fear is primarily a behavioral and physiological reaction to an immediate threat, in which the person responds to imminent danger. People respond to fearful stimuli with confrontation (e.g., fighting) or escape (e.g., flee-ing). We might experience fear when we discover that we are poorly prepared for an important exam. As we stare at the test, our pulse quickens, our breathing becomes shallow, and we may become dizzy or light-headed. Subjectively, we might experience a sense of panic or terror and a strong desire to flee the situation.

In contrast, worry is primarily a cognitive response to threat, in which the person considers and prepares for future danger or misfortune. We might worry about next week's exam, an upcoming job interview, or tomorrow's big game. The subjective experience of worry is a chronic state of psychological distress that can cause uneasiness, apprehension, and tension. Worry is typically accompanied by thoughts and self-statements about the future, such as "What is going to be on the exam?" "What should I wear to the interview?" or "What if I make a mistake and lose the game?" (Donovan, Holmes, & Farrell, 2016).

In most cases, anxiety is beneficial; it helps us deal with immediate threats to our integrity or motivates us to prepare for future danger. For example, a moderate amount of anxiety can help us stay alert and cautious while driving our car during a thunderstorm. Similarly, a moderate degree of apprehension before an important exam can motivate us to study.

Maladaptive anxiety can be differentiated from adaptive anxiety in at least three ways: (1) by its intensity, (2) by its chronicity, and (3) by its degree of impairment. First, maladaptive anxiety tends to be *intense and out of proportion* to the threat that triggered the anxiety response. For example, many students experience apprehension about giving an oral presentation in front of the class. In most cases, moderate anxiety is appropriate and adaptive; it can motivate us prepare for the presentation. However, apprehension becomes maladaptive when it causes intense feelings of distress or psychological discomfort. For example, a student's mind may "go blank" during the presentation, or she may become physically ill shortly before the presentation because of her anticipatory anxiety (Ramirez, Feeney-Kettler, Flores-Torres, Kraochwill, & Morris, 2006).

Second, maladaptive anxiety tends to be *chronic*. Worry about an upcoming exam is appropriate and adaptive when it motivates individuals to prepare for the exam and terminates after the exam's completion. Chronic worry, however, is maladaptive. Chronic worriers, who always anticipate disasters on the horizon, tend to experience long-standing agitation as well as physical and emotional discomfort.

Third, maladaptive anxiety *interferes* with people's ability to perform daily tasks. For example, most people experience moderate anxiety before a job interview. Anticipatory anxiety becomes maladaptive when people decide to keep their current, low-paying job in order to avoid the anxiety-provoking interview. Similarly, many people experience moderate apprehension before riding in an airplane. This apprehension becomes problematic if the person is unable to attend his best friend's wedding because of his fear of flying.

Anxiety in the Context of Development

Children's anxiety also exists on a continuum from developmentally expected and adaptive to developmentally divergent and maladaptive (see Table 11.1). At any given point in time, children's fears and worries reflect their present stage of cognitive, social, and emotional development (Pine & Klein, 2010). For example, a critical developmental task in infancy is to establish a sense of basic trust in a primary caregiver—someone who will provide safety and security in times of danger or distress. The natural emergence of object permanence (4–10 months), stranger anxiety (6–12 months), and separation anxiety (12–18 months) promotes the mastery of this social–emotional task. It is developmentally normative and expected that infants will display a wariness of strangers and anxiety upon being separated from their mothers. However, some children display separation anxiety of unusual intensity, chronicity, or impairment. Their fears might be out of proportion to the actual threat that might confront them (e.g., screaming or clinging to avoid separation at day care). Furthermore, their anxiety may extend beyond the typical developmental period (e.g., beyond toddlerhood). Finally, their anxiety may interfere with their ability to master other developmental tasks at later points in time. For example, a child who fears separation may refuse to play at a friend's home or attend sleepovers. These developmentally unexpected signs of anxiety might indicate an anxiety disorder (Wehry, Beesdo-Baum, Hennelly, Connolly, & Strawn, 2015).

A critical task in early adolescence is to develop a sense of social competence—that is, to establish close friendships and establish meaningful social roles in school, extracurricular activities, or sports. Adolescents' increased capacity for empathy and metacognition (e.g., thinking about their own thinking) helps their social interactions. However, these abilities also can elicit self-doubts and insecurities. For example, it is developmentally normative for young adolescents to show increased self-consciousness and a tendency to engage in egocentrism (Elkind & Bowen, 1979). However, some children's fears and doubts become unusually intense, extend beyond the typical developmental period, and interfere with their overall functioning. Their anxiety about school or interactions with teachers and peers can cause sleep problems, irritability, or avoidance of social situations. At that point, they might be classified with an anxiety disorder.

Children's fears, anxieties, and worries, therefore, exist along a continuum. On one end of this continuum is developmentally expected and adaptive anxiety that can help children achieve developmental tasks and interact effectively with the world. Anxiety helps children study for tests, prepare for important presentations, and seek safety in times of danger. At the other extreme is intense anxiety, fear, or worry that extends beyond the usual development period and interferes with children's capacities to meet the expected challenges along life's path (e.g., establishing trust in a primary caregiver, autonomy and independence at school, confidence in social situations). Many children fall somewhere in between these extremes. It takes both scientific knowledge and clinical skills to determine where normal anxiety ends and anxiety disorders begin (Ollendick, King, & Yule, 2013).

Table 11.1   A Continuum of Fears and Worries Across Childhood

Age	Developmentally Expected Fears/ Worries	Symptoms That Might Indicate a Disorder	Corresponding DSM-5 Anxiety Disorder
Toddlerhood (2–3 years)	Fears of separation from caregivers Shyness, anxiety with strangers	Extreme panic when separated after age 2 years, sleep disturbance, tantrums when separated; failure to talk with others outside the home	Separation anxiety disorder Selective mutism
Preschool (4–5 years)	Fear of separating from parents to go to preschool or day care Fear of thunderstorms, darkness, nightmares Fear of specific animals	Clinging to parents, crying, tantrums, freezing, sneaking into parents' bed at night, avoiding feared stimuli, sleep refusal, bed-wetting	Separation anxiety disorder/ selective mutism Specific phobia (natural environment) Specific phobia (animals)
Elementary School (6–8 years)	Fear of specific objects (animals, monsters, ghosts) Fear of germs or illnesses Fear of natural disasters or injuries Anxiety about school	Avoidance of feared stimuli, refusal to attend school, extreme anxiety/panic during tests, academic problems	Specific phobia (animals, situations)
Middle School (9–12 years)	Anxiety about school or tests, worry about completing assignments Worries about making and keeping friends, concerns about pleasing others	School refusal, academic problems, procrastination, insomnia, tension or restlessness, social withdrawal, timidity, extreme shyness in social situations, persistent worry	Social anxiety disorder Generalized anxiety disorder
High School (13–18 years)	Concerns about acceptance and rejection by peers, teachers Worries about grades, sports, relationships	Academic problems, persistent worry, sleep/appetite disturbance, depressed mood or irritability, substance abuse, recurrent panic attacks, social withdrawal	Social anxiety disorder Generalized anxiety disorder Panic disorder, agoraphobia

Review:

- Anxiety is a complex state of psychological distress that reflects emotional, behavioral, physiological, and cognitive reactions to threatening stimuli. Fear is primarily a behavioral and physiological reaction to immediate threat, whereas worry is primarily a cognitive reaction to the anticipation of future misfortune.
- Maladaptive anxiety can be differentiated from adaptive anxiety by its (1) intensity, (2) chronicity, and (3) degree of impairment.
- Children's anxiety symptoms reflect their level of cognitive and social–emotional development.

How Common Are Childhood Anxiety Disorders?

Onset

The *Diagnostic and Statistical Manual of Mental Disorders, Fifth Edition* (DSM-5; American Psychiatric Association,

2013) identifies seven anxiety disorders that can be diagnosed in children, adolescents, and adults (American Psychiatric Association, 2013). They are (1) separation anxiety disorder (SAD), (2) selective mutism, (3) specific phobia, (4) social anxiety disorder, (5) panic disorder, (6) agoraphobia, and (7) generalized anxiety disorder (GAD). These disorders tend to emerge at different periods in children's development (see Figure 11.1).

Four disorders typically emerge in early or middle childhood: (1) separation anxiety disorder, (2) selective mutism, (3) specific phobia, and (4) social anxiety disorder. These disorders are characterized by recurrent, unwanted fears of specific objects or situations. A child with SAD might fear leaving her parents to attend school, whereas a child with selective mutism might not speak at school with teachers or classmates. A child with specific phobia might fear snakes or spiders, and a child with social anxiety disorder might fear attending parties or other social gatherings. These disorders are usually considered "fear" disorders because they are characterized by

Figure 11.1 Separation anxiety disorder (SAD), selective mutism, specific phobia, and social anxiety disorder usually emerge in childhood. Generalized anxiety disorder (GAD), panic disorder, and agoraphobia tend to emerge in adolescence or adulthood.

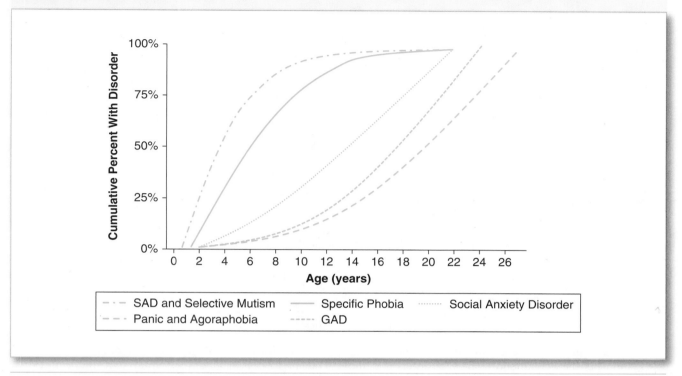

Source: Based on Higa-McMillan, Francis, and Chorpita (2014); Muris and Ollendick (2015); Simon (2016); and Zinbarg, Anand, Lee, Kendall, and Nunez (2015).

persistent, unwanted fears that greatly interfere with children's social–emotional functioning and quality of life.

The next two anxiety disorders, panic disorder and agoraphobia, are rare in children. These disorders tend to emerge in adolescence or adulthood. They are characterized by feelings of intense apprehension, dread, or panic. Panic disorder and agoraphobia often, but not always, co-occur. Adolescents and adults with panic disorder experience recurrent intense panic attacks, characterized by discrete episodes of severe, unpleasant autonomic arousal (e.g., rapid breathing, heart rate, and negative thoughts, feelings, and actions). Adolescents and adults with agoraphobia fear situations in which escape might be difficult or embarrassing (e.g., movie theaters, shopping malls). Often, adolescents fear having a panic attack in these situations and, consequently, avoid them.

The final anxiety disorder, GAD, is unlike the other anxiety disorders because it is characterized by persistent worry, rather than fear or panic. Youths with GAD do not fear specific situations, objects, or events; instead, they chronically worry about future misfortune. GAD usually does not develop until late childhood or adolescence because only older children have the cognitive capacity to contemplate (and worry about) events in the future.

Prevalence and Course

Anxiety disorders are among the most frequently diagnosed psychiatric conditions in children and adolescents (Essau & Petermann, 2013). Approximately 20% of children and adolescents will develop an anxiety disorder before reaching adulthood (see Figure 11.2). At any given time, approximately 5% of youths have an anxiety disorder. The prevalence of anxiety disorders is higher for adolescents than for children. The prevalence is also higher for girls than boys. The gender ratio of anxiety disorders tends to increase with age, reaching 1:2 or 1:3 by adolescence.

Anxiety disorders tend to persist across childhood and adolescence (Beesdo, Knappe, & Pine, 2009). The Early Developmental Stages of Psychopathology (EDSP) study followed a large group of children with anxiety disorders over time. On average 25% to 30% of children diagnosed with a specific anxiety disorder at baseline met diagnostic criteria for the same disorder 10 years later (homotypic continuity). Furthermore, more than 70% of children who met criteria for an anxiety disorder at baseline also met criteria for an anxiety or mood disorder a decade later (heterotypical continuity). Although the stability of individual anxiety disorders is modest, the stability of anxiety problems in general is high (Wigman et al., 2013).

Figure 11.2 The median prevalence of anxiety disorders in children and adolescents in the United States. At any point in time, approximately 5% of youths have at least one anxiety disorder.

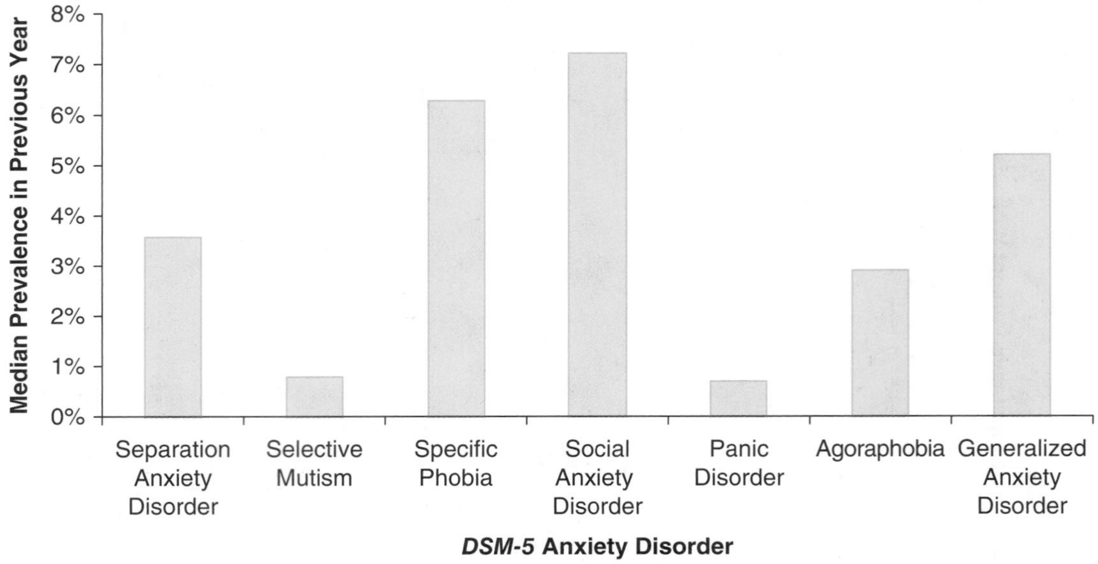

Source: Based on Connolly, Suarez, Victor, Zagoloff, and Bernstein (2015); Higa-McMillan et al. (2014); Simon (2016); and Zinbarg et al. (2015).

Several longitudinal studies have also demonstrated an association between childhood anxiety disorders and the development of depressive disorders in adolescence and young adulthood (Cummings, Caporino, & Kendall, 2014). Childhood anxiety disorders predict a litany of negative developmental outcomes including major depressive disorder (MDD), substance use disorder, and suicide attempts. On average, depression tended to emerge 5 years after the onset of anxiety. Certain childhood anxiety disorders, especially those characterized by chronic worry or extreme panic, are particularly predictive of later depression (Moffitt, Caspi, & Harrington, 2007). These findings have led many researchers to conclude that early problems with anxiety can adversely affect children's developmental paths (Pine & Klein, 2010).

Review:

- SAD, selective mutism, specific phobia, social anxiety disorder, and GAD typically emerge in childhood, whereas panic disorder and agoraphobia typically emerge in late adolescence or adulthood.
- Approximately 5% of youths have an anxiety disorder at any point in time; approximately 20% of youths will experience an anxiety disorder prior to adulthood.

What Is Separation Anxiety Disorder?

Description

Children with separation anxiety disorder (SAD) show excessive anxiety about leaving caregivers and other individuals to whom they are emotionally attached (see Table 11.2). Typically, these youths are preoccupied by fears that misfortune or harm will befall themselves or their caregivers during the separation period. For example, young children with SAD may believe that monsters might kidnap them while their parents are away. Older children might fear that their parents will become injured at work. Children with SAD usually insist that caregivers remain in close proximity, and they may become angry, distressed, or physically ill upon separation. Many refuse to attend school, summer camps, or activities with friends to avoid separation (American Psychiatric Association, 2013).

A certain degree of separation anxiety is adaptive and developmentally expected in infants and very young children (Bernstein & Victor, 2010). Fear of separation tends to emerge in infants at 6 months of age and peaks between 13 and 18 months. Older infants and toddlers show separation anxiety as they develop a sense of trust in the availability of their caregivers. Separation anxiety keeps infants in close proximity to caregivers and helps protect them from harm. Separation anxiety typically declines between the ages of 3 and 5. However, preschoolers and young school-age children continue to require reassurance from caregivers when scared, upset, or unsure. The tendency to seek out caregivers when scared or upset indicates that the young child expects her parents to provide comfort and care.

Periodic concerns about separation are also common among school-age children. Indeed, approximately 70% of school-age children admit to occasional anxiety when separating from parents, and 15% report occasional nightmares about being kidnapped or harm befalling

Table 11.2   Diagnostic Criteria for Separation Anxiety Disorder

A. Developmentally inappropriate and excessive fear or anxiety concerning separation from those to whom the individual is attached, as evidenced by at least three of the following:

  1. Recurrent excessive distress when anticipating or experiencing separation from home or from major attachment figures.

  2. Persistent and excessive worry about losing major attachment figures or about possible harm to them, such as illness, injuries, disasters, or death.

  3. Persistent and excessive worry about experiencing an untoward event (e.g., getting lost, being kidnapped, having an accident, becoming ill) that causes separation from a major attachment figure.

  4. Persistent reluctance or refusal to go out, away from home, to school, to work, or elsewhere because of fear of separation.

  5. Persistent and excessive fear of or reluctance about being alone or without major attachment figures at home or in other settings.

  6. Persistent reluctance or refusal to sleep away from home or to go to sleep without being near a major attachment figure.

  7. Repeated nightmares involving the theme of separation.

  8. Repeated complaints of physical symptoms (e.g., headaches, stomachaches, nausea, vomiting) when separation from major attachment figures occurs or is anticipated.

B. The fear, anxiety, or avoidance is persistent, lasting at least 4 weeks in children and adolescents and typically 6 months or more in adults.

C. The disturbance causes clinically significant distress or impairment in social, academic, occupational, or other important areas of functioning.

D. The disturbance is not better explained by another mental disorder, such as refusing to leave home because of excessive resistance to change in Autism Spectrum Disorder; refusal to go outside without a trusted companion in Agoraphobia; or worries about ill health or other harm befalling significant others in Generalized Anxiety Disorder.[1]

Source: Reprinted with permission from the *Diagnostic and Statistical Manual of Mental Disorders, Fifth Edition* (Copyright 2013). American Psychiatric Association.

[1] Agoraphobia and Generalized Anxiety Disorder are presented later in this chapter.

loved ones. However, only about 15% of school-age children report persistent fears about separation, and 3% to 4% meet diagnostic criteria for SAD. SAD is differentiated from developmentally expected fears of separation by the intensity of the fear, its persistence, and the degree to which the fear interferes with the child's overall functioning (Connolly et al., 2015).

The presentation of SAD varies by age (Higa-McMillan et al., 2014). Young children with SAD worry about physical harm befalling themselves or their parents, usually through unlikely means. For example, a 7-year-old boy with SAD might worry about being kidnapped on the way to school or his parents being abducted by robbers while at work. Young children with SAD may refuse to attend school and throw tantrums if forced to go. When their parents are home, young children may "shadow" them from room to room or engage in other clinging behavior. Parents often regard these children as excessively needy. They may become frustrated with their children's strong desire for reassurance. Young children with SAD often experience nightmares about harm befalling themselves or family members. They may have difficulty going to sleep, insist on a parent staying in their room, or ask to sleep in their parents' bed. If denied, some youths with SAD will sleep outside their parents' bedroom door in order to gain closer proximity.

Older children with SAD often worry about more realistic events that might separate them from parents. For example, a 12-year-old with SAD might worry about her parents contracting a terrible disease or getting into an auto accident. Adolescents with SAD often have diffuse fears of separation. They might report only a vague sense that "something bad will happen" if they are separated from their parents or loved ones. Consider Valerie, an adolescent with SAD.

Older children and adolescents with SAD usually tolerate separation better than younger children; however, older children still experience considerable anxiety and sadness when separated. Some become physically ill if forced to separate from parents. Others show severe social withdrawal, concentration problems, and signs of depression. Many older children and adolescents sacrifice time with peers to be near their families. Often, these fears of separation interfere with academic and social functioning (Ollendick et al., 2013).

Onset of SAD is usually between 7 and 9 years of age. Some children first show symptoms following a stressful event. Events that threaten the availability of parents or the child's security may be most likely to elicit SAD: illness of

SEPARATION ANXIETY DISORDER

Concerned About Dad

Source: ©iStockphoto.com/JacquiMoore

Valerie was a 14-year-old girl referred to our clinic because she persistently refused to go to school. According to her father, Valerie would feign sickness, lie, tantrum, and do "just about anything" to stay home. Her father explained, "Last week, she promised me that she would go. I watched her get on the bus, but she never made it to school. She was back home 25 minutes later saying that her stomach hurt."

Valerie's mother added, "It's getting to be a problem. All she wants to do is stay home. I ask her, 'Don't you want to go to Emily's house or shopping with your friends?' but she always prefers to be with us."

A psychologist at our clinic, Dr. Saunders, asked Valerie about her reluctance to go to school. "Did something bad happen at school? Are you having trouble there?" Valerie responded, "No. I get along fine with the other kids and I'm getting good grades. I just like being at home better, near my dad." Dr. Saunders learned that Valerie's school refusal began last autumn, shortly after her father had heart surgery. Valerie was asked to take care of her father, while her mother was at work, as he recovered from the surgery. Since that time, Valerie's father had worked from home, and Valerie showed especially strong attachment to him.

After several sessions, Dr. Saunders asked, "Are you worried that something bad might happen to your father, like maybe he'll have another heart problem?" Valerie responded, "Of course not! The doctors say he's fine." After a long pause, she added, "I just want to make sure."

a family member, parental divorce, a change in home or school. However, many families cannot identify a specific stressor associated with onset (Bernstein & Victor, 2010).

Experts disagree about the course of SAD. Most children experience a marked decrease in separation fears over time (Zinbarg et al., 2015). For example, longitudinal research indicates that only about 20% to 25% of youths initially diagnosed with SAD continue to meet full diagnostic criteria 18 months later. However, most children continue to show subthreshold symptoms that cause them (or their families) distress. In some instances, SAD can persist into adolescence and adulthood. Data from a large epidemiological study showed that 36% of adults who reported a history of SAD in childhood continued to report fears of separating from loved ones (Bögels, Knappe, & Clark, 2013).

Causes

Compared to other anxiety disorders, genetic factors play a relatively small role in the development of SAD. Genetic factors likely predispose children to SAD by increasing their level of autonomic arousal and general anxiety in novel situations. Consequently, these children often demand considerable reassurance and comfort from parents to help them regulate their physiological arousal and feel safe (Barlow et al., 2015).

The quality of parent–child interactions, especially early attachment relationships, likely plays an important role in the development of anxiety problems, including SAD (Goldberg, 2014). According to John Bowlby (1988), the purpose of caregiver–child attachment is to provide the child with a "secure base"—that is, a sense of safety and security from which to explore the world. Attachment behaviors, such as approaching the parent when scared, are evolutionarily adaptive; they keep children in close proximity to their caregivers.

Several prospective, longitudinal studies suggest that insecure attachment in infancy predicts anxiety problems during childhood and adolescence (Madigan, Atkinson, Laurin, & Benoit, 2013; Mikulincer & Shaver, 2012). Warren, Huston, Egeland, and Sroufe (1997) examined the relationship between the quality of the attachment relationship in infancy and the prevalence of anxiety disorders, including SAD, during adolescence. Infants who initially displayed insecure attachment relationships with their mothers at age 12 months were more likely to develop anxiety disorders during their teenage years. Furthermore, a particular pattern of insecure attachment predicted later anxiety. This pattern, called insecure–ambivalent attachment, is associated with inconsistent parental care. It is possible that children who receive inconsistent care from parents experience anxiety in times of stress because they do not know when (or if) parents will come to their aid. They seem to lack a secure base from which they can derive comfort and protection (Esbjørn, Bender, Reinholdt-Dunne, Munck, & Ollendick, 2012).

On the other hand, parents who provide their infants and young children with sensitive and responsive care may prevent the emergence of SAD and other anxiety problems later in childhood. Warren and Simmens (2005) examined the quality of parent–child interactions in families with infants who had difficult temperaments or high levels of shyness. The researchers found that infants whose parents provided sensitive and responsive care were less likely to have anxiety problems during toddlerhood.

Parents' own levels of anxiety and insecurity can contribute to the development of SAD in their children. The parents of children with SAD often appear overly involved, controlling, and protective of their children's behavior. Rather than encouraging independent play and exploration, these parents may model anxiety and fearfulness to their children and encourage their children to be excessively cautious. The tendency to parent in a highly controlling, overprotective manner is strongest among mothers with histories of insecure attachment relationships with their own parents (Kohlhoff, Barnett, & Eapen, 2015).

It is important to remember that insecure parent–child attachment relationships are not indicative of early child abuse or neglect. Children who develop insecure attachment relationships with their parents *are* attached to them—they love them, care about them, and experience distress when unexpectedly separated from them. These children simply feel less secure in their parents' ability to provide comfort and protection. In contrast, some children who are deprived of parental care during infancy and early childhood can fail to develop an attachment relationship to any caregiver. Infants raised in low-quality orphanages, toddlers who move from foster family to foster family, and severely neglected children may develop no attachment to any caregiver whatsoever (van IJzendoorn et al., 2011).

Review:

- SAD is characterized by a developmentally inappropriate and excessive fear of separation from attachment figures. It lasts at least 4 weeks in children and causes distress or impairment.
- Onset of SAD is typically in early childhood, although adolescents and adults can also develop SAD. It affects approximately 3% to 4% of school-age youths.
- Insecure attachment and perceived environmental threat can trigger the development of SAD in youths with genetic or biological risk for the disorder.

What Is Selective Mutism?

Description

Selective mutism is an anxiety disorder in which children consistently fail to speak in social situations where speaking is expected (see Table 11.3). Typically, the disorder is shown by preschool or young school-age children who refuse to speak at school or with strangers, but speak at home with close family members. Many of these children appear

Table 11.3 Diagnostic Criteria for Selective Mutism

A. Consistent failure to speak in specific social situations in which there is an expectation for speaking (e.g., at school) despite speaking in other situations

B. The disturbance interferes with educational achievement or social communication

C. The duration of the disturbance is at least 1 month (not limited to the first month of school)

D. The failure to speak is not attributable to a lack of knowledge of, or comfort with, the spoken language required in the social interaction

E. The disturbance is not better explained by a communication disorder (e.g., stuttering) and does not occur exclusively during the course of autism spectrum disorder, schizophrenia, or another psychotic disorder

Source: Reprinted with permission from the *Diagnostic and Statistical Manual of Mental Disorders, Fifth Edition* (Copyright 2013). American Psychiatric Association.

inhibited, inactive, or "frozen" in these social situations. This pattern of behavior must occur for at least 1 month and continue beyond children's first month in school, a time period during which many children are reluctant to participate in class. By definition, children's lack of speech interferes with their educational or social functioning. For example, children with selective mutism might fall behind in school because teachers cannot monitor their progress in certain academic subjects (e.g., reading) and because they are reluctant to ask for help. Similarly, they may fail to develop social skills because of their unwillingness to speak with peers (American Psychiatric Association, 2013). Consider Russell, a preschooler with selective mutism.

Selective mutism is only diagnosed when children's failure to speak is not attributable to a lack of knowledge or comfort with the language used in the specific situation. For example, immigrant children whose first language is not English might be reluctant to speak in school because of limited language proficiency or self-consciousness. Similarly, selective mutism must not be attributable exclusively to other psychiatric conditions, such as communication disorders or autism spectrum disorder (ASD). For example, some children might avoid speaking at school because they stutter or have poor articulation. Although many children with selective mutism have communication disorders, their failure to speak must not be due only to their communication problems (American Psychiatric Association, 2013).

Selective mutism is a rare condition, affecting less than 1% of young children in the general population. Some studies indicate that girls are twice as likely as boys to show the disorder. Mean age of onset is in toddlerhood or preschool (ages 2.7–4.2 years) although the disorder is typically not diagnosed until children first attend school

Reticent Russell

Source: ©iStockphoto.com/McIninch

Russell was a 3-year-old boy referred by his teacher for suspected language problems and possible developmental delays. Although Russell had attended preschool for 4 weeks, he had yet to say a word to his teacher or classmates.

"Russell is a shy but friendly child," his teacher reported. "He smiles and makes good eye contact but refuses to say anything." Instead of speaking, Russell communicated largely through gestures, grunts, and clicks.

Russell's mother reported that Russell met early developmental milestones on time. "Then," she added, "approximately one year ago—about the time his father and I separated—Russell stopped talking to other people. He speaks to me when we're alone. He'll also whisper or 'mouth' things to his brother. But Russell won't speak to his teacher, other people outside the house, or even his father."

His teacher commented, "Russell is such a sweet boy, but I'm worried about him. I can't help him develop good speech and language skills if he never talks in class. I also worry that he won't develop the social skills he needs for kindergarten. I hope there's something we can do."

Source: Based on Conn and Coyne (2014).

and refuse to speak to classmates and teachers. Before beginning school, children with selective mutism may not speak with strangers outside the family, day care providers, babysitters, or extended relatives like aunts, uncles, or grandparents (Gensthaler et al., 2016a).

Longitudinal studies indicate that selective mutism is a long-term condition. Without treatment, average duration of the condition is approximately eight years. Children with selective mutism are at risk for other psychiatric disorders later in childhood and adolescence. As many as 94% will develop social anxiety disorder, a condition characterized by anxiety and avoidance of social situations. Youths with selective mutism are also at risk for academic problems and peer rejection because of their failure to speak at school (Genstahler et al., 2016a).

Causes

Emerging data indicate that selective mutism arises from the interaction of genetics, temperament, and early social learning (Muris & Ollendick, 2015). Family studies suggest that the condition is heritable. Although selective mutism is uncommon, 9% of fathers, 18% of mothers, and 18% of siblings of children with the disorder displayed the disorder themselves. Furthermore, approximately 50% of parents of children with selective mutism have histories of extreme shyness in social situations. Geneticists have identified an allele for a certain gene, CNTNAP2, that predisposes children toward social anxiety and greatly increases their chance of developing selective mutism, social anxiety disorder, and similar problems (Genstahler et al., 2016b).

It is likely that these genetic risks predispose children toward a temperament characterized by high behavioral inhibition (Muris, Hendricks, & Bot, 2016). Behavioral inhibition is the tendency to inhibit play and vocalization, to withdraw, and to seek a parent when encountering unfamiliar people or situations. Jerome Kagan demonstrated that children with high behavioral inhibition experienced arousal and distress when presented with novel stimuli. For example, infants with high behavioral inhibition flailed their arms and legs and cried when presented with a mobile, whereas infants with low behavioral inhibition sat motionless, watching the mobile with interest. Kagan showed that infants with high behavioral inhibition (approximately 15% of all infants) tended to cope with this heightened arousal by avoiding or withdrawing from novel stimuli. In later childhood and adolescence, these children were at risk for extreme shyness in social situations (see Figure 11.3; Fox, Snidman, Haas, Degnan, & Kagan, 2015). Subsequent research has shown that children with selective mutism often show very high behavioral inhibition and social anxiety, more generally (Muris et al., 2016).

Mowrer's two-factor theory of anxiety can be used to explain the cause and maintenance of selective mutism in children (Mowrer, 1960). According to this theory, selective mutism arises because of classical conditioning, when children associate speaking in certain situations with heightened arousal and psychological distress. Selective mutism is maintained over time, however, because of operant conditioning (specifically negative reinforcement). These children learn that they can lower their arousal and avoid distress by remaining silent. Over

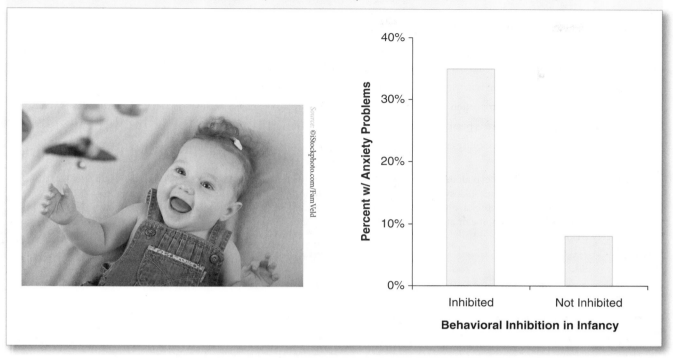

time, their habitual silence in certain situations can inhibit their speaking and social skills, making them increasingly less likely to break this cycle of negative reinforcement and speak out (Muris & Ollendick, 2015; Scott & Beidel, 2011).

Review:

- Selective mutism is characterized by a consistent failure to speak in certain social situations in which there is an expectation for speaking (e.g., at school). It lasts for at least 1 month and impairs functioning.
- Selective mutism tends to emerge in early childhood and affects less than 1% of preschoolers and young school-age children.
- Young children with temperaments characterized by high behavioral inhibition may be at risk for anxiety disorders in general and selective mutism in particular.

What Is Specific Phobia?

Description

Specific phobia is one of the most common, and most untreated, anxiety disorders in children and adolescents. Specific phobia is characterized by a marked fear of clearly discernible, circumscribed objects or situations (see Table 11.4). Although people can fear a wide range of stimuli, most phobias fall into five broad categories:

- *Animals*: fear of snakes, spiders, dogs, birds
- *Natural environment*: fear of thunderstorms, heights, water

- *Blood, injections, and injuries*: fear of receiving an injection, seeing blood
- *Specific situations*: fear of airplanes, elevators, enclosed places
- *Other stimuli*: fear of choking, contracting an illness, costumed characters

Individuals with specific phobia immediately experience anxiety when they encounter a feared situation or object. Sometimes, they may show extreme panic, characterized by racing heart, rapid and shallow breathing, sweaty palms, dizziness, and other somatic symptoms. Younger children might cry, tantrum, freeze, or cling to their parents. Often, individuals with specific phobia avoid situations in which they might encounter feared stimuli. For example, a child who is afraid of dogs might plan her walk to school in order to avoid encountering a neighbor's dog. Although some people with specific phobia recognize that their fears are excessive and unreasonable, many children do not have this degree of insight (American Psychiatric Association, 2013).

The fears displayed by people with specific phobia must be out of proportion to the actual danger posed by the specific object or situation. Usually, it is fairly easy for a parent or clinician to determine whether a fear is disproportionate to the threat of danger. A child who panics at the sight of a clown at her friend's birthday party is clearly showing a disproportionate degree of anxiety. In some instances, however, determining the appropriateness of

Table 11.4   Diagnostic Criteria for Specific Phobia

A. Marked fear or anxiety about a specific object or situation (e.g., flying, heights, animals, receiving an injection, seeing blood).

   Note: In children, the fear or anxiety may be expressed by crying, tantrums, freezing, or clinging.

B. The phobic object or situation almost always provokes immediate fear or anxiety.

C. The phobic object or situation is actively avoided or endured with intense fear or anxiety.

D. The fear or anxiety is out of proportion to the actual danger posed by the specific object or situation and to the sociocultural context.

E. The fear, anxiety, or avoidance is persistent, typically lasting for 6 months or more.

F. The fear, anxiety, or avoidance causes clinically significant distress or impairment in social, occupational, or other important areas of functioning.

G. The disturbance is not better explained by the symptoms of another mental disorder, including fear, anxiety, and avoidance of situations associated with panic-like symptoms or other incapacitating symptoms (as in Agoraphobia); objects or situations related to obsessions (as in Obsessive-Compulsive Disorder); reminders of traumatic events (as in Posttraumatic Stress Disorder); separation from home or attachment figures (as in Separation Anxiety Disorder); or social situations (as in Social Anxiety Disorder).[1]

Source: Reprinted with permission from the *Diagnostic and Statistical Manual of Mental Disorders, Fifth Edition* (Copyright 2013). American Psychiatric Association.

[1] Agoraphobia, Social Anxiety Disorder, and Obsessive-Compulsive Disorder are presented later in this chapter. Posttraumatic Stress Disorder is presented in Chapter 12.

the child's reaction is less straightforward. For example, a child's fear of storms might be appropriate if she lives in an area plagued by hurricanes or tornadoes (American Psychiatric Association, 2013).

Children are only diagnosed with specific phobia if (a) their anticipatory anxiety or fear significantly interferes with their day-to-day functioning or (b) their symptoms cause significant distress. An adolescent who fears the sight of blood and avoids watching gory movies might not be diagnosed with specific phobia because her fears do not seriously affect her daily activities. However, if she wants to become a doctor, but pursues another career path because of her fear of blood, then the diagnosis of specific phobia might be appropriate. Consider Mary, a girl with a specific phobia for dogs.

Specific phobias are seen in approximately 2% to 9% of children and adolescents (LeBeau et al., 2010). Animal phobia is the most common type; between 3% and 9% of youths show intense fear for at least one specific animal. Natural environment phobias are also common. Approximately 3% to 7% of youths fear natural stimuli, if we lump them all together into a single category (e.g., storms, water, heights). Fear of blood, injection, and injuries occurs in 3% to 4.5% of youths. Situational phobias are somewhat less common; they include fear of flying (2.7%) and fear of enclosed spaces (3.2%). Fear of the dark is especially common among younger children (3%–4%).

The fears shown by children and adolescents usually reflect their level of cognitive development (Warren & Sroufe, 2004). Young children tend to fear concrete objects such as animals and monsters. Indeed, animal phobias tend to emerge between 8 and 9 years of age, on average. Older children tend to fear situations that might result in injury to themselves or others. The mean age of onset for blood-injection-injury phobia is 9 to 10 years, whereas onset for natural disaster phobias is typically in early adolescence (13–14 years old). Adolescents' fears also reflect their interest in social interactions and achievement. Common phobias among adolescents include fear of being alone and fear of exams (LeBeau et al., 2010).

Girls are more likely than boys to develop most types of phobias. Fear of specific animals (91% girls), situations (87% girls), and natural disasters (70% girls) is much more common in girls. In contrast blood-injection-injury phobia is equally common among boys and girls (LeBeau et al., 2010).

When children with specific phobias confront feared stimuli, they show changes in cognition, physiology, and behavior. With respect to cognition, children make negative self-statements that maximize the danger of the situation (e.g., "That dog is going to bite me") and minimize their ability to cope (e.g., "There's nothing I can do to stop it"). With respect to physiological responses, children show changes in autonomic functioning, such as increased heart rate, rapid breathing, sweatiness, dizziness, or upset stomach. Finally, with respect to behavior, children may attempt to flee the situation. If they cannot flee, they may become clingy, panicky, or irritable (Kane, Braunstein, Ollendick, & Muris, 2015; Waters, Bradley, & Mogg, 2014).

Mary and Man's Best Friend

Source: ©iStockphoto.com/KathyDewar

Mary Valenta was a 6-year-old girl who was referred to our clinic because of her intense fear of dogs. Whenever Mary saw a dog, regardless of its size, Mary's body would tense, and she would immediately try to run away or cling to her parents. If she was forced to remain near a dog, she would cry, tantrum, and even hyperventilate! Mary's fear of dogs began 2 years ago when she saw a cocker spaniel bite her older brother.

Mrs. Valenta commented, "It seems silly, but Mary's fear of dogs really has had a negative effect on our family. She can't play with friends who have dogs as pets; Mary would have a fit. When we visit her grandmother's house, we have to be extra careful because she has a large black lab. Mary was constantly looking over her shoulder during the entire visit. She can't relax." Mary's phobia became even more salient because her family recently moved next door to a family that owns a Great Dane. Mrs. Valenta reported, "Now, Mary doesn't even want to go outside to play. We need to do something."

Phobias typically last 1 or 2 years and cause considerable distress and impairment if left untreated. Most childhood phobias do not persist into adulthood. However, children's phobias can develop into other anxiety, mood, and somatic problems later in life. Consequently, childhood phobias merit clinical attention if they cause significant impairment or distress (Higa-McMillan et al., 2014).

Causes

Genes play a relatively small role in the development of most phobias (Zinbarg et al., 2015). Fears of specific stimuli (e.g., dogs, clowns) usually do not run in families. Instead, people may inherit a general tendency toward anxiety, which can later develop into a specific fear.

In contrast, genetics seems to play a relatively greater role in the development of blood-injection-injury phobia than in other phobias. Individuals with blood-injection-injury phobia become dizzy or faint when confronted with blood, needles, or open wounds. Their reaction may be due to an unusual sensitivity of the vasovagal response, a physiological reaction that involves a rapid increase and sudden decrease in blood pressure. There is a strong relationship between parents' and children's fear of blood and needles, indicating that shared genetic factors could be partially responsible for blood-injection-injury phobia (Oar, Farrell, & Ollendick, 2015).

Many phobias are acquired through *classical conditioning*. Indeed, Watson and Rayner (1920) demonstrated that fear could be acquired in this way. In the famous "Little Albert" study, Watson and Rayner conditioned a fear response in an 11-month-old boy by pairing a white rat with a loud sound. Initially, the child was not afraid of the rat (neutral stimulus [NS]), but the loud noise (unconditioned stimulus [UCS]) produced an intense fear response (unconditioned response [UCR]). After repeated pairing of the rat and noise, the rat alone (conditioned stimulus [CS]) produced a fear response (conditioned response [CR]). Classical conditioning might explain some common childhood fears. For example, a child who is bitten by a dog or frightened by a mysterious noise at night might develop phobias of dogs or the dark, respectively.

An alternative means of fear acquisition is through *observational learning*. Children can acquire fears by watching other people respond with fear or avoidance to certain objects, events, or situations. For example, parents who avoid visiting the dentist or show fear while getting a flu shot can convey this anxiety to their children. Mary seemed to develop her fear of dogs after witnessing someone being bitten by a dog.

A third way of acquiring fears is through *informational transmission*. Children can learn to fear objects or situations by talking with others or overhearing others' conversations. For example, hearing about a friend's dog bite or reading a story about a child lost in the dark can contribute to the development of phobias.

Mowrer's two-factor theory of anxiety can also explain why children's phobias persist over time. According to this theory, phobias develop though classical conditioning and other forms of social learning, but they are maintained through negative reinforcement (Mowrer, 1960). A child who is bitten by a dog subsequently develops dog phobia. Whenever she encounters a dog, she experiences extreme fear. However, the child discovers that avoiding dogs causes a reduction in her anxiety. Through negative reinforcement, she learns to avoid dogs to manage this anxiety.

Although avoidance offers immediate benefits to the child (e.g., the child avoids anxiety), it interferes with her long-term functioning. For example, the child may not be able to visit friends or family members who have dogs, or she may have to walk home from school using a longer route to avoid dogs. In addition, avoidance of feared stimuli interferes with the child's development of coping strategies to deal with anxiety. If the child never confronts her fear of dogs, she may never be able to learn how to cope with other anxiety-provoking situations.

Review:

- Specific phobia is characterized by marked fear or anxiety about a specific object or situation. It persists for at least 6 months and must cause distress or impairment.
- Between 2% and 9% of youths meet criteria for specific phobia; fear of animals and natural environment stimuli are most common. Children's phobias usually reflect their level of cognitive development.
- Phobias can be acquired through classical conditioning, observational learning, or informational transmission. They are often maintained through negative reinforcement.

What Is Social Anxiety Disorder?

Description

Social anxiety disorder is characterized by a marked and persistent fear of social or performance situations in which scrutiny or embarrassment might occur (see Table 11.5). Like individuals with specific phobia, people with social anxiety disorder show immediate anxiety or panic symptoms when they encounter feared situations. For people with social anxiety disorder, feared situations involve social settings in which they might be judged, criticized, or negatively evaluated by others. These settings include public speaking, attending a party or social gathering, or performing in front of others. People with social anxiety disorder worry that they will be embarrassed in front of others, that others will think they are "crazy" or "stupid," or that others will notice their anxiety symptoms (e.g., shaking hands, sweaty palms). People with social anxiety disorder often avoid social or performance situations. If

---

Table 11.5   Diagnostic Criteria for Social Anxiety Disorder

A. Marked fear or anxiety about one or more social situations in which the individual is exposed to possible scrutiny by others. Examples include social interactions (e.g., having a conversation, meeting unfamiliar people), being observed (e.g., eating or drinking), and performing in front of others (e.g., giving a speech).

   Note: In children, the anxiety must occur in peer settings and not just during interactions with adults.

B. The individual fears that he or she will act in a way or show anxiety symptoms that will be negatively evaluated (i.e., will be humiliating or embarrassing; will lead to rejection or offend others).

C. The social situations almost always provoke fear or anxiety.

   Note: In children, the fear or anxiety may be expressed by crying, tantrums, freezing, clinging, shrinking, or failing to speak in social situations.

D. The social situations are avoided or endured with intense fear or anxiety.

E. The fear or anxiety is out of proportion to the actual threat posed by the social situation and to the sociocultural context.

F. The fear, anxiety, or avoidance is persistent, typically lasting 6 months or more.

G. The fear, anxiety, or avoidance causes clinically significant distress or impairment in social, occupational, or other important areas of functioning.

H. The fear, anxiety, or avoidance is not attributable to the physiological effects of a substance (e.g., a drug of abuse, a medication) or another medical condition.

I. The fear, anxiety, or avoidance is not better explained by the symptoms of another mental disorder, such as Panic Disorder[1] or Autism Spectrum Disorder.

J. If another medical condition (e.g., obesity, disfigurement from burns or injury) is present, the fear, anxiety, or avoidance is clearly unrelated or is excessive.

Specify if:

Performance only: If the fear is restricted to speaking or performing in public.

Source: Reprinted with permission from the *Diagnostic and Statistical Manual of Mental Disorders, Fifth Edition* (Copyright 2013). American Psychiatric Association.

[1]Panic Disorder is presented later in this chapter.

Erin's Social Anxiety

I've been dealing with social anxiety disorder since I was 10 or 11. I struggled all through middle school, crying every day, feeling like I had no friends, wondering why I couldn't just be normal! Meeting new people without other friends around to make me feel "normal" was extremely difficult. I hated parties, dances, interviews, class presentations, and get-to-know-you type of games. I dreaded any type of social setting.

I didn't ever want to share my writing in my composition class, even though I was friends with just about everyone in the class. I found that I had trouble being creative.... I edited all my ideas as being too "weird" or "stupid." I worried all the time about how I looked. I also worried about calling my friends or asking them to do things with me. I thought that I might be bothering them.

I kept a lot of things to myself and never told anyone what I felt. When they asked me what was wrong, I was sure that they would think that I was ridiculous.

Source: Used with permission of the author.

forced to attend social gatherings, they endure them with extreme distress. Consider Erin, a college student with social anxiety disorder since childhood.

Some people with social anxiety disorder only experience apprehension in performance situations; they do not fear other social settings. For example, an adolescent with social anxiety disorder might fear a piano recital, an athletic event, or an oral presentation for class. However, that same adolescent might be perfectly comfortable in nonperformance situations, such as parties or athletic events in which she is a spectator. In these instances, *DSM-5* instructs clinicians to diagnose the individual with "social anxiety disorder, performance situations only" to convey the nature of the person's fears (American Psychiatric Association, 2013).

Social anxiety disorder usually emerges in late childhood or early adolescence. Indeed, it is usually not diagnosed before age 10 (Mesa, Beidel, & Bunnell, 2014). The two most common situations that are feared by youths with social anxiety disorder are formal presentations and unstructured social interactions. Most youths with social anxiety disorder report intense discomfort reading aloud in class, giving a class presentation, performing for others on stage, or competing in an athletic event. Youths with social anxiety disorder often experience anxiety when initiating conversations with strangers, asking questions, or attending parties.

Any situation in which the person might be judged or evaluated negatively by others can potentially be a source of anxiety for a person with social anxiety disorder. Many children with social anxiety disorder experience distress while taking tests because they fear criticism by teachers. Some children experience anxiety eating in public because they believe others may be criticizing their diet or etiquette (see Figure 11.4)

Youths with social anxiety disorder experience considerable impairment in their social and emotional functioning. Usually, youths with social anxiety disorder avoid situations that elicit anxiety. Social avoidance is negatively reinforced by anxiety reduction. For example, by avoiding the school cafeteria, a child with social anxiety disorder will not experience anxiety associated with interacting with classmates. However, social avoidance also reduces children's contact with peers. Over time, peer avoidance can cause social impairment. Approximately 60% of youths with social anxiety disorder show school problems, 53% lack friends, and 27% report difficulty engaging in sports, clubs, and other leisure activities. Children with social anxiety disorder are at particular risk for depression, social isolation, and loneliness. Adolescents with social anxiety disorder are at additional risk for substance use problems (Connolly et al., 2015; Essau & Petermann, 2014)

Figure 11.4 Situations Feared by Children With Social Anxiety Disorder

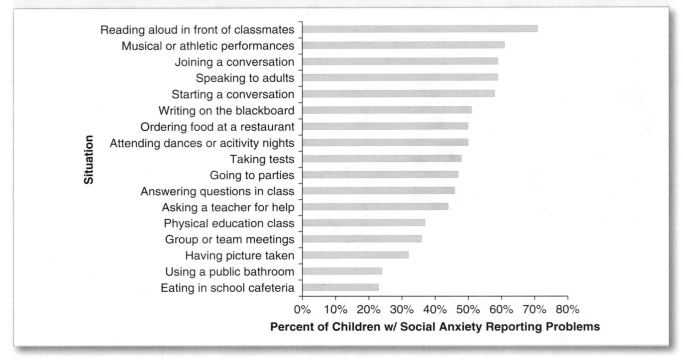

Causes

Genetic factors seem to underlie children's risk for developing social anxiety disorder. Twin studies indicate that 50% of the variance in children's symptoms of social anxiety disorder is attributable to genetics. Family studies indicate that the tendency to experience anxiety in social situations, and the diagnosis of social anxiety disorder in particular, runs in families (Higa-McMillan et al., 2014).

Many youths with social anxiety disorder displayed high behavioral inhibition in early childhood. It is likely that many of these youths cope with heightened physiological arousal in social situations by avoiding them. Over time, habitual avoidance is maintained through negative reinforcement. When social avoidance begins to interfere with children's schoolwork, afterschool activities, or peer relationships, it becomes social anxiety disorder (Gensthaler et al., 2016a).

Parent–child interactions can also contribute to the development of social anxiety disorder. The parents of children with social anxiety disorder are more likely to have problems with social anxiety themselves. Although this suggests a genetic transmission of anxiety from parent to child, it also indicates that anxious parents might teach anxiety responses to their children during parent–child interactions (Gulley, Oppenheimer, & Hankin, 2014).

First, the parents of children with social anxiety disorder are often described as more *controlling* than the parents of nonanxious children. For example, the parents of children with anxiety problems often intrude on their children's behavior and do not allow their children to make decisions for themselves. This highly controlling behavior may stifle the development of children's autonomy. Overcontrolling parents may communicate to children that they are not capable of coping with challenges in life. As a consequence, children of overcontrolling parents may require frequent reassurance when completing tasks or solving problems (Majdandžic, Möller, de Vente, Bögels, & van den Boom, 2014).

Second, the parents of children with social anxiety disorder are often described as *overprotective*—that is, they excessively restrict children's exploration and play because they fear harm befalling their children. For example, it is reasonable for a mother to prohibit her 14-year-old daughter from attending a party that might involve older boys, a lack of adult supervision, and alcohol consumption. However, it is probably not reasonable for a mother to prohibit her 14-year-old daughter from attending a similar party with same-age peers, responsible adult supervision, and nonalcoholic beverages. Although the world can be a dangerous place, overprotective parents can convey to their children an excessive degree of risk and worry. Children can learn to overestimate the degree of threat in their surroundings and become excessively inhibited (Budinger, Drazdowski, & Ginsburg, 2013).

Third, the parents of children with social anxiety disorder often show high levels of *hostile and critical* behavior toward their children. Not only are these parents highly controlling but they are also prone to criticizing and rejecting their children when they do not live up to their high expectations. Such critical behavior may communicate to children that the world is a hostile and dangerous place and that they should not expect sympathy from caregivers if they take risks and fail (Scanlon & Epkins, 2015).

Fourth, parents of children with social anxiety disorder may inadvertently *teach their children to be anxious* in social situations. Specifically, these parents may model anxiety and reinforce their children's anxiety reactions. Dadds and colleagues (Dadds, Barrett, Rapee, & Ryan, 1996) observed anxious children and their parents discussing hypothetical, ambiguous social situations. Some of the situations described people experiencing physical ailments, like an upset stomach. Other situations involved ambiguous social situations, like a group of peers laughing and joking. Youths with anxiety problems interpreted these ambiguous situations negatively. For example, they often interpreted the upset stomach as a sign of serious illness or the laughing peers as a sign of teasing or bullying. The parents of these anxious children also interpreted a great deal of danger and hostility in these ambiguous situations. Perhaps more important, the parents often supported children's decisions to overreact to these situations (Pereira, Barros, Mendonça, & Muris, 2014).

Fifth, parents can contribute to their children's social anxiety by *avoiding emotionally charged discussions*. Children's emotional well-being depends greatly on their ability to discuss and reflect upon their feelings. One way children learn to recognize, understand, and discuss their feelings is through interactions with their parents. Parents model emotional expression, teach children how to label emotions, and communicate socially acceptable ways to share emotions with others. However, the parents of anxious children often avoid discussions about their children's feelings. This lack of emotional expressiveness in the family can deprive children of opportunities to label, talk about, and process emotions and, consequently, it can contribute to their social anxiety.

Keep in mind that parent–child interactions are bidirectional (Ginsburg & Schlossberg, 2002). Although parents can contribute to children's anxiety, children's behavior can also cause their parents to be excessively controlling, protective, or critical. For example, young children with high levels of behavioral inhibition often demand considerable reassurance and protection from their parents. Children's behavioral inhibition also may elicit harsh, critical, and demanding parenting practices. It is likely that parent and child behaviors mutually influence each other across development and, together, contribute to children's emerging anxiety (Rapee, 2012; Yap, Pilkington, Ryan, Kelly, & Jorm, 2014).

Review:

- Social anxiety disorder is characterized by marked fear or anxiety about one or more social situations in which the individual is exposed to possible scrutiny by others. It lasts at least 6 months and causes distress or impairment.

- Social anxiety disorder usually emerges in late childhood or early adolescence. It affects 3% to 6% of youths.
- Approximately 50% of the variance in social anxiety disorder symptoms is attributable to genetics. Among children who inherit genetic risk, overprotective and highly controlling parenting behavior is associated with the emergence of this disorder.

What Is Panic Disorder?

Description

Panic disorder is a serious condition characterized by the presence of recurrent, unexpected panic attacks that cause the person significant distress or impairment (see Table 11.6). A panic attack is an acute and intense episode of psychological distress and autonomic arousal. During the attack, people experience signs and symptoms that fall into three broad clusters: (1) cognitive symptoms (e.g., thoughts of losing control or going crazy), (2) emotional symptoms (e.g., feelings of unreality or detachment), and (3) somatic symptoms (e.g., heart palpitations, chest pain, dizziness). People who experience panic attacks feel as if they are having a heart attack, believe that they are dying or going crazy, or experience a strong desire to flee the situation. Indeed, panic attacks can be extremely scary because they are so severe and because people seem to have little control over their onset (American Psychiatric Association, 2013).

Panic attacks may reach their peak intensity in adults in about ten minutes. However, many research studies indicate that adolescents show even more rapid onset. Several studies indicate that maximum heart rate is reached within 3 or 4 minutes after the onset of a panic attack in youths (Essau & Petermann, 2014).

Typically, adolescents and young adults who experience panic attacks report four or more symptoms. The most commonly reported symptoms are palpitations or "pounding heart" (78%–97%) and dizziness (73%–96%). The least common symptoms are numbness or tingling sensations (26%–29%) and choking (24%). The greater the number of symptoms experienced, the greater the likelihood an individual will seek treatment. In one study, an adolescent's risk of being taken to the emergency room increased 20% for every symptom he or she experienced beyond the four required by *DSM-5* (Craske et al., 2010).

The duration of panic attacks is variable. The median duration is approximately 12.6 minutes. However, average durations have ranged from 23.6 minutes to 45 minutes, depending on the study (Craske et al., 2010).

Typically, panic attacks are "unexpected"—that is, they come "out of the blue." For example, an adolescent might be working on her physics lab assignment when she suddenly begins to feel her heart race, her breathing to become shallow, and her palms to sweat. She might feel dizzy and hot and experience an urge to run out of the classroom. She might leave class, enter the bathroom,

Table 11.6   Diagnostic Criteria for Panic Disorder

A. Recurrent unexpected panic attacks. A panic attack is an abrupt surge of intense fear or intense discomfort that reaches a peak within ten minutes, and during which time four (or more) of the following symptoms occur:

  1. Palpitations, pounding heart, or accelerated heart rate.

  2. Sweating.

  3. Trembling or shaking.

  4. Sensations of shortness of breath or smothering.

  5. Feelings of choking.

  6. Chest pain or discomfort.

  7. Nausea or abdominal distress.

  8. Feeling dizzy, unsteady, light-headed, or faint.

  9. Chills or heat sensations.

  10. Paresthesias (numbness or tingling sensations).

  11. Derealization (feelings of unreality) or depersonalization (being detached from oneself).

  12. Fear of losing control or "going crazy."

  13. Fear of dying.

B. At least one of the attacks has been followed by one month (or more) of one or both of the following:

  1. Persistent concern or worry about additional panic attacks or their consequences (e.g., losing control, having a heart attack, "going crazy").

  2. A significant maladaptive change in behavior related to the attacks (e.g., behaviors designed to avoid panic attacks, such as avoidance of exercise or unfamiliar situations).

C. The disturbance is not attributable to the physiological effects of a substance (e.g., a drug of abuse, a medication) or another medical condition (e.g., hyperthyroidism, cardiopulmonary disorders).

D. The disturbance is not better explained by another mental disorder (e.g., panic disorders do not only occur in response to separation from attachment figures as in Separation Anxiety Disorder; in response to circumscribed phobic objects or situations as in Specific Phobia; in response to feared social situations as in Social Anxiety Disorder; or in response to reminders of traumatic events as in Posttraumatic Stress Disorder[1]).

Source: Reprinted with permission from the *Diagnostic and Statistical Manual of Mental Disorders, Fifth Edition* (Copyright 2013). American Psychiatric Association.

[1]Posttraumatic Stress Disorder is presented in Chapter 12.

and splash water on her face to cool down. Adolescents who experience unexpected attacks often report feeling as though they were having a heart attack or that they were overcome with terror. Consider Paul, an adolescent with recurrent panic attacks and possible panic disorder.

To get a sense of what an unexpected panic attack feels like, try to remember a time when you were driving and you suddenly saw the flashing lights of a police car in your rearview mirror. For an instant, you may have experienced many physiological symptoms of panic: pounding heart, rapid breathing, and dizziness. Perhaps you also had fleeting thoughts such as, "What did I do wrong?" or "Oh no, now

I'm in trouble." Now, imagine that these sensations came out of the blue, that is, that they emerged suddenly while you were driving, without ever seeing the police lights. You might ask yourself, "What's wrong with me? Am I going crazy or dying?" Finally, imagine that these feelings increased over the next 5 minutes and lasted for the next half hour.

To be diagnosed with panic disorder, an individual must have recurrent, unexpected panic attacks followed by (a) 1 month of persistent concern about having another panic attack, (b) worry about the implications of the attacks, or (c) a significant change in daily routines because of the attacks. For example, many people who have had a panic

Heart Attack at Age 16

Source: @iStockphoto.com/eurobanks

Paul was a 16-year-old boy who was sent to the emergency department (ED) of the hospital after two episodes of "heart problems" in one week. Paul's mother told the physician that Paul had experienced symptoms of a heart attack after dinner at home. Specifically, Paul's heart raced, his breathing became shallow, he experienced dizziness, and his skin became clammy to the touch.

"It came out of nowhere," Paul explained. "I felt like my heart was going to explode in my chest. Then, I got a terrible urge to run way, but I couldn't. I just froze. I was scared and shaking all over."

The physician at the hospital determined that Paul was medically healthy and showed no signs of heart problems. Dr. Dresser, a pediatric psychologist at the hospital, suggested that Paul had a panic attack.

"Do anxiety problems run in your family?" Dr. Dresser asked. Paul's father admitted to taking medication for both anxiety and depression. Paul worried, "Do you mean that I'm going to have more of these attacks?" Dr. Dresser replied, "That is a possibility. The important thing is that you learn to cope with them if they recur. Do you want to learn some techniques that can help?"

attack fear having another one. They might believe that the attacks are a sign of psychosis or serious physical illness. They may also avoid situations where they experienced attacks in the past to prevent their recurrence. Some people experience unexpected panic attacks but do not worry about them or change their day-to-day behavior because of them. If panic attacks do not cause the person significant distress or impairment, they do not meet the criteria for panic disorder (American Psychiatric Association, 2013).

Panic attacks are relatively common among adolescents. As many as 18% of teenagers have had at least one full-blown panic attack. Furthermore, 60% of adolescents may have had subthreshold panic symptom. Panic attacks are equally common in boys and girls, but they may be more severe in girls (Asselmann et al., 2014).

Although panic attacks occur relatively frequently, panic disorder is uncommon in adolescents and very rare in children. The onset of panic disorder is usually between the ages of 15 and 19. However, there are isolated instances of its onset occurring before puberty. Most cases of panic disorder in children and adolescents go undetected. Parents and physicians usually interpret panic symptoms as medical problems. Consequently, youngsters who are eventually diagnosed with panic disorder wait, on average, 12.7 years until their disorder is properly identified and treated (Zinbarg et al., 2015).

Researchers are not sure why panic disorder is seldom seen in prepubescent children. Clearly, young children can experience panic attacks. For example, a young child separated from her parents in a crowded department store might experience extreme panic. However, few children develop panic disorder. Some data indicate that young children do not develop panic disorder because they lack the cognitive capacity for metacognition—that is, the ability to think about their own thoughts and feelings. Indeed, younger adolescents who have had at least one panic attack worry less about having additional attacks and think less about the implications of these attacks than older adolescents and young adults. It is likely that younger children's cognitive immaturity protects them from thinking about (and worrying about) recurrent panic (Beran, 2012).

Panic disorder in adolescence or adulthood is also associated with childhood-onset SAD. Family studies indicate that adults with panic disorder are at elevated risk of having children who develop SAD. Furthermore, children with SAD are 3.5 times more likely to develop panic disorder in late adolescence or early adulthood. Indeed, both children with SAD and adults with panic disorder show subtle abnormalities in respiration that may make them susceptible to panic symptoms (i.e., rapid, shallow breathing). Some experts have argued that these two disorders are different developmental manifestations of the same underlying condition (Kossowsky et al., 2013).

Causes

The causes of panic disorder are complex; no single theory can adequately explain all of the features of this disorder. However, cognitive and behavioral models of panic disorder have received the most empirical support from studies involving adolescents. According to these models, biological, cognitive, and behavioral factors interact to produce recurrent panic attacks (Barlow et al., 2015).

Individuals prone to panic disorder may inherit a biological disposition toward anxiety sensitivity—that is, the tendency to perceive the symptoms of anxiety as extremely upsetting and aversive. For example, most people experience moderate anxiety before an important exam. A person with low anxiety sensitivity might be able to acknowledge her anxiety, cope with its symptoms (e.g., take deep breaths), and proceed with the exam. In contrast, a person with high anxiety sensitivity might experience pre-exam anxiety as extremely distressing and respond with fear. This unusual sensitivity can lead to panic (Taylor, 2014).

According to the expectancy theory of panic, people with high anxiety sensitivity are unusually sensitive to the physiological symptoms of anxious arousal. Specifically, individuals with high anxiety sensitivity pay special attention to the increase in heart rate and shallowness of breathing that characterizes the early signs of anxiety. Additionally, these individuals show characteristic ways of thinking that exacerbate their anxiety symptoms (Capron, Norr, & Schmidt, 2013).

First, these individuals tend to *personalize* negative events—that is, they blame themselves when bad events occur. For example, an adolescent with high anxiety sensitivity who experiences anxiety during an exam might blame herself for her anxiety: "I didn't study enough—it's my own fault that I'm not prepared." Personalization exacerbates the adolescent's anxiety and interferes with coping.

Second, adolescents with high anxiety sensitivity often engage in *catastrophic thinking*. When distressed, they anticipate the worst possible outcomes. For example, when an adolescent with high anxiety sensitivity experiences mild anxiety before an exam, she might expect her anxiety to escalate and become uncontrollable. She might think, "Oh no, I'm having one of those attacks again. I'm going to blank out and forget everything I studied! What am I going to do?" Catastrophic thinking is often self-fulfilling; it leads to an escalation of psychological distress.

Anxiety sensitivity, and the tendency to personalize and catastrophize negative events, can trigger a panic attack. Unfortunately, one panic attack can cause adolescents to pay excessive attention to early warning signs of future attacks. Consequently, these adolescents become sensitive to the mildest signs of anxious arousal. Even mild arousal can cause them to think, "Oh no! Am I going to have one of those attacks again?" (Bentley et al., 2013).

Review:

- Panic disorder is characterized by recurrent, unexpected panic attacks and 1 month of worry about future attacks or a change in behavior because of the attacks.
- Panic attacks affect approximately 18% of adolescents; however, panic disorder is relatively rare, affecting only 1% of youths.

- Youths with panic disorder often show unusually high anxiety sensitivity. They may worry about future panic attacks or modify their behavior in response to these attacks because they experience anxiety as unusually distressing.
- Cognitive distortions, such as personalization and catastrophic thinking, can exacerbate panic attacks and lead to panic disorder.

What Is Agoraphobia?

Description

Agoraphobia is characterized by recurrent anxiety about places or situations from which escape or help is not possible without considerable effort or embarrassment (see Table 11.7). The disorder gets its name from the word *agora*, which was the central meeting place in ancient Greek city-states. Indeed, some people with agoraphobia fear gathering places like shopping malls, movie theaters, or stadiums. However, people with agoraphobia can fear other places or situations, such as airplanes, subways, crowds, or simply being away from home alone (American Psychiatric Association, 2013).

In all cases, people with agoraphobia fear these situations because they believe escape might be difficult in the event of a panic attack, paniclike symptoms, or an embarrassing event. For example, a woman might avoid traveling on an airplane because she knows she cannot easily exit the plane in the event of a panic attack. The woman does not have specific phobia (i.e., a fear of flying); instead, she has a fear of places or situations in which escape might be impossible or extremely difficult. Similarly, a man with irritable bowel syndrome (IBS) might avoid sporting events in large stadiums because he fears incontinence. The man might love watching his favorite football team, but he avoids games because he worries that he might embarrass himself in the crowded stadium. The man does not have social anxiety disorder (i.e., a fear of social or performance situations); instead, he fears places or situations in which escape might be extremely difficult.

People with agoraphobia try to avoid feared situations. For example, an adolescent who fears leaving her home and attending school might tantrum, feign illness, or skip school in order to stay home. An adolescent who fears large, crowded public places might decline invitations from friends to go shopping or attend a concert. Agoraphobic avoidance can restrict adolescents' educational and social functioning. Agoraphobia limits adolescents' abilities to attend school, participate in afterschool activities, and spend time with friends.

Sometimes, adolescents with agoraphobia are forced into feared situations. For example, an adolescent who is afraid of leaving her home will eventually need to go to school; an adolescent afraid of certain modes of public transportation may eventually find herself on an airplane during a family vacation. In many cases, adolescents are

Table 11.7 Diagnostic Criteria for Agoraphobia

A. Marked fear or anxiety about two (or more) of the following five situations:

1. Using public transportation (e.g., buses, trains, ships, planes).
2. Being in open spaces (e.g., parking lots, marketplaces, bridges).
3. Being in enclosed places (e.g., shops, theaters, cinemas).
4. Standing in line or being in a crowd.
5. Being outside of the home alone.

B. The individual fears or avoids these situations because of thoughts that escape might be difficult or help might not be available in the event of developing panic-like symptoms or other incapacitating or embarrassing symptoms.

C. The agoraphobic situations almost always provoke fear or anxiety.

D. The agoraphobic situations are actively avoided, require the presence of a companion, or are endured with intense fear or anxiety.

E. The fear or anxiety is out of proportion to the actual danger posed by the agoraphobic situations and to the sociocultural context.

F. The fear, anxiety, or avoidance is persistent, typically lasting 6 months or more.

G. The fear, anxiety, or avoidance causes clinically significant distress or impairment in social, occupational, or other important areas of functioning.

H. If another medical condition is present, the fear, anxiety, or avoidance is clearly excessive.

I. The fear, anxiety, or avoidance is not better explained by the symptoms of another mental disorder—for example, the symptoms are not confined to fear of separation (as in Separation Anxiety Disorder); fear of specific objects or situations (as in Specific Phobia); fear of social situations (as in Social Anxiety Disorder); or reminders of traumatic events (as in Posttraumatic Stress Disorder[1]).

Source: Reprinted with permission from the *Diagnostic and Statistical Manual of Mental Disorders, Fifth Edition* (Copyright 2013). American Psychiatric Association.

Note: Agoraphobia is diagnosed irrespective of the presence of Panic Disorder. If an individual's presentation meets criteria for Panic Disorder and Agoraphobia, both diagnoses should be assigned.

[1]Posttraumatic Stress Disorder is presented in Chapter 12.

able to endure these situations with intense, emotional discomfort. In some cases, they rely on another person (e.g., parent, older sibling, close friend) to accompany them and provide them with reassurance and a sense of safety.

Agoraphobia is extremely rare in adolescents. Although the overall prevalence of agoraphobia is approximately 1.7%, the prevalence among adolescents is probably less than 0.5%. The typical age of onset for agoraphobia is between 18 and 29 years. Usually, the disorder emerges slowly as individuals come to fear an increasing number of places and situations. Without treatment, the disorder can last throughout adulthood (Connolly et al., 2015).

Causes

Agoraphobia is caused by the interaction of genetic risk and environmental factors (Wittchen, Gloster, Beesdo-Baum, Fava, & Craske, 2010). The heritability of agoraphobia is particularly high; as much as 61% of an individual's risk for agoraphobic avoidance can be attributed to genetic factors. Furthermore, youths who develop agoraphobia, like youths with many other anxiety disorders, often come from families characterized by low warmth, high demandingness, and overprotection. These parents place high expectations on their children yet often do not provide enough support to help them reach these expectations. Furthermore, they may communicate to their children that the world is a threatening place. The combination of genetic risk and authoritarian parenting places children at risk for this condition.

Between 50% and 75% of adolescents and young adults develop agoraphobia after a history of panic disorder. In these instances, agoraphobia occurs when individuals associate certain places or situations with a panic attack, through classical conditioning. For example, an adolescent who experiences a panic attack while shopping might avoid the mall. Similarly, a girl who experiences a panic attack at school might refuse to attend school. Agoraphobic avoidance is maintained through negative reinforcement. By avoiding the mall or school, these youths experience anxiety reduction. Consequently, they are more likely to avoid these places in the future. Consider Ryder, a boy who developed agoraphobia following repeated panic attacks.

Planning for an Emergency

Ryder was a 15-year-old boy who was referred to an anxiety disorders clinic in a large metropolitan area near his home. Several months ago, Ryder experienced a panic attack in the elevator of his apartment building. "My throat started to tighten and I couldn't breathe. It was terrible," he recalled. His mother added, "We were both very upset. I immediately took him to the hospital, but all of the tests came up negative."

Ryder experienced his second, unexpected panic attack 1 week later while sitting alone in his bedroom. He reported, "I had the same symptoms, but this time I also felt dizzy and nauseous." Since then, Ryder has experienced 12 more attacks. "I constantly worry about having more of them," he said.

Recently, Ryder has begun to limit his activities because of the attacks. Specifically, he refuses to ride in elevators, walking six flights of stairs to his apartment. He also refuses to ride the subway or buses, or go to the movies with friends. "He's saved his money to buy a new cell phone," his mother reported, "in case he needs to call 911. He's afraid to leave home without it."

Source: Adapted from the Anxiety Disorders Association of Canada (2016).

Experts used to believe that agoraphobic avoidance could only arise after a history of panic. Today, however, we know that between 25% and 50% of individuals with agoraphobia do not have a history of panic disorder or their panic symptoms emerged after their agoraphobic avoidance (Wittchen et al., 2010). How did these individuals develop agoraphobia?

Agoraphobia can develop in the absence of panic disorder in at least three ways (Hoffart, Hedley, Svanøe, Langkaas, & Sexton, 2016). First, some individuals experience paniclike symptoms but not true panic attacks. Paniclike symptoms include headaches, migraines, and gastrointestinal problems that cause distress or embarrassment. Through classical conditioning, individuals learn to associate these symptoms with specific situations. Through negative reinforcement, they learn to avoid these situations. For example, a child who develops migraines at school might develop agoraphobic avoidance of school because he fears their return. He would not be diagnosed with panic disorder because he has recurrent migraines, rather than panic attacks.

Second, some people develop agoraphobic avoidance of certain places or situations because they had an aversive experience in that place. For example, a child who is bullied at school or an adolescent who is teased at the swimming pool by peers might develop agoraphobia of those locations.

Third, some people who develop agoraphobia show chronically high anxiety and need for dependency. These individuals seem to worry a great deal about future misfortunes and doubt their ability to cope with psychosocial stress. They often report low self-efficacy and need frequent reassurance from others. These individuals may develop agoraphobic avoidance of certain places or situations if they are not accompanied by a family member or close friend who can provide reassurance. For example, an adolescent might insist that her older sister go with her to the grocery store or the shopping mall, because she doubts her ability to visit these places alone.

Review:

- Agoraphobia is characterized by marked anxiety about places or situations from which escape or help is not possible without considerable effort or embarrassment. It lasts at least 6 months and causes distress or impairment.
- Agoraphobia usually develops in early adulthood. Its prevalence among adolescents is less than 0.5%.
- Agoraphobia has high heritability.
- Between 50% and 75% of adolescents develop agoraphobia after a history of panic disorder. Agoraphobia can develop without comorbid panic attacks, however.

What Is Generalized Anxiety Disorder?

Description

Generalized anxiety disorder (GAD) is unlike the other anxiety disorders in two respects. First, GAD is characterized by worry rather than fear or panic. People with GAD do not fear specific objects, situations, or sensations; instead, they worry about future misfortune (Andrews et al., 2010). Second, GAD is more closely associated with depression than the other anxiety disorders. Children with GAD are especially likely to develop depression later in life. Adolescents with GAD often have co-occurring problems with depressed mood and dysphoria (Goldberg, Krueger, Andrews, & Hobbs, 2009).

The hallmark of GAD is apprehensive expectation—that is, excessive worry about the future (see Table 11.8). Adults with GAD worry about aspects of everyday life, such as completing tasks at work, managing finances, meeting appointments, and performing household chores. Children and adolescents with GAD also worry about activities and events in their day-to-day lives, especially exams, school assignments, athletics, and extracurricular activities. By definition, youths with GAD must worry about two or more activities or events. On average, however, most adolescents with GAD report many worries (Niles, Lebeau, Liao, Glenn, & Craske, 2012).

Worry is a cognitive activity characterized by repeated and increasingly elaborated thoughts about future negative events and their consequences. Children might worry about an upcoming exam, the possibility of not studying adequately for the exam, and the repercussions of earning a low grade or gaining the disapproval of teachers and parents. Children begin to show the ability to worry around age 4 or 5. However, the ability to think about and dwell upon negative events in the distant future does not seem to emerge until after age 8. The onset of GAD is usually after this cognitive capacity for worry develops—that is, between 8 and 10 years of age. As children's capacity for worry increases with age, so does the frequency and severity of GAD (Connolly et al., 2015).

Children and adolescents with GAD worry about the same topics as people without GAD, such as school, sports, relationships, and achieving goals for the future (Layne, Bernat, Victor, & Bernstein, 2009). The difference between the worries of people with and without GAD lies in their (a) number, (b) intensity, and (c) duration (see Figure 11.5). First, people with GAD report a greater *number* of worries than people without GAD. Second, people with GAD rate their worries as *more intense* or distressing than people without GAD. Furthermore, they often report greater impairment associated with worrying: daytime restlessness, sleep problems, fatigue, muscle tension, irritability, and difficulty concentrating. Third, people with GAD spend a greater *percentage of their day* worrying than most other individuals (Niles et al., 2012).

The worries shown by children with GAD interfere with their daily functioning. First, worry causes

---

Table 11.8   Diagnostic Criteria for Generalized Anxiety Disorder

A. Excessive anxiety and worry (apprehensive expectation), occurring more days than not for at least 6 months, about a number of events and activities (such as work or school performance).

B. The individual finds it difficult to control the worry.

C. The anxiety and worry are associated with three (more) of the following six symptoms (with at least some symptoms having been present for more days than not for the past 6 months):

   Note: Only one item is required in children.

   1. Restlessness or feeling keyed up or on edge.

   2. Being easily fatigued.

   3. Difficulty concentrating or mind going blank.

   4. Irritability.

   5. Muscle tension.

   6. Sleep disturbance (difficulty falling asleep or staying asleep, or restless unsatisfying sleep).

D. The anxiety, worry, or physical symptoms cause clinically significant distress or impairment in social, occupational, or other important areas of functioning.

E. The disturbance is not attributable to the physiological effects of a substance (e.g., a drug of abuse, a medication) or another medical condition (e.g., hyperthyroidism).

F. The disturbance is not better explained by another mental disorder (e.g., worry about separation from attachment figures as in Separation Anxiety Disorder; worry about negative evaluation as in Social Anxiety Disorder; or worry about having panic attacks as in Panic Disorder).

Source: Reprinted with permission from the *Diagnostic and Statistical Manual of Mental Disorders, Fifth Edition* (Copyright 2013). American Psychiatric Association.

Figure 11.5   Children With and Without GAD Worry About Similar Topics

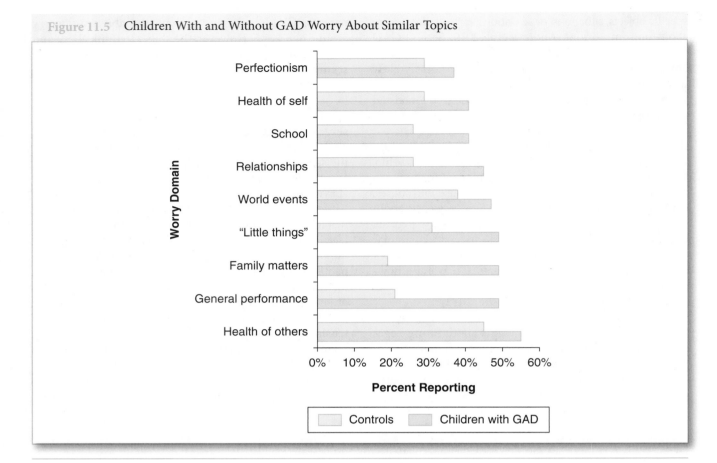

Source: Based on Layne and colleagues (2009).

Note: Children with GAD, however, report a greater number of worries and associated symptoms (e.g., restlessness, trouble concentrating, trouble sleeping) than their peers without GAD.

significant distress and consumes significant time and energy. Second, worry interferes with children's abilities to concentrate on important activities such as listening to parents or completing homework assignments. Third, worry can cause mood problems, frustration, and irritability. Fourth, worry can cause somatic problems, such as headaches, insomnia, or fatigue. Finally, worry can interfere with the development of more adaptive coping strategies. Children who frequently worry may not learn other ways to deal with anxiety, such as using relaxation or play, expressing negative emotions to parents or peers, or engaging in a sport or hobby. *DSM-5* requires children with GAD to experience at least one symptom as the result of their worrying. In contrast, adults with GAD must show at least three symptoms (American Psychiatric Association, 2013).

Children with GAD are often described by parents and teachers as "little adults" (Kendall, Krain, & Treadwell, 1999). These youths are often perfectionistic, punctual, and eager to please. They are usually quite self-conscious around others, especially adults and people in authority. They also tend to be highly conforming to rules and social norms. For these

reasons, Kendall and colleagues (1999) suggest that children with GAD create an "illusion of maturity" that makes them appear more emotionally competent than they really are.

Beneath this illusion of maturity, children with GAD harbor feelings of self-doubt, self-criticism, and uncertainty. They may strive for perfection when completing a homework assignment, preparing for a piano recital, or practicing for an athletic competition. However, they often require excessive reassurance from teachers, tutors, and coaches to make sure that they gain the approval of others. Children with GAD may also refuse to submit homework, play, or compete unless they know their performance will be perfect. They often interpret signs of imperfection (e.g., homework mistakes, misplayed notes, coming in second) as indicators of failure and worthlessness. Consider Tammie, a girl with GAD.

GAD is more closely associated with depression than any of the other anxiety disorders (Goldberg et al., 2009). Three lines of evidence indicate its close relationship to depression. First, GAD and MDD show high comorbidity in older children and adolescents. Approximately 50% of youths with GAD also have depression.

CASE STUDY

GENERALIZED ANXIETY DISORDER

Tammie's Sleepless Nights

Source: ©iStockphoto.com/-art-siberia-

Tammie was an 11-year-old girl who was referred to the hospital by her parents because of insomnia. Her mother explained, "A few months ago, Tammie started complaining about having problems falling asleep. We'd put her to bed, but she'd lie awake for several hours. Then, she'd wander out of her room and ask for a drink of water. Sometimes, she's not asleep until 11:30 or midnight, and then she's exhausted the next day."

Dr. Baldwin reviewed Tammie's developmental and medical history, her diet, and her habits before bed. However, he couldn't find any explanation for her sleep problems. Tammie's father said, "Tammie's never been a problem. She's very smart and does extremely well in school. She has a lot of friends. She's very mature for her age and almost always listens to her mother and me."

Dr. Baldwin interviewed Tammie: "When you're in bed at night, how do you feel?" Tammie replied, "At first I feel good, because I'm so tired. Then, I sort of tense up and feel nervous. I get tingly in my stomach." Dr. Baldwin asked, "Do you think about anything?" Tammie responded, "I start to think about all the things I need to do the next day for school. I worry about my homework, tests, volleyball . . . stuff like that. Then, I get more and more nervous and tingly. I just can't stop. I start to bite my lip or pick at my fingernails until they bleed. When I've had enough, I get out of bed."

Dr. Baldwin continued, "Is there anything you can do to make yourself relax and go to sleep?" Tammie responded, "If my mom or dad give me a hug or talk to me, I can usually stop worrying and think about other things and calm down. Sometimes, though, the worrying starts up again and I know it's going to be a long night."

Second, longitudinal research indicates that children with GAD are at particular risk for developing depression later in life. For example, Moffitt and colleagues (2007) examined a large sample of individuals with GAD and depression from adolescence through young adulthood. In most cases (68%), participants' anxiety problems preceded or appeared simultaneously with their depressive symptoms. Only about one-third of participants experienced anxiety problems after depression. On average, adolescents develop depressive symptoms 5 years after the emergence of their anxiety.

Third, factor analysis has shown that GAD and depressive symptoms tend to naturally co-occur in the general population (Michl, McLaughlin, Shepherd, & Nolen-Hoeksema, 2013). Factor analysis is a statistical technique that identifies underlying constructs, or "factors," that explain relationships between observable traits or symptoms. In this case, factor analysis is performed by identifying clusters of symptoms that tend to occur together. Several factor analytic studies have shown that children's internalizing symptoms can be explained by two factors (see Figure 11.6). A "fear" factor explains the relationship between most anxiety disorders characterized by anxiety, fear, and panic: specific phobia, social anxiety disorder, agoraphobia, and panic disorder. However, a second "anxious-misery" factor explains the relationship between GAD, MDD, and dysthymic disorder (another depressive

disorder). Children with GAD are more likely to show problems with depression than symptoms of fear or panic.

Causes

Many of the risk factors of anxiety disorders in general apply to GAD. For example, children with difficult temperaments, behavioral inhibition, and less-than-optimal parent–child interactions are at risk for GAD, in addition to the other anxiety disorders (Higa-McMillan et al., 2014; Simon, 2016).

GAD is different from the other anxiety disorders because it is characterized by worry rather than fear or panic. From a behavioral perspective, worrying seems to make little sense. Most people consider worrying to be an aversive activity; it appears to have no reinforcing properties. However, cognitive–behavioral theorists suggest that worrying serves a special purpose for children and adolescents with GAD. According to cognitive avoidance theory, worrying helps people avoid emotionally and physically arousing mental images (Borkovec & Inz, 1990; Roemer & Borkovec, 1993). Worry allows people to replace these emotion-laden images of imminent danger with more abstract, analytical thoughts about future misfortune. Worry, therefore, is a form of avoidance and is negatively reinforcing.

Figure 11.6   Children's Internalizing Symptoms

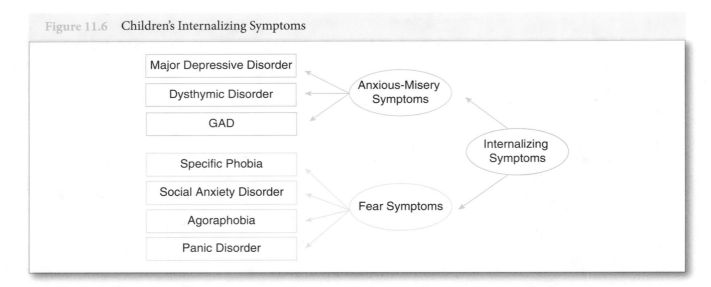

Source: Based on Goldberg and colleagues (2009).

Note: Children's internalizing symptoms can be divided into two groups based on how they typically co-occur: fear symptoms and anxious-misery symptoms. GAD tends to be more like depression than the other anxiety disorders.

To understand how worry can be negatively reinforcing, consider Elsa, a perfectionistic 12-year-old with GAD. Elsa's teacher has assigned her to work with three classmates on an important science project. As a group, the students must complete the project, write a poster, and present their findings at the school science fair. Most children would experience some apprehension when faced with this assignment; however, Elsa shows great distress. She imagines the group failing miserably in their experiment, making countless mistakes on their poster, and humiliating themselves during the presentation. Furthermore, she foresees chastisement and disapproval from her teacher and parents. To cope with these mental images, Elsa thinks about the situation in more abstract, verbal terms—she worries. She thinks to herself, "What if my classmates don't follow through with their part of the project?" or "I had better double-check our spelling on the poster" or "Maybe I'm not prepared enough for the oral presentation—I should rehearse one more time." These worries occupy Elsa's time and energy, but they also serve an important function: They allow Elsa to avoid imagining the terrible consequences of failing the project. To the extent that worry allows children like Elsa to avoid or escape distressing images, worry can be negatively reinforcing.

Most data supporting the cognitive avoidance theory of worry come from adults with GAD. However, several recent studies show that children and adolescents who experience excessive worrying engage in more cognitive avoidance strategies than youths who experience only moderate worry. For example, chronic worriers often use strategies like distraction (e.g., playing video games) or thought suppression (e.g., telling oneself not to think about a given topic) to avoid dealing with future problems. In contrast, low-level worriers tend to use more active problem-solving strategies that help them address problems directly (e.g., studying for an upcoming test). Furthermore, the number of avoidance strategies used by children predict the severity of their worrying (Dickson, Ciesla, & Reilly, 2012).

In fact, children with GAD worry to *avoid* thinking about problems, not to solve them. Most children use worrying to anticipate future problems and generate possible solutions ahead of time. For example, a child worrying about an upcoming exam might reason, "The test is going to be very hard, so I'm going to have to start studying right away—a little bit each night—in order to do well." In this case, worrying serves a positive, problem-solving function. In contrast, children with GAD show very little problem-solving while worrying (see Figure 11.7). Instead, these children simply ruminate about the negative event. For example, a child with GAD who is worrying about a future exam might think, "The exam is going to be really difficult. What if I fail? What will my mom say?" Because children with GAD are less likely to generate solutions for their worries, their worries persist uncontrollably (Ruscio et al., 2015).

Finally, many youths with GAD adopt cognitive distortions that exacerbate their worries. Weems and Watts (2005) identified three cognitive distortions seen in children with GAD: *catastrophizing, overgeneralizing,* and *personalizing.* Catastrophizing occurs when children expect disastrous outcomes from mildly aversive events. For example, a girl with GAD who has an upcoming dance recital might anticipate disaster: She might forget her dance shoes, trip on stage, and humiliate her family. Overgeneralizing

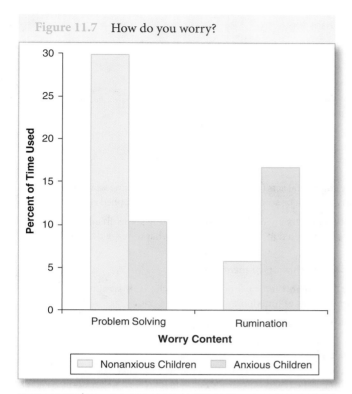

Figure 11.7   How do you worry?

Worry Content

Percent of Time Used

Nonanxious Children   Anxious Children

Source: Based on Szabo and Lovibond (2004).

Note: Children without anxiety disorders tend to generate solutions to future problems when they worry. In contrast, children with anxiety disorders, like GAD, tend to ruminate about potential trouble in the future.

occurs when children assume that a single setback is an indicator of future misfortune. For example, a child who makes a mistake in her first recital might anticipate mistakes in all subsequent performances. Finally, personalizing occurs when children blame themselves for misfortune. For example, a child who trips during a dance recital might attribute her mistake to her own clumsiness, rather than to a slippery floor. These distortions twist the reality of situations, making situations seem more threatening. Therefore, these distortions contribute to persistent worry, rumination, and negative affect.

Review:

- GAD is characterized by persistent worry that is difficult to control and associated with restlessness, poor concentration, fatigue, irritability, tension, and/or sleep problems. It lasts at least 6 months and causes distress or impairment.
- GAD differs from the other anxiety disorders because (a) it is characterized by worry and (b) it is most closely associated with depression.
- Cognitive avoidance theory posits that youths use worry to avoid emotionally and physically arousing negative mental images.
- Youths with GAD often engage in cognitive distortions that exacerbate their worries.

11.2 OBSESSIVE–COMPULSIVE AND RELATED DISORDERS

What Is Obsessive–Compulsive Disorder?

Description

Obsessive–compulsive disorder (OCD) is characterized by the presence of recurrent, unwanted obsessions or compulsions that are extremely time consuming, cause marked distress, or significantly impair daily functioning (see Table 11.9). Obsessions are "recurrent and persistent thoughts, urges, or images that are experienced as intrusive and unwanted" (American Psychiatric Association, 2013, p. 235). Obsessions include thoughts about contamination (e.g., touching "dirty" objects like door handles), repeated doubts (e.g., wondering whether someone left the door unlocked), need for order or symmetry (e.g., towels arranged a certain way), aggressive or horrific impulses (e.g., thoughts about swearing in church), and sexual imagery.

Most people with OCD attempt to ignore or suppress obsessions. However, ignoring obsessions usually causes an increase in anxiety, tension, or distress. To reduce these negative feelings, most people engage in compulsions. Compulsions are "repetitive behaviors or mental acts that an individual feels driven to perform in response to an obsession or according to rules that must be applied rigidly" (American Psychiatric Association, 2013, p. 235). Common compulsions include washing, cleaning, counting, checking, repeating, arranging, and ordering. Compulsions are usually performed in a rigid, stereotyped manner, often according to certain idiosyncratic rules. For example, an adolescent with recurrent obsessions involving sexual imagery may feel compelled to pray to alleviate anxiety or guilt. If she makes mistakes in her prayers, she may require herself to repeat them until they are recited flawlessly (see Figure 11.8).

Many adults and adolescents with OCD recognize that their unwanted thoughts, urges, or images are a product of their own mind; they are unlikely to "come true." However, younger children with OCD may be convinced that their obsessions will materialize. *DSM-5* requires clinicians to specify the person's insight into his or her obsessive–compulsive symptoms. Specification is important because people with good insight may be more motivated to participate in treatment than people with poor or absent insight (Geller, 2010; Piacentini, Chang, Snorrason, & Woods, 2014).

Approximately 1% to 2% of children and adolescents have OCD. Epidemiological studies suggest that at any given time, 90% of these children are not receiving treatment for the disorder. In childhood, OCD is more common among boys than girls, with a gender ratio of 2:1. By late adolescence, many girls begin to manifest the

Table 11.9   Diagnostic Criteria for Obsessive–Compulsive Disorder

A. The presence of obsessions, compulsions, or both:

Obsessions are defined by (1) and (2):

1. Recurrent and persistent thoughts, urges, or images that are experienced, at some time during the disturbance, as intrusive and unwanted, and that in most individuals cause marked anxiety or distress.

2. The individual attempts to ignore or suppress such thoughts, urges, or images, or to neutralize them with some other thought or action (i.e., by performing a compulsion).

Compulsions are defined by (1) and (2):

1. Repetitive behaviors (e.g., hand washing, ordering, checking) or mental acts (e.g., praying, counting, repeating words silently) that the individual feels driven to perform in response to an obsession or according to rules that must be applied rigidly.

2. The behaviors or mental acts are aimed at preventing or reducing anxiety or distress, or preventing some dreaded event or situation; however, these behaviors or mental acts are not connected in a realistic way with what they are designed to neutralize or prevent, or are clearly excessive.

Note: Young children may not be able to articulate the aims of these behaviors or mental acts.

B. The obsessions or compulsions are time-consuming (e.g., take more than 1 hour per day) or cause clinically significant distress or impairment in social, occupational, or other important areas of functioning.

C. The obsessive–compulsive symptoms are not attributable to the physiological effects of a substance (e.g., a drug of abuse, a medication) or another medical condition.

D. The disturbance is not better explained by the symptoms of another mental disorder (e.g., repetitive patterns of behavior as in Autism Spectrum Disorder; impulses as in Conduct Disorder; preoccupation with substances as in Substance Use Disorders; excessive worries as in Generalized Anxiety Disorder; hair pulling as in Trichotillomania[1]; skin picking as in Excoriation Disorder[1]; or guilty ruminations as in Major Depressive Disorder.[2]

Specify if:

With good or fair insight: The individual recognizes that obsessive–compulsive disorder beliefs are definitely or probably not true or that they may or may not be true.

With poor insight: The individual thinks that obsessive–compulsive disorder beliefs are probably true.

With absent insight: The individual is completely convinced that obsessive–compulsive disorder beliefs are true.

Specify if:

Tic-related: The individual has a current or past history of a Tic Disorder.

Source: Reprinted with permission from the *Diagnostic and Statistical Manual of Mental Disorders, Fifth Edition* (Copyright 2013). American Psychiatric Association.

[1]Trichotillomania and Excoriation Disorder are presented later in this chapter.

[2]Major Depressive Disorder is presented in Chapter 13.

disorder and the gender distribution becomes roughly equal (Geller, 2010).

Children's obsessions and compulsions differ somewhat from those of adults. First, it is not unusual for children to change obsessions and/or compulsions over time. Second, children's obsessions and compulsions are often more vague, magical, or superstitious than those of adults. Third, many children have difficulty describing their obsessions. For example, they might report fearing "bad things" rather than contamination or asymmetry. Fourth, some children who are able to articulate their obsessions are unwilling to do so because they fear that stating them aloud will make their feared consequences come true.

Technically, individuals can be diagnosed with OCD if they show *either* obsessions *or* compulsions. In reality, most children show both symptoms. Sometimes, children appear to display only obsessions because their compulsions involve mental rituals. For example, obsessions regarding harm befalling a loved one might be accompanied by ritualistic counting or praying. These mental acts might be easily overlooked by parents and clinicians who mistakenly conclude that no compulsions exist. Indeed, the treatment of mental compulsions is more difficult than the treatment of behavioral compulsions because they are difficult to detect and monitor. Consider Tony, a boy with OCD.

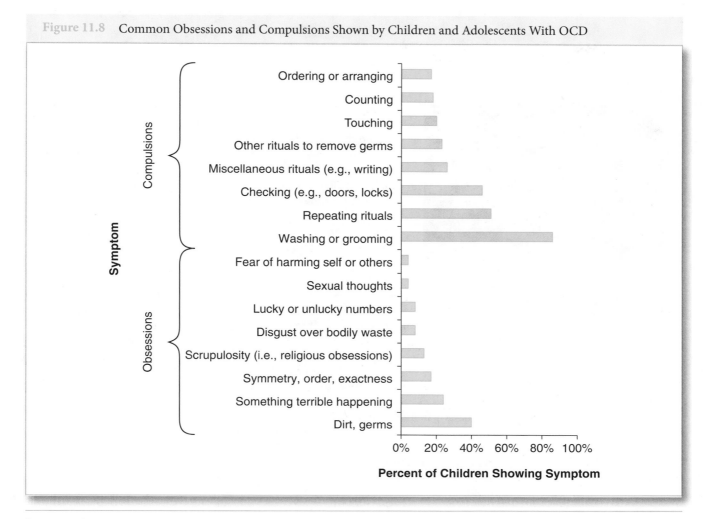

Source: Based on Rapoport and Shaw (2010).

Childhood OCD is a serious disorder that is persistent over time. On average, 41% of youths with OCD continue to meet diagnostic criteria for the disorder 5 years later. An additional 20% of youths continue to show subthreshold OCD symptoms. Youths with early symptom onset, longer duration of symptoms, and symptoms requiring hospitalization are most likely to show persistent problems. On the other hand, approximately 40% of youths with OCD show a marked reduction in symptoms in late adolescence or early adulthood. Many adolescents will experience complete symptom remission. Nevertheless, youths with OCD are at significantly greater risk for relationship, employment, and emotional problems in young adulthood compared to their typically developing peers (Geller & March, 2012).

Causes

OCD is best viewed as a neurodevelopmental disorder that is caused by a combination of genetic risk and abnormalities in brain structure and functioning (Rapoport & Shaw,

2010). OCD is heritable. Individuals who have first-degree relatives with OCD are at increased risk for developing OCD themselves. Approximately 10% to 25% of youths with OCD have at least one parent with the disorder. Twin studies indicate that genetic (45%–58%) and nonshared environmental (42%–55%) factors explain about the same amount of variance in OCD symptoms. Shared environmental experiences such as parenting style or socioeconomic status (SES) account for very little variance (Geller, 2010).

A neural pathway known as the cortico-basal-ganglionic circuit seems to be particularly important in OCD (see Figure 11.9). This circuit forms a feedback loop, involving three brain regions: (1) the orbitofrontal cortex; (2) the cingulate gyrus, and (3) a portion of the basal ganglia called the caudate.

The *orbitofrontal cortex* is responsible for detecting abnormalities or irregularities in the environment and initiating a behavioral response to correct these irregularities. For example, the orbitofrontal cortex might be activated when a person notices dirt on his hands. Signals

OBSESSIVE–COMPULSIVE DISORDER

Doing Things "Just Right"

Source: ©iStockphoto/spifoto

Tony Jeffries was a 12-year-old boy who was referred to our clinic by his mother after she noticed him repeatedly engaging in "strange rituals" around the house. Mrs. Jeffries first became aware of Tony's behavior when she noticed his persistent habit of turning lights on and off multiple times before entering or leaving a room. When she asked about this habit, Tony seemed embarrassed and dismissed it as "nothing." Mrs. Jeffries subsequently noticed other rituals. Tony avoided cracks in sidewalks, always entered rooms with his right foot, and always opened doors with his right hand. When Mrs. Jeffries confronted Tony, he admitted to performing these compulsions.

Later, Tony's therapist tried to gather information about possible obsessions. She asked, "Do any thoughts pop into your mind before you perform these acts?" Tony replied hesitatingly, "Yeah, but they're hard to describe. I feel tense. I feel like something bad is going to happen to me or to my mom . . . like maybe I'll get an F in school or my mom will lose her job. Then, I just feel like I need to do something in a certain way, like turn the lights on and off three times, or open and close a door three times, or enter and exit a room three times." His therapist asked "Always in threes?" Tony explained, "Yeah, it has to be in threes and just right so that I don't feel bad."

Figure 11.9 An overactive cortico-basal-ganglionic circuit often underlies OCD.

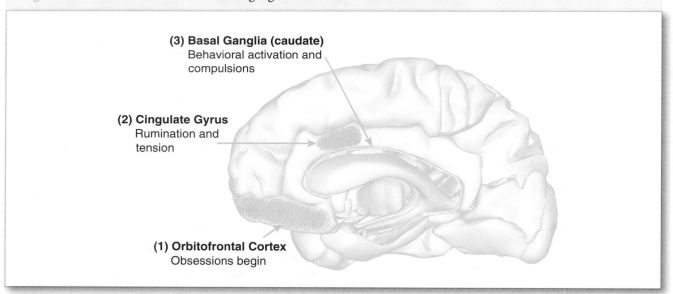

Source: From Brennan and colleagues (2015).

from the orbitofrontal cortex are sent to the *cingulate*, a portion of the limbic system. Activation of the cingulate is associated with cognitive rumination (e.g., "This dirt is really bothering me") and feelings of anxiety, apprehension, or tension. Finally, the neural signal is sent to the *caudate*, a portion of the basal ganglia located deep in the brain. The caudate prepares a behavioral response to

reduce these negative thoughts and feelings (e.g., wash your hands). Then, it provides feedback to the orbitofrontal cortex, telling it that the abnormality or irregularity has been fixed.

In healthy people, the caudate inhibits information from the orbitofrontal cortex and cingulate, regulating the amount of arousal a person experiences. However, people with OCD often show overactivity of the cingulate and a lack of inhibition by the caudate. Consequently, the person experiences unusually high levels of distress (Fullana et al., 2014).

It is noteworthy that the cortico-basal-ganglionic circuit is rich in serotonin. Consequently, serotonin is believed to play a major role in the development and treatment of OCD in children. As we will see, medications like fluoxetine (Prozac) that inhibit the reuptake of serotonin reduce OCD symptoms in many youths with the disorder. Furthermore, drugs that artificially increase serotonergic activity often exacerbate symptoms. Consequently, researchers believe that OCD symptoms are partially caused by excessively high levels of serotonin (Romanelli, Wu, Gamba, Mojtabai, & Segal, 2014).

Although genetic and biological factors might underlie OCD, the disorder is probably maintained through learning. Obsessions develop when people associate specific environmental stimuli with distressing thoughts or beliefs. For example, a door handle might be paired with thoughts of contamination. Later, the individual learns that washing alleviates these worries; consequently, he is more likely to wash his hands in the future. Compulsions, therefore, are negatively reinforced by the reduction of distress (Piacentini et al., 2014).

Furthermore, the way adolescents think can exacerbate their OCD symptoms. Two cognitive distortions seem particularly important. First, adolescents with OCD experience *inflated responsibility* for misfortune (Mathieu, Farrell, Waters, & Lightbody, 2015). For example, if the adolescent's mother is fired from her job or the adolescent's father experiences car trouble on the way home, the adolescent might blame herself for their misfortune. She might think, "My mother lost her job because I'm too much of a burden for her. She can't handle me and her job at once" or "My father had car trouble because I must have did something to it when I borrowed it last week. It must be my fault." These appraisals of misfortune contribute to feelings of guilt and self-doubt.

Second, adolescents with OCD often display *thought-action fusion*, the erroneous belief that merely thinking about an event will increase its probability (Bailey, Wu, Valentiner, & McGrath, 2014). For example, an adolescent girl with OCD might believe that simply thinking about her grandfather's death might increase the likelihood that he would get sick. Because the adolescent believes her thoughts can influence the external world, she attempts to control negative thoughts to prevent future misfortune. Thought-action fusion causes adolescents to feel great distress when they experience transient negative thoughts. Whereas most people dismiss such thoughts as "irrational" or "unlikely," an adolescent with OCD might take them seriously because she believes she has the ability to mentally influence occurrences in the real world (Piacentini et al., 2014).

Some cases of pediatric OCD are caused by a beta-hemolytic streptococcus infection (Swedo et al., 2015). The most common infection of this type is strep throat.

According to the Pediatric Autoimmune Neuropsychiatric Disorder Associated with Streptococcus (PANDAS) theory, a subset of children who show these infections develops rapid-onset OCD symptoms and tics (i.e., involuntary movements or vocalizations). These children may have other symptoms such as irritability, enuresis, anxiety, and deterioration in fine motor skills (e.g., handwriting). These symptoms are caused by an autoimmune reaction that interferes with the functioning of the brain. Antibiotic medication is not effective in preventing the onset of these symptoms. In most cases, children are later diagnosed with OCD and must receive treatment for the disorder (Ferretti, Stevens, & Fischetti, 2016).

Review:

- OCD is characterized by obsessions and/or compulsions that are time consuming and cause significant distress or impairment.
- Obsessions are recurrent and persistent thoughts, urges, or images that are experienced as intrusive and unwanted, whereas compulsions are repetitive behaviors or mental acts that a person feels driven to perform in response to an obsession or according to specific, rigid rules.
- OCD tends to emerge in late childhood or early adolescence. In children, it disproportionately affects boys. Approximately 1% to 2% of youths have OCD.
- The cortico-basal-ganglionic neural circuit likely underlies OCD. It consists of the (a) orbitofrontal cortex, (b) cingulate gyrus, and (c) caudate.
- Youths with OCD often show cognitive distortions, such as inflated sense of personal responsibility and thought-action fusion, which exacerbate their symptoms.

What Disorders Are Related to Obsessive–Compulsive Disorder?

OCD bears resemblance to three other *DSM-5* conditions sometimes seen in children and adolescents: (1) tic disorder and Tourette's disorder, (2) trichotillomania, and (3) excoriation disorder. Youths with these disorders, like youths with OCD, often report negative emotions such as anxiety, apprehension, frustration, or tension. These conditions have in common obsessive preoccupations, unwanted urges, and/or repetitive actions that cause great distress or impair day-to-day functioning (Stein, Craske, Friedman, & Phillips, 2011; Stein, Fineberg et al., 2010; Stein, Grant, et al., 2010).

Tic Disorders

Tics are sudden, rapid, nonrhythmic, and stereotyped behaviors that are involuntary. They can be either motoric (e.g., a facial grimace, neck twitch, or limb movement) or vocal (e.g., a grunt, chirp, or clearing of the throat). Tics can also be either simple or complex. *Simple tics* last a short duration (i.e., milliseconds) and consist of one type of motor behavior (e.g., eye blink, shrug) or vocalization (e.g., click, grunt). *Complex tics* last several seconds and usually consist of a combination of several simple tics (e.g., simultaneous head turning and shrugging). Some people with tics make sexual or obscene gestures (i.e., copropraxia), utter inappropriate slurs (i.e., coprolalia), imitate other people's movements (i.e., echopraxia), or repeat sounds or words (i.e., echolalia). In all cases, however, tics do not have a purpose and are done involuntarily (Chen et al., 2013).

Tics are similar to OCD; both disorders involve a sequence of events in which a stimulus is followed by a largely habitual response. In the case of OCD, the stimulus is an obsession, and the response is a compulsion. In the case of tics, the stimulus is a sudden, unwanted urge, and the response is the motor or vocal behavior. Furthermore, both tics and obsessions can be suppressed for brief periods of time but cause increasingly greater discomfort the longer they are held back (Leckman & Bloch, 2010).

OCD and tics also differ from one another. People with OCD almost always perform compulsions in response to certain obsessive thoughts or mental images. In contrast, not all people with tics report obsessive thoughts that prompt their motor or vocal behaviors (Phillips et al., 2010). Only about one-half of people with tic disorders report specific obsessions that occur prior to a tic. These obsessions often include thoughts about symmetry or order. However, between 50% and 80% of people with tic disorder report only premonitory urges prior to their tics. These urges are often described as having a "physical quality," much like an itch or muscle tension localized to a specific area of the body (Towbin, 2015).

Tics can range in severity from mild to severe. Many youths describe them as unwanted urges, similar to the feeling that you might get when you want to scratch your nose or sneeze. Usually, you can ignore or stifle this urge for a short period of time. However, suppressing the urge usually causes an increase in its intensity and feelings of discomfort. For this reason, tics are usually considered "largely involuntary"—youths are able to control tics only for short periods of time (Towbin, 2015).

There are several different tic disorders. *DSM-5* arranges them in a hierarchical fashion from least to most severe. First, provisional tic disorder is characterized by single or multiple motor or vocal tics (or both) lasting less than 1 year. Second, persistent motor or vocal tic disorder is defined by multiple motor or vocal tics (but *not* both) lasting for more than 1 year. Finally, Tourette's disorder is defined by multiple motor *and* vocal tics lasting for more than 1 year. Many people believe that Tourette's disorder is defined by coprolalia, the involuntary utterance of obscene words. In fact, less than 10% of individuals with Tourette's disorder engage in coprolalia (Leckman & Bloch, 2010).

The lifetime prevalence of Tourette's disorder ranges from 0.4% to 1.8%. Chronic tic disorder is more common, appearing in 2% to 4% of children and adolescents. Between 5% and 18% of youths experience transient tics, often at stressful times in their lives. Tics are 2 to 10 times more common in boys than in girls (Towbin, 2015).

Tic disorders and OCD often emerge in childhood or adolescence. The median age of onset for tics is 5.5 years; in contrast, OCD usually does not emerge until late childhood (in boys) or adolescence (in girls). Both disorders tend to wax and wane over time and are usually exacerbated by psychosocial stress. For example, before final exams or an important athletic competition, youths with these disorders often experience greater frequency and intensity of unwanted urges. Usually, symptoms peak in early to middle adolescence and decline by early adulthood (Bloch, Craiglow, & Landeros-Weisenberger, 2009).

Tic disorders are highly comorbid with OCD. Between 25% to 50% of youths with chronic tic or Tourette's disorder will develop OCD at some point in adolescence or early adulthood. Conversely, approximately 30% of youths with OCD also show tic or Tourette's disorder. Because tics are rare in the general population, their high comorbidity with OCD suggests a common underlying cause.

Indeed, both tic disorders and OCD are heritable conditions. The concordance of tic disorders among monozygotic (MZ) twins ranges from 77% to 94%, whereas the concordance for dizygotic (DZ) twins is only 23%. Furthermore, both conditions run in families. Children with tic disorders have a 15% to 53% likelihood of having a relative with a history of tics. Children with tic disorders are also 10 to 20 times more likely than unaffected children to have a family member with OCD (Towbin, 2015).

Trichotillomania

Youths with trichotillomania repeatedly pull out their hair, resulting in hair loss. For example, a girl might pull hair from the top of her head or bite and chew long hair dangling into her face. Alternatively, an adolescent boy might ritualistically pluck whiskers from his sideburns or chin. Although the person's hair loss may not be noticeable to others, the practice of hair pulling causes the person distress or interferes with his or her functioning. In the context of hair pulling, "distress" includes negative emotions, such as feeling a loss of control, embarrassment, or shame. For example, a child might become very upset because she feels like she cannot stop pulling her hair. Alternatively, an adolescent might be consistently late for school because she spends excessive time plucking hair in the morning. Many individuals with this condition pluck hair to alleviate anxiety (e.g., while studying for a test) or reduce boredom (e.g., while reading this book). Trichotillomania is only diagnosed when the person's hair pulling is recurrent and results in distress or impairment (American Psychiatric Association, 2013).

Clinical observations and recent research studies have identified two subtypes of trichotillomania. "Focused" hair pulling involves conscious, deliberate pulling, usually in response to unpleasant thoughts or feelings. Adolescents who engage in focused hair pulling tend to report distress immediately prior to pulling and relief immediately after the act. Focused hair pulling resembles many features of OCD. In contrast, "automatic" hair pulling involves habitual plucking, usually outside the person's awareness. Automatic pulling usually occurs while the adolescent is engaged in other tasks (e.g., completing homework, talking on the phone) and is usually not elicited by distress or negative affect (Stein, Grant, et al., 2010).

Like OCD, trichotillomania involves repetitive behaviors that can cause distress. Furthermore, many adolescents with trichotillomania engage in ritualistic behaviors associated with hair pulling. For example, some youths will remove hair from only certain parts of the body whereas other youths will "mouth" hair ritualistically before biting it off.

Trichotillomania differs from OCD in several respects. First, people with trichotillomania usually do not report obsessive thoughts or mental images. In contrast, nearly all patients with OCD report obsessions. Second, people with trichotillomania sometimes report pleasure or satisfaction from hair pulling. In contrast, people with OCD usually report relief (but not pleasure) after engaging in their compulsions. Third, people with trichotillomania usually recognize that their behavior is unusual, whereas some individuals with OCD (especially children) may not (Stein, Grant, et al., 2010).

Trichotillomania and OCD have a similar onset and course. Both disorders typically emerge in early adolescence. The mean age of onset for trichotillomania is 11.8 years, although it has been observed in toddlers and preschoolers. Onset is usually insidious (i.e., slow and increasingly more severe), and symptoms tend to worsen with psychosocial stress. Although symptoms of OCD tend to peak in late adolescence, symptoms of trichotillomania tend to peak slightly later, in young adulthood. Symptoms of trichotillomania and OCD are also comorbid. Although trichotillomania occurs in less than 1% of the general population, 9% of individuals with OCD have this condition.

Trichotillomania and OCD also have similar underlying causes. The two disorders tend to run in families. In one study, 5% of patients with trichotillomania had a relative with OCD; in contrast, <1% of healthy controls had a family member with OCD. Both disorders are also associated with dysfunction of the striatum. Interestingly, however, medications that are often effective for OCD (e.g., serotonin reuptake inhibitors) are less effective for trichotillomania, suggesting a possible difference between these two disorders (Phillips et al., 2010).

Excoriation Disorder

Excoriation disorder is new to *DSM-5*. It is characterized by recurrent skin picking that results in lesions. Individuals with excoriation disorder have made repeated attempts to decrease or stop their recurrent skin picking, but have been unable to do so. Their habitual picking, or inability to stop, causes them distress or impairment in school, work, or social functioning (American Psychiatric Association, 2013).

Skin picking is usually considered a minor problem or bad habit. In most cases, people pick at their skin in order to remove a blemish, tag, or other minor imperfection. Youths with excoriation disorder, however, repeatedly pick at their skin and find it difficult to stop. Between 2% and 5.4% of adolescents and young adults have excoriation disorder. Usually, individuals with this condition pick at skin on their face, head, or neck. Usually, picking is done with the fingernails, although some people use tweezers, scissors, nail files, or other objects. Repeated picking can cause lesions, abrasions, and scarring. Typically, youths with excoriation disorder are first referred to a pediatrician or dermatologist because of tissue damage. Sometimes, medication is necessary because of infection and, in rare cases, cosmetic surgery is needed to repair damage (Grant et al., 2012).

Excoriation disorder is similar to OCD because it is usually elicited by feelings of negative affect or distress. Many, but not all, individuals with excoriation disorder experience an urge to pick immediately following psychosocial stress and report alleviation of negative affect immediately after picking. Like people with OCD, individuals with excoriation disorder can spend hours each day engaged in their compulsive behavior. Their skin picking can greatly interfere with school, work, and friendships. Furthermore, adolescents with OCD and excoriation disorder are often embarrassed by their symptoms. Most will go to great lengths to avoid detection and are very reluctant to seek treatment.

Excoriation disorder often co-occurs with OCD, trichotillomania, depression, and anxiety disorders (Stein, Grant, et al., 2010). The comorbidity between excoriation disorder and these other conditions may be due to common genetic risks and neural pathways (Snorrason, Belleau, & Woods, 2012). Excoriation disorder is also seen in young adults with impulse-control problems, such as compulsive gambling, buying, and stealing (i.e., kleptomania) as well as compulsive sexual behavior (Odlaug et al., 2013).

Review:

- Tics are involuntary, rapid, nonrhythmic, stereotyped behaviors. They can be motoric or vocal. Tourette's disorder is defined by the presence of multiple motor and vocal tics lasting for more than 1 year.
- Trichotillomania is characterized by the repeated pulling out of hair, resulting in hair loss, which causes distress or impairment.
- Excoriation disorder is characterized by recurrent skin picking that results in lesions and causes distress or impairment.

11.3 EVIDENCE-BASED TREATMENT

How Can Behavior Therapy Be Used to Treat Phobias and Selective Mutism?

Almost all effective psychosocial treatments for childhood anxiety disorders involve exposure therapy (Graczyk &

Connolly, 2015). Recall that most anxiety disorders are maintained through negative reinforcement; children learn to avoid feared stimuli (e.g., dogs, speaking, social settings) in order to regulate negative emotions. Exposure therapy occurs when children confront these feared stimuli for discrete periods of time. Over time, and across multiple confrontations, their anxiety gradually dissipates. Exposure therapy can occur in many ways. Exposure can occur gradually (i.e., graded exposure) or rapidly (i.e., flooding). Children can confront real objects, people, or situations (i.e., in vivo exposure) or they can imagine the feared stimulus (i.e., imaginal exposure). Exposure can occur multiple times over a number of weeks (i.e., spaced exposure) or over the course of hours or days (e.g., massed exposure).

Behavioral treatments for children's phobias have existed for nearly 100 years. Mary Cover Jones (1924), a student of John Watson, used behavioral techniques to reduce fear in a 34-month-old child named Peter, who was afraid of rabbits. Jones used three techniques to reduce Peter's fear. First, she gradually exposed Peter to a rabbit for progressively longer periods of time. Initially, the rabbit remained on the other side of the room and in a cage. In subsequent sessions, assistants brought the rabbit closer to Peter, released it from the cage, and encouraged Peter to touch it. Second, Peter was provided with candy whenever he tolerated the rabbit's presence; that is, he was positively reinforced for coming into contact with the rabbit and not running away. Third, other children Peter's age, who were not afraid of rabbits, were asked to play with Peter while the rabbit was present. Peter observed these children pet the rabbit without fear. Over the course of several weeks, Peter's fear of the rabbit decreased (see Image 11.1).

Contingency Management

Behavioral techniques, like the ones used to treat Peter's phobia, are still used today. Jones's (1924) primary technique is now called contingency management. Contingency management is based on the principles of operant conditioning; it involves exposing the child to the feared stimulus and positively reinforcing the child contingent on the exposure. At the same time, the child is *not* allowed to avoid or withdraw from the feared stimulus. Jones progressively exposed Peter to the rabbit and reinforced his actions with candy. Furthermore, she prohibited him from running away.

Today, a therapist who wants to use contingency management would first meet with the family to establish a *behavioral contract*. The contract specifies exactly what actions the child is expected to perform and what reinforcement will be provided when the child meets these expectations. Usually, the child and his parents rank the child's behavior in a hierarchical fashion. Behaviors that elicit mild anxiety are introduced first, whereas behaviors that cause high anxiety are presented last.

The child is required to come into closer and closer contact with the feared stimulus for longer and longer periods of time. When the child successfully completes the required behavior, he is positively reinforced (e.g., given praise, access to toys and games). At the same time, he is not permitted to run away, tantrum, or otherwise avoid the feared stimulus. The child is encouraged to confront the feared stimulus until his anxiety dissipates.

Systematic Desensitization

A second behavioral technique to treat phobias is systematic desensitization, a technique based on the principle of classical conditioning. In systematic desensitization, children learn to associate a feared stimulus with a response that is incompatible with fear. Usually, this incompatible response involves relaxation.

Initially, parents and the child create a hierarchy of feared stimuli, just like in contingency management. The goal is to gradually progress up the fear hierarchy by exposing the child to the feared stimulus for longer periods of time. However, before exposure begins, the child is taught an incompatible response to use when confronting the feared stimulus. Some therapists teach children deep breathing techniques to help them relax. Other therapists teach children how to relax their muscles.

Then, children gradually progress up the fear hierarchy. When they experience anxiety, children use their relaxation skills to produce an incompatible (relaxation) response. Through classical conditioning, children come to associate the previously feared stimulus with the relaxation response.

Modeling

A final technique, also used by Jones (1924), involves observational learning or modeling. In modeling, the child watches an adult or another child confront the feared stimulus. For example, a child with dog phobia might watch his therapist approach, pet, and play with a dog during the therapy session. He might also see another child his age perform the same actions. The child sees that confronting the feared stimulus does not result in punishment (e.g., the model is not bitten by the dog) and often results in positive reinforcement (e.g., the model enjoys playing with the dog). Jones used modeling to extinguish Peter's fear; Peter watched other toddlers approach and play with the rabbit.

Modeling can occur in real life (i.e., in vivo modeling) or by watching videotapes (i.e., videotaped modeling). Some therapists use a third strategy called participant modeling. In participant modeling, the therapist first models the behavior for the child and then helps the child perform the behavior himself.

Efficacy of Behavioral Interventions

Research supports the efficacy of behavior therapy for youths with specific phobias (Connolly et al., 2015; Graczyk & Connolly, 2015). Behavioral techniques have been successfully used to reduce fears that range from the commonplace (e.g., animals, the dark, heights) to the atypical (e.g., menstruation, bowel movements).

Image 11.1 Mary Cover Jones (1924) used exposure therapy to reduce Peter's fear of rabbits. The techniques she used are still part of most evidence-based treatments today.

Source: Copyright.AlenaZamotaeva

Behavior therapy is also effective in treating young children with selective mutism (Oerbeck, Stein, Wentzel-Larsen, Langsrud, & Kristensen, 2014). For example, integrated behavior therapy is an evidence-based treatment in which clinicians use graded exposure and systematic desensitization to reduce children's fear of speaking in the clinic and at school (Bergman, Gonzalez, Piacentini, & Keller, 2013). Initially, the therapist works with parents and children to create a "talking ladder"—that is, a hierarchy of speaking situations that elicit low to high levels of anxiety. Then, clinicians help parents and teachers identify potential reinforcers that they can administer as children progress up the hierarchy. Early sessions might simply require children to mouth or whisper responses in the clinic whereas later sessions might involve speaking to teachers or classmates aloud at school. Sometimes, therapists use modeling and natural rewards to encourage children to speak. For example, children who are fearful of speaking might be invited to play "duck, duck, goose" or "red light, green light" with other children. As children watch their peers have fun playing these games (which require speaking), they might model their actions (Conn & Coyne, 2014; Klein, Armstrong, Skira, & Gordon, 2016).

Review:

- Exposure therapy is a behavioral intervention used to treat anxiety and related disorders. It involves repeatedly confronting feared stimuli for discrete periods of time until anxiety or negative affect decreases.

- Effective behavioral techniques include contingency management, systematic desensitization, and modeling.
- Behavioral interventions based on exposure are efficacious in reducing anxiety in children and adolescents.

How Can Cognitive–Behavioral Therapy Be Used to Treat Separation Anxiety Disorder, Generalized Anxiety Disorder, and Social Anxiety Disorder?

Cognitive–behavioral therapy (CBT) is an effective treatment for many childhood anxiety disorders, especially SAD, social anxiety disorder, and GAD. Recall that the underlying premise of CBT is that there is a close relationship between a person's thoughts, feelings, and actions. Changes in thinking can affect the way people feel and act. Similarly, changes in overt behavior can influence thought patterns and mood. In CBT, children with anxiety disorders are taught to recognize anxiety (feelings) and use cognitive and behavioral coping strategies to reduce the anxiety until it is more manageable (Graczyk & Connolly, 2015).

Philip Kendall and colleagues (Kendall, 2012) have examined the efficacy of a 16-week cognitive–behavioral treatment package for children. The program is divided into two phases: (1) education and (2) practice. In the first phase, children learn about the relationship between thoughts, feelings, and actions, and they are taught new ways to cope with anxiety and worry. Therapy is structured around a personalized FEAR plan. The steps in the plan are represented by the acronym FEAR: feelings, expectations, attitudes, and results (see Table 11.10). When the child confronts an anxiety-provoking situation, she uses the FEAR steps to manage her anxiety.

First, children learn to identify feelings and somatic sensations associated with anxiety. Children learn to ask themselves, "Am I feeling frightened?" Children are taught to use muscle relaxation when frightened as a way to reduce distress.

Next, children learn to recognize and modify negative thoughts or cognitive distortions that contribute to their anxiety. They ask themselves, "Am I expecting bad things to happen?" The therapist uses a workbook, games, and role-playing exercises to show how changes in thoughts can lead to changes in feelings and actions. For example, the *Coping Cat Workbook* (Kendall, Crawley, Benjamin, & Mauro, 2012) consists of a series of exercises designed to teach children to recognize and alter negative thoughts (see Figure 11.10).

Therapists help children reduce the frequency of negative self-statements (Keehn, Lincoln, Brown, & Chavira, 2013). Children with anxiety disorders engage in many more negative self-statements but the same number of positive self-statements as nonanxious children. The therapist's goal is not to increase the child's positive cognitions, that is, to help the child see the world through "rose-colored glasses." Rather, the therapist focuses on

Table 11.10 Sample FEAR Plan for a Socially Anxious Child Giving a Class Presentation

Step	Example
F: Feeling frightened	"Well, I have butterflies in my stomach and my palms are kind of sweaty."
E: Expecting bad things to happen	"I will mess up."
	"The other kids will make fun of me."
	"I'm going to look stupid and they'll laugh at me."
A: Attitudes and actions that will help	"I can practice beforehand and make sure I know what I'm going to say."
	"I didn't mess up the last time and the teacher said I did a good job."
	"Even if I mess up, it's not a big deal anyway because everybody messes up sometimes."
R: Results and rewards	"I was nervous in the beginning, but I felt OK by the end."
	"Nobody laughed at me."
	"I think I did a pretty good job and I tried really hard."
	"My reward is to go to the movies with Mom and Dad this weekend."

Source: Based on Kendall et al. (2005).

Figure 11.10 The Coping Cat

Some type of thoughts can help people deal with the situation, while other thoughts might make people feel more nervous or scared. Take a look at this cartoon scene. Circle the cat that would be most frightened. Why do you think he would feel more scared?

Source: From Kendall (1992). Used with permission.

Note: Children complete the *Coping Cat Workbook* to help them make connections between their thoughts and feelings.

helping the child see the world more realistically, rather than negatively or catastrophically. According to Kendall (1992), the goal of therapy is to teach children "the power of nonnegative thinking." Reductions in negative thoughts predict success in therapy.

In subsequent sessions, children learn cognitive problem-solving skills designed to cope with anxiety-provoking situations. They try to develop *attitudes that can help*. Problem-solving training is designed to help children view social situations or problems realistically, generate as many solutions to these problems as possible, consider the benefits and costs of each solution, and select the best course of action (Beidel & Reinecke, 2015).

Finally, in the *results and rewards* component of treatment, children are encouraged to realistically judge the effectiveness of their problem-solving and to reward themselves for addressing the feared situation. Since anxious children often place unrealistic expectations on themselves or exaggerate negative events, it is important for them to view outcomes in a realistic light and to take pride in attempting to cope with anxiety-provoking situations (Creswell, Waite, & Cooper, 2014; Kendall, 2012).

After children learn the FEAR plan in the clinic, they begin applying it in the community. Use of the FEAR steps in the community involves graded exposure. The type of exposure largely depends on the child's disorder. Children with social anxiety disorder might be asked to approach a group of children playing a game; adolescents with SAD might be encouraged to separate from their parents for 15 minutes during a shopping trip. Initially, children report intense anxiety following exposure. However, as children habituate to the anxiety-provoking situation, anxiety levels drop. Children learn that exposure does not result in catastrophe.

Several randomized controlled studies indicate that CBT is efficacious (Kendall, 2012). Research has typically involved children aged 7 to 13 diagnosed with social anxiety disorder, SAD, and GAD. CBT is associated with improvements in self-report, parent-report, and behavioral observations of children's anxiety symptoms, compared to controls. Furthermore, reductions in anxiety tend to be clinically significant; most children who participate in CBT no longer meet diagnostic criteria for anxiety disorders after treatment. Gains are maintained from 1 to 7 years later. CBT can also be administered to groups of children at the same time.

Recent research suggests that the two most important components of CBT are (1) exposing children to feared stimuli and (2) challenging their negative thoughts about these events. For example, Peris and colleagues (2015) assessed anxiety symptoms in children as they participated in CBT. Whereas children showed marked symptom reduction while learning to challenge cognitive distortions and exposing themselves to feared stimuli, they showed relatively little symptom reduction when taught simple relaxation techniques. These findings suggest that both cognitive and behavioral components are essential to the effectiveness of CBT (see Figure 11.11).

CBT treatment packages have been modified so that children and adolescents can participate via the computer (Spence, March, Vigerland, & Serlachius, 2016). A computer-administered version of *Coping Cat* has been developed for children with social anxiety disorder, SAD, and GAD. Other programs for children include *Camp Cope-A-Lot* and *BRAVE for Children*. Programs called *BRAVE for Adolescents* and *Cool Teens* have been developed for adolescents. Several studies indicate that these programs can be used to supplement traditional, face-to-face CBT, or as a substitute for families who do not have access to evidence-based CBT in their communities (Donovan, Spence, & March, 2013; Graczyk & Connolly, 2015).

Review:

- CBT involves the integration of cognitive and behavioral interventions to reduce psychological distress. It relies on the premise that changes in thoughts or overt actions can affect emotions.
- CBT consists of (a) learning the association between thoughts, actions, and feelings; (b) identifying and challenging cognitive distortions that exacerbate anxiety; and (c) altering environmental contingencies to promote adaptive coping.
- Children can develop FEAR plans to cope with anxious stimuli or situations.

How Can Cognitive–Behavioral Therapy Be Used to Treat Panic Disorder?

CBT for adolescents with panic disorder involves four components: (1) relaxation training, (2) interoceptive exposure, (3) cognitive restructuring, and (4) graded in vivo exposure (Connolly et al., 2015; Simon, 2016). In relaxation training, the adolescent learns ways to reduce physiological arousal when he begins to experience panic. Relaxation training is designed to combat the adolescent's anxiety sensitivity and tendency to overreact to stress. Most therapists teach breathing exercises, muscle relaxation, or calming self-statements to help clients relax.

Interoceptive exposure is a technique unique to the treatment of panic disorder. In interoceptive exposure, the adolescent learns to produce some of the physiological symptoms of panic and then use relaxation techniques to cope with these symptoms. Paniclike symptoms can be intentionally produced by spinning in a chair, hyperventilating into a paper bag, or running in place for 1 to 2 minutes. Mimicking panic symptoms has at least three benefits. First, adolescents recognize that panic symptoms can be intentionally produced and, therefore, are not always beyond their control. Second, adolescents learn that they will not die or pass out from panic. Although

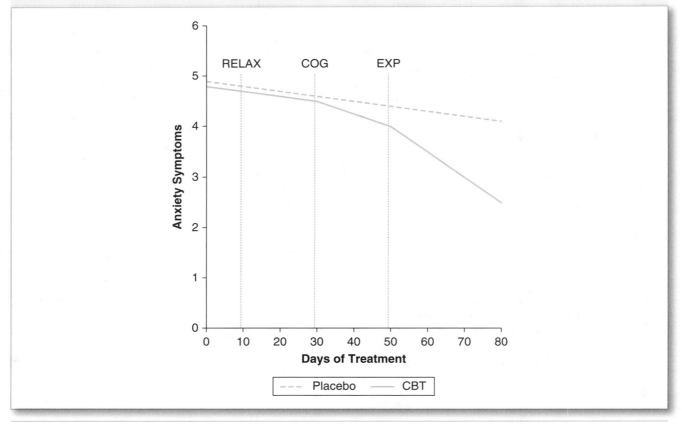

Figure 11.11   Researchers monitored children's symptom reduction during CBT. Youths showed greatest reduction after changing negative cognitions (COG) and exposing themselves to feared stimuli (EXP). Relaxation training (RELAX) was not as helpful.

Source: Based on Peris and colleagues (2015).

distressing, panic symptoms decrease over time. Third, adolescents learn that relaxation techniques can be used to effectively cope with panic symptoms.

Cognitive restructuring is also used to treat panic disorder. Cognitive restructuring techniques generally involve challenging cognitive biases and distortions that lead to panic attacks. The main target of cognitive restructuring is catastrophic thinking. Some therapists play the "detective game" with their adolescent clients to help them critically evaluate the likelihood of catastrophic events occurring during a panic attack. For example, a therapist might challenge her client's distorted beliefs by asking for evidence for and against those beliefs (see the following Research to Practice section).

The final component of CBT for panic disorder is graded exposure. Graded exposure is primarily used to correct agoraphobic avoidance. The therapist and adolescent create a hierarchy of situations or events that ranges from moderately distressing to highly upsetting. The adolescent is encouraged to face each feared situation until she experiences a reduction in panic.

Considerable evidence supports the efficacy of CBT and interoceptive exposure for individuals with panic

disorder (Barlow et al., 2015). Unfortunately, nearly all randomized controlled studies have involved adults, rather than children or adolescents. Furthermore, no randomized controlled trial has included more than 30 youths as participants. Consequently, CBT is believed to be the first-line treatment for youths with this disorder, but must be used carefully given the limited pediatric data that are available.

Review:

- Relaxation training is a cognitive–behavioral intervention designed to reduce physiological arousal and avoid panic. It often involves muscle relaxation, controlled breathing, and pleasant imagery.
- Interoceptive exposure is a behavioral intervention unique to the treatment of panic disorder. The person intentionally produces physiological symptoms of panic and then uses relaxation techniques to cope with these symptoms.
- Cognitive restructuring can be used to challenge biases and distortions that lead to panic. Clients learn to look at panic-inducing situations more realistically and less catastrophically.

CHALLENGING CATASTROPHIC THOUGHTS THAT LEAD TO PANIC

Marie: When I start to get those feelings, you know, with my heart beating fast and hyperventilating, I feel like I'm having a heart attack, like I'm going to die!

Therapist: What's the likelihood that you're *actually* going to die when you feel that way?

Marie: Pretty high; at least, it feels that way.

Therapist: Yes, but you've had a number of these attacks before.

Marie: Uh-huh.

Therapist: And you obviously haven't died from them.

Marie: No.

Therapist: And you've never even fainted or lost consciousness before, right?

Marie: No. I never have.

Therapist: So what's the likelihood that you will die, faint, or lose consciousness from an attack in the future?

Marie: I guess pretty low since it's never happened before.

Therapist: You're probably right. You can even tell yourself, when you feel an attack coming on, that you'll be OK, that you're not going to die or faint or pass out.

Marie: Yes. But it sure feels like I will.

Therapist: Yes, it does. But *feeling* like it will happen and *actually* fainting are two different things. Besides, what is the worst possible thing that could happen?

Marie: Well, I could sweat all over and hyperventilate and get all pale and clammy. I'd have to run out of class and go to the bathroom to feel better. The teacher and the other kids in class would think I was crazy.

Therapist: OK. So we agree that you'll probably not die or pass out, right?

Marie: Yeah, but I would probably make a fool out of myself.

Therapist: Well, if you saw another kid in your class suddenly look sweaty and clammy and then run out of class for the bathroom, what would you think?

Marie: I'd think she was sick.

Therapist: Would you think she was crazy?

Marie: No. I'd think she had the flu.

Therapist: Would you tease her after class or talk about her with your friends?

Marie: Of course not. I'd probably ask her if she was feeling OK.

Therapist: Don't you think your teacher and classmates would react the same way if they saw you do the same thing?

Marie: Yes. I suppose they would.

How Can Cognitive–Behavioral Therapy Be Used to Treat Obsessive–Compulsive Disorder and Related Disorders?

Treatment for Obsessive–Compulsive Disorder

CBT is currently the treatment of choice for youths with OCD (Geller & March, 2012; Olatunji, Davis, Powers, & Smits, 2015). Usually, CBT is administered as a treatment package consisting of three basic components: (1) information gathering, (2) exposure and response prevention (EX/RP), and (3) generalization.

First, the clinician interviews the parents and child to obtain information regarding the family's psychosocial history, the child's symptoms, and the onset and course of the disorder. It is important for the clinician to determine exactly what kinds of obsessions and compulsions the child experiences. For example, treating a child's ritualistic actions (e.g., hand washing, checking) would require different methods than addressing a child's mental rituals (e.g., counting, praying silently).

The next step is exposure and response prevention (EX/RP). Using information gathered during the interview, the child and clinician develop a hierarchy of feared stimuli. Over several weeks, the child exposes himself to each of the feared stimuli, gradually progressing up the hierarchy. At the same time, the child must not engage in the rituals he feels compelled to do after confronting the feared stimuli (Essau & Ozer, 2015).

To illustrate EX/RP, imagine a 10-year-old boy who obsesses about contamination. After he touches certain objects that he considers "dirty," he feels compelled to wash his hands. His obsession is contamination by "dirty" objects; his compulsion is ritualistic washing. The boy and his therapist develop a fear hierarchy, ranging from behaviors that elicit only mild anxiety (e.g., sitting in the therapist's chair) to strong anxiety (e.g., touching a public toilet). During each session, the boy and his therapist confront a different feared stimulus, gradually moving up the hierarchy. The therapist might teach the boy relaxation techniques, like controlled breathing, to help him cope with anxiety during the exposure. The therapist might also use modeling, positive reinforcement, and the strength of their therapeutic relationship to help the boy to successfully confront the stimuli. At the same time, the therapist prohibits the boy from washing. EX/RP works through the principle of extinction. Initially, exposure produces a rapid surge of distress. Over time, however, the child's distress gradually decreases and becomes more manageable.

Older children and adolescents with OCD might benefit from cognitive therapy in addition to EX/RP. Cognitive techniques usually do not reduce OCD behaviors directly; rather, they help some children engage in the EX/RP exercises. Many therapists use cognitive restructuring to help children view feared situations more realistically, rather than in an excessively negative light. For example, a child might initially think, "That chair is disgusting. It has germs all over it, and I'll get sick if I touch it." The therapist might challenge the child's thinking by asking, "Lots of other people have sat in that chair; have they all gotten sick?" Some therapists help children replace self-defeating, negativistic self-statements with more realistic statements. For example, after confronting a feared stimulus, a child might initially say, "I just can't stand it. I have to wash." The therapist might encourage him to say, "It's tough, but I can do it. I just need to hang in there" (Franklin, March, & Garcia, 2007).

The final component of CBT involves generalization training and relapse prevention. Parents play an important role in this part of treatment. The therapist teaches parents how to coach their children through the EX/RP tasks and asks parents and children to continue confronting feared stimuli outside the therapy setting. In the final sessions, the therapist, child, and parents discuss what to do in case symptoms return. Most therapists suggest viewing relapses as learning experiences, rather than as signs of failure. If relapses occur, the family can try using EX/RP techniques or they can call the therapist for additional support.

The efficacy of CBT for children and adolescents is supported by several randomized controlled studies. Overall, youths with OCD show 50% to 67% symptom reduction following initial participation in CBT. Furthermore, combining CBT with medication seems to help most youths who do not respond to CBT alone. Symptom reduction tends to persist after treatment. Most studies suggest that EX/RP is the most important component of treatment. Relaxation training and cognitive interventions that are often part of OCD treatment packages may be useful, but they do not seem to be critical for success (Skarphedinsson et al., 2015).

Treatment for Tics, Trichotillomania, and Excoriation

Two behavioral interventions are effective in reducing the frequency and severity of tics and related disorders in children and adolescents (Christophersen & Vanscoyoc, 2013). The first method is self-monitoring. Children, with the help of parents, are asked to monitor and record the frequency of tics during the course of the day. Families can use a small notebook or handheld clicker. Sometimes, children are not aware of the frequency of their tics. In these cases, self-monitoring raises awareness of their tics and decreases their frequency. In rare cases, however, self-monitoring can make children uncomfortable and actually exacerbate the problem. Even if self-monitoring does not alter children's behavior, it can provide baseline data regarding the frequency, time, and location of children's tics (Azrin & Peterson, 1988).

A second behavioral strategy is habit reversal training (Peterson & Azrin, 1992). Habit reversal training involves teaching the child to engage in a behavior that makes it impossible to produce the tic. For example, a boy with a neck or arm tic might be instructed to tense his muscles in such a way that it is physically impossible for him to engage in the tic. Alternatively, a girl with a vocal tic might be taught to breathe in a certain way that is incompatible with the tic. Habit reversal training can be highly effective in reducing the frequency of tics. Furthermore, habit reversal techniques are usually not noticeable by others. However, they take motivation to learn and practice to implement.

Review:

- EX/RP is a first-line behavioral treatment for OCD. It involves exposing oneself to stimuli that elicit obsessions and avoiding compulsions.
- Tics, trichotillomania, and excoriation can be treated using behavioral techniques such as self-monitoring and habit reversal training.

Is Medication Effective in Treating Childhood Anxiety Disorders?

Exposure-based, psychosocial interventions are the first-line treatment for most pediatric anxiety disorders. However, many children do not respond to exposure-based therapy, or symptom reduction may not occur fast enough to satisfy families. For these children, medication can sometimes be helpful (Connolly et al., 2015).

Medication for Childhood Anxiety Disorders

Several studies have demonstrated the effectiveness of selective serotonin reuptake inhibitors (SSRIs) for treating anxiety disorders in children and adolescents. The medications fluoxetine (Prozac), sertraline (Zoloft), fluvoxamine (Luvox), and paroxetine (Paxil) are superior to placebo in treating anxiety problems. For example, in the Research Unit on Pediatric Psychopharmacology Anxiety Study Group (2001), researchers randomly assigned 128 children and adolescents with SAD, social phobia, or GAD to receive either fluvoxamine (Luvox) or placebo. After 8 weeks, youths taking the medication showed greater symptom reduction than controls. In another study, researchers randomly assigned 74 children with SAD to receive either fluoxetine (Prozac) or placebo. Approximately twice as many youths taking the medication (61%) improved compared to youths in the placebo condition (35%). Across studies, approximately 45% to 65% of youths prescribed these medications show at least moderate improvement (Bernstein & Victor, 2010).

Combining CBT with medication will likely improve children's outcomes. The Child/Adolescent Anxiety Multimodal Study (CAMS) compared various treatments for 488 youths with SAD, social phobia, and GAD (Walkup et al., 2008). Youths were randomly assigned to one of four conditions: (1) sertraline (Zoloft) alone, (2) CBT alone, (4) sertraline plus CBT, or (4) placebo. All three treatments were more effective than placebo (see Figure 11.12). However, youths who received both medication and CBT were more likely to improve than youths who received either medication or CBT alone (Compton et al., 2010). It is noteworthy that medication is associated with a significant reduction in symptoms but not symptom remission. For example, in the CAMS

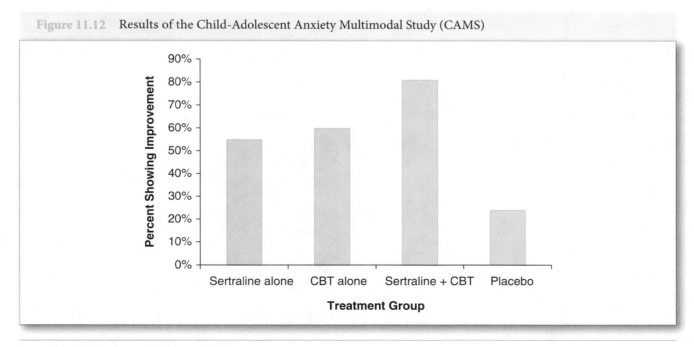

Figure 11.12   Results of the Child-Adolescent Anxiety Multimodal Study (CAMS)

Source: Based on Compton and colleagues (2010).

Note: CAMS showed that youths who received both sertraline (Zoloft) and CBT were more likely to experience a reduction in anxiety symptoms than youths receiving either treatment alone.

study, "improvement" was defined as a 30% reduction in symptom severity. Most youths who "improved" after taking medication continued to experience symptoms of anxiety (Bernstein & Victor, 2010).

SSRIs may be effective in helping young children with selective mutism. Overall, 84% of children with selective mutism show improvement after taking an SSRI. However, most studies supporting the usefulness of SSRIs have not included control groups. Therefore, results must be interpreted cautiously (Manassis, Oerbeck, & Overgaard, 2016).

Medication for Obsessive–Compulsive Disorder and Related Disorders

The Pediatric OCD Treatment Study (POTS; 2004) examined the relative efficacy of medication and CBT for childhood OCD. Researchers studied 112 youths (aged 7–12) with OCD. Children were assigned to one of four groups: (1) sertraline (Zoloft) alone, (2) CBT alone, (3) sertraline plus CBT, or (4) placebo. After 12 weeks of treatment, children who received combined CBT and medication showed greater symptom reduction than children who received either CBT or medication alone. Children who received either of the treatments alone showed approximately equal symptom reduction. Furthermore, youths who received either treatment alone showed greater symptom reduction than children who received a placebo (see Figure 11.13). The researchers also examined the percentage of children who no longer showed

significant OCD symptoms after treatment in each group. Results showed that 53.6% of children in the combined group, 38.3% in the CBT-only group, 21.4% in the medication-only group, and 3.6% in the placebo group recovered. These results suggest that both CBT and medication are efficacious at reducing OCD symptoms in children (Essau & Ozer, 2015).

The POTS study showed that combining CBT with medication was more effective than using medication alone. However, CBT can take many sessions to implement. Furthermore, there are not enough clinicians trained in using CBT for youths with OCD. The researchers wanted to know if providing children and parents with information about CBT and instructions on how to implement EX/RP might be as effective as actual CBT in alleviating OCD symptoms. To answer this question, the Pediatric OCD Treatment Study II (Franklin et al., 2011) team examined 124 children and adolescents with OCD, randomly assigned to one of three conditions: (1) youths taking sertraline alone, (2) youths taking sertraline and participating in CBT, and (3) youths taking sertraline who received information about OCD and instructions on EX/RP. Results showed that youths who received medication plus actual CBT were significantly more likely to improve (68.6%) than youths who received medication alone (30%) or medication plus instructions (34%). A trained cognitive–behavior therapist seemed to be essential to effective treatment.

Medication can also be used to supplement the behavioral treatment of tics and related disorders. The goal of pharmacotherapy is to reduce, not eliminate, tics.

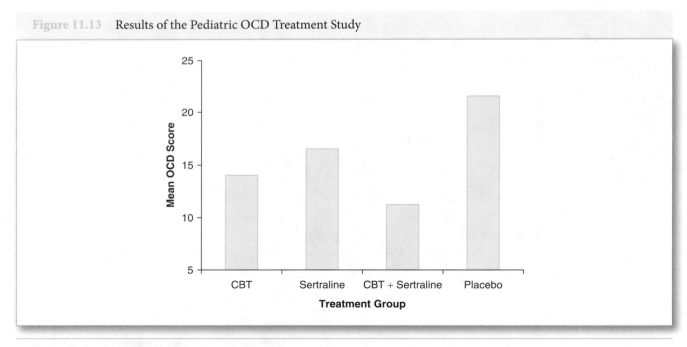

Figure 11.13   Results of the Pediatric OCD Treatment Study

Source: Based on Pediatric OCD Treatment Study Team (2004).

Note: After treatment, youths with OCD who participated in either CBT or pharmacotherapy showed greater improvement than youths who received a placebo. However, combining CBT with medication was associated with greater symptom reduction than either therapy or medication alone.

Physicians try to find a medication that reduces children's tics to a level that allows them to function at home, school, and with peers yet does not elicit too many side effects. Antipsychotic medications, which block dopaminergic activity in portions of the frontal-striatal neural circuit, are often recommended. Overall, older medications like haloperidol (Haldol) and pimozide (Orap), and newer medications like risperidone (Risperdal) and ziprasidone (Geodon), result in a 22% to 56% reduction in tics, compared to a 16% reduction with placebo. These medications are associated with sedation, weight gain, and metabolic problems. As many as 40% of youths discontinue them because of these side effects (Towbin, 2015).

A second class of medications used to treat tics include the alpha-2 adrenergic agonists. These medications affect serotonin and norepinephrine in a brain area called the median raphe nucleus, which, in turn, reduces dopamine activity. The effect is usually a reduction in tics without the side effects associated with antipsychotics. Studies investigating the efficacy of alpha-2 adrenergic agonists have

yielded mixed results. Some studies have shown a 20% to 31% reduction in tics when using medications like clonidine (Catapres) or guanfacine (Tenex), whereas others have shown no improvement associated with these medications. The chief side effects of alpha-2 adrenergic agonists are sedation and low blood pressure (Towbin, 2015).

Review:

- The Research Unit on Pediatric Psychopharmacology study showed that SSRIs, like fluoxetine (Prozac), reduce anxiety in children and adolescents.
- CAMS demonstrated that CBT with SSRI led to greater anxiety reduction than either treatment alone.
- POTS I and II showed that the combination of EX/RP and SSRI led to better OCD symptom reduction than either treatment alone. Furthermore, treatment was most effective when administered by trained therapists.
- Certain atypical antipsychotic medications (e.g., risperidone) and α2-adrenergic agonists (guanfacine) may be effective in reducing tics and related disorders.

KEY TERMS

Agoraphobia: A *DSM-5* disorder characterized by marked anxiety about places or situations from which escape or help is not possible without considerable effort or embarrassment; lasts at least 6 months and causes distress or impairment 357

Anxiety: An emotional state of psychological distress that reflects emotional, behavioral, physiological, and cognitive reactions to threatening stimuli 336

Anxiety sensitivity: The tendency to perceive anxiety symptoms as extremely upsetting and aversive; may explain a person's likelihood of developing Panic Disorder 354

Apprehensive expectation: An essential feature of GAD; excessive worry about the future 357

Attachment: A construct developed by John Bowlby to refer to the emotional bond between caregiver and child during the first few years of life; promotes safety and allows the child to explore his environment 392

Behavioral inhibition: The capacity to inhibit play and vocalization, to withdraw, and to seek a parent when encountering unfamiliar people or situations 344

Cognitive avoidance theory: Posits that worry (and GAD) is maintained through negative reinforcement; individuals replace images of imminent danger with more abstract, analytical thoughts about future misfortune 357

Cognitive–behavioral therapy (CBT): The integration of cognitive and behavioral interventions to produce behavior change; relies on the premise that changes in thoughts or overt actions can affect emotions 367

Cognitive restructuring: Cognitive interventions that involve challenging biases and distortions that lead to negative emotions by looking for objective evidence to support them 372

Compulsions: Repetitive behaviors or mental acts that an individual feels driven to perform in response to an obsession or according to specific, inflexible rules 361

Contingency management: A behavioral intervention in which a person receives positive reinforcement for confronting a feared stimulus and is not allowed to avoid or escape the stimulus 367

Cortico-basal-ganglionic circuit: A neural pathway that often underlies OCD; consists of the (a) orbitofrontal cortex; (b) cingulate gyrus, and (c) caudate 363

Excoriation disorder: A *DSM-5* disorder characterized by recurrent skin picking that results in lesions; causes distress or impairment 367

Expectancy theory of panic: An explanation for the emergence of panic disorder; posits that people with high anxiety sensitivity are prone to anxiety about panic attacks because of their heightened sensitivity to anxiety 354

Exposure therapy: A form of behavior therapy used to treat anxiety and related disorders; involves repeatedly confronting feared stimuli for discrete periods of time until anxiety or negative affect dissipates 368

Exposure and response prevention (EX/RP): A behavioral intervention used to treat OCD; involves exposing oneself to a series of stimuli that elicit obsessions and avoiding their corresponding compulsive behaviors 374

Fear: A behavioral and physiological reaction to immediate threat, in which the person responds to imminent danger by confrontation or escape 336

Generalized anxiety disorder (GAD): A *DSM-5* disorder characterized by persistent worry, that is difficult to control, and associated with restlessness, poor concentration, fatigue, 356 irritability, tension, and/or sleep problems; lasts at least 6 months and causes distress or impairment

Habit reversal training: A behavioral technique used to decrease unwanted behaviors; the person engages in a behavior that, when carried out, makes it impossible to produce the unwanted behavior 374

Interoceptive exposure: A behavioral intervention unique to the treatment of panic disorder; the person intentionally produces physiological symptoms of panic and then use relaxation techniques to cope with these symptoms 371

Maladaptive anxiety: Anxiety characterized by (a) intensity that is out of proportion to the perceived threat, (b) chronicity that lasts beyond removal of the immediate threat, and (c) impairment 337

Metacognition: The ability to think about one's own thoughts and feelings 353

Modeling: A behavioral intervention in which the child acquires a new behavior through imitating another (i.e., observational learning) 367

Mowrer's two-factor theory of anxiety: A general theory of anxiety that posits that disorders emerge through classical conditioning and are maintained through negative reinforcement 344

Obsessions: Recurrent and persistent thoughts, urges, or images that are experienced as intrusive and unwanted 361

Obsessive–compulsive disorder (OCD): A *DSM-5* disorder characterized by obsessions and/or compulsions that are time consuming and cause significant distress or impairment 361

Panic attack: An abrupt surge of intense fear or intense discomfort that reaches a peak within ten minutes and is characterized by heightened negative affect and physiological arousal; can occur by themselves or in the context of other anxiety disorders (e.g., panic disorder, posttraumatic stress disorder [PTSD]) 351

Panic disorder: A *DSM-5* disorder characterized by recurrent, unexpected panic attacks and 1 month of worry about future attacks or a change in behavior because of the attacks 351

Pediatric Autoimmune Neuropsychiatric Disorder Associated with Streptococcus (PANDAS) theory: An explanation for some causes of childhood OCD; posits that streptococcus infection leads to an autoimmune reaction that causes OCD-like symptoms, tics, and irritability 365

Relaxation training: A cognitive–behavioral intervention designed to reduce physiological arousal and avoid panic; usually involves muscle relaxation, controlled breathing, and pleasant imagery 371

Selective mutism: A *DSM-5* disorder characterized by consistent failure to speak in some specific social situations in which there is an expectation for speaking (e.g., at school); lasts for at least 1 month and impairs functioning 343

Self-monitoring: A behavioral intervention to treat unwanted actions; the individual observes and records the frequency of the actions during the course of the day 374

Separation anxiety disorder (SAD): A *DSM-5* disorder characterized by a developmentally inappropriate and excessive fear of separation from attachment figures; lasts at least 4 weeks in children and causes distress or impairment in functioning 340

Social anxiety disorder: A *DSM-5* disorder characterized by marked fear or anxiety about one or more social situations in which the individual is exposed to possible scrutiny by others; lasts at least 6 months and causes distress or impairment 348

Specific phobia: A *DSM-5* disorder characterized by marked fear or anxiety about a specific object or situation; persists for at least 6 months and causes distress or impairment 375

Systematic desensitization: A behavioral technique based on classical conditioning; the person associates a feared stimulus with a in incompatible response (e.g., relaxation) 365

Tics: Sudden, rapid, non-rhythmic, and stereotyped behaviors that are involuntary; can be motoric or vocal 365

Tourette's disorder: A *DSM-5* disorder characterized by the presence of multiple motor *and* vocal tics lasting for more than 1 year 366

Trichotillomania: A *DSM-5* disorder characterized by the repeated pulling out of hair, resulting in hair loss; causes distress or impairment 366

Vasovagal response: A physiological response that involves a rapid increase and sudden decrease in blood pressure; sometimes shown by individuals with blood-injection-injury phobias 347

Worry: A cognitive response to threat in which the person considers and prepares for future danger or misfortune 337

CRITICAL THINKING EXERCISES

1. Many children fear snakes, although relatively few children have ever been bitten by a snake. If a child has never been attacked by a snake, how can he or she develop snake phobia?

2. Mallorie is a 16-year-old girl who experienced two panic attacks while at school. Since that time, she has been reluctant to go to school. How can learning theory be used to explain Mallorie's school refusal?

3. Most people regard worry as very unpleasant. How can worry be negatively reinforcing?

4. Bryan is a 14-year-old boy who was recently diagnosed with OCD. His pediatrician suggests that Bryan take an SSRI for this condition and also participate in exposure therapy with a psychologist. Bryan and his mother agree to the medication but wonder

whether participating in therapy is also necessary. If you were Bryan's pediatrician, how might you respond to their concerns given the results of the POTS I and II studies?

5. Christian is a 14-year-old boy with GAD. During an important basketball game, Christian mistakenly passed the ball to an opponent, and his team lost the game. After the game, Christian thought, "How could I have been so incredibly stupid? The coach is never going to let me play again! I single-handedly ruined the game." Explain how Christian's thoughts about the event contribute to his negative feelings.

TEST YOURSELF AND EXTEND YOUR LEARNING

Videos, flash cards, and links to online resources for this chapter are available to students online. Teachers also have access to PowerPoint slides to guide lectures, case studies to prompt classroom discussions, and exam questions. Visit www.abnormalchildpsychology.org.

iStockphoto.com/Liderina

CHAPTER 12

Trauma-Related Disorders and Child Maltreatment

12.1 POSTTRAUMATIC STRESS DISORDER

On December 14, 2012, Adam Lanza fatally shot 20 children and six adult staff members at Sandy Hook Elementary School in Newtown, Connecticut. The incident was the deadliest shooting in an American elementary school. One 6-year-old girl survived by playing dead and fleeing the school after Lanza left her classroom. When she was reunited with her parents, she said, "Mommy, I'm okay but all of my friends are dead (see Image 12.1)."

Although terrible, massacres like the one at Sandy Hook can direct our attention away from other, more common traumatic experiences that can adversely affect children's well-being. Children are much more likely to be involved in a serious car accident or an at-home injury than a school shooting or terrorist attack. Sadly, children are also at surprisingly high risk for physical maltreatment, sexual victimization, and physical or emotional neglect. All of these experiences have the potential to negatively affect their development (Joshi, Cullins, & Southammakosane, 2015).

In this chapter, we will examine psychological problems that can arise from three types of psychosocial stressors: (1) traumatic experiences, (2) early social and emotional deprivation, and (3) child maltreatment. First, we will examine posttraumatic stress disorder (PTSD), an adverse reaction to a potentially life-threatening event, such as a car accident, home fire, or natural disaster. Then, we will discuss a rare, but equally traumatic experience for infants—social–emotional deprivation. Finally, we will study two of the most common psychosocial stressors experienced by children and adolescents throughout the world: child abuse and neglect.

Although these topics are not pleasant to study, they are extremely important. As many as 30% of youths are exposed to a serious, traumatic event at some point in their childhood, and roughly one third of these children will develop symptoms of PTSD (Yule & Smith, 2010). Furthermore, between 1% and 2% of children in the United States are confirmed victims of child maltreatment, to say nothing about the many children who are victimized but never brought to the attention of officials. We sorely need dedicated researchers to discover the best ways to identify and treat these youths, and caring practitioners to help children and families cope with these painful experiences (Brenner, 2016).

What Is Posttraumatic Stress Disorder?

Posttraumatic Stress Disorder in Older Children and Adolescents

Description

Posttraumatic stress disorder (PTSD) is defined by a characteristic set of behavioral, cognitive, emotional, and physiological symptoms that emerge following exposure to a serious or life-threatening event (see Table 12.1). By definition, a traumatic event is a psychosocial stressor that involves actual or threatened death, serious physical injury, or sexual violation. Events can be either intentional (e.g., a physical assault), accidental (e.g., a car crash), or natural (e.g., a fire). People need not show anxiety or distress during or immediately after the event, but they must show PTSD symptoms at some point after the trauma.

Note also that the traumatic event must occur either to the individual directly or to a close family member or friend. Hearing about a traumatic event occurring to an acquaintance or stranger (e.g., in the newspaper) does not satisfy this criterion. Similarly, watching a real or fictitious traumatic event on television or in a movie is insufficient for the diagnosis of PTSD.

After exposure to the traumatic event, people with PTSD show characteristic symptoms that fall into four clusters. First, they experience *intrusive symptoms* associated with the trauma; they persistently reexperience the event, often in the form of recurrent dreams, transient images, or unwanted thoughts. In some cases, people with PTSD experience dissociative reactions or "flashbacks"— that is, they temporarily feel as if the traumatic event is recurring in the present moment. An adolescent involved in an auto accident might have nightmares about the incident or have recurrent images of the accident pop into his mind while attending school. In contrast, a 7-year-old girl who witnessed a violent storm destroy her house might have persistent thoughts about the disaster. Her parents might observe her reenacting the event during play (e.g., with a doll house) or overhear her dolls "talking" to each other about the storm and their relocation to a new house.

Second, people with PTSD persistently *avoid stimuli associated with the trauma*. Avoidance might come in the form of an unwillingness to discuss the traumatic experience or visit people or places associated with the trauma. For example, a child who was sexually assaulted by a

Table 12.1   Diagnostic Criteria for Posttraumatic Stress Disorder

A. *Exposure* to actual or threatened death, serious injury, or sexual violence in one (or more) of the following ways:

   1. Directly experiencing the traumatic event(s).

   2. Witnessing, in person, the event(s) as it occurred to others.

   3. Learning that the traumatic event(s) occurred to a close family member o[r] close friend. In cases of actual or threatened death of a family member or friend, the event(s) must have been violent or accidental.

   4. Experiencing repeated or extreme exposure to aversive details of the traumatic event (e.g., first responders collecting human remains; police officers repeatedly exposed to details of child abuse).

   Note: Criterion A4 does not apply to exposure through electronic media, television, movies, or pictures, unless this exposure is work related.

B. Presence of one (or more) of the following *intrusion symptoms* associated with the traumatic event(s), beginning after the traumatic event(s) occurred:

   1. Recurrent, involuntary, and intrusive distressing memories of the traumatic event(s). Note: In children older than 6 years, repetitive play may occur in which themes or aspects of the traumatic event(s) and [*sic*] expressed.

   2. Recurrent or distressing dreams in which the content and/or affect of the dream are related to the traumatic event(s). Note: In children, there may be frightening dreams without recognizable content.

   3. Dissociative reactions (e.g., flashbacks) in which the individual feels or acts as if the traumatic event(s) were recurring. Note: In children, trauma-specific reenactment may occur in play.

   4. Intense or prolonged psychological distress at exposure to internal or external cues that symbolize or resemble an aspect of the traumatic event(s).

   5. Marked physiological reactions to internal or external cues that symbolize or resemble an aspect of the traumatic event(s).

C. *Persistent avoidance* of stimuli associated with the traumatic event(s), beginning after the traumatic event(s) occurred, as evidenced by one or both of the following:

   1. Avoidance of or efforts to avoid distressing memories, thoughts, or feelings about or closely associated with the traumatic event(s).

   2. Avoidance of or efforts to avoid external reminders (people, places, conversations, activities, objects, situations) that arouse distressing memories, thoughts, or feelings about or closely associated with the traumatic event(s).

D. *Negative alterations in cognitions and mood* associated with the traumatic event(s), beginning or worsening after the traumatic event(s) occurred, as evidenced by two (or more) of the following:

   1. Inability to remember an important aspect of the traumatic event(s).

   2. Persistent and exaggerated negative beliefs or expectations about oneself, others, or the world (e.g., "I am bad," "No one can be trusted," "The world is completely dangerous," "My whole nervous system is permanently ruined").

   3. Persistent, distorted cognitions about the cause or consequences of the traumatic event(s) that lead the individual to blame himself/herself or others.

   4. Persistent negative emotional state (e.g., fear, horror, anger, guilt, or shame).

   5. Markedly diminished interest or participation in significant activities.

   6. Feelings of detachment or estrangement from others.

   7. Persistent inability to experience positive emotions (e.g., inability to experience happiness, satisfaction, or loving feelings).

E. Marked *alterations in arousal and reactivity* associated with the traumatic event(s), beginning or worsening after the traumatic event(s) occurred, as evidenced by two (or more) of the following:

   1. Irritable behavior and angry outbursts (with little or no provocation) typically expressed as verbal or physical aggression toward people or objects.

   2. Reckless or self-destructive behavior.

   3. Hypervigilance.

   4. Exaggerated startle response.

   5. Problems with concentration.

   6. Sleep disturbance (e.g., difficulty falling or staying asleep or restless sleep).

F. Duration of the disturbance is more than 1 month.

G. The disturbance causes clinically significant distress or impairment in social, occupational, or other important areas of functioning.

H. The disturbance is not attributable to the physiological effects of a substance (e.g., medication, alcohol) or another medical condition.

Specify whether:

With dissociative symptoms: The individual's symptoms meet criteria for Posttraumatic Stress Disorder, and in addition, the individual experiences persistent or recurrent symptoms of either of the following:

1. Depersonalization: Persistent or recurrent experiences of feeling detached from, and as if one were an outside observer of, one's mental processes or body (e.g., feeling as though one were in a dream; feeling a sense of unreality of self or body or of time moving slowly).

2. Derealization: Persistent or recurrent experiences of unreality of surroundings (e.g., the world around the individual is experienced as unreal, dreamlike, distant, or distorted).

With delayed expression: If the full diagnostic criteria are not met until at least 6 months after the event (although the onset and expression of some symptoms may be immediate).

Source: Reprinted with permission from the *Diagnostic and Statistical Manual of Mental Disorders, Fifth Edition* (Copyright 2013). American Psychiatric Association.

Note: These criteria apply to adults, adolescents, and children older than 6 years. For children 6 years and younger, see corresponding criteria in Table 12.2.

relative will likely avoid thinking about or discussing the incident. He might also try to avoid that relative by refusing to visit him on a family outing or by feigning illness.

Third, PTSD causes *a negative alteration in the person's feelings or thoughts*. These alterations are sometimes referred to as emotional or cognitive "numbing." Emotional numbing might include the inability to experience joy or positive emotions, a lack of interest in activities that used to be pleasurable, or feelings of detachment or estrangement from others (Forbes et al., 2011). Individuals might also experience persistent negative emotions, such as anger, guilt, or shame, regarding the traumatic event. Cognitive numbing might manifest as problems in remembering details about the traumatic event, a tendency to blame oneself or others for the trauma, or a dramatic and negative change in the person's view of self, others, or the world. For example, a girl who is sexually assaulted might blame herself for being raped or view herself as "damaged goods" following the incident.

Fourth, individuals with PTSD show alteration in *physiological arousal* or reactivity. These symptoms include overactivity of the fight-or-flight response. Symptoms might include insomnia, irritability or aggression, concentration problems, and excessive vigilance. Some people with PTSD show an exaggerated startle response. For example, if an adolescent involved in an auto accident hears a loud noise similar to the sound of a crash, he might jump or panic (Nader & Fletcher, 2014).

PTSD symptoms must cause significant distress or interfere with the person's social interactions, capacity to work or attend school, and other activities like sports, clubs, or hobbies. Usually, PTSD greatly interferes with all aspects of an individual's life. Consider Preston, an adolescent with PTSD.

In the past, PTSD was considered an anxiety disorder, because clinicians believed that individuals reacted to traumatic events with fear, helplessness, or horror (Brewin, Lanius, Novac, Schnyder, & Galea, 2009). In the *Diagnostic and Statistical Manual of Mental Disorders, Fifth Edition* (*DSM-5*; American Psychiatric Association, 2013) however, PTSD is considered a trauma-related disorder because research has shown that people respond to catastrophic events in a variety of ways. A recent survey of parents indicated that most children react to traumatic events with anxiety (39.6%), sadness (39.6%), or fear (32.1%). However, some children also show excitement (22.6%), enjoyment (3.8%), or no emotion whatsoever (11.3%; Scheeringa, Zeanah, & Cohen, 2011).

Associated Features

Although not required for the diagnosis of PTSD, some people exposed to traumatic events also experience dissociative symptoms. Dissociative symptoms involve persistent or recurrent feelings of detachment from oneself or one's surroundings (American Psychiatric Association, 2013). Often, individuals use dissociative symptoms to cope with extremely traumatic events by cognitively or emotionally distancing themselves from memories of the event. Two types of dissociative symptoms are especially relevant to PTSD: (1) depersonalization and (2) derealization.

POSTTRAUMATIC STRESS DISORDER

Survivor's Guilt

Source: ©iStockphoto/bjalmeida

Preston was a 17-year-old boy referred to our clinic by his parents because of severe depression and self-injury. "He's been 'different' since the accident," reported his mother. "That night, three other mothers lost their sons, but I also lost my boy (pointing to her heart) here."

Preston was a tall, good-looking high school senior who excelled at cross country and had many friends. Preston had no history of emotional or behavioral problems before his car accident 3 months earlier.

Preston and three friends were driving home from a party on a rural highway. Although Preston had not been drinking, his friends had consumed several beers and were acting up. Preston, who was driving, became distracted. His car verged off the side of the road, entered a ditch, and rolled over. It finally stopped after hitting a utility pole. Preston broke his arm and clavicle. Two friends died instantly, and the third died in the hospital the next day.

"I don't really want to do anything anymore. Sometimes, I think I should have died that night like the others," Preston explained to Dr. Foster. "I know I'm to blame for the accident. It should have been me, not them."

Dr. Foster asked, "Do you think about the accident a lot?" Preston replied, "Actually, I try not to think about it. I try to keep myself distracted with school or work, but it's no use. I'm on Ambien because I can't sleep at night and I have terrible dreams. During the day, I snap at my parents and sister all the time. I can't concentrate at school. I keep thinking about their families. There's no way I can go to graduation."

"You were sent to me partially because you were cutting your arm," added Dr. Foster. After a long pause and heavy sigh, Preston replied, "It's really the only way I can feel anything at all."

Depersonalization describes persistent or recurrent experiences of feeling detached from one's own body or mental processes. People who experience episodes of depersonalization often feel like they are watching themselves in a movie, like they are in a dream, or like they are somehow disconnected from their own thoughts and actions. Some people report, "I felt as if I was floating away," "I felt disembodied, disconnected, or far away from myself," or "I could see and hear everything around me but couldn't respond."

Derealization involves persistent or recurrent thoughts and feelings that one's surroundings are not real. People who experience episodes of derealization see the world around them in an unusual or distorted manner. Some individuals report, "My surroundings seemed unreal and far away," "I felt like I was looking at everything through a strange lens or a glass," or "Objects seemed smaller than usual, drab, or artificial."

When individuals with PTSD also show dissociative symptoms, *DSM-5* instructs clinicians to add the specifier "with dissociative symptoms" to the PTSD diagnosis. This specifier provides additional information to other professionals regarding the person's symptoms (American Psychiatric Association, 2013).

Exposure to trauma is not uncommon among youths in the United States. Approximately 30% of adolescents

in the general population have experienced at least one serious trauma (Nader & Fletcher, 2014). The most common traumatic events involving youths include exposure to violent crime, auto accidents, home fires and injuries, natural disasters, domestic violence, physical and sexual abuse, and serious physical illnesses. Exposure to violence is especially common in urban settings. In one study of predominantly African American low-income children living in a large city, 39% had witnessed a shooting, 35% had seen a stabbing or physical assault, and 24% had observed an attempted killing. Nearly one half of the sample reported being a victim of violent crime.

Posttraumatic Stress Disorder in Preschoolers

Very young children exposed to traumatic events may not show PTSD in the same way as older children, adolescents, and adults. Young children often have difficulty articulating their thoughts and feelings. Consequently, it can be difficult for clinicians to use the same diagnostic criteria for PTSD with preschool-age children as they might with other individuals (Wheeler & Jones, 2015).

For example, when very young children experience an increase in sleep problems and frightening dreams following a traumatic event, it may be difficult or impossible to determine if the content of these dreams is connected to the trauma. Similarly, it is very unlikely that preschoolers will be able to describe symptoms of avoidance or negative changes in their thoughts and feelings—characteristics essential to PTSD in older children, adolescents, and adults. Instead, it is more likely that their parents will notice behaviors that suggest intrusive thoughts or dreams, avoidance of people or places associated with trauma, and negative changes in overt behavior and mood (Puff & Renk, 2015).

Because very young children manifest PTSD differently than adults, *DSM-5* includes specific criteria for PTSD in preschool children. These criteria (see Table 12.2) are similar to PTSD in adults; they require symptoms to follow a serious, traumatic event. Furthermore, they require the presence of at least one intrusive symptom, such as recurrent memories or thoughts about the event, unpleasant dreams, or distress when confronted with people or places associated with the trauma.

The criteria for PTSD in preschoolers differ from the criteria for older children, adolescents, and adults in three important ways. First, preschooler's symptoms are expressed in terms of actions or observable behaviors, because it is often difficult for preschoolers to express thoughts and feelings. For example, adults might report feeling detached or estranged from others and experience a lack of interest in activities they previously found enjoyable. In contrast, preschoolers might show social withdrawal and restricted play.

Second, preschoolers need to show only one persistent avoidance symptom *or* one negative alteration in cognition and mood symptom to meet criteria for PTSD. In contrast, adults must show one persistent avoidance symptom and two symptoms of negative alteration in cognition and mood to meet criteria. The lower symptom threshold for preschoolers reflects their difficulty in articulating their thoughts and feelings.

Table 12.2   Diagnostic Criteria for PTSD for Children 6 Years and Younger

A. In children 6 years and younger, *exposure* to actual or threatened death, serious injury, or sexual violence in one (or more) of the following ways:

   1. Directly experiencing the traumatic event(s).

   2. Witnessing, in person, the event(s) as it occurred to others, especially primary caregivers.

   Note: Witnessing does not include events that are witnessed only in electronic media, television, movies, or pictures.

   3. Learning that the traumatic event(s) occurred to a parent or caregiving figure.

B. Presence of one (or more) of the following *intrusion symptoms* associated with the traumatic event(s), beginning after the traumatic event(s) occurred:

   1. Recurrent, involuntary, and intrusive distressing memories of the traumatic event(s). Note: Spontaneous and intrusive memories may not necessarily appear distressing and may be expressed as play reenactment.

   2. Recurrent or distressing dreams in which the content and/or affect of the dream are related to the traumatic event(s). Note: It may not be possible to ascertain that the frightening content is related to the traumatic event.

   3. Dissociative reactions (e.g., flashbacks) in which the child feels or acts as if the traumatic event(s) were recurring. Trauma-specific reenactment may occur in play.

   4. Intense or prolonged psychological distress at exposure to internal or external cues that symbolize or resemble an aspect of the traumatic event(s).

   5. Marked physiological reactions to reminders of the traumatic event(s).

C. One (or more) of the following symptoms, representing either *persistent avoidance* of stimuli associated with the traumatic event(s), or *negative alterations in cognitions and mood* associated with the traumatic event(s), must be present, beginning after the traumatic event(s) occurred or worsening after the event(s):

   Persistent Avoidance of Stimuli

   1. Avoidance of or efforts to avoid distressing activities, places, or physical reminders that arouse recollections of the traumatic event(s).

   2. Avoidance of or efforts to avoid people, conversations, or interpersonal situations that arouse recollections of the traumatic event(s).

(Continued)

Table 12.2   (Continued)

Negative Alterations in Cognitions or Mood

1. Substantially increased frequency of negative emotional states (e.g., fear, guilt, sadness, shame, confusion).

2. Markedly diminished interest or participation in significant activities, including constriction of play.

3. Socially withdrawn behavior.

4. Persistent reduction in expression of positive emotions.

D. *Alterations in arousal and reactivity* associated with the traumatic event(s), beginning or worsening after the traumatic event(s) occurred, as evidenced by two (or more) of the following:

1. Irritable behavior and angry outbursts (with little or no provocation) typically expressed as verbal or physical aggression toward people or objects (including extreme temper tantrums).

2. Hypervigilance.

3. Exaggerated startle response.

4. Problems with concentration.

5. Sleep disturbance (e.g., difficulty falling or staying asleep or restless sleep).

E. Duration of the disturbance is more than 1 month.

F. The disturbance causes clinically significant distress or impairment in relationships with parents, siblings, peers, or other caregivers or with school behavior.

G. The disturbance is not attributable to the physiological effects of a substance (e.g., medication, alcohol) or another medical condition.

Source: Reprinted with permission from the *Diagnostic and Statistical Manual of Mental Disorders, Fifth Edition* (Copyright 2013). American Psychiatric Association.

Note: These criteria apply to children 6 years and younger.

Third, preschoolers' symptoms must cause them distress, interfere with their behavior at school, *or* impair their relationships with parents, siblings, or caregivers. In contrast, PTSD symptoms in older children, adolescents, and adults must cause distress or impairment to the individual themselves (not necessarily others).

DSM-5 also shows sensitivity to the ways preschoolers might express PTSD symptoms differently than adults. For example, young children with significant PTSD symptoms may not appear distressed immediately following a traumatic event. They might engage in repetitive play instead of experiencing intrusive memories of events. For example, a child who underwent a painful or frightening medical procedure might reenact the event with her dolls. Similarly, children with PTSD may experience nightmares after the traumatic experience, but they may not be able to connect their bad dreams to the experience itself. Other young children with PTSD show regressive behaviors. They might suck their thumb, refuse to go to bed at night, or tantrum. Still other preschoolers might experience anxiety problems, such as separation anxiety, fear of the dark, or monsters under the bed. Consider Ammar, a preschooler with signs of PTSD.

Review:

- PTSD is a *DSM-5* disorder that occurs following exposure to death, serious injury, or sexual violence. It is characterized by (a) intrusive symptoms, (b) avoidance of stimuli associated with the event, (c) negative alterations in thoughts or mood, and (d) alterations in arousal and reactivity that cause distress or impairment and last at least one month.
- Some people with PTSD show dissociative symptoms. Depersonalization involves feelings of detachment from one's own body whereas derealization involves distorted perceptions or sense of time.
- Preschoolers manifest PTSD differently than older children and adults. They may express symptoms as overt actions, they may show fewer signs/symptoms, and they may cause distress or impairment to family members (instead of experiencing it themselves).

How Common Is Posttraumatic Stress Disorder?

Prevalence

Approximately 25% to 30% of youths are exposed to a serious traumatic event at some point in their childhood. Data

PTSD IN A PRESCHOOL-AGE CHILD

Fleeing Syria

Source: ©iStockphoto/michaeljung

Ammar was a 5-year-old boy referred to our clinic because of sleep disturbance and anxiety. His parents fled the Syrian civil war in 2013, first arriving at a refugee camp in Turkey and then relocating to the United States. Like many refugees, Ammar and his family were exposed to atrocities at the hands of both the Syrian government and opposition forces. Ammar's father, a physician, treated wounded civilians in Aleppo before fleeing the region. Ammar himself witnessed the death of relatives and friends and the destruction of his neighborhood.

"We are most concerned with his sleep," reported his mother. "He insists on sleeping in our bed. If we refuse, he screams and tantrums." His father added, "And he has nightmares, usually several times each week. He says that he can't describe them, but he has mentioned that they involve fire and explosions.'"

Additional questioning revealed several other signs of early childhood PTSD. At school, Ammar behaved in a sad, withdrawn manner. "He seems to have no joy, no desire to play, like other kids his age," his teacher reported. "I've tried art, music, sports, special classroom privileges – anything to get him to open up – but he seems so closed off from the rest of us."

Ammar also displayed an exaggerated startle response. Loud noises easily cause him to jump, cry, or panic. "The Independence Day fireworks were terrible for him. He didn't even want to watch them on TV," his mother explained. "He frequently asks us, "Is everything OK?' We tell him, 'yes, you're in America now, everything's going to be fine, but he doesn't believe us."

from the National Center for PTSD indicate that the most common traumatic events include physical or sexual abuse, witnessing domestic violence, neighborhood violence (e.g., assaults, shootings), natural disasters (e.g., floods, hurricanes), human-made catastrophic events (e.g., fires, explosions), and motor vehicle accidents. Approximately one-third of these youths will develop at least some symptoms of PTSD (see Figure 12.1; Hamblen & Barnett, 2016).

The number of children who meet full criteria for PTSD is likely much smaller. The first population-based study examining PTSD in children showed a lifetime prevalence of less than 1% (Copeland, Keeler, Angold, & Costello, 2007). However, more recent data indicate that as many as 5% of older adolescents have experienced PTSD at some point in their lives (Hamblen & Barnett, 2016). This prevalence is closer to the lifetime prevalence among adults, approximately 8% (Scheeringa et al., 2011). Overall, girls (8%) are more likely to develop PTSD than boys (2.3%).

The prevalence of pediatric PTSD depends largely on the trauma to which children have been exposed. Children exposed to chronic or repeated traumatic events show the highest likelihood of PTSD. Between 40% to 60% of refugees from war-torn countries, chronic victims of physical or sexual abuse, and children who are repeatedly exposed to domestic violence meet diagnostic criteria for PTSD. The prevalence of PTSD among youths exposed to single-incident traumatic events is somewhat lower. For example, between 25%

and 30% of children caught in fires or involved in serious auto accidents develop PTSD. Rates of PTSD associated with single-incident household accidents are lower still. For example, between 14% and 26% of young children burned or otherwise injured at home later meet criteria for the disorder (DeYoung, Kenardy, & Cobham, 2011; Yule & Smith, 2010).

Course and Comorbidity

The course of PTSD is variable. Some adults with PTSD recover from the disorder without treatment. Retrospective studies indicate that two-thirds of adults who had PTSD as adolescents no longer experience the disorder in adulthood (Yule & Smith, 2010).

Prospective, longitudinal studies involving children reveal a different picture, however. These studies suggest that childhood PTSD often persists over time. For example, Meiser-Stedman and colleagues (Meiser-Stedman, Yule, Smith, Glucksman, & Dalgeish, 2005) conducted a prospective, longitudinal study of children involved in assaults or traffic accidents. Two to 4 weeks after the trauma, 20% of children showed significant PTSD symptoms. Six months after the incident, 12% met criteria for PTSD. Another study assessed children who developed PTSD after surviving a major hurricane (Shaw, Applegate, & Schorr, 1996). Although their symptoms decreased over time, 70% of children still met criteria for PTSD 21 months after the storm. Children who were victims of fires, car

Source: Based on DeYoung and colleagues (2011).

accidents, and other injuries showed similar persistence in symptoms (Scheeringa et al., 2011).

PTSD merits treatment for several reasons. First, many youths who "recover" from PTSD continue to show subthreshold PTSD symptoms and problems with depression and anxiety. Irritability and sleep disturbance are the most common lingering symptoms in children. Second, early treatment might prevent long-term problems or facilitate the recovery of PTSD once it emerges. Third, PTSD interferes with children's emotional well-being. Youths with PTSD often have other anxiety disorders, especially phobias. In most cases, phobias exist before the development of PTSD (Kruczek & Vitanza, 2015).

Moreover, depression and suicidal ideation are comorbid with PTSD. In one study of adolescents with PTSD, 41% met criteria for depression. As many as 46% of adolescents with PTSD develop alcohol use problems, while 25% abuse other drugs. Adolescents with PTSD seem to use substances to cope with anxiety and depression associated with the trauma (Nader & Fletcher, 2014).

Review:

- As many as 30% of youths witness a serious traumatic event such as physical or sexual abuse, domestic or neighborhood violence, disasters, or motor vehicle accidents.
- As many as 5% of youths may develop PTSD in childhood or adolescence. Prevalence is higher for girls (8%) than boys (2.3%).
- Although most children seem to recover from PTSD, many continue to show subthreshold symptoms or anxiety and mood problems.

What Predicts the Emergence of Posttraumatic Stress Disorder?

Many children are exposed to traumatic events, but relatively few develop PTSD. Although catastrophic events are necessary for the development of PTSD, they are not sufficient. In order to understand why some children exposed to trauma develop PTSD symptoms and others do not, researchers have developed a risk and resilience approach to understanding the disorder. Recall that risk factors increase the likelihood that children will develop a particular disorder, whereas resilience factors buffer children from the potential harmful effects of risk. Although our understanding of childhood PTSD is not complete, the emergence of the disorder depends largely on the complex interaction of risk and resilience.

Functioning Before the Trauma

One fairly consistent finding has been that children's social–emotional functioning before a traumatic event predicts the severity of their posttraumatic symptoms. Several studies have found that children with elevated anxiety and/or depression levels before the September 11, 2001, terrorist attacks in New York were more likely to develop distress and impairment after the attacks (Gil-Rivas, Holman, & Silver, 2004; Hock, Hart, Kang, & Lutz, 2004; Lengua, Long, Smith, & Meltzoff, 2005). In one study of New York schoolchildren, the relationship between exposure to the trauma and PTSD symptoms disappeared after researchers controlled for children's pretraumatic psychological functioning

(Aber, Gershoff, Ware, & Kotler, 2004). Similarly, children's emotional functioning *before* hurricane Katrina predicted their likelihood of PTSD, general anxiety, and depression after the hurricane (Weems et al., 2007). Collectively, these findings indicate that children already showing mood or anxiety disorders are most susceptible for developing PTSD following a traumatic event.

Proximity to the Trauma

The likelihood of developing PTSD depends on the child's proximity to the traumatic event (McKnight, Compton, & March, 2004). In 2001, a 15-year-old Santana High School student opened fire during the school day, killing two classmates and wounding 10 other people. Several months after the incident, researchers assessed PTSD symptoms among students at the high school (Wendling, 2009). In total, 247 students witnessed someone being shot or receiving medical treatment, 590 had heard or seen a shot fired from a distance, and 323 were not directly exposed to the trauma. The researchers found a dose-response relationship between proximity to the trauma and PTSD (see Figure 12.2). Overall, 4.9% of students met criteria for PTSD. Rates were highest

for students directly exposed to the trauma (9.7%) and lowest for students only indirectly exposed (3.4%). These findings indicate that the closer youths are to traumatic events, the greater their likelihood of PTSD. However, even youths more distally exposed to trauma can develop PTSD symptoms.

Children can also be traumatized by hearing about a catastrophic event occurring to their parents, relatives, or loved ones. Many children attending school near the World Trade Center on 9/11 were directly exposed to the terrorist attack (Hoven, Mandell, & Duarte, 2003). Data collected immediately after 9/11 demonstrated that children who were directly exposed to the trauma, or whose family members were directly exposed to the attack, were more likely to develop psychiatric problems than children who were only exposed to the attacks through television. For example, 87% of children who were exposed to the trauma (directly or through parents) displayed at least one PTSD symptom after the attacks. Almost 25% of these children showed intrusive thoughts, concentration problems, *and* sleep disturbance (Aber et al., 2004; Schlenger et al., 2002). After the attacks, approximately 27% of youths met diagnostic criteria for at least one anxiety or mood disorder. The most common psychiatric disorders were separation

---

Figure 12.2   The Relationship Between PTSD and Children's Proximity to Trauma

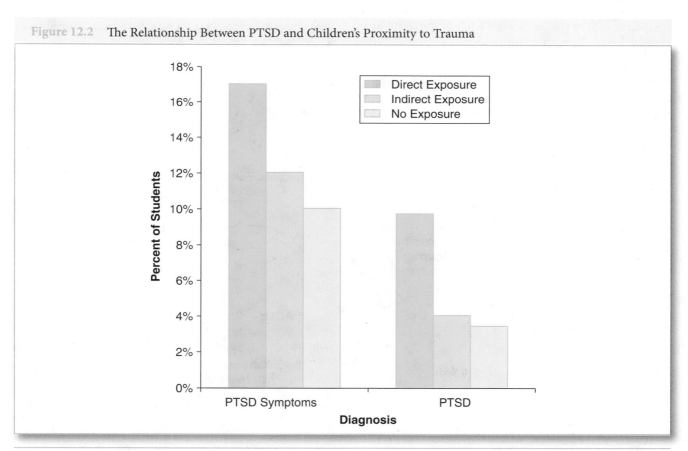

Source: Based on Wendling (2009).

Note: Children who saw a classmate shot or receiving medical treatment (direct exposure) were more likely to develop PTSD symptoms or to meet full criteria for PTSD than children who heard or saw shots only from a distance (indirect exposure) or who attended the school but did not witness the shooting.

anxiety disorder (SAD; 12.3%), PTSD (10.6%), generalized anxiety disorder (GAD; 12.3%), panic disorder (8.7%), and depression (8.1%; Stuber et al., 2005).

Brain and Endocrine Functioning

The body's stress response system is regulated by the HPA axis, a neuroendocrine feedback system that connects the hypothalamus, pituitary, and adrenal cortex. In healthy people, the amygdala is the starting point for this axis (see Figure 12.3). When a person encounters a stressful event, the amygdala causes the hypothalamus to release a hormone called corticotropin-releasing factor (CRF). CRF is detected by a second brain area, the pituitary, which releases the hormone corticotropin. Finally, corticotropin triggers the release of cortisol by the adrenal cortex. Cortisol, the body's primary stress hormone, activates the sympathetic nervous system and prepares the body for confronting or fleeing potential dangers. After the body has produced sufficient levels of cortisol to effectively deal with the stressful situation, the amygdala inhibits further activity (Daskalakis, McGill, Lehrner, & Yehuda, 2016).

Traumatic events can cause disruption in the body's stress response system. Immediately following a traumatic event, children who develop PTSD often show chronic overactivity of the HPA axis, even while at rest. HPA overactivity results in high baseline levels of cortisol, blood pressure, and heart rate, which can make these individuals unusually sensitive to threatening stimuli, hypervigilant, and prone to startle. The amygdala also plays a role in the formation of emotion-laden memories. Overactivity of the amygdala may be responsible for the unwanted thoughts or memories experienced by people with PTSD. Furthermore, some youths with PTSD show difficulty inhibiting cortisol secretion once it begins. In healthy people, the amygdala detects cortisol levels in the blood and inhibits production after a threat passes. However, in people with PTSD, this normal feedback loop is sometimes dysfunctional, causing the body's fight-or-flight response to be mobilized for an extended period of time (Frodl & O'Keane, 2013).

Interestingly, however, several studies indicate that children with chronic PTSD have *lower* resting cortisol levels than their peers. Furthermore, these traumatized youths often show a blunted corticotropin response to stress. Researchers believe that these unusually low cortisol levels reflect the body's way of compensating for chronic stress by down-regulating its stress-response system. This down-regulation helps the body cope with chronic stress, but it seems to be maladaptive in the long term. When children with low resting cortisol levels are exposed to another major stressor, they may show an exaggerated stress response, increasing their likelihood of greater distress and impairment (Lehrner, Daskalakis, & Yehuda, 2016; Simsek, Uysal, Kaplan, Yuksel, & Aktas, 2015).

Figure 12.3 The HPA axis regulates the body's response to stress

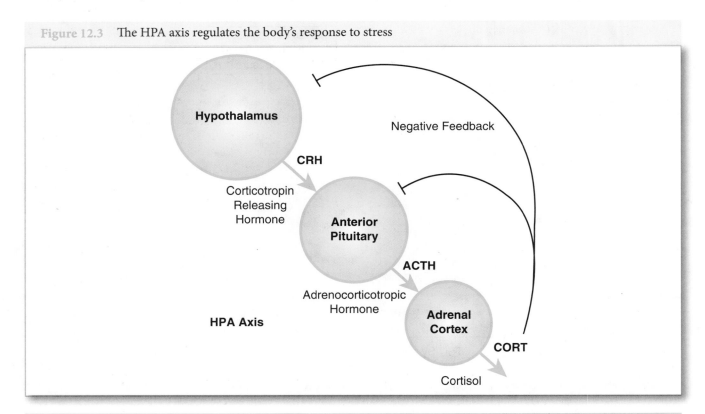

Source: From Brian M. Sweis.

Note: Children with PTSD often show dysregulation of this axis and abnormally high or low levels of cortisol, the body's main stress hormone.

Children's cognitive appraisal of traumatic events can greatly influence their response to these events (Yule & Smith, 2010). Cognitive appraisal theory asserts that the way people feel about situations depends on their evaluations (i.e., appraisals) of those situations. Children who experience trauma as personally relevant typically show more distress than children who cognitively distance themselves from catastrophic events (Brenner, 2016).

For example, children who knew someone involved in the 9/11 terrorist attacks or who believed that they or their families could be victims of a similar event in the future were likely to develop PTSD symptoms. This type of cognitive appraisal is called personalization. Consider the following statements of children who lived or attended school near the attacks (Hock et al., 2004):

- *It was scary. If they could do it to the World Trade Center, they could do it to our house. It bothered me because so many people died.*
- *I'm afraid that Dad might get drafted if they lose too many soldiers. My mom is a nurse so I kind of worry about her.*
- *The week after it happened my dad had to fly to [city name]. That made me scared.*

In contrast, children who believed that it was unlikely that their families would be harmed in subsequent attacks showed relatively few anxiety and mood problems. This type of appraisal is sometimes called distancing and can be seen in these statements made by children who witnessed the attacks (Hock et al., 2004):

- *There are a billion people in the world. It would be like a one in a billion chance that something like that would happen to me.*
- *No, I don't think something bad might happen to my parents. My dad doesn't work in a big building, only 20 stories, and my mom only works in a one-story building.*
- *It made me mad and I wished the USA could get revenge. It did not really cause me to worry. I've never been on an airplane before.*

Children's coping strategies immediately following a traumatic event can also greatly influence their behavioral and social–emotional functioning. Coping refers to thoughts and actions that protect oneself from psychological damage following a stressful event. Coping mediates the relationship between stress and a person's behavioral or emotional response. Most theories of coping assert that a person's coping strategy largely determines his or her response to a psychosocial stressor, rather than aspects of the stressor itself. Consequently, the same stressor can have different effects on different people.

Psychologists differentiate between two types of coping: (1) problem-focused and (2) escape-avoidance. Problem-focused coping is often considered more adaptive. It involves modifying or eliminating the conditions that gave rise to the psychosocial stressor or changing the perception of an experience in a way that reduces or neutralizes the problem. In many cases, children and adolescents cannot "fix" traumatic events once they occur; however, they can change the way they think about the stressor in order to make them feel more in control of the situation. For example, an adolescent who witnesses friends die in a serious car crash cannot change the accident itself. However, she may be able to reduce feelings of guilt or loss by talking to a loved one about the accident and realizing that she was not to blame.

In contrast, escape or avoidance coping involves disengaging from a stressful situation and its behavioral, cognitive, and emotional consequences. After a traumatic event, most people want to avoid people, places, thoughts, and feelings associated with the event. They might become increasingly isolated or try to distract themselves with other activities. Some people use medication, alcohol, and other drugs to cope with negative emotions, whereas others emotionally "shut down" in order to avoid any feeling whatsoever.

Escape-avoidance coping is negatively reinforcing because it temporarily reduces psychological distress. In the short term, escape-avoidance coping can also be adaptive; it can allow people to meet school, work, or family obligations immediately following a major stressor. In the long term, however, escape-avoidance coping predisposes people to social–emotional problems, especially anxiety disorders and PTSD. Because individuals do not confront people, situations, thoughts, and feelings associated with the stressor, negative emotions tend to linger, leading to long-term impairment. For example, adolescents who responded to the 9/11 terrorist attacks with social and emotional withdrawal displayed the poorest outcomes: depression, hopelessness, suicidal ideation, and PTSD. In contrast, youths who actively discussed their thoughts and feelings about the trauma with parents and friends were less likely to develop these emotional problems (Khamis, 2015; Marsac, Kassam-Adams, Delahanty, Widaman, & Barakat, 2014).

Review:

- By definition, youths must experience death, serious injury, or sexual violence to develop PTSD. Children's functioning before the traumatic event and proximity to the event, however, predict whether they will develop the disorder.
- PTSD is associated with dysregulation of the HPA axis, the body's main stress response system. Many youths with PTSD show lower cortisol secretion and blunted stress response over time.
- Children's cognitive appraisals of traumatic events predict their ability to cope with these events. Problem-focused coping (rather than avoidance) is often associated with better long-term outcomes.

What Evidence-Based Treatments Are Effective for Children with Posttraumatic Stress Disorder?

Psychological First Aid

Psychological First Aid (PFA) is an evidence-based intervention designed to prevent PTSD and other psychological problems in youths exposed to death, serious injury, or catastrophic events (Watson, Brymer, & Bonanno, 2011). PFA is typically administered by first responders or mental health professionals at the site of the trauma (see Image 12.2). PFA provides victims with a sense of safety and security and meets their immediate physical, social, and emotional needs (Tol et al., 2013).

PFA has several objectives: (a) fostering a sense of safety, (b) promoting a sense of calmness, (c) increasing self-efficacy, (d) achieving connectedness and social support, and (e) instilling hope for the future. Although providers of PFA are certainly willing to listen to victims' thoughts and feelings about the traumatic event, their focus is chiefly on meeting victims' immediate, tangile needs (Fox et al., 2012).

For example, a primary goal in working with traumatized children is to make sure that they feel safe, that they know their parents and loved ones are also safe, and that they will soon be reunited with their family (Koocher & LaGreca, 2010). The practitioner introduces herself to the child and tries to offer comfort and reassurance:

> Hi. I'm Lisa, and I'm here to try to help you and your family. Is there anything you need right now? There is some water and juice over there, and we have blankets in those boxes. Your mom is here, and many people are all working hard so that you and your family will be safe. Do you have any questions about what we're doing to keep you safe? (Brymer et al., 2006, p. 24).

Next, the individual providing PFA tries to determine other needs, besides safety, that the child might have and begins to develop a plan with the child and family to meet those needs:

> It sounds like you are really worried about several different things, like what happened to your house, when your dad is coming, and what will happen next. Those are all important things. Let's think about what's most important right now, and then make a plan. (Brymer et al., 2006, p. 66)

The practitioner will encourage the child to engage in active coping strategies, by talking with parents and other adults that are available to help. The goal is not to get the child to discuss the trauma but, rather, to know that adults are willing to listen and connect with her if she does need tangible or emotional support:

> You are doing a great job letting grown-ups know what you need. It is important to keep letting people know how they can help you. The more help you get, the more you can make things better. Even grown-ups need help at a time like this. (Brymer et al., 2006, p. 72)

Sometimes, PFA might involve teaching children simple relaxation strategies, such as focused breathing, to help them regulate their emotions. Relaxation is also useful in helping children sleep:

Image 12.2 Psychological first aid can be used by paraprofessionals to help families feel safe and make sure their immediate physical and psychological needs are met. This photograph shows counselors and volunteers helping victims of Hurricane Katrina.

Source: FEMA photo/Andrea Booher.

Let's practice a way of breathing that can help calm our bodies down. Put one hand on your stomach, like this [demonstrate]. Okay, we are going to breathe in through our noses. When we breathe in, we are going to fill up with a lot of air and our stomachs are going to stick out like this [demonstrate]. Then, we will breathe out through our mouths. When we breathe out, our stomachs are going to suck in and up like this [demonstrate]. We can pretend that we are a balloon, filling up with air and then letting the air out, nice and slow. We are going to breathe in really slowly while I count to three. I'm also going to count to three while we breathe out really slowly. Let's try it together. (Brymer et al., 2006, p. 83)

Finally, practitioners of PFA will attempt to normalize the child and family's stress response by explicitly stating that their emotional reactions are expected given the severity of the situation. Practitioners will usually provide families with the names and contact information of mental health professionals in case they need treatment.

The essential elements of the intervention are supported by research. For example, techniques such as active listening, supporting individuals through normalization, and providing informational, tangible, and emotional support to foster a sense of self-efficacy and control are all associated with enhanced coping (Bisson & Lewis, 2009). Future research needs to include randomized controlled studies of the entire treatment package to determine its effectiveness with children and families (Ritchie, Watson, & Friedman, 2015).

Trauma-Focused Cognitive–Behavioral Therapy

Trauma-focused cognitive–behavioral therapy (TF–CBT) involves exposing children to stimuli associated with traumatic events and then encouraging them to think about and cope with the trauma in more adaptive ways. TF–CBT has several important features (Cohen, Berliner, & Mannarino, 2010; Cohen, Mannarino, & Deblinger, 2013; Cohen, Mannarino, Kliethermes, & Murray, 2012).

First, early treatment sessions are used to teach families about PTSD. It is usually helpful for parents and children to know that PTSD symptoms are relatively common among individuals who experience trauma and that treatment can be effective in reducing children's distress.

Second, the therapist teaches the child coping skills to deal with negative emotions. Most therapists teach relaxation skills, such as deep breathing or muscle relaxation. Some therapists also teach children to engage in positive self-talk that is designed to give them greater confidence and security. For example, a child might practice saying to herself, "It's going to be okay" when she experiences distress or "I can do it" when she attempts to use relaxation techniques to combat anxiety.

Third, TF–CBT involves gradually exposing children to stimuli associated with the traumatic event. At a minimum, exposure usually involves the therapist encouraging the child to imagine the traumatic event in the safety and security of the therapy session. The therapist might ask the child to give a play-by-play account of the event and pay attention to sights, sounds, and feelings associated with the trauma. The goal is to expose the child to the anxiety-provoking stimuli for progressively longer intervals. Many therapists also ask the child to provide increasingly more detailed narratives of the traumatic event, either orally or in writing. Ideally, the child will eventually feel comfortable enough to share his narrative with others. If possible, some therapists use in vivo exposure to correct avoidance of situations associated with the trauma. For example, a child might avoid recess at school because he witnessed a classmate being severely injured in a car accident in the school parking lot. The therapist, with the help of parents and teachers, might encourage the child to visit the parking lot to overcome his anxiety (Cohen, 2005).

Fourth, TF–CBT involves identifying and changing children's maladaptive cognitions about the traumatic event. Many children believe they somehow caused the traumatic event or are to blame for the misery and hardship the event placed on others. For example, an adolescent who is sexually abused might assume blame for her maltreatment because she acquiesced to the demands of her abuser. Another child, whose mother died in an auto accident, might believe that he is to blame because he was arguing with his sister in the car when the accident occurred. The clinician identifies and challenges these maladaptive beliefs. For example, the therapist might ask children to provide evidence for their beliefs. A clinician might say to a sexually abused child, "It is true that you never told anyone about the abuse. However, didn't he threaten to kill you and your mother if you didn't give in to his demands? Were you really free to say 'no'?"

Several randomized controlled studies have investigated the efficacy of TF–CBT for children with PTSD. In general, children who participate in TF–CBT show reductions in PTSD symptoms and increases in social competence greater than youths who receive no treatment or nondirective counseling. For example, Smith and colleagues (2007) randomly assigned youths with PTSD following assault to either TF–CBT or a waitlist control condition. After treatment, 92% of youths who participated in TF–CBT no longer met criteria for PTSD compared to 42% of children on the waitlist. Children who received TF–CBT also showed significant reductions in anxiety and depression. These benefits remained 6 months after treatment. TF–CBT has since been effectively used to help children cope with natural disasters, chronic maltreatment, and the loss of a parent deployed overseas (Cohen & Mannarino, 2011; Cohen et al., 2013; Jaycox et al., 2010).

Eye Movement Desensitization and Reprocessing

Eye movement desensitization and reprocessing (EMDR) is a technique developed by Francine Shapiro to treat PTSD in adults. The technique involves asking an adult patient to generate a mental image related to the traumatic experience during the therapy session. With this image in mind, the patient is instructed to follow the therapist's finger as the therapist rapidly moves it across the patient's visual field, back and forth, for approximately thirty seconds. Then, the therapist asks the patient to report his or her current thoughts and feelings. The procedure is typically repeated several times during a single therapy session (Shapiro & Laliotis, 2015).

EMDR is as effective as CBT at alleviating PTSD in adults (National Institute for Health and Clinical Excellence, 2005). However, relatively few studies have investigated its efficacy with children. One team of researchers compared EMDR to CBT for 523 children involved in a fireworks disaster (de Roos et al., 2011). Although children improved in response to both treatments, EMDR yielded benefits in fewer sessions. Another group of researchers used EMDR to treat 32 children who did not respond to other forms of psychosocial interventions (Chemtob, Nakashima, & Carlson, 2002). In this study, three sessions of EMDR were associated with reductions in PTSD, anxiety, and depression.

The main drawback to EMDR is that the mechanism by which it reduces PTSD is unknown. Proponents claim that saccadic eye movements somehow integrate memories of traumatic events into individual's long-term memory, thereby, reducing intrusive thoughts, images, and dreams. However, several studies indicate that the effects of EMDR are attributable to exposing patients to memories of the trauma and allowing them to cognitively and emotionally process these events (Bisson et al., 2007; Seidler & Wagner, 2006). Although the mechanism by which EMDR "works" has yet to be determined, it is a promising treatment for children with the disorder (Yule & Smith, 2010).

Review:

- PFA is a first-line intervention for youths exposed to traumatic events. It emphasizes safety, self-efficacy, and social support.
- TF–CBT is effective in reducing PTSD symptoms in children and adolescents. Therapists help children recall traumatic experiences and use relaxation skills to cope with negative affect. Therapists also help youths identify and challenge cognitive distortions that might cause guilt or shame.
- EMDR involves repeated exposure to memories of traumatic events combined with rapid lateral eye movements. It appears to reduce PTSD in youths through its reliance on repeated exposure to memories of the event.

12.2 SOCIAL-EMOTIONAL DEPRIVATION IN INFANCY

There are few things more traumatic to young children than to be separated from their parents (Nelson, Fox, & Zeanah, 2016). Parents and other caregivers are a source of comfort, support, and reassurance. Children rely on parents for protection, nurturance, and direction. Moreover, humans are biologically predisposed to form attachment relationships with their caregivers and to rely on caregivers for support

in time of need. When caregivers are absent, infants and young children lack their primary sources of behavioral, social, and emotional support to help them cope effectively with their surroundings (Sroufe & Waters, 1977).

Approximately 8 million infants and children worldwide have no parent or primary caregiver (United Nations Children's Fund, 2016). Most of these youths are raised in orphanages, "baby centers," or other institutions (see Image 12.3). Many of these orphanages are located in countries ruled, or formerly ruled, by totalitarian regimes (e.g., Romania, Korea), plagued by war or disease (e.g., Mali, Sudan), or troubled by financial instability (e.g., portions of Latin America). Some institutions provide adequate physical care and cognitive stimulation to children, whereas the conditions of other orphanages have been described as "abusive" and "deplorable" (Nelson, Fox, & Zeanah, 2014; van IJzendoorn et al., 2011).

Image 12.3   Some Romanian orphans who were raised in institutions, like this boy, showed stereotypies, low cognitive functioning, inattention, and inappropriate social behavior. These problems often persisted even when children were adopted into loving homes in the United States, the United Kingdom, and other countries.

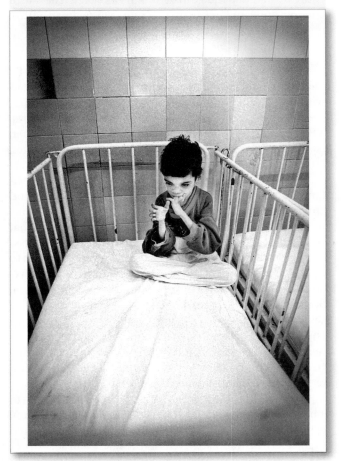

Source: Photo by Anglea Catlin.

Despite their heterogeneity, most of these institutions have the following characteristics in common:

- High child-to-caregiver ratios ranging from 1:8 to 1:31
- High caregiver turnover, with children exposed to 50 to 100 caregivers during their first 18 months of life
- High regimentation and periods of isolation; in one Greek orphanage children spent 3.5 hours per day at play and 17.5 hours per day in their cribs or beds
- Caregivers focusing chiefly on children's physical health (e.g., feeding, cleaning) rather than children's social–emotional well-being
- Caregivers providing little warmth, sensitivity, and responsiveness.

Even if institutionalized children are given adequate physical care and cognitive stimulation, these children lack attention and nurturance from a primary caregiver. Orphanages are no substitute for home-based care from loving families (Nelson et al., 2014; van IJzendoorn et al., 2011).

DSM-5 identifies two disorders that can develop in infants and young children when they lack developmentally appropriate care from parents or other primary caregivers early in life: (1) reactive attachment disorder (RAD) and (2) disinhibited social engagement disorder (DSED). Typically, these disorders are seen in infants and young children raised in orphanages, group homes, or multiple foster care settings. More rarely, severely abused and neglected children can also develop these disorders.

What Is Reactive Attachment Disorder?

Description

Reactive attachment disorder (RAD) is a rare condition seen almost exclusively in infants and young children who experience extreme deprivation (see Table 12.3). According to DSM-5, infants and young children with RAD show disturbed or developmentally inappropriate attachment behaviors. Most children display attachment behaviors when they are scared, upset, or unsure of their surroundings. Attachment behaviors, such as crying, clinging, and gesturing to be picked up, bring the child closer to his caregiver

---

Table 12.3   Diagnostic Criteria for Reactive Attachment Disorder

A. A consistent pattern of inhibited, emotionally withdrawn behavior toward adult caregivers, manifested by both of the following:

1. The child rarely or minimally seeks comfort when distressed.

2. The child rarely or minimally responds to comfort when distressed.

B. A persistent social and emotional disturbance characterized by at least two of the following:

1. Minimal social and emotional responsiveness to others.

2. Limited positive affect.

3. Episodes of unexplained irritability, sadness, or fearfulness that are evident even during nonthreatening interactions with adult caregivers.

C. The child has experienced a pattern of extremes in insufficient care as evidenced by at least one of the following:

1. Social neglect or deprivation in the form of persistent lack of having basic emotional needs for comfort, stimulation, and affection met by caregiving adults.

2. Repeated changes of primary caregivers that limit opportunities to form stable attachments (e.g., frequent changes in foster care).

3. Rearing in unusual settings that severely limit opportunities to form selective attachments (e.g., institutions with high child-to-caregiver ratios).

D. The care in criterion C is presumed to be responsible for the disturbed behavior in criterion A.

E. The criteria are not met for Autism Spectrum Disorder.

F. The disturbance is evident before age 5 years.

G. The child has a developmental age of at least 9 months.

Specify current severity:

Reactive Attachment Disorder is specified as severe when a child exhibits all symptoms of the disorder, with each symptom manifesting at relatively high levels.

Source: Reprinted with permission from the Diagnostic and Statistical Manual of Mental Disorders, Fifth Edition (Copyright 2013). American Psychiatric Association.

and help the child attain safety (Ainsworth, Blehar, Waters, & Wall, 1978; Bowlby, 1969). Children with RAD do not seek comfort from caregivers when distressed, and they do not respond effectively to comfort when it is provided. Instead, these children are inhibited and emotionally withdrawn from their caregivers. Caregivers sometimes describe these children as "emotionally absent" and lacking the usual social reciprocity that characterizes most parent–infant interactions. Furthermore, children with RAD often show very little positive affect (e.g., smiles, hugs, and kisses) but, instead, present as sad, anxious, or irritable (American Psychiatric Association, 2013).

By definition, RAD is caused by pathogenic care. In the United States, RAD is most often seen among international adoptees who spent their first 12 to 24 months of life in orphanages characterized by an absence of close caregiver–child interactions. RAD can also be seen in some infants exposed to extreme neglect and infants relocated to multiple foster homes during their first year of life (Glowinski, 2011).

RAD should not be diagnosed in children less than 9 months of age, because attachment relationships are not believed to develop until after this time period. Similarly, RAD should not be first diagnosed after age 5, because attachment relationships are typically formed during the first few years of life (American Psychiatric Association, 2013).

Early Studies on Infant Deprivation

During World War II, psychologists became interested in the development of infants and young children separated from their caregivers for prolonged periods of time (Spitz, 1965). Pioneering work was conducted by Anna Freud, who opened the Hampstead (England) War Nursery for children separated from their parents because of World War II (see Image 12.4). Some children were sent to the nursery to escape bombing raids over London (like the children in the book *The Lion, the Witch, and the Wardrobe*); others were separated from parents who were serving in the war effort (Burlingham & Freud, 1962). Later, Freud and her colleagues established a second residential facility for children who survived concentration camps. Freud (1956) published some of the first papers describing the harmful effects of maternal deprivation on these children's emotional health.

At about the same time, Rene Spitz and Katherine Wolf (1946) described the behavior of infants and toddlers abandoned by their parents and raised in orphanages. Although their physical care was adequate, these infants were given very little social stimulation from caregivers at these institutions. You can read their description of one of these children in the case study.

Spitz and Wolf (1946) described these infants as listless, withdrawn, and emotionally unresponsive. These infants did not show interest in seeking closeness with caregivers, even when they were scared or upset. Many infants failed to make normal gains in weight and some engaged in stereotypies, such as repetitive hand or body movements.

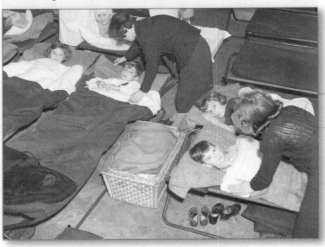

Image 12.4 Homeless and orphaned children settle down to sleep on beds in a British air raid shelter during World War II. The basket in the center of the photograph probably contains a small baby. Observations of children like these led to the development of attachment theory.

Spitz and Wolf believed these infants experienced "anaclitic depression," a sadness and withdrawal caused by the loss of their parents and the absence of an alternative caregiver with whom to bond.

Shortly after World War II, John Bowlby (1951) was asked by the World Health Organization to review research on the developmental outcomes of children who experienced parental deprivation in postwar Europe. Bowlby met with researchers and clinicians in the United States and Europe who worked with youths raised in orphanages, group homes, and other institutions. Bowlby also noticed a form of "depression" shown by infants and young children deprived of a primary caregiver during their first year of life. He described these children as "listless, quiet, unhappy, and unresponsive." They showed the following:

> . . . an emotional tone of apprehension and sadness. The child withdraws himself from all that is around him; there is no attempt to contact a stranger and no brightening if this stranger contacts him. The child often sits or lies inert in a dazed stupor. Lack of sleep is common and lack of appetite is universal. Weight is lost and there is a sharp drop in general development. (Bowlby, 1954, pp. 23–24)

Bowlby concluded that a "warm, intimate, and continuous relationship" between young children and a primary caregiver was essential to children's physical, cognitive, and social–emotional development.

Reactive Attachment Disorder and Parent–Child Attachment

Bowlby's observations of deprived children led to the development of attachment theory. Bowlby (1969, 1973) posited that infants are biologically disposed to form attachment

REACTIVE ATTACHMENT DISORDER

Anaclitic Depression

This is a moderately intelligent, unusually beautiful child with enormously big blue eyes and golden curls. At the end of the 11th month, the child, who never has been very active, began to lose even more interest in playing with the experimenter. In the following 2 weeks, the behavior was more marked. The child was not only passive but she also refused to touch any toys offered to her. She sat in a sort of daze, by the hour, staring silently into space. She did not even show the apprehensiveness in the presence of an approaching observer that was shown by other children. If a toy was put into contact with her, she would withdraw into the farthest corner of her bed and sit there wide-eyed, absent, and without contact, with an immobile, rigid expression on her beautiful face.

Source: From Spitz and Wolf (1946).

Image source: Wikipedia Commons.

relationships with one or a few primary caregivers over the first few years of life. Attachment is adaptive; it brings the infant in close proximity to the caregiver in times of danger or uncertainty.

Attachment theorists believe that children form internal working models (schemas or mental representations) of themselves and their caregivers (Bowlby, 1988; Main, Kaplan, & Cassidy, 1985). These models are based on the history of interactions between each child and his or her caregiver. Some infants develop models based on attachment security; they expect that their caregivers will provide care, comfort, and support in a sensitive and appropriate fashion when they are scared, upset, or unsure (Ainsworth et al., 1978). Other infants develop models based on attachment insecurity; they expect that their caregivers will be dismissive, inappropriate, and/or inconsistent in the care they provide. They may believe that in times of trouble they cannot rely on anyone, other than themselves, for help. Finally, some infants develop disorganized attachment models. These children do not have a coherent set of expectations for their caregivers when they are in distress. Sometimes, their caregivers might be helpful, but at other times, their caregivers might be unresponsive or even frightening.

Several points follow from Bowlby's conceptualization of attachment (Bretherton, 1992). First, parent–child attachment is an experience-expectant process. Because humans are biologically predisposed to form attachments and because attachments are evolutionarily adaptive, all infants who are exposed to a primary caregiver early in life will develop an attachment relationship with that caregiver. Even infants who are mistreated by their primary caregivers will form attachment relationships with these caregivers. The time period between 6 and 12 months of age appears to be a particularly *sensitive period* in attachment formation—that is, a time period in which

the human nervous system is especially prepared to organize itself in response to care from one or more attachment figures. Before 6 months, children show little preference for their primary caregiver, whereas after 6 months, children begin showing stranger anxiety and heightened attachment behaviors.

Second, Bowlby's theory asserts that attachment relationships vary in their quality; some relationships are secure, others are insecure, and others are disorganized. Whereas forming an attachment is experience-expectant and common to the entire human species, the quality of the attachment that is formed (secure, insecure, disorganized) is an experience-dependent process; it is unique to each caregiver–infant dyad and is based on the quality of their interactions over time (Nelson, Bos, Gunnar, & Sonuga-Barke, 2011; Nelson et al., 2014).

How does RAD fit into Bowlby's conceptualization of attachment? RAD occurs when infants are deprived of even minimal care from a primary caregiver during this sensitive period of attachment formation (i.e., after age 6 months). Such deprivation results in the absence of a clear attachment relationship and corresponding attachment behaviors (e.g., making eye contact, smiling, cuddling, using the caregiver as a means of comfort). Consequently, infants with RAD appear listless, withdrawn, and sad. RAD should not be confused with insecure or disorganized attachments. Whereas insecure or disorganized children have developed attachment relationships with a primary caregiver, children with RAD have absent or minimal attachments to any caregivers whatsoever (Nelson et al., 2011, 2014).

Review:

- RAD is a *DSM-5* disorder characterized by inhibited, emotionally withdrawn behavior toward caregivers caused by deprivation in infancy or early childhood.

The development of an attachment relationship is experience-expectant—that is, it is biologically predisposed and relies only on the presence of a caregiver. The quality of the attachment relationship is experience-dependent; it depends on the sensitivity and responsiveness of care over time.

RAD seems to be caused by a lack of attachment to a single caregiver in infancy. It should not be confused with insecure or disorganized attachment, in which children do have attachment relationships, although they are less than optimal.

What Is Disinhibited Social Engagement Disorder?

Description

Children with disinhibited social engagement disorder (DSED) show a pattern of culturally and developmentally inappropriate, overly familiar, behavior with strangers (see Table 12.4). Beginning at age 6 or 7 months, typically developing children begin showing wariness of strangers. In contrast, children with DSED do not. Instead, children with DSED readily approach and interact with unfamiliar adults. Unlike their same-age peers, children with DSED do not "check back" with their caregivers to make sure that they are safe and that their caregivers know their whereabouts. Perhaps most concerning, children with DSED will often talk to strangers, make inappropriate physical contact with strangers (e.g., sit on their laps, hold hands), and wander off with strangers without their caregivers' permission (American Psychiatric Association, 2013).

By definition, DSED is diagnosed only if children have a history of severe neglect or social–emotional deprivation. Many children with DSED have experienced deprivation in institutions. However, signs of DSED can also be seen among children who experienced frequent disruptions in their caregiving over the first year of life. For example, DSED is observed in some children who have been relocated to multiple foster homes and in children exposed to inconsistent care because of parental abuse or neglect.

Early Studies on "Indiscriminately Friendly" Children

In his research for the World Health Organization, Bowlby (1954) described a small group of children who showed "undiscriminating and shallow friendliness" (p. 29). These children sought social and emotional contact with almost all adults, including strangers. Although they appeared charming to adults in their orphanages, and often became "favorites"

Table 12.4   Diagnostic Criteria for Disinhibited Social Engagement Disorder

A. A pattern of behavior in which a child actively approaches and interacts with unfamiliar adults and exhibits at least two of the following:

   1. Reduced or absent reticence in approaching and interacting with unfamiliar adults.

   2. Overly familiar verbal or physical behavior (that is not consistent with culturally sanctioned and age-appropriate social boundaries).

   3. Diminished or absent checking back with adult caregiver after venturing away, even in unfamiliar settings.

   4. Willingness to go off with an unfamiliar adult with minimal or no hesitation.

B. The behaviors in criterion A are not limited to impulsivity (as in ADHD) but include socially disinhibited behavior.

C. The child has experienced a pattern of extremes in insufficient care as evidenced by at least one of the following:

   1. Social neglect or deprivation in the form of persistent lack of having basic emotional needs for comfort, stimulation, and affection met by caregiving adults.

   2. Repeated changes of primary caregivers that limit opportunities to form stable attachments (e.g., frequent changes in foster care).

   3. Rearing in unusual settings that severely limit opportunities to form selective attachments (e.g., institutions with high child-to-caregiver ratios).

D. The care in criterion C is presumed to be responsible for the disturbed behavior in criterion A.

E. The child has a developmental age of at least 9 months.

Specify current severity:

Disinhibited Social Engagement Disorder is specified as severe when the child exhibits all symptoms of the disorder, with each symptom manifesting at relatively high levels.

Source: Reprinted with permission from the *Diagnostic and Statistical Manual of Mental Disorders, Fifth Edition* (Copyright 2013). American Psychiatric Association.

among nursing staff, their relationships tended to be superficial and one-sided. Bowlby (1951, 1954) noted that many of these indiscriminately friendly children experienced frequent disruptions in their caregiving relationships over their first years of life. He also observed that these children experienced problems bonding with their biological or adoptive parents after leaving their institutions.

The first systematic, longitudinal study of infants raised in institutions corroborated Bowlby's findings. Barbara Tizard and colleagues (Tizard & Hodges, 1978; Tizard & Rees, 1974, 1976) studied 65 children who spent their first years in a London nursery. These children were provided with adequate nutrition, physical care, toys, and books. However, caregivers were explicitly told to avoid bonding with these children. Furthermore, caregiver turnover in the nursery was high; infants had few opportunities to form attachment relationships.

Tizard found that 18 out of 26 children reared in the institution until aged 4.5 years showed social–emotional problems. Eight "emotionally withdrawn and unresponsive" children did not seem to form attachment relationships with any caregiver, nor did they show distress or make bids for closeness and social engagement. Today, these children would likely be diagnosed with RAD.

However, Tizard also described 10 other children as "indiscriminate, attention seeking, and socially superficial." These children were "exceptionally affectionate" toward most caregivers, would beg for attention and physical proximity from anyone who entered the room, and showed no wariness of strangers. This "overly friendly and attention seeking" behavior persisted across development; even at the age of 16, these children continued to display superficial relationships with others (Hodges & Tizard, 1989). Tizard's description of these children formed the basis for the *DSM-5* conceptualization of DSED (Zeanah & Gleason, 2010).

Review:

- DSED is a *DSM-5* disorder in which the child repeatedly approaches and interacts with unfamiliar adults in a manner that is developmentally unexpected. The disorder is associated with insufficient care or deprivation in infancy or early childhood.
- Tizard described children with DSED as "indiscriminantly friendly" and attributed their behavior to being raised in orphanages.

What Causes Reactive Attachment Disorder and Disinhibited Social Engagement Disorder?

Reactive Attachment Disorder: An Absence of Attachment

Although RAD and DSED are both caused by early deprivation, they differ in several important ways (see Table 12.5; Zeanah & Smyke, 2008). To study these differences, researchers examined 136 children who spent their early years in impoverished Romanian orphanages (Fox, Almas, Degnan, Nelson, & Zeanah, 2011; Gleason et al., 2011; Nelson et al., 2014). Conditions in these orphanages were terrible. Many children were undernourished, staff-to-child ratios were extremely high, children were left unattended in cribs for long periods of time, and there was little to no social interaction between children and staff. Worse yet, Romania at that time, had no effective foster care system. Consequently, the researchers began the Bucharest Early Intervention Project (BEIP); they found foster homes for children in the orphanages and provided education and support to foster parents. Because there were not enough foster parents for all infants, the researchers randomly assigned

Table 12.5   Major Differences Between RAD and DSED

	RAD	DSED
Children's characteristics	Little interest in social interactions, passive, do not show preference for primary caregivers	Interested in social interactions, willingly approach and seek contact with strangers
Cause	Social deprivation in infancy	Social deprivation in infancy
Frequency	Rare in institutionalized children; almost never seen in children adopted out of institutions	Sometimes seen in institutionalized children, children adopted out of institutions, and maltreated children
Relationship to attachment	Child lacks clear attachment relationship to a caregiver	Child typically shows attachments to caregivers, attachment may be secure
Relationship to caregiving	Associated with a lack of sensitive and responsive care	Not associated with the quality of care
Associated disorders	Many children also show depressed mood, irritability	Some children show hyperactivity-impulsiveness
Course-Prognosis	Often persistent if child remains in institution; remits after child forms attachment to adoptive parents	Usually persists into childhood even if child is adopted

Source: Adapted from Zeenah & Gleason (2010).

Figure 12.4   Attachment Among Infants Raised in Romanian Orphanages

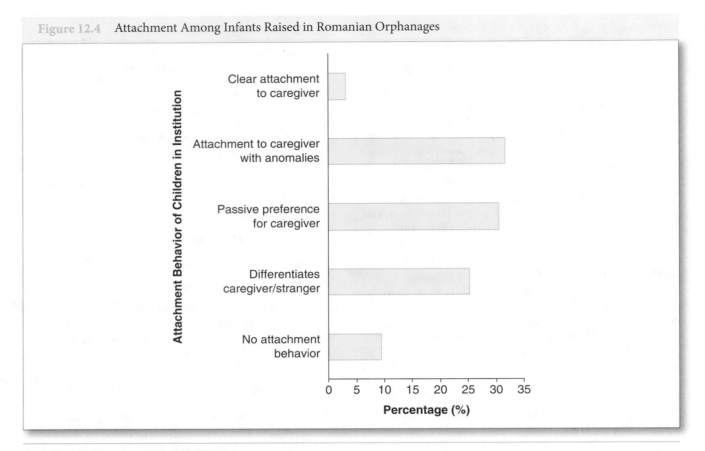

Source: Based on Zeanah and colleagues (2005).

infants to either foster placement or care as usual (i.e., staying in the orphanage). Then, the researchers examined children's development until age 54 months to determine their outcomes. Because the BEIP is a prospective, randomized controlled study, it allows us to examine the outcomes of institutionalized children over time and to see whether foster care improves the outcomes of these infants (McLaughlin et al., 2011; 2012; Zeanah, Fox, & Nelson, 2012).

The results of the BEIP provide strong evidence that the signs and symptoms of RAD are associated with a lack of attachment in infancy and early childhood (see Figure 12.4). The BEIP team compared three groups of children: (1) children raised in Romanian orphanages, (2) children initially raised in Romanian orphanages but placed in foster homes before age 24 months, and (3) Romanian children living with their families. At age 24 months, all of the noninstitutionalized children showed a clear attachment to their primary caregiver. In contrast, only 3.2% of institutionalized children showed a clear attachment pattern. Indeed, 9.5% of institutionalized children showed no attachment behavior toward caregivers and no differentiation between familiar and unfamiliar adults whatsoever. An additional 25.3% of institutionalized infants showed only slight preference for their primary caregiver over a stranger but no positive affect when interacting with their caregiver. The researchers also found that the severity of RAD was inversely associated with the quality of care infants received: The more sensitive

and responsive the care, the fewer signs of RAD children displayed (Gleason et al., 2011; Nelson et al., 2014).

On a more positive note, the BEIP team discovered that foster placement was helpful in reducing RAD over time. Whereas children who remained in the orphanage showed relatively stable RAD signs and symptoms into early childhood, children placed in foster care showed decreased RAD signs and symptoms over time. Altogether, the results of the BEIP and a similar study conducted in a Ukrainian institution (Bakermans-Kranenburg, Dobrova-Krol, & van IJzendoorn, 2012) suggest that most institutionalized children develop attachment relationships, even under conditions of extreme deprivation. However, a small percentage of children seem to lack attachment relationships altogether, appear emotionally flat, and act behaviorally passive. These children likely meet criteria for RAD. The good news is that if children are removed from the institution before age 24 months, they can form attachment relationships with foster parents. Furthermore, the quality of care largely predicts children's ability to overcome previous deprivation (Bos et al., 2011).

Disinhibited Social Engagement Disorder: A Lack of Inhibition

Many more (31.8%) infants in the BEIP showed symptoms of DSED. Curiously, DSED signs and symptoms were not consistently associated with the quality of care infants received in the institution or in foster homes. Furthermore, there was little relationship between infants' attachment security and DSED; even security-attached infants sometimes showed signs and symptoms of DSED. Later in childhood, infants with DSED displayed difficulty with attention and social inhibition—that is, controlling impulses in social situations.

Late infancy and early childhood may be a sensitive period for the development of social inhibition. Parents play a central role in helping infants and young children regulate their social behavior (Hofer, 2006). For example, parents direct young children's attention to social situations and cues, model and reinforce appropriate social interactions, and teach impulse control, especially in potentially dangerous situations. How many times did your parents warn, "Look both ways before crossing the street" or "Don't talk to strangers"? Young children deprived of parents may miss out on many of these social learning experiences. Consequently, they may show delays or deficits in social inhibition. Indiscriminately social behavior, such as touching or wandering off with strangers, may reflect these underlying deficits in social inhibition (Bakermans-Kranenburg et al., 2011).

To test this hypothesis, Bruce, Tarullo, and Gunnar (2009) measured the behavioral and social–emotional functioning of children adopted from orphanages and foster care settings in China, Eastern Europe, and South Korea. As expected, adoptees showed more problems with social inhibition than nonadopted children; furthermore, children who spent more time in institutions or foster care showed more "indiscriminately friendly" behavior at 7 years of age. Interestingly, "indiscriminately friendly" behavior was not correlated with children's attachment to parents; it was associated only with underlying problems with social inhibition.

Additional support for the social inhibition hypothesis came from a second study, which compared 93 maltreated children in foster care to 60 children living with their parents in the community (Pears, Bruce, Fisher, & Kim, 2010). Again, as expected, foster care children showed more symptoms of indiscriminately social behavior than controls. More importantly, children who had more changes in their foster care placements showed more indiscriminately social behavior. The most important finding was that children's social inhibition mediated the

relationship between the number of foster caregivers and their indiscriminately social behavior: A high number of different foster caregivers predicted problems with inhibition; problems with inhibition, in turn, predicted indiscriminately social behavior (see Figure 12.5).

Altogether, these data suggest that DSED does not reflect a disruption in attachment (Potter, Chevy, Amaya-Jackson, O'Donnell, & Murphy, 2009). Instead, indiscriminately social behavior may reflect underlying problems with social inhibition. Emerging evidence suggests that institutionalized children who show indiscriminately social behavior often have deficits in behavior control and regulation that are similar to (but not the same as) children with ADHD. Their tendency to indiscriminately seek physical contact from others and impulsively "wander off" with strangers may reflect this problem with social inhibition rather than attachment. Consequently, most children with DSED do not show significant improvement in their social behavior after being adopted by sensitive and responsive caregivers (Schechter, 2012).

Review:

- RAD is likely caused by a lack of attachment to a caregiver in infancy or early childhood. Children adopted from orphanages prior to 24 months did not show RAD whereas one-third of the children raised in orphanages developed the disorder.
- In contrast, DSED is not an attachment disorder. It is associated with underlying problems with social inhibition. Deprivation in infancy seems to disrupt children's capacity for inhibitory control.

What Evidence-Based Treatments Are Available for Youth Exposed to Deprivation?

Treatment for Reactive Attachment Disorder

Prognosis for children with RAD is good if these children are provided sensitive and responsive care by foster or adoptive parents. Outcomes seem to be especially positive if home placement occurs early in development. For example, Dozier, Dozier, and Manni (2002) asked foster mothers to

Figure 12.5 DSED Reflects Problems With Inhibitory Control

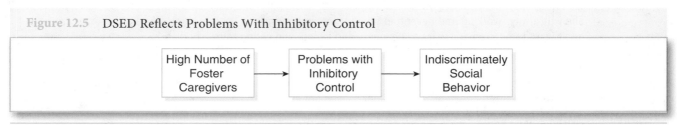

Source: Pears et al., 2010.

Note: Children placed in multiple foster care settings showed problems with inhibitory control. Problems with inhibitory control, in turn, predicted indiscriminately social behavior.

keep diaries about their interactions with their babies for 60 days after placement into their homes. Parents were asked to pay special attention to situations in which children experienced distress. The researchers coded parents' diaries in terms of the quality of parent–child interactions. Three findings emerged. First, parents and infants began forming attachments within days of children being placed in foster homes. Second, the security of attachment relationships was greatest when children were placed in foster homes before age 10 months. Third, mothers and babies showed reciprocity in their interactions; both mothers and babies influenced each other's actions. For example, mothers of overly passive babies often had difficulty reading their babies' signals and meeting their needs. Similarly, mothers of irritable babies often had trouble providing sensitive and patient care.

Based on the results of the diary study, Dozier developed an intervention to promote attachment security between infants and foster parents at risk for attachment problems. The intervention, Attachment and Biobehavioral Catch-Up (ABC), consists of 10, one-hour sessions for parent–child dyads (Bernard, Simons, & Dozier, 2015).

ABC has three components. First, parents are taught to meet their infants' needs even when these needs are not clearly communicated. Recall that many children with RAD are passive and show little interest in receiving care. Foster parents are taught the importance of providing warmth and nurturance to their children even when their children fail to ask for contact or actively spurn their efforts. For example, therapists ask parents to keep a record of instances in which their children avoided or resisted their attempts at nurturance. Therapists review this record with parents and help parents find ways to persist in offering sensitive and responsive care to their children despite their children's passivity or irritable behavior (Dozier & Roben, 2015).

Second, parents are encouraged to give their infants greater autonomy in parent–child interactions and to be sensitive and responsive to their needs and signals during play. Recall that many children with RAD symptoms have little experience being in control over their surroundings. Instead, they may view the world as unpredictable and caregivers as uncaring or intrusive. Foster parents are taught to interact with their children in ways that respect their emerging autonomy and self-direction. For example, parents and infants are asked to engage in structured activities designed to give children greater latitude in directing parent–child interactions. Activities include eating, looking at a picture book, and playing with blocks. Therapists provide real-time coaching to parents, encouraging them to let their children take the lead during play. Activities are also video recorded so that therapists and parents can review parents' attempts at sensitive and responsive care and monitor their progress.

Third, therapists help parents overcome barriers to meeting their children's needs in sensitive and responsive ways. Because foster children do not come with instruction manuals, parents often rely on their own caregiving experiences to decide how to interact with their infants. However, parents who have experienced neglectful or abusive parenting themselves may have difficulty meeting their infants' needs. Parents are taught to recognize when their caregiving histories interfere with their ability to provide sensitive care to their infants and find ways to overcome these negative experiences for the benefit of their children. Often, this involves helping parents identify negative thoughts that distort their perceptions of their

RESEARCH TO PRACTICE

EXPLORING A MOTHER'S THOUGHTS ABOUT HER OWN PARENTS

Therapist: When your baby cries, what goes through your mind?

Mother: I feel terrible. You know, completely helpless. I try to do everything I can think of to get her to settle down, but I can't.

Therapist: That's how you *feel*. Now, tell me what you *think*. Is there a thought or a picture that pops into your mind when she cries and cries?

Mother: It's funny, but I think about my own mom when I was a little girl. She was never really there for me very much. She was always working and never had time for me and my sister. I used to think, "When I become a mom, I don't want to be like her. I want to be warm, and loving, and caring to my children."

Therapist: And now you are a mom.

Mother: Yes. And no matter what I do, she doesn't seem to respond to me. She doesn't like to be cuddled or soothed. She doesn't seem to need me at all. I might as well not even be there.

Therapist: Like your mom.

Mother: Something like that.

children. Consider the exchange between a therapist and a new mother in the following Research to Practice section.

Therapists might teach mothers to recognize the ways their caregiving histories can negatively impact their current parent–child interactions, using the "shark music" analogy. In the movie *Jaws*, ominous music precedes each shark attack. When you hear the music, you instantly feel anxiety. Memories of negative caregiving experiences are like shark music; they compromise parents' abilities to attend to their children's needs and signals by producing anxiety, anger, or other negative emotions. Therapists help parents recognize situations that lead to shark music and cope with these situations with more objective (less distorted) thoughts (Dozier & Roben, 2015).

ABC can be efficacious in promoting secure parent–child attachment. Bernard and colleagues (2012) randomly assigned 120 foster parents of children between 11 and 31 months of age to either ABC or to a control group. All dyads were at risk for attachment problems because of domestic violence, parental substance abuse, neglect, or similar stressors. After treatment, more parent–child dyads who received ABC (52%) were securely attached than were dyads in the control group (33%). Furthermore, fewer dyads who participated in ABC showed disorganized attachment (32%) than did dyads in the control condition (57%).

Treatment for Disinhibited Social Engagement Disorder

For Children Living in Institutions

Providing children with sensitive and responsive foster parents may not be sufficient to reduce indiscriminately social behavior. Several longitudinal studies suggest that once indiscriminately social behaviors emerge in late infancy or early childhood, they often persist into late childhood or early adolescence (Gunnar, 2010).

Nearly all studies indicate that institutionalized infants who are adopted into nurturing homes prior to age 6 months do *not* develop significant symptoms of DSED. Therefore, prevention of DSED is best accomplished by home placement before age 6 months. Infants who remain socially deprived after age 6 months are at increased risk for indiscriminately social behavior. The number of different caregivers and disruptions to the caregiving environment between 6 and 24 months of age is associated with later social disinhibition (Zeanah, Berlin, & Boris, 2011). Consequently, researchers have tried to provide more stable and consistent care to institutionalized infants in the hope of reducing DSED (Rutter, Sonuga-Barke, & Castle, 2011; Rutter, Sonuga-Barke, Beckett et al., 2011).

Smyke and colleagues (Smyke, Dumitrescu, & Zeanah, 2002; Smyke, Zeanah, Fox, Nelson, & Guthrie, 2010) compared two groups of children living in Romanian orphanages: (1) children assigned to usual care and (2) children assigned to a pilot program designed to reduce the number of caregivers to whom each child was exposed. Children in both groups had the same child-to-caregiver ratio (1:12). However, children in the usual care group were exposed to a wide range of different caregivers whereas children in the pilot program saw the same caregivers each day. Over time, children in the pilot program displayed fewer symptoms of both RAD and social disinhibition than children receiving usual care.

A second study involved young infants living in Russian orphanages (McCall and St. Petersburg-USA Orphanage Research Team, 2008). Researchers compared three groups of children. The caretakers of children in the first group were specifically trained to provide sensitive and responsive care to their children; furthermore, the caregiver-to-child ratio for infants in their group was reduced. The caretakers of children in the second group received training only; these children had the same high caregiver-to-child ratio. Children in the third group received usual care in the orphanage. As expected, infants in the first group showed the best outcomes: more positive emotions, greater exploration and play, more attempts to gain proximity to caregivers, and less indiscriminately social behavior.

For Children Living in Foster Care

What can be done for children who already show a lack of social inhibition? Results of three large longitudinal studies suggest that socially disinhibited behavior often persists, even after children are adopted into nurturing homes (Zeanah et al., 2011). Although social disinhibition tends to decrease over time, it can continue to interfere with children's interactions with parents and peers in late childhood and early adolescence. Early deprivation likely takes its toll on the development of children's abilities for behavioral control. These underlying neurological deficits, once they appear, are resistant to change and may manifest themselves in hyperactivity, impulsiveness, and risk taking (Ghera et al., 2009).

Some researchers have suggested that indiscriminately social behaviors can be corrected by targeting the neurological deficits that likely underlie these behaviors, namely, problems with behavioral inhibition (Pears et al., 2010). For example, researchers have developed a computer program that fosters the development of attentional control in typically developing young children (Rueda, Rothbart, McCandliss, Saccomanno, & Posner, 2005). Children who completed the program showed increased capacity for inhibition and greater activation of brain areas believed responsible for inhibition, especially the prefrontal cortex. However, this program has not yet been used with children who have DSED. Clearly, more research must be directed at finding effective treatments for these youths.

Review:

- ABC is used to improve the quality of attachment between caregivers and young children; caregivers learn how to read their children's needs and signals and provide care in a sensitive, nonintrusive manner.

Therapists also help caregivers identify aspects of their own histories that might interfere with the quality of care they afford their children.

- DSED can be prevented if children are provided with stable, consistent care prior to 6 months of age. If children remain in orphanages, lowering the caregiver–child ratio and helping caregivers provide more sensitive or responsive care can be helpful.
- DSED is difficult to correct in toddlers and older children. Promising treatments target underlying problems with inhibitory control.

12.3 CHILD ABUSE AND NEGLECT

Although early deprivation is relatively rare in the United States, other forms of child maltreatment are, unfortunately, too common. Each year, approximately 2.6 million youths in the United States are referred to child protective services for suspected maltreatment. After review and investigation, almost 900,000 of these reported cases are substantiated. These statistics indicate that approximately 1.3% of children and adolescents are abused or neglected each year. This estimate does not include the vast number of maltreated youths who are never reported (Cicchetti & Toth, 2016).

Child maltreatment places considerable financial demands on society. Most obvious are the direct financial costs associated with child maltreatment: the cost of providing medical, mental health, and home placement services to victims; the cost of providing training and rehabilitative services to offending parents; and (in some cases) the cost of prosecuting and incarcerating adult offenders. Less noticeable are the indirect financial costs associated with maltreatment: lower academic and job attainment by victims, lost wages and productivity by parents, and the negative impact on the community caused by antisocial behavior shown by many maltreated youths who do not receive treatment. The estimated annual financial cost of child maltreatment in the United States is approximately $50 billion to $100 billion (Jud, Fegert, & Finkelhor, 2016).

Child maltreatment has less tangible, but no less important, emotional costs. Child victims typically experience considerable emotional pain and psychological distress, family members often report increased conflict and reduced quality of life, and perpetrators must face the consequences of their acts, ranging from humiliation to social ostracism to imprisonment. Child maltreatment seriously affects victims, families, and society.

What Is Child Maltreatment?

Public policy and research have been limited by a lack of consensus regarding the definition of child maltreatment. Put simply, experts cannot agree what behaviors constitute abuse and neglect. Indeed, definitions of child maltreatment vary from state to state and from professional to professional.

The first definition of child maltreatment was presented in the Child Abuse Prevention and Treatment Act of 1974 (PL 93–247). This act defined maltreatment as follows:

> The physical or mental injury, sexual abuse, exploitation, negligent treatment, or maltreatment of a child under the age of 18 . . . by a person who is responsible for the child's welfare under circumstances which indicate that the child's health or welfare is harmed or threatened.

Although somewhat vague, this definition is noteworthy because it identifies four types of child maltreatment: (1) physical abuse, (2) sexual abuse, (3) psychological abuse (i.e., "mental injury"), and (4) neglect.

DSM-5 also recognizes these same four domains of child maltreatment (see Table 12.6). However, abuse and neglect are not considered mental disorders in *DSM-5*. Children who are victims of maltreatment vary considerably in their outcomes: Some children develop disorders whereas others do not. Clinicians can describe a child as the victim of abuse or neglect and assign diagnoses if the child meets diagnostic criteria. For example, a child who experiences abuse might be diagnosed with PTSD, an anxiety disorder, or a sleep disorder depending on his symptoms (American Psychiatric Association, 2013).

Physical Abuse

Physical abuse includes deliberate actions that result in injury, or the serious risk of injury, to a child. Examples of physically abusive behavior include hitting, kicking, shaking, throwing, burning, stabbing, or choking. Consider Kayla's description of physical abuse.

States have different definitions of physical maltreatment. Some states use the "harm standard" to identify cases of physical abuse; that is, the abusive act must result in physical harm to the child. Other states apply the "endangerment standard," in which the *potential* for harm is sufficient to merit the classification of physical abuse. For example, dangling a small child over a balcony in order to punish him would be considered physical abuse according to the endangerment standard, even if the child did not experience physical injury (Wekerle, Wolfe, Dunston, & Alldred, 2014).

Sexual Abuse

There is no consensus regarding the definition of child sexual abuse (Furniss, 2013; Mrazek & Kempe, 2014). In fact, experts disagree about the precise meaning of each component of the term: *child*, *sexual*, and *abuse*.

Experts disagree regarding the age of "child" victims. Some professionals limit their definition of child sexual abuse to sexual acts committed against individuals 14 years of age and younger. Other experts, adopting a more liberal definition, classify all individuals under the age of 18 as "children." Still others consider the age difference between the victim and the perpetrator of the abuse.

Table 12.6 *DSM-5* Definitions of Child Maltreatment

Child Physical Abuse is nonaccidental physical injury to a child, ranging from minor bruises to severe fractures or death, occurring as a result of punching, beating, kicking, biting, shaking, throwing, stabbing, choking, hitting (with a hand, stick, strap, or other object), burning, or any other method that is inflicted by a parent, caregiver, or other individual who has responsibility for the child. Such injury is considered abuse regardless of whether the caregiver intended to hurt the child. Physical discipline, such as spanking or paddling, is not considered abuse as long as it is reasonable and causes no bodily injury to the child (American Psychiatric Association, 2013, p. 717).

Child Sexual Abuse encompasses any sexual act involving a child that is intended to provide sexual gratification to a parent, caregiver, or other individual who has responsibility for a child. Sexual abuse includes activities such as fondling a child's genitals, penetration, incest, rape, sodomy, and indecent exposure. Sexual abuse also includes noncontact exploitation, for example, forcing, tricking, enticing, threatening, or pressuring a child to participate in acts for the sexual gratification of others, without direct physical contact between child and abuser (American Psychiatric Association, 2013, p. 718).

Child Psychological Abuse is nonaccidental verbal or symbolic acts by a child's parent or caregiver that result, or have reasonable potential to result, in significant psychological harm to the child. Examples include berating, disparaging, or humiliating the child; threatening the child; harming/abandoning people or things that the child cares about; confining the child (as by tying the child's arms and legs together or binding a child to furniture, or confining a child to a small enclosed area [e.g., a closet]); egregious scapegoating of the child; coercing the child to inflict pain on himself or herself; and disciplining the child excessively (i.e., at an extremely high frequency or duration) through physical or nonphysical means (American Psychiatric Association, 2013, p. 719).

Child Neglect is defined as any confirmed or suspected egregious act or omission by a child's parent or other caregiver that deprives the child of basic age-appropriate needs and thereby results, or has reasonable potential to result, in physical or psychological harm to the child. Child neglect encompasses abandonment; lack of appropriate supervision; failure to attend to necessary emotional or psychological needs; and failure to provide necessary education, medical care, nourishment, shelter, and/or clothing (American Psychiatric Association, 2013, p. 718).

Source: *DSM-5*, American Psychiatric Association, 2013, pp. 717–719.

Note: Child maltreatment is not considered a mental disorder in *DSM-5*. Clinicians can describe a child as a victim of abuse or neglect (based on the definitions above) and then diagnose the child with one or more mental disorders, depending on his or her symptoms.

CASE STUDY

PHYSICAL ABUSE

Kayla's Story

My grandmother died when I was 12, and I was alone with my older brother, who is mentally handicapped, and my grandfather. I was beaten daily for almost a year. My grandfather used to scream at me . . . tell me I was worthless, and ugly, and a disappointment, stuff like that. I would take the blame for stuff my brother did just so that he might be spared from the pain I was forced to deal with.

One night, I was alone in my room, crying from the verbal abuse I'd just been subjected to. I picked up a razor blade and just started slicing my arms and wrists. For some reason, it made me feel better. I'd swallow painkillers to try and kill myself. I was hospitalized on one occasion, and a man from the local mental health center came to speak with me. I could not answer all his questions truthfully because my grandfather stood right next to me.

Source: ©iStockphoto/fasphotographic

Source: Used with permission of the author.

Experts also disagree about the types of sexual acts that constitute sexual abuse. Some individuals only consider penetration as sexually abusive. Others believe all sexual activity that involves physical contact merits the definition of sexual abuse (e.g., fondling, open-mouth kissing). Still other experts include sexual acts that do not involve physical touching in their definition of abuse so long as these acts are directed toward children and intended to sexually gratify the adult. From this perspective, voyeurism, exhibitionism, and the use of children for sexually explicit pictures or videos constitute sexual abuse.

Finally, experts disagree about the exact definition of abuse. Some individuals claim that physical force or coercion is necessary for a sexual act to be considered abusive. Other experts believe that *all* sexual activity toward children and adolescents is abusive, even those acts that are seemingly performed willingly by adolescents. Consider Angela, a girl referred to our clinic for a history of sexual maltreatment.

According to Lucy Berliner (2000), child sexual abuse involves any sexual activity with a child in which consent is not or cannot be given. Berliner's definition includes all sexual behavior regardless of whether the interactions are physical or nonphysical. Consequently, both physical contact (e.g., touching, penetration) and nonphysical sexual interactions (e.g., voyeurism, exhibitionism) with children can be considered sexual abuse (Fitzgerald & Berliner, 2014).

Berliner's definition of sexual abuse also includes all sexual interactions between adults and nonadults (i.e., children and adolescents). Adult sexual contact with children and adolescents is *always* abusive because nonadults are incapable of consenting to sexual activity. In order to consent, people must (a) understand all of the implications associated with their sexual behavior and (b) freely decide to engage in the sexual activity without any outside pressure. Most youths are unable to appreciate the full implications of engaging in sexual behavior with an adult. Furthermore, by virtue of their age and developmental status, children and adolescents are always at a power disadvantage in their interactions with adults. Consequently, they can *never* consent to sexual activity without adults influencing their decision.

Of course, there are gray areas in determining what constitutes child sexual abuse. For example, experts disagree

SEXUAL ABUSE

Unhappy Family

Source: ©iStockphoto/Halfpoint

Angela was a 13-year-old girl who was referred to our clinic because she was sexually abused. Before being placed in foster care, Angela lived with her mother, Mrs. Alosio, her stepfather, Mr. Valenta, and her three younger half sisters. Angela grew up in a tumultuous home. Angela's biological father had a history of aggressive and antisocial behavior. He was incarcerated for domestic violence at the time of the evaluation. Angela's mother had a history of alcohol abuse and had been arrested for selling narcotics on two occasions. Mrs. Alosio used alcohol, cocaine, and other drugs during her pregnancy with Angela. Angela was born prematurely and showed cognitive delays.

Angela's mother married Jason Valenta when Angela was 6 years old. Mr. Valenta appeared to provide a stable home and family life for Angela and her sisters. However, several weeks before Angela's referral, Mrs. Alosio discovered Mr. Valenta engaging in sexual intercourse with Angela. Shocked and repulsed, Mrs. Alosio yelled at both Mr. Valenta and Angela and ordered them to leave the house.

Angela had been repeatedly sexually abused for at least 5 years. Mr. Valenta eventually admitted to seeking out Mrs. Alosio, whom he described as "emotionally and financially vulnerable," to gain access to her daughters. Mr. Valenta instructed Angela never to tell anyone about the abuse because disclosure would cause his imprisonment, family disunification, and Mrs. Alosio's return to poverty and drug abuse.

In foster care, Angela showed problems with anxiety and depression. She displayed sleep difficulties, fear of the dark, and frequent nightmares associated with the abuse. Angela also had unwanted memories of abuse while in church. During the sermon, Angela showed extreme panic, ran from the congregation, and repeatedly cried, "I'm so bad!"

Angela preferred to play with the 6- and 7-year-old children in her foster home, rather than with girls her own age. She had few friends at school. Angela was reprimanded for kissing several boys during recess because "they asked her to." In foster care and at school, Angela tended to act helpless or to use "baby talk" to get special favors. Most of all, Angela seemed to need constant approval and reassurance from adults. Her foster mother described her as "needy" and "crushed by the slightest reprimand or criticism."

how to classify sexual contact between two children or two adolescents. Furthermore, experts disagree whether sexual contact between a minor adolescent (e.g., 16 years) and a young adult (e.g., 19 years) constitutes abuse. In these cases, professionals usually consider the age and developmental status of the two youths, their relationship to each other, and any power differentials that might have led to coercion.

Psychological Abuse

Child psychological abuse is more difficult to identify and substantiate than physical or sexual abuse. The American Professional Society on the Abuse of Children (APSAC) defines *psychological maltreatment* as a pattern of caregiver behavior that conveys to children that they are worthless, flawed, unloved, unwanted, endangered, or only of value in meeting another's needs (Myers, 2010). According to the APSAC definition, psychological maltreatment includes five broad types of behavior:

1. *Spurning*: Verbal and nonverbal acts that reject or degrade a child. Behaviors include ridiculing a child for showing normal emotions, humiliating a child in public, or showing extreme favoritism to one child at the expense of another.

2. *Terrorizing*: Threatening to hurt or abandon a child or his/her loved one. Examples include threatening to hurt or abandon a child if she does not obey, allowing a child to witness domestic violence, or threatening to kill a child's pet.

3. *Isolating*: Denying a child opportunities to interact with peers or adults outside the home. For example, a caregiver might refuse to allow a child to play with friends or have legal visitation with a parent.

4. *Exploiting*: Encouraging a child to adopt maladaptive, inappropriate behaviors. Examples include allowing a child to witness illegal acts or using the child to sell or transport drugs.

5. *Denying emotional responsiveness*: Ignoring the child's bids for attention and emotional interactions. For example, a caregiver might act cold or emotionally distant, rarely show affection, or refuse to give a child comfort when he is distressed.

Psychological maltreatment denies children the respect and dignity that is the inherent right of all human beings. Consider Dee's description of psychological abuse at the hands of her mother.

One particularly troubling form of psychological maltreatment deserves special mention: exposing children to domestic violence. In the United States, domestic violence occurs in approximately one-fourth of all long-term relationships. No one knows how many children witness acts of domestic violence each year. However, the effects of domestic violence on children are striking. Children exposed to violence in the home show a wide range of internalizing and externalizing behavior problems, especially depression, anxiety, conduct problems, and PTSD. Furthermore, many adults who physically abuse their partners also engage in child physical abuse (Lieberman & Chu, 2016).

CASE STUDY

PSYCHOLOGICAL ABUSE

Words Can Hurt, Too

Source: ©iStockphoto/JerryB7

One Saturday night, I went with my friend to a restaurant. My mother found out, and she came to the restaurant and yelled at me in front of my friends. She pulled me home, where she threw me to the floor and started kicking me and slapping me.

The next day, she called me to her bed and gave me a 2-hour lecture on how it was my fault that I had forced her to hit me because I wouldn't listen to her. I then had to write a sorry letter to her for forcing her to hit me. It was like that every time after we got hit. She would always make us tell her that we were sorry for forcing her to hit us, and we were forced to thank her for doing it because it was for our own good.

Every night we fell asleep, knowing sooner or later we would be awakened for a lecture about something we had done. It would go on for 2 to 3 hours. And just wanting it to end, we had to agree she was right. She forced us to repeat after her:

"I am a lazy, clumsy girl."

"I am stupid."

"I don't respect my parents enough."

Source: Used with permission of the author.

Lost Boy

Source: ©iStockphoto/mactrunk

Michael was a 6-year-old boy who was referred to our hospital by child protective services. Michael and his half siblings were removed from their grandmother's care because of neglect. The children were discovered living in a dirty apartment with little food and almost non-existent daytime supervision. They had an inconsistent history of medical care (e.g., immunizations, well-child checks), were malnourished, and were generally unkempt. All of the children were physically sick, and Michael's 2-year-old sister had extensive diaper rash that needed medical attention.

Michael displayed below average social and self-care skills. Upon arriving in foster care, he was unable to adequately wash his face, brush his teeth, and bathe. Michael hoarded food and displayed poor table manners. His teeth were decayed.

Michael displayed poor social skills at his foster home. He refused to share toys, wait his turn, pick up his clothes, or obey other rules of the home. He usually settled interpersonal disputes with physical violence. Ironically, Michael was expelled from Sunday School for punching a classmate. Michael's foster mother said that he intimidated and bullied the other children in the home.

"Michael is a needy kid," his foster mother explained. "He demands constant reassurance. He's always acting up and then asking us, 'Am I a good boy?'"

Neglect

Child neglect occurs when caregivers do not meet children's essential needs and when their negligence harms or threatens children's welfare. There are at least three ways caregivers can neglect children: (1) physically, (2) medically, and (3) educationally (Myers, 2010; Stoltenborgh, Bakermans-Kranenburg, & van IJzendoorn, 2013).

Physical neglect occurs when caregivers fail to protect children from danger or provide for their physical needs. Failing to provide food, shelter, and clothing is usually considered neglectful. Physical neglect is, perhaps, the most common form of neglect and the easiest to identify. However, it is sometimes difficult to differentiate parents who physically neglect their children from parents who, because of economic hardship, are unable to provide for their children's needs. Consider Michael, a boy exposed to physical neglect.

Medical neglect occurs when children's basic health care needs are unmet. Basic health care refers to medical procedures or treatments that, if not administered, would seriously jeopardize the health of the child. Medical neglect might include failing to provide children with necessary immunizations, not taking children for a medical examination when they display serious illness, or refusing to follow doctors' recommendations regarding the treatment or management of a severe illness (e.g., parents not helping a young child with diabetes management).

Educational neglect usually occurs when parents do not enroll their children in school or otherwise provide for their education. Educational neglect might also occur when parents repeatedly allow their children to skip school.

Summary:

- *DSM-5* and federal law recognizes four types of child maltreatment: (1) physical abuse, (2) sexual abuse, (3) psychological abuse, and (4) neglect.
- Sexual abuse is any sexual contact with a minor. It includes both physical contact (e.g., touching, penetration) and nonphysical contact (e.g., exhibitionism, voyeurism).
- Psychological abuse includes spurning, terrorizing, isolating, exploiting, and denying emotional responsiveness to children.
- There are three broad types of neglect: (1) physical, (2) medical, and (3) educational.

How Common Is Child Maltreatment?

Maltreatment in Children

The best data regarding the prevalence of child maltreatment come from the National Survey of Children's Exposure to Violence (Finkelhor, Vanderminden, Turner, Hamby, & Shattuck, 2014; Finkelhor, Turner, Shattuck, & Hamby, 2015), a population-based study involving children aged 0 to 17 and their caregivers. Overall, 12.1% of youths experienced at least one form of maltreatment at some point in their childhood or adolescence. This estimate is remarkably consistent with

Figure 12.6   Prevalence of Child Maltreatment in the United States.

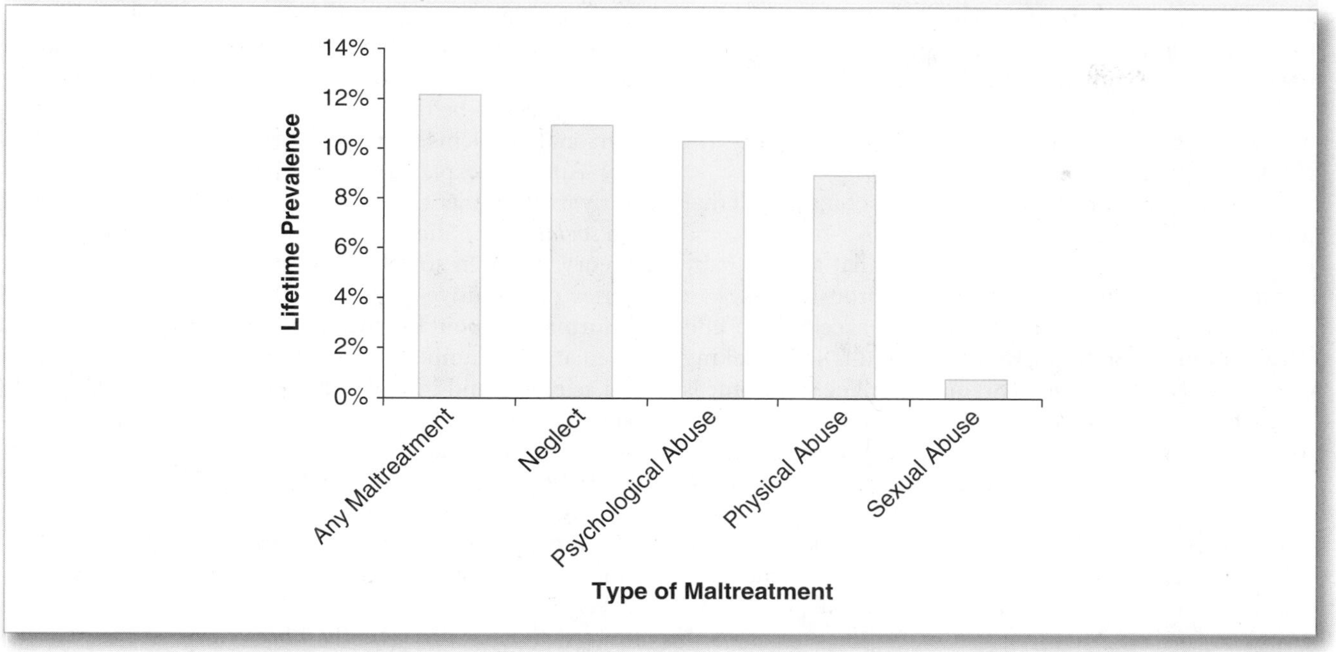

Source: Based on Finkelhor and colleagues (2014, 2015).

another meta-analysis that showed an overall lifetime prevalence of 12.7% (Jud et al., 2016). This percentage translates into approximately 9,000,000 youths in the United States alone (see Figure 12.6).

The most common form of child maltreatment is neglect (11.6%) followed by psychological abuse (10.3%) and physical abuse (8.9%). The prevalence of sexual maltreatment is much lower (0.7%). On average, the prevalence of physical abuse, psychological abuse, and neglect does not differ for boys and girls. The most likely perpetrators of these forms of abuse are biological parents or stepparents.

Girls are significantly more likely than boys to experience sexual abuse. The most common perpetrators of sexual abuse are biological fathers, stepfathers, and other men living in the child's house.

Sexual Abuse and Assault Among Adolescents

Data from the National Survey of Children's Exposure to Violence alone may not tell the whole story about child sexual abuse, however. Finkelhor, Shattuck, Turner, and Hamby (2014) also examined self-report data provided by older adolescents regarding their lifetime histories of sexual maltreatment. These data are noteworthy because they are based exclusively on adolescent self-reports, they include all forms of sexual maltreatment (e.g., fondling, touching, penetrating), and they take into account sexual maltreatment perpetrated by adults *and* peers.

Three important findings emerged. First, approximately 1 in 4 girls (26.6%) and 1 in 20 boys (5.1%) reported some form of sexual maltreatment. Second, the

sexual maltreatment rates increased dramatically for girls between the age of 15 and 17 years, indicating that late adolescence is a particularly vulnerable time for girls. Third, in most cases, youths were victimized by other adolescents rather than adults. The researchers describe peer-to-peer sexual victimization as "sexual assault" rather than "child abuse" because the perpetrators in these instances are other adolescents (e.g., a boyfriend or classmate). Although such acts of victimization may not meet the definition of child sexual abuse, they are events that threaten adolescents' social–emotional well-being and development.

Review:

- Epidemiological studies indicate that 12.1% of youths experience at least one form of maltreatment prior to adulthood.
- Neglect is the most common form of maltreatment.
- Approximately 26.6% of adolescent girls and 5.1% of adolescent boys report being the victim of sexual abuse or assault. Their sexual victimization tended to occur in late adolescence at the hands of peers.

What Are the Effects of Physical/ Psychological Abuse and Neglect?

Health Problems

Child physical abuse and neglect can take its toll on children's physical health. Severely neglected infants can exhibit nonorganic failure to thrive (FTT), which can cause long-term health and behavior problems or death.

Children who experience physical abuse often suffer bruises, broken bones, burns, and scars. These injuries are sometimes accompanied by neurological damage due to head trauma or abnormally elevated levels of stress hormone. Approximately one-third of physically abused children suffer serious injury that requires medical or psychiatric treatment to prevent long-term impairment (Finkelhor, Vanderminden et al., 2014).

One of the most serious and potentially lethal forms of child physical abuse is abusive head trauma (i.e., "shaken baby syndrome"). Recall that shaken baby syndrome occurs when a caregiver vigorously shakes an infant back and forth, causing a rapid acceleration and deceleration of the brain within the skull. This shaking can cause severe damage to brain tissue. The syndrome is characterized by initial drowsiness or sleepiness, failure to respond to outside stimulation, breathing problems, vomiting, seizures, coma, and death. Usually, symptoms are not apparent until hours or days after the damage has been inflicted. Between 33 and 38 out of every 100,000 infants are the victims of shaken baby syndrome each year (Shanahan, Zolotor, Parrish, Barr, & Runyan, 2013).

Behavior Problems

Children who experience physical abuse or neglect are at risk for developing disruptive behavior problems. Children with histories of maltreatment are frequently diagnosed with oppositional defiant disorder (ODD). At home, they are often spiteful and argumentative toward caregivers. At school, they are frequently disruptive and defiant. Most research indicates that this tendency toward negativistic, disruptive behavior continues throughout childhood and early adolescence. Children exposed to physical abuse or neglect also show increased risk for aggression, especially toward other children. Physically abused and neglected children tend to use aggression both proactively (i.e., to get what they want) and reactively (i.e., in response to frustration; N'zi & Eyberg, 2013; Wekerle et al., 2014).

Older children and adolescents with histories of physical abuse and neglect are at risk for conduct disorder (CD). Abused youths have greater likelihoods of engaging in serious antisocial behavior, especially stealing, cheating, being physically violent, and being chronically truant. Underlying deficits in moral reasoning may partially account for these antisocial tendencies. As adolescents, they are twice as likely as nonabused youths to be suspended from school, arrested, or involved in a violent crime. Boys who experience maltreatment show increased likelihood of developing antisocial personality disorder (ASPD) as adults. Girls who experience physical abuse or neglect show increased risk for underemployment and prostitution later in life (Klika, Herrenkohl, & Lee, 2013; van Vugt, Lanctôt, Paquette, Collin-Vézina, & Lemieux, 2014).

Why do maltreated children show increased likelihood of disruptive behavior later in life? One explanation is based on *learning theory*. Physically abused children

may model the hostile and aggressive behavior of caregivers. Indeed, children exposed to child maltreatment often witness other aggressive acts, such as domestic violence, parental antisocial behavior, and violent crime. Children may learn, through their observations, that disruptive and aggressive behavior is an effective way to solve interpersonal problems (Topitzes, Mersky, & Reynolds, 2012).

Another explanation for the relationship between early maltreatment and later disruptive behavior is based on *social information-processing theory*. According to this theory, children solve social problems by engaging in a series of cognitive steps: (a) taking in and interpreting information about the social situation, (b) generating and evaluating a number of possible ways of responding, and (c) selecting and implementing the best plan. Physically abused children show difficulty with all three steps, making them more likely to use hostile and aggressive means to solve interpersonal problems (Dodge, Godwin, & Conduct Problems Prevention, 2013).

First, physically abused children show hostile attributional biases when solving social problems. That is, they expect others to behave in a hostile and aggressive manner toward them. Consequently, they often misinterpret the benign behaviors of others as hostile and aggressive. Second, abused children usually have difficulty generating solutions to social problems; furthermore, the solutions that they are able to generate are usually hostile or aggressive in nature. Third, abused children impulsively select a plan of action— that is, they often do not consider the consequences of their behavior before they act. These social problem-solving deficits increase the likelihood that children will act aggressively in ambiguous social situations (Runions, Shapka, Dooley, & Modecki, 2013; Young & Widom, 2014).

What about neglected youths? How might they develop disruptive and antisocial behaviors? Children who experience neglect often have peer problems and low social functioning. Indeed, many neglected youths have few friends and are actively rejected by classmates. Because neglected children are often ostracized by prosocial peers, they may seek friendships with other rejected children. These rejected peers can introduce them to disruptive and antisocial behaviors, such as aggression, delinquency, and substance use. Furthermore, parents who neglect their children usually do not sufficiently monitor their children's activities. Consequently, neglected children are free to engage in antisocial activities with little adult supervision. Association with deviant peer groups and low parental monitoring are primary predictors of conduct problems (Merlo & Benekos, 2016).

Anxiety and Mood Disorders

Many physically abused and neglected children develop anxiety and mood problems disorders. Approximately 25% of youths exposed to physical abuse develop PTSD. Furthermore, approximately one-third of children who develop abuse-related PTSD continue to show symptoms

2 years after the end of their physical maltreatment (Shenk, Putnam, Rausch, Peugh, & Noll, 2014). Comorbid mood problems include major depressive disorder (MDD), persistent depressive disorder (dysthymia), and general feelings of hopelessness. Many psychologically maltreated children also report low self-esteem and self-efficacy. These mood problems are especially common in youths who experience multiple types of maltreatment and among girls (Cicchetti & Rogosch, 2014; Dunn, McLaughlin, Slopen, Rosand, & Smoller, 2013).

How does child abuse place children at risk for anxiety and mood disorders? One hypothesis is that child maltreatment adversely affects the development of children's capacity to cope with psychosocial stress. Although the exact physiological mechanisms are poorly understood, the timing of maltreatment seems to be important. Dunn and colleagues (2013) found that children who experienced physical abuse or neglect during the preschool years were 77% more likely to develop mood problems than youths who experienced maltreatment at other times (e.g., infancy, later childhood, adolescence). They suggested that children might be unusually sensitive to the effects of maltreatment during this sensitive period in their development.

Child maltreatment can cause children to adopt negative views of themselves, others, and the future. Compared to nonabused children, maltreated children are more likely to believe that they are inherently unworthy, bad, or flawed. The attributions children make about their maltreatment predict the severity of their internalizing symptoms. Children who blame themselves for their victimization show much greater mood disturbance than children who do not assume responsibility for their maltreatment (Harter, 2015).

Insecure and Disorganized Attachment

Abused and neglected children show greater likelihood of developing insecure attachment relationships with parents and other adults responsible for their care. Approximately two-thirds of maltreated children develop insecure attachment relationships with their caregivers, compared to approximately one-third of nonmaltreated children (Cicchetti & Doyle, 2016; Goldberg, Muir, & Kerr, 2013).

Insecure attachment might mediate the relationship between child maltreatment and problems later in development. Specifically, child maltreatment can lead children to adopt internal working models of themselves and others that are based on mistrust and self-doubt. Although rarely articulated, these working models might include the following beliefs: "The world is dangerous. I cannot trust others. I must rely on myself. I am not worthy of receiving help from others, anyway." These models subsequently color all of the child's future relationships and his self-view. The result could be disruptive behavior, social isolation, and a host of mood and anxiety problems (Erickson & Egeland, 2002; Wekerle et al., 2014).

Recall that maltreated children sometimes display disorganized patterns of attachment toward their caregivers (Main et al., 1985). Children who form disorganized attachments behave in bizarre, erratic, or unpredictable ways during the strange situation procedure. Some children who are classified as having disorganized attachment show considerable distress when separated from their mothers during the strange situation, but they attempt to flee from their mothers when their mothers reenter the room. Other children classified as having disorganized attachment also show distress during separation, but when their mothers return, they seek comfort from inanimate objects instead of their mothers. Still other children appear hesitant or fearful of their mothers. Disorganized attachment is most common among children who have experienced physical abuse or neglect. Maltreatment may cause children to expect that their parents will behave in unpredictable or threatening ways (Cicchetti, 2016b; Lyons-Ruth, 2015).

Review:

- Abusive head trauma (i.e., "shaken baby syndrome") affects 33 to 38 out of every 100,000 infants annually. It is a severe form of physical abuse.
- Youths exposed to maltreatment are at risk for conduct problems. Parents who engage in maltreatment can model and reinforce aggressive behavior or interfere with the development of youths' social information-processing skills.
- Child maltreatment, especially during the preschool years, is associated with increased risk for anxiety and depression. Abuse experiences can lead children to have negative views of themselves and others.
- Children who experience maltreatment often develop disorganized attachment relationships with their caregivers. Their internal working models for relationships are often built on mistrust and emotional distancing from others.

What Are the Effects of Sexual Abuse?

Sexually abused children sometimes show higher levels of sexualized behavior compared to nonabused peers (Kendall-Tackett, Williams, & Finkelhor, 1993). Sexualized behaviors are actions that are either not typical for the child's age and development or inappropriate to the social situation. Sexualized behaviors include excessive or public masturbation, preoccupation with sex, sexualized play with dolls, forced sexual activity with playmates, and seductive language and actions (Heiman & Heard-Davison, 2004).

It is sometimes difficult to differentiate normative and nonnormative sexualized behavior during childhood because little research has been conducted on typical sexual activity in children. Some sexualized behaviors are normative at certain ages. For example, many toddlers engage in self-stimulation, preschoolers try to look at adults while naked or undressing, and school-age children ask parents sex-related questions. However, other sexual behavior is usually never developmentally appropriate in childhood, such as sexualized play with dolls, forced sexual behavior, or the insertion of objects into sexual body parts.

Age-inappropriate sexual behavior is *not* a reliable indicator of child sexual abuse, however. Although many sexually abused children show sexualized behavior, most (66%) do not. Even the most problematic sexualized behaviors (e.g., a child forcing sexual activity on a playmate) differentiate sexually abused and nonabused children with only 75% accuracy. Instead, emerging data indicate that the presence of precocious sexual knowledge might better differentiate sexually abused and nonabused youths. Young, sexually abused children often have greater knowledge about sex than their nonabused peers (Wolfe & Gentile, 2013).

Child sexual abuse can also speed up sexual maturation, especially in girls. In one study, sexually abused girls who experienced vaginal penetration showed menarche approximately one year earlier than their nonabused peers. The mechanism by which child sexual abuse leads to early menarche is unknown, but researchers have suggested that the abuse experience could stimulate hormonal or biochemical (e.g., pheromone) secretions.

Sexually abused girls are at risk for being sexually victimized as adults. A meta-analysis investigating the association between sexual abuse in childhood and sexual victimization in adulthood revealed an average effect size (ES) of .59 for women (Roodman & Clum, 2001). Overall, women who were sexually abused as children were 2 to 3 times more likely to be sexually assaulted during adulthood than their nonabused peers (Rich, Combs-Lane, Resnick, & Kilpatrick, 2004).

Child sexual abuse can also lead to traumatic sexualization—that is, the development of anxiety or fear associated with one's sexuality or the establishment of relationships based largely on sexual activity. Traumatic sexualization can increase youths' risk for sexual disorders and risky sexual behavior as adults (Koenig & Clark, 2004; Rich et al., 2004). For example, sexually abused girls show higher rates of sexual arousal problems as adults than their nonabused peers (Laumann, Paik, & Rosen, 1999). Other women with histories of child sexual abuse display hypersexual behavior. Specifically, they are more likely to show sexual promiscuity, engage in unsafe sexual practices such as one-time-only sexual encounters, become involved in prostitution, and contract human immunodeficiency virus (HIV) than their nonabused peers (see Table 12.7).

The relationship between child sexual abuse and sexual revictimization is less clear for boys. Most research indicates that boys who are sexually abused are *not* more likely to be sexually assaulted as adults (Purcel, Malow, Dolezal, & Carballo-Dieguez, 2004). However, some data indicate that homosexual men with histories of child sexual abuse do show increased risk for adult sexual victimization by other men.

Men with histories of sexual abuse are also more likely to show sexual adjustment problems than their nonabused peers (Heiman & Heard-Davison, 2004; Purcel et al., 2004). Potential problems include sexual dysfunction (e.g., premature ejaculation, erectile dysfunction, low sexual desire), sexually coercive and aggressive behaviors toward their partners, sexual promiscuity, risky sexual behavior, and HIV infection.

Review:

- Early sexual maltreatment can lead to traumatic sexualization—that is, the development of anxiety or fear associated with one's sexuality or the establishment of relationships based largely on sexual activity.
- Precocious sexual knowledge is an indicator of sexual maltreatment in young children.

Table 12.7   Traumatic Sexualization

Adults with histories of sexual maltreatment are more likely to endorse items that indicate fear of sexual activity, a preoccupation with sex, or potentially problematic sexual behavior.	
Domain	*Examples*
Avoidance and Fear	*I avoid being sexually intimate.*
	I prefer nonsexual relationships over sexual relationships.
Preoccupation With Sex	*I have trouble keeping sexual thoughts out of my head.*
	Thoughts about sex interfere with my daily life.
Use of Sex	*I use sex to avoid loneliness.*
	I avoid rejection by having sex.
Attraction and Sexuality	*People are attracted to me because of sex.*
	My sexuality is what attracts people to me.

Based on McCallum and colleagues (2012).

What Treatments Are Effective for Children Exposed to Physical Abuse or Neglect?

Supportive Therapy for Children

The most common form of treatment for abused and neglected children is supportive therapy. The primary goal of supportive therapy is to help children cope with feelings and memories associated with their maltreatment and to improve their sense of self and relationships with others. William Friedrich (2002) has developed an integrated approach to the treatment of abused and neglected children. In his approach, treatment addresses three core areas of children's functioning: (1) attachment to caregivers, (2) behavioral regulation, and (3) self-perceptions (Leenarts, Diehle, Doreleijers, Jansma, & Lindauer, 2013).

Abuse and neglect can seriously jeopardize the security of the parent–child attachment relationship. Under optimal conditions, children expect sensitive and responsive care from parents when they are scared, upset, or unsure. However, acts of maltreatment rob children of that security. Physical and emotional neglect communicate to children that parents are not able or willing to provide for their basic material and psychological needs. Furthermore, parents who physically abuse children are, simultaneously, the source of danger and support. The result of maltreatment is an attachment relationship built on mistrust and doubt. In the worst cases, attachment is disorganized, as children learn to fear their caregivers.

Early in therapy, the clinician uses the therapeutic relationship as a source of support, care, and nurturance. The clinician's primary goal is to establish a sense of trust between himself and the maltreated child. Fostering trust is initially a difficult task because maltreated children often expect rejection and abandonment by others. Indeed, children may engage in disruptive behaviors and aversive emotional displays to elicit anger and resentment from the therapist and thereby confirm their expectations that others will reject them.

To establish a sense of trust, clinicians strive to provide a safe, consistent, and accepting therapeutic environment. Therapy sessions are typically used to help children process feelings associated with maltreatment. Some children harbor anger toward parents for their neglectful and abusive behavior. Other children resent the police, child protective services, and foster families for keeping them away from their parents. Still other children blame themselves for their mistreatment, believing they were somehow responsible for their caregivers' actions. Finally, a large number of children deny having problems altogether. The therapist tries to validate children's feelings by listening to them in a supportive, nonjudgmental way.

Later in therapy, the clinician might help children recognize their feelings and understand how these feelings affect their thoughts and actions. For example, feelings of anger and resentment could lead to aggressive outbursts at school and problems with teachers or peers. Peer problems, in turn, could contribute to additional feelings of loneliness, resentment, and hostility. The therapist might teach children more effective ways to cope with negative feelings, in order to avoid long-term emotional and social problems. Some therapists teach children relaxation techniques, others encourage participation in art or sports, while others ask children to keep journals about their memories and experiences.

The clinician hopes that the therapeutic relationship can become a corrective emotional experience for the child, perhaps the first relationship that the child has ever had in which her needs are placed above the needs of others. Establishing such a corrective relationship is usually quite difficult because many maltreated children are reluctant to trust or confide in another adult who they believe (based on previous experience) will reject, abandon, or mistreat them. By supporting the child, the clinician shows that the child is worthy of receiving care and attention from others. The experience of unconditional positive regard from the therapist can correct self-perceptions of worthlessness or guilt that interfere with the child's self-esteem and self-efficacy (Joshi et al., 2015; Wekerle et al., 2014).

Parent Training

Most caregivers who physically abuse or neglect children are offered therapy that involves behavioral parent training. Recall that the primary goal of parenting training is to teach parents more effective ways to socialize children. Specifically, parents are shown how to (a) attend to children's activities and positively reinforce appropriate behavior, (b) give clear and developmentally appropriate commands to maximize children's compliance, (c) ignore inappropriate behaviors and avoid hostile–aggressive displays, and (d) use noncoercive forms of discipline, such as time out (with young children) and response cost (with older children and adolescents).

Parent training can be administered either individually or in groups. Each week, the therapist introduces a new parenting skill and encourages parents to practice the skill at home with their children. The following week, parents provide feedback to the therapist and the therapist offers suggestions on how to tailor the treatment to meet parents' needs. When administered in groups, the therapist might use video demonstrations to elucidate parenting principles and tactics. The therapist might also encourage parents to discuss their experiences with each other (Barkley, 2014; Hembree-Kigin & McNeil, 2013; Webster-Stratton, 2016).

Parent training is efficacious in improving the quality of parent–child interactions. Specifically, parent training is associated with improvements in the quality of care parents provide their children, reductions in hostile and coercive parenting behaviors, and a decrease in children's behavior problems. The efficacy of parent training is based primarily on research involving children with disruptive behavior disorders, not abused and neglected children per se (Joshi et al., 2015).

Parent–child interaction therapy (PCIT) has been adapted for caregivers who have engaged in child maltreatment. Chaffin and colleagues (2004) randomly assigned parents to one of three treatment conditions: (1) PCIT, (2) PCIT plus individual therapy for parents, and (3) a traditional group-based parenting training program. Results showed that PCIT alone (Group 1) was superior to a traditional parenting program (Group 3) in decreasing re-referral to child protective services. These results indicate that the hands-on "coaching" approach used in PCIT may be especially useful to high-risk parents (see Figure 12.7). Interestingly, adding individual therapy to PCIT (Group 2) did not increase the efficacy of treatment; in fact, parents who participated in PCIT plus individual therapy showed *greater* likelihood of reabusing than parents who participated in PCIT alone. The researchers suggest that the addition of individual therapy may have diluted the efficacy of PCIT by decreasing parents' interest in treatment.

Later studies showed that increasing parents' motivation to participate in PCIT greatly increased it effectiveness. For example, Chaffin and colleagues (2009; Chaffin, Funderbunk, Bard, Valle, & Gurwitch, 2011) randomly assigned parents with histories of child maltreatment to receive either PCIT or PCIT plus a brief motivational session in which the therapist explained the rationale and importance of therapy. Results showed 21% of parents who received the combined motivational treatment reoffended compared to 47% of parents who received PCIT alone.

Most recently, Lanier, Kohl, Benz, Swinger, and Drake (2014) examined whether PCIT could prevent future maltreatment in a large sample of parents who previously engaged in physical abuse or neglect. Between 1 and 3 years after treatment, 12.5% of parents who participated in PCIT had reoffended compared to an overall reoffense rate of approximately 50%. Altogether, these findings support the use of PCIT as a first-line treatment of families with young children.

Cognitive–Behavioral Family Therapy

Parents

Many clinicians use a combination of behavioral parent training and cognitive therapy to help families who have experienced child maltreatment: cognitive–behavioral family therapy. Melissa Runyon and Esther Deblinger (2014) have developed a combined CBT program for parents who engaged in maltreatment and their children. Parent–child dyads participate in 16 weekly group therapy sessions, each lasting approximately 2 hours. Initially, parents and children are separated. Parents receive specific training in the causes and consequences of child maltreatment, child behavior management, stress reduction, and social problem-solving.

Figure 12.7   Parent–child interaction therapy (PCIT) is effective in preventing future abuse.

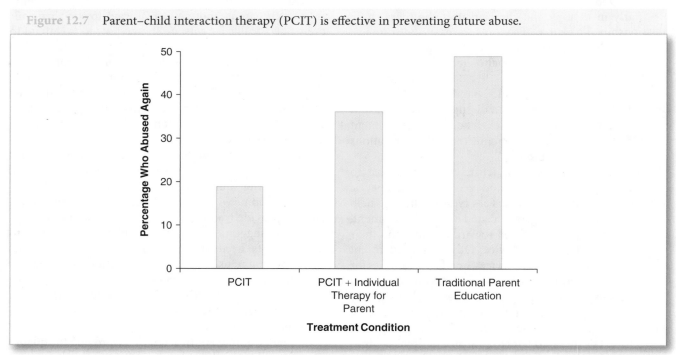

Source: Based on Chaffin and colleagues (2004).

Note: Interestingly, PCIT alone yielded better outcomes than more extensive forms of treatment.

One important aspect of cognitive therapy is to help parents form more realistic expectations for their children's behavior. Physically abusive parents often set extremely high and developmentally inappropriate expectations for their children. When their children fail to live up to these expectations, parents can become angry and respond with verbal or physical aggression.

Additionally, cognitive interventions for parents often involve challenging caregivers' cognitive distortions that lead to maltreatment. For example, a parent might think, "My child is always disrespectful; he never listens to me." The therapist might challenge this distorted belief by asking the parent to provide evidence for and against this claim. In fact, there are probably many instances each day in which the child obeys the parent, but these situations are often overshadowed by acts of noncompliance.

Another cognitive technique is to improve parents' problem-solving skills. Specifically, parents are taught to avoid blaming themselves or their children for children's misbehavior. Instead, parents are encouraged to look for alternative (and more benign) reasons for their children's acting out. For example, if the child becomes disruptive during a shopping trip, the parent might initially blame herself (e.g., "I'm a terrible parent") or the child (e.g., "He's a naughty kid"). Alternatively, the parent might attribute the child's misbehavior to situational factors (e.g., "He missed his nap today" or "He's bored and needs something to do"). Alternative attributions that do not place blame on the parent or child can reduce feelings of guilt, helplessness, or anger and, consequently, the likelihood of maltreatment.

Still another cognitive intervention involves improving parents' coping skills. Since distress, resentment, and anger usually precede child abuse, it is important for parents to learn ways to reduce these emotional states. The techniques that therapists use depend largely on the needs and preferences of parents. Some parents prefer breathing exercises, others respond to muscle relaxation, and still others like journaling. Most therapists also try to increase parents' social support as a way to buffer them against the harmful effects of parenting stress.

Children

While parents participate in cognitive therapy, their children simultaneously participate in group treatment. During the initial sessions, children learn about child abuse and neglect and the possible consequences that child maltreatment can have on children and families. In the early phase of treatment, therapists attempt to normalize children's feelings of anger, sadness, or anxiety. Therapists also help children identify and label their feelings and examine how feelings, thoughts, and actions are connected. This can be accomplished through games, role play, and discussion.

An important component of child therapy is the development of a trauma narrative. During this task, which occurs over the course of several sessions, children describe and reflect upon their personal experiences related to abuse or neglect. Older children are usually asked to write and illustrate a book about the trauma. Younger children and youths with developmental disabilities might instead enact a play using dolls. An important component of the trauma narrative is that the child describes the experience and is allowed to revisit the narrative (e.g., the book, a recording of the play) over time. The activity, therefore, is a variation of exposure therapy analogous to treatment used for PTSD (see the following Research to Practice section).

Later, children and therapists develop a safety plan. The safety plan is a specific strategy for dealing with future episodes of maltreatment. The safety plan involves (a) learning how to identify signs that abuse might occur (e.g., "Mom gets very angry and starts to threaten me; Dad starts drinking again"), (b) engaging in an immediate behavior to keep the child safe (e.g., leave the house), and (c) going to a trusted adult for help (e.g., grandmother, neighbor). Other child therapy sessions are designed to increase children's anger management, social skills, and problem-solving strategies.

After separate parent and child sessions, dyads participate in joint sessions that focus on the quality of parent–child interactions. For most of these combined sessions, parents practice behavior management skills with their children in the room, while they receive coaching from therapists. During some of these combined sessions, therapists encourage parents and children to openly discuss the abuse incident and to talk about ways to prevent it from happening in the future.

Several randomized controlled studies and other quasi-experimental studies support the effectiveness of cognitive–behavioral family therapy. Therapy reduces parenting stress, maladaptive parental cognitions, and hostile–coercive discipline practices. Moreover, treatment is associated with reductions in maltreated children's symptoms of anxiety, depression, PTSD, and disruptive behavior (Deblinger, Mannarino, Cohen, Runyon, & Heflin, 2015; Runyon & Deblinger, 2014).

Review:

- The primary goal of supportive therapy is to help the child establish a sense of trust in the therapist. The therapist tries to provide sensitive, responsive care to the child and, later, allow the child to discuss thoughts and feelings in the safety of their relationship.
- PCIT is effective in reducing recidivism in parents who previously engaged in child physical abuse or neglect. Overall, approximately 12.5% of parents who participate in PCIT reoffend compared to almost 50% of parents who do not receive PCIT.
- Cognitive–behavioral family therapy emphasizes the relationship between actions, thoughts, and feelings. Children construct trauma narratives to process their abuse experiences while parents learn to identify and correct maladaptive beliefs and negative emotions that can lead to maltreatment.

CREATING ABUSE NARRATIVES

Abuse narratives allow children to process thoughts and feelings about traumatic experiences. They also expose children to memories of these events and allow children to practice coping skills until negative emotions decrease. Some children are reluctant to write about their experiences directly. In these cases therapists can try other approaches:

- *Let's draw some pictures first. Then we'll add the words...*
- *Let's write a poem about what happened. What would be some good words to include?*
- *You're a guest star on a talk show and I'm going to interview you. Tell me about...*
- *Let's write a song about what happened. What instruments do we need?*
- *Let's play basketball. Each time you miss a shot, I get to ask you a question...*
- *Let's make a timeline about what happened, so we can keep it straight...*
- *Let's use my computer to draw a cartoon about what happened...*

Based on Runyon and Deblinger (2014).

What Treatments Are Effective for Children Exposed to Sexual Abuse?

Trauma-Focused Cognitive–Behavioral Therapy for Sexual Abuse

TF–CBT incorporates elements of exposure therapy, cognitive restructuring, parent training, and family support into a single treatment package for sexually abused children (Cohen et al., 2013; Kruczek & Vitanza, 2015). TF–CBT follows eight steps that can be remembered using the word PRACTICE (see Table 12.8).

The first phase of TF–CBT is to help children identify and manage negative emotions associated with the traumatic experience. Initially, therapists teach families about maltreatment, especially the tendency for people to avoid stimuli associated with traumatic experiences. Therapists also emphasize the need for parental support and consistency as they help their children recover.

Children also learn about the relationship between actions, thoughts, and feelings. Although they usually cannot directly change their feelings, they can alter their overt actions to improve their mood. For example, therapists might teach relaxation skills, such as deep breathing, to reduce anxiety. Alternatively, children and therapists might brainstorm other actions to reduce negative emotions, such as drawing, riding a bike, or taking their dog for a walk.

The second phase of treatment involves helping children use coping strategies as they confront memories of the traumatic event. Children also learn to challenge maladaptive thoughts about the event that might exacerbate negative emotions. Therapists usually begin by reading books about other children's traumatic experiences and talking about these children's thoughts and feelings. Later, children and therapists work on their own abuse narratives, each time providing more details. Gradually, therapists help children challenge and reframe maladaptive cognitions about the abuse experience. For example, a child might initially think, "It's my fault that I was abused. I let my stepfather do it, and I didn't tell anyone." The therapist might reframe this statement as, "It's not my fault; I was scared and felt like I couldn't tell anyone."

While children participate in therapy activities, non-offending parents also meet with clinicians for individual sessions. For the most part, parent sessions mirror the child sessions. For example, both children and parents learn to identify and accept feelings regarding the traumatic experience and to develop coping strategies to

Table 12.8   Trauma-Focused CBT for Families

P	Psychoeducation and Parenting Skills
R	Relaxation
A	Affective Regulation
C	Cognitive Coping
T	Trauma Narrative Development & Processing
I	In-vivo Gradual Exposure
C	Conjoint Parent-Child Sessions
E	Enhancing Safety and Future Development

Source: Wikipedia commons

From Cohen and collegaues (2013).

deal with negative affect and stress. In addition, parents participate in training designed to improve the support and consistency they give to their children and to teach effective ways of addressing children's behavior problems that might arise after the abuse.

In the final phase of therapy, children and nonoffending parents meet together. Children are encouraged to read their abuse stories to their parents and to discuss their thoughts and feelings about the trauma. Parents are asked to listen with acceptance and understanding and to answer children's questions regarding their abuse. Finally, parents and children develop new strategies to keep children safe. For example, parents might be encouraged to monitor their children more frequently, whereas children might pledge to come to parents immediately if they feel uncomfortable about a person or situation.

The efficacy of TF–CBT has been investigated in a number of randomized controlled studies. For example, Cohen and colleagues (Cohen, Mannarino, & Knudsen, 2005) examined 82 children and adolescents (ages 8–15 years) with histories of sexual abuse. Youths were randomly assigned to either TF–CBT or supportive therapy. Children's PTSD symptoms, behavior problems, and sexual behavior were assessed before treatment, after treatment, and at 6- and 12-month follow-up. Results showed that both forms of treatment were efficacious in reducing children's mood and anxiety symptoms. However, children were more likely to complete TF–CBT (73%) than supportive therapy (46%). Furthermore, at 12-month follow-up, children who participated in TF–CBT showed fewer problems with depression, anxiety, inappropriate sexual behaviors, and PTSD compared to children who received supportive therapy.

Several other randomized controlled trials have yielded similar results. These trials support the use of TF–CBT as a first-line treatment for sexually abused children who display PTSD, other mood and anxiety disorders, and maladaptive sexual behaviors (Mannarino, Cohen, & Deblinger, 2014).

Cognitive Restructuring for Sexually Abused Adolescents

Older children and adolescents who have been sexually abused often report negative thoughts about themselves, others, and the world that contribute to their anxiety and mood problems (Cohen et al., 2013; Deblinger et al., 2015). First, sexually abused children often hold negative appraisals of themselves. They may view themselves as worthless, as "damaged goods," or as unlovable by others. They may also blame themselves for the abuse, especially if they feel that they were somehow complicit.

Second, sexually abused children often hold negative views of others. They may view other people as untrustworthy, self-centered, and coercive. Consequently, they may be suspicious of others' motives and avoid asking others for help or support.

Finally, sexually abused children may adopt negative views of the world and the future. Abused children often view the world as a dangerous place. Some children report a pessimistic attitude toward the future and an inability to think about long-term plans.

The way children think about themselves, others, and the world can color their experiences and influence their feelings and actions. A child who believes "No one can be trusted" will likely have difficulty forming attachments with caregivers and friends. An adolescent who believes "I am worthless—even my own father mistreated me" may have problems with low self-esteem and self-efficacy. These negative beliefs, in turn, can cause individuals to distort interpersonal experiences to confirm their pessimistic and mistrustful schemas (Kruczek & Vitanza, 2015).

Therapists try to challenge cognitive distortions and help youths find ways to think about their abuse

CHALLENGING COGNITIVE DISTORTIONS

Therapist: When something reminds you of the abuse now, what feelings do you have?

Michelle: I guess I mostly feel bad.

Therapist: I'm not sure what you mean by "bad." Can you tell me a little more about which kind of bad feelings you have?

Michelle: Well, I just feel guilty about all of it.

Therapist: OK, remember how we said sometimes our thoughts influence how we are feeling? Can you tell me what you are thinking about when you feel guilty?

Michelle: I just feel like I must have done something to make my dad decide to do it to me.

Therapist: What do you think you might have done?

Michelle: I don't know. He used to always yell at me for the clothes I wore, so I guess maybe I wore the wrong kind of stuff.

Therapist: What do you think was wrong with your clothes?

Michelle: I don't really know. I dress like all the other kids, but he said I was trying to look too grown up, too sexy. He even said sometimes that I made him do it to me because of the way I walked around in really short shorts and miniskirts.

Therapist: Well, let's think about that carefully. You said that you dress like the other kids?

Michelle: Yeah, pretty much.

Therapist: And so, do you think that dressing like that also caused all of *them* to be sexually abused?

Michelle: Well, not all of them, no. Actually, I don't think this has happened to any of my friends.

Therapist: So, if dressing like that hasn't caused them to be sexually abused, it doesn't make sense that it caused you to be abused, does it?

Michelle: No, I guess not.

Source: From Heflin and Deblinger (2003). Used with permission.

experiences. Consider Michelle, a 14-year-old adolescent who was sexually abused by her father. In the Research to Practice section, the therapist identifies a cognitive distortion that may be contributing to Michelle's guilt. Then, the therapist asks Michelle to critically examine the validity of her distorted belief.

The negative cognitions evidenced by abused children contribute to their psychological and somatic symptoms. Cognitive therapy is designed to challenge these negative cognitions and help children view themselves, others, and the world more realistically.

Review:

- TF–CBT follows the PRACTICE model. Youths learn about common reactions to trauma, effective coping skills, and ways to identify and challenge maladaptive thoughts about their abuse experiences. Nonoffending parents are encouraged to provide sensitive care to their children.
- Cognitive restructuring involves identifying and challenging negative thoughts about self, others, and the world. Its goal is to see self, others, and situations in a more realistic, less threatening way.

Attachment and Biobehavioral Catch-Up (ABC): A treatment designed to improve attachment quality between parents and young children; caregivers learn to how to read their children's needs and signals and provide care in a sensitive, nonintrusive manner; helps caregivers identify aspects of their own histories that might interfere with the quality of care they afford their children 402

Bucharest Early Intervention Project (BEIP): A longitudinal study investigating the effects of institutionalization and later adoption on orphaned children; showed that RAD is likely caused by a lack of attachment to a caregiver in infancy or early childhood 399

Child neglect: An egregious act or omission by a child's parent or other caregiver that deprives the child of basic age-appropriate needs and thereby results, or has reasonable potential to result, in physical or psychological harm; includes lack of physical care and supervision, medical care, or education 405 408

Child physical abuse: Nonaccidental physical injury to a child, ranging from minor bruises to severe fractures or death, inflicted by a parent, caregiver, or other individual who has responsibility for the child 405

Child psychological abuse: Nonaccidental verbal or symbolic acts by a child's parent or caregiver that result, or have reasonable potential to result, in significant psychological harm to the child; includes spurning, terrorizing, isolating, exploiting, and denying emotional responsiveness 405 407

Child sexual abuse: Any sexual act involving a child that is intended to provide sexual gratification to a parent, caregiver, or other individual who has responsibility for a child; includes sexual contact and noncontact exploitation 405

Cognitive appraisal theory: A model for the development of anxiety disorders, PTSD, and mood disorders; asserts that the way people feel about situations depends on their evaluations of those situations 371

Cognitive–behavioral family therapy: A treatment for child maltreatment for both children and parents; emphasize the relationship between overt actions, thoughts, and feelings; children construct trauma narratives to process their abuse experiences while parents learn to identify and correct maladaptive beliefs that can lead to maltreatment 414

Coping: Actions and thoughts that protect a person from psychological damage following a stressful event; it mediates the relationship between stress and a person's behavioral or emotional response 371

Depersonalization: A dissociative symptom that involves feelings of detachment from one's body 384

Derealization: A dissociative symptom that involves distorted perceptions or sense of time 384

Disinhibited social engagement disorder (DSED): A *DSM-5* disorder shown by infants or young children who repeatedly approach and interact with unfamiliar adults in a manner that is developmentally unexpected; associated with early social–emotional deprivation 398

Dissociative symptoms: Persistent or recurrent feelings of detachment from oneself or one's surroundings; include depersonalization and derealization 383

Escape or avoidance coping: Disengaging from a stressful situation and its behavioral, cognitive, emotional consequences 391

Experience-dependent process: An aspect of development that is believed to depend greatly on the duration, nature, and/or quality of environmental stimuli (e.g., attachment, spoken language) 397

Experience-expectant process: An aspect of development that is believed to be biologically predisposed and relies only on the presence of minimal environmental stimuli (e.g., quality of attachment, which language the child learns to speak) 357

Eye movement desensitization and reprocessing (EMDR): A treatment for PTSD that involves repeated exposure to memories or traumatic events combined with rapid lateral eye movements 393

HPA axis: A neuroendocrine feedback system that connects the hypothalamus, pituitary, and adrenal cortex; regulates the body's stress response; may be dysregulated in youths with PTSD 390

Posttraumatic stress disorder (PTSD): A *DSM-5* disorder that occurs following exposure to death, serious injury, or sexual violence; characterized by (a) intrusive symptoms, (b) avoidance of stimuli associated with the event, (c) negative alterations in thoughts or mood, and (d) alterations in arousal and reactivity that cause distress or impairment and last at least 1 month 381

Precocious sexual knowledge: Awareness of sexual behavior that is beyond what might be expected given the child's age; a possible indicator of sexual maltreatment 412

Problem-focused coping: Modifying or eliminating the conditions that gave rise to a psychosocial stressor or changing the perception of an experience in a way that reduces or neutralizes the problem 391

Psychological First Aid (PFA): An evidence-based treatment for youths exposed to traumatic events; it emphasizes safety, self-efficacy, and social support immediately after the event 392

Reactive attachment disorder (RAD): A *DSM-5* disorder shown by infants and children who display inhibited, emotionally withdrawn behavior toward caregivers, a failure to respond to comfort, and episodes of irritability/negative affect; associated with early social–emotional deprivation 395

Safety plan: A strategy for dealing with future episodes of maltreatment; involves (a) identifying signs of potential abuse, (b) engaging in an immediate behavior to stay safe, and (c) going to a trusted adult for help 415

Sexualized behaviors: Sexual behaviors that are developmentally atypical or inappropriate to the social context 411

Supportive therapy: A treatment for child maltreatment in which the therapist tries to establish a safe, trusting therapeutic relationship in which the child can share thoughts and feelings about the abuse experience 413

Trauma-focused cognitive–behavioral therapy (TF–CBT): An evidence-based treatment for PTSD or child maltreatment in which therapists (1) help children gradually recall traumatic experiences, (2) use relaxation skills to cope with negative affect, and (3) identify and challenge cognitive distortions 313

Trauma narrative: A progressively more detailed description of traumatic experiences; may consist of a book, story, poem, or 415

other creative work that can be reviewed by the child; a component of many cognitive–behavioral treatments for youths with PTSD or exposed to maltreatment

Traumatic sexualization: The development of anxiety, fear, disgust, or other negative emotions associated with one's sexuality or the establishment of relationships based largely on sexual activity 412

CRITICAL THINKING EXERCISES

1. PTSD used to be considered an anxiety disorder. In *DSM-5*, however, PTSD is placed in a different category of disorders called trauma-related disorders. Why was PTSD reclassified in this manner?

2. Imagine that your friend's teenage son was involved in a serious car accident in which one of his friends died. Although the accident occurred 3 months ago, her son refuses to talk about the accident, despite the fact that it continues to cause him distress and interfere with his daily functioning. Your friend thinks it might be best to let him "put it in the past and move on with his life." How might you respond to her suggestion?

3. Angela and Brad are planning to adopt a child from Central America who was abandoned by her mother shortly after birth. The child, now 3 years old, received very poor care in an orphanage. Why might this child be at risk for social–emotional problems?

4. Beatrice is a 16-year-old girl who has engaged in a sexual relationship with a 25-year-old single man named Dante. Beatrice and Dante have dated for approximately six months. Is their relationship abusive? Why or why not?

5. What is the effectiveness of (a) behavioral parent training and (b) cognitive–behavioral family therapy for the treatment of physical abuse and neglect? If you were a therapist, which approach would you use?

TEST YOURSELF AND EXTEND YOUR LEARNING

Videos, flash cards, and links to online resources for this chapter are available to students online. Teachers also have access to PowerPoint slides to guide lectures, case studies to prompt classroom discussions, and exam questions. Visit www.abnormalchildpsychology.org.

iStockphoto.com/Liderina

Depressive Disorders and Suicide

After reading this chapter, you should be able to do the following:

13.1. Describe the key features of disruptive mood dysregulation disorder (DMDD), and differentiate DMDD from other conditions affecting young children.

Identify and give examples of evidence-based treatments for DMDD.

13.2. Describe the key features of major depressive disorder (MDD) and dysthymic disorder, and show how children might manifest these disorders differently than adults.

Analyze the major causes of depressive disorders in children and adolescents ranging from genetic–biological factors to social–cultural influences.

Evaluate the efficacy and safety of medication, psychosocial therapy, and combined treatment for youths with depressive disorders.

13.3. Differentiate suicidal and nonsuicidal self-injury (NSSI), and describe how the prevalence of self-injurious behaviors varies as a function of age, gender, and ethnicity.

Identify some of the main causes of suicide in youths and evidence-based techniques to prevent and treat suicidal behavior.

13.1 DISRUPTIVE MOOD DYSREGULATION DISORDER

Everyone has felt sad, down, or blue from time to time. Occasionally, we even experience prolonged episodes of dysphoria, perhaps after losing someone we love or experiencing a major life change. During these times, we may be less motivated to go to school or work, to spend time with friends and family, or to participate in sports or hobbies we typically enjoy. We may even feel tired and sluggish, be irritable or "crabby," and have difficulty eating, sleeping, or concentrating. Mood problems like these are common; however, they are also characteristics of depressive disorders. Determining when sadness ends and clinically significant depression begins is a major task facing mental health practitioners and the family and friends who refer individuals to their care.

Mood disorders occur when people experience emotional problems that are prolonged and cause distress or impairment. There are two broad classes of mood disorders: depressive disorders and bipolar disorders. **Depressive disorders** are characterized by predominantly depressed or irritable mood, a lack of interest in people and activities, and problems meeting the demands of everyday life. Sometimes, depressive disorders are called unipolar mood disorders, because people experience moods at the negative (i.e., depressed) end of the emotional spectrum. In contrast, bipolar disorders are characterized by discrete periods of mania or hypomania—that is, feelings of euphoria, energy, and grandiosity. Often (but not always), people with bipolar disorders also experience periods of depression; consequently, these disorders are called "bipolar" to reflect mood episodes at both ends of the emotional spectrum.

Depressive disorders in children and adolescents have only received serious attention from researchers and clinicians in the past few decades. A generation ago, many mental health professionals believed that children were incapable of developing depression. We now know that mood disorders not only exist in children and adolescents, but they are also fairly common. Advances in research and clinical practice are leading to new developments in how we diagnose and treat childhood depression (see Image 13.1).

In this chapter, we will examine three of the most common depressive disorders experienced by children and adolescents. First, we will learn about disruptive mood dysregulation disorder (DMDD), a condition typically seen in young children. Children with DMDD show persistently irritable mood and frequent tantrums. DMDD is important because it is upsetting to children and families and because many young children with this condition develop depression and anxiety. Second, we will discuss MDD, the most common mood disorder seen in older children and adolescents. Finally, we will examine persistent depressive disorder (dysthymia), a condition characterized by long-standing dysphoria.

We will also learn about a closely related phenomenon: suicide. Approximately 12% of older children and adolescents report suicidal thoughts, usually prompted by intense dysphoria (Curtin, Warner, & Hedegaard, 2016). Approximately 5,000 children and adolescents in the United States commit suicide each year, making it the second leading cause of death among youths (Centers for Disease Control and Prevention, 2016b).

What Is Disruptive Mood Dysregulation Disorder?

Disruptive mood dysregulation disorder (DMDD) is a mood disorder characterized by persistent irritability and recurrent temper outbursts (Table 13.1). Although many young children display temper tantrums, children with DMDD have outbursts that are out of proportion to the situation in terms of their intensity or duration. These outbursts can be verbal or behavioral. For example, many children with DMDD display sudden, intense verbal outbursts that observers describe as "rages" or "fits." They may scream, yell, and cry for excessively long periods of time, for no apparent reason. Other children with DMDD show intense physical aggression toward people or property. During an outburst, children may destroy toys or furniture; throw things; hit, slap, or bite others; or otherwise act in a harmful manner. Often, children's outbursts are both verbal and physical. In all cases, these outbursts are inconsistent with the child's developmental level. To be diagnosed with DMDD, temper outbursts must occur, on average, three or more times per week (American Psychiatric Association, 2013).

Image 13.1   Depressive disorders can be differentiated from sadness by their severity, duration, and degree to which they interfere with a person's daily life.

Source: Istockphoto ID: 47627466

Table 13.1   Diagnostic Criteria for Disruptive Mood Disregulation Disorder (DMDD)

A.   Severe recurrent temper outbursts manifested verbally (e.g., verbal rages) and/or behaviorally (e.g., physical aggression toward people or property) that are grossly out of proportion in intensity or duration to the situation or provocation.

B.   The temper outbursts are inconsistent with developmental level.

C.   The temper outbursts occur, on average, three or more times per week.

D.   The mood between temper outbursts is persistently irritable or angry most of the day, nearly every day, and is observable by others (e.g., parents, teachers, peers).

E.   Criteria A–D have been present for 12 months or more. Throughout that time, the individual has not had a period lasting 3 or more consecutive months without all of the symptoms in criteria A–D.

F.   Criteria A and D are present in at least two settings (i.e., at home, at school, with peers) and are severe in at least one of these.

G.   The diagnosis should not be made for the first time before age 6 years or after age 18 years.

H.   By history or observation, the age of onset of criteria A–E is before age 10 years.

I.   There has never been a distinct period lasting more than 1 day during which the full symptom criteria, except duration, for a manic or hypomanic episode have been met.

Note: Developmentally appropriate mood elevation, such as occurs in the context of a highly positive event or its anticipation, should not be considered as a symptom of mania or hypomania.

J.   The behaviors do not occur exclusively during an episode of Major Depressive Disorder and are not better explained by another mental disorder.

Note: This diagnosis cannot coexist with Oppositional Defiant Disorder (ODD) or Bipolar Disorder. Individuals who meet criteria for both DMDD and ODD should only be given the diagnosis of DMDD. If the individual has ever experienced a manic or hypomanic episode, the diagnosis of DMDD should not be assigned.

K.   The symptoms are not attributable to the physiological effects of a substance or to another medical or neurological condition.

Source: Reprinted with permission from the *Diagnostic and Statistical Manual of Mental Disorders, Fifth Edition* (Copyright 2013). American Psychiatric Association.

In addition to temper outbursts, children with DMDD display a persistently irritable or angry mood that is observable by others. Irritability is a feature of many childhood disorders. For example, children with behavior problems (e.g., oppositional defiant disorder [ODD]), anxiety disorders (e.g., generalized anxiety disorder [GAD]), and other mood disorders (e.g., major depressive disorder [MDD]) can show irritability. However, the irritability or anger displayed by children with DMDD is "persistent"—that is, it is shown nearly every day, most of the day. Parents, teachers, or classmates describe these children as habitually angry, touchy, grouchy, or easily "set off."

Children with DMDD, therefore, show persistently irritable or angry mood overlain with recurrent, severe temper outbursts. Consider the case of Reese, a girl with DMDD.

The *Diagnostic and Statistical Manual of Mental Disorders, Fifth Edition* (DSM-5; American Psychiatric Association, 2013) includes several additional diagnostic criteria that specify the chronicity, severity, and onset of DMDD:

1.   The outbursts and mood problems must be present for at least 12 months. This criterion highlights the *chronicity* of the problem and differentiates DMDD from mood disorders that are characterized by discrete episodes of dysphoria, irritability, or excitement such as MDD or bipolar disorder.

2.   The outbursts and mood problems must occur in at least two settings (e.g., home, school, with peers) and must be severe in at least one setting. This criterion highlights the *severity* of the problem and differentiates DMDD from disruptive behavior that might occur only in one setting (e.g., a child tantrums only at home to avoid chores, a child shows anger only at school because of learning problems).

3.   The disorder should be first diagnosed only between the ages of 6 and 18 years. Furthermore, symptom *onset* must occur prior to age 10 years. These criteria highlight the fact that DMDD is a childhood disorder that should not be diagnosed in toddlers or preschoolers. Very young children might show developmentally expected temper outbursts (e.g., tantrums to obtain a toy) that are not symptoms of DMDD. Furthermore, mood problems or temper outbursts that first emerge in adolescence likely reflect other problems besides DMDD, such as other mood disorders or difficulties adjusting to psychosocial stressors (Birmaher & Brent, 2015).

It is also important to differentiate developmentally expected temper tantrums from the tantrums shown by

DISRUPTIVE MOOD DYSREGULATION DISORDER

Mood Problems and Meltdowns

Reese was a 9-year-old who was referred to our clinic by her pediatrician. Her pediatrician had attempted to treat Reese's hyperactive and disruptive behavior for several years with various medications, to little effect. Reese's mother also participated in a parenting program to help her manage Reese's temper tantrums, but they seemed to be worsening rather than getting better.

Reese had a long-standing history of behavior problems. Her mother said Reese was a "colicky" infant who never seemed to be able to settle down. As a toddler, Reese would frequently throw tantrums, "sass," and disobey. About the same time, Reese began to show high-rate, disruptive behavior that interfered with her ability to pay attention and follow the rules at home and at preschool. In kindergarten, she was diagnosed with attention-deficit/hyperactivity disorder (ADHD) and ODD. Her pediatrician began prescribing stimulant medication to help Reese manage her hyperactivity; however, these medications had little effect on her behavior.

By the time Reese was in first grade, she had been expelled from two schools for throwing violent temper tantrums. During one tantrum, she threw a chair at her teacher; during another tantrum, she bit a classmate and stabbed a girl with a pencil. At the time of the interview, Reese was receiving special education for children with "emotional disturbance." Reese continued to throw tantrums multiple times each week, at home and at school. These tantrums usually lasted 30 minutes to two hours. During her "meltdowns," Reese would scream, cry, throw objects, destroy toys and clothing, and finally collapse from exhaustion.

Reese also had a history of mood problems. According to her mother, Reese was "always" irritable, spiteful, and "touchy." Reese often had crying spells in her room, which usually followed her tantrums.

Her mother stated, "I just don't know what to do about Reese. I'm so scared for her, and I don't know who to turn to for help. Everybody keeps saying, 'she just needs more discipline,' but I just don't think it's that simple."

children with DMDD. Among preschool-age children, tantrums are fairly common. In one recent survey, 83.7% of young children had a tantrum at home or school at least once in the previous month. However, frequent tantrums are *not* normative; only 8.6% of preschoolers had a tantrum every day (Wakschlag et al., 2012). Furthermore, temper displays seem to exist along a continuum, with most young children showing only mild displays of temper. Angry, aggressive, or destructive outbursts are rare, even among preschoolers. For example, many youths lose their temper when angry or frustrated and some children have a "short fuse" and yell at others when upset. However, less than 5% of children have severe tantrums or "meltdowns" that last until they are exhausted, tantrum with nonfamily members (e.g., teachers, babysitters), or hit, kick, or bite during tantrums. These severe and aggressive-destructive symptoms are not normative and may merit clinical attention.

Emerging data indicate that approximately 2% to 3% of school-age children have DMDD. However, DMDD is much more common among clinic-referred youths. In one large study, 47% of children referred to an outpatient clinic had a history of severe temper outbursts at home or school, and 14% displayed "rages" in both locations (Stringaris, 2011). In another study, 31% of children hospitalized for psychiatric problems met diagnostic criteria for DMDD, based on parental report, and 15.9% met criteria based on observations made by hospital staff (Margulies, Weintraub, Basile, Grover, & Carlson, 2012).

Review:

- DMDD is a mood disorder characterized by severe, recurrent temper outbursts and persistently irritable or angry mood. It is diagnosed in children between 6 and 18 years of age who show problems for at least 12 months in two or more settings.
- Approximately 2% to 3% of school-age children have DMDD. Prevalence is much higher among children receiving mental health treatment.

How Is Disruptive Mood Dysregulation Disorder Different From Other Childhood Disorders?

The irritability and temper outbursts shown by children with DMDD are often seen in children and with other psychiatric disorders. Therefore, differentiating DMDD from these other disorders can be difficult. Three disorders most closely resemble DMDD: ADHD, ODD, and bipolar disorder.

Attention-Deficit/Hyperactivity Disorder

ADHD is a neurodevelopmental disorder characterized by problems with inattention and/or hyperactivity–impulsivity. Children with DMDD often show several features of hyperactivity and impulsiveness common to ADHD. However, DMDD can be differentiated from ADHD in at least two ways. First, DMDD is a mood disorder, whereas ADHD is a disruptive behavior disorder. A salient feature of DMDD is the persistently angry or irritable mood shown by children with this condition. In contrast, children with ADHD do not typically display anger or irritability. Second, DMDD is characterized by severe, recurrent temper outbursts that are not characteristic of ADHD. Although many children with ADHD behave impulsively, they typically do not show verbal rages or physical aggression toward people or property.

In *DSM-5*, children with DMDD can also be diagnosed with ADHD. In fact, the two disorders frequently co-occur, despite the fact that they are separate conditions.

Oppositional Defiant Disorder

ODD is a disruptive behavior disorder characterized by oppositional, defiant, and/or spiteful behaviors directed at other people. Like DMDD, ODD emerges in childhood and is often characterized by both irritable mood and temper outbursts. Indeed, several diagnostic criteria of ODD closely resemble the diagnostic features of DMDD: (a) often loses temper, (b) is often angry or resentful, and (c) is often touchy or easily annoyed by others. Furthermore, the features of ODD and DMDD are persistent; children with these disorders show problems for months or years. ODD and DMDD are highly comorbid. Nearly all children with DMDD also meet criteria for ODD. However, only about 15% of children with ODD meet criteria for DMDD (*DSM-5* Childhood and Adolescent Disorders Working Group, 2010a, 2010b). This finding has led many experts to think of DMDD as a severe form of ODD in which emotional symptoms are predominant.

Despite their similarity, DMDD can be differentiated from ODD in several ways. First, the disruptive behavior shown by children with ODD is typically directed toward other people. For example, children with ODD may tantrum or defy a parent in order to avoid performing a chore. These defiant acts are usually directed toward specific people, based on the child's history of interactions with those people (e.g., the child tantrums only with mother, not with father). In contrast, children with DMDD direct anger and physical aggression to people *and* property. For example, a child with DMDD may break his own toys and destroy furniture in his own bedroom during a temper outburst. Furthermore, these tantrums are directed toward many people in many settings (e.g., toward parents at home and teachers at school).

Second, DMDD differs from ODD in the duration and severity of children's temper outbursts. Whereas a child with ODD may ignore parents' requests or stubbornly refuse to comply with their commands, a child with DMDD might yell, scream, hit, kick, and destroy objects to express anger. These outbursts may occur with little provocation and usually last much longer than expected.

A third, critical difference between ODD and DMDD come from longitudinal studies showing different developmental trajectories for youths with these disorders (Stringaris & Goodman, 2009). For example, researchers have found a relationship between DMDD in early childhood and anxiety and mood disorders in adolescence. In one study (Drabick & Gadow, 2012), researchers compared oppositional defiant children with and without angry outbursts. Compared to youths with behavior problems alone, youths with anger and irritability were at significantly greater risk for developing problems with anxiety and depression later in life.

In *DSM-5*, children cannot be diagnosed with both ODD and DMDD. If a child meets criteria for both disorders, only DMDD, the more serious disorder, is diagnosed.

Pediatric Bipolar Disorder

Bipolar disorder is a serious mood disorder characterized by the presence of discrete manic or hypomanic episodes. These episodes are usually characterized by feelings of euphoria, energy, and grandiosity. However, many children and adolescents with bipolar disorder also show periods of irritability and moodiness.

Beginning in the 1990s, clinicians began observing children and adolescents who showed hyperactivity, irritability, and severe temper outbursts that greatly impaired their lives at home, at school, and with friends (Leibenluft, 2011). Because other diagnoses, such as ADHD and ODD, did not seem to capture the severity of their irritability, anger, and disruptive behavior, many of these children were diagnosed with bipolar disorder. Some experts asserted that children and young adolescents manifested bipolar disorder differently than adults. Whereas adults with bipolar disorder typically display discrete episodes of mania and discrete episodes of depression lasting several weeks or months, they believed children with bipolar disorder might not show discrete manic and depressive episodes. Instead, these experts argued, children with "pediatric bipolar disorder" may show relatively persistent dysphoria with frequent, severe temper outbursts, or "rages." Furthermore, children's mood episodes may last only several hours or days. This "ultra-rapid" cycling of moods, the persistent irritability or anger, and the recurrent temper outbursts were thought to be unique features of the disorder in children (Biederman, Faraone, et al., 2004; Biederman, Kwon et al., 2004; Mick, Spencer, Wozniak, & Biederman, 2005). Because of this expanded definition of pediatric bipolar disorder, the number of children and adolescents diagnosed with the disorder increased dramatically (Leibenluft, Uher, & Rutter, 2012).

Recent research indicates that children with persistent irritability and angry outbursts do *not* have bipolar disorder, however (Leibenluft, 2011). Researchers conducted a series of longitudinal studies, examining children with chronic irritability and angry outbursts over time (Leibenluft, Charney, Towbin, Bhangoo, & Pine, 2003; Stringaris, Cohen, Pine, & Leibenluft, 2009; Stringaris et al., 2010). They found that youths with DMDD in childhood were 7 times more likely than typically developing youths to experience anxiety or depression in adulthood. However, very few children with DMDD (< 1%) developed bipolar disorder later in life.

Because of its close association with depression and anxiety, DMDD is classified as a depressive disorder. Clinicians are urged to diagnose children with persistent irritability and angry outbursts with DMDD and to reserve the diagnosis of bipolar disorder for those youths who show classic symptoms of mania (American Psychiatric Association, 2013).

Review:

- Children with DMDD always display mood problems; in contrast, children with ADHD typically do not display chronic anger or irritability.
- Children with DMDD typically direct their angry outbursts at people and objects; in contrast, children with ODD usually are oppositional toward specific people.
- Children with DMDD are at risk for anxiety and depression later in life; relatively few children with DMDD develop bipolar disorder.

What Causes Disruptive Mood Dysregulation Disorder?

Youths with DMDD often have difficulty attending, processing, and responding to negative emotional stimuli and social experiences. This difficulty may predispose them to anger and aggression in social settings (Leibenluft, 2011).

Youths with DMDD have problems interpreting social cues and the emotional expressions of others. Guyer and colleagues (2007) asked youths to label the emotional expressions shown in photographs of faces. Youths with DMDD made significantly more errors than youths with anxiety and depression or youths without emotional problems. Youths with DMDD were particularly bad at judging negative emotions such as sad, fearful, and angry. In a similar study using functional magnetic resonance imaging (fMRI), youths with DMDD showed underactivity of the amygdala during a facial perception task, compared to youths with ADHD, bipolar disorder, and healthy controls (Brotman et al., 2010). This finding is important because the amygdala is believed to play a role in the interpretation and expression of emotions. Deficits in processing emotional stimuli can cause youths to misinterpret social cues (e.g., misinterpret a smile as a smirk) and respond inappropriately or aggressively.

Children with DMDD may also have difficulty regulating negative emotions once they are elicited. Rich and colleagues (2011) asked older children and adolescents with DMDD to perform a simple, computerized task while their brain activity was monitored. Youths were asked to look at two boxes in a visual field and indicate whether a target stimulus appeared in the left-hand or right-hand box. Because the researchers were interested in how these youths processed negative emotions, they rigged the task so that youths often received false negative feedback, even when they gave the correct answer. The researchers were interested in what areas of the brain might be activated during this frustrating task. They also compared the brain activity of youths with DMDD with the brain activity of youths with bipolar disorder and healthy controls.

Two important findings emerged. First, youths with DMDD reported significantly less happiness and more agitation and negative arousal than comparison youths in the frustrating task. Furthermore, youths with DMDD showed significantly greater activation of the right *medial frontal gyrus (MFG)* and slightly greater activation in the left *anterior cingulate cortex (ACC)* than comparison youths. These brain regions are important because they are involved in evaluating and processing negative situations; monitoring one's own emotional state; and selecting an appropriate, effective behavioral response when upset, angry, or frustrated. The ACC, in particular, seems to be important in formulating a course of action in response to negative emotional stimuli. Altogether, these findings indicate that youths with DMDD are more strongly influenced by frustrating events than other youths. They may become more upset and select less effective and acceptable ways to deal with negative emotions than their peers (see Figure 13.1).

Deficits in inhibition, face perception, and emotional processing may lead to the development of DMDD in at least three ways. First, youths with DMDD may selectively attend to negative social cues that predispose them to anger, destructiveness, and aggression. For example, in social situations, these youths may attend to the most salient environmental (e.g., others scowling, teasing) or internal (e.g., feeling cheated, embarrassed) cues and minimize or ignore all other aspects of the event. Consequently, they may respond impulsively, selecting an emotional and behavioral response characterized by anger or aggression.

Second, youths with DMDD often show deficits in recognizing and interpreting others' emotional expressions. Consequently, these youths may misperceive benign social stimuli as hostile or threatening and respond with anger or aggression.

Third, youths with DMDD show marked problems monitoring their own emotions and behaviors, especially when they are angry, frustrated, or upset. Leibenluft (2011) uses the term *decreased context-sensitive regulation* to describe these deficits. That is, youths with DMDD do not modify or regulate their feelings and actions based on the context or situation. When their goals or objectives are blocked (e.g., a parent denies a request to stay up late; a coach asks the child to share the ball), these youths are unable to regulate their feelings and adjust their behavior. Instead, youths with DMDD experience these events as more distressing than most other children (Birmaher & Brent, 2015).

Figure 13.1   Brain Differences in Children With DMDD

Figure 13.1   Brain Differences in Children With DMDD

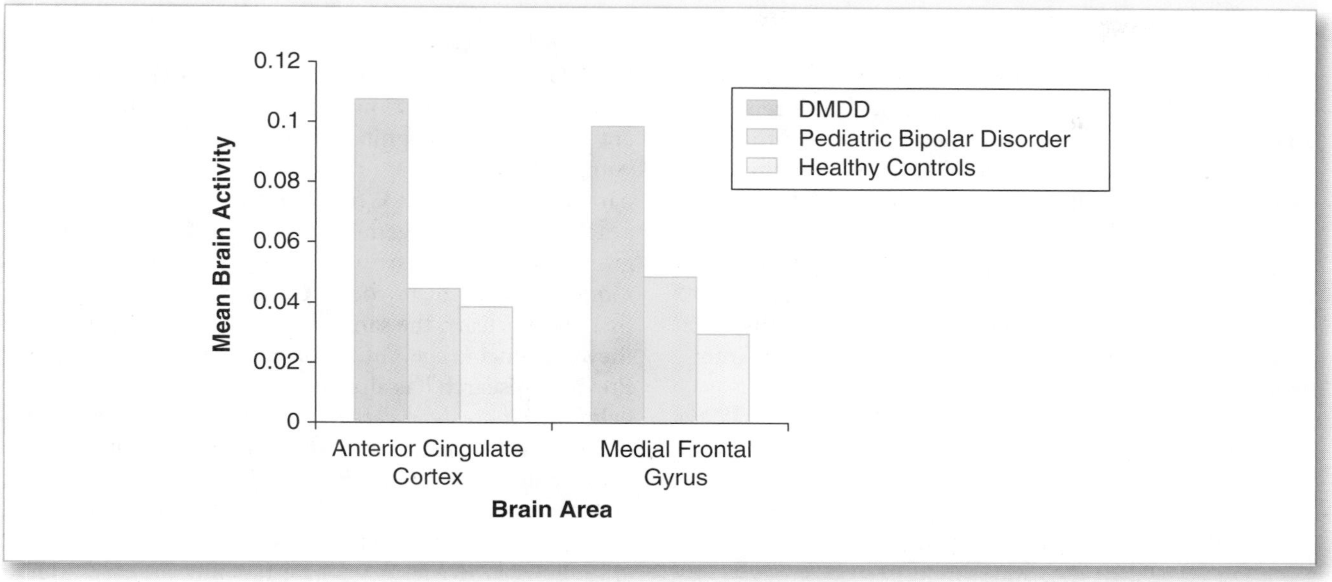

Source: Based on Rich and colleagues (2011).

Note: Youths with DMDD show over-activation of the anterior cingulate and medial frontal gyrus when performing a frustrating task. These brain regions are important when evaluating and processing negative situations, monitoring one's own emotional state, and selecting an appropriate, effective behavioral response when upset, angry, or frustrated.

Review:

- Youths with DMDD often selectively attend to negative social cues, making them more susceptible to anger and aggression.
- Youths with DMDD often show deficits in recognizing and interpreting emotional expressions in others, causing them to misperceive others' benign actions as hostile.
- Youths with DMDD often have difficulty regulating their own emotions. Overactivity of the MFG and ACC is associated with these emotion-regulation problems.

What Evidence-Based Treatments Are Available for Disruptive Mood Dysregulation Disorder?

Medication

Because the mood stabilizing medication lithium is effective in adults with bipolar disorder, psychiatrists have speculated that it might be useful for children with DMDD. However, when researchers randomly assigned youths with DMDD to receive either lithium or placebo, youths in both conditions failed to show improvement (Dickstein et al., 2009).

In contrast, the antipsychotic medication risperidone (Risperdal) has been shown to be effective in reducing irritability and depressed mood in older children and young adolescents with chronic irritability and anger (Krieger et al., 2011). However, approximately one-third of children taking this medication experience anxiety and excessive sleepiness.

Currently, most physicians recommend treating DMDD by using a combination of medications depending on the youth's symptom presentation (Jairam, Prabhuswamy, & Dullur, 2012). For youths with DMDD alone, many physicians recommend antidepressant medications to alleviate irritability and dysphoria. For youths with both DMDD and ADHD, stimulant medication may also be used to reduce hyperactivity and impulsivity.

Behavior Therapy

Because DMDD is a new disorder, our knowledge of effective psychosocial treatments is limited. However, several cognitive–behavioral interventions have been developed for youths with chronic irritability and temper outbursts that may be useful in treating DMDD. These treatments have typically involved one or more of the following three components: (1) parent training, to help caregivers manage children's disruptive behavior; (2) cognitive–behavioral interventions for youths, to help manage negative emotions and avoid angry outbursts; and (3) family therapy, to improve the quality of parent–child interactions.

Because many youths with DMDD tend to show problems with both ADHD and oppositional-defiant behavior, researchers initially attempted to treat these children with traditional parent training. Recall that parent training involves teaching caregivers to use contingency management (e.g., positive reinforcement for desired behavior, punishment for problem behavior) to increase compliance and decrease defiance at home. Researchers soon discovered that traditional parent training was not particularly effective for youths with DMDD, because it did not address these children's most salient problems: irritability and anger.

Researchers also attempted to treat youths with chronic irritability using therapeutic summer treatment programs, like the kind developed for children with ADHD. Recall that these summer treatment programs consist of psychoeducation, social skills training, and extracurricular activities (e.g., sports) in which children receive positive reinforcement for appropriate behavior and negative punishment (e.g., response cost) for inappropriate behavior. Although these therapeutic camps are effective for youths with ADHD, most youths with DMDD continued to show symptoms during this intervention (Waxmonsky et al., 2008).

Comprehensive Family Treatment

To address the irritability and angry outbursts of children with DMDD, some clinicians have used cognitive–behavioral interventions designed to improve anger management, social skills, and social problem-solving. Recall that youths with DMDD often show problems with controlling their impulses, interpreting others' emotions, and regulating their own emotions when their goals are blocked. These youths may selectively attend to negative events (e.g., focus on others laughing at them or teasing), interpret benign events as hostile or threatening (e.g., perceive a joke as a mean comment), and select responses to these events based on their immediate, negative emotional reactions rather than their long-term interests (e.g., hit someone rather than walk away).

Cognitive–behavioral interventions target these deficits by teaching youths anger management and social skills.

Waxmonsky and colleagues (2012) have developed a comprehensive treatment package for youths with DMDD and their parents (see Table 13.2). Their treatment includes education about DMDD, traditional parent training, and cognitive–behavioral interventions for youths. All sessions are run concurrently with groups of parents and children. While groups of children learn and practice anger management and social skills in one room, groups of parents learn similar child management techniques in an adjacent room. Concurrent sessions ensure that parents learn the same skills as their children so that they can encourage and reinforce these skills at home. Previous research has also shown that parent sessions are helpful in increasing caregivers' knowledge of their children's mood problems and increasing their motivation to participate in treatment. Parents also appreciate support and encouragement from each other during the parent sessions (Mendenhall, Fristad, & Early, 2009).

The treatment package consists of nine parent and child sessions (see Image 13.2). Parent sessions initially introduce caregivers to principles of contingency management. They stress the importance of attending to and praising appropriate behaviors, ignoring inappropriate behaviors, giving effective instructions, and using time-out or response cost to decrease inappropriate actions. Later, parents learn strategies to respond to children's outbursts. For example, parents learn how to recognize when their child is in a dysphoric mood, how to avoid triggers that might elicit an angry outburst, and how to cope with their own negative emotions that might exacerbate their children's tantrums.

Table 13.2 Comprehensive Family Therapy for DMDD

Parent Group	Child Group
1. Information about DMDD; introduction to contingency management	Icebreakers; identifying goals for a personal "fix it" kit
2. Attending to children's positive behavior	Recognizing emotions in self and others
3. Identifying anger in your child; using a daily report card to monitor child behavior	Anger I: What does anger look like?
	Rating the intensity of my anger
4. Helping children cope with anger; the importance of consistent "house rules"	Anger II: Coping to get calm
	Deep breathing, relaxation, guided imagery
5. Responding to problem behaviors; ignoring and using time-out	Anger III: How to stay in control
	Strategies to cope with teasing
6. Anger triggers and negative family cycles; negative parent–child interactions	Perspective taking, considering other people and consequences before acting
7. Improving parent–child communication	Being a good listener and communicator
8. Problem-solving skills	Problem-solving skills
9. Coping with depression in parents and kids	How to recognize and cope with depression
10. Review and graduation ceremony	Putting it together and awards ceremony

Source: Based on Waxmonsky et al. (2012).

Image 13.2 Family therapy may be effective for some children with DMDD. Parents learn to manage their children's tantrums while children learn emotion-regulation skills.

Still other sessions emphasize the need for consistency in caregiving. Parents discuss the value of regulating their children's sleep–wake cycles and daily activities. Skills are taught using a combination of videotaped vignettes of parent–child interactions and discussion.

Child sessions mirror the parent sessions. Children's behavior is monitored by therapists, and appropriate behavior is recognized and reinforced using a point system. Initial sessions focus on helping children accurately identify emotions in themselves and others. Subsequent sessions focus chiefly on anger: what it feels like, how to calm oneself when angry, and how to find nonaggressive solutions to social problems. Children learn to recognize situations, thoughts, and feelings that might elicit an angry outburst and cope with these potential "triggers" in effective ways. Skills are taught using a combination of semistructured physical activities, videotaped vignettes, games, and discussion.

An initial evaluation of the comprehensive treatment program indicated that families found it helpful in reducing children's disruptive behavior, alleviating depression, and improving the quality of parent–child interactions (Waxmonsky et al., 2012). Most children showed a marked reduction in disruptive behavior and angry outbursts, and approximately one-half of youths also showed improvements in depressive symptoms.

Sleep Enhancement

Children with DMDD often experience difficulty sleeping. In one large, epidemiological study, researchers identified youths who showed both severe mood problems and temper outbursts (Legenbauer, Heiler, Holtmann, Fricke-Oerkermann, & Lehmkuhl, 2012). These youths reported significant problems getting to sleep, staying asleep, and sleeping in a restful manner. We do not yet know if sleep problems cause irritability and anger, whether irritability has a deleterious effect on sleep, or whether a third variable, such as ADHD, might predispose youths to both angry outbursts and sleep problems.

Despite the limited data, several experts have argued that youths with DMDD should be assessed for sleep problems. If sleep difficulties exist, these youths may benefit from behavioral interventions to improve their sleep. Some basic interventions include establishing a consistent sleep–wake cycle, creating a relaxing routine prior to bedtime (e.g., washing face, brushing teeth, putting on pajamas, reading a book), and avoiding excessive stimulation that might delay sleep onset (e.g., drinking caffeinated beverages, watching television prior to bed). Clinicians hope that improving sleep hygiene and restfulness will lead to subsequent improvements in youths' ability to regulate their mood during the day.

Other experts have observed that youths with DMDD often have disrupted sleep–wake cycles (Heiler, Legenbauer, Bogen, Jensch, & Holtmann, 2011). Specifically, these youths often go to bed late, experience poor sleep quality, and have difficulty rising in the morning. To regulate these cycles and improve mood, these experts recommend chronotherapy. Chronotherapy is the deliberate, controlled presentation of light in order to regulate the sleep–wake cycle, establish better sleep quality, and improve emotional functioning.

Chronotherapy takes advantage of the fact that the human body responds physiologically to changes in the light–dark cycle. Specifically, changes in lightness and darkness are detected by the suprachiasmatic nucleus (SCN), which then regulates two hormones important to restfulness: melatonin and cortisol. Controlled studies have shown that when individuals are exposed to light immediately after waking, the light suppresses melatonin production and decreases cortisol levels, thereby, advancing the sleep–wake cycle and producing greater arousal and alertness over time. Chronotherapy, combined with improved sleep hygiene, is an effective component of the treatment for depression, bipolar disorder, and some types of anxiety. Experts hope it might be useful for youths with DMDD as well (Heiler et al., 2011).

Review:

- Traditional parent training has not been effective for youths with DMDD, because it does not specifically target children's angry outbursts and mood problems.
- Comprehensive family therapy, in which children and parents learn to manage children's tantrums and outbursts, is effective in improving children's behavior, mood, and the quality of parent–child interactions.
- Improving the quality of sleep may also help reduce DMDD symptoms although additional research is necessary.

13.2 MAJOR DEPRESSIVE DISORDER AND DYSTHYMIA
What Is Major Depressive Disorder?

To be diagnosed with major depressive disorder (MDD), a person must experience a "major depressive episode"—that is, a discrete period of dysphoria that lasts for at least 2 weeks (see Table 13.3). Specifically, people experiencing a major depressive episode must show five out of a possible nine symptoms. At least one of these symptoms must be either (a) depressed mood or (b) a diminished interest or pleasure in most activities.

1. *Depressed mood.* People with depression often feel sad, blue, or "down." Most people report these feelings directly. Other people show signs of sadness and emotional pain in their facial expressions and nonverbal behavior. Still others, especially children, express dysphoria through somatic complaints, such as headaches and upset stomach. Children and adolescents may show a predominantly irritable mood rather than a more traditional depressed mood. For example, children with depression may appear angry, touchy, easily upset, or annoyed. Parents and other adults may describe these children as crabby or cranky.

2. *Diminished interest or pleasure in most activities.* Most people with depression, regardless of age, also show a marked loss of interest or pleasure in activities they used to enjoy. Children with depression might drop out of sports or clubs. Adolescents with depression might avoid parties and other social gatherings. This loss of interest is often referred to as anhedonia—literally, a loss of pleasure.

3. *Significant change in appetite or weight.* Many people with depression show a marked decrease in appetite. These individuals often report that they "don't feel hungry," and they may need to be reminded and encouraged to eat. Their decreased appetite often leads to weight loss. In children and adolescents, failure to make age-expected weight gains meets this criterion. Some people with depression show increased appetite and weight gain. Increased appetite and weight gain are atypical and are more often seen in adults than in youths.

4. *Significant change in sleep.* The most common sleep problem among people with depression is insomnia. Typically, individuals with depression will wake in the middle of the night or during the early morning hours and be unable to return to sleep. Insomnia is one of the best predictors of mood problems in late childhood and early adolescence. In contrast, hypersomnia (i.e., sleeping too much) is more common among adults than among youths (van Lang, Ferdinand, & Verhulst, 2007).

5. *Psychomotor agitation or retardation.* Psychomotor agitation refers to a noticeable increase in motor activity. Children and adolescents with psychomotor agitation may appear restless, have problems sitting still, pace or wander about the room, or fidget with their hands or clothing. These behaviors seem to have no purpose, and they reflect an increase in children's usual activity level. Agitation must be severe enough to be observable by others. In some cases, individuals with depression show psychomotor retardation—that is, a general slowness or sluggishness in movement. Psychomotor retardation is more common in adults than in children and adolescents.

6. *Loss of energy or fatigue.* Most people with depression experience a loss of energy, tiredness, or fatigue. Adults and adolescents may report that even trivial daily tasks seem to require an enormous amount of effort. An adolescent with depression might have great difficulty getting ready for school or completing a short homework assignment. Children are less likely to report a loss of energy or fatigue than are adolescents and adults. Instead, they may appear unusually resistant or oppositional when asked to perform household chores and participate in activities with family members.

7. *Feelings of worthlessness or guilt.* Many people with depression are preoccupied by feelings of worthlessness or excessive feelings of guilt. Typically, these individuals ruminate on personal shortcomings or failures and overlook their strengths and successes. For example, a child with depression might get into frequent arguments with parents because of her irritable mood. Then, she might feel terribly guilty for having these arguments, believing that she is not worthy of her parents' love. Similarly, an adolescent with depression might fail to complete homework assignments or drop out of sports because he believes he is untalented or worthless.

Table 13.3   Diagnostic Criteria for MDD

A. Five (or more) of the following symptoms have been present during the same 2-week period and represent a change from previous functioning: at least one of the symptoms is either (1) depressed mood or (2) loss of interest or pleasure.

   1. Depressed mood most of the day, nearly every day, as indicated by either subjective report (e.g., feels sad, empty, hopeless) or observation made by others (e.g., appears tearful). Note: In children and adolescents, can be irritable mood.

   2. Marked diminished interest or pleasure in all, or almost all, activities most of the day, nearly every day (as indicated by either subjective account or observation).

   3. Significant weight loss when not dieting or weight gain (e.g., a change of more than 5% of body weight in a month), or decrease or increase in appetite nearly every day. Note: In children, consider failure to make expected weight gain.

   4. Insomnia or hypersomnia nearly every day.

   5. Psychomotor agitation or retardation nearly every day (observable by others, not merely subjective feelings of restlessness or being slowed down).

   6. Fatigue or loss of energy nearly every day.

   7. Feelings of worthlessness or excessive or inappropriate guilt nearly every day (not merely self-reproach or guilt about being sick).

   8. Diminished ability to think or concentrate, or indecisiveness, nearly every day (either by subjective account or as observed by others).

   9. Recurrent thoughts of death (not just fear of dying), recurrent suicidal ideation without a specific plan, or a suicide attempt or a specific plan for committing suicide.

B. The symptoms cause clinically significant distress or impairment in social, occupational, or other important areas of functioning.

C. The episode is not attributable to the physiological effects of a substance or to another medical condition.

   Note: Criteria A–C represent a major depressive episode.

D. The disturbance is not better explained by Schizophrenia or a psychotic disorder.[1]

E. There has never been a manic episode or hypomanic episode.

Specify course:

Single Episode: Only one major depressive episode.

Recurrent: Two or more major depressive episodes, with at least two months between episodes in which the individual does not meet criteria.

Specify current severity:

Mild: Few, if any, symptoms in excess of those required to make the diagnosis are present, the intensity of the symptoms is manageable, and the symptoms result in minor impairment.

Moderate: The number of symptoms, intensity of symptoms, and/or functional impairment are between those specified for "mild" and "severe."

Severe: The number of symptoms is substantially in excess of that required to make the diagnosis, the intensity of the symptoms is seriously distressing and unmanageable, and the symptoms markedly interfere with functioning.

Source: Reprinted with permission from the *Diagnostic and Statistical Manual of Mental Disorders, Fifth Edition* (Copyright 2013). American Psychiatric Association.

[1]Schizophrenia is presented in Chapter 14.

   8. *Thought and concentration problems.* People with depression often report problems with attention and concentration. They may be easily distracted, have problems thinking, or report difficulty making decisions. People with depression often show clouded judgment or lapses in memory. For example, adolescents with depression may have problems performing complex mental activities at school, such as writing a science report or performing a difficult musical arrangement. Children and adolescents with depression show increased difficulty in completing homework assignments and may experience a sudden drop in grades.

MAJOR DEPRESSIVE DISORDER

Hannah Misunderstood

Hannah was a 10-year-old girl who was sent to the emergency department of our hospital following a suicide attempt. The previous evening, Hannah had a fight with her mother, who had asked Hannah to clean her room. After 15 minutes of shouting, Hannah locked herself in the bathroom and swallowed an entire bottle of acetaminophen.

The pediatric psychologist at the hospital, Dr. Loebach, interviewed Hannah and her mother. According to her mother, Hannah had shown a gradual deterioration in her mood over the past several months. She had been increasingly irritable and cranky. Her mother said, "Hannah just flies off the handle for no apparent reason. I'll ask her to set the table or to turn off the TV and she'll scream, swear, or throw a tantrum. Then she'll run into her room and cry." Her mother was most concerned that Hannah might hurt herself. "Twice, I've had to stop her from banging her head against the wall. She kept crying, 'I want to die. I wish I was dead.'"

Hannah also showed problems with her behavior. In recent months, her appetite greatly decreased, and she had problems going to sleep. Hannah used to have many friends at school, but in recent months she stopped playing with peers. She dropped out of the Girl Scouts and the 4-H club, two activities that she formerly enjoyed. "She used to be the perfect child—getting good grades, helping around the house, trying to do everything to please me. Now, she deliberately tries to upset me."

Hannah's family life was stressful. Her mother had a history of depression and had attempted suicide on two occasions. Although she took antidepressant medication, she still admitted to periods of intense sadness and loneliness. Hannah's father, a photographer, had long-standing problems with alcohol dependence. According to her mother, "Hannah thinks the world of her dad, and why shouldn't she? He's really fun when he's drunk. Hannah hates me because I'm the one who makes her do her homework, pick up her room, and eat her vegetables."

Dr. Loebach attempted to interview Hannah. "I feel terrible," said Hannah, her mouth covered with charcoal residue. Dr. Loebach explained, "They needed to put that stuff in your stomach to get all the acetaminophen out of your system." Hannah said, "I didn't want to kill myself. I just wanted to show my mom that I'm serious. When I say no I mean no. She just doesn't understand how much my life sucks. No one understands."

9. *Recurrent thoughts of death or suicide.* Thoughts of death and suicide are common among people with depression, including children and adolescents. Consider Hannah, a girl with major depression.

Once a clinician determines whether a child or adolescent meets criteria for a major depressive episode, she assesses whether the child has ever experienced a depressive episode in the past. If the child's current depressive episode is the only period of time in which she experienced depression, she would be diagnosed with MDD, single episode. However, if the child had had a history of depression in the past, she would be diagnosed with MDD, recurrent. It is important to differentiate between single and recurrent depression because the latter is associated with poorer prognosis and is often more resistant to treatment (Birmaher & Brent, 2015).

Finally, the clinician determines the severity of the individual's most recent symptoms. Severity can be described as mild, moderate, or severe. Severity is based on the number of depressive symptoms the person experiences, the distress they cause, and the degree to which symptoms impair functioning (American Psychiatric Association, 2013).

Review:

- Children with MDD experience at least five symptoms of depression, including depressed mood or anhedonia, for at least 2 weeks. These symptoms cause distress or impair the child's functioning at home, school, or with friends.
- "After his ship was demasted by the enemy, the captain felt guilty." You can remember the symptoms of depression using the acronym DEMASTED + Guilt. D = depressed mood; E = eating problems; M = movement problems; A = anhedonia; S = sleep problems; T = thought/concentration problems; E = energy low; D = death/suicide + Guilt.

What Is Persistent Depressive Disorder (Dysthymia)?

In adults, persistent depressive disorder (dysthymia) is defined by the presence of chronically depressed mood, occurring most days for at least 2 years. In children and adolescents, dysthymia is characterized by chronically depressed or irritable mood that lasts at least 1 year (see Table 13.4).

Table 13.4   Diagnostic Criteria for Persistent Depressive Disorder

A. Depressed mood for most of the day, for more days than not, as indicated by either subjective account or observation by others, for at least 2 years. *Note:* In children and adolescents, mood can be irritable and duration must be at least one year.

B. Presence, while depressed, of two (or more) of the following:

1. Poor appetite or overeating.
2. Insomnia or hypersomnia.
3. Low energy or fatigue.
4. Low self-esteem.
5. Poor concentration or difficulty making decisions.
6. Feelings of hopelessness.

C. During the 2-year period (1 year in children and adolescents) of the disturbance, the individual has never been without the symptoms in criterion A and B for more than 2 months at a time.

D. Criteria for Major Depressive Disorder may be continuously present for 2 years.

E. There has never been a manic episode or a hypomanic episode, and criteria have never been met for Cyclothymic Disorder.[1]

F. The disturbance is not better explained by Schizophrenia or a psychotic disorder.[1]

G. The symptoms are not attributable to the physiological effects of a substance or another medical condition.

H. The symptoms cause clinically significant distress or impairment in social, occupational, or other important areas of functioning.

Specify if:

With pure dysthymic syndrome: Full criteria for a major depressive episode have not been met in the preceding two years.

With persistent major depressive episode: Full criteria for a major depressive episode have been met through the preceding 2-year period.

With intermittent major depressive episodes, with current episode: Full criteria for a major depressive episode are currently met, but there have been periods in the preceding 2 years with symptoms below threshold for a full major depressive episode.

With intermittent major depressive episodes, without current episode: Full criteria for a major depressive episode are not currently met, but there has been one or more major depressive episodes in the preceding 2 years.

Source: Reprinted with permission from the *Diagnostic and Statistical Manual of Mental Disorders, Fifth Edition* (Copyright 2013). American Psychiatric Association.

[1]Bipolar Disorders (including Cyclothymic Disorder) and Schizophrenia are presented in Chapter 14.

Children with dysthymia are often described as moody, sluggish, down, or cranky. Adolescents with dysthymia often regard themselves as uninteresting, unlikable, and ineffective. For example, an adolescent with dysthymia might not believe that classmates want to spend time with her or select her to be part of a group activity. Another adolescent with the disorder might doubt his ability to make a sports team or to gain admission to college. Youths with dysthymia are also prone to self-criticism. They might dwell upon their shortcomings, belittle themselves in front of others, and constantly doubt themselves and their abilities. They usually show poor self-esteem and express pessimism and hopelessness about the future.

As its name implies, persistent depressive disorder is a long-lasting condition. If we think of MDD as a severe bout of the flu, we might liken most cases of dysthymia to chronic problems with allergies. These symptoms are not as severe, but they last a long time, and they affect nearly all aspects of the person's life. The symptoms of dysthymia occur for so long that many people with the disorder do not even realize that they have mood problems. Some adults and adolescents with dysthymia see these symptoms as part of their personality, claiming, "I've always been this way" or "That's just how I am." Consider the case of Eppy.

Dysthymia can be differentiated from MDD by its onset, duration, severity, and (to some extent) its symptoms. Dysthymia usually begins gradually. In contrast, the onset of MDD is usually more rapid. By definition, dysthymia is a long-term condition, whereas MDD usually lasts for only a few months. Although MDD and dysthymia share some of the same symptoms, the symptoms of MDD are more severe. Certain symptoms like anhedonia

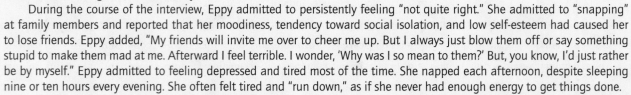

PERSISTENT DEPRESSIVE DISORDER (DYSTHYMIA)

Bad Genes

Eppy Andersen was a 16-year-old girl who was referred to our clinic by her mother. According to Mrs. Andersen, Eppy had been experiencing long-term problems with depressed mood and irritability. "For a while now," her mother explained, "Eppy's been withdrawn and moody. Sometimes, she just shuts herself in her room as soon as she gets home from school, and we don't see her again until the next morning. At other times, she just mopes around the house, never wanting to do anything with anyone. When we ask her what's wrong, she just snaps at us, 'Nothing! Can't you just leave me alone?'"

Eppy had to deal with many stressors in her childhood. Mrs. Andersen had a history of depression. Eppy's father abandoned Eppy and her mother when Eppy was in the second grade. Eppy had long-term academic problems. She earned mostly Cs and Ds, even though she studied very hard.

During the course of the interview, Eppy admitted to persistently feeling "not quite right." She admitted to "snapping" at family members and reported that her moodiness, tendency toward social isolation, and low self-esteem had caused her to lose friends. Eppy added, "My friends will invite me over to cheer me up. But I always just blow them off or say something stupid to make them mad at me. Afterward I feel terrible. I wonder, 'Why was I so mean to them?' But, you know, I'd just rather be by myself." Eppy admitted to feeling depressed and tired most of the time. She napped each afternoon, despite sleeping nine or ten hours every evening. She often felt tired and "run down," as if she never had enough energy to get things done.

Eppy denied suicidal thoughts, but she showed extreme pessimism about the future. "Nothing I do is ever good enough," she explained. "At home, my mom's always nagging me. At school, I work hard and never get anywhere. My friends don't care. I'll probably just end up like my mom—a basket case . . . or worse, like my dad." Her therapist asked, "How do you know that?" Eppy responded, "I just know. It's in the genes."

and suicidal ideation are characteristic of MDD but not dysthymia (American Psychiatric Association, 2013).

Review:

- Children with dysthymia experience chronically depressed or irritable mood for at least one year. They often regard themselves as unlikable and ineffective, are plagued by self-doubts and self-criticism, and are pessimistic about the future.
- Compared to MDD, dysthymia usually has a more gradual onset, longer duration, and lesser severity.

How Common Is Depression in Children and Adolescents?

Overall Prevalence

The prevalence of depression varies by age (Brent & Weersing, 2010). Approximately 1% to 2% of prepubescent children meet diagnostic criteria for MDD. In contrast, between 3% and 7% of adolescents have MDD at any given point in time. Moreover, as many as 20% of youths experience MDD at some time during adolescence (Birmaher & Brent, 2015).

The dramatic increase in the prevalence of depression from childhood to adolescence is largely due to a

marked increase in the number of adolescent girls with this disorder. Indeed, adolescent girls are twice as likely as adolescent boys to experience a depressive disorder. By age 18, as many as 28% of girls (compared to 14% of boys) have experienced either MDD or dysthymia (Costello, He, Sampson, Kessler, & Merikangas, 2014).

Depression in Girls

Depression is not only more common among adolescent girls but it may also be more impairing. Compared to boys, girls with depression show a greater number of symptoms, more severe symptoms, and greater likelihood of self-harm. Initial depressive episodes last longer for adolescent girls than boys and are more likely to lead to long-term mood problems (Costello & Angold, 2016).

Keenan and Hipwell (2005) developed a theoretical model to explain these gender differences. According to their model, girls who are at risk for depression have three personality characteristics that predispose them to mood problems.

First, some girls display *excessive empathy*—that is, they are unusually sensitive to the emotional well-being of others and may assume unwarranted responsibility for others' negative emotions. Consequently, girls may try to solve other people's problems and experience guilt and helplessness when they are unable to alleviate others' distress.

Second, some girls show *excessive compliance*—that is, they have a strong need to meet others' needs and to gain others' approval. Often, they sacrifice their own well-being and autonomy in order to please others. Excessive compliance can be problematic in two ways. First, depression can occur when girls comply with others' requests in situations when noncompliance might be more appropriate (e.g., a girl giving in to a boy's demands for sex). Second, depression can occur when girls repeatedly remain passive in interpersonal situations to meet the social expectations of others (e.g., a girl reluctant to speak up in class). Excessive compliance can stifle the development of autonomy and individuality and contribute to low self-esteem and self-worth.

Third, some girls show *problems with emotion regulation*—that is, have difficulty modifying and altering negative moods. Keenan and Hipwell (2005) argue that some girls have a limited number of coping strategies to deal with negative emotions. When these strategies are ineffective, they can become either excessively distressed or overcontrolled. Rather than displaying negative emotions in open and adaptive ways, these girls hide their feelings and develop mood problems.

A combination of biological and environmental factors can lead to excessive empathy, overcompliance, and emotional overcontrol in girls. Indeed, young girls are more likely than boys to display higher levels of all three risk factors (Keenan & Hipwell, 2005). These three characteristics limit girls' social and emotional competencies, especially their self-confidence, assertiveness, and emotional expressiveness. When they enter adolescence, they may be unprepared to cope with the biological and psychosocial stressors of puberty (Zahn-Waxler, 2000; Zahn-Waxler, Cole, & Barrett, 1991). Consequently, they may show rates of depression much higher than do boys.

Depression Over Time

Depressive symptoms also show moderate to high stability over time. If left untreated, the duration of depressive episodes ranges from 8 to 13 months in children and 3 to 9 months in adolescents. Relapse is fairly common (Birmaher, Arbelaez, & Brent, 2002; Birmaher et al., 2004). Approximately 60% of depressed youths have another depressive episode within 2 years after recovery, whereas 72% have another depressive episode within 5 years of recovery (Simons, Rohde, Kennard, & Robins, 2005).

Robert Post (2016) developed the kindling hypothesis to explain the tendency of depressed individuals to have recurrent depressive episodes. According to this hypothesis, early depressive episodes sensitize individuals to stressful life events and dysphoria. After multiple depressive episodes, less severe stressors can trigger major depressive symptoms. Support for the kindling hypothesis has been found in adults, but it remains largely untested in children.

In order to investigate the course of depression, researchers have conducted longitudinal studies assessing children's mood symptoms from childhood through adolescence. Based on this longitudinal research, researchers have identified four distinct patterns of mood functioning among youths (Brendgen, Wanner, Morin, & Vitaro, 2005).

First, 50% of children and adolescents show very low levels of depression across childhood and adolescence. These youngsters are at low risk for developing mood problems. Boys are the overwhelming majority of children in this group.

Second, 30% of youths show consistent but moderate levels of depressive symptoms throughout childhood and adolescence. These youths experience mild dysphoria, but their mood problems usually do not interfere with day-to-day activities. Boys outnumber girls in this group as well.

Third, 10% of youths show chronically high levels of depression, beginning in late childhood and continuing through adolescence. These youngsters are disproportionately girls with histories of early parent–child conflict and difficulties with emotion regulation. These girls often show difficult temperaments that interfere with their social and emotional functioning. They are at risk for long-term problems with mood and behavior.

The remaining 10% of youths show low levels of depressive symptoms in childhood but dramatically higher levels of depression in adolescence. These youngsters also tend to be girls with difficult temperaments and histories of parent–child conflict. However, they frequently experience peer rejection and social alienation during late childhood or early adolescence. It is likely that peer rejection and other psychosocial stressors of puberty exacerbate social and emotional problems in this group of children.

Taken together, these findings indicate that approximately 20% of youths will have mood problems during childhood or adolescence. This is consistent with other longitudinal research that suggests that 20% of youths show moderate to long-term mood problems. Indeed, youths with depression are 4 times more likely to experience mood disorders in adulthood compared to their nondepressed peers (Hammen, Rudolph, & Abaied, 2014).

Review:

- Approximately 1% to 2% of prepubescent children experience a depressive disorder. Prevalence increases markedly in adolescence, especially for girls; as many as 14% of adolescent boys and 28% of adolescent girls experience depression.
- Youths who experience a depressive episode are at risk for another depressive episode in the future.
- As many as 20% of youths experience depression in adolescence and are at risk for recurrent mood problems in adulthood.

What Genetic and Biological Factors Contribute to Childhood Depression?

Genes and Neurotransmitters

Depression is a heritable condition. The concordance of monozygotic (MZ) twins reared together ranges from 70%

to 85%. Moreover, the concordance of MZ twins reared apart is almost as high: between 65% and 70%. In contrast, dizygotic (DZ) twins reared together show only about 19% concordance for the disorder. Taken together, these findings indicate that genetic factors place individuals at considerable risk for depression. Having a parent with depression increases one's risk of developing the disorder threefold (Reinecke & Simons, 2005).

It is likely that genetic factors contribute to depression by affecting children's neurotransmitter functioning. The monoamine hypothesis for depression asserts that two neurotransmitters play roles in depressive disorders: (1) serotonin and (2) norepinephrine. These neurotransmitters are monoamines, hence the name of the hypothesis. According to the theory, depression is associated with dysregulation in one or both of these neurotransmitters.

Evidence for the monoamine hypothesis comes primarily from research with adults. The hypothesis is supported by the fact that antidepressant medications, which regulate serotonin and/or norepinephrine, can alleviate depression in adults. Adolescents treated with certain antidepressant medications can also show changes in serotonin functioning; furthermore, the magnitude of these changes is directly associated with the degree of adolescents' symptom reduction (Axelson et al., 2005).

Other evidence for the monoamine hypothesis comes from molecular genetics research. Eley and colleagues (2004) examined genes responsible for serotonergic functioning. They discovered a number of genes that predicted depression in adolescent girls. Furthermore, some of the genes predicted depression only when girls also experienced adverse life events. The authors argued that genes responsible for serotonergic activity play roles in the emergence of depression in youths. However, these genes may require certain adverse environmental conditions to produce their harmful effects.

Temperament

A second mechanism by which genes might contribute to the development of mood problems is through temperament. Recall that temperament refers to the physiological, emotional, and behavioral responses a child typically displays when she encounters novel stimuli (Stifter & Dollar, 2016). Temperament is largely genetically determined; however, it can be modified by children's early experiences.

Temperament can contribute to the development of mood disorders in at least three ways (Compas, Connor-Smith, & Jaser, 2004). First, difficult temperament can contribute to children's depressive symptoms by increasing negative emotions. Children with difficult temperament (e.g., excessive irritability, moodiness) often overreact to negative life events and have difficulty regulating their emotions. They may simply experience more frequent and intense levels of negative affect than other children their age.

Second, difficult temperament in childhood may elicit negative reactions from caregivers and peers. For example, irritability in early childhood might lead caregivers to adopt more angry, hostile, and coercive parenting tactics. These adverse parenting behaviors can cause parent–child conflict, behavior problems, and depression.

Third, children with difficult temperaments may show greater problems coping with early childhood stressors. These coping problems, in turn, can contribute to mood problems. For example, children with difficult temperaments may become overwhelmed when they encounter stressful life events. When faced with a psychosocial stressor, these children might show high levels of anger. Alternatively, other children with difficult temperaments may avoid coping with the stressor altogether by emotionally shutting down, withdrawing, or developing anxiety and depression.

Hypothalamus-Pituitary-Adrenal Dysregulation

Early childhood stressors can contribute to later mood problems by affecting the body's stress response system. Recall that the body's response to stress is regulated by the hypothalamus-pituitary-adrenal (HPA) axis. When the child encounters a psychosocial stressor, brain regions that process and regulate emotions (especially the amygdala and hippocampus) activate the HPA axis. When activated, components of the HPA axis cause a release of cortisol, the body's main stress hormone. Cortisol activates the sympathetic nervous system, initiates fight-or-flight response, and increases feelings of alertness and apprehension.

In typically developing individuals, cortisol flows through the bloodstream and is detected by the hypothalamus, pituitary, and hippocampus. These brain regions shut off production of cortisol, returning the body to a more relaxed state. However, adults with depression often show chronically high levels of cortisol. Furthermore, they often have difficulties stopping cortisol production once it starts. For example, if researchers give adults with depression a synthetic form of cortisol (i.e., dexamethasone), many adults do not show the normal "shutting off" of cortisol production. In fact, as many as 60% of depressed adults do not pass this dexamethasone suppression test (DST) and show chronically high levels of cortisol, even when not experiencing an immediate stressor. This dysregulation of the HPA axis is believed to partially explain their depressed mood (Shea, Walsh, MacMillan, & Steiner, 2005).

Depressed youths may also show dysregulation of the HPA axis. First, many depressed youths show elevated cortisol activity, even while at rest. Second, some depressed adolescents show structural abnormalities in parts of the HPA axis. Compared to healthy adolescents, depressed adolescents show smaller amygdalae and hippocampi, and enlarged pituitary (MacMaster & Kusumakar, 2004; Rosso et al., 2005).

Review:

- Depression is highly heritable; MZ twin concordance is approximately .70 to .85.

- The neurotransmitters most often implicated in childhood depression are the monoamines: serotonin and norepinephrine. Most antidepressant medications affect these neurotransmitters.
- Young children who inherit difficult temperaments are at risk for depression later in life, either directly (by increasing negative emotions) or indirectly (by affecting parent–child interactions or the child's coping skills).
- Some youths with depression show dysregulation of the HPA axis, the body's stress response system.

What Behavioral and Cognitive Factors Contribute to Childhood Depression?

Stressful Life Events

Stressful life events are associated with child and adolescent depression. Several studies have shown that major life stressors predict the onset of MDD. Furthermore, depressed children and adolescents report more frequent and serious stressful life events than their nondepressed peers. In fact, children's risk of depression is directly associated with the number of stressful life events that they encounter (Hammen et al., 2014). The timing of stressful life events may also be important. Events that occur during adolescence seem to be especially problematic (Ge, Coger, & Elder, 2001).

Although stressful life events are associated with depression in youths, they are not robust predictors of depression. On average, stressful life events explain only 2% of the variance in adolescents' depressive symptoms (Garber, Keiley, & Martin, 2002; Lewinsohn et al., 1994). Furthermore, the importance of stressful life events in triggering depressive episodes may diminish over time. Lewinsohn and colleagues (Lewinsohn, Allen, Gotlib, & Seeley, 1999) found that adolescents' first depressive episodes were strongly associated with a negative life event. However, later depressive episodes were less closely connected to psychosocial stressors.

Although stressful life events and depression are correlated, stressful life events may not necessarily *cause* adolescents to become depressed. Waaktaar, Borge, Fundingsrud, Christie, and Torgersen (2004) assessed adolescents' depressive symptoms and stressful life events at two times, approximately one year apart. Consistent with previous research, they found a moderate correlation between depressive symptoms and life stressors. Contrary to expectations, however, the researchers discovered that early symptoms of depression predicted *later* stressful life events.

The researchers suggested that the traditional view—that stressful events cause depression—is too simplistic. Instead, the relationship between stressful events and depression may be bidirectional. Of course, stressful events can contribute to depression. However, depressed youths may also elicit stressful events from the environment (Hammen, Shih, & Brennan, 2004). For example, children who are rejected by peers may experience depression.

Depression, in turn, can lead to social avoidance and increased feelings of loneliness.

Beck's Cognitive Theory of Depression

Contemporary models of child and adolescent depression emphasize the role of cognition in the emergence and maintenance of depressive symptoms (Reinecke & Simons, 2005). According to cognitive models, early stressful experiences adversely affect the way children think about themselves and their surroundings. These experiences also color the attributions they make about other people's behavior and the way they interpret events. Cognitions, in turn, can affect children's moods (Mezulis, Hyde, & Abramson, 2006).

Aaron Beck (1967, 1976) developed a model of depression that focuses primarily on people's cognitions. According to Beck, thoughts, feelings, and actions are intricately connected. The way people think influences the way they feel and act. Beck posited that individuals who are depressed show two characteristic ways of thinking that predispose them to negative emotions and maladaptive behaviors: cognitive biases and cognitive distortions.

First, people with depression often show *cognitive biases*. A bias is a cognitive shift toward looking at the world in a certain way. People with depression show a negative cognitive bias in their view of themselves, the world, and the future. Although these people encounter pleasant and unpleasant experiences every day, they tend to selectively attend to negative experiences while ignoring or dismissing positive aspects about themselves and their surroundings. For example, an adolescent with depression might dwell upon a low grade that she receives on a particular math exam rather than on her otherwise good performance in math class.

Second, people with depression show cognitive distortions. A cognitive distortion involves adjusting one's perceptions or interpretations of the world in a manner that is inconsistent with reality. Individuals with depression interpret events in an excessively negative light, causing them to feel helpless and hopeless (Wells, 2013). For example, after receiving a low grade on a math exam, an adolescent with depression might believe that she is "stupid" and that she will "never get into college." These distortions are untrue; one low math grade is not sufficient evidence that someone is stupid. Furthermore, one low grade will probably not affect one's chances of gaining college admission. These beliefs reflect distortions of reality that confirm the adolescent's view that she is worthless, that the world is cruel, and that the future is bleak.

According to Beck (1967, 1976), cognitive distortions are especially salient in people's negative automatic thoughts about themselves, the world, and the future. Automatic thoughts are transient self-statements or images that pop into people's minds immediately after they experience a psychosocial stressor. For example, after missing a game-winning free throw, a child might think to himself, "I'm such a loser" or "Nothing I do ever goes right." Alternatively, he might have a mental image of his friends or family members teasing or ostracizing him for missing the basket. These transient negative thoughts color people's interpretation of events and can contribute to feelings of depression.

Depressed children and adolescents show both cognitive biases and distortions. Furthermore, the number of cognitive biases and distortions shown by youths is associated with the severity of their depressive symptoms. Depressed youths typically report more negative automatic thoughts than their emotionally healthy peers. Furthermore, depressed youths tend to dwell upon their negative thoughts and personal failures. The negative automatic thoughts reported by depressed youths differ from the automatic thoughts reported by youths with other disorders. For example, depressed youths frequently report beliefs characterized by personal loss and failure, whereas anxious youths are more likely to report automatic thoughts about threat and personal vulnerability (Wells, 2013).

Depressogenic Attributions

Martin Seligman (1975) hypothesized that feelings of helplessness contribute to the emergence of depression. In a now-famous study, Seligman and colleagues attempted to condition fear in dogs by restraining them and administering a mild electrical shock. The researchers expected that when the restraints were removed, the dogs would actively avoid the shock by jumping away. To their surprise, the previously restrained dogs passively succumbed to shocks even when they were given the opportunity to escape or avoid them. Seligman believed the dogs learned to endure the shocks. Since the dogs had no control over the shocks, they were unmotivated to avoid the shocks later when given the opportunity.

Seligman proposed that learned helplessness might explain depression in humans (Hiroto & Seligman, 1975). He suggested that people who are exposed to stressful but apparently uncontrollable life events would become passive and depressed. They would not actively cope with stressors but, instead, succumb to feelings of pain and despair.

Later, Abramson, Seligman, and Teasdale (1978) adjusted the learned helplessness theory of depression to explain *how* negative life events can contribute to depressed mood. They suggested that the attributions we make about success and failure in our lives affect our mood. Specifically, depressed individuals attribute *negative* events to internal, stable, and global factors. For example, if an adolescent boy asks a girl for a date and she turns him down, he might attribute his rejection to internal, stable, and global factors. He might reason that he was rejected because he is ugly (internal); he will always be ugly (stable); and no one, no matter how desperate, will ever want to go out with someone as ugly as him (global). This depressogenic attributional style can lead to feelings of helplessness, hopelessness, and depression.

Depressed people also tend to attribute *positive* life events to external, unstable, and specific causes. For example, if a child with depression gets an A on an exam,

she might attribute her success to the fact that the teacher is an easy grader (external), that she was lucky (unstable), or that she just happened to study the information that was on the exam (specific). These attributions can contribute to her negative mood and low self-regard.

Most research has shown a relationship between depressogenic attributional styles and depressed mood in adults. Similarly, depressed children and adolescents show pessimistic attributions for negative events (Hammen, Hazel, Brennan, & Najman, 2014).

Only recently have researchers looked for the source of children's depressogenic attributions (Stevens & Prinstein, 2005). Available data indicate at least three possible causes. First, negative life events can cause youths to adopt depressogenic attributional styles (Gibb, Abramson, & Alloy, 2004). For example, children who are physically or sexually abused can erroneously blame themselves for their victimization and view maltreatment as stable and pervasive (Harkness, Bruce, & Lumley, 2006).

Second, depressed mood, itself, might cause depressogenic attributions (Nolen-Hoeksema, Girgus, & Seligman, 1992). When adolescents feel helpless, they may begin to attribute failure to internal, stable, and global causes and attribute success to external, unstable, and specific factors. Depression, therefore, may beget depressogenic thoughts.

Third, and perhaps most interestingly, depressogenic attributions can be acquired though friends. The peer contagion model posits that depression, like a cold, can be acquired through close contact with peers. As friends share secrets and talk about stressors in their lives, they may inadvertently model and reinforce depressive symptoms and depressogenic attributions. In one large study, sixth to eighth graders often adopted the depressive symptoms and attributional styles of their best friends. Friends maintain each others' depressive symptoms by corroborating depressogenic attributions or avoiding other positive social experiences (Stevens & Prinstein, 2005).

Review:

- Stressful life events are directly correlated with children's depressive symptoms.
- According to Beck's cognitive theory of depression, cognitive biases and distortions contribute to a negative view of self, world, and the future.
- The reformulated learned helplessness model posits that depression occurs when we attribute negative events to internal, stable, and global causes.

How Might Parents and Peers Contribute to Childhood Depression?

Children's relationship with parents can also affect their likelihood of developing depression. Although a number of parenting variables can place youths at risk for depression or buffer them from the deleterious effects of psychosocial stressors, three of the most important variables are (1) the quality of parent–child attachment, (2) parents' social–emotional health, and (3) conflict in the home (Yap, Pilkington, Ryan, Kelly, & Jorm, 2014).

Parent–Child Attachment

According to the principles of attachment theory, children construct mental representations or internal working models of caregivers during the first few years of life (Bowlby, 1969, 1980). These mental representations are based on the quality of parent–child interactions during infancy and childhood. Children whose parents provide sensitive and responsive care come to expect accessibility and responsiveness from others. In contrast, children whose parents provide intrusive or unresponsive care come to expect that others will be inaccessible or unavailable in times of stress or crisis.

As children grow, they apply the internal working models developed in infancy and early childhood to other important interpersonal relationships in their lives. Children who develop secure attachment relationships with early caregivers come to expect sensitive and responsive treatment from other adults, teachers, and peers. Alternatively, children who develop insecure relationships in early childhood may anticipate that others will be dismissive, unavailable, or uncaring. The internal working models, therefore, serve as social–emotional templates for understanding and predicting future relationships.

Attachment theorists have suggested that insecure attachments in infancy and early childhood predispose children to social–emotional problems later in life. Indeed, research has shown a significant correlation between insecure attachment and mood problems among children and adolescents (Hammen et al., 2014). Insecure attachment in infancy and early childhood can place youths at risk for mood problems in one of two ways. First, children and adolescents who hold insecure representations of caregivers also report feelings of low self-worth and low self-confidence (Hankin & Abela, 2005). These youngsters derive self-esteem from their accomplishments and approval by others, rather than from an intrinsic sense of self-worth (Shirk, Gudmundsen, & Burwell, 2005). They need attention and reassurance from caregivers to maintain a sense of worthiness and self-confidence (Abela et al., 2005).

Second, adolescents who hold insecure representations of caregivers do not rely on others for support in times of crisis (Shirk et al., 2005). Although these individuals appear self-reliant under usual circumstances, they may feel isolated and overwhelmed when negative events occur. Children with histories of insecure attachment may be reluctant to seek help from parents or teachers to solve personal problems. Adolescents with insecure attachment histories often underutilize social support networks. Excessive self-reliance predisposes youths to isolation, loneliness, and depression.

Maternal Depression

The children of depressed mothers are at risk for depression themselves. As many as 60% of the children of depressed parents show depression by young adulthood. The risk for depression is 6 times greater for the children of depressed mothers compared to the offspring of nondepressed women. The relationship between mother and child depression is complex and not fully understood. However, there are three general approaches to explaining the transmission of depression across generations (Pearson et al., 2013; Raposa, Hammen, Brennan, & Najman, 2014).

First, some research suggests there might be a genetic component to the relationship between parent and child depression. It is possible that depressed mothers and their offspring share similar genes that predispose them both to mood disorders (Lewis, Collishaw, Thapar, & Harold, 2014).

Second, maternal stress during pregnancy might compromise the development of children's neurological and endocrine systems. These developmental problems, in turn, can lead to childhood depression. For example, women's anxiety levels during gestation predict their offspring's ability to regulate cortisol during late childhood. Maternal stress hormones during pregnancy might adversely affect the development of their children's HPA axis. Furthermore, women's levels of depression shortly after delivery predicted their children's cortisol levels and regulation during childhood and adolescence. Being cared for by a depressed parent early in life places considerable stress on infants. This increased stress might lead to dysregulation of the HPA axis and later mood problems (Apter-Levi et al., 2016; Laurent et al., 2013).

The intergenerational interpersonal stress model of depression offers a third explanation for the relationship between parent and child depression. According to this model, children of depressed mothers experience two problems. First, they must face many of the same family stressors that contribute to their mothers' depression, such as high family conflict or socioeconomic hardship. Second, the children of depressed mothers are not taught effective problem-solving and social skills to cope with these stressors. Instead, depressed parents often model ineffective problem-solving skills and discipline their children in less-than-optimal ways. Consequently, the children of depressed mothers often display behavior problems and show difficulty in interpersonal relationships themselves. These difficulties, in turn, lead to their own problems with depression and low self-worth (Hammen et al., 2012).

Several studies have supported the intergenerational interpersonal stress model. For example, longitudinal research shows that maternal depression is associated with more hostile and less responsive parenting behavior. This negative parenting behavior subsequently predicts childhood depression. Furthermore, Hammen and colleagues (2004) found the relationship between maternal depression and children's mood problems was explained by mothers' tendencies to use parenting techniques characterized by low warmth and high hostility. Family stress and problematic parenting predicted adolescents' mood problems (Hammen et al., 2014).

Other researchers have examined the role that peers play in child and adolescent depression. Harry Stack Sullivan (1953) described the importance of peer relationships to the emotional well-being of children. He claimed that children develop the capacity for empathy and emotional autonomy through their friendships in late childhood and adolescence. Through interactions with peers, children learn the emotional give-and-take that characterizes healthy, intimate adult relationships. Children also learn about themselves and develop a sense of identity. For example, children compare themselves to peers to determine their strengths and weaknesses. They also derive self-esteem from friends' acceptance of their personality, values, and beliefs (Millings, Buck, Montgomery, Spears, & Stallard, 2013; Steiger, Allemand, Robins, & Fend, 2014).

Empirical research has shown that acceptance by peers is important to children's self-concept and emotional well-being. Children who are rejected or victimized by peers are more likely to show depressive symptoms. Both physical victimization (e.g., physical bullying) and relational aggression (e.g., teasing, spreading rumors) are associated with depression in boys and girls. In one study, relational aggression predicted adolescent depression better than physical aggression (LaGreca & Harrison, 2005). This finding contradicts the old saying about "sticks and stones." It also suggests that school-based interventions designed to reduce bullying must target both physical and verbal aggression in order to prevent children's mood problems (Litwack, Aikins, & Cillessen, 2012).

Prinstein and Aikins (2004) showed how the relationship between peer rejection and depression is moderated by adolescents' thoughts. As expected, peer rejection predicted later depressive symptoms in a sample of tenth graders. However, the relationship was strongest for adolescents who (a) also showed depressogenic attributional styles and (b) placed a great deal of importance on peer acceptance. The researchers suggested that adolescents who attribute peer rejection to internal, stable, and global causes (e.g., "I'm no good") are more likely to become depressed than adolescents who hold less pessimistic attributions for their rejection (e.g., "The other kids are jerks"). Furthermore, adolescents who are rejected, but who desperately want to be accepted by peers, may be especially prone to depression. The study is significant because it shows how cognitive factors can moderate the effects of psychosocial stressors on adolescents' moods.

Friendships and romantic relationships can also be stressful to adolescents. Friendships characterized by conflict or coercion can negatively affect the emotional well-being of adolescents and contribute to depression. Stressful romantic relationships during adolescence also predict depressive symptoms (Ha, Dishion, Overbeek, Burk, & Engels, 2014).

What about the positive effects of peer relationships? Can peers buffer adolescents from other psychosocial stressors by offering them a source of support? The answer appears to be no. In their review of the adolescent depression literature, Burton, Stice, and Seeley (2004) found very little evidence supporting the idea that positive peer relationships protect children from the effects of other psychosocial stress. However, problematic peer relationships did independently predict depression. Although the buffering effect of peer relationships seems intuitive, it may not have much empirical support (Chow, Ruhl, & Buhrmester, 2015).

Social Information Processing

In previous chapters, we examined how biases in children's information processing can lead to externalizing behavior problems. Dodge, Godwin, and the Conduct Problems Prevention Research Group (2013) found that aggressive boys tend to show hostile attributional biases when solving interpersonal problems. These boys interpret others' benign behavior as malevolent, and they rely on hostile strategies to resolve interpersonal disputes.

Recently, some authors have applied similar information-processing models to explain childhood depression (Prinstein, Cheah, & Guyer, 2005). According to the social information-processing theory of depression, children with depression display two types of biases when solving interpersonal problems (see Figure 13.2). First, like aggressive children, depressed children attribute hostile intentions to other people's ambiguous behavior. For example, imagine that a child is playing outside during recess. While playing, a peer kicks a soccer ball, and it hits the child in the head. The child might show a hostile attributional bias by believing that he was hit on purpose.

Second, children with depression often show internal and stable attributions—that is, they attribute social problems or failures to internal and stable causes. For example, the child who is hit by the soccer ball might blame himself for his perceived victimization (e.g., "He hit me in the head because he doesn't like me. I'm no fun to be with").

The social information-processing model of depression suggests that depressed children interpret others' behavior as hostile and attribute others' hostile actions to their own shortcomings. These cognitions can influence children's long-term self-perceptions and social behaviors. Children who adopt these information-processing biases are likely to avoid social situations and view themselves negatively. They are at risk for peer rejection and victimization, which, in turn, can lead to more hostile and depressogenic problem-solving (Black & Pössel, 2013).

Review:

- Children who develop insecure attachment relationships with their caregivers, or whose caregivers are depressed, are at risk for depression.
- Peer rejection can place youths at risk for depression.
- Children at risk for depression often show social information-processing biases; they may view others' actions as hostile and blame themselves for their own victimization.

Figure 13.2   Social Information-Processing Theory of Depression

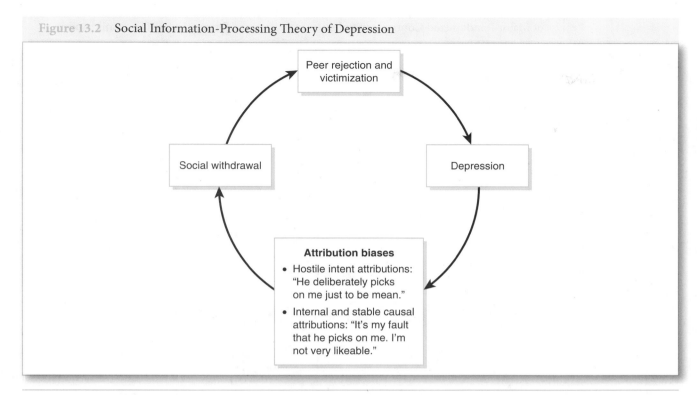

Source: Based on Prinstein et al. (2005).

Note: Children at risk for depression believe that (a) other people have hostile intentions and (b) other people's hostility is their fault. Consequently, these children withdraw from social situations, causing them to experience peer rejection, teasing, and depression.

Is Medication Effective and Safe for Children With Depression?

Effectiveness

Until the early 1990s, the pharmaceutical treatment of depression in children and adolescents was limited. Most physicians prescribed tricyclic antidepressants. These medications, which affect levels of serotonin and norepinephrine, included amitriptyline (Elavil), desipramine (Norpramin), and imipramine (Tofranil). Tricyclic antidepressants were effective in treating depression in adults. However, two meta-analyses revealed that tricyclic antidepressants were largely ineffective in reducing depressive symptoms in youths, especially prepubescent children. This is probably because the serotonin and norepinephrine neurotransmitter systems upon which these medications work are not fully developed until late adolescence or early adulthood. Researchers also discovered that tricyclic antidepressants caused severe side effects in some children, including cardiac arrhythmia, suicidal behavior, and death. In one study, 14% of youths taking imipramine reported cardiovascular side effects that caused them to discontinue the medication (Hazell & Mirzaie, 2013).

In the early 1990s, physicians began prescribing selective serotonin reuptake inhibitors (SSRIs) to youths with depression. These medications slow the reuptake of serotonin, allowing the neurotransmitter to remain in the synaptic cleft for longer periods of time. Meta-analysis indicates that SSRIs are superior to placebo in alleviating depression in children and adolescents (see Figure 13.3). On average, 60% of youths respond to SSRIs, whereas 49% improve with placebo. The overall effect size (ES) of SSRIs is small, mostly because approximately one-half of depressed children and adolescents improve when taking placebo rather than actual medication (Bridge et al., 2007).

Currently, the only SSRI that has received FDA approval for the treatment of depression in children is fluoxetine (Prozac). Three published studies of youths with depression have compared fluoxetine to placebo. All three studies have shown fluoxetine to be superior in reducing depressive symptoms with minimal side effects. Despite these results, the efficacy of fluoxetine in children and adolescents has been questioned. First, the magnitude of the difference between youths taking fluoxetine versus placebo is somewhat small. For example, in one study, approximately 65% of youths improved with fluoxetine compared to approximately 52% with placebo. Although fluoxetine decreases children's depressive symptoms, some of its benefits can be attributed to placebo. Second, the superiority of fluoxetine over placebo depends partially on *who* is reporting children's symptoms. In another study, medication was associated with symptom reduction when reported by clinicians, but *not* when reported by

Figure 13.3   Results of Major Randomized Controlled Studies Investigating the Efficacy of SSRIs on Child and Adolescent Depression

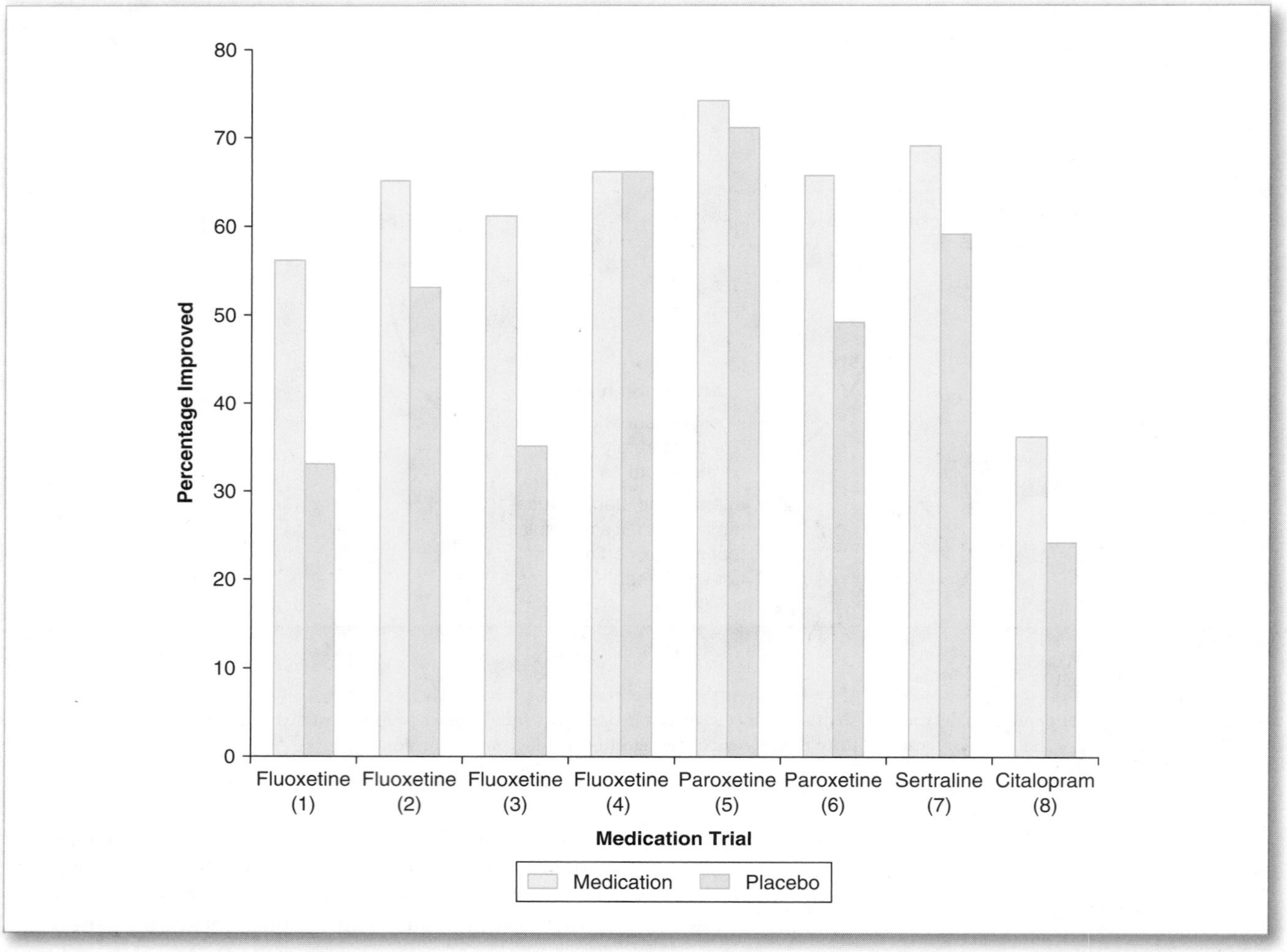

Source: Based on (1) Emslie et al. (1997); (2) Emslie et al. (2002); (3) TADS (2004); (4) Simeon, Dinicola, Ferguson, and Copping (1990); (5) Milin, Walker, and Chow (2003); (6) Keller et al. (2001); (7) Wagner et al. (2003); (8) Wagner, Berard et al. (2004).

Note: In general, only fluoxetine (Prozac) is associated with consistent improvement in depressive symptoms with minimal side effects. However, most SSRIs (including fluoxetine) perform only slightly better than placebo.

parents or children. Third, the superiority of fluoxetine over placebo may be largely due to its efficacy in reducing symptoms of comorbid anxiety, not depression per se (Hazell & Mirzaie, 2013).

Two other SSRIs have also been shown to be superior to placebo in treating pediatric depression. The first study showed that 69% of depressed children improved after using sertraline (Zoloft) compared to 59% of children receiving placebo. Again, the magnitude of the difference between children receiving the medication versus placebo was small. Furthermore, citalopram (Celexa) was more effective than placebo in reducing depression among children and adolescents. However, only 36% of the sample responded to citalopram. A second study of citalopram did not demonstrate its superiority over placebo (Hetrick, McKenzie, Cox, Simmons, & Merry, 2012).

Other antidepressant medications have *not* been shown to be superior to placebo in treating child or adolescent depression. Five large, randomized controlled studies of the SSRIs paroxetine (Paxil) and escitalopram (Lexapro) have shown these medications to be no better than placebo in reducing core depressive symptoms. Venlafaxine ER (Effexor), a medication that inhibits the reuptake of both serotonin and norepinephrine, has also been shown in two independent trials to be equivalent to placebo in treating childhood depression (Hazell & Mirzaie, 2013; Hetrick et al., 2012).

Safety

Approximately fifteen years ago, there was concern that certain antidepressant medications might increase the risk of suicidal thoughts and actions in youths with depression. In 2004, the US Food and Drug Administration (FDA) issued a public warning indicating children and adolescents prescribed SSRIs might be at increased risk for suicidal ideation and suicide attempts (Gibbons et al., 2015).

The National Institute of Mental Health (NIMH) subsequently reviewed the existing research literature on the association between antidepressants and suicidality. The researchers found no suicidal deaths among 2,200 children and adolescents prescribed SSRIs. However, 4% of youths taking SSRIs experienced increased suicidal thinking, a rate approximately twice as high as youths taking placebo. The researchers concluded that the benefits of SSRIs likely outweigh the risk of increased suicidality for youths with depression. However, youths taking SSRIs must be carefully monitored by their parents and physicians. In response, the FDA issued a "black-box" warning on antidepressants, indicating that these medications may increase suicidal thoughts in children and adolescents (see Image 13.4).

Other research confirms the benefits of SSRIs. In the largest clinical trial conducted so far, more youths with depression improved after receiving SSRI plus CBT (71%), or SSRI alone (61%), than either CBT alone (43%), or placebo (35%). Furthermore, the greatest reduction in suicidal thinking was seen among youths receiving SSRI plus CBT (Treatment for Adolescents With Depression Study Team, 2004).

More recently, researchers investigated the effects of antidepressants on adolescents who had previously attempted suicide. Results showed that youths who received medication, either with or without CBT, did not experience greater risk for suicidality than youths who received CBT alone. Furthermore, youths receiving any treatment experienced a reduction in depressive symptoms and suicidal thoughts (Tureki & Brent, 2016). Altogether, these findings indicate that SSRIs are effective in improving depression in children and adolescents, but must be used cautiously.

Review:

- On average, 60% of youths with depression respond to SSRIs whereas only 49% respond to placebo. Only fluoxetine (Prozac) is FDA approved for treating childhood depression.
- SSRIs are associated with a slightly higher risk for increased suicidal thoughts (4%) than placebo (2%).

What Evidence-Based Psychotherapies Are Available for Youths With Depression?

Cognitive–Behavioral Therapy for Children

Although cognitive–behavioral therapy (CBT) for depression is typically offered as a single treatment "package," it actually consists of two components. First, cognitive therapy for depression is based on the notion that maladaptive patterns in thinking contribute to people's depressed mood. In cognitive therapy, clients learn more realistic, flexible ways to perceive themselves, others, and the future (Beidel & Reinecke, 2015).

Second, behavior therapy for depression is based on the idea that depression is caused by a lack of response-contingent reinforcement (Lewinsohn, 1974). Specifically, people become depressed when they are unable to derive pleasure or satisfaction from their surroundings. For example, adolescents who lack adequate social or communication skills may frequently argue with parents and isolate themselves from peers. Consequently, they may spend much of their time alone, deriving little satisfaction from interpersonal relationships. Over time, they may become depressed and show even greater social isolation. Behavior therapists try to improve adolescents' social and communication skills, increase their level of social activity, and teach them to reward themselves for their successes and accomplishments.

Image 13.3   FDA Black-Box Warning for Antidepressant Medication

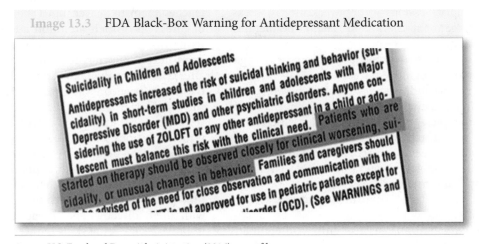

Source: U.S. Food and Drug Administration (2016); www.fda.org.

Image 13.4　Bullying and cyberbullying are unique predictors of suicidality. In contrast, youths who feel connected to their family, peers, and school are at low-risk for suicide and self-harm.

Source: Istockphoto.com: 63905383

There are many cognitive–behavioral interventions for youths with depression. We will examine two of the best-studied treatments: (1) Stark's CBT for school-age children and (2) the Adolescent Coping With Depression (CWD-A) course.

One of the first CBT packages developed for depressed children was created by Kevin Stark and colleagues (Stark & Kendall, 1996; Stark et al., 2005). The goal of treatment was to change children's problematic ways of thinking and to increase their satisfaction with themselves, others, and their surroundings. To accomplish this task, the therapist teaches children social, emotional, and behavioral skills so that they can effectively cope with negative feelings, solve problems, and interact with others. Treatment is conducted in small groups consisting of school-age children and a therapist. Sessions occur biweekly for 10 weeks.

In Stark's treatment (Stark et al., 2005), the therapist teaches four basic skills: (1) recognizing and understanding emotions, (2) solving social problems, (3) coping with negative feelings, and (4) cognitive restructuring. The first goal of therapy is to help children recognize and label emotions. Many children with depression have difficulty labeling their feelings. For example, some children can only differentiate "happy" and "sad." The therapist might use emotion flash cards, charades, or role play to teach children to differentiate within these mood states. For example, the facial expressions and physical sensations that accompany the feeling "embarrassed" are different from those that characterize feeling "angry" or "left out."

After children are able to recognize, differentiate, and label emotions, they learn basic problem-solving skills. That is, children must learn what to do when they feel embarrassed, angry, or left out. Many children with depression feel overwhelmed by their negative emotional states and withdraw from family and peers. Other children express their negative emotions directly, through acting out or aggression. The goal of problem-solving training is to help children actively address social problems and the mood states they engender.

In problem-solving training, children are taught to systematically identify a social problem, brainstorm possible solutions, evaluate each solution, select and implement the best course of action, and evaluate outcomes (Dodge et al., 2013). In addition, problem-solving training for children with depression has two unique components. First, when children identify the problem, the therapist teaches them to "psych-up" (Stark et al., 2005, p. 249), or direct all of their attention and energy to solving it. Psyching-up helps children feel more empowered to confront and solve social problems and less hopeless. Second, after children evaluate the consequences of their actions, the therapist encourages them to reward their problem-solving efforts. Children are encouraged to praise themselves for their attempts at solving social problems, even if their solutions are not 100% effective.

Cognitive–behavioral therapists also teach coping skills. Many children with depression lack the ability to regulate their emotions. When they feel sad or helpless, they ruminate on their feelings rather than try to cope with them directly. The therapist might help children improve their coping skills in three ways. First, she might teach specific coping strategies, like relaxation. Second, she might ask children to interview their nondepressed peers and find out how these children cope with negative moods and everyday hassles. Third, she might ask children to actively plan pleasurable activities during the week so that they can experience positive emotions. For example, she might encourage children to go to a movie with friends or to a sporting event with family (Beidel & Reinecke, 2015).

Finally, therapists use cognitive restructuring—that is, they attempt to challenge and alter the cognitive biases and distortions that maintain children's negative moods. Stark and colleagues (2005) discuss a number of games to help children look at themselves, others, and the future more objectively. In *What's the Evidence?*, children must provide empirical support for their negative thinking. If a child is earning a low grade in reading class, she might conclude that she is not very smart. The therapist might challenge her conclusion by asking her for evidence to support her claim and by challenging her to provide evidence to the contrary (i.e., that she *is* smart). Although she may have trouble in reading, she may be extremely talented in art or math.

In another cognitive game, *Alternative Interpretations*, the therapist challenges children's automatic thoughts about ambiguous events by asking them to consider other ways of viewing the event. If a child is ignored by her classmates while walking down the hallway at school, she might conclude that her classmates are upset with her. The therapist might challenge this cognitive distortion and encourage her to consider other possibilities for their behavior: Perhaps her friends were late for class and in a hurry, or perhaps they did not see her.

A third strategy is to use the *What If* technique. Therapists use this technique to combat the unreasonable expectations children place on themselves, and their tendency to engage in catastrophic thinking. For example, a boy who earns low grades might think, "Oh, no. Now I'll never make the honor roll, and my parents are going to kill me!" The therapist might ask *what if* he does not make the honor roll; will his parents actually kill him? Will they disown him? Will they stop loving him?

Controlled studies of CBT for children with depression have shown it to be more effective than placebo and nondirective therapy. However, CBT may be equally as effective as cognitive restructuring, problem-solving training, or relaxation training alone. In some studies, CBT was superior to these other treatments in the short term, but groups showed comparable outcomes at long-term follow-up. Overall, these results indicate that CBT is useful for reducing children's depressive symptoms. However, it is likely that certain components of the CBT package (i.e., problem-solving training, coping skills training) are sufficient to produce these benefits (Roberts, 2015).

Cognitive–Behavioral Therapy for Adolescents

The CWD-A course (Clarke, Lewinsohn, & Hops, 1990; Lewinsohn, Clarke, Hops, & Andrews, 1990) is a group treatment for older adolescents (14–16 years) with MDD or dysthymia. CWD-A was designed to be nonstigmatizing. It is conducted like a class, with the therapist playing the role of teacher. In class, adolescents learn and practice new skills to help them cope with depressive symptoms and daily stressors. Skills are taught using traditional instruction, role play and dialogue, workbook exercises, and quizzes. Adolescents complete homework to help generalize skills outside the therapy setting.

CWD-A is based heavily on the behavioral theory of depression developed by Lewinsohn and colleagues (Lewinsohn, Youngren, & Grosscup, 1979). According to this theory, adolescents become depressed because of a lack of positive reinforcement and an excess of punishment from their environments. When they succeed, these adolescents do not give themselves credit or enjoy their success. When they fail, they attribute their failure to personal faults and assign self-blame. Over time, they experience only failure and frustration and perceive themselves as helpless and powerless. They also begin to show certain maladaptive thought patterns that contribute to their depressed mood, such as cognitive biases and distortions.

In CWD-A, adolescents learn new skills to cope with depressive symptoms, increase self-efficacy and pleasure, and change maladaptive thought patterns. Each week, the therapist–teacher introduces a new skill, which is practiced in the session and at home. In the first phase of treatment, the therapist teaches adolescents *how to increase their energy levels and positive emotions*. First, adolescents learn to monitor their emotions and notice how changes in their actions can improve their mood. For example, adolescents might notice how riding a bike, playing a sport, or calling a friend on the telephone usually results in greater energy. Later in treatment, the therapist uses social skills training to teach adolescents how to make friends and engage in social activities (Roberts, 2015).

Finally, the therapist encourages adolescents to plan pleasurable activities in their daily lives. Specifically, the therapist encourages adolescents to identify activities that they formerly enjoyed and set realistic expectations for engaging in these activities. For example, a girl who formerly enjoyed going to school dances might plan on attending a dance over the weekend. An unrealistic expectation for the dance is that everyone would complement her on her appearance and that she would be the center of attention. Such an expectation would set the girl up for disappointment. A more realistic expectation would be to attend the dance and spend some time with friends. The therapist encourages adolescents to deliberately schedule pleasurable events into their weekly routine. As adolescents engage in these pleasurable activities, they may derive greater reinforcement from their environment and improve their mood.

In the second phase of CWD-A, the therapist *targets adolescents' negative moods*. First, the therapist teaches relaxation techniques, like deep breathing and muscle relaxation, to help adolescents cope with anxiety and dysphoria. Later, the therapist teaches adolescents to recognize cognitive biases and distortions, using cartoons and role playing exercises. Adolescents are also taught to modify their thoughts with more realistic cognitions. In fact, the ability to replace negative automatic thoughts with more realistic cognitions may be one of the primary mechanisms by which CWD-A reduces depressive symptoms. Finally, adolescents are taught communication and conflict-resolution skills to help them negotiate interpersonal disputes. Conflict-resolution training involves teaching adolescents how to listen to others with an open mind, avoid critical or accusatory comments, brainstorm possible solutions to interpersonal problems, and select a course of action that everyone can accept (Nolen-Hoeksema & Hilt, 2013).

The efficacy of CWD-A has been examined in a number of randomized controlled studies. The first two studies involved a total of 155 adolescents with MDD. Adolescents were randomly assigned to one of three treatment conditions. The first group participated in CWD-A. The second group participated in CWD-A, and their parents also participated in parallel parenting sessions. Adolescents in the third group served as waitlist controls. Adolescents' depressive symptoms were assessed before treatment, immediately after treatment, and 2 years after treatment. Results showed that adolescents who participated in CWD-A (e.g., the first two groups) showed greater symptom reduction than adolescents on the waitlist. However, the adolescents in the two treatment conditions showed comparable outcomes, indicating that adding the parent group to CWD-A may be desirable but not necessary (Nolen-Hoeksema & Hilt, 2013; Roberts, 2015).

Interpersonal Psychotherapy for Adolescents

The underlying premise of interpersonal psychotherapy is that depression is best understood in the context of youths' interpersonal problems. Adolescents with depression have usually experienced disruptions in their relationships or high levels of interpersonal stress. These interpersonal problems both contribute to and maintain their depressed mood. Interpersonal psychotherapy seeks to improve adolescents' interpersonal functioning by helping them develop more satisfying and meaningful relationships, cope with the separation and loss of loved ones, or alleviate social distress and isolation (Gunlicks-Stoessel & Mufson, 2015).

Early in treatment, the adolescent and therapist select one or two problems to be the focus of therapy. These problems usually center on one of the following interpersonal themes: (a) grief and loss, (b) interpersonal role disputes, (c) role transitions, or (d) interpersonal deficits (Young, Mufson, & Davies, 2006).

Some adolescents become depressed following *the loss of an important relationship*. Adolescents can grieve the death of a family member, the separation from a parent, or the departure of a friend. When a relationship with a loved one is disrupted, adolescents can experience feelings of insecurity and helplessness. From the perspective of attachment theory, these adolescents have lost a secure

base from which they derive comfort and confidence. As a result, some adolescents become anxious, fearful, or unsure of themselves. Others become withdrawn and lethargic. Still others act out. The interpersonal therapist helps adolescents mourn the loss of the relationship and develop alternative sources of support (McBride, Atkinson, Quilty, & Bagby, 2006).

Other adolescents become depressed due to *interpersonal role disputes*. Role disputes are usually between the adolescent and his parents; they typically reflect differences in values. Although parent–child disagreements are common during adolescence, they can become problematic if left unresolved. Adolescents who perceive their parents as unsympathetic or disinterested can feel low self-worth and helplessness. The interpersonal therapist teaches both parents and adolescents more effective communication skills and ways to resolve disagreements—ways that balance the authority of the parent with the autonomy of the adolescent.

Adolescents can also experience depression following a *major role transition* or psychosocial stressor. Adolescents experience considerable life transitions: entering junior and senior high school, beginning dating and serious romantic relationships, separating from family members, entering the workforce. At other times, life transitions are forced upon adolescents through the birth of a new sibling, an unexpected pregnancy, the deployment of a family member in the armed forces, or a chronic illness. The interpersonal therapist helps the adolescent define, accept, and cope with his new social role. Coping may involve grieving the loss of the old role and learning new skills (or adjusting one's lifestyle) to suit new responsibilities.

Finally, adolescents can become depressed because of *interpersonal deficits*. Adolescents who lack appropriate social skills may have difficulty making friends, dating, or participating in extracurricular activities. Since adolescents' self-concepts are heavily influenced by peers, problems in peer functioning can cause a lack of self-esteem, self-confidence, and social isolation. The therapist teaches social skills, usually through role play exercises.

Although a number of randomized controlled studies have supported the efficacy of interpersonal therapy (IPT) for adults with depression, less research has focused on adolescents. In one study, 48 adolescents with depression were randomly assigned to one of two groups (Mufson, Weissman, Moreau, & Garfinkel, 1999). The first group participated in 12 weeks of interpersonal psychotherapy. The second group met with a counselor but did not receive any active form of treatment. Results showed that adolescents who participated in interpersonal psychotherapy were more likely to complete treatment (88%) than adolescents in the control group (46%). Furthermore, adolescents who received interpersonal psychotherapy showed greater improvement in mood, overall functioning, and social problem-solving than controls. A second study (Rossello & Bernal, 2005), using a slightly different version of interpersonal psychotherapy, showed similar results.

Another study compared the effectiveness of interpersonal psychotherapy versus nondirective counseling

(Mufson et al., 2004). Sixty-three adolescents with depression who were attending schools in low-income neighborhoods were randomly assigned to two treatment groups. The first group received 12 sessions of interpersonal psychotherapy at school. The second group received nondirective counseling. After treatment, adolescents in both groups showed improvement in depressive symptoms and overall functioning. Clinician ratings indicated that interpersonal psychotherapy was superior to nondirective counseling in improving mood and functioning. Adolescents' self-reports indicated that interpersonal psychotherapy was superior to nondirective counseling in improving social functioning, but not in reducing depressive symptoms. Taken together, these results indicate that interpersonal psychotherapy is effective in treating adolescent depression. However, interpersonal psychotherapy may not always be superior to supportive psychotherapy in reducing adolescents' self-reported depressive symptoms.

Review:

- Stark's CBT is effective in reducing depression in children. Children learn to (a) recognize negative emotions, (b) solve social problems, (c) cope with negative feelings, and (d) challenge cognitive biases and distortions.
- CWD-A is a group therapy that is effective for adolescents. Initially, adolescents learn emotion recognition skills and techniques to increase positive affect. Later, adolescents learn relaxation skills and strategies to manage negative emotions and avoid conflicts.
- In IPT, adolescents target one of the following problems that can prompt depression: grief, role disputes, role transitions, or interpersonal deficits.

Should Medication and Psychotherapy Be Combined to Treat Depression?

Many experts recommend combining medication and psychotherapy to treat child and adolescent depression (Birmaher & Brent, 2015; Birmaher, Brent, & AACAP Work Group on Quality Issues, 2007). The rationale for combined treatment is threefold. First, combining medication and psychotherapy might provide a greater "dose" of treatment, thereby producing faster symptom reduction and greater treatment response. Second, medication plus psychotherapy might target different symptoms, thus, maximizing the range of symptoms that might be improved. For example, medication might target the physical symptoms of depression (e.g., fatigue, sleep, and appetite changes), whereas therapy might target cognitive symptoms (e.g., anhedonia, thoughts of death). Third, combined treatment might address a wider range of comorbid problems.

The Treatment for Adolescents With Depression Study (TADS; Treatment for Adolescents With Depression Study Team, 2004) was designed to investigate the relative merits of medication and psychotherapy in treating adolescent depression. In TADS, researchers compared the efficacy of medication and CBT in adolescents aged 12 to 17. Four hundred and thirty-nine adolescents with MDD were randomly assigned to one of four treatment groups: (1) fluoxetine (Prozac) only, (2) CBT only, (3) combined fluoxetine and CBT, and (4) placebo. All treatments were administered for 12 weeks. Researchers measured adolescents' depressive symptoms before and after treatment. They also measured adolescents' self-harm during the course of treatment.

Children in all groups showed reductions in their depressive symptoms, although children in the combined treatment group showed the greatest symptom reduction at the fastest rate (see Figure 13.4). At the end of treatment, the percentage of adolescents who showed significant improvement were 71% (combined treatment), 60.6% (medication only), 43.2% (CBT only), and 34.8% (placebo), respectively.

Follow-up tests revealed three important findings. First, the difference between adolescents who received combined treatment and adolescents who received medication alone was *not* statistically significant. In fact, another study published after TADS showed similar results: combining psychotherapy with medication yielded no better outcomes than medication alone (Clarke et al., 2005). Second, adolescents who received combined treatment or medication alone showed significantly greater improvement than adolescents who received either CBT alone or placebo. Third, adolescents who received CBT alone and adolescents who received placebo *did not* statistically differ.

Some children do not respond to antidepressant medication. In the Treatment of SSRI-Resistant Depression in Adolescents (TORDIA) study, researchers examined the effects of adding CBT to medication in adolescents who did not respond to medication alone (Brent et al., 2008; Kennard et al., 2009). This study involved a large sample of 12- to 18-year-olds with severe depression. Adolescents were randomly assigned to one of four conditions: (1) SSRI alone, (2) non-SSRI antidepressant alone, (3) SSRI and CBT, or (4) non-SSRI antidepressant and CBT. In this study, CBT included cognitive restructuring, problem-solving training, emotion regulation and social skills training, and parent–child sessions to improve family communication and problem-solving. After 12 weeks of treatment, the combination of any medication and CBT yielded greater reductions in depression than medication alone. Furthermore, problem-solving training seemed to be the most effective component of CBT. Unfortunately, 24 weeks after treatment the combination of medication and CBT was no longer superior to medication alone (Brent et al., 2008; Emslie et al., 2010).

The results of the TADS and TORDIA studies indicate that a combination of fluoxetine and CBT should be considered a first-line treatment for adolescent depression. However, the combination of CBT with medication may yield only modest benefits beyond medication alone. CBT alone may be a useful alternative for adolescents and families unwilling to participate in pharmacotherapy, especially in light of recent FDA warnings against SSRIs (Emslie, 2012).

Source: Based on TADS (2004).

Note: Adolescents who received medication (either with or without CBT) showed lowest depression scores after treatment. Adding CBT to medication did not produce significantly greater effects than using medication alone. Youths who participated in CBT alone showed similar outcomes as youths who received placebo.

Review:

- In the TADS study, depressed adolescents who received medication and therapy showed the greatest improvement.
- In the TORDIA study, severely depressed adolescents who did not initially respond to medication showed the greatest improvement when receiving both medication and therapy.

13.3 SUICIDE

Self-injurious behavior (SIB) refers to an action that is deliberately self-directed and results in injury or potential injury to oneself. SIBs range from cutting or burning oneself to self-inflicted suffocation, poisoning, or shooting. They do not include activities that are merely risky, such as alcohol and drug use, gambling, or speeding/reckless driving (Centers for Disease Control and Prevention, 2016b).

SIB can be suicidal or nonsuicidal. Suicidal self-injury is self-inflicted, results in injury or the potential for injury, and there is implicit or explicit evidence that the person intends to die. Examples include hanging/suffocation, running out into traffic, jumping from a tall building or bridge, or poisoning with intent to die (Capuzzi & Golden, 2014).

Nonsuicidal self-injury (NSSI) is self-inflicted, results in injury or potential for injury, but there is no evidence that the person intends to die. Instead, individuals typically engage in NSSI to alter their life circumstances (e.g., obtain attention or sympathy from others) or their emotional state

(e.g., reduce feelings of emotional pain). Examples include burning, cutting, or scratching oneself without intent to die (Hornor, 2016).

How Common Is Child and Adolescent Suicide?

The National Violent Death Reporting System estimates the number of youths who die by suicide each year (Perou et al., 2016). It is difficult to obtain an exact number because many suicides are attributed to accidental causes or the intent of victims is unknown. On average, approximately 5,000 youths die by suicide annually. For every 100,000 youths, approximately 2.1 older children (aged 10 to 14) and 14.5 adolescents and young adults (aged 15 to 24) commit suicide. These statistics make suicide the second leading cause of death among adolescents after accidental injuries (Centers for Disease Control and Prevention, 2016b).

The prevalence of suicide is increasing rapidly. Over the past 15 years, the suicide rate has increased 24% in the United States. The greatest increase has occurred among girls aged 10 to 14. Although the absolute number of suicide deaths among younger girls remains relatively low (approximately 1.5 deaths per 100,000 girls), the prevalence of suicide among young girls has increased nearly 200% (Curtin et al., 2016).

Suicidal thoughts and actions exist on a continuum ranging from ideation, planning, attempting, and death

(Carson, 2015). The best data that we have regarding the prevalence of suicidal thoughts and actions come from the National Comorbidity Survey, which includes information from a nationally representative sample of adolescents (Nock et al., 2013). Overall, 12.1% of adolescents reported a lifetime history of suicidal ideation, 4% claimed that they had formulated a suicide plan, and 4.1% attempted suicide at least once. The percentage of youths attempting suicide was slightly higher than the percentage of youths who formulated a suicide plan because some youths attempt suicide without planning their actions in advance.

These data indicate that suicidal thoughts, plans, and actions are relatively common among American youths. In a high school classroom of 25 students, on average, 3 students would have experienced suicidal ideation and 1 student may have planned or attempted suicide.

Review:

- In the United States, approximately 5,000 youths die by suicide each year.
- Suicide death is higher in adolescents (14.5/100,000 youths) than older children (2.1/100,000 youths).
- Approximately 12% of adolescents experience suicidal thoughts, and 4% report a suicide plan or past attempt.

How Does Suicide Vary as a Function of Gender, Age, and Ethnicity?

Gender

The prevalence of suicidal thoughts and actions depends on gender. On average, adolescent girls are 1.7 times more likely than boys to have suicidal thoughts or make suicidal plans, and 3 times more likely than boys to attempt suicide (Nock et al., 2013). Boys are 3 to 4 times more likely than girls to die from suicide, probably because boys select more lethal strategies (Curtin et al., 2016). For example, boys (45%) are more likely than girls (21%) to use a firearm, whereas girls (11%) and more likely than boys (3%) to use poison or prescription medication (Karch, Logan, McDaniel, Floyd, & Vagi, 2013).

Age

Prevalence also depends on age. Suicidal thoughts are uncommon among prepubescent children. Suicidal ideation becomes slightly more common between the ages of 10 and 12 years and then increases markedly between the ages of 15 and 18 years (eventually reaching about 12% of youths).

The prevalence of suicidal plans and actions remains very low through age 12 years; then it increases steadily during the early teenage years and eventually plateaus at age 17 or 18 years (eventually reaching about 4% of youths).

Recent data also tell us important information about the course of suicidal behavior. Most (68%) adolescents who experience suicidal thoughts formulate a plan within 1 year. Furthermore, the vast majority (88%) of adolescents who have a suicide plan attempt suicide within 1 year of developing that plan. Therefore, suicidal thoughts and plans are strong predictors of suicide attempts and should be taken seriously by clinicians, parents, and peers (Nock et al., 2013).

Ethnicity

Finally, prevalence varies as a function of ethnicity. Asian Americans report the highest rates of suicidal thoughts; they are approximately 1.5 to 2.0 times more likely than non-Latino, White adolescents to experience suicidal ideation. Latinas and American Indian girls are most likely to attempt suicide; they are approximately 1.5 times more likely than non-Latino, White adolescents to engage in suicidal acts. American Indian boys show the highest rates of suicide deaths; they are 2 to 3 times more likely to die by suicide than non-Latino, White adolescents (Goldston et al., 2015).

Interestingly, suicidal thoughts and actions are less common among African American adolescents. In fact, African American youths are one-half less likely than non-Latino, White youths to experience suicidal thoughts and two-thirds less likely than White youths to attempt suicide (Nock et al., 2013).

Many researchers believe that adolescents' cultures partially explain differences in suicidal behavior across ethnic groups. The beliefs and values of these adolescents, their families, and their communities can protect these youths from suicide or, conversely, increase their likelihood of self-harm. For example, religious beliefs and church involvement is often associated with decreased risk for suicide. Furthermore, African American girls and women report higher religious involvement than other ethnic groups. It is possible that religious involvement provides African American girls with the social support and sense of connectedness to others that protects them from suicidal thoughts and actions (Goldston, Weller, & Doyle, 2014).

In contrast, many Asian American families endorse communal values—that is, they prioritize the needs of the family or the community before their own. When these youths experience anxiety, depression, or anger, they may avoid talking about their problems because they worry they might burden or dishonor their family (Schwartz, Unger, Zamboanga, & Szapocznik, 2010).

Cultural differences may partially explain the high rate of suicide deaths among American Indian boys and young men. These youths often report a high degree of stigma and embarrassment associated with reporting psychological problems. Many also perceive mental health services as foreign to their community. Consequently, when they experience psychological problems, American Indian youths are often reluctant to seek help (Goldston et al., 2015).

Review:

- Girls are 3 times more likely than boys to attempt suicide, but boys are 3 to 4 times more likely than girls to die by suicide, perhaps because boys use more lethal means.
- The prevalence of suicidal thoughts and actions increases markedly after puberty.

- Latinas and American Indian boys and girls show the highest rates of suicide. African American youths show the lowest rates.

What Factors Predict Suicide in Children and Adolescents?

Previous Suicidal Thoughts or Actions

The best predictor of future behavior is past behavior. Previous suicidal thoughts and actions are among the best predictors of a future suicide attempt (King, Foster, & Rogalski, 2013). Approximately 88% of adolescents who attempt suicide experience suicidal thoughts prior to their attempts. Furthermore, 40% of adolescents who die by suicide have made at least one attempt in the past. These findings indicate that one of the best ways to screen for suicidal behavior, and prevent suicide attempts, is to ask adolescents about their current suicidal thoughts and past suicide attempts.

Mental Health Problems

Psychopathology is one of the most common risk factors for suicide. In one large study, 90% of youths who committed suicide had at least one psychiatric disorder (King et al., 2013). The most common disorder is depression. Approximately 61% of boys and 73% of girls who commit suicide experience major depression or dysthymia at the time of their deaths (Karch et al., 2013). The association between depression and suicide is likely not surprising given that one of the symptoms of MDD is recurrent thoughts about death or suicidal ideation (American Psychiatric Association, 2013).

Some adolescents who are depressed also experience hopelessness—that is, negative and pessimistic expectations about the future. Although often correlated with depression, hopelessness predicts suicide above and beyond depression alone. Consequently, most psychologists not only ask if their client is experiencing depression but also ask if he or she feels hopeless about the future. Hopelessness is also important because it is often malleable, that is, it can be changed in the process of psychotherapy. Indeed, many cognitive therapies challenge adolescents' hopeless thoughts and encourage them to think more rationally and realistically about the future (Goldston et al., 2014).

Bipolar disorder is also associated with increased suicide risk. Approximately one-third of children and adolescents with bipolar disorder report a history of attempting suicide. Prospective, longitudinal studies indicate that approximately 20% of adolescents who are hospitalized for bipolar disorder attempt suicide within one year after discharge. Furthermore, approximately 25% of youths hospitalized for bipolar disorder commit suicide within 10 years (Karch et al., 2013; King et al., 2013).

Finally, disruptive behavior disorders predict suicide in adolescents who also experience emotional distress. For example, approximately 18% of youths who die by suicide have ADHD and 20% to 25% of youths who commit suicide have ODD or conduct disorder (CD). Adolescents with these disorders often behave impulsively or erratically; consequently, they may be more likely to attempt suicide without first thinking about the consequences of their actions (Karch et al., 2013; King et al., 2013).

It is important to remember that most adolescents with mental disorders do *not* experience suicidal thoughts or actions. Mental disorders are general, not specific, predictors of suicide.

Substance Use Problems

Alcohol and other drug use is a proximal risk factor for suicidal actions. Approximately one-half of adolescents who commit suicide have used alcohol or other drugs immediately before their death. Alcohol, a depressant, increases adolescents' capacity to engage in suicide by lowering their inhibitions against self-injury. In contrast, stimulant drugs such as amphetamine and cocaine may increase adolescents' risk for suicide by exacerbating agitation and impulsive decision-making (King et al., 2013).

Substance use disorders are more distal risk factors for suicide. Adolescent boys and girls who have substance use disorders are 15 times and 3 times more likely to attempt suicide than their peers without substance use disorders, respectively. As you might image, an adolescents' risk for suicide increases even more when he or she misuses multiple substances and also experiences a mood disorder (King et al., 2013).

Psychosocial Stressors

Many adolescents experience a major psychosocial stressor immediately before they attempt suicide. In one study, researchers reviewed the suicide attempts of a large sample of adolescents to determine which stressful events were most likely to precede each attempt (Karch et al., 2013). The most common antecedent events were a relationship problem with a parent or friend (51%), a life stressor or crisis situation (42%), a problem with a romantic relationship or a possible pregnancy (27%), or a school-related problem (26%).

Family Problems

Adolescents whose parents committed suicide are at risk for suicide themselves. Specifically, suicide is five times more likely in adolescents whose mothers died by suicide and two times more likely in adolescents whose fathers died by suicide. Twin studies suggest that suicide risk is moderately heritable; furthermore, disorders associated with suicide (e.g., bipolar disorder, depression) show moderate to high heritability. Consequently, parents likely pass on genes that place their children at risk for suicidal behavior. At the same time, parents who engage in suicidal behavior often place considerable psychosocial stress on their children during development. This environmental stress, in turn, can lead to greater likelihood for depression and suicidal behavior in adolescence (King et al., 2013).

Indeed, parents who experience mental disorders (even in the absence of suicidal thoughts and actions) place their children at risk for suicide. Specifically, the adolescents of parents with mood disorders, substance use disorders, and personality disorders (i.e. long-standing problems with identity and social–emotional functioning) are at risk. These disorders likely compromise the care these parents afford their children, increase stress in the family, and contribute to the emergence of mental disorders in adolescents (King et al., 2013).

Adolescents who experience low parental attachment or support also report greater suicidal thoughts and actions. Interestingly, adolescents' perceptions of parental support are more predictive of suicide than the actual support that parents provide. It is likely that some depressed adolescents have distorted views of their parents and families—views that are pessimistic and fit their negative view of self, world, and others. For example, an adolescent might think, "My mom doesn't care if I live or die. Why should she?" These distortions are especially important predictors of adolescent suicide (King et al., 2013).

Child Maltreatment

Child maltreatment is an important predictor of adolescent suicide. Youths who report suicidal thoughts or actions often have histories of physical abuse, sexual abuse, or severe neglect. Furthermore, longitudinal studies show that children who experience maltreatment are at greatly increased risk for suicidal thoughts and actions during adolescence. Of all the forms of maltreatment, sexual abuse appears to be the most salient predictor of suicide later in life (Miller, Esposito-Smythers, Weismoore, & Renshaw, 2013).

Child maltreatment is also a *unique* predictor of later suicidal ideation and action. Even after controlling for adolescents' levels of depression or other psychosocial stressors, child maltreatment continues to predict suicide. Furthermore, the more severe the maltreatment, the greater the likelihood that youths will later experience suicidal thoughts or attempt self-harm (Miller et al., 2013).

Bullying and Cyberbullying

Bullying is also a specific risk factor for suicide in children and adolescents (Chu et al., 2015; see Image 13.5). Bullying is defined as intentional, repetitive, aggressive behavior that is directed from a person with higher power toward a person of lower power. Bullying can be physical (e.g., hitting, kicking, pinching), verbal (e.g., name-calling, teasing, intimidating), or relational (e.g., spreading rumors, excluding or ostracizing others). Approximately 20% to 30% of school-age children report problems with bullying (Holt, 2015).

Cyberbullying is a specific form of bullying in which youths use digital media to hurt, threaten, harass, or embarrass someone. Examples of cyberbullying include posting hurtful or embarrassing images on social media, making

online threats, or sending hurtful texts. Cyberbullying is particularly pernicious because attacks can be brutal, easily shared, and difficult to control. Approximately 10% to 30% of youths report problems with cyberbullying (Bauman, 2015).

Any form of bullying places youths at risk for suicide. The best available data indicate that the victims of traditional bullying or cyberbullying are approximately 1.7 to 1.9 times more likely than their nonbullied peers to attempt suicide. Interesting, bullies themselves are also at increased risk for suicide, suggesting that bullying hurts both victims and perpetrators (Bauman, 2015).

Bullying increases suicide risk in at least three ways. First, bullying is strongly associated with emotional problems among adolescents, especially anxiety, depression, and feelings of hopelessness (Kodish et al., 2016; Nickerson & Torchia, 2015). Some youths may contemplate suicide as a mean to alleviate emotional suffering. Second, bullying is associated with alcohol and other drug use problems. Some youths may use substances to cope with bullying; however, these substances may also make them more likely to act impulsively (and harmfully) when they experience negative emotions (Litwiller & Brausch, 2013). Third, bullying often makes youths feel rejected by their peers. Adolescents who feel ostracized are at particular risk for suicide (van Orden et al., 2010).

Sexual Minority Identification

Adolescents who identify as lesbian, gay, or bisexual are at elevated risk for suicide compared to their heterosexual peers. On average, lesbian, gay, or bisexual youths are 2 to 5 times more likely to report suicidal thoughts and 2 to 4 times more likely to attempt suicide than their heterosexual classmates. Suicidal ideation and attempts are highest among gay or bisexual boys and young men (Poteat & Rivers, 2015).

Gender nonconforming youths show even greater risk for suicidal thoughts and actions. As many as 83% of transgender youths report suicidal ideation, and approximately one-third of transgender youths have attempted suicide (Testa & Hendricks, 2015).

Why are sexual minority youths at increased risk for suicide? One culprit appears to be bullying. The National School Climate Survey showed that 80% to 90% of lesbian, gay, or bisexual youths experienced name-calling or other forms of verbal harassment at school. Furthermore, 55% experienced cyberbullying and 40% were physically harassed or assaulted because of their sexual orientation (Ybarra, Mitchell, Kosciw, & Korchmaros, 2015). Rates of peer rejection and bullying are also high among gender nonconforming youths. For example, 63% of transgender adolescents report a history of teasing and other forms of verbal abuse from peers, 45% experienced hostile or otherwise threatening comments at school, and 15% reported that their victimization was so severe that it prevented them from completing high school.

As we have seen, bullying is a powerful, unique predictor of suicidal thoughts and feelings. Youths who are bullied because of their sexual orientation or identity may feel rejected by peers, internalize feelings of worthlessness, and engage in suicidal actions to alleviate the pain of ostracism (Corona, Jobes, & Berman, 2015).

On the other hand, recent research indicates that sexual minority youths are at increased risk for suicide after controlling for the frequency and severity of their bullying. For example, in once large study, researchers found that gay adolescents were twice as likely as their heterosexual classmates to experience suicidal ideation even after controlling for their exposure to bullying. Similarly, lesbian adolescents were approximately 3.5 times more likely than their heterosexual peers to experience suicidal thoughts even after controlling for bullying. It appears that other factors, such as a lack of support from parents and family, also contribute to increased suicidal behavior among sexual minority youths (Mueller, James, Abrutyn, & Levin, 2015).

Review:

- Approximately 90% of youths who commit suicide have a history of a mental disorder, including MDD, bipolar disorder, substance use disorders, and ADHD.
- Many youths who attempt suicide have a history of maltreatment. Youths who feel that they are a burden on their families are at particular risk.
- Youths who are bullied, or identify as lesbian, gay, bisexual, or transgender, are at particular risk for suicide. Youths who feel like they do not belong in their family or peer group are at particular risk.

What Theories Help Explain Suicide in Children and Adolescents?

Hopelessness Theory

Researchers have developed theoretical models to explain how the risk factors for suicide relate to each other and predict suicidal thoughts and actions (Barzilay & Apter, 2014). One influential model is the hopelessness theory of suicide. This theory posits that a particular kind of depression, characterized by feelings of hopelessness, is a strong predictor of suicide (Abramson, Metalsky, & Alloy, 1989).

According to the theory, hopelessness begins when individuals experience a negative life event, such as the loss of a loved one, a transition to a new home or school, or rejection by peers. However, negative events alone are not sufficient to elicit hopelessness; individuals must also have a cognitive vulnerability, or characteristic way of thinking about these negative events, that elicit hopeless feelings (Hewitt, Caelian, Chen, & Flett, 2014). Specifically, people who experience hopelessness tend to think about negative events in three ways:

1. They *attribute negative events to stable and global causes*. For example, a girl might earn a low score on the SAT and believe her poor performance was caused by a lack of intelligence (i.e., a stable and global cause). She might feel hopeless because she believes there is nothing she can do to improve her score.

2. They *believe that the consequences of the negative event are extremely important*. For example, the girl might feel hopeless because she believes that her low SAT score will limit her ability to gain admission to her favorite college.

3. They *think that the negative event is an indicator of worthlessness*. For example, the girl might believe that she is worthless, or her parents will not value her, because she can't get into a good college.

These three ways of thinking—(1) attributing negative events to global and stable causes, (2) believing that negative events have important consequences, and (3) doubting one's self-worth because of the events—predict hopelessness. Hopelessness, in turn, predicts suicidal thoughts and actions (Abramson et al., 2000).

Note that hopelessness theory suggests avenues for prevention and treatment. Therapists can teach patients other ways of thinking that are less likely to generate hopeless feelings. For example, if a student attributes her low SAT score to unstable or situational causes (e.g., "I wasn't feeling well during the test"), views the importance of her test score more realistically (e.g., "Several excellent colleges, like Denison University, do not require me to submit SAT scores"), or sees her self-worth independent of her test score (e.g., "My mom would support me wherever I go to school), she may feel disappointed, but not hopeless (Steeg et al., 2016).

Interpersonal Theory

More recently, researchers have developed the interpersonal–psychological theory of suicide to explain how relationship problems can elicit suicidal thoughts and actions (Joiner, Van Orden, Witte, & Rudd, 2009). According to this theory, suicide is prompted by three factors: (1) perceived burdensomeness, (2) thwarted belongingness, and (3) capability for suicide (see Figure 13.5). First, youths at risk for suicide believe that they impose a *burden* on significant people in their lives, such as parents or peers. For example, a boy might think, "Why do I cause my mom such trouble? She'd be better off without me." Second, youths feel *a lack of belongingness* or connectivity to those around them. For example, a girl might feel ostracized by her friends at school or left out of family activities. Together, perceived burdensomeness and thwarted belongingness contribute to suicidal thoughts. The third factor, *capability for suicide*, explains how some adolescents act upon those thoughts. Specifically, as adolescents engage in SIBs (e.g., burning, cutting) or other actions that risk their physical health (e.g., illegal drug use, reckless driving, unprotected sex) their fear of death and dying is reduced. Consequently, they are more likely to attempt suicide (Cha & Nock, 2014).

Research generally supports the interpersonal–psychological theory of suicide. As we have seen, adolescents who feel estranged from their family and friends, who are mistreated by caregivers, or who are actively bullied by classmates are at elevated risk for suicide. In contrast, adolescents who feel connected to their families and

Figure 13.5 Interpersonal–psychological theory of suicide. Adolescents who view themselves as a burden and feel disconnected from parents and peers may experience suicidal thoughts. Self-injury and other risky behaviors increase their capability for suicide and may turn their thoughts into actions.

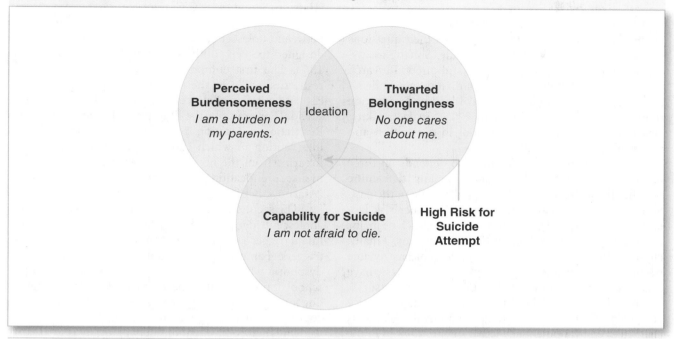

Source: Based on Joiner, Brown, and Wingate (2005).

communities may be protected from suicide and self-harm. Perceived burdensomeness and thwarted belong-ingness predict depression; depression, in turn, predicts suicidal ideation (Barzilay & Apter, 2014).

Empirical research also supports the notion that risky behaviors and previous self-injury reduces ado-lescents' inhibitions against suicide and increases their capability for self-harm. For example, adolescents who have experienced maltreatment, who misuse alcohol and other drugs, or who have attempted suicide in the past, are much more likely to transition from suicidal ideation to attempts (Cha & Nock, 2014).

However, some youths who engage in self-injury attempt suicide, but do *not* first experience suicidal ide-ation. Instead, these adolescents tend to act impulsively, without contemplating their situations or formulating a plan. Indeed, adolescents with disorders characterized by impulsivity and risky decision-making (e.g., ADHD, bipo-lar disorders, conduct problems, substance use problems) are at risk for suicidal behaviors (Barzilay et al., 2015).

Review:

- According to hopelessness theory, youths are at risk for suicide when they (a) attribute negative events to stable and global causes, (b) believe the consequences of the negative events are important, and (c) see themselves as worthless because of the event.
- According to interpersonal–psychological theory, youths are at risk for suicide when they (a) view

themselves as a burden to others, (b) feel like they do not belong to their family or peer group, and (c) feel capable of self-harm.

How Do Clinicians Assess Suicide Risk?

Mental health professionals who treat adolescents should routinely screen for suicidal thoughts and actions. Even if the adolescent does not present with depression, it is wise to determine if he is currently experiencing suicidal ide-ation or has made suicide attempts in the past. Typically, screening occurs during the diagnostic interview or one of the early sessions. Clinicians often begin with questions to assess thoughts about death and later transition to suicide plans and actions, if applicable (King et al., 2013):

Thoughts of death: I wonder if you've been so down that you've had thoughts about death or have wished that you were dead?

Suicide thoughts: It sounds like you've been really down. Sometimes, when people experience major disappointments like you have, they have thoughts of suicide. I wonder if you've had thoughts of suicide? How often? How long do they last? How hard is it to get them out of your mind?

Suicide plans: Have you had thoughts about how you would do it? Have you taken steps toward this plan?

Suicide attempt: Is there any part of you that wants to die? What stops you from suicide? What are some reasons for wanting to be living next week, next month, or next year?

Although clinicians ask about suicide in a sensitive, respectful manner, they do not sugarcoat their questions or use euphemisms to describe suicide. Suicide assessment requires clinicians to be clear and direct. Research has shown that asking adolescents directly about death and suicide does not increase their likelihood of suicide (Gould, Marrocco, & Kleinman, 2005). In fact, asking about suicidal behavior is essential to prevention and treatment (King et al., 2013).

Determining risk for suicide also depends on three other important factors. First, clinicians determine whether the adolescent has attempted suicide in the past. Second, clinicians assess the presence of other risk factors that increase the likelihood of suicide, such as major depression, substance use, or family problems. Finally, clinicians determine whether the adolescent has a viable means of committing suicide. For example, does he have access to a gun, pain medication, or antidepressants?

Based on the available information, clinicians estimate adolescents' acute risk for suicide (see). *Acute high risk* is characterized by a potentially lethal suicide attempt in the past, persistent suicidal thoughts with an intent to die, and an active plan to commit suicide. Youths at high risk are typically hospitalized to protect themselves until their risk decreases. *Acute moderate risk* is characterized by persistent suicidal thoughts and a potentially lethal plan, but no immediate intent to die. Youths at moderate risk may be hospitalized if parents are not able to protect them at home. If the adolescent goes home, the therapist provides emergency contact information to the family, develops a plan to keep the adolescent safe in the short-term, and schedules an appointment for therapy. *Acute low risk* is characterized by thoughts of death but no plan or intent to die. Youths at low risk are typically sent home with emergency contact information and an appointment for therapy.

Review:

- Suicide risk exists on a continuum from thoughts of death through existence of a current, feasible plan.
- A past suicide attempt is a specific, unique predictor of future suicide risk.

How Can Clinicians Help Youths Who Attempt Suicide?

Hospitalization and Safety Planning

Youths who made a recent suicide attempt or who are at acute high risk for suicide will be hospitalized. Although hospitalization is necessary to protect the youth's life, it is typically stressful for the adolescent, his or her family, and the clinician. The goal of hospitalization is to provide any medical treatment that is necessary because of the youth's suicide attempt, to keep the youth safe in the short term, and to develop a safety plan so the youth can return home (Hawton, Saunders, & O'Connor, 2012).

Safety plans are verbal and written agreements between adolescents, caregivers, and therapists that are designed to keep youths safe after discharge (see Figure 13.7). The first component of a safety plan is means restriction—that is, the therapist helps caregivers identify and restrict adolescents' access to lethal means of suicide. For example, the Emergency Department Means Restriction Education program is an evidence-based intervention in which caregivers are taught to remove firearms from the home, keep medications and alcohol in a secure location, and monitor adolescents' activities (Asarnow, Berk, Hughes, & Anderson, 2015).

The second component of a safety plan is to help the adolescent identify thoughts, feelings, or situations that might trigger a suicide attempt and ways to cope with these triggers. For example, an adolescent might experience dysphoria when he feels overwhelmed by coursework at school or problems at home. He might identify "taking my dog for a walk" or "going for a run" as two effective ways to cope with negative feelings (King et al., 2013).

The final component of safety planning is to identify sources of support for the adolescent in case of future crises. For example, the adolescent might list the names and phone numbers of friends or family members he can turn to when feeling overwhelmed. Similarly, the therapist would provide her own contact information and the number of a suicide prevention hotline. The adolescent might also identify people or objects that give meaning, purpose, or pleasure in his life (King et al., 2013).

The period immediately following hospitalization is especially dangerous. Approximately one-fourth of youths who attempt suicide will try again within 1 year. The greatest risk period is the first three months after discharge (Asarnow et al., 2015). One simple method to protect youths during this critical period is to remind them of support services in their area in case of crisis. For example, Carter and colleagues (Carter, Clover, Whyte, Dawson, & D'Este, 2013) conducted the Postcards from the EDge program, in which they periodically mailed postcards to individuals who were released from the emergency department (ED) because of self-poisoning. The postcards reminded them of crisis support services in the area. Individuals who received these postcards were half as likely to be readmitted for a suicide attempt as individuals who did not receive the postcards. Results indicate that even simple methods of support can be helpful in preventing future hospitalization.

Medication

As we have seen, SSRIs can be effective in helping youths with depression; however, some youths experience an increase in suicidal thinking after taking antidepressants.

Figure 13.6 Youth suicide risk exists on a continuum. As youths move along this continuum, their risk of death increases.

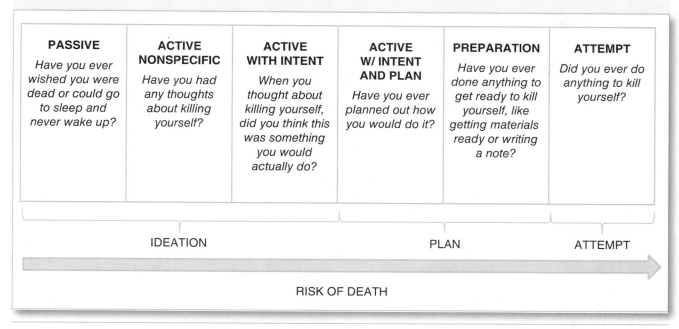

Source: Based on Carson (2015) and Posner (2016).

Consequently, it was initially unclear whether antidepressants would be helpful for youths at risk for suicidality.

The Treatment of Adolescent Suicide Attempters (TASA) study was designed to examine the effectiveness and safety of medication for suicidal youths. In this study, 124 adolescents who had attempted suicide received either medication (typically an SSRI), CBT (which included safety planning), or the combination of medication and CBT. During the 6-month study, 24% of youths experienced suicidal ideation or a suicide attempt, a percentage much lower than is typically reported by adolescents with a history of suicide attempts. Furthermore, risk for suicidality did not differ across the three conditions. Finally, all three treatments were effective in reducing depression (Brent et al., 2009; Vitiello et al., 2009).

The TASA study provides the first evidence that medication can be used safely and effectively for adolescents with a history of suicide. The study is limited by the fact that all youths received treatment (i.e., there was no control group) and youths were not randomly assigned to each treatment condition. Future research is necessary to determine whether the improvements shown in the TASA study are due to treatment or are partially due to placebo effects.

Family-Focused Treatments

The most promising, evidence-based treatments for suicidal youths involve families (Sharma & Sargent, 2015). One such intervention is Safe Alternatives for Teens and Youths (SAFETY; Asarnow et al., 2015). The SAFETY program was developed because most youths who attempt suicide never participate in outpatient therapy, or they receive inadequate support services. SAFETY provides services to adolescents who have attempted suicide, and their parents, shortly after discharge from the hospital.

Treatment is structured along a series of steps: (a) restricting adolescents' means of suicide at home, (b) improving communication and connectedness in the family, (c) identifying triggers for future suicidal thoughts and actions, and (d) developing better ways to cope with negative thoughts and feelings.

Therapists meet with adolescents and parents separately. Adolescents learn skills to prevent suicidal ideation and actions while parents learn skills to keep their adolescents safe, support them in times of crisis, and manage their own stress and negative affect. For example, in one session, adolescents build a "hope kit" that is filled with reasons for living and reminders to use effective coping strategies in times of distress. To complement this activity, parents create a "family album" in which they describe positive thoughts and feelings about their adolescents. Parents share the album with their adolescents to promote feelings of acceptance and belongingness. Parents and adolescents also practice communication and support skills together.

The SAFETY program is effective in reducing adolescents' feelings of hopelessness and preventing future suicidal thoughts and actions. Furthermore, both adolescents and their parents report improvements in depression and social functioning following treatment (Asarnow et al., 2015).

SAFETY PLAN

1. What are my triggers for suicidal thoughts or self-harmful behaviors? How might I recognize when I need to protect my well-being and remain safe?

   Triggers — when I feel alone; when no one seems to care about me

   Recognize — when I shut out my parents and family

2. The steps I will take when I experience these triggers, suicidal thoughts, or urges:

   - Try to relax by: *Playing my guitar; painting*
   - Do something physically active like: *playing lacrosse, running*
   - Distract myself by: *going for a drive, take my dog for a walk*
   - Use coping statements such as: *If I give myself time, I can usually think of a solution to my problems.*
   - Contact a family member, friend, or support person:

Grandma	*xxx-xxx-xxxx*
Aunt Jen	*xxx-xxx-xxxx*
Amelia	*xxx-xxx-xxxx*

   - Call my therapist or emergency numbers or go to the emergency department:

Emergency:	*911*
Psychologist/therapist:	*xxx-xxx-xxxx (Times: M-F 8AM – 5PM)*
Suicide prevention line:	*1-800-273-TALK (8255)*

   - Move away from any method or means of hurting myself; involve a family member or support person in limiting access to my means.

3. A couple of things that are very important to me and worth living for are:
   Spending time with my dog; visiting with my grandma on weekends

Client:	*Margaret Sellers*
Therapist:	*Dr. Williams*
Parent/Guardian:	*Jennifer Brown*

Source: Based on King, Foster, and Rogalski (2013).

Another family-focused intervention for suicidal youths is the Resourceful Adolescent Parent Program (RAP-P; Pineda & Dadds, 2013). The program consists of four, two-hour sessions for parents that are designed to reduce their adolescents' suicidal ideation and negative affect.

In Session 1, parents learn about adolescent suicide, practical strategies to reduce adolescents' suicidal thoughts and actions, and available mental health services in the community. In Session 2, parents identify positive aspects of their parenting style and ways to manage stress that might interfere with the care they offer their children. This session is especially helpful for parents who have mood problems themselves, or who feel discouraged by their adolescents' suicidal behavior. Session 3 focuses on identifying ways to increase adolescents' self-esteem and strategies to balance adolescents' need for independence with their desire for a close relationship with their parents. In Session 4, parents learn techniques to reduce family conflict.

The efficacy of RAP-P is supported by a study involving adolescents with depression who were referred to a hospital ED because of suicidal behavior (Pineda & Dadds, 2013; see Figure 13.8). In this study, families were randomly assigned to RAP-P plus routine care (e.g., medication) or routine care alone. After three months, youths whose parents participated in RAP-P reported less suicidal ideation and were rated by parents and therapists as having better social–emotional functioning than controls. Results were maintained 6 months later. Perhaps most interestingly, improvements in family functioning mediated the relationship between the RAP-P treatment

Figure 13.8 The RAP-P program improved family functioning. Better communication and problem-solving at home, in turn, led to fewer suicidal thoughts, plans, and actions among adolescents.

and improvement. RAP-P led to improvements in family communication and problem-solving that, in turn, led to improvements in adolescents' mood.

Review:

- Safety planning includes means restriction; identifying thoughts, feelings, and situations that might trigger a future suicide attempt; and finding sources of support in case of future crises.
- Results of the TASA study indicate that medication, especially SSRIs, are effective in preventing future suicide attempts among adolescents with a history of suicidal actions.
- In family-focused treatment, families learn how to (a) restrict youths' access to firearms, pills, or other means of suicide; (b) improve communication and connectedness in the family; and (c) identify and cope effectively with negative events, thoughts, and feelings. Examples are the SAFETY and RAP-P programs.

Can We Prevent Suicide in Children and Adolescents?

Of course, it is better to prevent suicidal ideation and behavior than to treat it. Most effective suicide prevention programs are administered through schools. The goal of most school-based prevention programs is to help students and staff members recognize risk factors for suicide, increase students' willingness to seek help for depression and other mental health problems that might lead to suicide, and create a school environment that is accepting of all students. Prevention programs may be directed at all students (i.e., universal prevention), subgroups of students who are at increased risk for suicide, such as the victims of bullying (i.e., selective prevention), or students who show the early signs and symptoms associated with suicide (i.e., indicated prevention; O'Connell, Boat, & Warner, 2009).

Prevention programs are often administered through schools for at least four reasons (Davidson & Linnoila, 2013; Surgenor, Quinn, & Hughes, 2016). First, students spend a great deal of time at school. Teachers, coaches, and other school personnel might be trained to recognize the

warning signs of suicide and provide early intervention. Gatekeeper training is a prevention strategy in which mental health providers train school personnel to recognize risk factors for suicidal behavior and to appropriately help students gain access to treatment (Joshi, Hartley, Kessler, & Barstead, 2016).

Second, students themselves can be taught to recognize emotional, behaviors, and substance use problems in themselves and their classmates—problems that place them at risk for suicide. Students can provide support to each other and refer at-risk classmates to professionals who can provide them with the services they need. Educational awareness programs are methods of prevention that help students recognize signs and symptoms of suicidal behavior in themselves and their classmates. For example, Youth Aware of Mental Health (YAM) is an educational awareness program that is associated with significant reductions in suicidal ideation and attempts (Wasserman et al. 2016). Awareness programs are designed to promote the use of mental health services and encourage students to seek professional help if they (or a classmate) experience suicidal thoughts (Freedenthal, 2010).

Third, the social climate of school can either place youths at risk for suicidal behavior or protect them from suicidal thoughts and actions. Prevention programs that reduce bullying and increase students' connectedness to school may be particularly effective. School climate programs attempt to establish a campus culture where students feel safe and welcomed (O'Brennan, Waasdorp, & Bradshaw, 2014). One important step toward a positive school climate is establishing clear rules and consequences for students who violate rules that may jeopardize another student's safety or ability to learn (O'Brennan, Waasdorp, Pas, & Bradshaw, 2015).

Finally, students contemplating suicide can benefit from talking with classmates who have experienced suicide in their own lives. Peer support programs are prevention strategies in which students who have experienced mental health problems in themselves or their families share their experiences with at-risk classmates and provide support and reassurance. These programs are based on social learning theory, the notion that modeling positive coping strategies (e.g., talking about one's feelings, seeking help from others) can increase students' willingness to report suicidal thoughts and obtain treatment. Examples include the Coping and Support Training (CAST), Linking Education and Awareness of Depression and Suicide (LEADS), and Lifelines programs. Several studies indicate that peer support programs can be effective in reducing suicidal thoughts and suicide attempts in adolescents (Reidenberg, 2014). Students also report significant improvement in their mood and feelings of acceptance and inclusion through their interactions with peer models (Petrova, Wyman, Schmeelk-Cone, & Pisani, 2015; Surgenor et al. 2016).

Review:

- Gatekeeper training, educational awareness programs, and school climate/peer support programs have demonstrated modest effectiveness in preventing suicide.

KEY TERMS

Anhedonia: Subjective decrease or loss of pleasure in people and events the individual used to find enjoyable 430

Attributions: Our explanation for events 438

Bipolar disorders: A group of *DSM-5* disorders characterized by discrete periods of mania or hypomania (i.e., feelings of euphoria, energy, and grandiosity); often associated with other periods of dysphoria or depression 422

Bullying: Intentional, repetitive, aggressive behavior that is directed from a person with higher power toward a person of lower power 451

Chronotherapy: The deliberate, controlled presentation of light in order to regulate the sleep–wake cycle, establish better sleep quality, and improve mood 429

Cognitive restructuring: A technique used in cognitive therapy in which the therapist attempts to change cognitive biases and distortions by asking clients to look at situations in more flexible, realistic ways 445

Cortisol: The body's main stress hormone; activates the sympathetic nervous system and initiates fight-or-flight behavior 436

Cyberbullying: A form of bullying in which individuals use digital media to hurt, threaten, harass, or embarrass someone 451

Depressive disorders: A group of *DSM-5* disorders characterized by predominantly depressed or irritable mood, negative affect and anhedonia, a lack of interest in people and activities, and problems meeting the demands of everyday life 421

Depressogenic attributional style: The tendency to attribute negative events to internal, stable, and global factors and positive events to external, unstable, and situational factors 438

Disruptive mood dysregulation disorder (DMDD): A *DSM-5* depressive disorder characterized by (a) severe and recurrent temper outbursts and (b) persistently angry or irritable mood; first diagnosed in children aged 6 to 18 only 422

Educational awareness programs: Suicide prevention programs that help students recognize signs and symptoms of suicidal behavior in themselves and their classmates

Gatekeeper training: A suicide prevention strategy in which mental health providers train school personnel to recognize risk factors and to appropriately help students gain access to treatment 457

Hopelessness: Negative and pessimistic expectations about the future; a unique predictor of suicide 450

Hopelessness theory of suicide: Suicide risk increases when people (a) attribute negative events to stable and global causes, (b) believe the event is important, and (c) believe that he or she is worthless 452

Hypothalamus-pituitary-adrenal (HPA) axis: The body's main stress response and regulatory system; regulates cortisol and operates as a feedback loop 436

Intergenerational interpersonal stress model: A theory of depression that suggests that children of depressed parents may become depressed themselves because of (a) family stressors and (b) poor coping skills modeled by their parents 439

Interpersonal–psychological theory of suicide: Posits that suicide is prompted by three factors: (1) perceived burdensomeness, (2) thwarted belongingness, and (3) capability for suicide 452

Kindling hypothesis: Posits that early depressive episodes sensitize individuals to stressful life events and make them more likely to experience depressive episodes in the future 435

Learned helplessness: Posits that people become depressed when they experience recurrent situations that are negative and uncontrollable; individuals succumb to pain and despair rather than cope effectively 438

Major depressive disorder (MDD): A *DSM-5* disorder characterized by depressed mood, anhedonia, and other indicators of dysphoria that last for at least 2 weeks and cause significant distress or impairment 430

Monoamine hypothesis: Posits that depression is caused by dysregulation of the neurotransmitters serotonin and norepinephrine 436

Negative automatic thoughts: In Beck's cognitive theory of depression, negative transient thoughts or images that arise immediately after some experiences a psychosocial stressor 437

Nonsuicidal self-injury (NSSI): Any action that is self-inflicted, results in injury or potential for injury, but there is no evidence that the person intends to die 448

Peer contagion model: A theory of depression in which peers are believed to model and reinforce depressive symptoms and depressogenic attributions to each other 438

Peer support programs: Suicide prevention strategies in which students who have experienced mental health problems provide support and reassurance to at-risk classmates 457

Persistent Depressive Disorder (Dysthymia): A *DSM-5* disorder characterized by chronically depressed and/or irritable mood for at least 2 years in adults or 1 year in children and cause significant distress or impairment 432

Resourceful Adolescent Parent Program (RAP-P): A brief parenting intervention to prevent the recurrence of suicidal behavior in adolescents; helps parents manage stress and improve the quality of parent–adolescent interactions 456

Response-contingent reinforcement: Pleasurable experiences or the alleviation/reduction of unpleasant experiences that is gained through one's actions 443

Safe Alternatives for Teens and Youths (SAFETY): A family therapy program for youths who attempt suicide; involves (a) restricting adolescents' means of suicide, (b) improving family communication, (c) identifying suicide triggers, and developing better ways to cope with (d) negative thoughts and (e) feelings 455

Safety plans: Verbal and written agreements between adolescents, caregivers, and therapists that are designed to reduce the likelihood of suicidal behavior 454

School climate programs: Suicide prevention programs that attempt to establish a campus culture where students feel safe and welcomed 457

Self-injurious behavior (SIB): Any action that is deliberately self-directed and results in injury or potential injury to oneself 448

Social information-processing theory of depression: Posits that depressed children (a) attribute hostile intentions to other people's ambiguous behavior and (b) show internal and stable causal attributions 490

Suicidal self-injury: Any action that is self-inflicted, results in injury or the potential for injury, and there is implicit or explicit evidence that the person intends to die 448

Suprachiasmatic nucleus (SCN): A centrally located brain region that regulates the sleep-wake cycle and the secretion of cortisol and melatonin 429

Treatment for Adolescents With Depression Study (TADS): A large, randomized controlled study that showed that medication and therapy yielded slightly better outcomes than medication alone for adolescents with depression 447

Treatment of Adolescent Suicide Attempters (TASA) study: A study that demonstrated that antidepressant medication reduced suicidal behavior in youths who previously attempted suicide 455

Treatment of SSRI-Resistant Depression in Adolescents (TORDIA) study: A large, randomized controlled study that indicated that medication and therapy was superior to medication alone for adolescents with treatment-resistant depression 447

CRITICAL THINKING EXERCISES

1. Imagine that you are a junior high school guidance counselor. You want to help the teachers in your school better recognize the signs and symptoms of depression in adolescents. Create a list of symptoms (with examples) that teacher could use to identify at-risk students.

2. Only trained professionals should evaluate someone's risk for suicide. However, it is often helpful for parents and other people who interact with youths to know suicide risk factors. What are some risk factors? If you were a teacher, coach, or mentor and you suspected an adolescent of suicidal thoughts, what would you do?

3. Kimberly is a 14-year-old girl who has been experiencing mood problems over the past 3 months. Kimberly feels terrible about herself, believes that she has no friends, and is angry and resentful toward her family. She was recently cut from the debate team (for missing practices) and her grades have dropped considerably. What attributions might Kimberly make about these negative events?

4. Imagine that you are a psychologist who has recently diagnosed a 15-year-old girl with MDD. Her parents want to know whether antidepressant medication might help her overcome her mood problems and whether antidepressant medication is safe. Based on the data presented in the text, what might you tell her parents?

5. Alida is participating in cognitive therapy for depression. During therapy, Alida comments, "I messed up on my math test yesterday and got a D-. I just can't make myself study. I'm just no good at anything." If you were Alida's therapist, how might you use cognitive restructuring to change her ways of thinking?

TEST YOURSELF AND EXTEND YOUR LEARNING

Videos, flash cards, and links to online resources for this chapter are available to students online. Teachers also have access to PowerPoint slides to guide lectures, case studies to prompt classroom discussions, and exam questions. Visit www.abnormalchildpsychology.org.

CHAPTER 14

Pediatric Bipolar Disorders and Schizophrenia

14.1 BIPOLAR DISORDERS IN CHILDREN AND ADOLESCENTS

What Are Bipolar Disorders?

Bipolar disorders are serious mood disorders—defined by the presence of manic symptoms. Mania refers to a discrete period of elevated, expansive, or irritable mood and increased level of energy and activity. All youths with bipolar disorders have at least some manic symptoms. Many (but not all) youths with bipolar disorders also show symptoms of depression. Consequently, these disorders are referred to as "bipolar" (i.e. manic-depressive) mood disorders, in contrast to "unipolar" depression.

The *Diagnostic and Statistical Manual of Mental Disorders, Fifth Edition (DSM-5*; American Psychiatric Association, 2013) recognizes three bipolar disorders that are relevant to children and adolescents: (1) bipolar I disorder, (2) bipolar II disorder, and (3) cyclothymic disorder. These disorders exist on a spectrum of severity. Bipolar I disorder, defined by the presence of full-blown mania, is most severe. In contrast, cyclothymic disorder, which is characterized by subthreshold mood problems, is least severe but longest lasting. All of the bipolar disorders are serious and can greatly disrupt the well-being of children who experience them and their families (Fitzgerald & Pavuluri, 2015).

To be diagnosed with bipolar I disorder, a person must have (or have had) at least one manic episode (see Table 14.1). A manic episode is "a distinct period of abnormally, persistently elevated, expansive, or irritable mood and persistently increased activity and energy" (American Psychiatric Association, 2013, p. 127). By definition, manic episodes last at least 1 week and symptoms are present most of the day, nearly every day. The duration criterion for mania (i.e., 1 week) is waived, however, if the person requires hospitalization.

During manic episodes, adults with bipolar I disorder describe their mood as euphoric, cheerful, high, or elated. They seem to have boundless energy and may describe themselves as powerful or "on top of the world." Children and adolescents also typically report expansive mood, elation, and increased energy. Most experts view the presence of elated mood and increased energy as the cardinal symptoms of bipolar I disorder. On average, 70% of youths with bipolar I disorder show uncharacteristically elated, expansive, or euphoric mood. Nearly 90% of these youths also show a dramatic increase in energy. These symptoms are highly specific to bipolar disorder—that is, they are common among youths with the disorder but relatively uncommon among youths with other psychiatric illnesses. Therefore, they are especially useful in identifying the disorder in children and adolescents (Youngstrom & Algorta, 2014).

Children and adolescents also frequently display irritable mood during manic episodes. Their mood is often described as touchy, angry, oppositional, or reactive. Young children with mania can be grouchy and easily set off. They may throw hour-long tantrums: yelling, crying, or acting physically aggressive toward others. Older children and adolescents sometimes display emotional outbursts or "affective storms." These tantrums often arise with little provocation (Van Meter, Burke, Kowatch, Findling, & Youngstrom, 2016).

Irritability is extremely common among youths with bipolar disorder, even those who also show expansiveness and increased energy. On average, 81% of youths with the disorder show a noticeable increase in irritability. However, irritability is not specific to bipolar disorder; it is a feature of pediatric depression, anxiety, and oppositional defiant disorder (ODD) as well. Therefore, many clinicians consider irritability to be a general indicator that "something's wrong," rather than a specific indicator of bipolar disorder. Irritability is analogous to a fever; it suggests that the child is sick but cannot specify which illness afflicts her (Youngstrom, Birmaher, & Findling, 2008).

Table 14.1   Diagnostic Criteria for Bipolar I Disorder

A. Criteria have been met for at least one manic episode. A manic episode is defined by the following:

- A distinct period of abnormally and persistently elevated, expansive, or irritable mood and abnormally and persistently increased goal-directed activity or energy, lasting at least one week and present most of the day, nearly every day (or any duration if hospitalization is necessary).
- During the period of mood disturbance and increased energy or activity, three (or more) of the following symptoms (four if the mood is only irritable) are present to a significant degree and represent a noticeable change from usual behavior:

  1. Inflated self-esteem or grandiosity.
  2. Decreased need for sleep (e.g., feels rested after only 3 hours of sleep).
  3. More talkative than usual or pressure to keep talking.
  4. Flight of ideas or subjective experience that thoughts are racing.
  5. Distractibility (i.e., attention too easily drawn to unimportant or irrelevant external stimuli), as reported or observed.
  6. Increase in goal-directed activity (either socially, at work or school, or sexually) or psychomotor agitation (i.e., purposeless, non-goal-directed activity).
  7. Excessive involvement in activities that have a high potential for painful consequences (e.g., engaging in unrestrained buying sprees, sexual indiscretions, or foolish business investments).

- The mood disturbance is sufficiently severe to cause marked impairment in social or occupational functioning or to necessitate hospitalization to prevent harm to self or others, or there are psychotic features.
- The episode is not attributable to the physiological effects of a substance (e.g., a drug of abuse, a medication) or to another medical condition.

B. The occurrence of the manic episode is not better explained by schizophrenia or another psychotic disorder.

Source: Reprinted with permission from the *Diagnostic and Statistical Manual of Mental Disorders, Fifth Edition* (Copyright 2013). American Psychiatric Association.

In addition to these changes in mood and energy, mania is characterized by at least three other signs or symptoms (or four symptoms, if the person shows only irritable mood). You can remember these signs and symptoms using the acronym GRAPES + D. On average, youths show five or six signs or symptoms during a manic episode (see Table 14.2; Diler & Birmaher, 2012).

Grandiosity or inflated self-esteem. In adults, grandiosity is characterized by unusually high self-confidence, exaggerated self-esteem, and overrated self-importance. Some adults hold erroneous beliefs that they have special abilities, talents, or skills. Youths with mania are also capable of grandiosity and inflated self-esteem. Children may manifest grandiose thinking by claiming that they are special, have superhuman abilities, or hold magical powers. For example, a child may try to jump off the roof of his house because he thinks that he has unusual athletic abilities. Older children and adolescents might tell their coaches how to run the team, or their teachers how to instruct the class, because they believe that they have special talents or intelligence.

Racing thoughts or flight of ideas. Adults with mania often report that their thoughts are "racing" or occurring too fast to articulate to others. Some patients describe the sensation as watching two or three television programs at once. Racing thoughts are sometimes referred to as a flight of ideas. Children and adolescents also report racing thoughts. For example, they may say that their minds are going "100 miles an hour" (Kowatch et al., 2005, p. 216).

Increased activity or psychomotor agitation. Adults with mania often show a marked increase in goal-directed activity—that is, they initiate a wide range of new activities and behaviors. For example, some adults with mania may decide to rebuild their car engine, write a novel, or start a new business with little preparation or training. Usually, these goal-directed activities are poorly planned and executed. Youths with mania can also show increased goal-directed activity. For example, children may draw, color, or build elaborate block towers. Older adolescents may begin a number of ambitious projects, like taking apart their computer. Youths with mania may also show psychomotor agitation—that is, they may appear hyperactive, restless, or impulsive. They often engage in short bursts of frenzied activity that do not have much purpose.

Pressured speech or more talkative than usual. Many adults with mania talk rapidly in an attempt to keep up with racing thoughts. Their speech is typically fast, loud, and difficult to understand. Youths with mania may also speak rapidly. Their speech seems pressured—that is, they seem to keep talking in order to avoid periods of silence. Sometimes, they transition rapidly from one topic to the next.

Excessive involvement in activities with high potential for painful consequences. Many adults with mania engage in pleasurable activities that are likely to have negative consequences. For example, some adults with mania go on shopping sprees, gambling trips, or risky sexual encounters. Youths with mania may also engage in pleasurable, but reckless, behaviors. Younger children may ride their bikes through dangerous intersections or perform stunts on their skateboards. Older children and adolescents may carelessly spend money, drive recklessly, steal items from a store, or indulge in alcohol and other drugs. Many youths with mania also show hypersexuality. Some show increased interest in pornography. Others engage in inappropriate, erotic behavior toward others. For example, some children dance suggestively, attempt to touch others' private parts, or open-mouth kiss family members. Youths with mania may show these hypersexual behaviors even if they have never experienced sexual abuse.

Decreased need for sleep. Many adults with mania may feel rested after only 3 hours of sleep. Others go for days without feeling sleepy or fatigued. Youths with mania also show decreased need for sleep. Many youths with mania sleep only 4 or 5 hours at night and wake in the early morning feeling full of energy. Some wander the house, play video games, or watch TV into the early morning hours.

Table 14.2   Signs and Symptoms of Mania

You can remember the *DSM-5* signs and symptoms of mania using the acronym GRAPES + D:

Grandiosity or inflated self-esteem

Racing thoughts or flight of ideas

Activity level increase or psychomotor agitation

Pressured speech or excessive talkativeness

Excessive involvement in potentially harmful activities

Sleep disturbance (i.e., decreased need for sleep)

Distractibility

From Diler and Birmaher (2012).

Distractibility. Adults with mania are easily distracted by irrelevant external stimuli or unimportant details. For example, an adult with mania may find it difficult to converse with another person because he is distracted by the pattern of the other person's tie or events occurring outside the room. Youths with mania almost always show distractibility. They may have problems concentrating on schoolwork or completing chores. Teachers and parents may describe them as disorganized or flighty. These problems with distractibility reflect a marked change in the youth's typical behavior, not a general problem with inattention or hyperactivity–impulsivity (i.e., not due to attention-deficit/hyperactivity disorder [ADHD]).

Three manic symptoms are particularly useful in identifying bipolar disorder in children: (1) grandiosity, (2) decreased need for sleep, and (3) involvement in high-risk sexual activity (Youngstrom et al., 2008). First, nearly 80% of youths with bipolar disorder show some form of grandiose thinking. If grandiosity coincides with increased elation and energy, it is a good indicator of mania.

Second, most (70%) youths with bipolar disorder show a decreased need for sleep. Typically, these youths feel rested after only a few hours of sleep. Decreased need for sleep is a good indicator of bipolar disorder because other disorders, such as anxiety and depression, are associated with problems falling asleep or staying asleep. Consider Emily, an adolescent experiencing her first manic episode.

Third, high-risk sexual activity is a relatively specific sign of bipolar disorder. A prepubescent child might begin acting or dressing in a sexually provocative manner at school, or an adolescent might engage in dangerous or exploitative sexual behavior with adults. A developmentally unexpected or marked change in sexual behavior is specific to only bipolar disorder and sexual abuse. Parents and clinicians who observe these changes in youths might suspect bipolar disorder, especially when the behavior is associated with increased elation and energy (Klimes-Dougan, Kennedy, & Cullen, 2016).

Bipolar II Disorder

To be diagnosed with bipolar II disorder, a person must have (or have had) at least one major depressive episode

---

CASE STUDY

BIPOLAR I DISORDER

Energetic Emily

Sixteen-year-old Emily Gellar was referred to our clinic by her parents. Mrs. Gellar said that Emily had been more reclusive, sullen, and moody in recent weeks. Emily was often disrespectful, irritable, and upset. When her mother asked her to clean up after dinner, Emily replied, "Why don't you just do it—that's all you're good for around here anyway!" In the previous 4 weeks, Emily dropped out of two of her favorite activities at school. She also slept very little, ate even less, and was generally sluggish and mopey around the house.

Emily reluctantly agreed to a "trial run" of therapy with Brenda Turner, a social worker at an our clinic. Brenda diagnosed Emily with depression and began to use interpersonal therapy (IPT) to improve Emily's mood. However, by the fourth session, Brenda noticed a dramatic change in Emily's affect and behavior. Emily arrived at the session in an unusually good mood. She spoke very fast: "I feel great today, Brenda, you know, like I can do anything. I think it's because I am in love." As Emily discussed her new boyfriend, Brenda noticed that her speech was extremely loud and her train of thought was difficult to follow. "Have you been drinking today?" Brenda asked. In a giddy tone, Emily responded, "Not today, I don't feel like I need to."

During the session, Brenda noticed how distractible Emily was. Emily fidgeted in her chair, paced about the room, and kept complaining how "boring" it was to sit and talk. She reported a sudden increase in energy and mood. She added, "You know, I think I'm cured. Maybe we don't have to meet anymore." Emily said she slept only about three or four hours in the previous 2 days but still did not feel tired. In fact, at 3:00 a.m. the night before, she decided to paint her room. "Thank God for Wal-Mart!" she said, "Do you know they're open 24 hours . . . and they sell paint?"

After the session, Brenda telephoned Mrs. Gellar to express her concern. Mrs. Gellar reported that Emily did, in fact, attempt to paint her bedroom in bright green but only managed to complete one and a half walls before moving on to another project. Emily also had been in trouble that week for skipping school, staying out all night, and going on a shopping spree with her mother's credit card. Mrs. Gellar stated, "She's been so distractible and flighty lately, I don't know what's gotten into her. Do you think she's just being a teenager?" Brenda answered, "No, I don't think so."

and at least one hypomanic episode (see Table 14.3). The prefix *hypo* means "below"; therefore, hypomania refers to less severe or prolonged manic symptoms. Like mania, hypomania is defined by a distinct period of elevated, expansive, or irritable mood and increased energy. Furthermore, the seven symptoms of hypomania are the same as the symptoms of mania. Hypomania differs from mania in three ways.

1. Hypomania lasts at least 4 days but less than 1 week.
2. Hypomania *does not* cause significant impairment in social, occupational, or academic functioning.
3. Hypomania *never* requires the person to be hospitalized.

By definition, a person cannot be diagnosed with bipolar II disorder if she has ever had a manic episode. If the person has had a manic episode, she would be diagnosed with bipolar I disorder instead. Many individuals initially diagnosed with bipolar II disorder eventually experience a manic episode and are subsequently diagnosed with bipolar I disorder.

Hypomania is somewhat difficult to assess in children and adolescents. By definition, it does not lead to marked distress or impairment in functioning and does not require hospitalization. Consequently, many parents do not refer their children to treatment because of hypomania. It is also difficult to differentiate hypomania from developmentally normative behavior. For example, many adolescents are impulsive, have rapid changes in mood, or adopt irregular sleep habits, but they do not have hypomania (Youngstrom, Van Meter, & Algorta, 2010).

By definition, youths with bipolar II disorder experience at least one major depressive episode. Depressive episodes are usually characterized by depressed mood, anhedonia, low energy, and irritability. They may take

Table 14.3   Diagnostic Criteria for Bipolar II Disorder

A. Criteria have been met for at least one hypomanic episode and at least one major depressive episode. A hypomanic episode is defined by the following:

- A distinct period of abnormally and persistently elevated, expansive, or irritable mood and abnormally and persistently increased activity or energy, lasting at least 4 days and present most of the day, nearly every day.
- During the period of mood disturbance and increased energy or activity, three (or more) of the following symptoms (four if the mood is only irritable) are present to a significant degree and represent a noticeable change from usual behavior:

    1. Inflated self-esteem or grandiosity.
    2. Decreased need for sleep (e.g., feels rested after only 3 hours of sleep).
    3. More talkative than usual or pressure to keep talking.
    4. Flight of ideas or subjective experience that thoughts are racing.
    5. Distractibility (i.e., attention too easily drawn to unimportant or irrelevant external stimuli), as reported or observed.
    6. Increase in goal-directed activity (either socially, at work or school, or sexually) or psychomotor agitation (i.e., purposeless, non-goal-directed activity).
    7. Excessive involvement in activities that have a high potential for painful consequences (e.g., engaging in unrestrained buying sprees, sexual indiscretions, or foolish business investments).

- The episode is associated with an unequivocal change in functioning that is uncharacteristic of the individual when not symptomatic.
- The disturbance in mood and the change in functioning are observable by others.
- The episode is not severe enough to cause marked impairment in social or occupational functioning or to necessitate hospitalization. If there are psychotic features, the episode is, by definition, manic.
- The episode is not attributable to the physiological effects of a substance (e.g., a drug of abuse, a medication) or to another medical condition.

B. There has never been a manic episode.

C. The occurrence of the hypomanic episode is not better explained by schizophrenia or another psychotic disorder.

D. The symptoms of depression or the unpredictability caused by frequent alteration between periods of depression and hypomania causes clinically significant distress or impairment in social, occupational, or other important areas of functioning.

Source: Reprinted with permission from the *Diagnostic and Statistical Manual of Mental Disorders, Fifth Edition* (Copyright 2013). American Psychiatric Association.

several months to resolve. Youths can experience depression before or after their hypomanic episode (Fitzgerald & Pavuluri, 2015).

Cyclothymic Disorder

Cyclothymic disorder is a bipolar disorder that is rarely diagnosed in children and adolescents (see Table 14.4). The disorder gets its name from the Greek words *kyklos* (cycle) and *thymos* (mood). It is defined by (a) periods of hypomanic symptoms that do not meet full criteria for a hypomanic episode and (b) periods of depressive symptoms that do not meet full criteria for a major depressive episode. Children and adolescents must experience these hypomanic and depressive symptoms for at least 1 year, and they must not be symptom free for more than 2 months.

Children and adolescents with cyclothymic disorder tend to describe their moods as a mixture of lethargy and low self-esteem, combined with racing thoughts and impulsivity. If bipolar I and II disorders are analogous to influenza, cyclothymic disorder would be analogous to the common cold—less severe but more long-lasting symptoms that cause distress or impairment. The most commonly

reported problems are irritability and excessive activity, which rise and fall in an episodic fashion over the course of at least one year. Because irritability and excessive activity are symptoms shared by many psychiatric disorders, and because they are sometimes shown by healthy children, cyclothymic disorder is often misdiagnosed or overlooked by practitioners (Van Meter, Youngstrom, Demeter, & Findling, 2012; Van Meter, Youngstrom, & Findling, 2012).

Distinguishing Among the Bipolar Disorders

Figure 14.1 provides a visual summary of the three main bipolar disorders. Let's review. Bipolar I disorder is defined by the presence of at least one manic episode. Although youths can also experience depression, a depressive episode is not required for the bipolar I disorder diagnosis.

Bipolar II disorder is defined by at least one hypomanic episode and at least one major depressive episode. However, youths must never have experienced a manic episode. Once a child or adolescent experiences a manic episode, he or she is diagnosed with bipolar I disorder instead.

Cyclothymic disorder is defined by hypomanic symptoms that do not meet criteria for a hypomanic episode and depressive symptoms that do not meet criteria for a major depressive episode. Furthermore, children's mood symptoms must last at least 1 year.

Review:

- Bipolar I disorder is a *DSM-5* condition characterized by at least one manic episode that results in marked impairment in functioning or requires hospitalization.
- Bipolar II disorder is a *DSM-5* condition characterized by at least one hypomanic episode and one major depressive episode that results in a marked change in functioning but does not lead to impairment or require hospitalization.
- Cyclothymic disorder is a *DSM-5* condition characterized by periods of hypomanic symptoms (but not a hypomanic episode) and depressive symptoms (but not a major depressive episode) lasting at least 1 year in children and adolescents.

What Problems Are Associated With Pediatric Bipolar Disorders?

Psychotic Features

Approximately 20% of youths with bipolar I disorder experience hallucinations or delusions during their manic episodes. **Hallucinations** are erroneous perceptions that do not correspond to reality. Although hallucinations can occur in any sensory modality, auditory hallucinations are most common. For example, children might hear voices telling them that they are special or possess unique talents. **Delusions** are erroneous beliefs that usually involve a misinterpretation of perceptions or experiences. Usually, these

---

Table 14.4 Diagnostic Criteria for Cyclothymic Disorder

A. For at least 2 years (at least one year in children and adolescents) there have been numerous periods with hypomanic symptoms that do not meet criteria for a hypomanic episode and numerous periods with depressive symptoms that do not meet criteria for a major depressive episode.

B. During the above 2 year period (one year in children and adolescents), the hypomanic and depressive periods have been present for at least half the time and the individual has not been without the symptoms for more than 2 months at a time.

C. Criteria for a major depressive, manic, or hypomanic episode have never been met.

D. The symptoms of criterion A are not better explained by schizophrenia or another psychotic disorder.

E. The symptoms are not attributable to the physiological effects of a substance (e.g., a drug of abuse, a medication) or another medical condition.

F. The symptoms cause clinically significant distress or impairment in social, occupational, or other important areas of functioning.

Source: Reprinted with permission from the *Diagnostic and Statistical Manual of Mental Disorders, Fifth Edition* (Copyright 2013). American Psychiatric Association.

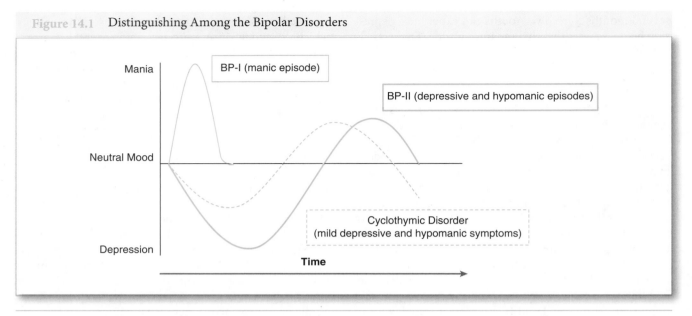

Figure 14.1   Distinguishing Among the Bipolar Disorders

Note: BP-I is defined by at least one manic episode. BP-II is defined by at least one major depressive episode and at least one hypomanic episode (but no manic episodes). Cyclothymic Disorder is defined by recurrent depressive and hypomanic symptoms (but no mood episodes).

beliefs are bizarre in nature or otherwise implausible. For example, an adolescent might believe that he is called to perform a special mission (i.e., delusions of reference) or has a special identity or power (i.e., delusion of grandiosity).

DSM-5 instructs clinicians to specify the presence of hallucinations and/or delusions when diagnosing bipolar I disorder. Specifying the presence of hallucinations and delusions is important because youths with bipolar I disorder who show psychotic symptoms tend to have poorer outcomes than their counterparts without these symptoms. As Hermione Granger once said to Harry Potter, "Even in the wizarding world, hearing voices isn't a good sign" (see Figure 14.2; Fristad, Arnold, & Leffler, 2011).

Mixed Features

The diagnostic criteria for bipolar disorders are the same for children, adolescents, and adults. However, the manifestation of these disorders depends on the person's age and level of development (Danielyan, Pathak, Kowatch, Arszman, & Johns, 2007; Masi et al., 2006, 2007). Most adults with bipolar disorders show classic, discrete episodes of mania and depression. A typical adult patient has reasonably good functioning before his first mood episode. Then, usually between the ages of 18 and 25, he experiences a clear manic episode marked by euphoria, inflated self-esteem and grandiosity, decreased need for sleep, racing thoughts and rapid speech, and risk-taking behavior. Following this clear-cut manic episode, which may last for a few weeks, he enters a period of major depression that can persist for weeks or months. Finally, his depression abates, and he shows a return to reasonably good functioning until his next mood episode.

Children and adolescents with bipolar disorders rarely show this classic presentation of mania and depression. Instead, youths often show mixed signs and symptoms during a single mood episode. A mixed mood occurs when youths meet criteria for either a manic or hypomanic episode and simultaneously show subthreshold symptoms of depression. Alternatively, a mixed mood can occur when youths meet criteria for a major depressive episode and simultaneously show subthreshold hypomanic symptoms (American Psychiatric Association, 2013).

How might a child or adolescent show both mania or hypomania *and* depression? To understand mixed moods, experts have likened them to desserts (see Figure 14.3; Youngstrom & Algorta, 2014). Some mixed moods are analogous to "chocolate milk"; symptoms of mania and depression are dissolved together into a homogenous state that is different from either component. These children display a blend of crankiness, irritability, anger, high energy, and excitability.

Other mixed moods are analogous to "fudge ripple"; chunks of manic and chunks of depressive symptoms remain identifiable in the child's behavior. During the course of the day, the child's mood might cycle from brief periods of elation and energy superimposed on more predominant instances of irritability, tearfulness, and lethargy. Some youths experience these mood fluctuations multiple times each day. In *DSM-5*, clinicians indicate the presence of mixed mood symptoms by adding a "with mixed features" specifier to the bipolar disorder diagnosis (American Psychiatric Association, 2013).

Mixed, fluctuating mood states are common among youths with bipolar disorders. In one study, 81% of children with bipolar disorders displayed mood shifts from hypomania

Figure 14.2   Bipolar I Disorder With and Without Psychotic Symptoms

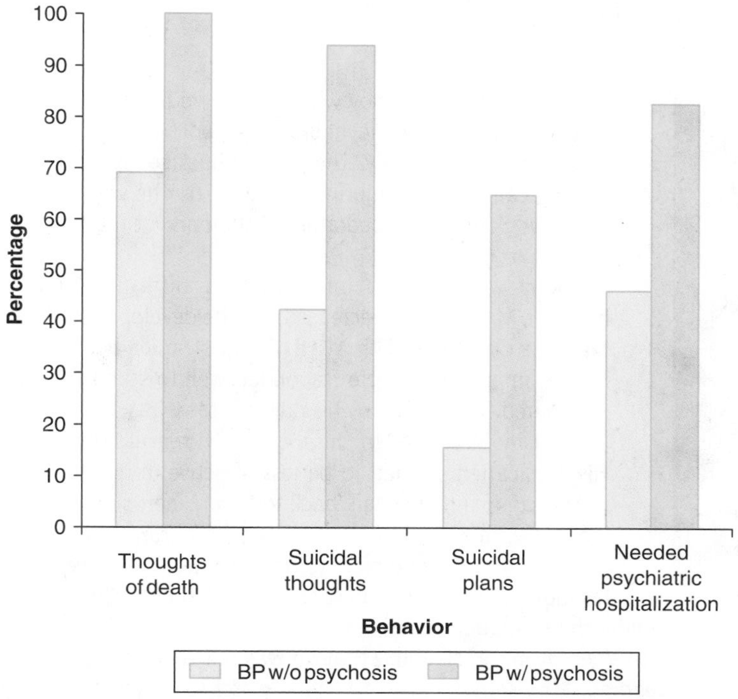

(Bar chart. Y-axis: Percentage, 0 to 100. X-axis: Behavior)

Behavior	BP w/o psychosis	BP w/ psychosis
Thoughts of death	~69	100
Suicidal thoughts	~42	~94
Suicidal plans	~15	~64
Needed psychiatric hospitalization	~45	~82

Source: Based on Caetano et al. (2006).

Note: Youths with Bipolar Disorders with Psychotic Symptoms show more severe impairment than youths with Bipolar Disorders alone.

Figure 14.3   Understanding Mixed Moods

How can children show both symptoms of mania and symptoms of depression?

The chocolate milk analogy:
A blend of crankiness, irritability, anger, high energy, & excitability

The fudge ripple analogy:
Brief periods of elation and energy superimposed on more predominant irritability, tearfulness, and lethargy

Source: Adapted from Youngstom and colleagues (2008). Images courtesy of pixabay.

to normal mood to depression during a single 24-hour period. In another study, approximately one third of adolescents with bipolar disorders displayed these rapid changes in mood. In contrast, rapid changes in mood are relatively rare among adults with bipolar disorders. Consider Max, a boy with mixed moods (Youngstrom & Algorta, 2014).

Review:

• Approximately 20% of youths with bipolar I disorder have psychotic features such as hallucinations or delusions. Youths with psychotic features are often more severely impaired than youths with bipolar I disorder alone.

BIPOLAR I DISORDER WITH MIXED FEATURES

Mixed Mood Max

Source: ©iStockphoto/eyecrave

Max was a 9-year-old boy who was referred to our hospital after an apparent suicide attempt. One day, while riding to school with his mother, Max began talking and laughing uncontrollably. Then, he unbuckled his seat belt and jumped out of their moving car, seriously injuring himself. After he was treated in the emergency department, Dr. Saunders, a pediatric psychologist at the hospital, interviewed Max and his mother.

Max was a "colicky" infant who was difficult to soothe. During his toddler years, however, Max's crying decreased, and he developed into an energetic, inquisitive child. Max was diagnosed with ADHD 3 years earlier, because of problems with hyperactivity and impulsiveness. He responded well to stimulant medication. Although he was considered "a handful" by his parents, Max was a likable, friendly boy.

Six months prior to the incident, however, Max's disposition began to change. His medication seemed to be less effective in managing his hyperactivity. He would whine, complain, and talk back to family members. Max began having problems falling asleep at night and eventually refused to go to bed when asked. In the morning, Max was irritable and cranky. Max also became a "weepy" child; on several occasions, his mother overheard him sobbing in his room, "Nobody loves me."

Max's mood deteriorated rapidly the week before his hospitalization. He was highly active and boisterous, both at home and at school. He refused to sleep at night, claiming that he was not tired, but during the day, he seemed moody and easily set off. Instead of sleeping, Max snuck out of his room, watched television, played video games, and even began disassembling his bicycle "to see how it worked." His mother also caught him viewing adult-oriented material on the computer.

Two days earlier, Max was suspended from school after starting a fight in the lunchroom. When a classmate would not allow Max to sit next to him, Max threw his food at the child and hit him with his tray. Max was taken to the principal's office, where he continued to scream and tantrum until his mother arrived an hour later.

Dr. Saunders asked Max about his apparent suicide attempt. Max said he did not want to kill himself. He explained, "I told my mom that I didn't want to go to school, and she wouldn't listen. So, I thought that if I just ran really fast, I could keep up with the car and hop out."

- Most youths with bipolar disorders experience mixed mood features. They show periods of mania with depressive or irritable mood or periods of major depression with hypomanic symptoms.

How Are Pediatric Bipolar Disorders Different From Other Childhood Disorders?

Externalizing Behavior Problems

Approximately 70% of children and 31% of adolescents with bipolar disorders also have ADHD (Birmaher et al., 2009). Some of this apparent comorbidity may be due to symptoms common to both ADHD and mania, such as talkativeness, distractibility, and excessive motor activity. However, it is clear that many youths legitimately experience both disorders. Despite symptom overlap, the two disorders can be

differentiated. A child with ADHD runs into the street because he forgot to look out for cars. A child with bipolar disorder runs out into the street because he believes he can outrun the cars (Fristad et al., 2011).

Although youths with bipolar disorders are at risk for ADHD, the converse is not true: Youths with ADHD are *not* at increased risk for developing bipolar disorders. In one large study of children and adolescents with ADHD, only one child met diagnostic criteria for a bipolar disorder (Hassan, Agha, Langley, & Thapar, 2011).

Disruptive behavior disorders are also comorbid conditions, although prevalence depends on age of onset (Birmaher et al., 2009). Youths with childhood-onset bipolar disorders are most likely to develop ODD (43%), whereas youths with adolescent-onset bipolar disorders are more likely to have conduct disorder (CD; 16%) or substance use problems (23%). Differentiating conduct problems and bipolar disorders can be challenging. In general, youths with conduct problems are deliberately noncompliant, whereas youths with bipolar disorders cannot comply because of their mood problems (Fristad et al., 2011).

The psychiatrist Emil Kraepelin was among the first diagnosticians to identify bipolar disorders in children and adolescents. Indeed, Kraepelin documented episodes of mania, depression, and irritability in approximately one hundred youths. Kraepelin saw the essential features of bipolar disorders in children and adolescents to be consistent with the features shown by adults with the disorder: severe mood episodes, which lasted several days or weeks, and marked impairment in functioning (Leibenluft, Charney, Towbin, Bhangoo, & Pine, 2003).

Despite Kraepelin's early observations, bipolar disorders came to be viewed as "adult" disorders—conditions rarely, if ever, shown by children. In the 1980s, however, Gabrielle Carlson described bipolar symptoms in prepubescent children, characterized by severe irritability and rapidly changing, mixed mood states. Carlson's description renewed interest among researchers and clinicians in pediatric bipolar disorders. Two views gradually emerged.

The first view, consistent with Kraepelin, was that the essential features of bipolar disorders were largely invariant across childhood, adolescence, and adulthood. All individuals with bipolar disorders, regardless of age, showed discrete mood episodes, characterized by manic (and often depressive) symptoms associated with marked impairment in functioning (Leibenluft et al., 2003).

The second view was that the definition of bipolar disorders should be expanded to include youths who showed *chronic* irritability and angry outbursts. According to this view, chronic mood problems, characterized by persistent irritability, anger, and violent or destructive tantrums, reflected an underlying mood disturbance consistent with bipolar disorders (Biederman, Milberger, & Faraone, 1995; Wozniak et al., 1995).

Expanding the definition of bipolar disorders caused a marked increase in the number of youths diagnosed with this condition. Increased diagnosis was also fueled by a *Time* magazine cover story and a lead article in the *New York Times Magazine* (Egan, 2008; Kluger & Song, 2002; Papolos & Papolos, 2000). These popular publications led many parents and clinicians to suspect that chronically angry, irritable, and moody children, who often displayed fits, tantrums, or "rages" might have bipolar disorders. Although the actual prevalence of bipolar disorders never changed, the frequency of the diagnosis increased markedly in outpatient clinics and hospitals (Parens & Johnston, 2010).

Although experts still disagree regarding the best conceptualization of pediatric bipolar disorders, research by Leibenluft and colleagues helped to resolve the issue (Leibenluft & Dickstein, 2008). Leibenluft and colleagues (2003) recognized that many children did show chronic problems with irritability and angry outbursts; however,

they argued, these children do not have pediatric bipolar disorders. Whereas bipolar disorder is an illness defined by mood *episodes*, these youths showed *chronic* problems with irritability, dysphoria, and anger. Prior to *DSM-5*, these children were "diagnostic orphans"—that is, youths with emotional problems who needed help, but did not fit any diagnostic category. Many clinicians diagnosed these youths with bipolar disorders so that they might receive treatment.

Rather than change *DSM* criteria to fit these children's symptoms, Leibenluft and colleagues (2003) created a new diagnostic classification, severe mood dysregulation (SMD), defined by the presence of *chronic* irritability or anger, violent or destructive temper outbursts, and hyperactivity–impulsivity. Researchers identified a large group of children with SMD and studied the presentation, course, and causes of this condition. They found that young children with SMD often developed depression and anxiety disorders in adolescence and early adulthood; almost none developed bipolar disorders. Furthermore, youths with SMD often had family members with depression or anxiety disorders, not bipolar disorders. The researchers concluded that chronic irritability and angry outbursts reflected depression, not bipolar disorders.

Because of this research, a new diagnosis was included in *DSM-5*: disruptive mood dysregulation disorder (DMDD). Recall that DMDD is a mood disorder characterized by persistent problems with irritability and frequent angry outbursts.

Both children with DMDD and children with bipolar disorders can show irritability and angry outbursts. However, children with DMDD show these problems persistently, whereas youths with bipolar disorders show a noticeable increase in these symptoms during mood episodes. DMDD is considered a depressive disorder, because it more closely resembles depression and anxiety than bipolar disorders (Fitzgerald & Pavuluri, 2015).

Review:

- Most children with bipolar disorders have ADHD; however, most youths with ADHD do not have bipolar disorders. Unlike youths with ADHD, youths with bipolar disorders show episodes of hyperactivity, decreased need for sleep, and risk taking.
- Children with DMDD show chronic problems with irritability and angry outbursts; in contrast, youths with bipolar disorders show episodic problems with irritability, grandiosity, and mood.

How Common Are Bipolar Disorders in Children and Adolescents?

Prevalence

There are very few epidemiological studies investigating the prevalence of bipolar disorders in children and adolescents.

Overall, the lifetime prevalence of bipolar I disorder ranges from 0% to 1.9% in youths, which is similar to the 1% lifetime prevalence seen in the adult population (Merikangas & Pato, 2009). However, the lifetime prevalence of all bipolar disorders may range from 3% to 4% (Youngstrom, Freeman, & Jenkins, 2009). Most adults with bipolar disorders report an age of onset either in childhood (15%–28%) or adolescence (50%–66%; Miklowitz, Mullen, & Chang, 2008).

The prevalence of bipolar disorders is much higher among children and adolescents referred for treatment compared to youths in the community. In outpatient mental health clinics, approximately 6% to 7% of youths have a bipolar disorder. Among youths receiving treatment in psychiatric hospitals, 26% to 34% have been diagnosed with this condition (Youngstrom et al., 2009).

Gender, Age, and Ethnicity

Data on gender differences in child and adolescent bipolar disorders are sparse. Adolescent and adult samples indicate that men and women are equally likely to develop bipolar I disorder. However, symptoms of bipolar disorders differ somewhat in men and women. Men tend to have earlier symptom onset and more frequent manic episodes than women. Women, on the other hand, tend to show higher frequency of mixed episodes and psychotic features than men. Bipolar II disorder may be more common in females. One epidemiological study showed a slightly increased prevalence of bipolar II in adolescent girls (3.3%) than boys (2.6%; Birmaher et al., 2009). This gender disparity may be due to the fact that depressive episodes are more common among females (Duax, Youngstrom, Calabrese, & Findling, 2007).

Adolescent boys and girls with bipolar disorders show different comorbid problems. Boys (91%) are somewhat more likely than girls (70%) to have comorbid ADHD. Girls (61%) are more likely than boys (46%) to have comorbid anxiety disorders (Biederman, Kwon et al., 2004).

Very few studies have investigated differences in pediatric bipolar disorders as a function of ethnicity. The prevalence of bipolar disorders among African Americans is similar to the prevalence of the disorder among non-Latino Whites. However, some data indicate that the *presentation* of bipolar disorders may vary across ethnic groups. African American adolescents with bipolar disorders are more likely to show psychotic symptoms, especially auditory hallucinations, than non-Latino, White adolescents with the disorder. Researchers are uncertain what causes these ethnic differences in symptom presentation (Patel, DelBello, Keck, & Strakowski, 2006).

Course and Outcomes

The onset of bipolar disorder is typically insidious (i.e., gradual and barely noticeable at first). Youths usually begin showing prodromal, subthreshold mood problems months or years before their first mood episode. In one study, 52%

of youths began experiencing minor mood problems 1 year before their first mood episode; only 4% of youths experienced sudden symptom onset. The most commonly reported mood problems are dysphoria, difficulty concentrating, irritability, and agitation. These problems are sometimes experienced by healthy youths from time to time, so they often go unnoticed and untreated (Luby & Navsaria, 2010).

Once youths experience a full-blown mood episode, symptoms usually persist for some time. The best data regarding the course of bipolar disorders in children and adolescents come from the Course and Outcome of Bipolar Youth (COBY) study. In this study, researchers recruited 413 youths (aged 7–17) with bipolar I, bipolar II, or subthreshold symptoms. All youths were receiving treatment, typically with medication. The researchers assessed the youths' emotional functioning every 9 months for 4 years in order to determine their outcomes (Birmaher et al., 2009).

Approximately two-and-a-half years after their first mood episode, most (81.5%) youths fully recovered. Average time to recovery was 124 weeks. However, 1.5 years later, at the end of the study, most (62.5%) had experienced another mood episode, usually depression. On average, the time from recovery to recurrence was 71 weeks. Approximately one-half of youths who experienced recurrence actually showed multiple mood episodes during the course of the 4-year study (see Figure 14.4).

The researchers also asked families to comment on children's emotional functioning from week to week. Children tended to show discrete mood episodes, usually long episodes of depression. When not experiencing these episodes, however, youths still tended to show subthreshold symptoms of depression and irritability. Even after recovery, youths remained symptomatic 60% of the time. Youths also tended to show mixed mood symptoms, with frequent changes in mood from excitability to irritability to sadness. On average, youths' moods changed polarity 12 times during the course of 1 year.

Individuals with childhood- and adolescent-onset bipolar disorders may have worse outcomes than individuals whose bipolar symptoms emerge during adulthood (Masi et al., 2007). Carlson, Bromet, and Sievers (2000) compared individuals with early and adult-onset bipolar disorders on a number of outcome variables. They found that individuals whose symptom onset occurred during adolescence showed greater frequency of manic symptoms, less remission of symptoms and more relapse over time, and a greater number of psychiatric hospitalizations than individuals whose onset occurred during adulthood. Furthermore, individuals with early onset bipolar disorders were more likely to have experienced educational, employment, and substance use problems than people whose symptoms emerged during adulthood.

Bipolar disorders can be debilitating if left untreated. Over time, patients who do not receive medication are at considerable risk for recurrent episodes of mania and depression, employment and relationship problems, legal

Figure 14.4   Results of the COBY Study on Childhood Bipolar Disorder

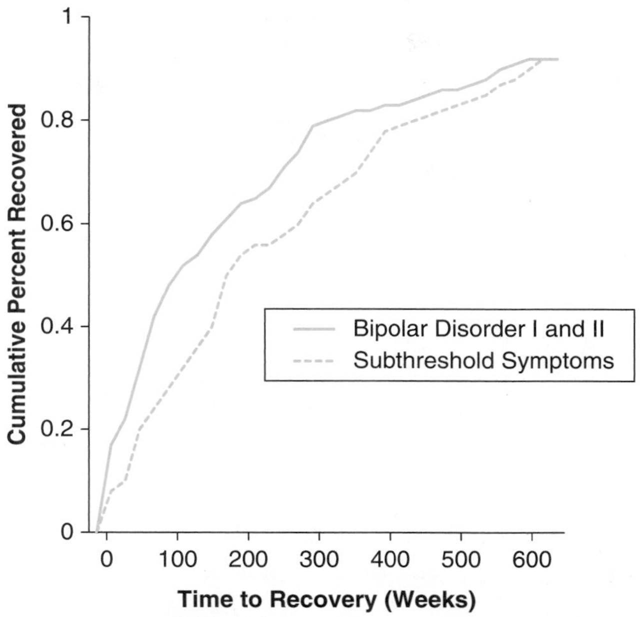

Source: Based on Birmaher, Axelson, Goldstein (2009).

Note: Most youths with bipolar disorders recover from their first mood episode, although average time to recovery is 124 weeks. Recovery is faster for youths with bipolar I or II disorder than for youths with subthreshold symptoms. Unfortunately, 62.5% of youths who recover will relapse within 18 months.

problems, hospitalizations, substance abuse, and suicide. These outcomes highlight the importance of identifying and managing bipolar disorders as early as possible (Youngstrom & Algorta, 2014).

Review:

- Approximately 1% of youths have bipolar I disorder; however, the prevalence of any bipolar disorder may range from 3% to 4% in children and adolescents.
- Girls with bipolar disorders are more likely to experience comorbid anxiety disorders whereas boys with bipolar disorders are more likely to experience comorbid ADHD.
- Bipolar disorders usually have an insidious onset with a long prodromal period marked by dysphoria, concentration problems, and irritability.
- The COBY study showed that most youths with bipolar disorders recovered from their initial manic or hypomanic episode, continued to experience mood problems, and experienced another mood episode within 1.5 years.

What Causes Bipolar Disorders in Youths?

Genetics

The single greatest risk factor for bipolar disorders is having a biologically related family member with a bipolar disorder (Birmaher et al., 2010). The average concordance rate for monozygotic (MZ) twins (.40) is much higher than the rate for dizygotic (DZ) twins (.05; Merikangas & Pato, 2009). Although the lifetime prevalence of bipolar disorders is appropriately 1%, the prevalence among the children of adults with bipolar disorders ranges from 5% to 10%. Furthermore, the children of adults with bipolar disorders are at increased risk for a wide range of psychiatric conditions (Klimes-Dougan et al., 2016).

In the Pittsburgh Bipolar Offspring Study (BIOS), researchers compared a large sample of children whose parents had bipolar disorders with a large sample of children from the community (Birmaher et al., 2009; 2010). After controlling for demographic variables, the children (aged 6–18) of adults with the illness showed increased risk of developing bipolar disorders, other mood disorders, and anxiety disorders. They were also twice as likely to develop psychiatric disorders as the children of healthy parents. Even preschool-age children (aged 2–5) of adults with bipolar disorders were at increased risk for psychiatric disorders, especially disruptive behavior problems (see Figure 14.5).

Brain Structure and Functioning

Several neuroimaging studies have compared the brains of youths with and without bipolar disorders. One of the most consistent neuroanatomical findings is that youths

Figure 14.5   The Pittsburgh Bipolar Offspring Study

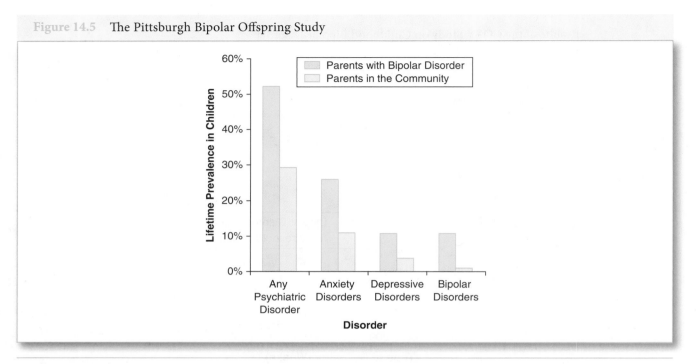

Source: Based on Birmaher, Axelson, Monk, Kalas, et al. (2009).

Note: The Pittsburgh Bipolar Offspring Study examined the children of adults with bipolar disorders. These children showed increased risk for developing bipolar disorders, anxiety, and depression.

with bipolar disorders often have smaller brains than unaffected youths. In several studies, adolescents with bipolar disorders showed a 5% reduction in total cerebral volume compared to adolescents without bipolar disorders. These findings suggest that genetic factors may cause irregular neurological development, which results in smaller brain size (Carlson, Pataki, & Meyer, 2015).

Since bipolar disorders are mood disorders, researchers have focused on areas of the brain responsible for emotional processing and regulation. Researchers have known for some time that children and adults with bipolar disorders often have problems correctly labeling others' facial expressions. When they are shown pictures of people displaying various emotions, they often misinterpret these expressions. Specifically, they tend to interpret benign facial expressions as sad, angry, or hostile. These problems with emotion recognition are seen even when youths are not experiencing mood episodes. As you might expect, problems identifying emotional expressions in others can interfere with their ability to interpret social situations and behave appropriately (Luby & Navsaria, 2010).

Youths with bipolar disorders also show abnormalities in brain areas responsible for emotion regulation. First, youths with bipolar disorders display hyperactivation of the amygdala, compared to healthy youths. Recall that the amygdala is part of the limbic system, a brain region that is critical to the experience and expression of negative emotions, especially fear and rage. When youths with bipolar disorders perceive negative facial expressions in others, they

experience more negative emotions themselves and show overactivity in this brain region.

Second, youths with bipolar disorders show hypoactivation in areas of the prefrontal cortex, during facial processing. Specifically, functional magnetic resonance imaging (fMRI) studies have shown underactivity in the dorsolateral and ventrolateral prefrontal cortices. Recall that the prefrontal cortex is the brain's "executive" area; it is involved in planning, considering the long-term consequences of our actions, and inhibiting behavior that might interfere with our long-term goals. The dorsolateral prefrontal cortex plays an important role in directing, shifting, and sustaining our attention. When presented with negative stimuli, the dorsolateral prefrontal cortex helps to inhibit our behavior and to regulate our emotions by directing our attention elsewhere. The ventrolateral prefrontal cortex partially regulates our peripheral nervous system, endocrine system, and motor system—body regions that become active during times of stress. Underactivity of the ventrolateral prefrontal cortex would lead to difficulty controlling these bodily reactions and greater behavioral and emotional arousal (see Figure 14.6; Luby & Navsaria, 2010).

Interestingly, the amygdala (and other limbic areas) are functionally connected to the prefrontal regions of the brain. Together, the available data indicate that youths with bipolar disorders often misinterpret the emotional expressions of others in a hostile or threatening way. They may have difficulty directing their attention away from these negative expressions in others and experience more

Figure 14.6   Brain Abnormalities in Children With Bipolar Disorders

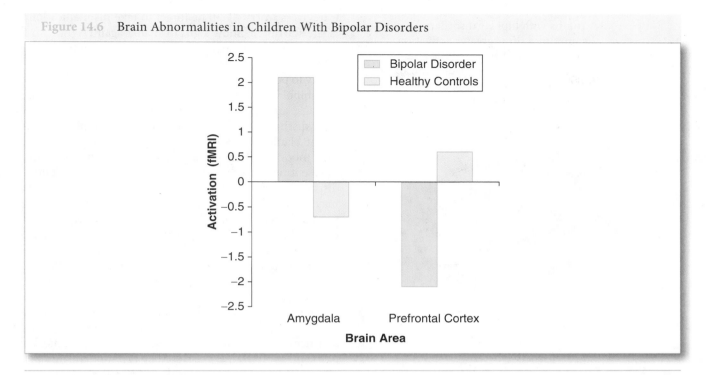

Source: Based on Garrett and colleagues (2012).

Note: Compared to healthy adolescents, youths with bipolar disorders show over-activation of the amygdala and underactivation of the prefrontal cortices while completing a frustrating task. These abnormalities are associated with high emotional reactivity to stress and problems regulating their emotions.

negative emotions themselves as a consequence. Once they begin experiencing fear, anger, or agitation, they may have trouble regulating these emotions and inhibiting their actions. Instead of thinking before acting, they may act out in an emotional or physical manner (Garrett et al., 2012).

Emotion Regulation

Other researchers have tried to explain why youths with bipolar disorders are so easily upset by seemingly minor stressors or setbacks. To answer this question, Rich and colleagues (2011) asked youths with and without bipolar disorders to play a simple computer game. The game required youths to press one of two buttons, depending on which side of the screen a stimulus was displayed. Correct answers were rewarded with money (e.g., "Correct! Win 25 cents"). Although the task was very easy, the game was rigged to frustrate participants. On slightly more than half of the trials, youths were told that their answer was incorrect, or "too slow," regardless of their response (e.g., "Wrong! Lose 25 cents"). While youths played the game, researchers recorded their brain activity.

Results showed marked differences in the brain activity of youths with and without bipolar disorders (Rich et al., 2011). As expected, youths with bipolar disorders reported more sadness and negative emotion during the rigged task than healthy youths. More importantly, youths with bipolar disorders showed much greater activity in the right superior frontal gyrus and much less activity in the

left insula brain region compared to controls. The superior frontal gyrus is a large area of the frontal lobe responsible for many activities, including attention and working memory. The insula is a more centrally located brain area, close to the limbic area, that plays a role in emotion regulation. Together, these findings indicate that youths with bipolar disorders may have problems directing their attention away from negative events and experiences. Once upset, they may also have difficulty modulating their emotions to deal effectively with problems (see Figure 14.7).

Of course, neuroimaging studies like these do not tell us whether these brain differences cause bipolar disorders; whether the symptoms of bipolar disorders cause deficits in emotion regulation; or whether a third variable, yet unidentified, might affect both brain and behavior. Longitudinal neuroimaging studies of youths with bipolar disorders are sorely needed to address these questions about causality (Carlson et al., 2015).

Stressful Life Events

Stressful events have also been shown to trigger manic and depressive episodes in adults with bipolar disorders. The death of a loved one, the loss of a job, or a crisis at home can lead to relapse. Interestingly, events do not always have to be negative to trigger relapse. Any life experience that seriously disrupts day-to-day routines can contribute to a change in mood. For example, adults with bipolar disorders who get married, change jobs,

Figure 14.7 Youths with bipolar disorders sometimes show greater activation of the superior frontal gyrus and less activation of the insula. These differences may underlie problems coping with negative events.

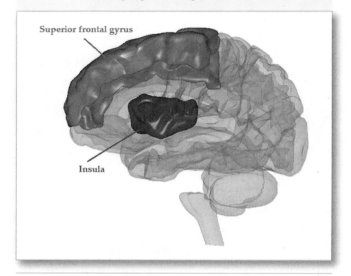

Superior frontal gyrus

Insula

Source: Based on Rich and colleagues (2011).

or have a baby may be at increased risk (Johnson et al., 2000).

Only recently have stressful life events been studied among children and adolescents with bipolar disorders. In the COBY study, youths with bipolar disorders reported a very high number of stressful life events. Indeed, the number of stressful events reported by youths with bipolar disorders was the same as the number reported by youths with depression. Furthermore, many of these negative events were a product of youths' own disruptive behavior. For example, an adolescent might get suspended from school or break up with his long-term girlfriend, during a manic episode. The fact that youths might contribute to their own negative life events might help explain the chronicity of youths' mood problems (Romero et al., 2009).

Youths with bipolar disorders also reported very few positive life events—even lower than the number reported by youths with depression. Furthermore, the scarcity of positive events in the lives of these youths seems to be dependent on their own behavior problems. For example, an irritable or depressed adolescent will likely have problems developing close relationships with family and friends. Limited social support and cohesive family ties, in turn, can exacerbate youths' mood problems (Romero et al., 2009).

Family Functioning

Individuals with bipolar disorders also frequently experience strained family relationships. Family tension typically arises in three ways. First, caring for a child or adolescent with a bipolar disorder can be extremely stressful to parents.

Caregivers worry, "Will he forget to take his medication? Is she starting to show signs of mania again? What am I going to do if he's suspended from school?" Parenting stress creates tension in the home and interferes with parents' ability to provide sensitive, consistent care. Second, youths with bipolar disorders frequently elicit negative thoughts, feelings, and actions from family members because of their disruptive mood and actions. For example, parents might blame youths for their dysphoric mood, viewing their mood problems as a sign of disrespect, disobedience, or resentment. To the extent that parents attribute youths' disruptive behavior to deliberate acts of malice, parents may be more likely to become angry, hostile, and resentful toward their children. Third, many youths with bipolar disorders often have parents with mood disorders themselves. Because of their own problems with depression or mania, parents may be less able to respond to their children's symptoms in effective ways (Youngstrom & Algorta, 2014).

Expressed emotion (EE) reflects the degree to which caregivers display criticism, hostility, or emotional overinvolvement (e.g., overprotectiveness, inordinate self-sacrifice) toward a family member with a mental health problem. Typically, EE is assessed by counting the number of *critical, hostile,* or emotionally *overinvolved* statements uttered by caregivers toward their children, during an interview or brief observation session. Here are some examples:

Criticism: Why can't you be responsible like other kids your age and remember to do your homework?

Hostility: I don't want to be around you when you act that way. You make me sick.

Overinvolvement: I lie awake at night, worrying about you. Are you safe? Who are you with?

EE is important because it predicts relapse in individuals with bipolar disorders, major depressive disorder (MDD), and schizophrenia. After discharge from psychiatric treatment, individuals from high-EE families are 2 to 3 times more likely to relapse over the course of 2 years than individuals from low-EE families (Miklowitz, 2012).

In contrast, warm, supportive parent–child interactions may prevent the return of mood episodes in youths with bipolar disorders (see Figure 14.8). Two years after recovering from a mood episode, youths were 4 times less likely to relapse in families characterized by high maternal warmth and responsiveness. Four years after recovery, children from high-warmth families (50.3%) were less likely to relapse than the children of low-warmth families (85.9%; Geller, Tillman, Craney, & Bolhofner, 2004).

Review:

- The children of individuals with bipolar disorders are at increased risk for bipolar disorders, other mood disorders, and anxiety disorders.
- Youths with bipolar disorders often show overactivity of the amygdala and underactivity of the prefrontal cortex.

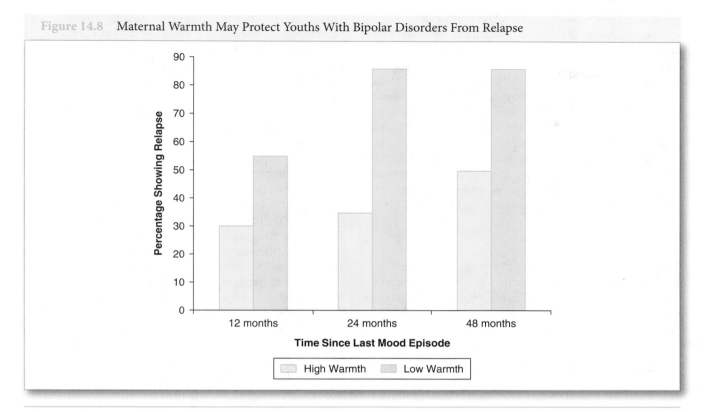

Source: Based on Geller et al. (2004).

Note: Children whose mothers showed high levels of sensitive and responsive care were less likely to relapse over a 4-year time period. Helping parents provide sensitive and responsive care and avoid conflict is a key component of most psychosocial treatments for pediatric bipolar disorders.

These abnormalities may be associated with problems regulating negative emotions.

- Abnormal functioning of the superior frontal gyrus and insula may explain the tendency of youths with bipolar disorders to have difficulty directing attention away from negative events and using coping strategies to reduce anger or irritability.
- High EE, characterized by critical, hostile, and emotionally overinvolved comments, predicts relapse in adolescents with bipolar disorders.

Is Medication Effective for Youths With Bipolar Disorders?

Medication is considered the primary form of treatment for bipolar disorders (Pfeifer, Kowatch, & DelBello, 2010). The American Academy of Child and Adolescent Psychiatry recommends that a single medication should be tried initially to treat the youth's most recent mood episode. If the child responds only partially, additional medications can be administered until a desired response is achieved. Three classes of medications are used to treat pediatric bipolar disorders: mood stabilizers (e.g., lithium), anticonvulsants (e.g., divalproex), and atypical antipsychotics (e.g., risperidone).

Mood Stabilizers and Anticonvulsants

The mood stabilizing medication lithium (Eskalith) was once considered the gold standard in treating pediatric bipolar disorders. Several randomized controlled studies demonstrated its efficacy in reducing mania in adults with the disorder. The mechanism by which lithium decreases mania and stabilizes mood is unknown. Lithium seems to reduce the action of the neurotransmitters norepinephrine and serotonin, which play important roles in mood and emotional expression (Carlson et al., 2015).

Unfortunately, few randomized, placebo-controlled studies investigating the efficacy of lithium on youths with bipolar disorders have been published (Liu et al., 2011). In one study, researchers compared lithium with several other medications used to treat bipolar disorders (Geller, Luby, & Joshi, 2012). The researchers found that only 35.6% of youths responded to lithium. Nearly as many youths, 32.2%, discontinued lithium and dropped out of the study before the end of the 8-week trial. Lithium was associated with side effects including nausea, headache, weight gain, thyroid dysfunction, diabetes, and tremor. For these reasons, lithium is usually not regarded as a first-line treatment for youths.

Anticonvulsants, medications designed to treat seizures, have also been used to treat mania in adults. These medications increase the inhibitory neurotransmitter gamma-aminobutyric acid (GABA) and/or decrease the excitatory neurotransmitter glutamate, causing a net decrease in neuronal activity, which may explain their effectiveness for both epilepsy and mania. The most widely studied anticonvulsant is divalproex (Depakote). Several studies suggest it may be effective in reducing mania in adolescents with bipolar disorders. Response rates vary from 24% to 53%, only slightly higher than placebo (Geller et al., 2012; Pfeifer et al., 2010). Common side effects include sedation, gastrointestinal problems, and weight gain. Rare but severe side effects are inflammation of the pancreas, liver toxicity, and polycystic ovary syndrome, which can cause infertility (Carlson et al., 2015).

Atypical Antipsychotics

Atypical antipsychotics are the most frequently prescribed medications for youths with bipolar disorders. Randomized controlled studies of atypical psychotics have shown them to be useful in reducing manic and mixed mood symptoms in children and adolescents (Singh,

Ketter, & Chang, 2010). Response rates range from 73% for quetiapine (Seroquel) to 49% for olanzapine (Zyprexa; Liu et al., 2011). Aripiprazole (Abilify), quetiapine (Seroquel), and risperidone (Risperdal) have been approved for children (aged 10–17), whereas olanzapine (Zyprexa) has been approved for adolescents (aged 13–17). Approximately half of youths who take these medications will show significant reduction in manic or mixed symptoms, compared to approximately one-fourth of youths who respond to placebo (see Figure 14.9).

Researchers conducted a head-to-head comparison of medications in the Treatment of Early Age Mania (TEAM) study. Specifically, 279 children and adolescents (aged 6–15) with bipolar disorders were randomly assigned to receive either the traditional mood stabilizer lithium (Eskalith), the anticonvulsant divalproex (Depakote), or the atypical antipsychotic risperidone (Risperdal). All youths were experiencing a manic episode but had not taken medication for bipolar disorders previously. After 8 weeks of treatment, 41.9% of youths responded to their medication. More youths responded to risperidone

Figure 14.9 Atypical Antipsychotics Are Currently the Treatment of Choice for Pediatric Bipolar Disorders

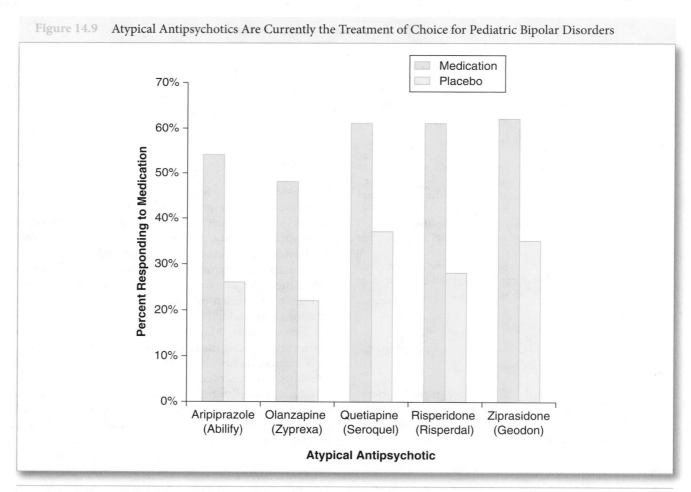

Source: Based on Singh and colleagues (2010).

Note: On average, 50% of youths with bipolar disorders will show a reduction in manic symptoms after taking these medications compared to 25% who respond to placebo.

(68.5%) than lithium (35.6%) or divalproex (24.0%). These findings supported the use of atypical antipsychotics in youths experiencing mania (Geller et al., 2012).

Atypical antipsychotics have several limitations. First, only about half of youths respond to these medications. Often, multiple medications must be administered to reduce symptoms. Second, although *response* rates are relatively high, complete *recovery* rates are low. Most youths show improvement while taking these medications, but most also continue to show symptoms. Third, side effects are common. The most common side effect is significant weight gain, which occurs in 7% to 42% of youths who take these medications (Singh et al., 2010).

Review:

- Lithium (Eskalith) is a mood-stabilizing medication that is used to treat bipolar disorders in adults. Approximately one-third of youths with bipolar disorders respond to this medication.
- Anticonvulsants, like divalproex (Depakote), reduce manic symptoms by increasing GABA and decreasing glutamate activity. Between 24% and 53% of youths show symptom reduction with these medications.
- The TEAM study showed that atypical antipsychotics, like risperidone (Risperdal), are more effective than either lithium or anticonvulsants in treating childhood bipolar disorder.

Is Psychotherapy Effective for Youths With Bipolar Disorders?

Psychosocial treatment for bipolar disorders is typically used in combination with medication. The primary purpose of psychosocial treatment is twofold: (1) to increase the child's compliance with medication and (2) to teaching coping skills to prevent another mood episode. The past decade has seen a marked increase in the number of evidence-based psychosocial interventions for youths with bipolar disorders. These treatments have several components in common:

Psychoeducation: Therapists teach clients about bipolar disorders, their causes, course, and treatment.

Family involvement: Therapy involves youths with bipolar disorders, primary caregivers, and (sometimes) siblings.

Reducing blame: Because family members often blame youths, or themselves, for their children's mood problems, therapists try to reduce blame and alleviate guilt.

Skill building: Therapists often teach skills that are deficient in children with bipolar disorders and their parents. Skills might include recognizing and regulating one's emotions, solving social problems, communicating within the family, and maintaining a consistent sleep-wake cycle.

Although several evidence-based interventions are currently available for youths with bipolar disorders, we will examine three that illustrate the use of psychosocial interventions across childhood and adolescence: (1) child- and family-focused cognitive–behavioral therapy (CFF-CBT), (2) psychoeducational psychotherapy (PEP), and (3) family-focused treatment for adolescents (FFT-A).

Child- and Family-Focused Cognitive–Behavioral Therapy

Mani Pavuluri and colleague (Fitzgerald & Pavuluri, 2015) developed child- and family-focused cognitive–behavioral therapy (CFF-CBT) for children aged 7 to 13 with bipolar disorders. Therapy consists of 12 sessions, some attended by children, some by parents, and some with children and parents together. Sessions provide information about bipolar disorders and teach cognitive behavioral strategies to improve children's mood and social problem-solving skills (see Table 14.5).

CFF-CBT is based on the assumption that children with bipolar disorders have disturbances in their neural systems responsible for processing and regulating emotions (West & Weinstein, 2012). These children usually want to behave appropriately at home and school, but their mood regulation problems prevent them from doing so. Treatment involves teaching children and parents strategies to help regulate children's emotions and decrease the frequency and severity of mood episodes.

First, therapists teach children to recognize and regulate negative emotions. Strategies include recognizing and labeling feelings; identifying and avoiding triggers that might elicit dysphoria; and developing tactics to cope with expansive, irritable, or sad mood states. Therapists also teach parents how to monitor their children's moods and prompt their children to use emotion-regulation skills in times of stress. Parents are also encouraged to develop stress-reduction techniques of their own, to help manage parenting stress.

Second, parents and children learn cognitive skills to improve the quality of parent–child interactions and children's social functioning. Some sessions focus on problem-solving skills, to help family members resolve disputes without anger and argument. Other sessions emphasize social skills. Through role play and discussion, parents and children learn how to listen to each other and communicate their feelings in positive ways.

Third, therapists teach parents behavior management strategies to cope with children's angry or irritable mood states. In traditional parent training, therapists teach parents to set limits on children's behavior, to give clear commands, and to immediately respond to instances of noncompliance. However, children with bipolar disorders may actually become more agitated by these tactics. Rather than strict limit-setting and punishment, children with bipolar disorders may respond to parenting strategies that defuse emotionally charged situations. Parents are

Table 14.5   Child- and Family-Focused Cognitive-Behavioral Therapy

R	Routine	To avoid mood problems, it is important for families to follow a routine. Waking, bedtime, meals, activities, and medication should be consistent. Transitions should be smooth and expected.
A	Affect Regulation	Parents and children should monitor children's moods each day. Families can decrease negative moods with coping strategies and parenting tactics to defuse situations.
I	I Can Do It!	Parents and children can solve disputes and arguments in positive ways. Parents can use a mixture of quiet confidence, calming tones, and a focus on empathy to help deescalate their children's negative moods.
N	No Negative Thoughts	Parents and children can identify and challenge cognitive distortions that contribute to negative moods. Negative thoughts (e.g., My child is terrible; nothing I do helps) can be reframed more realistically (e.g., My child's behavior is a problem that I can solve).
B	Be a Good Friend	Children are taught social skills to help them make and keep friends. Parents are encouraged to live a balanced lifestyle, to develop a social support network, and other ways to decrease stress.
O	Oh, How Can We Solve the Problem?	Parents and children can learn to use problem-solving strategies to deal with social problems. Breaking large problems into smaller steps, generating possible solutions, selecting and implementing the best solution, and evaluating outcomes can help.
W	Ways to Get Support	Children can identify family members, other adults, or friends who can help them when they have mood problems. Parents and therapists can advocate for their children at school to help them achieve.

Source: Based on West and Weinstein (2012).

Note: The acronym RAINBOW is used to remind families of the principles of treatment.

encouraged to use a calming voice, to modulate their own affect, and to emphasize an empathic and collaborative problem-solving approach to stressful situations.

The feasibility of CFF-CBT has been demonstrated in two open trials. In the first study, youths with bipolar disorders and their families participated in treatment. Participants reported a high degree of satisfaction with the program. Furthermore, children showed reductions in depression, mania, psychotic symptoms, and sleep problems as well as improvements in overall functioning over time (Pavuluri et al., 2004). Families were able to maintain these gains 3 years later (West et al., 2007).

In the second study, researchers examined the feasibility of treatment when administered to groups of parents and children. Children with bipolar disorders and their families participated in sessions together. After treatment, parents reported an increase in children's coping skills and a decrease in children's manic symptoms (West et al., 2009).

Psychoeducational Psychotherapy

Psychoeducational psychotherapy (PEP) was developed by Mary Fristad and colleagues (2011) to help children with bipolar and other mood disorders (see Table 14.6). It is designed for children aged 8 to 12 and their caregivers, although it is often used for older and younger children. PEP can be administered to individual families (IF-PEP), like CFF-CBT. PEP can also be administered to multiple families together (MF-PEP) in such a way that groups of children and groups of parents gain information, practice skills, and find support from one another.

As its name implies, PEP emphasizes psychoeducation. Considerable time is spent helping families understand mood disorders, their symptoms, course, causes, and treatments. Therapists conceptualize mood disorders as "no-fault brain disorders" that have biological underpinnings. Neither children nor parents are blamed for children's mood problems. The fundamental principle of PEP is reflected in the motto, "It's not your fault, but it's your challenge!" Although families do not cause bipolar disorders, the way they respond to children's symptoms can either alleviate or exacerbate children's problems (Mendenhall, Arnold, & Fristad, 2015).

A primary goal is to direct blame away from children by differentiating the child from his or her symptoms. Children participate in an activity called *Naming the Enemy* in which they are encouraged to see their mood problem as something external to themselves—something that needs to be targeted for treatment. Parents are also encouraged to differentiate their children from their children's symptoms and to pay attention to positive aspects of their children's behavior (see the Research to Practice section). They learn to monitor and record their children's mood symptoms and create practical goals for therapy.

A second component of PEP is emotion-regulation training. Initially, children learn basic skills to gain control of their emotions. For example, therapists teach three

Table 14.6   Components of Psychoeducational Psychotherapy (PEP)

1. Parents and children discuss the group's purpose and symptoms of mood disorders.

2. Parents and children are taught about medications used to treat mood disorders, expected benefits, and possible side effects. Parents and children learn to use medication logs to monitor medication effects.

3. Parents learn about systems of care; that is, how professionals at the child's school and clinic can work together to provide comprehensive treatment. Children create a "tool kit" of skills designed to help them cope with negative events and emotions. Coping skills include four areas: creative coping (e.g., dance), physical coping (e.g., sports), social coping (e.g., playing with a friend), and rest/relaxation coping (e.g., mom giving a back rub).

4. Parents learn how children's mood symptoms can cause conflict in the family. They participate in the "Naming the Enemy" exercise, in which they differentiate the child from his/her symptoms. This exercise demonstrates that symptoms can cover up the positive aspects and strengths of the child. Children participate in the thinking-feeling-doing exercise to learn the connection between thoughts, feelings, and actions. Therapists demonstrate how thoughts mediate the relationship between events and behavioral responses.

5. Parents and children learn to break down social problems into multiple steps: (1) Stop, (2) Think, (3) Plan, (4) Do, (5) Check.

6. Therapists and parents discuss "helpful" and "hurtful" forms of communication with children. Children learn this distinction through role play.

7. Parents learn specific symptom management skills. Children continue to learn and practice communication skills.

8. Families review what they have learned and receive feedback regarding family/child strengths. They are also given resource material (i.e., books, support groups in the community).

Source: From Kowatch and Fristad (2006). Used with permission.

breathing techniques (i.e., the three Bs) to reduce anxiety and anger: (1) belly breathing (e.g., deep breathing from the diaphragm), (2) bubble breathing (i.e., slow and steady release), and (3) balloon breathing (i.e., slow release with pursed lips). In later sessions, children build a "tool kit" of skills that they can use to cope with negative emotions. Coping skills in their tool kit fall into four categories that children remember by the acronym CARS: creative (e.g., drawing), active (e.g., playing outside), rest and relaxation (e.g., breathing), and social (time with friends).

Therapists also help children understand the relationship between their thoughts, feelings, and actions. In one exercise called *Thinking, Feeling, and Doing*, children learn that the way they think about a problem influences the way they feel about it (see Figure 14.10). If children change hurtful thoughts (e.g., She was mean to me on purpose) and actions (e.g., name-calling, yelling) with helpful thoughts (e.g., Maybe she didn't mean to hurt my feelings) or actions (e.g., smiling), they might feel better in stressful situations.

A third component of PEP is improving the family's problem-solving skills. Parents and children are encouraged to view children's mood disorders as a problem that needs to be addressed. Children learn simple problem-solving steps:

Stop: Take a moment to calm down.

Think: Define the problem and generate possible solutions.

Plan: Consider the best solution to use.

Do: Carry out the solution.

Check: Evaluate the outcome, and decide what to do next.

Parents practice responding to their children's mood symptoms without resorting to criticism, hostility, or blame. Although parents want to be empathetic and helpful, they often become frustrated when their efforts fail to regulate their children's behavior. Parents learn the "dos and don'ts" of responding to a moody child. They learn to recognize the early signs of anger, frustration, or guilt to avoid negative interactions with their children.

IF-PEP consists of 20 to 24 weekly family sessions, each lasting 45 to 50 minutes. Sessions typically alternate between parent-sessions and child-sessions. MF-PEP consists of 8 weekly sessions, each lasting 90 minutes. Typically, six to eight families (parents and children) meet together at the beginning and end of each session. For most of each session, however, children and parents meet separately in groups that address a similar theme for the week. In this manner, children can observe and practice skills with their peers while parents gain support from other caregivers (Davidson & Fristad, 2008).

Support for PEP comes from a large randomized controlled trial involving 165 children (aged 8–12) with mood disorders and their parents (Fristad, Verducci, Walters, & Young, 2009). Approximately 70% of children had bipolar disorders. Families were randomly assigned to receive eight sessions of MF-PEP immediately, or they were placed in a waitlist control group for 12 months.

NAMING THE ENEMY

Annie

Annie's Symptoms

Excellent drawer, artist	**Mania**
Good to animals (especially cats)	Doesn't sleep much, refuses to sleep
Wonderful smile	Acts goofy, silly, wild
Athletic-swimming, soccer, basketball	Talks a lot; won't sit still
Always willing to help younger brother	Tantrums, throws, breaks things
Good at sharing	**Depression**
Very affectionate	Irritable, cranky, "mouthy"
Funny, practical joker	Cries, weepy
Likes to help dad outside	Doesn't want to play sports or be with others

Source: Based on Fristad and colleagues (2011).

Note: Parents learn to differentiate the child from his or her symptoms in the Naming the Enemy activity, a component of psychoeducational psychotherapy for children with mood disorders. The child's mood disorder (not the child) is to blame.

Children in both groups were also allowed to take medication for their mood disorder. One year later, children who participated in MF-PEP showed significantly fewer mood symptoms than children on the waitlist. When children on the waitlist were also allowed to participate in MF-PEP, they, too, showed a reduction in mood symptoms. These findings indicate that MF-PEP is helpful in augmenting medication for pediatric bipolar disorders.

MF-PEP may also be effective in preventing (or at least delaying) the onset of bipolar disorders in young children at risk for developing the disorder. In one study, researchers administered MF-PEP to a large sample of children with depression and transient symptoms of mania. Youths and their parents either received MF-PEP immediately or were placed on a waitlist. Within 12 months, 12% of youths who received MF-PEP developed bipolar disorder compared to 45% of youths placed on the waitlist. Overall, MF-PEP was associated with a fourfold reduction in developing the illness. The researchers suggested that MF-PEP might prevent or delay bipolar disorder by helping families become better consumers of mental health care, by decreasing stress and increasing social support, and by improving family functioning (Nadkarni & Fristad, 2010).

Family-Focused Treatment for Adolescents

Family-focused treatment for adolescents (FFT-A) was developed by David Miklowitz (2012) and colleagues to treat adults with bipolar disorder. More recently, the therapy has been adapted to be used with adolescents and older children with the disorder (see Table 14.7). Ideally, FFT-A involves all family members, including parents and siblings. FFT-A is typically administered in 21 sessions spread over 9 months.

A primary goal of FFT-A is to reduce EE in the family. High-EE families often exacerbate their children's mood symptoms in three ways. First, families often attribute their children's disruptive behavior to internal, stable, and personal factors rather than to a medical illness. For example, they might blame their child for his disruptive actions, interpreting his misbehavior as a sign of disrespect or malice. Therefore, the first component of FFT-A is *education*. Families are taught about the symptoms, course, and causes

Figure 14.10   Thinking-Feeling-Doing Exercise

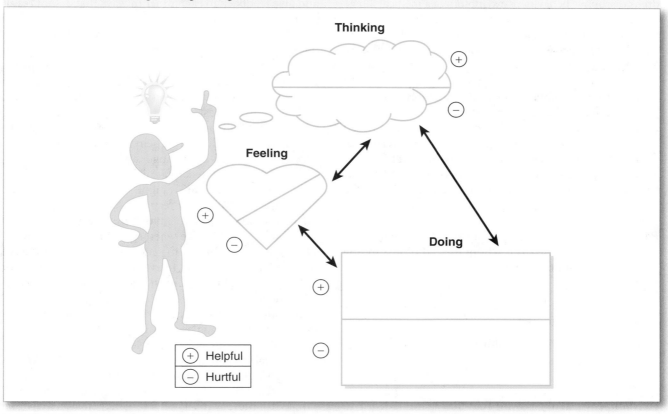

Source: From Goldberg-Arnold and Fristad (2003). Reprinted with permission.

Note: Children learn the connection between feelings (the heart), thoughts (the cloud), and actions (the box) in this game. Although it is unrealistic for children with mood problems to "wish" bad feelings away, they can change negative emotions by altering their actions or ways of thinking.

Table 14.7   Family-Focused Treatment for Adolescents With Bipolar Disorder

Sessions	Module	Description
1–9	Psychoeducation	Families learn about the causes, course, and treatment for Bipolar Disorder. Families learn that "genetics is not destiny"; adolescents can learn to avoid or reduce stressors that trigger mood episodes. Families develop a plan for relapse should it occur.
10–15	Communication Enhancement Training	Using role play, families practice four skills designed to improve communication at home: listening, expressing positive feelings, making positive requests for changes in others' behavior, and providing constructive negative feedback. Families identify and break negative communication cycles.
16–21	Problem-Solving Skills	Families learn steps to solve social problems and avoid arguments: break down problems into smaller steps, generate possible solutions, select and implement the best solution, and evaluate outcomes. Sessions may also focus on managing adolescents' disruptive behavior while respecting his or her emerging autonomy.
21+	Maintenance	Therapists periodically meet with families to trouble-shoot specific problems and review principles. Often, sessions involve the rehearsal of communication and problem-solving skills.

Source: Based on Miklowitz, Axelson, et al. (2008).

of bipolar disorders. Therapists help parents view their children's disruptive behavior as a symptom of a medical illness rather than as an act of irresponsibility or disrespect.

Youths with bipolar disorders often elicit negative thoughts, feelings, and actions from their parents. For example, when an adolescent skips school during a manic episode or yells at her parents during an episode of depression, parents might understandably react with feelings of anger or resentment. Often, families engage in a negatively escalating cycle of communication, in which criticism from one family member elicits countercriticism from another family member, until it is difficult to resolve amicably. Miklowitz (2008) calls this an "attack–counterattack" cycle of communication that usually follows a "three-volley sequence":

Parent: Why can't you pick up your things when you get home from school instead of just hiding in your room listening to music?

Adolescent: I wouldn't have to hide in my room if you didn't nag me so much and minded your own business.

Parent: Nag you? If I didn't nag, you wouldn't get anything done.

The second component of FFT is *communication enhancement training*. Using role play, parents learn to deescalate highly emotional, negative interactions with their children in order to avoid excessive displays of anger, hostility, or sadness. Families learn how to shift their attention away from immediate, negative feelings and instead to communicate their thoughts and feelings in constructive ways. Typically, communication enhancement training involves teaching families how to listen to each other, share positive feelings, make positive requests, and give feedback to each other in ways that do not result in criticism or condemnation.

Third, high-EE families often have difficulty solving social problems. When problems arise, families often resort to two ineffective strategies. Some families engage in criticism and hostility, as described previously. Instead of solving the problem directly, they emotionally attack each other. In contrast, other families use avoidance coping when dealing with problems. For example, a mother might ignore her child's disruptive behavior until it becomes so excessive she lashes out in anger and resentment.

FFT-A seeks to teach families *social problem-solving skills*. First, families are taught to take large, abstract problems (e.g., "We don't respect each other") and break them down into objective, smaller steps (e.g., "We need to use a lower tone of voice when speaking to each other"). Then, families are taught to generate possible solutions to real-life family problems, to evaluate the pros and cons of each possible solution, and to select the best solution to implement. Typically, problem-solving training is introduced during therapy sessions and practiced at home (see the Research to Practice section).

FFT has been evaluated in several randomized controlled trials of adults with bipolar disorders (Miklowitz, 2012). Overall, adults who participate in FFT are less likely to relapse (36%–46%) than adults assigned to traditional supportive therapy (60%) or emergency treatment (83%).

Furthermore, a randomized controlled study indicates that FFT-A may speed recovery of depression in adolescents with bipolar disorders. Miklowitz and colleagues (2009) assigned adolescents to either FFT-A plus medication or "enhanced care" plus medication. FFT-A consisted of 21 sessions spread across 9 months, involving adolescents, parents, and (sometimes) siblings. Enhanced care involved

RESEARCH TO PRACTICE

PROBLEM-SOLVING TRAINING FOR ADOLESCENTS WITH BIPOLAR SPECTRUM DISORDERS

Problem-solving training is an important component of therapy for adolescents with bipolar disorders. The therapist and adolescent might practice social problem-solving strategies on hypothetical situations created by the therapist or generated by the family:

This upcoming Saturday night is the big homecoming dance at our school. I am really excited because I am going to the dance with a person I really like. I don't know what to do because my date and all of my friends are allowed to stay out until 1:30 a.m. and my parents said that I have to be home by my normal curfew, which is midnight. My parents hate me—they want me to be unpopular! I am going to miss out on the big party after the dance because I have to go home! Everyone is going to think that I am so lame. I am thinking about just staying out and making up an excuse when I get home late. What do you think I should do? (Danielson et al., 2004)

By learning to engage in social problem-solving in a methodical way, families can weigh the strengths and weaknesses of each possible solution to the problem before acting. This can decrease the likelihood that youths will act in an impulsive fashion, get into trouble, and experience a negative mood state.

three weekly sessions during which families were provided information about bipolar disorders, medication management, and the importance of avoiding conflict in the home.

Two years after the beginning of the study, 91.4% of adolescents recovered from their initial mood episode. The recovery rates were similar for youths in both treatment conditions. However, youths who received FFT-A showed significantly faster reduction in depressive symptoms (10.2 weeks) than youths in the control condition (14.1 weeks). Youths who received FFT-A also showed faster recovery from mania (7.6 weeks) than youths in the control condition (13.8 weeks), although this difference only approached significance. The researchers suggested that the FFT-A focus on reducing family conflict, enhancing social support, and teaching interpersonal skills were responsible for its effectiveness in alleviating depression.

FFT-A may also be useful in preventing bipolar disorders in children at high risk for developing these conditions. In a pilot study, Miklowitz and colleagues (2011) administered a modified version of FFT-A to older children and young adolescents who had a biological parent with a bipolar disorder. These youths were selected for the study because they were at increased genetic risk for the disorder themselves. One year later, youths showed significant improvement in depression, hypomania, and psychosocial functioning. Because this study did not include a control group, we cannot be certain that these benefits are attributable to FFT-A. However, these findings do suggest that FFT-A may be an effective avenue for treatment and prevention.

Review:

- CFF-CBT is a treatment for children (aged 7–13) with bipolar disorders and their caregivers. Components include (a) monitoring and regulating emotions, (b) improving parent–child interactions, and (c) managing disruptive child behavior.
- PEP is a treatment for children (aged 8–12) with bipolar and other mood disorders and their caregivers. It can be administered to individual families or groups of families together. Therapists teach families about mood disorders, emotion regulation, and problem-solving skills.
- FFT-A is a family systems therapy for adolescents with bipolar disorders and their caregivers. Therapists improve parent–child communication and problem-solving and help adolescents avoid future mood episodes by decreasing EE in the family.

14.2 PEDIATRIC SCHIZOPHRENIA
What Is Schizophrenia?

Core Features

Schizophrenia is a psychotic disorder in which the person's thoughts, feelings, and actions reflect a lack of contact with reality. It is defined by the presence of two or more of the following psychotic symptoms: hallucinations,

delusions, disorganized speech, grossly abnormal behavior, and diminished emotional expression or lack of motor activity (see Table 14.8).

Although schizophrenia is usually thought of as an "adult" disorder, it can exist in children and adolescents (Palmen & van Engeland, 2012). Although rare, childhood- and adolescent-onset schizophrenia are conditions that greatly impact the lives of youths and families around the world.

The most common features of schizophrenia in children and adolescents are hallucinations. Hallucinations are "perception-like experiences that occur without an external stimulus" (American Psychiatric Associations, 2013, p. 87). Hallucinations are usually auditory, consisting of voices that may give commands, issue threats, or offer comments about the youths' thoughts or actions (see Figure 14.11). Sometimes, auditory hallucinations involve laughter, humming, whistling, or whispering. Visual hallucinations also occur frequently in children and adolescents with the disorder. Typically, youths see shadows, lights, or brief and unclear images. When children see clear images, they may be in the shape of animals (e.g., spiders), mythical figures (e.g., fairies), monsters, or cartoon characters. Olfactory (smell), gustatory (taste), and tactile or somatosensory (touch) hallucinations are rare in children and adolescents. If they do occur, they usually present alongside auditory and visual hallucinations (David et al., 2011).

Youths with schizophrenia also frequently experience delusions. Delusions are "fixed beliefs that are not amenable to change in light of conflicting evidence" (American Psychiatric Association, 2013). These beliefs usually reflect a misinterpretation of perceptions or experiences and may be bizarre in nature. Adolescents may report delusions that others are controlling their actions or thoughts (i.e., delusions of control), that others are out to get them (i.e., delusions of persecution), or that other people are sending them special messages or signals (i.e., delusions of reference). Sometimes, youths believe that they are special or called to perform a certain task (i.e., delusions of grandiosity) or that their body is defective or distorted in some way (i.e., somatic delusions). Although delusions like these are clearly atypical, their content may reflect developmentally appropriate concerns, such as a desire for autonomy, adolescent egocentrism, or preoccupation with appearance and the physical changes associated with puberty. Clearly developed and articulated delusions are relatively rare among children with schizophrenia. They become more common in adolescence as youths acquire more sophisticated cognitive abilities (Hollis, 2010).

Children and adolescents with schizophrenia often display peculiar speech and language (Clark, 2011). Some youths speak very little (i.e., poverty of speech) whereas others are extremely talkative (i.e., logorrhea). Other children repeat words and phrases (i.e., perseverations), use highly rigid, stereotyped language, or seem unusually preoccupied with certain topics. Some youths with

Table 14.8   Diagnostic Criteria for Schizophrenia

A. Two (or more) of the following, each present for a significant portion of time during a 1-month period (or less if successfully treated). At least one of these must be (1), (2), or (3):

   1. Delusions.

   2. Hallucinations.

   3. Disorganized speech (e.g., frequent derailment or incoherence).

   4. Grossly disorganized or catatonic behavior.

   5. Negative symptoms (i.e., diminished emotional expression or avolition).

B. For a significant portion of the time since the onset of the disturbance, level of functioning in one or more major areas, such as work, interpersonal relations, or self-care, is markedly below the level achieved prior to the onset (or when the onset is in childhood or adolescence, there is failure to achieve the expected level of interpersonal, academic, or occupational functioning).

C. Continuous signs of the disturbance persist for at least 6 months. This 6-month period must include at least 1 month of symptoms (or less if successfully treated), that meet criterion A (i.e., active-phase symptoms) and may include periods of prodromal or residual symptoms. During these prodromal or residual periods, the signs of the disturbance may be manifested by only negative symptoms or by two or more symptoms in attenuated form (e.g., odd beliefs, unusual perceptual experiences).

D. Depressive and Bipolar Disorder with psychotic features have been ruled out because either (1) no major depressive or manic episodes have occurred concurrently with the active-phased symptoms, or (2) if mood episodes have occurred during active-phase symptoms, they have been present for a minority of the total duration of the active and residual periods of the illness.

E. The disturbance is not attributable to the physiological effects of a substance (e.g., a drug of abuse, a medication) or another medical condition.

F. If there is a history of Autism Spectrum Disorder or a Communication Disorder of childhood onset, the additional diagnosis of Schizophrenia is made only if predominant delusions or hallucinations, in addition to the other required symptoms, are also present for at least 1 month (or less if successfully treated).

Source: Reprinted with permission from the *Diagnostic and Statistical Manual of Mental Disorders, Fifth Edition* (Copyright 2013). American Psychiatric Association.

schizophrenia repeat words or phrases uttered by others (i.e., echolalia). Still other children insert made-up words into their language (i.e., neologisms).

Children's language can give clues regarding their cognitive functioning. Youths with schizophrenia will often exhibit breaks in their train of thought (i.e., thought blockage), jump from one topic to another (i.e., knight's move thinking), discuss tangential or totally irrelevant topics, or use vague language. In rare cases, youths may complain that they can hear their own thoughts, as if they were spoken by someone else (i.e., thought echoing). Others report that people are inserting thoughts into their minds (i.e., thought insertion), that their thoughts are broadcast to others (i.e., thought broadcasting), or that someone has stolen their thoughts (i.e., thought withdrawal; Caplan, 2016).

Many youths with schizophrenia display disturbances in movement and coordination (Hollis, 2010). They may appear clumsy, engage in stereotypies, or show other compulsive actions or rituals. They may seem dejected and walk slowly. In rare instances, they may assume bizarre postures or remain motionless and unresponsive for long periods of time (i.e., catatonia).

Nearly all youths with schizophrenia show disturbances in affect. Youths with schizophrenia may show "diminished emotional expression"—that is, they do not show typical feelings through smiling, laughing, making eye contact, looking surprised, or becoming tearful when discussing sad topics. Youths may also display avolition—that is, a lack of drive, energy, or meaningful goal-directed behavior. They may seem "mopey" and uninterested in friends, sports, or hobbies. They may speak in a monotonous voice and seem lethargic or apathetic. Sometimes, youths show inappropriate affect. Inappropriate affect refers to emotional expressions that are incongruent with the content of speech. For example, a child might giggle while discussing her expulsion from school or a recent suicide attempt (Clark, 2011).

Youths with schizophrenia also frequently report mood problems. Some children describe their own mood as anxious, fearful, tense, or restless. Others experience listlessness and depression. Still others are touchy, angry, or irritable. Most experience considerable problems in interpersonal relationships and often avoid interactions with peers (Kuniyoshi & McClellan, 2014).

Source: Based on David and colleagues (2011).

Note: Auditory and visual hallucinations are most common. When other hallucinations occur, they usually accompany auditory and visual hallucinations.

To be diagnosed with schizophrenia, youths must show at least two of the five possible features of the illness: (1) hallucinations, (2) delusions, (3) disorganized speech, (4) abnormal behavior, and (5) diminished emotional expression. Furthermore, at least one of these symptoms must include delusions, hallucinations, or disorganized speech—the most salient features of the disorder. Usually, children with schizophrenia will show most, if not all, symptoms. Consider Mina, an adolescent who is beginning to show symptoms of schizophrenia.

DSM-5 also requires individuals with schizophrenia to show signs of the illness for at least 6 months. For at least 1 month, the psychotic symptoms must be present (e.g., delusions, hallucinations, disorganized speech). For the other 5 months, the individual can continue to show these psychotic symptoms, display less severe (i.e., attenuated) symptoms, or display only problems with diminished emotional expression.

Schizophrenia should not be diagnosed if youths experience a mood disorder at the same time they show psychotic symptoms. For example, some youths with MDD or bipolar I disorder experience auditory hallucinations. Clinicians only diagnose schizophrenia after they have ruled out the possibility that youths' psychotic symptoms are caused by depression or mania. Similarly, schizophrenia is not diagnosed when psychosis is caused by a medical illness, medication, or drug. As we shall see, many illnesses, medications, and drugs can mimic psychotic symptoms and can easily be mistaken for schizophrenia.

Finally, young children with schizophrenia often show several of the features of autism spectrum disorder (ASD), such as deficits in social communication and stereotypies. However, children with ASD typically do not have delusions or hallucinations that last for extended periods of time. Schizophrenia can be diagnosed in children with ASD only when these other positive symptoms are present (Kuniyoshi & McClellan, 2014).

Positive and Negative Symptoms

Clinicians often divide the symptoms of schizophrenia into two types: (1) positive and (2) negative (Crow, 1980). Positive symptoms reflect "behavioral over-expressions"; these symptoms are present in addition to or in excess of normal functioning. Examples of positive symptoms include hallucinations, delusions, disorganized behavior, excitement, grandiosity, suspiciousness, and hostility. Negative symptoms reflect behavioral "under-expressions"; they are absent or impoverished behavior with respect to normal functioning. Examples of negative symptoms include blunted or flat affect, avolition, social withdrawal, passivity or apathy, and a lack of spontaneity. Both positive and negative symptoms fluctuate over time (Kodish & McClellan, 2015).

Dividing symptoms into positive and negative types is useful to professionals for at least three reasons (Remschmidt & Theisen, 2012). First, positive and negative symptoms likely have different underlying neurobiological causes. For example, dopaminergic overactivity in central brain regions is associated with many positive symptoms, whereas underactivity in frontal brain regions is associated with many negative symptoms. Second, the prevalence and severity of

SCHIZOPHRENIA (ADOLESCENT-ONSET)

Mina's Macabre Visions

Source: ©iStockphoto/schmidt-z

Fifteen-year-old Mina was brought to the emergency department of our hospital by the police. According to the police report, Mina had assaulted her mother during a family argument. Dr. Harrington was asked to assess Mina's state of mind with respect to the incident and to recommend treatment.

Mina did not look up at Dr. Harrington when she entered the exam area. Although Mina was well-kempt, her behavior was calm, almost passive, and withdrawn. She responded to Dr. Harrington's questions with downcast eyes in a slow, monotone voice. Her affect was restricted; even while discussing the incident, her tone rarely fluctuated, and her facial expression remained unchanged. Mina stared at the hospital blankets on her bed as she spoke as if they were the most interesting objects in the world.

"I didn't want to hurt her," Mina reported. "But I felt like I had to. It's really the only way to make things stop."

Dr. Harrington replied, "Tell me about those things."

After a long pause, Mina continued, "It's the voice I hear, especially when things get bad. It's the voice of a bad man—a really raspy, quick voice. It tells me to hurt or kill other people. I know it's not real, but it keeps going on and on in my head, telling me to do things I know I shouldn't."

Dr. Harrington learned that Mina began experiencing auditory hallucinations at the age of 13. The hallucinations began as "whispers" which gradually became a male voice that told her to "hurt, kill, or choke" other people. Several months ago, Mina also began to experience brief, but vivid, visual hallucinations. Usually, she saw bloody, dismembered, or mutilated bodies or a corpse that had been stabbed or cut into several pieces. Each scene usually lasted 5 to 10 seconds but occurred multiple times each week. Understandably, the auditory and visual hallucinations caused Mina serious distress and interfered with her ability to do well at school and interact with family members and friends.

"Is there anything you can do to stop the voices or images?" Dr. Harrington asked.

Mina replied, "Sometimes, I don't know what to do. I just crawl into bed, under the covers, and try to hide from them. That usually doesn't work so well. I've thought about killing myself, but I'm too scared to do that. And I don't want to leave my mom all alone."

"Who else knows about the voice and the pictures you see?" Dr. Harrington asked.

"No one," Mina admitted, "I didn't want people to think I was crazy."

---

positive and negative symptoms often change during the course of the illness. Typically, psychotic episodes begin with predominantly positive symptoms, which are gradually replaced by predominantly negative symptoms. Third, positive and negative symptoms respond differentially to treatment. Although antipsychotic medications are often helpful in reducing positive symptoms, they are usually less effective in treating negative symptoms.

Review:

- Schizophrenia is a *DSM-5* psychotic disorder characterized by the presence of hallucinations, delusions, disorganized speech, disorganized actions, and/or diminished emotional expression which impair functioning for at least 6 months.
- The positive symptoms of schizophrenia reflect "behavioral over-expressions"—that is, aspects of behavior that are not seen in typically functioning individuals. They include hallucinations, delusions, disorganized behavior, excitement, grandiosity, suspiciousness, and hostility.
- Negative symptoms of schizophrenia reflect behavioral "under-expressions"—that is, a lack of functioning typically seen in individuals. They include flat affect, social withdrawal, passivity, apathy, and lack of spontaneity.

How Common Is Schizophrenia Among Children and Adolescents?

Prevalence

Researchers differentiate schizophrenia into three types, based on symptom onset. Adult-onset schizophrenia is most common; it is defined by onset after age 18. The lifetime

SCHIZOPHRENIA (CHILDHOOD-ONSET)

Caroline's Conversations

Eight-year-old Caroline was referred to our clinic by her pediatrician, who observed a marked decrease in her motor, language, and social functioning over the past 6 months. Her pediatrician was unable to find a cause for these problems despite a physical exam and extensive testing. Recently, Caroline had shown a dramatic decline in functioning: She was unable to dress herself, rarely made eye contact or spoke with others, and engaged in bizarre actions such as making unusual gestures and talking to herself.

Caroline showed delays in her motor and language development. She did not learn to walk until age 18 months and continued to show problems with balance, coordination, and clumsiness as a preschooler. She did not utter her first meaningful words until age 26 months or speak clear sentences until age 4. By kindergarten, Caroline had made some progress, but she was still physically, linguistically, and cognitively behind her peers.

"About one year ago, I noticed a change in her behavior," Caroline's mother explained. "She started talking to herself a lot—you know, carrying on conversations. They were usually accompanied by hand motions and other gestures. I thought, 'most kids have vivid imaginations' so I didn't worry about it at first. Then, I started hearing her say strange things during these conversations, like, 'My friend died, somebody killed him with a knife' or 'We need to find a grave and bury him.' I also heard her say scary things to the cat, like 'Oh, Roscoe (the cat), why do you have bugs coming from your mouth?' This made me worried."

As Caroline's unusual behavior increased, her mood and social skills declined. She began having problems falling asleep at night and complained of nightmares and fears associated with going to bed alone. She was often tearful or irritable during the day and would sometimes tantrum violently. She showed a marked increase in hyperactivity and defiance and gradually refused to do most things for herself, like dress in the morning, brush her hair and teeth, and eat meals. She also lost interest in school and playing with neighborhood friends.

Dr. Silverman observed Caroline and her mother together in the clinic playroom. Caroline made very little eye contact. When Dr. Silverman attempted to play with her, she looked at him with an empty, meaningless expression and turned away. Caroline spent most of the session talking to herself quietly.

Dr. Silverman questioned Caroline's mother about their family. Her mother replied, "Caroline lives with me and her younger half-brother. Her father really isn't in the picture anymore. He developed schizophrenia shortly after we were married, and we separated a few months later. We haven't had contact with him for several years."

prevalence of schizophrenia among adults in the general population is approximately 1%. Schizophrenia typically emerges between the ages of 20 to 24 in men and 25 to 29 in women (Gur et al., 2005).

Adolescent-onset schizophrenia (onset between ages 13 and 17) is much less common than adult-onset schizophrenia. Only about 5% of people who develop schizophrenia begin showing the disorder during adolescence. Although large epidemiological studies have not yet been conducted, the best estimate is that only 0.23% of all youths will develop schizophrenia during adolescence.

Childhood-onset schizophrenia (onset <12 years) is rarer still. Only about 1% of people who develop schizophrenia begin manifesting the illness before puberty. Overall, the likelihood of a child developing schizophrenia is approximately .0019%. Most clinicians will never

see a child with schizophrenia during their entire career (Remschmidt & Theisen, 2012). For a description of childhood-onset schizophrenia, consider Caroline.

Boys are approximately twice as likely as girls to develop schizophrenia in childhood or adolescence (Kodish & McClellan, 2015). This is probably because, on average, males begin showing symptoms 5 to 7 years earlier than females. By middle adulthood, the prevalence of schizophrenia across genders is similar (Nugent, Daniels, & Azur, 2012).

Course

People with schizophrenia typically progress through a series of stages over the course of several months or years. Each stage is characterized by a different cluster of symptoms

Figure 14.12   The Stages of Child- and Adolescent-Onset Schizophrenia

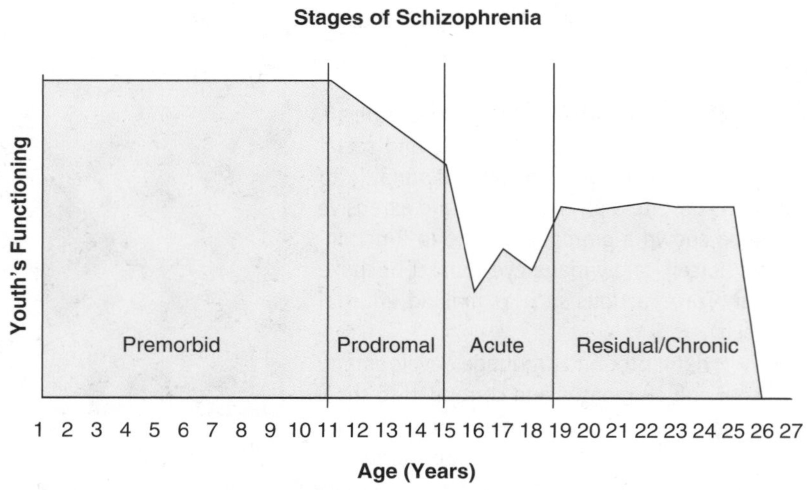

Source: Based on Gur and colleagues (2005).

Note: Motor, language, and cognitive delays are often seen during the premorbid stage. The prodromal stage is characterized by changes in behavior and mood. Psychotic symptoms define the acute stage. The residual stage usually lasts a long time and most youths do not return to their premorbid level of functioning.

and level of functioning (see Figure 14.12). Identifying the stage of a patient's illness is important, because treatment varies from stage to stage (Caplan, 2016).

The Premorbid Stage: Problems in Early Life

The premorbid stage lasts from gestation through the first signs of the illness. On the surface, children in the premorbid stage show no overt symptoms. However, several studies indicate that many youths who later develop schizophrenia display deficits in motor skills and social–emotional functioning during infancy and early childhood. Although these deficits are usually not recognized by parents and teachers at the time, they indicate that individuals with schizophrenia have neural abnormalities very early in life.

One way to assess early deficits in individuals later diagnosed with schizophrenia is to ask their parents to recall when they reached developmental milestones regarding basic motor skills and language. These retrospective studies reveal that infants and toddlers who later develop schizophrenia are slower to crawl, walk, manipulate objects, and toilet train than their peers. Similarly, they show marked delays in expressive language and the ability to converse with other children and adults. Many of these deficits are observed as early as the first year of life (Kodish & McClellan, 2015).

A chief problem with retrospective studies, however, is reporting bias. In hindsight, parents might magnify delays that were really quite minor to explain their children's current problems. To remedy this shortcoming of retrospective studies, researchers have examined the home movies of toddlers and preschoolers who later developed schizophrenia as adults (Walker & Lewine, 1990, 1993). Experts, who were not informed about the purpose of these studies, were asked to rate children's motor and social–emotional functioning based on the content of the films. Their ratings corroborated parents' reports; children who later developed schizophrenia showed delays in motor skills and social behavior in their home movies.

Longitudinal studies have replicated this association between early developmental delays and the later emergence of schizophrenia. In these studies, researchers periodically assessed the development of large samples of children, beginning in infancy and continuing through early adulthood. Infants who later developed schizophrenia in adulthood showed delays in sitting, standing, and walking. Their mothers reported delays in language acquisition. School personnel reported speech and language problems when these children began formal education. On average, 72% of youths later diagnosed with schizophrenia showed marked delays in early language acquisition, speech, and motor development. At the time, these delays did not greatly concern parents and school personnel; in hindsight, they provide the earliest warning signs for the disorder (Haut, Schvarcz, Cannon, & Bearden, 2016).

In primary school, children who later develop schizophrenia continue to show problems. Developmental tasks during elementary and middle school include the mastery of basic academic skills and the ability to make and keep friends. Unfortunately, children who later develop schizophrenia often show marked problems with both tasks. On average, their cognitive functioning is one standard deviation below average. Their academic performance tends to be poor. These youths also experience considerable difficulty in interpersonal relationships. Family members frequently notice their preference for solitary play and their lack of confidence when interacting with peers. Teachers and classmates often describe them as more touchy, irritable, or moody during social interactions. Although these problems often concern parents and teachers, they are almost never seen as the early indicators of schizophrenia. Indeed, academic and peer problems are so common in childhood, they lack the specificity to predict such an uncommon disorder (Gur et al., 2005).

The Prodromal Stage: Noticeable Changes

Prodromal symptoms may emerge 2 to 6 years before the youth's first psychotic episode. The prodromal stage is characterized by a marked change in youths' academic, behavioral, and social–emotional functioning. Although children and adolescents in the prodromal stage may not show positive symptoms of schizophrenia (e.g., hallucinations, delusions), family members usually notice a deterioration in their overall functioning. Many youths show significant problems with attention and concentration. They may seem restless and have difficulty completing their homework and studying for exams. Consequently, their grades in school decline. Parents usually describe their children as more "moody" or withdrawn. These youths may begin to avoid contact with family and friends, preferring to spend most of their time alone. They may quit clubs, sports, or other extracurricular activities. Sometimes, youths become more irritable and suspicious of others. Many youths begin to neglect their appearance or hygiene (Asarnow & Kernan, 2008).

The Acute Stage: Positive Symptoms and Impairment

The acute phase begins with the onset of positive symptoms. Young children typically experience insidious (i.e., slow, barely noticeable) onset. In contrast, onset is typically more rapid among adolescents. The acute phase typically lasts 1 to 6 months, depending on how rapidly medication can be administered and how responsive youths are to medication (Kodish & McClellan, 2015).

The Residual Stage: Chronic Problems

After a psychotic episode, most youths enter a residual stage that may last for several months or years. Functioning in this stage is variable. Some youths experience a noticeable improvement in behavior and social–emotional skills; their functioning returns to levels similar to before the prodromal phase. Sadly, however, most youths continue to show persistence of negative symptoms after a psychotic episode without a marked return to baseline functioning. These children remain withdrawn, moody, or irritable and experience long-term problems with relationships and school. Many of these youths will experience additional psychotic episodes later in adolescence or adulthood. With each subsequent episode, their functioning often deteriorates. Thus, these youths experience problems which persist over time.

Outcome

The short-term prognosis of youths with schizophrenia is poor. Psychotic symptoms usually persist for several months, even after they are recognized and treated. In one study, only 12% of individuals with schizophrenia recovered completely by the time they were discharged from the hospital. If recovery does occur, it tends to be within 3 months after onset. Only about one-fifth of patients have "good" outcomes, characterized by alleviation of positive symptoms, mild negative symptoms, and a general return to prepsychotic levels of functioning. Even among these patients, long-term problems in social functioning, friendships, and romantic relationships are common (Hollis, 2010).

Researchers have identified several variables that predict the long-term outcomes of youths with schizophrenia (see Table 14.9). One of the strongest predictors is age of onset. Most studies suggest that people who manifest the disorder during childhood or adolescence have poorer long-term outcomes than people who develop the disorder in adulthood. For example, Lay, Blanz, Hartmann, and

Table 14.9   Prognosis for Youths With Schizophrenia

Better Outcomes	Worse Outcomes
No family history of psychosis	First-degree relative with psychosis
Meets developmental milestones	Developmental delays in infancy and early childhood
Good functioning before onset of illness	Low premorbid functioning
Onset in late adolescence or adulthood	Onset in childhood or early adolescence
Short duration of first psychotic episode	Long duration of first psychotic episode
Symptoms identified and treated rapidly	Symptoms not identified or treated
Mild to moderate symptoms	Severe symptoms requiring hospitalization

Source: Based on Remschmidt & Theisen (2012).

Schmidt (2000) examined the outcomes of adolescents admitted to a psychiatric hospital because of schizophrenia. As adults, 66% had serious deficits in social functioning and interpersonal relationships; 75% were dependent on their family. A more recent, retrospective study showed similarly poor outcomes (Reichert, Kreiker, Mehler-Wex, & Warnke, 2008). Twenty-two percent were currently experiencing acute psychosis, 31% reported depression, and 37% admitted suicidal thoughts or actions. Most adults with adolescent-onset schizophrenia continued to live with their parents (48%) or in assisted living facilities (33%). Less than 19% completed high school.

A second important predictor is the duration of time between the onset of prodromal symptoms and the initiation of treatment. Youths who suffer through prodromal and early psychotic symptoms without medication and psychotherapy typically show more severe and persistent symptoms than youths who receive treatment in a timely manner (Remschmidt & Theisen, 2012).

Review:

- Approximately 0.0019% of youths develop schizophrenia in childhood whereas 0.23% develop schizophrenia in adolescence. The base rate for schizophrenia among adults in the general population is 1%.
- Youths later diagnosed with schizophrenia tend to experience delays in reaching developmental milestones in infancy and academic problems in early childhood.

- The prodromal phase of schizophrenia occurs 2 to 6 years prior to the first psychotic episode. It is marked by problems with attention and concentration, irritability and "moodiness," and deterioration in academic and social functioning.
- Individuals with child- or adolescent-onset schizophrenia have poorer outcomes than individuals whose symptoms begin in adulthood. Approximately 66% of youths with schizophrenia have long-term deficits in social functioning, and 77% are dependent on their family in adulthood.

What Causes Schizophrenia in Children and Adolescents?

Genetics

Schizophrenia is a heritable disorder (Helenius, Munk-Jorgensen, & Steinhausen, 2012). Every major study published since 1980 has shown that the disorder runs in families (see Figure 14.13). On average, individuals who have a first-degree family member with schizophrenia are significantly more likely (5.9%) to develop the disorder than individuals without an affected first-degree relative (0.5%). Twin studies provide additional evidence for the influence of genetics. The average concordance rate for MZ twins is 55.8%; concordance drops to 13.5% among DZ twins. Even more compelling evidence comes from children born to parents with schizophrenia, but adopted by adults without the disorder. Adopted children whose

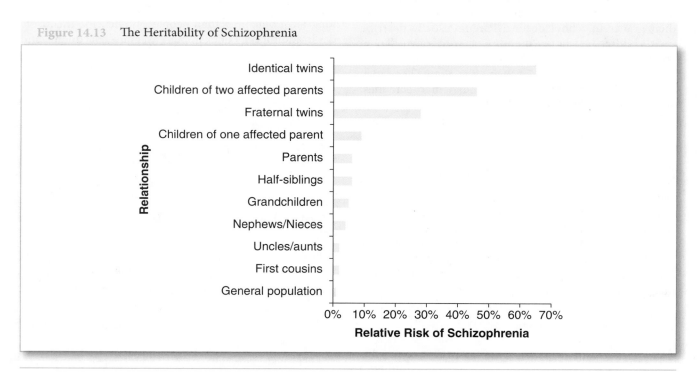

Figure 14.13   The Heritability of Schizophrenia

Source: Based on Walters, O'Donovan, and Owen (2011).

Note: The overall risk of developing schizophrenia is about 1%. The risk of schizophrenia increases if you have a biological relative with the disorder. However, even identical twins, who have 100% genetic similarity, are not 100% concordant for the disorder. Environmental factors are also important.

biological parents had schizophrenia were more likely to develop the disorder themselves than adopted children whose biological parents did not have the disorder (Escudero & Johnstone, 2014; Greenwood et al., 2016).

Knowledge of genetic risk has practical importance to couples with a positive family history of schizophrenia. For example, a woman without schizophrenia may have a father or brother with the disorder. She can use these data to determine the likelihood that she will have a child who will one day develop the disorder (i.e., a 2%–3% likelihood assuming her husband does not have a family history of schizophrenia). If the woman herself has schizophrenia, her child's risk increases to 7%. If both she and her husband have the disorder, their child's risk jumps to 27% (Corvin & Sullivan, 2016; Walters, O'Donovan, & Owen, 2011).

Researchers have identified several candidate genes that likely play roles in the development of schizophrenia. One of the most important genes in adolescent-onset schizophrenia is the catechol-O-methyltransferase (COMT) gene. The COMT gene produces an enzyme that regulates dopamine in several brain areas. It appears to produce excessive dopamine activity in brain regions responsible for positive symptoms and diminish dopamine activity in brain regions responsible for negative symptoms (Caspi, Moffitt, & Cannon, 2005).

Children with schizophrenia also have a higher rate of genetic abnormalities and mutations than their healthy peers. For example, young children with schizophrenia sometimes show deletions, duplications, or mutations of genetic material. Recall that researchers have discovered that several children with schizophrenia have a specific abnormality known as 22q11.2 deletion syndrome. Approximately 10% to 30% of youths who show this syndrome develop schizophrenia or psychotic disorders (Kuniyoshi & McClellan, 2014).

Although a genetic risk may be necessary for one to develop schizophrenia, it is not sufficient to explain the disorder. Even MZ twins, who have identical genetic similarity, are discordant for schizophrenia approximately one-half of the time. Consequently, researchers have explored early environmental influences that, along with genes, might more fully explain the emergence of the disorder.

Brain Development

Three decades of research have documented differences in the brain structure of adults with and without schizophrenia. Three abnormalities are most often replicated across studies. First, adults with schizophrenia often show increased volumes of the lateral ventricles, the canals in the center of the brain that are filled with cerebrospinal fluid (see Figure 14.14). Typically, individuals with schizophrenia show 40% greater ventricular enlargement than healthy adults. Second, adults with the disorder often show reductions in the total volume and thickness of the prefrontal, temporal, and parietal cortices. Overall, patients with schizophrenia show 10% less cortical volume than healthy controls. These areas are important because they are responsible for sensory-motor processes, language, and higher-order planning and reasoning. Third, adults with the disorder often display reductions in the size of the hippocampus and thalamus, two centrally located brain regions responsible for the integration of behavior. On average, the size of these brain regions is 5% to 10% smaller than in healthy adults (Hollis, 2010; Kuniyoshi & McClellan, 2014).

Figure 14.14   Adults with schizophrenia often show enlarged lateral ventricles, regions of the brain filled with cerebrospinal fluid.

Non-Schizophrenic Brain

Normal lateral ventricles

Schizophrenic Brain

Enlarged lateral ventricles

Lateral Ventricles

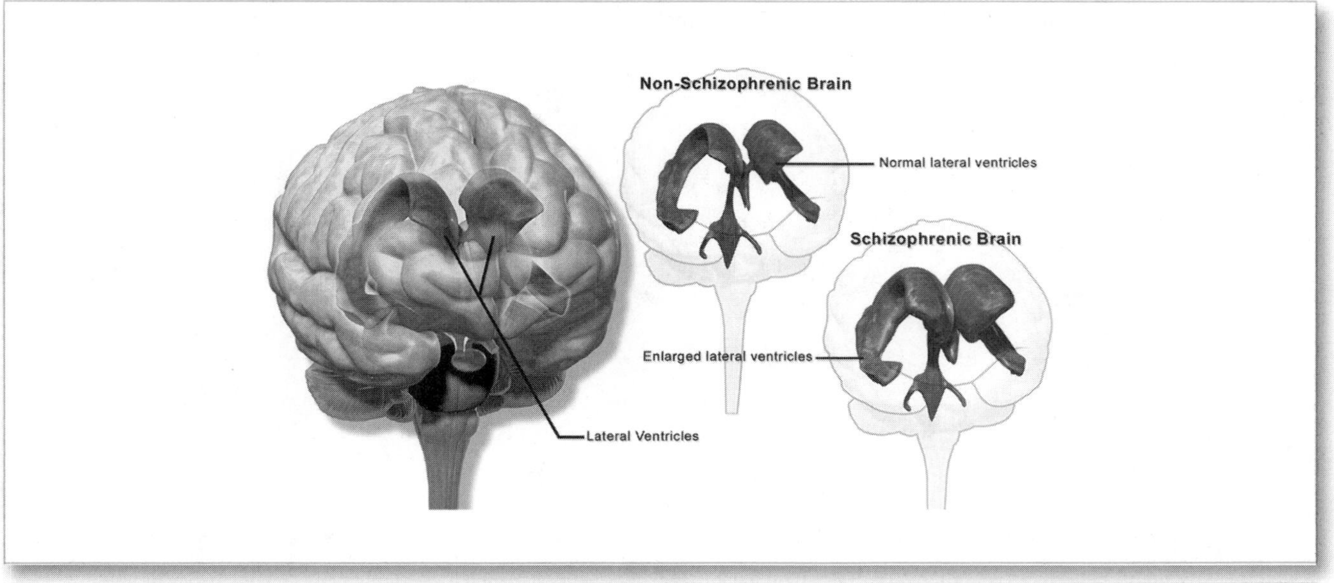

Source: Image courtesy of Blausen Medical (Wikimedia Commons).

Until recently, however, researchers did not know if these brain abnormalities were a cause of schizophrenia, a consequence of the disorder, or the result of a third variable such as antipsychotic medication. To answer these questions, researchers at the National Institute of Mental Health (NIMH) studied the brain structure and functioning of youths with childhood-onset schizophrenia from early childhood through young adulthood. Magnetic resonance imaging (MRI) scans of the brains of these youths were examined over time and compared to MRIs of the brains of healthy youths. Because patients were young, did not have extensive experience taking medication, and could be followed over time, the researchers could begin to determine the relationship between brain structure and psychotic symptoms (Kodish & McClellan, 2015).

The NIMH studies yielded three important findings. First, older children and adolescents with schizophrenia showed most of the same brain abnormalities as adults with the disorder. This finding was important because it suggested that youth-onset and adult-onset schizophrenia reflect the same disorder (Hollis, 2010).

Second, the abnormalities shown by young patients tended to occur early in the course of the disorder. This finding suggests that these brain abnormalities may cause many of the signs and symptoms of the illness that later emerge (Rapoport & Gogtay, 2011).

Third, and perhaps most importantly, young patients with schizophrenia showed dramatic reductions in gray matter that predict the onset of psychosis (Kuniyoshi & McClellan, 2014). Healthy children experience a dramatic overproduction of synaptic connections in infancy and early childhood. Later, these children show reduction of 1% to 2% of gray matter per year across late childhood and adolescence. This loss of gray matter reflects normal synaptic "pruning." Much like a bush that needs to be pruned to allow it to grow in the appropriate way, the neural connections that are not needed die off during adolescence, allowing the most important connections to work more efficiently. This pruning progresses from lower-order brain areas (central areas, parietal lobe) in childhood to higher-order brain areas (e.g., frontal lobe, prefrontal cortex) in adolescence and young adulthood. The outcome of normal neural pruning is adolescents' ability to engage in more complex, graceful, and efficient cognitive and social–emotional tasks (Kodish & McClellan, 2015; Whalley, 2016).

Children with schizophrenia, however, show more rapid, excessive neural pruning (see Figure 14.15). MRIs show a loss of 3% to 4% of gray matter per year on average. Furthermore, the loss of gray matter tends to occur shortly before the onset of the child's first psychotic episode. Interestingly, neural loss progresses in the same parietal-to-frontal pattern as it does in healthy children. However, youths with schizophrenia experience much more dramatic and rapid loss than would be developmentally expected. This loss in gray matter corresponds to the signs and symptoms of the disorder (Kuniyoshi & McClellan, 2014).

Neural Pathways

There are two brain pathways implicated in schizophrenia: (1) the mesolimbic pathway and (2) the mesocortical pathway (see Figure 14.16). The *mesolimbic pathway* is a dopamine-rich neural pathway that is involved in feelings of pleasure. It begins in the ventral tegmental area (VTA) of

Figure 14.15 Regions of greatest gray matter loss in children with schizophrenia (*shaded areas*). Brain scans conducted on the same children with schizophrenia between the ages of 12 and 16 years showed a progressive deterioration in gray matter not shown by healthy children. Notice how the gray matter loss moves from the parietal region to the frontal and temporal regions over time. This loss corresponds to the child's first psychotic episode.

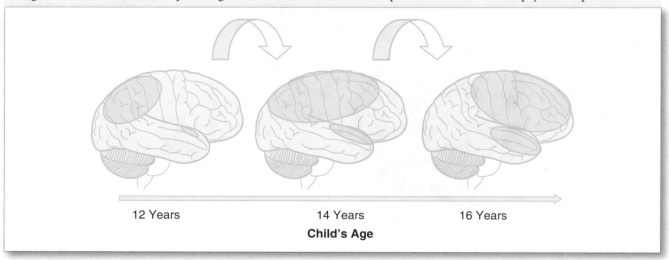

Source: Based on Rapoport and Gogtay (2011). Figure based on P. J. Lynch, Creative Commons.

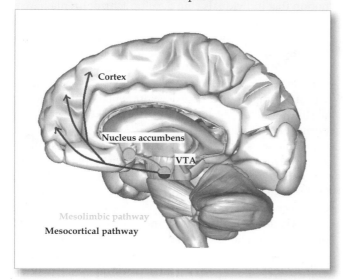

Figure 14.16 Youths with schizophrenia often show overactivity of the mesolimbic path and underactivity of the mesocortical path.

Cortex

Nucleus accumbens

VTA

Mesolimbic pathway
Mesocortical pathway

the midbrain and connects to several structures in the limbic system: the amygdala, hippocampus, and nucleus accumbens. It also connects to the striatum, an area deep within the brain responsible for coordination and movement.

The dopamine hypothesis posits that schizophrenia is caused by excessive stimulation of certain dopamine receptors (D2 receptors) along the mesolimbic pathway. Excessive dopaminergic activation is believed to produce many of the positive symptoms of schizophrenia, such as hallucinations and delusions. Evidence supporting this hypothesis comes from the fact that antipsychotic drugs, which reduce these positive symptoms, are D2 receptor antagonists. They block D2 receptors and reduce many positive psychotic symptoms. Furthermore, certain stimulant drugs (e.g., cocaine, methamphetamine) act as D2 agonists; they augment dopaminergic activity along this pathway and can produce hallucinations and delusions among individuals susceptible to the disorder (Asarnow & Kernan, 2008)

The *mesocortical pathway* is another dopaminergic neural path. It also begins in the VTA of the midbrain but connects to the dorsolateral prefrontal cortex. The dorsolateral area is believed to be responsible for motivation and the expression of emotions. Emerging evidence supports the hypofrontality hypothesis—that is, the notion that there is underactivity among certain dopamine receptors in the dorsolateral prefrontal region (D1 receptors). This underactivity is believed to be responsible for the negative symptoms of the disorder, including apathy and flat affect (Asarnow & Kernan, 2008).

The challenge in treating schizophrenia is to find medications that block excessive dopamine activity along

one pathway while simultaneously augmenting activity along the other pathway. To complicate matters, dopamine is involved in several other important activities of the central nervous system, such as the control of movement and the regulation of metabolism. Medications that affect dopamine receptors can adversely affect these other activities, producing side effects that make them intolerable to many patients (Kline et al., 2015).

Environmental Risks

Several early environmental risk factors are implicated in the development of schizophrenia. These include in utero maternal stress, exposure to disease, season of birth, and pre- or perinatal complications (Palmen & van Engeland, 2012). Recent longitudinal studies have shown that major life events also predict the onset of schizophrenia in individuals genetically predisposed to the illness. Events that are perceived as "uncontrollable" are particularly salient predictors of psychosis. Furthermore, both positive and negative events place individuals at risk. For example, leaving home and transitioning to college, which many adolescents regard as a positive event, can elicit symptoms in youths predisposed to the disorder (Kodish & McClellan, 2015).

Considerable research has been directed at the relationship between marijuana and schizophrenia in adolescents. Early studies showed a correlation between marijuana use in early adolescence and a greater likelihood of developing schizophrenia in later adolescence and early adulthood. For example, researchers examined cannabis use in a large sample of Swedish adolescents and young adults (>97% of the country's male population). They found a direct relationship between early cannabis use and schizophrenia 5 years later. Furthermore, there was a dose-dependent relationship between early cannabis use and later psychosis: The greater the use, the greater the likelihood of developing the disorder (Zammit, Allebeck, Andreasson, Lundberg, & Lewis, 2002). However, researchers could not tell whether marijuana caused later psychosis, whether prodromal symptoms led adolescents to use marijuana, or whether a third factor (such as impulsivity) might contribute to both marijuana use and schizophrenia.

To answer this question, Arseneault, Cannon, Witton, & Murray, (2004) reviewed the research literature on the causal relationship between cannabis and schizophrenia. They reached three conclusions. First, cannabis use in adolescence increased the likelihood of developing schizophrenia in early adulthood two- or threefold. Second, the earlier and more frequent the cannabis use in adolescence, the greater the likelihood of psychosis. Third, cannabis alone was not sufficient to cause schizophrenia; it only led to schizophrenia when adolescents were genetically at risk for the disorder (Milin, 2008).

Caspi and Moffitt (2006) conducted a prospective, longitudinal study to examine how adolescent cannabis use might interact with genes to place youths at risk for schizophrenia. The researchers examined a large cohort of individuals from Dunedin, New Zealand, aged 11 to 26. They assessed participants' psychotic symptoms in late childhood, cannabis use in adolescence, and subsequent psychotic symptoms in adulthood. They also collected DNA to study youths' genotype. The researchers discovered a significant gene–environment interaction that partially explains the relationship between cannabis use and psychosis.

The COMT gene has two variations (i.e., alleles): (1) the COMT valine allele and (2) the COMT methionine allele. Children can inherit two valine alleles, two methionine alleles, or one of each type. The researchers discovered that adolescents who avoided cannabis had lower risk of psychosis than adolescents who used cannabis, regardless of what alleles they inherited. However, adolescents who used cannabis and who inherited at least one COMT valine allele were significantly more likely to develop psychosis than adolescents who used cannabis but did not inherit a COMT valine allele. The COMT valine allele, which produces an enzyme that regulates dopamine, seems to place adolescents at risk for later schizophrenia but only if they use cannabis. In contrast, the COMT methionine allele seems to protect adolescents from psychosis, regardless of their cannabis exposure (see Figure 14.17).

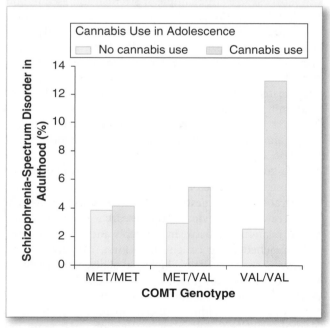

Figure 14.17 Cannabis in adolescence predicts later schizophrenia, but only among youths at genetic risk for the disorder.

Source: Based on Caspi and Moffitt (2006).

Note: Youths who use cannabis and inherit the VAL allele of the COMT gene are at increased risk. Youths with a family history of schizophrenia, therefore, should avoid cannabis.

The Neurodevelopmental Model

Today, most experts view childhood- and adolescent-onset schizophrenia as a neurodevelopmental disorder. The neurodevelopmental model for schizophrenia is based on the notion that individuals who develop schizophrenia have a diathesis for the disorder that is present at birth. Evidence for this claim comes from behavioral genetics research showing high heritability for the disorder and molecular genetics research suggesting specific genes that might place individuals at elevated risk. Genetic risk seems to be especially important for the development of schizophrenia; the likelihood of developing the disorder is 0.5% without a positive family history.

Genetic risk is not sufficient to explain the illness, however. The neurodevelopmental model posits that early environmental stressors, combined with biogenetic risk factors, lead to abnormalities in the organization and development of the central nervous system. Known environmental risk factors include maternal stress and illness during gestation, obstetric complications, malnutrition and poverty, and stressors associated with immigration and acculturation. It is likely that other risks will be discovered. Abnormalities of the central nervous system initially manifest themselves as premorbid differences. Toddlers and preschoolers who later develop schizophrenia often show deficits in language, social interaction, and motor skills.

Later, abnormalities in the organization and development of the brain manifest as prodromal signs and symptoms: marked decline in social behavior, mood, and cognitive functioning. These features, which often emerge years before the youth's first psychotic episode, correspond to the beginning of a documented pattern of excessive neural pruning that progresses from lower-level to higher-level brain regions. Indeed, the emergence of psychosis often coincides with dramatic reductions in gray matter in brain areas responsible for thinking, reasoning, and regulating emotions. The youth's first psychotic episode may be one step in a progression of events that began at (or before) birth (Rapoport & Gogtay, 2011).

Review:

- Schizophrenia is heritable. Individuals with a first-degree relative with schizophrenia are more likely to develop the disorder (5.9%) and individuals with no family history (0.5%).
- Youths with schizophrenia often experience dramatic neural pruning resulting in 3% to 4% loss of gray matter per year shortly before the onset of their first psychotic episode.
- Youths with schizophrenia show excessive dopaminergic activity along the mesolimbic pathway, which is associated with increased positive symptoms. However, they also show underactivity of the mesocortical pathway, which may underlie increased negative symptoms.
- Cannabis use in adolescence may elicit schizophrenia in individuals with a genetic susceptibility for the disorder.

Can Schizophrenia Be Predicted and Prevented?

Predicting Schizophrenia: Attenuated Psychosis Syndrome

Researchers are interested in identifying schizophrenia in children, adolescents, and young adults as early as possible (*DSM-5* Psychosis Work Group, 2013). Early identification is critical because long-term prognosis is related to the amount of time the disorder is left untreated. The sooner individuals with schizophrenia receive treatment, the better their outcomes.

Consequently, the *DSM-5* developers included a new disorder, attenuated psychosis syndrome (APS) as a "condition for further study." APS is diagnosed in children, adolescents, and young adults who experience the first signs and symptoms of psychosis, before the onset of full-blown schizophrenia. To be diagnosed, individuals must show at least one of the following:

- Delusions or delusional ideas
- Hallucinations or perceptual abnormalities
- Disorganized speech or communication

These features must be present at least once per week for the past month, and they must have started or worsened in the past year. Furthermore, these signs and symptoms must have caused enough distress or impairment to individuals or their families to prompt them to seek professional help (American Psychiatric Association, 2013).

The research that is available regarding APS is promising. Early studies indicate that it can be diagnosed reliably. Furthermore, APS is associated with later psychosis: 18% of individuals who meet criteria for APS develop psychosis within 6 months, 22% within 12 months, 29% within 24 months, and 36% within 36 months. Most (73%) patients who later experience psychosis develop schizophrenia; the remaining patients show mood disorders with psychotic features (e.g., bipolar I disorder).

McGorry and colleagues (2002) conducted a randomized controlled study to examine whether treatment delivered before the onset of psychotic symptoms might prevent those symptoms from emerging. The researchers identified a group of adolescents at genetic risk for developing schizophrenia; one or both of their biological parents had the disorder. Then, the researchers assigned youths to receive either a low dose of antipsychotic medication and psychotherapy or to "needs-based treatment." Youths in the latter condition received medication and therapy only after symptoms emerged. Immediately after treatment, patients who received early intervention were significantly less likely to develop psychotic symptoms than controls. At 12-month follow-up, differences between groups largely disappeared. However, outcomes were dependent on whether patients continued to take antipsychotic medication. Patients who adhered to their medication continued to show low rates of psychosis (see Figure 14.18). These findings speak to the importance of early treatment and adherence to medication in the prevention of psychosis.

Early Intervention Programs

Early identification and treatment programs for adolescents and young adults with prodromal or early psychotic symptoms have been developed in the United States and Europe. For example, in the United Kingdom, the Buckingham Integrated Mental Health Care Project was designed to identify individuals in the community showing the first indicators of the illness (Falloon, Wilkinson, Burgess, & McLees, 2016). Primary practice physicians were trained to routinely screen individuals for prodromal symptoms and to refer them to the early intervention program. The intervention itself consisted of low doses of antipsychotic medication, education about psychosis, and psychotherapy to help patients manage stress. The incidence of schizophrenia dropped from 7.4 per 100,000 people per year before the program to 0.75 per 100,000 per year after the program was initiated.

Early detection and prevention programs have also been developed at the Early Psychosis Prevention and Intervention Centre (EPPIC) in Australia. EPPIC works to identify youths at risk for developing schizophrenia before the onset of psychotic symptoms. The program then provides medication, education, and psychotherapy services to youths and their families to mitigate the effects of the illness. Staff members also offer support to help youths stay on track with regard to school and work. Youths who participate in EPPIC show better outcomes than individuals who do not receive these preventative and early intervention services. Specifically, youths show fewer positive symptoms, better adaptive functioning, fewer number of total psychotic episodes, and better vocational outcomes. These findings speak to the importance of early identification and intervention (Amminger et al., 2011).

Other early identification and prevention programs include the Treatment and Intervention in Psychosis Study (TIPS) project in Norway and the Portland Identification and Early Referral Program (PIER) in the United States. Evaluations of these programs indicate that prodromal and early psychotic symptoms can be identified in adolescents and young adults. Furthermore, early intervention, consisting of medication and counseling, is effective at delaying the onset of a major psychotic episode. However, these programs have not been shown to prevent the onset of psychosis altogether (Kline et al., 2015).

Review:

- APS is a condition for further study in *DSM-5*. It is diagnosed in youths who experience the first signs and symptoms of schizophrenia (e.g. delusions, hallucinations, disorganized speech) that occur weekly for at least 1 year, in the absence of a full psychotic episode.

Figure 14.18   Prevention of Schizophrenia in High-Risk Youths

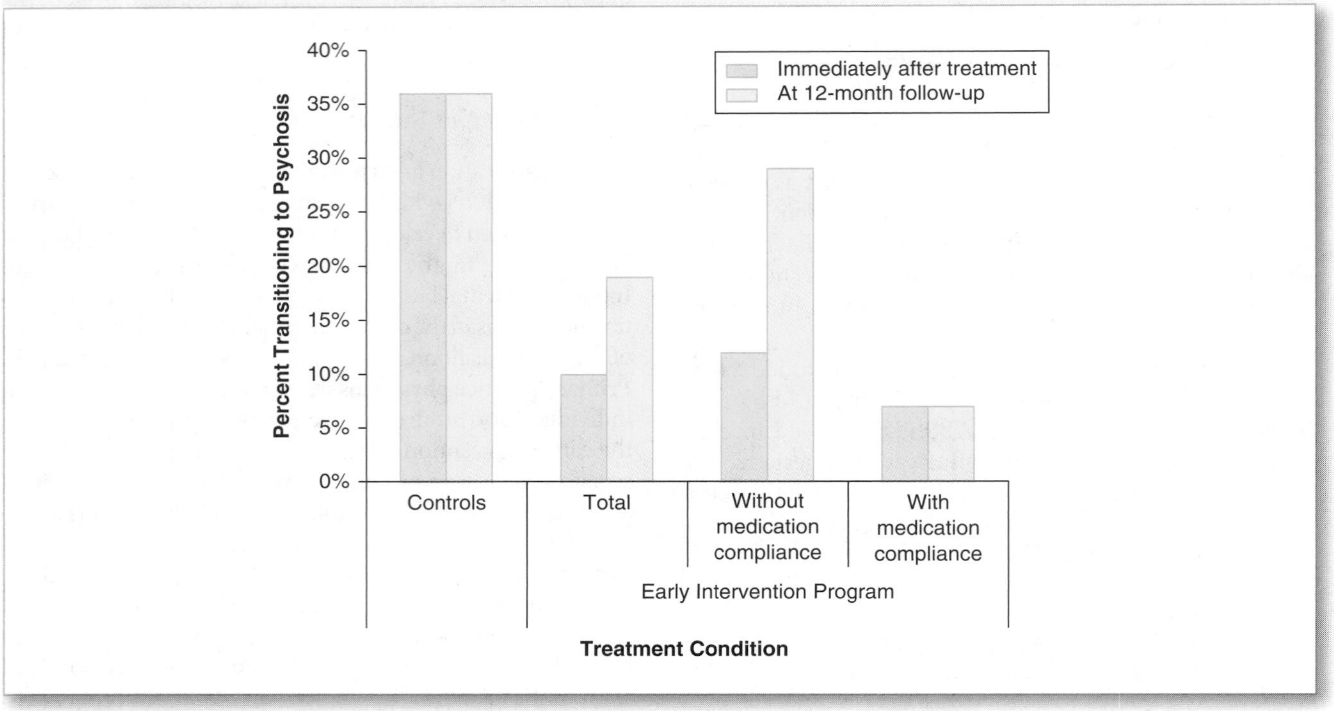

Source: Based on McGorry and colleagues (2002).

Note: Researchers examined the efficacy of early intervention to prevent schizophrenia in high-risk youths. Immediately after treatment, youths who received early intervention were less likely to develop psychotic symptoms than controls. One year later, most youths who received early intervention continued to remain symptom free—but only if they remained on antipsychotic medication. These findings highlight the importance of early intervention and compliance with medication.

- Early identification and intervention programs indicate that schizophrenia can be reliably detected in youths with genetic risk for the disorder and its onset can be delayed (but usually not prevented) with antipsychotic medication.

Is Medication Effective for Youths With Schizophrenia?

Conventional Antipsychotics

The first-line treatment for schizophrenia is antipsychotic medication. There are two broad classes of medications that are effective for the disorder: (1) conventional antipsychotics and (2) atypical antipsychotics.

Conventional antipsychotics have been used to treat adults with schizophrenia for more than 50 years. Conventional antipsychotics act as dopamine antagonists by binding to D2 receptors, particularly in the mesolimbic pathway. Consequently, they are especially effective in reducing the positive symptoms of schizophrenia, such as hallucinations and delusions. The most well-known conventional antipsychotics are haloperidol (Haldol), molindone (Moban), and perphenazine (Trilafon). Conventional antipsychotics are effective in reducing the

positive symptoms of schizophrenia in children and adolescents as well (Mattai, Hill, & Lenroot, 2010). Overall, 54% to 93% of youths experience symptom reduction while taking these medications compared to 0% to 38% taking placebo (Leucht et al., 2013; Rapoport, gogtay, & Shaw, 2008).

Conventional antipsychotics have two main drawbacks. First, they are less effective at reducing the negative symptoms of schizophrenia, such as apathy, restricted emotional expression, social withdrawal, and psychomotor problems. Second, and perhaps more importantly, they produce side effects in some patients that are distressing and occasionally life threatening.

Extrapyramidal side effects are most common. These effects are called extrapyramidal because they involve the extrapyramidal system, a neural network that regulates the body's control of movement. Brain regions in this system include the substantial nigra, basal ganglia, and cerebellum. Unfortunately, these regions are rich in dopamine receptors and can be adversely affected by antipsychotics that block dopamine.

Side effects include the inability to initiate movement (i.e., akinesia), intense feelings of restlessness and difficulty remaining motionless (i.e., akathisia), and tremors that resemble the symptoms of Parkinson's disease. Other involuntary motor movements include spasms of the muscles of the face and mouth, writhing of the hands or wrists, and minor tongue protrusion or lip smacking. In adults, tardive dyskinesia can occur, characterized by involuntary, purposeless, and repetitive movements of the face, mouth, and jaw (Leucht et al., 2013; Rapoport et al., 2008). A rare, but potentially life-threatening, side effect is neuroleptic malignant syndrome (NMS). Signs and symptoms include severe muscle rigidity, loss of motor control, elevated or highly fluctuating body temperature and blood pressure, and delirium (Rajamani, Kumar, & Rahman, 2016).

Atypical Antipsychotics

In the past 20 years, psychiatrists have begun using atypical antipsychotics to treat adults with schizophrenia. Like conventional antipsychotics, atypical antipsychotics act as dopamine antagonists and are effective in reducing positive symptoms of the disorder. Unlike conventional antipsychotics, they bind more weakly to dopamine receptors, resulting in reduced likelihood of extrapyramidal side effects. Moreover, most atypical antipsychotics have higher affinity for serotonin receptors, making them more effective at regulating mood and reducing negative symptoms (Harvey, James, & Shields, 2016; Harvey, Shields, & James, 2015).

The most frequently used atypical antipsychotics are aripiprazaole (Abilify), olanzapine (Zyprexa), paliperidone (Invega), quetiapine (Seroquel), risperidone (Risperdal), and ziprasidone (Geodon). Overall, 38% to 72% of youths show symptom reduction while taking atypical antipsychotic medication compared to 26% to 35% of youths who show symptom reduction taking placebo (Correll, 2015).

Because antipsychotic medications are newer and associated with fewer side effects, most physicians use these medications as the first-line treatment of schizophrenia (Correll, 2015). However, a large study called into question the superiority of atypical antipsychotics over conventional antipsychotics (Sikich et al., 2008). In the Treatment of Early Onset Schizophrenia Spectrum Disorders (TEOSS) study, 119 youths with schizophrenia were randomly assigned to receive one of three medications: (1) molindone, a conventional antipsychotic; (2) olanzapine, an atypical antipsychotic; or (3) risperidone, another atypical antipsychotic. The researchers assessed outcome 8 weeks after treatment. Overall, treatment gains were modest; between 20% and 34% of youths showed significant reduction in positive and negative symptoms. Furthermore, there were no significant differences in the percentage of youths who responded to molindone (50%), olanzapine (34%), and risperidone (46%; Findling et al., 2010).

Atypical antipsychotics also have side effects. Approximately one-half of children and adolescents prescribed olanzapine or risperidone still develop extrapyramidal side effects and approximately 5% to 10% develop akathisia. The most common nonmotor side effects are weight gain and sedation. Between 4% to 5% of adolescents show significant weight gain with aripiprazole, 15% to 16% with risperidone, and 45% to 46% with olanzapine. Weight gain is associated with other metabolic problems, such as risk for diabetes, obesity, and elevated triglycerides and cholesterol. Weight gain can also lead to teasing or ostracism by peers. The prevalence of sedation varies considerably across medications; prevalence is lowest for aripiprazole (0%–33%) and highest for olanzapine (46%–90%). Sedation can interfere with children's academic and social functioning. Atypical antipsychotics are also associated with abnormalities in liver enzymes in 22% to 35% of youths. Consequently, children's metabolism must be carefully monitored (Caccia, 2013; Correll, 2015).

Antipsychotic medication should be used for 6 to 18 months after the onset of psychotic symptoms. However, because of their side effects, most youths are reluctant to take these medications for long periods of time. One large study found that 71% to 77% of youths prescribed atypical antipsychotics for early onset schizophrenia stopped taking these medications in the first 180 days after they were first prescribed (Olfson, Blanco, Liu, Wang, & Correll, 2012). This high rate of discontinuation is important because it predicts relapse. On average, patients who discontinue their medication have a 7 to 28 times greater likelihood of having another psychotic episode compared to patients who remain adherent (Subotnik et al., 2011). Consequently, clinicians usually augment medication with psychotherapy to improve the likelihood of adherence (Kodish & McClellan, 2015).

Review:

- Conventional antipsychotics are effective in reducing the positive symptoms of schizophrenia in youths. Continued use is associated with extrapyramidal side effects and tardive dyskinesia.
- Atypical antipsychotic medication appears to be as effective as conventional antipsychotics for youths with schizophrenia. Atypical antipsychotics are also associated with fewer side effects.
- Results of the TEOSS study suggest that approximately one-third of youths will respond to antipsychotic medication.

Is Psychotherapy Effective for Youths With Schizophrenia?

Nearly all experts recommend that medication should be combined with psychosocial interventions to treat youths with schizophrenia (see Figure 14.19). Most psychosocial treatments have five components in common (Kline et al., 2015; Remschmidt & Theisen, 2012).

First, therapists provide *information* about the illness to youths and their families. Psychoeducation is critical to treatment success; family members often have many questions about the disorder and the best way to help youths

Figure 14.19 Multimodal Treatment for Pediatric Schizophrenia

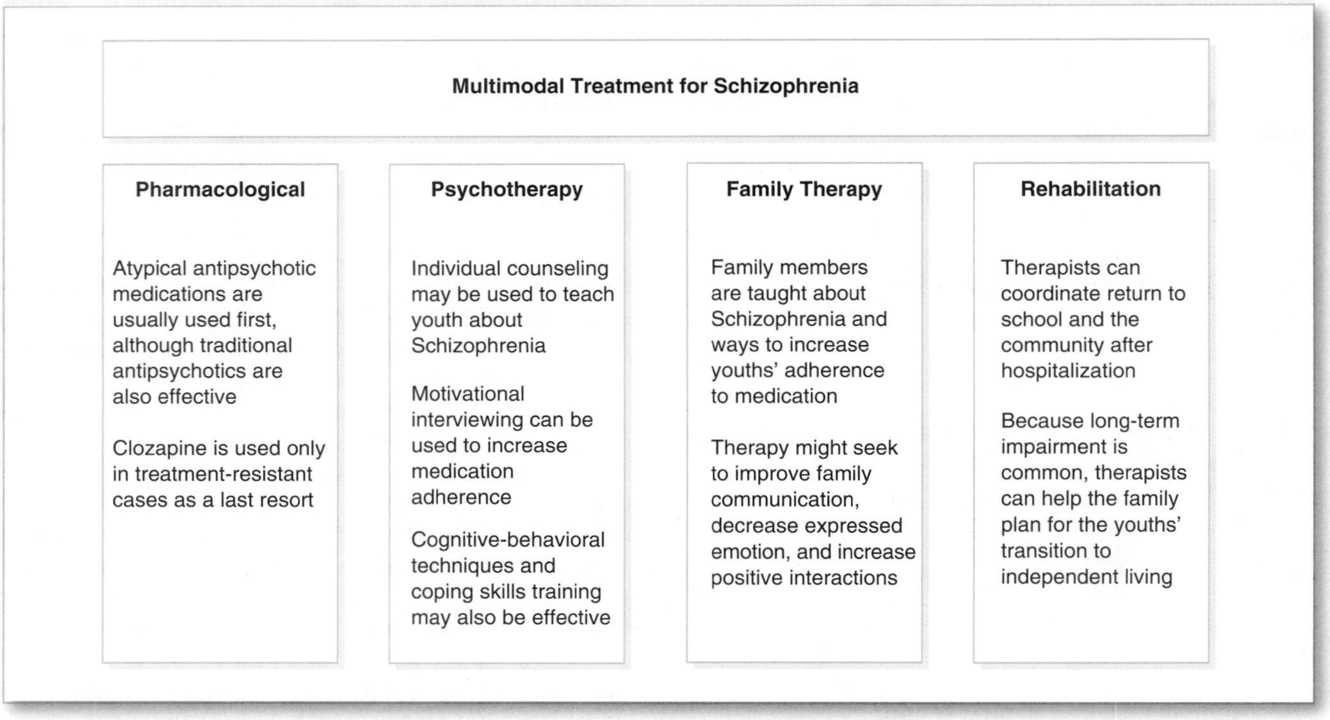

Multimodal Treatment for Schizophrenia

Pharmacological	Psychotherapy	Family Therapy	Rehabilitation
Atypical antipsychotic medications are usually used first, although traditional antipsychotics are also effective Clozapine is used only in treatment-resistant cases as a last resort	Individual counseling may be used to teach youth about Schizophrenia Motivational interviewing can be used to increase medication adherence Cognitive-behavioral techniques and coping skills training may also be effective	Family members are taught about Schizophrenia and ways to increase youths' adherence to medication Therapy might seek to improve family communication, decrease expressed emotion, and increase positive interactions	Therapists can coordinate return to school and the community after hospitalization Because long-term impairment is common, therapists can help the family plan for the youths' transition to independent living

Source: Based on Clark (2011).

Note: Nearly all treatment programs involve (a) medication, (b) individual psychotherapy, (c) family therapy, and (d) planning for the child's return to school and family life.

cope with symptoms. Therapists can also be instrumental in dispelling myths about schizophrenia and listening to families' concerns about caring for a youth with the disorder.

Second, therapists work with youths and their parents to encourage *medication adherence*. Because antipsychotic medications often have unpleasant side effects, such as weight gain, adolescents are often reluctant to take them for long periods of time. Nagging, pleading, and bribing on the part of parents are usually ineffective strategies to encourage compliance. Instead, therapists might use principles of motivational interviewing to help adolescents comply with pharmacotherapy. Instead of insisting that adolescents take their medication, therapists who use motivational interviewing acknowledge and try to understand adolescents' apprehension. Therapists also encourage youths to weigh the costs and benefits of medication adherence. Of course, therapists hope adolescents will decide that the benefits of adherence outweigh those of noncompliance. The goal of therapy is to slowly move adolescents from medication refusal to greater acceptance.

Third, adolescents with schizophrenia may benefit from *cognitive behavioral interventions*. For example, an adolescent with schizophrenia might feel as though she was treated unfairly by parents and teachers. A cognitive therapist might ask the adolescent for evidence of these beliefs and suggest alternative, more realistic ways to

interpret adults' behavior. Behavioral interventions might involve teaching specific communication skills to improve the quality of relationships with parents and teachers. For example, the therapist might teach and role-play ways the adolescent can express concerns to adults without starting an argument. Behavioral interventions might also involve introducing and practicing ways to cope with specific symptoms of schizophrenia. For example, the adolescent might learn to distract herself when she begins to hear voices or respond to them in more rational ways (e.g., "Oh, there are those voices again. I need to find a way to keep them in the background of my life.")

Fourth, treatment may involve *family-based interventions*. Although parents do not cause schizophrenia, the severity and course of the disorder may be influenced by the family system. Initially, family therapists try to establish a therapeutic alliance with family members. Typically, this involves listening empathically to the family's concerns, providing information, and offering emotional support to members. After forging an alliance with the family, therapists address areas of conflict or tension. For example, a family therapist might address parents' concerns that their adolescent avoids taking his medication because it produces side effects. The therapist might help balance the concerns of the parents with the developing autonomy of the adolescent. Similarly, a family therapist might address the feelings of a healthy sibling who feels "left out" because her brother with schizophrenia monopolizes her parents' attention and energy.

Fifth, therapy almost always involves rehabilitation and *integration back into the community*. Psychotic episodes are both distressing and disruptive to youths and their families. Some youths require hospitalization or residential treatment and may be separated from their families. Many youths will miss several weeks or months of school. Their relationships with teachers and friends may be greatly disrupted. Youths who play sports, are involved in extracurricular activities, or who hold part-time jobs may also suspend these activities. Therapists can be instrumental in helping youths transition from treatment to life at home, school, and the community (Remschmidt & Theisen, 2012).

Approximately 40% of youths who experience a psychotic episode do not return to their premorbid level of functioning. These youths continue to have problems with the negative symptoms of schizophrenia, especially dysphoria, apathy, and social withdrawal. For these youths, the goal of rehabilitation is not so much to return to their "old life" but to find new ways to cope with the illness moving forward.

Efficacy

Are psychosocial interventions effective for schizophrenia? Two reviews of cognitive behavioral interventions involving adults with schizophrenia have yielded disappointing results. In a qualitative review of the published research, Dickerson (2000) concluded that CBT was moderately effective in reducing positive symptoms of schizophrenia, especially among patients with clearly defined psychotic symptoms. However, she found little evidence that cognitive behavioral interventions were useful in alleviating negative symptoms or improving social functioning. Cormac, Jones, and Campbell (2014) conducted a meta-analysis of the effectiveness of various psychosocial interventions for schizophrenia. They found no overall differences in the effectiveness of CBT compared to supportive psychotherapy. Furthermore, when CBT was added to medication, it did not reduce relapse or the rate of hospitalization more than medication alone.

Unfortunately, there are no randomized controlled studies investigating the efficacy of cognitive behavioral interventions for youths with schizophrenia. However, two studies may be relevant. Lewis and colleagues (2002) studied the efficacy of treatment for adolescents and young adults who were experiencing their first psychotic episodes. Patients were randomly assigned to either CBT and medication, supportive therapy and medication, or medication alone. The intervention lasted only 5 weeks. Results showed modest benefits of CBT above and beyond the other two interventions in speeding recovery from the acute stage of the illness (see Figure 14.20).

A second study involved adolescents and adults recently released from the hospital following an acute psychotic

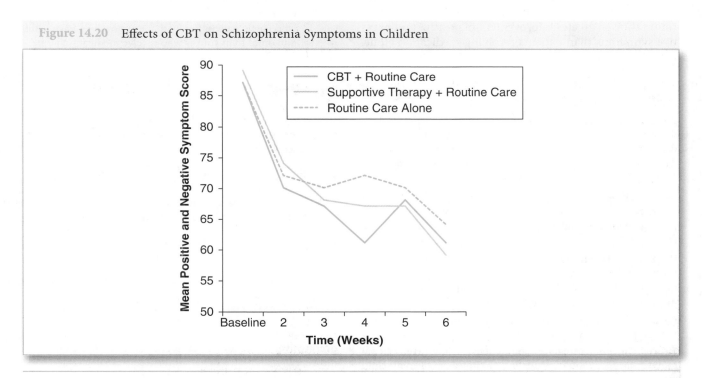

Figure 14.20   Effects of CBT on Schizophrenia Symptoms in Children

Source: Based on Lewis and colleagues (2002).

Note: Adding CBT to routine care (medication) modestly speeds recovery among adolescents with schizophrenia. Youths who received supportive therapy and medication or medication alone improved about as well as youths in CBT.

episode (Hogarty et al., 1997). Patients were randomly assigned to two psychosocial interventions: supportive therapy or behavioral skills training. Behavioral skills training consisted of progressively more complex skills to cope with psychosocial stress. For example, patients learned to recognize people and situations that might trigger negative emotions, to avoid these stimuli, and to use relaxation techniques. They also learned skills to improve social interactions and adjust to life in the community. Outcomes were assessed every 6 months for 3 years. Overall, approximately one-third of patients in both conditions relapsed. However, outcomes depended on whether patients lived with their families or independently during treatment. Skills training was very effective in reducing relapse among patients living with their families (only 13% relapsed). In contrast, skills training did not prevent relapse among patients living independently (44% relapsed). These findings suggest that the efficacy of therapy might depend on support from family and/or the stability of patients' lives outside the therapy setting.

Family therapy is almost universally recommended for children and adolescents with schizophrenia. Unfortunately, studies investigating the efficacy of family therapy for youths with schizophrenia are limited. One relevant study involved 547 newly diagnosed patients who were experiencing their first psychotic episodes; many were older adolescents and young adults (Petersen, Jeppesen, & Thorup, 2005). Researchers randomly assigned these youths to two treatment conditions: (1) medication alone or (2) medication plus family therapy. Patients who received family therapy in addition to medication showed greater improvement in positive and negative symptoms than patients receiving medication alone.

Patients who received family therapy were also less likely to use alcohol and other drugs, were more likely to adhere to medication, and were more satisfied with treatment.

There is also some evidence that family therapy can help younger patients with schizophrenia. In one study, youths with schizophrenia were randomly assigned to either (a) medication or (b) medication plus family therapy (Rund, 1994). Two years after treatment, overall functioning and relapse rates were better for youth who received medication plus family therapy. However, relapse was still quite high, supporting the notion that early onset schizophrenia is very resistant to treatment. Lenior, Dingemans, Linszen, de Haan, and Schene (2001) randomly assigned adolescents and young adults with schizophrenia to either standard treatment or standard treatment plus family therapy. Patients who received family therapy spent an average of 10 months less in residential care at follow-up than patients who received only standard treatment. Family therapy is a promising intervention for youths with schizophrenia. Clearly, more research is needed to maximize its effectiveness.

Review:

- Psychotherapy for youths with schizophrenia has five components: (1) education, (2) medication adherence, (3) challenging cognitive distortions, (4) family therapy to decrease EE, and (5) rehabilitation and return to school and the community.

- Approximately 40% of youths with schizophrenia do not return to their premorbid level of functioning. Youths who participate in family therapy, however, have better outcomes than youths who receive medication alone.

KEY TERMS

Attenuated psychosis syndrome (APS): A term used to describe the earliest signs and symptoms of psychosis (e.g. delusions, hallucinations, disorganized speech) occurring weekly for at least 1 year, in the absence of a psychotic episode; a "condition for further study" in *DSM-5*

Bipolar I disorder: A *DSM-5* disorder characterized by at least one manic episode that results in marked impairment in functioning, requires hospitalization, or is associated with psychotic features

Bipolar II disorder: A *DSM-5* disorder characterized by at least one hypomanic episode and one major depressive episode that results in a marked change in functioning but not lead to impairment or require hospitalization

Child- and family-focused cognitive–behavioral therapy (CFF-CBT): Treatment for children (aged 7–13) with bipolar disorders and their caregivers; components include (a) emotional monitoring and emotion regulation, (b) improving parent–child interactions, and (c) managing disruptive child behavior

Course and Outcome of Bipolar Youth (COBY) study: A large study of the course of bipolar disorders in children; it

showed that most youths with bipolar disorders recovered from their symptoms, continued to experience mood problems, and experienced another mood episode

Cyclothymic disorder: A *DSM-5* disorder characterized by periods of hypomanic symptoms (but not a hypomanic episode) and depressive symptoms (but not a major depressive episode) lasting at least 1 year in children and adolescents

Delusions: Erroneous, often bizarre, beliefs that usually involve a misinterpretation of perceptions or experiences

Dopamine hypothesis: Posits that the positive symptoms of schizophrenia are caused by excessive stimulation of certain dopamine receptors (D2 receptors) along the mesolimbic pathway

Expressed emotion (EE): Criticism, hostility, or emotional overinvolvement toward a family member with a psychiatric disorder

Extrapyramidal side effects: Side effects associated with the use of conventional antipsychotics; include problems initiating movements, feelings of restlessness, and tardive dyskinesia

Family-focused treatment for adolescents (FFT-A): A family systems therapy for adolescents with bipolar disorder and their caregivers; seeks to improve parent–child communication and problem-solving and avoid future mood episodes by decreasing expressed emotion

Flight of ideas: Racing thoughts often experienced by people with mania or hypomania

Goal-directed activity: A tendency to initiate a wide range of new behaviors

Grandiosity: Unusually high self-confidence, exaggerated self-esteem, and overrated self-importance

Hallucinations: Erroneous, often bizarre, perceptions that do not correspond to reality

Hypofrontality hypothesis: Posits that underactivity among certain dopamine receptors (D1 receptors) in the mesocortical pathway is responsible for the negative symptoms of schizophrenia

Hypomanic episode: A distinct period of abnormally, persistently elevated, expansive, or irritable mood and increased activity and energy, lasting at least 4 days, but less than 1 week, and occurring most of the day nearly every day

Insula: A centrally located region of the brain responsible for emotion regulation, self-awareness, and interpersonal functioning

Lateral ventricles: Canals in the center of the brain that are filled with cerebrospinal fluid; sometimes enlarged in adults with schizophrenia

Lithium (Eskalith): A mood stabilizing medication used to treat bipolar disorders in adults; regulates norepinephrine and serotonin

Mania: A discrete period of abnormally, persistently elevated, expansive, or irritable mood and increased level of energy and activity; an essential feature of all *DSM-5* bipolar disorders

Manic episode: A distinct period of abnormally, persistently elevated, expansive, or irritable mood and increased activity and energy, lasting at least 1 week and occurring most of the day nearly every day

Mixed mood: The presence of either a manic or hypomanic episode and subthreshold symptoms of depression or, alternatively, the presence of a major depressive episode and subthreshold hypomanic symptoms

Negative symptoms: Features of schizophrenia that reflect behavioral "under-expressions"; include flat affect, avolition, social withdrawal, passivity, apathy, and lack of spontaneity

Negatively escalating cycle of communication: Parent–child interaction in which criticism from one family member elicits countercriticism from another family member, until it is difficult to resolve; usually involves a three-volley sequence

Neurodevelopmental model for schizophrenia: Posits that early environmental stressors, combined with biogenetic risk factors, lead to abnormalities in the organization and development of the central nervous system; these abnormalities can be triggered to produce schizophrenia

Neuroleptic malignant syndrome (NMS): A rare condition caused by an initial, high dose of conventional antipsychotic medication; characterized by severe muscle rigidity, loss of motor control, fever, high blood pressure, and delirium

Pittsburgh Bipolar Offspring Study (BIOS): A large study showing that the children of individuals with bipolar disorders are at increased risk for bipolar disorders, mood disorders, and anxiety themselves

Positive symptoms: Features of schizophrenia that reflect "behavioral over-expressions"; include hallucinations, delusions, disorganized behavior, excitement, grandiosity, suspiciousness, and hostility

Prodromal: Signs or symptoms that occur before the onset of the disorder

Psychoeducational psychotherapy (PEP): A treatment for children (aged 8–12) with bipolar and mood disorders and their caregivers; can be administered to individual families or groups of families together; teaches families about mood disorders, emotion regulation, and problem-solving skills

Psychomotor agitation: Overt actions that are characterized by hyperactivity, restlessness, or impulsivity

Psychotic Disorders: A class of *DSM-5* disorders in which the person's cognitions, affect, and overt actions reflect a lack of contact or connection with their surroundings

Schizophrenia: A *DSM-5* psychotic disorder characterized by the presence of hallucinations, delusions, disorganized speech, disorganized actions, and diminished emotional expression or lack of motor activity which impair functioning for at least 6 months

Tardive dyskinesia: A side effect of prolonged use of conventional antipsychotics; characterized by involuntary, purposeless, and repetitive movements of the face, mouth, and jaw

Treatment of Early Age Mania (TEAM) study: A large study that showed atypical antipsychotics were more effective than traditional mood stabilizers for reducing bipolar symptoms in children and younger adolescents

Treatment of Early Onset Schizophrenia Spectrum Disorders (TEOSS) study: A large study showing significant, but modest, benefits for conventional and atypical antipsychotic medication in reducing children's psychotic symptoms

CRITICAL THINKING EXERCISES

1. Jody is a 15-year-old girl who has experienced a single manic episode, but she has never experienced a major depressive episode. Can she be diagnosed with bipolar I disorder?

2. Louisa is a 10-year-old girl with bipolar I disorder who is managing her symptoms with medication and family therapy. Her mother worries that Louisa's symptoms will return. Based on the results of the COBY study, are her mother's worries justified?

3. Jackson is a 13-year-old boy with a family history of schizophrenia. Jackson's father was diagnosed with the disorder as a young adult. Why might Jackson want to avoid cannabis during adolescence?

4. Maggie is a 17-year-old girl who is very involved in her religion. She prays multiple times each day, attends religious services regularly, and participates in religious youth group activities and charity events. Recently, she reported to her mother and her friends that she has "spoken" to God and that God is sending her messages about her life. Maggie has also reported seeing God and angels while praying. Her mother is becoming concerned about her vivid reports of these religious experiences. How might a clinician differentiate these experiences from delusions or hallucinations?

5. The inclusion of APS in *DSM-5* as a "condition for further study" was controversial. Why might a clinician *not* want to assign this label to an adolescent who is showing early features of schizophrenia?

TEST YOURSELF AND EXTEND YOUR LEARNING

Videos, flash cards, and links to online resources for this chapter are available to students online. Teachers also have access to PowerPoint slides to guide lectures, case studies to prompt classroom discussions, and exam questions. Visit www.abnormalchildpsychology.org.

PART V Health-Related Disorders

iStockphoto.com/Liderina

CHAPTER 15

Feeding and Eating Disorders

LEARNING OBJECTIVES

After reading this chapter, you should be able to do the following:

15.1. Differentiate among the most common feeding disorders affecting infants and young children.

Identify the main causes of feeding disorders and provide examples of evidence-based treatments for these problems.

15.2. Differentiate among anorexia nervosa, bulimia nervosa, and binge eating disorder.

Explain how eating disorders vary as a function of age, gender, ethnicity, and socioeconomic status (SES).

Outline some of the main causes of eating disorders ranging from genetic–biological factors to social–cultural influences.

15.3. Critically evaluate inpatient and outpatient treatment programs for adolescents with eating disorders.

Feeding and eating disorders are grouped together into a single diagnostic category in the *Diagnostic and Statistical Manual of Mental Disorders, Fifth Edition* (*DSM-5*; American Psychiatric Association, 2013). Feeding disorders are usually seen in infants, toddlers, and young children, although they may also be seen in children and adults with developmental disabilities. These disorders are characterized by marked disturbances in the ingestion of food, causing considerable distress to caregivers and placing children at risk for malnutrition or physical illness. In contrast, eating disorders are almost exclusively seen in older children, adolescents, and adults. These disorders are characterized by disturbances in eating that result in very low body weight, binge eating, and/or dangerous strategies to avoid weight gain. Eating disorders are among the most lethal of all mental disorders because of their effect on adolescents' health and their close relationship with depression, hopelessness, and self-harm (American Psychiatric Association, 2013).

In this chapter, we will first examine feeding disorders that typically present in infants and young children: pica, rumination disorder, and avoidant/restrictive food intake disorder (ARFID). Then, we will consider the three most common eating disorders in older children and adolescents: anorexia, bulimia, and binge eating disorder (BED).

15.1 FEEDING DISORDERS IN YOUNG CHILDREN

The transition from breast- or bottle-feeding to the consumption of solid foods occurs gradually over the first two years of life. Although this transition might seem effortless, it is highly dependent on the child's physical, motoric, and social–emotional development. First, the child's gustatory and digestive systems must be able to accept and digest increasingly solid food, of different tastes, textures, and appearances. Second, the child must have the capacity to bite, chew, and swallow, as well as coordinate movements to place food in his mouth, use a spoon, and drink from a cup. Third, the child must be able to regulate his attention, emotions, and behavior long enough to focus on mealtime, to accept food, and to consume sufficient calories. Finally, the child must recognize signals of hunger and satiety and negotiate with caregivers to perform feeding tasks (e.g., Who will hold the spoon?). Feeding is a social activity between caregiver and child; self-feeding is an important milestone in an infant's emerging autonomy and sense of self (Lyons-Ruth, Zeanah, Benoit, Madigan, & Mills-Koonce, 2014).

At its best, mealtime for 10-month-olds can be messy; at its worse, it can be a source of anxiety and frustration. Approximately 25% to 50% of parents report at least moderate feeding problems with their infant or toddler. Approximately 1% to 2% of young children have feeding disorders, severe feeding problems characterized by food avoidance, limited diet, inappropriate diet, or recurrent regurgitation (Chatoor & Ammaniti, 2007). Feeding disorders can elicit family distress and place children at risk for malnutrition, dehydration, growth suppression, and behavior problems (Chatoor, 2009).

What Are Pica and Rumination Disorder?

Two feeding disorders are most commonly seen among children with developmental disabilities: (1) pica and (2) rumination disorder. Pica refers to the persistent eating of nonnutritive, nonfood substances over the period of at least 1 month. The name "pica" comes from the Latin word for magpie, a bird known for eating both edible and inedible objects. Table 15.1 lists some of the substances consumed by children with pica. Some children with pica eat nonfood substances indiscriminately, whereas others prefer specific items. Pica is not diagnosed when the mouthing or consumption of nonfoods might be considered developmentally appropriate; for example, an infant who eats small objects she finds on the floor would not be diagnosed with pica (Lyons-Ruth et al., 2014).

Pica is most commonly associated with severe or profound intellectual disability (ID). Approximately 15% of individuals with ID have pica. It is possible that pica provides oral and gustatory stimulation to these individuals. Pica is also sometimes associated with iron or zinc deficiency. For example, children with medical disorders associated with these deficiencies (e.g., celiac disease, kidney and liver disease, sickle cell disease) sometimes show pica. Pregnant women with iron deficiency also may engage in pica. It is possible that these individuals eat substances to obtain necessary minerals. Pica is also associated with environmental stressors, such as major life events, impoverished home environments, or social neglect. Finally, some of the substances ingested by children with pica are intrinsically reinforcing. For example, many youths with pica ingest cigarette butts because of the nicotine they contain (Stiegler, 2005).

In typically developing children, pica usually remits spontaneously. In youths with developmental disabilities, pica tends to persist over time. In either case, pica should be treated because of the risks associated with eating nonfood substances. Common risks include intestinal and bowel blockage from eating impassible substances (e.g., hair, pebbles),

Table 15.1   Substances Most Often Consumed by Children With Pica

Burnt matches

Caulking, concrete, glass

Cigarette butts

Coins, nuts, bolts, screws

Crayons, chalk, glue, pencils

Dirt, sand, clay

Fibers, pillow/toy stuffing, carpet, cloth, sponge

Grass, leaves, acorns, pinecones

Hair

Insects

Laundry starch

Paint chips

Paper, toilet paper

Plastic toy parts

Rocks, gravel, pebbles

Wood, bark, twigs

Adapted from Stiegler (2005). Image courtesy of Pixabay.

ingestion of harmful bacteria and parasites, perforation of the digestive system caused by sharp objects (e.g., glass, nails), and lead toxicity following repeated consumption of lead-based paint chips (Sturmey & Williams, 2016).

Rumination disorder is also most often seen among children with developmental disabilities. Rumination involves the repeated regurgitation of stomach contents into the mouth. The regurgitated food may be rechewed, reswallowed, or spit out. Children are diagnosed with rumination disorder if this behavior is repeated over the course of at least 1 month. Youths with the disorder regurgitate out of habit; rumination disorder is not diagnosed if the child has a medical condition that might involve involuntary regurgitation, such as gastroesophageal reflux disease (GERD). Rumination disorder is also not diagnosed if the person regurgitates food to avoid weight gain, as in the case of some people with anorexia or bulimia (Silverman & Tarbell, 2009).

Rumination disorder typically develops in early childhood. It is 5 times more common among boys than girls. Operant conditioning, especially reinforcement, usually maintains regurgitation. Some children ruminate because they gain attention from caregivers or peers (i.e., social positive reinforcement). Other youths ruminate to avoid an undesirable task (i.e., social negative reinforcement); for example, a child who does not want to participate in a group activity might regurgitate to avoid social contact. Sometimes, rumination is a form of self-stimulation (i.e., automatic reinforcement). Although regurgitation probably does not sound pleasant to us, it may be stimulating to severely disabled youths (Bryant-Waugh & Watkins, 2015).

The repeated regurgitation of food can have physical and social consequences. The most common physical problems are weight loss and malnutrition, dental erosions because of stomach acid, and electrolyte imbalance because of fluid loss. Rumination disorder often results in negative social interactions with caregivers and rejection by peers. Over time, these negative social experiences can hinder the development of children's social skills and relationships (Lyons-Ruth et al., 2014).

Review:

- Pica is a *DSM-5* feeding disorder characterized by the persistent eating of nonnutritive, nonfood substances that is developmentally and culturally unexpected. It lasts at least 1 month.
- Rumination disorder is a *DSM-5* feeding disorder characterized by repeated regurgitation of food. It occurs over the period of at least 1 month and must not be attributable to a medical condition or an eating disorder.

What Is Avoidant/Restrictive Food Intake Disorder?

Avoidant/restrictive food intake disorder (ARFID) is a feeding disorder seen in typically developing children, children with developmental disabilities, and children with chronic health problems (see Table 15.2). Youths with ARFID show a lack of interest in eating, avoid certain foods based on their sensory characteristics (e.g., texture, color, smell) or are concerned about possible negative consequences of eating (e.g., nausea, choking, vomiting). By definition, all children with ARFID have persistent problems with meeting their nutritional or energy needs. For example, they may fail to gain weight or grow, develop nutritional deficiencies, or

---

Table 15.2   Diagnostic Criteria for Avoidant/Restrictive Food Intake Disorder

A.   An eating or feeding disturbance (e.g., apparent lack of interest in eating or food; avoidance based on the sensory characteristics of food; concern about the aversive consequences of eating) as manifested by persistent failure to meet appropriate nutritional and/or energy needs associated with one (or more) of the following:

1.   Significant weight loss (or failure to achieve expected weight gain or faltering growth in children).

2.   Significant nutritional deficiency.

3.   Dependence on enteral feeding or oral nutritional supplements.

4.   Marked interference with psychosocial functioning.

B.   The disturbance is not better explained by lack of available food or by an associated culturally sanctioned practice.

C.   The eating disturbance does not occur exclusively during the course of Anorexia Nervosa or Bulimia Nervosa, and there is no evidence of a disturbance in the way in which one's body weight or shape is experienced.

D.   The eating disturbance is not attributable to a current medical condition or not better explained by another mental disorder. When the eating disturbance occurs in the context of another condition or disorder, the severity of the eating disturbance exceeds that routinely associated with the condition or disorder and warrants additional clinical attention.

Source: **Reprinted with permission from the** *Diagnostic and Statistical Manual of Mental Disorders, Fifth Edition* (Copyright 2013). American Psychiatric Association.

need a feeding tube to acquire sufficient nutrition. They are also disruptive during meals; they may talk, cry, tantrum, arch their backs, throw food, or leave their seat—anything to avoid eating (Bryant-Waugh & Watkins, 2015).

There are three main subtypes of ARFID; each is associated with different causes and treatments:

1. Children who do not eat enough and show little interest in feeding (i.e., infantile anorexia)

2. Children who avoid certain foods because of their sensory characteristics, such as taste or texture (i.e., sensory food aversion)

3. Children who refuse foods because of a previous aversive experience associated with eating (i.e., posttraumatic feeding)

Children with all three subtypes would be diagnosed with ARFID (American Psychiatric Association, 2013).

Infantile Anorexia

Some children with feeding disorders show little interest in eating and rarely report feeling hungry (see Image 15.1). These children may accept a small bite of food or sip of milk and then indicate that they are full. They often turn away from food, attempt to leave the high chair or booster seat, or try to distract themselves or their parents from the meal. For example, they might play with food or utensils, talk, or tantrum. Because of their lack of interest in food and avoidance of meals, these children are often underweight or small for their age and gender (Norris, Spettigue, & Katzman, 2015).

Needless to say, most parents are concerned about their children's lack of interest in food, low body weight, and/or growth failure. Consequently, parents often attempt to use a variety of strategies to get their children to eat: coaxing, begging, distracting with toys, threatening with physical punishment, and force-feeding. Mealtime eventually becomes a stressful and time-consuming process during which children and parents struggle. Because these children show little interest in food and because they often fight with parents to assert their autonomy, these children have been described as having infantile anorexia, literally "a lack of interest in food."

Infantile anorexia tends to develop during the transition from breast- or bottle-feeding to the consumption of solid food (e.g., 6–36 months). During this time, children begin to develop great autonomy from their parents. They can wander away, say no, defy requests, and assume more control over metabolic functions, such as toileting and sleeping. Eating is another domain in which older infants and toddlers develop autonomy. Specifically, they must learn to recognize signals of hunger and satiety, signal to be fed, and effectively work with parents to obtain and consume desirable foods.

Unfortunately, children with infantile anorexia do not seem to develop these autonomous behaviors during this sensitive period in development. Consequently, their low interest in food persists over time. One longitudinal study followed infants with infantile anorexia into childhood. At 4 to 6 years of age, 68% showed mild–moderate malnutrition, and an additional 13% were

Image 15.1   Some children with avoidant/restrictive food intake disorder show little interest in food. Parents often become upset when their children do not appear hungry, are passive during meals, and fail to gain weight.

severely malnourished. By ages 7 to 8, only 21% showed weight within normal limits (Lucarelli, Cimino, Petrocchi, & Ammaniti, 2007). These children also showed increased rates of oppositional defiant behavior, anxiety, school refusal, and somatic problems.

What causes infantile anorexia? Chatoor's (2009) trans-actional model for feeding disorders posits that the disorder is caused by the interaction of child and caregiver characteristics over time. First, emerging data indicate that children with infantile anorexia often show high physiological arousal; they are active, need a great deal of cognitive stimulation, and are frequently "on the go." Consequently, they may be less sensitive to hunger signals (e.g., stomach contractions, empty feelings, fatigue). Second, these children often show temperaments that are described as "strong willed," making them more likely to engage in power struggles during mealtimes. Third, the parents of these children often report considerable anxiety about their children's eating and growth (see Figure 15.1). Consequently, with the best of intentions, they may try to trick, coerce, or force their children to eat. The result is that the child's eating becomes entirely regulated by the parent; the child never learns to recognize and respond to her own hunger signals. Treatment involves teaching the child to recognize hunger cues and rely on herself, rather than a parent, to feed and determine satiety (Owens & Burnham, 2009).

Sensory Food Aversion

Other children with ARFID report hunger and request food but accept only a limited diet. Most often, their diet consists of starches and grains, and it is often devoid of fruits, vegetables, and meats. They typically find certain foods aversive based on their taste, texture, temperature, or smell. In some cases, children will accept only certain brands of foods (e.g., only Tyson chicken nuggets), foods of a certain color (e.g., only "yellows" and "whites"), or foods in a certain package (e.g., McDonald's wrappers).

"Picky" eating is a common problem among toddlers and preschool-age children. As many as 50% of parents report that their children are selective eaters. However, children are not diagnosed with ARFID unless their selectiveness affects their health or causes severe disruption in the family (Norris et al., 2015).

There are many causes for children's food aversions. Some children seem to be hypersensitive to texture. Approximately 17% of infants who later show sensory food aversion have difficulty switching from milk to solids or from Stage 1 (pureed) to Stages 2 and 3 (slightly textured) foods. Other children seem to be unusually sensitive to certain tastes, especially bitterness, spiciness, and fattiness. This hypersensitivity to certain tastes is heritable and is associated with an unusual concentration

Figure 15.1 Mothers' worrying moderates the relationship between children's weight and interactions during feeding.

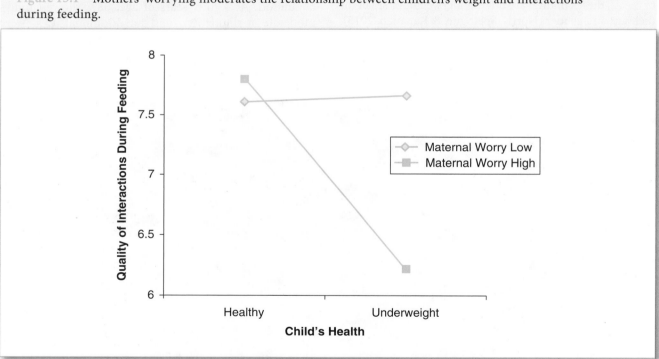

Source: Adapted from Gueron-Sela and colleagues (2011).

Note: The mothers of healthy infants provided structure and respected the autonomy of infants during meals. However, the feeding behavior of mothers of underweight children depended on the degree to which they worried about their children's weight. Parents who worried more about their children provided less structure and were more intrusive during mealtime.

of fungiform papillae and taste buds on the child's tongue. Many of these children also show hypersensitivity to other tactile stimuli; they may dislike getting their hands dirty, teeth brushed, or hair washed (Chatoor, 2009).

Food aversions and restricted diets often develop through classical conditioning and are maintained through operant conditioning. A parent may present a food that elicits a negative reaction (e.g., disgust, nausea). The pairing of the food and the negative reaction results in aversion to that food. Often, children generalize this learned association to food with similar texture, smell, or color. Understandably, the child avoids these foods in the future by crying, tantrumming, or engaging in other inappropriate actions. These inappropriate behaviors are maintained through negative reinforcement; the child learns to avoid ingesting the aversive foods. Parents' acquiescence is also maintained through negative reinforcement; they learn that they can stop or avoid children's inappropriate displays by serving only their children's favorite foods. Negative reinforcement maintains a coercive cycle of parent–child interactions. Treatment, therefore, involves breaking this cycle—teaching children that cries and tantrums will not allow them to escape or avoid healthy foods (Norris et al., 2015).

Posttraumatic Feeding

Other children develop feeding disorders following one or more traumatic insults to the mouth, throat, or gastrointestinal tract. For example, some infants have GERD, a condition in which stomach acid is involuntarily expelled into the esophagus. The acid produces irritation (similar to heartburn), nausea, coughing, or vomiting. These symptoms usually follow feeding and are very distressing to infants. Through classical conditioning, children associate feeding with the consequences of GERD (Eddy et al., 2015).

Posttraumatic feeding problems can also develop in the absence of medical illness. For example, some children aspirate, choke, or vomit on food as they transition from milk or formula to solids. In some cases, these negative events may become associated with feeding, causing children to refuse solids altogether.

Avoidance of feeding is maintained through negative reinforcement; children learn that they can avoid negative symptoms by abstaining from solids. Some children accept only milk, formula, or purees. Others, who are reluctant to eat even these substances, must be bottle-fed at night when they are sleepy and not aware that feeding is occurring. In severe cases, physicians may recommend nutrition through a gastric tube. Treatment for this feeding problem, similar to the treatment for posttraumatic stress disorder (PTSD), requires exposure therapy: the presentation of the feared stimulus (i.e., food) without refusal, escape, or avoidance (Fisher et al., 2014).

Prevalence

Approximately 1% to 2% of infants and young children have ARFID. The disorder is more common among children with medical illnesses (10%–49%), developmental disabilities (23%–43%), and physical disabilities (26%–90%). Approximately two-thirds of infants and toddlers with feeding disorders are classified as failure to thrive (FTT), a medical condition characterized by nutritional deficiency and weight below the fifth percentile for age and gender on standardized growth charts (Lyons-Ruth et al., 2014).

The various subtypes of ARFID are relatively distinct from one another. Most children with ARFID show only one subtype, probably because each subtype is associated with a specific cause. However, some children show symptoms of two or more subtypes. For example, 13% of children with feeding problems show both infantile anorexia and sensory food aversions. These children typically present with more serious feeding problems and are more resistant to treatment (Chatoor & Ammaniti, 2007).

Review:

- ARFID is a *DSM-5* feeding disorder characterized by (a) a lack of interest in feeding, (b) avoidance of food based on its sensory qualities, or (c) concerns about the negative consequences of eating. It is associated with weight loss, nutritional deficiencies, or other health/social impairment.
- The transactional model posits that feeding disorders arise through parent–child interactions characterized by children with (a) high physiological arousal, (b) difficult temperament, and (c) parents who are anxious about their child's food intake.
- Approximately 1% to 2% of infants and toddlers have ARFID. Prevalence is higher among children with medical illnesses, developmental disabilities, and physical disabilities.

What Treatments Are Effective for Feeding Disorders?

Treatment for Pica and Rumination Disorder

The treatment of pica and rumination disorder typically involves operant conditioning (Glasofer, Attia, & Timothy Walsh, 2015). Psychologists always try to use positive reinforcement first because it teaches developmentally appropriate behavior and is not aversive. One technique, *differential reinforcement of incompatible behavior (DRI)* is especially useful; children are positively reinforced for engaging in behavior that is incompatible with pica or rumination. For example, a child might be allowed to chew gum, which is both intrinsically reinforcing and incompatible with pica and rumination.

Another variation of positive reinforcement is *differential reinforcement of zero behavior (DRO)*; children are reinforced for not engaging in pica or rumination. For example, a caregiver might give the child a bite of a snack or a sip of a favorite beverage every minute he does not engage in the undesired behavior.

A final technique is to create a pica box. Parents and therapists identify the sensory properties of objects that are eaten by the child and replace these objects with foods that have similar properties. For example, a caregiver might substitute licorice for plastic toys, Grape-Nuts cereal for sand and pebbles, or beef jerky for bark and twigs. Food items are stored in a tackle box or similar carrier and provided to the child when he engages in pica (Sturmey & Williams, 2016).

If positive reinforcement is ineffective and the child's feeding problem places him at risk for serious injury, therapists might rely on punishment. Punishment is used only as a last resort and with the consent of parents. One method of positive punishment is *overcorrection*; the child is required to engage in a fairly long and mildly aversive series of actions, following pica or rumination. For example, a child who ruminates might be required to immediately brush his teeth, rinse with mouthwash, and wash his face.

Another method of positive punishment used to treat pica is facial screening; a child who engages in pica must wear a mask or bib over his mouth for a brief period of time. The screen is mildly uncomfortable and prohibits future pica. It is appropriate only with parental consent and when the child's feeding has a high likelihood of causing illness or injury (Stiegler, 2005; Sturmey & Williams, 2016).

Treatment for Avoidant/Restrictive Food Intake Disorder

As we have seen, ARFID can be conceptualized in terms of learning theory. Some children have not learned to recognize hunger and lack the skills necessary to eat independently. Others have learned to avoid certain foods based on their sensory qualities. Still others avoid solid foods altogether. Treatment, therefore, involves three components: (1) increasing children's motivation to eat, (2) changing the antecedents of eating to increase the likelihood that children will accept food, and (3) altering the consequences of children's eating to reinforce appropriate behavior and extinguish inappropriate behavior at mealtime.

Mild to moderate feeding disorders are typically treated on an outpatient basis; parents learn skills in a clinic and practice them at home with their children. Severe feeding disorders are best treated in a children's medical center. Hospitals allow medical professionals to monitor children's caloric intake and health and, if necessary, to provide supplemental fluid or nutrients. Hospitals also allow psychologists to carefully control the child's environment: when, how, and by whom food is presented. In this manner, psychologists have control over both the antecedents and consequences of feeding (Martin & Dovey, 2011).

Appetite Manipulation

Treatment involves three components: (1) appetite manipulation, (2) contingency management, and (3) parent counseling. Appetite manipulation is especially important for children who show little motivation to eat. In appetite manipulation, children are provided with fluids and essential electrolytes to maintain hydration but are prohibited from snacking. Children are offered food only during therapeutic meals, which are scheduled three to four times during the day, approximately 3 to 4 hours apart. Caloric restriction helps children recognize hunger and increases their motivation to eat when food is presented. Children learn that food provides its own reinforcement (Silverman & Tarbell, 2009).

Contingency Management

Contingency management is practiced during each meal. Initially, trained therapists feed children with parents absent from the room. Therapists are in complete control of the presentation of food (antecedents) and consequences of children's food refusal.

As we have seen, most feeding problems are maintained through operant conditioning, especially negative reinforcement. We know that operant conditioning maintains feeding problems because researchers have studied the responses of parents to children's food refusal and disruptive mealtime behavior (Vaz & Piazza, 2011). Most parents react in one of three ways: (1) they withdraw their demand that children eat the food, (2) they reprimand the child or express displeasure, or (3) they try to distract the child or provide the child with a toy or desired object. The first strategy (withdrawing the demand) is most common and negatively reinforces children for food refusal. The other two strategies are often positively reinforcing to children; parents present children with attention or access to a desired object, which increases their food refusal. Treatment, therefore, must involve the presentation of food, without the inadvertent use of positive or negative reinforcement (Piazza & Addison, 2007).

Escape extinction is critical to treatment. Escape extinction involves refusing to allow the child to escape or avoid eating through protests or tantrums. Escape extinction is typically implemented using (a) nonremoval of the spoon and (b) physical guidance. After the child is seated in a high chair, the therapist might place a small amount of food on a spoon and rest the spoon against the child's lips. The spoon is not removed until the child accepts the food. If the child does not accept the food in a few seconds, the therapist may apply gentle pressure to the child's lower mandibular joint to allow her to place the food in the child's mouth. Eventually, the child must accept the food and is not allowed to escape from the situation because of cries and protests (Linscheid, 2006).

Most therapists supplement escape extinction with positive reinforcement. Positive reinforcement might include giving praise, allowing access to a desired object, or watching a favorite video while feeding. These stimuli are contingent on the child's eating (Cornwell, Kelly, & Austin, 2010).

Some therapists also use time-out to reduce behavior problems during meals. Time-out is a form of negative punishment in which all positively reinforcing stimuli are momentarily withdrawn contingent on the child's food refusal. For example, if the child tantrums, the therapist might turn the child's high chair away for a few seconds and ignore the child's bids for attention. When the child is quiet, the therapist then reintroduces the food and requires the child to accept it (Linscheid, 2006).

Meals are limited to 20 to 25 minutes, regardless of the number of calories consumed by the child. The child must wait until the next session to eat again.

Parent Counseling

Nearly all professionals recognize the importance of including parents in treatment. Parents must be taught how to implement the behavioral feeding intervention and to avoid inadvertently reinforcing inappropriate mealtime behaviors. After the child accepts a variety of foods from the therapist, the therapist models the contingency management procedure to parents. Often, with parents present, children show a reemergence of food refusal. In behavioral terms, parents act as discriminative stimuli for children; children have learned that food refusal will be reinforced by parents but not by the therapist. The therapist's job is to teach parents to implement the contingency management program and reinforce their child only for appropriate feeding. Therapists coach parents until they are successful (Lyons-Ruth et al., 2014).

Parents may also benefit from individual counseling, which addresses thoughts and feelings that might compromise their ability to follow through with their child's treatment. For example, parents of children with feeding disorders often show a lack of sensitivity and responsiveness to their child's hunger and satiety cues, have unrealistic expectations regarding their children's eating habits, or have difficulty establishing meal schedules. Sometimes, these parents are too preoccupied by anxiety, depression, family or job stress, or their own caregiving histories to successfully implement treatment. Some parents exhibit deficits in problem-solving or emotion-regulation skills and have difficulty responding to children's food refusal in a patient, objective manner. Parents of malnourished or chronically ill children may be so concerned about their children's health, they may have difficulty restricting feeding to develop hunger motivation in their children. All of these parents would likely benefit from counseling to address their specific concerns (Bryant-Waugh & Watkins, 2015; Gueron-Sela, Atzaba-Poria, Meiri, & Yerushalmi, 2011).

Effectiveness

Most data supporting the behavioral treatment of feeding disorders come from single-subject research studies. Overall, these studies provide strong support for behavioral treatment, especially contingency management (Sharp, Jaquess, Morton, & Herzinger, 2010). The overall effect size (ES) for treatment is very large (ES = 2.46). Escape extinction seems to be essential to treatment; without it, few children show significant improvements. Gains are larger when escape extinction is paired with positive reinforcement and time-out.

Parent counseling also appears to be important for helping children generalize their feeding to the home environment (Groher & Crary, 2015).

Review:

- Positive reinforcement is the preferred treatment for pica and rumination. Positive punishment, such as overcorrection or facial screening, can be used with parental consent if positive reinforcement is not sufficient.
- The treatment of ARFID can include (a) appetite manipulation to increase children's motivation to eat, (b) contingency management to reinforce eating and avoid escape conditioning, and (c) parent counseling to help generalize skills to the home.
- Behavioral interventions are highly effective for young children with feeding disorders.

15.2 EATING DISORDERS IN OLDER CHILDREN AND ADOLESCENTS

What Eating Disorders Can Affect Children and Adolescents?

Anorexia Nervosa

Individuals with anorexia nervosa (AN) show three essential features (see Table 15.3). First, people with AN do not maintain normal body weight. Specifically, their weight is significantly below what is expected for their age, gender, and overall physical health (American Psychiatric Association, 2013).

Determining whether a person has "significantly low weight" requires both careful measurement and clinical judgment. *DSM-5* recommends that clinicians calculate an adult's body mass index (BMI): a ratio of weight to height squared (e.g., kg/m^2). Then, the adult's BMI can be compared to normative data gathered to determine if the person is significantly underweight compared to other people of the same age and gender. According to *DSM-5*, BMI scores <17 indicate significantly low weight. For example, a BMI of 17 corresponds to a weight of approximately 96 pounds for an 18-year-old, five-foot-three woman (World Health Organization, 2016).

In the case of children and adolescents, *DSM-5* recommends that clinicians also calculate the youth's BMI and compare his or her score to normative data. A score falling in the lowest fifth percentile, compared to youths of the same age and gender, would likely constitute significantly low weight. For example, a weight of approximately 87 pounds or less would fall in the lowest 5th percentile for a 14-year-old, five-foot-two girl (World Health Organization, 2016).

Clinicians must also be mindful of the person's developmental status and health history when determining if a person's low weight is attributable to AN. For example, an adolescent who falls slightly above the fifth percentile but who exhibits an unusual preoccupation with

Table 15.3 Diagnostic Criteria for Anorexia Nervosa

A. Restriction of energy intake relative to requirements, leading to a significantly low body weight in the context of age, sex, developmental trajectory, and physical health. *Significantly low weight* is defined as a weight that is less than minimally normal or, for children and adolescents, less than minimally expected.

B. Intense fear of gaining weight or of becoming fat, or persistent behavior that interferes with weight gain, even though at a significantly low weight.

C. Disturbance in the way in which one's body weight or shape is experienced, undue influence of body weight or shape on self-evaluation, or persistent lack of recognition of the seriousness of the current low body weight.

Specify current type:

Restricting type: During the past 3 months, the individual has not engaged in recurrent episodes of binge eating or purging behavior (i.e., self-induced vomiting or the misuse of laxatives, diuretics, or enemas). This subtype describes presentations in which weight loss is accomplished primarily through dieting, fasting, and/or excessive exercise.

Binge-eating/purging type: During the last 3 months, the individual has engaged in recurrent episodes of binge eating or purging behavior (i.e., self-induced vomiting or the misuse of laxatives, diuretics, or enemas).

Specify current severity:

The minimum level of severity is based, for adults, on current body mass index (BMI) or, for children and adolescents, on BMI percentile. The ranges below are derived from World Health Organization categories for thinness in adults; for children and adolescents, corresponding BMI percentiles should be used. The level of severity may be increased to reflect clinical symptoms, the degree of functional disability, and the need for supervision.

Mild: BMI $\geq$17 kg/m^2

Moderate: BMI 16–16.99 kg/m^2

Severe: BMI 15–15.99 kg/m^2

Extreme: BMI <15 kg/m^2

Source: Reprinted with permission from the *Diagnostic and Statistical Manual of Mental Disorders, Fifth Edition* (Copyright 2013). American Psychiatric Association.

eating and thinness might be diagnosed with the disorder. Alternatively, an adolescent with low weight who is recovering from a medical illness would not be diagnosed with AN.

Second, individuals with AN show excessive concern over their body shape and weight. Almost all adolescents with AN report that they are afraid of becoming fat. However, it might be more precise to say that they have an intense fear of gaining any weight whatsoever. The self-esteem of these adolescents is closely connected to their abilities to control their weight, appear attractive, and gain the approval and acknowledgment of others. Failure to control weight is seen as a sign of personal weakness and a risk to self-esteem. An adolescent with AN who gains even 1 pound might see herself on the path to obesity, peer rejection, and worthlessness.

Third, individuals with AN usually deny the seriousness of their low body weight. AN tends to be ego-syntonic—that is, people with the disorder usually do not think that their eating is problematic (Roncero, Belloch, Perpiñá, & Treasure, 2013). Instead, most adolescents with AN take pride in their ability to restrict their diet or avoid

weight gain. They often derive a certain degree of pleasure from resisting the temptation to eat even though they are severely malnourished. Resisting the temptation to eat is seen as a sign of control; dieting is regarded as a personal accomplishment. Severe dieting is doubly reinforced when other people, like parents or friends, comment on their willpower or slim figure. Since their self-esteem is dependent on their ability to avoid weight gain, they are usually resistant to treatment. Treatment, which would involve eating and gaining weight, would represent a loss of control and a reduction in self-worth. Consider Julie, a girl with AN.

DSM-5 requires clinicians to specify the severity of the individual's disorder, based on his or her BMI. Lower scores, indicative of severe weight loss, communicate an immediate need for intervention (American Psychiatric Association, 2013).

Bulimia Nervosa

The essential feature of bulimia nervosa (BN) is recurrent binge eating (see Table 15.4). Binge eating occurs when (a) a

Perfectly Normal

Source: ©iStockphoto/PhotoEuphoria

Julie was a 17-year-old girl who was referred to the hospital because of malnourishment and dehydration. Although Julie was five feet five inches tall, she weighed only 87 lbs. Her skin had a dry, yellow appearance and her clothes, which were stylish, hung from the frame of her body. Dr. Matyas escorted Julie and her mother to an examination room.

"We were brought to the hospital because Julie passed out after gym class at school," her mother explained. Julie interrupted her mother, "It was nothing. I just felt light-headed." Her mother interjected, almost in tears, "I'm very worried about her. She doesn't listen to me. She's irritable all the time."

Dr. Matyas asked, "Julie, what did you eat for breakfast and lunch today?" Julie replied, "A hard-boiled egg for breakfast . . . and I think that I had some yogurt at lunch."

Dr. Matyas noticed Julie's emaciated body. Her ribs and pelvic bones were clearly visible. Her hair was dry and brittle. On her face and arms, Julie had soft, downy hair to protect her from the cold. Dr. Matyas listened to Julie's heart and asked, "Do you have regular periods?" Julie responded, "Yes . . . well I used to, but now I don't."

"Julie," said Dr. Matyas, "do you know that you're underweight?"

Julie snapped, "If I was on television or in the movies, I'd be perfectly normal. It's just because I'm in high school that everybody thinks I'm too thin."

Dr. Matyas handed Julie her pen. Pointing to the exam table, she said, "I want you to imagine that you're sitting up there. I want you to use my pen to mark the width of your thighs on the exam table." With a sigh, Julie grabbed the pen and made two marks on the butcher-block paper spread out on the table. The distance was almost 4 feet.

---

person consumes an unusually large amount of food in a discrete period of time (e.g., within 2 hours), and (b) the person feels out of control while eating. During binge episodes, some people with BN consume 1,000 to 2,000 calories, roughly one half to one full day's caloric requirements. Most individuals with BN prefer foods that are high in sugar and fat like breads, cakes, pasta, and desserts (Stice, Marti, & Rohde, 2013).

By definition, people with BN also engage in some form of inappropriate compensatory behavior to prevent weight gain. Most people with BN purge—that is, they induce vomiting or misuse laxatives, diuretics, or enemas to avoid caloric absorption. Some individuals with BN do not purge. Instead, they avoid weight gain primarily through excessive fasting or exercise. For example, an adolescent who consumes 1,200 calories during a midnight binge might decide to "make up for it" by fasting the next day or running an extra 4 miles. Individuals with BN binge and use compensatory means of weight control regularly, at least twice each week. In extreme cases, individuals binge and show compensatory behaviors multiple times each day.

Like individuals with AN, people with BN show unusual preoccupation with body shape and weight. Indeed, the self-esteem and mood of individuals with BN is closely connected to their subjective impressions of their appearance. In contrast to AN, BN is usually an ego-dystonic disorder (Roncero et al., 2013). Individuals with BN usually regard their eating behavior as problematic. Indeed, people with BN often binge in private because bingeing produces guilt and shame. Adolescents will often go to great lengths to hide their bingeing and purging from family members, sometimes for months or years. Adolescents with BN usually seek treatment for their disorder only after they can no longer keep their eating habits a secret from loved ones (Stice et al., 2013).

One problem in diagnosing BN is identifying what constitutes a "binge." A binge is usually defined as an amount of food that is definitely larger than most people would eat during a similar period of time and under similar circumstances. However, two people's conceptualizations of a "large" amount of food might differ. A related problem with this definition is that many people with BN do not consume an extremely large amount of food when they binge. In one study, approximately one-third of patients with BN consumed fewer than 600 calories per binge, which is approximately one-third of their daily dietary requirement. Most experts believe that the subjective experience of feeling out of control over one's eating is more important to the diagnosis of BN than exactly how much a person eats during each

Table 15.4   Diagnostic Criteria for Bulimia Nervosa

A.   Recurrent episodes of binge eating. An episode of binge eating is characterized by both of the following:

  1.   Eating, in a discrete period of time (e.g., within any 2-hour period), an amount of food that is definitely larger than what most individuals would eat in a similar period of time under similar circumstances.

  2.   A sense of lack of control over eating during the episode (e.g., a feeling that one cannot stop eating or control what or how much one is eating).

B.   Recurrent inappropriate compensatory behaviors in order to prevent weight gain, such as self-induced vomiting; misuse of laxatives, diuretics, or other medications; fasting; or excessive exercise.

C.   The binge eating and inappropriate compensatory behaviors both occur, on average, at least once a week for 3 months.

D.   Self-evaluation is unduly influenced by body shape and weight.

E.   The disturbance does not occur exclusively during episodes of Anorexia Nervosa.

Specify current severity:

The minimum level of severity is based on the frequency of inappropriate compensatory behaviors. The level of severity may be increased to reflect other symptoms and the degree of functional disability.

Mild: An average of 1–3 episodes of inappropriate compensatory behaviors per week.

Moderate: An average of 4–7 episodes of inappropriate compensatory behaviors per week.

Severe: An average of 8–13 episodes of inappropriate compensatory behaviors per week.

Extreme: An average of 14 or more episodes of inappropriate compensatory behaviors per week.

Source: Reprinted with permission from the *Diagnostic and Statistical Manual of Mental Disorders, Fifth Edition* (Copyright 2013). American Psychiatric Association.

binge episode. Consequently, some experts use the term *subjective binge* to describe the feeling of being out of control while eating, even if the number of calories consumed is relatively small (Watson, Fursland, Bulik, & Nathan, 2013).

Binge Eating Disorder

Binge eating disorder (BED) is characterized by recurrent episodes of binge eating *without* inappropriate compensatory behaviors to avoid weight gain (see Table 15.5). During binges, people with BED feel out of control with their eating and find it very difficult to stop. For example, a boy with BED might consume a large bag of pretzels, an entire canister of potato chips, several handfuls of crackers, and a bowl of ice cream in a 30-minute period of time (American Psychiatric Association, 2013).

Often, people with BED are not subjectively hungry when they binge. For example, a girl with BED may eat dinner and binge an hour later in her bedroom while completing her homework. Individuals with BED often eat until they are uncomfortably full. Then they may feel disgusted, ashamed, or guilty for consuming so many calories and for their lack of control.

Most people with BED are embarrassed about their eating behavior; consequently, they typically binge alone.

It is not uncommon for a child or adolescent with BED to hide the disorder for months before being detected. Consider Mateo, a boy with BED.

Binges must occur at least once a week for 3 months for someone to be diagnosed with BED. This frequency and duration criteria are identical to BN. Unlike people with BN, however, individuals with BED do not engage in compensatory behaviors to avoid weight gain. Because of their compensatory behaviors, most people with BN are average or slightly above average in weight. In contrast, most people with BED are overweight or obese (American Psychiatric Association, 2013).

Differentiating Disorders

Anorexia vs. Bulimia

Many people believe that AN is defined by excessive dieting while BN is defined by bingeing and purging. In fact, neither disorder is defined in this way. Individuals with AN are classified into two subtypes, based on their current symptom presentation. Individuals with AN–restricting type maintain their low body weight through caloric restriction—that is, through extreme dieting or fasting. In contrast, individuals with AN–binge eating/purging type maintain low body weight primarily

Table 15.5   Diagnostic Criteria for Binge Eating Disorder

A.   Recurrent episodes of binge eating. An episode of binge eating is characterized by both of the following:

    1.   Eating, in a discrete period of time (e.g., within any 2-hour period), an amount of food that is definitely larger than what most individuals would eat in a similar period of time under similar circumstances.

    2.   A sense of lack of control over eating during the episode (e.g., a feeling that one cannot stop eating or control what or how much one is eating).

B.   The binge-eating episodes are associated with three (or more) of the following:

    1.   Eating much more rapidly than normal.

    2.   Eating until feeling uncomfortably full.

    3.   Eating alone because embarrassed by how much one is eating.

    4.   Feeling disgusted with oneself, depressed, or very guilty afterward.

C.   Marked distress regarding binge eating is present.

D.   The binge eating occurs, on average, at least once a week for 3 months.

E.   The binge eating is not associated with the recurrent use of compensatory behavior as in Bulimia Nervosa and does not occur exclusively during the course of Bulimia Nervosa or Anorexia Nervosa.

Specify current severity:

The minimum level of severity is based on the frequency of episodes of binge eating. The level of severity may be increased to reflect other symptoms and the degree of functional disability.

Mild: 1–3 binge-eating episodes per week.

Moderate: 4–7 binge-eating episodes per week.

Severe: 8–13 binge-eating episodes per week.

Extreme: 14 or more binge-eating episodes per week.

Source: Reprinted with permission from the *Diagnostic and Statistical Manual of Mental Disorders, Fifth Edition* (Copyright 2013). American Psychiatric Association.

through binge eating and purging (American Psychiatric Association, 2013).

Similarly, individuals with BN can exhibit either purging or nonpurging behavior. Most people with BN purge; they regularly induce vomiting or misuse laxatives, diuretics, or enemas to avoid weight gain. However, some people with BN use other compensatory behaviors, such as excessive fasting or exercise, to avoid weight gain.

The difference between AN and BN is *not* based on whether the person fasts or purges. In fact, some people with AN binge and purge while some people with BN seldom purge at all.

Instead, AN and BN can be differentiated in two ways. First, all individuals with AN show unusually low body weight. In contrast, low body weight is not required for the diagnosis of BN. In fact, most individuals with BN have weight within the normal range, and some people with BN are overweight. Second, all individuals with BN show recurrent binge eating. In contrast, not all people with AN binge (American Psychiatric Association, 2013).

Binge Eating Disorder vs. Anorexia Nervosa and Bulimia Nervosa

AN is differentiated from BED by low body weight. By definition, individuals with AN have very low body weight; in contrast, people with BED are usually overweight or obese. BN is differentiated from BED in that people with BN engage in purging or other compensatory strategies to avoid weight gain. In contrast, people with BED do not purge, fast, or engage in excessive exercise after bingeing. People with BN also tend to spend a great deal of time thinking about food and dieting. In contrast, people with BED usually do not show obsessive interests in food and may even view food negatively (Wilson & Sysko, 2009).

Although BED and BN are separate disorders, some individuals may transition from one disorder to the other over time (Bryant-Waugh & Watkins, 2015). It is most common for individuals with BED to begin purging or engaging in other compensatory behaviors. For example, Fichter and Quadflieg (2007) studied 60

BINGE EATING DISORDER

Ants!

Source: ©iStockphoto/Ruslanshug

Mateo was a 10-year-old boy referred to our outpatient clinic by his mother because of his unusual eating habits. A short and overweight boy, Mateo refused to enter the psychologist's office at the time of his appointment, preferring instead to remain in the waiting room.

His mother explained, "I've always tried to keep a neat house and insist that Mateo keep his room clean. Then, I noticed ants in the house. We've never had an ant problem before, so I thought this was strange. I followed the ants to Mateo's room where I found what was hidden under his bed: wrappers from cookies, crackers, candy bars, cheese curls, and lots of crumbs. I even found wrappers from Halloween candy from several months ago! I asked him about it, but he blamed his little brother."

Eventually, the psychologist was able to coax Mateo into her office and interview him alone. She said, "So I guess you know why you're here." Mateo responded, "Yeah. It's about my bed. My mom gets upset about everything."

The psychologist replied, "She told me about the different kinds of foods you eat. Maybe you can tell me when you eat them." Mateo answered, "I eat mostly when I get home from school. I'm hungry, and I need some snacks to keep me going until dinner."

"That seems reasonable," the psychologist commented. "Do you eat at other times, too?" Mateo replied, "Then, I eat in my room after dinner, while I watch TV or play video games. Sometimes, I just feel bored so I eat. Sometimes, I need to take my mind off school and things. I just keep eating and eating and can't seem to stop. I even tell myself, 'Okay that's enough' but I keep on going."

"How do you feel afterward?" the psychologist asked. Mateo answered, "Terrible. Like I want to throw up." The psychologist replied, "Do you?" Mateo answered, "No. That's gross."

---

people with BED for 2 years. Although none of the patients developed AN, many later met criteria for BN. Transitioning from BN to BED appears to be less common. Only 10% of women with BED report a history of BN (Hilbert et al., 2014).

Review:

- AN is a *DSM-5* eating disorder characterized by (a) caloric restriction leading to significantly low body weight, (b) intense fear of gaining weight or becoming fat, and (c) disturbance in one's body weight or shape.
- BN is a *DSM-5* eating disorder characterized by (a) recurrent episodes of binge eating, (b) recurrent inappropriate compensatory behaviors to prevent weight gain, and (c) self-evaluation that is unduly influenced by one's body shape or weight. It occurs at least once a week for at least 3 months.
- BED is a *DSM-5* eating disorder characterized by (a) recurrent episodes of binge eating, (b) associated features (e.g., eating rapidly, eating when depressed, feeling ashamed), and (c) marked distress. It occurs at least once a week for at least 3 months.

What Conditions Are Associated With Eating Disorders?

Physical Health Problems

Anorexia/Bulimia

Eating disorders can cause serious health problems (Smolak, Striegel-Moore, & Levine, 2013). A frequent and serious medical complication associated with eating disorders is electrolyte imbalance. Electrolytes are minerals found in the body; they include calcium, sodium, and potassium. These minerals help maintain proper fluid levels throughout the body. They also regulate important metabolic functions, such as heart rate and brain activity. Activities that cause the body to lose excessive amounts of fluids (e.g., vomiting, excessive use of diuretics or laxatives) can lead to electrolyte imbalance.

Electrolyte imbalance can cause cardiac arrhythmias (i.e., irregular heart rate) and death. A serious condition called hypokalemia, caused by low potassium levels, can be fatal. People with AN are especially vulnerable to cardiac arrhythmias when they attempt to gain weight during treatment. In fact, physicians use the term refeeding syndrome to describe the cardiac and other health-related problems shown by patients with AN during the first 7 to 10 days of treatment. Because of the danger of arrhythmia, refeeding is conducted slowly and under medical supervision.

Another serious medical complication associated with AN is osteopenia—that is, reduced bone mass. In healthy girls, bone density increases during childhood and early adolescence. Approximately 60% of a girl's bone density is acquired during her early adolescent years. However, AN interferes with this increase in bone density. The combination of poor nutrition, decreased estrogen levels caused by amenorrhea, and excessive exercise can lead to significantly lower bone density. Bone density loss is greatest in the spine and hips. Approximately 90% of adolescents and young adults with AN show osteopenia, placing them at risk for osteoporosis and hip fractures later in life. Bone loss may be irreversible.

Other medical complications associated with AN seem to be temporary. AN seems to disrupt hormone and endocrine functioning, which can lead to disturbances in appetite, physical growth, heart rate, and temperature regulation. Lack of body fat sometimes causes the development of fine downy hair (i.e., lanugo) on the midsection, limbs, and face. These soft hairs help conserve body temperature. Hair on the head can become brittle, and skin may adopt a yellow color. Malnutrition associated with AN also seems to cause problems with concentration, memory, and problem-solving.

Medical complications associated with BN are largely due to bingeing and purging. As mentioned previously, hypokalemia is the most serious medical risk factor associated with BN. Frequent vomiting can cause enlargement of the salivary glands, erosion of dental enamel, and damage to the esophagus. Some individuals who use their fingers to induce vomiting show temporary scarring of the skin tissue up to the second or third knuckle (see Image 15.2). Frequent laxative use can contribute to gastrointestinal problems, especially constipation (Sarafino & Smith, 2014).

Binge Eating Disorder

Approximately 41.7% of individuals with BED are obese, compared to 15.8% of people without BED. Obesity is associated with a wide range of health-related problems. These problems include diabetes, high blood pressure, high cholesterol, heart disease, and other forms of chronic pain (Kessler et al., 2013).

BED also interferes with obesity treatment (Wonderlich, Gordon, Mitchell, Crosby, & Engel, 2009). Individuals with BED who participate in weight loss programs lose less weight and are more likely to drop out than individuals without BED. Furthermore, adults who receive bariatric surgery to lose weight are more likely to regain their weight following surgery than their counterparts

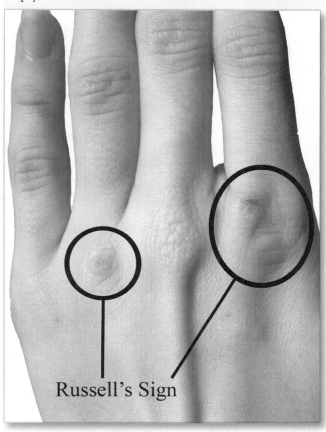

Image 15.2 Some people with AN or BN develop calluses on their knuckles due to repeated self-induced vomiting. The calluses arise when the knuckles repeatedly make contact with the incisor teeth. They are called "Russell's sign" after the British psychiatrist Gerald Russell who first described them.

Russell's Sign

without BED. These difficulties with weight loss are due to their frequent binges.

Because most youths with BED are overweight or obese, they are at risk for teasing and ostracism by peers. They frequently report avoidance of social situations, low self-esteem, and low self-confidence. Unfortunately, these negative feelings can contribute to depression and anxiety and elicit future binge episodes.

Indeed, children and adolescents with BED are at risk for anxiety, depression, and other internalizing disorders (Bryant-Waugh & Watkins, 2015). Researchers examined the prevalence of binge eating in obese adolescents who sought weight loss treatment. Approximately 30% met criteria for BED. Furthermore, adolescents with BED showed more concerns about eating, body shape, and weight than obese adolescents without BED. Furthermore, adolescents with BED also showed significantly more problems with depression and anxiety and adolescents who were obese but did not binge (see Figure 15.2).

Figure 15.2   Adolescents With BED Report Body Concerns

Note: Obese adolescents who seek treatment for weight loss report concerns about their eating behavior, shape, and weight. However, obese adolescents with BED report more concerns than obese adolescents without BED.

Mental Health Problems

Approximately 80% of adolescents with eating disorders meet diagnostic criteria for at least one other mental health problem. The most common comorbid disorders are depression, anxiety, and substance use problems (Herpertz-Dahlmann, 2015).

Depression and Suicide

The most common comorbid psychiatric condition among adolescents with eating disorders is major depressive disorder (MDD). The lifetime prevalence of depression for individuals with eating disorders is approximately 50% to 60%. The prevalence of depression among adolescents with eating disorders is much higher than in the general adolescent population. However, the prevalence of depression among adolescents with eating disorders is similar to rates of depression among other clinic-referred children without eating problems (Hughes et al., 2013).

In the case of AN and BN, depression usually emerges after the onset of the eating disorder and often persists after treatment of the eating problem. In one study, nearly 70% of individuals who previously suffered from AN subsequently developed depression (Halmi et al., 1991). Depression, therefore, is often a consequence of AN and BN, not a primary cause of these conditions.

Adults with BED also typically experience depression and other emotional problems after the onset of their binge eating. However, children and adolescents with BED tend to show depression *before* the onset of their binges. Children with BED tend to be obese and are often alienated and teased by peers because of their weight or body shape. They are also more likely than children without BED to have parents with mental health problems, low self-esteem, and depression themselves. Many of these children use food to cope with feelings of loneliness and other negative moods (Faulconbridge et al., 2013; Kessler et al., 2013).

Individuals with eating disorders are also at elevated risk for suicidal behavior (see Figure 15.3). Approximately 40% of adolescents with eating disorders report suicidal ideation, 10% report crafting a suicide plan, and 15% admit to attempting suicide on at least one occasion. The fact that more adolescents report suicide attempts than suicide plans suggests that many of these youths engage in impulsive acts of self-harm. Indeed, self-harm is particularly prevalent among youths with BN, a disorder associated with impulsivity and emotion-regulation deficits (Swanson, Crow, Le Grange, Swendsen, & Merikangas, 2011).

Anxiety Disorders

Social anxiety disorder affects 30% to 50% of females with eating disorders. Social anxiety disorder usually predates the emergence of AN and BN and persists after treatment. Many adolescent girls and women with eating disorders are extremely sensitive to criticism by others and have histories of avoiding situations in which they might be

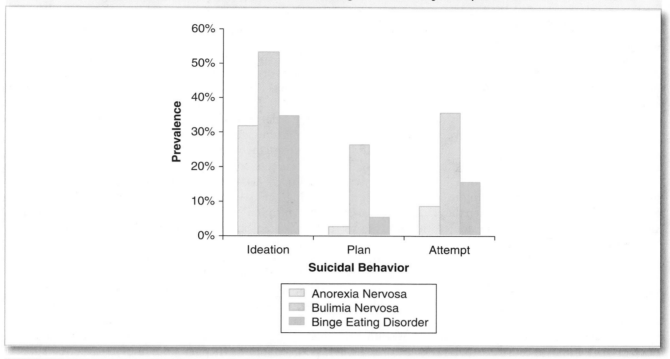

Figure 15.3 Suicidal behavior among adolescents with eating disorders. Suicide attempts are highest among youths with BN. These youths often show problems with emotion-regulation and impulsivity.

Source: Based on Swanson and colleagues (2011).

negatively evaluated by others. These individuals also frequently show a high need for approval by peers. Some may use dietary restriction and/or purging to assume physical appearances that meet the approval of others and enhance their social standing. Over time, these behaviors can lead to AN or BN (Levinson et al., 2013).

Approximately 30% to 40% of people with eating disorders show OCD. Most research indicates that perfectionism and OCD symptoms often precede the development of eating problems. Females with eating disorders often have long-standing problems with rigid, obsessive thinking. It is possible that a rigid cognitive style places these individuals at risk for eating problems (Halmi et al., 2005).

Common genetic or environmental factors might partially account for the co-occurrence of eating disorders and anxiety disorders. Keel, Klump, Miller, McGue, and Iacono (2005) examined 14 monozygotic (MZ) twins, aged 16 to 18, discordant for eating disorders; one of the twins had an eating disorder, while the other twin did not. Then, the researchers examined the prevalence of anxiety disorders among the twins who did not have an eating disorder. They found that these discordant twins were twice as likely to have an anxiety disorder as individuals in the general population. These findings suggest that common factors underlie both eating and anxiety disorders. However, we do not know whether these factors are predominantly genetic, environmental, or (most likely) a combination of the two (Levinson & Rodebaugh, 2012).

Substance Use Disorders

Substance use problems frequently occur with eating disorders. Adolescents and young adults with AN or BN most often use nicotine, alcohol, marijuana, and prescription pain medications. Overall, 20% to 25% of individuals with eating disorders show comorbid substance use disorders (Mann et al., 2014).

The prevalence of substance use disorders varies, depending on the subtype of eating disorder. Specifically, individuals who frequently engage in binge eating are 3 times more likely to show comorbid substance use problems than individuals with eating disorders who do not binge. Experts believe that underlying problems with impulsivity account for both the tendency to binge and the tendency to misuse alcohol and other drugs. In most cases, substance use disorders emerge during or after the onset of the eating disorder. Consequently, many individuals with eating disorders seem to use alcohol and other drugs to reduce anxiety and dysphoria (Bulik, 2004).

Personality

A central personality characteristic of AN is perfectionism, a personality trait characterized by the rigid and unrealistic pursuit of absolute standards of behavior. More than 40 years ago, Hilde Bruch (1973) described adolescents with AN as excessively compliant, eager to please, and lacking an autonomous sense of self. Subsequent research on adolescents with AN has generally confirmed Bruch's impressions.

Even before they meet diagnostic criteria for AN, these adolescents are usually described as perfectionistic, driven, and goal oriented. They are often overachievers, popular, and academically successful. They tend to be very conscientious about their appearance and the way they present themselves to others. They are often reluctant to take risks because they do not want to make mistakes or lose the approval of family or peers (Levine, Piran, & Jasper, 2015).

A second, related personality characteristic of adolescents with AN is rigidity and overcontrol (Roswell, MacDonald, & Carter, 2015). Adolescents with AN often show rigidity in their actions, feelings, and thoughts. With respect to actions, many of these individuals say that they need to have things "their way" in order to feel comfortable. They may become upset when they lack control over situations. Other people describe adolescents with AN as "obsessive" or excessively organized.

With respect to their feelings, adolescents with AN are often guarded and emotionally reserved. They are especially reluctant to express sadness, frustration, and anger directly, preferring to keep these feelings hidden or to deny them altogether.

With respect to their cognitions, adolescents with AN often engage in dichotomous (black-or-white) thinking—that is, they view themselves, others, and situations as either "good" or "bad." This type of dichotomous thinking causes them to see the world in rigid, harsh, and overly simplistic ways. For example, if they gain one pound, they might regard themselves as "worthless" or "a complete failure" (Alberts, Thewissen, & Raes, 2012; Egan et al., 2013).

Perhaps the most salient characteristic of adolescents with BN is their low self-evaluation. In contrast to adolescents with AN, adolescents with BN tend to be more emotionally labile and impulsive. Adolescents with BN often show problems with temper and acting out. Some engage in self-harm or misuse alcohol and other drugs. Many youths with BN show chronic problems with emotion regulation (Pisetsky, Utzinger, & Wonderlich, 2015).

Family Problems

Research has consistently shown problems in the family functioning of girls with eating disorders. Adolescents with AN often come from highly rigid, overprotective homes. The parents of adolescents with AN typically adopt authoritarian parenting strategies: They place high demands on their children's behavior, but they show low responsiveness to their children's needs. Parents usually assume considerable control over their children's lives and do not allow their adolescents to take much part in decision-making.

Adolescents with BN also tend to come from homes that place a premium on obedience and achievement. However, their homes are usually chaotic and stress filled. These adolescents often report a high degree of family conflict and, sometimes, domestic violence. Adolescents

with BN tend to have higher rates of insecure attachment compared to adolescents without eating problems.

Diet, weight, and body shape are given considerable attention in the families of girls with eating disorders (Levine et al., 2015). Girls with AN often report that their parents frequently dieted in order to lose weight and made periodic comments about their weight and physical appearance. Many girls have a first-degree family member with an eating disorder. In contrast, the family members of girls with BN are sometimes obese or overweight. These girls often report considerable tension during mealtime, parents who encourage them to lose weight, or family members who tease them about their weight, shape, or appearance.

Parents' comments about weight and body shape predict body dissatisfaction, low self-esteem, and unhealthy eating habits in girls (Levine et al., 2015). In one study, 23% of middle school girls said that at least one parent teased them about their appearance (Keery, Boutelle, van den Berg, & Thompson, 2005). Teasing by fathers was associated with body dissatisfaction, dietary restriction, and symptoms of BN. Teasing by mothers was associated with depression. Even mothers' comments about *their own* weight were associated with their daughters' body dissatisfaction. Although these associations do not necessarily mean that parents' comments cause girls to feel poorly about their appearance, they suggest that parents' comments about shape and weight are connected with their daughters' feelings about their own bodies (Bauer, Bucchianeri, & Neumark-Sztainer, 2013).

Review:

- Medical complications associated with AN or BN include electrolyte imbalance, osteopenia, cardiac problems, malnutrition, dry skin, lanugo, enlarged salivary glands, and damage to the esophagus and teeth. Youths with BED are at risk for obesity.
- Adolescents with AN or BN are at risk for depression and self-injury, anxiety and obsessive–compulsive behaviors, and substance use problems.
- Adolescents with AN often show perfectionism, a personality trait characterized by a rigid and unrealistic pursuit of absolute standards. These youths may also engage in dichotomous (black-or-white) thinking.
- Girls with AN or BN often come from families characterized by low autonomy, high conflict, and preoccupation with body shape and weight.

How Common Are Eating Disorders in Children and Adolescents?

Prevalence

It is difficult to estimate the prevalence of eating disorders among adolescents for two reasons. First, most people with eating disorders, especially adolescents, are reluctant to admit their symptoms. Even anonymous surveys may

Figure 15.4   Prevalence of Eating Disorders in Adolescents and Adults.

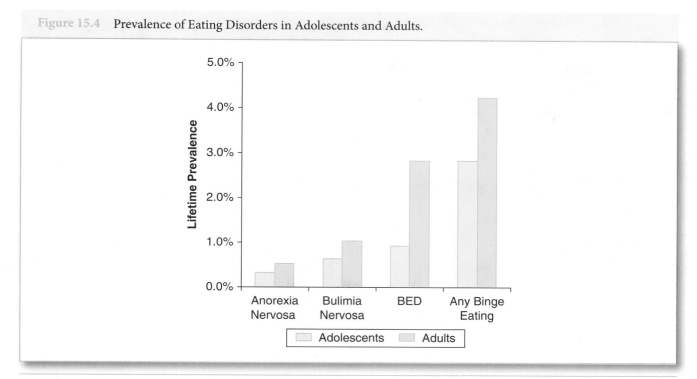

Source: Based on von Ranson and Wallace (2014).

underestimate prevalence. Second, eating disorders are relatively rare, especially among adolescents. Therefore, researchers need to gather data from large numbers of people in order to obtain precise estimates.

The best available data come from the National Comorbidity Survey Replication studies. These studies relied on nationally representative samples of adults and adolescents, respectively (see Figure 15.4). Results show that relatively few adolescents meet diagnostic criteria for AN (0.3%), BN (0.9%), or BED (2.5%) prior to reaching adulthood. Prevalence among adults is slightly higher, suggesting that most eating disorders have their onset in late adolescence or early adulthood (Swanson et al., 2011).

Although eating disorders are relatively rare among adolescents, maladaptive eating behavior is common (see Figure 15.5). One-fifth of 5-year-old girls, one-third of 9-year-old girls, and one-half of preadolescent girls report concerns about their weight. As many as 80% of adolescent girls report dissatisfaction with their body shape or weight, 77% have dieted to lose weight, and 16% have purged on at least one occasion. Nearly 14% of adolescent girls show eating problems that fall just short of diagnostic criteria (von Ranson & Wallace, 2014).

Gender Differences

On average, girls are more likely to develop eating disorders than boys. Data from the National Comorbidity Survey Replication studies showed that boys and girls are equally likely to meet diagnostic criteria for AN (0.3%).

However, girls (1.5%) are much more likely to have subthreshold AN symptoms than boys (0.1%).

Similarly, adolescent girls (1.3%) are almost 3 times more likely than adolescent boys (0.5%) to develop BN prior to adulthood. Similarly, adolescent girls (2.3%) are almost 3 times more likely than adolescent boys (0.8%) to meet diagnostic criteria for BED (Swanson et al., 2011).

Instead of AN and BN, some adolescent boys are at risk for eating problems caused by a desire to *gain* weight, body mass, and muscle. Many boys attempt to gain body mass and muscle in appropriate ways, such as by eating healthy foods and exercising. However, some boys rely on risky strategies such as overeating, excessive exercise, or reliance on dietary supplements. Between 25% and 50% of adolescent boys admit to using dietary supplements (e.g., protein shakes, creatine, ephedrine) to increase mass. Between 3% and 12% have used anabolic steroids to build muscle. Approximately 5% of adolescent boys exercise more than seven times each week, exercise despite pain and injury, or experience guilt or depression on days they are unable to exercise.

Culture, Ethnicity, and Socioeconomic Status

Cross-Cultural Differences

For years, experts believed that eating disorders were found only in Western, industrialized countries, predominantly in high socioeconomic groups. Today, we know that eating disorders exist across all cultures and socioeconomic strata (von Ranson & Wallace, 2014).

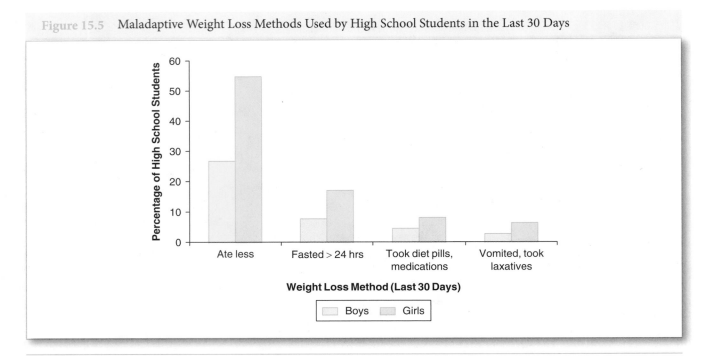

Source: Based on the Youth Risk Behavior Surveillance System (Centers for Disease Control, 2016).

Note: Data are based on a sample of approximately 14,000 adolescents in ninth through 12th grades. Although most youths do not have eating disorders, many (especially girls) use risky methods to lose weight.

AN and BN appear to be universal phenomena, existing across countries and cultures. For example, eating disorders have been identified in Asia, Africa, the Middle East, the Caribbean, the Pacific Islands, and Eastern Europe, in addition to Western Europe and North America. However, eating disorders are more prevalent among Western societies and industrialized nations than non-Western and preindustrialized countries. For example, the prevalence of eating disorders in Eastern Europe, Japan, Singapore, South Africa, and Israel is generally equivalent to the prevalence of these disorders in the United States. In non-Western and preindustrialized countries like Nigeria and Belize, prevalence is lower (Anderson-Frye & Becker, 2004).

Considerable evidence indicates that globalization has spread eating disorders from industrialized countries to developing nations. For example, eating disorders were largely unknown in the island of Fiji in the South Pacific a generation ago. However, the prevalence of eating disorders rose dramatically after Western culture was introduced to the island by television and other media. Similarly, adolescents who immigrate to the United States from developing countries initially show low rates of eating disorders. However, after years of living in the United States, their likelihood of eating disorders increases dramatically (Anderson-Frye & Becker, 2004; Polivy, Herman, Mills, & Wheeler, 2003). Consider Grace, an immigrant to the United States with emerging symptoms of BN.

Experts disagree as to how Western culture or industrialization might contribute to an increase in eating disorders. One popular explanation is that girls and women in non-Western and developing cultures compare themselves to the images of models and actresses portrayed in Western media. These comparisons cause girls in non-Western and developing countries to become dissatisfied with their bodies, to diet, and to engage in unsafe practices to lose weight.

An alternative hypothesis is that girls and women notice a relationship between the physical attractiveness of Western models and other indicators of wealth, social status, and happiness. In order to enhance their social status, they attempt to emulate these models and actresses by losing weight. For example, shortly after the introduction of Western media in Fiji, many girls expressed a desire to lose weight. They reasoned that if they were more attractive, like the models and actresses on television, they might be able to lead more successful lives (Becker, Burwell, Gilman, Herzog, & Hamburg, 2002). In other developing countries, girls and women most at risk for eating disorders tend to come from upwardly mobile families. For example, in Curacao and Belize, girls and women who had aspirations of achieving wealth and social status, or who had economic ties to Western culture through tourism, showed rates of eating disorders similar to those of females in the United States. Upwardly mobile Black females living in South Africa show greater prevalence of eating disorders than their White South African counterparts. For some girls and women, AN and BN may reflect a maladaptive attempt to emulate Western culture in order to share in its social and economic prosperity (Anderson-Frye & Becker, 2004).

BULIMIA NERVOSA AND CULTURE

Eye of the Beholder

Source: ©iStockphoto/valeriebarry

Grace was a 14-year-old girl who immigrated to the United States with her parents from the African nation of Rwanda following the civil war that occurred in that country. Although Grace's family was a member of the majority Hutus, her father aided and protected members of the minority Tutsis who were slaughtered by extremist Hutu militia. Fearing retribution, the family fled the country and eventually sought asylum in the United States.

In Africa, Grace was viewed as an intelligent and beautiful girl. In the United States, however, she had difficulty gaining acceptance from her peers because of her appearance. By Western standards, Grace was short and overweight. She was unaccustomed to being teased by other girls at school and ostracized by classmates. Within 6 months of enrolling in high school, Grace developed symptoms of bulimia. She began to binge and purge multiple times each week. Her parents finally sought help for her because of her maladaptive dieting, bingeing and purging, and depressed mood.

In the United States

Some experts have suggested that ethnic minorities in the United States are less likely to develop eating disorders than White adolescents. These experts argue that because ethnic minority adolescents come from subcultures that place less emphasis on slenderness, they may be less likely to diet and engage in problematic eating. In fact, Latina and African American adolescent girls tend to be more tolerant than non-Latina, White adolescent girls of a heavier and more curvaceous body shape. Furthermore, Latina and African American girls are often less concerned about weight gain than their non-Latina, White counterparts (McKnight Risk Factor Study, 2003).

However, eating disorders exist across all ethnic groups in the United States, and the culturally specific preferences regarding weight and shape may not protect minority girls from developing eating disorders.

Data from the National Comorbidity Survey Replication studies indicated that AN is most prevalent among non-Latina, White adolescents (0.4%) and least common among African American adolescents (0.1%). On the other hand, Latina adolescents (1.6%) are more likely to be diagnosed with BN than non-Latina, White adolescents (0.7%). Similarly, a greater percentage of Latina adolescents (2.4%) develop BED prior to adulthood than do African American (1.5%) or non-Latina, White adolescents (1.4%).

Overall, the prevalence of eating disorders does not vary as a function of SES. For example, prevalence does not differ significantly as a function of parents' education, marital status, or household income (Swanson et al., 2011).

Course of Anorexia and Bulimia

AN and BN usually begin during early adolescence. The most recent data suggest that symptoms of all three eating disorders typically emerge between 10 and 14 years of age. The typical age of first diagnosis is bimodal for AN, with girls most often identified either in early adolescence (11–14 years) or early adulthood (18–24 years). In contrast, BN and BED are typically first diagnosed in late adolescence or early adulthood (17–25 years). Although eating disorders can emerge at any age, they are rare among prepubescent children, and they usually do not emerge after age 25 (Swanson et al., 2011).

The course of AN is variable. Approximately 50% of individuals with AN recover from the disorder, 30% improve but continue to meet diagnostic criteria for either AN or BN, and 10% to 20% have chronic symptoms of AN. Individuals with chronic symptoms are most at risk for death, either from malnourishment or suicide. Adolescents with AN who receive treatment shortly after symptom onset have the best chance of recovery (Smink, Van Hoeken, & Hoek, 2012; 2013).

The prognosis for BN is somewhat better than for AN. In one large study of individuals previously diagnosed with BN, 15% continued to meet diagnostic criteria for the disorder 5 years later. Unfortunately, 36% of patients continued to show subthreshold eating problems while 41% met diagnostic criteria for major depression, instead. While the chance of recovery is greater for BN than AN, the majority of people diagnosed with either eating disorder continue to show psychiatric problems years later (Smink et al., 2012, 2013).

A significant percentage of adolescents with eating problems change diagnostic classification over time, a phenomenon called diagnostic migration. For example, individuals might initially meet diagnostic criteria for AN and later be diagnosed with BN. In one large study, 36% of patients with AN later showed BN. Furthermore, 27% of patients with BN later developed AN (Bryant-Waugh & Watkins, 2015). Diagnostic migration is especially common among adolescents with eating disorders, and it usually occurs within 5 years after the initial diagnosis.

Course of Binge Eating Disorder

Recent research indicates that youths manifest BED differently than adults (Fairburn & Gowers, 2010). Marcus and Kalarchian (2003) differentiate between early onset and late-onset BED. Early onset BED tends to emerge between 11 and 13 years of age. Youths with early onset BED, like Mateo, usually have weight problems or obesity in childhood. They typically begin binge eating in late childhood (mean age = 12 years) and begin dieting a few years later (mean age = 14 years). They often have problems with depression and anxiety and tumultuous family relationships. They are at risk for BN as adults.

In contrast, late-onset BED tends to emerge in early adulthood. People with late-onset BED tend to have weight problems or obesity in early adulthood rather than in childhood (mean age = 19 years). Furthermore, they often begin dieting (mean age = 20 years) *before* they engage in binge eating (mean age = 28 years). Late-onset BED is less closely associated with BN.

These findings suggest that BED in children and adolescents is closely associated with emotional problems, such as depression and anxiety. Food and eating may be a method of emotion regulation for these youths. In contrast, BED in adults is more closely associated with dietary restriction. Adults with BED may binge to alleviate feelings of hunger, emptiness, and dysphoria while dieting (Marcus & Kalarchian, 2003).

People are more likely to recover from BED than other eating disorders. Fairburn, Cooper, Doll, Norman, and O'Connor (2000) found that 85% of young women with BED no longer met criteria for the disorder 5 years after their initial diagnosis. A second longitudinal study also found high rates of recovery 2 years (65%) and 6 years (78%) after diagnosis (Fichter & Quadflieg, 2007).

Review:

- The lifetime prevalence of AN is 0.5% to 1% of females and less than 0.3% of males. The lifetime prevalence of BN is 1.5% to 4% of females and less than 0.5% of males. The lifetime prevalence of BED is 2.6%.
- Recent research suggests that eating disorders exist across countries and cultures. Adoption of western cultural values and acculturation into the United States is associated with increased prevalence.

- Onset of AN is typically in early adolescence or early adulthood. Onset of BN is typically in late adolescence or early adulthood. AN is associated with more severe and lasting impairment.
- The course of BED often depends on the age of symptom onset. Childhood-onset BED is associated with a history of childhood obesity, binge eating, and dieting as well as greater risk for depression and family problems in later adolescence and adulthood.

What Causes Child/ Adolescent Eating Disorders?

Genetic Risk

Genes play a role in the development of eating disorders (Bulik, 2004). Behavioral geneticists have determined that eating disorders run in families. Females who have a first-degree relative with an eating disorder are 4 to 11 times more likely to develop an eating disorder themselves compared to females with no family history of eating problems (Strober, Freeman, Lampert, Diamond, & Kaye, 2000). This increased genetic risk for eating disorders is not specific to AN or BN. For example, a family member with BN places other biological relatives at risk for *all* eating disorders, not BN per se.

Behavioral geneticists have also tried to determine how much of the variance of eating disorders can be explained by genetic versus environmental factors. Twin studies indicate that the heritability of AN is between 48% and 74%, depending on the sample (Bulik, 2004). Twin studies indicate that the heritability of BN is roughly the same: between 59% and 83%. The remaining variance is largely explained by nonshared environmental factors—that is, events and experiences unique to the adolescent and not her twin (e.g., different friends, teachers, sports, or hobbies). Shared environmental factors (e.g., same parents, house, SES) seem to play relatively little role in explaining either AN or BN.

Molecular geneticists have tried to locate specific genes that might be responsible for placing individuals at risk for eating pathology (Bulik, 2004). Unfortunately, this line of research has produced inconsistent results. So far, researchers have been unable to identify a single gene or set of genes that are consistently associated with either AN or BN. Some evidence suggests that chromosome 1 may be involved in the development of AN–restricting type as well as in the tendency to obsess over thinness. Other data indicate that chromosome 10 may play a role in the development of purging behavior, especially vomiting. More research is needed.

Serotonin and Cholecystokinin

The neurotransmitter serotonin may be involved in the development of eating disorders, especially AN. In healthy individuals, serotonin is involved in regulating metabolism, mood, and personality. With respect to metabolism, serotonin plays a crucial role in appetite; it is partially responsible for feelings of satiety. With respect to mood, serotonin plays a major role in emotion regulation. Abnormalities in serotonergic functioning are likely involved in depression. With respect to personality, high levels of serotonin are associated with sensitivity to psychological stress, perfectionism, and a need for order and organization.

Some individuals with eating disorders show a disturbance in serotonin levels. For example, people with AN often show unusually high levels of serotonin, even after they have recovered from the disorder. Similarly, individuals with BN show abnormalities in serotonin levels both during their illness and after recovery. Kaye, Bastiani, and Moss (1995) suggest that elevated serotonin may make certain individuals prone to psychological distress, anxiety, and perfectionism. Restrictive dieting can temporarily decrease serotonin levels, causing a reduction in negative affect. Thus, dietary restriction is negatively reinforced and maintained over time (Castellini et al., 2013).

Serotonin disturbance has also been suggested as a cause for bingeing and purging. In healthy individuals, serotonin plays a role in inhibiting eating. Individuals with BN, however, often show a dysregulation of serotonin. Dysregulation can produce feelings of dysphoria that might prompt binge eating and purging. Interestingly, individuals who recover from BN often show more regulated serotonin levels, indicating that recovery is partially dependent on changes in serotonergic activity (Goethals et al., 2014).

Some people with BN show low levels of a hormone called cholecystokinin (CCK). In healthy individuals, CCK is produced after eating a large meal. This hormone triggers satiety and regulates the amount of food consumed. However, people with BN produce much less CCK when they eat, perhaps allowing them to binge without experiencing satiety (Rigamonti et al., 2014).

Studies showing an association between serotonin, CCK, and eating disorders have relied on cross-sectional designs. These studies cannot tell us whether abnormalities in neurotransmitters or hormones are a cause or a consequence of eating disorders. For example, individuals with AN often have elevated levels of another neurotransmitter, norepinephrine. However, recent studies indicate that reductions in norepinephrine are the result of severe weight loss, and do not cause the disorder. Although it is tempting to infer causal relationships from correlational data, such inferences can lead to an inaccurate understanding of eating disorders (Hannon-Engel, Filin, & Wolfe, 2013).

Sexual Development and Sexual Maltreatment

Pubertal Timing

Experts have given considerable attention to the role of puberty in the emergence of eating disorders. Research has consistently shown that eating disorders usually develop sometime during or after puberty, and they rarely emerge before puberty or after age 25.

One explanation for the association between puberty and eating disorders is that the physical changes that characterize puberty are particularly stressful to adolescent girls. Before puberty, girls tend to have slender figures that are relatively low in body fat. Their body weight and shape are relatively close to the socially sanctioned ideal body promoted by Western society. With the onset of puberty, girls gain weight and body fat, making their bodies less compatible with this Western ideal. This increase in weight and change in shape can lead to body dissatisfaction in some girls, causing them to diet in order to regain their prepubescent shape (Smolak et al., 2013).

A related hypothesis is that the timing of puberty might be important in the development of eating disorders. Specifically, girls who mature earlier may be at particular risk for body dissatisfaction and eating pathology. These girls will not only violate socially sanctioned ideals regarding weight and shape but they will do so when their peers are not developing in similar ways. Some early maturing girls may be teased because of their precocious physical development.

Empirical studies have not consistently supported these hypotheses regarding the association between puberty, body dissatisfaction, and eating *problems*. Some studies have shown significant associations between pubertal development, pubertal timing, and body dissatisfaction; however, the strength of these associations has been relatively modest. Other studies have failed to support an association between pubertal development, pubertal timing, and body dissatisfaction altogether. Indeed, the only longitudinal study to test this hypothesis did not support the notion that puberty contributes to later body dissatisfaction (Rohde, Stice, & Marti, 2015).

Research investigating the association between pubertal development, pubertal timing, and eating *disorders* has also yielded mixed results. Pubertal development and timing is associated with dieting in some studies but not others. However, pubertal development and timing tends to be weakly correlated with the likelihood of eating disorders. Taken together, these findings indicate that puberty may be a developmental time frame during which adolescents are vulnerable to the emergence of body dissatisfaction and eating pathology. However, it is unlikely that puberty, by itself, *causes* eating problems or eating disorders.

Child Sexual Abuse

Some experts have speculated that sexual victimization during childhood can lead to the development of eating pathology, especially BN (Oppenheimer, Howells, Palmer, & Chaloner, 2013). According to these theorists, the experience of sexual abuse makes girls feel helpless and shameful. Maltreated girls may be disgusted by their bodies or view their bodies as "tainted" by the abusive act. Some girls may express this shame and disgust by harming their bodies through starvation, bingeing, and purging. Other girls attempt to regain a sense of control over their bodies by dieting. In any case, girls place themselves at risk for developing eating disorders as a consequence of their abuse.

There is considerable evidence that child sexual abuse is associated with eating disorders, especially BN. Studies involving abused children, adolescents with eating disorders, and youths in the community have shown that girls who are sexually maltreated show increased likelihood of developing eating disorders later in life. Furthermore, adolescents and adults with eating disorders often report that their sexual victimization occurred before the onset of their eating problems (Pérez-Fuentes et al., 2013).

On the other hand, child sexual abuse seems to place children at risk for a host of psychiatric problems, not eating disorders per se. Fairburn, Cooper, Doll, and Welch (1999) conducted a series of studies involving 102 women with BN, 102 women with other psychiatric disorders (usually depression), and 204 women with no mental health problems. Results showed that women with BN or another psychiatric disorder were more likely to have been sexually abused than women without a current mental illness. However, history of sexual abuse was as common among women with BN as among women with other psychiatric problems (Fairburn et al., 1999; Welch & Fairburn, 1996). These findings indicate that child sexual abuse is a risk factor for many psychiatric illnesses, but it is not a specific cause of eating pathology (Pérez-Fuentes et al., 2013).

Cognitive–Behavioral Theory

The cognitive–behavioral conceptualization of eating disorders is based on the notion that thoughts, feelings, and actions are closely connected. Each component

of behavior affects the others. Cognitive–behavioral theorists believe eating disorders are caused by a disturbance among these three factors: an *affective* disturbance characterized by low self-esteem; a *cognitive* disturbance characterized by distorted perceptions of weight, shape, and body image; and a *behavioral* disturbance marked by maladaptive eating habits (Pike, Devlin, & Loeb, 2004).

At the heart of the cognitive–behavioral model for eating disorders is low self-esteem. Adolescents at risk for AN and BN are believed to have underlying problems with dysphoria. Although the source of this low self-esteem is unknown, it likely stems from a combination of genetic and environmental factors. For example, individuals at risk for eating disorders tend to have personality dispositions that make them sensitive to psychological distress and critical of themselves and others. Furthermore, many youths with eating disorders come from disruptive or stressful family environments that can contribute to their feelings of low self-worth. Because of these negative emotions, adolescents may place considerable value on their physical appearance, especially their weight and body shape. They may believe that by attaining a certain weight or shape, they can overcome feelings of low self-esteem and self-worth (see Figure 15.6).

Most adolescents diet to attain ideal weight and shape. Severe dieting is negatively reinforced by the reduction of low self-esteem. Adolescents feel temporarily better about themselves and their appearance as they lose weight and receive compliments from others. Unfortunately, severe dieting usually exacerbates adolescents' dysphoria over time. First, adolescents usually hold such unrealistic ideals of weight and shape that no amount of dieting can allow

Figure 15.6 Cognitive–behavioral theory for bingeing and purging. Bingeing is negatively reinforced by a reduction in hunger and emptiness; purging is negatively reinforced by a reduction of guilt.

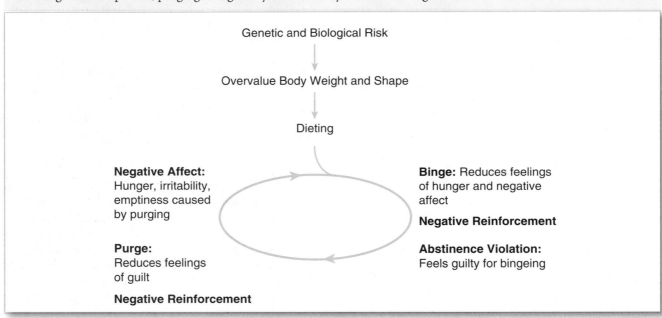

them to reach their goals. Second, dietary restriction causes feelings of hunger, irritability, and fatigue.

To compensate for feelings of frustration, hunger, and fatigue, many adolescents break their diets and binge. Binges are negatively reinforced by temporary reductions in negative affect. However, binges are quickly followed by more lasting feelings of guilt, disgust, and physical discomfort.

To alleviate guilt and avoid weight gain, some adolescents will engage in inappropriate compensatory behaviors. At first, these behaviors include fasting or extra exercise. Fasting is negatively reinforced by reductions in guilt and anxiety about weight gain. However, fasting also produces long-term feelings of dysphoria and hunger. Other adolescents purge in order to avoid weight gain. Purging is also negatively reinforced by temporary reductions of anxiety. However, purging usually exacerbates feelings of guilt and disgust over time. Furthermore, after purging, adolescents often feel the same sense of emptiness and dysphoria that existed before the binge.

In summary, low self-esteem and dysphoria form the basis for the cognitive–behavioral model of eating disorders. Dietary restriction causes a temporary reduction in dysphoria (negative reinforcement) but long-term feelings of frustration and hunger. Binge eating reduces feelings of hunger (negative reinforcement) but produces guilt and anxiety about weight gain. Fasting and purging can alleviate guilt and fears of weight gain (negative reinforcement) but exacerbate feelings of low self-worth. Eating disorders, therefore, are caused by underlying mood problems and maintained by problematic thoughts and a cycle of negative reinforcement.

Social–Cultural Theories

Dual Pathway Model

Other researchers are interested in how social and cultural factors might contribute to the emergence of eating disorders. Stice (2016) has offered one of the most influential social–cultural models to explain binge eating: the dual pathway model. According to the dual pathway model, eating disorders develop through two pathways: (1) dietary restriction and (2) negative affect (Rohde et al., 2015).

At the center of the dual pathway model is the notion that society places great demands on adolescent girls to lose weight and appear attractive. Many girls internalize the socially sanctioned thin ideal because they are reinforced by others when they conform to this ideal and punished when their appearance violates this standard. For example, adolescent girls often praise peers who lose weight and ostracize peers who are overweight. As anyone who has seen the movie *Mean Girls* knows, praise (positive reinforcement) and teasing or ostracism (punishment) can be powerful motivators.

Idealization of thinness contributes to body dissatisfaction, even in very young girls (Smolak et al., 2013).

When girls are dissatisfied with their bodies, they may engage in dietary restriction to lose weight and achieve their ideal size and shape. Unfortunately, dieting is an ineffective means of long-term weight control. Instead, dieting usually produces feelings of hunger, irritability, and fatigue. Furthermore, failure to lose weight and achieve the thin ideal contributes to low self-esteem, frustration, and negative affect (see Image 15.3).

In some girls, dietary restriction and negative affect lead to binge eating. Bingeing causes a temporary reduction in both hunger and negative emotions. Indeed, binge foods tend to be high in fat and carbohydrates—comfort foods. However, as described by the cognitive–behavioral model of eating disorders, bingeing also elicits increased guilt and the likelihood of purging or other compensatory behaviors.

Image 15.3 Brittany stands next to her body tracing during a therapy session for girls with eating disorders. The body tracing exercise allows her to see the distortion between her actual body, traced by the therapist, and her perceived body image.

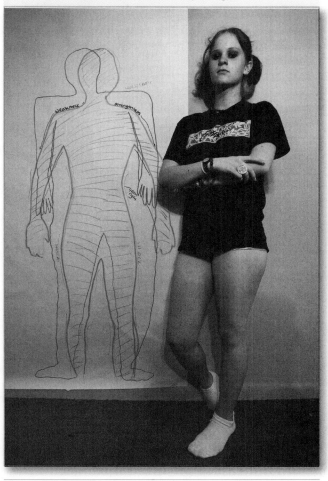

An alternative social–cultural model for the development of eating disorders is the tripartite influence model (Keery, van den Berg, & Thompson, 2004; Rodgers, McLean, & Paxton, 2015). According to this model, three social–cultural factors influence adolescent girls' eating behavior: (1) peers, (2) parents, and (3) the media (see Figure 15.7).

Peers can influence adolescent girls' eating when they place importance on weight and body shape, tease other girls about their appearance, or diet themselves. Parents affect a girl's eating behavior when they make comments about their own weight, shape, or appearance, when they diet, or when they criticize their daughter's appearance or urge her to lose weight. The media can also affect girls' eating behavior. Models on television, in movies, and in magazines can convey the importance of physical attractiveness to girls' well-being. Similarly, television and magazines can provide girls with maladaptive ideas about dieting, exercise, and weight loss (see Image 15.4).

According to the tripartite influence model, peers, parents, and the media can lead to the development of eating problems in three ways. First, they can directly affect eating behavior by motivating a girl *to diet*. For example, a girl who sees her mother, her best friend, and her favorite singer dieting might regard dieting as a developmentally normative and socially expected means of losing weight. She might decide to diet in order to appear more like these significant people in her life. As we have seen before,

however, dietary restriction is not an effective, long-term means of weight control. In fact, it often causes negative affect and can lead to binge eating.

Second, the relationship between these three social–cultural factors and girls' eating might be mediated by girls' *internalization of the thin ideal*. Messages from peers, parents, and the media about body shape, weight, or attractiveness might cause girls to internalize the unrealistic standards for beauty conveyed in Western culture. For example, girls who read fashion magazines might internalize the standards for body shape and weight conveyed by the models in these magazines. Girls who internalize these standards, in turn, might experience dissatisfaction with their own shape and weight. Such body dissatisfaction can lead to dieting, negative emotions, and bulimic symptoms.

Third, the relationship between these three social–cultural factors and girls' eating might be mediated by girls' tendency *to compare their appearance with others*. For example, peers might make comments about classmates who are exceptionally thin and attractive or overweight and unattractive. Adolescent girls, in turn, might compare their own weight and body shape to these attractive and unattractive classmates. These social comparisons, in turn, might cause girls to feel dissatisfied with their bodies. Body dissatisfaction can contribute to dieting, emotional problems, and eating disorders.

Data from adolescents and adults indicate that the tripartite influence model might be a useful way of explaining the potential influences of peers, parents, and the media on the emergence of dieting and eating

Figure 15.7   Tripartite Influence Model of Eating Disturbance

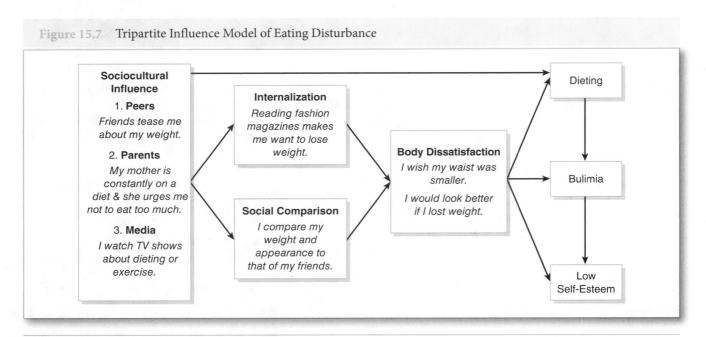

Source: From Shroff and Thompson (2006). Used with permission.

Note: Social-cultural factors lead to body dissatisfaction and BN in two ways: (a) by causing girls to internalize the thin ideal and (b) by causing girls to compare their appearance to others.

Image 15.4   According to the tripartite influence model, social-cultural factors (peers, parents, media) can lead to the development of eating problems in girls. Girls who internalize the "thin ideal" may be at particular risk.

pathology (Keery et al., 2004; Rodgers et al., 2015). Future research will likely be directed at examining the relative importance of these three social–cultural influences in girls of various ages. For example, older adolescents may be greatly influenced by peers, whereas younger adolescents may be influenced more heavily by parents.

Theories for Child/Adolescent Binge Eating Disorder

Individuals with BED almost certainly inherit a genetic diathesis for the disorder. Twin studies indicate heritability for binge eating to be .39. Furthermore, approximately 50% of adults with BED have a family member with obesity or BED. Unfortunately, no genetic markers have been consistently identified, although most evidence suggests abnormalities in the serotonin and dopamine transporter genes (Wonderlich et al., 2009).

Neuroimaging studies have also yielded mixed results, regarding the biological underpinnings of BED. Most research suggests that people with BED may be unusually sensitive to certain properties of food (e.g., color, smell, texture, taste) that make it more likely they will binge. For example, two studies have shown hyperactivation of the frontal and prefrontal lobes when presented with appealing foods (e.g., foods high in carbohydrates, fats, and salt; Wonderlich et al., 2009).

Children with BED are usually overweight or obese. Longitudinal data indicate these children often have weight problems in childhood, before they begin bingeing. Furthermore, these children often have parents with

weight problems and family members who make negative comments about their shape, weight, or eating habits. Furthermore, parents of children with BED often have strict rules about eating. They insist that children "clean their plates" at mealtime or severely restrict children's access to snacks or sweets. Longitudinal studies indicate that parental preoccupation with their own weight, their children's weight, or their children's diet predicts the development of maladaptive eating in children. For example, children whose parents severely restrict their access to snacks in kindergarten tend to overeat later in childhood (Osborn et al., 2013).

BED in children and adolescents is closely associated with depression and anxiety. Unlike adults with BED, youths with the disorder typically begin bingeing several years *before* they begin dieting. Children with BED are often alienated and teased by peers because of their weight or body shape. They are also more likely than children without BED to have negative childhood experiences or have parents with mental health problems (Marcus & Kalarchian, 2003).

It is likely that bingeing is negatively reinforced by the alleviation of anxiety, depression, worry, or boredom. Johnson, Cohen, Kotler, Kasen, and Brook (2002) prospectively studied children from late childhood through early adulthood. They found that depression at baseline predicted bingeing in adolescence and adulthood. Similarly, Stice, Becker, and Yokum (2014) followed a large sample of adolescent girls over time. They found that negative affect predicted the onset of bingeing but not purging. These findings suggest that youths with

BED may binge to alleviate anxiety, depression, or dysphoria.

Review:

- Both AN and BN have heritability estimates ranging from approximately .50 to .75. The neurotransmitter serotonin is implicated in both AN and BN and may explain why selective serotonin reuptake inhibitors (SSRIs) are effective in reducing anxiety and negative affect associated with these disorders.
- Child sexual abuse is a nonspecific risk factor for eating disorders; sexual maltreatment predicts a wide range of disorders, not only eating problems.
- The cognitive–behavioral model posits that bingeing is negatively reinforced by a reduction in hunger whereas purging is negatively reinforced by an alleviation of guilt.
- Social–cultural theories for eating disorders include the dual pathway model (i.e., dietary restriction, negative affect) and the tripartite influence model (i.e., peers, parents, media). At the center of both models is an adolescent's pursuit of an unrealistic thin ideal.

15.3 EVIDENCE-BASED TREATMENT FOR EATING DISORDERS

What Treatments Are Effective for Youths With Anorexia Nervosa?

Inpatient Treatment

Inpatient treatment for AN initially focuses on changing the adolescent's eating behavior, rather than on providing relief for the adolescent's emotional distress (Petti, 2015). The primary goal of treatment is to monitor the adolescent's physical health and to help her gain weight. Since rapid weight gain is dangerous to severely malnourished patients, physicians monitor the refeeding process. Typically, adolescents with AN are required to consume 1,500 calories per day for the first few days of inpatient treatment. Then, their target caloric intake is increased by about 500 calories every other day until the target reaches 3,500 calories daily (almost twice the amount of daily calories needed for weight maintenance). Consumption of 3,500 calories per day usually results in a gain of two to four pounds per week (Linscheid & Butz, 2003).

Most adolescents with AN are resistant to inpatient treatment because they fear any weight gain, no matter how small. Rigid, black-or-white thinking leads these adolescents to believe that if they gain even one pound, they have lost all control over their eating behavior and are on the road to obesity. Furthermore, adolescents with AN often derive self-worth from their ability to control their weight. To these adolescents, gaining weight means a loss of identity and self-esteem.

To help girls gain weight, the treatment team administers a behavioral protocol that reinforces caloric intake and participation in the treatment program. Usually, this behavioral protocol is based on the notion that girls with AN are afraid of weight gain. In order to overcome this fear, they are required to consume a wide variety of foods during regularly scheduled mealtimes and avoid behaviors designed to limit weight gain (e.g., purging, exercise).

Meal completion is positively reinforced by hospital staff. Upon entering treatment, adolescents are denied most of the privileges they enjoyed at home: watching television; viewing social media; taking telephone calls and visits from friends; and having access to makeup, favorite clothes, and accessories. Adolescents can earn these privileges by eating meals and participating in other aspects of the treatment program.

Patients are also prohibited from engaging in compensatory behaviors to avoid weight gain. Initially, staff members monitor patients to ensure that they do not purge or engage in covert exercise.

Group Therapy

In most inpatient treatment programs, adolescents participate in group therapy (Pretorius et al., 2012; Voriadaki, Simic, Espie, & Eisler, 2015). Groups consist of adolescents who are new to the inpatient program as well as adolescents nearing completion. Supportive confrontation between patients is encouraged by the group therapist. In supportive confrontation, senior group members are encouraged to challenge the cognitive distortions and food obsessions of newer members. For example, a new group member who complains that the food she is forced to consume will make her fat might be challenged by the other group members to avoid "fat talk" during the session. Attempts to lose weight or outsmart staff are discouraged by the group and lead to peer rejection. The therapist uses peer pressure during the session to promote healthy eating in the same way peer pressure likely contributed to the adolescent's eating problems outside of treatment.

Group therapy is structured along several tasks designed to teach adolescents about eating disorders, manage emotions and cope with low self-esteem, develop social skills, maintain a healthy diet, and recognize and challenge beliefs that lead to problematic eating (see Table 15.6). Individuals with eating disorders often show two types of cognitive distortions. First, many erroneously believe that their self-worth is directly associated with their weight. They think, "If it is good to be thin, then you are the best if you are the thinnest" (Linscheid & Butz, 2003, p. 645). The second distortion involves dichotomous (i.e., black-or-white) thinking. Specifically, they believe that if they start eating, they will be unable to stop (Linscheid & Butz, 2003). Therapists try to teach patients to recognize and critically evaluate these faulty beliefs.

There is limited evidence supporting the efficacy of inpatient group therapy for AN. Some researchers

Table 15.6 Group Therapy for Adolescent Eating Disorders

Topic	Description
Psychoeducation	Provides adolescents with information about eating disorders
Behavioral recovery	Teaches adolescents to recognize and challenge cognitive distortions that lead to eating problems; promotes weight gain and healthy eating using supportive confrontation between group members
Relaxation training	Teaches adolescents relaxation and emotion-regulation skills, such as deep breathing, imagery, yoga, and meditation
Nutrition	Teaches adolescents about basic nutrition, the risks associated with dieting, and alternative ways to manage weight and consume healthy foods
Meal planning	Helps adolescents select balanced meals and healthy portions; teaches social skills while eating
Body image	Teaches adolescents to correct maladaptive beliefs about their bodies, to critically evaluate images of women's bodies on TV and in magazines
Self-esteem	Provides adolescents with assertiveness training and communication skills training to improve self-confidence
Family issues	Helps adolescents understand how family relationships can lead to healthy or problematic eating; allows adolescents to develop more healthy patterns of interaction with family
Relapse prevention	Teaches adolescents to recognize and avoid environmental events or mood states that trigger problematic eating; helps adolescents plan for their return to family and school

Source: Based on Guarda and Heinberg (2004).

Note: Most inpatient treatment programs for adolescents with eating disorders require patients to participate in group therapy. Patients in the Johns Hopkins Eating Disorders Program participate in three group sessions daily. Each session covers one of the topics listed above.

believe that individuals with AN are too malnourished to fully participate in group therapy. For example, problems with concentration and problem-solving, caused by malnourishment, can interfere with adolescents' abilities to recognize and critically evaluate cognitive distortions (Linscheid & Butz, 2003).

Structural Family Therapy

After adolescents with AN gain sufficient weight, most professionals recommend family therapy as the first line of psychosocial treatment (Levine et al., 2015). Although many kinds of family therapy are available, the most well-known and widely used approach is structural family therapy.

Structural family therapy focuses primarily on the quality and patterns of relationships between family members. Therapists place little emphasis on the adolescent's eating behavior, per se. In fact, the adolescent's symptoms are believed to serve a diversionary function. As long as family members concentrate their energy and efforts on the adolescent's problematic eating, they do not have to focus on the real source of the problem: family relationships and communication. Family therapists see their "client" as the entire family system, not just the adolescent with the eating disorder (Minuchin, Rosman, & Baker, 1978).

The developer of structural family therapy, Salvador Minuchin, believed that adolescents with AN belong to highly controlling, overprotective families. He used the term *enmeshment* to describe family relationships in which boundaries between parents and children were blurred or diffuse. In enmeshed families, parents control too many aspects of their adolescents' lives and do not allow adolescents to express developmentally appropriate levels of autonomy. For example, parents might place excessive demands on adolescents' choice of afterschool activities, show a lack of respect for the adolescents' privacy, and insist on strict obedience to rigid family rules. At the same time, parents of adolescents with AN are overly concerned with the appearance of the family to others. Family members avoid conflict with one another, preferring to ignore family problems rather than to discuss them openly. Minuchin believed that adolescents from enmeshed families develop AN as a means to assert autonomy over the only aspect of their lives that they are able to control: their bodies (see Image 15.5).

Structural family therapists have two main goals. First, they try to improve communication among family members. Specifically, therapists help family members realize how their adolescent's eating pathology might distract them from other relationship problems in the family, such as a mother's excessive alcohol use or a father's

Image 15.5   Structural family therapy helps reduce family conflict and improve parent–adolescent communication.

tendency toward anger. Improved communication between family members, especially between parents, will decrease overall tension in the family that can contribute to the adolescent's eating problems.

Second, the therapist helps the family recognize the adolescent's emerging needs for autonomy and find developmentally appropriate ways for her to show self-direction. For example, parents might agree to knock on their adolescent's bedroom door before entering, avoid snooping through her room when she is not home, or resist listening to her telephone calls without her knowledge. They might also give their daughter more freedom to select classes and extracurricular activities. At the same time, the therapist might help the adolescent express concerns to her parents in direct and mature ways in order to reduce family conflict.

Data on the efficacy of family therapy are extremely limited. Minuchin's idea that adolescents with AN come from highly controlling, enmeshed families has not been adequately tested. Furthermore, structural family therapy has not been sufficiently evaluated using randomized controlled trials. Uncontrolled trials of structural family therapy indicate that 66% to 86% of adolescents with AN show improvements in weight gain following family treatment (Lock & Le Grange, 2015). Despite its popularity, more research is needed to establish structural family therapy as an efficacious treatment for AN.

The Maudsley Hospital Approach

Although structural family therapy is a popular form of outpatient treatment for AN, another variant of family therapy developed at Maudsley Hospital in London has received considerably more empirical support. Indeed, several randomized controlled trials have been conducted investigating the Maudsley Hospital approach to treatment, making it the best studied family approach to treating AN (Lock & Le Grange, 2005; Wallis et al., 2013).

On the surface, the Maudsley Hospital approach to family therapy is quite different from structural family therapy. Initially, clinicians using the Maudsley approach target the adolescent's eating disorder symptoms, rather than communication patterns in the family. During the first phase of treatment, the therapist encourages parents to take control of their adolescent's eating behavior and develop a plan for helping her gain weight. The therapist is usually not concerned with the tactics parents use to take control of their adolescent's eating, so long as both parents work together. At the same time, the therapist blames the adolescent's weight loss on the eating disorder itself, not on the parents or family-related problems. The goal of the initial phase of treatment is to help parents feel empowered over the adolescent's eating and to allow the adolescent to gain weight.

Under the surface, the initial phase of the Maudsley approach resembles that of structural family therapy. Both schools of therapy require parents to solidify their relationship and communicate with each other. Structural family therapists make this goal explicit, by focusing on communication patterns between parents. Practitioners of the Maudsley approach keep this goal implicit, by encouraging parents to find ways to "refeed" their adolescent. Accomplishing the refeeding task requires parents to open lines of communication and work together to solve a common problem.

In the second phase of the Maudsley approach, parents are encouraged to gradually shift responsibility for refeeding to their adolescent. Again, it is more important that families work out for themselves how to transfer this responsibility than it is for the therapist to tell families the "right way" to do it. Accomplishing this task requires families to give their adolescent progressively greater freedom and autonomy over her eating behavior.

The third phase of treatment begins when the adolescent has achieved sufficient weight. In this phase, treatment focuses less on the adolescent's eating behavior and more on her developing autonomy. Parents and adolescents work together to help adolescents negotiate rights and responsibilities within the family that satisfy all family members.

The Maudsley approach to family therapy takes approximately one year. Randomized controlled trials indicate that the Maudsley approach is efficacious in treating adolescents who show relatively recent onset of AN. Furthermore, the Maudsley approach is associated with more rapid weight gain than individual psychotherapy (Lock & Le Grange, 2015).

Review:

- The primary goal of inpatient treatment for AN is weight gain. Staff members administer behavioral protocols that usually involve positive reinforcement for eating and response cost for failing to achieve caloric goals.
- Group therapy for AN often relies on supportive collaboration in which senior group members challenge the cognitive distortions and food obsessions of newer members.
- Structural family therapy is sometimes used to improve parent–adolescent communication and to help parents meet adolescents' needs for greater autonomy.
- The Maudsley Hospital approach to treatment involves (a) initial refeeding by parents, (b) family therapy to improve communication, and (c) increased autonomy for the adolescent.

What Treatments Are Effective for Youths With Bulimia Nervosa?

Cognitive–Behavioral Therapy

Cognitive–behavioral therapy (CBT) is one of the most frequently used outpatient treatments for BN (Waller et al., 2014). Recall that cognitive–behavioral therapists conceptualize BN as reflecting a disturbance in mood, cognition, and eating (Pike et al., 2004). All three aspects of functioning are interrelated. Adolescents initially diet to achieve a highly idealized and unattainable weight or shape. By acquiring this ideal body, they believe that they will overcome feelings of low self-worth. Unfortunately, dieting often leads to binge eating, which causes adolescents to feel guilty and out of control. Many adolescents engage in further dietary restriction to alleviate these negative feelings, but continued dieting produces only more negative emotions. Other adolescents purge to reduce fears of weight gain, but purging exacerbates guilt and low self-esteem. The bulimic cycle is maintained through negative reinforcement. Binges are negatively reinforced by temporary reductions in hunger, irritability, and fatigue brought on by severe dieting. Purging is negatively reinforced by temporary reductions in guilt and dysphoria brought on by binges.

The goal of CBT is to break this cycle of negative reinforcement by exposing girls to normal amounts of food and prohibiting them from purging or engaging in other maladaptive means of avoiding weight. Clients initially experience considerable discomfort ingesting food and avoiding weight loss strategies; over time, however, anxiety is reduced and compensatory behaviors are no longer negatively reinforced.

CBT for bulimia is typically conducted in 20 weekly sessions and is divided into three phases. In the first phase, the therapist introduces the cognitive–behavioral model for BN and shows how the client's emotions, thoughts, and eating behaviors are closely connected. Early in treatment, the therapist asks the adolescent to identify situations or events that do and do not trigger bingeing or purging. Consider the following transcript in which Sara's therapist helps her identify these triggers (see the following Research to Practice section).

Another early goal is to increase the adolescent's motivation to change her eating behavior. Although adolescents with BN usually recognize that they have an eating disorder, they may be unwilling to give up purging because they fear becoming fat. The therapist might ask the adolescent to complete a cost–benefit analysis. First, the therapist might ask the adolescent to consider the positive and negative consequences of maintaining her present eating habits. A perceived benefit might be to lose weight, while a perceived cost might be feeling that she is out of control. Second, the therapist asks the adolescent to consider the benefits and costs of changing her eating habits. A possible benefit might be to feel less guilty about bingeing and purging. A potential drawback might be that she gains weight.

After the adolescent completes the cost–benefit analysis, the therapist asks the adolescent to critically evaluate perceived benefits of maintaining her present eating habits and perceived costs associated with reducing her bingeing and purging. The cost–benefit analysis often increases adolescents' willingness to participate in therapy. Consider the interaction between Becca and her therapist, as they weigh the costs and benefits of purging (see the following Research to Practice section).

In the second phase of treatment, therapy focuses primarily on identifying and challenging dysfunctional thoughts that contribute to the adolescent's eating

IDENTIFYING TRIGGERS FOR BINGEING AND PURGING

Therapist: OK. Now I'd like you to complete the following form with me about the times when you binge and the times you make yourself throw up. Tell me about situations that almost always cause you to binge.

Sara: Well, you know, I binge a lot when I'm alone in the house. Like, before my brother gets home from school and my parents get home from work.

Therapist: What do you mean by "a lot"? Do you mean all of the time?

Sara: No, maybe about half of the time. Maybe three or four times each week.

Therapist: OK. Then let's say that being home alone triggers a binge about 50% of the time. What kinds of situations or feelings *almost always* cause you to binge?

Sara: Feelings?

Therapist: Yes. Sometimes you might find that certain emotions cause you to binge.

Sara: Like, whenever I get into an argument with my boyfriend or I feel like he doesn't care about me or is angry with me.

Therapist: That almost always causes you to binge?

Sara: All of the time. I feel terrible inside, you know, depressed. And then I eat.

Therapist: OK. And in what sorts of situations do you *never* binge?

Sara: Well, I never binge when other people are around, like with my friends or family. I also never binge when I'm having fun with the other kids.

Therapist: OK. So you never binge when you're with other people, especially when you're having fun with friends?

Sara: Yeah.

Therapist: OK. So you see that certain situations and feelings often cause you to binge, like when you're alone or feeling depressed about your boyfriend. When you're in other situations or in a good mood, you never binge. Do you see how situations and feelings can affect your likelihood of bingeing?

Sara: Yeah.

Therapist: Also, do you see your bingeing is not completely out of control? After all, in some situations you never binge, right?

Sara: Yes. I guess I never thought about it that way.

---

disorder. Adolescents are taught that situations and events do not directly affect behavior. Instead, beliefs mediate the relationship between antecedent events and behavioral consequences. Many therapists teach adolescents the ABC approach to analyzing the relationship between antecedent events, beliefs, and consequences. Consider the dialogue between Heather and her therapist (see the following Research to Practice section).

The therapist spends the majority of the second phase of treatment teaching adolescents to recognize and challenge distorted thoughts that lead to bingeing and purging. In the example above, Heather displays dichotomous thinking. She sees herself in black-and-white terms, either all good or all bad. Therefore, she believes that if she

violates her diet, she is a terrible person who lacks control over her eating.

In the final phase of treatment, the therapist and client prepare for termination and plan for the possibility of relapse. Since relapse is common among individuals with BN, the therapist openly talks about the possibility that some time in the future, the adolescent might binge and purge. The therapist encourages the adolescent to anticipate high-risk situations that might trigger relapse. Then, the therapist and client develop strategies to manage those high-risk situations.

Several randomized controlled trials have demonstrated the efficacy of CBT in treating BN (Pike et al., 2004). CBT is associated with reductions in bingeing, purging,

THE COSTS AND BENEFITS OF PURGING

Therapist: So, you said that you'd like to stop purging, but purging helps you lose weight. Is that right?

Becca: Yeah. If I stop throwing up or exercising and stuff, I'll probably gain 50 lbs. like that.

Therapist: Well, let's look at that belief for a minute. Right now you're bingeing and purging pretty frequently . . . usually once or twice a day. How much weight have you lost over the last month?

Becca: Well, none. But I haven't gained any either.

Therapist: So purging hasn't caused you to lose weight?

Becca: No.

Therapist: Well, let's look at the alternative. If you stopped purging, would you really gain 50 lbs "just like that"?

Becca: Maybe not 50. Maybe 25.

Therapist: If you gained 25 lbs., do you think your friends would reject you?

Becca: I don't know. I worry about that.

Therapist: Well, if your best friend, Marcie, gained that much weight, would you stop being her friend or tease her or do something else mean like that?

Becca: Of course not.

Therapist: So you wouldn't do that to Marcie, but she might do that to you?

Becca: I guess not. I guess my real friends wouldn't do that to me even if I gained the weight.

dietary restraint, and concern over shape and weight. Furthermore, CBT leads to clinically meaningful reductions in these symptoms; after treatment, many adolescents no longer meet diagnostic criteria for BN (Lundgren, Danoff-Burg, & Anderson, 2004). CBT appears to be most effective in reducing dieting and purging, while it is somewhat less effective in reducing bingeing and concerns about weight and shape (see Figure 15.8).

Although CBT is currently the treatment of choice for adolescents with BN, it is not a panacea (Agras, Crow et al., 2000; Agras, Walsh, Fairburn, Wilson, & Kraemer, 2000). Approximately 20% to 30% of individuals who begin CBT withdraw before completion. Among those who complete CBT, 50% are not able to abstain from bingeing and purging after treatment. Finally, most studies have examined the efficacy of CBT with older adolescents and adults. More research is needed to confirm its utility with younger adolescents.

Interpersonal Therapy

Although CBT is currently the treatment of choice for adolescents with BN, not all patients respond to CBT. An alternative treatment is interpersonal therapy (IPT). Recall that interpersonal therapists focus on the quality of their client's relationships. Although they do not necessarily believe that interpersonal problems *cause* eating disorders,

therapists recognize that eating disorder symptoms are sometimes connected to adolescents' social functioning. Consequently, interpersonal therapists focus primarily on the adolescent's relationships with family members and friends, rather than on her eating disorder symptoms (Murphy, Straebler, Basden, Cooper, & Fairburn, 2012).

IPT is based on the medical model of psychopathology—that is, clients are told that BN is a medical illness that is interfering with their physical, psychological, and social well-being. Adolescents are allowed to assume the sick role. They are not blamed for having an eating disorder, nor are their symptoms interpreted as indicators of personal weakness.

The therapist initially teaches the adolescent about BN and demonstrates how interpersonal problems frequently coincide with (and sometimes elicit) maladaptive eating. Indeed, 75% of people with eating disorders experience a significant interpersonal stressor shortly before the onset of their eating problem. The therapist offers to help the adolescent improve the quality of her interpersonal relationships so that she might feel better about herself and more in control of her eating.

Interpersonal therapists target one or two areas of interpersonal functioning that are associated with the adolescent's eating disorder. These problems can be loosely classified into four interpersonal problem areas: (1) grief, (2) role transitions, (3) role disputes, and

THE A-B-C'S OF EATING PROBLEMS

Therapist: So you said that you binged a lot this week and felt totally out of control?

Heather: Yeah. I was doing real well, you know, on my diet. I went two days eating very little. Just some low-fat yogurt and steamed vegetables and stuff like that. Then, I was so hungry and feeling sort of bored, and I started to eat some potato chips. They tasted real good at first, but then I felt so guilty for breaking my diet. But I just couldn't stop, so I ate the whole bag, and I kept on eating until I was stuffed. That was Wednesday, when my parents were out. Afterward, I felt terrible, like a pig. I felt, you know, real dirty and bloated. So I threw up. That made me feel even worse because I had been so good lately, and then, I was hungry again.

Therapist: OK. So let's look at the situation a little more closely. You were hungry and bored, so you started eating the potato chips? That was the event that started the binge?

Heather: Yeah. Then, I just kept right on eating.

Therapist: Actually, something occurred in between. What was going through your mind when you started eating the chips?

Heather: I don't know . . . nothing.

Therapist: You said you felt so guilty for breaking your diet?

Heather: Yeah. I guess I thought, "Oh well, what the hell, I might as well eat the whole bag and pig out since I broke my diet."

Therapist: That's what I mean. Eating one potato chip didn't cause you to eat the whole bag and all the rest of the food. Your *thought* caused you to binge. You thought, "Well, I'm terrible for breaking my diet, so I might as well pig out." That's what caused you to binge.

Heather: I guess so.

Therapist: Well, if you had another thought at the time, a different thought, might you have acted differently? For example, if you'd thought, "Well, I ate a few chips and broke my diet a little, but I was really hungry. Maybe I should eat something healthy now," maybe you wouldn't have binged.

Heather: Yeah. Probably not.

---

(4) interpersonal deficits. First, some adolescents' symptoms are associated with grief, specifically, the death of a loved one or separation from a family member. For example, an adolescent might show severe depression and moderate symptoms of BN after her mother is sent overseas to serve in the army. In her mother's absence, she may have assumed many of the housekeeping and caregiving duties in the home and was not able to process the negative feelings associated with separation from her mother. An interpersonal therapist would help this adolescent grieve the loss of her mother's companionship.

Second, eating disorder symptoms may be associated with role transitions in the adolescent's life. Life-changing experiences, such as beginning a new school, moving to a new neighborhood, or coping with parental divorce, require adolescents to assume new roles. Often, these roles threaten the adolescent's self-esteem. For example, an adolescent who begins high school must abandon the old, comfortable roles that she played in junior high and create a new social niche. For some adolescents, this transition can be threatening. The interpersonal therapist helps the adolescent mourn the loss of her old social roles and embrace the challenges of her new surroundings. The therapist acts as a source of support as the adolescent begins to develop new areas of social competence.

Third, adolescent eating disorders may be associated with interpersonal role disputes. Role disputes usually occur when adolescents and their parents have mismatched expectations for each other's behaviors. For example, a 15-year-old adolescent might believe that she is old enough to start dating; however, her parents might believe that she should wait at least one more year and then only date boys with their approval. The adolescent might view herself as an emerging adult who deserves certain rights and responsibilities. Her parents, however, might still view the adolescent as a child who needs

Figure 15.8   Effectiveness of CBT for Bulimia Nervosa

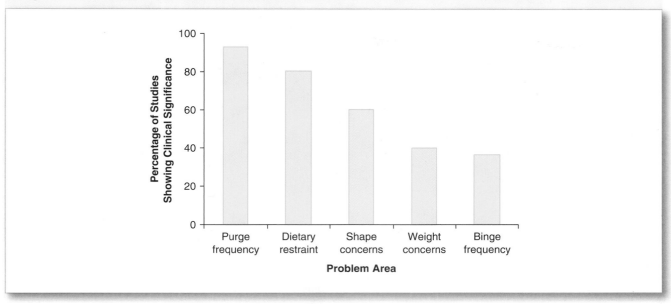

Source: Based on Lundgren et al. (2004).

Note: CBT is most effective in reducing purging and dietary restraint and least effective at reducing weight concerns and frequency of binges.

protection and guidance. Role disputes can lead to tension in the home, leaving the adolescent feeling misunderstood and unfairly treated. If role disputes are successfully resolved, they can lead to stronger parent–adolescent relationships. The interpersonal therapist's goal is to facilitate parent–adolescent communication so that both parties can achieve a greater understanding of each other's perspectives.

Fourth, eating disorders can be tied to adolescents' interpersonal deficits. Some adolescents lack adequate social skills to make and keep friends. Other adolescents are rejected by peers because they are socially withdrawn or disruptive. For example, an extremely shy adolescent might desperately want friends, but she might be unsure how to join peer groups. She might believe that if she were more attractive, she would gain social standing. Consequently, she might begin dieting or purging to lose weight. An interpersonal therapist might help her develop assertiveness skills so that she might feel more comfortable meeting peers and expanding her social network.

Preliminary evidence indicates that IPT is efficacious in reducing symptoms of BN, especially the frequency of bingeing and purging (Murphy et al., 2012). A large randomized controlled study directly compared CBT and IPT (Agras, Walsh et al., 2000). In this study, 220 women and girls with BN received either CBT or IPT over the course of 20 weeks. Outcomes were assessed immediately after treatment and at 1-year follow-up. Immediately after treatment, clients who participated in CBT showed greater improvement than clients who participated in

IPT. At follow-up, however, clients who participated in IPT continued to improve and showed comparable levels of functioning to clients who participated in CBT. These findings indicate that IPT may be a viable alternative for adolescents who do not respond to CBT (see Figure 15.9).

Medication

Antidepressant medications are often used to treat AN. Physicians have speculated that antidepressant medications may be effective for three reasons. First, there is high comorbidity between eating disorders and depression; as many as 80% of individuals with eating disorders show significant mood problems. Second, many people believe low self-esteem and dysphoria underlie eating disorder symptoms. Decreasing dysphoria with medication might alleviate eating disorder symptoms. Third, serotonin is involved in both mood regulation and satiety. Antidepressant medications that affect serotonin might improve mood and eating (Bühren et al., 2014).

Unfortunately, randomized controlled trials of tricyclic antidepressants and SSRIs have shown them to be largely ineffective in treating anorexia (de Vos et al., 2014). Both medications are generally equivalent to placebo in producing weight gain. One study indicates that the SSRI fluoxetine (Prozac) might be useful in preventing relapse after patients had already gained adequate weight. However, another study suggests that patients treated with both SSRIs and psychotherapy showed poorer outcomes than patients treated with psychotherapy alone.

Figure 15.9   Comparison of CBT and IPT in Treating Bulimia Nervosa

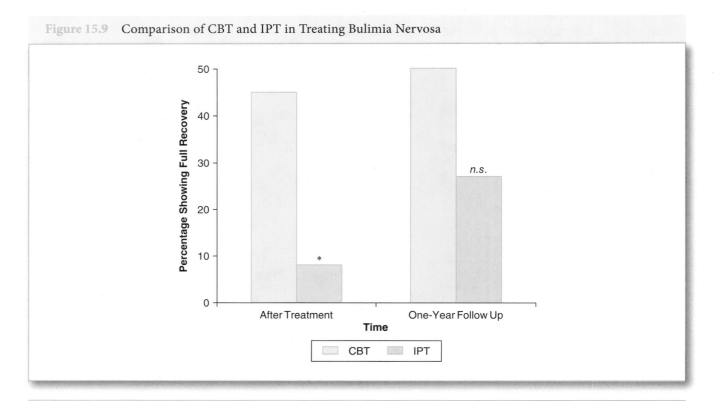

Source: Based on Wilson, Fairburn, Agras, Walsh, and Kraemer (2002).

Note: Immediately after treatment, more people improved after receiving CBT. One year later, people who received CBT and IPT showed similar outcomes.

*p < .05, n.s. = not significant.

Consequently, medication is not regarded as a first-line treatment for AN.

Antidepressant medications are effective in controlling BN (Flament, Furino, & Godart, 2005). Two randomized controlled trials, involving more than 700 patients with BN, showed that fluoxetine (Prozac) was superior to placebo in reducing bingeing and purging (Fluoxetine Bulimia Nervosa Collaborative Study Group, 1992; Goldstein, Wilson, & Thompson, 1995). A second SSRI, fluvoxamine (Luvox), has been shown to prevent relapse in patients who have already recovered from BN (Fichter, Kruger, Rief, Holland, & Dohne, 1996). Unfortunately, the vast majority of patients treated with medication do not stop bingeing or purging. Approximately 75% to 80% of patients remain symptomatic even while taking the medication. Medication can reduce, but not eliminate, symptoms (see Figure 15.10).

Additional data indicate that antidepressants should not replace psychotherapy (Flament et al., 2005). Four randomized controlled studies that have compared CBT to antidepressant medication have found CBT to be superior to medication alone. Some recent data indicate that combining antidepressant medication with psychotherapy, especially CBT, may be slightly more efficacious than providing CBT alone. Consequently, medication is probably used best as an adjunct to CBT or as a means to prevent relapse after treatment.

Review:

- The primary goals of CBT are (a) to expose youths to normal food intake while restricting compensatory behaviors and (b) to identify and challenge cognitive distortions that might elicit negative emotions and trigger maladaptive eating.
- IPT is based on the notion that relationship problems often coincide with and exacerbate eating disorders. Therapists help youths identify and overcome dysphoria related to (a) grief, (b) role transitions, (c) rule disputes, and (d) interpersonal deficits.
- SSRIs are effective in reducing symptoms of BN in adolescents. Combining SSRIs with CBT is more effective than administering SSRIs alone.

What Treatments Are Effective for Youths With Binge Eating Disorder?

Cognitive–Behavioral Therapy

Very few studies have examined the treatment of BED in children and adolescents. However, several evidence-based

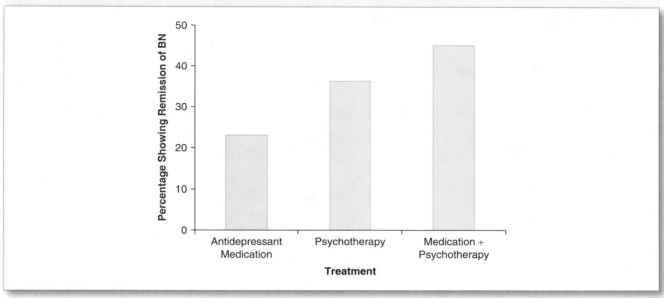

Source: Based on Bacaltchuk, Trefiglio, Oliveira, Hay, Lima, and Mari (2000).

Note: Combining SSRIs and psychotherapy (especially CBT) was slightly more effective in reducing BN than using therapy alone. Medication alone resulted in poorest outcomes.

treatments for adult BED have been identified. It is possible that these treatments might be modified for children and adolescents until interventions for youths are developed (Campbell & Peebles, 2014).

CBT is the treatment of choice for older adolescents and young adults with BED (Vocks et al., 2010). Therapy for BED resembles treatment for BN. An initial goal of therapy is to teach clients to recognize the situations, feelings, and thoughts that often prompt a binge episode. Consider the interaction in which Margo's therapist helps her identify the antecedents for Margo's binges (see the following Research to Practice section).

Later, clients and therapists work on altering these antecedent events and negative thoughts and feelings.

RESEARCH TO PRACTICE

IDENTIFYING ANTECEDENTS TO BED

Therapist: So this week, for homework, you kept a record of the times you binged, where you were when you binged, and what you were doing and feeling. I'm really glad you followed through with this assignment.

Margo: Yeah. I binged three times this week.

Therapist: Did you see any patterns in your bingeing? Did you always binge at the same time every day?

Margo: No, but I always binged in my room while I was using my computer. (Looks at notebook.) Once I was on Facebook. The other two times I was doing my homework.

Therapist: And how were you feeling during those times?

Margo: Depressed mostly. I was looking at an old friend's profile. We're not friends anymore because she was mean to me last year. I kind of missed her and was feeling pretty bad.

Therapist: And the other times?

(Continued)

(Continued)

Margo: I was feeling frustrated. You know I'm not very good at school, and I really didn't want to be working on homework. I just started eating and couldn't stop.

Therapist: OK. So, this past week, you always binged in your room while on your computer or doing your homework. You also felt depressed or frustrated before you binged. How can you use that information to make a plan for *this* week?

Margo: Well. I know I won't binge if I'm with someone else. I mean, I really can't binge if my mom or sister are around.

Therapist: Can you bring your laptop to the kitchen table and work there?

Margo: I guess so. It'll be a little distracting, but at least I won't binge. But there's not much I can do about my feelings.

Therapist: Maybe you can make a promise to yourself: If you feel depressed or frustrated, you'll promise to leave your room and talk with someone about it. Do you have anyone to talk to?

Margo: Yes. I've got two good friends. I guess I can try this plan for a week and see how it goes.

Figure 15.11 Cognitive-behavior therapy can reduce binge eating and weight concerns in people with BED.

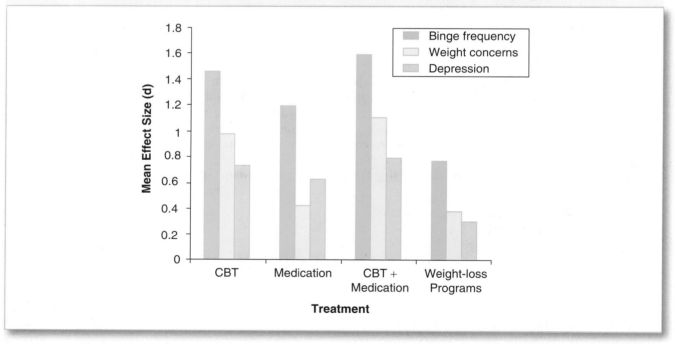

Source: Based on a meta-analysis by Vocks and colleagues (2010).

Note: Combining CBT with medication yields only slightly greater benefits than CBT alone. Weight-loss programs, those that do not target maladaptive thoughts and feelings, show lower effectiveness.

Specifically, sessions focus on identifying and challenging specific automatic thoughts about eating and body image that might elicit bingeing. Therapy can also include family sessions to improve the quality of parent–child interactions.

Meta-analysis indicates that CBT is efficacious in reducing binge eating in adults with BED (Vocks et al., 2010). On average, clients showed a 1.5 standard deviation decrease in binge eating compared to controls. Furthermore, medication (antidepressants in most studies) also reduced bingeing, but effects were smaller than for CBT. Combining CBT and medication yielded only slightly greater benefits than CBT alone.

Figure 15.12 Interpersonal therapy identifies and alleviates interpersonal problems that contribute to depression and binge eating.

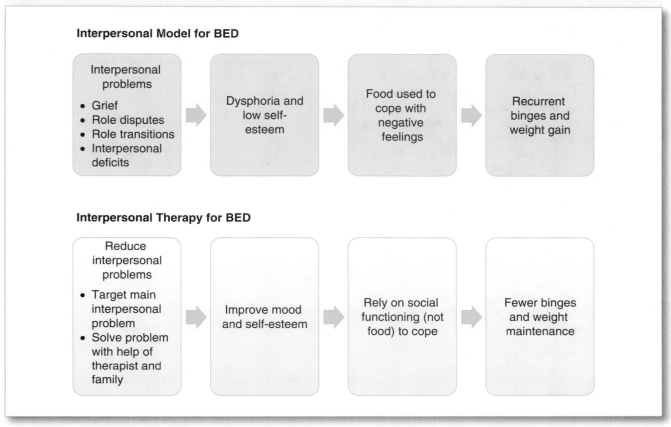

Source: Based on Tanofsky-Kraff and colleagues (2007).

Note: It may be especially useful for children and adolescents whose mood depends on relationships with family and friends.

Vocks and colleagues (2010) also examined the effects of behavioral weight loss programs on people with BED (see Figure 15.11). These programs focus on weight loss, rather than the dysphoric mood states or maladaptive cognitions that might elicit bingeing. Overall, the effects of weight loss programs on BED were moderate and about one-half the magnitude of the effects of CBT. This finding indicates that therapies for BED should address the psychosocial stressors, thoughts, and feelings that precipitate bingeing, rather than focus on dietary habits alone (Wonderlich et al., 2009).

Interpersonal Therapy

Denise Wilfley and colleagues (Wilfley, Frank, Welch, Spurrell, & Rounsaville, 1998) have adapted IPT to help children and adolescents with BED (see Figure 15.12). IPT may be particularly useful for youths with BED because interpersonal problems, such as conflicts with parents or rejection by peers, are often closely related to their binge eating. These problems elicit depression and low self-esteem. Youths may binge to temporarily alleviate these negative feelings. Bingeing usually results in greater dysphoria and weight gain over time. If IPT can alleviate the interpersonal problems that contribute to dysphoria and low self-esteem, it may be helpful in reducing bingeing and weight gain.

At the core of IPT is the identification of the youth's interpersonal problems that might be associated with her low self-esteem and bingeing. The therapist helps the child identify one interpersonal problem area for therapy. Then, therapist and client collaborate to solve the interpersonal problem and improve the client's mood and social functioning.

For example, a 12-year-old girl with BED might report frequent arguments with her mother. Specifically, her mother frequently nags her about her weight, poor school performance, and sloppy appearance. These arguments cause the girl to feel sad and tense at home. She uses food as a means to relax and gain a sense of satisfaction. An interpersonal therapist might conceptualize the girl's problem as a "role dispute" between herself and her mother. The goal of therapy might be to help the girl avoid arguments with her mother and, if arguments arise, to remain calm. Therapy might focus on improving the girl's communication skills. At first, the girl and therapist might role-play more effective ways to interact with her mother at home—ways to avoid yelling, screaming, and sarcasm. Later, the therapist might invite the girl's mother to join the sessions and practice communication skills together.

Another child might be socially isolated from peers and teased because of his weight. He might have few friends and no hobbies or interests outside of school. His ostracism makes him feel lonely and depressed, and he often uses food to cope with these feelings. An interpersonal therapist might view the boy as having an "interpersonal deficit." The goal of therapy might be to help him overcome this deficit by learning how to make and keep friends. Initially, sessions might focus on basic social skills, such as how to introduce yourself to a peer group, how to join a game or activity, or how to respond to teasing. Later, with the help of parents, the child and therapist might identify ways the boy might be more involved in after-school activities. For example, if he is a poor athlete but an excellent artist, he might take a drawing class rather than join the school basketball team.

IPT has been shown to be as effective as CBT in alleviating BED in adults. Furthermore, it is more effective than behavioral weight loss programs at reducing bingeing. IPT seems to help clients by improving self-esteem and reducing dysphoria. Additional research is necessary to demonstrate its usefulness with children (Cooper et al., 2016; Fairburn et al., 2015).

Review:

- CBT is effective in reducing symptoms of BED in children and adolescents. Therapy typically involves helping youths identify situations and negative emotions that trigger binge eating and challenging cognitive distortions that can lead to negative affect.
- IPT is also effective in reducing binge eating. Therapists help youths overcome interpersonal problems that can cause depression, loneliness, or social isolation that lead to binges.

KEY TERMS

Anorexia nervosa (AN): A *DSM-5* eating disorder characterized by (a) caloric restriction leading to significantly low body weight, (b) intense fear of gaining weight or becoming fat, and (c) disturbance in one's body weight or shape

Appetite manipulation: Children are provided with fluids and essential electrolytes to maintain hydration but are prohibited from snacking between meals; increases the motivation of children with ARFID to eat

Avoidant/restrictive food intake disorder (ARFID): A *DSM-5* feeding disorder characterized by (a) a lack of interest in feeding, (b) avoidance of food based on its sensory qualities, or (c) concerns about the negative consequences of eating; causes weight loss, nutritional deficiencies, or other health/social impairment

Binge eating disorder (BED): A *DSM-5* eating disorder characterized by (a) recurrent episodes of binge eating, (b) associated features (e.g., eating rapidly, eating when depressed, feeling ashamed), and (c) marked distress; occurs at least once a week for at least 3 months

Bulimia nervosa (BN): A *DSM-5* eating disorder characterized by (a) recurrent episodes of binge eating, (b) recurrent inappropriate compensatory behaviors to prevent weight gain, and (c) self-evaluation that in unduly influenced by one's body shape or weight; occurs at least once a week for at least 3 months

Cholecystokinin (CCK): A hormone that is secreted by the small intestines that signals satiety and reducing eating in healthy individuals

Diagnostic migration: The tendency of people with eating disorders to change diagnostic classification over time, most commonly from AN to BN

Dichotomous (black-or-white) thinking: A cognitive distortion in which the individual rigidly views herself, others, and the world as either all "good" or all "bad"

Dual pathway model: Posits that eating disorders develop through two pathways: (1) dietary restriction and (2) negative affect

Ego-dystonic: A term used to describe a condition or disorder that the person views as problematic, shameful, or is inconsistent with the person's goals and values

Ego-syntonic: A term used to describe a condition or disorder that the person does not view as problematic or is consistent with the person's goals and values

Electrolyte imbalance: Disturbance in the minerals found in the body (e.g., calcium, sodium, potassium) that regulate hydration and metabolism; can be caused by purging

Enmeshment: A term used by structural family therapists to describe family relationships in which boundaries between parents and children were blurred or diffuse

Facial screening: A form of positive punishment sometimes used to treat pica; the mouth is temporarily screened with a bib or loose-fitting mask to avoid substance ingestion; used only with caregiver assent when other interventions have failed and ingestion is potentially harmful

Failure to thrive (FTT): A medical condition characterized by nutritional deficiency and weight below the fifth percentile for age and gender on standardized growth charts

Feeding disorders: A class of *DSM-5* disorders characterized by a persistent disturbance in eating-related behavior that results in altered consumption or absorption of food and that interferes with physical health; includes pica, rumination disorder, and ARFID

Hypokalemia: Low potassium levels; potentially fatal; associated with recurrent purging

Maudsley Hospital approach: A method of treating youths with AN; components include (a) initial refeeding by parents, (b) structural family therapy to improve communication, and (c) increased autonomy for the adolescent

Osteopenia: Reduced bone mass; often seen in individuals with anorexia

Perfectionism: A personality trait sometimes shown by youths with anorexia; characterized by a rigid and unrealistic pursuit of absolute standards of behavior (athletics, academics, social); associated with excessive compliance, a strong desire to please others, and a lacking an autonomous sense of self

Pica: A *DSM-5* feeding disorder characterized by persistent eating of nonnutritive, nonfood substances over a period of at least 1 month; must be developmentally and culturally unexpected

Pica box: A box containing foods that have similar sensory properties as objects that are eaten by the child with pica

Refeeding syndrome: Cardiac and other health-related problems shown by patients with anorexia during the first 7 to 10 days of treatment

Rumination disorder: A *DSM-5* feeding disorder characterized by repeated regurgitation of food over the period of at least 1 month; must not be attributable to a medical condition or purging behavior shown by people with eating disorders

Supportive confrontation: A technique sometimes used in inpatient group therapy for eating disorders; senior group members are encouraged to challenge the cognitive distortions and food obsessions of newer members

Thin ideal: According to social–cultural theories of eating disorders, an unrealistic and culturally constructed notion of the perfect female body that is perpetrated in the media and through social interactions

Transactional model for feeding disorders: Posits that feeding disorders arise through parent–child interactions characterized by children with (a) high physiological arousal and (b) difficult temperament, and (c) parents who are anxious about their child's food intake

Tripartite influence model: Posits three risk factors for the development of eating disorders: (1) peers, (2) parents, and (3) the media; these factors lead to internalization of the thin ideal, social comparison, and body dissatisfaction over time

CRITICAL THINKING EXERCISES

1. Behavior therapy is typically considered the treatment of choice for infants and toddlers with feeding disorders. Why might it also be important for a therapist to provide cognitive or supportive therapy to the parents of children with feeding disorders?

2. Why is appetite manipulation often used in the treatment of ARFID? Why might some clinicians be opposed to appetite manipulation?

3. Is it possible for a 14-year-old girl who binges and purges to have AN? Is it possible for a 15-year-old girl to have BN but never purge?

4. Savannah is a 16-year-old girl with BN who feels out of control over her eating. However, she is afraid to participate in therapy because she feels she might gain weight. If you were Savannah's therapist, how might you perform a cost–benefit analysis to increase her motivation to change?

5. Ronnie is a 15-year-old girl with early signs of BN. In therapy, she explained to her counselor, "After I ate the pizza, ice cream, and soda, I felt disgusting—like I was an ugly slob with no self-control. I knew the other girls thought so too because they were watching me. So I went into the bathroom and threw it all up." If you were Ronnie's counselor, how might you challenge her ways of thinking?

TEST YOURSELF AND EXTEND YOUR LEARNING

Videos, flash cards, and links to online resources for this chapter are available to students online. Teachers also have access to PowerPoint slides to guide lectures, case studies to prompt classroom discussions, and exam questions. Visit www.abnormalchildpsychology.org.

iStockphoto.com/Liderina

CHAPTER 16

Health-Related Disorders and Pediatric Psychology

If you asked young parents to list their main concerns regarding their children, two items would likely be at the top: (1) toilet training and (2) sleeping. Although not glamorous, toilet training and "sleeping through the night" are two important developmental tasks that all young children must face and overcome. The way in which parents help their children reach these milestones—and children's ease in doing so—can greatly affect children's autonomy and self-efficacy as well as parents' competence and well-being (Christophersen & Vanscoyoc, 2013).

Elimination (i.e., toileting) and sleep disorders have at least three features in common. First, they are both best conceptualized as *deviations from typical development*. Over the first years of life, most children acquire bowel and bladder control and the ability to soothe themselves to sleep. However, elimination and sleep disorders reflect a fundamental delay or deviation from the typical developmental trajectory shown by most children. In some cases, children may have missed opportunities to acquire these skills during sensitive periods in their development. For example, children who experience disruptions to family routines during the time that toilet training usually occurs may not acquire this skill in early childhood and may be resistant to learning later on. Treatment of these disorders, therefore, involves helping children acquire the skills possessed by typically developing peers and correcting early developmental delays or deficits (Lyons-Ruth, Zeanah, Benoit, Madigan, & Mills-Koonce, 2014).

Second, elimination and sleep disorders illustrate the complex *interrelationship between children's physical and behavioral health*. For example, many children with encopresis have chronic problems with constipation. However, treating constipation alone rarely solves their soiling problems. Instead, treatment typically involves both medication and techniques to teach children toileting skills (e.g., recognizing the "need to go") and reducing embarrassment, resistance, or fear. The assessment and treatment of these disorders almost always involves both medical and behavioral professionals (Sulik & Sarvet, 2015).

Third, the development of children's elimination and sleeping skills occurs *within the context of their relationships with caregivers*. These disorders are probably best viewed as existing between parents and children rather than within children themselves. For example, many children have difficulty falling asleep. They may delay bedtime by asking for a drink of water, an additional story, or a trip to the bathroom. These sleep problems are often maintained by parents who intermittently reinforce their children for "stalling." These sleep problems reflect a pattern of interaction between parents and children. Treatment, therefore, involves both members of the parent-child dyad (Ivanenko & Johnson, 2015).

In this chapter, we will focus on the most common elimination and sleep disorders seen in infants, toddlers, and children. Then, we will discuss the field of pediatric psychology, an area of clinical child psychology concerned with helping children cope with medical illness and injury. Throughout the chapter, pay attention to how children's problems reflect a deviation in typical development, the interaction between children's physical and psychological well-being, and the importance of parent–child interactions in treatment.

16.1 ELIMINATION DISORDERS
What Is Enuresis?

Description

On average, children attain daytime control of urination by age 2.5 and nighttime continence by the end of age 3 (Houts, 2010). However, approximately 10 million children in the United States have difficulty with daytime or nighttime wetting and approximately 4% to 5% meet

diagnostic criteria for enuresis (Shreeram, He, Kalaydjian, Brothers, & Merikangas, 2009).

Enuresis is defined as the repeated voiding of urine into the bed or clothes in children aged 5 or older (see Table 16.1). Voiding must occur at least twice a week for at least 3 consecutive months to meet diagnostic criteria. Furthermore, the voiding must not be caused by medications, such as diuretics or selective serotonin reuptake inhibitors (SSRIs), which are known to cause increased urination. Enuresis can be nocturnal (i.e., occurring only at night), diurnal (i.e., occurring only during the day), or both nocturnal and diurnal (Friman, 2008).

Although not part of the diagnostic criteria, most clinicians specify whether enuresis is primary or secondary. Primary enuresis is seen in children who have never been able to stay dry during the night or day. Secondary enuresis is seen in children who had previously been toilet trained for at least 6 months and then began to show enuresis. Approximately 75% to 80% of children with enuresis have primary enuresis; the remainder show secondary enuresis (Friman, Resetar, & DeRuyk, 2009). Consider Trevor, a boy with primary enuresis.

The distinction between primary and secondary enuresis is important because it provides clinicians with clues regarding the cause of children's wetting. For example, whereas children with primary enuresis usually do not have other behavior or emotional problems, children with secondary enuresis sometimes show attention-deficit/hyperactivity disorder (ADHD) and oppositional behavior (Garralda & Rask, 2015). Furthermore, secondary enuresis sometimes follows a stressful event in children's lives, such as moving to a new home, the birth of a sibling, or parental separation. In one study, 81% of children experienced a stressful life event one month prior to the onset of secondary enuresis (Friman, 2008; Friman et al., 2009).

Table 16.1   Elimination Disorders in Children

Enuresis	Encopresis
Repeated voiding of urine into bed or clothes, whether involuntary or intentional	Repeated passage of feces into inappropriate places (e.g., clothing, floor), whether involuntary or intentional
Occurs either twice weekly for 3 months or causes distress/impairment	Occurs at least once per month for 3 months
Child is at least 5 years of age (or equivalent developmental level)	Child is at least 4 years of age (or equivalent developmental level)
Not attributable to a medication or medical condition	Not attributable to a medication (e.g., laxatives) or a medical condition except one causing constipation

Specify: Nocturnal only
            Diurnal only
            Nocturnal and diurnal
	Specify: With constipation and overflow incontinence
	            Without constipation and overflow incontinence

Source: Based on American Psychiatric Association (2013).

ENURESIS

No Sleepovers

©iStockphoto/JBryson

Trevor was a 9-year-old boy referred to our clinic by his pediatrician because of enuresis. Although Trevor never had accidents during the day, he was rarely able to remain dry at night. At first, his wetting caused his parents a great deal of trouble. They repeatedly checked on Trevor, woke him in the middle of the night when he was wet, and cleaned his bedding. For several months, his parents tried to keep him dry by restricting his fluids after dinner, waking him in the middle of the night to urinate, and offering rewards. When these tactics did not work, his parents allowed Trevor to sleep in Pull-Ups and kept a protective pad on his bed in case of leaks. Most nights, Trevor wet the bed an hour or two after falling asleep and did not wake until morning.

Trevor's mother explained, "It's easier to let him sleep in Pull-Ups. When we tried to train him to stay dry, it was really disruptive to our family. My husband and I were tired all the time, Trev was drowsy during the day at school, and his brother (who shares a room with him) always woke because of the commotion." Trevor's father added, "We'd really like him to be able to stay dry, but he can't."

Later, when the psychologist was able to interview Trevor alone, he asked, "Does wearing Pull-Ups at night bother you?" Trevor replied, "Not really. I got used to them, and my family doesn't say anything about it." He paused and then added, "But, my friends have invited me to three sleepovers this past year, and I couldn't go. One was my best friend's birthday party, and I missed it. He asked, 'Don't you like me? Is that why you're not coming to my party?' but I couldn't tell him the truth."

The psychologist asked, "So it would make things a lot easier if you could learn to stay dry? Maybe we can find a way."

Epidemiology

About 1 in 10 children experience occasional problems with daytime or nighttime wetting (Houts, 2010). In any given year, approximately 4.5% of children between the ages of 8 and 11 meet diagnostic criteria for enuresis. Enuresis is much more common among boys (6.2%) than girls (2.5%), perhaps because of delays in the maturation of the nervous and excretory systems of boys. The frequency of enuresis decreases with age. Whereas the prevalence of enuresis is 7.8% among 8-year olds, it drops to 3.8% among 9-year-olds and continues to decrease thereafter (Shreeram et al., 2009). Every year, approximately 15% of children will recover from enuresis without any treatment, perhaps because of physical maturation. However, approximately 1% to 2% of adolescents and 1% of adults have enuresis, indicating that the disorder is persistent in some people (Brown, Pope, & Brown, 2010; Mikkelsen, 2015).

Associated Problems

Early theories of enuresis were based on psychodynamic theory and suggested that enuresis reflected social–emotional disturbance. Recent, empirical research has not supported this hypothesis. Overall, children with and without enuresis do not differ in the number of social or emotional problems reported by parents and teachers. When children do show emotional problems, such as low self-esteem, it is typically a consequence rather than a cause of enuresis. As children with enuresis grow older, their self-esteem worsens. Social–emotional problems are most likely to be present in girls, in youths with secondary enuresis, and in children who wet during the day (Garralda & Rask, 2015).

On the other hand, several studies indicate that enuresis is associated with ADHD (Ghanizadeh, 2010). Approximately 35% of children with enuresis also show significant ADHD symptoms, and children with ADHD are almost 3 times more likely to have enuresis than their unaffected peers. ADHD is most often seen in boys with daytime enuresis. Problems with arousal probably underlie both disorders: Children with ADHD have difficulty with arousal and attention whereas children with enuresis often have difficulty recognizing and responding to indicators of a full bladder at night and during daytime activities (Elia et al., 2009; Shreeram et al., 2009).

Bed-wetting is stressful to all members of a family. Children often feel embarrassed or ashamed about their nighttime incontinence. Parents, too, may blame themselves or their children for their children's bed-wetting. Furthermore, bed-wetting can interfere with families' sleep cycles and lead to marital conflict. Enuresis places greater strain on families already experiencing psychosocial stress, such as single-parent or low-socioeconomic status (SES) families (Houts, 2010).

Although parents do not cause enuresis, they can maintain or exacerbate children's bed-wetting. Some parents attribute children's enuresis to laziness or defiance. Others believe that they have little control over their children's wetting and feel helpless as parents. Consequently, they may respond to their children's accidents in hostile and coercive ways, such as by yelling, spanking, or inducing guilt (e.g., "Why do you make so much work for me? Don't you care?"). Such attributions interfere with parents' abilities to reduce children's enuresis. These thoughts also increase parent–child conflict and elicit stress and negative affect (Cobussen-Boekhorst, van Genugten, Postma, Feitz, & Kortmann, 2013; Friman, 2008).

Sometimes, parents try to treat their children's enuresis in ways that are counterproductive (van Dommelen et al., 2009). For example, many parents allow younger children with nocturnal enuresis to wear diapers or Pull-Ups to bed. Because these underclothes absorb urine and keep children comfortable, these children usually do not learn to awaken when wet. Consequently, they never learn to detect feelings of a full bladder or inhibit bladder contractions to avoid wetting as typically developing children do. Other well-intentioned parents restrict children's fluids after dinner to decrease nighttime wetting. Although fluid restriction may reduce or delay wetting, it prohibits children from learning to recognize and respond to feelings of a full bladder. Finally, some parents engage in "lifting"—that is, when they discover a child has wet the bed, they lift or guide the child to the toilet and/or clean him without waking him. Although lifting spares children embarrassment, it also prohibits them from learning to stay dry at night (Christophersen & Friman, 2010; van Herzeele, De Bruyne, De Bruyne, & Walle, 2015).

Review:

- Enuresis is a *DSM-5* disorder characterized by the repeated voiding of urine into the bed or clothes, either involuntarily or intentional. A child with enuresis must be at least 5 years of age, and the act must occur at least twice per week for 3 months and cause distress or impairment.
- Approximately 4.5% of children have enuresis; boys outnumber girls approximately 3 to 1.
- Enuresis is most often associated with ADHD and minor psychosocial stressors. Enuresis can be exacerbated by harsh or critical discipline and well-intentioned but ineffective strategies to correct the problem.

What Causes Enuresis?

Causes of Nocturnal Enuresis

Approximately 85% of children with nocturnal enuresis show monosymptomatic primary enuresis (MPE): They wet only at night, have never been able to stay dry at night for longer than 6 months, and have no known medical cause for their wetting (Houts, 2010). Children with MPE usually wet soon after falling asleep, void a normal amount of urine, and often do not wake up after urination. These children usually do not show other behavioral or emotional problems (Mikkelsen, 2015).

Most research points to four causes for MPE. First, MPE is highly heritable. Indeed, one of the best predictors of the age at which children will attain nighttime dryness is the age at which their parents accomplished the same feat as children. If both parents have a history of enuresis, 77% of children will develop the disorder. In contrast, when one parent has a history of enuresis, the prevalence of enuresis in their children drops to 44% (Christophersen & Friman, 2010).

Second, approximately 20% of children with MPE show reduced secretion of arginine vasopressin (AVP), a hormone that increases urine concentration and reduces total urine volume. Low AVP secretion may cause nighttime urine production to exceed children's functional bladder capacity, leading children to wet the bed (Rittig & Kamperis, 2015).

Third, nearly all children with MPE have difficulty responding to signals of a full bladder during sleep. Although parents often describe these children as "deep sleepers," sleep studies indicate that MPE occurs at all stages of sleep, and children with MPE do not display atypical sleep patterns. However, most children with MPE do have problems arousing from sleep. Arousal is important because it allows children to recognize their bladder is full so that they can (a) inhibit the flow of urine and/or (b) wake and use the toilet. However, children with MPE are often unaware that their bladder is full and may even remain asleep after wetting the bed (Houts, 2010).

Fourth, nearly all children with MPE have difficulty inhibiting urination during sleep. By age 4.5, most children learn to detect a full bladder and inhibit urination during sleep by contracting muscles of the pelvic floor. However, children with MPE typically do not actively inhibit nighttime urination; consequently, they wet the bed. This lack of inhibition is probably caused by genetically influenced delays in physical maturation, increased urine production, a lack of awareness of a full bladder, and relatively few learning experiences that allow children to associate a full bladder with the contractions necessary to inhibit urination. The treatments for MPE involve helping children inhibit nighttime urination by recognizing sensations of a full bladder and responding to these sensations with inhibition (Houts, 2010; Mikkelsen, 2015).

Approximately 15% of children who wet at night have polysymptomatic nocturnal enuresis (PSNE). In contrast to children with MPE, children with PSNE tend to wet throughout the night, void small amounts of urine, and wake after wetting. Children with PSNE also tend to wet during the day and often complain of frequent, sudden urges to wet.

PSNE is a complex disorder that can be caused by a wide range of biological and psychosocial factors. However, two factors are most common. First, approximately one-third of children with PSNE have bladder instability—that is, they have uninhibited bladder contractions during the night, which prompt them to release urine. Second, some children with PSNE also have small functional bladder capacities; they are able to hold less urine before feeling the need for excretion. Consequently, children with PSNE often report "an urge to go" both during the day and at night (Brown et al., 2008).

Causes of Daytime Enuresis

The overall prevalence of daytime wetting (i.e., diurnal enuresis) is unknown. However, approximately 1% to 2% of children between the ages of 5 and 7 have frequent daytime accidents (Christophersen & Friman, 2010). Children engage in daytime wetting for different reasons. Most children who engage in daytime wetting have bladder instability (i.e., uninhibited bladder contractions) during the day and night. They experience a sudden, unexpected urge to urinate and typically show PSNE. Daytime wetting caused by bladder instability is more common in girls, is sometimes associated with medical problems such as a urinary tract infection, and may be brought on by psychosocial stress.

Another reason for daytime wetting is voiding postponement. As most parents and teachers know, some children (mostly boys) have daytime accidents because they are engrossed in daily activities and are not aware that their bladder is full. Others are hyperactive and impulsive and may not take time to use the bathroom. Children who engage in voiding postponement are conspicuous; they urinate infrequently, engage in holding maneuvers (e.g., crossing their legs, fidgeting), and must be prompted by adults to use the toilet (Christophersen & Friman, 2010).

A very small number of children, mostly girls, engage in daytime wetting because they lack coordination of the muscles responsible for urination. These children contract (instead of relax) the external urethral sphincter muscles that permit urination. The result is that they strain to urinate, their flow of urination is interrupted, and residual urine is often excreted after leaving the toilet (Garralda & Rask, 2015).

Review:

- The most common causes of MPE are (a) genetic risk, (b) reduced vasopressin, (c) insensitivity to a full bladder, and (d) problems inhibiting urine flow during sleep.
- The most common causes of PSNE are (a) insensitivity to a full bladder and (b) small functional bladder capacity.
- Daytime enuresis is often caused by voiding postponement.

What Treatments Are Effective for Children With Enuresis?

Treatment of Nocturnal Enuresis

Is enuresis a serious problem? Does it deserve treatment? Although most children with enuresis will eventually develop continence, recovery is often slow and stressful. Enuresis lowers children's self-esteem and quality of life, interferes with children's social activities (e.g., camps, sleepovers), and burdens parents. Furthermore, most children are able to significantly reduce daytime and/or nighttime wetting with treatment, and effective treatment can improve children's self-esteem and social functioning. Still, many parents view enuresis as a condition that children will outgrow. Only 36% of children with enuresis in the United States receive treatment (Brown et al., 2008; Shreeram et al., 2009).

The successful treatment of enuresis depends on collaboration between physicians, behavioral health professionals, and families (van Herzeele et al., 2015). Before treatment, pediatricians should assess children to determine whether their wetting might be caused by a medical condition. For example, urinary tract infections, diabetes, and SSRIs are sometimes associated with enuresis in children. Constipation can also contribute to enuresis, as fecal matter may place pressure on the bladder. In very rare instances, children have anatomical abnormalities that contribute to their wetting. In 90% to 95% of cases, however, children's wetting is not attributable to medical causes and, consequently, a behavioral intervention is warranted (Campbell, Cox, & Borowitz, 2009; Williams, Jackson, & Friman, 2007).

Behavioral interventions depend greatly on the resources and motivation of families. Therapists typically spend their first sessions with families assessing the nature of children's wetting as well as the family's ability and willingness to participate in behavioral treatment. Because behavioral treatments typically require time and energy on the part of parents and children (including lost sleep in the case of nocturnal enuresis), it is important for families to understand and commit to behavioral treatment. Often, therapists ask parents and children to sign a behavioral contract—that is, a written statement that describes what each family member is expected to do to participate in treatment (Mikkelsen, 2015).

Behavioral Treatment

The treatment of choice for nocturnal enuresis is the use of a urine alarm (Perrin, Sayer, & While, 2015). A urine alarm is a small mechanical device worn in children's underpants in an area most likely to become wet during the night (see Figure 16.1). The device is battery operated and connects to a small alarm that is clipped to children's pajamas. When children wet, urine completes an electrical circuit in the mechanical device, which triggers the alarm. The alarm typically wakes children, who become aware of their nighttime wetting (Axelrod, Tornehl, & Fontanini-Axelrod, 2014).

The urine alarm is believed to stop urination through classical conditioning. The alarm naturally startles the child, causing contraction of the muscles on the pelvic floor. This contraction inhibits urination. The classically

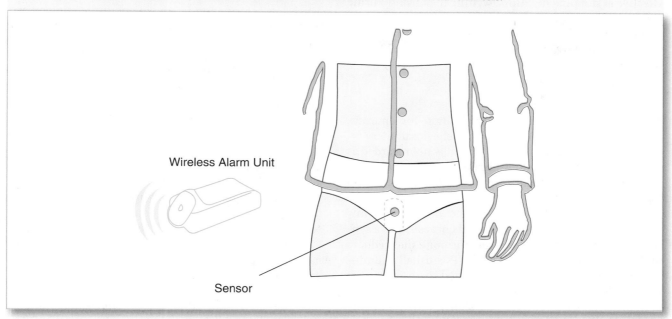

Wireless Alarm Unit

Sensor

conditioned response (CR) is maintained through negative reinforcement or avoidance learning. Over time, the child learns to avoid signaling the alarm by contracting the pelvic floor muscles when he or she senses a full bladder. Contraction during sleep delays urination until morning (Lyons-Ruth et al., 2014).

Approximately 59% to 78% of children who use a urine alarm stop bed-wetting in 8 to 14 weeks. Most children who do not improve do not wake to the alarm or eventually habituate to it (Houts, 2010). If a urine alarm alone is ineffective, clinicians may turn to full spectrum home training (FSHT; Mellon & Houts, 2007). FSHT has five components: (1) education and behavioral contracting, (2) urine alarm training, (3) cleanliness training, (4) retention control training, and (5) overlearning.

First, the therapist teaches families about the anatomy and physiology of nighttime urination. A behavior therapist will likely describe nocturnal enuresis as a problem in learning to associate a full bladder with the inhibition of urine during sleep. Treatment involves teaching the child to make this association by waking him using the alarm. Parents are told never to blame or scold their child for nighttime accidents but, rather, to acknowledge accidents in a matter-of-fact way: "Oh, you wet the bed. Let's get to work cleaning it up." Parents are also told to avoid restricting children's fluids or allowing them to use Pull-Ups at night—two strategies that can interfere with learning. Finally, the therapist asks family members to sign a behavioral contract that describes each family member's role in treatment.

Second, families begin using a urine alarm at home. Families use a wall chart to record children's ability to stay dry each night. The goal is for the child to stay dry for 14 consecutive nights. Each night the child remains dry, he is praised and receives a sticker or small reward. If the child wets and activates the alarm, the parents must make sure that the child immediately wakes and turns the alarm off. Once awake, the child is expected to go to the toilet and urinate.

Third, after waking from the alarm, parents begin cleanliness training exercises. Depending on the child's age, parents ask him to remove his bedding and pajamas and place them in the laundry. Then, he is expected to put on fresh pajamas and bedding and reactivate the urine monitor before returning to bed. Responding to the alarm and engaging in cleanliness training may occur multiple times each night, depending on the frequency of the child's wetting.

Fourth, children participate in retention control training. The purpose of retention control training is to increase the child's functional bladder capacity so that he can wait longer before urinating. During the day, parents ask the child to drink a large glass of water and refrain from using the toilet for 3 minutes. If he accomplishes this task, he is given a small reward. Each day, the duration for waiting is increased by 3 minutes until the child is able to delay urination for 45 minutes.

Fifth, after the child has remained dry for 24 consecutive nights, parents begin the overlearning procedure. Overlearning is designed to prevent relapse by giving children more practice associating full bladder sensations with the contractions needed to inhibit urination. Initially, parents ask the child to drink 4 ounces of water 15 minutes before bed and to refrain from wetting. If the child is able to accomplish this task, parents gradually increase the amount of water consumed prior to bedtime until the child is able to drink 8 to 10 ounces without wetting during the night.

Evaluations of FSHT indicate that it is slightly more effective at stopping nighttime wetting than using a urine alarm alone (see Table 16.2). Moreover, multicomponent treatments, like FSHT, are much better than urine alarm training alone at preventing relapse (Houts, 2010; Murphy & Carr, 2013).

Medication

Many physicians recommend medication for enuresis, either alone or in combination with behavioral interventions. However, medications are generally not regarded as long-term treatment options because they do not always reduce wetting and usually only work as long as children take them (Mikkelsen, 2015).

Desmopressin (DDAVP) is the most commonly prescribed medication for nocturnal enuresis. It is a synthetic version of vasopressin, the hormone that reduces nighttime urine production. DDAVP is usually administered as a nasal spray or freeze-dried medication that melts in the mouth. Approximately 25% to 60% of children prescribed DDAVP stay dry shortly after taking the medication; however, only about 20% remain dry after discontinuing it. DDAVP is also expensive; consequently, it is typically used on a short-term basis (e.g., during a sleepover) or in treatment-resistant cases (Chua et al., 2016; Mikkelsen, 2015).

Two other medications are less commonly used. Atomoxetine (Strattera), a selective norepinephrine reuptake inhibitor typically used to treat ADHD, has been prescribed for children with nocturnal enuresis. Atomoxetine increases arousal, allowing children to become more aware of full bladder sensations and thus inhibit nighttime urination. In a randomized controlled study, atomoxetine led to a small but significant reduction in nighttime wetting compared to placebo (Sumner, Schuh, Sutton, Lipetz, & Kelsey, 2006). Oxybutynin (Ditropan) is an antispasmic medication that is used to reduce the involuntary bladder contractions of children who engage in daytime wetting. Like DDAVP, however, oxybutynin is effective only when actively taken; relapse after discontinuation is 85% (Mellon & Houts, 2007).

Treatment of Daytime Enuresis

Much less information is known about the etiology and treatment of daytime wetting. Most children with diurnal enuresis are simply not cognizant of the fact that their bladder is full until it is too late. Even when parents and teachers prompt them to visit the bathroom because they are fidgeting, they seem largely unaware that they need to urinate. Prolonged use of Pull-Ups seems to keep incontinence outside children's awareness and decrease their motivation to remain dry (Christophersen & Friman, 2010).

Treatment for daytime wetting, therefore, has three main components: (1) help children recognize feelings of a full bladder, (2) increase their control over pelvic floor muscles so that they can inhibit urination until they reach the toilet, and (3) increase their functional bladder capacity so that they can delay urination for longer periods of time.

To increase children's awareness of their need to urinate, most clinicians ask children to engage in scheduled bathroom breaks during the course of the day. Children who remain dry during a discrete time period (e.g., all morning) are reinforced for this accomplishment. If possible, scheduled toileting should also occur at school. The child can be given "bathroom passes" during the school day. To discourage their abuse, reinforcement may be awarded for unused passes at the end of the day. Some children may also wear a urine monitor during the day so that even small amounts of daytime urination cannot go unnoticed.

To strengthen the muscles of the pelvic floor, clinicians might teach children to practice Kegel exercises—that is, repeatedly stopping and starting the flow of urine during a toileting episode (see Image 16.1). Kegel exercises, practiced at least three times a day, increase children's ability to inhibit urination.

To increase functional bladder capacity, children may engage in retention control training. Retention control training may help children hold more urine before excretion, thereby decreasing the frequency of urination. On weekends, some clinicians also suggest overlearning exercises—that is, asking children to drink progressively larger amounts of fluid during the day and avoid accidents (Christophersen & Friman, 2010).

Table 16.2   Effective Long-Term Treatment for Nocturnal Enuresis

Treatment	Success Rate (Dry 14 Consecutive Nights)	
	Immediately After Treatment	*One Year Later*
Urine alarm only	59–78%	34–43%
Multicomponent treatment	64–86%	45–75%

Source: Based on Houts (2010).

Note: Supplementing a urine alarm with cleanliness training, retention control training, and overlearning (e.g., multicomponent treatment) seems to reduce the likelihood of relapse.

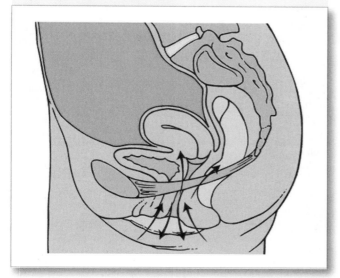

Image 16.1   Kegel exercises consist of repeatedly contracting and relaxing the muscles that form part of the pelvic floor, sometimes called the "Kegel muscles." Strengthening these muscles can help children reduce incontinence during the day.

Review:

- The treatment of enuresis requires coordination by medical and mental health professionals. Medical professionals must rule out physical causes for children's wetting prior to behavioral treatment.
- A urine alarm is the most effective single treatment for nocturnal enuresis. Secondary treatment can involve FSHT: (a) education and behavioral contracting, (b) urine alarm, (c) cleanliness training, (d) retention control training, and (e) overlearning.
- DDAVP, a synthetic vasopressin, is the most frequently used medication for nocturnal enuresis. It is effective in the short term, but most children experience relapse after discontinuation.

What Is Encopresis?

Description

Encopresis is the repeated passage of feces into inappropriate places, such as clothing or the floor. In most cases, the passage of feces is involuntary. However, some children's encopresis is intentional (e.g., defecating to upset parents). By definition, children must defecate inappropriately at least once a month for at least 3 months. Furthermore, they must be at least 4 years old. By definition, encopresis cannot be caused by a medication that typically causes incontinence, such as a laxative. Furthermore, it cannot be caused by a medical disorder, such as a bacterial or viral illness, that might result in accidents.

Although not part of the *Diagnostic and Statistical Manual of Mental Disorders* (*DSM-5*; American Psychiatric Association, 2013) diagnostic system, many clinicians differentiate primary encopresis from secondary encopresis. Primary encopresis is seen in children who have no history of controlling bowel movements. In contrast, secondary encopresis is characterized by the emergence of encopresis following a period of normal toilet use. It is important to determine the degree of volition and course of a child's encopresis, because this information can provide the clinician with clues regarding its cause and treatment. For example, a child with primary encopresis who has accidents during the day might benefit from systematic toilet training. In contrast, a child with secondary encopresis who deliberately defecates in his baby sister's crib might benefit from an intervention designed to address sibling rivalry or family stress (Mikkelsen, 2015).

Epidemiology

Approximately 3% of school-aged children in the United States meet diagnostic criteria for encopresis (Friman, 2008). Approximately 1.4% of 7-year-old children soil once a week, whereas 6.8% soil only occasionally (von Gontard, 2011). Boys are 4 to 6 times more likely than girls to develop the disorder (Campbell et al., 2009).

Associated Problems

Studies investigating the psychosocial functioning of children with encopresis have yielded mixed results. Some research indicates that these children are more likely to have behavioral or social–emotional problems than their peers without encopresis (Friman et al., 2009). Children with primary encopresis sometimes report less satisfying relationships, greater sadness, and more anxiety related to separation and social activities. Children with secondary encopresis and/or those who engage in deliberate defecation sometimes have experienced a recent stressful life event or show problems with oppositional and defiant behavior. All children with encopresis are at risk for low self-esteem and social problems, given the negative reactions they elicit from family and peers (Friman et al., 2009).

Approximately 30% of children with encopresis also show enuresis. Often, both disorders are caused by an enlarged colon, a result of prolonged constipation. The enlarged colon places pressure on the bladder, which contributes to wetting (Campbell et al., 2009).

What Causes Encopresis?

In 80% to 95% of cases, encopresis is caused by constipation and overflow incontinence (see Figure 16.2). Constipation usually develops because children do not defecate for a prolonged period of time. The reasons for delayed defecation are many: Children may be distracted by other activities (e.g., games, sports), children may not have easy access to a toilet (e.g., at school), children's diet may be restricted or irregular (e.g., too little fiber), or children may be experiencing periods of prolonged stress (e.g., moving). Oppositional and defiant children may simply refuse to use the toilet. Other children may feel embarrassed, ashamed, or unusually vulnerable when toileting. Still other children may experience discomfort or pain during a bowel movement and may subsequently avoid using the toilet (Friman, 2008).

Whatever the reason, fecal matter is retained in the anal canal, and the rectal wall is stretched to accommodate this mass. Retention has two consequences: (1) The rectum becomes enlarged, and (2) the nerves that line the rectum and allow the child to detect when it is full become less sensitive. Although fecal matter accumulates in the canal, children lose the normal sensation that they need to expel its contents.

Over time, water in the fecal mass is reabsorbed by the body. The mass becomes rocklike and difficult to pass. Through classical conditioning, the child quickly associates bowel movements with pain, increasing his avoidance of the toilet (Lyons-Ruth et al., 2014).

As new fecal matter continues to accumulate behind the fecal mass, it unexpectedly seeps around the mass, soiling the child's clothes. This new fecal matter usually resembles diarrhea. Consequently, many parents mistakenly administer antidiarrheal medication, which exacerbates the child's constipation (Mikkelsen, 2015).

As you might imagine, children who show constipation with overflow incontinence have little control over their encopresis. However, because they seldom complain of constipation, many parents misattribute their soiling to stubbornness, laziness, or defiance. Punitive discipline almost always increases children's frustration and decreases the likelihood that children will cooperate with parents to resolve the problem.

Approximately 15% of children with encopresis do not have constipation. Most of these children have primary nonretentive encopresis; they have never achieved bowel control and often have accidents in their clothing. These children often have developmental disabilities or neurological conditions that interfere with their ability to use the toilet. A few children, however, show secondary, nonretentive encopresis; they have bowel control but deliberately defecate in inappropriate places. These children are predominantly boys with histories of oppositional defiant behavior. However, some children develop encopresis following major life events, such as parental separation, hospitalization, or sexual abuse. Although sexual abuse is a possible cause of encopresis, children are more likely to have encopresis for other reasons. Encopresis is not routinely an indicator of sexual victimization (Friman, 2008).

Review:

- Encopresis is a *DSM-5* disorder characterized by the repeated passage of feces into inappropriate places whether involuntary or intentional. Children with encopresis must be at least 4 years of age, and the act must occur at least once per month for 3 months and cause distress or impairment.

Figure 16.2   Encopresis is usually caused by constipation with overflow.

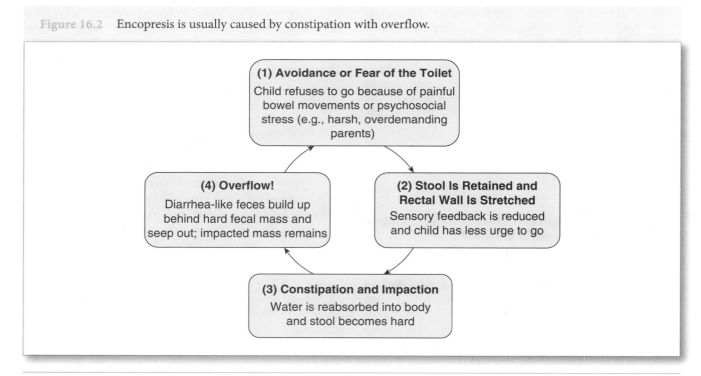

Source: Based on Butler (2008).

Note: Treatment involves relieving constipation and teaching children to use the toilet regularly.

- Most (80% to 95%) cases of encopresis are caused by constipation with overflow incontinence. Retention of feces leads to constipation, rectal stretching, and insensitivity. Children avoid passing feces because of pain, but experience involuntary discharge over time.
- Some youths have secondary, nonretentive encopresis. They have bowel control but voluntarily defecate in inappropriate places. These youths are predominantly boys with histories of oppositional defiant behavior.

What Treatments Are Effective for Children With Encopresis?

Treating encopresis caused by constipation involves collaboration among physicians, therapists, and families. Before treatment begins, the child should be evaluated by his pediatrician to rule out the possibility that his encopresis is caused by one of several rare medical disorders. For example, Hirschsprung's disease is a rare condition in which the nerves that control the muscles that line the colon wall are absent, causing a lack of sensory input (Williams et al., 2007). The pediatrician can also determine whether the child is suffering from constipation and, if so, prescribe a laxative or enema to relieve this condition. After the child's colon is cleaned, the physician will likely recommend a mild laxative (e.g., Miralax) for daily use to soften stools, increase motility in his digestive system, and decrease the likelihood of constipation in the future (Campbell et al., 2009).

Behavior therapy usually begins with an explanation of the causes of encopresis, specifically, constipation with overflow. Then, the therapist provides a rationale for treatment. Read the following Research to Practice section to see a portion of an initial discussion with a parent.

To get the child's "colon into shape," the therapist will likely recommend dietary changes that include increased fruits, vegetables, and whole grains; decreased dairy; and plenty of water.

Then, the child will be required to participate in scheduled toilet sitting. Approximately 15 to 20 minutes after breakfast and dinner, the child will be required to sit on the toilet for no more than 5 to 10 minutes with the intention to defecate. Parents should provide privacy and make the bathroom inviting to the child, perhaps by allowing him to read books or listen to music. It is also important for the toilet to be the correct size for the child and to have the child's feet supported to increase comfort.

To increase compliance with scheduled toileting, parents may provide small rewards for each successful time the child sits and larger rewards for successful defecation (Boles, Roberts, & Vernberg, 2010). To discourage soiling, parents may use cleanliness training and response cost. Cleanliness training requires the child to clean up after soiling (e.g., removing clothes and placing them in the laundry). Response cost involves withdrawing reinforcement following an accident. Parents may also engage in positive practice following an accident, to emphasize appropriate toilet sitting. For example, parents might require children to practice running to the toilet and sitting down numerous times (Friman et al., 2009).

Several randomized controlled studies indicate that combining behavioral treatments, like scheduled toilet sitting and positive reinforcement, is effective at reducing encopresis caused by constipation. Furthermore, behavioral interventions used in combination with laxatives often reduce encopresis more than the use of laxatives alone (Brazzelli, Griffiths, Cody, & Tappin, 2011).

Treatment for nonretentive encopresis (i.e., not caused by constipation) depends on the cause of the disorder. Children with primary nonretentive encopresis will usually benefit from toilet training. Recall that many

RESEARCH TO PRACTICE

EXPLAINING ENCOPRESIS TO FAMILIES

Therapist:	So, over time, Brad's colon has become enlarged and distended—it's much bigger and more stretchy than it should be. Also, the nerves surrounding it don't work right—they don't tell the brain when it's full. The result is that Brad can't tell when he needs to go.
Mom:	So, it's not his fault when he goes in his underwear?
Therapist:	No. He probably doesn't even know until it happens. Right?
Brad:	(Nods)
Therapist:	So, rewarding Brad for staying clean all day or punishing him for having an accident won't do any good. Making him feel bad about the accident also won't be helpful. Instead, we need to get his colon back into shape. Right now, it's like an out-of-shape, soft, flabby athlete who can't perform very well. We need Brad to train his colon to get back into shape so it can perform at the top of its game. He can do that by doing some exercises every day. You (Mom) can help him.

children who show this type of encopresis have developmental delays; consequently, the therapist must make sure that they have the cognitive ability to follow multiple-step commands necessary to successfully use the toilet (e.g., sit, wipe, wash). Children with secondary nonretentive encopresis should receive interventions that address possible causes of their soiling, before treating the encopresis itself. For example, oppositional defiant children, fearful children, or sexually abused children should receive treatment specific to these problems (Mikkelsen, 2015).

Review:

- The treatment of primary encopresis usually involves (a) education, (b) alleviation of constipation using laxatives, (c) dietary modification, and (d) scheduled toilet sitting with positive reinforcement.
- Treatment of secondary, nonretentive encopresis usually focuses on children's oppositional defiant behavior.

16.2 SLEEP–WAKE DISORDERS IN CHILDREN

What Are Sleep–Wake Disorders?

Although sleep is a natural process, the ability to fall asleep independently, stay asleep during the course of the night, and gain enough sleep to feel rested are skills that children must develop over the first few years of life. The development of these skills depends greatly on the maturation of their nervous system, children's temperament and behavior, and their parent's ability to foster healthy sleeping habits. Typically developing children show changes in their sleeping behavior and their sleep architecture (i.e., central nervous system activity) from birth through adolescence. As children's sleep patterns and architecture develop, sleep problems may emerge (see Table 16.3). Sleep–wake disorders are a large class of *DSM-5* conditions that are characterized by disruptions in a person's sleep patterns or dissatisfaction regarding the quality, timing, or amount of sleep. By definition, these disorders cause distress or impairment during the day (American Psychiatric Association, 2013; Lyons-Ruth et al., 2014).

Sleep disorders are identified using several methods. Usually, children's sleep problems are assessed through parental report. Psychologists may interview families about children's sleep habits, quality, and environment (Cortese et al., 2013). To screen for possible sleep disorders, some professionals use the acronym BEARS:

- Are there *bedtime difficulties* or problems going to sleep?
- Does the child seem *excessively sleepy* during the day?
- Does the child *awaken during the night* and can't go back to sleep?
- Does the child have a *regular sleep–wake schedule*?
- Does the child *snore* or have trouble breathing during sleep?

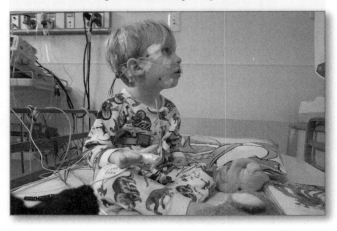

Image 16.2 This boy is preparing for a sleep study to determine the cause of his sleep problems. Polysomnography will measure his brain activity (EEG), eye movements (EOG), muscle activity or skeletal muscle activation (EMG), heart rhythm (ECG), and respiration during sleep.

Source: Photo courtesy of Robert Lawton.

Parents may also complete a sleep log or diary to record children's sleeping and waking. To obtain a more objective estimate of children's sleep duration and quality, children may wear an actometer. This small device attaches to the child's leg or child's arm and provides a reliable and accurate measure of nighttime activity.

The "gold standard" for assessing sleep is a polysomnogram (PSG) or "sleep study" (Crabtree & Williams, 2009). To perform a PSG, children must spend the night in the hospital while their sleep is monitored (see Image 16.2). Brain activity (electroencephalogram, or EEG), eye movements (electrooculogram, or EOG), muscle activation (electromyograph, or EMG), and heart rhythm (electrocardiogram, or ECG) are assessed. A PSG can assess sleep duration and quality, detect abnormalities in sleep architecture, and identify breathing-related sleep problems (Miano et al., 2016). For example, Figure 16.3 shows the sleep architecture of a typically developing child. Physicians can monitor the child's sleep cycle and notice periods in this cycle where sleep–wake disorders are most likely to emerge.

Sleep disorders can cause distress and impairment in children (O'Brien, 2009). Older children and adolescents with sleep disorders may exhibit the same signs and symptoms as adults (e.g., yawning, drowsiness). Most younger children show paradoxical symptoms such as overactivity, impulsiveness, and irritability. Sleep problems are associated with impairment in attention, concentration, and problem-solving. Not surprisingly, youths with sleep problems sometimes experience behavioral and academic difficulties in school (Mindell & Owens, 2015).

Sleep disorders can be equally disruptive to parents. The caregivers of children with sleep disorders often

Table 16.3   Sleep Behavior, Architecture, and Possible Problems Across Development

Age	Behavior	Architecture	Possible Problems
Newborn	Sleeps in 3–4 hour segments spread evenly across a 34–hour period; sleeps 16–18 hours/day	Enters REM after falling asleep; most sleep is spent in REM; other stages are indistinct	Depends on parents to fall asleep and return to sleep, but this is considered normal
2–4 months	At 3 months, infants become entrained to a 24 hour sleep-wake cycle; they can sleep more during the night than day; they can self-soothe and return to sleep if awakened during the night	Infants begin entering non-REM after falling asleep; less time is spent in REM	Infants may have problems falling asleep without parent's help
6–12 months	By 9 months, most children sleep through the night (6–7 hours); total sleep is 14–15 hours with 2–3 daytime naps	By 6 months, infants have circadian rhythm that remains stable until puberty; non-REM stages are distinct (like adults)	Infants may have problems falling asleep or returning to sleep without parent's help; night wakings or problems "sleeping through the night"
1–2 years	Total sleep is 12–14 hours with one daytime nap	REM declines to 30% of child's total sleep time by age 3 years	Child shows separation anxiety; may refuse separations at bedtime
3–5 years	Total sleep is 11–12 hours; napping stops in 75% of children by age 5 years	Sleep cycle increases to 90 minutes (like adults)	Cognitive development makes nighttime fears common; children may refuse going to bed; arousal disorders may occur; some children show sleep apnea
6–12 years	Children require 10–11 hours of sleep but usually do not get enough; sleep latency (time till sleep) is about 20 minutes	By late childhood, most children show adult-like sleep cycle	Children may stall or refuse to go to bed; some children show insomnia due to anxiety
12–18 years	Adolescents need 9–11 hours of sleep but usually do not get enough; delay in circadian rhythm causes a desire to stay up late and rise later in the day	With puberty, adolescents show phase delay in melatonin which delays circadian rhythm	Adolescents may show anxiety-related insomnia; school and other activities encroach on sleep time causing daytime sleepiness

Source: Adapted from Owens and Burnham (2009) and Reite, Weissberg, and Ruddy (2009).

report many of the same symptoms as their children: daytime drowsiness and fatigue, concentration problems, irritability, and dysphoria. Parenting a child with sleep problems can be extremely stressful, especially when parents are plagued by other psychosocial hardships (e.g., marital discord, single-parent status, irregular work schedules). The relationship between children's sleep problems and parental distress is also bidirectional: Children's problems cause, and are exacerbated by, parenting stress (Ivanenko & Johnson, 2015).

Approximately 25% of children experience a sleep problem at some point in their development. *DSM-5* recognizes 20 sleep–wake disorders. We will focus on five disorders most frequently seen in children: (1) insomnia disorder, (2) circadian rhythm sleep disorder, (3) sleep arousal disorders, (4) nightmare disorder, and (5) obstructive sleep apnea hypopnea (Ivanenko & Johnson, 2015).

Review:

- Sleep–wake disorders are a class of *DSM-5* disorders characterized by disruptions in sleep patterns or dissatisfaction regarding the quality, timing, or amount of sleep. They cause distress or impairment during the day.
- A child's sleep architecture can be assessed using a PSG that assesses brain activity (EEG), eye movements (EOG), muscle activation (EMG), and heart rhythm (ECG) over the course of the night.

What Is Pediatric Insomnia?

Description

Insomnia disorder is the most common sleep problem experienced by youths. It is defined by dissatisfaction with the quantity or quality of sleep (see Table 16.4). It is

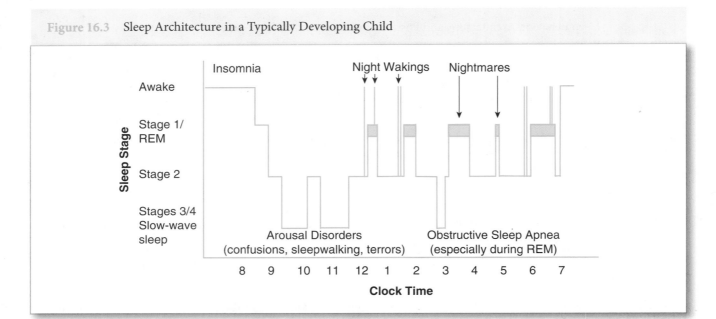

Figure 16.3   Sleep Architecture in a Typically Developing Child

Source: Adapted from Leu & Rosen (2008).

Note: The sleep cycle (relaxed awake, non-REM, REM) repeats throughout the night with periodic night waking and returning to sleep. Possible sleep disorders by title describe where cyclic disruptions most frequently occur.

Table 16.4   Diagnostic Criteria for Insomnia Disorder

A.   A predominant complaint of dissatisfaction with sleep quantity or quality, associated with one (or more) of the following symptoms:

   1.   Difficulty initiating sleep. (In children, this may manifest as difficulty initiating sleep without caregiver intervention.)

   2.   Difficulty maintaining sleep, characterized by frequent awakening or problems returning to sleep after awakenings. (In children, this may manifest as difficulty returning to sleep without caregiver intervention.)

   3.   Early-morning awakening with inability to return to sleep.

B.   The sleep disturbance causes clinically significant distress or impairment in social, occupational, educational, academic, behavioral, or other important areas of functioning.

C.   The sleep difficulty occurs at least 3 nights per week.

D.   The sleep difficulty is present for at least 3 months.

E.   The sleep difficulty occurs despite adequate opportunity for sleep.

F.   The insomnia is not better explained by and does not occur exclusively during the course of another sleep-wake disorder.

G.   The insomnia is not attributable to the physiological effects of a substance (e.g., a drug of abuse, a medication).

H.   Coexisting mental disorders and medical conditions do not adequately explain the predominant complaint of insomnia.

Source: Reprinted with permission from the *Diagnostic and Statistical Manual of Mental Disorders, Fifth Edition* (Copyright 2013). American Psychiatric Association.

noteworthy that dissatisfaction can be reported by either the child or her parents. Because infants and younger children typically do not report sleep problems, the diagnosis of insomnia depends on the degree to which children's sleep problems affect parents. Two children might show the same problems with bedtime refusal or nighttime waking; however, only one child (whose parent is upset by her child's sleep habits) might be diagnosed (Meltzer & Mindell, 2014).

Insomnia depends on the age and development of the child. Infants and toddlers typically have problems going to sleep and returning to sleep when they awaken during the night. Preschoolers and school-aged children may stall during bedtime or refuse to go to sleep. Older children and adolescents may have difficulty with anxiety, which interferes with their ability to sleep (Reid, Huntley, & Lewin, 2009).

Sleep problems must occur at least 3 nights per week. Furthermore, problems must persist for at least 3 months to qualify for "persistent" insomnia. Sleep problems of shorter duration are labeled as either acute (< 1 month) or subacute (1–3 months).

Epidemiology

Sleep problems are common among children. Approximately 25% to 50% of parents report at least occasional problems with their children's sleep. Sleep disorders are more prevalent in early childhood and decline with development. For example, the prevalence of significant sleep problems in infants and toddlers (25%), preschoolers and school-age children (10%), and adolescents (5%) declines with age. Sleep problems are especially common among youths with intellectual disability (ID; 30%–80%), autism spectrum disorder (ASD; 50%–70%), and chronic health problems (Ivanenko & Johnson, 2015).

Review:

- Insomnia is a *DSM-5* sleep–wake disorder characterized by difficulty or dissatisfaction with sleep quantity or quality. It is associated with problems going to sleep, remaining sleep, or returning to sleep. It occurs at least 3 nights per week for 3 months and causes distress or impairment.
- Approximately 25% of infants and toddlers, 10% of preschoolers and school-age children, and 5% of adolescents experience problems with insomnia.

What Causes Insomnia in Children?

Insomnia manifests itself in various ways, depending on children's age and development. Consequently, there is no single cause for insomnia. Nevertheless, several comprehensive models for childhood insomnia have been developed. These models assume that insomnias depend on characteristics of the child, characteristics of the parent, and the interactions between both members of the dyad (see Figure 16.4). For example, certain children are at risk for sleep problems, such as infants who have trouble falling asleep because of difficult temperament, children who wake during the night because of medical problems, and adolescents with generalized anxiety disorder (GAD) who worry while lying in bed. Certain parents are also less likely to respond effectively to their children's sleep difficulties. For example, some parents might not recognize the importance of sleep to children's health and well-being. Other parents who

experience psychosocial stress (e.g., single parents, parents working multiple jobs), might have trouble establishing regular bedtime routines. Indeed, children's sleep disorders are associated with parental risk factors, such as stress, fatigue, poor physical health, depression, and family disruption (Badin, Haddad, & Shatkin, 2016; Reid et al., 2009).

Difficulty Falling Asleep Alone

The most common sleep problem shown by infants is difficulty falling asleep independently. Between birth and 6 months of age, most infants rely on parents to regulate their behavior and emotions sufficiently to fall asleep. At 6 or 7 months of age, however, healthy infants begin to develop the capacity for self-soothing, which allows them to fall asleep on their own.

Problems occur when parents do not allow their children to acquire self-soothing skills. Approximately 12% to 30% of older infants and toddlers in the United States sleep in their parents' bed. Although the acceptability of co-sleeping varies considerably based on families' cultural backgrounds and child-rearing histories, co-sleeping is a risk factor for childhood insomnia. Parents may condition their infants to fall asleep while being held, rocked, carried, cuddled, or fed. Through classical conditioning, infants learn to associate sleep with these external stimuli and are unable to fall asleep without them. Co-sleeping or putting the infant or toddler to bed after she falls asleep is associated with problems falling asleep independently, more nighttime waking, and overall reduced sleep quality (Mindell, Sadeh, Kwon, & Goh, 2013; Reid et al., 2009).

Night Waking

Infants who are conditioned to fall asleep only with the help of their parents are likely to experience problems with night waking. Most infants and toddlers wake four to six times each night—that is, about every 90 to 120 minutes. These brief wakings correspond to their sleep cycles. Most older infants and children are able to rely on self-soothing techniques (e.g., sucking on fingers, cuddling with a blanket) and return to sleep. However, children who have been conditioned to fall asleep only with parental help will have difficulty returning to sleep. Instead, they may wake parents several times during the night, expecting their assistance. This behavior results in not only fragmented sleep on the part of the infant but also sleep loss on the part of the parent (Owens, Chervin, & Hoppin, 2014).

Bedtime Resistance or Struggles

After children are mobile and verbal, they may exhibit sleep refusal. Typically, bedtime resistance begins when children make seemingly reasonable requests to parents shortly before or after bedtime: Can you read one more story? Can you talk with me just a little longer? Can I have a drink of water? It is not unusual for children to make

Figure 16.4   Understanding Childhood Insomnia

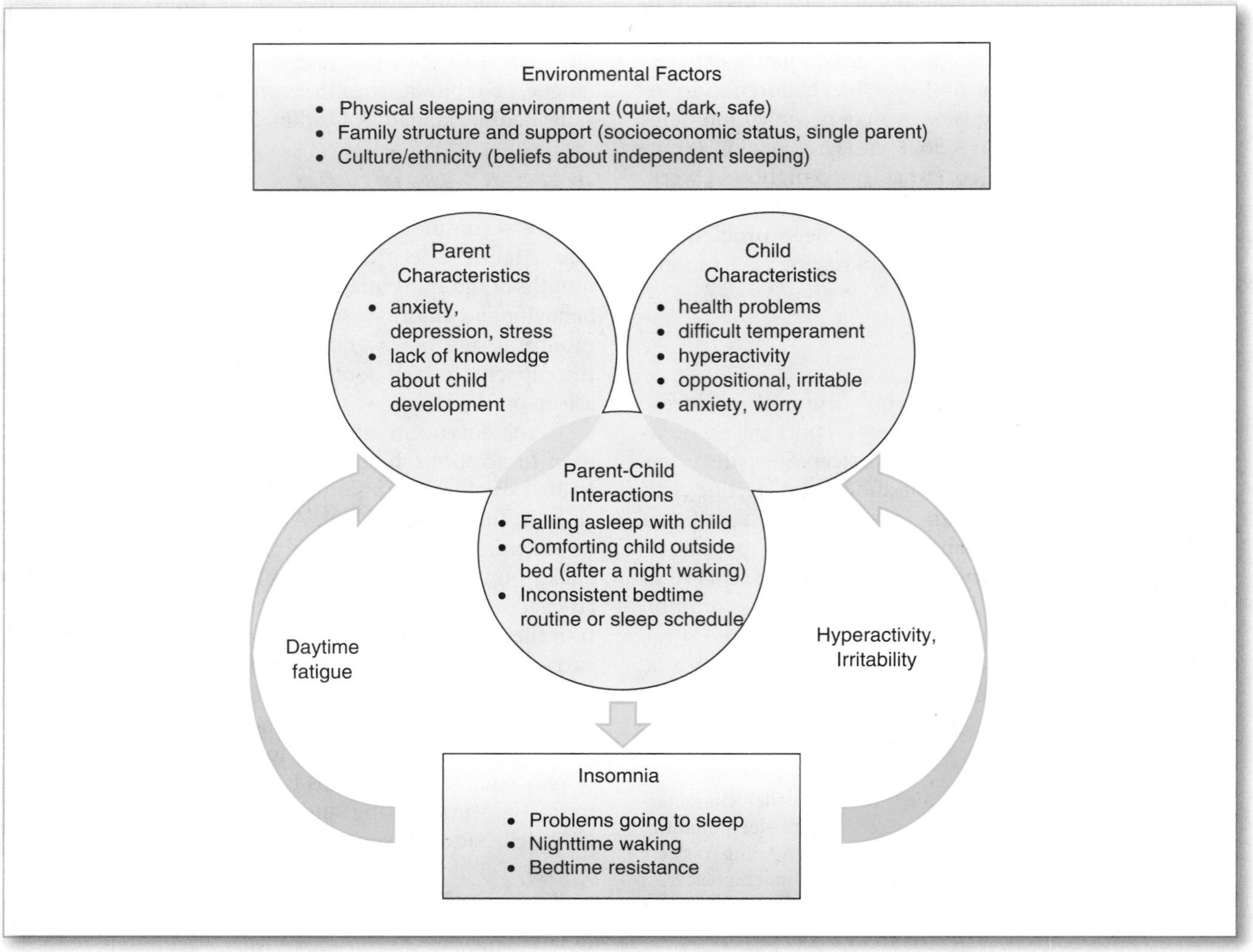

Source: Adapted from Owens & Burnham (2009) and Reite et al. (2009).

Note: Children's problems going to sleep and staying sleep depend on characteristics of the parent, child, and environment.

multiple "curtain calls" after being put to bed. These requests typically delay sleep onset and cause sleep loss (Ivanenko & Johnson, 2015).

Problems arise when parents occasionally give in to children's requests. When parents acquiesce, children are positively reinforced for their resistant behavior on a variable ratio schedule (the most difficult type to extinguish). Furthermore, parents are negatively reinforced for giving in to their children's requests: They temporarily satisfy their children and keep them quiet! Inconsistent bedtime schedules and routines exacerbate bedtime refusal. Parents inadvertently train their children to delay or refuse bedtime (Lyons-Ruth et al., 2014).

Even moderate delays in children's bedtimes, if they occur repeatedly, can adversely affect their daytime functioning. In an experimental study, researchers assessed the sleep habits and cognitive functioning of school-aged children for 2 days. On the third day of the study, families were randomly assigned to two treatment conditions. Some parents were told to keep their children up 1 hour later than usual; the parents of other children were told to put their children to bed 1 hour earlier than usual. After 3 days of either restricted or extended sleep, the researchers reassessed children's functioning. They found that the sleep-restricted children had poorer sleep quality and more night wakings than children who went to bed early. Furthermore, sleep-restricted children scored significantly lower on several measures of attention and concentration. Allowing children to stay up for "one more TV show" each night can take its toll over time (Ivanenko & Johnson, 2015).

Anxiety or Impulsivity

Older children and adolescents often have difficulty falling asleep because of anxiety. Children with separation anxiety disorder (SAD) may fear harm befalling their parents. Adolescents with GAD may worry about events scheduled for the following day. Even youths without anxiety disorders may adopt maladaptive ways of thinking that predispose them to anxiety and arousal. During the day, these youths can distract themselves from anxiety with school, social activities, extracurricular involvement, and media. At night, when lying in bed, these anxiety-provoking cognitions may emerge (Alfano, Zakem, Costa, Taylor, & Weems, 2009).

The most common cognitive distortion is *catastrophizing*—the tendency to expect the worst possible outcomes from a specific situation. For example, a child might worry about failing a test the following day and losing the respect of his parents and teacher. Another common error is *selective abstraction*, a cognitive bias in which events are taken out of context in a way that emphasizes their negative elements and downplays their positive elements. For example, an adolescent remembering a party that she attended that evening might recall only an embarrassing interaction with a former boyfriend rather than the good time she had with friends. A third cognitive error is *personalization*, in which the person erroneously attributes a negative event to her own actions. For example, an older adolescent might believe that her boyfriend did not call her that evening because he is mad at her when, in actuality, her boyfriend was simply working late (Gregory et al., 2009).

Adolescents often try to cope with bedtime anxieties by remaining in bed and forcing themselves to sleep. However, anxiety and sleep are antithetical processes: They cannot occur simultaneously. Sleep requires relaxation and inhibition; it makes us vulnerable to our surroundings. In contrast, anxiety makes us aroused, apprehensive, and vigilant. Adolescents who try to force themselves to sleep often experience increased frustration and tension. Other adolescents attempt to distract themselves by watching TV, using social media, or texting friends. Stimulating activities like these usually increase arousal, prolong sleep onset, and increase sleep loss (Hysing, Pallesen, Stormark, Lundervold, & Siversten, 2013).

Of course, children's sleep problems emerge in the context of their broader social and cultural surroundings. These environmental factors include the physical sleeping environment (e.g., Does the child have a safe, quiet, and dark room in which to sleep?), family structure and resources (e.g., Does Mom need to get up early the next morning for work?), and cultural or ethnic beliefs and values (e.g., Is it appropriate to allow children to sleep in their parents' bed?). Even within the United States, families from different cultural backgrounds report diverse values and habits regarding children's sleep (Giannotti & Cortesi, 2009).

Approximately 30% of children with ADHD also have problems falling and staying asleep (Mayes, Calhoun, Bixler, & Vgontzas, 2009). There are three possible explanations for this high comorbidity. First, problems with behavioral inhibition, which underlie ADHD symptoms, may also interfere with children's ability to soothe themselves to sleep. Indeed, most parents of children with ADHD report that their children have problems with repetitive movements and restlessness during sleep. However, sleep studies have usually not shown differences in the sleep architecture of youths with and without ADHD. Second, stimulant medication used to treat ADHD may cause insomnia. In these cases, insomnia is caused by the treatment of ADHD, not ADHD itself. Third, the effects of medication used to treat ADHD typically lose their efficacy in the evening. It is possible that as the medication wears off, symptoms of hyperactivity–impulsivity emerge and interfere with sleep (Corkum, Davidson, Tan-MacNeill, & Weiss, 2014; Gregory, Agnew-Blais, Matthews, Moffitt, & Arseneault, 2016).

Review:

- Infants and toddlers may develop insomnia if they rely on parents to fall asleep or return to sleep during the night.
- Younger children often exhibit bedtime refusal. Parents may positively reinforce their bids to stay up past their bedtime or allow children to sleep with them.
- Older children may experience insomnia because of anxiety exacerbated by cognitive distortions. Insomnia is also frequently seen in children with ADHD.

What Treatments Are Effective for Youths With Insomnia?

Behavior Therapy for Infants and Young Children

Infants must be taught to fall asleep independently and return to sleep when they awaken during the night. To help them learn this skill, parents should enforce a consistent bedtime routine that helps infants relax (e.g., bathing, dressing, changing). Infants should be put to bed at the same time each night. Furthermore, parents should place the infant awake, but drowsy, in the crib and leave the room. Parents may also give an older infant a transitional object, such as a small blanket or doll to help the child soothe himself to sleep (Owens & Burnham, 2009).

Mindell, Telpfski, Wiegand, and Kurtz (2009) demonstrated the efficacy of consistency in improving the sleep quality of infants and toddlers. A large sample of mothers of children (aged 7–18 months) were randomly assigned to two conditions. Half of the sample were instructed to put their children to bed at a consistent time each night, using a bedtime routine. The other half served as a no-treatment control group. After 3 weeks, infants and toddlers in the intervention group showed improved sleep habits: less time spent falling asleep, fewer and shorter night wakings, and better moods when rising in the morning. Furthermore, mothers of children in the intervention group experienced significant improvement in their mood and energy levels compared to mothers in the control group. The simple intervention benefited both members of the dyad!

Consistency alone will not correct all problems with insomnia. Other interventions should be used, depending on the child's age and specific problem. Extinction appears to be most effective in treating infants and toddlers who have problems falling asleep independently or returning to sleep after waking during the night. Recall that these problems arise through classical conditioning; infants associate falling asleep with the presence of a certain person (parent), object (bottle), or condition (being held) and they cannot fall asleep alone. Extinction involves placing the child in the crib without the stimulus he associates with sleep. The goal is for the child to learn self-soothing techniques so that he can fall asleep independently (Mindell & Owens, 2015).

Parents can practice extinction in several ways. The quickest treatment method is *planned ignoring*. Parents simply place their fed, dry, and drowsy infant in the crib and leave the room. The infant will likely cry because he is not provided with the conditions he has learned are necessary for sleep (e.g., mom, bottle). The parents ignore the infant's cries until sleep overcomes the infant. Needless to say, planned ignoring is stressful on parents and infants. Indeed, many infants will show an extinction burst—that is, an initial increase in the intensity or duration of their cries after the implementation of the extinction procedure. The parent's job is to extinguish these cries by continuing to ignore the infant until he falls asleep independently. After several nights of training, infants are usually able to fall asleep (or return to sleep) alone (Mindell & Owens, 2015).

Many parents find it difficult to ignore their infant's cries. In fact, some parents will initially allow their infants to cry, only later giving in to their protests and providing them with comfort or food. The practice of initially ignoring and then reinforcing children is problematic. In effect, parents are reinforcing children on an intermittent schedule, training them to cry longer and louder to receive the comfort they demand (Owens & Burnham, 2009).

An alternative, slightly less aversive technique is *graduated ignoring*. In graduated ignoring, parents place their fed, dry, and drowsy child in the crib and leave the room. Then, they ignore the infant's cries for a specified period of time

(e.g., 5 minutes). After that time, they may enter the room, check in on their infant, and briefly provide comfort (e.g., kiss, caress). Parents then leave the room again and ignore the child's cries for another specified period of time. The process repeats until the child falls asleep. It is important to note that the parent's decision to enter the room is based on time intervals; it is not contingent on the infant's crying. The infant is never reinforced for his protests. Some therapists recommend increasing the time intervals gradually over the course of a single night (e.g., 5 minutes until the first check-in, 10 minutes until the next check-in). Other therapists recommend increasing the intervals each night (e.g., 5-minute intervals on Monday, 10-minute intervals on Tuesday).

A third option is *bedtime fading*. This technique uses the infant's need for sleep to help her overcome her insomnia. Parents put their infant in the crib 30 minutes after her usual bedtime. If the infant does not fall asleep quickly, parents remove her from the crib for another 30 minutes and then put her back to bed. This process is repeated until the child falls asleep quickly when placed in the crib. The next night, the child is placed in the crib 30 minutes earlier than she fell asleep the night before. The child's bedtime is gradually "faded" to her regular bedtime on each subsequent night.

Considerable research supports the use of all three behavioral treatments. Overall, 94% of children show clinically significant improvement in sleep after families implement these interventions. Furthermore, 80% of children maintain these improvements in sleep duration and quality over time. Planned ignoring typically works more quickly than graduated ignoring and bedtime fading. Treatment for insomnia is also associated with improvements in parents' sleep quality, sleep duration, daytime mood and behavior, and interactions with their children (Owens & Burnham, 2009).

Cognitive–Behavioral Therapy for
Older Children and Adolescents

Cognitive–behavioral interventions may be especially helpful in treating insomnia in older children and adolescents. Recall that anxiety often interferes with the ability of these

Table 16.5   Sleep Hygiene for Families

Make sure the child's bedroom is safe, dark, and quiet

Establish a regular bedtime routine which may include bathing, putting on pajamas, and story time

No arousing stimuli before bed (e.g., television, video games, bright lights, sports)

Put the child to bed at the same time, 7 days/week (no late nights on weekends)

For infants, put the child to bed drowsy but awake so she learns to fall asleep independently

Put the child to bed without a bottle, music, or television

Maintain daytime naps through age 3 or 4 to avoid sleep deprivation

For children and adolescents, avoid caffeine in the evening

Source: Adapted from Owens and Burnham (2009).

adolescents to fall asleep or return to sleep when awakened. Consequently, treatment targets the behavior and thoughts that elicit anxiety (Alvaro, Roberts, & Harris, 2014).

Nearly all therapists begin treatment by helping adolescents establish effective sleep hygiene—that is, the behaviors and environmental conditions that promote restful sleep (see Table 16.5). It is especially important (and difficult) for older children and adolescents to have predictable sleep–wake schedules, to avoid caffeine and other substances that might inhibit sleep, and to refrain from highly stimulating activities prior to bedtime (e.g., exercise, video games).

In addition, cognitive–behavior therapists incorporate several other components into treatment (Dewald-Kaufmann, Oort, & Meijer, 2014; Meltzer et al., 2014):

- *Relaxation training*: Adolescents might learn anxiety-reduction techniques, such as progressive muscle relaxation, focused breathing, or guided imagery. These techniques would be taught during therapy sessions, practiced at home, and used prior to bedtime.
- *Stimulus control*: If adolescents do not fall asleep within 20 to 30 minutes of going to bed, they are instructed to leave the bedroom and engage in another quiet activity (e.g., reading) until they feel sleepy. Stimulus control is designed to help adolescents associate the bedroom with sleeping (not homework, eating, socializing) and to extinguish the association between the bedroom and feelings of anxiety or frustration.
- *Sleep restriction*: Sleep restriction involves limiting the total amount of time the adolescent is in bed. First, the adolescent monitors her usual sleep habits and determines the total number of hours she sleeps each night. Then, the adolescent is told to limit the number of hours she spends in bed to the average number of hours she sleeps. Sleep restriction and stimulus control, together, improve sleep efficiency—that is, the number of hours the adolescent is in bed *and* asleep.

RESEARCH TO PRACTICE

CHALLENGING IRRATIONAL BELIEFS ABOUT SLEEP

Lindsay:	When I lie in bed at night I can hear the clock ticking in the hallway, and I know I've been in bed for hours. I just can't stop myself from thinking about the day and the things that I need to do tomorrow.
Therapist:	The things you *need* to do tomorrow? Like what?
Lindsay:	You know. I promised to call Jessie and talk with her about our service project that's scheduled for next week. I'm also supposed to help Savannah with a Spanish assignment she's having trouble with. Then, there's my own homework to worry about!
Therapist:	That's a lot of things to remember. But I wonder if what you said is true?
Lindsay:	What did I say?
Therapist:	You said you start thinking about all the things you *need* to do the next day. I'm wondering if that's true. Do you really *need* to do all those things?
Lindsay:	Of course! Otherwise, I'll let everyone down and look like a bad friend.
Therapist:	Okay. Let's look at it more carefully—and clearly. Would you want Jessie or Savannah staying up all night worrying about all the things they promised to do for you?
Lindsay:	Of course not.
Therapist:	If Jessie or Savannah forgot to call or help you and then apologized the next day for forgetting, would you be really angry? Would you think they were bad friends?
Lindsay:	No, of course not. I'd understand that they have a lot going on.
Therapist:	But you hold yourself up to a higher standard. You think that these tasks are things that you *need* to do rather than things you would *like* to do.
Lindsay:	Yes, I'd like to do these things and be a good friend . . .
Therapist:	But you don't absolutely *need* to do them. You can still be a good friend if you forget sometimes or don't get around to it because of your schedule.
Lindsay:	I wouldn't like it, but I guess you're right.
Therapist:	So tonight, when you're thinking about all the things you *need* to do tomorrow, try changing the word "need" to "like"—all the things you'd *like* to do tomorrow. And if you don't get to them, it's okay. Your friends will understand. Let's practice right now.

- *Cognitive restructuring:* Adolescents learn to correct maladaptive thoughts that elicit anxiety and interfere with sleep. Cognitive restructuring involves three steps: (1) identifying distorted or irrational beliefs, (2) challenging the validity of these beliefs, and (3) replacing these incorrect beliefs with more rational, realistic beliefs. Consider the following Research to Practice section in which a therapist helps her adolescent client challenge irrational thoughts that keep her awake.

Psychologists also recommend interventions to combat nighttime worries. For example, adolescents might be encouraged to keep a to-do list for important tasks. If a task is on the list, they do not need to worry about it at bedtime. Similarly, adolescents may keep a "worry diary"—a journal in which they describe their worries. Adolescents set aside time each day to update the diary. If they find themselves worrying at bedtime, they remind themselves, "Now's not the time for that; I'll worry about that in my journal tomorrow." Other psychologists teach adolescents guided imagery to help them direct their attention to positive, relaxing events before bedtime. For example, adolescents might imagine hiking in the mountains, relaxing on the beach, or swimming in a coral reef (Buckhalt, Wolfson, & El-Sheikh, 2009; Newman, Llera, Erickson, Przeworski, & Castonguay, 2013).

Medication

Medication is the most commonly used treatment for pediatric insomnia. In a recent, epidemiological study, physicians were much more likely to prescribe medication to treat pediatric sleep problems (81%) than recommend behavior or cognitive therapy (22%). Unfortunately, there are no medications approved by the US Food and Drug Administration (FDA) to treat insomnia in children and adolescents. Furthermore, there is very little research supporting the efficacy of these medications with children. Nevertheless, physicians often recommend these medications to help children sleep (Pelayo & Huseni, 2016).

The most frequently prescribed medications for pediatric insomnia are alpha-adrenergic agonists, such as clonidine (Catapres). These medications are typically used to treat hypertension in adults. They decrease blood pressure by lowering heart rate and relaxing blood vessels. They have sedating effects and, consequently, are helpful in promoting sleep. These medications are most often used to help children with ADHD and other neurodevelopmental disorders fall asleep. Side effects include lightheadedness, dry mouth, and dizziness. Children can overdose from these medications, so their use must be carefully monitored by their physician and parents (Owens & Moturi, 2009).

The most frequently used over-the-counter medications for children's sleep problems are antihistamines. Histamines are neurotransmitters that regulate the body's immune system. They increase vascular permeability, causing fluid to escape from capillaries into bodily tissues. Consequently, they produce runny nose and watery eyes.

Most antihistamines block histamine receptors, reducing these effects. Antihistamines, such as diphenhydramine (Benadryl), produce drowsiness and sedation, which make them conducive to sleep. These medications are generally not appropriate for the long-term treatment of insomnia because they can lead to daytime drowsiness and can impair the quality of sleep if used habitually (Ivanenko & Johnson, 2010).

A third group of medications are the benzodiazepines (Neubauer, 2014). These medications act on receptors for gamma-aminobutyric acid (GABA), the body's most important inhibitory neurotransmitter. Traditional benzodiazepines, such as temazepam (Restoril), estazolam (ProSom), and quazepam (Doral), bind to major GABA receptors and produce marked sedation. Newer benzodiazepines bind only to specific GABA receptors. They produce sedation and anxiety reduction; consequently, they are referred to as "hypnotics." Examples of these newer medications are eszopiclone (Lunesta), zaleplon (Sonata), and zolpidem (Ambien). Unfortunately, all of these medications can reduce the quality of sleep when used habitually. Furthermore, individuals can develop tolerance for these medications and experience increased sleep problems after discontinuing their use.

Review:

- Behavior therapy for infants and toddlers often includes planned or graduated ignoring in which the child's bids to stay up are extinguished over time. Although effective in the long term, treatment can cause families distress in the short term.
- Most interventions for older children and adolescents' sleep problems begin with improving sleep hygiene. Techniques might include restricting caffeine and electronic devices prior to bedtime; engaging in a bedtime ritual; and sleeping in a dark, quiet environment.
- Cognitive–behavioral therapy (CBT) for older children and adolescents involves (1) relaxation training, (2) stimulus control, (3) sleep restriction during the day, and (4) cognitive restructuring to reduce anxiety.
- Alpha-adrenergic agonists and antihistamines are sometimes used for pediatric insomnia. Benzodiazepines are effective as a short-term treatment for insomnia but can cause tolerance and withdrawal if used habitually.

What Other Sleep–Wake Disorders Can Affect Children?

Circadian Rhythm Sleep–Wake Disorder

By early childhood, children become entrained to a sleep–wake cycle that causes them to rise and sleep at approximately the same times each day. This circadian (i.e., "about a day") rhythm is regulated by environmental cues and hormones that influence fatigue and arousal, such as melatonin and cortisol (Abbott, Reid, & Zee, 2015).

Many adolescents experience a delay in melatonin and cortisol secretion shortly after the onset of puberty. This delay can cause a corresponding phase delay in the circadian rhythm. We can see this phase delay in adolescents (including college students) who prefer to stay up until 2:00 or 3:00 a.m. and wake at 10:00 or 11:00 a.m. Problems arise when there is a mismatch between the adolescent's endogenous circadian rhythm and the sleep–wake cycle required by his social environment. High school students and younger college students know the difficulty of going to bed late and waking for an early morning class after only a few hours of sleep!

Circadian rhythm sleep–wake disorder describes the recurrent inability to fall asleep and wake at conventionally appropriate times. These sleep patterns lead to insomnia and/or daytime sleepiness and impairment in the youth's daytime functioning (American Psychiatric Association, 2013).

Approximately 7% to 10% of adolescents meet diagnostic criteria for circadian rhythm sleep–wake disorder. It can cause adolescents considerable distress and impairment. Some adolescents become upset when they cannot fall asleep at an appropriate hour because they know they need to rise early the next morning. Other adolescents, who wake up early for school, experience accumulated sleep loss, resulting in daytime fatigue, attention–concentration problems, and academic difficulties. Frustration over their sleep schedule and accumulated sleep loss can also contribute to dysphoria (Leu & Rosen, 2008).

The treatment of circadian rhythm sleep–wake disorder involves matching the adolescent's internal sleep–wake cycle to the expectations of his social environment (e.g., school or work). Some psychologists refer to this adjustment in the adolescent's sleep–wake cycle as chronotherapy. Chronotherapy can be performed in two ways. One method involves gradually advancing the adolescent's bedtime in 15-minute intervals over the course of several weeks. For example, an adolescent who feels the need to sleep at 2:00 a.m. might establish a bedtime of 1:45 a.m. for several nights until he falls asleep at that time. Then, he would move his bedtime forward another 15 minutes until eventually he is able to fall asleep at the desired hour (Burgess & Emens, 2016).

A second method is to delay bedtime by several hours each night until the desired bedtime is achieved. For example, an adolescent who feels the need to sleep at 2:00 a.m. might delay bedtime until 7:00 a.m. On each successive night, he might delay bedtime an additional 4 hours (i.e., 11:00 a.m., 3:00 p.m., 7:00 p.m.) until he reaches his desired bedtime. Although effective, this method can be very disruptive to the adolescent's daytime activities.

Many therapists supplement chronotherapy with synthetic melatonin supplements and light stimulation. Melatonin, a dietary supplement sold at many health food stores, mimics the body's natural sleep hormone. At low doses, it may produce mild drowsiness and promote sleep. It is typically taken shortly before bedtime. Upon waking, adolescents are instructed to expose themselves to an array of high-intensity artificial light (or natural sunlight if available) to increase arousal (Buckhalt et al., 2009).

Some data suggest that chronotherapy is effective in treating circadian rhythm sleep–wake disorder in adolescents. Data regarding the effectiveness of melatonin and light therapy for this disorder are more mixed. Furthermore, the safety of melatonin for children and adolescents has not been established. Consequently, these components of treatment should be used only under professional supervision, cautiously, and in conjunction with chronotherapy (Ivanenko & Johnson, 2015).

Some communities try to prevent adolescent sleep problems by avoiding early school start times. When researchers compare adolescents who begin school early (e.g., before 7:15 a.m.) and later (e.g., after 8:40 a.m.), several findings emerge:

- Adolescents go to bed at approximately the same time, regardless of when they need to wake and be at school. Therefore, adolescents who attend schools with early start times get less sleep on average.
- Schools with earlier start times have greater absenteeism.
- Adolescents attending schools with early start times show more problems with attention, concentration, daytime sleepiness, and lower academic achievement.

Delaying school start times is associated with improvements in adolescents' functioning (Buckhalt et al., 2009).

Several researchers have advocated for later school start times and more education about sleep hygiene and the importance of sleep. For example, the Young Adolescent Sleep-Smart Pacesetter Program is a school-based prevention program designed for middle school students. Adolescents learn to keep consistent sleep–wake schedules, to develop a relaxing bedtime routine, to regulate sleep and arousal by reducing light exposure in the evening and maximizing it in the morning, and to avoid caffeine and other stimulating substances that might interfere with sleep. This program is effective in helping adolescents increase their total sleep time, develop more consistent sleep schedules, and improve confidence in their ability to get sufficient sleep (Blunden, Chapman, & Rigney, 2012; Wolfson & Montgomery-Downs, 2013).

Sleep Arousal Disorders

Sleep arousal disorders are *DSM-5* conditions that occur when children have recurrent episodes of "incompletely awakening" from non-REM sleep. There are two types of arousal disorders: (1) sleepwalking and (2) sleep terrors. Both disorders have the following features in common (Meltzer & McLaughlin Crabtree, 2015):

- They usually occur 60 to 90 minutes after sleep onset.
- They occur during slow-wave (i.e., non-REM, or "deep") sleep.
- Children are generally unresponsive during an arousal episode.
- Episodes are relatively brief in duration (10–30 minutes).
- Children usually fall back to sleep after the episode.

- Children usually have no memory of the episode the following morning.

Sleepwalking is most common among children aged 4 to 8 years. Children typically leave the bed and wander about the house. Occasionally, they may engage in disruptive behaviors (e.g., urinating on the floor) or potentially dangerous acts (e.g., leaving the house). Because sleepwalking occurs during non-REM sleep, sleepwalking children are not dreaming, nor are they acting out dreams. If parents discover their child sleepwalking, they can usually lead the child to bed and allow her to return to sleep. Most episodes of sleepwalking last approximately 10 to 20 minutes. Sleepwalkers typically have no memory of the event (Arya & Jain, 2013).

Sleep terrors are seen in 3% of prepubescent children. Children typically emit a blood-curdling scream early in the sleep cycle. They may sit up in bed, open their eyes, and cry inconsolably. They are usually unresponsive to parents' offers of comfort. Because sleep terrors occur during non-REM sleep, they do not occur during dreaming; consequently, children are usually unable to describe the source of their terror. Sleep terrors typically pass in 10 to 30 minutes, after which children return to restful sleep. Children usually have no memory for the event the next day (Nevsimalova, Prihodova, Kemlink, & Skibova, 2013).

How is it possible for children to be "incompletely awake"? Disorders of arousal occur when the child transitions from slow-wave sleep to the beginning of her first REM episode. The child presents in a mixed state of sleep: She appears unresponsive to her surroundings,

disoriented, and has no memory of the event, like people in deep, slow-wave sleep, but she also shows a high degree of autonomic activity, like people in REM sleep. Children with sleep arousal disorders seem to be stuck between these two sleep states for a brief period of time until the episode passes (Meltzer & McLaughlin Crabtree, 2015).

Researchers are not completely sure what causes this mixed state. Sleep arousal disorders are highly heritable (see Figure 16.5). Twin and family studies indicate high prevalence in first-degree relatives. It appears that children inherit problems transitioning smoothly from slow-wave sleep to REM. These children also have immature neural networks that are responsible for inhibiting autonomic arousal and motor activity. Consequently, they sometimes show both autonomic arousal and movement even though they are largely unresponsive to others. As their nervous systems mature, inhibition becomes complete and children outgrow the disorder. Finally, environmental stressors may precipitate the disorder. Sleep deprivation, changes to the child's sleep–wake cycle, and psychosocial stress often occur before an episode (Petit et al., 2015).

The exact prevalence of sleep arousal disorders is unknown. A conservative estimate is that 15% of children experience sleepwalking or sleep terrors at some point during childhood. These problems are equally prevalent in boys and girls (Bloomfield & Shatkin, 2009).

Sleep arousal disorders are not associated with emotional problems. Parents of children with this disorder can be reassured that the disorder is not associated with neurological impairment, mood or anxiety disorders, or

Figure 16.5   Sleepwalking is heritable.

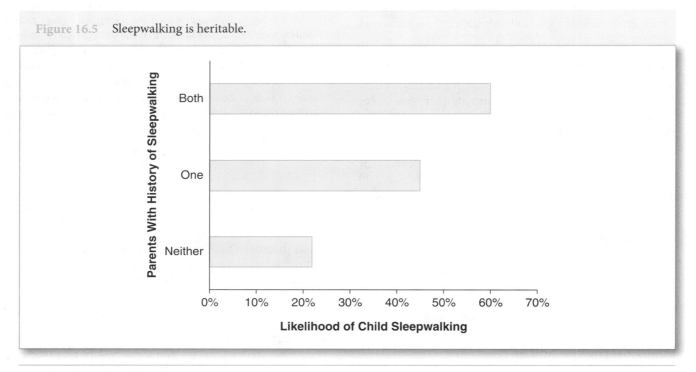

Source: Based on Reite et al. (2009).

Note: A child's likelihood of sleepwalking is correlated with his or her parent's history of sleepwalking as a child.

trauma. Children usually outgrow the disorder by late childhood or adolescence (Arya & Jain, 2013).

Nightmare Disorder

Nightmares are extremely common in children and adolescents. Approximately 2% to 11% of children report nightmares "always or often" whereas an additional 15% to 31% experience them "now and then." The content of nightmares often mirror the cognitive development of children. For example, preschoolers, who engage in preoperational thought, tend to dream about magical creatures or events (e.g., monsters, witches) whereas school-age children, whose thought is largely restricted to concrete operations, may dream of actual physical dangers (e.g., wild animals, storms). The formal operations attained by adolescents allow them to incorporate more abstract content into their nightmares (e.g., abandonment, death; Arya & Jain, 2013).

Youths may be diagnosed with nightmare disorder if their nightmares are recurrent, they reflect actual dreams that involve threats to their survival or well-being, and they cause significant distress or impairment (e.g., sleep loss, daytime fatigue). Although nightmares are common, relatively few children are formally treated for nightmare disorder (American Psychiatric Association, 2013).

Nightmares differ from sleep terrors in several ways. First, nightmares occur during REM sleep, whereas sleep terrors occur during non-REM sleep. Second, children who experience nightmares can be awakened during their dreams, either by themselves or their parents. Children who have sleep terrors are difficult to wake. Third, once awake, children can immediately recall the content of their nightmare. In contrast, children are usually unable to recall content associated with a sleep terror. Fourth, after a nightmare, most children have difficulty returning to sleep. In contrast, children usually return to restful sleep after a sleep terror. Finally, recurrent nightmares are sometimes experienced by children exposed to psychosocial stress or trauma. In contrast, anxiety, stress, and trauma are not associated with sleep terrors (Owens & Mohan, 2016).

Recurrent nightmares that cause distress or disrupt family functioning merit treatment. These nightmares occasionally reflect other sources of anxiety in children's lives. Professional treatment of nightmare disorder typically involves the assessment of possible psychosocial stressors that might elicit the nightmares, improving the child's sleep hygiene, and teaching children relaxation and coping skills. One interesting intervention, nightmare imagery rehearsal therapy, involves asking children to rewrite the nightmare in a manner that emphasizes mastery or resilience and then mentally rehearse the dream daily. Younger children may be asked to draw pictures of their nightmare's content, changing it to produce a positive or benign outcome (Kotagal, 2009; van Schagen, Lancee, de Groot, Spoormaker, & van den Bout, 2015).

Obstructive Sleep Apnea Hypopnea

Approximately 1.2% of children may have obstructive sleep apnea hypopnea, a condition in which the child's airway is constricted or blocked during sleep (Bixler et al., 2009). An apnea is a temporary cessation of breathing, whereas a hypopnea refers to slow or shallow breathing. These breathing problems cause children to wake frequently during the night to increase their intake of oxygen, reducing the quality of their sleep. Children's breathing problems are often caused by enlarged adenoids or tonsils, obesity, facial abnormalities, or thick tongue (as seen in some children with Down syndrome). The symptoms of apnea include snoring, disrupted or restless sleep, unusual sleeping positions (e.g., arching the head and neck to improve airflow), daytime fatigue, and daytime behavior problems, such as irritability, hyperactivity, and inattention. Parents and children are usually not aware that children have sleep apnea, so the disorder is often unrecognized or may be misdiagnosed as ADHD.

Treatment for sleep apnea in children often involves removal of the adenoids or tonsils. Adenotonsillectomy is 80% effective in reducing childhood apnea. Older children may be treated using a continuous positive air pressure (CPAP) device. The child wears a mask connected by a tube to a small ventilator. The ventilator delivers continuous airflow to the child, opening his airway and reducing the obstruction. Although using a CPAP device is the treatment of choice for apnea in adults, it is less often used with children because some youths find the device uncomfortable or embarrassing (Marcus et al., 2013).

Treatment for obstructive sleep apnea hypopnea is important because breathing problems can interfere with the quality of children's sleep and lead to behavioral, cognitive, or social–emotional impairment during the day. Treatment, either with surgery or a CPAP device, improves children's sleep, daytime behavior, school performance, and overall quality of life (Marcus et al., 2012).

Review:

- Circadian rhythm sleep–wake disorder is a *DSM-5* condition characterized by a persistent or recurrent pattern of sleep problems caused by a mismatch between the youth's typical sleep–wake cycle and the schedule required by her school or work. It is often treated with chronotherapy.
- Sleep arousal disorders are *DSM-5* conditions characterized by recurrent episodes of incomplete awakening during non-REM sleep resulting in either (a) sleepwalking or (b) sleep terrors. Children do not experience dreams during these episodes or have memory of the episodes the next day. Nevertheless, they cause distress or impairment.
- Nightmare disorder is a *DSM-5* condition characterized by repeated, extended, and upsetting dreams that occur during REM sleep.
- Obstructive sleep apnea hypopnea is a *DSM-5* condition characterized by recurrent breathing disruptions (apneas) or episodes of shallow breathing (hypopneas)

during sleep that lead to breathing disturbance (e.g., gasping, snoring) or daytime sleepiness. In children, this disorder is usually treated by surgery or a CPAP device.

16.3 PEDIATRIC PSYCHOLOGY

What Is Pediatric Psychology?

Pediatric psychology is an interdisciplinary field concerned with the application of psychology to the domain of children's health. Pediatric psychologists are scientists and practitioners who promote the physical and psychological health and development of youths. Most pediatric psychologists (63%) work in medical facilities, such as academic hospitals, children's hospitals, or rehabilitation centers. They collaborate with medical staff to help children cope with physical illness. Some pediatric psychologists (22%) work in private practice settings, often helping children and families with a wide range of behavioral, social–emotional, and medical problems. Pediatric psychologists work in a variety of other settings including universities, outpatient clinics, and schools (Buckloh & Greco, 2009).

Most pediatric psychologists are clinical or counseling psychologists with specialized training in the intersection of children's mental and physical health and development. Pediatric psychologists are involved in wide range of professional activities; however, most of their activities fall into three categories (Kazak, Sood, & Roberts, 2016):

Inpatient consultation-liaison: Pediatric psychologists work in hospitals to address the needs of children and adolescents with acute psychological problems. They also collaborate with medical staff to help patients participate in medical procedures, adhere to treatment, and cope with their illness.

Chronic conditions: Pediatric psychologists work on interdisciplinary teams in hospitals and outpatient clinics to help children cope with long-term medical problems. For example, a pediatric psychologist might help children with severe asthma, cancer, or diabetes to adhere to medical procedures related to their illness; address feelings of anxiety, depression, or anger associated with their medical problems; and improve their interactions with parents, siblings, and friends.

Specialized care: Pediatric psychologists work in outpatient clinics to help children with behavior problems that require coordinated psychological and medical treatment. For example, children with feeding disorders, elimination disorders, and sleep disorders typically require treatment by both psychologists and physicians.

Review:

- Pediatric psychology is an interdisciplinary field concerned with the application of psychology to the domain of children's health.

- Pediatric psychologists are typically clinical psychologists who work in medical settings. They engage in inpatient consultation-liaison, help youths with chronic medical conditions, and work in specialty clinics with children who have specific medical problems.

What Is Inpatient Consultation-Liaison?

Many pediatric psychologists who work in hospitals engage in consultation and liaison with medical staff (Carter, Kronenberger, Scott, & Ernst, 2009; Piazza-Waggoner, Roddenberry, Yeomans-Maldonado, Noll, & Ernst, 2013). Consultation occurs when a health care professional is treating a child with a behavioral, cognitive, or social–emotional problem that interferes with the child's medical treatment. The health care professional might ask the pediatric psychologist for her recommendations regarding how to address the child's psychological problems. For example, an adolescent might be brought to the emergency department (ED) because she swallowed a bottle of over-the-counter pain medicine. Her physicians might ask the psychologist to assess the adolescent and recommend a course of action after the girl is medically stable (e.g., Should she go home or stay for observation?).

Alternatively, a physician might request that the psychologist provide a service to help the child participate in treatment more effectively. For example, a child might be required to have a lumbar puncture to determine whether he has meningitis. This procedure involves inserting a needle into the lower spine to collect a small sample of cerebrospinal fluid. Because this procedure can be frightening and uncomfortable, the child might understandably refuse to participate. A psychologist might be asked to meet with the child and his family, discuss the procedure, and teach the child relaxation strategies so that he can undergo the procedure with less fear and pain (Kullgren et al., 2015).

Consultation is analogous to "firefighting." The psychologist's primary job is to address an immediate problem, to help solve the problem, or to recommend a course of action based on her knowledge of psychological science and child development.

Pediatric psychologists also act as liaisons between medical and psychological staff for children with chronic illnesses. Rather than focus on specific problems, liaisons usually work as part of an interdisciplinary team of medical and behavioral professionals who serve youths with specific illnesses. Rather than fighting specific "fires," the liaison's job is to "fireproof" the medical procedures and hospital environment to avoid problems.

For example, a psychologist might work on the hospital's pediatric oncology team, helping medical staff find ways to facilitate the diagnosis, treatment, and recovery of children with cancer. When a child is newly diagnosed, the psychologist might provide support services to parents, to help them address emotions associated with their children's illness. The psychologist might also teach relaxation and coping strategies to children in the unit to help them participate in medical procedures. Before children leave the hospital, the psychologist might help them prepare for their return to school and interactions with peers (Sulik & Sarvet, 2015).

Pediatric psychologists who practice consultation-liaison engage in a wide variety of activities; no two days are exactly alike. Carter and von Weiss (2005) classified these activities into five groups—the five Cs of consultation-liaison (see Figure 16.6):

1. *Crisis:* Psychologists help children and families who are initially admitted to the hospital or newly diagnosed with an illness. They attempt to normalize the family's fears and help them take steps to address children's medical problems.

2. *Coping:* Psychologists help children and families cope with anxiety, fear, and discomfort associated with medical procedures in the hospital. They also work with families to help children adjust their lifestyles in response to the illness (e.g., a child with diabetes learning to limit his sugar intake).

3. *Compliance:* Psychologists help children follow medical recommendations, such as taking medication, monitoring health, altering behavior, or participating in checkups and medical procedures. Many professionals also refer to this activity as promoting adherence.

4. *Communication:* Psychologists act as liaisons between medical staff and families. They educate children and families about medical procedures and help them cope with stressors associated with medical care.

5. *Collaboration:* Psychologists function as part of an interdisciplinary team of professionals, which often include physicians; nurses; occupational, recreational, and physical therapists; social workers; dieticians; and family life experts. These professionals have a shared goal of promoting the health and well-being of children.

Adherence (sometimes called compliance) is a common reason for psychological consultation. Adherence refers to the degree to which children and families follow the recommendations of medical staff. Many youths are unwilling to participate in medical procedures that might involve unknown situations, separation from parents, or physical discomfort. Other children are reluctant to change their diet or lifestyle to manage their illness. Only half of youths with chronic illnesses adhere to the recommendations of their physicians (Wu et al., 2013).

Children's cognitive and social–emotional development influences their likelihood of adherence. For example, younger children may resist parental separation or painful procedures whereas adolescents may avoid medication that limits their social activities. Families can also influence children's adherence. For example, families with greater knowledge about their children's

Figure 16.6   The Five Cs of consultation-liaison in pediatric psychology.

illness, coping and problem-solving skills, and tangible resources may be best able to address their children's needs and respond to their anxiety, frustrations, and fears (Pinsky, Rausch, & Abrams, 2015)

Review:

- Pediatric psychologists frequently engage in consultation, providing professional advice or assistance to medical professionals regarding an aspect of a child's behavior that interferes with treatment.
- Pediatric psychologists may also act as liaisons between members of an interdisciplinary health care team and children's family/school. Their goal is to enhance communication and quality of care.
- Many pediatric psychologists work with families to promote adherence—that is, the degree to which families agree with, understand, and follow the recommendations of medical staff.

How Do Pediatric Psychologists Help Youths With Health Problems?

Approximately 10% of children and adolescents have chronic medical conditions that necessitate ongoing care. Pediatric psychologists provide support for these children and their families during their stay in the hospital and after returning to their homes. Children with chronic illnesses may be at risk for behavioral and social–emotional problems (Roberts, Aylward, & Wu, 2015).

Asthma

Asthma is a chronic condition caused by inflammation of the airways and intermittent periods of difficulty breathing. Approximately 6% of children have recurrent asthma attacks that interfere with life activities (e.g., school, sports, family events). It is the most common chronic illness afflicting youths.

Children with asthma manage their symptoms by avoiding situations or activities that might trigger an asthma attack. Children also typically take medication and carry inhalers for asthmatic episodes. Some children resent limitations placed on their daily activities or are embarrassed to use medications or inhalers in front of peers. Other children develop anxiety problems because they fear future attacks (see Image 16.3).

Pediatric psychologists might educate families about asthma and help modify the home environment to prevent attacks (e.g., install a hypoallergenic filter, avoid smoking). Psychologists might help parents and children establish a behavioral contract that designates the responsibilities of both parties in managing children's asthma. For example, parents might agree to allow their child to attend a scout camping trip if she agrees to carry her inhaler at all times. For children with anxiety, psychologists might teach relaxation exercises, such as deep breathing or guided imagery, to help youths cope with asthmatic episodes should they occur (Miadich, Everhart, Borschuk, Winter, & Fiese, 2015).

Cancer

Cancer is the leading cause of death by disease for children in the United States. Although cancer is relatively rare in children, almost 16,000 youths are diagnosed each year. Acute lymphoblastic leukemia (ALL) and malignant brain tumors are most common among children. Cancer, especially ALL, is usually curable in children; however, the medical procedures needed to diagnose and treat cancer often cause physical, cognitive, and social–emotional problems.

Pediatric psychologists can be involved in all aspects of children's cancer treatment. Initially, they may help families cope with fears and worries associated with children's diagnoses. Later, psychologists might work with families to reduce conflict and increase cohesion during children's treatment. Psychologists may also teach children ways to manage pain and nausea associated with treatment or to distract themselves to cope with medical procedures. Psychologists might help children plan for their return to school and cope with missed work. Psychologists can also counsel children who experience specific problems, such as depression or possible sterility, following radiation therapy (Kazak & Noll, 2015).

Cystic Fibrosis

Cystic fibrosis is an inherited condition that causes thick mucus to be present in the airways and lungs. Foreign

Image 16.3   Pediatric psychologists help children with asthma manage their symptoms. This girl uses an inhaler to breathe more easily.

particles in the air, such as dust, pollen, or pollutants, can accumulate in this mucus causing lung infections. Cystic fibrosis affects 1 in 3,500 children; most youths are diagnosed in infancy or early childhood. Besides respiratory problems, children with cystic fibrosis must participate in frequent exercises to clear their airways and lungs. These exercises can be time consuming, laborious, and distressing to children and their families (Quittner, Abbott, et al., 2016).

Pediatric psychologists often help children and their families adhere to physicians' recommendations regarding the frequency of exercises. Young children may become oppositional and refuse to participate. In this case, psychologists might teach parents to use positive reinforcement and other behavioral techniques to increase adherence. Older children and adolescents, in contrast, may become depressed. They may believe that the exercises will not appreciably prolong their life span or improve their life satisfaction. Pediatric psychologists might challenge the maladaptive cognitions that rob these adolescents' of their motivation to manage their condition (Quittner, Saez-Flores, & Barton, 2016).

Diabetes Mellitus

Diabetes mellitus is a chronic disease caused by a deficiency in insulin, the hormone needed to regulate blood sugar. Type 1 diabetes, most often seen in children, is caused by the absence or destruction of cells in the pancreas responsible for manufacturing insulin. Type 2 diabetes, seen in 10% to 20% of youths with diabetes, occurs when the body develops a resistance to insulin and no longer uses it properly to control blood sugar. Approximately 1 in 600 children and adolescents has diabetes (Kichler, Harris, & Weissberg-Benchell, 2014).

Diabetes can cause severe problems if children allow blood sugar levels to remain unregulated. Hypoglycemia (low blood sugar) occurs when children allow blood glucose to drop to dangerously low levels, usually resulting in fatigue, dizziness, and possible damage to internal organs. Hypoglycemia can occur when children skip meals or take too much insulin. In contrast, diabetic ketoacidosis occurs when blood glucose levels are unusually high. It usually occurs when children eat a large (or sugary) meal and do not take sufficient insulin to metabolize their blood glucose. Over time, failure to regulate blood glucose can cause heart disease, stroke, and damage to the kidneys and eyes.

The chief problem with diabetes is adherence (see Image 16.4). Younger children might avoid the frequent needle pricks necessary to monitor blood sugar. Older children and adolescents might be embarrassed about their condition or might resent having to monitor and restrict their diet to manage blood glucose. Pediatric psychologists try to increase compliance in ways that are developmentally appropriate. For example, they might teach younger children strategies to reduce pain associated with glucose testing or respond to teasing from peers. They might also teach children to monitor and record their glucose levels over time and encourage parents to reinforce children for accepting responsibility for this task. Psychologists might also work with parents to find ways to avoid arguments about adolescents' diet and allow adolescents to take ownership of the management of their illness (Kazak et al., 2016).

Gastrointestinal Problems

Abdominal pain and gastrointestinal problems are fairly common among children and adolescents. Approximately 6% of older children and 14% of adolescents have symptoms of irritable bowel syndrome (IBS), a disorder characterized by abdominal discomfort and altered bowel functioning. Youths with IBS often experience diarrhea and/or constipation. Youths will IBS often miss school and must forgo activities with family and peers because of these chronic symptoms.

The cause of IBS is unknown, although most evidence points to a hypersensitivity of the nerve endings surrounding the bowel. However, stress and behavior can greatly affect the timing and severity of symptoms. Consequently, treatment usually involves medical and psychological

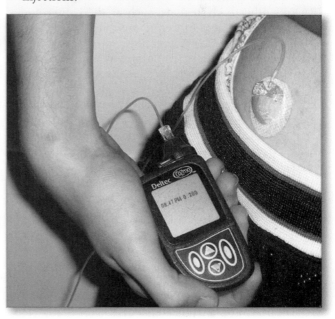

Image 16.4 Psychologists can help children with diabetes avoid high-risk foods and adhere to medication. This adolescent girl has an insulin pump which administers insulin to her after meals. Pumps like these are often more convenient than insulin injections.

interventions. With respect to psychological treatment, pediatric psychologists may teach children relaxation skills, pain reduction techniques, and other ways to manage stress (Reed-Knight, Claar, Schurman, & van Tilburg, 2016; Reed-Knight, Squires, Chitkara, & van Tilburg, 2016).

Inflammatory bowel disease (IBD) is a more serious disorder characterized by diarrhea, rectal bleeding, abdominal cramping, weight loss, fatigue, and fever. Crohn's disease is probably the best known example of IBD; it is caused by severe inflammation of the digestive tract, especially the intestinal wall. The cause of IBD is unknown, although it is likely influenced by genetics, exposure to bacteria or viruses, and/or problems with the body's immune system.

Understandably, children with IBD are at risk for anxiety, depression, poor social relationships, and difficulty with school attendance. Their self-reported quality of life is often poor. Adherence is often a problem, because children must frequently take medication to manage their symptoms. Psychologists can help children and families adhere to medication, overcome anxiety and mood problems, improve social competence and skills, and adjust to missed schooling (Gray, Denson, Baldassano, & Hommel, 2012; Mackner et al., 2013).

Juvenile Rheumatoid Arthritis

Juvenile rheumatoid arthritis (JRA) is a leading cause of physical disability among children and adolescents. It is characterized by inflammation of the musculoskeletal system, blood vessels, and skin. In particular, children with JRA show synovitis, inflammation of the synovial membrane of a joint. The result is chronic pain, restricted range of motion, and possible growth problems. JRA is diagnosed based on whether it affects only certain joints, such as the ankles and knees (pauciarticular JRA); many joints including the hands, wrists, and neck (polyarticular JRA); or other body regions, such as the lymph nodes, spleen, liver, and heart (systemic-onset JRA).

The treatment of JRA typically involves long-term use of anti-inflammatory medication such as ibuprofen (Advil), occasional use of corticosteroids in severe cases, and daily therapeutic exercises to maintain range and ease of motion. Pediatric psychologists are typically involved in the care of youths with JRA in three ways. First, psychologists may help patients manage chronic pain. Second, psychologists can develop ways to increase children's adherence to medication and their physical therapy program. Third, psychologists may work with parents and siblings to help reduce stress and conflict within the family, frequently caused by the child's chronic illness (Fuchs et al., 2013; Rapoff, Lindsley, & Karlson, 2009).

Sickle Cell Disease

Sickle cell disease is a medical disorder characterized by abnormal, sickle-shaped red blood cells. The unusual shape of the cells can cause problems with blood flow. The disease also causes anemia (i.e., a deficiency of red blood cells), episodes of acute pain, and risk of infections and damage to vital organs.

Sickle cell disease is a recessive genetic disorder (see Figure 16.7). Children develop the disease when they inherit two recessive genes for the disorder, one from each parent. If children inherit only one recessive gene, they will carry the disorder but not show symptoms. If they have children with another person who carries the recessive gene, their likelihood of having a child with sickle cell disease is 25%. Sickle cell is especially prevalent in African American youths. Whereas the prevalence of sickle cell disease is approximately 1 in 10,000 youths in the general population, approximately 1 in 365 African American children have the illness. Approximately 1 in 13 African Americans are carriers (Hassell, 2016; Homer & Oyeku, 2016).

Psychologists typically teach youths with sickle cell disease techniques to manage pain. Strategies such as deep breathing, guided imagery, and positive self-statements are often effective. Psychologists may also help children and families cope with other stressors associated with the disease, such as missed school, sleep problems, and restricted social activities (Anie & Green, 2016).

Review:

- Pediatric psychologists work with children and families experiencing medical problems. They help youths adhere to treatment; manage pain or discomfort; and cope with emotional, social, or educational problems associated with their illness.

What Psychological Treatments Are Often Used in Medical Settings?

Behavior Therapy for Children Undergoing Medical Procedures

Behavioral interventions used by pediatric psychologists are based on classical conditioning, operant conditioning, and observational learning. Systematic desensitization is a common intervention used to help children cope with painful procedures, such as injections, or uncomfortable situations, such as participating in an MRI (Brown, 2014).

In the context of pediatric psychology, systematic desensitization involves four steps. First, the psychologist teaches the child how to relax. Typically, relaxation is achieved through progressively tightening and relaxing muscle groups (e.g., arms, legs, middle) and concentrating on slow, deep breathing. Relaxation is introduced during a therapy session and practiced until it is achieved relatively quickly. Second, the child lists stimuli that elicit anxiety and orders them in a hierarchical fashion from least to most anxiety provoking. For example, seeing a picture of a hypodermic needle might elicit low anxiety, seeing an actual needle might elicit moderate anxiety, and seeing a needle while smelling the alcohol swab a nurse uses to clean the skin shortly before an injection might elicit high anxiety. Third, the child engages in imaginal exposure; after the child is relaxed, the psychologist asks him to imagine the stimulus that elicits the least anxiety. Imagined exposure continues until the child's anxiety is manageable. The child gradually progresses up the hierarchy, pairing relaxation with more anxiety-provoking stimuli. Fourth, the child engages in *in vivo* (real-life) exposure; after the child is relaxed, the psychologist presents an actual stimulus that elicits the least amount of anxiety (e.g., a picture of a needle). Once the child can tolerate this stimulus, he gradually progresses up the hierarchy until he can successfully undergo the medical procedure.

Pediatric psychologists often rely on operant conditioning to increase children's adherence. Three frequently used procedures are positive reinforcement, negative reinforcement, and response cost. For example, when a child is diagnosed with type 1 diabetes, physicians usually recommend that families keep a record of the child's diet, exercise, blood glucose, and insulin throughout the day. The record allows the physician and family to determine the best timing and amount of insulin for the child. However, the glucose tests are slightly painful and recordkeeping can be bothersome.

Rather than nag children, parents might award the child one point each time he correctly records information and bonus points for doing so with minimal prompting or complaining. These points can be used to buy small toys or privileges. Awarding points to increase compliance is

Figure 16.7 Sickle cell disease is caused by a recessive gene. Two parents who carry the gene have a 1 in 4 chance of having a child with the disorder.

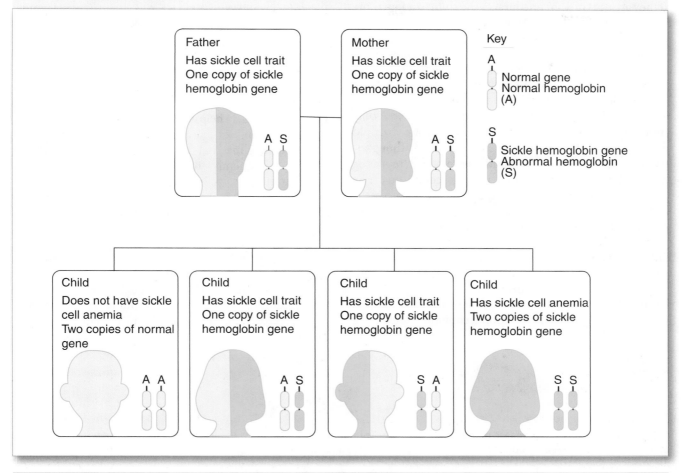

Source: Image courtesy of Wikimedia Commons and University of Michigan Medical School.

an example of positive reinforcement: the presentation of a stimulus resulting in an increase in behavior. As an additional incentive, if the child accurately records information throughout the entire day, he might be excused from a chore, such as taking out the garbage. Excusing a child from a chore to increase compliance is an example of negative reinforcement: the removal or avoidance of a stimulus resulting in an increase in behavior. Finally, if the child fails to record information, he might be penalized points. The removal of points is an example of response cost, a form of negative punishment in which a stimulus is withdrawn, resulting in a decrease in behavior.

Pediatric psychologists also rely on principles of observational learning. One particularly useful technique is participant modeling; the psychologist demonstrates the desired behavior, and a child is encouraged to imitate the action. For example, a child afraid of entering an MRI machine might be more likely to do so if he saw the psychologist (or parent) demonstrate the procedure.

Cognitive Therapy to Help
Youths Adhere to Treatment

Pediatric psychologists often use both cognitive and behavioral interventions to help older children with chronic illnesses. The underlying premise of CBT is the notion that children's thoughts, feelings, and actions are connected; each affects and is affected by the other. Therefore, changing the way children think about their medical condition, a procedure, or treatment can influence the way they feel and act. Cognitive interventions typically work better with older children who have the ability to engage in metacognition—that is, to think about their own thinking. Consequently, these interventions are most often used for school-aged children and adolescents (Wu et al., 2013).

Cognitive restructuring is a technique used to change distorted, inflexible thoughts to more realistic, flexible cognitions. The psychologist helps the child become aware of thoughts, beliefs, assumptions, or self-statements that cause him to become sad, anxious, or angry. The psychologist helps the child identify potentially problematic thoughts and test them empirically, to see if they are true. If they are not true, she encourages the child to adopt more accurate, rational beliefs in future situations. These more accurate, rational beliefs may reduce negative feelings and actions. For example, in the following Research to Practice section, a pediatric psychologist helps Lewis challenge negative thoughts about his diabetes.

Cognitive therapists also use role play and self-statements to help children adopt more accurate, rational thoughts. During role play, the psychologist and the child act out a situation that often elicits negative thoughts, feelings, and actions. The child can practice replacing distorted thoughts with more realistic cognitions. The psychologist might also teach the child to practice self-statements—short and simple phrases that the child can say when he experiences negative emotions.

Two other cognitive interventions are guided imagery and refocusing. In guided imagery, the child is taught to replace thoughts about a medical procedure or illness with thoughts about a pleasant, peaceful situation (e.g., lying on the beach, flying a kite). Guided imagery is often used in combination with other relaxation techniques. Refocusing involves redirecting the child's attention from the stressful or painful event to more relaxing or entertaining stimuli. For example, a child with chronic pain might be asked to think about celebrating his last birthday, eating a favorite meal, or playing video games with his friends (Forsner, Norström, Nordyke, Ivarsson, & Lindh, 2014).

Family Therapy to Foster Coping and Resiliency

Structural Family Therapy

Families with strong support, cohesion, and communication are best able to help children cope with medical illness. In contrast, families characterized by distress and conflict are less able to marshal their resources to meet children's needs. Consequently, many pediatric psychologists integrate family therapy into their practice. Family therapy is based on systems theory, the idea that an individual's ability to cope with his environment is dependent on the many relationships he has with other people in his life. Changing one of these relationships will necessarily affect all of the other relationships because they are interrelated. Family therapists view the entire family as their "client" rather than a single child. Their goal is to improve family functioning with the understanding that it will lead to a corresponding improvement in the child's behavior (Wendel & Gouze, 2015).

RESEARCH TO PRACTICE

COGNITIVE RESTRUCTURING FOR KIDS WITH DIABETES

Psychologist:	Your mom was pretty angry at you for going to the party and eating all of that pizza and soda. She worries about you because she sees you're not watching your blood sugar.
Lewis:	Well, I don't like the fact that all the other kids can eat what they want and drink what they want and I can't. Nobody has this problem but me.
Psychologist:	Let's look at that statement for a second: "Nobody has this problem but me." Do you think that's really true?
Lewis:	Of course, I feel like I'm the only one who has to worry about blood sugar and diet and stuff like that.
Psychologist:	I'm sure that's how you *feel*—like you're the only one, like you're singled out. Now tell me what you *think*. Are you really the only kid with diabetes in the world?
Lewis:	Of course not.
Psychologist:	Are you the only kid with diabetes at your school?
Lewis:	No. I know other kids who have it.
Psychologist:	What about kids in your school who have other dietary restrictions? It's not exactly the same thing, but do any of your friends have allergies or food restrictions?
Lewis:	Sure. Will and James are lactose intolerant. Sam's allergic to peanuts. Another kid can't eat breads or anything with wheat.
Psychologist:	So there's no need to feel resentful or angry or singled out. There are other kids who have to watch their diet too.
Lewis:	I guess I never thought about it before.

There are many schools of family therapy. Each school places different emphasis on certain relationships between family members or divisions between the family and the outside world. One of the best known approaches is structural family therapy. Recall that structural family therapy is chiefly concerned with special relationships, or *alliances,* between parents and children. Problems occur when parents show too much involvement (i.e., enmeshment) or too little involvement (i.e., disengagement) in the child's life. For example, enmeshed parents might assume too much control over their child's illness and deny the child any say in its management. The child, in turn, might resent parental overcontrol and assert her autonomy by sabotaging treatment. Alternatively, a father might feel left out of a relationship between a mother and a child with chronic illness. The father's disengagement might cause family strain and communication problems.

Structural family therapists are also concerned with *boundaries* between the family and the outside world. Ideally, boundaries should be flexible. They should clearly divide family activities from other important domains of life (e.g., school, friends, work) while also being open to involvement with these domains. Problems occur when boundaries become excessively rigid or diffuse. For example, families of chronically ill children need to work effectively with medical professionals, therapists, schools, and other people in children's lives (e.g., coaches, friends). Families who refuse to interact with these different groups or who become too preoccupied with extrafamily activities may experience a lack of coherence (Wendel & Gouze, 2015).

Structural therapists typically meet with parents and children together. They seek to understand relationships between family members and identify problematic alliances and boundaries. When problematic relationships are found, the therapist often tries to disrupt these relationships. For example, in an enmeshed family, the therapist might try to give the child greater autonomy and responsibility for managing her illness. Alternatively, in a family with rigid boundaries, the therapist might challenge the family's underlying mistrust for the outside world. Overall, structural family therapy is associated with improved coherence and communication among family members and reductions in children's behavior problems.

Behavior and Multisystemic Family Therapies

Behavior family systems therapy (BFST) combines cognitive–behavioral interventions with elements of structural family therapy. The primary goal of BFST is to reduce conflict and increase communication among family members. First, therapists provide problem-solving and communication skills training to families. Specifically, families are taught to solve disputes in ways that respect each family member's autonomy, thoughts, and feelings. A primary goal is to avoid coercive parent–child interactions, such as yelling, threatening, or inducing guilt. Second, therapists try to identify and challenge distorted beliefs held by family members that contribute to family conflict. For example, parents might misattribute an adolescent's frustration as "a lack of respect" whereas adolescents might misattribute parents' concern as "overcontrolling." A therapist might relabel these behaviors to help parents and children view interactions more accurately and avoid unnecessary conflict. Third, therapists attempt to identify and correct alliances or boundaries in the family in ways similar to structural family therapists (Falloon, 2015).

Multisystemic family therapy (MFT) has also been used to improve family cohesion and communication. Recall that MFT is typically used to treat antisocial adolescents; however, recent studies have demonstrated its effectiveness for families of children with chronic illness, such as diabetes. MFT is similar to other family therapies in that the goal is to improve relationships between family members. Therapists seek to reduce conflict, miscommunication, and coercive parent–child interactions. In addition, MFT is concerned with the family's relationships with the outside world, especially schools, medical professionals, and peers. Therapists who practice MFT emphasize the "ecological validity" of their interactions—that is, they want to make sure that their treatments will generalize to "the real world." Consequently, MFT therapists will consult with children's teachers, physicians, dieticians, and leaders of extracurricular activities to help identify and resolve problems that interfere with the management of their illness (Naar-King et al., 2014).

Group and Peer-Assisted Therapy to Enhance Social Support

Some therapists offer treatment to groups of children with similar pediatric disorders. Group therapy can be helpful in at least three ways. First, children with medical illnesses often feel emotionally isolated, that their illness or problems are unique, and that no one else can understand the stressors they experience. Group therapy allows children to encounter youths with similar medical problems and reduce feelings of isolation. Second, some children with chronic illness have deficits in problem-solving and social skills. Group therapy gives these children a chance to practice skills with each other. Third, group therapy allows children to receive feedback from their peers regarding their own behavior. For example, group members might notice that a particular child often appears angry and resentful or frequently blames others for his troubles. The group might mention this to the child saying, "Maybe you don't have many friends because you're always in a bad mood?" Although interpersonal feedback like this might be initially off-putting, a skillful therapist might be able to use this feedback to help youths learn about themselves and change their behavior.

The brief transcript in the following Research to Practice section illustrates two principles of group therapy.

GROUP THERAPY: GETTING FEEDBACK FROM PEERS

Hannah:	Maybe you don't have many friends, Kylie, because you're always in a bad mood?
Therapist:	What do you think, Kylie? Is there any truth to that?
Kylie:	No, that's dumb. (To Hannah) It's even stupid to say such a thing.
Therapist:	Hannah, how do you feel right now, after what Kylie said?
Hannah:	Not very good. Like I don't want to be around her.
Therapist:	(To the group) Anyone else? How do you feel?
Molly:	Me, too.
Therapist:	So, if these girls don't want to be around you when you get mad, maybe others don't, too. These girls want to be your friend, but they're being scared away.

First, group therapists focus chiefly on the *process* of therapy (i.e., the pattern of interactions between group members) rather than the *content* of therapy (i.e., what is being said). Second, whenever possible, group therapists focus on participants' immediate thoughts, feelings, and actions, rather than events that happened in the past or outside the therapy session. Group therapists often focus on the "here and now" rather than on the "there and then." Focusing on immediate interactions between group members allows members to give and receive feedback regarding their own interpersonal behavior.

Plante, Lobato, and Engel (2001) conducted a meta-analysis of the effectiveness of group therapy for children with chronic illness. They found that group therapies that focus chiefly on managing children's symptoms and fostering social and problem-solving skills were associated with the largest improvements in children's functioning. Groups that focused chiefly on providing facts about specific illnesses were less effective.

Two new group interventions for children with chronic illness have emerged in recent years: (1) summer treatment programs and (2) peer group interventions. Summer treatment programs usually consist of groups of children with similar medical problems who participate in several days' worth of psychoeducational and skill-building activities in the context of a summer camp. Camps have been developed for children with conditions such as asthma, cancer, diabetes, and gastrointestinal problems. Overall, these camps are associated with reductions in anxiety and depression, improvements in positive affect and self-efficacy, and more satisfying interactions with friends and family (Brown, 2014). Peer group interventions involve children with chronic illness and their best friends or classmates. Friends and classmates learn about children's illnesses and ways they can help them adhere to medical recommendations and support them through tough times. For example, a peer group intervention for children with diabetes might teach friends the importance of monitoring blood sugar and diet as well as ways to manage stress.

Effectiveness of Pediatric Interventions

Several meta-analyses indicate that individual, family, and group interventions for children with chronic illness are efficacious. Overall, mean effect sizes (ESs) from published studies range from .71 to .87, indicating moderate to large differences between children who participate in therapy and those who do not. Treatment efficacy does not seem to depend on the type of illness; children with a range of illnesses seem to benefit equally. However, some evidence indicates that therapies which focus primarily on symptom management and skills training yield greater benefits than therapies that provide only information and education. Finally, some data indicate that the effects of treatment are fairly long lasting, with benefits seen 12 months after termination (Fisher et al., 2014; Gayes & Steele, 2014; Meltzer & Mindell, 2014).

Review:

- Behavior therapy may be used to help youths cope with medical procedures. For example, systematic desensitization is effective in reducing anxiety that can exacerbate discomfort or interfere with a child's ability to participate in treatment.
- Older children and adolescents can benefit from cognitive restructuring to help them manage negative thoughts about their medical problems.
- Family therapy is often used to improve communication between caregivers and youths with chronic medical problems. A primary goal is to reduce hostile–coercive interactions and allow youths age-appropriate autonomy over the management of their illness.
- Group therapy can reduce feelings of isolation in youths with medical problems. In group therapy, youths can also practice effective coping and problem-solving skills and receive support from their peers.

Adherence: In the field of pediatric psychology, the degree to which children and families agree with, understand, and follow the recommendations of medical staff

Antihistamines: Medications that block the naturally occurring neurotransmitter histamine and cause drowsiness and sedation; examples are diphenhydramine (Benadryl) and hydroxyzine (Vistaril)

Arginine vasopressin (AVP): A naturally occurring hormone that increases urine concentration and reduces its total volume

Benzodiazepines: Medications that augment GABA and produce marked sedation; can cause tolerance and withdrawal symptoms; examples include temazepam (Restoril), estazolam (ProSom), and quazepam (Doral)

Chronotherapy: A behavioral treatment for circadian rhythm sleep–wake disorder; involves gradually advancing or delaying bedtime until the person's sleep–wake cycle is aligned with his or her daily schedule

Circadian rhythm sleep–wake disorder: A *DSM-5* disorder characterized by a persistent or recurrent pattern of sleep problems caused by a mismatch between the person's typical sleep–wake pattern and the schedule required by the person's school or work

Cleanliness training: A version of overcorrection used to treat nocturnal enuresis; children must wake, change their pajamas and bedding, and reactivate the urine alarm prior to returning to bed

Consultation: In the field of pediatric psychology, providing professional advice or assistance to a medical professional regarding an aspect of a child's behavior that interferes with treatment

Continuous positive air pressure (CPAP) device: A small mask connected to a tube and ventilator that provides constant air pressure to keep the individual's airway open during sleep

Desmopressin (DDAVP): The most commonly prescribed medication for nocturnal enuresis; a synthetic version of vasopressin, the hormone that reduces nighttime urine production

Encopresis: A *DSM-5* disorder characterized by the repeated passage of feces into inappropriate places whether involuntary or intentional; the individual must be at least 4 years of age, and the act must occur at least once per month for 3 months and cause distress or impairment

Enuresis: A *DSM-5* disorder characterized by the repeated voiding of urine into bed or clothes, either involuntarily or intentional; the individual must be at least 5 years of age and the act must occur at least twice per week for 3 months and cause distress or impairment

Full spectrum home training (FSHT): Comprehensive behavior treatment of nocturnal enuresis; includes (a) education and behavioral contracting, (b) urine alarm training, (c) cleanliness training, (d) retention control training, and (e) overlearning

Insomnia disorder: A *DSM-5* disorder characterized by predominant difficulty or dissatisfaction with sleep quantity or quality associated with problems going to sleep, remaining sleep, or returning to sleep; occurs at least 3 nights per week for 3 months and causes distress or impairment

Kegel exercises: Contracting and relaxing pelvic floor muscles in order to stop and start the flow of urine during voiding; used to treat daytime enuresis

Liaisons: In the field of pediatric psychology, mental health professionals who help members of an interdisciplinary health care team coordinate treatment and communicate with each other and the child's family or school

Monosymptomatic primary enuresis (MPE): A term used to describe children who wet only at night, have never been able to stay dry each night for longer than 6 months, and have no known medical cause for their wetting

Nightmare disorder: A *DSM-5* disorder characterized by repeated, extended, and upsetting dreams that occur during REM sleep, typically involve threats to personal security, and cause distress or impairment; the person can be easily awakened and has vivid memory of the dream

Nightmare imagery rehearsal therapy: A cognitive treatment for nightmare disorder, children rewrite the nightmare in a manner that emphasizes mastery or resilience and then mentally rehearsing the dream daily

Obstructive sleep apnea hypopnea: A *DSM-5* sleep–wake disorder characterized by recurrent breathing disruptions (apneas) or episodes of shallow breathing (hypopneas) during sleep that leads to breathing disturbance (e.g., gasping, snoring) or daytime sleepiness

Overlearning: A component of full spectrum home training; after remaining dry at night for 24 consecutive nights, a child continues to drink large amounts of fluids and delay voiding to prevent the return of nocturnal enuresis

Pediatric psychology: An interdisciplinary field concerned with the application of psychology to the domain of children's health

Polysomnogram (PSG): Assessment of a child's sleep architecture during the course of the night; involves the monitoring of brain activity (EEG), eye movements (EOG), muscle activation (EMG), and heart rhythm (ECG)

Polysymptomatic nocturnal enuresis (PSNE): A term used to describe children who wet throughout the night, void small amounts of urine, and wake after wetting; these children also frequently experience sudden urges to urinate during the day

Primary encopresis: A term used to describe encopresis exhibited by a child who has no history of bowel control

Primary enuresis: A term used to describe enuresis exhibited by a child who has never been able to stay dry at night

Retention control training: A component of full spectrum home training; children with enuresis drink increasing larger amounts of fluids and delay voiding for longer periods of time to become sensitive to a full bladder and to increase functional bladder capacity

Secondary encopresis: A term used to describe encopresis exhibited by a child who formerly showed appropriate toilet use

Secondary enuresis: A term used to describe enuresis exhibited by a child who was previously toilet trained for at least 6 months and then began to show enuresis

Sleep architecture: An activity of the central nervous system during sleep in typically developing individuals of a certain age; consists of a series of stages of non-REM sleep usually followed by a REM episode when repeat over the course of the night

Sleep arousal disorders: *DSM-5* disorders characterized by recurrent episodes of incomplete awakening during non-REM sleep resulting in either (a) sleepwalking or (b) sleep terrors; the child experiences no dreams during the episode or memory of the episode the next day, but the episode does lead to distress or impairment

Sleep hygiene: Developmentally appropriate behaviors and environmental conditions that promote restful sleep

Sleep terrors: A type of sleep arousal disorder characterized by recurrent episodes of abrupt panic and autonomic arousal during non-REM sleep; the child typically lacks responsiveness and is unable to be consoled during the episode; causes distress or impairment during the day

Sleep–wake disorders: A class of *DSM-5* disorders characterized by disruptions in a person's sleep patterns or dissatisfaction regarding the quality, timing, or amount of sleep; causes distress or impairment during the day

Sleepwalking: A type of sleep arousal disorder characterized by the tendency to leave the bed and walk during non-REM sleep; the person usually has reduced responsiveness to others and is difficult to wake

Urine alarm: A small mechanical device worn in children's underpants or placed in bedding that detects urine and wakes the child with a noise and/or vibration

Voiding postponement: A cause of daytime wetting in young children; children avoid voiding in the toilet because they are engrossed in other activities

CRITICAL THINKING EXERCISES

1. Many parents try to treat their children's nocturnal enuresis by restricting fluids after dinner. Why is this usually not effective in fixing the problem?

2. A urine alarm is typically used to treat nocturnal enuresis. However, experts disagree on how the alarm decreases nighttime wetting. How might you use classical conditioning to explain its effectiveness in decreasing enuresis? Alternatively, how might you use negative reinforcement to explain its effectiveness?

3. Many parents blame children for encopresis. To what extent is encopresis volitional? How might blaming or punishing children exacerbate the problem?

4. The treatment of insomnia in infants and toddlers typically involves extinction through planned ignoring. Why might some parents have difficulty implementing this treatment? How might parents' social and cultural backgrounds affect their willingness to use planned ignoring?

5. One of the Five Cs of pediatric psychology is "collaboration." Why is it important that pediatric psychologists collaborate with parents, teachers, physicians, and other health care providers? Give two examples of how collaboration might be critical to the treatment of children with chronic illness.

TEST YOURSELF AND EXTEND YOUR LEARNING

Videos, flash cards, and links to online resources for this chapter are available to students online. Teachers also have access to PowerPoint slides to guide lectures, case studies to prompt classroom discussions, and exam questions. Visit www.abnormalchildpsychology.org.

Appendix

A Primer on Research Methods in Abnormal Child Psychology

How Do Psychological Scientists Study Behavior?

Science is the systematic search for order in the natural world. Scientists seek to identify meaningful relationships between observable events in order to describe, predict, explain, or control these events. Physical scientists focus chiefly on the principles of matter and movement. Biological scientists concentrate on relationships within and between living systems. Psychological scientists direct their attention to the structure and functioning of behavior—that is, to people's thoughts, feelings, and actions (Kendall & Comer, 2014).

Science can be differentiated from nonscientific approaches to understanding the world in at least three ways (Newsom & Hovanitz, 2005).

1. Scientists generate hypothesis to understand natural phenomena.

2. Scientist's hypotheses are verifiable; that is, they can be tested.

3. Scientists test their hypotheses using carefully collected, empirical data.

First, to help organize their understanding of nature, scientists *generate hypotheses* about natural phenomena. Hypotheses are initial explanations or accounts about the natural world that are based on observation, previous research, and theory. Hypotheses are stated clearly and unambiguously, using either mathematical formulas or verbal statements. When scientists express hypotheses verbally, they provide operational definitions—that is, carefully crafted descriptions of how phenomena can be measured. For example, a behavioral scientist might operationally define the term *aggressive* as "getting into physical fights at least three times per month." Operational definitions translate hypotheses into clear, observable terms and allow scientists to communicate with one another precisely and consistently.

Second, scientists *generate testable hypotheses*. The statements that scientists make about the natural world must be open to evaluation by others. Specifically, hypotheses must be falsifiable, or capable of being disconfirmed.

Technically speaking, scientists do not seek to prove their hypotheses. Instead, they seek to examine the possibility that their hypotheses might be wrong. Once scientists generate a hypothesis, they reword the hypothesis as a statement that can be disconfirmed. This falsifiable hypothesis is often called the null hypothesis. For example, if a psychologist's hypothesis is "Disruptive adolescents will show higher levels of depression than nondisruptive adolescents," her null hypothesis might be "Disruptive adolescents will show levels of depression *equal* to nondisruptive adolescents." Then, the psychologist examines whether the null hypothesis can be rejected. Rejecting the null hypothesis can provide support for the psychologist's ideas, but it does not *prove* that her ideas are correct (Barker & Pistrang, 2015).

Finally, scientists systematically evaluate hypotheses using *empirical data*. Empirical data can come from direct observations of others' actions, physiological measures, or self- and other-reports. One goal of hypothesis testing is to determine causal relationships between two or more events (McBride, 2015). To establish that Variable A causes Variable B, three conditions must be met:

1. *Variable A and Variable B must show covariation;* that is, a change in the presence or strength of Variable A must be associated with a corresponding change in the presence or strength of Variable B. For example, if we say that child physical abuse causes depression, then children who experience abuse should also show greater likelihood of becoming depressed.

2. *Variable A must precede Variable B.* For example, if child abuse causes depression, then we would expect children who experience abuse to subsequently show depression. We would not expect depression to exist before the onset of abuse.

3. *Alternative causes for the covariation of Variables A and B must be ruled out.* For example, children who have experienced abuse may become depressed, but this covariation does not necessarily imply that abuse *causes* depression. Other variables may account for both abuse and children's depressive symptoms. One alternative explanation is that mothers who are depressed may be more likely to mistreat their children. Furthermore, mothers with depression may pass on genes that predispose their children to problems with depression.

What Are Correlational Studies?

Description

Most psychological research examines association between two or more variables. For example, a researcher might examine whether children who have histories of abuse in early childhood (i.e., Variable A) show greater likelihood of depression in later childhood or adolescence (i.e., Variable B). Similarly, researchers might examine whether the size or functioning of a certain brain region (i.e., Variable A) is associated with the severity of children's autistic symptoms (i.e., Variable B). Correlational studies allow researchers to determine the relationship between variables (Kazdin, 2017).

Researchers usually quantify the magnitude of the association between variables, using a correlation coefficient. The Pearson product–moment correlation coefficient (r) is the most commonly used statistic (see Figure A.1). Correlation coefficients range from 1.0 to –1.0. The *strength* of association is determined by the absolute value of the coefficient. Coefficients near 1.0 or –1.0 indicate strong covariation between variables, whereas coefficients near 0 indicate weak or absent covariation. The *direction* of the association is determined by the sign of the coefficient. Positive values indicate a direct association between variables (i.e., as one variable increases, the other increases), whereas negative values indicate an inverse association (i.e., as one variable increases, the other decreases).

Correlations and Causality

Correlational studies allow researchers to notice associations between variables, but they do not allow researchers to infer causal relationships between variables (Howell, 2016). Why?

First, a correlation between two variables does not tell us the temporal relationship between the variables. Imagine that researchers notice that the size of a certain brain area is negatively correlated with the severity of children's autistic symptoms: The smaller the brain region, the greater the child's symptoms. We might be tempted to infer a causal relationship between brain and behavior—specifically, that an underdevelopment of this brain region causes autism. However, it is also possible that autistic symptoms, over time, cause this part of the brain to atrophy. Correlations do not allow us to determine temporal relationships between variables. Consequently, they do not allow us to infer causality.

The second reason we cannot infer causal relationships from correlational data is that correlational studies do not rule out alternative explanations for covariation. If we notice a correlation between the size of a brain region and the severity of children's autistic symptoms, we might be tempted to conclude that brain structure influences behavior or behavior affects brain structure. However, an alternative possibility is that a third factor might account for both a reduction in brain size and an increase in autistic symptoms (see Figure A.2). For example, children exposed to certain toxins during gestation might show both brain abnormalities and features of autism. Correlational studies do not control for these alternative explanations; consequently, they cannot be used to infer causal relationships.

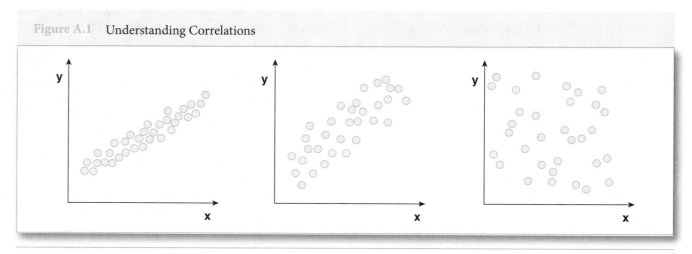

Figure A.1 Understanding Correlations

Note: The relationship between two variables is plotted on the X and Y axes respectively. Plots 1 and 2 show positive correlations. The association between variables is stronger for plot 1 ($r = .76$) than plot 2 ($r = .56$). Plot 3 shows no association between the two variables ($r = .00$).

Figure A.2 Correlation does not imply causality

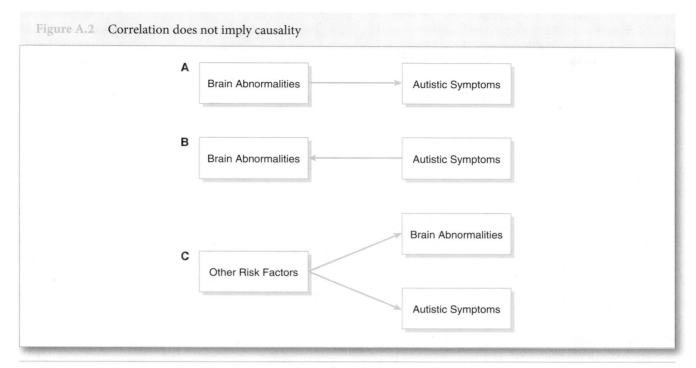

Source: Based on Baron-Cohen (2005) and Lawrence, Lott, and Haier (2005).

Note: Although there is a correlation between brain structure and autistic symptoms, we do not know if (a) brain abnormalities cause autistic behaviors, (b) autistic behaviors lead to abnormal brain development, or (c) other risk factors, like exposure to toxins, cause both brain abnormalities and autism.

Types of Correlational Studies

There are two types of correlational research designs that are especially relevant to scientists who examine the causes of childhood disorders: (1) cross-sectional and (2) longitudinal (Lane & Sándor, 2016). In a cross-sectional study, researchers examine the association between variables at the same point in time. For example, researchers might examine the brain structure of children with autism. At the same time, they might ask parents to complete a questionnaire regarding the severity of their children's autistic symptoms. Cross-sectional studies can be conducted relatively quickly. However, because data are collected at the same point in time, researchers cannot determine the temporal relationship between the variables.

In a longitudinal study, researchers specify the temporal relationship between variables by measuring variables at different times. In a prospective longitudinal study, researchers measure a hypothesized causal variable at Time 1 and measure its expected outcome at Time 2. For example, researchers might hypothesize that certain brain abnormalities lead to later autistic symptoms. To test this hypothesis, they might assess brain structure during toddlerhood and autistic symptoms 1 or 2 years later. Prospective longitudinal studies have the advantage over cross-sectional studies of testing temporal relationships between variables.

Prospective longitudinal studies are difficult to conduct because participants often drop out of studies before their completion and researchers must wait a long time to test their hypotheses. Consequently, some researchers use other types of longitudinal designs to test hypotheses about the etiology of disorders. In a retrospective longitudinal study, researchers examine individuals with known disorders and ask them (or their parents) to recall events in the past that might have caused the disorder. For example, researchers might ask the parents of children with autism to recall social deficits that their children showed during infancy and that might have preceded the emergence of the disorder. The chief limitation of retrospective longitudinal studies is that they depend on the accuracy of people's memories for events in the past.

In a follow-back study, researchers examine the case histories, school records, or medical records of individuals with known disorders to determine whether events in their past may have contributed to the emergence of the disorder. For example, Osterling and Dawson (1994) reviewed videotapes of the first birthday parties of children later diagnosed with autism. Compared to typically developing children, 1-year-olds later diagnosed with autism showed deficits during their birthday parties. Although parents usually did not notice these deficits at the time, they were observable on the videotape to researchers. The researchers suggested that early deficits in social and language functioning, often not noticeable by others, may contribute to the development of autism. Follow-back studies, like the one conducted by Osterling and Dawson (1994), do not rely on parents' memories of past events. However, obtaining high-quality records of children's developmental histories is often difficult.

Moderators and Mediators

Psychologists have long recognized the complexity of child development. Rarely is there a one-to-one correspondence between a single risk factor and a particular developmental outcome. Instead, researchers are often interested in identifying the conditions under which one variable is associated with another (Krull, Cheong, Fritz, & MacKinnin, 2016; Maric, van Steensel, & Bögels, 2015).

A moderator is a variable that affects the nature of the relationship between two other variables (Baron & Kenny, 1986; Hayes, 2013). For example, considerable research indicates that child maltreatment is a significant, unique predictor for adolescent suicide. Prospective, longitudinal studies have shown that children who experience sexual abuse are at increased risk for suicidal thoughts and actions later in adolescence. However, children's gender moderates the relationship between child sexual abuse and later suicidality. Specifically, child sexual abuse predicts suicidal thoughts and actions for boys but not for girls (see Figure A.3; Miller, Esposito-Smythers, Weismoore, & Renshaw, 2013).

Moderators affect the direction or strength of the association between two variables. In this case, gender moderates the relationship between abuse in childhood and suicidality in adolescence. Moderator variables tend to be categorical variables. Some frequently studied moderator variables in child psychopathology research are gender (i.e., boy, girl), age (e.g., child, adult), ethnicity (i.e., African American, non-Latino White), socioeconomic status (SES; e.g., low-income, middle class), and diagnostic status (e.g., attention-deficit/hyperactivity disorder [ADHD], non-ADHD).

Sometimes, researchers want to know the mechanism by which one variable affects another variable. A mediator is a variable that may explain the relationship between two other variables (Baron & Kenny, 1986; Hayes, 2013). In the field of developmental psychopathology, a mediator might explain how one variable (e.g., a risk factor) might influence another variable (e.g., a disorder).

For example, we know that child maltreatment predicts suicidal thoughts and actions in adolescence. A mediator is a variable that explains why this relationship occurs. One such mediator is children's interpersonal relationships in middle school. Specifically, children who experience maltreatment tend to have less trusting and satisfying peer relationships in middle school. These interpersonal problems, in turn, contribute to feelings of isolation, rejection and suicidal ideation in later adolescence (Miller et al., 2013).

Mediators explain the mechanism by which a risk factor (e.g., child maltreatment) leads to a developmental outcome or disorder (e.g., suicide). In this case, interpersonal relationships mediate the relationship between child maltreatment

Figure A.3   Moderation and Mediation

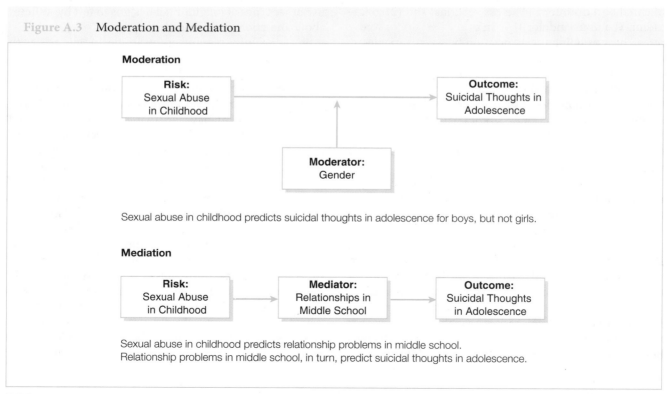

Moderation

Sexual abuse in childhood predicts suicidal thoughts in adolescence for boys, but not girls.

Mediation

Sexual abuse in childhood predicts relationship problems in middle school.
Relationship problems in middle school, in turn, predict suicidal thoughts in adolescence.

and adolescent suicide. Mediators tend to be continuous variables—that is, they range from low to high and everywhere in between. Mediators are important because they indicate how one variable might influence another variable and can suggest ways to prevent or treat childhood disorders. For example, one way to prevent suicide among maltreated children is to help them develop strong peer relationships (Klimes-Dougan, Klingbeil, & Meller, 2013).

What are Experiments?

Description

Researchers are usually not satisfied with knowing that variables correlate. They also want to determine whether a change in one variable *causes* a corresponding change in another variable. The best way to establish causality between two variables is to conduct an experimental study (Kazdin, 2017). In an experiment, researchers randomly assign participants to two or more groups. Then, they manipulate one variable (i.e., the independent variable) and notice the effects of this manipulation on a second variable (i.e., the dependent variable). Experiments allow causal inferences because researchers randomly assign participants to treatment and control groups at the onset of the study and treat both groups identically throughout the duration of the study (except for the manipulation of the independent variable).

In the field of abnormal child psychology, experimental research is most frequently used to examine the effectiveness of treatment. For example, a researcher might be interested in determining the efficacy of a new treatment designed to improve the verbal skills of children with autism. She might randomly assign children with autism to two groups. Children in the treatment group might receive 30 weeks of the new treatment (i.e., the independent variable), while children in the control group might be assigned to a waiting list. After 30 weeks, the researcher examines differences in children's language skills (i.e., the dependent variable) across groups. Differences between groups on the dependent variable might indicate that the new treatment has an effect on children's verbal skills (Kendall & Comer, 2014).

A randomized controlled trial is a special type of experiment used to test the effectiveness of treatment. Researchers identify a group of individuals with the same disorder. Typically, individuals are recruited from the community, mental health clinics, or hospitals. Then, participants are randomly assigned to at least two groups. One group, the treatment group, receives the intervention. The other group, the control group, is used for comparison. Random assignment implies that each participant has an equal chance of being assigned to the treatment or the control group. By randomly assigning participants, the researcher decreases the likelihood that groups differ in meaningful ways before the treatment.

Random assignment is essential to experimental research. Without random assignment, differences between groups that emerge at the end of the study might be attributable to differences that existed before the study, rather than to the treatment itself.

Many randomized controlled trials are double-blind. In a double-blind study, neither researchers nor participants know to what group participants have been assigned. Double-blind studies reduce biases on the part of researchers and participants. For example, researchers might behave differently toward participants in the treatment versus the control group if they know the group status of participants. Differences in researchers' behaviors toward members of these groups might affect the results of the evaluation.

Participants might also behave differently if they know whether they have been assigned to the treatment or control group. The placebo effect refers to the tendency of people to show improvement when they believe they are receiving treatment. Typically, people who believe that they are receiving treatment pay greater attention to their health and behavior, take better care of themselves, and are more optimistic about their outcomes. Researchers must control for placebo effects; they need to be able to attribute symptom reduction to the treatment itself, not to participants' expectations for improvement (Holmbeck, Zebracki, & McGoron, 2009).

Types of Control Groups

A critical decision in randomized controlled studies is what to do with participants in the control group (Kazdin, 2017). Many researchers compare the treatment group to a *no-treatment control group*. In this type of study, participants in the control group receive no treatment whatsoever. The primary shortcoming of using a no-treatment control group is that participants assigned to this group will clearly know that they are not receiving treatment. Consequently, differences between controls and participants in the treatment group can be attributable to placebo effects rather than the treatment per se. A second problem with using a no-treatment control group is that it is often unethical to withhold treatment from people with mental health problems, even for the sake of testing the efficacy of a new therapy. For example, it would be unethical to assign children with learning disorders to a no-treatment control group. By denying children treatment, we would be contributing to their academic delays.

Other researchers compare participants in the treatment group to participants assigned to a *waitlist control group*. In this type of study, participants assigned to the control group are placed on a waiting list to receive treatment. Treatment is delayed but not altogether withheld from participants. Waitlist control groups are usually more ethically justifiable than no-treatment control groups. However, they also have the limitation that participants assigned to the waitlist clearly know that they are not receiving treatment.

A third type of control group used in many randomized controlled studies is the *attention-placebo control group*. In an attention-placebo controlled study, participants assigned to the control group receive a theoretically inert form of treatment that resembles the treatment received by participants in the treatment group. For example, participants in an attention-placebo group might have weekly meetings with a therapist who listens to their concerns and responds in an empathic manner. Participants in the control group would likely believe that they were receiving the active treatment, thereby controlling for placebo effects between groups. However, participants in the attention-placebo group would not receive any specific form of treatment. For example, they would not be taught specific behavioral or cognitive techniques designed to reduce symptoms.

Finally, some researchers compare participants who receive the experimental treatment with participants who receive a treatment that is already available. For example, if a researcher develops a new treatment for ADHD, this new treatment might be compared to a treatment that already exists. Use of a *standard treatment control group* is the most stringent test of a new form of therapy. The new treatment must show that it reduces symptoms *and* that its benefits match or exceed those offered by existing therapies. A variant of the use of standard treatment controls is to compare an experimental treatment with "treatment as usual" (TAU). In this case, participants assigned to the treatment group receive the new therapy while participants assigned to the control group are referred to clinicians in the community and receive whatever form of care these clinicians recommend (i.e., treatment as usual).

A study conducted by Ronald Rapee and colleagues illustrates a randomized controlled trial. Rapee, Abbott, and Lyneham (2006) recruited 267 children with anxiety disorders and randomly assigned them to one of three conditions. The first group received a cognitive–behavioral therapy (CBT) program for youths with anxiety problems. The second group received bibliotherapy; that is, their parents were given a book that described ways to treat childhood anxiety problems and parents were encouraged to use the techniques described in the book with their children at home. Children in the third group were placed on a waiting list. Three months after the beginning of the study, researchers examined the percentage of children in each group who no longer met diagnostic criteria for an anxiety disorder (see Figure A.4). Results showed that significantly more children who participated in bibliotherapy (25.9%) were free of an anxiety disorder than children assigned to the waitlist control condition (6.7%). However, children who received CBT were more likely to be free of their anxiety problems (61.1%) than children assigned to either of the other two groups. Results indicate that bibliotherapy is effective in reducing childhood anxiety; however, CBT is preferable to bibliotherapy as a primary form of treatment.

What Are Quasi-Experimental Studies?

In some cases, random assignment is not possible. For example, researchers might want to examine the effectiveness of a new form of therapy to treat adolescents with severe depression and suicidal thoughts. It would be inappropriate to randomly assign youths to a control group that did not receive the best treatment possible. When random assignment is not possible, the research design is said to be quasi-experimental (Raulin & Lilienfeld, 2014).

Quasi-experimental studies cannot be used to infer causal relationships between variables because improvement in symptoms can be attributable to other factors, not the treatment per se (Maughan & Rutter, 2010). For example, if adolescents with severe depression participate in a new treatment and they show significant symptom alleviation, we might say that the treatment was *associated with* symptom reduction; however, it would be inappropriate to infer that treatment *caused* the adolescents' improvement in functioning.

The internal validity of a research study refers to the degree to which we can attribute changes in the dependent variable (e.g., symptom reduction) to manipulation of the independent variable (e.g., treatment). When other factors, besides treatment, can explain symptom reduction, researchers say these factors threaten the internal validity of the study.

What factors, besides treatment, might cause symptom reduction and threaten the internal validity of a study? Kazdin (2017) identifies at least five threats to internal validity that limit the causal inferences we can make from quasi-experimental research.

First, *maturation* can compromise the internal validity of a treatment study. Maturation refers to changes in the child that occur as a result of the passage of time. For example, in most adolescents, an episode of major depression lasts approximately two to nine months. Over time, depressive symptoms usually decrease even if no treatment is provided. Consequently, a researcher who administers a new therapy to adolescents with severe depression over the course of 6 months might erroneously conclude the treatment is effective if adolescents' symptoms decrease over time. Unless the researcher compares adolescents who received treatment with adolescents in a control group, the effects of treatment cannot be distinguished from maturation.

Second, events in the *surrounding environment* can threaten the internal validity of research. Events might include major news stories (e.g., terrorist attacks); natural disasters (e.g., hurricanes); changes in family environment or schools (e.g., a new teacher); or more subtle changes in temperature, weather, or the quality of the child's life. For example, a researcher might administer a new treatment for adolescent depression beginning in February and ending in May. The researcher might notice that adolescents' depression scores decrease over the course of treatment.

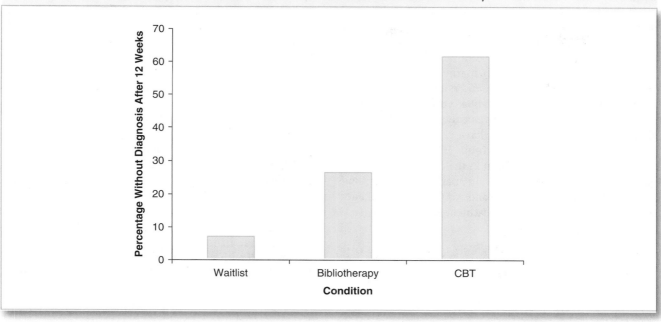

Source: Based on Rapee et al. (2006).

Note: Youths with anxiety disorders were randomly assigned to one of three conditions: (a) waitlist, (b) bibliotherapy, or (c) cognitive-behavioral therapy (CBT). Results showed that youths responded best to CBT; however, bibliotherapy was superior to the waitlist control.

She might erroneously attribute symptom reduction to her treatment. However, environmental changes across the duration of treatment might also be responsible for symptom alleviation. For example, adolescents might experience an improvement in mood simply because of more pleasant weather, greater opportunities for outdoor recreational activities, or anticipation of summer vacation.

A third threat to internal validity is *repeated testing.* The act of repeatedly assessing children can cause them to show improvement in their functioning over time. For example, a researcher might administer a 10-week treatment program to youths with math difficulties. To assess his treatment, he might ask the children to complete a math achievement test before the intervention, halfway through the treatment, and again upon completion. Children might show improvement in their math scores over time not because they benefited from the intervention but because they were exposed to the same math problems on three different occasions.

Fourth, in quasi-experimental studies, a *lack of random assignment* can lead to selection biases. Selection biases refer to systematic differences between treatment and control groups that emerge when groups are not randomly assigned at the beginning of the study. Imagine that a researcher investigates the efficacy of a new treatment for depression by recruiting adolescents with depression from hospitals and clinics. She assigns the first 25 adolescents who agree to participate in the study to the treatment group, and she places the remaining 25 adolescents on a

waiting list to serve as controls. After 10 weeks of treatment, the researcher notices greater mood improvement among adolescents who received treatment. The researcher cannot attribute these differences to the treatment itself. Instead, selection biases before treatment might account for symptom differences after treatment. For example, the first 25 adolescents who agreed to participate in the study may have been more motivated to participate in treatment than the latter 25 assigned to the control group.

Finally, *attrition* can threaten the validity of all treatment outcome studies, especially studies that involve quasi-experimental designs. Attrition refers to the loss of participants over the course of the study. Attrition most often occurs because participants decide to withdraw from the study or simply stop attending follow-up appointments. When a large percentage of participants who receive treatment withdraw from a study, researchers may not be able to attribute symptom reduction to treatment. For example, a researcher might notice differences between treatment and control groups following a 10-week trial of a new therapy for depression. However, if 50% of participants assigned to the treatment group withdrew from the study before its completion, the researcher cannot be certain whether the 50% who remained in the study were representative of the treatment group as a whole. It is possible that the 50% who withdrew showed an *increase* in depression, prompting them to drop out.

A study by Walker, Roffman, Stephens, Wakana, and Berghuis (2006) illustrates how a lack of random assignment to a control group can threaten internal validity. The researchers randomly assigned 97 high school students who frequently used marijuana to two conditions. The first group received a brief form of CBT called motivational enhancement therapy (MET). The second group was assigned to a waiting list. After 3 months, researchers assessed adolescents' marijuana use (see Figure A.5). Youths who received MET showed significant reduction in marijuana use. However, youths in the control group, who did not receive treatment, showed a similar reduction in marijuana use. The researchers hypothesized that the act of repeatedly asking adolescents about their marijuana use may have caused a decrease in marijuana smoking across both groups. If the researchers had failed to include a control group in their study, they would have only noticed the decrease in marijuana use among adolescents who received MET and would have mistakenly attributed this decrease to the treatment itself.

What Are Single-Subject Studies?

A third way to investigate the efficacy of treatment is to conduct a single-subject research study. In a single-subject study, the same individual's behavior is compared before and after treatment. Differences in behavior during or after treatment provide evidence for treatment efficacy. Single-subject studies are sometimes called time-series studies because the same individual's behavior is studied across time (Kazdin, 2017).

The simplest way to evaluate treatment effectiveness is to collect data regarding the frequency and/or severity of the child's problematic behavior before and after the intervention. This method is called an *AB design*. The *A* refers to the level of problematic behavior at baseline while the *B* refers to the level of problematic behavior after the intervention. For example, children with autism sometimes engage in high-rate, stereotyped behaviors, such as hand flapping or rocking back and forth, which can be distracting to teachers and classmates. To collect baseline data, a therapist might observe the number of times a child with autism flaps his hands during 1 hour of class on 3 consecutive days. Then, he instructs the child's classroom aide to reinforce the child with eye contact and

Figure A.5   The Importance of Using Control Groups

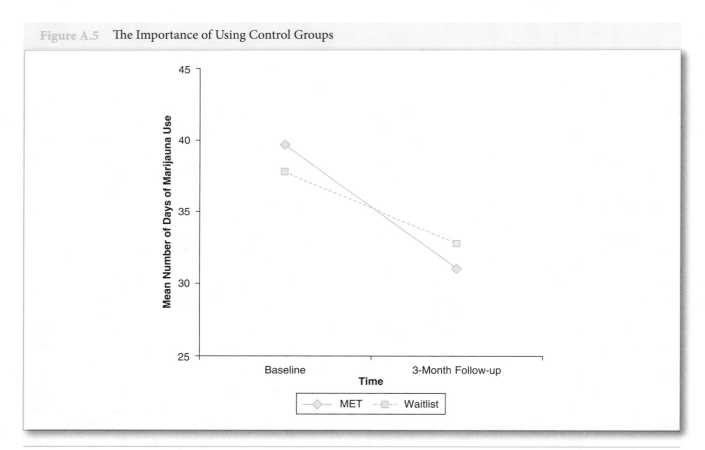

Source: Based on Walker et al. (2006).

Note: Researchers randomly assigned adolescents who frequently used marijuana to one of two conditions: (a) motivational enhancement therapy (MET) or (b) a waiting list. Youths who participated in MET showed a reduction in marijuana use. However, youths assigned to the waiting list also showed a reduction in marijuana use, even though they did not receive treatment.

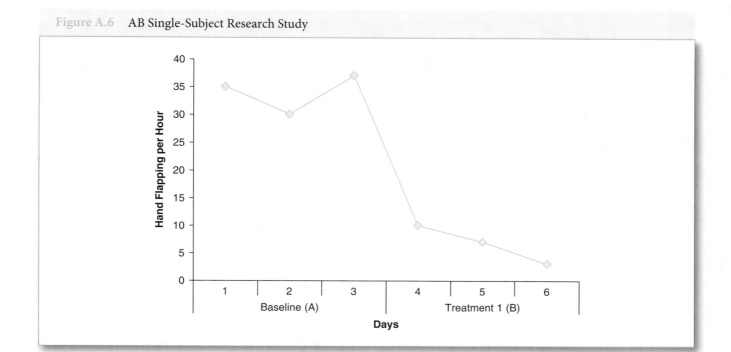

Note: In this study, a child with autism is observed for 3 days to gather baseline data on the frequency of hand flapping (A). Then, the therapist reinforces the child for keeping his hands at his side (B). The reduction in hand flapping suggests that positive reinforcement is effective to treat this problem.

a light touch each minute he keeps his hands in his pockets or on his lap. Finally, he observes the child's behavior in the classroom for another 3 consecutive days after treatment. A decrease in frequency of the child's hand flapping suggests improvement in functioning (see Figure A.6).

The chief limitation of the AB design is that it suffers from the same threats to internal validity as quasi-experimental research. Without a control group for comparison, clinicians cannot be sure that changes in the child's behavior can be attributed to treatment (Raulin & Lilienfeld, 2014).

To provide better evidence for a causal relationship between treatment and symptom reduction, many researchers use *ABAB designs*, also called reversal designs. First, the therapist collects data at baseline and after the intervention, just as in an AB design. Then, she temporarily withdraws treatment and notices any change in the child's behavior (the second A). If the intervention is responsible for improvement in the child's behavior, then withdrawal of the intervention should result in the temporary return of the child's behavior problems. Finally, the therapist would reinstate the intervention (the second B). If the intervention works, the child's behavior problems should subsequently decrease (see Figure A.7).

The chief limitation of the ABAB design is that it is sometimes unethical to withdraw treatment. Imagine that a therapist is treating a young child with severe intellectual disability (ID) for head banging; the boy repeatedly bangs his head against the wall when he becomes frustrated,

angry, or bored. First, the therapist monitors the rate of the child's head banging at baseline (A). Then, the therapist contingently interrupts the child's head banging by misting him with water from a spray bottle when he begins to engage in the behavior (B). To establish a causal connection between the water mist and the decrease in head banging, the clinician would need to withdraw use of the water mist and observe a subsequent increase in head banging. However, because head banging carries serious risks, withdrawal of treatment is unethical.

A third way to examine the effectiveness of treatment is to conduct a *multiple-baseline design*. Here, the therapist identifies two behavior problems and targets them one at a time. For example, a boy with autism might show both hand flapping and rocking in the classroom. First, the therapist collects baseline data regarding the frequency of both behaviors for 1 hour on 3 consecutive days (baseline). Then, he targets the child's hand flapping by instructing the classroom aide to reinforce the child for keeping his hands in his pockets. He observes the child for another 3 days. If the intervention is effective, he should notice a reduction in the child's hand flapping but not a reduction in the child's rocking. Next, the therapist targets the child's rocking. As the teacher continues to reinforce the child for keeping his hands in his pockets, the therapist instructs the child's classroom aide to reinforce him with a light touch on the shoulders every minute he does not rock. The therapist subsequently observes behavior for an additional 3 days. If the second intervention

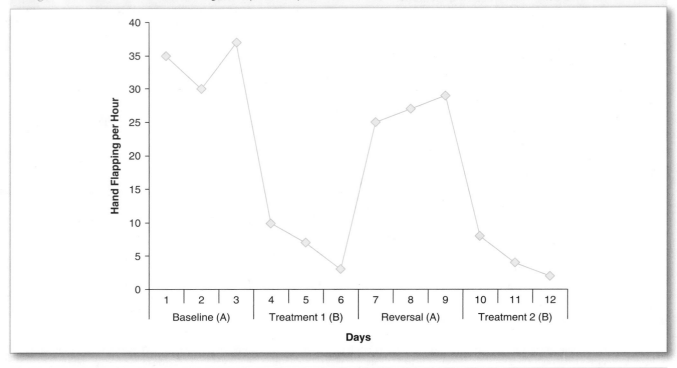

Note: In this study, the therapist collects baseline data on the child's hand flapping (A) and then provides reinforcement contingent on keeping hands at side (B). In the reversal phase (second A), reinforcement is removed, resulting in an increase in hand flapping. Finally, reinforcement is reapplied (second B) to again reduce the behavior.

is effective, the child should show a reduction in both behavior problems.

The chief limitation of all single-subject research designs is that causal inferences are based on data from only one client. Consequently, it is often unclear whether the results of a single-subject study are applicable to other individuals with similar problems.

The external validity of a study refers to the degree to which results generalize to other people and situations. To establish the external validity of findings generated from single-subject research, results must be replicated, or repeated, with other individuals and in other settings.

KEY TERMS

Correlational studies: Research designs that allow inferences about the relationship between variables but do not allow causal inferences

Cross-sectional study: A correlational study in which researchers examine the association between variables at the same point in time

Double-blind study: Neither researchers nor participants know to what group participants have been assigned; controls for placebo/expectancy effects

External validity: The degree to which results generalize to other people and situations

Falsifiable: Capable of being disconfirmed by empirical testing; a characteristics of a scientific hypothesis

Follow-back study: A study in which researchers examine the educational or medical records of individuals with known

disorders to determine whether events in their past may have contributed to the emergence of the disorder

Hypotheses: Initial accounts or explanations about natural phenomena that are based on observation, previous research, and theory

Internal validity: The degree to which we can attribute changes in the dependent variable (symptom reduction) to manipulation of the independent variable (treatment)

Mediator: A variable that may explain the relationship between two other variables; usually a continuous variable (e.g., severity of depression, IQ score)

Moderator: A variable that affects the nature of the relationship between two other variables; usually a categorical variable (e.g., gender, ethnicity)

Null hypothesis: A version of the researcher's hypothesis that assumes no relationships or effects between variables

Operational definitions: Clear descriptions of constructs that indicate how they will be observed and measured

Pearson product–moment correlation coefficient (r): A measure of the linear association between two variables; provides a value between +1 and −1 in which the value indicates the strength of the association and the sign indicates its direction

Placebo effect: The tendency of people to show improvement when they believe they are receiving treatment and expect such improvement

Prospective longitudinal study: A study in which researchers measure a hypothesized variable at Time 1 and measure its expected outcome at Time 2

Quasi-experimental studies: A study in which two or more groups are compared, but the study lacks random assignment; consequently, causality cannot be inferred

Random assignment: An essential feature of an experiment; each participant has an equal chance of being assigned to the treatment group or control group

Randomized controlled trial: An experimental study in which participants are assigned by chance to either a treatment condition or comparison (control) condition; the researchers manipulate treatment (independent variable [IV]) and notice changes in outcome (dependent variable [DV]) holding all other factors constant across the conditions

Retrospective longitudinal study: A study in which researchers examine individuals with known disorders and ask them (or their parents) to recall events in the past that might have caused the disorder

Single-subject research study: A design in which the same child's behavior is compared before and after treatment with all other variables held constant; changes in behavior provide evidence for treatment efficacy

References

Abbeduto, L., McDuffie, A., Brady, N., & Kover, S. T. (2012). Language development in Fragile X syndrome. In J. A. Burack, R. M. Hodapp, G. Iarocci, & E. Zigler (Eds.), *The Oxford handbook of intellectual disability and development* (pp. 200–216). New York, NY: Oxford University Press.

Abbott, S. M., Reid, K. J., & Zee, P. C. (2015). Circadian rhythm sleep–wake disorders. *Psychiatric Clinics of North America, 38*(4), 805–823.

Abela, J. R. Z., Hankin, B. L., Haigh, E. A. P., Adams, P., Vinokuroff, T., & Trayhern, L. (2005). Interpersonal vulnerability to depression in high-risk children. *Journal of Clinical Child and Adolescent Psychology, 34*, 182–192.

Aber, J. L., Gershoff, E. T., Ware, A., & Kotler, J. A. (2004). Estimating the effects of September 11th and other forms of violence on the mental health and social development of New York City's youth. *Applied Developmental Science, 8*, 111–129.

Abikoff, H., Hechtman, L., Klein, R. G., Gallagher, R., Fleiss, K., Etcovitch, J., . . . Pollack, S. (2004a). Social functioning in children with ADHD treated with long-term methylphenidate and multimodal psychosocial treatment. *Journal of the American Academy of Child and Adolescent Psychiatry, 43*, 820–829.

Abikoff, H., Hechtman, L., Klein, R. G., Weiss, G., Fleiss, K., Etcovitch, J., . . . Pollack, S. (2004b). Symptomatic improvement in children with ADHD treated with long-term methylphenidate and multimodal psychosocial treatment. *Journal of the American Academy of Child and Adolescent Psychiatry, 43*, 802–811.

Abramson, L. Y., Alloy, L. B., Hogan, M. E., Whitehouse, W. G., Gibb, B. E., & Hanklin, B. L. (2000). *Suicide science*. New York, NY: Kluwer.

Abramson, L. Y., Metalsky, G., & Alloy, L. (1989). Hopelessness depression: A theory-based subtype of depression. *Psychological Review, 96*, 358–372.

Abramson, L. Y., Seligman, M. E., & Teasdale, J. D. (1978). Learned helplessness in humans. *Journal of Abnormal Psychology, 87*, 49–74.

Acar, C., Tekin-Iftar, E., & Yikmis, A. (2016). Effects of mother-delivered social stories and video modeling in teaching social skills to children with autism spectrum disorders. *Journal of Special Education*. Advance online publication. doi:10.1177/0022466916649164

Achenbach, T. M. (2009). *The Achenbach System of Empirically Based Assessment (ASEBA)*. Burlington: University of Vermont Research Center.

Achenbach, T. M. (2015). Developmental psychopathology. In T. P. Beauchaine & S. P. Hinshaw (Eds.), *The Oxford handbook of externalizing spectrum disorders* (pp. 488–512). Oxford, England: Oxford University Press.

Achenbach, T. M. (2016). *ASEBA research updates from around the world*. Retrieved August 15, 2016, from http://www.aseba.org/research/research.html

Achenbach, T. M., McConaughy, S. H., & Howell, C. T. (1987). Child/adolescent behavioral and emotional problems: Implications of cross-informant correlations for situational specificity. *Psychological Bulletin, 101*, 213–232.

Achenbach, T. M., & Rescorla, L. A. (2016). Developmental issues in assessment, taxonomy, and diagnosis of psychopathology. In D. Cicchetti (Ed.), *Developmental psychopathology* (Vol. 1, pp. 46–93). New York, NY: Wiley.

Adams, G., & Carnine, D. (2003). Direct instruction. In H. L. Swanson, K. R. Harris, & S. Graham (Eds.), *Handbook of learning disabilities* (pp. 403–416). New York, NY: Guilford Press.

Agras, W. S., Crow, S. J., Halmi, K. A., Mitchell, J. E., Wilson, G. T., & Kraemer, H. C. (2000). Outcome predictors for the cognitive behavior treatment of bulimia nervosa. *American Journal of Psychiatry, 757*, 1302–1308.

Agras, W. S., Walsh, B. T., Fairburn, C. G., Wilson, G. T., & Kraemer, C. H. (2000). A multi-center comparison of cognitive-behavioral therapy and interpersonal psychotherapy for bulimia nervosa. *Archives of General Psychiatry, 57*, 459–466.

Ainsworth, M. D. S., Blehar, M. C., Waters, E., & Wall, S. (1978). *Patterns of attachment: A psychological study of the strange situation*. Hillsdale, NJ: Erlbaum.

Akinbami, L. J., Liu, X., Pastor, P. N., & Reuben, C. A. (2011). *Attention deficit hyperactivity disorder among children aged 5–17 in the United States*. Washington, DC: US Department of Health and Human Services.

Al-Yagon, M., & Margalit, M. (2012). Children with Down syndrome: Parents' perspectives. In J. A. Burack, R. M. Hodapp, G. Iarocci, & E. Zigler (Eds.), *The Oxford handbook of intellectual disability and development* (pp. 349–365). New York, NY: Oxford University Press.

Alarcon, R. D. (2009). Culture, cultural factors and psychiatric diagnosis. *World Psychiatry, 8*, 131–139.

Alberts, H. J. E. M., Thewissen, R., & Raes, L. (2012). Dealing with problematic eating behaviour. *Appetite, 58*, 847–851.

Alfano, C. A., & Gamble, A. L. (2009). The role of sleep in childhood psychiatric disorders. *Child and Youth Care Forum, 38*, 327–340.

Alfano, C. A., Zakem, A. H., Costa, N. M., Taylor, L. K., & Weems, C. F. (2009). Sleep problems and their relation to cognitive factors, anxiety, and depressive symptoms in children and adolescents. *Depression and Anxiety, 26*, 503–512.

Alvaro, P. K., Roberts, R. M., & Harris, J. K. (2014). The independent relationships between insomnia, depression, subtypes of anxiety, and chronotype during adolescence. *Sleep Medicine, 15*, 934–941.

Aman, M. G., De Smedt, G., Derivan, A., Lyons, B., Findling, R. L., & Risperidone Disruptive Behavior Study Group. (2002). Double-blind, placebo-controlled study of risperidone for the treatment of disruptive behaviors in children with subaverage intelligence. *American Journal of Psychiatry, 159*, 1337–1346.

Ameis, S. H., & Szatmari, P. (2016). Common psychiatric comorbidities and their assessment. In E. Anagnostou & J. Brian (Eds.), *Clinician's manual on ASD* (pp. 19–32). New York, NY: Springer.

American Academy of Child and Adolescent Psychiatry. (2016). *Practice parameters*. Retrieved August 19, 2016, from http://www.jaacap.com/content/pracparam

American Academy of Pediatrics Subcommittee on ADHD. (2011). Clinical practice guideline for the diagnosis, evaluation, and treatment of attention-deficit/hyperactivity disorder in children and adolescents. *Pediatrics, 128*, 1–16.

American Counseling Association. (2014). *ACA code of ethics*. Alexandria, VA: Author.

American Psychiatric Association. (1968). *Diagnostic and statistical manual of mental disorders* (2nd ed.). Washington, DC: Author.

American Psychiatric Association. (1980). *Diagnostic and statistical manual of mental disorders* (3rd ed.). Washington, DC: Author.

American Psychiatric Association. (1987). *Diagnostic and statistical manual of mental disorders* (3rd ed., text revision). Washington, DC: Author.

American Psychiatric Association. (2013). *Diagnostic and statistical manual of mental disorders* (5th ed.). Washington, DC: Author.

American Psychological Association. (2010). *Ethical principles of psychologists and code of conduct*. Washington, DC: Author.

American School Counselor Association. (2010). *Ethical standards for school counselors*. Alexandria, VA: Author.

American Speech-Language-Hearing Association. (2016). *Augmentative and alternative communication (AAC)*. Rockville, MD: ASHA.

Amminger, G. P., Henry, L. P., Harrigan, S. M., Harris, M. G., Alvarez-Jimenez, M., Herrman, H., . . . McGorry, P. D. (2011). Outcome in early-onset schizophrenia revisited. *Schizophrenia Research, 131*, 112–119.

Anastasi, A., & Urbina, S. (1997). *Psychological testing*. Upper Saddle River, NJ: Prentice Hall.

Anastopoulos, A. D., Shelton, T. L., & Barkley, R. A. (2005). Family-based psychosocial treatments for children and adolescents with attention-deficit/hyperactivity disorder. In E. D. Hibbs & P. S. Jensen (Eds.), *Psychosocial treatments for child and adolescent disorders* (pp. 327–350). Washington, DC: American Psychological Association.

Anderson-Frye, E. P., & Becker, A. E. (2004). Sociocultural aspects of eating disorders. In J. K. Thompson (Ed.), *Handbook of eating disorders and obesity* (pp. 565–589). Hoboken, NJ: Wiley.

Andersson, U. (2010). Skill development in different components of arithmetic and basic cognitive functions. *Journal of Educational Psychology, 102*, 115.

Andrews, G., Hobbs, M. J., Borkovec, T. D., Beesdo, K., Craske, M. G., Heimberg, R. G., . . . Stanley, M. A. (2010). Generalized worry disorder: A review of *DSM-IV* generalized anxiety disorder and options for *DSM-5*. *Depression and Anxiety, 27*, 134–147.

Andrews, G., Slade, T., & Peters, L. (2009). Classification in psychiatry: ICD versus *DSM*. *British Journal of Psychiatry, 174*, 3–5.

Angell, C. A. (2009). *Language development and disorders*. Boston, MA: Jones & Bartlett.

Angelman, H. (1965). "Puppet children": A report on three cases. *Developmental Medicine and Child Neurology, 7*, 681–688.

Angold, A., Erkanli, A., Copeland, W., Goodman, R., Fisher, P. W., & Costello, E. J. (2012). Psychiatric diagnostic interviews for children and adolescents: A comparative study. *Journal of the American Academy of Child & Adolescent Psychiatry, 51*, 506–517.

Anie, K. A., & Green, J. (2015). Psychological therapies for sickle cell disease and pain. *The Cochrane database of systematic reviews, 2*, CD001916-CD001916.

Anie, K. A., & Green, J. (2016). Psychological therapies for sickle cell disease and pain. *Cochrane Database Systematic Review*.

Ansel, L. L., Barry, C. T., Gillen, C. T., & Herrington, L. L. (2015). An analysis of four self-report measures of adolescent callous-unemotional traits. *Journal of Psychopathology and Behavioral Assessment, 37*, 207–216.

Antshel, K. M., Hier, B. O., & Barkley, R. A. (2014). Executive functioning theory and ADHD. In S. Goldstein & J. Naglieri (Eds.), *Handbook of executive functioning* (pp. 107–120). New York, NY: Springer.

Anxiety Disorders Association of Canada. (2016). *Panic disorder and agoraphobia*. Vancouver, BC: Author.

Appleton, R., & Baldwin, T. (2006). *Management of brain injured children*. New York, NY: Oxford University Press.

Apter-Levi, Y., Pratt, M., Vakart, A., Feldman, M., Zagoory-Sharon, O., & Feldman, R. (2016). Maternal depression across the first years of life compromises child psychosocial adjustment; relations to child HPA-axis functioning. *Psychoneuroendocrinology, 64*, 47–56.

Arbuthnot, J., & Gordon, D. A. (1986). Behavioral and cognitive effects of a moral reasoning development intervention for high-risk behavior-disordered adolescents. *Journal of Consulting and Clinical Psychology, 54*, 208–216.

Archer, R. P. (2016). *Assessing adolescent psychopathology: MMPI-A/MMPI-A-RF*. New York, NY: Routledge.

Arkowitz, H., Miller, W. R., & Rollnick, S. (2015). *Motivational interviewing in the treatment of psychological problems*. New York, NY: Guilford Press.

Arnold, L. E., Hodgkins, P., Kahle, J., Madhoo, M., & Kewley, G. (2016). Long-term outcomes of ADHD. *Journal of Attention Disorders*.

Aro, T., Poikkeus, A. M., Laakso, M. L., Tolvanen, A., & Ahonen, T. (2015). Associations between private speech, behavioral self-regulation, and cognitive abilities. *International Journal of Behavioral Development, 39*, 508–518.

Arseneault, L., Cannon, M., Witton, J., & Murray, R. M. (2004). Causal association between cannabis and psychosis. *British Journal of Psychiatry, 184*, 110–117.

Arya, R., & Jain, S. V. (2013). Sleepwalking in children and adolescents. In S. V. Hothare (Ed.), *Parasomnias* (pp. 97–113). New York, NY: Springer.

Asarnow, J. R., & Kernan, C. L. (2008). Childhood schizophrenia. In T. P. Beauchaine & S. P. Hinshaw (Eds.), *Child and adolescent psychopathology* (pp. 614–642). New York, NY: Wiley.

Asherson, P., & Gurling, H. (2011). Quantitative and molecular genetics of ADHD. In C. Stanford & R. Tannock (Eds.), *Behavioral neuroscience of attention deficit hyperactivity disorder and its treatment* (pp. 239–272). New York, NY: Springer.

Asselmann, E., Pané-Farré, C., Isensee, B., Wittchen, H. U., Lieb, R., Höfler, M., & Beesdo-Baum, K. (2014). Characteristics of initial fearful spells and their associations with *DSM-IV* panic attacks and panic disorder in adolescents and young adults from the community. *Journal of Affective Disorders, 165*, 95–102.

Augustyniak, K., Murphy, J., & Phillips, D. K. (2006). Psychological perspectives in assessing mathematics learning needs. *Journal of Instructional Psychology, 32*, 277–286.

Autism and Developmental Disabilities Monitoring Network. (2016). *Identified prevalence of autism spectrum disorder*. Washington, DC: Centers for Disease Control and Prevention.

Axelrod, M. I., Tornehl, C., & Fontanini-Axelrod, A. (2014). Enhanced response using a multicomponent urine alarm treatment for nocturnal enuresis. *Journal for Specialists in Pediatric Nursing, 19*, 172–182.

Axelson, D. A., Perel, J. M., Birmaher, B., Rudolph, G., Nuss, S., Yurasits, L., . . . Brent, D. A. (2005). Platelet serotonin reuptake inhibition and response to SSRIs in depressed adolescents. *American Journal of Psychiatry, 162*, 802–804.

Aylward, B. S., Bender, J. A., Graves, M. M., & Roberts, M. C. (2009). Historical developments and trends in pediatric psychology. In M. C. Roberts & R. G. Steele (Eds.), *Handbook of pediatric psychology* (pp. 3–18). New York, NY: Guilford Press.

Azrin, N. H., & Peterson, A. L. (1988). Habit reversal for the treatment of Tourette syndrome. *Behavior Research and Therapy, 26*, 347–351.

Babinski, D. E., Waxmonsky, J. G., & Pelham, W. E., Jr. (2014). Treating parents with attention-deficit/hyperactivity disorder. *Journal of abnormal child psychology, 42*, 1129–1140.

Badin, E., Haddad, C., & Shatkin, J. P. (2016). Insomnia: The sleeping giant of pediatric public health. *Current Psychiatry Reports, 18*, 1–8.

Bailey, B. E., Wu, K. D., Valentiner, D. P., & McGrath, P. B. (2014). Thought–action fusion: Structure and specificity to OCD. *Journal of Obsessive-Compulsive and Related Disorders, 3*, 39–45.

Bakermans-Kranenburg, M. J., Dobrova-Krol, N., & van IJzendoorn, M. (2012). Impact of institutional care on attachment disorganization and insecurity of Ukrainian preschoolers. *International Journal of Behavioral Development, 36*, 11–18.

Bakermans-Kranenburg, M. J., Steele, H., Zeanah, C. H., Muhamedrahimov, R. J., Vorria, P., Dobrova-Krol, N. A., . . . Gunnar, M. R. (2011). Attachment and emotional development in institutional care. *Monographs for the Society for Research in Child Development, 76*, 62–91.

Balboni, G., Tassé, M. J., Schalock, R. L., Borthwick-Duffy, S. A., Spreat, S., Thissen, D., . . . Navas, P. (2014). The Diagnostic Adaptive Behavior Scale: Evaluating its diagnostic sensitivity and specificity. *Research in Developmental Disabilities, 35*, 2884–2893.

Bandura, A., Ross, D., & Ross, S. A. (1961). Transmission of aggression through imitation of aggressive models. *Journal of Abnormal & Social Psychology, 63*, 575–582.

Bargh, J. A. (2013). *Social psychology and the unconscious.* New York, NY: Psychology Press.

Baribeau, D., & Anagnostou, E. (2015). Neuroimaging in autism spectrum disorders. In S. H. Fatemi (Ed.), *The molecular basis of autism* (pp. 117–152). New York, NY: Springer.

Barker, C., & Pistrang, N. (2015). *Research methods in clinical psychology.* New York, NY: Wiley.

Barkley, R. A. (2010). Deficient emotional self-regulation: A core component of attention-deficit/hyperactivity disorder. *Journal of ADHD and Related Disorders, 1*, 5–37.

Barkley, R. A. (2013a). *Defiant children: A clinician's manual for assessment and parent training.* New York, NY: Guilford Press.

Barkley, R. A. (2013b). Distinguishing sluggish cognitive tempo from ADHD in children and adolescents. *Journal of Clinical Child and Adolescent Psychology, 42*, 161–173.

Barkley, R. A. (2013c). *Taking charge of ADHD: The complete, authoritative guide for parents.* New York, NY: Guilford Press.

Barkley, R. A. (2014). *Attention-deficit hyperactivity disorder: A handbook for diagnosis and treatment.* New York, NY: Guilford Press.

Barkley, R. A. (2016). Sluggish cognitive tempo: A (misnamed) second attention disorder? *Journal of the American Academy of Child & Adolescent Psychiatry, 55*, 157–158.

Barkley, R. A., Shelton, T. L., Crosswait, C., Moorehouse, M., Fletcher, K., Barrett, S., . . . Metevia, L. (2000). Multi-method, psychoeducational intervention for preschool children with disruptive behavior. *Journal of Child Psychology and Psychiatry, 41*, 319–332.

Barlow, D. H. (2014). *Clinical handbook of psychological disorders.* New York, NY: Guilford Press.

Barlow, D. H., Conklin, L. R., & Bentley, K. H. (2015). Psychological treatments for panic disorders, phobias, and social and generalized anxiety disorders. In P. E. Nathan & J. M. Gorman (Eds.), *A guide to treatments that work* (pp. 409–461). Oxford, England: Oxford University Press.

Barnard, L., Stevens, T., To, Y. M., Lan, W. Y., & Mulsow, M. (2010). The importance of ADHD subtype classification for educational applications of DSM-5. *Journal of Attention Disorders, 13*, 573–583.

Baron, R. M., & Kenny, D. A. (1986). The moderator-mediator variable distinction in social psychological research. *Journal of Personality and Social Psychology, 51*, 1173–1182.

Baron-Cohen, S. (2005). Autism and the origins of social neuroscience. In A. Easton & N. Emery (Eds.), *The cognitive neuroscience of social behavior* (pp. 239–255). New York, NY: Psychology Press.

Baron-Cohen, S., Leslie, A. M., & Frith, U. (1985). Does the autistic child have a "theory of mind"? *Cognition, 21*, 37–46.

Baron-Cohen, S., Lombardo, M., Tager-Flusberg, H., & Cohen, D. (2013). *Understanding other minds: Perspectives from developmental social neuroscience.* Oxford, England: Oxford University Press.

Barrouillet, P. (2015). Theories of cognitive development: From Piaget to today. *Developmental Review, 38*, 1–12.

Barry, C. T., Frick, P. J., Grooms, T., McCoy, M. G., Ellis, M. L., & Loney, B. R. (2000). The importance of callous-unemotional traits for extending the concept of psychopathy to children. *Journal of Abnormal Psychology, 109*, 335–340.

Barzilay, S., & Apter, A. (2014). Predictors of suicide in adolescents and adults with mood and common comorbid disorders. *Neuropsychiatry,4*, 81–93.

Bauer, K. W., Bucchianeri, M. M., & Neumark-Sztainer, D. (2013). Mother-reported parental weight talk and adolescent girls' emotional health, weight control attempts, and disordered eating behaviors. *Journal of Eating Disorders, 1*, 45–66.

Baumeister, A. A., & Bacharach, V. R. (1996). A critical analysis of the Infant Health and Development Program. *Intelligence, 23*, 79–104.

Baumeister, A. A., & Bacharach, V. R. (2000). Early generic educational intervention has no enduring effect on intelligence and does not prevent mental retardation: The Infant Health and Development Program. *Intelligence, 28*, 161–192.

Baumrind, D. (1991). The influence of parenting style on adolescent competence and substance use. *Journal of Early Adolescence, 11*, 56–95.

Beavers, G. A., Iwata, B. A., & Lerman, D. C. (2013). Thirty years of research on the functional analysis of problem behavior. *Journal of Applied Behavior Analysis, 46*, 1–21.

Beck, A. T. (1967). *Depression: Clinical, experimental, and theoretical perspectives.* New York, NY: Harper & Row.

Beck, A. T. (1976). *Cognitive therapy and the emotional disorders.* New York, NY: International Universities Press.

Beck, S. J., Hanson, C. A., Puffenberger, S. S., Benninger, K. L., & Benninger, W. B. (2010). A controlled trial of working memory training for children and adolescents with ADHD. *Journal of Clinical Child and Adolescent Psychology, 39*, 825–836.

Becker, A. E., Burwell, R., Gilman, S. E., Herzog, D., & Hamburg, P. (2002). Eating behaviors and attitudes following prolonged exposure to television among ethnic Fijian adolescent girls. *British Journal of Psychiatry, 180*, 509–514.

Becker, S. P., Leopold, D. R., & Burns, L. (2016). The internal, external, and diagnostic validity of sluggish cognitive tempo: A meta-analysis and critical review. *Journal of the American Academy of Child and Adolescent Psychiatry, 55*, 163–178.

Beesdo, K., Knappe, S., & Pine, D. S. (2009). Anxiety and anxiety disorders in children and adolescents. *Psychiatric Clinics of North America, 32*, 483–524.

Beidel, D. C., & Reinecke, M. A. (2015). Cognitive-behavioral treatment for anxiety and depression. In M. K. Dulcan (Ed.), *Dulcan's textbook of child and adolescent psychiatry* (pp. 973–991). Washington, DC: American Psychiatric Publishing.

Bellini, S., Gardner, L., & Markoff, K. (2015). Social skills interventions. In F. R. Volkmar (Ed.), *Handbook of autism and pervasive developmental disorders* (pp. 887–905). New York, NY: Wiley.

Bentley, K. H., Gallagher, M. W., Boswell, J. F., Gorman, J. M., Shear, M. K., Woods, S. W., & Barlow, D. H. (2013). The interactive contributions of perceived control and anxiety sensitivity in panic disorder. *Journal of Psychopathology and Behavioral Assessment, 35*, 57–64.

Beran, M. J. (2012). *Foundations of metacognition.* Oxford, England: Oxford University Press.

Berger, N. I., & Ingersoll, B. (2015). An evaluation of imitation recognition abilities in typically developing children and young children with autism spectrum disorder. *Autism Research, 8*, 442–453.

Bergman, R. L., Gonzalez, A., Piacentini, J., & Keller, M. L. (2013). Integrated behavior therapy for selective mutism. *Behaviour Research and Therapy, 51*, 680–689.

Berkeley, S., Scruggs, T. E., & Mastropieri, M. A. (2010). Reading comprehension instruction for students with learning disabilities: A meta-analysis. *Journal of Learning Disabilities, 31*, 423–436.

Berliner, L. (2000). What is sexual abuse? In H. Dubowitz & D. DePanfilis (Eds.), *Handbook for child protection* (pp. 18–22). Thousand Oaks, CA: Sage.

Bernard, K., Dozier, M., Bick, J., Lewis-Morrarty, E., Lindheim, O., & Carlson, E. (2012). Enhancing attachment organization among maltreated children. *Child Development, 83,* 623–636.

Bernard, K., Simons, R., & Dozier, M. (2015). Effects of an attachment-based intervention on child protective services–referred mothers' event-related potentials to children's emotions. *Child Development, 86,* 1673–1684.

Bernard, P. B., & Benke, T. A. (2015). Early life seizures: Evidence for chronic deficits linked to autism and intellectual disability across species and models. *Experimental Neurology, 263,* 72–78.

Bernier, R., & Dawson, G. (2016). Autism spectrum disorders. In D. Cicchetti (Ed.), *Developmental psychopathology* (Vol. 3, pp. 81–115). New York, NY: Wiley.

Bernknopf, A. (2011). Guanfacine (Intuniv) for attention-deficit/ hyperactivity disorder. *American Family Physician, 83,* 468–475.

Bernstein, G. A., & Victor, A. M. (2010). Separation anxiety disorder and school refusal. In M. K. Dulcan (Eds.), *Child and adolescent psychiatry* (pp. 325–338). Washington, DC: American Psychiatric Publishing.

Bettelheim, B. (1967). *The empty fortress: Infantile autism and the birth of self.* New York, NY: Free Press.

Biederman, J., Faraone, S. V., Wozniak, J., Mick, E., Kwon, A., & Aleardi, M. (2004). Further evidence of unique developmental phenotypic correlates of pediatric bipolar disorder. *Journal of Affective Disorders, 82S,* S45–58.

Biederman, J., Kwon, A., Wozniak, J., Mick, E., Markowitz, S., Fazio, V., & Faraone, S. V. (2004). Absence of gender differences in pediatric bipolar disorder. *Journal of Affective Disorders, 83,* 207–214.

Biederman, J., Milberger, S., & Faraone, S. V. (1995). Family-environmental risk factors for attention-deficit hyperactivity disorder. *Archives of General Psychiatry, 52,* 464–470.

Biederman, J., Petty, C. R., Clarke, A., Lomedico, A., & Faraone, S.V. (2011). Predictors of persistent ADHD. *Journal of Psychiatric Research, 45,* 150–155.

Biederman, J., Petty, C. R., Evans, M., Small, J., & Faraone, S.V. (2010). How persistent is ADHD? *Psychiatry Research, 177,* 299–304.

Biederman, J., Spencer, T. J., Petty, C., Hyder, L. L., O'Connor, K. B., Surman, C. B., & Faraone, S. V. (2012). Longitudinal course of deficient emotional self-regulation CBCL profile in youth with ADHD. *Neuropsychiatric Disease and Treatment, 8,* 267–276.

Biklen, D. (1993). *Communication unbound: How facilitated communication is challenging traditional views of autism and ability-disability (Special education series).* New York, NY: Teachers Collge Press.

Binet, A., & Simon, T. (1916). *The development of intelligence in children.* Baltimore, MD: Williams & Wilkins.

Birkeland, S., Murphy-Graham, E., & Weiss, C. (2005). Good reasons for ignoring good evaluation: The case of the drug abuse resistance education (D.A.R.E.) program. *Evaluation and Program Planning, 28,* 247–256.

Birmaher, B., Arbelaez, C., & Brent, D. (2002). Course and outcome of child and adolescent major depressive disorder. *Child and Adolescent Psychiatric Clinics of North America, 11,* 619–637.

Birmaher, B., Axelson, D., Goldstein, B., Monk, K., Kalas, C., Obreja, M., . . . Kupfer, D. (2010). Psychiatric disorders in preschool offspring of parents with bipolar disorder. *American Journal of Psychiatry, 167,* 321–330.

Birmaher, B., Axelson, D., Goldstein, B., Strober, M., Gill, M. K., Hunt, J., . . . Keller, M. (2009). Four-year longitudinal course of children and adolescents with bipolar spectrum disorder: The course and outcome of bipolar youth (COBY) study. *American Journal of Psychiatry, 166,* 795–804.

Birmaher, B., & Brent, D. A. (2015). Depressive and disruptive mood regulation disorders. In M. K. Dulcan (Ed.), *Dulcan's textbook of child and adolescent psychiatry* (pp. 245–276). Washington, DC: American Psychiatric Publishing.

Birmaher, B., Brent, D., & AACAP Work Group on Quality Issues. (2007). Practice parameter for the assessment and treatment of children and adolescents with depressive disorders. *Journal of the American Academy of Child and Adolescent Psychiatry, 46,* 1503–1526.

Birmaher, B., Williamson, D. E., Dahl, R. E., Axelson, D. A., Kaufman, J., Dorn, L. D., & Ryan, N. D. (2004). Clinical presentation and course of depression in youth: Does onset in childhood differ from onset in adolescence? *Journal of the American Academy of Child and Adolescent Psychiatry, 43,* 63–70.

Bishop, D., & Rutter, M. (2010). Neurodevelopmental disorders: Conceptual issues. In M. Rutter (Ed.), *Child and adolescent psychiatry* (pp. 32–41). Malden, MA: Blackwell.

Bisson, J. I., Ehlers, A., Matthews, R., Pilling, S., Richards, D., & Turner, S. (2007). Psychological treatments for chronic post-traumatic stress disorder. *British Journal of Psychiatry, 190,* 97–104.

Bisson, J. I., & Lewis, C. (2009). *Systematic review of psychological first aid.* Cardiff, Wales: World Health Organization.

Bitter, J. (2013). *Theory and practice of family therapy and counseling.* Boston, MA: Cengage.

Bixler, E. O., Vgontzas, A. N., Lin, H. M., Liao, D., Calhoun, S., Vela-Bueno, A., . . . Graff, G. (2009). Sleep disordered breathing in children in a general population sample. *Sleep, 32,* 731–736.

Black, J. J., Clark, D. B., Martin, C. S., Kim, K. H., Blaze, T. J., Creswell, K. G., & Chung, T. (2015). Course of alcohol symptoms and social anxiety disorder from adolescence to young adulthood. *Alcoholism, 39,* 1008–1015.

Black, S. W., & Pössel, P. (2013). The combined effects of self-referent information processing and ruminative responses on adolescent depression. *Journal of Youth and Adolescence, 42,* 1145–1154.

Blackwell, A. K., Harding, S., Babayiğit, S., & Roulstone, S. (2015). Characteristics of parent–child interactions: A systematic review of studies comparing children with primary language impairment and their typically developing peers. *Communication Disorders Quarterly, 36,* 67–78.

Blair, C., Raver, C. C., & Finegood, E. D. (2016). Self-regulation and developmental psychopathology. In D. Cicchetti (Ed.), *Developmental psychopathology* (Vol. 2, pp. 484–522). New York, NY: Wiley.

Bloch, M. H., Craiglow, B. G., & Landeros-Weisenberger, A. (2009). Predictors of early adult outcome in pediatric-onset obsessive-compulsive disorder. *Pediatrics, 124,* 1085–1093.

Bloomfield, E. R., & Shatkin, J. P. (2009). Parasomnias and movement disorders in children and adolescents. *Child and Adolescent Psychiatric Clinics of North America, 18,* 947–965.

Blunden, S. L., Chapman, J., & Rigney, G. A. (2012). Are sleep education programs successful? *Sleep Medicine Reviews, 16,* 355–370.

Boesch, M. C., Wendt, O., Subramanian, A., & Hsu, N. (2013). Comparative efficacy of the Picture Exchange Communication System (PECS) versus a speech-generating device. *Autism Spectrum Disorders, 7,* 480–493.

Bögels, S. M., Knappe, S., & Clark, L. A. (2013). Adult separation anxiety disorder in DSM-5. *Clinical Psychology Review, 33,* 663–674.

Boles, R. E., Roberts, M. C., & Vernberg, E. M. (2010). Treating nonretentive encopresis with rewarded scheduled toilet visits. *Behavior Analysis in Practice, 1,* 68–72.

Bond, L., Toumbourou, J. W., Thomas, L., Catalano, R., & Patton, G. C. (2005). Individual, family, school and community risk and protective factors for depressive symptoms in adolescents. *Prevention Science, 6,* 73–88.

Borkovec, T. D., & Inz, J. (1990). The nature of worry in generalized anxiety disorder. *Behaviour Research and Therapy, 28,* 153–158.

Bornstein, M. H. (2016). Determinants of parenting. In D. Cicchetti (Ed.), *Developmental psychopathology* (Vol. 4, pp. 180–270). New York, NY: Wiley.

Bos, K., Zeanah, C. H., Fox, N. A., Drury, S. S., McLaughlin, K. A., & Nelson, C. A. (2011). Psychiatric outcomes in young children with a history of institutionalization. *Harvard Review of Psychiatry, 19,* 15–24.

Bottema-Beutel, K., Yoder, P., Woynaroski, T., & Sandbank, M. P. (2015). Targeted interventions for social communication symptoms in preschoolers with autism spectrum disorders. In F. R. Volkmar (Ed.), *Handbook of autism and pervasive developmental disorders* (pp. 788–811). New York, NY: Wiley.

Bowers, H., Manion, I., Papadopoulos, D., & Gauvreau, E. (2013). Stigma in school-based mental health. *Child and Adolescent Mental Health, 18,* 165–170.

Bowlby, J. (1951). *Maternal care and mental health.* New York, NY: Schocken.

Bowlby, J. (1954). *Child care and the growth of love.* New York, NY: Penguin.

Bowlby, J. (1969). *Attachment and loss, Vol. 1: Attachment.* New York, NY: Basic Books.

Bowlby, J. (1973). *Attachment and loss, Vol. 2: Separation.* New York, NY: Basic Books.

Bowlby, J. (1980). *Attachment and loss: Vol. 3. Loss: Sadness and depression.* New York, NY: Basic Books.

Bowlby, J. (1988). *A secure base: Parent–child attachment and healthy human development.* New York, NY: Basic Books.

Boyd, C. J., Veliz, P. T., & McCabe, S. E. (2015). Adolescents' use of medical marijuana. *Journal of Adolescent Health, 57,* 241–244.

Boyd, G. M., Howard, J., & Zucker, R. A. (2013). *Alcohol problems among adolescents.* New York, NY: Psychology Press.

Boyle, C. A., Boulet, S., Schieve, L. A., Cohen, R. A., Blumberg, S. J., & Yeargin-Allsopp, M. (2011). Trends in the prevalence of developmental disabilities in US children. *Pediatrics, 127,* 1023–1042.

Bozkus-Genc, G., & Yucesoy-Ozkan, S. (2016). Meta-analysis of pivotal response training for children with autism spectrum disorder. *Education and Training in Autism and Developmental Disabilities, 51,* 13–27.

Bradley, C. (1937). The behavior of children receiving benzedrine. *American Journal of Psychiatry, 94,* 577–581.

Bradshaw, J., Steiner, A. M., Gengoux, G., & Koegel, L. K. (2015). Feasibility and effectiveness of very early intervention for infants at-risk for autism spectrum disorder. *Journal of Autism and Developmental Disorders, 45,* 778–794.

Brännström, L., Kaunitz, C., Andershed, A. K., South, S., & Smedslund, G. (2016). Aggression replacement training (ART) for reducing antisocial behavior in adolescents and adults: A systematic review. *Aggression and Violent Behavior, 27,* 30–41.

Brasil, P., Pereira, J. P., Jr., Raja Gabaglia, C., Damasceno, L., Wakimoto, M., Ribeiro Nogueira, R. M., . . . Nielsen-Saines, K. (2016, March 4). Zika virus infection in pregnant women in Rio de Janeiro. *New England Journal of Medicine, 375,* 2321–2334.

Brazzelli, M., Griffiths, P. V., Cody, J. D., & Tappin, D. (2011). Behavioural and cognitive interventions with or without other treatments for the management of faecal incontinence in children. *Cochrane Reviews* doi: 10.1002/14651858.CD002040.pub4.

Brendgen, M., Wanner, B., Morin, A. J. S., & Vitaro, F. (2005). Relations with parents and with peers, temperament, and trajectories of depressed mood during early adolescence. *Journal of Abnormal Child Psychology, 33,* 579–594.

Brennan, B. P., Tkachenko, O., Schwab, Z. J., Juelich, R. J., Ryan, E. M., Athey, A. J., . . . Rauch, S. L. (2015). An examination of rostral anterior cingulate cortex function and neurochemistry in obsessive–compulsive disorder. *Neuropsychopharmacology, 40,* 1866–1876.

Brennan, L. M., Shaw, D. S., Dishion, T. J., & Wilson, M. (2012). Longitudinal predictors of school-age academic achievement. *Journal of Abnormal Child Psychology, 40,* 1289–1300.

Brenner, J. D. (2016). Traumatic stress from a multilevel developmental psychopathology perspective. In D. Cicchetti (Ed.), *Developmental psychopathology* (pp. 386–423). New York, NY: Wiley.

Brent, D., Emslie, G., Clarke, G., Wagner, K. D., Asarnow, J. R., Keller, M., . . . Birmaher, B. (2008). Switching to another SSRI or to venlafaxine with or without cognitive behavioral therapy for adolescents with SSRI-resistant depression: The TORDIA randomized controlled trial. *JAMA, 299,* 901–913.

Brent, D. A., Greenhill, L. L., Compton, S., Emslie, G., Wells, K., Walkup, J. T., . . . Kennard, B. D. (2009). The Treatment of Adolescent Suicide Attempters study (TASA). *Journal of the American Academy of Child and Adolescent Psychiatry, 48,* 987–996.

Brent, D., & Weersing, V. R. (2010). Depressive disorders in childhood and adolescence. In M. Rutter (Ed.), *Rutter's child and adolescent psychiatry* (pp. 587–612). Malden, MA: Blackwell.

Bretherton, I. (1992). The origins of attachment theory. *Developmental Psychology, 28,* 759–775.

Brewin, C. R., Lanius, R. A., Novac, A., Schnyder, U., & Galea, S. (2009). Reformulating PTSD for *DSM-5. Journal of Traumatic Stress, 22,* 366–373.

Bridge, J., Iyengar, S., Salary, C. B., Barbe, R. P., Birmaher, B., Pincus, H., . . . Brent, D. A. (2007). Clinical response and risk of reported suicidal ideation and suicide attempts in pediatric antidepressant treatment. *JAMA: Journal of the American Medical Association, 297,* 1683–1696.

Briggs-Gowan, M. J., Godoy, L., Heberle, A., & Carter, A. S. (2016). Assessment of psychopathology in young children. In D. Cicchetti (Ed.), *Developmental psychopathology* (Vol. 1, pp. 1–45). New York, NY: Wiley.

Bronfenbrenner, U., McClelland, P. D., Wethington, E., Moen, P., & Ceci, S. (1996). *The state of the Americas: This generation and the next.* New York, NY: Free Press.

Bronfenbrenner, U., & Morris, P. A. (1998). The ecology of developmental process. In W. Damon (Ed.), *Handbook of child psychology* (Vol. 1, pp. 993–1028). New York, NY: Wiley.

Brookshire, R. H., & McNeil, M. R. (2014). *Neurogenic communication disorders.* New York, NY: Elsevier.

Brotman, M. A., Rich, B. A., Guyer, A. E., Lunsford, J. R., Horsey, S. E., Reising, M. M., . . . Leibenluft, E. (2010). Amygdala activation during emotion processing of neutral faces in children with severe mood dysregulation versus ADHD or bipolar disorder. *American Journal of Psychiatry, 167,* 61.

Brown, M. L., Pope, A. W., & Brown, E. J. (2010). Treatment of primary nocturnal enuresis in children. *Child: Care, Health, and Development, 37,* 153–160.

Brown, R. (2014). *Handbook of pediatric psychology in school settings.* Mahwah, NJ: Erlbaum.

Brown, R.T., Ellis, D., & Naar-King, S. (2014). Health-related and somatic symptom disorders. In E.J. Mash & R.A. Barkley (Eds.), *Child psychopathology* (pp. 897–943). New York: Guilford.

Brown, R. T., Antonuccio, D. O., DuPaul, G. J., Fristad, M. A., King, C. A., Leslie, L. K., . . . Vitiello, B. (2008). Schizophrenia spectrum disorders. In *Childhood mental health disorders: Evidence based and contextual factors for psychosocial, psychopharmacological, and combined interventions* (pp. 97–103). Washington, DC: American Psychological Association.

Bruce, J., Tarullo, A. R., & Gunnar, M. R. (2009). Disinhibited social behavior among internationally adopted children. *Development and Psychopathology, 21,* 157–171.

Bruch, H. (1973). *Eating disorders.* New York, NY: Basic Books.

Brumbaugh, K. M., & Smit, A. B. (2013). Treating children ages 3–6 who have speech sound disorder. *Language, Speech, and Hearing Services in Schools, 44,* 306–319.

Brutten, E. J., & Shoemaker, D. (1967). *The modification of stuttering.* Englewood Cliffs, NJ: Prentice Hall.

Bryant-Waugh, R., & Watkins, B. (2015). Feeding and eating disorders. In M. A. Thapar (Ed.), *Rutter's Child and Adolescent Psychiatry* (pp. 1016–1034). Malden, MA: Blackwell.

Brymer, M., Jacobs, A., Layne, C., Pynoos, R., Ruzek, J., Steinberg, A., . . . Watson, P. (2006). *Psychological first aid*. Durham, NC: National Child Traumatic Stress Network.

Buckhalt, J. A., Wolfson, A. R., & El-Sheikh, M. (2009). Children's sleep and school psychology practice. *School Psychology Quarterly, 24*, 60–69.

Buckley, S. (1999). Promoting the cognitive development of children with Down syndrome. In J. A. Rondal, J. Perera, & L. Nadel (Eds.), *Down's syndrome: A review of current knowledge* (pp. 99–110). London, England: Whurr.

Buckley, S., Dodd, P., Burke, A., Guerin, S., McEvoy, J., & Hillery, J. (2006). Diagnosis and management of attention-deficit hyperactivity disorder in children and adults with and without learning disability. *Psychiatric Bulletin, 30*, 251–253.

Buckloh, L. M., & Greco, P. (2009). Professional development, roles, and practice patterns. In M. C. Roberts & R. G. Steele (Eds.), *Handbook of pediatric psychology* (pp. 35–51). New York, NY: Guilford Press.

Budinger, M. C., Drazdowski, T. K., & Ginsburg, G. S. (2013). Anxiety-promoting parenting behaviors: A comparison of anxious parents with and without social anxiety disorder. *Child Psychiatry and Human Development, 44*, 412–418.

Bufferd, S. J., Dyson, M. W., Hernandez, I. G., & Wakschlag, L. S. (2016). Explicating the "developmental" in preschool psychopathology. In D. Cicchetti (Ed.), *Developmental psychopathology* (Vol. 3, pp. 152–186). New York, NY: Wiley.

Buhr, A. P., Jones, R. M., Conture, E. G., & Kelly, E. M. (2015). The function of repeating: The relation between word class and repetition type in developmental stuttering. *International Journal of Language & Communication Disorders, 51*, 128–136.

Bühren, K., Schwarte, R., Fluck, F., Timmesfeld, N., Krei, M., Egberts, K., . . . Herpertz-Dahlmann, B. (2014). Comorbid psychiatric disorders in female adolescents with first-onset anorexia nervosa. *European Eating Disorders Review, 22*, 39–44.

Bukstein, O. G. (2005). Practice parameter for the assessment and treatment of children and adolescents with substance use disorders. *Journal of the American Academy of Child and Adolescent Psychiatry, 44*, 609–621.

Bukstein, O. G. (2011). Attention deficit hyperactivity disorder and substance use disorders. In C. Stanford & R. Tannock (Eds.), *Behavioral neuroscience of attention deficit hyperactivity disorder and its treatment* (pp. 145–172). New York, NY: Springer.

Bukstein, O. G. (2015). Substance use disorders and addictions. In M. K. Dulcan (Ed.), *Dulcan's textbook of child and adolescent psychology* (pp. 219–244). Washington, DC: American Psychiatric Publishing.

Bukstein, O. G., & Deas, D. (2010). Substance abuse and addictions. In M. K. Dulcan (Ed.), *Dulcan's textbook of child and adolescent psychology* (pp. 241–258). Washington, DC: American Psychiatric Publishing.

Bulik, C. M. (2004). Genetic and biological risk factors. In J. K. Thompson (Ed.), *Handbook of eating disorders and obesity* (pp. 3–16). Hoboken, NJ: Wiley.

Buntinx, W. (2016). Adaptive behavior and support needs. In A. Carr (Ed.), *The handbook of intellectual disability and clinical psychology practice* (pp. 107–135). New York, NY: Routledge.

Burgess, H. J., & Emens, J. S. (2016). Circadian-based therapies for circadian rhythm sleep-wake disorders. *Current Sleep Medicine Reports, 1*, 1–8.

Burke, J. D. (2012). An affective dimension within oppositional defiant disorder symptoms among boys: Personality and psychopathology outcomes into early adulthood. *Journal of Child Psychology and Psychiatry, 53*, 1176–1183.

Burke, J. D., Hipwell, A. E., & Loeber, R. (2010). Dimensions of oppositional defiant disorder as predictors of depression and conduct disorder in preadolescent girls. *Journal of the American Academy of Child and Adolescent Psychiatry, 49*, 484–492.

Burleson, J. A., & Kaminer, Y. (2005). Self-efficacy as a predictor of treatment outcome in adolescent substance use disorders. *Addictive Behaviors, 30*, 1751–1764.

Burlingham, D., & Freud, A. (1962). *Infants without families*. London, England: International Universities Press.

Burt, K. B., Coatsworth, J. D., & Masten, A. S. (2016). Competence and psychopathology in development. In D. Cicchetti (Ed.), *Developmental psychopathology* (Vol. 4, pp. 435–484). New York, NY: Wiley.

Burt, S. A., McGue, M., DeMarte, J. A., Krueger, R. F., & Iacono, W. G. (2006). Timing of menarche and the origins of conduct disorder. *Archives of General Psychiatry, 63*, 890–896.

Burton, E., Stice, E., & Seeley, J. R. (2004). A prospective test of the stress-buffering model of depression in adolescent girls. *Journal of Consulting and Clinical Psychology, 72*, 689–697.

Buschmann, A., Jooss B., & Rupp A., (2008). Children with developmental language delay at 24 months of age. *Developmental Medicine and Child Neurology, 50*, 223–229.

Butcher, N. J., Chow, E. W., Costain, G., Karas, D., Ho, A., & Bassett, A. S. (2012). Functional outcomes of adults with 22q11.2 deletion syndrome. *Genetics in Medicine, 14*, 836–843.

Caccia, S. (2013). Safety and pharmacokinetics of atypical antipsychotics in children and adolescents. *Pediatric Drugs, 15*, 217–233.

Calkins, S. D., & Perry, N. B. (2016). The development of emotion regulation. In D. Cicchetti (Ed.), *Developmental psychopathology* (Vol. 3, pp. 187–242). New York, NY: Wiley.

Callaghan, R. C., Hathaway, A., Cunningham, J. A., Vettese, L. C., Wyatt, S., & Taylor, L. (2005). Does stage-of-change predict dropout in a culturally diverse sample of adolescents admitted to inpatient substance-abuse treatment? *Addictive Behaviors, 30*, 1834–1847.

Campbell, K., & Peebles, R. (2014). Eating disorders in children and adolescents: State of the art review. *Pediatrics, 134*, 582–592.

Campbell, L., Vasquez, M., Behnke, S., & Kinscherff, R. (2010). *APA ethics code commentary and illustrations*. Washington, DC: American Psychological Association.

Campbell, L. K., Cox, D. J., & Borowitz, S. M. (2009). Elimination disorders. In M. C. Roberts & R. G. Steele (Eds.), *Handbook of pediatric psychology* (pp. 481–490). New York, NY: Guilford.

Canino, G., Polanczyk, G., Bauermeister, J. J., Rohde, L. A., & Frick, P. J. (2010). Does the prevalence of CD and ODD vary across cultures? *Social Psychiatry and Psychiatric Epidemiology, 45*, 695–704.

Capaldi, D. M., & Eddy, J. M. (2015). Oppositional defiant disorder and conduct disorder. In T. P. Gullotta, R. W. Plant, & M. Evans (Eds.), *Handbook of adolescent behavioral problems* (pp. 265–286). New York, NY: Springer.

Caplan, R. (2016). Childhood schizophrenia. In D. Cicchetti (Ed.), *Developmental psychopathology* (Vol. 3, pp. 950–996). New York, NY: Wiley.

Capron, D. W., Norr, A. M., & Schmidt, N. B. (2013). Risk of co-occuring psychopathology: Testing a prediction of expectancy theory. *Journal of Anxiety Disorders, 27*, 79–83.

Capuzzi, D., & Golden, L. (2014). *Preventing adolescent suicide*. Boston, MA: Routledge.

Cardon, T. A. (2016). Do as I'm doing: Video modeling and autism. In T. A. Cardon (Ed.), *Technology and the treatment of children with autism spectrum disorders* (pp. 87–96). New York, NY: Springer.

Carey, S., Zaitchik, D., & Bascandziev, I. (2015). Theories of development. *Developmental Review, 38*, 36–54.

Carlier, M., & Roubertoux, P. L. (2015). Genetic and environmental influences on intellectual disability in childhood. In D. Finkel (Ed.), *Behavior genetics of cognition across the lifespan* (pp. 69–101). New York, NY: Springer.

Carlson, C. D., & Francis, D. J. (2002). Increasing the reading achievement of at-risk children through direct instruction. *Journal of Education for Students Placed at Risk, 7*, 141–166.

Carlson, G. A., Bromet, E. J., & Sievers, S. (2000). Phenomenology and outcome of subjects with early and adult-onset psychotic mania. *American Journal of Psychiatry, 157,* 213–219.

Carlson, G. A., Pataki, C., & Meyer, S. E. (2015). Bipolar disorder. In M. K. Dulcan (Ed.), *Dulcan's textbook of child and adolescent psychiatry* (pp. 277–304). Washington, DC: American Psychiatric Publishing.

Carroll, J. B. (1997). Psychometrics, intelligence, and public perception. *Intelligence, 24,* 25–52.

Carson, G. (2015). Suicide and self-injurious behaviors. In F. Haddad & R. Gerson (Ed.), *Helping kids in crisis* (pp. 35–51). Washington, DC: American Psychiatric Publishing.

Carter, B. D., Kronenberger, W. G., Scott, E., & Ernst, M. M. (2009). Inpatient consultation-liaison. In M. C. Roberts & R. G. Steele (Eds.), *Handbook of pediatric psychology* (pp. 114–129). New York, NY: Guilford Press.

Carter, B. D., & von Weiss, R. T. (2005). Inpatient pediatric consultation-liaison. In R. G. Steele & M. C. Roberts (Eds.), *Handbook of mental health services for children, adolescents, and families* (pp. 63–83). New York, NY: Springer.

Casey, R. J., & Berman, J. S. (1985). The outcome of psychotherapy with children. *Psychological Bulletin, 98,* 388–400.

Caspi, A., Harrington, H., Moffitt, T. E., & Milne, B. J. (2002). Males on the life-course-persistent and adolescence-limited antisocial pathways: Follow-up at age 26 years. *Development and Psychopathology, 14,* 179–207.

Caspi, A., McClay, J., Moffitt, T. E., Mill, J., Martin, J., Craig, I. W., . . . Poulton, R. (2003). Role of genotype in the cycle of violence in maltreated children. *Science, 297,* 851–854.

Caspi, A., & Moffitt, T. E. (2006). Gene–environment interactions in psychiatry. *Nature Reviews Neuroscience, 7,* 583–590.

Caspi, A., Moffitt, T. E., & Cannon, M. (2005). Moderation of the effect of adolescent-onset cannabis use on adult psychosis by a functional polymorphism in the catechol-O-methyltransferase gene. *Biological Psychiatry, 57,* 1117–1127.

Caspi, A., & Shiner, R. (2010). Temperament and personality. In M. Rutter (Ed.), *Rutter's child and adolescent psychiatry* (pp. 182–198). Malden, MA: Blackwell.

Castellanos, F. X., Lee, P. P., Sharp, W., Jeffries, N. O., Greenstein, D. K., Clasen, L. S., . . . Rapoport, J. L. (2002). Developmental trajectories of brain volume abnormalities in children and adolescents with attention-deficit/hyperactivity disorder. *Journal of the American Medical Association, 288,* 1740–1748.

Castelli, F., Happe, F., Frith, U., & Frith, C. (2000). Movement and mind: A functional imaging study of perception and interpretation of complex intentional movement patterns. *Neuroimage, 12,* 314–325.

Castellini, G., Ricca, V., Lelli, L., Bagnoli, S., Lucenteforte, E., Faravelli, C., . . . Nacmias, B. (2013). Association between serotonin transporter gene polymorphism and eating disorders outcome. *American Journal of Medical Genetics, 159,* 491–500.

Catalano, R. F., Hawkins, J. D., Wells, E. A., Miller, J., & Brewer, D. (2009). Evaluation of the effectiveness of adolescent drug abuse treatment, assessment of risks for relapse, and promising approaches for relapse prevention. *International Journal of the Addictions, 25,* 1085–1140.

Centers for Disease Control and Prevention. (2012). *Ethan's house gets healthier.* Washington, DC: Author.

Centers for Disease Control and Prevention. (2016a). *ADHD state-based prevalence data.* Washington, DC: Author.

Centers for Disease Control and Prevention. (2016b). *National Health Interview Survey.* Washington, DC: Author.

Centers for Disease Control and Prevention. (2016c). *Prevalence of autism spectrum disorder.* Washington, DC: Author.

Centers for Disease Control and Prevention. (2016d). *Prevention tips for lead exposure.* Washington, DC: Author.

Centers for Disease Control and Prevention. (2016e). *Summary of autism spectrum disorder prevalence studies.* Washington, DC: Author.

Centers for Disease Control and Prevention. (2016f). *Zika and pregnancy.* Washington, DC: Author.

Chacko, A. K., Feirsen, N., Rajwan, E., Zwilling, A., Pelham, W. E., & Kapalka, G. M. (2015). Attention-deficit/hyperactivity disorder. In G. M. Kapalka (Ed.), *Treating disruptive disorders* (pp. 71–98). New York, NY: Routledge.

Chaffin, M., Funderburk, B., Bard, D., Valle, L. A., & Gurwitch, R. (2011). A combined motivation and parent–child interaction therapy package reduces child welfare recidivism in a randomized dismantling field trial. *Journal of Consulting and Clinical Psychology, 79,* 84–95.

Chaffin, M., Silovsky, J. F., Funderburk, B., Valle, L. A., Brestan, E. V., Balachova, T., . . . Bonner, B. L. (2004). Parent-child interaction therapy with physically abusive parents. *Journal of Consulting and Clinical Psychology, 72,* 500–510.

Chaffin, M., Valle, L. A., Funderburk, B., Gurwitch, R., Silvosky, J., Bard, D., . . . Kees, M. (2009). A motivational intervention can improve retention in PCIT for low-motivation child welfare clients. *Child Maltreatment, 14,* 356–368.

Chang, L. Y., Foshee, V. A., Reyes, H. L. M., Ennett, S. T., & Halpern, C. T. (2015). Direct and indirect effects of neighborhood characteristics on the perpetration of dating violence across adolescence. *Journal of Youth and Adolescence, 44,* 727–744.

Chang, L. Y., Wang, M. Y., & Tsai, P. S. (2016). Neighborhood disadvantage and physical aggression in children and adolescents: A systematic review and meta-analysis of multilevel studies. *Aggressive Behavior.* Advance online publication. doi: 10.1002/ab.21641

Chapman, R. S., & Bird, E. K. (2012). Language development in childhood, adolescence, and young adulthood in persons with Down syndrome. In J. A. Burack, R. M. Hodapp, G. Iarocci, & E. Zigler (Eds.), *The Oxford handbook of intellectual disability and development* (pp. 167–183). New York, NY: Oxford University Press.

Charach, A., Yeung, E., Climans, T., & Lillie, E. (2011). Childhood attention-deficit/hyperactivity disorder and future substance use disorders. *Journal of the American Academy of Child and Adolescent Psychiatry, 50,* 9–21.

Chase, C. D., Osinowo, T., & Pary, R. J. (2002). Medical issues in patients with Down syndrome. *Mental Health Aspects of Developmental Disabilities, 5,* 34–45.

Chassin, L. (2015). Self-regulation and adolescent substance use. In G. Oettinger & P. M. Gollwitzer (Eds.), *Self-regulation in adolescence* (pp. 266–287). New York, NY: Cambridge University Press.

Chassin, L., Colder, C. R., Hussong, A., & Sher, K. J. (2016). Substance use and substance use disorders. In D. Cicchetti (Ed.), *Developmental psychopathology* (Vol. 3, pp. 833–897). New York, NY: Wiley

Chassin, L., Sher, K. J., Hussong, A., & Curran, P. (2013). The developmental psychopathology of alcohol use and alcohol disorders. *Development and Psychopathology, 25,* 1567–1584.

Chaste, P., & Devlin, B. (2016). Architecture for the genetic risk for autism. In M. Leboyer & P. Chaste (Eds.), *Autism spectrum disorders* (pp. 80–96). Basel, Switzerland: Karger.

Chatoor, I. (2009). *Diagnosis and treatment of feeding disorders in infants, toddlers, and young children.* Washington, DC: National Center for Infants, Toddlers, and Families.

Chatoor, I., & Ammaniti, M. (2007). Classifying feeding disorders of infancy and early childhood. In W. E. Narrow (Ed.), *Age and gender considerations in psychiatric diagnosis* (pp. 227–242). Arlington, VA: American Psychiatric Association.

Chaudry, M., & Dissanayake, C. (2015). Pretend play in children with autism spectrum disorders. In S. Douglas (Ed.), *Children's play, pretense, and story* (pp. 31–50). New York, NY: Routledge.

Chawarska, K., Macari, S., Volkmar, F. R., Kim, S. H., & Shic, F. (2015). ASD in infants and toddlers. In F. R. Volkmar (Ed.), *Handbook of autism and pervasive developmental disorders* (pp. 121–146). New York, NY: Wiley.

Chemtob, C., Nakashima, J., & Carlson, J. (2002). Brief treatment for elementary school children with disaster-related posttraumatic stress disorder. *Journal of Clinical Psychology, 58*, 99–112.

Chen, D., Drabick, D. A., & Burgers, D. E. (2015). A developmental perspective on peer rejection, deviant peer affiliation, and conduct problems among youth. *Child Psychiatry and Human Development, 46*, 823–838.

Chen, M. H., Su, T. P., Chen, Y. S., Hsu, J. W., Huang, K. L., Chang, W. H., & Bai, Y. M. (2013). Attention deficit hyperactivity disorder, tic disorder, and allergy. *Journal of Child Psychology and Psychiatry, 54*, 545–551.

Chess, S., Thomas, A., & Birch, H. G. (1965). *Your child is a person.* New York, NY: Viking.

Chirdkiatgumchai, V., Xiao, H., Fredstrom, B. K., Adams, R. E., Epstein, J. N., Shah, S. S., . . . Froehlich, T. E. (2013). National trends in psychotropic medication use in young children. *Pediatrics, 132*, 615–623.

Chow, C. M., Ruhl, H., & Buhrmester, D. (2015). Romantic relationships and psychological distress among adolescents. *International Journal of Social Psychiatry, 61*, 711–720.

Christensen, D. L., Bilder, D. A., Zahorodny, W., Pettygrove, S., Durkin, M. S., Fitzgerald, R. T., . . . Yeargin-Allsopp, M. (2016). Prevalence and characteristics of autism spectrum disorder among 4-year-old children in the Autism and Developmental Disabilities Monitoring Network. *Journal of Developmental & Behavioral Pediatrics, 37*, 1–8.

Christophersen, E. R., & Friman, P. C. (2010). *Elimination disorders in children and adolescents.* Cambridge, MA: Hogrefe.

Christophersen, E. R., & Vanscoyoc, S. M. (2013). *Treatments that work with children.*, DC: American Psychological Association.

Christophersen, E. R., & Vanscoyoc, S. M. (2013). *Treatments that work with children: Empirically supported strategies for managing childhood problems.* Washington, DC: American Psychological Association.

Chronis, A. M., Fabiano, G. A., Gnagy, E. M., Onyango, A. N., Pelham, W. E., Lopez-Williams, A., . . . Seymour, K. E. (2004). An evaluation of the summer treatment program for children with attention-deficit/hyperactivity disorder using a treatment withdrawal design. *Behavior Therapy, 35*, 561–585.

Chua, M. E., Silangcruz, J. M., Chang, S. J., Williams, K., Saunders, M., Lopes, R. I., . . . Yang, S. S. (2016). Desmopressin withdrawal strategy for pediatric enuresis: A meta-analysis. *Pediatrics, 138*, 1–18.

Chung, T., Martin, C. S., Armstrong, T. D., & Labouvie, E. W. (2002). Prevalence of *DSM-IV* alcohol diagnoses and symptoms in adolescent community and clinical samples. *Journal of the American Academy of Child and Adolescent Psychiatry, 41*, 546–554.

Cicchetti, D. (2015). Neural plasticity, sensitive periods, and psychopathology. *Development and Psychopathology, 27*, 319–320.

Cicchetti, D. (2016a). *Developmental psychopathology, Vol.1: Theory and method.* New York, NY: Wiley.

Cicchetti, D. (2016b). *Developmental psychopathology, Vol, 4: Risk Resilience, and intervention.* New York, NY: Wiley.

Cicchetti, D., & Curtis, W. J. (2006). The developing brain and neural plasticity: Implications for normality, psychopathology, and resilience. In D. Cicchetti & D. J. Cohen (Eds.), *Developmental psychopathology* (Vol. 2, 2nd ed., pp. 1–64.). Hoboken, NJ: Wiley.

Cicchetti, D., & Doyle, C. (2016). Child maltreatment, attachment and psychopathology. *World Psychiatry, 15*, 89–90.

Cicchetti, D., & Rogosch, F. A. (2014). Genetic moderation of child maltreatment effects on depression and internalizing symptoms by serotonin transporter linked polymorphic region (5-HTTLPR), brain-derived neurotrophic factor (BDNF), norepinephrine transporter (NET), and corticotropin releasing hormone receptor 1 (CRHR1) genes in African American children. *Development and Psychopathology, 26*, 1219–1239.

Cicchetti, D., & Toth, S. L. (2016). Child maltreatment and developmental psychopathology. In D. Cicchetti (Ed.), *Developmental psychopathology* (Vol. 4, pp. 457–511). New York, NY: Wiley.

Clark, A. F. (2011). Schizophrenia and schizophrenia-like disorders. In C. Gillberg, R. Harrington, & H. Steinhausen (Eds.), *A clinician's handbook of child and adolescent psychiatry* (pp. 79–109). Cambridge, England: Cambridge University Press.

Clarke, G. N., Debar, L., Lynch, F., Powell, J., Gale, J., O'Connor, E., . . . Hertert, S. (2005). A randomized effectiveness trial of brief cognitive-behavioral therapy for depressed adolescents receiving antidepressant medication. *Journal of the American Academy of Child and Adolescent Psychiatry, 44*, 888–898.

Clarke, G. N., Lewinsohn, P. M., & Hops, H. (1990). *Instructor's manual for the adolescent coping with depression course.* Retrieved August 10, 2016, from http://www.kpchr.org/public/acwd/ acwd.html

Clayton, R., Cattarello, A. M., & Johnstone, B. M. (1996). The effectiveness of drug abuse resistance education (project D.A.R.E.): 5-Year follow up results. *Preventative Medicine, 25*, 307–318.

Cleave, P. L., Becker, S. D., Curran, M. K., Van Horne, A. J. O., & Fey, M. E. (2015). The efficacy of recasts in language intervention: A systematic review and meta-analysis. *American Journal of Speech-Language Pathology, 24*, 237–255.

Clemens, N. H., Keller-Margulis, M. A., Scholten, T., & Yoon, M. (2016). Screening assessment within a multi-tiered system of support. In S. R. Jimerson (Ed.), *Handbook of response to intervention* (pp. 187–213). New York, NY: Springer.

Cobussen-Boekhorst, H. J., van Genugten, L. J., Postma, J., Feitz, W. F., & Kortmann, B. B. (2013). Treatment response of an outpatient training for children with enuresis in a tertiary health care setting. *Journal of Pediatric Urology, 9*, 516–520.

Coghill, D., & Seth, S. (2011). Do the diagnostic criteria for ADHD need to change? *European Child and Adolescent Psychiatry, 20*, 75–81.

Cohen, J. (1988). *Statistical power analysis for the behavioral sciences.* Hillsdale, NJ: Erlbaum.

Cohen, J. A. (2005). Treating traumatized children. *Journal of Trauma and Dissociation, 6*, 109–121.

Cohen, J. A., Berliner, L., & Mannarino, A. (2010). Trauma focused CBT for children with co-occurring trauma and behavior problems. *Child Abuse and Neglect, 34*, 215–224.

Cohen, J. A., & Mannarino, A. P. (2011). Trauma-focused CBT for traumatic grief in military children. *Journal of Contemporary Psychotherapy, 41*, 219–227.

Cohen, J. A., Mannarino, A. P., & Deblinger, E. (2013). *Trauma-focused CBT for children and adolescents.* New York, NY: Guilford Press.

Cohen, J. A., Mannarino, A. P., Kliethermes, M., & Murray, L. A. (2012). Trauma-focused CBT for youth with complex trauma. *Child Abuse amd Neglect, 36*, 528–541.

Cohen, J. A., Mannarino, A. P., & Knudsen, K. (2005). Treating sexually abused children: 1 year follow-up of a randomized controlled trial. *Child Abuse and Neglect, 29*, 135–145.

Cohen, M. A., & Piquero, A. R. (2009). New evidence on the monetary value of saving a high risk youth. *Journal of Quantitative Criminology, 25*, 25–49.

Cohen, R. J., Swerdlik, M., & Sturman, E. (2013). *Psychological testing and assessment.* Columbus, OH: McGraw-Hill.

Cohn, A. M., & Adesman, A. (2016). Oppositional defiant disorder and conduct disorder. In L. A. Adler (Ed.), *Attention-deficit/ hyperactivity disorder in adults and children* (pp. 139–148). Cambridge, England: Cambridge Publishing.

Colalillo, S., Williamson, D., & Johnston, C. (2014). Attributions for parents' behavior by boys with and without attention-deficit/hyperactivity disorder. *Child Psychiatry and Human Development, 45*, 765–775.

Cole, P. M. (2016). Emotion and the development of psychopathology. In D. Cicchetti (Ed.), *Developmental psychopathology* (Vol. 1, pp. 265–324). New York, NY: Wiley.

Coll, C. G., & Magnuson, K. (2014). The psychological experience of immigration: A developmental perspective. In *The New Immigrant and the American Family: Interdisciplinary Perspectives on the New Immigration.* New York, NY: Routledge.

Collins, S. E., & Witkiewitz, K. (2013). Abstinence violation effect. *Encyclopedia of Behavioral Medicine* (pp. 8–9). New York, NY: Springer.

Compas, B. E., Connor-Smith, J., & Jaser, S. S. (2004). Temperament, stress reactivity, and coping. *Journal of Clinical Child and Adolescent Psychology, 33,* 21–31.

Compton, S. N., Walkup, J. T., Albano, A. M., Piacentini, J. C., Birmaher, B., Sherrill, J. T., . . . March, J. S. (2010). Child/adolescent anxiety multimodal study (CAMS). *Child and Adolescent Psychiatry and Mental Health, 4,* 1–15.

Conger, R. D., Ge, X. J., Elder, G. H., Lorenz, F. O., & Simons, R. L. (1994). Economic stress, coercive family process, and developmental problems of adolescents. *Child Development, 65,* 541–561.

Conn, B. M., & Coyne, L. W. (2014). Selective mutism in early childhood: Assessment and treatment of an African American preschool boy. *Clinical Case Studies, 1,* 1–14.

Conners, C. K. (2015). *Conners Third Edition: DSM-5 update.* Ontario, Canada: MHS.

Connolly, S. D., Suarez, L. M., Victor, A. M., Zagoloff, A. D., & Bernstein, G.A. (2015). Anxiety disorders. In M. K. Dulcan (Eds.), *Dulcan's textbook of child and adolescent psychiatry* (pp. 305–344). Washington, DC: American Psychiatric Publishing.

Connors, G. J., DiClemente, C. C., Velasquez, M. M., & Donovan, D. M. (2012). *Substance abuse treatment and the stages of change.* New York, NY: Guilford Press.

Cook, B. L., Barry, C. L., & Busch, S. H. (2013). Racial/ethnic disparity trends in children's mental health care access and expenditures. *Health Services Research, 48,* 129–149.

Cooke, D. J., Forth, A. E., & Hare, R. D. (2012). *Psychopathy: Theory, research and implications for society.* New York, NY: Springer.

Cooper, Z., Allen, E., Bailey-Straebler, S., Basden, S., Murphy, R., O'Connor, M. E., & Fairburn, C. G. (2016). Predictors and moderators of response to enhanced cognitive behaviour therapy and interpersonal psychotherapy for the treatment of eating disorders. *Behaviour Research and Therapy, 84,* 9–13.

Copeland, W. E., Keeler, G., Angold, A., & Costello, E. J. (2007). Traumatic events and posttraumatic stress in childhood. *Archives of General Psychiatry, 64,* 577–584.

Coppus, A., Evenhuis, H., Verberne, G., Visser, F., van Gool, P., Eikelenboom, P., & van Duijin, C. M. (2006). Dementia and mortality in persons with Down's syndrome. *Journal of Intellectual Disability Research, 50,* 768–777.

Corkum, P., Davidson, F. D., Tan-MacNeill, K., & Weiss, S. K. (2014). Sleep in children with neurodevelopmental disorders. *Sleep Medicine Clinics, 9,* 149–168.

Cornish, K., Cole, V., Longhi, E., Karmiloff-Smith, A., & Scerif, G. (2013). Mapping developmental trajectories of attention and working memory in Fragile X syndrome. *Development and Psychopathology, 25,* 365–376.

Cornwell, S. L., Kelly, K., & Austin, L. (2010). Pediatric feeding disorders: Effectiveness of multidisciplinary inpatient treatment of gastronomy-tube dependent children. *Children's Health Care, 39,* 214–231.

Correll, C. U. (2015). Antipsychotic medications. In M. K. Dulcan (Eds.), *Dulcan's textbook of child and adolescent psychiatry* (pp. 795–846). Washington, DC: American Psychiatric Publishing.

Corrigan, P. W., Bink, A. B., Schmidt, A., Jones, N., & Rüsch, N. (2016). What is the impact of self-stigma? *Journal of Mental Health, 25,* 10–15.

Corsini, R. J. (2005). Introduction to current psychotherapies. In R. J. Corsini & D. Wedding (Eds.), *Current psychotherapies* (pp. 1–14). Belmont, CA: Brooks/Cole.

Cortese, S., Brown, T. E., Corkum, P., Gruber, R., O'Brien, L. M., Stein, M.,, . . . Owens, J. (2013). Assessment and management of sleep problems in youths with attention-deficit/hyperactivity disorder. *Journal of the American Academy of Child and Adolescent Psychiatry, 52,* 784–796.

Corvin, A., & Sullivan, P. F. (2016). What next in schizophrenia genetics for the psychiatric genomics consortium?. *Schizophrenia Bulletin, 42,* 538–541.

Costa Dias, T. G., Iyer, S. P., Carpenter, S. D., Cary, R. P., Wilson, V. B., Mitchell, S. H., . . . Fair, D. A. (2015). Characterizing heterogeneity in children with and without ADHD based on reward system connectivity. *Developmental Cognitive Neuroscience, 11,* 155–174.

Costa Dias, T. G., Wilson, V. B., Bathula, D. R., Iyer, S. P., Mills, K. L., Thurlow, B. L., . . . Fair, D. A. (2013). Reward circuit connectivity relates to delay discounting in children with attention-deficit/hyperactivity disorder. *European Neuropsychopharmacology, 23,* 33–45.

Costantino, G., Malgady, R. G., & Cardalda, E. (2005). TEMAS narrative treatment. In E. D. Hibbs & P. S. Jensen (Eds.), *Psychosocial treatments for child and adolescent disorders* (pp. 717–742). Washington, DC: American Psychological Association.

Cortiella, C., & Horowitz, S. H. (2014). *The state of learning disabilities.* New York, NY: National Center for Learning Disabilities.

Costello, E. J., & Angold, A. (2016). Developmental epidemiology. In D. Cicchetti (Ed.), *Developmental psychopathology* (Vol. 1, pp. 94–128). New York, NY: Wiley.

Costello, E. J., He, J., Sampson, N. A., Kessler, R. C., & Merikangas, K. R. (2014). Services for adolescents with psychiatric disorders. *Psychiatric Services, 65,* 359–366.

Courtad, C. A., & Bakken, J. P. (2011). History of learning disabilities. *History of Special Education, 21,* 61–87.

Coyne, P., Pisha, B., Dalton, B., Zeph, L. A., & Smith, N. C. (2012). Literacy by design. *Remedial and Special Education, 33,* 162–172.

Crabtree, V. M., & Williams, N. A. (2009). Normal sleep in children and adolescents. *Child and Adolescent Psychiatric Clinics of North America, 18,* 799–811.

Crapanzano, A. M., Frick, P. J., & Terranova, A. M. (2010). Patterns of physical and relational aggression in a school-based sample of boys and girls. *Journal of Abnormal Child Psychology, 38,* 433–445.

Craske, M. G., Kircanski, K., Epstein, A., Wittchen, H.-U., Pine, D. S., Lewis-Fernández, R., & Hinton, D. (2010). Panic disorder: A review of *DSM-IV* panic disorder and proposals for *DSM-5. Depression and Anxiety, 27,* 93–112.

Creswell, C., Waite, P., & Cooper, P. J. (2014). Assessment and management of anxiety disorders in children and adolescents. *Archives of Disease in Childhood, 99,* 674–678.

Crick, N. R. (1995). Relational aggression. *Development and Psychopathology, 7,* 313–322.

Crick, N. R. (1997). Engagement in gender normative versus nonnormative forms of aggression. *Developmental Psychology, 33,* 610–617.

Crick, N. R., & Dodge, K. A. (1994). A review and reformulation of social information-processing mechanisms in children's social adjustment. *Psychological Bulletin, 115,* 74–101.

Crick, N. R., & Dodge, K. A. (1996). Social information-processing mechanisms in reactive and proactive aggression. *Child Development, 67,* 993–1002.

Crick, N. R., & Grotpeter, J. K. (1995). Relational aggression, gender, and social-psychological adjustment. *Child Development, 66,* 710–722.

Critchley, H. D., Daly, E. M., Bullmore,E. T., Williams, S. C. R., van Amelsvoort, T., Robertson, D.M. . . .Murphy, D. G. M. (2000). The functional neuroanatomy of social behaviour: Changes in cerebral blood flow when people with autistic disorder process facial expressions. *Brain: A Journal of Neurology.* doi: http://dx.dpi.org/10.1093/brain/123.11.2003

Crome, I., & Bloor, R. (2005). Substance misuse and psychiatric comorbidity in adolescents. *Current Opinion in Psychiatry, 18*, 435–439.

Cronbach, L. J., & Meehl, P. E. (1955). Construct validity in psychological tests. *Psychological Bulletin, 52*, 281–302.

Crow, T. J. (1980). Molecular pathology of schizophrenia: More than one disease process? *British Medical Journal, 280*, 66–69.

Cuckle, H., Pergament, E., & Benn, P. (2015). Maternal serum screening for chromosomal abnormalities and neural tube defects. In A. Milunsky & J. M. Milunsky (Eds.), *Genetic disorders and the fetus* (pp. 483–540). New York, NY: Wiley.

Cuckle, H., Wald, N., & Thompson, S. (1987). Author's reply. *BJOG: An International Journal of Obstetrics & Gynaecology, 94*: 1226–1227. doi 10.111/j.1471-0528.1987.tb02329.x

Cummings, C. M., Caporino, N. E., & Kendall, P. C. (2014). Comorbidity of anxiety and depression in children and adolescents: 20 years after. *Psychological Bulletin, 140*, 816–845.

Cummings, J. R., Wen, H., & Druss, B. G. (2013). Improving access to mental health services for youth in the United States. *JAMA: Journal of the American Medical Association, 309*, 553–554.

Cunningham, C. E., & Boyle, H. (2002). Preschoolers at risk for attention-deficit hyperactivity disorder and oppositional defiant disorder: Family, parenting, and behavioral correlates. *Journal of Abnormal Child Psychology, 30*, 555–569.

Cupples, B. (2011). Language disorders in children. In R. B. Hoodin (Ed.), *Intervention in child language disorders* (pp. 33–44). Boston, MA: Jones & Bartlett.

Curry, J., Silva, S., Rohde, P., Ginsburg, G., Kennard, B., Kratochvil, C., . . . March, J. (2012). Onset of alcohol or substance use disorders following treatment for adolescent depression. *Journal of Consulting and Clinical Psychology, 80*, 299–312.

Curtin, S. C., Warner, M., & Hedegaard, H. (2016). Increase in suicide in the United States. *NCHS Data Brief, 241*, 1–8.

Curtis, D. F., Elkins, S. R., Miller, S., Areizaga, M. J., Brestan-Knight, E., & Thornberry, T. (2016). Oppositional defiant disorder. In G. M. Kapalka (Ed.), *Treating disruptive behavior disorders* (pp. 99–119). New York, NY: Routledge.

Cyphers, L. (2015). *Meet the little girl who wiped out government use of the R-word.* Boston, MA: ESPN Magazine.

Dadds, M. R., Barrett, P. M., Rapee, R. M., & Ryan, A. (1996). Family process and child anxiety and aggression: An observational analysis. *Journal of Abnormal Child Psychology, 24*, 715–734.

Dadds, M. R., Moul, C., Hawes, D. J., Mendoza Diaz, A., & Brennan, J. (2016). Individual differences in childhood behavior disorders associated with epigenetic modulation of the cortisol receptor gene. *Child Development, 86*, 1311–1320.

Dalsgaard, S., Nielsen, H. S., & Simonsen, M. (2013). Five-fold increase in national prevalence rates of attention-deficit/hyperactivity disorder medications for children and adolescents with autism spectrum disorder, attention-deficit/hyperactivity disorder, and other psychiatric disorders. *Journal of Child and Adolescent Psychopharmacology, 23*, 432–439.

Dandreaux, D. M., & Frick, P. J. (2009). Developmental pathways to conduct problems: A further test of the childhood and adolescent-onset distinction. *Journal of Abnormal Child Psychology, 37*, 375–385.

Danielyan, A., Pathak, S., Kowatch, R. A., Arszman, S. P., & Johns, E. S. (2007). Clinical characteristics of bipolar disorder in very young children. *Journal of Affective Disorders, 97*, 51–59.

Daskalakis, N. P., McGill, M. A., Lehrner, A., & Yehuda, R. (2016). Endocrine aspects of PTSD. In C. R. Martin (Ed.), *Comprehensive guide to post-traumatic stress disorders* (pp. 245–260). New York, NY: Springer.

David, C. N., Greenstein, D., Clasen, L., Gochman, P., Miller, R., Tossell, J. W., . . . Rapoport, J. L. (2011). Childhood onset schizophrenia: High rate of visual hallucinations. *Journal of the American Academy of Child and Adolescent Psychiatry, 50*, 681–686.

Davidson, K. H., & Fristad, M. A. (2008). Psychoeducational psychotherapy. In B. Geller & M. P. DelBello (Eds.), *Treatment of bipolar disorder in children and adolescents* (pp. 184–201). New York, NY: Guilford Press.

Davis, N. O, & Carter, A. S. (2015). Social development in autism. In F. R. Volkmar (Ed.), *Handbook of autism and pervasive developmental disorders* (pp. 212–228). New York, NY: Wiley.

de Haan, M., & Johnson, M. H. (2016). Typical and atypical human functional brain development. In D. Cicchetti (Ed.), *Developmental psychopathology* (Vol. 2, pp. 632–653). New York, NY: Wiley.

de Nil, L., Kroll, R., Lafaille, S., & Houle, S. (2003). A positron emission tomography study of short- and long-term treatment effects on functional brain activation in adults who stutter. *Journal of Fluency Disorders, 28*, 357–380.

de Roos, C., Greenwald, R., den Hollander-Gijsman, M., Noorthoorn, E., van Buuren, S., & de Jongh, A. (2011). A randomised comparison of cognitive behavioural therapy (CBT) and eye movement desensitisation and reprocessing (EMDR) in disaster exposed children. *European Journal of Psychotraumatology, 2*, 1–11.

de Vos, J., Houtzager, L., Katsaragaki, G., van de Berg, E., Cuijpers, P., & Dekker, J. (2013). Meta analysis on the efficacy of pharmacotherapy versus placebo on anorexia nervosa. *Journal of Eating Disorders, 2*, 27–27.

Deblinger, E., Mannarino, A. P., Cohen, J. A., Runyon, M. K., & Heflin, A. H. (2015). *Child sexual abuse.* Oxford, England: Oxford University Press.

Delaney-Black, V., Chiodo, L. M., Hannigan, J. H., Greenwald, M. K., Janisse, J., Patterson, G., & Sokol, R. J. (2010). Just say "I don't": Lack of concordance between teen report and biological measures of drug use. *Pediatrics, 126*, 887–893.

Denckla, M. B., & Rudel, R. G. (1976). Rapid automatized naming (RAN): Dyslexia differentiated from other learning disorders. *Neuropsychologia, 14*, 471–479.

Dennis, M., Godley, S. H., Diamond, G., Tims, F. M., Babor, T., Donaldson, J., . . . Funk, R. (2004). The Cannabis Youth Treatment (CYT) study: Main findings from two randomized trials. *Journal of Substance Abuse Treatment, 27*, 197–213.

Dennis, M. L., Titus, J. C., Diamond, G., Donaldson, J., Godley, S. H., Tims, F. M., . . . C. Y. T. Steering Committee. (2002). The Cannabis Youth Treatment (CYT) experiment. *Addiction, 97*, 16–34.

Dewald-Kaufmann, J. F., Oort, F. J., & Meijer, A. M. (2014). The effects of sleep extension and sleep hygiene advice on sleep and depressive symptoms in adolescents: A randomized controlled trial. *Journal of Child Psychology and Psychiatry, 55*, 273–283.

DeYoung, A. C., Kenardy, J. A., & Cobham, V. E. (2011). Diagnosis of posttraumatic stress disorder in preschool children. *Journal of Clinical Child and Adolescent Psychology, 40*, 375–384.

Dhalla, S., Zumbo, B. D., & Poole, G. (2011). A review of the psychometric properties of the CRAFFT instrument. *Current Drug Abuse Review, 4*, 57–64.

Diamond, G., Godley, S. H., Liddle, H. A., Sampl, S., Webb, C., Tims, F. M., & Meyers, R. (2002). Five outpatient treatment models for adolescent marijuana use. *Addiction, 97*, 70–83.

Dick, D. M., & Todd, R. D. (2006). Genetic contributions. In D. Cicchetti & D. J. Cohen (Eds.), *Developmental psychopathology* (Vol. 2, pp. 16–28). Hoboken, NJ: Wiley.

Dickerson, F. B. (2000). Cognitive behavioral therapy for schizophrenia. *Schizophrenia Research, 43*, 71–90.

Dickson, D. J., Richmond, A. D., Brendgen, M., Vitaro, F., Laursen, B., Dionne, G., & Boivin, M. (2015). Aggression can be contagious. *Aggressive Behavior, 41*, 455–466.

Dickson, K. S., Ciesla, J. A., & Reilly, L. C. (2012). Rumination, worry, cognitive avoidance, and behavioral avoidance: Examination of temporal effects. *Behavior Therapy, 43*, 629–640.

Dickstein, D. P., Towbin, K. E., Van Der Veen, J. W., Rich, B. A., Brotman, M. A., Knopf, L., . . . Leibenluft, E. (2009). Randomized, double-blind, placebo-controlled trial of lithium in youths with severe mood dysregulation. *Journal of Child and Adolescent Psychopharmacology, 19,* 61–73.

Didden, R., Sturmey, P., Sigafoos, J., Lang, R., O'Reilly, M. F., & Lancioni, G. E. (2012). Nature, prevalence, and characteristics of challenging behavior. In J. L. Matson (Ed.), *Functional assessment for challenging behavior* (pp. 25–44). New York, NY: Springer.

Diler, R. S., & Birmaher, B. (2012). Bipolar disorder in children and adolescents. In J. M. Rey (Ed.), *IACAPAP e-textbook of child and adolescent mental health.* Geneva, Switzerland: International Association for Child and Adolescent Psychiatry and Allied Professions.

Dimitropoulos, A., Feurer, I. D., Butler, M. G., & Thompson, T. (2001). Emergence of compulsive behavior and tantrums in children with Prader-Willi syndrome. *American Journal on Mental Retardation, 106,* 39–51.

Dishion, T. J., Kim, H., & Tein, J. Y. (2015). Friendship and adolescent problem behavior: Deviancy training and coercive joining as dynamic mediators. In T. P. Beauchaine & S. P. Hinshaw (Eds.), *The Oxford handbook of externalizing spectrum disorders* (pp. 303–242). New York, NY: Oxford University Press.

Dishion, T. J., & Patterson, G. R. (2016). The development and ecology of antisocial behavior. In D. Cicchetti (Ed.), *Developmental psychopathology* (Vol. 3, pp. 647–678). New York, NY: Wiley.

Dishion, T. J., & Snyder, J. J. (2016). *The Oxford handbook of coercive relationship dynamics.* Oxford, England: Oxford University Press.

Dodd, B. (2013). *Differential diagnosis and treatment of children with speech disorder.* New York, NY: Wiley.

Dodd, B. (2014). Differential diagnosis of pediatric speech sound disorder. *Current Developmental Disorders Reports, 1,* 189–196.

Dodge, K. A. (2003). Do social information-processing patterns mediate aggressive behavior? In B. B. Lahey, T. E. Moffitt, & A. Caspi (Eds.), *Causes of conduct disorder and juvenile delinquency* (pp. 254–274). New York, NY: Guilford Press.

Dodge, K. A., Godwin, J., & Conduct Problems Prevention Research Group. (2013). Social-information-processing patterns mediate the impact of preventive intervention on adolescent antisocial behavior. *Psychological Science, 24,* 456–465.

Dodge, K. A., & Pettit, G. S. (2003). A biopsychosocial model of the development of chronic conduct problems in adolescence. *Developmental Psychology, 39,* 349–371.

Donovan, C. L., Holmes, M. C., & Farrell, L. J. (2016). Investigation of the cognitive variables associated with worry in children with Generalized Anxiety Disorder and their parents. *Journal of Affective Disorders, 192,* 1–7.

Donovan, C. L., Spence, S. H., & March, S. (2013). Using new technologies to deliver cognitive behaviour therapy with children and adolescents. In P. Graham & S. Reynolds (Eds.), *Cognitive behavior therapy for children and families* (pp. 351–369). Cambridge, England: Cambridge University Press.

Dopp, A. R., Borduin, C. M., Wagner, D. V., & Sawyer, A. M. (2014). The economic impact of multisystemic therapy through midlife: A cost–benefit analysis with serious juvenile offenders and their siblings. *Journal of Consulting and Clinical Psychology, 82,* 694–705.

Dowrick, P. W. (2015). Autism. In T. P. Gullotta, R. W. Plant, & M. Evans (Eds.), *Handbook of adolescent behavior problems* (pp. 329–344). New York, NY: Springer.

Dozier, M., Dozier, D., & Manni, M. (2002). Attachment and biobehavioral catch-up. *Zero to Three, 11,* 7–13.

Dozier, M., & Roben, C. K. (2015). Attachment-related preventive interventions. In J. A. Simpson & W. S. Rholes (Eds.), *Attachment theory and research* (pp. 374–392). New York, NY: Guilford Press.

Drabick, D. A. G., & Gadow, K. D. (2012). Deconstructing oppositional defiant disorder: Clinic-based evidence for an anger/irritability phenotype. *Journal of the American Academy of Child and Adolescent Psychiatry, 51,* 384–393.

Drabick, D. A. G., & Goldfried, R. (2000). Training the scientist-practitioner for the 21st century. *Journal of Clinical Psychology, 56,* 327–340.

DSM-5 Childhood and Adolescent Disorders Working Group. (2010a). *Issues pertinent to a developmental approach to bipolar disorder in DSM-5.* Washington, DC: American Psychiatric Association.

DSM-5 Childhood and Adolescent Disorders Working Group. (2010b). *Justification for temper dysregulation disorder with dysphoria.* Washington, DC: American Psychiatric Association.

DSM-5 Psychosis Work Group. (2013). *Attenuated psychosis syndrome proposal.* Washington, DC: American Psychiatric Association.

Duax, J. M., Youngstrom, E. A., Calabrese, J. R., & Findling, R. L. (2007). Sex differences in pediatric bipolar disorder. *Journal of Clinical Psychiatry, 68,* 1565–1573.

Dukes, R. L., Stein, J. A., & Ullman, J. B. (1997). Long-term impact of drug abuse resistance education (D.A.R.E.): Results of a 6-year follow-up. *Evaluation Review, 21,* 483–500.

Dulcan, M. K. (2015). *Dulcan's textbook of child and adolescent psychiatry.* Washington, DC: American Psychiatric Publishing.

Dulcan, M. K., & Ballard, R. (2015). *Helping parents and teachers understand medications for behavioral and emotional problems.* Washington, DC: American Psychiatric Publishing.

Dunlosky, J., Rawson, K. A., Marsh, E. J., Nathan, M. J., & Willingham, D. T. (2013). Improving students' learning with effective learning techniques: Promising directions from cognitive and educational psychology. *Psychological Science in the Public Interest, 14,* 4–58.

Dunn, E. C., McLaughlin, K. A., Slopen, N., Rosand, J., & Smoller, J. W. (2013). Developmental timing of child maltreatment and symptoms of depression and suicidal ideation in young adulthood. *Depression and Anxiety, 30,* 955–964.

DuPaul, G. J., Gormley, M. J., & Laracy, S. D. (2013). Comorbidity of LD and ADHD. *Journal of Learning Disabilities, 46,* 43–51.

Durand, V. M. (2015). Behavioral therapies. In S. H. Fatemi (Ed.), *The molecular basis of autism* (pp. 195–210). New York, NY: Springer.

Durkin, M. S., Maenner, M. J., Meaney, F. J., Levy, S. E., DiGuiseppi, C., Nicholas, J. S., . . . Schieve, L. A. (2010). Socioeconomic inequality in the prevalence of autism spectrum disorder. *PLOS ONE, 5,* e11551.

Dwight, D. M. (2006). *Hands-on core skills in speech-language pathology.* San Diego, CA: Plural.

Dykens, E. M. (1995). Measuring behavioral phenotypes. *American Journal on Mental Retardation, 99,* 522–532.

Dykens, E. M. (2003). Anxiety, fears, and phobias in persons with Williams syndrome. *Developmental Neuropsychology, 23,* 291–316.

Dykens, E. M., & Cassidy, S. B. (1999). Prader-Willi syndrome. In S. Goldstein & C. R. Reynolds (Eds.), *Handbook of neurodevelopmental and genetic disorders in children* (pp. 525–554). New York, NY: Guilford Press.

Dykens, E. M., Cassidy, S. B., & King, B. H. (1999). Maladaptive behavior differences in Prader-Willi syndrome due to paternal deletion versus maternal uniparental disomy. *American Journal on Mental Retardation, 104,* 66–77.

Dykens E. M., & Hodapp, R. M. (2001). Research in mental retardation: Toward an etiologic approach. *Journal of Child Psychology and Psychiatry, 42,* 49–71.

Dykens, E. M., Hodapp, R. M., & Evans, D. W. (2006). Profiles and development of adaptive behavior in children with Down syndrome. *Down Syndrome: Research & Practice, 9,* 45–50.

Dykens, E. M., & Kasari, C. (1997). Maladaptive behavior in children with Prader-Willi syndrome, Down syndrome, and nonspecific mental retardation. *American Journal on Mental Retardation, 102,* 228–237.

Dykens, E. M., & Shah, B. (2003). Psychiatric disorders in Prader-Willi syndrome. *CNS Drugs, 17,* 167–178.

Eadie, P., Morgan, A., Ukoumunne, O. C., Ttofari Eecen, K., Wake, M., & Reilly, S. (2015). Speech sound disorder at 4 years. *Developmental Medicine and Child Neurology, 57,* 578–584.

EAGALA: Equine Assisted Growth and Learning Association (2016). Equine-assisted therapy: *How it works.* Retrieved August 15, 2016, from http://www.eagala.org

Eddy, K. T., Thomas, J. J., Hastings, E., Edkins, K., Lamont, E., Nevins, C. M., . . . Becker, A. E. (2015). Prevalence of *DSM-5* avoidant/restrictive food intake disorder in a pediatric gastroenterology healthcare network. *International Journal of Eating Disorders, 48,* 464–470.

Egan, J. (2008, September). The bipolar puzzle. *New York Times Magazine.*

Egan, S. J., Watson, H. J., Kane, R. T., McEvoy, P., Fursland, A., & Nathan, P. R. (2013). Anxiety as a mediator between perfectionism and eating disorders. *Cognitive Therapy and Research, 37,* 905–913.

Eid, A., & Zawia, N. (2016). Consequences of lead exposure, and its emerging role as an epigenetic modifier in the aging brain. *Neurotoxicology, 56,* 254–261.

Einfeld, S. L. (2005). Behavior problems in children with genetic disorders causing intellectual disability. *Educational Psychology, 25,* 341–346.

Einfeld, S. L., Piccinin, A. M., Mackinnon, A., Hofer, S. M., Taffe, J., Gray, K. M., . . . Tonge, B. J. (2006). Psychopathology in young people with intellectual disability. *Journal of the American Medical Association, 296,* 1981–1989.

Elbe, D., McGlanaghy, E., & Oberlander, T. F. (2016). Do we know if they work and if they are safe? In N. DiPietro (Ed.), *The science and ethics of antipsychotic use in children* (pp. 27–64). New York, NY: Academic Press.

Elia, J., Takeda, T., Deberardinis, R., Burke, J., Accardo, J., Ambrosini, P. J., . . . Hakonarson, H. (2009). Nocturnal enuresis: A suggestive endophenotype marker for a subgroup of inattentive attention-deficit/hyperactivity disorder. *Journal of Pediatrics, 155,* 239–244.

Elkind, D., & Bowen, R. (1979). Imaginary audience behavior in children and adolescence. *Developmental Psychology, 15,* 38–44.

Elkins, I. J., Malone, S., Keyes, M., Iacono, W. G., & McGue, M. (2011). The impact of attention-deficit/hyperactivity disorder on preadolescent adjustment may be greater for girls than for boys. *Journal of Clinical Child and Adolescent Psychology, 40,* 532–545.

Elliott, D. S., Huizinga, D., & Menard, S. (2012). *Multiple problem youth: Delinquency, substance use, and mental health problems.* New York, NY: Springer.

Ellis, A. (2005). *The myth of self-esteem.* Amherst, NY: Prometheus Books.

Ellis, A. (2011). Rational emotive behavior therapy. In R. J. Corsini & D. Wedding (Eds.), *Current psychotherapies* (pp. 196–234). Belmont, CA: Brooks/Cole.

Ellis, A., & Harper, R. A. (1961). *A guide to rational living.* Hollywood, CA: Wilshire Books.

Elsabbagh, M., & Johnson, M. H. (2016). Autism and the social brain: The first-year puzzle. *Biological Psychiatry, 80*(2), 94–99.

Elsabbagh, M., & Karmiloff-Smith, A. (2012). The contribution of developmental models toward understanding gene-to-behavior mapping. In J. A. Burack, R. M. Hodapp, G. Iarocci, & E. Zigler (Eds.), *The Oxford handbook of intellectual disability and development* (pp. 20–41). New York, NY: Oxford University Press.

Emsell, L., Van Hecke, W., & Tournier, J. D. (2016). Introduction to diffusion tensor imaging. In W. Van Hecke (Ed.), *Diffusion tensor imaging* (pp. 7–19). New York, NY: Springer.

Emslie, G. J. (2012). The psychopharmacology of adolescent depression. *Journal of Child and Adolescent Psychopharmacology, 22,* 2–4.

Emslie, G. J., Croarkin, P., Chapman, M. R., & Mayes, T. L. (2015). Antidepressants. In M. Dulcan (Eds.), *Dulcan's textbook of child and adolescent psychiatry* (pp. 737–768). Washington, DC: American Psychiatric Publishing.

Emslie, G. J., Mayes, T., Porta, G., Vitiello, B., Clarke, H., Wagner, K. D., . . . Brent, D. (2010). Treatment of resistant depression in adolescents (TORDIA): Week 24 outcomes. *American Journal of Psychiatry, 167,* 782–791.

Ennett, S. T., Tobler, N. S., Ringwalt, C. L., & Flewelling, R. L. (1994). Resistance education? A meta-analysis of Project D.A.R.E. outcome evaluations. *American Journal of Public Health, 84,* 1394–1401.

Erickson, M. F., & Egeland, B. (2002). Child neglect. In J. E. B. Meyers, L. Berliner, J. Briere, C. T. Hendrix, C. Jenny, & T. A. Reid (Eds.), *The APSAC handbook on child maltreatment* (pp. 3–20). Thousand Oaks, CA: Sage.

Erikson, E. H. (1963). *Childhood and society.* New York, NY: Norton.

Esbjørn, B. H., Bender, P. K., Reinholdt-Dunne, M. L., Munck, L. A., & Ollendick, T. H. (2012). The development of anxiety disorders: Considering the contributions of attachment and emotion regulation. *Clinical Child and Family Psychology Review, 15,* 129–143.

Escudero, I., & Johnstone, M. (2014). Genetics of schizophrenia. *Current Psychiatry Reports, 16,* 1–6.

Essau, C. A., & Ozer, B. U. (2015). Obsessive-compulsive disorder. In T. P. Gullotta, R. W. Plant, & M. Evans (Eds.), *Handbook of adolescent behavioral problems* (pp. 235–263). New York, NY: Springer.

Essau, C. A., & Petermann, F. (Eds.). (2013). *Anxiety disorders in children and adolescents: Epidemiology, risk factors and treatment.* New York, NY: Routledge.

Essau, C. A., Sasagawa, S., & Frick, P. J. (2006). Callous-unemotional traits in a community sample of adolescents. *Assessment, 13,* 454–469.

Evans, S. W., Langberg, J. M., Schultz, B. K., Vaughn, A., Altaye, M., Marshall, S. A., & Zoromski, A. K. (2016). Evaluation of a school-based treatment program for young adolescents with ADHD. *Journal of Consulting and Clinical Psychology, 84,* 15.

Evans, S. W., Owens, J. S., & Bunford, N. (2014). Evidence-based psychosocial treatments for children and adolescents with attention-deficit/hyperactivity disorder. *Journal of Clinical Child and Adolescent Psychology, 43,* 527–551.

Ewing, J. A. (1984). Detecting alcoholism: The CAGE questionnaire. *JAMA: Journal of the American Medical Association, 252,* 1905–1907.

Eyberg, S. M. (2006). Oppositional defiant disorder. In J. E. Fisher & W. T. O'Donohue (Eds.), *Practitioner's guide to evidence-based psychotherapy* (pp. 461–468). New York, NY: Springer.

Eysenck, H. J. (1959). *Behavior therapy and the neuroses.* Oxford, England: Pergamon.

Fabiano, G. A., Pelham, W. E., Coles, E. K., Gnagy, E. M., Chronis-Tuscano, A., & O'Connor, B. C. (2009). A meta-analysis of behavioral treatments for attention-deficit/hyperactivity disorder. *Clinical Psychology Review, 29,* 129–140.

Fabiano, G. A., Schatz, N. K., & Pelham, W. E. (2014). Summer treatment programs for youth with ADHD. *Child and Adolescent Psychiatric Clinics of North America, 23,* 757–773.

Fairburn, C. G., Bailey-Straebler, S., Basden, S., Doll, H. A., Jones, R., Murphy, R., . . . Cooper, Z. (2015). A transdiagnostic comparison of enhanced cognitive behaviour therapy (CBT-E) and interpersonal psychotherapy in the treatment of eating disorders. *Behaviour Research and Therapy, 70,* 64–71.

Fairburn, C. G., Cooper, Z., Doll, H. A., Norman, P., & O'Connor, M. (2000). The natural course of bulimia nervosa and binge eating disorder in young women. *Archives of General Psychiatry, 57,* 659–665.

Fairburn, C. G., Cooper, Z., Doll, H. A., & Welch, S. L. (1999). Risk factors for anorexia nervosa. *Archives of General Psychiatry, 56,* 468–476.

Fairburn, C. G., & Gowers, S. G. (2010). Eating disorders. In M. Rutter (Ed.), *Rutter's child and adolescent psychiatry.* Malden, MA: Blackwell.

Falck-Yttr, T., Fernell, E., Hedvall, A.L., von Vofsten, C., & Gillberg, C. (2012). Gaze performance in children with autism spectrum disorder when observing communicative actions. *Journal of Autism and Developmental Disorders*, 42, 2236–2245.

Falloon, I. (2015). *Handbook of behavioural family therapy*. New York, NY: Routledge.

Falloon, I., Wilkinson, G., Burgess, J., & McLees, S. (2016). Evaluation in psychiatry. In D. Milne (Ed.), *Evaluating mental health practice* (pp. 203–240). New York, NY: Routledge.

Faraone, S. V. (2009). Using meta-analysis to compare the efficacy of medications for attention-deficit/hyperactivity disorder in youths. *Pharmacy and Therapeutics*, 34, 678.

Farmer, C., & Aman, M. (2011). Aggressive behavior in a sample of children with autism spectrum disorders. *Research in Autism Spectrum Disorders*, 5, 317–323.

Faulconbridge, L. F., Wadden, T. A., Thomas, J. G., Jones-Corneille, L. R., Sarwer, D. B., & Fabricatore, A. N. (2013). Changes in depression and quality of life in obese individuals with binge eating disorder. *Surgery for Obesity and Related Diseases*, 9, 790–796.

Feeley, K. M., & Jones, A. (2006). Addressing challenging behavior in children with Down syndrome. *Down Syndrome: Research & Practice*, 11, 64–77.

Feindler, E. L., & Engel, E. C. (2011). Assessment and intervention for adolescents with anger and aggression difficulties in school settings. *Psychology in the Schools*, 48, 243–253.

Feinstein, A. (2010). *A history of autism: Conversations with the pioneers*. New York, NY: Wiley-Blackwell.

Ferretti, J. J., Stevens, D. L., & Fischetti, V. A. (2016). Pediatric autoimmune neuropsychiatric disorders associated with streptococcal infections (PANDAS). In J. J. Ferretti (Ed.), *Streptococcus pyogenes*. Oklahoma City: Oklahoma Health Sciences Center.

Fichter, M. M., Kruger, R., Rief, W., Holland, R., & Dohne, J. (1996). Fluvoxamine in prevention of relapse in bulimia nervosa. *Journal of Clinical Psychopharmacology*, 16, 9–18.

Fichter, M. M., & Quadflieg, N. (2007). Long-term stability of eating disorder diagnoses. *International Journal of Eating Disorders*, 40, 61–66.

Findling, R. L., Johnson, J. L., McClellan, J., Frazier, J. A., Vitiello, B., Hamer, R. M., . . . Sikich, L. (2010). Double-blind maintenance safety and effectiveness findings from the treatment of early-onset schizophrenia spectrum (TEOSS) study. *Journal of the American Academy of Child and Adolescent Psychiatry*, 49, 583–594.

Findling, R. L., Kafantaris, V., Pavuluri, M., McNamara, N. K., Frazier, J. A., Sikich, L., . . . Taylor-Zapata, P. (2013). Post-acute effectiveness of lithium in pediatric bipolar I disorder. *Journal of Child and Adolescent Psychopharmacology*, 23, 80–90.

Finegersh, A., & Homanics, G. E. (2014). Paternal alcohol exposure reduces alcohol drinking and increases behavioral sensitivity to alcohol selectively in male offspring. *PLOS ONE*, 9, e99078.

Finkelhor, D., Shattuck, A., Turner, H. A., & Hamby, S. L. (2014). The lifetime prevalence of child sexual abuse and sexual assault assessed in late adolescence. *Journal of Adolescent Health*, 55, 329–333.

Finkelhor, D., Turner, H. A., Shattuck, A., & Hamby, S. L. (2015). Prevalence of childhood exposure to violence, crime, and abuse. *JAMA Pediatrics*, 169, 746–754.

Finkelhor, D., Vanderminden, J., Turner, H., Hamby, S., & Shattuck, A. (2014). Child maltreatment rates assessed in a national household survey of caregivers and youth. *Child Abuse and Neglect*, 38, 1421–1435.

First, M. B., & Wakefield, J. C. (2010). Defining mental disorder in *DSM-5*. *Psychological Medicine*, 40, 1779–1782.

Fisher, E., Heathcote, L., Palermo, T. M., de C Williams, A. C., Lau, J., & Eccleston, C. (2014). Systematic review and meta-analysis of psychological therapies for children with chronic pain. *Journal of Pediatric Psychology*, 39, 763–782.

Fiske, S. T., & Taylor, S. E. (2013). *Social cognition*. Thousand Oaks, CA: Sage.

Fitzgerald, J., & Pavuluri, M. (2015). Bipolar disorder. In T. P. Gullotta, R. W. Plant, & M. Evans (Eds.), *Handbook of adolescent behavioral problems* (pp. 193–208). New York, NY: Springer.

Fitzgerald, M. M., & Berliner, L. (2014). Psychosocial consequences and treatments for maltreated children. In J. E. Korbin & R. D. Krugman (Ed.), *Handbook of child maltreatment* (pp. 377–392). Dordrecht, The Netherlands: Springer Netherlands.

Flament, M. F., Furino, C., & Godart, N. (2005). Evidence-based pharmacotherapy of eating disorders. In D. J. Stein (Ed.), *Evidence-based psychopharmacology* (pp. 204–254). London, England: Cambridge University Press.

Flanagan, D. P., Fiorello, & Ortiz, S. O. (2010). Enhancing practice through application of Cattell-Horn-Carroll theory and research. *Psychology in the Schools*, 47, 739–760.

Flanagan, D. P., & Harrison, P. L. (Eds.). (2012). *Contemporary intellectual assessment*. New York, NY: Guilford Press.

Flanagan, D. P., Ortiz, S. O., & Alfonso, V. C. (2013). *Essentials of cross-battery assessment*. New York, NY: Wiley.

Flore, L. A., & Milunsky, J. M. (2012). Updates in the genetic evaluation of the child with global developmental delay or intellectual disability. *Seminars in Pediatric Neurology*, 19, 173–180.

Fluoxetine Bulimia Nervosa Collaborative Study Group. (1992). Fluoxetine in the treatment of bulimia nervosa. *Archives of General Psychiatry*, 49, 139–147.

Fombonne, E. (2005). Epidemiological studies of pervasive developmental disorders. In F. R. Volkmar, R. Paul, A. Klin, & D. Cohen (Eds.), *Handbook of autism and pervasive developmental disorders* (Vol. 1, pp. 42–69). Hoboken, NJ: Wiley.

Fontanella, C. A., Hiance, D. L., Phillips, G. S., Bridge, J. A., & Campo, J. V. (2014). Trends in psychotropic medication use for Medicaid-enrolled preschool children. *Journal of Child and Family Studies*, 23, 617–631.

Forbes, D., Fletcher, S., Lockwood, E., O'Donnell, M., Creamer, M., Bryant, R. A., . . . Silove, D. (2011). Requiring both avoidance and emotional numbing in *DSM-5* PTSD: Will it help? *Journal of Affective Disorder*, 130, 483–486.

Forsner, M., Norström, F., Nordyke, K., Ivarsson, A., & Lindh, V. (2014). Relaxation and guided imagery used with 12-year-olds during venipuncture in a school-based screening study. *Journal of Child Health Care*, 18(3), 241–252.

Forth, A. E., Kosson, D. S., & Hare, R. D. (2014). *Hare psychopathy checklist, youth version: PCL: YV*. New York, NY: Springer.

Fox, J. H., Burkle, F. M., Bass, J., Pia, F. A., Epstein, J. L., & Markenson, D. (2012). The effectiveness of psychological first aid as a disaster intervention tool. *Disaster Medicine and Public Health Preparedness*, 6, 247–252.

Fox, N. A., Almas, A. N., Degnan, K. A., Nelson, C. A., & Zeanah, C. H. (2011). The effects of severe psychosocial deprivation and foster care intervention on cognitive development at 8 years of age. *Journal of Child Psychology and Psychiatry*, 52, 919–928.

Fox, N. A., Snidman, N., Haas, S. A., Degnan, K. A., & Kagan, J. (2015). The relations between reactivity at 4 months and behavioral inhibition in the second year. *Infancy*, 20, 98–114.

Fox, S. E., Levitt, P., & Nelson III, C. A. (2010). How the timing and quality of early experiences influence the development of brain architecture. *Child Development*, 81, 28–40.

Frances, A. (2009). Whither *DSM-5*? *British Journal of Psychiatry*, 195, 391–392.

Frank, J. D. (1973). *Persuasion and healing*. Baltimore, MD: Johns Hopkins University Press.

Frank, J. D., & Frank, J. (2004). Therapeutic components shared by all psychotherapies. In A. Freeman, M. J. Mahoney, P. DeVito, & D. Martin (Eds.), *Cognition and psychotherapy* (pp. 45–78). New York, NY: Springer.

Franklin, M., March, J. S., & Gracia, A. (2007). Treating obsessive-compulsive disorder in children and adolescents. In M. M. Antony, C. Purdon, & L. J. Summerfeldt (Eds.), *Psychological* treatment of obsessive compulsive disorders (pp. 253–266). Washington, DC: American Psychological Association.

Franklin, M., Sapyta, J., Freeman, J. B., Khanna, M., Compton, S., Almirall, D., . . . March, J. S. (2011). Cognitive behavior therapy augmentation of pharmacotherapy in pediatric obsessive-compulsive disorder: *JAMA: Journal of the American Medical Association, 306*, 1224–1232.

Frenkel, T. I., Fox, N. A., Pine, D. S., Walker, O. L., Degnan, K. A., & Chronis-Tuscano, A. (2015). Early childhood behavioral inhibition, adult psychopathology and the buffering effects of adolescent social networks: A twenty-year prospective study. *Journal of Child Psychology and Psychiatry, 56*, 1065–1073.

Freud, A. (1936). *The ego and the mechanisms of defense.* New York, NY: International Universities Press.

Freud, A. (1956). *Research at the Hampstead Child-Therapy Clinic.* New York, NY: International University Press.

Freud, S. (1961). The ego and the id. In J. Strachey (Ed. & Trans.), *The standard edition of the complete psychological works of Sigmund Freud* (Vol. 19). London, England: Hogarth Press. (Original work published 1923)

Frey, K. S., Higheagle Strong, Z., & Onyewuenyi, A. C. (2016, June 2). Individual and class norms differentially predict proactive and reactive aggression. *Journal of Educational Psychology.* Advance online publication. doi:10.1037/edu0000118

Frick, P. J. (2012). Developmental pathways to conduct disorder. *Journal of Clinical Child and Adolescent Psychology, 41*, 378–389.

Frick, P. J. (2013). *Conduct disorders and severe antisocial behavior.* New York, NY: Springer.

Frick, P. J., Cornell, A. H., Barry, C. T., Bodin, S. D., & Dane, H. A. (2003). Callous-unemotional traits and conduct problems in the prediction of conduct problem severity, aggression, and self-report of delinquency. *Journal of Abnormal Child Psychology, 31*, 457–470.

Frick, P. J., Lahey, B. B., Loeber, R., Tannenbaum, L. E., Van Horn, Y., Christ, M. A. G., . . . Hanson, K. (1993). Oppositional defiant disorder and conduct disorder: A meta-analytic review of factor analyses and cross-validation in a clinic sample. *Clinical Psychology Review, 13*, 319–340.

Frick, P. J., & Loney, B. R. (2002). Understanding the association between parent and child antisocial behavior. In R. J. McMahon & R. De V. Peters (Eds.), *The effects of parental dysfunction on children* (pp. 105–126). New York, NY: Kluwer.

Frick, P. J., & Moffitt, T. E. (2010). *A proposal to the DSM-5 childhood disorders and the ADHD and disruptive behavior disorders work groups to include a specifier to the diagnosis of conduct disorder based on the presence of callous-unemotional traits.* Washington, DC: American Psychiatric Association.

Frick, P. J., & Nigg, J. T. (2012). Current issues in the diagnosis of attention deficit hyperactivity disorder, oppositional defiant disorder, and conduct disorder. *Annual Review of Clinical Psychology, 8*, 77.

Frick, P. J., Ray, J. V., Thornton, L. C., & Kahn, R. E. (2014). A developmental psychopathology approach to understanding callous-unemotional traits in children and adolescents with serious conduct problems. *Journal of Child Psychology and Psychiatry, 55*, 532–548.

Frick, P. J., & Shirtcliff, E. A. (2016). Children at risk for serious conduct problems. In M. Cima (Ed.), *The handbook of forensic psychopathology and treatment.* New York, NY: Routledge.

Frick, P. J., Wall, T. D., Barry, C. T., & Bodin, S. D. (2015). Applying the concept of psychopathy to children. In C. B. Gacono (Ed.), *The clinical and forensic assessment of psychopathy: a practitioner's guide.* New York, NY: Routledge.

Fried, R., Chan, J., Feinberg, L., Pope, A., Woodworth, K. Y., Faraone, S. V., & Biederman, J. (2016). Clinical correlates of working memory deficits in youth with and without ADHD. *Journal of Clinical and Experimental Neuropsychology, 38*, 487–496.

Friedman, R. A. (2014). Antidepressants' black-box warning: 10 years later. *New England Journal of Medicine, 371*, 1666–1668.

Friedrich, W. N. (2002). An integrated model of psychotherapy for abused children. In J. E. B. Meyers, L. Berliner, J. Briere, C. T. Hendrix, C. Jenny, & T. A. Reid (Eds.), *The APSAC handbook on child maltreatment* (pp. 141–158). Thousand Oaks, CA: Sage.

Frijters, J. C., Lovett, M. W., Steinbach, K. A., Wolf, M., Sevcik, R. A, & Morris, R. D. (2011). Neurocognitive predictors of reading outcomes for children with reading disabilities. *Journal of Learning Disabilities, 44*, 150–166.

Friman, P. C. (2008). Encopresis and enuresis. In D. Reitman (Ed.), *Handbook of psychological assessment, case conceptualization, and treatment* (pp. 589–621). New York, NY: Wiley.

Friman, P. C., Resetar, J., & DeRuyk, K. (2009). Encopresis: Biobehavioral treatment. In W. O'Donohue & J. E. Fisher (Eds.), *General principles and empirically supported techniques of cognitive behavior therapy* (pp. 285–294). New York, NY: Wiley.

Fristad, M. A., Arnold, J. S. G., & Leffler, J. M. (2011). *Psychotherapy for children with bipolar and depressive disorders.* New York, NY: Guilford Press.

Fristad, M. A., Verducci, J. S., Walters, K., & Young, M. E. (2009). Impact of multifamily psychoeducational psychotherapy in treating children aged 8 to 12 years with mood disorders. *Archives of General Psychiatry, 66*, 1013–1021.

Frodl, T., & O'Keane, V. (2013). How does the brain deal with cumulative stress? *Neurobiology of Disease, 52*, 24–37.

Frommlet, F., Bogdan, M., & Ramsey, D. (2016). *A primer in genetics.* London, England: Springer.

Frost, L., & Bondy, A. (2002). *The picture exchange communication system training manual.* Newark, DE: Pyramid Educational Products.

Fuchs, C. E., Van Geelen, S. M., Hermans, H. J. M., Van De Putte, E. M., Van Geel, R., Sinnema, G., & Kuis, W. (2013). Psychological intervention for adolescents with juvenile idiopathic arthritis: for whom and when?. *The Journal of rheumatology, 40*(4), 528–534.

Fuchs, C. E., Van Geelen, S. M., Hermans, H. J. M., Van De Putte, E. M., Van Geel, R., Sinnema, G., & Kuis, W. (2013). Psychological intervention for adolescents with juvenile idiopathic arthritis: For whom and when? *Journal of Rheumatology, 40*, 528–534.

Fulford, K. W. M. (1994). Closet logics: Hidden conceptual elements in the *DSM* and ICD classification of mental disorders. In J. Z. Sadler, O. P. Wiggins, & M. A. Schwartz (Eds.), *Philosophical perspectives on psychiatric diagnostic classification* (pp. 211–232). Baltimore, MD: Johns Hopkins University Press.

Fullana, M. A., Cardoner, N., Alonso, P., Subirà, M., López-Solà, C., Pujol, J., . . . Soriano-Mas, C. (2014). Brain regions related to fear extinction in obsessive-compulsive disorder and its relation to exposure therapy outcome. *Psychological Medicine, 44*, 845–856.

Funderburk, B. W., & Eyberg, S. (2011). Parent-child interaction therapy. In J. C. Norcross (Ed.), *History of psychotherapy* (pp. 415–420). Washington, DC: American Psychological Association.

Furniss, T. (2013). *The multiprofessional handbook of child sexual abuse.* New York, NY: Routledge.

Galanter, M., Kleber, H. D., & Brady, K. (2014). *The American Psychiatric Publishing textbook of substance abuse treatment.* Washington: DC, American Psychiatric Publishing.

Ganzel, B., & Morris, M. H. (2016). Typical and atypical brain development across the lifespan in a neural network model of psychopathology. In D. Cicchetti (Ed.), *Developmental psychopathology* (Vol. 2, pp. 557–631). New York, NY: Wiley.

Garb, H. N., & Boyle, P. A. (2004). Understanding why some clinicians use pseudoscientific methods. In S. O. Lilienfeld, S. J. Lynn, & J. M. Lohr (Eds.), *Science and pseudoscience in clinical psychology* (pp. 17–38). New York, NY: Guilford Press.

Garber, J., Keiley, M. K., & Martin, N. C. (2002). Developmental trajectories of adolescents' depressive symptoms. *Journal of Consulting and Clinical Psychology, 70*, 79–95.

Garcia-Barrera, M. A., & Davidow, J. H. (2015). Anticipation in stuttering. *Journal of Fluency Disorders, 44*, 1–15.

Garcia-Barrera, M. A., & Moore, W. R. (2013). History taking, clinical interviewing, and the mental status examination in child assessment. In D. H. Saklofske, C. R. Reynolds, & V. L. Schwean (Eds.), *The Oxford Handbook of Child Psychological Assessment* (pp. 423–445). Oxford, England: Oxford University Press.

Gardner, D. M., & Gerdes, A. C. (2015). A review of peer relationships and friendships in youth with ADHD. *Journal of Attention Disorders, 19*, 844–855.

Garland, A. F., Haine-Schlagel, R., Brookman-Frazee, L., Baker-Ericzen, M., Trask, E., & Fawley-King, K. (2013). Improving community-based mental health care for children. *Administration and Policy in Mental Health and Mental Health Services Research, 40*, 6–22.

Garner, A. A., Mrug, S., Hodgens, B., & Patterson, C. (2012). Do symptoms of sluggish cognitive tempo in children with ADHD symptoms represent comorbid internalizing difficulties? *Journal of Attention Disorders, 17*, 510–518.

Garralda, M. E., & Rask, C. U. (2015). Somatiform and related disorders. In A. Thapar (Ed.), *Rutter's child and adolescent psychiatry* (pp. 1035–1053). Malden, MA: Blackwell.

Garrett, A. S., Reiss, A. L., Howe, M. E., Kelley, R. G., Singh, M. K., Adleman, N. E., . . . Chang, K. D. (2012). Abnormal amygdala and prefrontal cortex activation to facial expressions in pediatric bipolar disorder. *Journal of the American Academy of Child and Adolescent Psychiatry, 51*, 821–831.

Gathercole, S. E., & Baddeley, A. D. (2014). *Working memory and language.* New York, NY: Psychology Press.

Gatzke-Kopp, L. M., Greenberg, M., & Bierman, K. (2015). Children's parasympathetic reactivity to specific emotions moderates response to intervention for early-onset aggression. *Journal of Clinical Child & Adolescent Psychology, 44*, 291–304.

Gayes, L. A., & Steele, R. G. (2014). A meta-analysis of motivational interviewing interventions for pediatric health behavior change. *Journal of Consulting and Clinical Psychology, 82*, 521.

Ge, X., Coger, R. D., & Elder, G. H. (2001). Pubertal transition, stressful life events, and the emergence of gender differences in adolescent depressive symptoms. *Developmental Psychology, 37*, 404–417.

Geary, D. C. (2010). Mathematical disabilities. *Learning and Individual Differences, 20*, 130–133.

Geary, D. C. (2011). Consequences, characteristics, and causes of mathematical learning disabilities and persistent low achievement in mathematics. *Journal of Developmental and Behavioral Pediatrics, 32*, 250–263.

Geary, D. C. (2013). Early foundations for mathematics learning and their relations to learning disabilities. *Current Directions in Psychological Science, 22*, 23–27.

Geary, D. C., Bailey, D. H., & Hoard, M. K. (2009). Predicting mathematical achievement and mathematical learning disability with a simple screening tool. *Journal of Psychoeducational Assessment, 27*, 265–279.

Geary, D. C., Hoard, M. K., & Bailey, D. H. (2011). How SLD manifests in mathematics. In D. P. Flanagan & V. C. Alfonso (Eds.), *Essentials of specific learning disability identification* (pp. 43–64). Hoboken, NJ: Wiley.

Geary, D. C., Hoard, M. K., Nugent, L., & Bailey, D. H. (2012). Mathematical cognition deficits in children with learning disabilities and persistent low achievement. *Journal of Educational Psychology, 104*, 206–223.

Geary, D. C., Hoard, M. K., Nugent, L., & Rouder, J. N. (2015). Individual differences in algebraic cognition: Relation to the approximate number and sematic memory systems. *Journal of Experimental Child Psychology, 140*, 211–227.

Geller, B., Luby, J. L., & Joshi, P. (2012). A randomized controlled trial of risperidone, lithium, or divalproex for initial treatment of bipolar I disorder, manic or mixed phase, in children and adolescents. *Archives of General Psychiatry, 69*, 515–528.

Geller, B., Tillman, R., Craney, J. L., & Bolhofner, K. (2004). Four-year prospective outcome and natural history of mania in children with a prepubertal and early adolescent bipolar disorder phenotype. *Archives of General Psychiatry, 61*, 459–467.

Geller, D. A. (2010). Obsessive-compulsive disorder. In M. K. Dulcan (Eds.), *Child and adolescent psychiatry* (pp. 349–363). Washington, DC: American Psychiatric Publishing.

Geller, D. A., & March, J. (2012). Practice parameter for the assessment and treatment of children and adolescents with obsessive-compulsive disorder. *Focus, 10*, 360–373.

Gelman, R., & Gallistel, C. R. (1978). *The child's understanding of number.* Cambridge, MA: Harvard University Press.

Gengoux, G. W., Berquist, K. L., Salzman, E., Schapp, S., Phillips, J. M., Frazier, T. W., . . . Hardan, A. Y. (2015). Pivotal response treatment parent training for autism. *Journal of Autism and Developmental Disorders, 45*, 2889–2898.

Gensthaler, A., Khalaf, S., Ligges, M., Kaess, M., Freitag, C. M., & Schwenck, C. (2016a). Selective mutism and temperament: the silence and behavioral inhibition to the unfamiliar. *European Child and Adolescent Psychiatry, 18*, 1–8.

Gensthaler, A., Maichrowitz, V., Kaess, M., Ligges, M., Freitag, C. M., & Schwenck, C. (2016b). Selective mutism: The fraternal twin of childhood social phobia. *Psychopathology, 49*, 95–107.

Gerdes, A. C., Lawton, K. E., Haack, L. M., & Hurtado, G. D. (2014). Assessing ADHD in Latino Families. *Journal of Attention Disorders, 17*, 128–140.

Gersten, R., Chard, D. J., Jayanthi, M., Baker, S. K., Morphy, P., & Flojo, J. (2009). Mathematics instruction for students with learning disabilities: A meta-analysis of instructional components. *Review of Educational Research, 79*, 1202–1242.

Ghaemi, S. Z., Khakshour, A., Abasi, Z., & Hajikhani Golchin, N. A. (2015). Effectiveness of school-based program to preventing mental disorders in school age children. *Reviews in Clinical Medicine, 2*, 118–124.

Ghanizadeh, A. (2010). Comorbidity of enuresis in children with attention-deficit/hyperactivity disorder. *Journal of Attention Disorders, 13*, 464–467.

Ghera, M. M., Marshall, P. J., Fox, N. A., Zeanah, C. H., Nelson, C. A., Smyke, A. T., & Guthrie, D. (2009). The effects of foster care intervention on socially deprived institutionalized children's attention and positive affect. *Journal of Child Psychology and Psychiatry, 50*, 246–253.

Giannotti, F., & Cortesi, F. (2009). Family and cultural influences on sleep development. *Child and Adolescent Psychiatric Clinics of North America, 18*, 849–861.

Gibb, B. E., Abramson, L. Y., & Alloy, L. B. (2004). Emotional maltreatment from parents, verbal peer victimization, and cognitive vulnerability to depression. *Cognitive Therapy and Research, 28*, 1–21.

Gibbons, R. D., Coca Perraillon, M., Hur, K., Conti, R. M., Valuck, R. J., & Brent, D. A. (2015). Antidepressant treatment and suicide attempts and self-inflicted injury in children and adolescents. *Pharmacoepidemiology and Drug Safety, 24*, 208–214.

Gibbs, J. C. (2010). *Moral development and reality.* Boston, MA: Pearson.

Giedd, J. N., & Denker, A. H. (2015). The adolescent brain: Insights from neuroimaging. In *Brain Crosstalk in Puberty and Adolescence* (pp. 85–96). Cham, Switzerland: Springer International Publishing.

Giedd, J. N., Raznahan, A., Alexander-Bloch, A., Schmitt, E., Gogtay, N., & Rapoport, J. L. (2015). Child psychiatry branch of the national institute of mental health longitudinal structural magnetic resonance imaging study of human brain development. *Neuropsychopharmacology, 40*, 43–49.

Giedd, J. N., Shaw, P., Wallace, G., Gogtay, N., & Lenroot, R. K. (2006). Anatomic brain imaging studies of normal and abnormal brain development in children and adolescents. In D. Cicchetti & D. J. Cohen (Eds.), *Developmental psychopathology* (Vol. 2, pp. 127–196). Hoboken, NJ: Wiley.

Gil, A. G., Vega, W. A., & Turner, R. J. (2002). Early and mid-adolescence risk factors for later substance abuse by African-Americans and European Americans. *Public Health Reports, 177,* 15–29.

Gilissen, C., Hehir-Kwa, J. Y., Thung, D. T., van de Vorst, M., van Bon, B. W., Willemsen, M. H., . . . Veltman, J. A. (2014). Genome sequencing identifies major causes of severe intellectual disability. *Nature, 511*(7509), 344–347.

Gillies, D., Sinn, J. K., Lad, S. S., Leach, M. J., & Ross, M. J. (2012). Polyunsaturated fatty acids (PUFA) for attention deficit hyperactivity disorder (ADHD) in children and adolescents. *The Cochrane Library.*

Gil-Rivas, V., Holman, E. A., & Silver, R. C. (2004). Adolescent vulnerability following the September 11th terrorist attacks. *Applied Developmental Science, 8,* 130–142.

Ginsburg, G. S., & Schlossberg, M. C. (2002). Family-based treatment of childhood anxiety disorders. *International Journal of Psychiatry, 14,* 142–153.

Glasofer, D. R., Attia, E., & Timothy Walsh, B. (2015). Feeding and eating disorders. In A. Tasman (Ed.), *Psychiatry* (pp. 1231–1249). New York, NY: Wiley.

Gleason, M. M., Fox, N. A., Drury, S., Smyke, A. T., Egger, H. L., Nelson, C. A., . . . Zeanah, C. H. (2011). Validity of evidence-derived criteria for reactive attachment disorder. *Journal of the American Academy of Child and Adolescent Psychiatry, 50,* 216–231.

Glick, B., & Gibbs, J. C. (2011). *Aggression replacement training.* Champaign, IL: Research Press.

Glidden, L. M. (2012). Family well-being and children with developmental disability. In J. A. Burack, R. M. Hodapp, G. Iarocci, & E. Zigler (Eds.), *The Oxford handbook of intellectual disability and development* (pp. 303–317). New York, NY: Oxford University Press.

Glowinski, A. L. (2011). Reactive attachment disorder. *Journal of the American Academy of Child and Adolescent Psychiatry, 50,* 210–212.

Goethals, I., Vervaet, M., Audenaert, K., Van de Wiele, C., Ham, H., Vandecapelle, M., . . . van Heeringen, C. (2014). Comparison of cortical 5-HT2A receptor binding in bulimia nervosa patients and healthy volunteers. *The American Journal of Psychiatry, 161,* 1916–1918.

Goforth, A. N., Pham, A. V., & Carlson, J. S. (2011). Diathesis-stress model. In S. Goldstein & J. Naglieri (Eds.), *Encyclopedia of child behavior and development* (pp. 502–503). New York, NY: Springer.

Goldberg, D. P., Krueger, R. F., Andrews, G., & Hobbs, M. J. (2009). Emotional disorders: Cluster 4 of the proposal meta-structure for *DSM-5* and ICD-11. *Psychological Medicine, 39,* 2043–2059.

Goldberg, S. (2014). *Attachment and development.* New York, NY: Routledge.

Goldberg, S., Muir, R., & Kerr, J. (2013). *Attachment theory.* New York, NY: Routledge.

Goldsmith, S. (2012). *Universal design.* Oxford, England: Architectural Press.

Goldstein, A. L., Faulkner, B., & Wekerle, C. (2013). The relationship among internal resilience, smoking, alcohol use, and depression symptoms in emerging adults transitioning out of child welfare. *Child Abuse and Neglect, 37,* 22–32.

Goldstein, A. P., & Martens, B. K. (2000). *Lasting change: Methods for enhancing generalization of gain.* Champaign, IL: Research Press.

Goldstein, D. J., Wilson, M. G., & Thompson, V. L. (1995). Long-term fluoxetine treatment of bulimia nervosa. *British Journal of Psychiatry, 166,* 660–667.

Goldston, D. B., Daniel, S. S., Erkanli, A., Heilbron, N., Doyle, O., Weller, B., . . . Faulkner, M. (2015). Suicide attempts in a longitudinal sample of adolescents followed through adulthood. *Journal of Consulting and Clinical Psychology, 83,* 253–264.

Goldston, D. B., Weller, B. E., & Doyle, O. (2014). Suicide. In F. Leong (Ed.), *APA handbook of multicultural psychology* (pp. 361–376). Washington, DC: American Psychological Association.

Golmaryami, F. N., & Frick, P. J. (2015). Callous-unemotional traits and the development of externalizing spectrum disorders. In T. P. Beauchaine & S. P. Hinshaw (Eds.), *The Oxford handbook of externalizing spectrum disorders* (pp. 360–374). Oxford, England: Oxford University Press.

Gonzales, N. A., Lau, A. S., Murray, V. M., Pina, A. A., & Barrera, M. (2016). Culturally adapted preventative interventions for children and adolescents. In D. Cicchetti (Ed.), *Developmental psychopathology* (Vol. 4, pp. 874–933). New York, NY: Wiley.

Goodman, E., & Capitman, J. (2000). Depressive symptoms and cigarette smoking among teens. *Pediatrics, 706,* 748–755.

Goods, K.S., Ishijima, E., Chang, Y., Kasari, C. (2013). Preschool based JASPER intervention in minimally verbal children with autism. *Journal of Autism and Developmental Disorders.*

Goodwin, R. D., Fergusson, D. M., & Horwood, L. J. (2004). Association between anxiety disorders and substance use disorders among young persons. *Journal of Psychiatric Research, 38,* 295–304.

Goodwin, R. D., Lieb, R., Hoefler, M., Pfister, H., Bittner, A., Beesdo, K., & Wittchen, H.-U. (2005). Panic attack as a risk factor for severe psychopathology. *American Journal of Psychiatry, 161,* 2207–2214.

Gottlieb, G., & Willoughby, M. T. (2006). Probabilistic epigenesis of psychopathology. In D. Cicchetti & D. J. Cohen (Eds.), *Developmental psychopathology* (Vol. 1, pp. 673–700). Hoboken, NJ: Wiley.

Gracious, B. L., Danielyan, A., & Kowatch, R. A. (2015). Mood stabilizers. In M. Dulcan (Eds.), *Dulcan's textbook of child and adolescent psychiatry* (pp. 769–793). Washington, DC: American Psychiatric Publishing.

Graczyk, P. A., & Connolly, S. D. (2015). Anxiety disorders. In T. P. Gullotta, R. W. Plant, & M. Evans (Eds.), *Handbook of adolescent behavioral problems* (pp. 107–130). New York, NY: Springer.

Graham, P., & Reynolds, S. (2013). *Cognitive behavior therapy for children and families.* Cambridge, England: Cambridge University Press.

Graham, S., Harris, K. R., & Chambers, A. B. (2016). Evidence-based practice and writing instruction. In C. A. MacArthur (Ed.), *Handbook of writing research* (pp. 215–242). New York, NY: Guilford Press.

Graham, S., McKeown, D., Kiuhara, S. A., & Harris, K. R. (2012). A meta-analysis of writing instruction for students in the elementary grades. *Journal of Educational Psychology, 104,* 879–896.

Grant, J. E., Odlaug, B. L., Chamberlain, S. R., Keuthen, N. J., Lochner, C., & Stein, D. J. (2012). Skin picking disorder. *American Journal of Psychiatry, 169,* 1143–1149.

Grapel, J. N., Cicchetti, D. V., & Volkmar, F. R. (2015). Sensory features as diagnostic criteria for autism. *Yale Journal of Biology and Medicine, 88,* 69–71.

Gray, J. A. (1982). *The neuropsychology of anxiety.* New York, NY: Oxford University Press.

Gray, J. A. (1987). *The psychology of fear and stress.* Cambridge, England: Cambridge University Press.

Gray, J. A. (1994). Three fundamental emotion systems. In P. Ekman & R. J. Davidson (Eds.), *The nature of emotion* (pp. 243–247). New York, NY: Oxford University Press.

Gray, W. N., Denson, L. A., Baldassano, R. N., & Hommel, K. A. (2012). Treatment adherence in adolescents with inflammatory bowel disease: The collective impact of barriers to adherence and anxiety/depressive symptoms. *Journal of Pediatric Psychology, 37,* 282–291.

Gray, W. N., Resmini, A. R., Baker, K. D., Holbrook, E., Morgan, P. J., Ryan, J., . . . & Hommel, K. A. (2015). Concerns, barriers, and recommendations to improve transition from pediatric to adult

IBD care: Perspectives of patients, parents, and health professionals. *Inflammatory bowel diseases, 21*(7), 1641–1651.

Graziano, P. A., Slavec, J., Hart, K., Garcia, A., & Pelham, W. E., Jr. (2014). Improving school readiness in preschoolers with behavior problems: Results from a summer treatment program. *Journal of Psychopathology and Behavioral Assessment, 36*, 555–569.

Greenhill, L. L. (2005). The science of stimulant abuse. *Psychiatric Annals, 35*, 210–214.

Greenough, W. T., & Black, J. E. (2013). Induction of brain structure by experience. In *Developmental behavioral neuroscience* (pp. 155–168). New York, NY: Psychology Press.

Greenwood, T. A., Lazzeroni, L. C., Calkins, M. E., Freedman, R., Green, M. F., Gur, R. E., . . . Radant, A. D. (2016). Genetic assessment of additional endophenotypes from the Consortium on the Genetics of Schizophrenia Family Study. *Schizophrenia Research, 170*, 30–40.

Gregory, A. M., Agnew-Blais, J. C., Matthews, T., Moffitt, T. E., & Arseneault, L. (2016). ADHD and sleep quality. *Journal of Clinical Child & Adolescent Psychology.*

Gregory, A. M., Cox, J., Crawford, M. R., Holland, J., Haravey, A. G., & The STEPS Team. (2009). Dysfunctional beliefs and attitudes about sleep in children. *Journal of Sleep Research, 18*, 422–426.

Greydanus, D. E., Kaplan, G., & Patel, D. R. (2015). Pharmacology of autism spectrum disorder. In S H. Fatemi (Ed.), *The molecular basis of autism* (pp. 173–193). New York, NY: Springer.

Gridley, N., Hutchings, J., & Baker-Henningham, H. (2015). The Incredible Years Parent–Toddler Program and parental language. *Child: Care, Health and Development, 41*, 103–111.

Grigorenko, E. L., Bick, J., Campbell, D. J., Lewine, G., Abrams, J., Nguyen, V., & Chang, J. T. (2016). The trilogy of GxE. In D. Cicchetti (Ed.), *Developmental psychopathology* (Vol. 2, pp. 287–338). New York, NY: Wiley.

Groher, M. E., & Crary, M. A. (2015). *Dysphagia: Clinical management in adults and children.* St. Louis, MO: Elsevier.

Grossman, K. E., Bretherton, I., Waters, E., & Grossman, K. (Eds.). (2016). *Maternal sensitivity: Mary Ainsworth's enduring influence on attachment theory, research, and clinical applications.* Boston, MA: Routledge.

Groth-Marnat, G. (2003). *Handbook of psychological assessment.* New York, NY: Wiley.

Gruber, R., Michaelsen, S., Bergmame, L., Frenette, S., Bruni, P., Fontil, L., & Carrier, J. (2012). Short sleep duration is associated with teacher-reported inattention and cognitive problems in healthy school-age children. *Nature and Science of Sleep, 4*, 33–40.

Gueron-Sela, N., Atzaba-Poria, N., Meiri, G., & Yerushalmi, B. (2011). Maternal worries about child underweight mediate and moderate the relationship between child feeding disorders and mother-child feeding. *Journal of Pediatric Psychology, 36*, 827–836.

Gulley, L. D., Oppenheimer, C. W., & Hankin, B. L. (2014). Associations among negative parenting, attention bias to anger, and social anxiety among youth. *Developmental Psychology, 50*, 577.

Gunlicks-Stoessel, M. L., & Mufson, L. (2015). Interpersonal psychotherapy for depressed adolescents. In M. K. Dulcan (Ed.), *Dulcan's textbook of child and adolescent psychiatry* (pp. 959–971). Washington, DC: American Psychiatric Publishing.

Gunnar, M. R. (2010). Reversing the effects of early deprivation after infancy. *Frontiers of Neuroscience, 4*, 1–2.

Gur, R. E., Andreasen, N., Asarnow, R., Gur, R., Jones, P., Kendler, K., et al. (2005). Schizophrenia. In *Treating and preventing adolescent mental health disorders* (pp. 77–156). Oxford, England: Oxford University Press.

Gustafson, K. E., & McNamara, J. R. (2010). Confidentiality with minor clients. In D. N. Bersoff (Ed.), *Ethical conflicts in psychology* (pp. 192–196). Washington, DC: American Psychological Association.

Guyer, A. E., McClure, E. B., Adler, A. D., Brotman, M. A., Rich, B. A., Kimes, A. S., . . . Leibenluft, E. (2007). Specificity of facial expression labeling deficits in childhood psychopathology. *Journal of Child Psychology and Psychiatry, 48*, 863–871.

Ha, T., Dishion, T. J., Overbeek, G., Burk, W. J., & Engels, R. C. (2014). The blues of adolescent romance: Observed affective interactions in adolescent romantic relationships associated with depressive symptoms.*Journal of Abnormal Child Psychology, 42*, 551–562.

Hair, N. L., Hanson, J. L., Wolfe, B. L., & Pollak, S. D. (2015). Association of child poverty, brain development, and academic achievement. *JAMA Pediatrics, 169*(9), 822–829.

Hale, J., Alfonso, V., Berninger, V., Bracken, B., Christo, C., Clark, E., . . . Yalof, J. (2010). Critical issues in response-to-intervention, comprehensive evaluation, and specific learning disabilities identification and intervention. *Learning Disabilities Quarterly, 33*, 223–235.

Halmi, K. A., Eckert, E., Marchi, P., Sampagnaro, V., Apple, R., & Cohen, J. (1991). Comorbidity of psychiatric diagnoses in anorexia nervosa. *Archives of General Psychiatry, 48*, 712–718.

Halmi, K. A., Tozzi, F., Thornton, L. M., Crow, S., Fichter, M. M., Kaplan, A. S., . . . Bulik, C. M. (2005). The relation among perfectionism, obsessive compulsive personality disorder and obsessive compulsive disorder in individuals with eating disorders. *International Journal of Eating Disorders, 38*, 371–374.

Hamblen, J., & Barnett, E. (2016). *PTSD in children and adolescents.* Washington, DC: National Center for PTSD.

Hamilton, J., Daleiden, E., & Youngstrom, E. (2015). Evidence-based practice. In M. K. Dulcan (Ed.), *Dulcan's textbook of child and adolescent psychiatry* (pp. 523–537). Washington, DC: American Psychiatric Publishing.

Hamilton, J. L., Stange, J. P., Abramson, L. Y., & Alloy, L. B. (2015). Stress and the development of cognitive vulnerabilities to depression explain sex differences in depressive symptoms during adolescence. *Clinical Psychological Science, 3*, 702–714.

Hammen, C., Hazel, N. A., Brennan, P. A., & Najman, J. (2012). Intergenerational transmission and continuity of stress and depression. *Psychological Medicine, 42*, 931–942.

Hammen, C. L., Rudolph, K. D., & Abaied, J. L. (2014). Child and adolescent depression. In E. J. Mash & R. A. Barkley (Eds.), *Child psychopathology* (pp. 225–263). New York, NY: Guilford Press.

Hammen, C., Shih, J. H., & Brennan, P. A. (2004). Intergenerational transmission of depression. *Journal of Consulting and Clinical Psychology, 72*, 511–522.

Hankin, B. L., & Abela, J. R. Z. (2005). *Development of psychopathology: A vulnerability-stress perspective.* Thousand Oaks, CA: Sage.

Hanley, G. P., Iwata, B. A., & McCord, B. E. (2003). Functional analysis of problem behavior. *Journal of Applied Behavior Analysis, 36*, 147–185.

Hanna, S. E., Rosenbaum, P. L., Bartlett, D. J., Palisano, R. J., Walter, S. D., Avery, L., & Russell, D. J. (2009). Stability and decline in gross motor function among children and youth with cerebral palsy aged 2 to 21 years. *Developmental Medicine and Child Neurology, 51*, 295–302.

Hannon-Engel, S. L., Filin, E. E., & Wolfe, B. E. (2013). CCK response in bulimia nervosa and following remission. *Physiology and Behavior, 122*, 56–61.

Harford, T. C., Grant, B. F., Yi, H., & Chen, C. M. (2005). Patterns of *DSM-IV* alcohol abuse and dependence criteria among adolescents and adults. *Alcoholism, 20*, 810–828.

Harford, T. C., Yi, H., Faden, V. B., & Chen, C. M. (2009). The dimensionality of *DSM-IV* alcohol use disorders among adolescent and adult drinkers and symptom patterns by age, gender, and race/ethnicity. *Alcoholism, 33*, 868–877.

Harkness, K. L., Bruce, A. E., & Lumley, M. N. (2006). The role of childhood abuse and neglect in the sensitization to stressful life events in adolescent depression. *Journal of Abnormal Psychology, 115*, 730–741.

Harris, J. C., & Greenspan, S. (2016). Definition and nature of intellectual disability. In *Handbook of evidence-based practices in intellectual and developmental disabilities* (pp. 11–39). New York, NY: Springer.

Harris, K. R., & Graham, S. (2016). Self-regulated strategy development in writing policy implications of an evidence-based practice. *Policy Insights from the Behavioral and Brain Sciences, 3*, 77–84.

Harris, K. R., Graham, S., & Adkins, M. (2015). Practice-based professional development and self-regulated strategy development for Tier 2, at-risk writers in second grade. *Contemporary Educational Psychology, 40*, 5–16.

Harris, K. R., Lane, K. L., Graham, S., Driscoll, S. A., Sandmel, K., Brindle, M., & Schatschneider, C. (2012). Practice-based professional development for self-regulated strategies development in writing. *Journal of Teacher Education, 63*, 103–119.

Hart, K. J., Nelson, W. M., & Finch, A. J. (2006). Comparative treatments of conduct disorder: Summary and conclusions. In W. M. Nelson, A. J. Finch, & K. J. Hart (Eds.), *Conduct disorders: A practitioner's guide to comparative treatments* (pp. 321–343). New York, NY: Springer.

Harter, S. (2015). *The construction of the self*. New York, NY: Guilford Press.

Hartley, S. L., & Sikora, D. M. (2009). Sex differences in autism spectrum disorder. *Journal of Autism and Developmental Disorders, 39*, 1715–1722.

Harvey, R. C., James, A. C., & Shields, G. E. (2016). A systematic review and network meta-analysis to assess the relative efficacy of antipsychotics for the treatment of positive and negative symptoms in early-onset schizophrenia. *CNS Drugs, 30*(1), 27–39.

Harvey, R. C., Shields, G. E., & James, A. C. (2015). Antipsychotics for treatment of pediatric schizophrenia: A systematic review and network meta-analysis of symptom control, weight gain and discontinuation due to adverse events. *Value in Health, 3*, 115–116.

Hassan, A., Agha, S. S., Langley, K., & Thapar, A. (2011). Prevalence of bipolar disorder in children and adolescents with attention-deficit hyperactivity disorder. *British Journal of Psychiatry, 198*, 195–198.

Hassell, K. L. (2016). Sickle cell disease. *American Journal of Preventive Medicine, 51*, S1–S2.

Haut, K. M., Schvarcz, A., Cannon, T. D., & Bearden, C. E. (2016). Neurodevelopmental theories of schizophrenia. In D. Cicchetti (Ed.), *Developmental psychopathology* (Vol. 2, pp. 885–930). New York, NY: Wiley.

Hawes, D. J., Price, M. J., & Dadds, M. R. (2014). Callous-unemotional traits and the treatment of conduct problems in childhood and adolescence. *Clinical Child and Family Psychology Review, 17*, 248–267.

Hawton, K., Saunders, K. E., & O'Connor, R. C. (2012). Self-harm and suicide in adolescents. *The Lancet, 379*, 2373–2382.

Hay, D. F. (2016). Early peer relations and their impact on children's development. In M. Boivin (Ed.), *Early child development*. Montreal, Quebec: CEECD.

Hayden, E. P., & Mash, E. J. (2014). Child psychopathology: A developmental-systems perspective. In E. J. Mash & R. A. Barkley (Eds.), *Child psychopathology* (pp. 3–72). New York, NY: Guilford Press.

Hayes, A. F. (2013). *Introduction to mediation, moderation, and conditional process analysis*. New York, NY: Guilford Press.

Hayes, J., & Flower, L. (1980). Identifying the organization of writing processes. In L. Gregg & E. Steinberg (Eds.), *Cognitive processes in writing* (pp. 3–30). Hillsdale, NJ: Erlbaum.

Hazell, P., & Mirzaie, M. (2013). Tricyclic drugs for depression in children and adolescents. *The Cochrane Database of Systematic Reviews, 6*, 1–48.

Heal, D. J., Smith, S. L., & Findling, R. L. (2011). ADHD: Current and future therapies. In C. Stanford & R. Tannock (Eds.), *Behavioral neuroscience of attention deficit hyperactivity disorder and its treatment* (pp. 361–390). New York, NY: Springer.

Health Care Cost Institute. (2012). *Health care cost and utilization report*. Washington, DC: Author.

Healy, O., Lydon, S., & Murray, C. (2014). Aggressive behavior. In P. Sturmey & R. Didden (Eds.), *Evidence-based practice and intellectual disabilities* (pp. 103–132). New York, NY: Wiley.

Heath, A., Ganz, J., Parker, R., Burke, M., & Ninci, J. (2015). A meta-analytic review of functional communication training across mode of communication, age, and disability. *Review Journal of Autism and Developmental Disorders, 2*, 155–166.

Heath, A., Lynskey, M. T., & Waldron, M. (2010). Substance use and substance use disorder. In M. Rutter (Ed.), *Rutter's child and adolescent psychiatry* (pp. 565–586). Malden, NJ: Blackwell.

Hebb, D. O. (1949). *The organization of behavior*. New York, NY: Wiley.

Hechtman, L., Abikoff, H., Klein, R. G., Greenfield, B., Etcovitch, J., Cousins, L., . . . Pollack, S. (2004a). Children with ADHD treated with long-term methylphenidate and multimodal psychosocial treatment: Impact on parental practices. *Journal of the American Academy of Child and Adolescent Psychiatry, 43*, 830–838.

Hechtman, L., Abikoff, H., Klein, R. G., Weiss, G., Respitz, C., Kouri, J., . . . Pollack, S. (2004b). Academic achievement and emotional status of children with ADHD treated with long-term methylphenidate and multimodal psychosocial treatment. *Journal of the American Academy of Child and Adolescent Psychiatry, 43*, 812–819.

Hecker, L., & Sori, C. F. (2010). Ethics in therapy with children in families. In L. Hecker (Ed.), *Ethics and professional issues in couple and family therapy* (pp. 51–70). New York, NY: Routledge.

Hedge, M. N. (2008). *Hedge's pocket guide to communication disorders in children*. Clifton Park, NY: Delmar.

Hedge, M. N., & Maul, C. A. (2006). *Language disorders in children*. Boston, MA: Pearson.

Hedges, K., & Korchmaros, J. D. (2016). Pubertal timing and substance abuse treatment outcomes. *Journal of Child and Adolescent Substance Abuse, 25*(6), 598–605.

Heflin, A. H., & Deblinger, E. (2003). Treatment of a sexually abused adolescent with posttraumatic stress disorder. In M. A. Reinecke, F. M. Dattilio, & A. Freeman (Eds.), *Cognitive therapy with children and adolescents* (pp. 214–246). New York, NY: Guilford Press.

Heiler, S., Legenbauer, T., Bogen, T., Jensch, T., & Holtmann, M. (2011). Severe mood dysregulation: In the "light" of circadian functioning. *Medical Hypotheses, 77*, 692–695.

Heilskov Rytter, M. J., Andersen, L. B., Houmann, T., Bilenberg, N., Hvolby, A., Mølgaard, C., . . . Lauritzen, L. (2015). Diet in the treatment of ADHD in children. *Journal of Psychiatry, 69*, 1–18.

Heiman, J. R., & Heard-Davison, A. R. (2004). Child sexual abuse and adult sexual relationships: Review and perspective. In L. J. Koenig, L. S. Doll, A. O'Leary, & W. Pequegnat (Eds.), *From child sexual abuse to adult sexual risk: Trauma, revictimization, and intervention* (pp. 13–47). New York, NY: American Psychological Association.

Helenius, D., Munk-Jorgensen, P., & Steinhausen, H. (2012). Family load estimates of schizophrenia and associated risk factors in a nationwide population study of former child and adolescent patients up to forty years of age. *Schizophrenia Research, 139*, 193–188.

Helzer, J. E. (2011). A proposal for incorporating clinically relevant dimensions into *DSM-5*. In D. A. Reiger (Ed.), *The conceptual evolution of DSM-5* (pp. 81–96). Washington, DC: American Psychiatric Publishing.

Hembree-Kigin, T. L., & McNeil, C. (2013). *Parent-child interaction therapy*. New York, NY: Springer.

Hendershot, C. S., Witkiewitz, K., George, W. H., & Marlatt, G. A. (2011). Relapse prevention for addictive behaviors. *Substance Abuse Treatment, Prevention, and Policy, 6*, 1–17.

Henderson, C. E., Dakof, G. A., Greenbaum, P. E., & Liddle, H. A. (2010). Effectiveness of multidimensional family therapy with higher severity substance-abusing adolescents. *Journal of Consulting and Clinical Psychology, 78,* 885–897.

Hendrick, C. E., Cance, J. D., & Maslowsky, J. (2016). Peer and individual risk factors in adolescence explaining the relationship between girls' pubertal timing and teenage childbearing. *Journal of Youth and Adolescence, 45,* 916–927.

Henggeler, S. W., & Lee, T. (2003). Multisystemic treatment of serious clinical problems. In A. E. Kazdin & J. R. Weisz (Eds.), *Evidence-based psychotherapies for children and adolescents* (pp. 301–322). New York, NY: Guilford Press.

Henggeler, S. W., & Schaeffer, C. M. (2016). Multisystemic therapy: Clinical overview, outcomes, and implementation research. *Family Process, 55*(3), 514–528.

Herpertz-Dahlmann, B. (2015). Adolescent eating disorders: Update on definitions, symptomatology, epidemiology, and comorbidity. *Child and Adolescent Psychiatric Clinics of North America, 24,* 177–196.

Herrenkohl, T. I., Hong, S., Klika, J. B., Herrenkohl, R. C., & Russo, M. J. (2013). Developmental impacts of child abuse and neglect related to adult mental health, substance use, and physical health. *Journal of Family Violence, 28,* 191–199.

Hess, M., & Scheithauer, H. (2015). Bullying. In T. P. Gullotta, R. W. Plant, & M. Evans (Eds.), *Handbook of adolescent behavioral problems* (pp. 429–443). New York, NY: Springer.

Hetherington, E. M. (Ed.). (2014). *Coping with divorce, single parenting, and remarriage: A risk and resiliency perspective.* New York, NY: Psychology Press.

Hetrick, S. E., McKenzie, J. E., Cox, G. R., Simmons, M. B., & Merry, S. N. (2012). Newer generation antidepressants for depressive disorders in children and adolescents. *The Cochrane Library.*

Heyman, R. E., Slep, A. M. S., Beach, S. R., Wamboldt, M. Z., Kaslow, N. J., & Reiss, D. (2009). Relationship problems and the DSM. *World Psychiatry, 8,* 7–14.

Higa-McMillan, C. K., Francis, S. E., & Chorpita, B. F. (2014). Anxiety disorders. In E. J. Mash & R. A. Barkley (Eds.), *Child psychopathology* (pp. 345–428). New York, NY: Guilford Press.

Hilbert, A., Pike, K. M., Goldschmidt, A. B., Wilfley, D. E., Fairburn, C. G., Dohm, F. A., & Walsh, B. T. (2014). Risk factors across the eating disorders. *Psychiatry Research, 220,* 500–506.

Hill, C. E. (2014). *Helping skills.* Washington, DC: American Psychological Association.

Hill, C. J., Gormley, W. T., & Adelstein, S. (2015). Do the short-term effects of a high-quality preschool program persist? *Early Childhood Research Quarterly, 32,* 60–79.

Hill, D. E., Yeo, R. A., Campbell, R. A., Hart, B., Vigil, J., & Brooks, W. (2003). Magnetic resonance imaging correlates of attention-deficit/hyperactivity disorder in children. *Neuropsychology, 17,* 498–506.

Hill, K., & Toth, T. L. (2016). Epigenetic mechanisms in the development of behavior. In D. Cicchetti (Ed.), *Developmental psychopathology* (Vol. 2, pp. 416–441). New York, NY: Wiley.

Hinshaw, S. P., & Beauchaine, T. P. (2015). The developmental psychopathology perspective on externalizing behavior dimensions and externalizing disorders. In T. P. Beauchaine & S. P. Hinshaw (Eds.), *The Oxford handbook of externalizing spectrum disorders* (pp. 90–102). Oxford, England: Oxford University Press.

Hinshaw, S. P., Klein, R. G., & Abikoff, H. B. (2002). Childhood attention-deficit hyperactivity disorder: Nonpharmacological treatments and their combination with medication. In P. E. Nathan & J. M. Gorman (Eds.), *A guide to treatments that work* (pp. 3–23). New York, NY: Oxford University Press.

Hiroto, D. S., & Seligman, E. (1975). Generality of learned helplessness in man. *Journal of Personality and Social Psychology, 31,* 311–327.

Hock, E., Hart, M., Kang, M. J., & Lutz, W. J. (2004). Predicting children's reactions to terrorist attacks: The importance of self-reports and preexisting characteristics. *American Journal of Orthopsychiatry, 74,* 253–262.

Hodapp, R. M., & DesJardin, J. L. (2002). Genetic etiologies of mental retardation: Issues for interventions and interventionists. *Journal of Developmental and Physical Disabilities, 14,* 323–338.

Hodapp, R. M., & Dykens, E. M. (2006). Mental retardation. In K. A. Renninger, I. E. Sigel, W. Damon, & R. M. Lerner (Eds.), *Handbook of child psychology* (pp. 453–496). Hoboken, NJ: Wiley.

Hodapp, R. M., Zakemi, E., Rosner, B. A., & Dykens, E. M. (2006). Mental retardation. In D. A. Wolfe & E. J. Marsh (Eds.), *Behavioral and emotional disorders in adolescents* (pp. 383–409). New York, NY: Guilford Press.

Hodges, J., & Tizard, B. (1989). Social and family relationships of ex-institutional adolescents. *Journal of Child Psychology and Psychiatry, 30,* 77–97.

Hofer, M. A. (2006). Psychobiological roots of early attachment. *Current Directions in Psychological Science, 15,* 84–88.

Hoffart, A., Hedley, L. M., Svanøe, K., Langkaas, T. F., & Sexton, H. (2016). Agoraphobia with and without panic disorder. *Journal of Nervous and Mental Disease, 204,* 100–107.

Hoffmann, H. (1845). *Struwwelpeter.* Project Gutenberg.

Hogarty, G. E., Kornblith, S. J., Greenwald, D., DiBarry, A. L., Cooley, S., Ulrich, R. F., . . . Flesher, S. (1997). Three-year trials of personal therapy among schizophrenic patients living with or independent of family. *American Journal of Psychiatry, 154,* 1504–1513.

Hogue, A., & Dauber, S. (2013). Assessing fidelity to evidence-based practices in usual care: The example of family therapy for adolescent behavior problems. *Evaluation and Program Planning, 37,* 21–30.

Hogue, A., Dauber, S., Henderson, C. E., Bobek, M., Johnson, C., Lichvar, E., & Morgenstern, J. (2015). Randomized trial of family therapy versus nonfamily treatment for adolescent behavior problems in usual care. *Journal of Clinical Child and Adolescent Psychology, 44,* 954–969.

Hogue, A., Liddle, H. A., Dauber, S., & Samuolis, J. (2004). Linking session focus to treatment outcome in evidence-based treatments for adolescent substance abuse. *Psychotherapy: Theory, Research, Practice, Training, 41,* 83–96.

Hollis, C. (2010). Schizophrenia and allied disorders. In M. Rutter (Ed.), *Rutter's child and adolescent psychiatry* (pp. 737–758). Malden, MA: Blackwell.

Holmbeck, G. H., Zebracki, K., & McGoron, K. (2009). Research design and statistical applications. In M. C. Roberts & R. G. Steele (Eds.), *Handbook of pediatric psychology* (pp. 52–70). New York, NY: Guilford Press.

Homer, C. J., & Oyeku, S. O. (2016). Sickle cell disease. *American Journal of Preventive Medicine, 51,* S3–S4.

Hornor, G. (2016). Nonsuicidal self-injury. *Journal of Pediatric Health Care, 30,* 261–267.

Horwitz, S. M., Kelleher, K., Boyce, T., Jensen, P., Murphy, M., Perrin, E., . . . Weitzman, M. (2002). Barriers to health care research for children and youth with psychosocial problems. *JAMA: Journal of the American Medical Association, 288,* 1508–1512.

Houts, A. C. (2010). Behavioral treatment for enuresis. In J. R. Weisz & A. E. Kazdin (Eds.), *Evidence-based psychotherapies for children and adolescents* (pp. 359–374). New York, NY: Guilford Press.

Hoven, C. W., Mandell, D. J., & Duarte, C. S. (2003). Mental health of New York City public school children after 9/11. In S. W. Coates, J. L. Rosenthal, & D. S. Schechter (Eds.), *September 11: Trauma and human bonds* (pp. 51–74). Hillsdale, NJ: Analytic Press.

Howard, K. I., Kopta, S. M., Krause, M. S., & Orlinsky, D. E. (1986). The dose-effect relationship in psychotherapy. *American Psychologist, 41,* 159–164.

Howell, D. C. (2016). *Fundamental statistics for the behavioral sciences.* Boston, MA: Nelson Education.

Howie, L. D., Pastor, P. N., & Lukacs, S. L. (2014). Use of medication prescribed for emotional or behavioral difficulties among children aged 6–17 years in the United States. *NCHS Data Brief, 148,* 1–8.

Howlin, P. (2015). Outcomes in adults with autism spectrum disorder. In F. R. Volkmar (Ed.), *Handbook of autism and pervasive developmental disorders* (pp. 97–115). New York, NY: Wiley.

Hoza, B., Mrug, S., Gerdes, A. C., Hinshaw, S. P., Bukowski, W. M., Gold, J. A., . . . Arnold, L. E. (2005). What aspects of peer relationships are impaired in children with attention-deficit/hyperactivity disorder? *Journal of Consulting and Clinical Psychology*, 73, 411–423.

Hughes, E. K., Goldschmidt, A. B., Labuschagne, Z., Loeb, K. L., Sawyer, S. M., & Grange, D. L. (2013). Eating disorders with and without comorbid depression and anxiety. *European Eating Disorders Review*, 21, 386–394.

Huguet, G., Benabou, M., & Bourgeron, T. (2016). The genetics of autism spectrum disorders. In P. Sassone-Corsi & Y. Christian (Eds.), *A time for metabolism and hormones* (pp. 101–129). New York, NY: Springer.

Humeniuk, R., Henry-Edwards, S., Ali, R., Poznyak, V., & Monteiro, M. G. (2010). *The Alcohol, Smoking and Substance Involvement Screening Test (ASSIST)*. Geneva, Switzerland: World Health Organization.

Humphreys, K. L., Eng, T., & Lee, S. S. (2013). Stimulant medication and substance use outcomes: A meta-analysis. *JAMA Psychiatry*, 70, 740–749.

Hurwitz, S., & Minshawi, N. F. (2012). Methods of defining and observing behaviors. In J. L. Matson (Ed.), *Functional assessment for challenging behavior* (pp. 91–103). New York, NY: Springer.

Hyman, S. E. (2011). Repairing a plane while it is flying: Reflections on Rutter (2011). *Journal of Child Psychology and Psychiatry*, 52, 661–662.

Hysing, M., Pallesen, S., Stormark, K. M., Lundervold, A. J., & Sivertsen, B. (2013). Sleep patterns and insomnia among adolescents: A population-based study. *Journal of Sleep Research*, 22, 549–556.

Iarocci, G., & Petrill, S. A. (2012). Behavioral genetics, genomics, intelligence, and mental retardation. In J. A. Burack, R. M. Hodapp, G. Iarocci, & E. Zigler (Eds.), *The Oxford handbook of intellectual disability and development* (pp. 13–29). New York, NY: Oxford University Press.

Ibanez, L. V., Stone, W. L., & Coorod, E. E. (2015). Screening for autism in young children. In F. R. Volkmar (Ed.), *Handbook of autism and pervasive developmental disorders* (pp. 585–607). New York, NY: Wiley.

Ingersoll, B. (2010a). Pilot randomized controlled trial of reciprocal imitation training or teaching elicited and spontaneous imitation to children with autism. *Journal of Autism and Developmental Disorders*, 40, 1154–1160.

Ingersoll, B. (2010b). Teaching social communication: A comparison of naturalistic behavioral and developmental social pragmatic approaches for children with autism spectrum disorders. *Journal of Positive Behavioral Interventions*, 12, 33–43.

Ingersoll, B. (2012). Effect of a focused imitation intervention on social functioning in children with autism. *Journal of Autism and Developmental Disorders*, 42, 1768–1773.

Ingersoll, B., & Dvortcsak, A. (2010). *Teaching social communication to children with autism*. New York, NY: Guilford Press.

Insel, T. R., & Lieberman, J. A. (2013). *DSM-5 and RDoC shared interests*. Washington, DC: NIMH.

Isaacs, L., Webb, A., Jerome, S., & Fabiano, G. A. (2015). Inclusion and engagement of fathers in behavioral parent training for ADHD: An update and recommendations. *The ADHD Report*, 23, 1–7.

Ivanenko, A., & Johnson, K.P. (2015). Sleep disorders. In M.K. Dulcan (Ed.), *Dulcan's textbook of child and adolescent psychiatry* (pp. 495–519). Washington, DC: American Psychiatric Press.

Ivanenko, A., & Johnson, K. P. (2015). Sleep disorders. In M. K. Dulcan (Ed.), *Dulcan's textbook of child and adolescent psychiatry*. Washington, DC: American Psychiatric Publishing.

Iwata, B. A., Dorsey, M. F., Slifer, K. J., Bauman, K. E., & Richman, G. S. (1994). Toward a functional analysis of self-injury. *Journal of Applied Behavior Analysis*, 27, 197–209.

Jackson, E. S., Yaruss, J. S., Quesal, R. W., Terranova, V., & Whalen, D. H. (2015). Responses of adults who stutter to the anticipation of stuttering. *Journal of Fluency Disorders*, 45, 38-51.

Jacob, S., & Kleinheksel, M.M. (2012). School psychology. In S. J. Knapp (Ed.), *APA handbook of ethics in psychotherapy* (Vol. 2, pp. 125–148). Washington, DC: American Psychological Association.

Jacobson, J. W., & Mulick, J. A. (1996). *Manual of diagnosis and professional practice in mental retardation*. Washington, DC: American Psychological Association.

Jacobus, J., & Tapert, S. F. (2013). Neurotoxic effects of alcohol in adolescence. *Annual Review of Clinical Psychology*, 9, 703–721.

Jaffee, S. R. (2016). Quantitative and molecular behavioral genetic studies of gene-environment correlation. In D. Cicchetti (Ed.), *Developmental psychopathology* (Vol. 2, pp. 242–286). New York, NY: Wiley.

Jairam, R., Prabhuswamy, M., & Dullur, P. (2012). Do we really know how to treat a child with bipolar disorder or one with severe mood dysregulation? *Depression Research and Treatment, 2012*, 1–9.

Jaycox, L. H., Cohen, J. A., Mannarino, A. P., Walker, D. W., Langley, A. K., Gegenheimer, K. L., . . . Schonlau, M. (2010). Children's mental health care following Hurricane Katrina. *Journal of Traumatic Stress*, 23, 223–231.

Jenkins, J. M., Farkas, G., Duncan, G. J., Burchinal, M., & Vandell, D. L. (2016). Head Start at ages 3 and 4 versus head start followed by state pre-K which is more effective? *Educational Evaluation and Policy Analysis*, 38, 88–112.

Jennings, W. G., & Fox, B. H. (2015). Neighborhood risk and development of antisocial behavior. In T. P. Beauchaine & S. P. Hinshaw (Eds.), *The Oxford handbook of externalizing spectrum disorders* (pp. 313–322). Oxford, England: Oxford University Press.

Jensen, P. S., Hoagwood, K., & Zitner, L. (2006). What's in a name? Problems versus prospects in current diagnostic approaches. In D. Cicchetti & D. J. Cohen (Eds.), *Developmental psychopathology* (Vol. 1, pp. 24–40). New York, NY: Wiley.

Jimerson, S. R., Burns, M. K., & VanDerHeyden, A. M. (2016). From response to intervention to multi-tiered systems of support: Advances in the science and practice of assessment and intervention. In S. R. Jimerson (Ed.), *Handbook of response to intervention* (pp. 1–6). New York, NY: Springer.

Jocson, R. M., & McLoyd, V. C. (2015). Neighborhood and housing disorder, parenting, and youth adjustment in low-income urban families. *American Journal of Community Psychology*, 55, 304–313.

Johnson, E. S., Humphrey, M., Mellard, D. F., Woods, K., & Swanson, H. L. (2010). Cognitive processing deficits and students with specific learning disabilities: A selective meta-analysis of the literature. *Learning Disability Quarterly*, 33, 3–18.

Johnson, J. G., Cohen, P., Kotler, L., Kasen, S., & Brook, J. S. (2002). Psychiatric disorders associated with risk for the development of eating disorders during adolescence and early adulthood. *Journal of Consulting and Clinical Psychology*, 70, 1119–1128.

Johnson, M. H., & de Haan, M. (2006). Typical and atypical human functional brain development. In D. Cicchetti & D. J. Cohen (Eds.), *Developmental psychopathology* (Vol. 2, pp. 197–215). Hoboken, NJ: Wiley.

Johnson, S. L., Sandrow, D., Meyer, B., Winters, R., Miller, I., Solomon, D., & Keitner, G. (2000). Increases in manic symptoms after life events involving goal attainment. *Journal of Abnormal Psychology*, 109, 721–727.

Johnston, C. (2005). The importance of parental attributions in families of children with attention-deficit/hyperactivity and disruptive behavior disorders. *Clinical Child and Family Psychology Review*, 8, 167–182.

Johnston, L. D., O'Malley, P. M., Miech, R. A., Bachman, J. G., & Schulenberg, J. E. (2016a). *Demographic subgroup trends among adolescents in the use of various illicit drugs.* Ann Arbor: University of Michigan.

Johnston, L. D., O'Malley, P. M., Miech, R. A., Bachman, J. G., & Schulenberg, J. E. (2016b). *Monitoring the future II: Overview, key findings on adolescent drug use.* Ann Arbor: University of Michigan.

Joiner, T. E., Brown, J. S., & Wingate, L. R. (2005). The psychology and neurobiology of suicidal behavior. *Annual Review of Psychology, 56,* 287–314.

Jonas, B. S., Gu, Q., & Albertorio-Diaz, J. R. (2013). Psychotropic medication use among adolescents: United States. *NCHS Data Brief, 135,* 1–8.

Jonas, R., Nguyen, S., Hu, B., Asarnow, R. F., LoPresti, C., Curtiss, S., . . . Mathern, G. W. (2004). Cerebral hemispherectomy. *Neurology, 62,* 1712–1721.

Jones, M., Onslow, M., Harrison, E., & Packman, A. (2000). Treating stuttering in young children. *Journal of Speech, Language, and Hearing Research, 43,* 1440–1450.

Jones, M. C. (1924). A laboratory study of fear: The case of Peter. *Pedagogical Seminary, 31,* 308–315.

Jones, W., Carr, K., & Klin, A. (2008). Absence of preferential looking to the eyes of approaching adults predicts level of social disability in 2-year-old toddlers with autism spectrum disorder. *Archives of General Psychiatry, 65,* 946–954.

Joseph, L., Soorya, L., & Thurm, A. (2015). *Autism spectrum disorders.* Boston, MA: Hogrefe.

Joshi, P. T., Cullins, L. M., Southammakosane, C. A. (2015). Child abuse and neglect. In M. K. Dulcan (Ed.), *Dulcan's textbook of child and adolescent psychiatry* (pp. 539–558). Washington, DC: American Psychiatric Publishing.

Jud, A., Fegert, J. M., & Finkelhor, D. (2016). On the incidence and prevalence of child maltreatment. *Child and Adolescent Psychiatry and Mental Health, 10,* 1–12.

Kaderavek, J. N. (2014). *Language disorders in children.* Boston, MA: Pearson.

Kagan, J. (2014). Temperamental contributions to the development of psychological profiles. In S. G. Hofman & P. M. DiBartolo (Eds.), *Social anxiety: Clinical, developmental, and social perspectives.* New York, NY: Academic Press.

Kahn, R. E., Frick, P. J., Youngstrom, E., Findling, R. L., & Youngstrom, J. K. (2012). The effects of including a callous–unemotional specifier for the diagnosis of conduct disorder. *Journal of Child Psychology and Psychiatry, 53,* 271–282.

Kahng, S., Iwata, B. A., & Lewin, A. B. (2002). Behavioral treatment of self-injury. *American Journal on Mental Retardation, 107,* 212–221.

Kaminer, Y., & Bukstein, O. G. (2005). Treating adolescent substance abuse. In R. J. Frances, S. I. Miller, & A. H. Mack (Eds.), *Clinical textbook of addictive disorders* (pp. 559–587). New York, NY: Guilford Press.

Kamphaus, R. W., & Frick, P. J. (2002). *Clinical assessment of child and adolescent personality and behavior.* Boston, MA: Allyn & Bacon.

Kamphaus, R. W., Reynolds, C. R., & Dever, B. V. (2014). Behavioral and mental health screening. In R. J. Kettler (Ed.), *Universal screening in educational settings* (pp. 249–273). Washington, DC: American Psychological Association.

Kane, E. J., Braunstein, K., Ollendick, T. H., & Muris, P. (2015). Relations of anxiety sensitivity, control beliefs, and maternal overcontrol to fears in clinic-referred children with specific phobia. *Journal of Child and Family Studies, 24,* 2127–2134.

Kanne, S., & Mazurek, M. (2011). Aggression in children and adolescents with ASD. *Journal of Autism and Developmental Disorders, 41,* 926–937.

Kanner, L. (1943). Autistic disturbances of affective contact. *Nervous Child, 2,* 217–250.

Karch, D. L., Logan, J., McDaniel, D. D., Floyd, C. F., & Vagi, K. J. (2013). Precipitating circumstances of suicide among youth aged 10–17 years by sex. *Journal of Adolescent Health, 53,* S51–S53.

Karila, L., Roux, P., Rolland, B., Benyamina, A., Reynaud, M., Aubin, H. J., & Lançon, C. (2014). Acute and long-term effects of cannabis use: A review. *Current Pharmaceutical Design, 20,* 4112–4118.

Karmiloff-Smith, A., Doherty, B., Cornish, K., & Scerif, G. (2016). Fragile X syndrome as a multilevel model for understanding behaviorally defined disorders. In D. Cicchetti (Ed.), *Developmental psychopathology* (Vol. 3, pp. 68–80). New York, NY: Wiley.

Kasari, C., Freeman, S., & Paparella, T. (2006). Joint attention and symbolic play in young children with autism. *Journal of Child Psychology and Psychiatry, 47,* 611–620.

Kasari, C., Gulsrud, A. C., Freeman, S., Paparella, T., & Hellemann, G. (2012). Longitudinal follow-up of children with autism receiving targeted interventions on joint attention and play. *Journal of the American Academy of Child and Adolescent Psychiatry, 51,* 487–495.

Kasari, C., Gulsrud, A., Paparella, T., Hellemann, G., & Berry, K. (2015). Randomized comparative efficacy study of parent-mediated interventions for toddlers with autism. *Journal of Consulting and Clinical Psychology, 83,* 554–563.

Kasari, C., Gulsrud, A. C., Wong, C., Kwon, S., & Locke, J. (2010). Randomized controlled caregiver mediated joint engagement intervention for toddlers with autism. *Journal of Autism and Developmental Disorders, 40,* 1045–1056.

Kashdan, T. B., Adams, L. M., Kleiman, E. M., Pelham, W. E., & Lang, A. R. (2013). Stress-induced drinking in parents of boys with attention-deficit-hyperactivity disorder. *Journal of Abnormal Child Psychology, 41,* 919–927.

Kaufman, A. S., & Raiford, S. E. (2016). *Intelligent testing with the WISC-V.* New York, NY: Wiley.

Kawabata, Y., Tseng, W. L., & Crick, N. R. (2014). Adaptive, maladaptive, mediational, and bidirectional processes of relational and physical aggression, relational and physical victimization, and peer liking. *Aggressive Behavior, 40,* 273–287.

Kaye, W. H., Bastiani, A. M., & Moss, H. (1995). Cognitive style of patients with anorexia nervosa and bulimia nervosa. *International Journal of Eating Disorders, 18,* 287–290.

Kazak, A. E., & Noll, R. B. (2015). The integration of psychology in pediatric oncology research and practice. *American Psychologist, 70,* 146.

Kazak, A. E., & Noll, R. B. (2015). The integration of psychology in pediatric oncology research and practice: Collaboration to improve care and outcomes for children and families. *American Psychologist, 70*(2), 146–158.

Kazak, A. E., Sood, E., & Roberts, M. C. (2016). Pediatric psychology. In J. C. Norcross (Ed.), *APA handbook of clinical psychology* (pp. 81–106). Washington, DC: American Psychological Association.

Kazak, A. E., Sood, E., & Roberts, M. C. (2016). Pediatric psychology. In J.C. Norcross (Ed.); APA handbook of clinical psychology (pp. 81–106). Washington, DC: American Psychological Association.

Kazdin, A. E. (2005). Child, parent, and family-based treatment of aggressive and antisocial child behavior. In E. D. Hibbs & P. S. Jensen (Eds.), *Psychosocial treatments for child and adolescent disorders* (pp. 445–476). Washington, DC: American Psychological Association.

Kazdin, A. E. (2010). Problem-solving skills training and parent management training for oppositional defiant disorder and conduct disorder. In J. R. Weisz & A. E. Kazdin (Eds.), *Evidence-based psychotherapies for children and adolescents* (pp. 211–226). New York, NY: Guilford.

Kazdin, A. E. (2017). *Research design in clinical psychology.* Boston, MA: Pearson.

Kazdin, A. E., Bass, D., Ayers, W. A., & Rodgers, A. (1990). Empirical and clinical focus of child and adolescent psychotherapy research. *Journal of Consulting and Clinical Psychology, 58,* 729–740.

Keehn, R. H. M., Lincoln, A. J., Brown, M. Z., & Chavira, D. A. (2013). The coping cat program for children with anxiety and autism spectrum disorder. *Journal of Autism and Developmental Disorders, 43*, 57–67.

Keel, P. K., Klump, K. L., Miller, K. B., McGue, M., & Iacono, W. G. (2005). Shared transmission of eating disorders and anxiety disorders. *International Journal of Eating Disorders, 38*, 99–105.

Keenan, K., & Hipwell, A. E. (2005). Preadolescent clues to understanding depression in girls. *Clinical Child and Family Psychology Review, 8*, 89–105.

Keenan, K., & Shaw, D. S. (2003). Starting at the beginning: Exploring the etiology of antisocial behavior in the first years of life. In B. B. Lahey, T. E. Moffitt, & A. Caspi (Eds.), *Causes of conduct disorder and juvenile delinquency* (pp. 153–181). New York, NY: Guilford Press.

Keenan, K., & Wakschlag, S. (2004). Are oppositional defiant and conduct disorder symptoms normative behaviors in preschoolers? *American Journal of Psychiatry, 161*, 356–358.

Keery, H., Boutelle, K., van den Berg, P., & Thompson, J. K. (2005). The impact of appearance-related teasing by family members. *Journal of Adolescent Health, 37*, 120–127.

Keery, H., van den Berg, P., & Thompson, J. K. (2004). An evaluation of the tripartite influence model of body dissatisfaction and eating disturbance with adolescent girls. *Body Image, 1*, 237–251.

Kelly, J. F., Yeterian, J. D., Cristello, J. V., Kaminer, Y., Kahler, C. W., & Timko, C. (2016). Developing and testing twelve-step facilitation for adolescents with substance use disorder. *Substance Abuse: Research and Treatment, 10*, 55–64.

Kendall, P. C. (1992). *Coping cat workbook*. Ardmore, PA: Workbook Publishing.

Kendall, P. C. (2012). Anxiety disorders in youth. In P. C. Kendall (Ed.), *Child and adolescent therapy* (pp. 143–189). New York, NY: Guilford Press.

Kendall, P. C., & Comer, J. S. (2014). Research methods in clinical psychology. In D. H. Barlow (Ed.), *The Oxford handbook of clinical psychology* (pp. 52–75). Oxford, England: Oxford University Press.

Kendall, P. C., Crawley, S., Benjamin, C., & Mauro, C. (2012). *Brief coping cat: The 8-session therapist manual*. Ardmore, PA: Workbook Publishing.

Kendall, P. C., Krain, A., & Treadwell, K. (1999). Generalized anxiety disorders. In R. T. Ammerman, M. Hersen, & C. G. Last (Eds.), *Handbook of prescriptive treatments for children and adolescents* (pp. 155–171). Needham Heights, MA: Allyn & Bacon.

Kendall-Tackett, K. A., Williams, L. M., & Finkelhor, D. (1993). Impact of sexual abuse on children. *Psychological Bulletin, 113*, 164–180.

Kendler, K. S., Chen, X., Dick, D., Maes, H., Gillespie, N., Neale, M. C., & Riley, B. (2012). Recent advances in the genetic epidemiology and molecular genetics of substance use disorders. *Nature Neuroscience, 15*, 181–189.

Kennard, B. D., Clarke, G. N., Weersing, V. R., Asarnow, J. R., Shamseddeen, W., Porta, G., Brent, D. A. (2009). Effective components of TORDIA cognitive-behavioral therapy for adolescent depression. *Journal of Consulting and Clinical Psychology, 77*, 1033–1041.

Kerig, P. K. (2016). Family systems from a developmental psychopathology perspective. In D. Cicchetti (Ed.), *Developmental psychopathology* (Vol. 1, pp. 580–630). New York, NY: Wiley.

Kerr, A., & Archer, H. (2011). Rett disorder. In P. A. Howlin (Ed.), *The SAGE handbook of developmental disorders* (pp. 147–169). Thousand Oaks, CA: Sage.

Kerstjens, J. M., DeWinter, A. F., Bocca-Tjeertes, I., Bos, A. F., & Reijnveld, S. A. (2013). Risk of developmental delay increases exponentially as gestational age of preterm infants decreases. *Developmental Medicine and Child Neurology, 54*, 1096–2101.

Kessler, R. C., Avenevoli, S., Costello, E. J., Georgiades, K., Green, J. G., Gruber, M. J., . . . Merikangas, K. R. (2012a). Prevalence, persistence, and sociodemographic correlates of DSM-IV disorders in the National Comorbidity Survey Replication–Adolescent Supplement. *Archives of General Psychiatry, 69*, 372–380.

Kessler, R. C., Avenevoli, S., Costello, J., Green, J. G., Gruber, M. J., McLaughlin, K. A., . . . Merikangas, K. R. (2012b). Severity of 12-month DSM-IV disorders in the national comorbidity survey replication adolescent supplement. *Archives of General Psychiatry, 69*, 381–389.

Kessler, R. C., Berglund, P. A., Chiu, W. T., Deitz, A. C., Hudson, J. I., Shahly, V., . . . Xavier, M. (2013). The prevalence and correlates of binge eating disorder in the World Health Organization World Mental Health Surveys. *Biological Psychiatry, 73*, 904–914.

Kessler, R. C., Berglund, P., Dernier, O., Jin, R., & Walters, E. (2005). Lifetime prevalence and age-of-onset distributions of *DSM-IV* disorders in the National Co-morbidity Survey replication. *Archives of General Psychiatry, 62*, 593–602.

Key, A. P. F., & Thornton-Wells, T. A. (2012). Brain-based methods in the study of developmental disabilities. In J. A. Burack, R. M. Hodapp, G. Iarocci, & E. Zigler (Eds.), *The Oxford handbook of intellectual disability and development* (pp. 149–166). New York, NY: Oxford University Press.

Khamis, V. (2015). Coping with war trauma and psychological distress among school-age Palestinian children. *The American Journal of Orthopsychiatry, 85*, 72–79.

Kichler, J. C., Harris, M. A., & Weissberg-Benchell, J. (2014). Contemporary Roles of the Pediatric Psychologist in Diabetes Care. *Current diabetes reviews, 11*(4), 210–221.

Kichler, J. C., Harris, M. A., & Weissberg-Benchell, J. (2015). Contemporary roles of the pediatric psychologist in diabetes care. *Current Diabetes Reviews, 11*, 210–221.

Kim, S. H., Paul, R., Tager-Flusberg, H., & Lord, C. (2015). Language and communication in autism. In F. R. Volkmar (Ed.), *Handbook of autism and pervasive developmental disorders* (pp. 230–261). New York, NY: Wiley.

Kimonis, E. R., Fanti, K. A., Frick, P. J., Moffitt, T. E., Essau, C., Bijttebier, P., & Marsee, M. A. (2015). Using self-reported callous-unemotional traits to cross-nationally assess the DSM-5 'With Limited Prosocial Emotions' specifier. *Journal of Child Psychology and Psychiatry, 56*, 1249–1261.

King, C. A., Foster, C. E., & Rogalski, K. M. (2013). *Teen suicide risk: A practitioner guide to screening, assessment, and management*. New York, NY: Guilford Press.

Kingston, M., Huber, A., Onslow, M., Jones, M., & Packman, A. (2003). Predicting treatment time with the Lidcombe program. *International Journal of Language and Communication Disorders, 38*, 165–177.

Kirby, R. S. (2015). Epidemiological features of ASD. In S. H. Fatemi (Ed.), *The molecular basis of autism* (pp. 23–31). New York, NY: Springer.

Kirk, S. A. (1962). *Educating exceptional children*. Boston, MA: Houghton Mifflin.

Klein, E. R., Armstrong, S. L., Skira, K., & Gordon, J. (2016). Social Communication Anxiety Treatment (S-CAT) for children and families with selective mutism. *Clinical Child Psychology and Psychiatry*. Advance online publication. doi:10.1177/1359104516633497

Klerman, G. L., & Weissman, M. M. (1993). Interpersonal psychotherapy for depression: Background and concepts. In G. L. Klerman & M. M. Weissman (Eds.), *New applications of interpersonal psychotherapy* (pp. 3–26). Washington, DC: American Psychiatric Press.

Klika, J. B., Herrenkohl, T. I., & Lee, J. O. (2013). School factors as moderators of the relationship between physical child abuse and pathways of antisocial behavior. *Journal of Interpersonal Violence, 28*, 852–867.

Klimes-Dougan, B., Kennedy, K. P., & Cullen, K. R. (2016). Bipolar disorder from a developmental psychopathology perspective. In D. Cicchetti (Ed.), *Developmental psychopathology* (Vol. 3, pp. 898–949). New York, NY: Wiley.

Klimes-Dougan, B., Klingbeil, D. A., & Meller, S. J. (2013). The impact of universal suicide-prevention programs on the help-seeking attitudes and behaviors of youths. *Crisis, 34*, 82–97.

Klimes-Dougan, B., & Kopp, C. B. (1999). Children's conflict tactics with mothers: A longitudinal investigation of the toddler and preschool years. *Merrill-Palmer Quarterly, 45*, 226–241.

Klin, A. (2000). Attributing social meaning to ambiguous visual stimuli in higher functioning autism and Asperger syndrome: The social attribution task. *Journal of Child Psychology, Psychiatry and Allied Disciplines, 33*, 763–769.

Klin, A., Jones, W., Schultz, R. T., & Volkmar, F. R. (2003). The enactive mind: From actions to cognition. *Philosophical Transactions of the Royal Society, Biological Sciences, 358*, 345–360.

Kline, E., Thompson, E.C., Wilson, C. S., Ereshefsky, S., Reeves, G., & Schiffman, J. (2015). Schizophrenia. In T. P. Gullotta, R. W. Plant, & M. Evans (Eds.), *Handbook of adolescent behavioral problems* (pp. 361–380). New York, NY: Springer.

Klinger, L. G., Dawson, G., Barnes, K., & Crisler, M. (2014). Autism spectrum disorder. In E. J. Mash & R. A. Barkley (Eds.), *Child psychopathology* (pp. 531–572). New York, NY: Guilford Press.

Kluger, J., & Song, S. (2002). Young and bipolar. *Time, 160*, 38.

Knapp, S. J., Gottlieb, M. C., & Handelsman, M. M. (2015). *Ethical dilemmas in psychotherapy*. Washington, DC: American Psychological Association.

Knight, J. R., Shrier, L. A., Bravender, T. D., Farrell, M., Vander Bilt, J., & Shaffer, H. J. (1999). A new brief screen for adolescent substance abuse. *Archives of Pediatrics and Adolescent Medicine, 153*, 591.

Kobrynski, L. J., & Sullivan, K. E. (2007). Velocardiofacial syndrome, DiGeorge syndrome: The chromosome 22q11. 2 deletion syndromes. *The Lancet, 370*, 1443–1452.

Kochanska, G., & Kim, S. (2013). Difficult temperament moderates links between maternal responsiveness and children's compliance and behavior problems in low-income families. *Journal of Child Psychology and Psychiatry, 54*, 323–332.

Kodish, I., & McClellan, J. M. (2015). Early-onset schizophrenia. In D. Reitman (Ed.), *Handbook of psychological assessment, case conceptualization, and treatment* (pp. 405–443). New York, NY: Wiley.

Koegel, L. K., Koegel, R. L., & Brookman, L. I. (2005). Child-initiated interactions that are pivotal in intervention for children with autism. In E. D. Hibbs & P. S. Jensen (Eds.), *Psychosocial treatments for child and adolescent disorders* (pp. 633–657). Washington, DC: American Psychological Association.

Koehne, S., Hatri, A., Cacioppo, J. T., & Dziobek, I. (2016). Perceived interpersonal synchrony increases empathy: Insights from autism spectrum disorder. *Cognition, 146*, 8–15.

Koenig, K., & Tsatsanis, K. D. (2005). Pervasive developmental disorders in girls. In D. J. Bell, S. L. Foster, & E. J. Mash (Eds.), *Handbook of behavioral and emotional problems in girls* (pp. 211–237). New York, NY: Kluwer.

Koenig, L. J., & Clark, J. (2004). Sexual abuse of girls and HIV infection among women: Are they related? In L. J. Koenig, L. S. Doll, A. O'Leary, & W. Pequegnat (Eds.), *From child sexual abuse to adult sexual risk* (pp. 69–92). Washington, DC: American Psychological Association.

Kohlhoff, J., Barnett, B., & Eapen, V. (2015). Adult separation anxiety and unsettled infant behavior: Associations with adverse parenting during childhood and insecure adult attachment. *Comprehensive Psychiatry, 61*, 1–9.

Koob, G. F., & LeMoal, M. (2006). *Neurobiology of addiction*. Amsterdam, Netherlands: Elsevier.

Koocher, G. P. (2008). Ethical challenges in mental health services to children and families. *Journal of Clinical Psychology, 64*, 601–612.

Koocher, G. P., & Daniel, J. H. (2012). Treating children and adolescents. In S. J. Knapp (Ed.), *APA handbook of ethics in psychotherapy* (Vol. 2, pp. 3–14). Washington, DC: American Psychological Association.

Koocher, G. P., & LaGreca, A. M. (2010). *The parents' guide to psychological first aid*. Oxford, England: Oxford University Press.

Kopta, S. M. (2003). The dose-effect relationship in psychotherapy: A defining achievement for Dr. Kenneth Howard. *Journal of Clinical Psychology, 59*, 727–733.

Kornilov, S. A., & Grigorenko, E. L. (2016). Molecular genetics methods for developmental scientists. In D. Cicchetti (Ed.), *Developmental psychopathology* (Vol 2., pp. 378–415). New York, NY: Wiley.

Kornilov, S. A., Rakhlin, N., Koposov, R., Lee, M., Yrigollen, C., Caglayan, A. O., . . . Grigorenko, E. L. (2016). Genome-wide association and exome sequencing study of language disorder in an isolated population. *Pediatrics, 137*, 1–16.

Koskentausta, T., Iivanainen, M., & Almqvist, F. (2007). Risk factors for psychiatric disturbance in children with intellectual disability. *Journal of Intellectual Disability Research, 51*, 43–53.

Kossowsky, J., Pfaltz, M. C., Schneider, S., Taeymans, J., Locher, C., & Gaab, J. (2013). The separation anxiety hypothesis of panic disorder revisited: A meta-analysis. *American Journal of Psychiatry, 170*, 768–781.

Kosten, T. R., George, T. P., & Kleber, H. D. (2005). The neurobiology of substance dependence. In R. J. Frances, S. I. Miller, & A. H. Mack (Eds.), *Clinical textbook of addictive disorders* (pp. 3–15). New York, NY: Guilford Press.

Kotagal, S. (2009). Parasomnias in childhood. *Sleep Medicine Reviews, 13*, 157–168.

Kovacs, M. (2011). *Children's Depression Inventory-2 manual*. North Tonawanda, NY: MHS.

Kovelman, I., Norton, E. S., Christodoulou, J. A., Gaab, N., Lieberman, D. A., Triantafyllou, C., . . . Gabrieli, J. D. (2012). Brain basis of phonological awareness for spoken language in children and its disruption in dyslexia. *Cerebral Cortex, 22*, 754–764.

Kowatch, R. A., Fristad, M., Birmaher, B., Wagner, K. D., Findling, R. L., & Hellander, M. (2005). Treatment guidelines for children and adolescents with bipolar disorder. *Journal of the American Academy of Child & Adolescent Psychiatry, 44*, 213–235.

Koyama, M. S., Di Martino, A., Castellanos, F. X., Ho, E. J., Marcelle, E., Leventhal, B., & Milham, M. P. (2016). Imaging the "at-risk" brain. *Journal of the International Neuropsychological Society, 22*, 164–179.

Kratochwill, T. R. (2014). *Single subject research*. New York, NY: Academic Press.

Krieger, F. V., Pheula, G. F., Coelho, R., Zeni, T., Tramontina, S., Zeni, C. P., & Rohde, L. A. (2011). An open-label trial of risperidone in children and adolescents with severe mood dysregulation. *Journal of Child and Adolescent Psychopharmacology, 21*, 237–243.

Kruczek, T., & Vitanza, S. (2015). Posttraumatic stress disorder. In T. P. Gullotta, R. W. Plant, & M. Evans (Eds.), *Handbook of adolescent behavioral problems* (pp. 131–150). New York, NY: Springer.

Krueger, R. F., & Bezdjian, S. (2009). Enhancing research and treatment of mental disorders with dimensional concepts. *World Psychiatry, 8*, 5–6.

Krull, J. L., Cheong, J., Fritz, M. S., & MacKinnin, D. P. (2016). Moderation and medication in interindividual longitudinal analysis. In D. Cicchetti (Ed.), *Developmental psychopathology* (Vol. 1, pp. 922–985). New York, NY: Wiley.

Kullgren, K. A., Tsang, K. K., Ernst, M. M., Carter, B. D., Scott, E. L., & Sullivan, S. K. (2015). Inpatient pediatric psychology consultation-liaison practice survey. *Clinical Practice in Pediatric Psychology, 3*, 37–47.

Kumin, L. (1994). Intelligibility of speech in children with Down syndrome in natural settings. *Perceptual and Motor Skills, 78*, 307–313.

Kuniyoshi, J., & McClellan, J. M. (2014). Early-onset schizophrenia. In E. J. Mash & R. A. Barkley (Eds.), *Child psychopathology* (pp. 573–592). New York, NY: Routledge.

Kuppens, S., Laurent, L., Heyvaert, M., & Onghena, P. (2013). Associations between parental psychological control and relational aggression in children and adolescents. *Developmental Psychology, 49,* 1697.

Lacourse, E., Nagin, D. S., Vitaro, F., Cote, S., Arseneault, L., & Tremblay, R. E. (2006). Prediction of early-onset deviant peer group affiliation. *Archives of General Psychiatry, 63,* 562–568.

LaGreca, A. M., & Harrison, M. (2005). Adolescent peer relations, friendships, and romantic relationships. *Journal of Clinical Child and Adolescent Psychology, 34,* 49–61.

Lahey, B. B., McBurnett, K., & Loeber, R. (2000). Are attention-deficit/hyperactivity disorder and oppositional defiant disorder developmental precursors to conduct disorder? In A. J. Sameroff, M. Lewis, & S. M. Miller (Eds.), *Handbook of developmental psychopathology* (pp. 431–446). New York, NY: Kluwer Academic/Plenum.

Lam, Y. G. (2015). Symbolic play in children with autism. In V. B. Patel (Ed.), *Comprehensive guide to autism* (pp. 551–567). New York, NY: Springer.

Lambert, M. J. (2013). Outcome in psychotherapy: The past and important advances. *Psychotherapy, 50,* 42–51.

Lambert, M. J., & Ogles, B. M. (2004). The efficacy and effectiveness of psychotherapy. In M. J. Lambert (Ed.), *Bergin and Garfield's handbook of psychotherapy and behavior change* (pp. 139–193). New York, NY: Wiley.

Lambert, N. M., & Hartsough, C. S. (1998). Prospective study of tobacco smoking and substance dependencies among samples of ADHD and non-ADHD participants. *Journal of Learning Disabilities, 31*(6), 533–544.

Lancioni, G. E., Singh, N. N., O'Reilly, M. F., Sigafoos, J., & Didden, R. (2012). Function of challenging behaviors. In J. L. Matson (Ed.), *Functional assessment for challenging behavior* (pp. 45–64). New York, NY: Springer.

Landau, B. (2012). The organization and development of spatial representation: Insights from Williams Syndrome. In J. A. Burack, R. M. Hodapp, G. Iarocci, & E. Zigler (Eds.), *The Oxford handbook of intellectual disability and development* (pp. 61–88). New York, NY: Oxford University Press.

Landrum, R. E., & Davis, S. F. (2014). *The psychology major.* New York, NY: Pearson.

Lane, D. M., & Sándor, A. (2016). *Methodological issues and strategies in clinical research.* Washington, DC: American Psychological Association.

Langberg, J. M., Becker, S. P., & Dvorsky, M. R. (2014). The association between sluggish cognitive tempo and academic functioning in youth with attention-deficit/hyperactivity disorder (ADHD). *Journal of Abnormal Child Psychology, 42,* 91–103.

Langberg, J. M., Dvorsky, M. R., Molitor, S. J., Bourchtein, E., Eddy, L. D., Smith, Z., . . . Evans, S. W. (2016). Longitudinal evaluation of the importance of homework assignment completion for the academic performance of middle school students with ADHD. *Journal of School Psychology, 55,* 27–38.

Langberg, J. M., Evans, S. W., Schultz, B. K., Becker, S. P., Altaye, M., & Girio-Herrera, E. (2016). Trajectories and predictors of response to the challenging horizons program for adolescents with ADHD. *Behavior Therapy, 47,* 339–354.

Lanier, P., Kohl, P. L., Benz, J., Swinger, D., & Drake, B. (2014). Preventing maltreatment with a community-based implementation of parent–child interaction therapy. *Journal of Child and Family Studies, 23,* 449–460.

Latimer, W. W., Ernst, J., Hennessey, J., Stinchfield, R. D., & Winters, K. C. (2004). Relapse among adolescent drug abusers following treatment: The role of probable ADHD status. *Journal of Child and Adolescent Substance Abuse, 13,* 1–16.

Laugeson, E. A., Gantman, A., Kapp, S. K., Orenski, K., & Ellingsen, R. (2015). A randomized controlled trial to improve social skills in young adults with autism spectrum disorder. *Journal of Autism and Developmental Disorders, 45,* 3978–3989.

Laugeson, E. A., & Park, M. N. (2014). Using a CBT approach to teach social skills to adolescents with autism spectrum disorder and other social challenges. *Journal of Rational-Emotive and Cognitive-Behavior Therapy, 32,* 84–97.

Laumann, E. O., Paik, A., & Rosen, R. C. (1999). Sexual dysfunction in the United States. *Journal of the American Medical Association, 281,* 537–544.

Laurent, H. K., Leve, L. D., Neiderhiser, J. M., Natsuaki, M. N., Shaw, D. S., Harold, G. T., & Reiss, D. (2013). Effects of prenatal and postnatal parent depressive symptoms on adopted child HPA regulation. *Developmental Psychology, 49,* 876–886.

Lawrence, C. J., Lott, I., & Haier, R. J. (2005). Neurobiology of autism, mental retardation, and Down syndrome. In C. Stough (Ed.), *Neurobiology of exceptionality* (pp. 125–142). New York, NY: Kluwer.

Lawton, K., & Kasari, C. (2012). Teacher-implemented joint attention intervention. *Journal of Consulting and Clinical Psychology, 80,* 687–693.

Lay, B., Blanz, B., Hartmann, M., & Schmidt, M. (2000). The psychosocial outcome of adolescent schizophrenia: A 12-year follow-up. *Schizophrenia Bulletin, 26,* 801–816.

Layne, A. E., Bernat, D. H., Victor, A. M., & Bernstein, G. A. (2009). Generalized anxiety disorder in a nonclinical sample of children. *Journal of Anxiety Disorders, 23,* 283–289.

LeBeau, R. T., Glenn, D., Liao, B., Wittchen, H., Beesdo-Baum, K., Ollendick, T., & Craske, M. G. (2010). Specific phobia: A review of *DSM-IV* specific phobia and preliminary recommendations for *DSM-5. Depression and Anxiety, 27,* 148–167.

Leckman, J. F., & Bloch, M. H. (2010). Tic disorders. In M. Rutter (Ed.), *Rutter's child and adolescent psychiatry* (pp. 719–736). Malden, MA: Blackwell.

Lee, C. M., Horvath, C., & Hunsley, J. (2013). Does it work in the real world? The effectiveness of treatments for psychological problems in children and adolescents. *Professional Psychology: Research and Practice, 44,* 81–89.

Lee, E. S., & Findling, R. L. (2015). Principles of psychopharmacology. In M. K. Dulcan (Eds.), *Dulcan's textbook of child and adolescent psychiatry* (pp. 691–708). Washington, DC: American Psychiatric Publishing.

Lee, S. S., Humphreys, K. L., Flory, K., Liu, R., & Glass, K. (2011). Prospective association of childhood attention-deficit/hyperactivity disorder (ADHD) and substance use and abuse/dependence. *Clinical Psychology Review, 31,* 328–341.

Leenarts, L. E., Diehle, J., Doreleijers, T. A., Jansma, E. P., & Lindauer, R. J. (2013). Evidence-based treatments for children with trauma-related psychopathology as a result of childhood maltreatment. *European Child and Adolescent Psychiatry, 22,* 269–283.

Lees, D. G., & Fergusson, D. M. (2015). A study to assess the acceptability of adding Home Parent Support along with the Incredible Years parent programme. *Psychology, 44,* 40–44.

Legenbauer, T., Heiler, S., Holtmann, M., Fricke-Oerkermann, L., & Lehmkuhl, G. (2012). The affective storms of school children during night time. *Journal of Neural Transmission, 119,* 989–998.

Lehrner, A., Daskalakis, N., & Yehuda, R. (2016). Cortisol and the hypothalamic-pituitary-adrenal axis in PTSD. In J. D. Bremner (Ed.), *Posttraumatic stress disorder* (pp. 265–290). New York, NY: Wiley.

Leibenluft, E. (2011). Severe mood dysregulation, irritability, and the diagnostic boundaries of bipolar disorder. *American Journal of Psychiatry, 168,* 129–142.

Leibenluft, E., Charney, D. S., Towbin, K. E., Bhangoo, R. K., & Pine, D. S. (2003). Defining clinical phenotypes of juvenile mania. *American Journal of Psychiatry, 160,* 430–437.

Leibenluft, E., & Dickstein, D. P. (2008). Bipolar disorder in children and adolescents. In M. Rutter (Ed.), *Rutter's child and adolescent psychiatry* (pp. 613–627). Malden, MA: Blackwell.

Leibenluft, E., Uher, R., & Rutter, M. (2012). Disruptive mood dysregulation with dysphoria disorder. A proposal for ICD-11. *World Psychiatry, 11S*, 77–81.

Leijten, P., Raaijmakers, M. A., Orobio de Castro, B., van den Ban, E., & Matthys, W. (2015). Effectiveness of the incredible years parenting program for families with socioeconomically disadvantaged and ethnic minority backgrounds. *Journal of Clinical Child and Adolescent Psychology*, 1–15.

Lengua, L. J., Long, A. C., Smith, K. I., & Meltzoff, A. N. (2005). Pre-attack symptomatology and temperament as predictors of children's responses to the September 11 terrorist attacks. *Journal of Child Psychology and Psychiatry, 46*, 631–645.

Lenior, M., Dingemans, P., Linszen, D., de Haan, L., & Schene, A. (2001). Social functioning and the course of early-onset schizophrenia: Five-year follow-up of a psychosocial intervention. *British Journal of Psychiatry, 179*, 53–58.

Leu, R. M., & Rosen, C. L. (2008). Sleep and pediatrics. In H. R. Smith (Ed.), *Sleep medicine* (pp. 208–223). Cambridge, England: Cambridge University Press.

Leucht, S., Cipriani, A., Spineli, L., Mavridis, D., Örey, D., Richter, F., . . . Kissling, W. (2013). Comparative efficacy and tolerability of 15 antipsychotic drugs in schizophrenia: A multiple-treatments meta-analysis. *The Lancet, 382*, 951–962.

Leukefeld, C. G., Marks, K. R., Stoops, W. W., Reynolds, B., Lester, C., Sanchez, L., & Martin, C. A. (2015). Substance use and misuse. In T. P. Gullotta, R. W. Plant, & M. Evans (Eds.), *Handbook of adolescent behavioral problems* (pp. 495–513). New York, NY: Springer.

Levine, M. P., Piran, N., & Jasper, K. (2015). Eating disorders. In T. P. Gullotta, R. W. Plant, & M. Evans (Eds.), *Handbook of adolescent behavioral problems* (pp. 305–328). New York, NY: Springer.

Levinson, C. A., & Rodebaugh, T. L. (2012). Social anxiety and eating disorder comorbidity: The role of negative social evaluation fears. *Eating Behaviors, 13*, 27–35.

Levinson, C. A., Rodebaugh, T. L., White, E. K., Menatti, A. R., Weeks, J. W., Iacovino, J. M., & Warren, C. S. (2013). Social appearance anxiety, perfectionism, and fear of negative evaluation. *Appetite, 67*, 125–133.

Levy, S. E., Giarelli, E., Lee, L., Schieve, L. A., Kirby, R. S., Cunniff, C., . . . Rice, C. E. (2010). Autism spectrum disorder and co-occurring developmental, psychiatric, and medical conditions among children in multiple populations in the United States. *Journal of Developmental Behavioral Pediatrics, 31*, 267–275.

Lewandowski, L. J., & Lovett, B. J. (2014). Learning disabilities. In E. J. Mash & R. A. Barkley (Eds.), *Child psychopathology* (pp. 625–669). New York, NY: Wiley.

Lewinsohn, P. M. (1974). A behavioral approach to depression. In R. J. Friedman, & M. M. Katz (Eds.), *The psychology of depression* (pp. 157–184). Washington, DC: Winston-Wiley.

Lewinsohn, P. M., Allen, N. B., Gotlib, I. H., & Seeley, J. R. (1999). First onset versus recurrence of depression. *Journal of Abnormal Psychology, 108*, 483–498.

Lewinsohn, P. M., Clarke, G. N., Hops, H., & Andrews, J. (1990). Cognitive-behavioral group treatment of depression in adolescents. *Behavior Therapy, 21*, 385–401.

Lewinsohn, P. M., Roberts, R. E., Seeley, J. R., Rohde, P., Gotlib, I. H., & Hops, H. (1994). Adolescent psychopathology: II. Psychosocial risk factors for depression. *Journal of Abnormal Psychology, 103*, 302–315.

Lewinsohn, P. M., Youngren, M. A., & Grosscup, S. J. (1979). Reinforcement and depression. In R. A. Dupue (Ed.), *The psychobiology of depressive disorders* (pp. 291–316). New York, NY: Academic Press.

Lewis, G., Collishaw, S., Thapar, A., & Harold, G. T. (2014). Parent–child hostility and child and adolescent depression symptoms: The direction of effects, role of genetic factors and gender. *European Child and Adolescent Psychiatry, 23*, 317–327.

Lewis, S., Tarrier, N., Haddock, G., Bentall, R., Kinderman, P., Kingdon, D., . . . Dunn, G. (2002). Randomized controlled trial of cognitive-behavioral therapy in early schizophrenia. *British Journal of Psychiatry, 181*, s91–s97.

Li, D., Sulovari, A., Cheng, C., Zhao, H., Kranzler, H. R., & Gelernter, J. (2014). Association of gamma-aminobutyric acid A receptor α2 gene (GABRA2) with alcohol use disorder. *Neuropsychopharmacology, 39*, 907–918.

Libby, A. M., Orton, H. D., Novins, D. K., Spicer, P., Buchwald, D., Beals, J., . . . AI-SUPERPFP Team. (2004). Childhood physical and sexual abuse and subsequent alcohol and drug use disorders in two American-Indian tribes. *Journal of Studies on Alcohol, 65*, 74–83.

Libby, A. M., Orton, H. D., Stover, S. K., & Riggs, P. D. (2005). What came first, major depression or substance use disorder? *Addictive Behaviors, 30*, 1649–1662.

Liddle, E. B., Hollis, C., Batty, M. J., Groom, M. J., Totman, J. J., Liotti, M., . . . Liddle, P. F. (2011). Task-related default mode network modulation and inhibitory control in ADHD. *Journal of Child Psychology and Psychiatry, 52*, 761–771.

Liddle, H. A. (2004). Family-based therapies for adolescent alcohol and drug use. *Addiction, 99*, 76–92.

Liddle, H. A. (2016). Multidimensional family therapy. In T. J. Sexton & J. Lebow (Eds.), *Handbook of family therapy* (pp. 231–249). New York, NY: Routledge.

Liddle, H. A., & Rowe, C. L. (2006). *Adolescent substance abuse.* New York, NY: Cambridge University Press.

Lieberman, A. F. & Chu, A. T. (2016). Childhood exposure to interpersonal trauma. In D. Cicchetti (Ed.), *Developmental psychopathology, maladaptation and psychopathology* (pp. 425–456). New York, NY: Wiley.

Lilienfeld, S. O., & Treadway, M. T. (2016). Clashing diagnostic approaches: *DSM–ICD versus RDoC. Annual Review of Clinical Psychology.*

Lindheim, O., Bennett, C. B., Hipwell, A. E., & Pardini, D. A. (2015). Beyond symptom counts for diagnosing oppositional defiant disorder and conduct disorder? *Journal of Abnormal Child Psychology, 43*, 1379–1387.

Linscheid, T. R. (2006). Behavioral treatments for pediatric feeding disorders. *Behavior Modification, 30*, 6–23.

Linscheid, T. R., & Butz, C. (2003). Anorexia nervosa and bulimia nervosa. In M. C. Roberts (Ed.), *Handbook of pediatric psychology* (pp. 636–651). New York, NY: Guilford Press.

Lipton, J. S., & Spelke, S. (2003). Origins of number sense: Large-number discrimination in human infants. *Psychological Science, 14*, 396–401.

Litwack, S. D., Aikins, J. W., & Cillessen, A. H. (2012). The distinct roles of sociometric and perceived popularity in friendship implications for adolescent depressive affect and self-esteem. *The Journal of Early Adolescence, 32*, 226–251.

Liu, H. Y., Potter, M. P., Woodworth, K. Y., Yorks, D. M., Petty, C. R., Wozniak, J. R., . . . Biederman, J. (2011). Pharmacologic treatments for pediatric bipolar disorder. *Journal of the American Academy of Child and Adolescent Psychiatry, 50*, 749–762.

Lochman, J. E., Boxmeyer, C., Powell, N., & Dishion, T. J. (2016). Child-focused cognitive-behavioral interventions designed to reduce aggression. In T. J. Dishion & J. J. Snyder (Eds.), *Oxford handbook of coercive relationship dynamics* (pp. 273–285). Oxford, England: Oxford University Press.

Lock, J., & Le Grange, D. (2015). *Treatment manual for anorexia nervosa: A family-based approach.* New York, NY: Guilford Press.

Lofland, K. B. (2016). The use of technology in the treatment of autism. In T. A. Cardon (Ed.), *Technology and the treatment of children with autism spectrum disorders* (pp. 27–35). New York, NY: Springer.

Lopez-Tamayo, R., LaVome Robinson, W., Lambert, S. F., Jason, L. A., & Ialongo, N. S. (2016). Parental monitoring, association with externalized behavior, and academic outcomes in urban African-American youth. *American Journal of Community Psychology*.

Lord, C., Corsello, C., & Grzadzinski, R. (2015). Diagnostic instruments in autistic spectrum disorders. In F. R. Volkmar (Ed.), *Handbook of autism and pervasive developmental disorders* (pp. 609–660). New York, NY: Wiley.

Lord, C., Rutter, M. Dilavore, P., Risi, S., Gotham, K., & Bishop, S. (2015). *Autism Diagnostic Observation Schedule*. Torrance, CA: WPS.

Lovaas, O. I. (1987). Behavioral treatment and normal educational and intellectual functioning in young autistic children. *Journal of Consulting and Clinical Psychology, 55*, 3–9.

Lovaas, O. I., & Smith, T. (2003). Early and intensive behavioral intervention in autism. In A. E. Kazdin & J. R. Weisz (Eds.), *Evidence-based psychotherapies for children and adolescents* (pp. 325–340). New York, NY: Guilford Press.

Lovejoy, M. C., Weis, R., O'Hare, E., & Rubin, E. C. (1999). Development and initial validation of the Parent Behavior Inventory. *Psychological Assessment, 11*, 534–545.

Luby, J. L. (2015). Poverty's most insidious damage: The developing brain. *JAMA Pediatrics, 169*, 810–811.

Luby, J. L., & Navsaria, N. (2010). Pediatric bipolar disorder: Evidence for prodromal states and early markers. *Journal of Child Psychology and Psychiatry, 51*, 459–471.

Lucarelli, L., Cimino, S., Petrocchi, M., & Ammaniti, M. (2007). Infantile anorexia: A longitudinal study on maternal and child psychopathology. *Scientific Program and Abstracts, 12*, 25–27.

Luman, M., van Meel, C. S., Oosterlaan, J., & Geurts, H. M. (2012). Reward and punishment sensitivity in children with ADHD. *Journal of Abnormal Child Psychology, 40*, 145–157.

Lundahl, B., Risser, H. J., & Lovejoy, M.C. (2006). A meta-analysis of parent training. *Clinical Psychology Review, 26*, 86–104.

Lundgren, J. D., Danoff-Burg, S., & Anderson, D. A. (2004). Cognitive-behavioral therapy for bulimia nervosa. *International Journal of Eating Disorders, 35*, 262–274.

Luthar, S. S. (2006). Resilience in development. In D. Cicchetti & D. J. Cohen (Eds.), *Developmental psychopathology* (Vol. 3, pp. 739–795). Hoboken, NJ: Wiley.

Luthar, S. S., & Latendresse, J. (2005). Children of the affluent: Challenges to well-being. *Current Directions in Psychological Science, 14*, 49–53.

Lynch, G. T. F. (2016). AAC for individuals with autism spectrum disorder. In T. A. Cardon (Ed.), *Technology and the treatment of children with autism spectrum disorder* (pp. 3–25). New York, NY: Springer.

Lyons-Ruth, K. (2015). Dissociation and the parent–infant dialogue: A longitudinal perspective from attachment research. *Attachment, 9*(3), 253–276.

Lyons-Ruth, K., Zeanah, C. H., Benoit, D., Madigan, S., & Mills-Koonce, W. R. (2014). Disorder and risk for disorder during infancy and toddlerhood. In E. J. Mash & R. A. Barkley (Eds.), *Child psychopathology* (pp. 673–736). New York, NY: Routledge.

Lyons-Ruth, K., Zeanah, C.H., Benoit, D., Madigan, S., & Mills-Koonce, W.R. (2014). Disorder and risk for disorder during infancy and toddlerhood. In E.J. Mash & R.A. Barkley (Eds). *Child psychopathology* (pp. 673–736). New York: Wiley.

Lyst, M. J., & Bird, A. (2015). Rett syndrome: A complex disorder with simple roots. *Nature Reviews Genetics, 16*, 261–275.

MacArthur, C.A. (2016). Instruction in evaluation and revision. In C.A. MacArthur (Ed.), *Handbook of writing research*. New York, NY: Guilford Press.

MacArthur, C. A., Philippakos, Z. A., & Graham, S. (2016). A multicomponent measure of writing motivation with basic college writers. *Learning Disability Quarterly, 39*, 31-43.

MacArthur, C. A., Philippakos, Z. A., Graham, S., & Harris, K. (2012). Writing instruction. In B. Wong & D. Butler (Eds.), *Learning about learning disabilities* (pp. 247–270). New York, NY: Elsevier.

Machalicek, W., Raulston, T., Knowles, C., Ruppert, T., Carnett, A., & Alresheed, F. (2016). Challenging behavior. In J. L. Matson (Ed.), *Comorbid conditions among children with autism* (pp. 137–170). New York, NY: Springer.

Mackner, L. M., & Crandall, W. V. (2013). Psychological Aspects of IBD in Children and Adolescents. In P. Maula (Ed.), *Pediatric Inflammatory Bowel Disease* (pp. 483–490). New York: Springer.

Mackner, L. M., Greenley, R. N., Szigethy, E., Herzer, M., Deer, K., & Hommel, K. A. (2013). Psychosocial issues in pediatric inflammatory bowel disease. *Journal of Pediatric Gastroenterology and Nutrition, 56*, 449–458.

MacMaster, F. P., & Kusumakar, V. (2004). MRI study of the pituitary gland in adolescent depression. *Journal of Psychiatric Research, 38*, 231–236.

MacWhinney, B., & William, O. (2015). *The handbook of language emergence*. New York, NY: Wiley.

Madigan, S., Atkinson, L., Laurin, K., & Benoit, D. (2013). Attachment and internalizing behavior in early childhood. *Developmental Psychology, 49*, 672–689.

Madson, M. B., Moorer, K. D., Zeigler-Hill, V., Bonnell, M. A., & Villarosa, M. (2013). Alcohol expectancies, protective behavioral strategies, and alcohol-related outcomes. *Drugs: Education, Prevention and Policy, 20*, 286–296.

Magaña, S., Lopez, K., Aguinaga, A., & Morton, H. (2013). Access to diagnosis and treatment services among Latino children with autism spectrum disorders. *Intellectual and Developmental Disabilities, 51*, 141–153.

Magee, T. (2016). Common genetic disorders. In B. Richardson (Ed.), *Pediatric primary care* (pp. 59–70). Burlington, MA; Jones & Bartlett.

Maglione, M., Gans, D., Das, L., Timbie, J., & Kasari, C. (2012). Nonmedical interventions for children with ASD. *Pediatrics, 130*, s169–s178.

Magnuson, K.A., Kelchen, R., Duncan, G. J., Schindler, H. S., Shager, H., & Yoshikawa, H. (2016). Do the effects of early childhood education programs differ by gender? *Early Childhood Research Quarterly, 36*, 521–536.

Main, M., Kaplan, K., & Cassidy, J. (1985). Security in infancy, childhood and adulthood: A move to the level of representation. In I. Bretherton & E. Waters (Eds.), *Growing points of attachment theory and research, Monographs of the Society for Research in Child Development, 50*, 66–104.

Main, M., & Solomon, J. (1986). Discovery of an insecure-disorganized/disoriented attachment pattern. In T. B. Brazelton (Ed.), *Affective development in infancy* (pp. 95–124). Westport, CT: Ablex.

Majdandžić, M., Möller, E. L., de Vente, W., Bögels, S. M., & van den Boom, D. C. (2014). Fathers' challenging parenting behavior prevents social anxiety development in their 4-year-old children. *Journal of Abnormal Child Psychology, 42*, 301–310.

Mak-Fan, K. M., Taylor, M. J., Roberts, W., & Lerch, J. P. (2012). Measures of cortical grey matter structure and development in children with autism spectrum disorder. *Journal of Autism and Developmental Disorders, 42*, 419–427.

Manassis, K., Oerbeck, B., & Overgaard, K. R. (2016). The use of medication in selective mutism. *European Child and Adolescent Psychiatry, 25*, 571–578.

Mann, A. P., Accurso, E. C., Stiles-Shields, C., Capra, L., Labuschagne, Z., Karnik, N. S., & Le Grange, D. (2014). Factors associated with substance use in adolescents with eating disorders. *Journal of Adolescent Health, 55*, 182–187.

Mannarino, A. P., Cohen, J. A., & Deblinger, E. (2014). Trauma-focused cognitive-behavioral therapy. In *Evidence-based approaches for the treatment of maltreated children* (pp. 165–185). New York, NY: Springer.

Marcus, C. L., Brooks, L. J., Draper, K. A., Gozal, D., Halbower, A. C., Jones, J., . . . Shiffman, R. N. (2012). Diagnosis and management of childhood obstructive sleep apnea syndrome. *Pediatrics, 130,* 714–755.

Marcus, C. L., Moore, R. H., Rosen, C. L., Giordani, B., Garetz, S. L., Taylor, H. G., . . . Redline, S. (2013). A randomized trial of adenotonsillectomy for childhood sleep apnea. *New England Journal of Medicine, 368,* 2366–2376.

Marcus, M. D., & Kalarchian, M. A. (2003). Binge eating in children and adolescents. *International Journal of Eating Disorders, 34,* 47–57.

Maric, M., van Steensel, F. J., & Bögels, S. M. (2015). Parental involvement in CBT for anxiety-disordered youth revisited. *Journal of Attention Disorders.* Advance online publication. doi:10.1177/1087054715573991

Margret, C. P., & Ries, R. K. (2016). Assessment and treatment of adolescent substance use disorders. *Child and Adolescent Psychiatric Clinics of North America, 25,* 411–430.

Margulies, D. M., Weintraub, S., Basile, J., Grover, P. J., & Carlson, G. A. (2012). Will disruptive mood dysregulation disorder reduce false diagnosis of bipolar disorder in children? *Bipolar Disorders, 14,* 488–496.

Marlatt, G. A., Larimer, M. E., & Witkiewitz, K. (2012). *Harm reduction: Pragmatic strategies for managing high-risk behaviors.* New York, NY: Guilford Press.

Marsac, M. L., Kassam-Adams, N., Delahanty, D. L., Widaman, K. F., & Barakat, L. P. (2014). Posttraumatic stress following acute medical trauma in children. *Clinical Child and Family Psychology Review, 17,* 399–411.

Marshall, E. J. (2014). Adolescent alcohol use: Risks and consequences. *Alcohol and Alcoholism, 49,* 160–164.

Marshall, S. A., Evans, S. W., Eiraldi, R. B., Becker, S. P., & Power, T. J. (2014). Social and academic impairment in youth with ADHD, predominately inattentive type and sluggish cognitive tempo. *Journal of Abnormal Child Psychology, 42,* 77–90.

Martin, C., & Dovey, T. M. (2011). Intensive intervention for childhood feeding disorders. In A. Southall & C. Martin (Eds.), *Feeding problems in children* (pp. 277–293). Oxon, England: Radcliffe.

Martin, R. R., Kuhl, P., & Haroldson, S. (1972). An experimental treatment with two preschool stuttering children. *Journal of Speech and Hearing Research, 15,* 743–752.

Martinez, A. G., & Hinshaw, S. P. (2016). Mental health stigma. In D. Cicchetti (Ed.), *Developmental psychopathology* (Vol. 4, pp. 997–1039). New York, NY: Wiley.

Mascolo, J. T., Alfonso, V. C., & Flanagan, D. P. (2014). *Essentials of planning, selecting, and tailoring interventions for unique learners.* New York, NY: Wiley.

Maser, J. D., Norman, S. B., Zisook, S., Everall, I. P., Stein, M. B., Schettler, P. J., . . . Judd, L. L. (2009). Psychiatric nosology is ready for a paradigm shift in *DSM-5. Clinical Psychology: Science and Practice, 16,* 24–40.

Masi, G., Perugi, G., Millepiedi, S., Mucci, M., Toni, C., Bertini, N., . . .Pari, C. (2006). Developmental differences according to age at onset in juvenile bipolar disorder. *Journal of Child and Adolescent Psychopharmacology, 16,* 679–685.

Mason, L. H., & Hagaman, J. L. (2012). Highlights in reading comprehension intervention research for students with learning disabilities. In B. Wong & D. Butler (Eds.), *Learning about learning disabilities* (pp. 191–215). New York, NY: Elsevier.

Masten, A. S., & Cicchetti, D. (2016). Resilience in development. In D. Cicchetti (Ed.), *Developmental psychopathology* (Vol. 4, pp. 271–333). New York, NY: Wiley.

Masterpasqua, F. (2009). Psychology and epigenetics. *Review of General Psychology, 13,* 194–201.

Mather, N., & Wendling, B. J. (2011). *Essentials of dyslexia assessment and intervention.* New York, NY: Wiley.

Mathieu, S. L., Farrell, L. J., Waters, A. M., & Lightbody, J. (2015). An observational study of parent–child behaviors in pediatric OCD. *Journal of Obsessive-Compulsive and Related Disorders, 6,* 132–143.

Matson, J. L., Sipes, M., Horovitz, M., Worley, S., Shoemaker, M., & Kozlowski, A.M. (2011). Behaviors and corresponding functions addressed via functional assessment. *Research in Developmental Disabilities, 32,* 625, 629.

Mattai, A. K., Hill, J. L., & Lenroot, R. K. (2010). Treatment of early-onset schizophrenia. *Current Opinion in Psychiatry, 23,* 304–310.

Maughan, B., & Rutter, M. (2010). Development and psychopathology: A life course perspective. In M. Rutter (Ed.), *Rutter's child and adolescent psychiatry* (pp. 160–182). Malden, NJ: Blackwell.

Mayes, S. D., Calhoun, S., Bixler, E. O., & Vgontzas, A. N. (2009). Sleep problems in children with autism, ADHD, anxiety, depression, acquired brain injury, and typical development. *Sleep Medicine Clinics, 4,* 19–25.

Maziak, W. (2014). Harm reduction at the crossroads: The case of e-cigarettes. *American Journal of Preventive Medicine, 47,* 505–507.

Mazumdar, M., Bellinger, D. C., Gregas, M., Abanilla, K., Bacic, J., & Needleman, H. L. (2011). Low-level environmental lead exposure in childhood and adult intellectual function. *Environmental Health, 10,* 24–24.

McBride, C., Atkinson, L., Quilty, L. C., & Bagby, R. M. (2006). Attachment as moderator of treatment outcome in major depression. *Journal of Consulting and Clinical Psychology, 74,* 1041–1054.

McBride, D. (2015). *The process of research in psychology.* Thousand Oaks, CA: Sage.

McCall, R., & St. Petersburg-USA Orphanage Research Team (2008). The effects of early social-emotional and relationship experience on the development of young orphanage children. *Monographs of the Society for Research in Child Development, 73,* 1–297.

McCallum, E. B., Peterson, Z. D., & Mueller, T. M. (2012). Validation of the traumatic sexualization survey for use with heterosexual men. *Journal of Sex Research, 49,* 423–433.

McEachin, J. J., Smith, T., & Lovaas, O. I. (1993). Long-term outcome for children with autism who received early intensive behavioral treatment. *American Journal on Mental Retardation, 97,* 359–372.

McFall, R. M. (1991). Manifesto for a science of clinical psychology. *The Clinical Psychologist, 44,* 75–88.

McGilloway, S., NiMhaille, G., Bywater, T., Leckey, Y., Kelly, P., Furlong, M., . . . Donnelly, M. (2014). Reducing child conduct disordered behaviour and improving parent mental health in disadvantaged families. *European Child and Adolescent Psychiatry, 23,* 783–794.

McGinnis, E. (2011a). *Skillstreaming the adolescent.* Champaign, IL: Research Press.

McGinnis, E. (2011b). *Skillstreaming the elementary school child.* Champaign, IL: Research Press.

McGorry, P. D., Yung, A. R., Phillips, L. J., Yuen, H. P., Francey, S., Cospgrave, E. M., . . . Jackson, H. (2002). Randomized controlled trial of interventions designed to reduce the risk of progression to first-episode psychosis in a clinical sample with subthreshold symptoms. *Archives of General Psychiatry, 59,* 921–928.

McKeague, I. W., Brown, A. S., Bao, Y., Hinkka-Yli-Salomäki, S., Huttunen, J., & Sourander, A. (2015). Autism with intellectual disability related to dynamics of head circumference growth during early infancy. *Biological Psychiatry, 77,* 833–840.

McKeganey, N. (2012). Harm reduction at the crossroads and the rediscovery of drug user abstinence. *Drugs: Education, Prevention and Policy, 19,* 276–283.

McKenzie, R. G. (2009). Obscuring vital distinctions: The oversimplification of learning disabilities within RTI. *Learning Disability Quarterly, 32,* 203–215.

McKnight, C. D., Compton, S. N., & March, J. S. (2004). Posttraumatic stress disorder. In T. L. Morris & J. S. March (Eds.), *Anxiety*

REFERENCES   615

disorders in children and adolescents (pp. 241–262). New York, NY: Guilford Press.

McKnight Risk Factor Study. (2003). Risk factors for the onset of eating disorders in adolescent girls. *American Journal of Psychiatry, 160,* 248–254.

McLaren, J., & Bryson, E. (1987). Review of recent epidemiological studies of mental retardation. *American Journal on Mental Retardation, 92,* 243–254.

McLaughlin, K. A., Fox, N. A., Zeanah, C. H., Sheridan, M. A., Marshall, P., & Nelson, C. A. (2011). Delayed maturation in brain electrical activity partially explains the association between early environmental deprivation and symptoms of attention-deficit/hyperactivity disorder. *Biological Psychiatry, 68,* 329–336.

McLaughlin, K. A., Green, J. G., Gruber, M. J., Sampson, N. A., Zaslavsky, A. M., & Kessler, R. C. (2012). Childhood adversities and first onset of psychiatric disorders in a national sample of US adolescents. *Archives of General Psychiatry, 69,* 1151–1160.

McMahon, R. J., & Frick, J. (2005). Evidence-based assessment of conduct problems in children and adolescents. *Journal of Clinical Child and Adolescent Psychology, 34,* 477–505.

McMahon, R. J., Witkiewitz, K., & Kotler, J. S. (2010). Predictive validity of callous-unemotional traits measured in early adolescence with respect to multiple antisocial outcomes. *Journal of Abnormal Psychology, 119,* 752–763.

McPartland, J. C., Reichow, B., & Volkmar, F. R. (2012). Sensitivity and specificity of proposed DSM-5 diagnostic criteria for autism spectrum disorder. *Journal of the American Academy of Child & Adolescent Psychiatry, 51,* 368–383.

Meiser-Stedman, R., Yule, W., Smith, P., Glucksman, E., & Dalgeish, T. (2005). Acute stress disorder and posttraumatic stress disorder in children and adolescents involved in assaults or motor vehicle accidents. *American Journal of Psychiatry, 162,* 1381–1383.

Mellon, M. W., & Houts, A. C. (2007). Nocturnal enuresis: Evidenced-based perspectives in etiology, assessment and treatment. In J. E. Fisher & W. T. O'Donohue (Eds.), *Practitioner's guide to evidence-based psychotherapy* (pp. 432–441). New York, NY: Springer.

Meltzer, L. J., Brimeyer, C., Russell, K., Avis, K. T., Biggs, S., Reynolds, A. C., & Crabtree, V. M. (2014). The children's report of sleep patterns. *Sleep Medicine, 15,* 1500–1507.

Meltzer, L. J., & McLaughlin Crabtree, V. (2015). *Confusional arousals, sleep terrors, and sleepwalking.* Washington, DC: American Psychological Association.

Meltzer, L. J., & Mindell, J. A. (2014). Systematic review and meta-analysis of behavioral interventions for pediatric insomnia. *Journal of Pediatric Psychology, 39*(8), 932–948.

Mendenhall, A. N., Arnold, L. E., & Fristad, M. A. (2015). Parent counseling, psychoeducation, and parent support groups. In M. K. Dulcan (Ed.), *Dulcan's textbook of child and adolescent psychiatry* (pp. 875–899). Washington, DC: American Psychiatric Publishing.

Mendenhall, A. N., Fristad, M. A., & Early, T. J. (2009). Factors influencing service utilization and mood symptom severity in children with mood disorders: Effects of Multifamily Psychoeducation Groups (MFPGs). *Journal of Consulting and Clinical Psychology, 77,* 463–473.

Mendola, A., & Gibson, R. L. (2016). Addiction, 12-step programs, and evidentiary standards for ethically and clinically sound treatment recommendations. *American Medical Association Journal of Ethics, 18,* 646–655.

Merikangas, K. R., & He, J. (2014). Epidemiology of mental disorders in children and adolescents. *From Research to Practice in Child and Adolescent Mental Health, 19,* 22–41.

Merikangas, K. R., & Pato, M. (2009). Recent developments in the epidemiology of bipolar disorder in adults and children. *Clinical Psychology: Science and Practice, 16,* 121–133.

Merlo, A. V., & Benekos, P. J. (2016). Maltreatment and delinquency: Breaking the cycle of offending. In M. D. McShane & M. Cavebnaugh (Eds.), *Understanding juvenile justice and delinquency* (pp. 5–21). Santa Monica, CA: ABC-CLIO.

Mervis, C. B. (2012). Language development in Williams Syndrome. In J. A. Burack, R. M. Hodapp, G. Iarocci, & E. Zigler (Eds.), *The Oxford handbook of intellectual disability and development* (pp. 217–237). New York, NY: Oxford University Press.

Mesa, F., Beidel, D. C., & Bunnell, B. E. (2014). An examination of psychopathology and daily impairment in adolescents with social anxiety disorder. *PLOS ONE, 9,* e93668.

Mesibov, G., Howley, M., & Naftel, S. (2015). *Accessing the curriculum for learners with autism spectrum disorders: Using the TEACCH program to help inclusion.* London, England: Routledge.

Mesibov, G. B., Shea, V., & Schopler, E. (2005). *The TEACCH approach to autism spectrum disorders.* New York, NY: Springer.

Messenger, M., Packman, A., Onslow, M., Menzies, R., & O'Brian, S. (2015). Children and adolescents who stutter: Further investigation of anxiety. *Journal of Fluency Disorders, 46,* 15–23.

Metz, K. (2016). *Careers in mental health.* New York, NY: Wiley.

Meyer, J. S., & Quenzer, L. F. (2005). *Psychopharmacology: Drugs, the brain, and behavior.* Sunderland, MA: Sinauer Associates.

Mezulis, A. H., Hyde, J. S., & Abramson, L. Y. (2006). The developmental origins of cognitive vulnerability to depression. *Developmental Psychology, 42,* 1012–1025.

Miadich, S. A., Everhart, R. S., Borschuk, A. P., Winter, M. A., & Fiese, B. H. (2015). Quality of life in children with asthma. *Journal of Pediatric Psychology, 40,* 672–679.

Miadich, S. A., Everhart, R. S., Borschuk, A. P., Winter, M. A., & Fiese, B. H. (2015). Quality of Life in Children With Asthma: A Developmental Perspective. *Journal of Pediatric Psychology, 40*(7), 672–679.

Miano, S., Esposito, M., Foderaro, G., Ramelli, G. P., Pezzoli, V., & Manconi, M. (2016, June 3). Sleep-related disorders in children with attention-deficit hyperactivity disorder. *CNS Neuroscience and Therapeutics.* Advance online publication. doi:10.1111/cns.12573

Michelson, L., Sugai, D. P., Wood, R. P., & Kazdin, A. E. (2013). *Social skills assessment and training with children.* New York, NY: Springer.

Michl, L. C., McLaughlin, K. A., Shepherd, K., & Nolen-Hoeksema, S. (2013). Rumination as a mechanism linking stressful life events to symptoms of depression and anxiety. *Journal of Abnormal Psychology, 122,* 339–352.

Mick, E., Spencer, T., Wozniak, J., & Biederman, J. (2005). Heterogeneity of irritability in attention-deficit/hyperactivity disorder subjects with and without mood disorders. *Biological Psychiatry, 58,* 576–582.

Miech, R. A., Johnston, L. D., O'Malley, P. M., Bachman, J. G., & Schulenberg, J. E. (2016). *Monitoring the future I: Secondary school students.* Ann Arbor: University of Michigan.

Mikami, A. Y., Griggs, M. S., Lerner, M. D., Emeh, C. C., Reuland, M. M., Jack, A., & Anthony, M. R. (2013). A randomized trial of a classroom intervention to increase peers' social inclusion of children with attention-deficit/hyperactivity disorder. *Journal of Consulting and Clinical Psychology, 81,* 100–113.

Mikami, A. Y., Jia, M., & Na, J. J. (2014). Social skills training. *Child and Adolescent Psychiatric Clinics of North America, 23,* 775–788.

Mikami, A. Y., & Normand, S. (2015). The importance of social contextual factors in peer relationships of children with ADHD. *Current Developmental Disorders Reports, 2,* 30–37.

Mikkelsen, E. J. (2015). Elimination disorders. In M. K. Dulcan (Ed.), *Dulcan's textbook of child and adolescent psychiatry.* Washington, DC: American Psychiatric Publishing.

Mikkelsen, E.J. (2015). Elimination disorders. In M.K. Dulcan (Ed.), *Dulcan's textbook of child and adolescent psychiatry* (pp. 479–493). Washington, DC: American Psychiatric Press.

Miklowitz, D. J. (2008). *Bipolar disorder: A family-focused treatment approach.* New York, NY: Guilford Press.

Miklowitz, D. J. (2012). Family-focused treatment for children and adolescents with bipolar disorder. *International Journal of Psychiatry and Related Sciences, 49,* 95–103.

Miklowitz, D. J., Axelson, D. A., Birmaher, B., George, E. L., Taylor, D. O., Schneck, C. D., . . . Brent, D. A. (2009). Family-focused treatment for adolescents with bipolar disorder. *Archives of General Psychiatry, 65,* 1053–1061.

Miklowitz, D. J., Chang, K. D., Taylor, D. O., George, E. L., Singh, M. K., Schneck, C. D., . . . Garber, J. (2011). Early psychosocial intervention for youth at risk for bipolar I or II disorder. *Bipolar Disorders, 13,* 67–75.

Miklowitz, D. J., Mullen, K. L., & Chang, K. D. (2008). Family-focused treatment for bipolar disorder in adolescence. In B. Geller & M. P. DelBello (Eds.), *Treatment of bipolar disorder in children and adolescents* (pp. 166–183). New York, NY: Guilford Press.

Mikulincer, M., & Shaver, P. R. (2012). An attachment perspective on psychopathology. *World Psychiatry, 11,* 11–15.

Milekic, M. H., Xin, Y., O'Donnell, A., Kumar, K. K., Bradley-Moore, M., Malaspina, D., . . . Gingrich, J. A. (2015). Age-related sperm DNA methylation changes are transmitted to offspring and associated with abnormal behavior and dysregulated gene expression. *Molecular Psychiatry, 20,* 995–1001.

Milin, R. (2008). Comorbidity of schizophrenia and substance use disorders in adolescents and young adults. In Y. Kaminer & O. G. Bukstein (Eds.), *Adolescent substance abuse* (pp. 355–378). New York, NY: Routledge.

Miller, A. B., Esposito-Smythers, C., Weismoore, J. T., & Renshaw, K. D. (2013). The relation between child maltreatment and adolescent suicidal behavior: A systematic review and critical examination of the literature. *Clinical Child and Family Psychology Review, 16,* 146–172.

Miller, E. (2015). Controversies and challenges of vaccination. *BMC Medicine, 13,* 1–5.

Miller, R., & Prosek, E. A. (2013). Trends and implications of proposed changes to the *DSM-5* for vulnerable populations. *Journal of Counseling and Development, 91,* 359–366.

Miller, V. A., Schreck, K. A., Mulick, J. A., & Butter, E. (2012). Factors related to parents' choices of treatments for their children with autism spectrum disorders. *Research in Autism Spectrum Disorders, 6,* 87–95.

Miller, W. R., & Rollnick, S. (2012). *Motivational interviewing.* New York, NY: Guilford Press.

Millichap, J. G. (2010). *Attention deficit hyperactivity disorder handbook.* New York, NY: Springer.

Millings, A., Buck, R., Montgomery, A., Spears, M., & Stallard, P. (2012). School connectedness, peer attachment, and self-esteem as predictors of adolescent depression. *Journal of Adolescence, 35,* 1061–1067.

Millon, T. (2014). Developmental pathogenesis. In P. H. Blaney (Ed.), *Oxford textbook of psychopathology* (pp. 71–99). Oxford, England: Oxford University Press.

Miltenberger, R. G., Miller, B. G., & Zerger, H. M. (2015). Applied behavior analysis. In C. M Nezu & A. M. Nezu (Eds.), *Oxford handbook of cognitive and behavioral therapies* (pp. 79–95). Oxford, England: Oxford University Press.

Mindell, J. A., & Owens, J. A. (2015). *A clinical guide to pediatric sleep.* Philadelphia, PA: Lippincott.

Mindell, J. A., Sadeh, A., Kwon, R., & Goh, D. Y. (2013). Cross-cultural differences in the sleep of preschool children. *Sleep Medicine, 14,* 1283–1289.

Mindell, J. A., Telpfski, L. S., Wiegand, B., & Kurtz, E. S. (2009). A nightly bedtime routine: Impact on sleep in young children. *Sleep, 32,* 599–606.

Minuchin, S. (1974). *Families and family therapy.* Cambridge, MA: Harvard University Press.

Minuchin, S., Rosman, B., & Baker, I. (1978). *Psychosomatic families: Anorexia nervosa in context.* Cambridge, MA: Harvard University Press.

Moeschler, J. B., Shevell, M., Saul, R. A., Chen, E., Freedenberg, D. L., Hamid, R., . . . Tarini, B. A. (2014). Comprehensive evaluation of the child with intellectual disability or global developmental delays. *Pediatrics, 134,* e903–e918.

Moffitt, T. E. (2003). Life-course persistent and adolescence-limited antisocial behavior. In B. B. Lahey, T. E. Moffitt, & A. Caspi (Eds.), *Causes of conduct disorder and juvenile delinquency* (pp. 49–75). New York, NY: Guilford Press.

Moffitt, T. E., Caspi, A., & Harrington, H. (2007). Generalized anxiety disorder and depression: Childhood risk factors in a birth cohort followed to age 32. *Psychological Medicine, 37,* 441–452.

Moffitt, T. E., Caspi, A., Rutter, M., & Silva, P. A. (2001). *Sex differences in antisocial behaviour: Conduct disorder, delinquency, and violence in the Dunedin Longitudinal Study.* Cambridge, England: Cambridge University Press.

Mohammadzaheri, F., Koegel, L. K., Rezaei, M., & Bakhshi, E. (2015). A randomized clinical trial comparison between pivotal response treatment and adult-driven applied behavior analysis intervention on disruptive behaviors in public school children with autism. *Journal of Autism and Developmental Disorders, 45,* 2899–2907.

Molina, B. S., Hinshaw, S. P., Arnold, L. E., Swanson, J. M., Pelham, W. E., Hechtman, L., . . . Greenhill, L. L. (2013). Adolescent substance use in the multimodal treatment study of attention-deficit/hyperactivity disorder (ADHD)(MTA) as a function of childhood ADHD, random assignment to childhood treatments, and subsequent medication. *Journal of the American Academy of Child and Adolescent Psychiatry, 52,* 250–263.

Molina, B. S., Hinshaw, S. P., Swanson, J. M., Arnold, L. E., Vitiello, B., Jensen, P. S., . . . MTA Cooperative Group (2009). The MTA at 8 years: Prospective follow-up of children treated for combined-type ADHD in a multisite study. *Journal of the American Academy of Child and Adolescent Psychiatry, 48,* 484–500.

Monti, P. M., Barnett, N. P., O'Leary, T. A., & Colby, S. M. (2001). Motivational enhancement for alcohol-involved adolescents. In P. M. Monti, S. M. Colby, & T. A. O'Leary (Eds.), *Adolescents, alcohol, and substance abuse* (pp. 145–182). New York, NY: Guilford Press.

Monti, P. M., Colby, S. M., Barnett, N. P., Spirito, A., Rohsenow, D. J., Myers, M., . . . Lewander, W. (1999). Brief intervention for harm reduction with alcohol-positive older adolescents in a hospital emergency department. *Journal of Consulting and Clinical Psychology, 67,* 989–994.

Moore, D. S. (2015). *The developing genome.* Oxford, England: Oxford University Press.

Morris, R. D., Lovett, M. W., Wolf, M., Sevcik, R. A., Steinbach, K. A., Frijters, J. C., & Shapiro, M. B. (2012). Multiple-component remediation for developmental reading disabilities. *Journal of Learning Disabilities, 45,* 99–127.

Mowrer, O. (1960). *Learning theory and behavior.* New York, NY: Wiley.

Mrazek, P. B., & Kempe, C. H. (2014). *Sexually abused children and their families.* Oxford, England: Pergamon.

Mrug, S., Molina, B. S., Hoza, B., Gerdes, A. C., Hinshaw, S. P., Hechtman, L., & Arnold, L. E. (2012). Peer rejection and friendships in children with attention-deficit/hyperactivity disorder. *Journal of Abnormal Child Psychology, 40,* 1013–1026.

MSSNG. (2016). *About MSSNG.* Retrieved August 21, 2016, from https://www.mss.ng

MTA Cooperative Group. (1999). A 14-month randomized clinical trial of treatment strategies for attention-deficit/hyperactivity disorder. *Archives of General Psychiatry, 56,* 1073–1086.

Mufson, L., Pollack Dorta, K., Wickramaratne, P., Nomura, Y., Olfson, M., & Weissman, M. M. (2004). A randomized effectiveness trial of interpersonal psychotherapy for depressed adolescents. *Archives of General Psychiatry, 61,* 577–584.

Mufson, L., Weissman, M. M., Moreau, D., & Garfinkel, R. (1999). Efficacy of interpersonal psychotherapy for depressed adolescents. *Archives of General Psychiatry, 56,* 573–579.

Mundy, P. (2016). *Autism and joint attention.* New York, NY: Guilford Press.

Muris, P., Hendriks, E., & Bot, S. (2016). Children of few words: Relations among selective mutism, behavioral inhibition, and (social) anxiety symptoms in 3-to 6-year-olds. *Child Psychiatry and Human Development, 47,* 94–101.

Muris, P., & Ollendick, T. H. (2015). Children who are anxious in silence: A review on selective mutism, the new anxiety disorder in *DSM-5. Clinical Child and Family Psychology Review, 18,* 151–169.

Murphy, E., & Carr, A. (2013). Enuresis and encopresis. In A. Carr (Ed.), *What works with children and adolescents?* (pp. 49–64) London, England: Routledge.

Murphy, R., Straebler, S., Basden, S., Cooper, Z., & Fairburn, C. G. (2012). Interpersonal psychotherapy for eating disorders. *Clinical Psychology and Psychotherapy, 19,* 150–158.

Murray, D. W., Arnold, L. E., Swanson, J., Wells, K., Burns, K., Jensen, P., . . . Strauss, T. (2008). A clinical review of outcomes of the multimodal treatment study of children with attention-deficit/hyperactivity disorder. *Current Psychiatry Reports, 10,* 424–431.

Murray-Close, D., Nelson, D. A., Ostrov, J. M., Casas, J. F., & Crick, N. R. (2016). Relational aggression. In D. Cicchetti (Ed.), *Developmental psychopathology.* (Vol. 4, pp. 660–722). New York, NY: Wiley.

Musser, E. D., Galloway-Long, H. S., Frick, P. J., & Nigg, J. T. (2013). Emotion regulation and heterogeneity in attention-deficit/hyperactivity disorder. *Journal of the American Academy of Child & Adolescent Psychiatry, 52,* 163–171.

Myers, B. J., Mackintosh, V. H., & Goin-Kochel, R. P. (2009). "My greatest joy and my greatest heart ache:" Parents' own words on how having a child in the autism spectrum has affected their lives and their families' lives. *Research in Autism Spectrum Disorders, 3,* 670–684.

Myers, J. E. B. (2010). *The APSAC handbook on child maltreatment.* Thousand Oaks, CA: Sage.

Myers, S. M., & Johnson, C. P. (2007). Management of children with autism spectrum disorders. *Pediatrics, 120,* 1162–1182.

N'zi, A. M., & Eyberg, S. M. (2013). Tailoring parent–child interaction therapy for oppositional defiant disorder in a case of child maltreatment. In W. O'Donohue & S. O. Lilienfeld (Eds.), *Case studies in clinical psychological science.* Oxford, England: Oxford University Press.

Naar-King, S., Ellis, D., King, P. S., Lam, P., Cunningham, P., Secord, E., . . . Templin, T. (2014). Multisystemic therapy for high-risk African American adolescents with asthma. *Journal of Consulting and Clinical Psychology, 82,* 536–545.

Naar-King, S., Ellis, D., King, P. S., Lam, P., Cunningham, P., Secord, E., . . . & Templin, T. (2014). Multisystemic Therapy for high-risk African American adolescents with asthma: A randomized clinical trial. *Journal of consulting and clinical psychology, 82*(3), 536.

Nader, K., & Fletcher, K. E. (2014). Childhood posttraumatic stress disorder. In E. J. Mash & R. A. Barkley (Ed.), *Child psychopathology* (pp. 476–528). New York, NY: Guilford Press.

Nadkarni, R. B., & Fristad, M. A. (2010). Clinical course of children with a depressive spectrum disorder and transient manic symptoms. *Bipolar Disorders, 12,* 494–503.

Nagy, P., & Armstrong, S. (2015). Motivational interviewing. In M. K. Dulcan (Ed.), *Dulcan's textbook of child and adolescent psychiatry* (pp. 993–1006). Washington, DC: American Psychiatric Publishing.

Nagy, T. F. (2011). *Essential ethics for psychologists.* Washington, DC: American Psychological Association.

Nathan, P. E., & Gorman, J. M. (2015). *A guide to treatments that work.* Oxford, England: Oxford University Press.

National Association of School Psychologists. (2010). *Principles for professional ethics.* Bethesda, MD: Author.

National Center for Educational Statistics. (2015). *National assessment of educational progress.* Washington, DC: US Department of Education.

National Institute for Health and Clinical Excellence. (2005). *Post traumatic stress disorder.* London, England: Author.

National Institute on Drug Abuse. (2013). *ASSIST.* Bethesda, MD: Author.

National Professional Development Center on Autism Spectrum Disorders. (2016). *Evidence-based practice for ASD.* Chapel Hill, NC: FPG Child Development Institute.

National Reading Panel. (2000). *Teaching children to read: An evidence-based assessment of the scientific research literature on reading and its implications for reading instruction.* Washington, DC: National Institute of Child Health and Human Development.

Nele, D., Ellen, D., Petra, W., & Herbert, R. (2015). Social information processing in infants at risk for ASD at 5 months of age. *Research in Autism Spectrum Disorders, 17,* 95–105.

Nelson, C. A., Bos, K., Gunnar, M. R., & Sonuga-Barke, E. J. (2011). V. The neurobiological toll of early human deprivation. *Monographs of the Society for Research in Child Development, 76,* 127–146.

Nelson, C. A., Fox, N. A., & Zeanah, C. H. (2014). *Romania's abandoned children.* Cambridge, MA: Harvard University Press.

Nelson, C. A., Fox, N. A., & Zeanah, C. H. (2016). The effects of early psychosocial deprivation on brain and behavioral development. In D. Cicchetti (Ed.), *Developmental psychopathology* (Vol. 4, pp. 934–970). New York, NY: Wiley.

Nelson, T. (2016). An insider's look at technology and autism. In T. A. Cardon (Ed.), *Technology and the treatment of children with autism spectrum disorders* (pp. 147–149). New York, NY: Springer.

Neubauer, D. N. (2014). New and emerging pharmacotherapeutic approaches for insomnia. *International Review of Psychiatry, 26,* 214–224.

Nevsimalova, S., Prihodova, I., Kemlink, D., & Skibova, J. (2013). Childhood parasomnia: A disorder of sleep maturation? *European Journal of Paediatric Neurology, 17,* 615–619.

Newcorn, J. H., Harpin, V., Huss, M., Lyne, A., Sikirica, V., Johnson, M., . . . Robertson, B. (2016). Extended-release guanfacine hydrochloride in 6–17-year olds with ADHD. *Journal of Child Psychology and Psychiatry, 57*(6), 717–728.

Newman, M. G., Llera, S. J., Erickson, T. M., Przeworski, A., & Castonguay, L. G. (2013). Worry and generalized anxiety disorder: A review and theoretical synthesis of evidence on nature, etiology, mechanisms, and treatment. *Annual Review of Clinical Psychology, 9,* 275–297.

Newsom, C., & Hovanitz, C. A. (2005). The nature and value of empirically validated interventions. In J. W. Jacobson, R. M. Foxx, & J. A. Mulick (Eds.), *Controversial therapies for developmental disabilities* (pp. 31–44). Mahwah, NJ: Erlbaum.

Niec, L. N., Barnett, M. L., Prewett, M. S., & Shanley, C. J. (2016). Group parent-child interaction therapy: A randomized control trial for the treatment of conduct problems in young children. *Journal of Consulting and Clinical Psychology, 84*(8), 682–698.

Nigg, J. T. (2006). Temperament and developmental psychopathology. *Journal of Child Psychology and Psychiatry, 47,* 395–422.

Nigg, J. T. (2016a). Attention and impulsivity. In D. Cicchetti (Ed.), *Developmental psychopathology* (Vol. 3, pp. 591–646). New York, NY: Wiley.

Nigg, J. T. (2016b). Where do epigenetics and developmental origins take the field of developmental psychopathology? *Journal of Abnormal Child Psychology, 44,* 405–419.

Nigg, J. T., & Barkley, R. A. (2014). Attention-deficit/hyperactivity disorder. In E. J. Mash & R. A. Barkley (Eds.), *Child psychopathology* (pp. 75–144). New York, NY: Guilford Press.

Niles, A. N., Lebeau, R. T., Liao, B., Glenn, D. E., & Craske, M. G. (2012). Dimensional indicators of generalized anxiety disorder severity for *DSM-5*. *Journal of Anxiety Disorders, 26,* 279–286.

Nissley-Tsiopinis, J., Krehbiel, C., & Power, T. J. (2016). Attention-deficit hyperactivity disorder. In T. P. Gullotta, R. W. Plant, & M. Evans (Eds.), *Handbook of adolescent behavioral problems* (pp. 151–171). New York, NY: Springer.

Nock, M. K., Green, J. G., Hwang, I., McLaughlin, K. A., Sampson, N. A., Zaslavsky, A. M., & Kessler, R. C. (2013). Prevalence, correlates, and treatment of lifetime suicidal behavior among adolescents. *JAMA Psychiatry, 70,* 300–310.

Nolen-Hoeksema, S., & Hilt, L. M. (2013). *Handbook of depression in adolescents.* New York, NY: Routledge.

Nolen-Hoeksema, S., Girgus, J. S., & Seligman, M. E. (1992). Predictors and consequences of childhood depressive symptoms: A 5-year longitudinal study. *Journal of Abnormal Psychology, 101,* 405–422.

Norbury, C. F. (2014). Practitioner review: Social (pragmatic) communication disorder conceptualization, evidence and clinical implications. *Journal of Child Psychology and Psychiatry, 55,* 204–216.

Norcross, J. C., & Sayette, M. A. (2016). *Insider's guide to graduate programs in clinical and counseling psychology.* New York, NY: Guilford Press.

Norris, M. L., Spettigue, W. J., & Katzman, D. K. (2015). Update on eating disorders: Current perspectives on avoidant/restrictive food intake disorder in children and youth. *Neuropsychiatric Disease and Treatment, 12,* 213–218.

Norton, E. S., & Wolf, M. (2012). Rapid automatized naming (RAN) and reading fluency. *Annual Review of Psychology, 63,* 427–452.

Novaco, R. W. (1975). *Anger control: The development and evaluation of an experimental treatment.* Lexington, MA: Heath.

Nugent, K. L., Daniels, A. M., & Azur, M. J. (2012). Correlates of schizophrenia spectrum disorders in children and adolescents cared for in community settings. *Child and Adolescent Mental Health, 17,* 101–108.

Nussbaum, R. L. (2016). *Thompson & Thompson genetics and medicine.* New York, NY: Elsevier.

O'Brien, B. A., Wolf, M., & Lovett, M. W. (2012). A toxometric investigation of developmental dyslexia subtypes. *Dyslexia, 18,* 16–39.

O'Brien, C. P., Anthony, J. C., Carroll, K., Childress, A. R., Dackis, C., Diamond, G., . . . Spoth, R. (2005). Substance use disorders. In D. L. Evans, E. B. Foa, R. E. Gur, H. Hendin, C. P. O'Brien, M. E. P. Seligman, et al. (Eds.), *Treating and preventing adolescent mental health disorders* (pp. 335–426). New York, NY: Oxford University Press.

O'Brien, L. M. (2009). The neurocognitive effects of sleep disruption in children and adolescents. *Child and Adolescent Psychiatric Clinics of North America, 18,* 813–823.

O'Brien, W. H., Haynes, S. N., & Kaholokula, J. K. A. (2015). Behavioral assessment and the functional analysis. In C. M Nezu & A. M. Nezu (Eds.), *Oxford handbook of cognitive and behavioral therapies* (pp. 44–61). Oxford, England: Oxford University Press.

O'Driscoll, C., Heary, C., Hennessy, E., & McKeague, L. (2012). Explicit and implicit stigma towards peers with mental health problems in childhood and adolescence. *Journal of Child Psychology and Psychiatry, 53,* 1054–1062.

O'Handley, R. D., Radley, K. C., & Whipple, H. M. (2015). The relative effects of social stories and video modeling toward increasing eye contact of adolescents with autism spectrum disorder. *Research in Autism Spectrum Disorders, 11,* 101–111.

Oar, E. L., Farrell, L. J., & Ollendick, T. H. (2015). One session treatment for specific phobias: An adaptation for paediatric blood–injection–injury phobia in youth. *Clinical Child and Family Psychology Review, 18,* 370–394.

Odlaug, B. L., Lust, K., Schreiber, L. R. N., Christenson, G., Derbyshire, K., & Grant, J. E. (2013). Skin picking disorder in university students. *General Hospital Psychiatry, 35,* 168–173.

Odle, T. (2016). Emotional development in children and adolescents. *Education.*

Odom, S. L., Boyd, B. A., Hall, L. J., & Hume, K. A. (2015). Comprehensive treatment models for children and youth with autism spectrum disorders. In F. R. Volkmar (Ed.), *Handbook of autism and pervasive developmental disorders* (pp. 770–787). New York, NY: Wiley.

Oerbeck, B., Stein, M. B., Wentzel-Larsen, T., Langsrud, O., & Kristensen, H. (2014). A randomized controlled trial of a home and school-based intervention for selective mutism. *Child and Adolescent Mental Health, 19,* 192–198.

Office of Juvenile Justice and Delinquency Prevention. (2016). *Prevalence and development of child delinquency.* Washington, DC: US Department of Justice.

Ojodu, J., Hulihan, M.M., Pope, S,N., & Grant, A.M. (2014). Incidence of sickle cell trait. *Morbidity and Mortality Weekly Report, 63,* 1155–1158.

Olatunji, B. O., Davis, M. L., Powers, M. B., & Smits, J. A. (2013). Cognitive-behavioral therapy for obsessive-compulsive disorder: A meta-analysis of treatment outcome and moderators. *Journal of Psychiatric Research, 47,* 33–41.

Olfson, M., Blanco, C., Liu, S. M., Wang, S., & Correll, C. U. (2012). National trends in the office-based treatment of children, adolescents, and adults with antipsychotics. *Archives of General Psychiatry, 69,* 1247–1256.

Olfson, M., Blanco, C., Wang, S., Laje, G., & Correll, C. U. (2014). National trends in the mental health care of children, adolescents, and adults by office-based physicians. *JAMA Psychiatry, 71,* 81–90.

Olfson, M., Druss, B. G., & Marcus, S. C. (2015). Trends in mental health care among children and adolescents. *New England Journal of Medicine, 372,* 2029–2038.

Olfson, M., Gameroff, M. J., Marcus, S. C., & Jensen, P. S. (2003). National trends in the treatment of attention deficit hyperactivity disorder. *American Journal of Psychiatry, 160,* 1071–1077.

Olfson, M., He, J. P., & Merikangas, K. R. (2013). Psychotropic medication treatment of adolescents: Results from the National Comorbidity Survey–Adolescent Supplement. *Journal of the American Academy of Child and Adolescent Psychiatry, 52,* 378–388.

Ollendick, T. H., King, N. J., & Yule, W. (2013). *International handbook of phobic and anxiety disorders in children and adolescents.* New York, NY: Springer.

Oppenheimer, R., Howells, K., Palmer, R. L., & Chaloner, D. A. (2013). Adverse sexual experience in childhood and clinical eating disorders. *Anorexia Nervosa and Bulimic Disorders: Current Perspectives, 19,* 357–361.

Osborn, R., Miller, R., Vanucci, A., Goldschmindt, A. B., Boutelle, K., & Tanofsky-Kraff, M. (2013). Loss of control and binge eating in children and adolescents. In J. Alexander (Ed.), *A clinician's guide to binge eating disorder* (pp. 170–181). New York, NY: Routledge.

Osterling, J., & Dawson, G. (1994). Early recognition of children with autism. *Journal of Autism and Developmental Disorders, 24,* 247–257.

Owens, J., & Burnham, M. M. (2009). Sleep disorders. In C. H. Zeanah (Ed.), *Handbook of infant mental health* (pp. 362–391). New York, NY: Guilford Press.

Owens, J., Chervin, R. D., & Hoppin, A. G. (2014). *Behavioral sleep problems in children.* New York, NY: Klewer.

Owens, J., & Mohan, M. (2016). Behavioral interventions for parasomnias. *Current Sleep Medicine Reports, 2,* 81–86.

Owens, J. A., & Moturi, S. (2009). Phramacologic treatment of pediatric insomnia. *Child and Adolescent Psychiatric Clinics of North America, 18,* 1001–1016.

Owens, R. E. (2013). *Language disorders.* Boston, MA: Pearson.

Ozonoff, S., Cook, I., Coon, H., Dawson, G., Joseph, R. M., Klin, A., . . . Wrathall, D. (2004). Performance on Cambridge Neuropsychological Test automated battery subtests sensitive to frontal lobe function in people with autistic disorder. *Journal of Autism and Developmental Disorders, 34,* 139–150.

Ozonoff, S., Young, G. S., Belding, A., Hill, M., Hill, A., Hutman, T., . . . Iosif, A. M. (2014). The broader autism phenotype in infancy. *Journal of the American Academy of Child and Adolescent Psychiatry, 53,* 398–407.

Palmen, S., & van Engeland, H. (2012). The relationship between autism and schizophrenia. In M. E. Garralda & J. Raynaud (Eds.), *Brain, mind, and developmental psychopathology in childhood* (pp. 123–143). Lanham, MD: Aronson.

Pandolfi, C., & Magyar, C.I. (2016). Psychopathology. In J. L. Matson (Ed.), *Comorbid conditions among children with autism spectrum disorders* (pp. 171–186). New York, NY: Springer.

Papolos, D., & Papolos, J. (2000). *The bipolar child.* New York, NY: Broadway.

Pardini, D. A., & Fite, P. J. (2010). Symptoms of conduct disorder, oppositional defiant disorder, attention-deficit/hyperactivity disorder, and callous-unemotional traits as unique predictors of psychosocial maladjustment in boys. *Journal of the American Academy of Child and Adolescent Psychiatry, 49,* 1134–1144.

Parens, E., & Johnston, J. (2010). Controversies concerning the diagnosis and treatment of bipolar disorder in children. *Child and Adolescent Psychiatry and Mental Health, 4,* 1–14.

Parloff, M. B. (1984). Psychotherapy research and its incredible credibility crisis. *Clinical Psychology Review, 4,* 95–109.

Pasco Fearon, R. M., Groh, A. M., Bakermans-Kranenburg, M. J., van IJzendoorn, M. H., & Roisman, G. I. (2016). Attachment and developmental psychopathology. In D. Cicchetti (Ed.), *Developmental psychopathology* (Vol. 1, pp. 325–384). New York, NY: Wiley.

Patel, N. C., DelBello, M. P., Keck, P. E., & Strakowski, S. M. (2006). Phenomenology associated with age at onset in patients with bipolar disorder at their first psychiatric hospitalization. *Bipolar Disorders, 8,* 91–94.

Patterson, G. R. (2016). Coercion theory: The study of change. In T. J. Dishion & J. J. Snyder (Eds.), *Oxford handbook of coercive relationship dynamics* (pp. 7–22). Oxford, England: Oxford University Press.

Patterson, G. R., & Capaldi, D. M. (1991). Antisocial parents: Unskilled and vulnerable. In P. A. Cowan & E. M. Hetherington (Eds.), *Family transitions* (pp. 195–218). Hillsdale, NJ: Erlbaum.

Patterson, G. R., Reid, J. B., & Dishion, T. J. (1992). *Antisocial boys.* Eugene, OR: Castalia.

Patterson, H. O., & O'Connell, D. F. (2003). Recovery maintenance and relapse prevention with chemically dependent adolescents. In M. A. Reinecke, F. M. Dattilio, & A. Freeman (Eds.), *Cognitive therapy with children and adolescents* (pp. 70–94). New York, NY: Guilford Press.

Patton, G. C., Coffey, C., Carlin, J. B., Degenhardt, L., Lynskey, M. T., & Hall, W. D. (2002). Cannabis use and mental health in young people. *British Medical Journal, 525,* 1195–1198.

Pavuluri, M. N., Graczyk, P. A., Henry, D. B., Carbray, J. A., Heidenreich, J., & Miklowitz, D. J. (2004). Child- and family-focused cognitive-behavioral therapy for pediatric bipolar disorder. *Journal of the American Academy of Child and Adolescent Psychiatry, 43,* 528–537.

Peacock, G. G., & Ervin, R. A. (2012). *Practical handbook of school psychology.* New York, NY: Guilford Press.

Pears, K. C., Bruce, J., Fisher, P. A., & Kim, H. K. (2010). Indiscriminate friendliness in maltreated foster children. *Child Maltreatment, 15,* 64–75.

Pearson, R. M., Evans, J., Kounali, D., Lewis, G., Heron, J., Ramchandani, P. G., . . . Stein, A. (2013). Maternal depression during pregnancy and the postnatal period. *JAMA Psychiatry, 70,* 1312–1319.

Pelayo, R., & Huseni, S. (2016). Pharmacotherapy of insomnia in children. *Current Sleep Medicine Reports, 2,* 38–43.

Pelham, W. E., Fabiano, G. A., Gnagy, E. M., Greiner, A. R., & Hoza, B. (2005). The role of summer treatment programs in the context of comprehensive treatment for attention-deficit/hyperactivity disorder. In E. D. Hibbs & P. S. Jensen (Eds.), *Psychosocial treatments for child and adolescent disorders* (pp. 377–409). Washington, DC: American Psychological Association.

Pelham, W. E., Fabiano, G. A., Waxmonsky, J. G., Greiner, A. R., Gnagy, E. M., Pelham, W. E., . . . Murphy, S. A. (2016). Treatment sequencing for childhood ADHD. *Journal of Clinical Child and Adolescent Psychology, 45,* 396–415.

Pelham, W. E., Gnagy, E. M., Greiner, A. R., Hoza, B. Hinshaw, S. P., Swanson, J. M., . . . McBurnett, K. (2000). Behavioral vs. behavioral and pharmacological treatment in ADHD children attending a summer treatment program. *Journal of Abnormal Child Psychology, 28,* 507, 526.

Pena-Brooks, A., & Hedge, M. N. (2007). *Assessment and treatment of articulation and phonological disorders in children.* Austin, TX: Pro-Ed.

Penner, M., Zwaigenbaum, L., & Roberts, W. (2015). Diagnosis: Screening, surveillance, assessment, and formulation. In E. Anagnostou & J. Brian (Eds.), *Clinician's manual on autism spectrum disorder* (pp. 5–17). New York, NY: Springer.

Pereira, A. I., Barros, L., Mendonça, D., & Muris, P. (2014). The relationships among parental anxiety, parenting, and children's anxiety. *Journal of Child and Family Studies, 23,* 399–409.

Pérez-Fuentes, G., Olfson, M., Villegas, L., Morcillo, C., Wang, S., & Blanco, C. (2013). Prevalence and correlates of child sexual abuse. *Comprehensive Psychiatry, 54,* 16–27.

Peris, T. S., Compton, S. N., Kendall, P. C., Birmaher, B., Sherrill, J., March, J., . . . Piacentini, J. (2015). Trajectories of change in youth anxiety during cognitive-behavior therapy. *Journal of Consulting and Clinical Psychology, 83,* 239–252.

Perou, R., Bitsko, R. H., Blumberg, S. J., Pastor, P., Ghandour, R. M., Gfroerer, J. C., . . . Huang, L. N. (2016). Mental health surveillance among children. *Morbidity and Mortality Weekly Report, 62,* 1–36.

Perrin, N., Sayer, L., & While, A. (2015). The efficacy of alarm therapy versus desmopressin therapy in the treatment of primary monosymptomatic nocturnal enuresis: A systematic review. *Primary Health Care Research & Development, 16,* 21–31.

Peter, C. J., Reichenberg, A., & Akbarian, S. (2015). Epigenetic regulation in autism. In S. H. Fatemi (Ed.), *The molecular basis of autism* (pp. 67–92). New York, NY: Springer.

Peters-Scheffer, N., Didden, R., & Lang, R. (2016). Intellectual disability. In J. L. Matson (Ed.), *Comorbid conditions among children with autism* (pp. 283–300). New York, NY: Springer.

Petersen, L., Jeppesen, P., & Thorup, A. (2005). A randomized, multicenter trial of integrated versus standard treatment for patients with a first episode of psychotic illness. *British Medical Journal, 331,* 602.

Peterson, A. L., & Azrin, N. H. (1992). Behavioral and pharmacological treatments for Tourette syndrome. *Applied and Preventive Psychology, 2,* 231–242.

Petit, D., Pennestri, M. H., Paquet, J., Desautels, A., Zadra, A., Vitaro, F., . . . Montplaisir, J. (2015). Childhood sleepwalking and sleep terrors: A longitudinal study of prevalence and familial aggregation. *JAMA Pediatrics, 169,* 653–658.

Petti, T. A. (2015). Milieu treatment. In M. K. Dulcan (Ed.), *Dulcan's textbook of child and adolescent psychiatry* (pp. 1027–1046). Washington, DC: American Psychiatric Publishing.

Pfeifer, J. C., Kowatch, R. A., & DelBello, M. P. (2010). Pharmacotherapy of bipolar disorder in children and adolescents. *CNS Drugs, 24,* 575–593.

Pfiffner, L. J., & Kaiser, N. M. (2015). Behavioral parent training. In M. K. Dulcan (Ed.), *Dulcan's textbook of child and adolescent psychiatry* (pp. 901–935). Washington, DC: American Psychiatric Publishing.

Pfuntner, A., Wier, L. M., & Stocks, C. (2013). *Most frequent conditions in US hospitals. Healthcare costs and utilization.* Rockville, MD: National Institutes of Health.

Phillips, D. A., & Meloy, M. C. (2016). High-quality school-based Pre-K can boost early learning for children with special needs. *Exceptional Children, 78,* 1–20.

Phillips, K. A., Stein, D. J., Rauch, S. L., Hollander, E., Fallon, B. A., Barsky, A., . . . Leckman, J. (2010). Should obsessive-compulsive spectrum grouping of disorders be included in *DSM-5? Depression and Anxiety, 27,* 528–555.

Piacentini, J., Chang, S., Snorrason, I., & Woods, D. W. (2014). Obsessive-compulsive spectrum disorders. In E. J. Mash & R. A. Barkley (Eds.), *Child psychopathology* (pp. 429–475). New York, NY: Guilford Press.

Piazza, C. C., & Addison, L. R. (2007). Function-based assessment and treatment of pediatric feeding disorders. In P. Sturmey (Ed.), *Functional analysis in clinical treatment* (pp. 129–149). Burlington, MA: Elsevier.

Piazza-Waggoner, C., Roddenberry, A., Yeomans-Maldonado, G., Noll, J., & Ernst, M. M. (2013). Inpatient pediatric psychology consultation-liaison program development. *Clinical Practice in Pediatric Psychology, 3,* 37–47.

Pickard, K. E., & Ingersoll, B. R. (2015). High and low level initiations of joint attention, and response to joint attention. *Journal of Autism and Developmental Disorders, 45,* 262–268.

Pickles, A., & Hill, J. (2006). Developmental pathways. In D. Cicchetti & D. J. Cohen (Eds.), *Developmental psychopathology* (Vol. 1, pp. 211–243). Hoboken, NJ: Wiley.

Picon, F., Volpe, U., Sterzer, P., & Heinz, A. (2016). Translational neuroimaging. In A. Fiorillo, U. Volpe, & D. Bhugra (Eds.), *Psychiatry in Practice: Education, Experience, and Expertise.* Oxford, England: Oxford University Press.

Pierce, K. (2015). Neurodevelopmental disorders. In M. K. Dulcan (Ed.), *Dulcan's textbook of child and adolescent psychiatry* (pp. 157–171). Washington, DC: American Psychiatric Publishing.

Pierce, K., & Redcay, E. (2009). Fusiform function in children with an autism spectrum disorder is a matter of "who." *Biological Psychiatry, 64,* 552–560.

Pike, K. M., Devlin, M. J., & Loeb, K. L. (2004). Cognitive-behavioral therapy in the treatment of anorexia nervosa, bulimia nervosa, and binge eating disorder. In J. K. Thompson (Ed.), *Handbook of eating disorders and obesity* (pp. 130–162). Hoboken, NJ: Wiley.

Pindzola, R. H., Plexico, L. W., & Haynes, W. O. (2015). *Diagnosis and evaluation in speech pathology.* Boston, MA: Pearson.

Pine, D. S. (2006). A primer on brain imaging in developmental psychopathology. *Journal of Child Psychology and Psychiatry, 47,* 983–986.

Pine, D. S., Costello, E. J., Dahl, R., James, R., Leckman, J. F., Leibenluft, E., . . . Zeanah, C. H. (2011). Increasing the developmental focus in *DSM-5.* In D. A. Reiger (Ed.), *The conceptual evolution of DSM-5* (pp. 305–321). Washington, DC: American Psychiatric Publishing.

Pine, D. S., & Klein, R. G. (2010). Anxiety disorders. In M. Rutter (Ed.), *Rutter's child and adolescent psychiatry* (pp. 628–647). Malden, MA: Blackwell.

Pinsky, E., Rauch, P. K., & Abrams, A. N. (2015). Pediatric consultation and psychiatric aspects of somatic disease. In A. Thapar (Ed.), *Rutter's child and adolescent psychiatry* (pp. 586–598). New York, NY: Wiley.

Pisetsky, E. M., Utzinger, L. M., & Wonderlich, S. A. (2015). Personality disorders as comorbidities in eating disorders. In T. Wade (Ed.), *Encyclopedia of feeding and eating disorders* (pp. 1–4). New York, NY: Springer.

Plante, W. A., Lobato, D., & Engel, R. (2001). Review of group interventions for pediatric chronic conditions. *Journal of Pediatric Psychology, 26,* 435–453.

Pliszka, S. R. (2015). Attention-deficit/hyperactivity disorder. In M. K. Dulcan (Ed.), *Dulcan's textbook of child and adolescent psychiatry* (pp. 173–193). Washington, DC: American Psychiatric Publishing.

Pliszka, S. R. (2016). Conceptual issues in understanding comorbidity in ADHD. In L. A. Adler (Ed.), *Attention-deficit/hyperactivity disorder in adults and children* (pp. 63–71). Cambridge, England: Cambridge Publishing.

Polivy, J., Herman, P. C., Mills, J. S., & Wheeler, H. B. (2003). Eating disorders in adolescence. In G. R. Adams & M. D. Berzonsky (Eds.), *Blackwell handbook of adolescence* (pp. 523–549). Malden, MA: Blackwell.

Pontifex, M. B., Saliba, B. J., Raine, L. B., Picchietti, D. L., & Hillman, C. H. (2013). Exercise improves behavioral, neurocognitive, and scholastic performance in children with attention-deficit/hyperactivity disorder. *Journal of Pediatrics, 162,* 543–551.

Popova, S., Lange, S., Shield, K., Mihic, A., Chudley, A. E., Mukherjee, R. A., . . . Rehm, J. (2016). Comorbidity of fetal alcohol spectrum disorder: A systematic review and meta-analysis. *Lancet, 387,* 978–987.

Posner, K. (2016). Evidence-based assessment to improve assessment of suicide risk, ideation, and behavior. *Journal of the American Academy of Child and Adolescent Psychiatry, 55,* S95.

Post, R. M. (2016). The kindling/sensitization model and the pathophysiology of bipolar disorder. In J. C. Soares & A. Young (Eds.), *Bipolar disorders* (pp. 204–218). Cambridge, England: Cambridge University Press.

Potter, D., Chevy, C., Amaya-Jackson, L., O'Donnell, K., & Murphy R. A. (2009). *Reactive attachment disorder.* Washington, DC: American Academy of Child and Adolescent Psychiatry.

Poulton, R., Moffitt, T. E., & Silva, P. A. (2015). The Dunedin Multidisciplinary Health and Development Study: Overview of the first 40 years, with an eye to the future. *Social Psychiatry and Psychiatric Epidemiology, 50,* 679–693.

Powers, M. D., Palmieri, M. J., Egan, S. M., Rohrer, J. L., Nulty, E. C., & Forte, S. (2015). Behavioral assessment of individuals with autism. In F. R. Volkmar (Ed.), *Handbook of autism and pervasive developmental disorders* (pp. 695–735). New York, NY: Wiley.

Pretorius, N., Dimmer, M., Power, E., Eisler, I., Simic, M., & Tchanturia, K. (2012). Evaluation of a cognitive remediation therapy group for adolescents with anorexia nervosa. *European Eating Disorders Review, 20,* 321–325.

Pringsheim, T., & Steeves, T. (2012). Pharmacological treatment for attention deficit hyperactivity disorder (ADHD) in children with comorbid tic disorders. *Evidence-Based Child Health, 4,* 1196–1230.

Prinstein, M. J., & Aikins, W. (2004). Cognitive moderators of the longitudinal association between peer rejection and adolescent depressive symptoms. *Journal of Abnormal Child Psychology, 32,* 147–158.

Prinstein, M. J., Cheah, C. S. L., & Guyer, A. E. (2005). Peer victimization, cue interpretation, and internalizing symptoms: Preliminary concurrent and longitudinal findings for children and adolescents. *Journal of Clinical Child and Adolescent Psychology, 34,* 11–24.

Prinstein, M. J., & Giletta, M. (2016). Peer relations and developmental psychopathology. In D. Cicchetti (Ed.), *Developmental psychopathology* (Vol. 1, pp. 527–579). New York, NY: Wiley.

Prochaska, J. O. (2013). Transtheoretical model of behavior change. *Encyclopedia of behavioral medicine.* New York, NY: Springer.

Prochaska, J. O., & Norcross, J. C. (2009). *Systems of psychotherapy: A transtheoretical analysis.* Belmont, CA: Brooks/Cole.

Puff, J., & Renk, K. (2015). Preschool PTSD treatment (PPT) for a young child exposed to trauma in the Middle East. *Clinical Case Studies, 14,* 388–404.

Purcel, D. W., Malow, R. M., Dolezal, C., & Carballo-Dieguez, A. (2004). Sexual abuse of boys. In L. J. Koenig, L. S. Doll, A.

O'Leary, & W. Pequegnat (Eds.), *From child sexual abuse to adult sexual risk* (pp. 93–114). New York, NY: American Psychological Association.

Querne, L., Fall, S., Le Moing, A. G., Bourel-Ponchel, E., Delignières, A., Simonnot, A., . . . Berquin, P. (2016). Effects of methylphenidate on default-mode network/task-positive network synchronization in children with ADHD. *Journal of Attention Disorders*. Advance online publication. doi:10.1177/1087054713517542

Quittner, A. L., Abbott, J., Georgiopoulos, A. M., Goldbeck, L., Smith, B., Hempstead, S. E., . . . International Committee on Mental Health. (2016). Cystic Fibrosis Foundation and European Cystic Fibrosis Society consensus statements for screening and treating depression and anxiety. *Thorax*, 71, 26–34.

Quittner, A. L., Abbott, J., Georgiopoulos, A. M., Goldbeck, L., Smith, B., Hempstead, S. E., . . . & Crossan, A. (2016). International Committee on Mental Health in Cystic Fibrosis: Cystic Fibrosis Foundation and European Cystic Fibrosis Society consensus statements for screening and treating depression and anxiety. *Thorax*, 71(1), 26–34.

Quittner, A. L., Saez-Flores, E., & Barton, J. D. (2016). The psychological burden of cystic fibrosis. *Current Opinion in Pulmonary Medicine*, 22, 187–191.

Quittner, A. L., Saez-Flores, E., & Barton, J. D. (2016). The psychological burden of cystic fibrosis. *Current opinion in pulmonary medicine*, 22(2), 187–191.

Rajamani, B., Kumar, Y., & Rahman, S. M. (2016). Neuroleptic malignant syndrome. *Journal of Family Medicine and Primary Care*, 5, 178–180.

Rajwan, E., Chacko, A., Wymbs, B. T., & Wymbs, F. A. (2014). Evaluating clinically significant change in mother and child functioning: Comparison of traditional and enhanced behavioral parent training. *Journal of Abnormal Child Psychology*, 42, 1407–1412.

Ramirez, S. Z., Feeney-Kettler, K. A., Flores-Torres, L., Kratochwill, T. R., & Morris, R. J. (2006). Fears and anxiety disorders. In G. G. Bear & K. M. Minke (Eds.), *Children's needs III: Development, prevention, and intervention* (pp. 267–279). Washington, DC: National Association of School Psychologists.

Ramo, D. E., Anderson, K. G., Tate, S. R., & Brown, S. A. (2005). Characteristics of relapse to substance use in comorbid adolescents. *Addictive Behaviors*, 30, 1811–1823.

Rao, U., Daley, S. E., & Hammen, C. (2000). Relationship between depression and substance use disorders in adolescent women during the transition to adulthood. *Journal of the American Academy of Child and Adolescent Psychiatry*, 39, 215–222.

Rapee, R. M. (2012). Family factors in the development and management of anxiety disorders. *Clinical Child and Family Psychology Review*, 15, 69–80.

Rapee, R. M., Abbott, M. J., & Lyneham, H. J. (2006). Bibliotherapy for children with anxiety disorders using written materials for parents. *Journal of Consulting and Clinical Psychology*, 74, 436–444.

Rapoff, M. A., Lindsley, C. B., & Karlson, C. (2009). Medical and psychosocial aspects of juvenile rheumatoid arthritis. In M. C. Roberts & R. G. Steele (Eds.), *Handbook of pediatric psychology* (pp. 366–380). New York, NY: Guilford Press.

Rapoff, M., & Lindsley, C. B. (2015). Pain and Its Assessment. In R.E. Petty (Ed.), *Textbook of Pediatric Rheumatology* (pp. 88-94). Philadelphia, PA: Elsevier.

Rapoport, J. L., & Gogtay, N. (2011). Childhood onset schizophrenia: Support for a progressive neurodevelopmental disorder. *International Journal of Developmental Neuroscience*, 29, 251–258.

Rapoport, J. L., Gogtay, N., & Shaw, P. (2008). Schizophrenia and psychotic illness. In R. L. Findling (Ed.), *Clinical manual of child and adolescent psychopharmacology* (pp. 337–373). Washington, DC: American Psychiatric Association.

Rapoport, J. L., & Shaw, P. (2010). Obsessive-compulsive disorder. In M. Rutter (Ed.), *Rutter's child and adolescent psychiatry* (pp. 696–718). Malden, MA: Blackwell.

Raposa, E., Hammen, C., Brennan, P., & Najman, J. (2014). The long-term effects of maternal depression: early childhood physical health as a pathway to offspring depression. *Journal of Adolescent Health*, 54, 88–93.

Rasmussen, S. A., Jamieson, D. J., Honein, M. A., & Petersen, L. R. (2016). Zika virus and birth defects. New *England Journal of Medicine*, 374, 1981–1987.

Ratner, N. B., & Guitar, B. (2006). Treatment of very early stuttering and parent-administered therapy. In N. B. Ratner & J. Tetnowski (Eds.), *Current issues in stuttering research and practice* (pp. 99–124). Mahwah, NJ: Erlbaum.

Ratner, N. B., & Tetnowski, J. A. (2014). *Current issues in stuttering research and practice*. New York, NY: Psychology Press.

Ratto, A. B., Reznick, J. S., & Turner-Brown, L. (2015). Cultural effects on the diagnosis of autism spectrum disorder among Latinos. *Focus on Autism and Other Developmental Disabilities*, 17, 1–9.

Raulin, M. L., & Lilienfeld, S. O. (2014). Conducting research in the field of psychopathology. In P. H. Blaney (Ed.), *Oxford textbook of psychopathology* (pp. 100–129). Oxford, England: Oxford University Press.

Ray, J. V., Thornton, L. C., Frick, P. J., Steinberg, L., & Cauffman, E. (2016). Impulse control and callous-unemotional traits distinguish patterns of delinquency and substance use in justice involved adolescents. Journal of Abnormal Child Psychology, 44, 599–611.

Ray, L. A., Bujarski, S., & Roche, D. J. (2016). Subjective response to alcohol as a research domain criterion. *Alcoholism: Clinical and Experimental Research*, 40, 6–17.

Ray, R., & Dhawan, A. (2011). Diagnostic orphans. *Addiction*, 106, 867–868.

Rayner, K., Foorman, B. R., Perfetti, C. A., Pesetsky, D., & Seidenberg, M. S. (2001). How psychological science informs the teaching of reading. *Psychological Science in the Public Interest*, 2, 31–74.

Raz, M. H. (1995). *Help me talk right: How to teach a child to say the "L" sound in 15 easy lessons*. Scottsdale, AZ: Gerstenweitz.

Realmuto, G.M. (2015). Autism spectrum disorder: Diagnostic considerations. In S. H. Fatemi (Ed.), *The molecular basis of autism* (pp. 15–21). New York, NY: Springer.

Reed-Knight, B., Claar, R. L., Schurman, J. V., & van Tilburg, M. A. (2016). Implementing psychological therapies for functional GI disorders in children and adults. *Expert Review of Gastroenterology & Hepatology*. Onlinefirst.

Reed-Knight, B., Claar, R. L., Schurman, J. V., & van Tilburg, M. A. L. (2016). Implementing psychological therapies for functional GI disorders in children and adults. *Expert Review of Gastroenterology and Hepatology*, 10(9), 981–984.

Reed-Knight, B., Squires, M., Chitkara, D. K., & van Tilburg, M. A. L. (2016). Adolescents with irritable bowel syndrome report increased eating-associated symptoms, changes in dietary composition, and altered eating behaviors: A pilot comparison study to healthy adolescents. *Neurogastroenterology & Motility*. Advance online publication. doi:10.1111/nmo.12894

Reichert, A., Kreiker, S., Mehler-Wex, C., & Warnke, A. (2008). The psychopathological and psychosocial outcome of early-onset schizophrenia. *Child and Adolescent Psychiatry and Mental Health*, 2, 1–6.

Reid, G., Huntley, E. D., & Lewin, D. S. (2009). Insomnias of childhood and adolescence. *Child and Adolescent Psychiatric Clinics of North America*, 18, 979–1000.

Reid, R. R., Harris, K. R., Graham, S., & Rock, M. (2012). Self-regulation among students with LD and ADHD. In B. Wong & D. Butler (Eds.), *Learning about learning disabilities* (pp. 141–173). New York, NY: Elsevier.

Reidenberg, D. J. (2014). Suicide. In T. P. Gullotta (Ed.), *Handbook of adolescent behavior problems* (pp. 209–234). New York, NY: Springer.

Reinecke, M. A., & Simons, A. (2005). Vulnerability to depression among adolescents: Implications for cognitive-behavioral treatment. *Cognitive and Behavioral Practice*, 12, 166–176.

Reiss, S. (1990). Prevalence of dual diagnosis in community-based day programs in the Chicago metropolitan area. *American Journal on Mental Retardation, 94,* 578–585.

Remschmidt, H., & Theisen, F. (2012). Early-onset schizophrenia. In M. E. Garralda & J. Raynaud (Eds.), *Brain, mind, and developmental psychopathology in childhood* (pp. 145–172). Lanham, MD: Aronson.

Rende, R., & Waldman, I. (2006). Behavioral and molecular genetics and developmental psychopathology. In D. Cicchetti & D. J. Cohen (Eds.), *Developmental psychopathology* (Vol. 2, pp. 427–464). Hoboken, NJ: Wiley.

Renz, K., Lorch, E. P., Milich, R., Lemberger, C., Bodner, A., & Welsh, R. (2003). On-line story representation in boys with attention deficit hyperactivity disorder. *Journal of Abnormal Child Psychology, 31,* 93–104.

Reschly, A. L., & Coolong-Chaffin, M. (2016). Contextual influences and response to intervention. In S. R. Jimerson (Ed.), *Handbook of response to intervention* (pp. 441–453). New York, NY: Springer.

Reschly, D. J., & Bergstrom, M. K. (2009). Response to intervention. In T. B. Gutkin & C. R. Reynolds (Eds.), *Handbook of school psychology* (pp. 434–460). Hoboken, NJ: Wiley.

Research Unit on Pediatric Psychopharmacology Anxiety Study Group. (2001) Fluvoxamine for the treatment of anxiety disorders in children and adolescents. *New England Journal of Medicine, 344,* 1279–1285.

Reynolds, C. R., & Kampaus, R. W. (2014). *Behavior assessment system for children, third edition manual (BASC-3).* Boston, MA: Pearson.

Rich, B. A., Carver, F. W., Holroyd, T., Rosen, H. R., Mendoza, J. K., Cornwell, B. R., . . . Leibenluft, E. (2011). Different neural pathways to negative affect in youth with pediatric bipolar disorder and severe mood dysregulation. *Journal of Psychiatric Research, 45,* 1283–1294.

Rich, C. L., Combs-Lane, A. M., Resnick, H. S., & Kilpatrick, D. G. (2004). Child sexual abuse and adult sexual revictimization. In L. J. Koenig, L. S. Doll, A. O'Leary, & W. Pequegnat (Eds.), *From child sexual abuse to adult sexual risk* (pp. 49–68). Washington, DC: American Psychological Association.

Richards, S., & Goswami, U. (2015). Auditory processing in specific language impairment. *Journal of Speech, Language, and Hearing Research, 58,* 1292–1305.

Rigamonti, A. E., Sartorio, A., Scognamiglio, P., Bini, S., Monteleone, A. M., Mastromo, D., . . . Monteleone, P. (2014). Different effects of cholestyramine on postprandial secretions of cholecystokinin and peptide YY in women with bulimia nervosa. *Neuropsychobiology, 70,* 228–234.

Rimland, B. (1964). *Infantile autism: The syndrome and its implications for a neural theory of behavior.* New York, NY: Appleton-Century-Crofts.

Ringeisen, H., Casanueva, C. E., Urato, M., & Stambaugh, L. F. (2015). Mental health service use during the transition to adulthood for adolescents reported to the child welfare system. *Psychiatric Services, 60,* 1084–1091.

Riou, E. M., Ghosh, S., Francoeur, E., & Shevell, M. I. (2009). Global developmental delay and its relationship to cognitive skills. *Developmental Medicine and Child Neurology, 51,* 600–606.

Rissanen, A., Niemimaa, M., Suonpää, M., Ryynänen, M., & Heinonen, S. (2007). First trimester Downs Syndrome screening shows high detection rate for trisomy 21, but poor performance in structural abnormalities. *Fetal Diagnosis and Therapy, 22,* 45–50.

Ritchie, E. C., Watson, P. J., & Friedman, M. J. (2015). *Interventions following mass violence and disasters.* New York, NY: Guilford Press.

Rittig, S., & Kamperis, K. (2015). Pathophysiology of nocturnal enuresis. In I. Franco (Ed.), *Pediatric incontinence* (pp. 209–219). New York, NY: Wiley.

Roberts, C. (2015). Depression. In T. P. Gullotta, R. W. Plant, & M. Evans (Eds.), *Handbook of adolescent behavioral problems* (pp. 173–191). New York, NY: Springer.

Roberts, M. C., Aylward, B. S., & Wu, Y. P. (2015). *Clinical practice of pediatric psychology.* New York, NY: Guilford Press.

Robins, D. L., Casagrande, K., Barton, M., Chen, C. M. A., Dumont-Mathieu, T., & Fein, D. (2014). Validation of the modified checklist for autism in toddlers, revised with follow-up (M-CHAT-R/F). *Pediatrics, 133,* 37–45.

Robins, E., & Guze, S. B. (1970). Establishment of diagnostic validity in psychiatric illness. *American Journal of Psychiatry, 126,* 983–987.

Rodgers, R. F., McLean, S. A., & Paxton, S. J. (2015). Longitudinal relationships among internalization of the media ideal, peer social comparison, and body dissatisfaction. *Developmental Psychology, 51,* 706–713.

Roodman, A. A., & Clum, G.A. (2001). Revictimization rates and method variance: A meta-analysis. *Clinical Psychology Review, 21,* 183–204.

Roemer, L., & Borkovec, T. D. (1993). Worry: Unwanted cognitive activity that controls unwanted somatic experience. In D. M. Wegner & J. W. Pennebaker (Eds.), *Handbook of mental control* (pp. 220–238). Englewood Cliffs, NJ: Prentice Hall.

Rogers, C. R. (1957). The necessary and sufficient conditions of therapeutic personality change. *Journal of Consulting Psychology, 21,* 95–103.

Rogers, S. J., & Vismara, L. (2015). Interventions for infants and toddlers at risk for autism spectrum disorder. In F. R. Volkmar (Ed.), *Handbook of autism and pervasive developmental disorders* (pp. 739–768). New York, NY: Wiley.

Rohde, P., Stice, E., & Marti, C. N. (2015). Development and predictive effects of eating disorder risk factors during adolescence. *International Journal of Eating Disorders, 48,* 187–198.

Rohrbach, L. A., Sussman, S., Dent, C. W., & Sun, P. (2005). Tobacco, alcohol, and other drug use among high-risk young people. *Journal of Drug Issues, 35,* 333–356.

Romanelli, R. J., Wu, F. M., Gamba, R., Mojtabai, R., & Segal, J. B. (2014). Behavioral therapy and serotonin reuptake inhibitor pharmacotherapy in the treatment of obsessive–compulsive disorder. *Depression and Anxiety, 31,* 641–652.

Romero, S., Birmaher, B., Axelson, D. A., Iosif, A., Williamson, D. E., Gill, M. K., . . . Keller, M. (2009). Negative life events in children and adolescents with bipolar disorder. *Journal of Clinical Psychiatry, 70,* 1452–1460.

Roncero, M., Belloch, A., Perpiñá, C., & Treasure, J. (2013). Ego-syntonicity and ego-dystonicity of eating-related intrusive thoughts in patients with eating disorders. *Psychiatry Research, 208,* 67–73.

Rosenbaum, D. P., Gordon, S., & Hanson, S. (1998). Assessing the effects of school-based drug education: A six-year multilevel analysis of project D.A.R.E. *Journal of Research in Crime and Delinquency, 35,* 381–412.

Rosenberg, R. E., Daniels, A. M., Law, J. K., Law, P. A., & Kaufmann, W. E. (2009). Trends in autism spectrum disorder diagnoses. *Journal of Autism and Developmental Disorders, 39,* 1099–1111.

Rosenzweig, S. (1936). Some implicit common factors in diverse methods of psychotherapy. *American Journal of Orthopsychiatry, 6,* 412–415.

Rossello, J., & Bernal, G. (2005). New developments in cognitive-behavioral and interpersonal treatments for depressed Puerto Rican adolescents. In E. D. Hibbs & P. S. Jensen (Eds.), *Psychosocial treatments for child and adolescent disorders* (pp. 187–217). Washington, DC: American Psychological Association.

Rosso, I. M., Cintron, C. M., Steingard, R. J., Renshaw, P. F., Young, A. D., & Yurgelun-Todd, D. A. (2005). Amygdala and hippocampus volumes in pediatric major depression. *Biological Psychiatry, 57,* 21–26.

Rowsell, M., MacDonald, D. E., & Carter, J. C. (2015). Emotion regulation difficulties in anorexia nervosa. *Journal of Eating Disorders, 4,* 17–31.

Roth, F. P., & Worthington, C. K. (2015). *Treatment resource manual for speech language pathology.* New York, NY: Cengage.

Rousseau, D. M., & Gunia, B. C. (2016). Evidence-based practice. *Annual Review of Psychology*, 67, 667–692.

Rubin, K. H., & Asendorpf, J. B. (2014). *Social withdrawal, inhibition, and shyness in childhood*. New York, NY: Psychology Press.

Rudolph, K. D., Lansford, J. E., & Rodkin, P. C. (2016). Interpersonal theories of developmental psychopathology. In D. Cicchetti (Ed.), *Developmental psychopathology* (Vol. 3, pp. 243–311). New York, NY: Wiley.

Rudolph, K. E., Stuart, E. A., Glass, T. A., & Merikangas, K. R. (2014). Neighborhood disadvantage in context. *Social Psychiatry and Psychiatric Epidemiology*, 49, 467–475.

Rueda, M. R., Rothbart, M. K., McCandliss, B. D., Saccomanno, L., & Posner, M. I. (2005). Training, maturation, and genetic influences on the development of executive attention. *Proceedings of the National Academy of Sciences*, 41, 14931–14936.

Rumpf, H. J., Wohlert, T., Freyer-Adam, J., Grothues, J., & Bischof, G. (2012). Screening questionnaires for problem drinking in adolescents: Performance of AUDIT, AUDIT-C, CRAFFT and POSIT. *European Addiction Research*, 19, 121–127.

Rund, B. R. (1994). The relationship between psychosocial and cognitive functioning in schizophrenic patients and expressed emotion and communication deviance in their parents. *Acta Psychiatrica Scandinavica*, 90, 133–140.

Runions, K., Shapka, J. D., Dooley, J., & Modecki, K. (2013). Cyber-aggression and victimization and social information processing. *Psychology of Violence*, 3, 9–26.

Runyon, M. K., & Deblinger, E. (2014). *Combined parent-child cognitive behavioral therapy: An approach to empower families at-risk for child physical abuse*. Oxford, England: Oxford University Press.

Ruscio, A. M., Gentes, E. L., Jones, J. D., Hallion, L. S., Coleman, E. S., & Swendsen, J. (2015). Rumination predicts heightened responding to stressful life events in major depressive disorder and generalized anxiety disorder. *Journal of Abnormal Psychology*, 124, 17–26.

Russo, D. C. (2015). Pioneers in pediatric psychology: Environments shape behavior. *Journal of Pediatric Psychology*, 40, 487–491.

Rutter, M. (1978). Diagnosis and definition of childhood autism. *Journal of Autism and Child Schizophrenia*, 8, 139–161.

Rutter, M. (2011). Child psychiatric diagnosis and classification. *Journal of Child Psychology and Psychiatry*, 32, 647–660.

Rutter, M., Lecouteur, A., & Lord, C. (2015). Autism Diagnostic Interview–Revised. Torrance, CA; WPS.

Rutter, M., Sonuga-Barke, E. J., Beckett, C., Castle, J., Kreppner, J., Kumsta, R., . . . Bell, C. A. (2011). Deprivation-specific psychological patterns. *Monographs of the Society for Research in Child Development*, 75, 1–252.

Rutter, M., Sonuga-Barke, E. J., & Castle, J. (2011). Investigating the impact of early institutional deprivation on development. *Monographs of the Society for Research in Child Development*, 75, 1–20.

Rutter, M., & Sroufe, A. (2000). Developmental psychopathology: Concepts and challenges. *Development and Psychopathology*, 12, 265–296.

Rutter, M., & Thapar, A. (2015). Genetics of autism spectrum disorders. In F. R. Volkmar (Ed.), *Handbook of autism and pervasive developmental disorders* (pp. 411–422). New York, NY: Wiley.

Sacco, R., Stefano G., & Persico, A. M. (2015). Head circumference and brain size in autism spectrum disorder. *Neuroimaging*, 234, 239–251.

Sadock, B., & Sadock, V. (2015). *Kaplan & Sadock's synopsis of psychiatry*. Philadelphia, PA: Lippinott.

Saldana, L., & Henggeler, S. W. (2006). Multisystemic therapy in the treatment of adolescent conduct disorder. In W. M. Nelson, A. J. Finch, & K. J. Hart (Eds.), *Conduct disorders* (pp. 217–258). New York, NY: Springer.

Salvy, S. J., Mulick, J. A., Butter, E., Bartlett, K. K., & Linscheid, T. R. (2004). Contingent electric shock (SIBIS) and a conditioned punisher eliminate severe head banging in a preschool child. *Behavioral Interventions*, 19, 59–72.

Sambrano, S., Springer, J. F., Sale, E., Kasim, R., & Hermann, J. (2005). Understanding prevention effectiveness in real-world settings. *American Journal of Drug and Alcohol Abuse*, 31, 491–513.

Samek, D. R., Elkins, I. J., Keyes, M. A., Iacono, W. G., & McGue, M. (2015). High school sports involvement diminishes the association between childhood conduct disorder and adult antisocial behavior. *Journal of Adolescent Health*, 57, 107–112.

Samek, D. R., Keyes, M. A., Iacono, W. G., & McGue, M. (2013). Peer deviance, alcohol expectancies, and adolescent alcohol use. *Behavior Genetics*, 43, 286–296.

Sameroff, A. J. (2000). Developmental systems and psychopathology. *Development and Psychopathology*, 12, 297–312.

Samms-Vaughn, M. (2006). Learning disorders. In C. A. Essau (Ed.), *Child and adolescent psychopathology* (pp. 271–289). New York, NY: Routledge.

Santiago, C. D., Kaltman, S., & Miranda, J. (2013). Poverty and mental health. *Journal of Clinical Psychology*, 69, 115–126.

Sarafino, E. P., & Smith, T. W. (2014). *Health psychology*. New York, NY: Wiley.

Sattler, J. M. (2014). *Foundations of behavioral, social, and clinical assessment of children*. La Mesa, CA: Author.

Sauer-Zavala, S., Burris, J. L., & Carlson, C. R. (2014). Understanding the relationship between religiousness, spirituality, and underage drinking: The role of positive alcohol expectancies. *Journal of Religion and Health*, 53, 68–78.

Saxbe, C., & Barkley, R. A. (2014). The second attention disorder? Sluggish cognitive tempo vs. attention-deficit/hyperactivity disorder. *Journal of Psychiatric Practice*, 20, 38–49.

Saywitz, K. J., & Camparo, L. B. (2014). Interviewing children. In *Handbook of child research* (pp. 371–390). Thousand Oaks, CA; Sage.

Scanlon, N. M., & Epkins, C. C. (2015). Aspects of mothers' parenting: Independent and specific relations to children's depression, anxiety, and social anxiety symptoms. *Journal of Child and Family Studies*, 24, 249–263.

Scarr, S., & McCartney, K. (1983). How people make their own environments. *Child Development*, 54, 424–435.

Schaeffer, C. M., & Borduin, M. (2005). Long-term follow-up to a randomized clinical trial of multisystemic therapy with serious and violent juvenile offenders. *Journal of Consulting and Clinical Psychology*, 73, 445–453.

Schalock, R. L., Borthwick-Duffy, S. A., Bradley, V. J., Buntinx, W. H., Coulter, D. L., Craig, E. M., . . . Shogren, K. A. (2010). *Intellectual disability: Definition, classification, and systems of supports*. Washington, DC: AAIDD.

Schalock, R. L., & Luckasson, R. (2015). A systematic approach to subgroup classification in intellectual disability. *Intellectual and Developmental Disabilities*, 53, 358–366.

Schalock, R. L., Tassé, M. J., & Balboni, G. (2015). *Diagnosing intellectual disability using the DABS*. Washington, DC: AAIDD.

Schechter, D. S. (2012). The developmental neuroscience of emotional neglect, its consequences, and the psychological interventions that can reverse them. *American Journal of Psychiatry*, 169, 452–454.

Scheeringa, M. S., Zeanah, C. H., & Cohen, J. A. (2011). PTSD in children and adolescents: Toward an empirically based algorithma. *Depression and Anxiety*, 28, 770–782.

Schlenger, W. E., Caddell, J. M., Ebert, L., Jordan, B. K., Rourke, K. M., Wilson, D., . . . Kulka, R. A. (2002). Psychological reactions to terrorist attacks. *JAMA: Journal of the American Medical Association*, 288, 581–588.

Schneider, H. E., Lam, J. C., & Mahone, E. M. (2016). Sleep disturbance and neuropsychological function in young children with ADHD. *Child Neuropsychology*, 22, 493–506.

Schrieks, I. C., Stafleu, A., Kallen, V. L., Grootjen, M., Witkamp, R. F., & Hendriks, H. F. (2014). The biphasic effects of moderate alcohol consumption with a meal on ambiance-induced mood and autonomic nervous system balance. *PLOS ONE, 9*, e86199.

Schroeder, S. R., Oster-Granite, M. L., Berkson, G., Bodfish, J. W., Breese, G. R., Cataldo, M. F., . . . Wong, D. F. (2001). Self-injurious behavior: Gene-brain-behavior relationships. *Mental Retardation and Developmental Disabilities Research Reviews, 7*, 3–12.

Schultz, R. T., Grelotti, D. J., Klin, A., Kleinman, J., Van der Gaag, C, Marois, R., & Skudlarski, P. (2003). Autism and movement disturbance. In U. Frith & E. Hill (Eds.), *Autism: Mind and brain* (pp. 267–293). New York, NY: Oxford University Press.

Schultz, R. T., & Robins, D. L. (2005). Functional neuroimaging studies of autism spectrum disorders. In F. R. Volkmar, R. Paul, A. Klin, & D. Cohen (Eds.), *Handbook of autism and pervasive developmental disorders* (Vol. 1, pp. 515–533). Hoboken, NJ: Wiley.

Schumann, C. M., & Amaral, G. (2006). Stereological analysis of amygdala neuron number in autism. *Journal of Neuroscience, 26*, 7674–7679.

Schwartz, S. J., Unger, J. B., Zamboanga, B. L., & Szapocznik, J. (2010). Rethinking the concept of acculturation. *American Psychologist, 65*, 237–251.

Scott, S., & Beidel, D. C. (2011). Selective mutism: An update and suggestions for future research. *Current Psychiatry Reports, 13*, 251–257.

Sedky, K., Bennett, D. S., & Carvalho, K. S. (2014). Attention deficit hyperactivity disorder and sleep disordered breathing in pediatric populations: A meta-analysis. *Sleep Medicine Reviews, 18*, 349–356.

Seligman, M. E. P. (1975). *Helplessness: On depression, development, and death*. San Francisco, CA: Freeman.

Sexton, T. L., & Lebow, J. (2015). *Handbook of family therapy*. New York, NY: Routledge.

Shaahinfar, A., Whitelaw, K. D., & Mansour, K. M. (2015). Update on abusive head trauma. *Current Opinion in Pediatrics, 27*, 308–314.

Shaffer, D., Fisher, P., Lucas, C. P., Dulcan, M. K., & Schwab-Stone, M. E. (2000). The NIMH diagnostic interview schedule for children version IV (DISC-IV). *Journal of the American Academy of Child and Adolescent Psychiatry, 39*, 28–38.

Shah-Kulkarni, S., Ha, M., Kim, B. M., Kim, E., Hong, Y. C., Park, H., . . .Ha, E. H. (2016). Neurodevelopment in early childhood affected by prenatal lead exposure and iron intake. *Medicine, 95*, e2508.

Shanahan, M. E., Zolotor, A. J., Parrish, J. W., Barr, R. G., & Runyan, D. K. (2013). National, regional, and state abusive head trauma: Application of the CDC algorithm. *Pediatrics, 132*, 1546–1553.

Shapiro, D. A., & Shapiro, D. (1982). Meta-analysis of comparative therapy outcome studies. *Psychological Bulletin, 92*, 581–604.

Shapiro, F., & Laliotis, D. (2015). EMDR therapy for trauma-related disorders. In *Evidence based treatments for trauma-related psychological disorders* (pp. 205–228). New York, NY: Springer.

Sharp, W. H., Jaquess, D. L., Morton, J. F., & Herzinger, C. V. (2010). Pediatric feeding disorders: A quantitative synthesis of treatment outcomes. *Child and Family Psychology Review, 13*, 348–365.

Shaw, J., Applegate, B., & Schorr, C. (1996). Twenty-one month follow-up study of school-age children exposed to Hurricane Andrew. *American Journal of Child and Adolescent Psychiatry, 35*, 359–364.

Shaw, P., Stringaris, A., Nigg, J., & Leibenluft, E. (2014). Emotion dysregulation in attention deficit hyperactivity disorder. *American Journal of Psychiatry, 171*, 276–293.

Shaywitz, B. A., Shaywitz, S. E., Blachman, B. A., Pugh, K. R., Fulbright, R. K., Skudlarski, P., . . . Gore, J. C. (2004). Development of left occipitotemporal systems for skilled reading in children after a phonologically-based intervention. *Biological Psychiatry, 55*, 926–933.

Seidler, G., & Wagner, F. (2006). Comparing the efficacy of EMDR and trauma-focused cognitive-behavioral therapy in the treatment of PTSD: A meta-analytic study. *Psychological Medicine, 36*, 1515–1522.

Shea, A., Walsh, C., MacMillan, H., & Steiner, M. (2005). Child maltreatment and HPA axis dysregulation. *Psychoneuroendocrinology, 30*, 162–178.

Shenk, C. E., Putnam, F. W., Rausch, J. R., Peugh, J. L., & Noll, J. G. (2014). A longitudinal study of several potential mediators of the relationship between child maltreatment and posttraumatic stress disorder symptoms. *Development and Psychopathology, 26*, 81–91.

Sher, K. J. (1991). *Children of alcoholics: A critical appraisal of theory and research*. Chicago, IL: University of Chicago Press.

Sher, K. J., Grekin, E. R., & Williams, N. A. (2005). The development of alcohol use disorders. *Annual Review of Clinical Psychology, 1*, 493–523.

Sherman, R., & Dinkmeyer, D. (2014). *Systems of family therapy: An Adlerian integration*. New York, NY: Routledge.

Shevell, M. I. (2008). Global developmental delay and mental retardation or intellectual disability. *Pediatric Clinics of North America, 55*, 1071–1084.

Shevell, M. I. (2010). Present conceptualization of early childhood neurodevelopmental disabilities. *Journal of Child Neurology, 25*, 120–126.

Shevell, M. I., Ashwal, S., Donley, D., Flint, J., Gingold, M., Hirtz, D., . . . Sheth, R. D. (2003). Evaluation of the child with global developmental delay. *Neurology, 60*, 367–380.

Shifrer, D., Muller, C., & Callahan, R. (2011). Disproportionality and learning disabilities. *Journal of Learning Disabilities, 44*, 246–257.

Shiner, R. L., & Tackett, J. L. (2014). Personality disorders in children and adolescents. In E. J. Mash & R. A. Barkley (Eds.), *Child psychopathology* (pp. 848–883). New York, NY: Guilford Press.

Shipley, K., & McAfee, J. (2015). *Assessment in speech-language pathology: A resource manual*. Boston, MA: Nelson Education.

Shirk, S. R., Gudmundsen, G. R., & Burwell, R. A. (2005). Links among attachment-related cognitions and adolescent depressive symptoms. *Journal of Clinical Child and Adolescent Psychology, 34*, 172–181.

Shreeram, S., He, J., Kalaydjian, A., Brothers, S., & Merikangas, K. R. (2009). Prevalence of enuresis and its association with Attention-Deficit/Hyperactivity Disorder among US children. *Journal of the American Academy of Child and Adolescent Psychiatry, 48*, 35–41.

Shumaker, D., & Medoff, D. (2013). Ethical and legal considerations when obtaining informed consent for treating minors of high-conflict divorced or separated parents. *Family Journal, 21*, 318–327.

Sibley, M. H., Ross, J. M., Gnagy, E. M., Dixon, L. J., Conn, B., & Pelham, W. E., Jr. (2013). An intensive summer treatment program for ADHD reduces parent–adolescent conflict. *Journal of Psychopathology and Behavioral Assessment, 35*, 10–19.

Siegel, B., & Ficcaglia, M. (2006). Pervasive developmental disorders. In R. T. Ammerman (Ed.), *Comprehensive handbook of personality and psychopathology* (pp. 254–271). Hoboken, NJ: Wiley.

Sigafoos, J., O'Reilly, M. F., Lancioni, G. E., Lang, R., & Didden, R. (2014). Self-injurious behavior. In P. Sturmey & R. Didden (Eds.), *Evidence-based practice and intellectual disabilities* (pp. 133–162). New York, NY: Wiley.

Sikich, L., Frazier, J. A., McClellan, J., Findling, R. L., Vitiello, B., Ritz, L., . . . Lieberman, J. A. (2008). Double-blind comparison of first- and second-generation antipsychotics in early-onset schizophrenia and schizoaffective disorder. *American Journal of Psychiatry, 165*, 1420–1431.

Sikorski, J. B., & Kuo, A. D. (2015). Legal and ethical issues. In M. K. Dulcan (Ed.), *Dulcan's textbook of child and adolescent psychiatry* (pp. 653–668). Washington, DC: American Psychiatric Publishing.

Silasi, M., Cardenas, I., Kwon, J. Y., Racicot, K., Aldo, P., & Mor, G. (2015). Viral infections during pregnancy. *American Journal of Reproductive Immunology, 73*, 199–213.

Silverman, A. H., & Tarbell, S. (2009). Feeding and vomiting problems in pediatric populations. In M. C. Roberts & R. G. Steele (Eds.), *Handbook of pediatric psychology* (pp. 429–445). New York, NY: Guilford Press.

Simon, D. J. (2016). *School-centered interventions*. Washington, DC: American Psychological Association.

Simon, P., & Olson, S. (2014). *Building capacity to reduce bullying*. Washington, DC: National Academies Press.

Simons, A. D., Rohde, P., Kennard, B. D., & Robins, M. (2005). Relapse and recurrence prevention in the treatment for adolescents with depression study. *Cognitive and Behavioral Practice, 12*, 240–251.

Simsek, S., Uysal, C., Kaplan, I., Yuksel, T., & Aktas, H. (2015). BDNF and cortisol levels in children with or without post-traumatic stress disorder after sustaining sexual abuse. *Psychoneuroendocrinology, 56*, 45–51.

Singh, M. K., Ketter, T. A., & Chang, K. D. (2010). Atypical antipsychotics for acute manic and mixed episodes in children and adolescents with bipolar disorder. *Drugs, 70*, 433–442.

Skarphedinsson, G., Weidle, B., Thomsen, P. H., Dahl, K., Torp, N. C., Nissen, J. B., . . . Ivarsson, T. (2015). Continued cognitive-behavior therapy versus sertraline for children and adolescents with obsessive–compulsive disorder that were non-responders to cognitive-behavior therapy. *European Child and Adolescent Psychiatry, 24*, 591–602.

Skinner, B. F. (1974). *About behaviorism*. New York, NY: Knopf.

Smile, S., & Anagnostou, E. (2015). Pharmacotherapy in autism spectrum disorder. In E. Anagnostou & J. Brian (Eds.), *Clinician's manual on ASD* (pp. 43–62). New York, NY: Springer.

Smink, F. R., Van Hoeken, D., & Hoek, H. W. (2012). Epidemiology of eating disorders: Incidence, prevalence and mortality rates. *Current Psychiatry Reports, 14*, 406–414.

Smink, F. R., van Hoeken, D., & Hoek, H. W. (2013). Epidemiology, course, and outcome of eating disorders. *Current Opinion in Psychiatry, 26*, 543–548.

Smith, I. M., & Bryson, S. E. (2015). Behavioral and educational interventions. In E. Anagnostou & J. Brian (Eds.), *Clinician's manual on ASD* (pp. 63–76). New York, NY: Springer.

Smith, I. M., Flanagan, H. E., Garon, N., & Bryson, S. E. (2015). Effectiveness of community-based early intervention based on pivotal response treatment. *Journal of Autism and Developmental Disorders, 45*, 1858–1872.

Smith, J. D., Dishion, T. J., Shaw, D. S., Wilson, M. N., Winter, C. C., & Patterson, G. R. (2014). Coercive family process and early-onset conduct problems from age 2 to school entry. *Development and Psychopathology, 26*, 917–932.

Smith, M. L., & Glass, G. V. (1977). Meta-analysis of psychotherapy outcome studies. *American Psychologist, 32*, 752–760.

Smith, P., Yule, W., Perrin, S., Tranah, T. Dalgeish, T., & Clark, D. M. (2007). A randomized controlled trial of cognitive behavior therapy for PTSD in children and adolescents. *Journal of the American Academy of Child and Adolescent Psychiatry, 46*, 1–51–1061.

Smith, P. J., Humiston, S. G., Marcuse, E. K., Zhao, Z., Dorell, C. G., Howes, C., & Hibbs, B. (2011). Parental delay or refusal of vaccine doses, childhood vaccination coverage at 24 months of age, and the Health Belief Model. *Public Health Reports, 126S2*, 135–146.

Smith, T., Groen, A. D., & Wynn, J. W. (2000). Randomized trial of intensive early intervention for children with pervasive developmental disorder. *American Journal on Mental Retardation, 105*, 269–285.

Smith-Bell, M., & Winslade, W. J. (2008). Privacy, confidentiality, and privilege in psychotherapeutic relationships. In D. N. Bersoff (Ed.), *Ethical conflicts in psychology* (pp. 151–155). Washington, DC: American Psychological Association.

Smolak, L., Striegel-Moore, R. H., & Levine, M. P. (2013). *The developmental psychopathology of eating disorders*. New York, NY: Routledge.

Smolkowski, K., & Cummings, K. D. (2016). Evaluation of the DIBELS diagnostic system for the selection of native and proficient english speakers at risk of reading difficulties. *Journal of Psychoeducational Assessment, 34*, 103–118.

Smyke, A. T., Dumitrescu, A., & Zeanah, C. H. (2002). Attachment disturbances in young children. *Journal of the American Academy of Child and Adolescent Psychiatry, 41*, 972–982.

Smyke, A. T., Zeanah, C. H., Fox, N. A., Nelson, C. A., & Guthrie, D. (2010). Placement in foster care enhances quality of attachment among young institutionalized children. *Child Development, 81*, 212–223.

Snorrason, I., Belleau, E. L., & Woods, D. W. (2012). How related are hair pulling disorder (trichotillomania) and skin picking disorder? A review of evidence for comorbidity, similarities and shared etiology. *Clinical Psychology Review, 32*, 618–629.

Snyder, J., Reid, J., & Patterson, G. (2003). A social learning model of child and adolescent antisocial behavior. In B. B. Lahey, T. E. Moffitt, & A. Caspi (Eds.), *Causes of conduct disorder and juvenile delinquency* (pp. 27–48). New York, NY: Guilford Press.

Snyder, J. J. (2016). Coercive family process and the development of child social behavior and self-regulation. In T. J. Dishion & J. J. Snyder (Eds.), *Oxford handbook of coercive relationship dynamics* (pp. 101–113). Oxford, England: Oxford University Press.

Snyder, J. J., & Dishion, T. J. (2016). Coercive social process. In T. J. Dishion & J. J. Snyder (Eds.), *Oxford handbook of coercive relationship dynamics* (pp. 1–6). Oxford, England: Oxford University Press.

Snyder, J. J., Schrepferman, L. P., Bullard, L., McEachern, A. D., & Patterson, G. R. (2012). Covert antisocial behavior, peer deviancy training, parenting processes, and sex differences in the development of antisocial behavior during childhood. *Development and Psychopathology, 24*, 1117–1138.

Snyder, J.J., Schrepferman, L., Oeser, J., Patterson, G., Stoolmiller, M., Johnson, K., & Snyder, A. (2005). Deviancy training and association with deviant peers in young children. *Development and Psychopathology, 17*, 397–413.

Snyderman, M., & Rothman, S. (1987). Survey of expert opinion on intelligence and aptitude testing. *American Psychologist, 42*, 137–144.

Society of Clinical Child and Adolescent Psychology. (2016). *Evidence-based mental health treatment for children and adolescents*. Retrieved August 22, 2016, from http://effectivechildtherapy.org

Solanto, M. V., Wasserstein, J., Marks, D. J., & Mitchell, K. J. (2013). Diagnosis of ADHD in adults: What is the appropriate *DSM-5* symptom threshold for hyperactivity-impulsivity? *Journal of Attention Disorders, 16*, 631–634.

Solso, S., Xu, R., Proudfoot, J., Hagler, D. J., Campbell, K., Venkatraman, V., . . . Courchesne, E. (2017). Diffusion tensor imaging provides evidence of possible axonal overconnectivity in frontal lobes in autism spectrum disorder toddlers. *Biological Psychiatry, 79*, 676–684.

Sonuga-Barke, E. J. S., Brandeis, D., Cortese, S., Daley, D., Ferrin, M., Holtmann, M., . . . European ADHD Guidelines Group. (2013). Nonpharmacological interventions for ADHD. *American Journal of Psychiatry, 170*, 275–289.

Southam-Gerow, M. A., & Prinstein, M. J. (2014). The evolution of the evaluation of psychological treatments for children and adolescents. *Journal of Clinical Child and Adolescent Psychology, 43*, 1–6.

Spence, S. H., March, S., Vigerland, S., & Serlachius, E. (2016). Internet-based therapies for child and adolescent emotional and behavioral problems. In *Guided Internet-based treatments in psychiatry* (pp. 197–217). New York, NY: Springer.

Spencer, D., Marshall, J., Post, B., Kulakodlu, M., Newschaffer, C., Dennen, T., . . . Jain, A. (2014). Psychotropic medication use and polypharmacy in children with autism spectrum disorders. *Pediatrics, 132*, 833–840.

Spencer, T., Heiligenstein, J. H., Biederman, J., Faries, D. E., Kratochvil, C. J., Conners, C. K., & Potter, W. Z. (2002). Results from 2 proof-of-concept, placebo-controlled studies of atomoxetine in children with attention-deficit/hyperactivity disorder. *Journal of Clinical Psychiatry, 63*, 1140.

Spencer, T. J., Biederman, J., & Wilens, T. E. (2015). Medications used for attention-deficit/hyperactivity disorder. In M. K. Dulcan (Eds.), *Dulcan's textbook of child and adolescent psychiatry* (pp. 709–735). Washington, DC: American Psychiatric Publishing.

Spitz, R. A. (1965). *The first year of life: A psychoanalytic study of normal and deviant development of object relations.* Oxford, England: International Universities Press.

Spitz, R. A., & Wolf, K. M. (1946). Anaclitic depression. *Psychoanalytic Study of the Child, 2*, 313–342.

Sroufe, L. A. (1997). Psychopathology as an outcome of development. *Development and Psychopathology, 9*, 251–268.

Sroufe, L. A., & Waters, B. (1977). Attachment as an organizational construct. *Child Development, 49*, 1184–1199.

Srour, M., & Shevell, M. (2014). Genetics and the investigation of developmental delay/intellectual disability. *Archives of Disease in Childhood, 99*, 386–389.

Stark, K. D., Hoke, J., Ballatore, M., Valdez, C., Scammaca, N., & Griffin, J. (2005). Treatment of child and adolescent depressive disorders. In E. D. Hibbs & P. S. Jensen (Eds.), *Psychosocial treatments for child and adolescent disorders* (pp. 239–265). Washington, DC: American Psychological Association.

Stark, K. D., & Kendall, P. C. (1996). *Treating depressed children.* Ardmore, PA: Workbook.

Starkey, P., & Cooper, R. G. (1980). Perception of number by human infants. *Science, 210*, 1033–1035.

Steedly, K., Dragoo, K., Arafeh, S., & Luke, S. D. (2008). Effective mathematics instruction. *Evidence for Education, 3*, 1–12.

Steiger, A. E., Allemand, M., Robins, R. W., & Fend, H. A. (2014). Low and decreasing self-esteem during adolescence predict adult depression two decades later. *Journal of Personality and Social Psychology, 106*, 325–338.

Stein, D. J., Craske, M. G., Friedman, M. J., & Phillips, K. A. (2011). Meta-structure issues for the *DSM-5. Current Psychiatry Reports, 13*, 248–250.

Stein, D. J., Fineberg, N. A., Bienvenu, O. J., Denys, D., Lochner, C., Nestadt, D., . . . Phillips, K. A. (2010). Should OCD be classified as an anxiety disorder? *Depression and Anxiety, 27*, 495–506.

Stein, D. J., Grant, J. E., Franklin, M. E., Keuthen, N., Lochner, C., Singer, H. S., & Woods, D. W. (2010). Trichotillomania (hair pulling disorder), skin picking disorder, and stereotypic movement disorder: Toward *DSM-5. Depression and Anxiety, 27*, 611–626.

Stein, D. J., Keating, J., Zar, H. J., & Hollander, E. (1994). A survey of the phenomenology and pharmacotherapy of compulsive and impulsive-aggressive symptoms in Prader-Willi syndrome. *Journal of Neuropsychiatry and Clinical Neurosciences, 6*, 23–29.

Stein, D. J., Phillips, K. A., Bolton, D., Fulford, K. W. M., Sadler, J. Z., & Kendler, K. S. (2010). What is a mental/psychiatric disorder? *Psychological Medicine, 40*, 1759–1765.

Stemple, J. C., & Fry, L. T. (2010). *Voice therapy.* San Diego, CA: Plural.

Stenseng, F., Belsky, J., Skalicka, V., & Wichstrøm, L. (2016). Peer rejection and attention deficit hyperactivity disorder symptoms. *Child Development, 87*, 365–373.

Stephenson, J., & Limbrick, L. (2015). A review of the use of touchscreen mobile devices by people with developmental disabilities. *Journal of Autism and Developmental Disorders, 45*, 3777–3791.

Stevens, E. A., & Prinstein, J. (2005). Peer contagion of depressogenic attributional styles among adolescents. *Journal of Abnormal Child Psychology, 33*, 25–37.

Stevens, L. J., Kuczek, T., Burgess, J. R., Hurt, E., & Arnold, L. E. (2011). Dietary sensitivities and ADHD symptoms. *Clinical Pediatrics, 50*, 279–293.

Stevens, S. J., & Morral, A. R. (2014). *Adolescent substance abuse treatment in the United States.* New York, NY: Routledge.

Stevenson, R. E., Schwartz, C. E., & Rogers, R. C. (2012). *Atlas of X-linked intellectual disability syndromes.* Oxford, England: Oxford University Press.

Stice, E. (2016). Interactive and mediational etiologic models of eating disorder onset. *Annual Review of Clinical Psychology, 12*, 359–381.

Stice, E., Becker, C. B., & Yokum, S. (2014). Eating disorder prevention. *International Journal of Eating Disorders, 46*, 478–485.

Stice, E., Kirz, J., & Borbely, C. (2002). Disentangling adolescent substance use and problem use within a clinical sample. *Journal of Adolescent Research, 17*, 122–142.

Stice, E., Marti, C. N., & Rohde, P. (2013). Prevalence, incidence, impairment, and course of the proposed DSM-5 eating disorder diagnoses in an 8-year prospective community study of young women. *Journal of Abnormal Psychology, 122*, 445–457.

Stiegler, L. N. (2005). Understanding pica behavior. *Focus of Autism and Other Developmental Disabilities, 20*, 27–38.

Stiffler, M. C., & Dever, B. V. (2015). *Mental health screening at school.* New York, NY: Springer.

Stifter, C., & Dollar, J. (2016). Temperament and developmental psychopathology. In D. Cicchetti (Ed.), *Developmental psychopathology* (Vol. 4, pp. 546–607). New York, NY: Wiley.

Stock, M. L., Gibbons, F. X., Gerrard, M., Houlihan, A. E., Weng, C. Y., Lorenz, F. O., & Simons, R. L. (2013). Racial identification, racial composition, and substance use vulnerability among African American adolescents and young adults. *Health Psychology, 32*, 237.

Stoltenborgh, M., Bakermans-Kranenburg, M. J., & van IJzendoorn, M. H. (2013). The neglect of child neglect: A meta-analytic review of the prevalence of neglect. *Social Psychiatry and Psychiatric Epidemiology, 48*, 345–355.

Stover, C. S., Zhou, Y., Kiselica, A., Leve, L. D., Neiderhiser, J. M., Shaw, D. S., . . . Reiss, D. (2016). Marital hostility, hostile parenting, and child aggression: Associations from toddlerhood to school age. *Journal of the American Academy of Child & Adolescent Psychiatry, 55*, 235–242.

Strang, J. F. (2016). Scope and prevalence of the problem. In J. L. Matson (Ed.), *Comorbid conditions among children with autism* (pp. 27–42). New York, NY: Springer.

Stringaris, A. (2011). Irritability in children and adolescents: A challenge for *DSM-5. European Child and Adolescent Psychiatry, 20*, 61–66.

Stringaris, A., Baroni, A., Haimm, C., Brotman, M., Lowe, C. H., Myers, F., . . . Leibenluft, E. (2010). Pediatric bipolar disorder versus severe mood dysregulation. *Journal of the American Academy of Child and Adolescent Psychiatry, 49*, 397–405.

Stringaris, A., Cohen, P., Pine, D. S., & Leibenluft, E. (2009). Adult outcomes of adolescent irritability: A 20-year community follow-up. *American Journal of Psychiatry, 166*, 1048–1054.

Stringaris, A., & Goodman, R. (2009). Three dimensions of oppositionality in youth. *Journal of Child Psychology and Psychiatry, 50*, 216–223.

Strober, M., Freeman, R., Lampert, C., Diamond, J., & Kaye, W. (2000). Controlled family study of anorexia nervosa and bulimia nervosa. *American Journal of Psychiatry, 157*, 393–401.

Strohl, M. P. (2011). Bradley's benzedrine studies on children with behavioral disorders. *The Yale Journal of Biology and Medicine, 84*, 27–33.

Stromme, P., & Hagberg, G. (2000). Etiology in severe and mild mental retardation. *Developmental Medicine and Child Neurology, 42*, 76–86.

Stromme, P., & Magnus, P. (2000). Correlations between socioeconomic status, IQ and etiology in mental retardation. *Social Psychiatry and Psychiatric Epidemiology, 35*, 12–18.

Stuber, J., Galea, S., Pfefferbaum, B., Vandivere, S., Moore, K., & Fairbrother, G. (2005). Behavior problems in New York City's children after the September 11, 2001, terrorist attacks. *American Journal of Orthopsychiatry, 75,* 190–200.

Sturmey, P. (2014a). Adaptive behavior. In P. Sturmey & R. Didden (Eds.), *Evidence-based practice and intellectual disabilities* (pp. 29–60). New York, NY: Wiley.

Sturmey, P. (2014b). Maladaptive behavior. In P. Sturmey & R. Didden (Eds.), *Evidence-based practice and intellectual disabilities* (pp. 62–84). New York, NY: Wiley.

Sturmey, P., & Didden, R. (2014). Mood disorders. In P. Sturmey & R. Didden (Eds.), *Evidence-based practice and intellectual disabilities* (pp. 261–279). New York, NY: Wiley.

Sturmey, P., Lindsay, W. R., Vause, T., & Neil, N. (2014). Anxiety disorders. In P. Sturmey & R. Didden (Eds.), *Evidence-based practice and intellectual disabilities* (pp. 235–260). New York, NY: Wiley.

Sturmey, P., & Williams, D. E. (2016). *Pica in individuals with developmental disabilities.* New York, NY: Springer.

Substance Abuse and Mental Health Services Administration. (2007). *Results from the National Survey on Drug Use and Health.* Rockville, MD: Author.

Sullivan, H. S. (1953). *The interpersonal theory of psychiatry.* New York, NY: Norton.

Sullivan, K., Hooper, S., & Hatton, D. (2007). Behavioral equivalents of anxiety in children with Fragile X syndrome. *Journal of Intellectual Disability Research, 51,* 54–65.

Sullivan, J. R., Ramirez, E., Rae, W. A., Razo, N. P., & George, C. A. (2010). Factors contributing to breaking confidentiality with adolescent clients. In D. N. Bersoff (Ed.), *Ethical conflicts in psychology* (pp. 197–202). Washington, DC: American Psychological Association.

Subotnik, K. L., Nuechterlein, K. H., Ventura, J., Gitlin, M. J., Marder, S., Mintz, J., . . . Singh, I. R. (2011). Risperidone nonadherence and return of positive symptoms in the early course of schizophrenia. *American Journal of Psychiatry, 168,* 286–292.

Sulik, L. R., & Sarvet, B. (2015). Collaborating with primary care. In M. K. Dulcan (Ed.), *Dulcan's textbook of child and adolescent psychiatry* (pp. 245–276). Washington, DC: American Psychiatric Publishing.

Sumner, C. R., Schuh, K. J., Sutton, V. K., Lipetz, R., & Kelsey, D. K. (2006). Placebo-controlled study of the effects of atomoxetine on bladder control in children with nocturnal enuresis. *Journal of Child and Adolescent Psychopharmacology, 16,* 699–711.

Swanson, H. L. (2015). Cognitive strategy interventions improve word problem solving and working memory in children with math disabilities. *Frontiers in Psychology, 6,* 1099.

Swanson, H. L., Lussier, C. M., & Orosco, M. J. (2015). Cognitive strategies, working memory, and growth in word problem solving in children with math difficulties. *Journal of Learning Disabilities, 48,* 339–358.

Swanson, H. L., & Stomel, D. (2012). Learning disabilities and memory. In B. Wong & D. Butler (Eds.), *Learning about learning disabilities* (pp. 27–57). New York, NY: Elsevier.

Swanson, J. M., Kraemer, H. C., Hinshaw, S. P., Arnold, L. E., Conners, C. K., Abikoff, H. B., . . . Wu, M. (2001). Clinical relevance of the primary findings of the MTA. *Journal of the American Academy of Child and Adolescent Psychiatry, 40,* 168–179.

Swanson, S. A., Crow, S. J., Le Grange, D., Swendsen, J., & Merikangas, K. R. (2011). Prevalence and correlates of eating disorders in adolescents. *Archives of General Psychiatry, 68,* 714–723.

Swedo, S. E., Seidlitz, J., Kovacevic, M., Latimer, M. E., Hommer, R., Lougee, L., & Grant, P. (2015). Clinical presentation of pediatric autoimmune neuropsychiatric disorders associated with streptococcal infections in research and community settings. *Journal of Child and Adolescent Psychopharmacology, 25,* 26–30.

Swineford, L. B., Thurm, A., Baird, G., Wetherby, A. M., & Swedo, S. (2015). Social (pragmatic) communication disorder: A research review of this new *DSM-5* diagnostic category. *Journal of Neurodevelopmental Disorders, 6,* 1–8.

Szymanski, L. S., & Kaplan, L. C. (2006). Mental retardation. In M. K. Dulcan & J. M. Weiner (Eds.), *Essentials of child and adolescent psychiatry* (pp. 121–152). Washington, DC: American Psychiatric Publishing.

Tackett, J. L., Krueger, R. F., Iacono, W. G., & McGue, M. (2005). Symptom-based subfactors of DSM-defined conduct disorder: Evidence for etiologic distinctions. *Journal of Abnormal Psychology, 114,* 483–487.

Tamm, L., Garner, A. A., Loren, R. E., Epstein, J. N., Vaughn, A. J., Ciesielski, H. A., & Becker, S. P. (2016). Slow sluggish cognitive tempo symptoms are associated with poorer academic performance in children with ADHD. *Psychiatry Research, 242,* 251–259.

Tamm, L., Menon, V., & Reiss, A. L. (2006). Parietal attentional system aberrations during target detection in adolescents with attention deficit hyperactivity disorder. *American Journal of Psychiatry, 163,* 1033–1043.

Tanguay, P. E., & Lohr, W. D. (2015). Autism spectrum disorders. In M. K. Dulcan (Ed.), *Dulcan's textbook of child and adolescent psychiatry* (pp. 135–155). Washington, DC: American Psychiatric Publishing.

Tannock, R. (2013). Rethinking ADHD and LD in *DSM-5. Journal of Learning Disabilities, 46,* 5–25.

Tassé, M. J., Schalock, R. L., Balboni, G., Bersani, H., Jr., Borthwick-Duffy, S. A., Spreat, S., . . . Zhang, D. (2012). The construct of adaptive behavior. *American Journal on Intellectual and Developmental Disabilities, 117,* 291–303.

Taylor, E., & Sonuga-Barke, E. (2010). Disorders of attention and activity. In M. Rutter (Ed.), *Rutter's child and adolescent psychiatry* (pp. 521–542). Malden, MA: Blackwell.

Taylor, L. E., Swerdfeger, A. L., & Eslick, G. D. (2014). Vaccines are not associated with autism: An evidence-based meta-analysis of case-control and cohort studies. *Vaccine, 32,* 3623–3629.

Taylor, R. D., & Wang, M. C. (2013). *Social and emotional adjustment and family relations in ethnic minority families.* New York, NY: Routledge.

Taylor, S. (2014). *Anxiety sensitivity: Theory, research, and treatment of the fear of anxiety.* New York, NY: Routledge.

Temple, C. M., & Sherwood, S. (2002). Representation and retrieval of arithmetic facts: Developmental difficulties. *Quarterly Journal of Experimental Psychology, 55,* 733–752.

Terr, L. (2015). Individual psychotherapy. In M. K. Dulcan (Ed.), *Dulcan's textbook of child and adolescent psychiatry* (pp. 849–874). Washington, DC: American Psychiatric Publishing.

Tervo, R. C. (2012). Developmental and behavior problems predict parenting stress in young children with global delay. *Journal of Child Neurology, 27,* 291–296.

Thapar, A., Cooper, M., Eyre, O., & Langley, K. (2013). What have we learnt about the causes of ADHD? *Journal of Child Psychology and Psychiatry, 54,* 3–16.

Therrien, W. J., Wickstrom, K., & Jones, K. (2006). Effect of a combined repeated reading and question generation intervention on reading achievement. *Learning Disabilities Research and Practice, 21,* 89–97.

Thomas, C. R. (2015). Oppositional defiant disorder and conduct disorder. In M. K. Dulcan (Ed.), *Dulcan's textbook of child and adolescent psychiatry* (pp. 195–217). Washington, DC: American Psychiatric Publishing.

Thomas, P., Zahorodny, W., Peng, B., Kim, S., Jani, N., Halperin, W., & Brimacombe, M. (2012). The association of autism diagnosis with socioeconomic status. *Autism, 16,* 201–213.

Thomeer, M. L., Lopata, C., Volker, M. A., Toomey, J. A., Lee, G. K., Smerbeck, A. M., . . . Smith, R. A. (2012). Randomized clinical trial replication of a psychosocial treatment for children with high-functioning autism spectrum disorders. *Psychology in the Schools, 49,* 942–954.

Thompson, T., & Caruso, M. (2002). Self-injury: Knowing what we're looking for. In S. R. Schroeder, M. L. Oster-Granite, & T. Thompson (Eds.), *Self-injurious behavior* (pp. 1–21). Washington, DC: American Psychological Association.

Tirosch, E., & Jaffe, M. (2011). Global developmental delay and mental retardation. *Developmental Disabilities Research Reviews, 17*, 85–92.

Tizard, B., & Hodges, J. (1978). The effect of early institutional rearing on the development of eight year old children. *Journal of Child Psychology and Psychiatry, 19*, 99–118.

Tizard, B., & Rees, J. (1974). A comparison of the effects of adoption, restoration to the natural mother, and continued institutionalization on the cognitive development of four-year-old children. *Child Development, 45*, 92–99.

Tizard, B., & Rees, J. (1976). The effect of early institutional rearing on the behavior problems and affectional relationships of four-year-old children. *Journal of Child Psychology and Psychiatry, 16*, 61–73.

Tolan, P. H. (2016). Community violence exposure and developmental psychopathology. In D. Cicchetti (Ed.), *Developmental psychopathology* (Vol. 4, pp. 43–85). New York, NY: Wiley.

Toll, S. W. M., van der Ven, S. H. G., Kroesbergen, E. H., & van Luit, J. E. H. (2011). Executive functions as predictors of math learning disabilities. *Journal of Learning Disabilities, 44*, 521–532.

Toolan, J. M. (1962). Suicide and suicidal attempts in children and adolescents. *American Journal of Psychiatry, 118*, 719–724.

Topitzes, J., Mersky, J. P., & Reynolds, A. J. (2012). From child maltreatment to violent offending: An examination of mixed-gender and gender-specific models. *Journal of Interpersonal Violence, 27*, 2322–2347.

Toth, K., deLacy, N., & King, B. H. (2015). Intellectual disability. In M. K. Dulcan (Ed.), *Dulcan's textbook of child and adolescent psychiatry*. Washington, DC: American Psychiatric Publishing.

Towbin, K. E. (2015). Tic disorders. In M. K. Dulcan (Ed.), *Dulcan's textbook of child and adolescent psychiatry* (pp. 461–478). Washington, DC: American Psychiatric Publishing.

Treatment for Adolescents With Depression Study Team. (2004). Fluoxetine, cognitive-behavioral therapy, and their combination for adolescents with depression: Treatment for Adolescents With Depression Study (TADS) randomized controlled trial. *JAMA: Journal of the American Medical Association, 292*, 807–820.

Trierweiler, S. J., & Stricker, G. (2013). *The scientific practice of professional psychology*. New York, NY: Springer.

Tucker, J. S., Ellickson, P. L., Orlando, M., Martino, S. C., & Klein, D. J. (2005). Substance use trajectories from early adolescence to emerging adulthood. *Journal of Drug Issues, 35*, 307–332.

Turecki, G., & Brent, D. A. (2016). Suicide and suicidal behaviour. *The Lancet, 387*, 1227–1239.

Turkheimer, E., & Horn, E. E. (2015). Interactions between SES and components of variation in cognitive ability. In D. Finkel (Ed.), *Behavior genetics of cognition across the lifespan* (pp. 41–68). New York, NY: Springer.

United Nations Children's Fund. (2016). *Orphans*. Washington, DC: Author.

US Food and Drug Administration. (2012). *Pediatric provisions in the Food and Drug Administration Safety and Innovation Act (FDASIA)*. Silver Spring, MD: Author.

van der Stouwe, T., Asscher, J. J., Stams, G. J. J., Deković, M., & van der Laan, P. H. (2014). The effectiveness of Multisystemic Therapy (MST): A meta-analysis. *Clinical Psychology Review, 34*, 468–481.

Van Dommelen, P., Kamphuis, M., van Leerdam, F., deWilde, J. A., Rijpstra, A., Campagne, A. E., & Verkerk, P. H. (2009). The short- and long-term effects of simple behavioral interventions for nocturnal enuresis in young children. *Journal of Pediatrics, 154*, 662–666.

van Empelen, R., Jennekens-Schinkel, A., Buskens, E., Helders, P. J. M., & van Nieuwenhuizen, O. (2004). Functional consequences of hemispherectomy. *Brain, 127*, 2071–2079.

van Ewijk, H., Heslenfeld, D. J., Zwiers, M. P., Faraone, S. V., Luman, M., Hartman, C. A., . . . Oosterlaan, J. (2014). Different mechanisms of white matter abnormalities in attention-deficit/hyperactivity disorder. *Journal of the American Academy of Child and Adolescent Psychiatry, 53*, 790–799.

van Ewijk, H., & Oosterlaan, J. (2015). Attention deficit hyperactivity disorder. In P. H. Blaney (Ed.), *Oxford textbook of psychopathology* (pp. 513–529). Oxford, England: Oxford University Press.

Van Hecke, A.V., Oswald, T., & Mundy, P. (2016). Joint attention and the social phenotype of autism spectrum disorder. In D. Cicchetti (Ed.), *Developmental psychopathology* (Vol. 3, pp. 116–151). New York, NY: Wiley.

van Herzeele, C., De Bruyne, P., De Bruyne, E., & Walle, J. V. (2015). Challenging factors for enuresis treatment. *Journal of Pediatric Urology, 11*, 308–313.

van IJzendoorn, M. H., & Bakermans-Kranenburg, M. J. (2014). Confined quest for continuity: The categorical versus continuous nature of attachment. *Monographs of the Society for Research in Child Development, 79*, 157–167.

van IJzendoorn, M., Palacios, P., Sonuga-Barke, E. J. S., Gunnar, M. R., Vorria, P., McCall, R. B., . . . Juffer, F. (2011). Children in institutional care. *Monographs for the Society for Research in Child Development, 76*, 8–30.

van Lang, N. D. J., Ferdinand, R. F., & Verhulst, F. C. (2007). Predictors of future depression in early and late adolescence. *Journal of Affective Disorders, 97*, 137–144.

van Lier, P. A., Vitaro, F., Barker, E. D., Brendgen, M., Tremblay, R. E., & Boivin, M. (2012). Peer victimization, poor academic achievement, and the link between childhood externalizing and internalizing problems. *Child Development, 83*, 1775–1788.

Van Meter, A. R., Burke, C., Kowatch, R. A., Findling, R. L., & Youngstrom, E. A. (2016). Ten-year updated meta-analysis of the clinical characteristics of pediatric mania and hypomania. *Bipolar Disorders, 18*, 19–32.

Van Meter, A. R., Youngstrom, E. A., Demeter, C., & Findling, R. L. (2012). Examining the validity of cyclothymic disorder in a youth sample. *Journal of Abnormal Child Psychology, 41*, 367–378.

Van Meter, A. R., Youngstrom, E. A., & Findling, R. L. (2012). Cyclothymic disorder: A critical review. *Clinical Psychology Review, 32*, 229–243.

van Ryzin, M. J., Fosco, G. M., & Dishion, T. J. (2012). Family and peer predictors of substance use from early adolescence to early adulthood. *Addictive Behaviors, 37*, 1314–1324.

van Schagen, A. M., Lancee, J., de Groot, I. W., Spoormaker, V. I., & van den Bout, J. (2015). Imagery rehearsal therapy in addition to treatment as usual for patients with diverse psychiatric diagnoses suffering from nightmares. *Journal of Clinical Psychiatry, 76*, 1105–1113.

van Schooneveld, M. M., Braun, K. P., van Rijen, P. C., van Nieuwenhuizen, O., & Jennekens-Schinkel, A. (2016). The spectrum of long-term cognitive and functional outcome after hemispherectomy in childhood. *European Journal of Pediatric Neurology, 20*, 376–384.

van Vugt, E., Lanctôt, N., Paquette, G., Collin-Vézina, D., & Lemieux, A. (2014). Girls in residential care: From child maltreatment to trauma-related symptoms in emerging adulthood. *Child Abuse and Neglect, 38*, 114–122.

Vandermeer, J., Beamish, W., Milford, T., & Lang, W. (2015). iPad-presented social stories for young children with autism. *Developmental Neurorehabilitation, 18*, 75–81.

Vaz, P. C. M., & Piazza, C. C. (2011). Behavioral approaches to the management of pediatric feeding problems. In A. Southall & C. Martin (Eds.), *Feeding problems in children* (pp. 53–73). Oxon, England: Radcliffe.

Velasquez, M. M., Crouch, C., Stephens, N. S., & DiClemente, C. C. (2015). *Group treatment for substance abuse: A stages-of-change therapy manual*. New York, NY: Guilford Press.

Verhoeven, L., & Vermeer, A. (2006). Literacy achievement of children with intellectual disabilities and differing linguistic backgrounds. *Journal of Intellectual Disability Research, 50,* 725–738.

Virues-Ortega, J., Julio, F. M., & Pastor-Barriuso, R. (2013). The TEACCH program for children and adults with autism: A meta-analysis of intervention studies. *Clinical Psychology Review, 33,* 940–953.

Visser, S. N. (2016). National and state-specific patterns of attention deficit/hyperactivity disorder treatment among insured children aged 2–5 years. *Morbidity and Mortality Weekly Report, 65,* 443–450.

Visser, S. N., Bitsko, R. H., Danielson, M. L., Ghandour, R. M., Blumberg, S. J., Schieve, L. A., . . . Cuffe, S. P. (2015). Treatment of attention deficit/hyperactivity disorder among children with special health care needs. *Journal of Pediatrics, 166,* 1423–1430.

Visser, S. N., Danielson, M., & Bitsko, R. (2014). Trends in the parent-report of health care provider-diagnosis and medication treatment for ADHD. *Journal of the American Academy of Child and Adolescent Psychiatry, 53,* 34–46.

Vocks, S., Tuschen-Caffier, B., Pietrowsky, R., Rustenbach, S. J., Kersting, A., & Herpertz, S. (2010). Meta-analysis of the effectiveness of psychological and pharmacological treatments for binge eating disorder. *International Journal of Eating Disorders, 43,* 205–217.

Volkmar, F. R., & Pelphrey, K. (2015). Autism and autism spectrum disorders. In F. R. Volkmar (Ed.), *Handbook of autism and pervasive developmental disorders* (pp. 530–539). New York, NY: Wiley.

Volkmar, F. R., Reichow, B., Westphal, A., & Mandell, D. S. (2015). Autism and the autism spectrum. In F. R. Volkmar (Ed.), *Handbook of autism and pervasive developmental disorders* (pp. 3–26). New York, NY: Wiley.

Volkow, N. D., Baler, R. D., Compton, W. M., & Weiss, S. R. (2014). Adverse health effects of marijuana use. *New England Journal of Medicine, 370,* 2219–2227.

Volkow, N. D., Swanson, J. M., Evins, A. E., DeLisi, L. E., Meier, M. H., Gonzalez, R., . . . Baler, R. (2016). Effects of cannabis use on human behavior, including cognition, motivation, and psychosis. *JAMA Psychiatry, 73,* 292–297.

Vollmer, T. R., Bosch, A. B., Ringdahl, J. E., & Rapp, J. T. (2014). Stereotypic behavior. In P. Sturmey & R. Didden (Eds.), *Evidence-based practice and intellectual disabilities* (pp. 163–197). New York, NY: Wiley.

Volpe, J. J. (2008). Brain injury in premature infants. *Lancet Neurology, 8,* 110–124.

von Gontard, A. (2011). Elimination disorders: A critical comment on *DSM-5* proposals. *European Child and Adolescent Psychiatry, 20,* 83–88.

von Ranson, K. M., & Wallace, L. M. (2014). Eating disorders. In E. J. Mash & R. A. Barkley (Eds.), *Child psychopathology* (pp. 801–841). New York, NY: Routledge.

von Stumm, S., & Plomin. (2015). Socioeconomic status and the growth of intelligence from infancy through adolescence. *Intelligence, 48,* 30–36.

Voriadaki, T., Simic, M., Espie, J., & Eisler, I. (2015). Intensive multi-family therapy for adolescent anorexia nervosa: Adolescents' and parents' day-to-day experiences. *Journal of Family Therapy, 37,* 5–23.

Vorstman, J. A., Breetvelt, E. J., Duijff, S. N., Eliez, S., Schneider, M., Jalbrzikowski, M., . . . International Consortium on Brain and Behavior in 22q11.2 Deletion Syndrome. (2015). Cognitive decline preceding the onset of psychosis in patients with 22q11.2 deletion syndrome. *JAMA Psychiatry, 72,* 377–385.

Vygotsky, L. S. (1978). *Mind in society: The development of higher psychological processes.* Cambridge, MA: Harvard University Press.

Waaktaar, T., Borge, A. I. H., Fundingsrud, H. P., Christie, H. J., & Torgersen, S. (2004). The role of stressful life events in the development of depressive symptoms in adolescence. *Journal of Adolescence, 27,* 153–163.

Wade, T. J., & Cairney, J. (2006). Sociological contributions. In R. T. Ammerman (Ed.), *Comprehensive handbook of personality and psychopathology* (Vol. 3, pp. 44–63). Hoboken, NJ: Wiley.

Wadsworth, M. E., Evans, G. W., Grant, K., Carter, J. S., & Duffy, S. (2016). Poverty and the development of psychopathology. In D. Cicchetti (Ed.), *Developmental psychopathology* (Vol. 4, pp. 136–179). New York, NY: Wiley.

Wagner, D. V., Borduin, C. M., Sawyer, A. M., & Dopp, A. R. (2014). Long-term prevention of criminality in siblings of serious and violent juvenile offenders. *Journal of Consulting and Clinical Psychology, 82,* 492–499.

Wagner, E. F., & Austin, A. M. (2006). Substance use disorders. In R. T. Ammerman (Ed.), *Comprehensive handbook of personality and psychopathology* (Vol. 3, pp. 348–366). Hoboken, NJ: Wiley.

Wakefield, A. J., Murch, S. H., Anthony, A., Linnell, J., Casson, D. M., Malik, M., . . . Walker-Smith, J. A. (1998). Ileal lymphoid-nodular hyperplasia, non-specific colitis, and pervasive developmental disorder in children. *Lancet, 351,* 637–641.

Wakefield, J. C. (1992). Disorder as harmful dysfunction. *Psychological Review, 99,* 232–247.

Wakefield, J. C. (1997). When is development disordered? *Development and Psychopathology, 9,* 269–290.

Wakschlag, L. S., Choi, S. W., Carter, A. S., Hullsiek, H., Burns, J., McCarthy, K., . . . Briggs-Gowan, M. J. (2012). Defining the developmental parameters of temper loss in early childhood. *Journal of Child Psychology and Psychiatry, 53,* 1099–1108.

Walker, D. D., Roffman, R. A., Stephens, R. S., Wakana, K., & Berghuis, J. (2006). Motivational enhancement therapy for adolescent marijuana users. *Journal of Consulting and Clinical Psychology, 74,* 628–632.

Walker, E., & Lewine, J. (1990). Prediction of adult-onset schizophrenia. *American Journal of Psychiatry, 147,* 1052–1056.

Walker, E., & Lewine, R. R. (1993). Sampling biases in studies of gender and schizophrenia. *Schizophrenia Bulletin, 19,* 1–7.

Walkup, J. T., Albano, A. M., Piacentini, J., Birmaher, B., Compton, S. N., Sherrill, J. T., . . . Kendall, P. C. (2008). Cognitive behavioral therapy, sertraline, or a combination in childhood anxiety. *New England Journal of Medicine, 359,* 2753–2766.

Waller, G., Gray, E., Hinrichsen, H., Mountford, V., Lawson, R., & Patient, E. (2014). Cognitive-behavioral therapy for bulimia nervosa and atypical bulimic nervosa. *International Journal of Eating Disorders, 47,* 13–17.

Waller, R., Hyde, L. W., Grabell, A. S., Alves, M. L., & Olson, S. L. (2015). Differential associations of early callous-unemotional, oppositional, and ADHD behaviors: multiple domains within early-starting conduct problems? *Journal of Child Psychology and Psychiatry, 56,* 657–666.

Wallis, A., Alford, C., Hanson, A., Titterton, J., Madden, S., & Kohn, M. (2013). Innovations in Maudsley family-based treatment for anorexia nervosa at the Children's Hospital at Westmead. *Journal of Family Therapy, 35,* 68–81.

Walter, H. J. (2015). School-based interventions. In M. K. Dulcan (Ed.), *Dulcan's textbook of child and adolescent psychiatry* (pp. 1049–1074). Washington, DC: American Psychiatric Publishing.

Walters, J. T. R., O'Donovan, M., & Owen, M. J. (2011). The genetics of schizophrenia. In W. Gaebel (Ed.), *Schizophrenia: Current science and clinical practice* (pp. 109–140). New York, NY: Wiley.

Walton, J. R., & Coury, D. L. (2016). Medical comorbidities in ASD. In E. Anagnostou & J. Brian (Eds.), *Clinician's manual on ASD* (pp. 33–41). New York, NY: Springer.

Wang, Y., Wang, P., Xu, X., Goldstein, J., McConkie, A., Cheung, S. W., & Jiang, Y. H. (2015). Genetics of autism spectrum disorders. In *The molecular basis of autism* (pp. 33–66). New York, NY: Springer.

Waring, R., & Knight, R. (2013). How should children with speech sound disorders be classified? *International Journal of Language and Communication Disorders, 48,* 25–40.

Warren, S. L., Huston, L., Egeland, B., & Sroufe, L. A. (1997). Child and adolescent anxiety disorders and early attachment. *Journal of the American Academy of Child and Adolescent Psychiatry, 36,* 637–644.

Warren, S. L., & Simmens, J. (2005). Predicting toddler anxiety/depressive symptoms. *Infant Mental Health Journal, 26,* 40–55.

Warren, S. L., & Sroufe, L. A. (2004). Developmental issues. In T. H. Ollendick & J. S. March (Eds.), *Phobic and anxiety disorders in children and adolescents* (pp. 92–115). New York, NY: Oxford University Press.

Waters, A. M., Bradley, B. P., & Mogg, K. (2014). Biased attention to threat in paediatric anxiety disorders as a function of 'distress' versus 'fear' diagnostic categorization. *Psychological Medicine, 44,* 607–616.

Watson, H. J., Fursland, A., Bulik, C. M., & Nathan, P. (2013). Subjective binge eating with compensatory behaviors: A variant presentation of bulimia nervosa. *International Journal of Eating Disorders, 46,* 119–126.

Watson, J. B., & Rayner, R. (1920). Conditioned emotional reactions. *Journal of Experimental Psychology, 3,* 1–14.

Watson, P. J., Brymer, M. J., & Bonanno, G. A. (2011). Postdisaster psychological intervention since 9/11. *American Psychologist, 66,* 482–494.

Waxmonsky, J., Pelham, W. E., Gnagy, E., Cummings, M. R., O'Connor, B., Majumdar, A., . . . Robb, J. A. (2008). The efficacy and tolerability of methylphenidate and behavior modification in children with attention-deficit/hyperactivity disorder and severe mood dysregulation. *Journal of Child and Adolescent Psychopharmacology, 18,* 573–588.

Waxmonsky, J. G., Wymbs, F. A., Pariseau, M. E., Belin, P. J., Waschbusch, D. A., Baboscai, L., . . . Pelham, W. E. (2012). A novel group therapy for children with ADHD and severe mood dysregulation. *Journal of Attention Disorders, 17,* 527–541.

Weaver, I. C., Cervoni, N., Champagne, F. A., D'Alessio, A. C., Sharma, S., Seckl, J. R., . . . Meaney, M. J. (2004). Epigenetic programming by maternal behavior. *Nature Neuroscience, 7,* 847–854.

Webster-Stratton, C. (2016). The Incredible Years series. In M. van Ryzin (Ed.), *Family-based prevention programs for children and adolescents* (pp. 42–67). New York, NY: Routledge.

Webster-Stratton, C., Reid, M. J., & Beauchaine, T. P. (2013). One-year follow-up of combined parent and child intervention for young children with ADHD. *Journal of Clinical Child and Adolescent Psychology, 42,* 251–261.

Wechsler, D. (1958). *The measurement and appraisal of adult intelligence.* Baltimore, MD: Williams & Wilkins.

Wechsler, D., Raiford, S. E., & Holdnack, J. A. (2014). *WISC-V technical and interpretive manual.* Bloomington, MN: PsychCorp.

Weeks, J. (2016). *Evidence-based assessment for ASD.* Washington, DC: US Department of Education.

Weems, C. F., Graham, R. A., Scott, B. G., Banks, D. M., & Russell, J. D. (2013). Suppressor effects and age differences in the expression of anxious emotion. *Personality and Individual Differences, 55,* 283–287.

Weems, C. F., Pina, A. A., Costa, N. M., Watts, S. E., Taylor, L. K., & Cannon, M. F. (2007). Predisaster trait anxiety and negative affect predict posttraumatic stress in youths after hurricane Katrina. *Journal of Consulting and Clinical Psychology, 75,* 154–159.

Weems, C. F., & Watts, S. E. (2005). Cognitive models of childhood anxiety. In C. M. Velotis (Ed.), *Anxiety disorder research* (pp. 205–232). Hauppauge, NY: Nova Science.

Wehry, A. M., Beesdo-Baum, K., Hennelly, M. M., Connolly, S. D., & Strawn, J. R. (2015). Assessment and treatment of anxiety disorders in children and adolescents. *Current Psychiatry Reports, 17,* 1–11.

Weis, J. R., & Ross, S. (2015). Substance use. In F. Haddad & R. Gerson (Eds.), *Helping kids in crisis* (pp. 147–169). Washington, DC: American Psychiatric Publishing.

Weis, R., & Pucke, E. R. (2013). Aggression replacement training for disruptive adolescents. In E. Trejos-Castillo (Ed.), *Youth: Practices, perspectives and challenges* (pp. 179–206). Hauppauge NY: Nova.

Weis, R., Speridakos, E. C., & Ludwig, K. (2014). Community college students with learning disabilities. *Journal of Learning Disabilities, 47,* 556–568.

Weis, R., & Toolis, E. E. (2010). Parenting across cultural contexts in the USA. *Early Child Development and Care, 180,* 849–867.

Weismer, S. E. (2008). Speech perception in specific language impairment. In D. B. Pisoni, R. E. Remez, & S. E. Weismer (Eds.), *The handbook of speech perception* (pp. 567–588). Malden, MA: Blackwell.

Weiss, D. C., & Chorpita, B. F. (2011). *Revised Children's Anxiety and Depression Scale.* Los Angeles, CA: UCLA Child First.

Weiss, L. H., & Schwarz, J. C. (1996). The relationship between parenting types and older adolescents' personality, academic achievement, adjustment, and substance use. *Child Development, 67,* 2101–2114.

Weisz, J. R. (1990). Cultural-familial mental retardation. In R. M. Hodapp, J. A. Burack, & E. Zigler (Eds.), *Issues in the developmental approach to mental retardation* (pp. 137–168). New York, NY: Cambridge University Press.

Weisz, J. R. (2014). Building robust psychotherapies for children and adolescents. *Perspectives on Psychological Science, 9,* 81–84.

Weisz, J. R., Doss, A. J., & Hawley, K. M. (2005). Youth psychotherapy outcome research: A review and critique of the evidence base. *Annual Review of Psychology, 56,* 337–363.

Weisz, J. R., & Jensen, A. L. (2001). Child and adolescent psychotherapy in research and practice contexts. *European Child & Adolescent Psychiatry, 10,* S12–S18.

Weisz, J. R., Jensen, A. L., & McLeod, B. D. (2005). Development and dissemination of child and adolescent psychotherapies. In E. D. Hibbs & P. S. Jensen (Eds.), *Psychosocial treatments for child and adolescent disorders* (pp. 9–39). Washington, DC: American Psychological Association.

Weisz, J. R., Weiss, B., Alicke, M. D., & Klotz, M. L. (1987). Effectiveness of psychotherapy with children and adolescents: A meta-analysis for clinicians. *Journal of Consulting and Clinical Psychology, 55,* 542–549.

Weisz, J. R., Weiss, B., Han, S. S., Granger, D. A., & Morton, T. (1995). Effects of psychotherapy with children and adolescents revisited: A meta-analysis of treatment outcome studies. *Psychological Bulletin, 117,* 450–468.

Wekerle, C., Wolfe, D. A., Dunston, J., & Alldred, T. (2014). Child maltreatment. In E. J. Mash & R. A. Barkley (Eds.), *Child psychopathology* (pp. 737–798). New York, NY: Guilford Press.

Welch, S. L., & Fairburn, C. G. (1996). Childhood sexual and physical abuse as risk factors for the development of bulimia nervosa. *Child Abuse and Neglect, 20,* 633–642.

Wells, A. (2013). *Cognitive therapy of anxiety disorders.* New York, NY: Wiley.

Wendel, R., & Gouze, K. R. (2015). Family-based assessment and treatment. In M. K. Dulcan (Ed.), *Dulcan's textbook of child and adolescent psychiatry* (pp. 937–958). Washington, DC: American Psychiatric Publishing.

Wendling, P. (2009). PTSD can present months after a shooting. *Clinical Psychiatry News, 21,* 20–21.

West, A. E., Jacobs, R. H., Westerholm, R., Lee, A., Carbray, J., Heidenreich, J., & Heidenreich, J. (2009). Child and family-focused cognitive-behavioral therapy for pediatric bipolar disorder. *Journal of the Canadian Academy of Child and Adolescent Psychiatry, 18,* 239–246.

West, A. E., & Weinstein, S. M. (2012). A family-based psychosocial treatment model. *International Journal of Psychiatry and Related Sciences, 49,* 86–94.

Westen, D. (2012). Prototype diagnosis of psychiatric syndromes. *World Psychiatry, 11,* 16–21.

Weyandt, L., Swentosky, A., & Gudmundsdottir, B. G. (2013). Neuro-imaging and ADHD: fMRI, PET, DTI findings, and methodological limitations. *Developmental Neuropsychology, 38,* 211–225.

Whalley, K. (2016). Psychiatric disorders: Linking genetic risk to pruning. *Nature Reviews Neuroscience, 17,* 199.

Wheeler, N., & Jones, K. D. (2015). DSM-5 PTSD in children six years and younger. *Journal of Child and Adolescent Counseling, 1,* 119–134.

White, H. R., Labouvie, E. W., & Papadaratsakis, V. (2005). Changes in substance use during the transition to adulthood. *Journal of Drug Issues, 35,* 281–306.

Wigman, J. T., Nierop, M. V., Vollebergh, W. A., Lieb, R., Beesdo-Baum, K., Wittchen, H. U., & Os, J. V. (2013). Evidence that psychotic symptoms are prevalent in disorders of anxiety and depression, impacting on illness onset, risk, and severity. *Schizophrenia Bulletin, 38,* 247–257.

Wilens, T. E., & Zulauf, C. A. (2015). Attention-deficit/hyperactivity disorder and substance use disorders. In Y. Kaminer (Ed.), *Youth substance abuse and co-occurring disorders* (pp. 103–130). Arlington, VA: American Psychiatric Press.

Wilfley, D., Frank, M., Welch, R., Spurrell, E., & Rounsaville, B. (1998). Adapting interpersonal psychotherapy to a group format (IPT-G) for binge eating disorder. *Psychotherapy Research, 8,* 379–391.

Wilczynski, S., McIntosh, D. E., Tullis, C. A., Cullen, J., & Querim, A. (2016). Autism spectrum disorder in adolescents. In T. P. Gullotta, R. W. Plant, & M. Evans (Eds.), *Handbook of adolescent behavioral problems* (pp. 345–360). New York, NY: Springer.

Willcutt, E. G., Nigg, J. T., Pennington, B. F., Solanto, M. V., Rohde, L. A., Tannock, R., . . . Lahey, B. B. (2012). Validity of DSM-IV attention deficit/hyperactivity disorder symptom dimensions and subtypes. *Journal of Abnormal Psychology, 121,* 991–1010.

Williams, C. A. (2005). Neurological aspects of the Angelman syndrome. *Brain and Development, 27,* 88–94.

Williams, J. F., Smith, V. C., & Committee on Substance Abuse. (2015). Fetal alcohol spectrum disorders. *Pediatrics, 135,* 1395–1406.

Williams, W. L., Jackson, M., & Friman, P. C. (2007). Encopresis and enuresis. In P. Sturmey (Ed.), *Functional analysis in clinical treatment* (pp. 171–190). Burlington, MA: Academic Press.

Wilson, G. T., & Sysko, R. (2009). Frequency of binge eating episodes in bulimia nervosa and binge eating disorder. *International Journal of Eating Disorders, 42,* 603–610.

Wilson, J. J., & Levin, R. (2005). Attention-deficit/hyperactivity disorder and early-onset substance use disorders. *Journal of Child and Adolescent Psychopharmacology, 15,* 751–763.

Winters, K. C., Martin, C. S., & Chung, T. (2011). Commentary on O'Brien: Substance use disorders in *DSM-5* when applied to adolescents. *Addiction, 106,* 882–897.

Wittchen, H., Gloster, A. T., Beesdo-Baum, K., Fava, G. A., & Craske, M. G. (2010). Agoraphobia: A review of the diagnostic classification position and criteria. *Depression and Anxiety, 27,* 113–133.

Witwer, A. N., Lawton, K., & Aman, M. G. (2014). Intellectual disability. In E. J. Mash & R. A. Barkley (Eds.), *Child psychopathology* (pp. 593–624). New York, NY: Guilford Press.

Witwer, A. N., & Lecavalier, L. (2008). Examining the validity of autism spectrum disorder subtypes. *Journal of Autism and Developmental Disorders, 38,* 1611–1624.

Wolf, M., Barzillai, M., Gottwald, S., Miller, L., Spencer, K., Norton, E., . . . Morris, R. (2009). The RAVE-O intervention. *Mind, Brain, and Education, 3,* 84–91.

Wolf, M., & Bowers, P. G. (1999). The double-deficit hypothesis for the developmental dyslexias. *Journal of Educational Psychology, 91,* 415–438.

Wolf, M., Gottwald, S., & Orkin, M. (2009). Serious word play: How multiple linguistic emphasis in RAVE-O instruction improve multiple reading skills. *Mind, Brain, and Education, 3,* 21–24.

Wolf, M., Miller, L., & Donnelly, K. (2000). Retrieval, Automaticity, Vocabulary, Elaboration, Orthography (RAVE-O). *Journal of Learning Disabilities, 33,* 375–386.

Wolfe, V. V., & Gentile, C. (2013). Psychological assessment of sexually abused children. *The Sexual Abuse of Children, 2,* 143–187.

Wolfson, A. R., & Montgomery-Downs, H. E. (2013). *The Oxford handbook of infant, child, and adolescent sleep and behavior.* Oxford, England: Oxford University Press.

Wolpe, J. (1958). *Psychotherapy by reciprocal inhibition.* Stanford, CA: Stanford University Press.

Wonderlich, S. A., Gordon, K. H., Mitchell, J. E., Crosby, R. D., & Engel, S. G. (2009). The validity and clinical utility of binge eating disorder. *International Journal of Eating Disorders, 42,* 687–705.

World Health Organization. (2016). *Global database on body mass index.* Geneva, Switzerland: Author.

Wozniak, J., Biederman, J., Kiely, K., Ablon, J. S., Faraone, S. V., Mundy, E., & Mennin, D. (1995). Mania-like symptoms suggestive of childhood-onset bipolar disorder in clinically referred children. *Journal of the American Academy of Child and Adolescent Psychiatry, 34,* 867–876.

Wright, C. A., & Kaiser, A. P. (2016). Teaching parents enhanced milieu teaching with words and signs using the teach-model-coach-review model. *Topics in Early Childhood Special Education, 16,* 1–13.

Wu, L. T., & Blazer, D. G. (2015). Substance use disorders and co-morbidities among Asian Americans and Native Hawaiians/Pacific Islanders. *Psychological Medicine, 45,* 481–494.

Wu, L. T., Blazer, D. G., Gersing, K. R., Burchett, B., Swartz, M. S., Mannelli, P., & Workgroup, N. A. (2013). Comorbid substance use disorders with other Axis I and II mental disorders among treatment-seeking Asian Americans, Native Hawaiians/Pacific Islanders, and mixed-race people. *Journal of Psychiatric Research, 47,* 1940–1948.

Wu, P., Hoven, C. W., Liu, X., Cohen, P., Fuller, C. J., & Shaffer, D. (2005). Substance use, suicidal ideation and attempts in children and adolescents. *Suicide and Life-Threatening Behavior, 34,* 408–420.

Wu, T., Howells, N., Burger, J., Lopez, P., Lundeen, R., & Sikkenga, A. V. (2016). Conduct disorder. In G. M. Kapalka (Ed.), *Treating disruptive behavior disorders* (pp. 120–143). New York, NY: Routledge.

Wynn, K. (1992). Addition and subtraction by human infants. *Nature, 358,* 749–750.

Xu, F., & Spelke, E. S. (2000). Large-number discrimination in 6-month-old infants. *Cognition, 74,* B1–B11.

Yairy, E., & Seery, C. H. (2016). *Stuttering foundations and clinical applications.* New York, NY: Pearson.

Yap, M. B. H., Pilkington, P. D., Ryan, S. M., Kelly, C. M., & Jorm, A. F. (2014). Parenting strategies for reducing the risk of adolescent depression and anxiety disorders. *Journal of Affective Disorders, 156,* 67–75.

Yeargin-Allsop, M., Boyle, C., & van Naarden, K. (2008). The epidemiology of developmental disabilities. In P. J. Accardo (Ed.), *Neurodevelopmental disabilities in infancy and childhood* (pp. 61–100). Baltimore, MD: Brookes.

Yoshikawa, H., Weiland, C., Brooks-Gunn, J., Burchinal, M. R., Espinosa, L. M., Gormley, W. T., . . . Zaslow, M. J. (2013). *Investing in our future.* Washington, DC: SRCD.

Yoshimasu, K., Barbaresi, W. J., Colligan, R. C., Voigt, R. G., Weaver, A. L., & Katusic, S. K. (2016). Mediating and moderating role of depression, conduct disorder or attention-deficit/hyperactivity disorder in developing adolescent substance use disorders. *PLOS ONE, 11,* e0157488.

Young, J. C., & Widom, C. S. (2014). Long-term effects of child abuse and neglect on emotion processing in adulthood. *Child Abuse and Neglect, 38,* 1369–1381.

Young, J. F., & Mufson, L. (2003). *Manual for interpersonal psychotherapy-adolescent skills training (IPT-AST)*. New York, NY: Columbia University.

Young, J. F., Mufson, L., & Davies, M. (2006). Efficacy of interpersonal psychotherapy-adolescent skills training: An indicated preventive intervention for depression. *Journal of Child Psychology and Psychiatry, 47*, 1254–1262.

Young, S., & Amarasinghe, M. (2010). Non-pharmacological treatments for ADHD. *Journal of Child Psychology and Psychiatry, 51*, 116–133.

Youngstrom, E. A., & Algorta, G. P. (2014). Pediatric bipolar disorder. In E. J. Mash & R. A. Barkley (Eds.), *Child psychopathology* (pp. 264–314). New York, NY: Routledge.

Youngstrom, E. A., Birmaher, B., & Findling, R. L. (2008). Pediatric bipolar disorder: Validity, phenomenology, and recommendations for diagnosis. *Bipolar Disorders, 10*, 194–214.

Youngstrom, E. A., Freeman, A. J., & Jenkins, M. M. (2009). The assessment of children and adolescents with bipolar disorder. *Child and Adolescent Psychiatric Clinics of North America, 18*, 353–390.

Youngstrom, E. A., Van Meter, A., & Algorta, G. P. (2010). The bipolar spectrum: Myth or reality? *Current Psychiatry Reports, 12*, 479–489.

Yssledyke, J., Burns, M., Scholin, S., & Parker, D. (2010). Instructionally valid assessment within response to intervention. *Teaching Exceptional Children, 42*, 54–61.

Yule, W., & Smith, P. (2010). Post-traumatic stress disorder. In M. Rutter (Ed.), *Rutter's child and adolescent psychiatry* (pp. 686–697). Malden, MA: Blackwell.

Zablotsky, B., Black, L. I., Maenner, M. J., Schieve, L. A., & Blumberg, S. J. (2015). Estimated prevalence of autism and other developmental disabilities following questionnaire changes in the 2014 National Health Interview Survey. *National Health Statistics Reports, 87*, 1–21.

Zahn-Waxler, C. (2000). The development of empathy, guilt, and internalization of distress. In R. J. Davidson (Ed.), *Anxiety, depression, and emotion* (pp. 222–265). Oxford, England: Oxford University Press.

Zahn-Waxler, C., Cole, P. M., & Barrett, K. C. (1991). Guilt and empathy: Sex differences and implications for the development of depression. In J. Garber & K. A. Dodge (Eds.), *The development of emotion regulation and dysregulation* (pp. 243–272). Cambridge, England: Cambridge University Press.

Zammit, S., Allebeck, P., Andreasson, S., Lundberg, I., & Lewis, G. (2002). Self reported cannabis use as a risk factor for schizophrenia in Swedish conscripts. *British Medical Journal, 7374*, 1199–2011.

Zapolski, T. C., Pedersen, S. L., McCarthy, D. M., & Smith, G. T. (2014). Less drinking, yet more problems: Understanding African American drinking and related problems. *Psychological Bulletin, 140*, 188–223.

Zeanah, C. H., Berlin, L. J., & Boris, N. W. (2011). Clinical applications of attachment theory and research for infants and young children. *Journal of Clinical Child Psychology and Psychiatry, 52*, 819–833.

Zeanah, C. H., Fox, N. A., & Nelson, C. A. (2012). The Bucharest Early Intervention Project. *Journal of Nervous and Mental Disease, 200*, 243–247.

Zeanah, C. H., & Gleason, M. M. (2010). *Reactive attachment disorder: A review for DSM-5*. Washington, DC: American Psychiatric Association.

Zeanah, C. H., & Smyke, A. T. (2008). Attachment disorders in family and social context. *Infant Mental Health Journal, 29*, 219–233.

Zigler, E. (1969). Developmental versus difference theories of mental retardation and the problem of motivation. *American Journal of Mental Deficiency, 73*, 536–556.

Zigler, E., Balla, D., & Hodapp, R. M. (1986). On the definition and classification of mental retardation. *American Journal of Mental Deficiency, 89*, 215–230.

Zinbarg, R. E., Anand, D., Lee, J. K., Kendall, A. D., & Nunez, M. (2015). Generalized anxiety disorder, panic disorder, social anxiety disorder, and specific phobias. In P. H. Blaney (Ed.), *Oxford textbook of psychopathology* (pp. 133–162). Oxford, England: Oxford University Press.

Zisser, A. R., & Eyberg, S. M. (2012). Maternal ADHD: Parent-child interactions and relations with child disruptive behavior. *Child and Family Behavior Therapy, 34*, 33–52.

Zuckerman, M. (2007). Sensation seeking and substance use and abuse: Smoking, drinking, and drugs. In M. Zuckerman (Ed.), *Sensation seeking and risky behavior* (pp. 107–143). Washington, DC: American Psychological Association.

Cannabis Youth Treatments Study, 330
Carbamazepine (Tegretol), 90
Caregiver support, 147–148
Catastrophic thinking, 331, 354, 360–361, 372, 373, 559
Catechol-O-methyltransferase (COMT) gene, 491, 494
Categorical classification, 78
Celexa (citalopram), 442
Cerebellum, 42
Cerebral palsy, 118
Challenging behaviors, children with intellectual disabilities, 119–122
    intervention approaches, 144–147, 178
Challenging Horizons Program, 257
Chelation therapy, 136
Child- and family-focused cognitive-behavioral therapy (CFF-CBT), 477–478
Child development
    adolescent stages of change, 326
    anxiety and, 337
    bioecological systems theory, 55–57
    central nervous system, 40–44
    cognitive, 47–48
    emotional, 48–49
    individual differences, 21
    interpersonal relationships and, 54
    milestones, 117t
    parent-child attachment, 50–52. See also Attachment
    parenting styles and, 52–53
    sociocultural influences, 55–57
    See also Developmental psychopathology
Childhood-onset conduct disorder, 272–273, 290–291
Childhood-onset fluency disorder, 198–203
Childhood psychological disorders
    defining "abnormal behavior," 10–12
    DSM-5 definitional considerations, 12–14
    prevalence of, 3–5
    stability over time, 18–21
    See also Developmental psychopathology; specific disorders
Child life experts, 100
Child maltreatment, 404
    causes of intellectual disabilities, 138–139
    comorbid mood problems, 411
    DSM-5 definitions, 405t
    effects of, 409–412, 413
    later depression and, 36
    later substance use disorders and, 319
    prevalence, 408–409
    psychological abuse, 405t, 407
    suicide risk and, 451
    See also Child neglect; Physical abuse; Sexual abuse; Social-emotional deprivation in infancy
Child maltreatment, treatments
    cognitive-behavioral family therapy, 414–415
    cognitive restructuring, 417–418
    parent training, 413–414
    safety plan, 415
    supportive therapy, 413
    trauma-focused cognitive-behavioral therapy, 416–417
Child neglect, 408
    DSM-5 definition, 405t
    effects of, 409–411

treatments interventions, 413–415
    See also Child maltreatment
Children's Depression Inventory, Second Edition (CDI-2), 76
Children with disabilities, school-based support for, 142–144
Cholecystokinin (CKK), 525
Chorionic villus sampling, 140
Chromosomal abnormalities, 125–131
    22q11.2 deletion syndrome, 130–131, 491
    X-linked disorders, 119, 122–123, 125, 131–132
    See also Genetics
Chromosomal microarray (CMA) screening test, 118–119
Chromosomal mosaicism, 125
Chromosomes, 32–33
Chronic health problems, helping children with, 567–570
Chronosystems, 57
Chronotherapy, 429, 563
Cigarette smoke exposure, 246
Cingulate gyrus, 363–365
Circadian rhythm sleep-wake disorder, 562–563
Citalopram (Celexa), 442
Classical conditioning, 45
    cognitive-behavioral therapy for substance abuse, 323
    insomnia intervention, 560
    pediatric psychology applications, 570
    phobias and, 347
    selective mutism and, 344
    two-factor theory of stuttering, 201–202
    urinary incontinence intervention, 548–549
Cleanliness training, 549, 553
Clinical behavior therapy, 254–255
Clonidine, 322, 377, 562
COACHES program, 25
Cocaine, 302
Codes of ethics, 101
Coercive family process, 282–284
Cognition assessment, 64
Cognitive appraisal theory, 391
Cognitive-behavioral family therapy, 414–415, 427–428
Cognitive-behavioral therapy (CBT)
    anxiety disorder interventions, 369–375
    bipolar disorder intervention, 477–478
    child- and family-focused CBT, 477–478
    depression treatments, 443–446
    disruptive mood dysregulation disorder intervention, 427–428
    eating disorder treatments, 533–535, 538–541
    medication combination, 375, 376, 447
    OCD treatments, 374–375
    pediatric psychology applications, 571–572
    PTSD treatments, 393
    schizophrenia interventions, 499–500
    substance use disorder interventions, 323–326, 330
    trauma-focused CBT, 393, 416–417
Cognitive biases and distortions, depressive disorders and, 437
Cognitive development, 47–48
    intellectual disabilities and, 124
    interpersonal relationships and, 54
    socioeconomic relationships, 139
Cognitive distortion, 92
Cognitive function assessment
    academic achievement, 67–70
    intelligence, 66–67

D.A.R.E. program, 321
Daydreaming, 248–249
Daytrana, 88, 251
Decomposition, 226
Default mode network, 248–249
DEFENDS strategy, 223
Delay technique in language therapy, 195
Delirium tremens, 317
Delta-9-tetrahydrocannabinol (THC), 302, 317
Delusions, 465–466, 483
Depakote (Divalproex), 90, 475, 476
Depersonalization, 384
Depressive disorders, 421–422
    age-related differences, 6
    anxiety disorders and, 340, 357, 358–359
    assessment tools, 76
    bipolar disorders and, 465, 466, 469
    child maltreatment comorbidity, 411
    conduct problems and, 278
    coping skills, 444
    course, 435
    disruptive mood dysregulation disorder, 49, 422–427, 469
    eating disorders and, 518, 529
    gender differences, 6, 434
    hopelessness, 450
    major depressive disorder, 422, 430–432
    masked depression theory, 278
    maternal, 439
    persistent depressive disorder or dysthymia, 422, 432–434
    prevalence, 434
    PTSD and, 388, 390
    severe mood dysregulation, 469
    substance use and, 305, 309–310, 319
    suicidal ideation and, 422, 431, 450
    See also Bipolar disorders; Disruptive mood dysregulation
        disorder; specific types
Depressive disorders, causes and risk factors
    attribution theory, 437–438
    Beck's cognitive theory, 437–438
    child maltreatment history, 36
    genes and neurotransmitters, 435–436
    hypothalamus-pituitary-adrenal dysregulation, 436
    intergenerational interpersonal stress model, 439
    interpersonal relationships, 446
    kindling hypothesis, 435
    Lewinsohn's behavioral theory, 445
    maternal depression, 439
    parent-child attachment, 439
    peers, 438, 440
    response-contingent reinforcement, 443
    social information processing, 440, 441f
    stressful life events, 436
    temperament, 436
Depressive disorders, treatments
    cognitive-behavioral therapy for adolescents, 445–446
    cognitive-behavioral therapy for children, 443–445
    interpersonal psychotherapy, 446–447
    medication, 6, 441–443. See also Antidepressant medications
    medication and psychotherapy combination, 447
Depressogenic attributional style, 438
Derealization, 384

Desensitization, eye movement desensitization and reprocessing
    (EMDR), 393–394
Desipramine (Norpramin), 441
Desmopressin (DDAVP), 550
Detoxification, 322
Developmental disabilities, 110–111
Developmental pathways, 18–20
Developmental psychopathology, 15–16
    adaptive vs. maladaptive development, 16–18
    autism spectrum disorder model, 170
    developmental pathways, 18–20
    disorder stability over time, 18–21
    DSM-5 vs. earlier versions, 80–81
    eating disorders, 525
    epigenetics, 38–39
    genetic factors and, 32–38. See also Genetics
    global developmental delay, 117–119
    individual differences, 21
    levels of analysis, 31–32
    normal brain development, 40–44
    pathways toward conduct problems, 290–291
    protective factors, 23–24
    risk factors, 22–24, 55
    sexual abuse consequences, 412
    See also Child development; Intellectual disabilities;
        specific disorders
Developmental stage theory, 47–48
Deviance-prone pathway, 319–321
Deviancy training, 288
Dexedrine, 251, 311
Diabetes mellitus, 569, 570
Diagnosis, 60
    DSM-5 diagnostic approach, 77–80
    International Classification of Diseases (ICD), 81
    possible benefits of, 81–82
    potential limitations of, 82–83
    Research Domain Criteria, 83–84
    signs and symptoms, 77
Diagnostic Adaptive Behavior Scale (DABS), 113
Diagnostic and Statistical Manual of Mental Disorders, Fifth
    Edition (DSM-5)
    ADHD in earlier editions, 233
    child maltreatment definitions, 405t
    criticism of classification approach, 82–83
    Cross-Cutting Symptom Measure, 79
    defining mental disorders, 12–14
    diagnostic approach, 77–80
    differences from earlier versions, 80–81
    See also specific disorders
Diagnostic and Statistical Manual of Mental Disorders, Fourth
    Edition (DSM-IV), 80–81
Diagnostic interview, 62–65
Diagnostic Interview Schedule for Children, 64
Diagnostic overshadowing, 122
Diagnostic specifiers, 79–80
Dialects, 197
Diathesis–stress model, 35–36
Dichotomous (black-or-white) thinking, 520, 530
Dietary interventions
    children with ADHD, 258
    children with encopresis, 553

EMDR (eye movement desensitization and reprocessing), 393–394
Emotional arousal, low, conduct problems and, 281
Emotional development, 48–49, 54
Emotional expression
    affect assessment, 64
    conduct disorder and limited prosocial emotions, 273–275, 281
    expressed emotion and family tensions, 474
    normal development, 48
    parental modeling, 351
    PTSD and emotional numbness, 383
    schizophrenia and, 484
Emotional reactivity, 50, 280–281, 320
Emotion regulation
    ADHD and, 239, 250
    bipolar disorders and, 472–473
    bipolar disorder treatments, 478–480
    brain abnormalities, 472
    conduct problems and, 280–281
    depressive disorders and, 444
    eating disorders and, 49
    executive function development, 250
    normal development, 49
    parent-child attachment, 50–52. See also Attachment
    problems for some girls, 435
Empathy, 168
    conditions for therapeutic change, 91
    excess in some girls, 434
    normal development, 47, 48
Encephalitis, 138
Encopresis, 551–554
    causes, 551–552
    constipation and, 544, 551, 553
    treatments, 553–554
Endogenous opioids, 121, 316
Endorphins, 121, 316
English as a second language children, 215
Enhanced reinforcement pathway, 318–319
Enmeshment, 531
Enuresis, 545–551
    causes, 547–548
    prevalence, 546
    treatments, 548–550
Environmental toxins, 55, 134–136
Epidemiological research methods, 4
Epidemiologists, 3
Epigenetics, 38–39, 163
Epilepsy, 159
Equifinality, 21
Equine-assisted therapy, 183
Escape extinction, 510
Escape or avoidance coping, 391
Escitalopram (Lexapro), 442
Eskalith, 90, 475
Estazolam (ProSom), 562
Eszopiclone (Lunesta), 562
Ethics, 25–26, 101
    APA Ethics Code, 101
    consent, 102–103, 327
    four Cs, 101–106

Ethnic or racial differences, 8–9, 55
    ADHD prevalence, 243
    autism prevalence, 161
    bipolar disorders prevalence, 470
    childhood disorder identification, 14–15
    eating disorders, 523
    learning disability prevalence, 214
    speech sound disorder and, 197
    substance use prevalence, 312, 313f
    suicidal thoughts or actions prevalence, 449
    treatments access, 9
    See also Cultural differences
Event recording, 144
Evidence-based practice, 24–27
Evidence-based treatments, 3, 25–27. See also Treatments; specific disorders or treatments
Excoriation disorder, 367
Executive functioning, 43
    ADHD and, 249–251
    autism and, 166
    four basic functions, 249–251
    neurobiology of, 248
    See also Emotion regulation; Working memory
Exercise interventions, 258–259
Exosystems, 56
Expectancy theory of panic, 354
Experience-expectant process, 397
Experiments, 581–582
Exposure and response prevention (EX/RP), 374
Exposure therapy, 367–368
Expressed emotion (EE), 474
Expressive One-Word Picture Vocabulary Test, 187
External validity, 586
Extinction, 45, 146, 283, 510, 560
Extrapyramidal side effects, 496
Eye contact, 132, 154, 166, 167, 172, 205
Eye movement desensitization and reprocessing (EMDR), 393–394

Facial screening, 510
Facilitated communication, 27
Failure to thrive (FTT), 409, 509
False belief task, 169
Family-focused treatments for adolescents (FFT-A), 480–483
Family-related problems. See Parent-child interactions
Family suicide history, 450–451
Family systems therapy, 94–95
Family therapists, 100
Family therapy
    behavior family systems therapy, 573
    bipolar disorder treatments, 477–483
    disruptive mood dysregulation disorder intervention, 427–428
    eating disorder treatments, 531–533
    Maudsley Hospital approach, 532–533
    multidimensional, 329
    multisystemic, 573
    pediatric psychology applications, 572–573
    psychoeducational psychotherapy, 478–480
    schizophrenia interventions, 498, 500
    structural, 94, 531–532, 572–573
    substance abuse interventions, 328–330

Haldol (haloperidol), 377, 496
Hallucinations, 465–466, 483, 485f
Hallucinogens, 302
Haloperidol (Haldol), 377, 496
Hand-over-hand assistance, 176
Harmful dysfunction, 11–12
Head injuries, 138–139, 410
Health care settings. *See* Pediatric psychology
Hepatitis B, 134
Herpes simplex virus type 2 (HSV-2), 134
Heterotypic continuity, 20
Hippocampus, 42, 316, 491
Histamines, 562
Histones, 32, 38
HIV/AIDS, 134
Homotypic continuity, 20
Hopelessness theory of suicide, 450, 452
Hostile-coercive parenting behavior, 282, 291
Human chorionic gonadotropin, 140
Hyperactivity, 233–235
Hyperphagia, 127
Hypnotics, 302, 562
Hypoglycemia, 569
Hypokalemia, 517
Hypothalamus-pituitary-adrenal (HPA) axis, 390, 436
Hypotheses, 577

Illnesses, chronic, pediatric psychology, 567–570
Illnesses or injuries, causes of intellectual disabilities, 138–139
Imipramine (Tofranil), 441
Imitation training, 177
Immature speech, 197
Immigrant families, 8, 14
Inattention, ADHD diagnosis and presentation, 233–238
Incidence, 3
Incidental teaching, 195
Inclusion, 142–143
Incontinence. *See* Encopresis; Enuresis
Incredible Years program, 294–295
Individual differences in development, 21, 49–50
Individualized Education Program (IEP), 143, 210–211
Individuals with Disabilities Education Improvement Act (IDEIA), 143, 210–211, 243
Indulgent parents, 53
Infant failure to thrive (FTT), 409, 509
Infant genetic or metabolic screening tests, 118–119, 139–140
Infant screening for autism, 172
Infant social-emotional deprivation, 394–399
Inflammatory bowel disease (IBD), 569
Informed consent, 102–103
Inhalants, 302
Inpatient consultation-liaison, 566–567
Inpatient eating disorder treatment programs, 530
Inpatient substance abuse disorder treatment programs, 323
Insight, 64
Insomnia disorder, 555–562
  causes, 557–559
  DSM-5 diagnostic criteria, 556t
  prevalence, 557
  treatments, 559–562

Institutionalized infants, social-emotional deprivation consequences, 343, 394–395, 396, 399, 403
Instruction approaches for math, 226–228
Integrated behavior therapy, 368–369
Intellectual disabilities (IDs), 110–113
  adaptive functioning assessment, 112–113
  Angelman syndrome, 128–129
  autism and, 157
  challenging behaviors and, 119–122, 144–147
  comorbid disorders, 122. *See also specific disorders*
  diagnostic criteria, 112
  global developmental delay, 117–119
  harmful terminology, 112
  infant screening, 118–119, 139–140
  IQ tests, 112, 116
  needed supports, 115–116
  pica disorder and, 505
  Prader-Willi syndrome, 126–128
  prevalence of, 122
  Rosa's Law, 111
  severity of, 114–115
  sleep problems and, 557
  support for parents/caregivers, 147–148
  22q11.2 deletion syndrome, 130–131
  Williams syndrome, 129–130
  See also Down syndrome; Learning disabilities
Intellectual disabilities (IDs), causes
  behavioral phenotypes, 124
  childhood illness or injury, 138–139
  chromosomal abnormalities, 119, 125–131
  cultural-familial ID, 139
  environmental toxins, 134–136
  maternal illness, 134, 138
  maternal substance use during pregnancy, 136–137
  metabolic disorders, 119, 133, 139–140
  organic vs. cultural-familial types, 123–125
  perinatal complications, 138
  premature or low birth weight infants, 138
  similar sequence/similar structure hypotheses, 124
Intellectual disabilities (IDs), prevention and treatments
  early intervention programs, 141–142
  educational inclusion and support services, 142–144
  reducing challenging behaviors, 144–147
Intelligence, 66–67
  genetic factors and, 33–34
  tests, 66–67, 117
  See also IQ test scores
Intergenerational interpersonal stress model, 439
Internal consistency, 75
Internalized speech, 250
Internal validity, 582–583
Internal working model, 51
International Classification of Diseases (ICD), 81
Interoceptive exposure, 371
Interpersonally dependent stressors, 7
Interpersonal-psychological theory of suicide, 452–453
Interpersonal psychotherapy (IPT), 446–447
Interpersonal therapy (IPT), 93–94, 535–537, 541–542
Inter-rater reliability, 75
Interval recording, 144
Intoxication, 304, 306t

eating disorders and, 518
hopelessness theory, 450, 452
interpersonal-psychological theory, 452–453
interventions, 453–457
pharmacological intervention, 454, 456
prevalence, 448–449
prevention programs, 457–458
PTSD and, 388
risk factors, 450–452
safety plans, 454, 455f
substance use problems and, 310, 450
Suicide history of family, 450–451
Suicide prevalence, 448–449
Suicide prevention, 457–458
Sullivan, Harry Stack, 54, 93
Summer Treatments Program (STP) for children
    with ADHD, 256
Supportive confrontation, 530
Supports Intensity Scale, 116
Suprachiasmatic nucleus (SCN), 429
Sylvian fissure, 191
Symbolic play, 167–168, 178
Symptoms, 77
Synapses, 41
Synaptic pruning, 42, 492
Synaptogenesis, 44
Syphilis, 134
Systematic desensitization, 368, 570
Systems theory, bioecological, 55–57

Tacts, 193
Tardive dyskinesia, 497
TEACCH, 176–177
Teacher rating scales for children's functioning, 71, 73
Temazepam (Restoril), 562
Temperament, 49–50
    conduct problems and, 280–282
    depressive disorders and, 436
    See also Emotion regulation
Temper outbursts, disruptive mood dysregulation disorder,
    422–427
Temporal lobe, 43
Tenex, 377
Test-retest reliability, 75
Tetrahydrocannabinol (THC), 302, 317
Text enhancements, 221
Thalamus, 491
Theory of mind, 47, 168–170
Thin ideal, 527, 528
Thinking, Feeling, and Doing exercise, 479
Thought content, 64
Thought process, 64
Tic disorders, 254, 365–366, 374–375, 376–377
Time-out, 146–147, 293, 510–511
Tobacco, 302
Tofranil (imipramine), 441
Toileting-related disorders, 544, 545. *See also* Encopresis; Enuresis
Tolerance, 302, 304, 306, 316–317
TORCH, 134
Touch screen communication systems, 182
Tourette's syndrome, 254, 366

Toxoplasma, 134
Transactional model for feeding disorders, 508
Transactional nature of development, 15–16
Transference, 95
Translocation, 125
Trauma-focused cognitive-behavioral therapy (TF-CBT), 393,
    416–417
Trauma narrative, 415
Trauma-related disorders. *See* Child maltreatment; Posttraumatic
    stress disorder; Sexual abuse
Traumatic sexualization, 412
Treatment and Education of Autistic and Related
    Communication-Handicapped Children (TEACCH), 176
Treatment of Adolescent Suicide Attempters (TASA) study, 456
Treatment of Early Age Mania (TEAM), 476
Treatment of Early Onset Schizophrenia Spectrum Disorders
    (TEOSS) study, 497
Treatments, 60, 86
    access to, 9
    adherence, 87, 567, 569, 570–572
    assessment for progress monitoring, 61
    barriers to, 3, 9–10
    benefits of diagnosis for, 82
    ethics considerations, 25–27, 101–105
    evidence-based, 3, 25–27
    harm reduction approach, 327
    limited prosocial emotions and, 275
    medication, 87–90
    parental consent for, 327
    professional practice, 99–101
    psychotherapy, 91–99
    See also Behavior therapy; Cognitive-behavioral therapy;
        Family therapy; Medication; Psychotherapy; *specific*
        disorders, therapeutic approaches
Trichotillomania, 366–367
Tricyclic antidepressants, 88, 441, 537. *See also* Antidepressant
    medications; *specific drugs*
Trilafon (perphenazine), 496
Trileptal, 90
Tripartite influence model, 528
Triple test, 140
Trisomy 21, 125
Twelve-step programs, 323
22q11.2 deletion syndrome, 130–131, 491
Twin studies, 34. *See also* Genetics
Two-factor theory of stuttering, 201–202
Type I diabetes, 569, 570
Type II diabetes, 569

UCLA Young Autism Project, 173
Ultrasound, 140
Underextension, 191
Uninvolved parents, 53
Universal design, 143–144
Urinary incontinence. *See* Enuresis
Urine alarm, 548–549
US Food and Drug Administration (FDA), 87

Vaccines and autism, 27
Validity, 76–77, 582–583, 586
Valproate (Depakote), 90